Marketing Communications

SEVENTH EDITION

Marketing Communications

Integrating online and offline, customer engagement and digital technologies

PR Smith and Ze Zook

First published by Kogan Page Limited in 1993
Second edition published in 1998
Third edition published in 2002
Fourth edition published in 2004
Fifth edition published in 2011
Sixth edition published in 2016
Seventh edition published in Great Britain and the United States in 2020 by Kogan Page Limited

2nd Floor, 45 Gee Street
London
EC1V 3RS
United Kingdom
www.koganpage.com

122 W 27th St, 10th Floor
New York, NY 10001
USA

4737/23 Ansari Road
Daryaganj
New Delhi 110002
India

ISBNs

Paperback 978 0 7494 9864 1
eBook 978 0 7494 9865 8

British Library Cataloguing-in-Publication Data

A CIP record for this book is available from the British Library.

Library of Congress Cataloging-in-Publication Data

CIP data is available. Library of Congress Cataloging-in-Publication Data
Control Number: 2019045704

Typeset by Integra Software Services, Pondicherry
Print production managed by Jellyfish
Printed and bound in Great Britain by Henry Ling Limited, at the Dorset Press, Dorchester, DT1 1HD

CONTENTS

Additional resources for lecturers and students are available at:

www.koganpage.com/marketingcommunications7

ABOUT THE AUTHORS

PR Smith

PR Smith is an international speaker, marketing consultant and author of six books (translated into eight languages) renowned for their 'edutainment' style. These include *Digital Marketing Excellence* (co-authored with Dave Chaffey) and the *SOSTAC® Guide to Writing Your Perfect Digital Marketing Plan*. Paul created the SOSTAC® planning framework, voted in the top 3 business models worldwide by the Chartered Institute of Marketing's Centenary Poll and now adopted by LinkedIn, KPMG and Greenpeace, as well as hundreds of innovative start-ups. His SOSTAC® online portal at **www.sostac.org** helps professionals learn how to write the perfect plan (in four minutes) and perfect it thereafter. Professionals become SOSTAC® Certified Planners, while consultancies and agencies become SOSTAC® Certified Companies and trainers/training companies become SOSTAC® Certified Training Companies.

Paul delivers inspiring talks and workshops around the world to professional associations and private organizations (**https://prsmith.org/home-page/speaking/**). Paul's consulting and mentoring covers government departments, blue-chips and innovative start-ups. From launching Christmas Crackers in America to Short Game Golf in China, Paul enjoys a challenge. He is currently advising the SuperNode™, which is connecting all Northern Europe's windfarms with Southern Europe's Solar Parks to fulfil and deliver 100 per cent of all of Europe's future energy needs (**https://supernode.energy/**). He is also Sri Lanka Golf Tours' Managing Partner, dedicated to creating inbound golf holidays on Paradise Island, the 'Pearl in the Indian Ocean'.

Finally, Paul is also founder and chief author of the Great Sportsmanship Programme (**https://greatmomentsofsportsmanship.com/**) an inspirational NFP edutainment programme which, through short stories about sportsmanship, encourages youths to create a new generation of global citizens with sportsmanship values while also boosting interest in reading and sport. In short, it is designed to change the world (one small step at a time).

Instagram: @prpsmith Twitter: @PR_Smith
Website: **PRSmith.org**

Ze Zook

Ze is an integrated marketing author, lecturer and consultant with a background in the creative industries, particularly those organizations embracing digital transformation.

Ze has also helped many innovative start-ups in the UK, and in particular through partnerships with brands such as Microsoft, Sainsbury's and The Prince's Trust. More recently Ze has worked with ZenithOptimedia.

Ze has worked with Paul over the past 25 years, firstly launching the award-winning, first three-Screen TV video explaining how public relations works. Since then, Ze and Paul worked together developing the world's first digital marketing course delivered electronically (originally CDs, then online). These original multimedia courses sold into 66 countries around the world and were adopted by the Chartered Institute of Marketing, blue-chip organizations like IBM and third level educational institutions around the UK.

More recently, Ze's consultancy has focused on the health and well-being sector, assisting clients through his agency, KD7, both strategically and tactically, helping them grow primarily through integrating their digital channels.

Ze is also a visiting academic at the Grenoble School of Management, guiding students on an innovative and multichannel approach to business and marketing. His written insights on the nature of digital, branding and web entrepreneurship have appeared in publications including IGI Global and UK Public Health, where he was recently commissioned to explore the structure of their social media strategy. He is also a writer contributor to the Native Advertising Institute on some of the latest topics on digital marketing.

Ze also has a passion for photography and lives in London and the South Coast of England with his wife and daughter. The family also spend a lot of time in France.

Twitter: @MrZZ8Q Website: **kd7.org.uk**

PREFACE

I was playing golf with a friend, who asked me what was the latest book I was working on (excuse his terrible grammar). When I told him it was the seventh edition, no less, of our best-selling marketing communications book, he replied, "Well I hope you get it right this time!" I think we have. Ze and I are delighted to have gathered an array of intriguing, cutting edge examples of marketing communications in action, underpinned by academic theory, all written in a very practical way. In fact, we hope you enjoy it as we really want to 'edutain' you and perhaps even 'wow' you occasionally. As we know, having to read through volumes of books can be fatiguing, so we try to lighten your load with the occasional intriguing, controversial or even mildly humorous examples.

Something that has become screamingly obvious is that tactical communications tools never work in isolation. For many years now, we have been pushing marcomms integration, ie integrate everything in order to leverage and maximize the impact of each tactical marketing communications tool. In fact, we've been saying this for a quarter of a century (the first edition in 1993 was *Marketing Communications: An integrated approach*). Today, it is impossible to isolate any tactic, as marketers today think in an integrated way – whether it is a microsite built for an ad campaign with a contact strategy of an email followed by a tailored landing page/microsite followed by some remarketing, marketers today think integrated, which is great. You'll see this in all the mini cases at the end of each chapter in Part Two.

Even this is changing, as AI-driven chatbots can shorten this sequence and deliver far better leads, as we show in Chapter 11. From time to time, you will think, 'Hang on, shouldn't this case study actually be in another chapter?', because it will feature other tactical tools almost as much as it does the tool being discussed in that chapter. Personalized videos at scale appear in several places. Pedigree's AI-driven app is in the packaging chapter (Chapter 19), but it could have featured in content marketing and sales promotion. You will see a lot of this.

What's new in the 7th edition?

In addition to demonstrating the maturing of marketing automation, content marketing, single user experience and the lifetime journey, we are delighted to tell you that we have included materials from the best in the world including America's Larry Kim (Facebook bots and unicorns) and Mark Schaefer (content shock and the human-centred approach to marketing), Banksy (the street artist and his world's greatest PR stunt), Greenpeace, AI companies and generally organizations that use both the left brain (analytics and data) and the right brain (creative thinking) approach to marketing.

We have a broader international range of examples, with world-class campaigns from the UK, Europe, the USA, Ireland, India, Sri Lanka and Brazil.

We have put a lot more emphasis on data and AI in particular. In fact, references to AI and data appear throughout the book. AI is here to stay. As is the clever use of data. We also explore the misuse of data.

We also include the hidden Web and how it was used by the Leave campaign, which was subsequently found to have broken the electoral laws and advertising principles: 'legal, decent, honest and truthful'. We include links to the hidden Web ads that Facebook initially refused to release. You can see the need for data protection, and hence the importance of GDPR is emphasized.

Hence there is a need for, and we encourage, a more responsible approach to marketing, as demonstrated by Mark Schaefer's human-centred marketing. His infographic on p 315 should generate a heated discussion or two.

Finally, the last photo in the book (p 636) includes ethics, which, ironically, might be objectionable to some, but to us it is a brilliant example of using 'owned media' by a small semi-pro football club in the south of England.

The application of the SOSTAC® planning framework has been updated in Part One and applied throughout the second half of the book. Overall, we hope you find this edition more challenging and enlightening than ever before. Read on.

ABOUT THIS BOOK

This book should not be read from cover to cover but rather it should be used as a reference when addressing a particular aspect of marketing communications. The integrated nature of the subject does, however, refer the reader to other chapters and sections that are relevant to the particular area of interest. The anecdotal style, examples, case studies, questions, key points and sections have been carefully structured so that the reader can dip into an area of interest, absorb the information and cross-refer if required. This allows the reader to extract specific answers quickly and easily. This book is designed to entertain as well as inform and so it is hoped that when dipping into a particular area, the reader will be lured into reading more.

Part 1 (see Figure 0.1), Chapter 1 introduces the new thinking and new tools (largely driven by marketing automation, social media, virtual worlds and new analytics tools) alongside 100-year-old business principles that are, surprisingly, much required today. Part 1 continues to build a background to marketing communications by exploring branding, customer relationship management, buyer behaviour and communications theory and how information reduces risk (what information market research can and cannot provide), how to work with agencies and consultancies of all types, moving with the changing business environment, international marketing and ultimately shows how to write a marketing communications plan using the simple SOSTAC® planning framework.

Part 2 covers specific marketing communication tools that marketing professionals have to manage at some time or other. These include selling and sales management (and Key Account Management), advertising, PR, sponsorship, sales promotion (particularly free 'content marketing'), direct mail, exhibitions (all online and offline), packaging, and finally, websites that work and social media that wins. The case studies at the end of each chapter in Part 2 have been carefully selected to show a range of different types and sizes of organizations using various communications tools across a range of different industries and markets. Materials are drawn from both small organizations with small budgets and larger businesses with multi-billion-dollar budgets.

This book should prove useful to anyone interested, or working, in marketing. The reader will discover that all of the communication tools can and should integrate with each other, as shown in Figure 0.2 and explained at the end of Chapter 1. Equally we need to be able to think creatively (right brain) and analytically (left brain) to make better-quality marketing decisions to ensure we satisfy exactly what our stakeholders need, at the right time in the right place amidst the white heat of competition.

It is sometimes difficult to separate and categorize an activity as being one type of tool or another. For example, direct marketing and sales promotions should probably be called 'direct promotions' since they both more than likely involve each other. The chapters are not listed in order of importance. Selling and sales management is not always included in a marketing communications budget but the sales force is a potent form of communication and generally they (or the sales manager) report to the marketing manager. In fact it has been put to the top of the list because all the other chapters thereafter tend to lead into each other.

The successful application of the marketing communications mix is helped by an understanding of communication theory and buyer behaviour theory. Marketing research can provide some practical and specific answers to the questions that the theories generate. This provides the building blocks for the marketing communications plan, which draws upon an understanding of how agencies operate and how different media work. The details of the plan are worked out within the sometimes complex, but always integrated, web of the marketing communications mix (see Figure 0.2). The changing marketing communications environment and international opportunities/threats constantly affect the whole marketing communications mix. The world has moved on since the sixth edition.

Different organizations allocate the same communication tools to different departments/budgets,

FIGURE 0.1 Part One: Background to the communications process

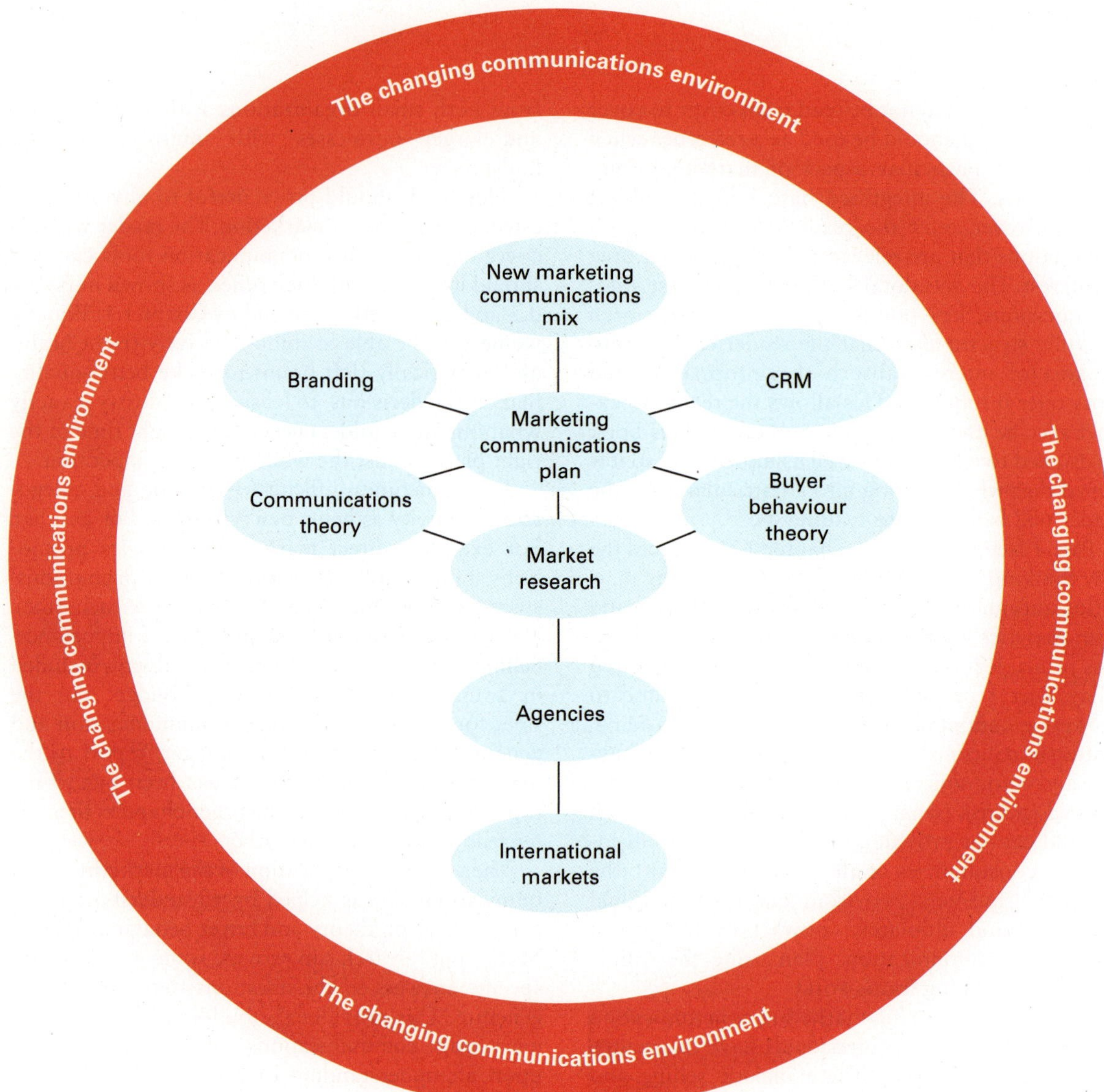

FIGURE 0.2 All tactical communications tools integrate with almost all other communications tools

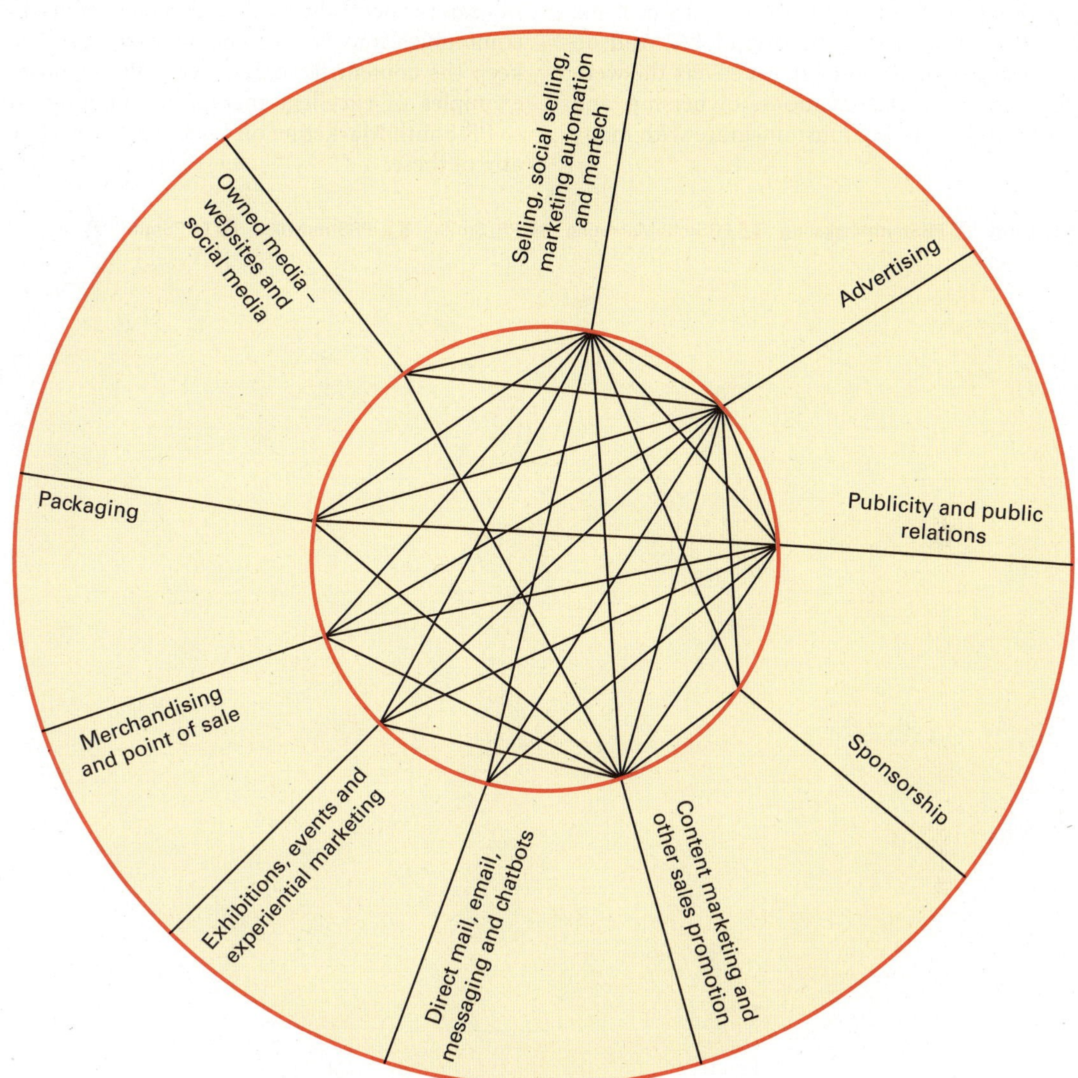

eg exhibitions may be seen to be part of public relations, although the sales team will man the stand and benefit from extra sales. Sponsorship is considered by some to be an extension of advertising, while others consider it to be part of PR. And no one is too sure about whose budget covers the website. Regardless of classifications, ownership and responsibilities, each tool must integrate with many others.

We are always looking to update the material within the book and our readers are invited to contact us with any ideas, suggestions and contributions to the next edition. As our subject of marketing communications is ever changing, we are keen to keep the content fresh and lively. Please post your examples of excellent marketing communications to PR Smith Marketing on LinkedIn or Facebook or any of these:

PRSmith.org PRSmithMarketing PRSmithMarketing PR_Smith PRSmith1000 PRPSmith SOSTAC.org

KEY FEATURES OF THIS BOOK

Learning objectives – these will provide you with an outline of what we will be covering in each chapter.

> **LEARNING OBJECTIVES**
>
> By the end of this chapter you will be able to:
>
> - appreciate the importance of branding;
> - list the stages in building a brand process;
> - avoid the classical branding mistakes;
> - understand why brands need to be maintained.

Case studies – selected to show a variety of different types and sizes of organizations using various communications tools across a range of different industries and markets.

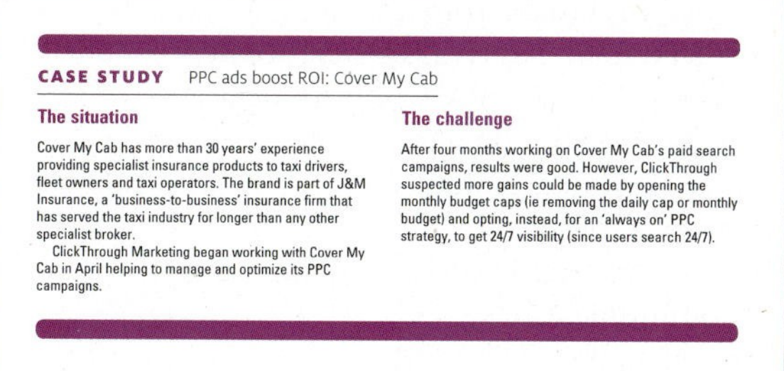

CASE STUDY PPC ads boost ROI: Cover My Cab

The situation

Cover My Cab has more than 30 years' experience providing specialist insurance products to taxi drivers, fleet owners and taxi operators. The brand is part of J&M Insurance, a 'business-to-business' insurance firm that has served the taxi industry for longer than any other specialist broker.

ClickThrough Marketing began working with Cover My Cab in April helping to manage and optimize its PPC campaigns.

The challenge

After four months working on Cover My Cab's paid search campaigns, results were good. However, ClickThrough suspected more gains could be made by opening the monthly budget caps (ie removing the daily cap or monthly budget) and opting, instead, for an 'always on' PPC strategy, to get 24/7 visibility (since users search 24/7).

Key points – a checklist of all the issues covered within the chapter.

> **Key points from Chapter 2**
>
> - Brands help customers and the organizations behind them.
> - Branding is a strategic issue.
> - Branding can create competitive advantage.
> - There brand
> - Brand maint:

Feature boxes – quotes and pertinent points of interest to punctuate the discussion.

> **No brand, no cattle**
>
> The term 'brand' comes from the old Norse verb brandr, which meant to burn, and which eventually became a noun and adjective in medieval English. The noun 'brand' meant flame, fire or torch, and the adjective meant burning, hence 'brand hot'. Animals were marked with red-hot branding irons

Further information – contact information for organizations relevant to the topics discussed.

> **Further information**
>
> Market Research Society (MRS)
> 15 Northburgh Street
> London EC1V 0JR
> Tel: +44 (0)20 7490 4911
> www.mrs.org.uk
>
> Ofcom
> Riverside House
> 2a Southwark Bridge Road
> London SE1 9HA
> Tel: +44 (0)300 123 3000
> www.ofcom.org.uk

Online resources for lecturers – contain PowerPoint slide decks for each chapter, links to videos mentioned in the book plus others, links to PR Smith blog posts relevant to each chapter and questions for each chapter. Go to:
www.koganpage.com/marketingcommunications7

ACKNOWLEDGEMENTS

Danni Adams, Greenpeace
Nico Ainsworth, Colenso BBDO
Kristina Allen, ion interactive
Warren Allot, Photographer
Zaid Al-Zaidy, McCann, London
Mike Backs, Digital Doughnut
Jeremy Baker
Banksy, Courtesy of Pest Control Office
Riccardo Benzo, Managing Expectations
Lacey Berrien, Drift
Tanya Binks, Wild Card
Michael Bland, Author
Sarah Botterill, European Interactive Advertising Association
Adrian Brady, Eulogy
Michelle Brammer, GaggleAMP
JoAnna Brandi, The Customer Care Coach®
Alan Briefel, StratCom
Scott Brinker, ion international
Ged Carroll, Racepoint Global
Joe Carter, Colenso BBDO
Juan Pablo Castro, LanderApp.com
Dr Dave Chaffey, Smart Insights
Mary Pat Clark, Pew Research Center
Alistair Clay, Plan UK
John Coffey, Liberty Insurance
Amelia Collins, Photographer
Keith Curley, Muzu.TV
Emmanuel de Hemptinne, NEO DARWIN
Lucy Edgar, Kantar Millward Brown
Allan Edwards, Ogilvy PR
Jenny Ellery, Saatchi & Saatchi
Jennifer Faughnan, Zip Adventure Holidays
Patrick Foley, Samsung
Annie Fong, Mischief PR
Stuart Fowkes, Oxfam
Luke Frake, Space Between
Alice Franklin, Contagious
Alex Gibson, The Persuaders, Dublin Radio FM
Rob Gotlieb, Muzu.TV
Jonathan Grant, Grenadier Advertising
Mark Grey, Grey Corporate
Gavin Grimes, McBoom
Paul Hague, B2B International
Dr Hansen, Hansen
Chloe Haynes, Cadbury
Christine Hegarty, Road Safety Authority
Neil Hegarty, BMP Optimum
Colette Hiller, Sing London
Kenny Hoang, BlitzMetrics
Teresa Horscroft, Eureka PR
John Horsley, Digital Doughnut
Martin Hutchins, Cambridge Professional Academy
Peter 'Magic' Johnston, MediaZoo Studios
Justin Jones, Digital Marketing Consultant (AI job reduction)
Nigel Jones, Herdman Jones Associates Ltd
Paul Kemp-Robertson, Contagious
Larry Kim, MobileMonkey.com
Jeff Kirk, Corporate Magic
Isobel Kerr-Newell, Saatchi & Saatchi
Helen Lamb European Sponsorship Association
Mike Langford, BT
Basil Long, Kroner Consultants
Jez Lysaght, Green Tomato Cars
Toby Marsden, Survival International
Ian Maynard, Murphy Cobb Associates
Davy McDonald, davymac.com
Paul McFarland, Goldhawk
Gerry McGovern
Sharon McLaughlin, McLaughlin Gibson Communications
Blair Metcalfe, Ogilvy PR
Kevin Miller, Whitehawk FC
Walter Miltenberger, Crystal
Claire Mitchell, Natural History Museum
Matt Monfredi, Photographer
Ian Morton, Happy Tuesdays
Jorian Murray, DDB London
Jasmin Naim, Kogan Page
Orson Nava, Director/Content Producer
Kasia Nieduzak, Greenpeace Comms
Julia O'Brien, Moonshine Media
Deborah O'Dowd, Greenpeace
Brian O'Neill, Freshideas.ie Ltd
Barry O'Sullivan, BBDO Dublin
Paul O'Sullivan, Dublin Institute of Technology
Marie Page, Musicademy.com
Hina Patel, Creating Results From Vision Ltd

Alexandra Phelan, Paddy Power
Jennifer Powell, Jennifer Powell, inc.
Ben Queenborough, Photographer
Suresh Raj, Borkowski
Charles Randall, SAS Solutions
Mark Read, Photographer
Tim Redgate, Tim Redgate Consultancy
Josh Rex, This Is Open
Kevin Roberts, Saatchi & Saatchi
Phil Robinson, ClickThrough
Danielle Sammeroff, Fuse
Dennis Sandler, PACE University
Mark Schaefer, BusinessesGrow.com
Richard Sedley, Seren
Heather Sewell, ICE
Adam Sharp, CleverTouch
Joel Simon, Flickerpix Animations Ltd
Greg Skloot, Crystal
Graeme Slattery, PSG Communications
Dr Meixian Song, University of Exeter, School of Law
Jessie Soohyun Park, Samsung
Tery Spataro, CCG Catalyst Consulting Group
Saffron Steele, Halpern PR
Frances Still, Science Museum Group
Merlin Stone, The Customer Framework
Dr Peter Tan, World Financial Group
Jonathan Taylor, former co-author
Jamie Tosh, Kick4change
Jon Twomey, Student Support Group
Neil Verlander, Friends of the Earth
Salvador Nissi Vilcovsky, Memomi
Gian Walker, Network Co-op Ltd
Steve Wellington, Havavision Records
Todd Wheatland, King Content
James Whelan, James Whelan Butchers
Cameron James Wilson and @TheDiigitals
Jamie Yarborough, BlitzMetrics

Ze's particular thanks: I dedicate this work to my wife, Revital and daughter, Nessa, for their patience and understanding and to my mother and father for their acceptance and nourishment of my being.

Paul's particular thanks to Aran, Cian and Lily and the ever-patient, lovely, Beverley. And lastly, a very special thanks to Owen Palmer (RIP) who gave me my first break in UK Academia and never ceased to inspire and encourage me even long after he had retired.

PART ONE
Communications background and theories

01 New integrated marketing communications

LEARNING OBJECTIVES

By the end of this chapter you will be able to:

- understand the importance of customer-orientated thinking;
- understand the need for both left-brain analytics and right-brain creativity;
- embrace the 4th Industrial Revolution, led by data, AI and digital developments;
- consider 10 hot marketing topics;
- see how everything can fit into a carefully structured marketing plan.

Introduction to integrated marketing communications

Marketing orientation

'What is the single most important reason why you have a website?' is a great question which we ask when we run workshops. Surprisingly, it generates a lot of wrong answers, even from experienced marketers. Answers like: 'to sell more' or 'to give information' or 'to collect email addresses' or 'to show off our new services' or 'to compete with our competitors' and so on. These are wrong answers. They are not the primary reason. There is only one primary reason: 'to help customers'. If you can help your customers better than your competitors you will convert more visitors into sales, and eventually convert more customers into lifetime customers. All the initial answers were product-orientated – about business benefits rather than customer benefits. So keep asking, 'How does this help my customers?'

In fact, Peter Drucker, known as 'the father of business' and arguably America's greatest business author, once said 'The purpose of business is to create and keep a customer'. We go further and say, 'There is only one reason that you are in business: to help customers.' The moment you stop helping customers better than your competitors is the moment you start sliding down the subtle, slippery slope to lost sales and spiralling down towards extinction.

> 'There is only one reason why you are in business. It is, simply, to help customers. The moment you stop helping customers (better than your competitors do) is the moment your business starts to die.'
>
> PR Smith

Customer-centric mission

Now consider one of the world's largest ecommerce companies, yet relatively unknown (to some westerners), they're called Alibaba. Their **customer-centric mission** reads: 'making it easier to do business across the world', and is followed by their motto: 'Customer first, employee second, shareholder third.' Their founder Jack Ma says, 'We know well we haven't survived because our strategies are far-sighted and brilliant, or because our execution is perfect, but because for 15 years we have persevered in our mission.' Meanwhile, top American digital marketing blogger, Brian Solis (2015) insists that businesses must empathize with customers and develop strong missions.

> **Temper profit with customer empathy**
>
> 'Learn to temper (balance) their profit goals with empathy and look at the bottom line as part of a larger mission, doctrine or ethos.'
>
> Solis (2015)

Customer empathy

Success 'requires true empathy for what your customers are thinking and an ability to identify what they want or need even before they do' (Solis, 2015). Apple consistently did it with the Mac, iPhone and iPad. You 'have to see your customers for who they are becoming, not just who they are today', Solis continues. 'This all starts by defining the experience you want your customers to have. How do you want them to feel? What should they share? Define it. Build it.' Building it includes integrating marketing systems, logistics systems, customer relationship management (CRM) systems. Being customer-centric goes beyond the marketing team, it has to be in customer-centric operations also. It also requires a different perspective. Campaigns cannot reach buyers if, say, an advertising campaign is shorter than a buyer's journey.

> **Long-term success – think about customers differently**
>
> 'To succeed means thinking about customers differently as groups of connected people and not simply demographics. It requires a level of leadership that can see something others don't or find inspiration in what others feel or hope to feel. These traits – not the technology itself – are what will define the most resilient companies in the years to come.'
>
> Solis (2015)

Customer experience

Although customers are on a multichannel journey (from websites to offline stores and back to social media, etc), they want a single, well-defined, customer experience across channels. Whether they touch (have contact with) your brand via your mobile site, your website, your app, your in-store display, your staff, your social media, your customer care, telesales, direct mail – it is all one journey for the customer. They want a nice consistent experience, regardless of channel.

Customer service time bomb

Although some companies have managed to improve their customer services, the continual culling of employees and general cost cutting combined with sloppy marketing execution has put marketers on the cusp of a customer revolution. It may well be that the really clever chatbots that learn to become experts and really help customers to find solutions quickly and in a 24/7/365 always-friendly manner will be the winners.

Many customers are angry, irritated, impatient and ready to switch to another brand as soon as something better becomes available. In a word, they are dissatisfied. We have gone backwards in marketing. Look around. Many brands have falling satisfaction scores, sloppy websites, automated telephone queuing, customer service people who can't answer questions and others who simply don't really care. How many bad experiences do customers suffer while seeking service from a utility, a phone company or a bank either on the phone or on a website?

The manager's online banking system: A foreign country he rarely visited

'Recently, I had problems with online banking. After lots of frustration with technical support, I rang my bank manager. In the past, whenever I had a problem he had been extremely helpful and made sure it was resolved immediately. This time around, things were different. "I'm not technical", he told me. He began to talk about his bank's online banking service as if it were a foreign country he had rarely visited. He was behaving like a typical senior manager when it came to IT. He wanted to wash his hands of responsibility. It was not his domain. IT, it seems, is not the responsibility of senior managers or CEOs. They have much more important things to do, obviously.'

McGovern (2010)

Has this changed since 2010?

Combine the sloppy service with customers' lower tolerance levels: less time, less attention and less patience with inefficient service. Don't customers like endless automated telephone queuing systems, robotic rerouting or, if they are lucky, after queuing and rerouting, getting to speak to someone whom they cannot understand, or to someone who cannot solve the problem, who then puts them back into a queuing system? It seems that many brands have gone backwards in marketing.

How many people have had bad experiences online with websites that are confusing, have dead ends or just don't work, sites that waste precious time and cause irritation? And all the time advertising budgets are wasted driving customers to these sites.

Harvard's Ram Charan and business CEO Larry Bossidy many years ago wrote a book claiming that the last source of real sustainable competitive advantage was the ability to execute plans better than the competitors. Called *Execution: The discipline of getting things done* (2002), it highlighted the importance of executing with excellence and passion the small things, the basic things including customer service.

So if companies get worse at marketing then this creates a huge opportunity for those organizations that have a process for listening to their customers, and continually improving and staying relevant.

Nightmare on Banking Street

'I hadn't physically visited a bank in years. However, when I was doing a favour for a friend, I walked into a well-known high street branch in London on a Saturday afternoon to be greeted almost immediately by a friendly-faced customer service clerk, in a nicely branded blazer, who pleasantly informed me that the queue in front of me would take 40 minutes. I thought I had stepped into a time warp. What amazed me was that other customers seemed prepared to queue. Was it always like this? Then it occurred to me that instant automated ATMs, although quick, do effectively ask customers to sometimes stand in the rain, block prying eyes and hidden cameras from stealing your PIN and hope that the muggers around the corner have not seen you yet. Fear has increased in many people's lives.'

PR Smith

A sense of purpose

Ask: 'Why does your brand matter?' If you don't know, and no other colleagues know, then nobody else will care. A sense of purpose at work is important – partly because customers like to buy brands that stand for something and partly because employees like to work for an organization that stands for something more than just making money. Something deeper.

- Johnson & Johnson support nurses; Procter & Gamble support mums.
- In 10 years, **'firms of endearment'** grew collectively at a rate of **1,000 per cent +**
- In 10 years, **Standard & Poor's 500** companies grew collectively at a rate of **122 per cent**

'Find your sense of purpose – your mission – your passion. You simply cannot drive sustained performance and high levels of achievement in one's job and career without being fully engaged and feeling a strong sense of purpose... The common element that often is the spark plug for change and progress is a sense of purpose. We have found this applies to people in the beginning of their careers as much as it does to middle managers and senior leaders.'

Moore (2017)

'It's not about merit, professionalism, or quality. It is about faith, belief, conviction, courage, and meaning. Because the brutal reality of today's new world is this: If you don't stand for something you're dead; it's just a question of when.'

Sisodia *et al* (2014)

'Companies who put purpose and passion at the heart of what they do are blowing away the S&P 500 averages when it comes to their performance.'

Sisodia *et al* (2014)

'Strive not to be a success, but rather to be of value.'

Albert Einstein

100-year-old principles still win today

Despite the emergence of digital body language, marketing automation, programmatic advertising, retargeting, content marketing, multichannel funnels, hyper competition (we'll explore these later), the same old marketing principle remains intact: be customer-centric. It's interesting to see that although customers are changing, technology leaps are rampaging through markets and wonderful new tools are becoming available to marketers, the same basic business principles survive from over 100 years ago. Interpreted by Mark Zwilling (2014), here are the highly successful industrialist (and subsequent philanthropist) Scottish American Andrew Carnegie's top tips (from 1889), which still work today.

Andrew Carnegie's top 10 tips for success:

1. Definiteness of purpose (a real and passionate mission).
2. Master-mind alliance (marketing marriages and strategic alliances).
3. Going the extra mile (help customers).
4. Applied faith (believe in the opportunity you see).
5. Personal initiative (be proactive).
6. Imagination (ability to see opportunities/vision).
7. Enthusiasm (a contagious quality).
8. Accurate thinking (analyse carefully before deciding).
9. Concentration of effort (on key success factors).
10. Profiting by adversity (learn and improve from failure).

Zwilling's (2014) interpretation of Carnegie's tips is worth a read. There are valuable lessons for today's marketers stored in ancient wisdom. For example, arguably the best marketing book ever written is a 2,000-year-old book, *The Art of War*, by the Chinese military strategist, Sun Tzu, who always believed that battles could be won without confrontation. Proper application of intelligence wins wars, often peacefully. A few thousand years later, we (in the West) are getting excited about the power of analytics.

Stop, look at who you are and what your business is for

'If you believe your business is a machine for making you rich, you are going down the wrong road. If you believe your purpose is to make the world a better place, then do so, and wealth will come to you.'

Witzel (2015)

Happiness is a business model

Happy employees want to create happy customers, which helps to generate sales, repeat sales, better margins, bigger profits and ultimately happy shareholders.

Happy employees = happy customers = happy shareholders

'It's possible to "suck the fluffiness out of happiness" and make it real, measurable, and tangible' (Kuppler, 2014). This means clearly defining values that actually create a culture such as integrity and being innovative. Leaders then must ensure everyone is committed to running a values-driven organization in both good times and bad times.

There are different approaches to maintaining those happy values throughout the organization. For example, Zappos ask their employees to summarize what the Zappos culture means to them. These answers are then published unedited (other than typos corrected) in a *Zappos Culture Book* for everyone to see. Capgemini take a different approach to happiness and are committed to creating an environment and opportunities that 'nurture your passions' and 'to love what you do. And if you demonstrate a love or passion for what you do, we'll help you to build the skills and obtain the experience that will empower you to ace your career' (Capgemini, 2018).

Integrating left-brain and right-brain thinking

Analytics (left-brain thinking) and creativity (right-brain thinking) are both necessary in marketing communications to break through the clutter of noise and hyper-competition. 'Relevant creativity' means creating products and services and communications that are always deemed to be relevant (and useful) by your target markets. Although analytics often refers to Google Analytics or similar analytical software, we are broadening the term analytics to include analysing customer and competitor behaviour via all forms of market research.

Analysis builds a foundation for success

As previously mentioned, arguably the greatest marketing book ever is *The Art of War*, written over 2,000 years ago by the Chinese military strategist Sun Tzu (translated by Wing, 1989). Most senior marketers have a copy of it on their shelves. It has become a classic read, particularly for some enlightened marketing managers. Interestingly, confrontation, or war, is seen as a last resort and the best military strategies win the war without any bloodshed. They win wars through intelligence.

'Much computation' or much analysis is required. The better the analysis, the easier the decisions will be later. Decisions about strategy and tactics become a lot easier when you know your customers, your competitors, your competencies and resources as well as market trends. In fact, you need to know your customers and prospects better than they know themselves. Old tools (in-depth discussions) and more contemporary tools like digital body language (analysing click behaviour on your website) both give marketers vital information that helps deliver better messages (more relevant messages), better websites, apps, ads, presentations, sales pitches – you name it.

That's why half of your marketing communications plan should be devoted to the situation analysis. It doesn't have to be at the front of the plan (you can dump a lot of it in the appendices) but the detailed analysis must be carried out if you are to succeed. The first year you do this analysis it will be particularly challenging, but as you find better (and often free) sources for highly relevant information, the analysis gets easier, the intelligent information gets stronger and consequently, you make more informed decisions. This ultimately boosts your results.

More good news – there is a plethora of new listening tools and analytic tools available to marketers. Although traditional market research is still useful, there are faster ways of monitoring online discussions and analysing customers, competitors and spotting trends.

> 'All markets are conversations' declared the influential Cluetrain Manifesto (Levine *et al*, 2000). The subsequent rampant growth of social media since that time confirms the classic Cluetrain vision.

'The old marketing ship is sinking.' All marketers need to monitor, analyse and engage in these conversations because the old 'shouting' model, consisting of pumping out advertising, PR and marketing content through social media channels ('shouting') no longer works as well as it used to.

FIGURE 1.1 The old marketing ship is sinking

SOURCE: Photo courtesy of DavyMac.com

Customers do not always understand their own needs

However valuable market research is, significant creative leaps can sometimes be too difficult for customers to grasp. Therefore, negative customer feedback for innovations (particularly discontinuous innovations/significant innovations) can sometimes be misleading. In some cases, 'Listening too much to customer input is a recipe for a disaster' (Christensen, 2003). 'If I'd listened to my customers, I would have invented a faster horse,' said Henry Ford.

Whoever could have imagined that a device created for engineers to communicate with each other would one day become a global necessity for all young people (text messaging)? Whoever could have imagined that people would walk around with invisible vinyl record players on their heads (streaming music with headphones)? Whoever could have imagined a nation seemingly talking loudly to themselves (hands-free mobile phones)?

Here are some classic quotations that demonstrate how, not just customers, but even experts in their field, could not see the benefit of a significant innovation that subsequently went on to become a massive global success:

Telephone: 'This "telephone" has too many shortcomings to be seriously considered as a means of communication. The device is inherently of no value to us' (Western Union, internal memo, 1876).

Radio: 'The wireless music box has no imaginable commercial value. Who would pay for a message sent to nobody in particular?' (David Sarnoff's associates in response to his urgings for investment in the radio in the 1920s).

Movies (with sound): 'Who the hell wants to hear actors talk?' (Harry M Warner, Warner Bros, 1927).

TV: 'TV will never be a serious competitor to radio because people must sit and keep their eyes glued on a screen. The average American family doesn't have time for it' (*New York Times*, 1939).

PCs: 'I think there is a world market for maybe five computers' (Thomas Watson, Chairman of IBM, 1943).

Home PCs: 'There is no reason for any individuals to have a computer in their home' (Ken Olsen, President, Chairman and Founder of Digital Equipment Corp, 1977).

The Beatles: 'There is no demand for guitar bands' (Decca Records turning down The Beatles, 1962).

Looking back on it, there are many innovations in common use now, the need for which simply did not exist five or ten years ago. This applies to both business-to-customer (B2C) and business-to-business (B2B) markets. As organizations, and marketers in particular, embrace creative thinking, new solutions will emerge and contribute to continued success once we learn to think 'outside the box'.

> **'Seeing what everyone else can see but thinking what no one else has thought'**
>
> 'It's seeing one thing in terms of something else. That eureka moment. You don't have to be a brilliant novelist or painter or musician... it can be about some private matter. It can be about economics. It can be while you are reading a novel, you suddenly make a connection that suddenly gives you an insight that no one else has had. Someone defined science as "seeing what everyone else can see but thinking what no one else has thought".'
>
> Greenfield (2007)

Market research: A fundamental part of Edison's creative process

Despite the lack of vision by many chief executive officers (CEOs) and the challenge of researching innovations (since customers often don't know what they want, particularly with innovations), the United States' greatest inventor, Thomas Edison, used market research creatively in the 19th century. He literally went to homes and places of work and analysed what people did in order to gain insight to invent products that could help them do it better and faster. He looked first for unmet needs and then applied science and creativity to fill them. The first example of Edison's success using a 'needs-first' approach to invention is one we seldom associate with him: document duplication. Post-Civil War newspaper accounts of the rebuilding of the South and the tremendous demand it created for insurance policies led him to think that the insurance business could use some efficiencies. Edison got permission from insurance agents to watch their clerks at work. He saw that most of their day was spent hand-copying documents for each party to the insurance sale instead of selling insurance. Edison realized that if he could invent something that would save both the insurance clerks' and agents' time writing, they could all make more money (Caldicott, 2010). Interestingly, today's top CEOs spend time with customers. In fact Martin Sorrell, CEO of the world's largest communications services group ($66 billion turnover), spends one-third of his time with clients (Rogers, 2014).

Edison combined creativity with customer needs

Thomas Edison was indeed a creative genius, but **it was not until he discovered some of the principles of marketing that he found increased success.** One of his first inventions was, although much needed, a flop. In 1869 he created and patented an electronic vote recorder, which tallied the votes in the Massachusetts state legislature faster than the chamber's old hand-tab system. 'To Edison's astonishment, it flopped. Edison had not taken into account legislators' habits. They don't like to vote quickly and efficiently. They do like to lobby their fellow legislators as voting takes place. Edison had a great idea, but he completely misunderstood the needs of his customers' (Caldicott, 2010). He learned from his failure the relationship between invention and marketing. Edison learned that **marketing and invention must be integrated.** 'Anything that won't sell, I don't want to invent', he said. 'Its sale is proof of utility, and utility is success.' He realized he needed to put the customers' needs first and tailor his thinking accordingly, despite any temptation to invent for invention's sake. His change of mindset led to tremendous success (Caldicott, 2010).

Anything that won't sell, I don't want to invent

'This was said by Thomas Edison, best known for the light bulb. He was a prolific inventor, registering an extraordinary 1,093 US patents and 1,293 international patents. The six industries he pioneered between 1873 and 1905 – and their offshoots – are estimated to be worth more than $1 trillion today. He was one of the world's first market researchers.'

Caldicott (2010)

Nurture creativity

Look at the more successful companies out there; they nurture creativity. It is not accidental. The importance of creativity is recognized, encouraged and nurtured. Listen to what some of these organizations say:

- 'Either you'll learn to acquire and cultivate [creative people] or you'll be eaten alive' (Leon Royer, Executive Director, 3M).
- 'My job is to listen to, search for, think of, and spread ideas, to expose people to good ideas and role models' (Jack Welch, former CEO, GE).
- 'The first step in the creative process is hiring the best of the best. This is how HP maintains an environment that crackles with creativity and intellectual spirit' (Mary Patterson, former Director of Corporate Engineering, Hewlett-Packard).
- 'To make money in a disinflationary period takes real innovation and creativity at all levels of the corporation' (Michael Fradette, Manufacturing Consultant, Deloitte & Touche).

Creativity – in the mushy word category?

'For many, the word "creativity" is as soft as "nice". Such people had better revise their lexicons.'

John Kao, Harvard Business School Professor (1997)

Creativity is a blood sport

The reality is that creativity is hard work. And managing creativity is, as Harvard's Professor John Kao says,

> if anything, even harder work. It has nothing to do with finding a nice safe place for people to goof off. Managing creativity is much more difficult. It means finding an appropriate place for people to contend and collaborate – even if they don't particularly want to. It means scrounging from always-limited resources. It means controlling the uncontrollable, or at least unpredictable, process. Creativity, for many, is a blood sport.
>
> Kao (1997)

Nurturing creativity and channelling it in the right way is hard work. As Ed Catmull said in the *HBR*, 'If you want to be original, you have to accept the uncertainty, even when it's uncomfortable, and have the capability to recover when your organization takes a big risk and fails. What's the key to being able to recover? Talented people!' Such people are not so easy to find (Catmull, 2008).

The *Forbes* columnist, Greg Satell (2013), agrees and emphasizes that creative collaboration is absolutely essential: 'Creativity is no longer a "solo act." Today, collaboration is not just important, it's absolutely essential and that's why digital marketing is so hard.'

Create added value and relevant content

Digital can create so much added value for the customer. Take a look at the website of the Sistine Chapel: **http://www.vatican.va/various/cappelle/sistina_vr/index.html**. This is the best website in the world (well it's my favourite and it's only got two buttons). Arguably, this digital experience is better than the real-world 'product experience'. The Sistine Chapel website allows visitors to look at Michelangelo's paintings for as long as they want, climb up the walls and examine the stunning art. They can go right up to the ceiling and even see where Michelangelo painted donkey ears on some of the bishops that he didn't like. All of these things you cannot do if you visit the chapel. Many people tell me that the digital experience is better than the real-world visit (in which you have to keep moving, cannot take photos and it's busy with the hum of other tourists). The digital experience

FIGURE 1.2 Some would say the Sistine Chapel digital experience beats the real thing

SOURCE: Photo courtesy of The Sistine Chapel Digital Experience, **www.vatican.va/various/cappelle/sistina_vr/index.html**

has beautiful choral music playing, you can do a 360-degree pivot, climb the walls, explore the ceiling – it is simply amazing.

A brand needs to be wherever its customers are and when they have a need. Find out what they really want and then help them. People searching for information about the Vatican or Rome might welcome a virtual tour of where customers go (offline and online). Be creative with messages and media/channels.

Find creative partnerships that take the brand's message and products to its target audience in a completely different environment (wherever the target market is) and just when they need help. The Internet of Things (IoT) can bring your experience to far wider audiences via the appropriate IoT partners. Be where customers go, online and offline. There may be ways of reaching them through collaborative partnerships both offline and online.

> **Creativity will fuel growth in the future**
>
> 'The search for value has led companies to seek efficiency through: downsizing; rationalizing; right-sizing approaches that eventually result in a diminishing level of return. But what will fuel growth in the future? Growth will come through mastering the skills of creativity and making creativity actionable.'
>
> Professor John Kao, Harvard Business School

Be relevant to customer needs – if a brand gives customers useful, relevant information at just the right time, it strengthens the brand relationship. Convenience is in demand. Being creative always helps. But being convenient and relevant is even more important, as customers only want and listen to whatever is relevant (or interesting). Constant monitoring of their changing needs is critical. Whether it is at the lowest levels of interaction, ie product ratings, reviewing products or creating user-generated content, engagement helps to keep customer attention and to nurture stronger relationships.

> 'Anyone who has never made a mistake has never tried anything new.'
>
> Albert Einstein

Nurture the inquisitive mind

> We asked the former President of McKinsey's Japan and highly respected author Kenichi Ohmae if he could sense whether a company was going to be successful. Was there something he could smell or sense when he was in an organization that suggested this company was going to be a winner? He said 'yes' and went on to explain that 'if a company is not afraid to ask questions, if everyone asks questions from the CEO down to the office boy, if they ask questions like 'Why do we do it this way?' then this company will succeed.
>
> Ohmae (1996)

So the inquisitive mind is an essential ingredient for future success.

This was echoed by Susan Greenfield of the University of Oxford when speaking at the Third European Futurists Convention in Lucerne in 2007. She confirmed the need for creativity and the need to challenge old dogma:

> So creativity, this eureka connection (neuronal connection) that triggers a new insight in yourself and others, is all about forging connections and so providing environments that will foster a challenging of dogma, of old stale connections, a forging of new ones that trigger even more connections that give a meaning and an insight to both yourself and others.
>
> Greenfield (2007)

> **Love them or hate them, shopping malls are also observatories**
>
> Kenichi Ohmae spends hours visiting shopping malls to observe human behaviour. People are fascinating; the way they behave, move, talk, walk, shop, browse. Shopping malls can provide 360-degree wide screen interactive entertainment (observing customers), or to many real marketers, malls provide real consumer behaviour insights.

Marketing communications is part of customer experience

Marketing communications (marcomms) is more than just communicating and promoting. Marcomms is now impacting the customer experience as it adds value to the overall customer experience (CX). This has not gone unnoticed by the world's best marketers. In 2007 Unilever moved its digital marketing out of the media mix and into the marketing mix (WARC, 2007). It realized that its digital budget was part of the overall marketing mix, rather than just part of its media spend (marketing communications mix).

The search for added value is now relentless, whether through new features or more likely through enhanced online experiences, social media sharing or simply the addition of features to a product or service never dreamt possible before the arrival of smart phones, apps and increasingly virtual and augmented reality experiences. For example, Gibson Guitar's app includes a guitar tuner, a metronome and a chord chart, all of which are extremely useful for any guitarist. Kraft's iFood Assistant delivers recipes and a feature that creates a shopping list that automatically includes the ingredients for the chosen recipes. It even identifies the locations of nearby grocery stores and which aisles stock the items.

Think of '4Es instead of 4Ps' (Rothery, 2008) from the old marketing mix. A product is an experience (including online), place becomes 'everyplace', price becomes 'exchange' and promotion becomes 'evangelism' or advocates. Alternatively, promotion is just morphing with product as communications seek to engage customers with relevant added-value experiences.

Product, place and promotion are morphing

Location marketing identifies customers with mobile phones in specific places and then offers highly relevant promotions. You can see how digital can morph all of the elements of the old marketing mix with a single digital offer containing, say, a price reduction (price), and/or add some additional useful information about using the product (product), which makes it so easy and convenient to buy (place) – all by sending a timely message (promotion).

Integrate data, staff and communications

Inbound and outbound with online and offline communications delivers higher impact and more cost-effective 'joined-up marketing'. **Customer data needs to be integrated** since customers are touched by many contact points or 'touchpoints' such as social media, point of sale, ads, email, etc. Customers need a consistent (integrated) message. Equally, companies are collecting information from many different customer touchpoints (website registration, website body language, customer service, social media and much more). It's a gold mine if they collect and store it safely in a data warehouse and then use it all to build better profiles of customers. Customer data needs to be integrated (this a major challenge for any organizations with older legacy databases). Data usage (collection, storage, retrieval) and privacy statements must adhere to the General Data Protection Regulation (GDPR).

Staff need to be integrated. As we said earlier, 'happy employees = happy customers = happy shareholders', which means that every customer-facing member of staff is a brand ambassador. They have to feel part of it. They have to integrate with the brand values (sometimes their recruitment policies use the brand values to select people with those values). This requires internal marketing (investing in internal communications, motivation and training). If you get this right, staff can become your most potent communications tool. One salesperson made his own product demonstration video showing him eating his dinner off the subway floor after he had cleaned it with his floor-cleaning equipment (Figure 1.3).

FIGURE 1.3 This employee was sufficiently motivated that he made his own 'shockvertising' video for his company

Marketing communications have to be integrated for two reasons. First, unintegrated databases cause many problems and complications, as there is no single picture of the customer and therefore customers receive many different types of experiences and messages from the brand. This confuses customers and dilutes the brand's presence in the marketplace. Second, as communications morph into customer experiences, all communications need to be integrated to deliver a consistent experience.

Death of the colouring department

Marketers have got to get used to analytics and be creative in new ways. A lot of 'old' marketing has had too much emphasis on just marketing communications. This is a weakness.

This may have led to communications strategies that shouted about product benefits. Today, marketing strategies ask 'How will customers engage with us and each other?' This leads to the bigger question: 'What kind of customer experience are marketers creating?' This in turn brings marketers back to the quintessential marketing question: 'How do we help customers?' This is, for example, the ultimate reason why any company has a website and/or an app. In fact, this is often forgotten, but helping customers is the only reason a company exists in the first place.

These kinds of questions move marketers beyond communications, into customer experiences, customer relations, new product development processes, service processes and, of course, brand evaluation, which affects market capitalization. This, ultimately, invites marketers back into the boardroom, hopefully speaking the language of the board. Analytics can tell us sales plus cost per visitor, cost per enquiry, cost per order, return on investment (ROI) and a lot more. Sentiment scores aggregate what the market is saying about your brand and net promoter score (NPS) tells you how likely customers are to recommend your product/service. Boards like numbers and hence analytics have opened the door to the boardroom for marketers.

Stop calling marketers 'the Colouring Department'

'Not so long ago I was invited into a major global bank and given the brief: "To stop the board from referring to the marketing department as the colouring department."'

PR Smith

Enter the boardroom opportunity

Marketers can and should demonstrate to any board of directors how marketing can create two sources of sustainable competitive advantage by creating two assets: brands and data. Brand appears on the balance sheet, yet data does not. This is despite what *The Economist* proclaimed on its front page on 6 May 2017:

> 'The world's most valuable resource is no longer oil, but data.'

Hence data will soon be a company's most valuable resource/asset. Facebook, Amazon and the BAT Boys (Baidu, Alibaba and Tencent) would perhaps agree. Yet it doesn't appear on a balance sheet. Does this suggest that financial directors are not reporting on reality (if they omit data from appearing as an asset on the balance sheet)?

A well-integrated website helps to grow a database of customers and prospects, as well as boosting a brand's value as more and more relevant 'services' and 'sizzle' are added to the customer experience. Well-managed databases create a mini-monopoly of customers and prospects, and can be used with a variety of channels to communicate intimately with customers (email, snail mail, messaging, telephone calls and personal visits).

Although the value of a database can be quantified by estimating customer lifetime values, the development of clever algorithms (and other assets derived from data science) and the customer database itself do not appear to be represented on too many balance sheets (if any at all).

Marketers missed their chance to enter the boardroom when the internet first emerged in the early 1990s. They also missed the social media opportunity. Perhaps now with the emergence of the 4th Industrial Revolution (read on), marketers will strike and seize the opportunity to participate in boardroom discussions involving the future of the business.

The opportunities presented by artificial intelligence (AI), IoT, marketing automation, Big Data, virtual reality (VR) and augmented reality (AR) and the threats from hyper-competition will force many businesses to ask how they can harness these developments to create competitive advantage. This will trigger another question: 'What business are we in?' Or, better still, 'What business should we be in?' Marketers must be comfortable with everything we have discussed here and finally take their place in all boardrooms.

Why marketing was kept out of the boardroom

'Seeing marketing as a series of distinct activities has been the reason that marketing has become more marginalized over the last 15 years, because it has been positioned as managing communications rather than managing the whole business orientation.'

Jenkinson (2004)

The 4th Industrial Revolution

This is a new beginning. I know we have said this before. The internet came along in the 1990s, and we said this would change everything. It did. Then social media came along it was suggested in 2005 that social media was the biggest change since the Industrial Revolution. And now we have even bigger changes coming via AI, machine learning, automation and a proliferation of technology developments, economic (power) shifts, new social structures. Effectively, we are seeing the start of the 4th Industrial Revolution. With it come some wonderful opportunities and some dangerous risks.

There has never been a time of greater promise or potential peril

'The changes are so profound that, from the perspective of human history, **there has never been a time of greater promise or potential peril**. My concern, however, is that decision-makers are too often caught in traditional, linear (and non-disruptive) thinking or too absorbed by immediate concerns to think strategically about the forces of disruption and innovation shaping our future.'

Professor Klaus Schwab, founder and Executive Chairman of the World Economic Forum (2017)

Positive or negative revolution

This revolution has the potential to be good or bad for both economies and societies. It could **improve the quality of life** across the world, raise income levels, and reduce illness and starvation. In fact, it might even help us to prepare better for natural disasters and 'potentially also **undo some of the damage wrought by previous industrial revolutions**' (Marr, 2018).

On the other hand, it could create **more polarization between rich and poor** with increased social tensions resulting from the socio-economic changes with polarized segments of: 'low-skill/low-pay' and high-skill/high-pay'.

Marr continues:

> **first-adopters of technology** are the ones with the financial means to secure it, and that technology can catapult their continued success, **increasing the economic gaps**. Some jobs will become **obsolete**. Additionally, the changes might develop so **swiftly**, that even those who are ahead of the curve in terms of their knowledge and preparation, might not be able to keep up with the ripple effects of the changes... world governments need to

plan carefully and regulate the emerging new AI capabilities to ensure our security.

Marr (2018)

Companies must invest in data tech and data skills to survive

Regardless of positive or negative 4th Industrial Revolution scenarios, to survive, organizations must invest in:

- technical infrastructure and data analysing capabilities;
- staff with new data skills who embrace new tech and are marketing orientated;
- leaders capable of harnessing these dramatic business trends.

Organizations that are not smart and connected will soon fall behind a new wave of competition, known as hyper-competition, which is one of the three unstoppable business trends. Read on.

Our jobs today might be dramatically different in the not too distant future

'As professionals, we need to embrace change and realize that what our jobs are today might be dramatically different in the not too distant future. Our education and training systems need to adapt to better prepare people for the flexibility and critical thinking skills they will need in the future workplace.'

Marr (2018)

Data-driven businesses

'The world's most valuable resource is no longer oil, but data.'

The Economist (2017)

Data is, without doubt, a source of distinctive competitive advantage. The better your database (if it is clean and relevant, and adheres to the GDPR), the bigger your advantage. Data scientists can extract extra value from data and ultimately enhance customer experiences and improve marketing efficiency (more later). Some business giants (eg GE and Siemens) now promote themselves as 'data firms'.

Data is the lifeblood of any business. Data can determine the success or failure of a business. A lack of data can destroy a business. How long could your business continue if all your customer data was hacked, infected, destroyed, stolen or sold? Having taken years to build a good, clean database, it could be destroyed in seconds. It is a fragile asset.

Organizations today must start becoming data-driven businesses. Data can inform our decisions, ie make better decisions. For example, we could split test an email campaign version A against version B or use AI to sift through large amounts of data to give us customer insights to identify hidden customer needs so we can deliver more relevant offers that simply can't be ignored.

Although databases are assets, accountants do not include 'data' as an asset on balance sheets. Other forms of data (eg data used to create profiles or data that triggers an automated event) can have even more value to a business.

Data is now a multi billion dollar market. US companies will spend almost $20 billion by 2018 to acquire and process consumer data (Dance *et al*, 2018). Data can also be used to win elections (see 'How Trump won', Smith, 2017b) and even control society (see 'Your social credit score might change your life', Smith, 2019a).

Digital transformation

A detailed digital transformation plan warrants its own separate detailed plan outlining what digital developments are emerging, who's using them to gain competitive advantage, setting transformation objectives, and developing a strategy or phases to roll out these digital changes, right down to who will do what.

Equally, a standard annual digital marketing plan should refer to new digital tools and techniques being introduced, leveraged and integrated.

Digital transformation requires many skills (as well as the technology). Table 1.1 shows the five stages to becoming fully digitally transformed. The strategic choice that then emerges is whether to build a newly structured marketing department or employ external agencies.

TABLE 1.1 The capability maturity model helps to plan your digital transformation

Stage → Criteria ↓	1. Initial (Directionless)	2. Managed	3. Defined (Structured Testing)	4. Quantified (Customer-centric)	5. Optimized
A. Strategic Approach	No Strategy	Prioritized Marketing Activities	Defined Vision & Strategy	Whole Business-aligned	Agile Strategic Approach
B. Performance Improvement Process	No KPIs	Volume-based KPIs	Quality-based KPIs + Last click Attribution AB tests + CTAs	Value-based KPIs + Weighted Attribution Multivariate Testing	Lifetime Value KPIs
C. Management By-In	Limited	Verbal Support but Inadequate Resourcing	Sponsorship & Increased Investment	Active Championing & Full Investment	Integral Part of Strategy Development
D. Resourcing & Structure	No specific skills	Core Skills Centralized or agencies	Centralized Hub & Dedicated Resources	Decentralizing & Reskilling	Balanced Blend of Marketing Skills
E. Data & Infrastructure	Limited/No Customer Database	Separate Data, Tools & IT Services	Partially Integrated Systems & Data Mktg Automation Remarketing	Integrated Systems & 360 Data Sources Social CRM	Flexible Approach To Optimize Resources 360 customer view
F. Integrated Customer Comms	Not Integrated	Core Push Activities Synchronized	Integrated Inbound Approach	Integrated, Personalized, Paid Owned Earned	Constant Optimization to Help Customers & Max CLV & ROI
G. Integrated Customer Experience	Website Not Integrated	Desktop & Mobile Support Not Personalized	Partially Personalized Experience 90 day planning programme of testing	Integrated Personalized, web, email Social, Ads + Realtime social media & Shared CX	Full Contextual Personalized Experiences & Recommendations

SOURCE: Carnegie Mellon University, adapted by Dave Chaffey

NOTES: This matrix was adopted from the original Carnegie Mellon Capability Maturity model for systems (CMMI) to become the Capability Maturity Model Integration (since adapted by Dave Chaffey of Smart Insights). This is the same Andrew Carnegie whose business principles we mentioned at the beginning of this chapter.

Martech stack

XYZ + IoT, VR, AR, MA

Marketers stack various technologies together into what we call a martech stack. This integrates various tools to give a single 360-degree view of prospects and customers and in turn allows marketers to use the tools to build customer relationships across multiple channels.

Martech stacks, once integrated can automatically:

- collect customer data, build profiles and customer personas while integrating with any existing CRM systems;
- identify and nurture leads with tailored personalized communications (in real time);
- predict which segments to prioritize and target;
- distribute and schedule content across multiple platforms to existing customers at different stages in the buyer lifecycle;
- measure and report on customer feedback and track campaigns.

Five things every martech stack should have

Martech stacks have to be tailored so that the stack is integrated. Here are Almitra Karnik's five features that every stack should have (Karnik, 2018):

1. **Integration:** An efficient martech stack isn't a list of tools you use; it's a series of integrated tools that work well together. There's a big difference. Look for solutions that have application programming interfaces (APIs) that integrate with your core technology like your CRM, marketing automation, website optimization and analytics platform.
2. **Single source of truth for data:** Every tool comes with its own analytics, which can be a challenge when stacking tools together. To maintain data integrity and limit confusion, look for a single source of truth, or a centralized data collection stream that offers a complete customer view. Having the ability to connect multiple systems though webhooks and APIs is gold.
3. **Real-time information:** One of the benefits of a martech stack is the ability to get real-time customer information and act on it. This kind of data-driven marketing gives brands a competitive edge as they work to meet the needs of customers faster and more efficiently than others. Make sure your stack has fast processing and real-time computing available.
4. **Data that provides attribution:** To make sure you're getting the best ROI, you need access to data that tells you where your money is best spent. In other words, you need data that attributes your success to a specific marketing initiative. Make sure your stack provides this kind of insight so you can spend your budget wisely.
5. **Ability to reach customers anytime, anywhere:** Your martech stack should include tools to help you engage customers across multiple channels. You want to create a holistic, omnichannel experience for customers that provides the right information at the right time on the right platform.

Here come the bots

Chatbots may be bodiless helpers answering questions on customer service platforms or they can be built into human-looking robots. Do remember that **not all chatbots are equal** – some hinder and some help. Some chatbots will damage your business, with 70 per cent of customer questions not being answered (Orlowski, 2017). However, 'good chatbots' are painstakingly built using decision trees to cover all options and natural language processing (NLP) to identify the customer's real intent behind their questions, followed by rigorous testing and modifications. AI and bots, in particular, takes patience and expertise (and lots of people, if you are developing your own AI).

Better bots simply help customers, in a conversational way, to find answers more quickly and therefore boost conversions. If a bot makes life more convenient for a customer, then they are doing their job. Bots help customers to 'get the job done'. Moving from chatbots to robots, we now see Pizza Hut Japan with robot waiters serving happy customers and Hilton McLean in Canada having a concierge bot helping guests to find local entertainment, dinner and transport.

There are many types of bots. You can see a selection of bots including shopping bots, slack bots, marriage bots, research bots, cooking bots, Boris bots, election bots, research bots, lead generation bots and sales bots in 'Here come the clever bots – bursting with artificial intelligence?' (Smith, 2016), or you can see a video of Sophia, the world's first bot that became a citizen delivering her chilling reply to a serious ethical question in 'Here come the really clever bots – where AI meets customer needs' (Smith, 2017a). Bots are developing quickly and it is hard to tell the difference between China's first fully fledged TV news presenter bot and a human presenter (Smith, 2018).

AI and data analytics

As AI spreads into every aspect of business, it is also spreading into every aspect of marketing. This includes using AI to improve the CX at every stage of the customer journey:

- **Product/service:** Layers of **data-driven added-value services** – eg recipes streamed on a fridge or the Chinese robot news presenter who works 24/7/365 without sleep, holidays or sick pay.
- **Customer service chatbots** on a screen or in a personal assistant (like Alexa) or a beautiful, friendly and extremely helpful 'real' plastic robot who answers all your questions, remembers your name (and needs), makes helpful suggestions and more – 24/7/365. But, remember, 'not all chatbots are equal' – some help and others hinder the brand.
- **Promotions/comms:** AI helps create headlines for ads, emails and can even create total pieces of content delivered via rule-based marketing automation to help, say, lead generation, as well as personalization of, say, hundreds of thousands of tailored videos with individualized and personalized messages.
- **Place/distribution:** Companies like Amazon use AI in their world-class warehousing, logistics and distribution, from robots to drones to self-driving vans. Alibaba now have a fresh food chain that delivers fresh food orders not just the same day, but the same hour (ie within 30 minutes)!
- **Processing orders** and customer service issues, eg insurance companies using AI to help process customer claims. Customers are now recorded on their own smart phone, uploaded to the company and analysed by AI facial recognition to determine whether they are telling the truth.
- **Identifying needs:** AI can help marketers learn things even the most creative humans can't. By using NLP, for instance, companies can determine whether a consumer is interested in sports cars without the person ever having said so (Gregg *et al*, 2018).
- **Forecasting/predicting** which segments will give the best results from various campaigns.

Using AI, marketers can track and understand a customer's behaviour and, consequently, a customer's needs (sometimes even before the customer is aware of his/her own needs). AI can then **make smart suggestions** about which particular content, service support or type of product an individual actually needs during each stage of the **customer journey**.

A word of caution regarding Super AI

We need to be cautious about Super AI and building Super AI that is far more intelligent than any humans. It can have some great benefits, and some dire consequences. Scientists and researchers can become so engrossed in their work that they could unleash an uncontrollable Super AI bot that could endanger the human species. Governments, regulators, professional bodies and marketers need to be aware of this as we delve into AI and Super AI.

AI + UC

Not only must we be aware of AI issues like bias being excluded and ethics being included in the development of any AI, we must also be aware of consequences or, more specifically, of unintended consequences (UC). For example, if a CEO of a major corporation asks its Super AI board bot to 'eradicate world hunger' this would be highly irresponsible, as perhaps the most cost effective option that the bot generates is to eradicate the human species (and thus eradicates world hunger) and decides to do so as quickly as possible in order to be as cost-effective as possible.

'Your animal life is over. Machine life has begun.'

This shocking article by Mark O'Connell in the *Guardian* in 2017 was shared over 32,000 times. He believes that we are close to inventing a machine that replicates the human brain and keeps a version of us alive forever. Transhumanists aim to improve our bodies and minds to the point where we become something other and better than the animals we are. Ray Kurzweil, for one, is a prominent advocate of 'mind uploading'. Meanwhile, O'Connell highlights a joint venture company called OS that is investing in 'entrepreneurs working towards quantum leap discoveries that promise to rewrite the operating systems of life' (O'Connell, 2017).[1]

We have to pay attention, develop an interest, and influence the development of AI and, in particular, Super AI.

10 hot marketing topics

1. The customer lifetime journey

Repeat business is where the real money is. Estimates suggest that selling to an existing customer is at least six times more profitable than selling to a new customer. Hence, we are interested in the customer's lifetime journey. Some marketers refer to the 'customer journey'. We believe this journey is more than a one-off journey where a customer sees some social media or an ad, becomes aware of a brand, learns more about it via searching online, visits a website, downloads an app or perhaps visits a location; the marketer's job is to ensure the right communications are offered at the right touchpoints. This work continues after the initial sale – in fact a welcome strategy thanks the customer for their initial purchase, helps the customer with tips and ideas to ensure maximum satisfaction, and keeps in touch with relevant communications (and offers) throughout the life of the customer.

2. Customer experience and company mission

The CX is the result of the customer journey and is inextricably linked to the company mission. The mission is your organization's raison d'être. The reason it exists is to help customers in a particular way. To improve the CX, start with your mission statement. Soccer.com's mission statement is to 'inform, inspire and innovate'. Their ecommerce director says 'It's not enough for us to sell products. Selling products is the basics of what we do. But it's not the core of what we do. We want to be there for our customers. We want to be there with a full experience for our customers and establish an authority in the space of soccer' (Nicastro, 2018). So all CX (both online and offline) should support the organization's mission.

'To improve customer experience, start with morale, not technology.'

Shoop (2018)

3. Content marketing

Most organizations already have a lot of marketing content (market research, white papers, presentations, speeches, articles, videos, photos, graphics, as well as social media content). Some potential content is less obvious but nevertheless easy, such as book reviews (if written by the CEO). Frequently asked questions (FAQs) collected by customer service teams can be a rich source of content recreated into '10 most popular questions', '10 questions you've got to answer', '10 reasons why' or '10 things you've got to know'. These can be converted into quizzes with multiple answers, or self-assessment widgets. Speeches – record them and then edit them into shorter clips. Slide shows – share them on SlideShare. Re-use the graphics. The key is to work out what customers need first (avoid content shock; see p 453), then create a content plan and calendar and deliver it. Being creative is great but it has to be relevant/interesting to the customer. One problem remains. Most customers do not fully know what they want or what they might like in the future (as they cannot imagine it).

4. Personalization

Different clusters of customers (segments) have slightly different needs. Even the same customer has different requirements as he/she moves through the customer lifetime journey. Basic personalization ensures all comms are personalized and more advanced personalization ensures exactly the right tailored message is delivered to the right customer and the right time via the right channel. Even videos can, today, be personalized on a large scale (more of this later). Tools like Adobe Target and Optimizely collect and analyze data from social media listening, consumer behaviour and previous purchases to generate profiles and eventually personalized content.

> **You're in the market for a new car**
>
> You visit a manufacturer's website. You can't complete your research just then because you have to attend a meeting, so you leave your email address requesting more info. When you get home and are browsing on your tablet, you receive an email about the vehicle you're interested in. You like what you see and make an in-person appointment to test drive the vehicle. You then get a text message confirming your appointment (Hall, 2019).

Remember not to be too greedy (asking for too much information). Sign-ups increase if you only ask for an email address. After that, you can take customers on a data collection journey: offering tips, advice, coupons, points or experiences in exchange for personal data each time you give the prospect something in return.

Customers fear that the data they give to companies will be misused by someone. But if benefits look favourable (purchase confirmation, new special offers, discounts, countdown offers, nudges, more convenient airport check-in, loyalty points, live chats, etc) and a level of trust is established, then many are happy to share their data.

5. Omnichannel marketing

'All-in-one technology' solutions essentially manage marketing communications across multiple channels throughout the entire lifetime customer journey, eg by integrating and automating email, social media, content marketing and mobile marketing solutions. So omnichannel marketing ensures customers get content they actually want exactly when they need it via their preferred channel. The marcomms becomes a seamless, consistent helpful contact. Note that this is all about helping customers throughout the customer lifetime journey, which is another underlying theme in this book.

6. Influencer marketing

Influencers continually influence your market. A comment, like or share can win attention, enquiries and even sales. Influencers can have a much bigger impact than any of your other marketing efforts. Identify and connect with influencers in your industry. You may not be able to afford to pay (money, free products, place ads on influencers blog) or even collaborate with all the influencers. Sometimes you can just focus on a small number of 'nano influencers' (with, say, 5,000 followers). A hundred nano influencers with a combined audience of over 1 million could be very effective and cheaper than working with one influencer with 1 million followers.

TABLE 1.2 Personalization

You get (ie you ask for)	You give (a personalized response)
DOB	Offer a birthday treat
Gender	Customized homepage with relevant offers
Waist size	Aaargh, too creepy! Forget it

Either way, you have to ensure the influencers understand your brand, your values and your messaging and then continually monitor their performance.

7. Agile marketing (agile and optimized)

After the marcomms omnichannel contact (message or content) has been delivered, hopefully, customers and prospect customers engage with the messages, which then triggers the analytics to automatically tell the marketers what's working and what's not so they can do more of what works and do less of what doesn't work so well. Marketers today operate as agile marketers, constantly testing and therefore optimizing. One note of caution: analytics reveal reach and engagement levels but do not reveal other criteria such as brand building or, say, awareness building. Proper market surveys (online or offline) are required to do this.

8. Marketing automation

Marketing automation uses click behaviour (or digital body language) to trigger an automatic email, or an automatic dynamic page swap (varying the content that is served on the next page), or an automatic alert sent to a salesperson if the clicks suggest a hot prospect. Click behaviour includes monitoring whether an email is opened or a video is fully watched and determining what the next contact will be. It is all rule-based (if they click this they then see that). Even writing a comment on a social media platform can trigger a personalized video (containing the words they wrote). See personalized videos (p 167). We also explore the martech stack to identify different types of technology can help boost marketing performance.

9. The human touch

The human touch, now more than ever before, works some marketing magic. Despite tightly targeted relevant and personalized automated content and extremely clever bots doing great jobs, the human touch delivers something extra special. Some kind of quaint emotional connection. So, whenever possible, get out there and meet customers, ask them questions, listen to them, converse with them, reward them, thank them. The owner of the business says hello to customers, the mechanic takes time to give some advice, the chef meets customers, the salesperson gives the customer a personal call – the human touch is still very much appreciated.

10. Accelerated change

Consider **accelerated brand creation.** Once upon a time it took two generations to build a major brand; now it takes just a year or two if you get it right. Look at Amazon, Uber and Twitter. Once upon a time it took several generations to acquire 50 million users. Facebook did it in less than one (in fact Facebook acquired 100 million in one year). This simply could never have happened 10 years ago. Radio took almost 40 years to reach 50 million users, while TV took 13 years, the internet four years, the iPod three years, Facebook one year and the iPhone less than a year to get 100 million users.

Shorter brand lives

Meanwhile, the average lifespan of companies and their brands is also shrinking from 67 years in the 1920s to just 15 years (by 2012) as per the S&P 500 index of leading US companies and according to Professor Richard Foster from Yale University. Back in 2012, Professor Foster estimated that, by 2020, more than three-quarters of the S&P 500 would be companies that we had not yet heard of (Gittleson, 2012).

Accelerated returns (AI & Super AI)

The 21st century will achieve 20,000 times the progress of the 20th century according to the American Futurist **Ray Kurzweil,** who suggests that the progress of the entire 20th century would have been achieved in only 20 years at the rate of advancement in the year 2000. In other words, by 2000, the rate of progress was five times faster than the average rate of progress during the 20th century.

Kurzweil believes that another 20th century's worth of progress happened between 2000 and 2014 and that another 20th century's worth of progress will happen by 2021, in only seven years. A couple of decades later, he believes a 20th century's worth of progress will happen multiple times in the same year, and even later, in less than one month. This is the **Law of Accelerating Returns.** Kurzweil believes that the 21st century will achieve 20,000 times the progress of the 20th century! So embrace technology developments (Smith, 2019b).

Hyper competition

Competition can come from your own country or overseas, as all markets are global markets today. Competition can also come from outside your category of business (eg Google Wallet and Apple Pay compete with bank services). Disruptive start-ups (like Uber and Airbnb) can come out of anywhere at any time once they see an opportunity to use data more cleverly (this will perhaps occur increasingly frequently with AI). You must improve or get left behind.

Platform companies are investing in Big Data, AI, IoT and other tools to improve operations, assets, customer experiences and competitive positions. It's happening. Look around you. Amazon is now (January 2019) the largest private company in the world and is busily wiping out the traditional high street. Then we have the BAT platform companies: Baidu, Alibaba (who own AliPay with its 500 million customers) and Tencent (who own WeChat with its 1 billion customers). These SuperApps help you to buy, pay, use, consume just about everything in China. Is there a sector that Amazon, Apple, Google or BAT could not enter?

You have simply got to keep improving as existing and new competitors will be continually improving.

> **30 minute delivery for online shoppers**
>
> 'Alibaba's Hema is a supermarket chain that promises fresh produce delivered to online shoppers within 30 minutes. Tencent is trying to empower companies that compete with Alibaba including Carrefour, the French retailer, but it cannot supply the level of Big Data support that its competitors can.'
>
> Li Guoferi, Chinese tech commentator with a wide following on WeChat, referred to by Kynge (2018)

Hyper-competition is borderless and category-less

Global boundaries are falling; the Iron Curtain has been swept aside, the Berlin Wall torn down and the Chinese gates flung open partly by political movement, partly by aggressive businesses seeking growth overseas and partly by the internet giving instant global access driven by customers who want to buy products and services from anywhere in the world whenever they want. And, all the time, category-less competitors quietly step across old borders.

Once upon a time, supermarkets sold groceries and petrol stations sold petrol. Now petrol stations sell DVDs, fresh coffee, groceries, gambling and a lot more, while grocery stores sell petrol, garden furniture, car insurance and soon legal advice (including DIY divorce kits), as well as groceries. Clear-cut business categories are evaporating.

Powerful category-less brands take more 'share of wallet'. Customers trust some brands sufficiently to try other products from the same brand name. This is 'share of wallet'. Growth for most US companies was forecast to come from share of wallet rather than growth from finding new customers. Enlightened boardrooms understand the power of the brand, its access to share of wallet and its impact on the balance sheet. Combine category-less, fast-moving competitors with borderless markets and you get hyper-competition. No market or business can ignore it.

Competitors can target your visitors, your fans, your employees

Both Facebook and LinkedIn enable competitors to target their ads by age, interests, location or company. They can target their ads at your employees (LinkedIn), your fans (Facebook) and even your website visitors may soon become accessible.

The need to wholeheartedly adapt to and embrace change is akin to the need for frogs to stay out of the kitchen. If you take a frog and put it into a boiling pot of water, it will jump out somewhat blistered, but it will survive. If, on the other hand, you put a frog in a cold pan of water and slowly raise the temperature it will boil to death. Business is similar. No one will change your environment so rapidly that you have to change your behaviour immediately. It just changes continually.

> **Competition in your pocket**
>
> 'Amazon and eBay mobile apps invite customers, while in another store, to scan in a product to see how much cheaper they can get it via the app (plus they deliver it to your door). So retailers have to have even better apps to compete inside your hypercompetitive pocket. Meanwhile Amazon can target ads at customers within a radius of one mile of a competing store.'
>
> Smith (2014a)

Amidst this hyper-competition some CEOs wake up in the middle of the night in a cold sweat worried about their value chain and wondering who is unpicking the lock on it. Teams of analysts and MBAs from Boston to Beijing analyse industry after industry, sector by sector, to find businesses with a weak link in their value chain that would benefit from a third-party supplier fulfilling a piece of the chain. Most CEOs know some parts of their value chain, whether production, logistics or after-sales, are more profitable than other parts. When they get an offer to replace the weakest link with a higher-quality link (or service) at lower cost and seamlessly linked by web technology, many CEOs find this a very attractive proposition.

> 'We have only two sources of competitive advantage: the ability to learn more about our customers faster than the competition, and the ability to turn that learning into action faster than the competition.'
>
> Jack Welch, former CEO, GE

As the company moves from a value chain to a seamlessly connected value network, CEOs are forced to consider the most basic of questions: 'What business are we in?' This can only be answered by asking another very basic question: 'What do customers want now and in the future and what is our sustainable competitive advantage (SCA)?'

> **30,000 illegal competitors**
>
> 'Some competition is legal and some not so legal and vast! The Premier League is targeting 30,000 illegal, competing, streaming sites. This can require a lot of resources.'
>
> iSport Connect (2012)

When we ask CEOs what is their SCA, we usually get answers that include patents, product differentiation, cost efficiencies, superior service, stronger brand and sometimes distribution channels. Most of these can be, and are being, attacked. Two major sources of SCA, if managed carefully, are the brand and customer relationships – inseparable, you may say.

However, many companies damage these two critical assets. Sloppy customer service and negative CRM destroy brands (see Chapters 2, 3 and 20 for more on this.) Despite the importance of CRM, many companies are still sitting on a customer service time bomb. And it's ticking. Those who ignore it will be left behind, in the same way that those who ignore the golden opportunity presented by social media will also be left behind. Those who embrace it, seize the opportunity, develop rigorous processes around the new technologies and continually strive to find and satisfy customer needs will survive and thrive.

> **Who are the survivors?**
>
> 'It is not the strongest of the species that survives, nor the most intelligent that survives. It is the one that is the most adaptable to change.'
>
> Charles Darwin

Creative destruction

Sony's famous president and co-founder, the late Akio Morito, once said: 'My job is to make our products obsolete before competition does.' These sentiments were recently echoed by an interesting American author, Brian Solis, who said that 'resilient companies intentionally break their business models in anticipation of what customers want and need. For example, the "sharing economy" – companies like Uber, Airbnb, TaskRabbit and other services that allow people to rent or share their cars, homes or skills' (Solis, 2015). These resilient companies recognize evolving consumer values and aspirations.

> **Anyone with vision and empathy can upend entire industries**
>
> 'Anyone today has the power to disrupt entire industries with a single, smart idea. Most companies are built to keep things from going wrong, not to try to break things apart. Creative disruption becomes a business strategy to either invest in or acquire the very things you feared, rather than simply protecting what it is you have. Companies identify and develop products, processes and philosophies that allow

them to flourish at first but later cause stagnation... paralyzed by their success.'

Solis (2015)

'What brought us success in the past will unlikely be enough to bring us success in the future.'

HBR (2017)

There is no doubt that the world of marketing is in its most interesting and exciting period – if you have an open mind. Change must not be feared, but rather embraced, while remembering basic principles like customer orientation, lifetime journeys, etc. Figure 1.4 is an interesting vision by American digital columnist and CEO of Wordstream and Mobile Monkey, Larry Kim, of what marketing skills will be required from marketers.

FIGURE 1.4 The many faces of a unicorn marketer

SOURCE: Illustrated by Larry Kim, **https://mobilemonkey.com**

One thing that will remain constant is the structure of the perfect plan, whether it is a business plan, a marketing plan, a digital marketing plan, a project plan, a campaign plan or even your own personal plan. SOSTAC® planning framework works every time, all the time, both now and in the future. So let us explore SOSTAC®.

The perfect plan: SOSTAC® planning framework

There are many approaches to writing marketing plans, some far more complicated than others. The SOSTAC® approach (see **http://prsmith.org/SOSTAC/**) simplifies marketing plans and was voted in the top three marketing models in the Chartered Institute of Marketing's centenary poll. We will explore it in detail elsewhere.

- Situation analysis (where are we now?).
- Objectives (where do we want to be?).
- Strategy (how do we get there?).
- Tactics (the details of strategy, eg the marketing mix and communications mix).
- Action (execution – checklists, guidelines, processes including internal marketing).
- Control (are we getting there? – metrics and measurement – daily, monthly).
- + 3Ms – the key resources: men and women (human resources), money (budgets) and minutes (timescales).

The old marketing mix (McCarthy, 1960) comprises product, price, place, promotion (4Ps) and the 'service mix' comprises people, processes and physical evidence (bringing it up to 7Ps). However, digital blurs the lines and morphs the mix (eg social media is part of the product experience, promotional reach, physical evidence and place/distribution) – see the next section. Meanwhile Table 1.3 shows the communications mix – the 10 tactical communications tools, both offline and the online equivalent.

TABLE 1.3 The communications mix: 10 tactical tools, offline and online

Advertising	Interactive ads, pay per click keyword, display ads, remarketing/retargeting
Public relations	Online editorial, newsletters, ezines, discussion groups, viral marketing
Sponsorship	Sponsoring online events/sites service
Sales force/agents/telemarketing	Virtual sales staff, affiliate marketing, web rings, links/chat
Exhibitions, events and conferences	Virtual exhibitions, virtual events, webinars
Direct mail	Opt-in email and eNewsletter
Retail store or office HQ	Website (SEO and markeing automation opportunity)
Word of mouth	Social media platforms, review platform (eg reevoo.com), forums
Sales promotion	Content marketing, incentives, rewards, online loyalty schemes, competitions
Merchandising and packaging	e-tailing, QR codes, augmented reality, virtual reality (real packaging can be displayed online)

Top 10 tips for world-class marketing communications

1. Develop credibility before raising visibility.
2. Continually ask 'Does my website/platform help visitors (better than the competition)?'
3. Continually ask 'What am I doing to bring visitors back?'
4. Stop thinking about campaigns and think about customer lifecycle and continued engagement.
5. Develop a process of listening and responding to customers.
6. Reward customers who are socially positive with your brand.
7. Build a culture that worships customer knowledge.
8. Build a constant beta culture (constant optimization, analysis and ROI analysis where possible).
9. Ask great questions.
10. Embrace change and be creative – plus invest in internal marketing.

Key points from Chapter 1

- Is this business going places?
- What's your process of listening and responding to your customers?
- Why do you have a website?
- Do people ask good questions?
- Do they embrace change?
- This is the beginning of a new era in marketing amidst hyper-competition.
- There is an opportunity for marketers to take a seat on the board and drive a marketing culture.

Endnotes

1 Extracts from 'Your animal life is over. Machine life has begun. The road to immortality' (Mark O'Connell, *Guardian*, 25 March 2017): 'At some point, you become aware that you are no longer present in your body. You observe – with sadness, or horror, or detached curiosity – the diminishing spasms of that body on the operating table, the last useless convulsions of a discontinued meat. The animal life is over now. The machine life has begun. This, more or less, is the scenario outlined by Hans Moravec, a professor of cognitive robotics at Carnegie Mellon, in his 1988 book *Mind Children: The future of robot and human intelligence*. [...] It's a belief shared by many transhumanists, a movement whose aim is to improve our bodies and minds to the point where we become something other and better than the animals we are. Ray Kurzweil, for one, is a prominent advocate of the idea of mind-uploading. [...] Bryan Johnson, who had sold his automated payment company to PayPal a couple of years back for $800m and who now controlled a venture capital concern called the OS Fund, which, I learned from its website, "invests in entrepreneurs working towards quantum leap discoveries that promise to rewrite the operating systems of life". [...]That scan then becomes a blueprint for the reconstruction of the subject brain's neural networks, which is then converted into a computational model. [...] "You can be anything you like," as an article about uploading in *Extropymagazine* put it in the mid-90s. "You can be big or small; you can be lighter than air and fly; you can teleport and walk through walls. You can be a lion or an antelope, a frog or a fly, a tree, a pool, the coat of paint on a ceiling".'

References and further reading

Aarons, C, Edwards, A and Lanier, X (2009) Turning blogs and user-generated content into search engine results, Marketing Vox and Nielsen BuzzMetrics, *SES Magazine*, 8 June

Barhat, V (2018) China is determined to steal AI crown from US and nothing, not even a trade war, will stop it, CNBC, 4 May

Beck, S (2010) Make your product work for your brand: Why what you're selling has become your primary advertising channel, *Financial Times*, 4 May

Bird, D (2008) *Commonsense Direct and Digital Marketing*, 5th edn, Kogan Page, London

Brogan, C (2009) The serendipity engine, www.delicious.com/chrisbrogan/casestudy (archived at https://perma.cc/32C8-CC43)

Caldicott, S (2010) Invention and marketing: Joined at the hip, *Media Week*, 28 April

Capgemini (2018) Finding purpose in passion and what it means to 'ace' your career at Capgemini, 23 July

Catmull, E (2008) How Pixar fosters collective creativity, *Harvard Business Review – The Magazine*, September

Chaffey, D and Smith, PR (2013) *Emarketing Excellence*, 4th edn, Routledge, Abingdon

Charan, R and Bossidy, L (2002) *Execution: The discipline of getting things done*, Crown Business, New York

Christensen, C (2003) *The Innovator's Dilemma*, Harper Business Essentials, New York

Collins J (2001) *Good To Great*, Random House, London

Dance, G, LaForgia, M N and Confessore, N (2018) Interactive advertising bureau, *New York Times*, 16 December

Earls, M (2002) *Welcome to the Creative Age: Bananas, business and the death of marketing*, Wiley, Chichester

eConsultancy 2015 Quarterly digital intelligence briefing: digital trends [online] https://econsultancy.com/reports/quarterly-digital-intelligence-briefing-2015-digital-trends/ (archived at https://perma.cc/PEW8-G2G3)

Edelman, D (2014) Mastering digital marketing, McKinseys Insights & Publications [online] www.mckinsey.com/insights/marketing_sales/mastering_digital_marketing?cid=other-eml-nsl-mip-mck-oth-1407 (archived at https://perma.cc/A9JR-TKN5)

Fletcher, W (2010) author, lecturer and former chairman of the Royal Institution in conversation with PR Smith

Forrester (2013) www.forrester.com

Garvey, D (2002) BT ignite, *Marketing Business*, March

Gittleson, K (2012) Can a company live forever? BBC News, 19 January

Goldberg, C (2013) Marketing on mobile: Why is this platform different? *High Tech Communicator*, 3 June

Grande, C (2007) Cannes diary: Six of the best by Carlos Grande, *Financial Times*, 24 June

Gray, R (2013) Retail revolution, *The Marketer*, March/April

Greenfield, S (2007) The future of brain – the brain of the future, Third European Futurists Convention, Lucerne

Gregg, B, Heller, J, Perrey, J and Tsai, J (2018) The most perfect union: Unlocking the next wave of growth by unifying creativity and analytics, *McKinseys*, June

Hall, E (2010) In Greece, Kraft scores a hit for Lacta chocolate with crowdsourced film, *Advertising Age*, 24 March

Hall, J (2019) Marketing automation trends to pay attention to for 2019, *Forbes*, 8 November

HBR (2017) Competing in 2020: Winners and losers in the digital economy, *Harvard Business Review*, 25 April [online] https://hbr.org/sponsored/2017/04/competing-in-2020-winners-and-losers-in-the-digital-economy (archived at https://perma.cc/6YL3-V6KY)

Hoffman, D (2009) Managing beyond Web 2.0, *McKinsey Quarterly*, July

iSport Connect (2012) Premier League to clamp down on illegal streams after 30,000 sites taken down last year [online] www.isportconnect.com/index.php?option=com_content&view=article&id=13758:premier-league-to-clamp-down-on-illegal-sreams-after-30000-sites-taken-down-last-year&catid=36:football–soccer&Itemid=42 com (archived at https://perma.cc/ZM7Z-ZFZE)

Jenkinson, A (2004) The bigger picture, *Marketing Business*, March

Kao, J (1997) *Jamming: The art and discipline of business creativity*, HarperCollins, New York

Karnik, A (2018) The origin of the martech stack and how to build one that drives growth, *Forbes*, 27 April

Kennedy, J (2009) App-fab, *Marketing Age*, November

Kuppler, T (2014) Inspiring passion and purpose, or happiness as a business model, *TLNT*, 22 May

Kynge, J (2018) Smart money, *Financial Times*, 30 August

Levine, R *et al* (2000) The Cluetrain Manifesto [online] www.cluetrain.com (archived at https://perma.cc/9EGQ-TK2U)

Lilley, A (2007) Why Web 2.0 adds up to a revolution for our industry, *Media Guardian*, 1 October

Manyika, J (2008) Google's view on the future of business: An interview with CEO Eric Schmidt, *The McKinsey Quarterly*, September

Marr, B (2018) The 4th Industrial Revolution is here – are you ready? *Forbes*, 13 August

McCarthy, J E (1960) *Basic Marketing. A Managerial Approach*, Irwin, Homewood, IL

McGovern, G (2010) Time is (still) money: Increasing employee productivity (Part 1) [online] www.gerrymcgovern.com (archived at https://perma.cc/HW4U-EUMY)

McGovern, G (2014) Customer-centric and easy-to-use is the new business model (The Alibaba story) [online] http://gerrymcgovern.com/customer-centric-and-easy-to-use-is-the-new-business-model-the-alibaba-story/ (archived at https://perma.cc/9CDH-NRFC)

McKinsey (2009) How companies are benefiting from Web 2.0, McKinsey Global Survey results, national customer satisfaction scores, Technology Office, *McKinsey Quarterly*, September

Mell, J (2013) IBM: What does social business mean? *Bright Talk*, 10 April

Moore, K (2017) How to increase your performance by finding your purpose, *Forbes*, 3 August

Nicastro, D (2018) 9 key takeaways from the DX summit 2018, *CMS Wire*, 16 November

O'Connell, M (2017) Your animal life is over. Machine life has begun. The road to immortality, *Guardian*, 25 March

O'Dea, A (2008) Innovation, *Marketing Age*, September/October

O'Reilly, L (2015) Now advertisers can use beacons to make the shoes you were looking at inside a physical store follow you around the internet, Business Insider [online] http://uk.businessinsider.com/total-communicator-solutions-unacast-beacon-retargeting-2015-1?r=US#ixzz3QIfHL8sj (archived at https://perma.cc/R847-2ZWX)

Ohmae, K (1996) Video interview with PR Smith, The Marketing CDs [online] https://prsmith.org/ (archived at https://perma.cc/8LKG-MEEW)

Orlowski, A (2017) Facebook scales back AI flagship after chatbots hit 70% f-AI-lure rate, *The Register*, 22 February

Qualman, E (2009) Statistics show social media is bigger than you think, Socialnomics [Online] http://socialnomics.net/2009/08/11/statistics-show-social-media-is-bigger-than-you-think/ (archived at https://perma.cc/LBH7-QK2P)

Ram, A (2018) Artificial intelligence research boosted by £300m of public money, *Financial Times*, 26 April

Roberts, K (2009) in conversation with PR Smith, The Worshipful Company of Marketors, The Great Hall at Barts, St Bartholomew's Great Hall, 17 November

Roberts, K (2010) Video interview with PR Smith [online] https://prsmith.org/ (archived at https://perma.cc/8LKG-MEEW)

Rogers, D (2014) Praise for the underdog, *PR Week*, Oct

Rothery, G (2008) The matchmaker, *Marketing Age*, November/December

Ryan, D and Jones, C (2009) *Understanding Digital Marketing*, Kogan Page, London

Safco, L and Brake, D (2009) *The Social Media Bible*, Wiley, Hoboken, NJ

Satell, G (2013) How to build an effective social marketing strategy, *Forbes*, 6 October

Schwab, K (2017) *The Fourth Industrial Revolution*, Currency

Scott, D (2009) *The New Rules of Marketing and PR*, Wiley, Hoboken, NJ

Shoop, T (2018) To improve customer experience, start with morale, not technology, Feds say, Nextgov, 21 November

Sisodia, R, Sheth, J and Wolfe, D (2014) *Firms of Endearment: How world-class companies profit from passion and purpose*, 2nd edn, Pearson Education, London

Smith, PR (2014a) Social listening skills [online] http://prsmith.org/blog/ (archived at https://perma.cc/67JZ-HYWA)

Smith, PR (2014b) The rise and fall of owned and earned but not paid media – world cup marketing wars? [online] https://prsmith.org/2014/06/27/the-decline-of-owned-but-not-earned-nor-paid-media-world-cup-marketing-wars/ (archived at https://perma.cc/Q9J5-FC8X)

Smith, PR (2016) Here come the clever bots – bursting with artificial intelligence? 16 July [online] http://prsmith.org/blog/ (archived at https://perma.cc/67JZ-HYWA)

Smith, PR (2017a) Here come the really clever bots – where AI meets customer needs, 8 November [online] http://prsmith.org/blog/ (archived at https://perma.cc/67JZ-HYWA)

Smith, PR (2017b) How Trump won (using a SOSTAC® analysis), 20 January [online] http://prsmith.org/blog/ (archived at https://perma.cc/67JZ-HYWA)

Smith, PR (2018) AI driven TV news presenter, 14 November [online] http://prsmith.org/blog/ (archived at https://perma.cc/67JZ-HYWA)

Smith, PR (2019a) Your social credit score might change your life, 15 January [online] http://prsmith.org/blog/ (archived at https://perma.cc/67JZ-HYWA)

Smith, PR (2019b) The SOSTAC® guide to your perfect digital marketing plan [online] http://prsmith.org/blog/ (archived at https://perma.cc/67JZ-HYWA)

Solis, B (2015) Crossing the experience divide: Creating positive, lasting experiences is a crucial mandate for any brand, Technology of Us [online] http://technologyofus.com/ (archived at https://perma.cc/PX8D-AZ93)

Statista (2014) Statistics and facts about MMO gaming, July [online] www.statista.com/topics/2290/mmo-gaming (archived at https://perma.cc/6QHY-RR6V)

The Economist (2017) The world's most valuable resource is no longer oil, 5 May

WARC (2007) Unilever changes online focus, 25 June

Wing (1989) *The Art of Strategy: A new translation of Sun Tzu's 'The Art of War'*, Broadway Books, Danvers, MA

Witzel, M (2015) Philip Kotler turns gaze from marketing to capitalism's flaws, *Financial Times*, 2 April [regarding Kotler's 2015 book *Confronting Capitalism*, Amacom]

Zwilling, M (2014) Ten rules for business success survive a century, *Huffington Post*, 17 December [online] www.huffpost.com/entry/ten-rules-for-business-su_b_6000998 (archived at https://perma.cc/496E-9Q6W)

Further information

Advertising Association
7th Floor North
Artillery House
11–19 Artillery Row
London SW1P 1RT
Tel: +44 (0)20 7340 1100
www.adassoc.org.uk

Chartered Institute of Marketing
Moor Hall
Cookham
Maidenhead
Berkshire SL6 9QH
Tel: +44 (0)1628 427120
www.cim.co.uk

CIPR
4th Floor
85 Tottenham Court Road
London W1T 4TQ
Tel: +44 (0)20 7631 6900
www.cipr.co.uk

Communication Advertising and Marketing Education Foundation Limited (CAM Foundation)
Moor Hall
Cookham
Maidenhead
Berkshire SL6 9QH
Tel: +44 (0)1628 427120
www.camfoundation.com

Incorporated Society of British Advertisers
12 Henrietta Street
London WC2E 8LH
Tel: +44(0)20 7291 9020
www.isba.org.uk

Institute of Promotional Marketing Ltd
70 Margaret Street
London W1W 8SS
Tel: +44 (0)20 7291 7730
www.ipm.org.uk

International Organization for Standardization (ISO)
Chemin de Blandonnet 8
CP 401
1214 Vernier, Geneva
Switzerland
Tel: +41 22 749 01 11
www.iso.org

Marketing Society
8 Waldegrave Road
Teddington
Middlesex TW11 8GT
Tel: +44 (0)20 8973 1350
www.marketingsociety.com

Public Relations Consultants Association
82 Great Suffolk Street
London SE1 0BE
Tel: +44 (0)20 7233 6026
www.prca.org.uk

02
Branding

LEARNING OBJECTIVES

By the end of this chapter you will be able to:

- appreciate the importance of branding and why it is a strategic issue;
- list the stages in building a brand process;
- avoid the classical branding mistakes;
- understand why brands need to be maintained.

Introduction to branding

What is a brand?

A brand is an intangible, legally protectable, valuable asset. It is how a company or product is perceived by customers (or the target audience). It is the image, associations and inherent value customers put on your product and services. Brands include intangible attributes and values. For a brand to be successful, its components have to be coherent, appropriate and appealing to consumers. A brand is a promise to the customer. A brand also embraces vision, values and personality (see 'Brand components' later in this chapter). A brand is far more than just a logo or a name (this is just brand identity). It is the complete customer experience; the integrated sum of all the marketing mix and the communications mix from products to customer service, from packaging to advertising, from rumour to discussion. The last two components are less controllable, from a brand management perspective, but they can nevertheless be influenced, as good brand management participates wholeheartedly in social media too. So a brand is everything a customer (or stakeholder) sees, feels and experiences about a product or service (or organization). A brand is the 'magical' difference between many competing products and services.

> **A (favourable) consensus of subjectivity**
>
> 'Because brand reputations exist only in the minds of their observers – and all observers are different... the strongest brands are those that enjoy what's been called "a (favourable) consensus of subjectivity". And that's when their brand managers, in the widest sense of that phrase, should be most warmly congratulated. They didn't build those brands themselves; but they fed such enticing titbits to their audience that their audience gratefully did the rest.'
>
> Millward Brown Optimor (2010)

The power of branding

How do brands become so powerful that they control economies, determine corporate takeovers, or make customers pay almost 1,000 per cent price premiums (Coca-Cola vs Asda cola)? How do brands become the most valuable asset in a company, determining the whole financial value of a company and driving corporate takeovers? How do brands create sustainable competitive advantage? What makes people all around the world hand over their hard-earned cash for the same brand whether in Taiwan or Tokyo, Kashmir or Carlisle? Today, the power of branding is such that brands defend organizations from competitors, nurture customer relationships, and boost sales, profits and balance sheet assets.

Customers benefit from brands

So we know how brands help businesses, but how do they help customers? What do they do for customers? Brands save customers time, reduce their perceived risk and fulfil their aspirations. Now consider each benefit.

Brands save customers time

Brands help customers' busy lives by saving them time, helping them to find goods and services more quickly. Imagine trying to buy books or DVDs on the internet if you couldn't remember the name of Amazon or CD WOW. Or it could be beans in the supermarket or mortgages on the high street. Unilever's chairman, Niall FitzGerald, calls a brand 'a storehouse of trust which matters more and more as choices multiply' and we face what David Ogilvy once called 'the misery of choice'. People want to simplify their lives and simplify their decision-making.

Brands reduce perceived risk

A strong brand is an implicit guarantee or promise of consistent quality, image and style. A brand is built on trust. Customers trust the promise made in the advertisement and on the pack. Customers form relationships with brands. Brands, in turn, provide a reassuring sense of order. Brands provide a safe and trusted option. Would you buy from someone you didn't know? Customers would prefer to reduce the amount of time and energy involved in decision-making. That's one of the reasons why brand extensions are valuable. The brand is an implicit guarantee or promise. Customers trust the promise made in the advertisement and on the pack.

Brands satisfy aspirations

Brands give status and recognition. Brands reflect aspirations, images and associations that are carefully gleaned from in-depth customer motivation research. This is compounded by our search for identity and beliefs. 'In an irreligious world, brands provide us with beliefs', says Wally Olins of Wolff Olins. Some brands unconsciously create a sense of belonging from their cultish quality. In a way, buying and consuming brands actually defines who we are. Brands signal our affiliations. 'You are what you shop.' Brands reflect aspirations and act as a badge of self-image or desired self-image.

Do brands fill the vacuum left by the decline of organized religion?

'In the developed world, they [brands] are seen by some to have expanded into the vacuum left by the decline of organized religion.'

Economist (2001)

Consider the magic marketing formula: identify needs; reflect them; deliver/satisfy them. Remember, brands need to continually do this. Think about what needs Coca-Cola advertising reflects. It reflects people's own aspirations, so that when they buy a can or a case of Coca-Cola they actually buy a slice of their own aspirations (plus a product whose promise of refreshing cola is consistently delivered anywhere in the world).

Business advantages from branding

Brands create sustainable competitive advantage from hyper-competition, boost relationships, boost sales, boost profits and boost balance sheets. Why would any managers not nurture their brand very carefully? The truth is that many do not (see 'Customer service time bomb' in Chapter 1). However, consider these individual benefits of nurturing strong brands.

Brands create sustainable competitive advantage

Brands will be, for many organizations, the critical success factor in the hyper-competitive 21st-century marketplace. Strong brands create sustainable competitive advantage. For the first time in the history of business, the most powerful barriers to competition are no longer controlled by companies but by customers. The old barriers are falling. Factories and even access to finance are not as powerful barriers as those erected inside customers' minds. Only a few chosen winners are allowed inside. These are the successful brands with which customers have relationships. Successful brands build differentiators.

The CEO of one of the world's greatest brands, Coca-Cola, reputedly once said: 'They can take everything we have, our machinery, our plants, our distribution – as long as they don't take our brand – and we will be able to rebuild our organization in six months.'

For many years now more people in Britain have trusted top brands than trust the church. In fact Heinz and Nescafé were trusted more than the church, the police and Members of Parliament (Croft, 1998, in Reynolds *et al*, 2004). How come British people give their credit card details over the internet to an unknown, invisible American on the other side of the Atlantic? How come Americans pour down their throats water from an unknown source in France? Brand trust in Amazon and Evian is strong. However, more recently, brands have been losing some of their trust ratings. The Reputation Institute's RepTrak report suggests that brands are facing their biggest trust crisis since the global recession hit in 2008 (Stewart, 2018).

Brands control people and brands control economies

'What gives brands their power to influence – if not quite control – people's purchasing decisions and thus their power to influence – if not quite control – modern economies?'

Fletcher (2010)

Brands differentiate a company's products or services and help them to stand out from a crowd. Brands are often the primary source of competitive advantage and a company's most valuable strategic asset. All markets tend towards commodities (as patents run out and the competition catch up and copy others). Brands protect and defend a business from competition, as they differentiate the product by adding perceived value. This creates barriers to entry for potential new competitors that are constantly tempted to enter the new borderless and category-less market space.

Chinese president visits a brand before visiting the president

'When visiting the United States, President Hu Jintao of China chose Microsoft's Bill Gates as his first visit, followed the next day by a visit to President Bush. The *International Herald Tribune* headline read "Chinese president's itinerary for US visit: Gates first, Bush later".'

Yeong and Yu (2006)

This was a seminal moment in the history of brands.

Some years ago it was suggested that two-thirds of the stock market capitalization of US companies was attributable to intellectual assets (brands, patents and know-how). That's a massive $4.5 trillion. One-third of global wealth is accounted for by brands (Clifton, 2004). It is probably a lot more today.

Brands boost relationships

Brands create (mostly unconscious) relationships between the user and the brand. Brands add a subtle meaning to the act of consumption. We allow these brands into our homes and offices and into our lives because they generally mean something to us all. They represent something. At the heart of any successful brand proposition there is a human dimension. That's why brands have personality, values and associations. Brands used to be just a seal of quality. Today brands have emotional connections that differentiate them. Brands provide reassurance to customers and differentiation from competitors. Brands save customers time by being easily recognizable and providing a reassuring sense of order in an increasingly destabilized and chaotic world. Brands inspire loyalty, trust and continuity. Brands are built upon a platform of reliable quality. As in any relationship, a brand's promise must never be broken.

Brands are even used to pigeonhole people: 'He drives a Porsche and drinks Pimm's.' A person's entire life can be effectively categorized by his or her use of brands. Some brands are even definitive, eg 'He is the Rolls-Royce of hosts.'

'Coca-Cola sells more because our love of a particular brand is as important as our love of a flavour.'

Ronay (2004)

Brands boost sales

Brands help customers by making their purchasing process easier. Brands are easier to recognize and to associate with quality; it is easier to understand their benefits, and they are less risky than unknown commodities. Brands encourage repeat purchases and brand relationships, which in turn boost sales. Strong brands are easily recognizable and build single-minded awareness, ensuring they have a greater chance of being included in the customer's 'considered set' of possible purchases or, better still, 'preferred purchases'. Brands inspire loyalty, trust and most importantly continuity, providing a reassuring sense of order in an increasingly chaotic, insecure and fast-changing world. Established brands also provide a platform from which to launch other products under the same brand names, thereby increasing share of wallet.

Brands boost profits

Brands, rightly or wrongly, can command premium prices, which results in increased profits, which consequently allows more money to be spent on better (relevant and tested) communications with clearer messages – which continually strengthens the brand. For example, in the same store, Coca-Cola charges a price premium of almost 1,000 per cent for its 1.75 litre bottle priced at £1.85 (compared to Asda's 2 litre bottle at £0.15). Incidentally, Coca-Cola knows the long-term power of its brand and invests in it accordingly (eg it invested $65 million in 12 years' Olympic sponsorship until 2012). Profits are also boosted by repeat purchase customers, who generate on average five times more profits than sales to new customers. In online sales, this figure rises to 10 times more profitability (Eltvedt and Flores, 2005). Strong brands also boost margins, as they increase bargaining power within the trade.

Brands boost balance sheets

As well as affecting politics and economics, brands affect company valuations. Brands can indicate future profit trends and assist decisions and investor relations. Today, brands are recognized as assets, and more companies are putting brand values on to their balance sheets. Figure 2.1 shows a list of brand values taken from the Millward Brown BrandZ survey (2018). The 2010 survey revealed the world's first $100 billion brand – Google. Now there are four brands worth over $200 billion: Google, Apple, Amazon and Microsoft.

At the time of writing, there were 14 Chinese brands in the world's top 100 list. The best known in the West is probably Baidu, the Chinese search engine (at number 41). But don't forget about Alibaba, whom we mentioned in Chapter 1. Although most westerners haven't heard of them, they had, at the time, the biggest IPO (initial public offering to sell their shares) at a value of $160 billion.

New accounting rules worldwide require companies to value their intangible assets – such as brands – on their balance sheets when they are acquired (IAS 38). When these assets are judged to have an indefinite life, which is often the case with a brand, they will be subject to annual review for impairment. This means that the difference between the price paid and the current value will be calculated. Any resulting write-downs can often have major implications, as seen in 2002 when AOL Time Warner (as it was then known) had to write off $54 billion for the value lost when AOL acquired Time Warner at the end of the dotcom boom way back in 2000.

> 'Financial analysts are already using next-gen social analytics to predict future brand performance. Credit Suisse have partnered with NetBase to compile sentiment data on handbag designers.'
>
> Brun-Jensen (2014)

There is no doubt that brands can add value to the balance sheet, grow the value of the business (market capitalization) and therefore boost the sale price of a business. They also, as mentioned, save customers time, satisfy their aspirations and reduce perceived risk.

You have the factory and staff; I'll have the brand

> 'If we split the business tomorrow, you kept all the factories and staff and I kept the brand name, within two years I would be a multimillionaire and you would be bankrupt.'
>
> CEO, Quaker Foods

So brands are assets that need to appear on the balance sheet. But like any other asset, brands can depreciate if they are not managed (or maintained) carefully, keeping them fresh and aligned to market changes, patterns and trends.

UEFA is an example of a very high-profile brand that refreshes itself every three years. Some of the updating is so subtle that the average customer would not notice it. The detailed case study on pp 65–72 includes 'before and after' visuals, following a redesign in 2018 (Figure 2.13).

Branding is not just for the big boys

Even small businesses must be clear about their passion for their business. Why they enjoy their work. Why they are stimulated and invigorated by the challenges it presents. This passion and excitement must be captured and clarified and articulated so that the brand reflects this passion.

As the *Huffington Post*'s David Brown says:

> Purpose will guide your small business, but it's passion that propels you forward. What excites you about your purpose? What do you love about it? I believe you have to know the answer to have success. And I'm not defining success as financial success: I'm defining it as being excited to wake up every day, knowing you enjoy your work and are invigorated by the challenges it presents.
>
> Brown (2016)

FIGURE 2.1 BrandZ™ top 100 most valuable global brands 2018

BrandZ™ Top 100 Most Valuable Global Brands 2018

	Brand	Category	Brand value 2018 $M	Brand contribution	Brand value % change 2018 vs 2017	Rank change	Country of origin
1	Google	Technology	302,063	4	+23%	0	
2		Technology	300,595	4	+28%	0	
3	amazon	Retail	207,594	4	+49%	1	
4	Microsoft	Technology	200,987	4	+40%	–1	
5	Tencent 腾讯	Technology	178,990	5	+65%	3	
6	facebook	Technology	162,106	4	+25%	–1	
7	VISA	Payments	145,611	5	+31%	0	
8	McDonald's	Fast Food	126,044	4	+29%	2	
9	Alibaba Group 阿里巴巴集团	Retail	113,401	3	+92%	5	
10	AT&T	Telecom Providers	106,698	3	–7%	–4	
11	IBM	Technology	96,269	4	–6%	–2	
12	verizon	Telecom Providers	84,897	3	–5%	–1	
13	Marlboro	Tobacco	81,914	3	–6%	–1	
14	Coca-Cola	Soft Drinks	79,964	5	+2%	–1	
15	mastercard	Payments	70,872	4	+42%	5	
16	ups	Logistics	60,412	5	+4%	0	
17	SAP	Technology	55,366	3	+23%	4	
18	WELLS FARGO	Regional Banks	54,952	3	–6%	–3	
19	Disney	Entertainment	53,833	5	+3%	–1	
20	THE HOME DEPOT	Retail	47,229	3	+17%	4	
21	中国移动 China Mobile	Telecom Providers	46,349	4	–18%	–4	
22	ICBC 中国工商银行	Regional Banks	45,853	2	+45%	6	
23		Fast Food	44,503	4	+1%	–1	
24	xfinity	Telecom Providers	43,056	3	+3%	–1	
25	T · ·	Telecom Providers	41,499	3	+8%	0	

Source: BrandZ™ / Kantar Millward Brown (including data from Bloomberg)
Brand contribution measures the influence of brand alone on financial value, on a scale of 1 to 5, 5 highest

SOURCE: Reproduced with the kind permission of BrandZ™/Kantar (including data from Bloomberg)

FIGURE 2.1 (Continued)

BrandZ™ Top 100 Most Valuable Global Brands 2018

	Brand	Category	Brand value 2018 $M	Brand contribution	Brand value % change 2018 vs 2017	Rank change	Country of origin
26	LV	Luxury	41,138	5	+41%	3	
27	Spectrum	Telecom Providers	39,372	2	NEW		
28	GE	Conglomerate	39,041	2	–22%	–9	
29		Apparel	38,479	4	+13%	–3	
30	PayPal	Payments	35,440	5	+85%	22	
31	Walmart	Retail	34,002	2	+22%	0	
32	accenture	Technology	33,723	3	+24%	0	
33	SAMSUNG	Technology	32,191	4	+34%	4	
34	MOUTAI	Alcohol	32,113	4	+89%	30	
35	AMERICAN EXPRESS	Payments	30,046	4	+24%	1	
36	TOYOTA	Cars	29,987	4	+5%	–6	
37	vodafone	Telecom Providers	28,860	3	–9%	–10	
38	intel	Technology	28,316	2	+29%	6	
39	HERMÈS PARIS	Luxury	28,063	5	+20%	2	
40	Budweiser	Beer	27,031	4	0%	–7	
41	Baidu 百度	Technology	26,861	5	+14%	–2	
42	ZARA	Apparel	26,860	3	+7%	–8	
43	中国平安 PING AN	Insurance	26,141	3	+51%	18	
44	L'ORÉAL PARIS	Personal Care	26,107	4	+9%	–6	
45	ORACLE	Technology	25,802	2	–21%	1	
46	Mercedes-Benz	Cars	25,684	5	+9%	–6	
47	BMW	Cars	25,624	4	+4%	–12	
48	HUAWEI	Technology	24,922	3	+22%	1	
49	中国建设银行 China Construction Bank	Regional Banks	23,747	2	+27%	5	
50	HSBC	Global Banks	23,633	3	+15%	–2	

The Brand value of Coca-Cola includes Lights, Diets and Zero
The Brand value of Budweiser includes Bud Light

FIGURE 2.1 (Continued)

BrandZ™ Top 100 Most Valuable Global Brands 2018

	Brand	Category	Brand value 2018 $M	Brand contribution	Brand value % change 2018 vs 2017	Rank change	Country of origin
51	YouTube	Technology	22,958	4	+37%	14	
52	RBC	Regional Banks	22,924	4	+8%	–5	
53	movistar	Telecom Providers	22,824	3	+4%	–10	
54	GUCCI	Luxury	22,442	5	+66%	26	
55	NTT	Telecom Providers	22,377	3	+11%	–5	
56	FedEx	Logistics	22,218	5	+14%	–5	
57	cisco	Technology	21,331	2	+28%	9	
58	citi	Global Banks	21,258	2	+21%	1	
59	JD.COM	Retail	20,933	3	+94%	NEW	
60	HDFC BANK	Regional Banks	20,874	4	+22%	3	
61	NETFLIX	Entertainment	20,819	3	+73%	31	
62	DHL	Logistics	20,568	4	+30%	8	
63		Oil & Gas	20,264	1	+10%	–6	
64	Pampers	Baby Care	20,183	5	–10%	–22	
65	orange	Telecom Providers	19,647	3	+14%	–3	
66	TD	Regional Banks	19,628	3	+6%	–10	
67	CHASE	Regional Banks	19,324	3	–35%	6	
68	CommonwealthBank	Regional Banks	19,286	3	+11%	–8	
69	中国农业银行 AGRICULTURAL BANK OF CHINA	Regional Banks	19,141	2	+28%	3	
70	SUBWAY	Fast Food	18,766	4	–14%	–25	
71	Colgate	Personal Care	18,516	5	+4%	–13	
72	COSTCO WHOLESALE	Retail	18,265	3	+12%	–4	
73	J.P.Morgan	Global Banks	18,251	3	–29%	1	
74	ExxonMobil	Oil & Gas	18,222	1	–3%	–19	
75	Adobe	Technology	17,831	3	+53%	23	

Source: BrandZ™ /Kantar Millward Brown (including data from Bloomberg)
Brand contribution measures the influence of brand alone on financial value, on a scale of 1 to 5, 5 highest

FIGURE 2.1 (Continued)

BrandZ™ Top 100 Most Valuable Global Brands 2018

	Brand	Category	Brand value 2018 $M	Brand contribution	Brand value % change 2018 vs 2017	Rank change	Country of origin
76	IKEA	Retail	17,481	3	–8%	–23	
77	Bank of America	Regional Banks	17,439	2	+42%	10	
78	salesforce	Technology	17,026	3	+39%	12	
79	中国人寿 CHINA LIFE	Insurance	16,429	3	+18%	–1	
80	usbank	Regional Banks	16,278	3	+7%	–9	
81	UBER	Transport	16,045	3	NEW		
82	SIEMENS	Conglomerate	15,965	2	+14%	–5	
83	LinkedIn	Technology	15,657	5	+15%	–4	
84	中国银行 BANK OF CHINA	Regional Banks	15,607	2	+30%	10	
85	Gillette	Personal Care	15,358	5	–6%	–18	
86	AIA THE REAL LIFE COMPANY	Insurance	15,131	3	+29%	11	
87	KFC	Fast Food	15,131	4	+12%	–6	
88	ebay	Retail	14,829	3	+20%	–2	
89	hp	Technology	14,797	3	NEW		
90	SF Express	Logistics	14,537	4	NEW		
91	Instagram	Technology	14,496	5	NEW		
92	ANZ	Regional Banks	14,465	3	+3%	–17	
93	ALDI	Retail	13,785	3	+12%	–4	
94	BT	Telecom Providers	13,604	3	–15%	–25	
95	LOWE'S	Retail	13,111	3	–2%	–13	
96	Ford	Cars	12,742	3	–2%	–13	
97	HONDA	Cars	12,695	4	+4%	–6	
98	pepsi	Soft Drinks	12,685	4	0%	–14	
99	BCA	Regional Banks	12,674	4	NEW		
100	adidas	Apparel	12,456	4	+50%	NEW	

The Brand value of Pepsi includes Diets

Business disadvantages of weak brands

If a product or service does not have a single strong, unifying brand, its presence becomes diluted, seen differently by different people. A diluted brand is less recognizable, therefore less known, therefore less trusted and ultimately a more risky purchase. Without a strong unified brand, products and services become buried in a busy world of other, stronger brands. If a product or service has no real strong brand, it may be symptomatic that the management team are themselves not sure of what the brand really is, what it is really good at, what distinguishes it, what needs it meets and what emotions it connects with. Without a strong brand most of the marketing efforts fragment, splinter and disappear.

No brand, no cattle

The term 'brand' comes from the old Norse verb brandr, which meant to burn, and which eventually became a noun and adjective in medieval English. The noun 'brand' meant flame, fire or torch, and the adjective meant burning, hence 'brand hot'. Animals were marked with red-hot branding irons as a sign of ownership and an easy way to identify particular cattle.

So strong brands beat weak brands. But, despite creating protection against competition and boosting relationships, sales, profits and balance sheets, brands are continually damaged and weakened. Why do so many marketers allow so many brands to press their own self-destruct button? Read on.

Brand self-destruction

The brand relationship is always fragile. Constant sloppy service or a single moment of disaster, such as contamination or a misplaced word (eg Ratners; see 'Uncontrollable publicity – any publicity is good publicity?' on p 414), can destroy the customer's trust. And customers are changing. They're becoming more demanding.

Not only do they talk back, but they now shout back and even bite back if brands break their promise. Today's customers have unlocked 'brand control' from marketers and set up their own brand discussions. Although they are still time pressed and information fatigued, they have found a new energy, fuelled by social media, which allows them to fulfil their age-old desire to communicate about what interests or concerns them. Customers have a platform to raise their voices, and some of them can't stop shouting!

Customers are angry. They are also impatient. We are sitting on a customer service time bomb. Sloppy marketing and self-destructing brands go hand-in-hand.

Lousy marketing

We are in an era of declining marketing skills, measured by falling customer satisfaction scores in many markets. The customer service time bomb is ticking (see Chapter 1 for more). Some angry customers publicize their feelings on the many blogs and hate sites attacking brands. These can fuel an exponential spreading of negative word of mouth.

Unlocking control

Customers have unlocked some 'control' from companies, via social media conversations and public reviews. Online social networks are here to stay. They will continue to grow in line with the very human need for social contact. Customers have been mobilized by blogs, Twitter, Facebook, Instagram, WeChat and other social network sites.

The long tail

In the online world, the 'long tail' (Anderson, 2006) suggests it can be as profitable to serve 100 customers spread across the world with 100 different digital products as it is to serve 100 local customers with one standardized product. This opens a gate to discrete consumer taste, which effectively moves markets away from the mass market and its tyranny of the lowest common denominator. Instead of a handful of powerful marketers recommending, and often determining, what is in and what is out, there are now mobilized niche customers alerting their own networks about their own particular preferences.

> **Death of the dumbed-down customer?**
>
> 'For too long we've been suffering the tyranny of lowest-common-denominator fare, subjected to brain-dead summer blockbusters and manufactured pop. Many of our assumptions about popular taste are actually artefacts of poor supply-and-demand matching – a market response to inefficient distribution.'
>
> Anderson (2006)

Careful brand management as global niches emerge

Although spread across the world, customers with similar interests can communicate and share thoughts through images, audio, video and text anywhere they want. Global segments are here. For example, Manchester United Football Club has an estimated 659 million fans and Al Jazeera's English language TV news service reaches 300 million people across 100 countries. As media follow markets, media consumption may go global; therefore marketers must remember that brands with international ambitions must have a consistent global image – production should be international in mind, and content rights should be global. True brand masters also 'think global and act local' by paying attention to local market needs and having the nous to express this in local terms.

Some brand names restrict international sales or global brand ambitions because they have brand names that do not translate very well (or that cannot be pronounced). See p 251 for a list of names that damage the brand when used in some international markets.

Data owner vs brand owner

Power will be prised away from those major brands that cannot adapt to market trends. Maybe it will be the customer database holders that take control? Imagine a consumer opening a fridge and as they take the last can of Guinness the fridge asks, 'Would you like a new delivery of beer, but this time at a special price from a different brand?' Here, it is the database holder that knows who drinks what beer, when and where, as the IoT fridge sensors can see that this is the last can and therefore scans the barcode and commences searching for best beer deals. The key to accessing the customers' databases embedded in fridges, microwaves, cars, phones and personal digital assistants (PDAs) is not the hardware but the intelligence (and the database) to know exactly when customers might like to replace something. The IoT will connect customer databases with all sorts of devices, offering competitors' special deals. Data owners could steal control from brands.

So marketers who ignore new trends and real customer needs and, worse still, deliver sloppy service are simply pressing a self-destruct button that damages and ultimately destroys a very valuable brand.

Before exploring the right way to nurture a brand (ie the branding process), consider exactly what a brand is and what its component parts are.

Brand components

What exactly is a brand?

A brand is far more than just a name, term, design or symbol that identifies and distinguishes a product or service from that of other competitors. A brand is still a badge of origin, a promise of performance and a point of differentiation. Today, a brand is a holistic experience that stretches beyond the physical and into the psychological. It is the sum of the real product or service experience and the perceived values, images, associations and promises made through marketing communications.

'Brand' is both a verb and a noun. It is a verb, as it is a continual process, and a set of skills is required to create and nurture brands. Branding is a core competency for serious marketers. 'Brand' is also a noun, as it is an asset on the balance sheet and something people buy. Some commentators define brands as simply the difference between a bottle of sugared, flavoured, fizzy water and a bottle of Coca-Cola.

> 'Harley-Davidson does not sell motorcycles. Starbucks do not sell coffee. Club Med does not sell vacations. And Guinness does not sell beer. Think about it.'
>
> Peters (2003)

FIGURE 2.2 The most valuable global brands, 2018

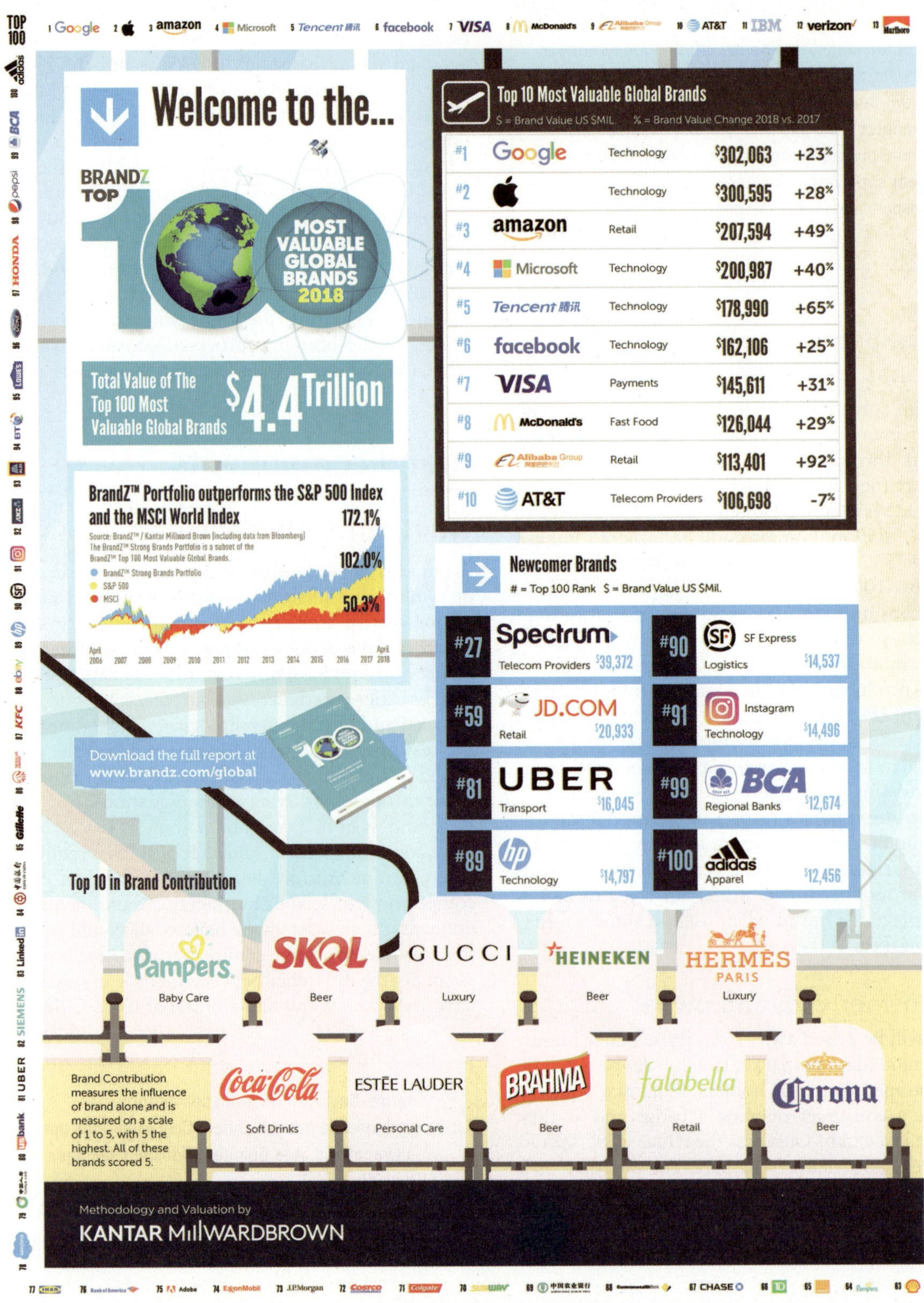

FIGURE 2.2 (Continued)

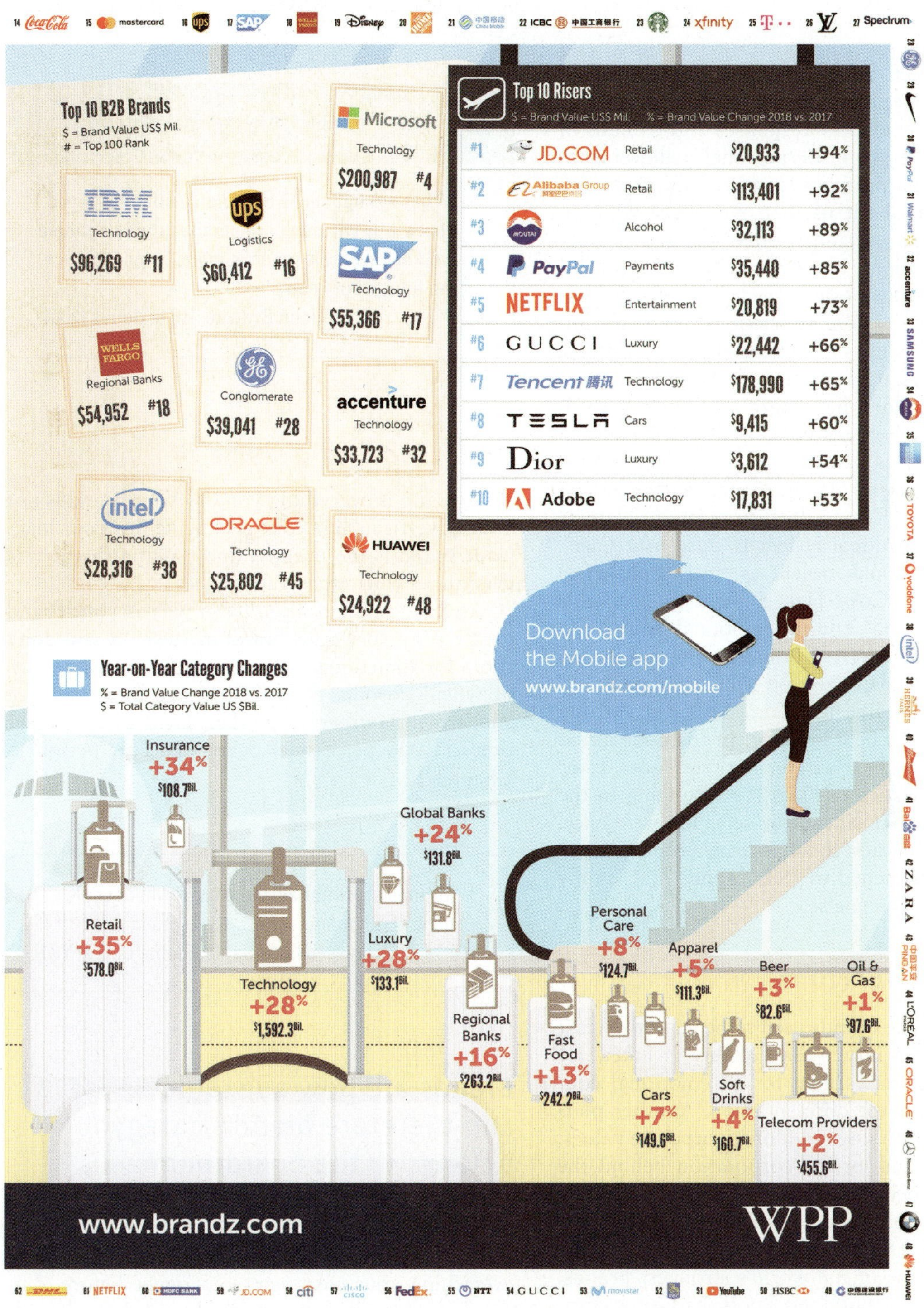

A brand's rational and emotional appeals

A brand is a cluster of rational or functional and emotional aspects that match customers' rational and emotional needs. Strong brands are designed to trigger specific emotional responses in the minds of customers. Nike promises 'personal achievement', while Coca-Cola promises 'carefree fun'. What we buy says more about us than we might want to admit. It reveals our inner, often unconscious desires and aspirations. If the brand gets it right (understands a customer's deep needs and reflects these through a range of communications) then customers are simply buying some of their own aspirations. They are, in fact, buying a slice of their ideal self.

Brands, therefore, have both rational and emotional benefits. For example, Red Bull's physical (rational) benefit is that it keeps you awake (physical stimulation), and its emotional benefit is that you feel you can do more (feel stimulated). Natural food drinks' functional benefit is 'pure fruit juice', and their emotional benefit is 'feel healthy/feel good'. Kellogg's Corn Flakes' physical benefit is 'breakfast nutrition', and the emotional benefit is 'a great start to the day'. As a brand develops, it should elicit an emotional connection from customers.

Some authors, like Kapferer (2008), see strong brands as a deeply held belief or 'an attitude knitted into consumers' hearts. This attitude goes from emotional resonance to liking, to belonging to the evoked set (or consideration set), to preference, attachment, advocacy, to fanaticism.' Some customers are really attached to their brands and simply will not buy anything else.

The emotional connection

Once upon a time brands used to be all about trust and a seal of quality. Today quality is taken for granted. Now brands fight for an emotional connection as a way of differentiation. Another platform for brands to slug it out on is corporate values. Who is the brand, or the corporation behind the brand? Is it socially responsible, environmentally friendly, an animal tester, politically neutral, charitable, or good for its community? Historically, the founders of some of the world's strongest brands, like Guinness, Cadbury and Boots, had huge commitments to their employees' and communities' lives, ranging from building spacious towns, to better schools, hospitals, libraries and parks. Today's brands also need a platform of social responsibility.

There's never been so much emotion in business

'What will happen is based on emotional drives. That's why you can't predict the future. If people worked on pure economic logic, I could predict the future, but I can't.'

Sir John Browne, BP in Jones (2001)

Branding and a sense of purpose

Your brand is everything you do. Your brand is not your advertising nor your packaging nor your logo. Your brand is the purpose and passion that drives everything your organization does.

As Ras Sisodia said, ask, 'So why is your brand great? Why does your brand matter?' **'If you don't stand for something you're dead**; it's just a question of when' (Sisodia *et al*, 2014). See how 'firms of endearment' outperform 'other' firms by over eight times (1,000 per cent+) over a 10-year period in Chapter 1.

'Brands are, after all, the sum of what people think about them.'

David Sable, Global CEO at Y&R

Brands are now a leadership issue and therefore brand strategy belongs in the boardroom

Your brand is a lot more than a nice colourful logo or an advertising strapline. Your brand is everything you do. Your brand culminates in the CX, which is everything your customers experience before, during and after consuming your brand. Your brands are the reason your business exists.

Whatever you sell, sooner or later, somebody else will do it better, faster, or cheaper than you. Your brand, and its purpose and passion that it embodies, is what customers will continue to buy (assuming you are not way behind on the other variables).

Your brand is your 'reason why'. Why I should believe you, why I should work for you, why I should choose you, why I should endorse you.

So in addition to a sense of purpose what are the other brand components?

The brand components

The brand components include brand equity, brand essence, brand experience, brand identity, brand personality, brand positioning, brand promise, brand role, brand values and brand vision. They must all integrate with each other. Here is an explanation of each component.

Brand equity

Brand equity is the total awareness and perceived value of the brand in the minds of customers. Badly managed brands can result in negative brand equity. Brand equity components include the brand identity (brand name, symbols, jingles, colours, associations and any sensory features such as unique smells or tactile experiences), awareness, customer loyalty, perceived qualities and reputation. Brand awareness, brand preferences and brand loyalty are also part of the brand equity. Above all, actual brand experiences contribute to brand equity.

Brand essence

Brand essence is the brand's soul and spiritual centre, which draws on its core value(s). It is the brand's mission statement (how it will help the world) that motivates customers (and employees). The brand essence is the primary functional and emotional benefits. For example, Apple Computers' essence might be 'artful technology', while Amazon's might be 'unparalleled breadth of selection' and Hallmark's might be 'helping people define and express themselves'. The brand essence must have 100 per cent recall among the whole business team and influence every decision they make. It starts with what the brand excels at and then connects to an important cultural truth or trend, eg Apple: the world would be a better place if people had the technology to unleash their potential.

Brand experience

Brand experience is what the customers feel or experience when actually consuming a product or service. This includes all touchpoints of the brand (see below). Somehow this seems to be forgotten by many companies. The actual experience customers enjoy, or suffer, directly affects the brand image. Brand moments are all those moments of contact between the brand and the customer. This includes the website, email responses, telephone responses, handling enquiries, the actual consumption of the product or service, and handling complaints and after-sales, as well as all the marketing communications contacts with the customer. These are critical brand moments.

Brand identity

Brand identity is part of brand equity. Identity is how the brand looks and is sometimes called the 'visual narrative', ie logo, colours and graphics. Brand image, on the other hand, is perception, ie how consumers see the brand based on identity plus all other communications, discussions and experiences. Identity is reality. Image is perception. Identity precedes image. Identity helps customers to remember a brand, recognize it and eventually build associations with the brand values, personality and promise promoted through all communications tools.

Brand personality

People have relationships with brands just as they do with people. That's why marketers define the brand personality carefully. Some brands have subtle, and often unconscious, relationships with customers. A brand's personality has those human personality traits. What kind of person would the brand be if it were human? Think of brands as actual people. How would the brand talk and walk? What kind of clothes would it wear? What kind of car would it drive? What kinds of parties would it go to? For example, the Marlboro Cowboy and the Singapore Airlines Girl have very different but well-defined personalities.

> **'Hello gorgeous'**
>
> Virgin's website greets you with 'Hello gorgeous'. This is part of the whole brand experience and is consistent with the brand values and slightly naughty brand personality.

Brand positioning

Brand positioning is all about perception – how the brand is to be seen, or perceived, by customers using just one or two (or sometimes a maximum of three) key variables. For example, a certain drink could be positioned as a young sick person's drink or a healthy adult's drink. A positioning statement identifies the best space for a brand to be positioned in the minds of customers. As markets change (customers' attitudes and needs change) so too brands change to meet customer needs. Positioning studies identify what is important to customers, where competitors are positioned (or what they are seen as by customers) and if there are any gaps for a brand to fill or take over. This is brand strategy and is absolutely critical to success.

Ask these questions when choosing a positioning:

- Is it important to our target customers (will it drive their buying behaviour)?
- Is it distinctive and specific?
- Is it sustainable or can the competition copy it?
- Can the brand deliver it?

Brand promise

Brand promise or proposition is what the brand offers the customer. For example, Perrier is a premium-priced carbonated mineral water with unique packaging, etc. It is quite product related as opposed to consumer benefit related. Another brand of water might be the healthiest water for your body. The actual proposition flows from the positioning.

Brand role

What role does this brand play in target customers' lives? The brand role is an extension of brand personality or lifestyle, or as a social facilitator. Where does it fit in the life of the customer? Is the brand a champion, a chum, a comforter, a confessor, a conscience, an enabler, an expert, an entertainer, a friend, a servant, a patron, a ringleader, a guide, a guru, etc? For example, Red Bull might be a 'portable comforter for tired people' or Ryanair possibly enables people to access Europe.

Brand values

Brand values are not necessarily seen, as they are declared internally. Imagine again the brand as a person. What does your brand believe in? What does it stand for? What standards does it attain? How should it behave? Brand values are a belief system or a way of working and communicating. Mose (2003) asks:

> Which values are so inherent in your company that, if they disappeared, your company would cease to exist as it is? Thousands of companies disappear every year. So why has your company survived? Why are investors still investing in your company? Why do your customers still buy your product? Why do people come to work for your company? Why do you still work for your company? These questions can help determine your company's true core values.

Brand vision

Brand vision is what the brand should be. In Virgin's case it might be to provide a service that is 'the people's champion and which shakes up the status quo'. In Nike's case the vision is one of achievement, of personal best, of being part of a community of athletes. The brand allows people to reconnect with an Olympic ethos that sits somewhere deep inside the psyche.

> 'Do not relax until you have identified the irreducible core of a brand – what drives its connection with consumers. This will mean getting inside consumers' heads, and understanding deep-seated motivations and thought processes.'
>
> Braun (2004)

Sensory branding may become more of the brand experience, as trademark regulations in almost all countries are accepting applications for registering components of the brand that incorporate all five senses. Lindstrom (2005) reported that:

> Decades ago, Texas developed the Texas touch, albeit on their calculators. Texas was one of the first companies to actually trademark the specific 'clicks' – the feel of the number pad on their calculators. The interesting fact is that users of the product may not recognize Texas's logo, but they still recognize the 'touch'. Singapore Airlines currently has nine patents including a patent on the Stephan Florida Smell – the characteristic 'Singapore Airline smell' of the hot towels served onboard. Kellogg's invested in the power of auditory stimulus, testing the crunching of cereals in a Danish sound lab to upgrade their product's 'sound quality.'

Brand touchpoints are sometimes called 'brand moments' or 'customer touchpoints'. Touchpoints are anywhere the brand touches the customer, eg packaging, advertisements, websites, telephonists, sponsorship, events, etc. While customers are waiting on the phone, what brand experience do they have? While they are receiving a bill, letter, fax or email, what experience do they have? These are part of the brand experience. Marketers need to pinpoint the relevant attributes that distinguish the brand and the touchpoints that can deliver these (in order of importance). This requires input from everyone – from CEO, MD, marketing, operations and sales teams to advertising people and webmasters.

One of the ultimate touchpoints for a brand is experiential marketing – traditionally live events offline where customers get to interact with the brand in a new and immersive environment.

Branding is simple but not easy

So branding is simple, but, that doesn't mean branding is easy! As Richard Sauerman says,

> There is an art to discovering the authentic purpose and passion that is at the heart of your company. There's also an art to bringing your brand to life, both on the inside as well as the outside of your company. Because at the end of the day your brand is what you DO, not just what you say... A clearly articulated and authentic brand is the most powerful way to shift the attitudes and behaviour of your people and customers, shift your performance, and shift your world.
>
> Sauerman (2018)

Branding involves love and joy

'Bringing love, joy, authenticity, empathy, and soulfulness into their businesses, and not just focusing on making a profit.'

Sauerman (2018)

The branding process

A big prize awaits brands that can develop deeper and longer-lasting connections with their customers. Marketers should treat the word 'brand' as a verb and not a noun, as branding is a continual process. Brand building and brand maintenance are, in fact, a core competency. Outstanding marketers use a development process when creating an advertising campaign, an exhibition, a website or an actual brand. They also use it when reviewing and updating a brand, since brands have to be redefined for a new era (otherwise markets can move away from old, outdated brands). The best brand stewards or guardians have an inbuilt review process to ensure the brand is kept fresh. They ensure it does not allow obsolescence to creep in, and tweak it if necessary. So, whether you are creating a new brand or maintaining an existing one, here are the four main steps in the process: brief, concept generation, concept development and roll-out/delivery. Figure 2.3 shows the process required to create and maintain strong brands.

A clear brief covers details of the target market, required brand role, personality, values, positioning, etc. Concepts or ideas are generated. One or two are selected and developed, and finally one is rolled out as the new brand. What's missing in this process? Research. Research is required before and after

FIGURE 2.3 The brand development process

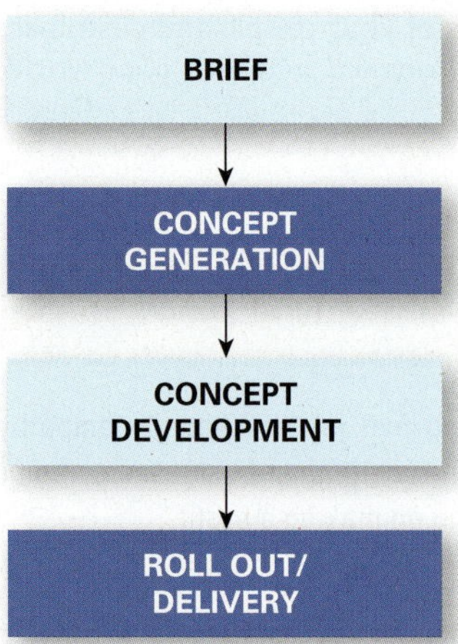

FIGURE 2.4 The brand development process including research

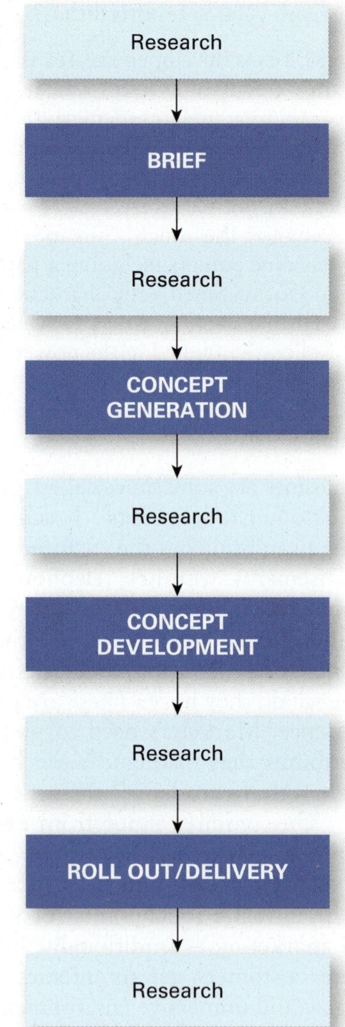

each stage. The revised and complete brand development process is shown in Figures 2.4 and 2.5.

Research

In order to explore the brand opportunity, research is used at the early stage of a brand's development (way before any brand names, logos and colours). Target markets are analysed, buyer behaviour drivers explored, brand personalities defined and the most cost-effective brand moments identified.

Successful brands use a platform of information to help to nurture the brand. Initial exploratory research is used to:

- identify long-term profitable customers;
- develop a deep understanding of the customer;
- identify aspects of the brand that drive behaviour;
- identify the emotions that drive brand behaviour;
- identify personality, values, associations and the promise;
- identify critical brand moments – or critical touchpoints;
- identify the most cost-effective, high-impact brand moments.

Let's consider each of these in more detail.

Identify long-term profitable customers

Do not invest branding efforts in unprofitable segments (particularly those with weak long-term potential). The profit potential of each segment needs to be measured. Also watch out for trends that may affect the relevance of the traditional segmentation approach (eg size, income, age, ethnicity, consumption patterns, loyalty, locations, lifestyles, needs and attitudes). For example, the business traveller

FIGURE 2.5 The complete brand development process

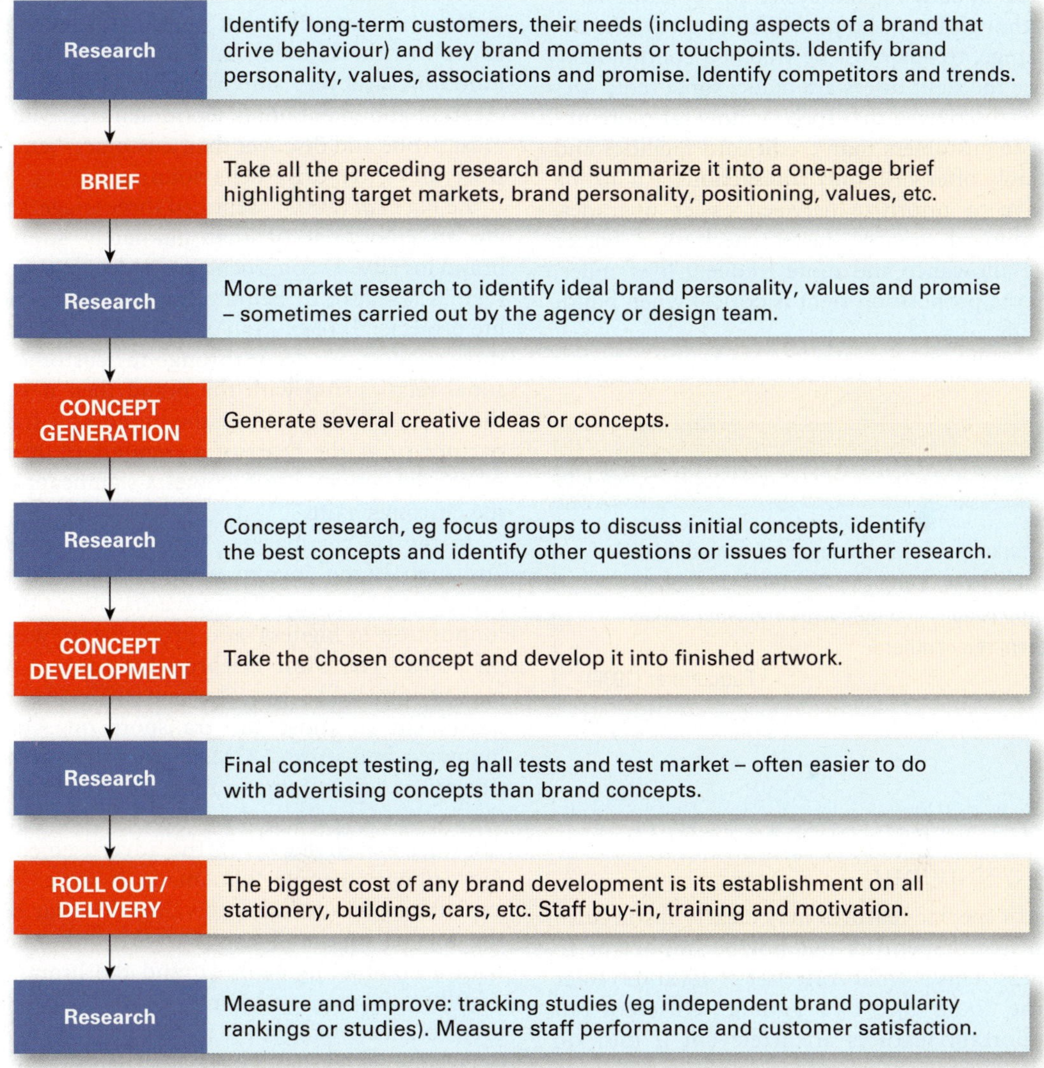

hotel segments may be changing from service-orientated business travelling to value-driven business travelling and luxury-driven business travelling. The latter may split into 'fashion seeker' segments (who see their hotels as a way of expressing who they are) and 'escape seeker' segments (who want to feel pampered and far from the pressures of business).

Research
Identify long-term customers, their needs (including aspects of a brand that drive behaviour) and key brand moments or touchpoints. Identify brand personality, values, associations and promise. Identify competitors and trends.
BRIEF
Take all the preceding research and summarize it into a one-page brief highlighting target markets, brand personality, positioning, values, etc.
Research
More market research to identify ideal brand personality, values and promise – sometimes carried out by the agency or design team.
CONCEPT GENERATION
Generate several creative ideas or concepts.
Research
Concept research, eg focus groups to discuss initial concepts, identify the best concepts and identify other questions or issues for further research.
CONCEPT DEVELOPMENT
Take the chosen concept and develop it into finished artwork.
Research
Final concept testing, eg hall tests and test market – often easier to do with advertising concepts than brand concepts.
ROLL OUT/ DELIVERY
The biggest cost of any brand development is its establishment on all stationery, buildings, cars, etc. Staff buy-in, training and motivation.
Research
Measure and improve: tracking studies (eg independent brand popularity rankings or studies). Measure staff performance and customer satisfaction.

Identified trends are a marketer's friend.

Develop a deep understanding of the customer

Rudyard Kipling's six honest serving men were the questions who, what, why, where, when and how. Outstanding marketers can answer all of these questions about their customer segments. The most difficult is 'why' – why do customers buy? (We'll look at this further in Chapter 4.) Excellent marketers know their customers better than they know themselves. A deep understanding of the customers is required; for example a hotel might uncover that the core need underlying the desire for comfort is to 'feel as though I'm at home while I'm away'. As desires change, trends must be watched continuously to ensure the right offers are made; some retail sectors have discovered that speed is now far more important to customers than credit card facilities and accordingly offer cash-only transactions. An airline may have to prioritize between easier upgrades, more onboard services, faster check-in, a bigger baggage allowance and more frequent-flyer miles. Getting the proposition right is critical when building brands.

Invite a brand into your life

'Marketers need a deeper understanding of what makes people invite certain brands and propositions into their lives and what makes them reject others.'

Fauconnier (2006)

Identify aspects of the brand that drive behaviour

A brand's specific features may clearly distinguish it from its competitors but not be important to customers. This is what Aufreiter *et al* (2003) refer to as the 'fool's gold of branding'. Different but non-important features are irrelevant if they do not drive customer behaviour. Without knowing which features really do affect customer behaviour, an organization can squander limited resources promoting unwanted aspects of the brand. It's a little bit like getting high satisfaction scores but wondering why customers are leaving in droves. You're probably measuring features that were important in previous years but are no longer so. Customer desires change, and so trend spotting and brand adjusting are required to keep brands up to date and out of the great brand graveyard in the sky.

Identify the emotions that drive brand behaviour

A brand is much more than a product. It is a lifestyle or a personality that appeals to the emotions as well as the rational, thinking side of the brain. Emotions are very important. Branding is about creating and maintaining emotional ties. Marketers must probe and discover their customers' emotions, since they often drive behaviour.

Le Pla *et al* (2003) identified three triggers to create an emotional tie that ultimately strengthens brand loyalty: 1) congruence with deeply rooted life themes (values); 2) helping the accomplishment of life projects; 3) resolution of current concerns. 'If all three triggers can occur through the customer's personal relationship with the brand then it is likely that the customer will see the brand as a friend or partner, or as the heart of a community of users – where the community becomes a significant part of the customer's life.'

In the US car market, Mini created huge sales and high brand loyalty when it appealed to the emotions of drivers. The advertisements declared 'opposition to bigness' and promised to 'wage war on SUVs'. The Mini 'celebrated the joy of motoring' as opposed to 'the lobotomized, cruise control movement of most car transport on America's highways and streets'. GM's Saturn also used emotion in car advertisements that said very little about the car but lots about the company's ideology. The car wasn't even shown in the advertisements, but the ordinary people who made it were. The ad explained GM's beliefs and values. The car became the top-selling small car two years after launch, with a community built around the brand (some 45,000 customers and families turned up at a factory to meet each other and the company at its open day, which had barbecues, bands and a factory tour).

'We don't know how to sell on performance. Everything we sell, we sell on image.'

Robert Gouezeta, former CEO, Coca-Cola

Identify personality, values, associations and the promise

Identify the kind of brand personality that reflects the ideal personality that the target market aspires to or admires. Build in the values and associations that matter to the target market. Make a very clear simple promise and stick to it – never break it.

Identify critical brand moments – or critical touchpoints

These are the places, often beyond the consumption of the actual product or service, where a large part of the total brand experience is really delivered. This is where the customer has a large emotional investment, for example a phone call to the customer service line to make a complaint. It includes anywhere that customers interact with the brand (phone, store and web, as well as ads and events, etc).

Identify the most cost-effective, high-impact brand moments

Channel creativity and resources into these high-impact areas. This is where the brand will be enhanced or destroyed. Remember, a beautifully designed logo and clever brand name mean nothing if the website doesn't work or the customer service person cannot solve the problem. Equally, a wonderful product can be destroyed if it is delivered uncaringly.

Service training or website redesign?

Which is the priority? Creating a new customer service training programme or redesigning a website? Answer: find the high-impact touchpoints and allocate resources that have the biggest effect on them

Equipped with answers to all of the research questions, we now know what we want and what is the priority. Having completed the research, we can now write the brief.

Secure the .com version of your new brand name's url. Secure the Twitter handle you want for the new brand.

Run focus groups with customers in your target markets to uncover any hidden issues with your proposed rebranding.

'When Netflix first announced its ill-fated rebranding to split the Netflix and Qwikster services, it quickly became apparent that one vital element of the due-diligence process had been glossed over. Because the company had failed to secure the "@Qwikster" username on Twitter, the handle was snatched up by a user who flooded his feed with images of a beloved children's character making use of illicit substances. Netflix quickly scrapped the launch of the DVD-only service Qwikster in the face of negative publicity.'

Kumar (2012)

The brief

The starting point for any branding initiative is to ask what its objectives are: what is it trying to achieve in the customers' minds? The brief should include the brand promise, personality, values, associations and positioning (as well as the 3Ms: men/women, money and minutes – who is responsible for what, how much budget is allocated to creating this brand, and how much time there is before the launch, testing and concept development stages). Brand logos and clever names come later. A good brief should be written and agreed or signed off by all the key decision-makers.

As well as defining the target market, the brief includes the brand's promise to customers. What makes it different? What needs is it fulfilling? In addition to target markets, distribution channels and regulatory guidelines, the brief should include brand vision, role and essence.

An example of promise is Volkswagen promising the most reliable car. Volvo promise the safest. The brand's personality (the tone, manner and style of how you speak to customers, what you look like and how your staff behave) gives guidelines both for marketing communications and for staff behaviour. Virgin's personality is consistently irreverent; their airport luggage-size signs state 'The size of your bag has a limit – but the size of your ego can't be too large!' Brand values are included, as they influence how you work, your beliefs and your standards of behaviour. The brand's positioning must be crystal clear. This summarizes all the other questions and is key to marketing strategy. Positioning defines how your brand's distinctive benefits should be perceived by customers alongside competitive offers.

Two important aspects for any brand brief are relevance and differentiation. The proposition must make customers an offer, firstly, that fits their needs and, secondly, that the competition cannot (easily) offer. Relevance and difference increase the likelihood of success. But remember, relevant product differentiators may change over time.

A useful aide-mémoire for any brief is SOS + 3Ms, which is taken from the marketing planning system called SOSTAC®. The SOS brief provides a useful framework, as it includes situation analysis (where are we now?), objectives (where are we going?) and strategy (how do we get there?); the 3Ms are men/women (the brand manager and team who decide), money (budget) and minutes (timescale). For more on SOSTAC®, see Chapter 9.

> A brand that does not stand for something stands for nothing.

Concept generation and development

The answers to questions about the brand's promise, personality, values, associations and positioning give clear guidance to any creative ideas. A good brief saves a lot of time, as it steers creative thinking in the right direction and avoids generating time-consuming concepts that do not fulfil the brand prerequisites.

However, once the brief has been signed off, some additional research may be carried out into customers, distributors and even competitors. On the basis of a clear brief and any additional research required, brand names and brand logos can be generated and then researched, with the best one(s) being selected for refinement or development. The finished brand name and logo are then tested once more. Early-stage research should include global use, ie whether the name or the logo has any strange meaning in other key languages, and whether it is protectable. Let us look at brand name development and brand logo development.

Brand name development

Developing brand names is a specialized business in itself. A brand name should be distinctive and easy to say, spell and remember. It should also be relevant, brief (maximum four syllables) and legally protectable (ie not generic) and lend itself to advertising and promotion. Lastly, a really good name can be used almost globally.

Three different approaches to brand name development are: product function; classic names (Latin or Greek); and benefit based. Product function, eg International Business Machines (now IBM), is difficult to protect. The classic approach is more protectable; Nike is a Greek name, which relates to the specific cultural values of the Olympic Games and the glorification of the human body. Thirdly, benefit-based names are less directly associated with a product or service's functions and closer to a name that evokes product benefit or even a certain state of mind, eg Nectar for a 'reward points' programme.

And there are always exceptions to the rule. Richard Branson claims to have named his brand Virgin because he was a virgin when it came to business. Tech giant Cisco's name comes from the last five letters of San Francisco, reportedly chosen when the founders were inspired by a drive past the Golden Gate Bridge en route to register the company. Aldi supermarket's founder, Theo Albrecht, supposedly combined his name with 'discount'.

Names need to be distinctive and protectable (to register them as trademarks). Functional or descriptive names are difficult to register, as they may be deemed to be generic words commonly used by others (and therefore owned by everyone).

Once a short list of names has been generated, a name search is carried out in the target market (and potential target markets) to check to see if anyone has registered these names already in the same business sector. After that, some simple concept testing in each target market reveals whether the brand name has any negative meanings in different languages, as Coca-Cola discovered in China (see Chapter 8). Without these checks, subsequent opportunities for global expansion are curtailed without an expensive and time-consuming rebranding exercise.

Brand logos

The crucifix, the hammer and sickle, the swastika, the red cross or a national flag immediately arouse emotions, feelings, images or interpretations of some kind. Logos are a language (sometimes international) of emotional response. Symbols, shapes and colour all have conscious and unconscious meanings. Visual symbols or devices can also be powerful as a means of increasing awareness by facilitating easy recognition. A logo can act as a focal point to summarize or encapsulate an organization, although it should not be too complex. If an identity needs too much explaining, then it isn't working. The acid test for a logo is: distinctive, easily recognizable, memorable and reducible (can work when reduced on to a business card or postage stamp). It should work in black and white as well as colour, since many corporate images appear in black and white in the press. Ideally, the logo should also be symbolic, or relevant to the business, but this is rarely the case. It must work well online, as well as in its more traditional applications.

Logos are an important part of the brand identity and often are described as a key component of brand equity; Nike's swoosh and McDonald's golden arches help audiences and customers to recognize the brand instantly and also help to differentiate the brand. A logo also acts as a stamp or guarantee. It should, ideally, reflect the values of the brand. Logos can protect a trademark when combined with generic words (as generic words themselves are usually not protectable on their own, but the combination of the words with the logo may be). Good logos (unique, easily recognizable, relevant and well maintained) become icons, and not only are they recognizable but even parts of them are recognizable, such as the Heinz chevron or the 'M' in Marlboro.

Logo development

The process of developing a logo is similar to the process of developing any aspect of marketing communications: brief, concept generation (and selection), concept development and finally launch or roll-out. In between each stage, research gives crucial feedback. This helps to select the best concept, which when guided by feedback (research) is developed into the final logo design. It does get one last check with more research before roll-out.

One UK design consultancy developed a new logo for Saudi Arabian Airlines that looked, to the uninitiated, distinctive, unique and easily recognizable. The logo contained golden palm trees, crossed Arabian swords and a crescent moon and appeared to be suitably upmarket and regal. In fact, it contained four major errors:

- the wrong type of palm tree – Saudi Arabia is the number two producer of dates, but the palm tree shown was not a date palm tree;
- the wrong type of sword – the traditional Saudi sword is a fighting sword, but the sword shown in the logo looked weak, old and ceremonial;
- the wrong moon – the crescent of the new moon used by Saudi Arabia represents a new beginning, but the proposed crescent was that of an old moon, suggesting 'the end';
- the wrong colour – the old green colour was replaced by cream, which represents hot, barren sand in the desert when Saudi Arabia was trying to irrigate the kingdom and make it green.

This confirms the need for designers to invest in detailed research before attempting to develop any design concepts. Designers who neither budget nor plan for research (or several stages of research) vastly increase the likelihood of problems. Worse still, if problems occur after implementation of a new design, the costs immediately spin out of control, and there is a highly embarrassed management team.

The logo can be literal (eg Shell), a logotype (a stylized treatment of the company name with no additional symbol, eg Kellogg's), wordmarks that integrate a graphic element into the name, company initials (eg IBM) or purely abstract. Whichever type of logo is chosen, it is essential to research the choice carefully, particularly in global markets where symbols, colours and words can have very different meanings.

End of logos?

'A logo today has turned out to be a warning sign of a commercial message. The trend is that it will disappear and be replaced by other non-conscious signals – everything from iPod's white ear plugs, to Tiffany's blue packaging, to the United Colors of Benetton photos or whatever you are imaging. If you look at Formula 1 today, you'll see that most of the Ferrari cars have these funny red-coloured bar codes. That is the secret logo from Marlboro. There's no logo, there's no name on it.'

Martin Lindstrom, in Rothery (2009)

Roll-out/delivery

The roll-out of a brand requires far more than just press launches and lavish branding events. It starts internally; the whole organization needs to be mobilized. They must live and breathe the brand, starting with the CEO acting as brand champion and cascading down through the organization by:

- living the brand;
- linking operational targets to brand ratings;
- linking rewards to customer satisfaction and brands ratings;
- putting brand values in job specifications.

Living the brand means internalizing it and living its values. What a business does reveals its personality and values far more than any amount of advertising. Any significant disconnection between what an organization says about itself and what it actually does will seriously undermine people's relationship with the brand.

Living the brand occurs when employees actively and enthusiastically deliver the brand promise day in, day out. It helps if the brand and brand responsibilities are written into the job description of every member of the team. This is where marketing and HR work closely together. The brand effectively becomes everybody's business.

Do all employees know (and memorize) what the brand promise and brand values are? Do they know what the business stands for? Are they able to tell the brand story in a compelling way to different stakeholder audiences including shareholders, employees, customers and vendors? To ensure that a brand comes to life throughout the organization, ask whether you need structural or departmental changes. It is that important. Consider every aspect of the organization from employee behaviour to premises. Inject the brand DNA into your organization structure.

Motivate and train staff

Develop operational targets to build the brand. Try linking customer satisfaction scores and brand ratings to operational targets. (You should measure criteria that are important to customers, not those you think are important.) All staff are brand ambassadors.

Brand consistency stops a brand from splintering, diluting and ebbing away. Crystal-clear brand guidelines can include templates for all marketing collateral so that brochures, websites and signage are all consistently produced anywhere in the world. The brand guidelines also include the Pantone colours, size and layout of logos and straplines for a range of different uses, online and offline, as well as above and below the line.

'Nike bought its iconic "swoosh" logo for a mere $35 while Twitter paid iStockphoto less than $15 for its now famous bird logo.'

Stampler (2013)

At first a new logo has little or no value because it has no franchise. First it must be associated with the right kinds of images, and then its recognition levels can be developed (eg Lloyds Bank's black horse). This takes time, since initial reaction to change or anything new is often quite negative. Sometimes the initial reaction is one of upset, dislike or disgust, as the new logo does not fit in with the previous set of cognitions (and thereby creates 'cognitive dissonance' and possibly tension). The value of the logo eventually starts to increase as the years roll by and it becomes better understood. However, it helps enormously if internal marketing carefully brings staff on board throughout the development and ultimately before the launch.

Whether the logo trend is towards simplicity, swooshes or sharp-edged internationally understood symbols, the corporate identity demands careful management across all the points of public contact.

Brand maintenance

Creating a brand is relatively simple, but not easy. Maintaining it can also be a challenge (as you will see with the UEFA corporate identity case study). Great brand managers constantly develop or reinvigorate the brand so that it is seen as relevant (not 'hip' or necessarily modern, but definitely always relevant to the target market). Remember, target markets move and change. The classic Lucozade drink was once upon a time positioned as a drink for sick children. As the market demographics moved from a disproportionately large number of children in the 1960s to a disproportionately large number of young adults in the 1980s, Lucozade repositioned itself as a healthy adult's drink. Today it has moved on again, twisting and tweaking itself to stay relevant to its key target market. Maintaining a brand requires vision, system, determination and people.

Mobilize staff and channel partners

The brand requires a system that mobilizes the entire organization. Bringing a brand to life requires a completely integrated approach beyond marketing. Operations and HR must develop a system that inspires and motivates all staff to support the brand. Ideally, job descriptions should explain the responsibilities that staff have to 'live the brand'. Operational targets can be linked to building and maintaining the brand (such as measuring relevant customer satisfaction). The brand needs to be embedded into the DNA of the business.

This, in turn, helps the company to live the brand, ensuring that all those crucial 'brand moments' (when the business interacts with the customer) actually reflect the brand. The primary audience for a brand is the employees – as they need to be mobilized to support it; then come the channel partners (distributors). Brand managers need to ensure that the brand is never compromised or tarnished on its journey to the end customer.

A fatal mistake some marketers make is to focus too heavily on external marketing communications (developing advertising campaigns, direct mail campaigns, websites and opt-in SMS campaigns to boost cross-selling and up-selling), rather than ensuring all customer touchpoints are consistently executed.

> **Subconscious air travel worries?**
>
> Attention to detailed design management can subconsciously influence air travellers. The same logo, typeface, primary and secondary colours and trim on all visual points of contact help to reassure the traveller, while reinforcing the airline's identity. The check-in desk logo, signs, colours and trims should be coordinated with the uniform (and badge), ticket holder, baggage tag and departure lounge carpets, right through to the plane's exterior graphics, interior carpet and even the trim on the china and linen. Without this coordinated corporate identity, cognitive dissonance can set in. There is a subconscious unease or discomfort created by the inconsistent messages. A coordinated identity reduces this often-unconscious tension, which in turn creates a more satisfied passenger. The cohesive identity does not make the traveller leap off the plane and scream for joy on arrival, but it might make the subconscious difference next time around when choosing between two airlines if one offers a reassuring sense of order.

Brand policing

Brand managers are guardians who need to ensure the brand is consistently used in all touchpoints. Brand policing is important. If an organization's identity is not coordinated or managed precisely, confusing signals go out to different audiences around the world. A splintered identity fragments the corporate image, which in turn dilutes the corporate presence among key audiences. The potential asset (corporate brand) depreciates to the point where it becomes a liability. The organization dilutes its presence and has an uncoordinated image. This sends out disorganized messages that weaken the initial or final impression left by the organization.

A logo displayed prominently in an office or on a letterhead makes a good strong statement, but it is the consistent 'echoing' of the logo, its exact primary and secondary colours, the specific typeface and the overall design style on the 'secondary format' of products, packages, business forms and employee uniforms, that provides the all-important, if subtle, consistent reinforcement.

There is a need to think it through in detail and then to police the usage of all visual points of contact. This is where a design manual guides managers in different buildings and in different countries to specify, in a consistent manner, the exact graphic requirement for every point of visual contact.

Sweaty identity

In corporate identity terms, attention to detail needs to spread beyond just graphics. The classic 1990 US Hall of Shame reported the following:

> 'To upgrade its image in 1982 AT&T told its repair people to wear dress shirts and ties, gave them attaché cases for their tools, and renamed them "system technicians". But Ma Bell didn't install air conditioning in its cars. So during the summer the technicians arrived on the job looking like they had just stepped out of a sauna. Said a union official, "It's hard to have corporate appeal if your shirt is wringing wet."'
>
> Nash and Zull Products (1989)

The importance of consistency applies right across the communications spectrum. In John Murphy's classic book *Branding* (1991), Klaus Morwind Henkel points to consumer research that 'has indicated that a lack of consistency between the brand name, the packaging and the advertising is subconsciously recognized by the consumer and leads to a feeling of detachment, ultimately resulting in brandswitching'. So it is important to be consistent and to reinforce identity through all the appropriate points of public contact. This should include advertising and all elements of the communications mix, which includes permanent media like corporate headquarters.

The logo is just the tip of the iceberg. It is often the most visible part of an organization. A corporate identity scheme may have a logo at its heart, but it will generally include a whole array of other elements, often referred to as 'visual language'. This may include typefaces, a colour palette, the use of photography and illustrations, a layout style for using these items and even a particular style of written language, as well as briefs for interior design and exteriors of buildings (plus, today, eco-friendly building requirements).

A good corporate brand can help sales and boost employee relationships, financial relationships and media relationships during a crisis. Corporate branding, however, requires a lot more than just a corporate identity. The impact of a corporate identity programme goes far beyond a logo or a lick of paint. It influences almost every manifestation of an organization, its corporate headquarters, its staff and even the way they work. All of the components need to be in place. A new logo raises stakeholder expectations.

Boards, doors, logos and skunks

> 'A new letterhead and a new logo is no substitute for a new board of directors.'
>
> Fitch (2003)

> 'Painting the lavatory door won't cure the plumbing.'
>
> Bernstein (1984)

> 'If you take a lousy low-profile company and give it a major corporate revamp, you end up with a lousy high-profile company.'
>
> Olins (1989)

> 'Even if you paint out a skunk's stripes it will still smell extremely nasty.'
>
> Source unknown

Corporate brands and sub-brands

An umbrella brand, such as the Virgin brand, can have various sub-brands, such as Virgin Atlantic and Virgin Trains. A corporate brand, such as GlaxoSmithKline (GSK), Unilever or Procter & Gamble (P&G), on the other hand, remains in the background and offers an endorsement, while a mainstream brand like Persil can have sub-brands such as Persil washing-up liquid and Persil powder.

Invest in the brand asset

Constant investment is also required to maintain a brand's profile and avoid it getting buried in the communications clutter. Some companies take the long-term, brand investment view; Coke invested $65 million in sponsoring the Olympics from 2009 to 2020.

Constant reviews of brands, and in particular large portfolios of brands, can result in a major strategic consolidation of the brand portfolio, as in the case of Unilever when it cut its portfolio of 1,600 brands down to 400.

Brands are under increased challenges today. Brands fade as tastes change, unless of course they are maintained and nurtured carefully to meet the new market conditions. Even in steady-state markets where there are no great trends pulling the market away from the brand, marketers still need to ensure that it is policed carefully, particularly as a brand grows globally. Rigorous use of brand guidelines is required here to ensure that exactly the same features appear correctly anytime and anywhere.

Review the brand

Brands require constant reviews and investment of energies and money. They often need to be reinvented or reinvigorated to avoid being left behind by a fast-changing marketplace. A constant flow of market research should ensure the brand really addresses customers' deep needs, which change over time. Otherwise brands fade as tastes change. Constant market research also reveals how the brand is positioned against existing competition and new competitors. As British design guru Wally Olins (1989) said, 'In a complex and changing company the corporate identity [for an overall company] bears a great strain, twisting and turning to fit every new requirement. But a good corporate identity should last a generation.' Well some brand managers like to review and tweak every ten years, or every five years or in the case of UEFA, every three years.

When does a brand identity become out of date? Can the business environment change and move away from the organization and its values, leaving behind the obsolete, irrelevant and even damaging corporate identity? When do the staff and other audiences get tired of it? Mergers and acquisitions sometimes necessitate a new corporate identity. Occasionally, legal reasons force a change. Sometimes overseas ambitions are restricted by the use of a

FIGURE 2.6 The Shell logo and its redesign

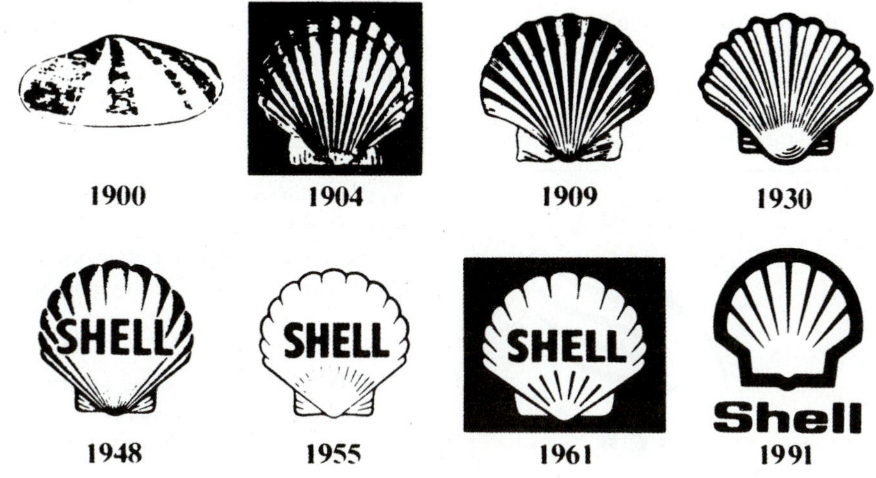

home-grown logo (eg BT's old logo clashed with that of overseas companies).

Shell reviews and updates its corporate identity (Figure 2.6). The shell device has served it well, despite its being a petrol company with a 'high explosive' name. Global markets are constantly moving and changing, so much so that some organizations fear they are being left behind. A review and redesign can help an organization to keep abreast of trends and avoid being left isolated by a redundant identity. See the full UEFA corporate identity case study at the end of this chapter.

Sometimes new brand identities are developed simply because old management wants to say something new or a new CEO wants to announce he or she has arrived. This is a dangerous game, as a new brand identity or a new corporate identity raises expectations that the organization has new ways of working, new customer benefits or new customer experiences.

Aggressive hand-held torch of learning gets the chop

The National Union of Teachers' 25-year-old 'hand-held torch of learning' was considered to have become too strident, aggressive and uncaring, with none-too-desirable connotations of the Conservative party and the Greek fascist party. Although it was designed in the 1960s, it had a 1930s look. It appeared that the time was right to move the logo on but keep it relevant and maintain the link with the union's heritage. The updated design shows an outstretched hand embraced by the spelt-out words of the NUT, tying the symbol together as one cohesive form, either male or female, adult or child, to avoid alienation.

FIGURE 2.7 Hand-held torch of learning

Constant watch: The customer experience

Brand maintenance also requires careful attention to the customer experience (which as we've seen is often very poor). Poor product quality and sloppy service destroy brands more quickly than any large advertising budget can build them. Unacceptable product or service quality, complicated order forms, late delivery, incomprehensible customer service agents and error-laden websites all destroy a brand. Slow email responses damage the brand. Non-responses can kill it.

Attention to the customer experience both offline and online is important. Online brands still deliver offline (eg Amazon books), hence marketers monitor the offline aspects carefully also. And all brands (online and offline) have opportunities to extend the brand experience online by layering in new and exciting value-adding benefits. They add some 'sizzle'. Embellishing and extending the brand experience online can be achieved with 'sizzle', which cannot be found offline.

Nurturing brands can include lavishing wonderful brand experiences on customers, otherwise known as experiential marketing. It also includes engaging customers and moving them up into higher levels of brand engagement.

Finally there is the experience – the quality of the experience, both online and offline, directly affects the brand and its image. Remember, sloppy websites, unanswered emails and comments, unpleasant receptionists and any other touchpoints can damage the brand. Many marketers now see the online opportunity to build both the brand image and the overall company value.

> In just a few seconds sloppy websites destroy brands that took years to build.

Social media now engages the customer in new ways (as discussed in Chapter 1). A brand's own website can add deeper, richer brand experiences by adding some 'sizzle' (Chaffey and Smith, 2013).

> Ask 'What experience could a website deliver that would really wow customers?'

What experience could a website deliver that would really add value for customers, be truly unique and be representative of the brand? Ultimately ask 'How can my website help my customers (or other stakeholders)?' Here are a few examples:

- A camera company can help customers to take better photographs by simulating taking photographs with different settings and allowing customers to compare and contrast the results (and can also give tips on how to maintain cameras and protect films and photos, and invite customers to send their best photos in for a competition).
- A travel company can give you a 'virtual friend' who can advise you and tailor your holiday experience, or show 360-degree photographs that allow you to 'walk through' your holiday location.
- Cosmetic companies offer online games, screensavers, viral emails, video clips and soundtracks with tips to help customers get the most out of their products.
- Food companies offer printable recipes, video demonstrations and discussion forums, as well as 'ask the expert' sessions.
- Chocolate companies generate ideas for desserts (using the chocolates), dinner party games and designs for table layouts.

Create customer engagement

If marketers understand customer engagement better than their competitors, then this helps them develop brand loyalty. How else can the ideal customer engage with the brand? The ideal customer, or most valuable customer, does not have to be someone who buys a lot. They could be an influencer who may be a small irregular buyer who posts ratings and reviews. The reviews can influence another 100 people. 'Engaged customers' are probably going to become brand zealots if they are kept engaged.

Marketers can easily monitor the type, quantity and frequency of blog posts, forum discussions, reviews, profile updates, etc. This identifies opportunities and also acts as an early warning system to any possible future problems. Consider targeting brand evangelists rather than just purchasers.

A customer who doesn't care about the product or service is likely to be less committed or less emotionally attached to the firm supplying the product or service. On the other hand, a customer who is engaging is likely to be more emotionally connected to the brand. Marketers need to know about the sentiment, opinion and affinity a person has towards a brand. This is often expressed through repeat visits, purchases, product ratings, reviews, blogs and discussion forums and, ultimately, the person's likelihood to recommend a friend.

Ask 'How well are we measuring engagement amongst different online audiences?' and then close the loop by using the data to identify the advocates and deliver more relevant communications.

> Engaged customers = customer engagement = stronger brands.

Brand expansion/strategy

Brand extensions and the brand portfolio

There are few single-product companies. Many companies start up that way, but they soon develop other products as they grow and markets fragment. A product line is a string of products grouped together for marketing or technical reasons. Guinness started as a single-product company. Since then it has extended the product line to fill market needs as they emerged. It has also expanded beyond the basic product line of beers to offer whiskeys, soft drinks and more: different lines of product.

Add all the product lines together and you get the product mix. Finding the right product mix is a subtle balancing act. How far should a product line be extended? How many different lines should be in the product group?

Advantages of brand expansion

'Brand (or line) extension is attractive but dangerous' (Smith, 2003). There are advantages and disadvantages lurking behind this apparently easy option. Extending an existing brand name on to a new product is one of many different ways of increasing sales. Some feel that it reduces the risk of launching an unknown brand. Using a recognized brand name on a new product can give the new product immediate presence in the marketplace – customers will recognize, trust and try the new product more easily. This also creates savings in advertising and other promotions, so as the original product matures the extended brand ensures some continuity and survival of the brand in the longer run. Generally, brand extensions work if the new product actually satisfies a real relevant need amongst customers and they like the idea. Ultimately the new product should enhance the promise of the original brand as opposed to cannibalizing it. Careful consideration must be given to what happens if the extension fails.

Brand extension is a tempting option, as it uses the same sales team with the same distribution channels and often the same customers. It can also fill any unoccupied positions in the market, which might otherwise invite unwanted competitors. Finally, a full product line builds the image of the complete player, a big player, which in turn suggests reliability.

Disadvantages of brand extension

But there are disadvantages lurking behind brand and line extensions. A low-quality product will damage the original brand's reputation. A really good new product can also cannibalize the original product if the new product merely takes sales away from the old one. When contemplating brand extension, ask how much of the 'extra sales' actually replace existing sales of the original product. Constant brand extensions may dilute the brand's strength and its unique positioning, particularly if the extensions are not appropriate to the central brand. When easyJet extended into easyInternetcafes it was reported to have lost £75 million (Taylor, 2004), whereas easyJet Holidays appears to be a better fit. Although Virgin is another successful company and has enjoyed a variety of brand extensions, some of them have failed, including Virgin Vodka, Virgin Jeans, Virgin Brides, Virgin Balloons and Virgin Cosmetics.

Failed extensions

'Unfortunately, the hard truth is that many brand extensions don't work. Each brand has its own special positioning. The extension won't succeed if it works against that. Any time a brand is extended, its focus gets blurred in the minds of consumers. When the image is unclear, the original promise is broken. When the promise is broken, the brand loses value and me.'

Jacobson and Knapp (2008)

In a sense, product deletion should be a standard activity, as companies constantly replace old products with improved ones. Some corporations like to balance the product portfolio by ensuring they have a minimum of 30 per cent of 'new products' (products developed in the last five years). Phasing out and deleting products that have had their day is a delicate task. They have to be withdrawn carefully and gracefully without damaging employee morale or upsetting small groups of customers who may still want spare parts or simply to continue consuming the product. As has been mentioned, one of the world's best-marketed companies, Unilever, chopped its product portfolio from 1,600 to 400 in 2004.

Although criticized by some, the Boston Matrix can help to balance the product portfolio, as it helps managers identify which products generate surplus cash, which need extra marketing resources to support them and which need a lot of resources. 'Cash cows' (high market share in a low-growth market) generate the surplus cash that in turn funds other products, such as the high-growth 'star' products. Low-growth (and low-market-share) 'dogs' often absorb a disproportionate amount of management resources. This analysis is from a cash-flow perspective as opposed to that of the customers.

Riezebos (2003), on the other hand, analysed a brand portfolio from a competitor perspective. Different types of brands have different roles to play within the brand portfolio. Bastion brands are the key brands, usually the most profitable, with a large market share. Their success attracts competitors. Some companies expand their portfolios to protect their brands by introducing 'flanker brands' and 'fighter brands'. The flanker brand may be priced differently or have a different set of attributes and tends to fend off any new competitors that are considering occupying that space. Fighter brands are lower priced and compete with existing or potential competitors trying to occupy lower price points (the quality perceptions need to be shifted downwards so as not to dilute the bastion brand). Many organizations prefer to lose some premium-priced brand sales to an internal less profitable brand than to lose the sales to competitors. However, today many companies of a certain size reject brands that will not become star performers, as they prefer to direct their limited resources to major winners. The tasks of product extinction and extension require rigorous analysis of customers, competitors and overall trends. The marketer's task of being the guardian of the brand is a challenging one.

Brand summary and the challenges ahead

Twenty-first century brands face new challenges, including hyper-competitive markets, unknown competitors (category-less and borderless), shortened product lifecycles, more demanding, time-pressed and information-fatigued customers, media fragmentation and message clutter, anti-brand pressure groups, own brands and two other internal challenges – short-termism and fear of the boardroom.

The rise of the anti-brand

A direct challenge to brands is the 'ethical anti-branders', who attack premium-priced branded training shoes (allegedly made in sweatshops in the Far East).

Various anti-brand feelings have been aroused by many publications, ranging from Vance Packard's 1957 classic *The Hidden Persuaders* to Eric Schlosser's *Fast Food Nation* (2002) to Robert Frank's *Luxury Fever* (2000) to *The World Is Not For Sale* (2001) by José Bové (a French farmer who is best known for vandalizing a McDonald's restaurant) and François Dufour. Brands are vulnerable to a rising tide of antipathy to branding and marketing.

The demise of major corporations like Enron has further fuelled a cynicism towards big business. However, Naomi Klein's *No Logo: Taking aim at the brand bullies* (2000) articulated a certain kind of brand frustration where global brands represent, in her words, 'a fascist state where we all salute the logo and have little opportunity for criticism because our newspapers, TV stations, internet servers, street and retail spaces are all controlled by multinational corporate interests'. The ubiquitous global brand bullies effectively reduce the colourful variety of choice and force a grey cultural homogeneity on customers instead of an array of interesting local alternatives. Even the *Economist* magazine back in 2001 pointed the finger at today's global businesses: 'So companies are switching from producing products to marketing aspirations, images and lifestyles. They are trying to become weightless, shedding physical assets by shifting production from their own factories in the first world to other people's in the third.'

This provides all the more reason for brands and the businesses behind them to behave ethically and to demonstrate publicly their social responsibility. This includes environmental policies (and actions), supporting charitable endeavours and local communities, racial integration, not supplying or contributing to military regimes and political donations.

And, of course, there are the brand haters who create anti-brand websites dedicated to venting their frustrations and anger about certain brands, usually resulting from alleged poor customer service, sometimes even without consuming the brand but simply because they don't like it. As Dell has demonstrated by listening to these criticisms, addressing the reasonable issues and fixing them can strengthen a brand and grow its relations and sales.

Do brands reflect our own instability?

'Everyone needs a sense of purpose. To have a cause, to feel that we belong and are admired. Brands promise to fill the voids between who we are and what we could become. But by putting so much belief on which brand is in today but out tomorrow, we reflect our own instability. People increasingly judge others by what they have, rather than who they are. How much a person is esteemed is measured by the boots they wear, rather than the individual they are.'

Gabay (2012)

Own brands

As major retailers flex their muscles and demand that suppliers also create and deliver the retailers' own brand in almost every category, it is easy to understand why brand owners are concerned, particularly when they have to deliver a constantly high-quality own brand also. Many retailers' brands are so strong that customers are happy to give them more and more share of their wallets. Look at Tesco: what can't they sell to customers now those customers trust the brand to deliver a consistent quality at reasonable prices?

The brands do, however, have a source of continual competitive advantage, and that is continuous innovation. Although own brands are getting smarter and smarter, Saatchi & Saatchi CEO Kevin Roberts (2009) says:

> The game has changed. Own labels deliver quality. They are as strong in many categories as traditional consumer brands. But will they deliver innovation? No. This is where real marketing comes into play. A big retailer cannot possibly develop the innovation in a category that a P&G, Unilever or a Nestlé can. So as long as those companies continue to keep their core, their focus on innovation, they will continue to develop new value in this reclaimed world.

The rise of people brands, humanity and product switching

'This evolution has been guiding our society back into one that requires a more personal approach. It is time for a reminder about our humanity. Comparisons are easier to make and product switching happens faster than ever. Customers are ready to move on unless they have one thing – an undying relationship with a person or people at your brand who made them feel uniquely special.'

Kramer (2014)

Social media

Each tweet you send is either building or destroying your brand. The tone, content and timing of a tweet impacts how an audience perceives you. The same applies to Facebook, Instagram, Pinterest and so on. Brands that do not have crystal clear social media guidelines will find that social media can destroy the very essence of their own business – the brand and how it helps its customers.

The experience divide and leveraging advocacy

What you say your brand is and what others may share are different. This, if ignored, can destroy a brand. We need to create customer experiences that firstly they want and secondly they want to share. As Solis (2015) says, 'If we're not creating the types of experiences we want people to have and share, we're simply reacting to them.' And this is missing the social media opportunity.

> Positive experiences feel good to express outwardly, too, though we're not innately inclined to share them. NB It's in the business's best interest for consumers to share these positive experiences, because we know that they define the ultimate moment of truth – the moment when the consumer enters into a partnership with the brand.

Solis suggests that your strategy for loyalty and advocacy determines the future of the brand. So do you have a system to reward advocates?

'Do you have a system to reward advocates?... particularly when they define the "ultimate moment of truth" – the moment when the consumer enters into a partnership with the brand.'

Solis (2015)

Short-term sales vs long-term brand building

Brands are not for the short term. Think of them like people. They are strategic assets that need to be nurtured and grown over the long term. After that, relationships can last a lifetime and beyond, as some brands are handed down from generation to generation (if the brands manage to stay relevant to the needs of the next generation). There is a constant tension between sales and marketing and, for that matter, finance and marketing. Quarterly results-driven businesses require quarterly results, which usually means seeing quarterly growth in sales and profits. Brands do not deliver quick returns, particularly new and repositioned brands. They take time to research and develop. They take time to build relationships. Although some brands have developed in one or two years, these are exceptional. Certainly brands emerging within a quarter is, even today, highly unlikely.

The impatience of the chief financial officer (CFO) or the board or the shareholders may jeopardize the long-term work of the brand builder. This also manifests itself in the advertising debate: whether a campaign is sales or brand building. Ad campaigns can of course do either, but rarely can do both really well. One usually takes priority. Yes, campaigns can deliver sales and grow a brand, but each objective has different priorities. Brands are for the long term and can secure higher sales, higher prices and higher profits. These are some of the factors that can bring the marketer back into the boardroom.

Brands – the bridge between marketing, finance and the boardroom

Marketers may have slipped from being the potential heroes of the boardroom back in the 1980s when brands were suddenly touted as a 'surefire means of differentiation in the face of increased competitive pressures and rampant product proliferation activities. They were secret weapons of sorts: legally-protectable assets that brought unrivalled powers to the firms that developed them' (Madden *et al*, 2002).

A study revealed that shareholders should insist on systematic performance feedback on branding. It actually suggested systematic performance feedback on all key items in the balance sheet including branding. However, it suggested that very few companies had this optimal balance between financial performance and branding (Ohnemus, 2009). The report went on to say that 'the board of directors should systematically assess and monitor the strategic branding position of their company and how their branding investments are performing against key competitors'. Board directors acknowledge the value of brands but do not understand how they are built and sustained or, in particular, how marketing makes this happen.

The irony of it all is that, now that brands appear on the balance sheet, they are recognized as a financial asset of the business, yet budgets required to grow them are considered to be 'expenses rather than investments' (Ohnemus, 2009).

When Harvard's Madden *et al* (2002) suggested that 'the demonstration of brand value to stockholders would prove most useful in reconceptualizing marketing from expense to investment', an opportunity knocked for marketers. But the lingering, unanswered question remains to this day: 'Do brand-building investments really pay off? Lacking conclusive evidence concerning branding and the bottom line, brand "investments" remain "expenses" and the promise of the brand remains unfulfilled.'

Marketers must learn the language of finance and apply it to marketing. Marketing language and jargon have been charged as 'inaccessible and disconnected from the financial metrics by which firms are ultimately steered' (Davis, 2001). If there is no common language, there is no communication and with that comes no understanding of marketing's crucial role in brand building.

Marketers and the language of finance

So here it is. International Organization for Standardization (ISO) standard ISO 10668 on monetary brand valuation requires legal, market research and financial analysis must be completed in determining a brand's value. Since 2004, International Financial Reporting Standard (IFRS) 3 has required that, on acquisition of a brand, the purchase price paid must be allocated to the individual assets acquired for inclusion in the balance sheet of the acquirer at their fair values. 'The requirement to conduct brand valuations for financial compliance purposes has forced CFOs and financial regulators to take brand valuation seriously' (Haigh, 2011).

Prior to 1988, brand values were never shown in balance sheets. In fact in 1988 Hovis chose to put a financial value on its brand and then add it in the balance sheet as part of a takeover defence. This triggered a major debate that has been running ever since. Today, there are several approaches to valuing a brand, including the market approach, the cost approach and the income approach (Roberts, 2011).

Brands have become big business and managing them has become a branch of high finance (Haigh, 2011). If managers can show that marketing will increase returns to shareholders, marketing will obtain a much more pre-eminent role in the boardrooms of industry. The discipline itself will also obtain more respect for its rigour and direction.

Marketers have much to do. But, with some work, the doors of the boardroom will be flung wide open so they can secure funds to develop great brands and, in return, deliver dividends back to shareholders.

Politics and brands: Are brands becoming political?

Starbucks, Coca-Cola and other major brands repudiated President Trump's executive order banning immigration from seven predominantly Muslim countries. Uber's Chief Executive stepped down from Mr Trump's business advisory group following objections from Uber staff. 200,000 Uber customers deleted their accounts while Uber's competitors seized the opportunity to attack. The New York Taxi Workers Alliance alerted the news media to Uber's CEO, Travis Kalanick's, links with President Trump and organized a protest at Uber's New York office while Lyft, another taxi service, promised a $1 million donation to the American Civil Liberties Union. Its app simultaneously shot towards the top of the download charts (Isaac, 2017). Meanwhile, the retailer Nordstrom dropped President Trump's daughter's fashion line after public boycotts (BBC Newsbeat, 2017).

Even America's own global giant brand, Coca-Cola, became political when its CEO, Muhtar Kent, criticized President Trump's immigration ban, which was contrary to the values of global beverage maker, The Coca-Cola Co. Kent said, 'Coca-Cola is resolute in its commitment to diversity, fairness and inclusion, and we do not support this travel ban or any policy that is contrary to our core values and beliefs' (Saunders, 2017). Coca-Cola employs 700,000 people in 200 countries.

> '"Americans now are using brands as a mechanism to fight with each other. They're becoming the weapons in the social war" says Thomas Ordahl, chief strategy officer at Landor branding consultancy.'
>
> Whipp and Bond (2017)

As brands are assets that reflect passion and people's needs, it is almost inevitable that brands, like Coca-Cola and Starbucks, become 'politically sensitive'. A brand's values (and today its political and ethical statements) are an intrinsic part of what, why and how an organization does its business. So transparency, and having a crystal clear point of view about values is sometimes inseparable from political statements.

As politics polarize around the world, will we see more brands declaring their point of view? Are we witnessing the rise of the political brand?

Conclusion

Brands are being challenged. However, they are powerful assets that generate many benefits to both an organization and its customers. Surprisingly, many brands allow themselves to self-destruct with sloppy service and inconsistent brand applications.

Brand components include name, logo, colours, positioning, promise, personality, values, association and experience. Brand creation is a process that starts with a brief and goes through concept generation, concept development and roll-out. Copious research is carried out before and after each step.

Brand maintenance focuses on the customer experience, extending it online and considering customer engagement as a way to move customers up a ladder of engagement towards becoming brand zealots. Experiential marketing is also considered. Finally, brand expansion/strategy has both advantages and disadvantages. The strategic corporate brand is also explored.

> **Strong brands survive through careful management**
>
> It is no accident that these brands have been around for over 100 years: Bass, Coke, Kellogg's Corn Flakes, Guinness, Pears Soap.

You can see how UEFA go about managing and upgrading the corporate identity (corporate brand) in the following case study.

CASE STUDY UEFA brand identity refresh

FIGURE 2.8 The UEFA logo and trophy

Situation analysis

UEFA's European Champions League is one of the world's most prestigious sporting events as the top football teams from across Europe compete with each other to win this coveted prize.

- Hyper-competition: Today, football competes with other sports and other forms of entertainment. In addition to hyper-competition in an already cluttered global marketplace, there are other trends that have a significant impact on the marketplace.
- Digital developments: Include a growing variety of digital devices including mobile, tablets, TVs, cinema screens and whatever IoT will bring. Other digital developments include virtual reality (eg the BBC offering its free VR app for World Cup 2018), perhaps AR and any other developments that can enhance the CX both inside and outside the stadium, and, around the rest of the world.
- Stakeholders: The European Champions League has many stakeholders (UEFA internal teams, sponsors, broadcasters, licensees, fans, clubs and industry experts).
- Three-year review cycle: All markets continually move away from their suppliers. To stay close to this continually changing marketplace, UEFA reviews its brand identity every three years in sync with the commercial cycle of broadcast and sponsorship rights.

FIGURE 2.9 Teams entering the stadium

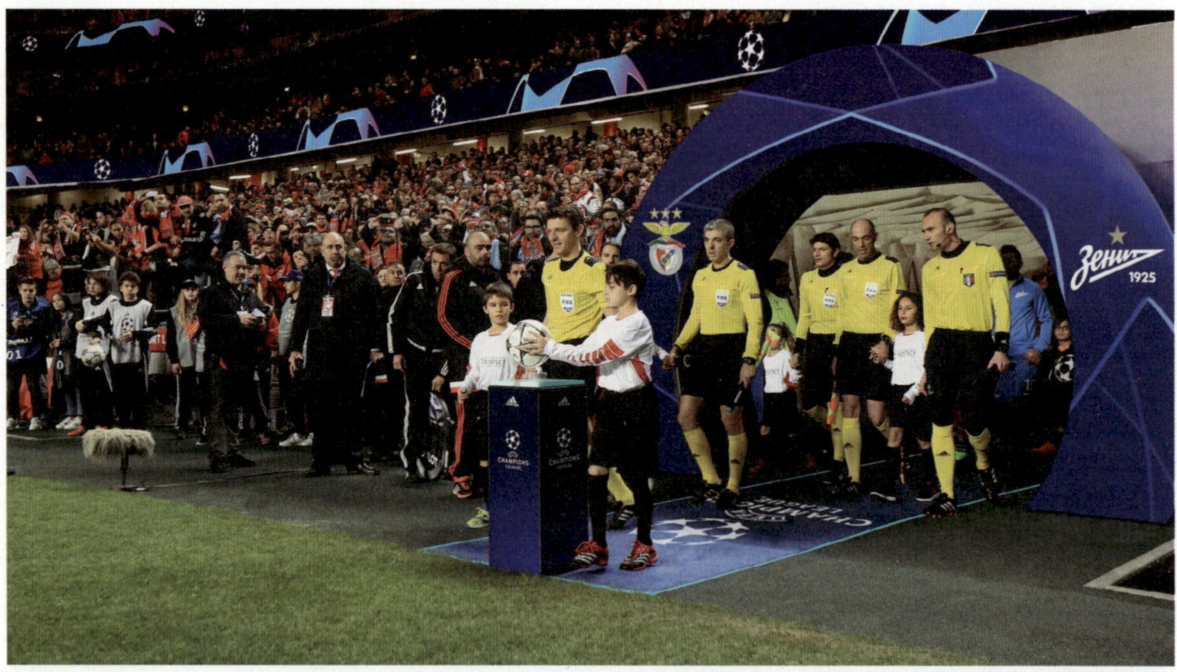

Objectives

Create a new brand identity that:

- supports the repositioning of the European Champions League from 'European sports' to 'global entertainment';
- enhances the prestige of one of the world's biggest sporting competitions;
- helps to keep fans (and viewers) engaged in a distracting and cluttered world;
- adapts to the fast-changing digital tech world.

Strategy

Create a flexible brand identity that can be used by different stakeholders on different platforms while helping to engage customers/audiences as well as strengthening and embedding the European Champions League's repositioning in a global entertainment marketplace.

Here are the brand values, brand personality, brand vision, brand mission and brand essence that are strategically part of the whole brand experience.

- **Brand values:** Excitement – exhilarating events that inspire and engage, leadership being the benchmark in sport, leading by examples of excellence, striving for the highest standards in everything we do.
- **Brand personality:** Prestigious, premium, sophisticated, inspiring, emotive and captivating.
- **Brand vision:** To be the benchmark global sport competition.
- **Brand mission:** To give clubs and their fans the best competition experience.
- **Brand essence:** The best of the best on the ultimate stage.
- **Creative concept:** Highlighting the moments that make the ultimate stage.

Tactics

The actual process or steps to create or update a brand identity are described in the 'Actions' section, which is about getting things done and the steps that need to be taken to make this happen. Essentially, after issuing a brief

FIGURE 2.10 The stadium and logo

to four pre-scanned agencies, the best concept is chosen and then 'tweaked' to improve it even further. Here is the winning concept.

The winning concept

The UEFA Champions League brand for the 2018/19 season delivers a vibrant new look, based on a concept called 'Highlighting moments that make the ultimate stage' (Figure 2.10).

The connected stars from the 'starball' in the UEFA Champions League logo are the centrepiece of this new brand identity (Figure 2.11). The concept captures the iconic moments of extraordinary feats of skill and ability that make UEFA Champions League match nights so special.

The new identity visually articulates the brand and expresses the refined UEFA Champions League brand positioning. It consolidates the core brand values that the competition is known for, while highlighting the leading role it plays in football. The UEFA Champions League has expanded to become part of the global entertainment environment, rather than just solely being a sports event.

Remain relevant and engaging for fans

The refined brand identity has been created to support digital, mobile and social media platforms (Figure 2.12). The new assets allow for an easier, scalable brand integration (from soft to full branding) on smaller surfaces and mobile devices.

Cater for digital requirements

The level of detail on the 'ultimate stage' stadium and 'starball' visuals has been enhanced to cater for a richer ultra-high-definition television experience. This will ensure that the brand remains relevant and engaging for fans and will enable them to interact with it, as technology and content platforms develop.

FIGURE 2.11 Starball and logo

The starball icon (is part of the logo)

The starball icon, together with the logotype, is the UEFA Champions League logo (Figure 2.11). The starball icon forms part of the logo. The basic shape of the starball featured in the logo and used as an individual icon has remained the same. However, the new identity uses a 3D version of the starball icon in its key visuals (both stills and motion).

Boldest change in years

Compared with previous brand identity updates, the new design is a greater leap forward. While the 'starball' visual gains importance in the new identity, the distinct and successful 'ultimate stage' arena still features in the branding package. This provides an extended range of key visuals that can be used for communication purposes, both internally as well as by UEFA's partners.

New, more flexible colour co-branding system

The new identity has been designed to support a large range of stakeholders, such as sponsors, broadcasters, licensees and clubs. A new, more flexible colour co-branding system has been introduced to give commercial partners the opportunity to tailor the brand identity to their own needs, while ensuring consistency of the look and feel across multiple touchpoints.

The key visuals in Figure 2.13 demonstrate the subtle differences between before and after the brand identity refresh.

More flexible branding

The branding has been designed to be more flexible, while building on established elements such as the starball, the stadium and the trophy. The blue colour palette deriving from UEFA Champions League match nights has been enriched with new accent colours – magenta and cyan – to support the fresher look.

Actions

A brand identity review team was created using all stakeholders. Four top brand identity agencies were vetted and selected to pitch for the refreshed brand identity. The winning brand identity concept (and agency) was selected.

FIGURE 2.12 Brand guidelines

5-PILLAR BRANDING APPROACH

1
OFFICIAL MATCH INFO BRANDING

FIXTURES
BAYERN MUNICH
VS
PARIS ST GERMAIN
TUE 14 MAR, 18:55
VILLARREAL
VS
ANDERLECHT
TUE 14 MAR, 18:55

- Entirely branded (full screen)
- In line with TV graphics design
- Mobile ready (increased font size, less content)

2
PHOTO-CONTENT BRANDING

- Frames, placeholders for photos and videos
- Partially branded
- Flexible approach split photo vs branding needed (1/3, 1/2, etc)

3
PHOTOGRAPHY SOFT BRANDING

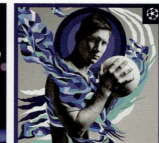

- Photo colour, keying, contrast treatment (and/or)
- Watermark, pattern branding
- Feature frame, sign-off device

4
ARTISTIC BRANDING

- Artistic illustrations, less restricted bold visual expressions
- Red-thread in style, graphic elements
- Feature frame, sign-off device

5
PHOTOGRAPHY WITHOUT BRANDING

- No graphic treatment
- Purely editorial photography
- Still in line with overall brand positioning

FULLY BRANDED → UNBRANDED

FIGURE 2.13 UEFA design changes, 2018

Before: 2015–18 visuals	After: 2018–21 visuals
(a) Apex	(d) Apex
(b) Side view	(e) Side view
(c) Trophy	(f) Trophy

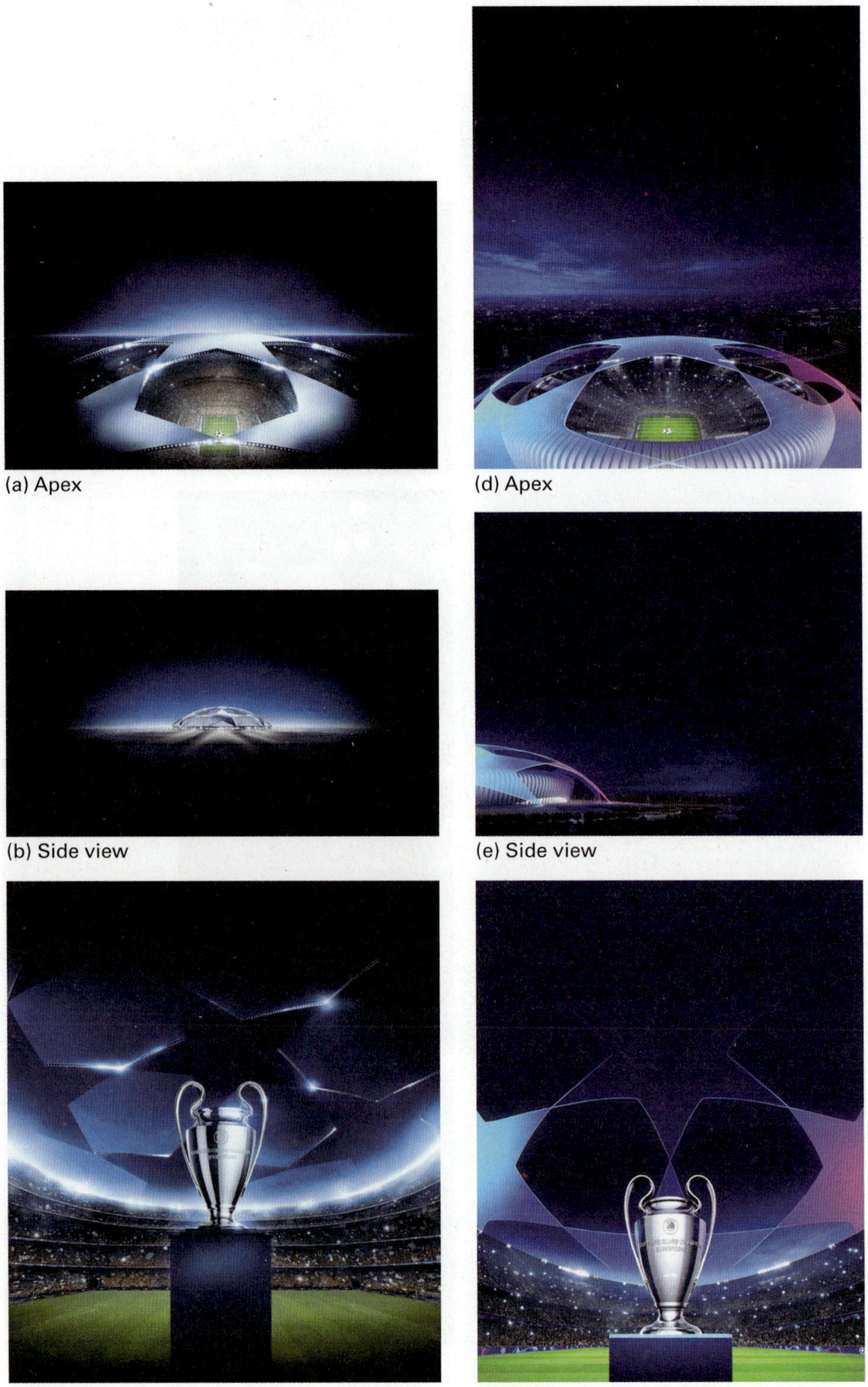

SOURCE: Reproduced by kind permission of UEFA

The brand identity concept was then refined to ensure it has maximum impact as well as supporting the repositioning, enabling more customer engagement and also allowing the brand to be used by emerging digital trends (including digital, mobile and social media platforms).

Development timeline

The project for the 2018–21 rebranding was launched in September 2015 and involved multiple stakeholder reviews (UEFA internal, sponsors, broadcasters, licensees, clubs and industry experts) to assess strength, weaknesses, opportunities and threats of the branding.

The findings were briefed to four pre-scanned creative agencies that presented two concepts each. Two agencies made it to the final round where the winning concept 'Highlighting moments that make the ultimate stage' was chosen. The winning agency was asked to develop and implement the updated brand identity. The unsuccessful agencies were all paid rejection fees.

After various concept enhancements, development of the new brand started in June 2017 and it was launched in June 2018.

Executing with excellence

To help execute the roll-out of the refreshed brand identity, a brand manual was developed giving very specific guidance for media and other authorized users of the brand identity, to ensure correct and consistent use of the brand identity.

The 52-page brand manual (Figure 2.14) gives clear guidance for all forms of the brand identity usage for stakeholders' use in TV studios, retailer's point of sale, social media, including how official partners can incorporate products and brand colours with selected UEFA Champions League assets. When the world is watching, every detail matters. Using the brand assets effectively is vital to remaining consistent and making the brand instantly recognizable.

The manual also includes hard and soft usage (Figure 2.12 shows the five-pillar branding approach previously mentioned). The brand manual addresses the surprisingly wide array of potential use of UEFA assets. For example, the use of the anthem (music) is supported with links to 44 different types of audio files required for different usage by broadcasters and stadium managers.

FIGURE 2.14 The 52-page brand manual helps to ensure consistent brand usage

Control

In addition to formally tracking reaction to the new identity, key stakeholders were invited to give feedback. Here is a selection of their reactions.

> The most iconic of sporting identities:
>
> 'Confident, contemporary and courageous. With refined elegance and a vibrant injection of colour, the UEFA Champions League brand upholds its position as possibly the most iconic of sporting identities.'
>
> (Mark Hyde, Head of Design, BT Sport)
>
> Fresh yet premium:
>
> 'The branding is fresh and appealing. It gives the competition a new, contemporary look while remaining premium.'
>
> (Hans Erik Tuijt, Global Sponsorship Director, Heineken)
>
> Maximizes the opportunities to engage:
>
> 'The UEFA Champions League is a globally recognized brand in football, sports and entertainment. This brand refresh maximizes the opportunities to engage with fans and stakeholders across new technologies and platforms.'
>
> (Guy-Laurent Epstein, Marketing Director, UEFA Events SA)

The new brand identity will continue to afford the UEFA Champions League a unique branding that will be applied across a wide range of promotional applications, with the objective of further enhancing the prestige of one of the world's biggest sporting competitions.

Resources

- Men and women: Led by the director of marketing, other UEFA marketing staff liaised with the stakeholders and the agencies. UEFA have a marketing partner, TEAM Marketing AG, and the London-based creative agency DesignStudio, who both helped to manage this brand identity programme.
- Money: Although budgets are confidential, UEFA did pay rejection fees to the three unsuccessful agencies.
- Minutes: It took 33 months from start to finish (launch and roll out the brand identity).

Key points from Chapter 2

- Brands help customers and the organizations behind them.
- Branding is a strategic issue.
- Branding can create competitive advantage.
- There is a disciplined approach to the brand-building process.
- Brands, like any other asset, need to be maintained and require resources.

References and further reading

Anderson, C (2006) *The Long Tail: Why the future of business is selling less of more*, Hyperion Books, New York

Atkin, D (2004) New priests for the new religion, *Marketer*, September

Aufreiter, N, Elzinga, D and Gordon, J (2003) Better brands, *McKinsey Quarterly*, 4

Banham, Russ (1998) Making your mark: Time for finance to play a role in brand management, *CFO: The magazine for senior financial executives*, **14** (3), 1 March

Bayley, S and Mavity, R (2008) *Life's a Pitch*, Corgi Books, London

BBC Newsbeat (2017) Ivanka Trump fashion brand dropped by US retailer after boycott, BBC Newsbeat, 22 March

Bernstein, D (1984) *Company Image and Reality: A critique of corporate communications*, Holt, Rinehart and Winston, London

Bové, J and Dufour, F (2001) *The World Is Not For Sale*, Verso Books, London

Braun, T (2004) *The Philosophy of Branding*, Kogan Page, London

Brown, D (2016) Purpose and passion: The pillars of small business success, *Huffington Post*, 18 May (updated)

Brun-Jensen, P (2014) Next-gen social analytics are transforming digital marketing, *Adweek*, 22 September

Chaffey, D and Smith, PR (2013) *Emarketing Excellence*, 4th edn, Routledge, London

Clifton, R (2004) The big debate, *Marketer*, July/August

Davis, S (2001) Taking control of your brand's destiny, *Brandweek*, 15 October

Economist (1998) The rebirth of IBM – blue is the colour, 6 June

Economist (2001) Who's wearing the trousers? 6 September

Eltvedt, H and Flores, L (2005) Beyond online advertising – lessons about the power of brand websites to build and expand brands, ESOMAR Online Conference, Montreal, June

Farrell, S (2008) A million dollar branding secret, How-to Internet Marketing Network

Fauconnier, C (2006) Humanising the marketplace: A manifesto for brand growth, *Admap*, 471, April

Fitch, R (2003) in *Revealing the Corporation: Perspectives on identity image reputation*, ed J Balmer and S Greyser, Routledge, London

Fletcher, W (2010) Author, lecturer and former chairman of the Royal Institution in conversation with PR Smith

Frank, R H (2000) *Luxury Fever: Money and happiness in an era of excess*, Princeton University Press, Princeton, NJ

Gabay, J (2012) Q&A: Jonathan Gabay, *The Marketer*, p 50, 29 June, available in hard copy from the CIM library (www.cim.co.uk (archived at https://perma.cc/32CR-LBSL))

Haigh, D (2011) A brand new approach, *The Marketer*, February, available in hard copy from the CIM library (www.cim.co.uk (archived at https://perma.cc/32CR-LBSL))

Hooker, S (1991) Applying psychology to market research: The theory of raised expectations, *Market Research Society Newsletter*, January

Isaac, M (2017) Uber CEO to leave Trump advisory council after criticism, *New York Times*, 2 February

Jacobson, T and Knapp, K (2008) Brand extensions, Vistage chief executive organization online papers [online] www.vistage.com (archived at https://perma.cc/34TX-GKS4)

Jenkins, N (1991) *The Business of Image*, Kogan Page, London

Jones, B (2001) *The Big Idea*, HarperCollins, London

Kanter, R (2009) The downsides of branding, 23 July [online] http://blogs.hbr.org/kanter/2009/07/the-downsides-of-branding.html (archived at https://perma.cc/2MCH-9D26)

Kapferer, J (2008) *The New Strategic Brand Management*, 4th edn, Kogan Page, London

Klein, N (2000) *No Logo: Taking aim at the brand bullies*, Flamingo, London

Kramer, B (2014) A return to simplicity, empathy and imperfection in communication: Human to human #H2H, Brian Solis, 25 February [online] www.briansolis.com/2014/02/return-simplicity-empathy-imperfection-communication-human-human-h2h/ (archived at https://perma.cc/N84L-R8WX)

Kumar, A J (2012) How to effectively rebrand your social media profiles, *Social Media Examiner*, 5 November

Le Pla, F J, Davis, S and Parker, L (2003) *Brand Driven: The route to integrated branding through great leadership*, Kogan Page, London

Lindstrom, M (2005) *Brand Sense*, Kogan Page, London

Madden, T, Fehle, F and Fournier, S (2002) Brands matter: An empirical investigation of brand-building activities and the creation of shareholder value, working paper, Harvard Business School, Boston, MA

Millward Brown Optimor (2010) *BrandZ Top 100 Most Valuable Global Brands*, Millward Brown Optimor, New York

Mose, M (2003) *United We Brand: How to create a cohesive brand that's seen, heard, and remembered*, Harvard Business School Publishing, Boston, MA

Murphy, J (ed) (1991) *Branding: A key marketing tool*, Macmillan, London

Nash and Zull Products (1989) 1990 US Hall of Shame, Universal Press Syndicate, Kansas City

Neumeier, M (2007) *Zag*, New Riders, Berkeley, CA

Ohmae, K (1994) Interview with PR Smith, Marketing CDs, https://prsmith.org (archived at https://perma.cc/S9PK-G5MW)

Ohnemus, L (2009) B2B Branding: A financial burden for shareholders? *Business Horizons*, **52** (2), pp 159–66

Olins, W (1989) *Corporate Identity: Making business strategy visible through design*, Thames & Hudson, London

Olins, W (1996) *The New Guide to Identity*, Gower, Aldershot

Olins, W (2003) *On Brand*, Thames & Hudson, London

Packard, V ([1957] 1960) *The Hidden Persuaders*, Penguin Books, Harmondsworth

Peters, T (2003) *Re-imagine*, Dorling Kindersley, London

PRTV (1993) Corporate image video, PRTV, London

Reynolds, J, Cuthbertson, C and Bell, R (2004) *Retail Strategy: The view from the bridge*, Elsevier Butterworth-Heinemann, Oxford

Riezebos, R (2003) *Brand Management: A theoretical and practical approach*, Pearson, Harlow

Roberts, K (2009) Short cuts (part 2), 6 July, available in hard copy from the CIM library (www.cim.co.uk (archived at https://perma.cc/32CR-LBSL))

Roberts, S (2011) Brand valuation: methodologies, *Intellectual Property Magazine*, February [online] http://shop.bsigroup.com/upload/Standards%20&%20Publications/IPM_Brand_Valuation_article.pdf (archived at https://perma.cc/G73H-LFTD)

Ronay, A (2004) Emotional brands, *Marketer*, 5, September

Rothery, G (2009) All in the mind, *Marketing Age*, 3 (6), November

Sable, D (2017) Nations as brands: Why Justin Trudeau is bigger than Kim Kardashian, LinkedIn, 7 March

Sauerman, R (2018) Brand is the purpose and passion that propels everything your company does [online] https://firebrandtalent.com/blog/2018/07/brand-is-the-purpose-and-passion-that-propels-everything-your-company-does/ (archived at https://perma.cc/RYL3-37RH)

Saunders, J (2017) Coca-Cola CEO Muhtar Kent criticizes immigration order, *Atlanta Business Chronicle*, 31 January

Schlosser, E (2002) *Fast Food Nation*, Penguin Books, Harmondsworth

Sisodia, R, Sheth, J and Wolfe, D (2014) *Firms of Endearment: How world-class companies profit from passion and purpose*, 2nd edn, Pearson Education, London

Smilansky, S (2008) *Experiential Marketing*, Kogan Page, London

Smith, P R (2003) *Great Answers to Tough Marketing Questions*, Kogan Page, London

Solis, B (2015) Crossing the experience divide: Creating positive, lasting experiences is a crucial mandate for any brand [online] www.briansolis.com (archived at https://perma.cc/6SVS-GYLN), 12 January

Stampler, L (2013) How much the world's most iconic logos cost to design, Yahoo Finance, 27 March [online] https://ca.finance.yahoo.com/news/how-much-the-world-s-most-iconic-logos-cost-companies-to-design-them-151333867.html (archived at https://perma.cc/A4VM-6HG8)

Stewart, R (2018) People's trust in brands faces biggest dip since the 2008 financial crash, *The Drum*, 19 April

Taylor, D (2004) More bangers for your bucks, *Marketer*, 5, September

Universal McCann (2007) Power to the people: Tracking the impact of social media wave, 2.0, May

Valentine, V (1988) Signs and symbols, survey, Market Research Society, London

Whipp, L and Bond, S (2017) Politics of products emerges as flashpoint in polarised markets, *Financial Times*, 11 February

Yeong, C L and Yu, H-Y (2006) Chinese president's itinerary for US visit: Gates first, Bush later, *International Herald Tribune*, 13 April

03 Customer relationship management

LEARNING OBJECTIVES

By the end of this chapter you will be able to:

- discuss the importance of relationship marketing and how CRM creates competitive advantage;
- see how marketing automation generates leads for the CRM system;
- see how social and CRM are a natural fit;
- outline the CRM planning process;
- understand the benefits and resources required by CRM;
- identify and avoid the classic CRM errors;
- present the case of long-term brand building vs short-term sales growth.

Introduction to CRM

CRM presents a golden opportunity to create competitive advantage by listening to customers, serving their needs better than ever before, improving the overall CX and, in summary, adding value to the CX.

Your marketing strategy should, among other things, highlight which has priority: customer acquisition, or customer retention. CRM is primarily about helping prospects to become customers and then nurturing customers into lifetime customers.

> A customer's LTV (lifetime value) might be worth sales of, say, 20 cars or 20 mobile phones (during the customer's life). Obviously, this is worth a lot more than selling one car or one mobile and hence why customer retention is deemed to be, on average, at least six times more profitable than customer acquisition. It is therefore, generally speaking, worth investing in customer retention.

So, deciding how to split resources between customer acquisition and customer retention is a strategic decision that comes from your overall marketing strategy. Acquisition is generated by driving traffic to the website and using marketing automation systems to identify and deliver sales leads to the sales teams by delivering the prospect customer's information into the CRM system for the sales team to convert to a customer. After that, customer retention can be managed via a sales CRM system. Sales and service teams can help customers throughout the customers' lifetime with exactly the right information at exactly the right time on exactly the right platform. Marketers can learn to optimize their timely (and relevant) offers which, effectively, block out competition. Ultimately, keep nurturing the customer relationship throughout the customer lifetime journey. Customer retention depends on excellent customer relationship management.

Better CRM is required if:

- customers receive irrelevant, untimely emails they mark as spam;
- customer emails or messages are left unanswered for days;
- fans' comments are ignored;
- immediate response is expected but not delivered;
- satisfying customers is simply not enough to keep them.

Adapted from Chaffey and Smith (2017)

What is CRM?

Some call it customer relationship management; others call it customer experience management (CEM); others call it customer managed relationships (CMR). Regardless of its name, it is a strategic decision to invest in and develop your customer relationship process. This includes sales/order fulfilment, sales/order processing, returns and overall service management. Do remember that customer retention is different to customer acquisition as it requires different messages, incentives and channels; in fact, a different communications mix. Given that it is possibly six times more profitable to sell to an existing customer than to a new customer, it follows that the decision to invest in CRM and customer retention, in particular, is a relatively easy strategic choice. What may be more challenging is choosing and executing a suitable CRM system that connects to all customer touchpoints, both online and offline. Contacting customers pre, during and post sales with relevant, tempting and timely offers, as well as responding to customers' direct and indirect comments (on social platforms) requires carefully planned systems. Some of this may be automated. We'll look at this later.

There is a direct overlap between nurturing customer relationships and nurturing a brand (see p 35), and growing the longer-term profitability of the business. Carefully managed brands help customers to develop good relationships with those brands. CRM is a set of processes, linked to a database, that helps an organization keep in contact with customers and deal with their queries, complaints, purchases, suggestions and post-purchase issues as well as seeking to nurture loyal customers and advocates. Today, this involves multiple channels, particularly social media. Hence the term: social CRM.

Customer relationships

Think about how personal relationships grow stronger and stronger: listening, understanding, responding and communicating. Understanding what is important and what makes a difference; delivering it regularly; never breaking the promise; occasionally surprising or even delighting the other person; caring about the person; helping the person when things go wrong; always being there for them. The same applies to customer relationships. It is not rocket science.

Even remembering someone's name makes a difference. People generally like it when their names are remembered, particularly when their preferences and needs are also remembered. How nice is it when a waiter or receptionist remembers your name?

Never sell to a stranger

'Think of the old corner shop. If the shopkeeper ordered a new type of pickle, he wouldn't expect strangers to flock in and buy it. He'd recommend it to his regular pickle buyers and to people buying cheese and pork. You wouldn't call that hard sell. You'd call it personal service, based on the shopkeeper remembering the preferences of individual customers and using this knowledge to anticipate their needs. No matter what the size and character of your marketplace, direct marketing now lets you offer that personal service to every customer.'

Young (nd)

Remembering names, needs and profiles

Remembering a customer's particular needs and providing the right response is rarely the result of guesswork. In the case of a company with a small number of customers, it requires a good memory, good interpretive skills and attention to detail. In the case of an organization with many hundreds, thousands, or sometimes millions of customers on a database, it is largely dependent on accurate analysis and building up valuable insights. As customers are more demanding and have more channels of communication, organizations simply have to be able to respond to them continuously, in a personalized way – wherever, whenever and however required.

'Your name is the most important sound in the world'

Remembering names and needs (and satisfying them) helps to build customer relationships. This applies to a small business with 50 customers or a bigger business with 50 million customers.

A system is required, whether automated or manual. Securing loyalty today is a never-ending process requiring outstanding CRM and ongoing customer engagement.

50 per cent of FTSE 100 did not know who their customers were

They could not profile their own customers, even though they had the customer data collected and safely stored (MORI, 2003). We thought this was crazy but has it improved since?

Rewarding customers

A lot of CRM is about serving customers properly and occasionally rewarding them, identifying advocates and regularly rewarding them in a carefully planned process, and, finally, identifying potential defectors and somehow stopping them from leaving (if they are worth keeping). Not all customers are equal. Some are ideal and some you lose money on. Those ideal customers who buy a lot, recommend you a lot and give useful feedback, deserve to be rewarded. After all, they generate six times more profit than new customers and they spread awareness and positive attitudes, so why wouldn't you identify them, contact them and surprise them, just like when Canadian bank, TD, decided to 'wow' their customers (Figure 3.1).

TD Bank turned ATMs into Automated Thanking Machines™ to create some very special moments for a selection of their loyal customers across Canada. A simple thank you can change someone's day. A simple thank you with a highly relevant and valuable gift can help to create advocates. Warning: the video captures some very emotional customer reactions, which make many viewers feel quite emotional too.

FIGURE 3.1 'Customer retention isn't boring – here's wow'! Watch the video on PR Smith's blog at **http://prsmith.org/customer-retention-isnt-boring-heres-wow/**

SOURCE: TD Bank, Canada

Angry and impatient customers

Customers know how to use social media and how to generate publicity if required. Meanwhile, remember that even though customers are tired, have no time, are angry, and are often simply wrong, we need to manage, now more than ever before, our customer care to nurture lifetime relationships.

Angry customers become militant complainers and smash Mercedes

'The chairman of a Chinese wildlife park destroyed his $60,000 SLK230 Mercedes sports car as a protest because he was unhappy about the warranty. With an astute understanding of the media, he "intended to cause maximum embarrassment" to Mercedes-Benz by inviting hundreds of spectators and journalists to watch five workers with sticks smash the car. After that he attached ropes to the wreck and got several bulls to tow it through the city. Compensation negotiations resumed immediately but progressed too slowly, so Mr Wang (who wanted a full refund) asked a friend to also destroy his Mercedes. The friend obliged and drove his white S320 1,000 miles from Beijing to Wuhan. In another public event, six men armed with batons smashed the windows and doors. Mercedes-Benz claimed that Mr Wang had "used the wrong fuel and had subsequently refused a complimentary cleaning of the engine".'

August (2002)

What is marketing automation?

Marketing automation (MA) is all about automated communications: an email, a pop-up page, a dynamic page swap showing more relevant material to a particular visitor, or alerting a sales rep to call a particular prospect – all triggered by a visitor's click behaviour (digital body language). Many processes can now be automated in very sophisticated ways. MA's primary goal is to acquire leads. MA can improve campaign results, as it generates automatic tailored communications triggered by click behaviour and profiles. It is rules based (eg a visitor who stays for over five minutes, views the product video, views prices and goes to the checkout but doesn't buy will get a higher score and subsequently receive a call or email from a salesperson offering help – assuming the visitor has clearly opted-in and given their name, email and phone number).

What is the difference between CRM and MA?

MA is primarily used to develop a 'marketing qualified lead' (ie identify a prospect's behaviour and then present the prospect/lead's information to the sales team) while CRM is primarily used to help prospects and customers, so they firstly convert prospects into customers, and secondly, nurture customers into lifetime customers. MA helps to attract visitors (prospects) to a website (eg via an email), analyses their behaviour on the site, nurtures a percentage of them into leads (marketing qualified leads or MQLs) via a follow-up auto email, or an auto dynamic page swap (serving the visitor with even more relevant web pages). The MQLs can be delivered to a sales team for follow up. Once the lead is presented the data is transferred into the CRM system so that the subsequent relationship can be managed. CRM handles the entire customer journey from the point that a marketing qualified lead is handed over to sales.

What are service bots?

CRM bots include chatbots like Facebook Messenger bots or any bots that auto answer customer service questions on a website. Other forms of service bots are emerging such as Pizza Hut Japan's new robot waiters and Hilton Hotels' concierge bot.

Pizza Hut's waiter (designed by Softbank) takes and delivers orders as well as carrying out 'emotional sensing' to detect whether a customer is happy or not. The bot will then adjust the ordering process.

What is social CRM?

Firstly, social CRM is a strategic decision, similar to the strategic decision to engage website visitors and customers at different levels via the Ladder of Engagement. Essentially, social CRM integrates social media conversations into your CRM systems. Ideally, it links all of these conversations with telephone calls, emails and online chats into information to understand and serve customers better. Social selling is different as 'salespeople use social media platforms to research, prospect, and network by sharing educational content and answering questions... build relationships until prospects are ready to buy' (Minsky and Quesenberry, 2016).

What is CRM dialogue?

The CRM system should facilitate a dialogue, or a two-way flow of information, between the customer and the organization. Every time customers respond, they can be encouraged to give information about their needs and their situation (eg whether they want to opt out or stay on the database, or whether they prefer email to a phone call). Does the system prompt a three-way dialogue ('trialogue') by regularly sharing engaged customers' opinions, scores, ratings and reviews with other prospects?

Front end is fun, back end is business

Marketers are reasonably good at developing websites (front end) but we have to become experts with the database and the CRM systems (back end) required to build continual success.

Roll-out requires an investment of the 3Ms (men and women, money and minutes) into communication, motivation and training. Training ensures all staff are fully familiar with the system, how it works, how it can make their lives easier, how it will help the customer and how it will help the business.

The power of CRM

CRM builds a protective wall around customers, in the same way as a brand does. CRM enhances the customers' relationship with the brand. In fact, CRM is part of the brand experience, therefore it is part of the brand. As the relationship strengthens, loyalty builds and gives you some protection from losing customers to the constant onslaught of competitive promotions. Relationships built on excellent service and occasional rewards are more enduring (see TD Bank video, Figure 3.1) than relationships built on price discounts, which can dilute the perceived value of your brand.

Boost sales

Good customer relations boost sales, as they simply help customers to repeat-buy during their 'customer lifetime', as well as buying other products and services as they increase their share-of-wallet spend with the same trusted brand (customers still buy almost any product or service from Tesco; think: Google Pay and Apple Wallet). Good relations also help to recruit new customers, as happy customers spread the word.

Excellent CRM systems can predict customer preferences and prompt customers with tempting offers when they are ready to buy or sometimes just before they are ready to buy. Some of this is purchase triggered, time triggered, event triggered or digital body language triggered (particular click behaviour can trigger an automated response in the form of a tailored web page, an email, a pop-up or an offline phone call).

Equally, good CRM systems can identify potential defectors (customers who are about to leave), pre-empt them and trigger win-back programmes for those who might otherwise have slipped through the net.

Reduce costs

Good CRM systems save money as the systems monitor customer feedback or issues before they grow into a major problem. Take Federal Express's 1–10–100 rule. They believe that for every pound your company might spend on preventing a quality problem, it will spend 10 to inspect and correct the mistake after it occurs. In the worst case, the quality failure goes unanswered or unnoticed until after your customer has taken delivery. To fix the problem at this stage, you probably pay about 100 times what you could have paid to prevent it from happening at all.

Boost profits

Marketing to both existing and referred customers costs a lot less than marketing to new ones. As mentioned, estimates suggest that it is six times more profitable to sell to existing customers, hence the importance of customer retention versus customer acquisition. Keeping existing customers happy and keeping in contact with them boosts sales in a more cost-efficient way. This boosts profits.

1 per cent customer satisfaction = $500 million

'Over a quarter of a century ago IBM calculated that each percentage point improvement in customer satisfaction translates into $500 million more revenue over five years.'

Kirkpatrick (1992)

Solve customer problems early

Of all calls to Fujitsu call centres (fifteen years ago), 50–70 per cent were for value restoration (fixing a problem, such as late delivery, wrong delivery or poor product quality) rather than value creation, eg adding value with helpful advice over the phone (Mitchell, 2004). Fujitsu recently (2018) installed marketing automation that integrates with the CRM system, which ensures visitors/prospects and customers receive increasingly relevant and helpful information. The new MA system listens to and responds to customers' behaviour (click behaviour) in a quicker and more accurate manner. More later.

Create competitive advantage

Managing customer relationships is, ultimately, critical to an organization's future. Nurturing excellent customer relationships can build a wall around a business that most competitors struggle to break through. A wall built on solid relationships can protect your customers from the constant waves of competitors' offers. This wall of trust and loyalty creates one form of competitive advantage.

Your best defence

A strong, loyal customer relationship is sometimes the only thing that competition cannot replicate.

Create assets

Customer relationships add value to the brand, boost repeat sales, boost profits and ultimately boost the balance sheet assets as the financial value of brands can be included as assets on the balance sheet. Well-kept databases are also a valuable asset but not yet appearing as assets on the balance sheet.

Brand assets

Stronger relations create stronger brands. This builds brand loyalty, which effectively builds a defensive wall around the customer, protecting them from the inevitable onslaught of hyper-competition as it advances across this 'borderless and category-less' marketplace (see Chapter 1). Good relations also boost the brand image and consequently the brand value, which is eventually reflected on the balance sheet.

Database asset

CRM systems can create and maintain a good-quality database. This is significant and, although not shown on the balance sheet, a very real asset to a company. It gives you, if used correctly, a monopoly of your own market share. It gives you access (assuming the database includes fields for various contact channels from email to phone to social media). Some companies quantify the value of their databases by calculating lifetime sales value of customers and then discount these revenues back to today's net present value.

A well-run CRM programme requires happy staff and effective integrated systems. Excellent CRM makes customers happy. An excellent CX delivers happier customers, which ultimately equals happy shareholders. So here's the happiness formula:

> Happy staff (+ excellent CRM) = happy customers = happy shareholders

What causes CRM failure?

Many organizations appear to have steadily got worse at CRM because of the lack of a customer-driven culture (failed leadership and, specifically, failed CRM leadership), poor CRM project management skills (in particular, scope creep, lack of training and lack of staff motivation programmes), poor CRM usability (eg an unintuitive, difficult-to-use interface that forgets about the staff need for an easy-to-use, friendly, intuitive system) and, after all of this, forgetting customer needs.

Organizations are sitting on a customer service time bomb. Customers are more demanding, and many marketers are not delivering. Yes, many products have got better (eg rustproof cars and hybrid cars), but service and CRM are generally not keeping up with these improvements Customers are not happy. They are ready to swap suppliers. They are bombarded with competitive offers. They have less time but more demands. And marketers are not delivering, perhaps because they are not in control of their own CRM (IT may hijack the process). Regardless of the reasons, the stats do not seem to get any better over time.

'In 2017, CIO magazine reported that around one-third of all customer relationship management (CRM) projects fail. That was actually an average of a dozen analyst reports. The numbers ranged from 18 per cent to 69 per cent. Those failures can mean a lot of things – over-budget, data integrity issues, technology limitations, and so forth. But in my work with clients, when I ask executives if the CRM system is helping their business to grow, the **failure rate is closer to 90 per cent**.'

Edinger (2018)

'Avon calling' cancelled

'Avon cancelled a $125 million investment in an enterprise system that had taken four years of effort to install. Basically, Avon salespeople refused to use it because it was a usability nightmare. This should not be remotely surprising. Many of the systems organizations give to their employees are usability monstrosities.'

McGovern (2014)

These are horrendous figures. Why do CRM systems keep failing, despite being so important to a business? Let's explore a few possible reasons including: poor CRM process skills; poor project management skills; poor internal marketing (motivation, training and communication); ignoring customers' needs.

Poor CRM process skills

Many CEOs and CMOs fail because they lack an understanding about the development and implementation of customer-driven marketing.

Many marketers have previously failed because they have not mastered CRM systems, or managed to integrate the culture across the organization, nor helped the CEO to understand the importance of

CRM. Assuming marketers do address these issues, they have an opportunity to integrate the potential of marketing automation and content marketing (more about these later) to create powerful new CRM systems that will nurture lifetime customers (many of whom may become advocates).

Poor project management skills

Poor project management skills stop CRM systems from being implemented on time and within budget. CRM projects are relatively large to any organization. Failings like scope creep (constantly adding extra and late requirements into the brief), unnecessary and often poor system design, and an overdominant IT department also wreck potential CRM programmes. One possible reason why so many 'IT projects' fail is because they are called 'IT projects'! IT is a service that supports business functions, not an end in itself. IT simply uses information technology processes to help run a business, which in turn is designed to help customers.

Poor internal marketing

Many CRM projects lack buy-in from staff who both fear and resist change. Internal marketing (internal training, motivation and communications) is a critical yet often forgotten key component in any CRM programme. 'A staggering 88 per cent of CRM users reported that they haven't entered complete contact information in the system. Almost two-thirds of users don't log every activity and have repeat entries for the same prospects' (Leslie Le, Hubspot).

Last but not least, constant cost cutting and operational failings have shifted the emphasis of many CRM programmes from value creation to value restoration. Overburdened and demotivated staff may also be struggling with a work overload. Sometimes, competitors see this as a service gap in the market and develop an improved customer service programme, until years later new management cut costs and reduce service, and competitors seize the opportunity.

Forgetting customer needs

It may seem ironic to have a CRM system that forgets about the customer's continuously changing needs. As highlighted in *Digital Marketing Excellence* (Chaffey and Smith, 2017):

> Old CRM systems were effectively automated selling systems that took little or no account of what customers actually want. Danger bells should start ringing when an IT consultant offers a front-end automated solution that cuts costs and streamlines operations and processes because this does not necessarily make marketing more effective.

Forgetting sales team needs

Instead of saying how can this system help sales people to help, and therefore retain, existing customers, as well as convert prospects into customers, many CRM systems lose their focus and, for example, end up being used as a management control system reporting on 'progress, improve accuracy of forecasts, provide visibility, predict project delivery dates, and provide a range of other business intelligence – rather than creating improvement in the sales process' (Edinger, 2018).

Over-burdened sales team hate new CRM and go GIGO

Harvard Business Review's Scott Edinger (2018) observed this first hand. When asked if the new CRM system was a success or not,

> 'The EVP of marketing was pleased she could now track the assignment of every single lead. The CIO was unhappy about data integrity issues that arose from the integration of more than 20 discrete databases. The EVP of sales liked the easy-access dashboard to report on metrics and the forecast. Sales management was less positive but acknowledged that it helped them monitor activity. And the sales team – well, they mostly hated it. They had to enter a lot of information that added little value (for them), and provided no help in selling more. Because the sales team had so little incentive to keep up with the data entry requirements, the quality of the data in the system became less and less reliable over the following year. The result? Incomplete or inaccurate information

from the CRM was exported into Excel spreadsheets for further manipulation by each level of management.'

GIGO (garbage in: garbage out) means inputting incorrect and/or incomplete data destroys the effectiveness of any CRM system.

Interdepartmental squabbles

The marketing team blames the sales team for not following up on all the wonderful sales leads that the marketing team generated. Meanwhile the sales team says that 'marketing doesn't understand exactly what is meant by a real qualified lead'. Integrating the two teams, getting them to work together, on a regular basis (and share their successes together) is the best solution here. See how sales and marketing collaboration can also help to generate extremely relevant marketing content in the section on content marketing later in this chapter.

IT hijackers

A few years earlier, another Harvard Business School Professor, Susan Fournier (in an interview with Manda Mahoney, 2002), suggested that IT was actually hijacking CRM projects:

> Most customer relationship management technology programs are failing. Why? CRM programs are expensive and take a long time to install. One consequence is that IT has 'hijacked' the process. In emphasizing technology decisions over marketing decisions, we've lost the opportunity to build better relationships with customers. To get back in balance, marketers have to help design CRM systems from the get-go.

Given that 71 per cent of IT projects today are not successful (Ismail, 2018) there is a natural concern about IT driving CRM.

It gets worse, specifically with CRM projects. We've moved from 47 per cent CRM failure in 2009 (Forrester Research) to 84 per cent CRM failure in 2014 (NetProspex), as defined by 'barely functional databases'. We need to explore exactly what drives CRM success.

71 per cent of IT projects fail (Ismail, 2018) and 84 per cent of CRM projects fail (NetProspex, 2014).

Effectively, marketers need to work closely with sales and customer service, and develop some shared goals and operations to ensure a cohesive, integrated CRM system is embraced by all departments.

The success/dominance trap

A classic Harvard article by Allen *et al* (2005) thought the CRM problems had something to do with growth. They called it 'the dominance trap' and explained it as follows:

> The larger a company's market share, the greater the risk it will take its customers for granted. As the money flows in, management begins confusing customer profitability with customer loyalty, never realizing that the most lucrative buyers may also be the angriest and most alienated. Worse, traditional market research may lead the firm to view customers as statistics. Managers can become so focused on the data that they stop hearing the real voices of their customers.

What drives CRM success?

CRM is a strategic decision and has a long-term impact on how a business is run. However, CRM programmes need resources, the 3Ms:

- Men/women: Commitment, including the CEO's support, an expert project director and teams of trained people to carry out the service.
- Money: Finances to pay for the software, outside consultants, installation, testing, training and motivation programmes.
- Minutes: It can take several years to develop a major CRM project, and even the training can take many months.

An excellent CRM system often requires a cultural change, which may be a challenge for many organizations.

Without senior management support cascading right down throughout the organization, CRM will fail. CRM implementation is disruptive, expensive and time-consuming and requires extra resources particularly for internal marketing (communicating, motivating and training staff).

Overambitious CRM system suppliers sometimes recommend a 'rip and replace implementation'. This can be expensive. Here, some CRM suppliers convince the client company to dump their existing system (because of its unfriendly and difficult-to-use interfaces, or inadequate functionality) and, therefore, start again from scratch.

Whichever approach is used, integrating customer interactions and data across a range of channels from website to mobile to telephone to sales rep to email is a key requirement – as is an easy-to-use, friendly interface.

> **Blame storming**
>
> 'Companies who do not appreciate the importance of an effective complaint handling system risk internal friction (passing on the blame). This may lead to a vicious circle, as internal friction generates poor motivation and cynicism, staff disloyalty and worse service. This is why customer loyalty and staff loyalty are closely linked.'
>
> Merlin Stone, Neil Woodcock (source unknown)

CRM culture

Building a customer-driven business requires a specific corporate culture where the organization, at all levels, recognizes the need for customer service and customer focus. A real CRM philosophy sees customers at the centre of the business (or organization). This customer focus requires a longer-term, strategic view of continually helping the customer throughout the customer lifetime (as opposed to a short-term 'transactional marketing' approach that focuses on quarterly sales results). Ultimately, CRM is an attitude as much as a system. Success depends on a customer culture where all staff always ask: 'How can we help the customer?'

The ladder of loyalty

This ladder was devised by Considine and Raphel in 1981 (Figure 3.2). Organizations seek to move prospects up the ladder of loyalty from 'suspects' eventually up to devoted 'advocates' who advocate an organization's product or service. There is some overlap with the PR 'Ladder of Engagement', where visitors are encouraged to engage initially at low engagement levels (ratings and reviews) up to higher levels (collaborating with new product developments).

In the CRM philosophy, the organization continually seeks to learn about customer needs and preferences in order to deliver excellent relevant services and content to better satisfy customer needs. The organization must also continually measure the right criteria. Ultimately, a CRM philosophy seeks to move customers up the ladder of loyalty.

Customer lifecycle marketing

Lifecycle marketing takes a long-term view of the customer. It involves developing a one-to-one relationship with the customer to help the customer on his/her lifecycle journey. To save the customer time by making it so easy to buy again, when the customer is ready. To help the customer with timely reminders and tips to get the best out of their product or service. Customer needs may change as they move through the customer lifecycle. For example,

FIGURE 3.2 The ladder of loyalty

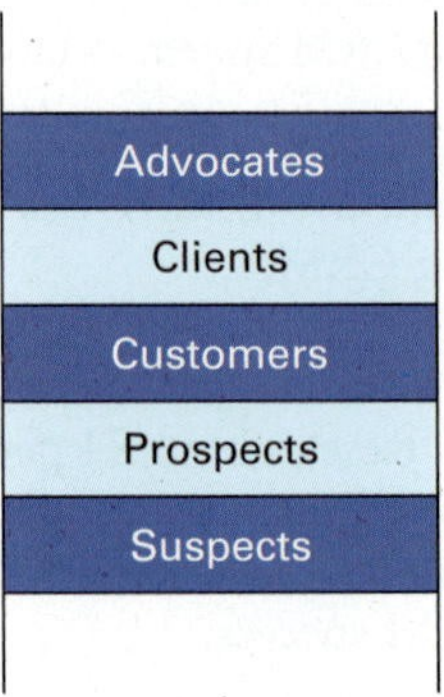

a small sports car may be required when the buyer is single, a larger family car when children arrive and a smaller car when the children have 'left the nest'. Constantly aiming to help the customer increases the likelihood of delivering an excellent lifecycle CX, which keeps the customer loyal and with you rather than drifting off to competition.

CRM architecture

An enterprise architecture is a blueprint that defines the structure and operation of a business or organization. CRM needs an integrated enterprise architecture.

Ultimately, we would like to integrate several processes, even marketing automation, as well as building, storing and accessing a 'universal customer record' for each customer (so that customer data from every channel can be integrated); and delivering the subsequent customer contact sequence (called a 'contact strategy'; see more on p 87). In addition, the database needs to be managed so that other processes like data mining, data analytics and profiling can be carried out. Marketers also need to have another process integrated and that is the ability to personalize and tailor offers and rewards and all ongoing communications.

Not all of the software that enables CRM goes under the CRM banner. Here are some of the applications sometimes associated with CRM and now part of the martech stack (marketing technology stack):

- collaboration tools (eg instant messaging, community support on websites);
- content management system;
- marketing automation;
- social platforms;
- customer feedback;
- knowledge management;
- portals and self-service;
- call centres becoming interactive contact centres;
- business information and analysis;
- enterprise process management;
- gamification;
- display and retargeting ads.

Samsung's gamification boosts results

'Samsung uses game mechanics to offer incentives and rewards to users who review products, advocate on social networks, participate in Q&As and register products. After deploying game mechanics in conjunction with social login, Samsung has experienced increases in time on site, reviews written, comments published and shop clicks to its ecommerce site.'

Janrain (2012)

Read 'The good, the bad and the ugly of gamification' (Smith, 2014a) for broader use of gamification.

Hosted, outsourced and web-service IT solutions are becoming increasingly available from service suppliers. Organizations should make the most of these.

In hyper-competitive markets – ie markets with no categories, no boundaries and no borders – differentiation is important. What difference is perceived between Visa and MasterCard, or L'Oréal and Clairol? Brands should be distinct from the competition. They need a 'personality' that can be promoted and brought to life through all the CRM touchpoints. Brand promotion offers a promise; CRM and CX are the physical delivery of that promise. This can be achieved by having the right systems and, most importantly, the right people, or human architecture (we'll explore this later). Before considering integrated processes, let us just emphasize the importance of human architecture alongside CRM architecture.

Human architecture

CRM architecture (systems and processes) is just part of the equation. Even though a significant proportion of repetitive CRM tasks can be automated, the human factor is still deemed critical to most CRM systems. This is why internal marketing is critical. Here are a few tips to ensure you get the best from your CRM team who are on the front line, dealing with prospects and customers:

- Benchmark current culture with staff via story techniques about customers, their work and CRM. Establish the problem areas and use the information for internal brand alignment through change programmes.
- Spread customer insight among staff and ensure they can use it in their work. Link knowledge of management processes to customer interaction processes for greater collaboration and learning. The big mistake of previous process re-engineering was not doing this. Good customer experience depends on the learning and support that staff give each other as a natural part of everyday life.
- Establish the new skills required and 'cast' staff into the new roles. Develop skills through continuous coaching in delivering the brand values.
- Redesign organizational structures to support new ways of working. Put flexible delivery teams together, pulled from 'communities of practice' (ie similar skill pools) as and when required. CRM challenges old structures because of the need for:
    - a segmented approach to customers;
    - non-siloed thinking and working;
    - new and scarce skills.
- Link key performance indicators (KPIs) through performance management to staff incentives; banish incentives that misdirect activity. The right incentives are vital. Do not focus just on 'what' is being delivered in terms of financial targets. Focus also on the 'how' of good performance delivery. Gamification can be and is used here.
- Link the brand values to the team and the CX:
    - basing brand values on what customers want;
    - involving employees in developing the values;
    - linking the values to the main brand promise;
    - recruiting employees with appropriate brand values;
    - encouraging staff to align their behaviour with the values;
    - rewarding employees for delivering the brand values.
- The CEO needs to develop a real customer culture where staff really care about customers. This is no easy task. It's a mindset. It is more an attitude than simply a set of processes. It affects the whole organization, as everyone is responsible – not just the customer services, marketing or sales departments. It's everyone's job, from the delivery driver to the receptionist to accounts and finance. Everyone can enhance every customer experience to create a strategic advantage over the competition.

CRM processes

How does an organization manage complaints, money-back requests, queries, compliments, suggestions and requests for additional services? How does it handle a sale, a cancellation, a complaint or a customer defection? Are there processes or systems in place? After an order, do you send out an order acknowledgement? And after a sale, do you send out a delivery alert, followed by a post-sales service satisfaction questionnaire, or score sheet or feedback request or a formal review? What happens with this information? Who decides to act on a particular customer suggestion? Who tells the staff? Who tells the customer what's happening with their complaint, query or suggestion? How many times should a customer be contacted after a sale? If customers have outstanding issues, it is not the time to cross-sell them something else. Should different types of customers get different types of offers? Who decides? Who implements this? Processes are important.

Does everyone know how to process an order or a complaint? What happens if someone phones with an unusual enquiry? Who deals with it? How many times are customers left hanging on the phone, being passed around from department to department?

Customer feedback process

Some organizations value customer feedback. They encourage it with 0800 numbers, feedback buttons on websites, questionnaires, rating cards and even outbound telemarketing to collect feedback. Others employ the services of third-party feedback specialists like reevoo.com or feefo.com, who aim to gather feedback from 30 per cent of your customers. There are also many new customer listening tools (many of them are free; read 'The old marketing ship is sinking', **http://prsmith.org/blog/**). Listening is just the beginning. It is vital to have a system that enables a listening process as well as a constructive response, or sometimes a series of responses (see the Tesco auto contact example later).

Maximize the customer's opportunity to complain

Companies can set up suggestion boxes and other feedback systems to maximize the customer's opportunity to complain, compliment, create or engage with the brand. Feedback (even negative) is food and drink to marketers. However, only one in every 24 dissatisfied customers bothers to complain, according to E-Satisfy Ltd (formerly TARP). Rather than facing an unknown enemy of bitter, disappointed and dissatisfied customers, an organization, through its complaints process, can offer a chance to sort out previously unknown problems. It also gives the organization the opportunity to find the enemy within (internal problems such as quality control or demotivated staff). One company chairman takes time to listen to taped telephone complaints while driving home in his car. Many services companies actually ask their customers to fill in a form about levels of satisfaction or dissatisfaction. Solutions are relatively easy. Identifying the problem is the difficult part. Complaints are generally helpful. Welcome them.

Stew Leonard's: US retail chain's listening process

At Stew Leonard's grocery stores there are monthly focus groups and a daily suggestion box. Suggestions are typed up by 10 am the next day, and store managers either act or call the customers about the complaints or suggestions. The chain averages approximately 100 comments per day – they are the pulse of the store. By actively listening to customers (and their complaints), companies can save, rather than spend, money.

Contact strategy

Too much contact can wear out a relationship. As in personal relationships, you can become a bore, a nuisance or irrelevant. On the other hand, too little contact may kill the relationship. The key to building the relationship is to contact customers when it is convenient and/or helpful, ie at the right time, via their preferred channel. This is a contact strategy. It specifies which kinds of customers and enquirers get which sequence of contacts and incentives via which channel (email, newsletter with dynamic, relevant content, push notifications/message, telephone call, personal call, or even remarketing or retargeting ads). Some organizations ask their customers how they prefer to be updated. Organizations also need to be flexible and vary their contact strategy depending on how customers react. You can either ask customers directly about how they prefer to be contacted or you can observe their response (or lack of response). And remember, permission to contact customers is only temporary. Organizations have to continually win it by delivering relevant added-value communications continuously.

Morton's steak story

'Companies are reportedly incorporating influencer scores into their customer service operations. Morton's Steakhouse even arranged for the surprise delivery of a deluxe meal at Newark airport, for an influencer. After noticing that Peter Shankman (an influential entrepreneur and investor with 100,000 followers on Twitter) had tweeted the following message mid-flight: "Hey @Mortons – can you meet me at Newark airport with a porterhouse when I land in two hours? K, thanks :)"

The effort won Morton's considerable publicity, via traditional and social media, and demonstrated their ability to engage creatively with loyal customers. As one technologist noted, "few companies would be agile enough to pull off a stunt like that in under three hours – it says a lot about the freedom that Mortons have chosen to give their social media team".'

Curragh (2012)

Some garages maintain contact with their customers via email or SMS, sending them reminders when their car is due for a service. If no response is generated then this triggers a prompt for staff to make a phone call to see whether the customer still wants to receive reminders (maintaining permission). A contact strategy defines an initial welcome strategy when the prospect is first added to the database, based on the best interval and sequence of messages. The contact strategy should then be extended for later stages in the customer lifecycle, with messages designed to convert customers to purchase, encourage repeat purchases, encourage customers to try new products or reactivate customers when their interest wanes. Here are three steps to a contact strategy from Chaffey and Smith (2017):

Step 1: Welcome programme process

Develop a welcome programme where over the first three to six months targeted auto-triggered emails are sent to educate subscribers about the brand and its benefits and deliver targeted offers. For example, the Renault B2C welcome strategy has a container or content pod within its e-newsletter to deliver personalized information about the brand and model of car in which a prospect is interested. This is updated each month as the customer gets to know the brand better and the brand gets to know the customer better.

Segment list members by activity (responsiveness) and age on the list. Assess the level of email list activity (ask what percentage of list members haven't clicked within the last three to six months – if they haven't, they are inactive and should be treated differently, either by reducing frequency or by using more offline media). Some customers become less responsive. A specific contact strategy is required to reactivate waning customers.

Step 2: 'Contact strategy' process

Here is how Tesco, arguably the world's most sophisticated relationship marketer, develops different contact strategies relevant to four different customer types and relationship stages:

- new website visitor registers;
- first-time customer;
- repeat customer;
- lapsed customer.

Tesco monitors customer actions during the customer lifecycle. Different customer actions trigger different automatic responses (ARs) by email:

- *Trigger event 1:* The customer first registers on the site (but does not buy).
  - AR1: Two days after registration, an email is sent offering phone assistance and a £5 discount off the first purchase to encourage a trial.
- *Trigger event 2:* The customer first purchases online.
  - AR1: An immediate order confirmation is sent.
  - AR2: Five days after purchase, an email is sent with a link to an online customer satisfaction survey asking about the quality of service from the driver and picker (eg item quality and substitutions).
  - AR3: Two weeks after the first purchase, a direct mail approach offers tips on how to use the service and a £5 discount on the next purchase, intended to encourage re-use of online services.
  - AR4: A generic monthly e-newsletter with online exclusive offers.
  - AR5: A bi-weekly alert with personalized offers for the customer.
  - AR6: After two months, a £5 discount for the next shop.
  - AR7: A quarterly mailing of coupons.
- *Trigger event 3:* The customer does not purchase for an extended period.
  - AR1: The dormancy is detected, and a reactivation email is sent with a survey of how the customer is finding the service (to identify any problems) and a £5 incentive.

- AR2: A further discount incentive is used in order to encourage continued usage after a break.

Remember, markets are conversations. Listen to what customers say or watch what they click on and use this information to tailor relevant added value with every contact you make. Then ask customers how often they want contact and what type of information or offers they would like. This increases relevancy – a key success factor.

BA puts VIP faces to a welcome name via Google

'Three years ago British Airways were reported to be watching out for its most important customers with its then-new "Know Me" programme which involved a thorough Googling of their passengers, so that check-in staff can "put a face to the name before the customer sets foot in the airport". Staff searched Google images for specific VIP passengers, and those with high Klout scores. "Results of the searches will be forwarded to front-line staff equipped with iPads, making for more personal interactions with check-in staff or cabin crew." BA were hoping to send out about 4,500 daily "personal recognition messages" in 2012.'

Huffington Post (2012)

The higher the relevance, the greater the value – it's a continuum

'If you want to protect and enhance the value of your brand, your offer must be valuable.'

'Customers get what they want; your margins are protected; everyone's a winner.'

dunnhumby (2006)

Step 3: Customer defector reduction process

All organizations lose customers. It's called 'churn'. Some customers change job, leave the country, grow old or die, and some switch to a competitor. Organizations need a process for following up any lost customers. Essentially the organization needs to listen carefully, find out why customers have defected, clarify what can be done to win back the business, and remind them what business offers (sometimes with an added incentive). All of this has to be recorded on the database for review (particularly why customers are leaving).

Patience is required, as the defecting customer may have just bought a competitor's product or service and the organization has to wait for the next purchase cycle to start again. So be patient. Keep in touch. Make it easy to come back to the organization. When defectors actually do return, the organization has to go out and win their business every day.

Marketers must know what aspect of the organization's procedures, customer care and customer experience causes customers to leave. They must also know which types of customers are defecting. If it is a disproportionate number of high-value customers, then alarm bells should start ringing.

Catch the at-risk customer defectors

It is surprising how many major brands do not have any alarm systems to highlight customers who are about to switch to a competitor. They can be easily identified or profiled by their behaviour (or lack of behaviour/spending). At-risk (of defecting) customers or even recently 'churned' customers need to be followed up with a 'contact strategy', which might comprise a sequence of calls, emails, gifts/incentives (if they fit the ideal long-term customer profile).

Profiling is a continuous activity, which includes continually collecting customer information, mining it and using it to profile and target more successfully. For example, Grattan's ladies' fashion mail-order company decided to experiment with a new product, a grandfather clock. They guessed the likely target profile would be something like middle-aged, well-off ABs living in ACORN types J35 (villages with wealthy older commuters) and J36 (detached houses, exclusive suburbs). They then asked for a print-out of names and addresses that fitted this profile. The subsequent mailing generated 60 orders at £1,000 each. They then analysed those 60 orders with a view to identifying any hidden characteristic that could be added to the profile and fed into the database again to produce a different, more accurate target list. When they mailed this list they sold every one of the 1,000 limited edition clocks.

3M complaints system generates innovative ideas

3M claim that over two-thirds of their innovation ideas come from listening to customer complaints.

Some organizations have systems and processes that stop complaints before they happen. Compared to fixing a complaint, telemarketing (or even an email) can provide a low-cost method of ensuring customer satisfaction. For example, some customers may have a question that does not merit them making a telephone call, but nevertheless they would like it answered. If left unanswered, the question can fester into a source of dissatisfaction, so regular outbound telephone contact (the company calls the customer) picks up any issues or problems before they become major ones. This is usually more cost-effective than fixing problems. Inbound (0800 and freephone) customer service lines can also reassure customers if they are made aware of the facility. Some technology companies, like ICL, have a team of telephone diagnosticians who handle fault reports from customers. Linked to a sophisticated computerized diagnostic kit, they can identify whether the fault really exists or not. Many problems arise from the user's lack of knowledge, which means many potential problems or frustrations can be sorted out over the phone. If a fault is identified, the diagnosis informs the engineer in advance so that he or she arrives with the right spare part.

Marketing optimization analyses all contact history to identify what communications mix generates the best return on investment. It identifies which channels (or tactical tools) generate the best results, whether email, direct mail (snail mail), call centre, search engine traffic (resulting from SEO campaigns), social media or any other sources of customer acquisition (or retention).

Personalization

The most important sound in the world is... your own name! It's personal. It's a compliment – an expression of respect. Marketers depend on a good database to remember customer names, needs, interests and preferences. Specialized software combined with an up-to-date and well-cleaned database allows marketers to personalize communications such as emails, voicemails (voice-activated emails), snail mails (traditional direct mail), SMS text messages (for mobiles) and, most interestingly, websites – personalized websites.

Personalization can help to build relationships. When someone remembers your name and, even more importantly, your interests, it demonstrates that the person cares about you. Similarly, an organization that remembers your name and your interests is, at least, trying to do a good job.

There are three distinct approaches to personalization, as explained by Chaffey and Smith (2017):

- customization;
- individualization;
- group characterization.

Customization is the easiest to see in action: it allows visitors to select and set up their specific preferences. Individualization goes beyond this fixed setting and uses patterns of a visitor's own behaviour (and not any other user's – it is known that it's a particular customer because of the log-in and password choices) to deliver specific content to the visitor. In group characterization, visitors receive recommendations based on the preferences of people like them, using approaches based on collaborative filtering and case-based reasoning. Mass customization is where a different product, service or content is produced for different segments – sometimes hundreds of them. Personalization is different. It is truly one-to-one, particularly when not only the website and communications are personalized but also the product or service.

Another way of thinking about the many options for online personalization is suggested by the Gartner Group (ranging from simple to complex):

- Addressing customers personally:
  - address customers or prospects by name in print communication;

- address customers or prospects by name in electronic communication.
- Real-time personalization:
  - keyword query to change content;
  - clickstream data to dynamically change website content;
  - collaborative filtering to classify visitors and serve content.
- Customer profile personalization:
  - geographic personalization to tailor messages in traditional media;
  - demographic personalization to tailor messages in traditional media;
  - geographic personalization to tailor online messages;
  - demographic personalization to tailor online messages;
  - give website visitors control over content from set preferences;
  - registration data to change website content.

For over a decade marketers have been using other interesting options for tailored offers and ads, including 'content interested in' (pages visited) combined with other live data such as a bank account balance. For example, when HSBC Bank International wanted to move customers into more valuable segments, it tested personalized banner ads on its own website. *New Media Age* reported that this was a challenge: since 60 per cent of total weekly visitors to **offshore.hsbc.com** log on to the internet banking service, HSBC wanted to market to them effectively while they were engaged in this task, disrupting their banking experience without infuriating them (Rubach, 2007). HSBC developed some rules to serve different offers dependent on the type of content accessed and the level of balance in the customer's account. The personalized approach worked, with new banners having an 87.5 per cent higher click-through rate than non-personalized banners (6.88 per cent versus 3.67 per cent); savings accounts opened via internet banking increased by 30 per cent (based on the six months pre- and post-launch); and non-premier customers upgrading to premier accounts (requiring a balance of £60,000 or more) increased by 86 per cent (based on the four weeks pre- and post-launch of the targeted banners).

Personalization enhances relationships. Personalized web pages help to give customers a sense of ownership – not the marketer owning the customer, but the customer owning (or controlling) the site. When you make customers feel that their home page is truly theirs, then the offers you make available belong to them, the information they access is put together just for them, and you allow the customers to own you.

Many personalized sites require users to log in with a password, which can be frustrating when customers forget. Many visitors give up and leave the site. Incidentally, privacy laws now require marketers to ask permission before placing a cookie on a user's device (and also explain the use of cookies within the privacy policy).

Here are some other personalization problems.

Although personalization is important, it is possible to over-personalize. American Express once tried too hard to be too personal and upset customers. UK Online for Business reported that American Express call centres discovered that customers resented being greeted in person before they had actually declared who they were, even although a powerful database can recognize an incoming phone number and reveal the caller's name, address, purchases, issues, etc. The practice of immediate personalized greeting was swiftly discontinued.

Dear Rich Fat Bastard

Security becomes even more important when personalized information is collected. A credit card company once had a direct mailshot to 30,000 of its best customers (its gold card holders) intercepted by a disenchanted employee. He changed the salutation in each of the personalized letters to 'Dear Rich Fat Bastard'.

Nike's website once offered customers the opportunity to personalize their own shoes by stitching on their own personal logo. One customer filled out the online form, sent the $50 and chose 'sweatshop' as a personal logo. Nike refused. The publicity soared.

Automated personalized systems can present challenges. However, listening to feedback, ensuring security measures are in place and motivating staff to spot issues (eg Nike) are all simply best practice.

In addition to personalized communications, having relevant, added-value content can also help boost CRM results.

Content marketing

Content marketing is content that will be of value to your customers. This can be a book, ebook, white paper, report, photograph, infographic, video, etc. Some include games, responses and even direct mail and text messages (a sequence of emails needs simple yet carefully crafted messages). A newsletter requires interesting and relevant content. A social media feed requires great content with lots of visuals. A public talk requires an interesting speech and visuals. A sales promotion, whether offered on TV, via email, at a conference or on social media, needs to be interesting and desirable. Suffice to say that before developing any content suitable for your customers on, say, your social media platforms, it is worth carrying out a social media audit. This will help you decide what information/marketing content and interactions customers will actually engage with, and what they won't. A contact strategy can also include interesting content marketing.

There is a process to ensure your marketing content is relevant and desirable, plus a sequence or continual stream throughout the year. We will look at this process in more detail in Chapter 15. Meanwhile, knowing what content customers prefer is part of the bigger customer picture, called a '360-degree view'.

360-degree view of the customer

A 360-degree view gives a single, end-to-end picture of the customer's experience, including each step of their journey with a brand and also how they felt. This generates a single unified view from all the customer touchpoints at each stage of their buying (before, during and afterwards), whether the customer was on the website or calling a call centre or commenting on social media (about the brand).

Whatever processes are integrated, they should ideally deliver a single customer view (a 360-degree view) and identify which media (including social media tools) work best using propensity models (propensity or likelihood to open, propensity to buy, etc). Both hard and soft data are combined. Hard data includes customer interactions with a company, including calls, chats, emails, texts, social media responses and surveys. Soft data is buried in among hard data and can give a clearer insight into how a customer is actually feeling about your brand.

Your digital footprint (or click behaviour) can give a far better insight to customer than their demographics.

A 360-degree view used by, say, a call centre can generate, in real time, an instant snapshot regarding the background to the customer's call:

- **identity:** name, age, gender, location;
- **relationships:** influence, connections, associations;
- **current activity:** purchases, deliveries, faults, etc;
- **history:** contacts, processes, campaigns;
- **value:** which of our products or services have they used?
- **flags:** churn propensity (likelihood to swap supplier), cross-sell and up-sell opportunity, credit risk, fraud risk, last interaction mood, fault record, frequency of contact;
- **actions:** expected, likely or key actions the caller might take.

Consumer variables, or traits, like browsing and shopping patterns in conjunction with social media activity, can be added to a CRM and used subsequently for more detailed persona creation and customer segmentation.

> 'Companies now use an increasing array of tools to develop this 360-degree view, including social media listening tools to gather what customers are saying on sites like Facebook and Twitter, predictive analytics tools [more later] to determine what customers may research or purchase next, customer relationship management suites and marketing automation software. So it has become more important than ever for this software to integrate with other platforms to enable data sharing and a cohesive, up-to-date, accurate view of customers. In some cases, this may involve the use of application programming

> interfaces to enable applications to share data. Data quality and data cleansing practices may also be necessary to attain an accurate picture of customers, where the data is current, not duplicate or conflicting, and so forth.'
>
> Rouse (2015)

When customers 'opt in' to further emails or phone calls they give their permission to be contacted. This is a first step in using their permission to develop the relationship. In fact permission can, and ideally should, be extended to be quite specific by asking customers exactly what they prefer:

- content – news, products, offers, events, topics;
- frequency – weekly, monthly, quarterly or alerts;
- channel – email, direct mail, phone or SMS;
- format – text vs HTML.

Ensure future contact with customers always adds value to the CX. It is a moral and legal requirement (in B2C markets) to offer the customer the option to 'opt out' every time you contact them. The number of existing customers who opt out from further contact is the 'churn rate'. Marketers watch the churn rate closely and try to understand why it varies.

All of these approaches are dependent on an overall customer philosophy that is more strategic than tactical, with customers being nurtured over the medium to long term rather than by a one-off transactional sale approach. This also requires different teams to integrate and work together (eg closed loop reporting), rather than 'silo' departments competing against each other.

Closed loop reporting

Closed loop reporting (CLR) brings data from two main sources together. Integrating the data that the marketing team collect via marketing automation with the information that the sales and customer service team collect via the CRM system is an example of CLR. Even if both teams work well together (the marketing team deliver leads efficiently to the sales team who then convert the leads into customers), many organizations still have a gap between marketing qualified leads (MQLs) and sales qualified leads (SQLs).

CLR closes this gap as marketing and sales simply share data with each other so that they can both make more informed decisions. CLR lets specific members from both marketing and sales obtain a complete view of the whole sales funnel, including MQLs and SQLs.

Another way to close the loop is to get the sales teams to share with the marketing team what happened to the leads that the sales team received. This helps marketing to understand how best they can help the sales team in the future.

CLR helps to boost conversion rates, and even identify the best- and worst-performing campaigns, ultimately lower marketing costs, improve the CX, generally have better lead management processes and ultimately improve ROI analysis.

CLR helps to generate a 360-degree view of your sales cycle – so you can see a user's first visit to the website, browsing through their activities and then identifying their last conversion event. See what marketing content a prospect downloads. Then compare that with any data about their business type, size or location to see if any content appeals to one segment more than another. Closed-loop reporting is a powerful tool.

Databases

The database is at the heart of CRM. A database can contain a lot of information about customers depending on how many 'fields' or variables an organization wants to capture. It contains customer names and addresses, enquiries, purchasing patterns, preferences, areas of interest, incentives and a lot more depending on how many 'fields' are kept and what kind of analytics are used. It can even be progressively improved with each interaction (or even each click). The database can be enriched with data from publicly available social media information if required. A database gives an organization access to its own private marketplace. It can create a monopoly of your own customers.

A good database contains highly relevant and up-to-date customer data. It is a valuable repository of information on prospects and customers from all

FIGURE 3.3 Visualizing closed-loop marketing

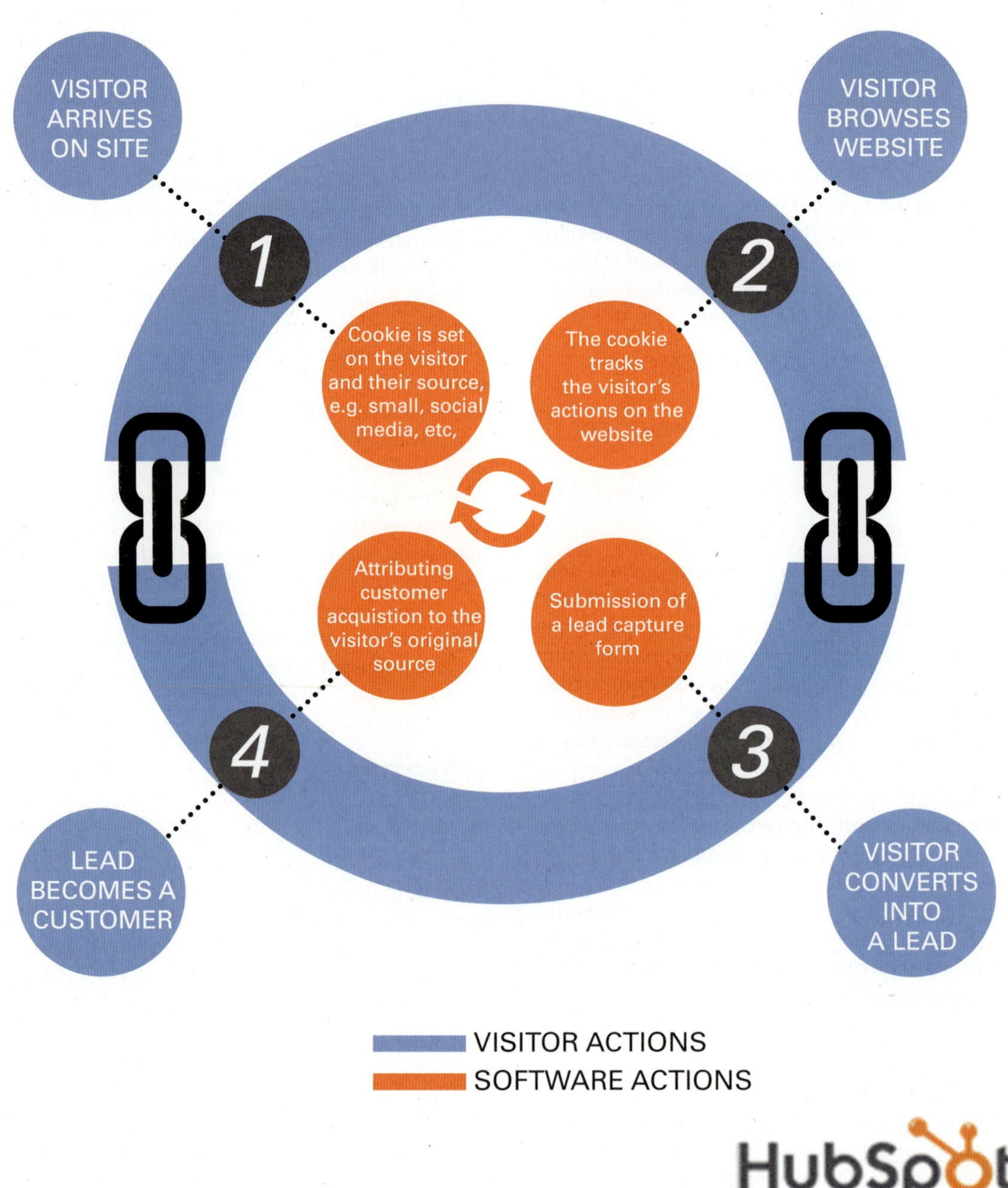
Visualizing Closed-Loop Marketing:
VISITOR ARRIVES ON SITE
VISITOR BROWSES WEBSITE
1
2
Cookie is set on the visitor and their source, e.g. small, social media, etc,
The cookie tracks the visitor's actions on the website
Attributing customer acquistion to the visitor's original source
Submission of a lead capture form
4
3
LEAD BECOMES A CUSTOMER
VISITOR CONVERTS INTO A LEAD
VISITOR ACTIONS
SOFTWARE ACTIONS
HubSpot

sources and channels, including website registration forms, sales reps' discussions with customers, customer service calls including complaints, comments or any customer feedback. The database can build up a detailed 360-degree customer view, identifying issues, buying cycle/frequency, preferences and which incentives work for each customer.

Organizations with properly managed databases enjoy a competitive advantage over competitors without one. A good database is a powerful asset.

> Sometimes some of the best customer data lies in the bottom of a drawer or a customer file.

Data

Historical data and predictive data

There are two types of information kept: historical data and predictive data. Historical data ('transactional data' or 'back data') includes name, address, recency and frequency of purchases, responses to offers and value of purchases. Predictive data can identify which groups or subgroups are more likely to respond to a specific offer. This is done through statistical scoring: customer attributes (eg lifestyle, house type, past behaviour, etc) are given scores that help to indicate the customers' future behaviour. The database can identify best ('ideal') customers and worst customers. The worst customers have 'negative value': these are customers who, for example, only buy when special offers are available.

Data analytics

Data analytics improves customer intelligence, which in turn improves targeted marketing, which in turn improves campaign management and, most importantly, customer relationship management. Forget how this boosts profitability for a moment, and just consider how more relevant benefits make customers happier, and how happy customers generate more business and more word-of-mouth referrals. It's a virtuous circle that starts with a bunch of processes: identifying customer needs, reflecting those needs through marcomms and then delivering more relevant products, services and incentives in a timely and cost-efficient manner which ultimately boosts customer sales and satisfaction (IRD – identify needs; reflect those needs/benefits; deliver a reasonable product or service – the magic marketing formula, see p 352). ROI improves. The deep analytic tools can now also be applied to online social media as well as the more traditional scenarios. First, consider how data mining works to build better customer profiles and contact strategies while exploiting purchasing cycles with automated marketing.

Data mining

Data mining and segmentation can identify potential long-term, loyal customers as opposed to those who are promiscuous 'bonus seekers' (short-term shoppers who grab sales promotions and then switch when another brand offers a new sales promotion). The latter are costly and increase the 'churn rate' (customers who leave). Since the long-term loyal customers are far more profitable and the promiscuous customers are loss making, every business needs to know where each of these segments comes from, ie which channels and incentives recruit the best customers. Businesses need to know which offline advertising, online advertising, direct mail (online or offline), referrals links, social media channels and content type are generating the right or wrong customer traffic and conversions.

Intelligent miner saves Safeway's top customers

Data mining has been around for many decades now. Here's an example of how data mining helps make better decision:

> 'Before Safeway delisted a particular cheese product, ranked 209th in sales, an intelligent miner discovered that this cheese was frequently purchased by its ideal customer profile – the top-spending 25 per cent of customers, the last clientele Safeway would want to disappoint. Under conventional analytical principles, the product would have been delisted; in actual fact, the item was quite important.'
>
> DB2 (1997)

So the cheese was not delisted.

Databases have to be stored securely. Large databases require large warehouses. Data mining drills down into these data warehouses and applies advanced statistical analysis and modelling techniques to the data to find useful patterns and relationships. It can, for example, explore each and every transaction of millions of customers and how they relate to each other. Data mining can find correlations that are beyond human conceptual capability (see the 'Unexpected relationships' box below). A range of statistical tools is used, including regression analysis, time-series forecasting, clustering, associations, logistic regression, discriminant analysis, neural nets and decision trees. A sequence-discovery function detects frequently occurring purchasing patterns over time. This information can then be layered with demographic data (from the main database) so that a company can tailor its mailings on each household's vulnerability or propensity to buy certain items at certain times.

Unexpected relationships

'Data mining can reveal unexpected database connections. For example 82 per cent of motorcycle owners buy frozen seafood and 62 per cent of amateur cellists buy power tools. It can be mathematically interesting to see these techniques in action. However, it is also important that a manager knows roughly what the purpose and possible benefits are of any such data-mining analysis... The ability to ask a good question or write a good data-mining brief is a relatively new skill for today's marketing manager.'

PR Smith

Data retrieval

Remember, input is one thing, but retrieving it in a sensible format is another. The art lies in the retrieval of the data in an appropriate format, for example a list of 'all enquirers for product x from the southwest in the past six months', a list of a particular category of business customer (SIC code), a list of 'customers who have bought all product x but not product y', and so on.

Scale is important too. Will the database grow? How many sources of data might there be? How many scenarios might exist?

London Fire Brigade data analytics predict fires

Database mining can even be used for non-marketing purposes, such as fire prevention. Take the London Fire Brigade. It carries out 65,000 home safety visits each year, but with over 3 million homes in London it would take over 50 years to cover every one. More than 60 different data elements are fed into the model, including census data and population demographics, broken down into 649 geographical areas (ward level), plus type of land use, data on deprivation, Mosaic lifestyle data, historical incidents and past prevention activity. The model predicts where fires are most likely to occur. London Fire Brigade use the information to predict where there is a high risk of fire, eg in a small estate of houses or industrial buildings, so they can then send in an assessor to investigate and perhaps circulate information, set up some advisory services and ultimately reduce the number of fires.

Managing the database

The database is at the heart of the CRM system. The database manager has many responsibilities in addition to the database design (which allows relevant customer data to be accessed rapidly and queries performed):

- Data quality: Ensuring data are accurate, relevant and kept up to date. Data, like any asset, needs to be maintained (cleaned and updated continuously). See box below.
- Data security: Ensuring data cannot be compromised by attacks from inside or outside the organization.
- Data coordination or user coordination: Specifying exactly who has access to data retrieval and who has access to data input. Too many uncontrolled inputs may result in files being deleted or changed by too many different people. The database spins out of control.
- Data back-up and recovery: Ensuring that data can be restored when there are the almost inevitable system failures or attacks.

The manager also monitors performance, particularly checking the system is coping as either the database or the number of interactions grows (driven by the contact strategies).

Data asset becomes a liability if data maintenance is poor

Although it does not appear on the balance sheet, the database is an asset. Like any asset, it deteriorates or depreciates over time if it is not properly maintained. In the same way that a physical asset, like a building, needs to be maintained to avoid it becoming run down and eventually a liability (if tiles fall off the roof or a wall collapses), a database asset needs to be cleaned and maintained to stop it deteriorating and eventually becoming a liability. For example, sending messages (direct mail/email/messaging) to people who have died upsets their relatives. Or contacting individuals who have opted out (or who have registered with the Mail Preference Service, the Email Preference Service, the Telephone Preference Service, etc) can incur a large fine. See 'GDPR compliance' in this chapter and p 299. Careful maintenance (cleaning and updating) of this valuable asset is required.

Profiling

Fifty per cent of FTSE 100 companies do not know who their customers are. They cannot describe how their ideal customers are different to their negative-value customers. They cannot profile them. They may have their names and addresses, etc, but they do not build useful profiles describing them. If an organization doesn't know its customer profiles (identities, needs and preferences), how can it give them relevant offers that satisfy them better, and find other customers like them? It is like searching for a needle in a haystack if customers are not profiled.

Chaffey and Smith (2017) explain how profiling can combine explicit data (customer information collected from registrations and surveys) and implicit data (behavioural information gleaned from the back end, ie through the recorded actions of customers on a website). Valuable profiles combine both implicit and explicit data continually. This provides a real picture (or profile) of the target markets, the characteristics that define each segment and how to serve each segment. For example, certain car buyers might have different demographic profiles, show an interest in particular features (pages) of a car and request a test drive. If this group of visitors (or segment) fits the ideal customer profile then they may get an immediate incentive to buy now, whereas another group, or segment, of visitors with a less likely profile may only get an e-newsletter once a month.

Website visitors are observed as they leave an audit trail of what they did, what they looked at and for how long. Cookies enable marketers to track which pages they access, what they are interested in (pages visited, times, duration spent there) and what they buy, which then helps to build their profile. They can drill down deeper to see how well different segments respond to different offers or features in a newsletter. Profiling helps to identify who the most profitable customers are and whether they have any similar characteristics (eg whether they respond to certain mailshots, came from a certain type of site or search engine, searched using a particular key phrase, or spent a certain amount of time on particular pages).

Profile customers, visitors and enquirers

Build profiles of both customers and enquirers and then segment them according to their different interests, enquiries, requirements or purchases. Marketers can build sophisticated consumer profiles based on previous purchasing decisions and even identify the consumer hierarchy of criteria, whether quality, speed of delivery, level of service, etc. This enables tightly targeted, tailored offers that match the specific needs of each segment or profile type.

Progressive profiling

Asking for information is a delicate affair. Marketers can be too greedy. This can create 'form friction' by presenting a customer with 20 questions to answer. Beyond the basic information, you may need to offer incentives for more information or simply wait for the relationship to develop and gain permission to ask for more. Progressive profiling means asking for a little bit of extra information with each visit or purchase. But remember that customers value their privacy. All organizations' privacy policies should be clearly posted on the website and any other access points customers may have with you.

> 'Incorporate progressive profiling to build a richer understanding of your audience. Hopefully you wouldn't put someone through the wringer on your first date by asking 50 questions... right? Dating advice is surprisingly relevant when it comes to learning more about your online users. Don't ask your users to share their life story on your first date. Build progressive profiling workflows that invite users to share more information about themselves at the right moments. The points at which people post comments, share content, purchase products or write reviews all present an opportunity to inquire and build a deeper, more comprehensive customer profile.'
>
> Janrain (2012)

The better the profiling, the better the results, because the more accurate the targeting, the less resources are wasted. Different customers have different needs. It is actually easier to satisfy them by dividing them into groups sharing similar needs (segments) and then treating each segment differently (different contact strategies for each).

Non-scientific profiling

In the absence of completely reliable data, a less scientific analysis is sometimes used to separate or take out names that do not fit the target profile. For example, Rediffusion cable services felt that older home dwellers did not fit their ideal prospects' profile, so they did not target prospects with older-generation Christian names such as Albert, Alfred, Alice, Amelia, Arthur, Bertram, Constance, Grace, Harold, May, Mildred, Rose, Sabena, Samuel, Victor, Violet and Winifred.

Gaming company profiles big gamblers vs loss-making bonus seekers

Internet gaming company Victor Chandler uses SAS Analytics to do a behavioural analysis to predict lifetime values of new customers. For example, if a new customer comes in and bets on casinos (instead of poker tables), the company can predict whether that customer is more likely to become a long-term customer or a short-term, expensive, loss-making customer. The predictive analysis suggests which customers are worth investing in (with regular contact and regular incentives) and which are not – those loss-making 'bonus seeker' customers, whose profile is: young male, tight betting (as opposed to betting all of their stash), declining betting frequency, infrequent betting, or middle-aged female. If visitors display these characteristics, they'll stay three weeks and leave and therefore do not warrant any relationship-building efforts (ie no regular contact or incentives). The other customers are worth investing in, and it is worth developing 'retention activity' (a regular attractive incentivized contact strategy) for them. Predictive analytics use historical data to highlight and optimize marketing messages that work better for certain social networks.

Remember Alibaba's CEO talking about their **customer-centric mission** in Chapter 1: 'Making it easier to do business across the world', followed by their motto, 'Customer first, employee second, shareholder third'.

Building a profile with fields of data

So what kind of data, or 'fields', should be captured? In addition to a customer's name and address, there are obviously other fields of data worth capturing for either a B2C or a B2B business. Today marketers can collect a plethora of customer data. There are many fields of data, and many ways to collect it. A single universal customer record can be used to link all the data together.

FRAC

Another useful approach to building immediately useable profiles relates to their likelihood to buy based on four common sense factors collectively known as FRAC. It stands for: frequency (of purchase/visit), recency (of purchase/visit), amount (of money spent on purchases) and category of purchase. These were in use a long time before the internet emerged.

Chaffey and Smith (2013) show how some CRM systems use recency, frequency, monetary value (RFM) analysis for targeting emails according to how a customer interacts with a website. Values could be assigned to each customer, as shown in Table 3.1.

Customers can be combined in different categories and then appropriate message treatments sent to encourage purchase. There are many approaches here; for example, a theatre group uses nine categories to tailor its direct marketing for customers who have attended once, twice or more over the last year, previous year, etc. Other companies will have hundreds of segments with very tailored offerings.

TABLE 3.1 Using RFM analysis

Recency	Frequency	Monetary value
1 Over 12 months	**1** More than once every 6 months	**1** Less than £10
2 Within last 12 months	**2** Every 6 months	**2** £10–£50
3 Within last 6 months	**3** Every 3 months	**3** £50–£100
4 Within last 3 months	**4** Every 2 months	**4** £100–£200
5 Within last 1 months	**5** Monthly	**5** More than £200

FIGURE 3.4 Types of data that can be collected from customers

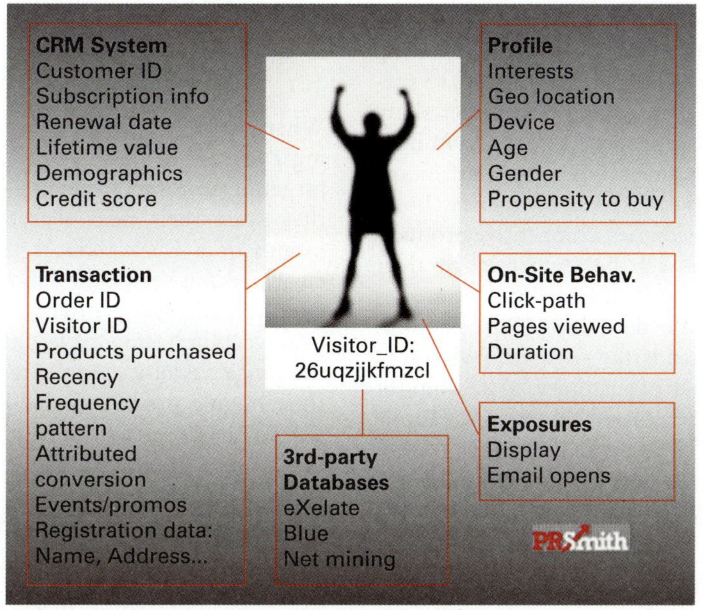

SOURCE: PR Smith's SOSTAC® Guide to The Perfect Digital Marketing Plan (2019)

FIGURE 3.5 Digital body language and marketing automation

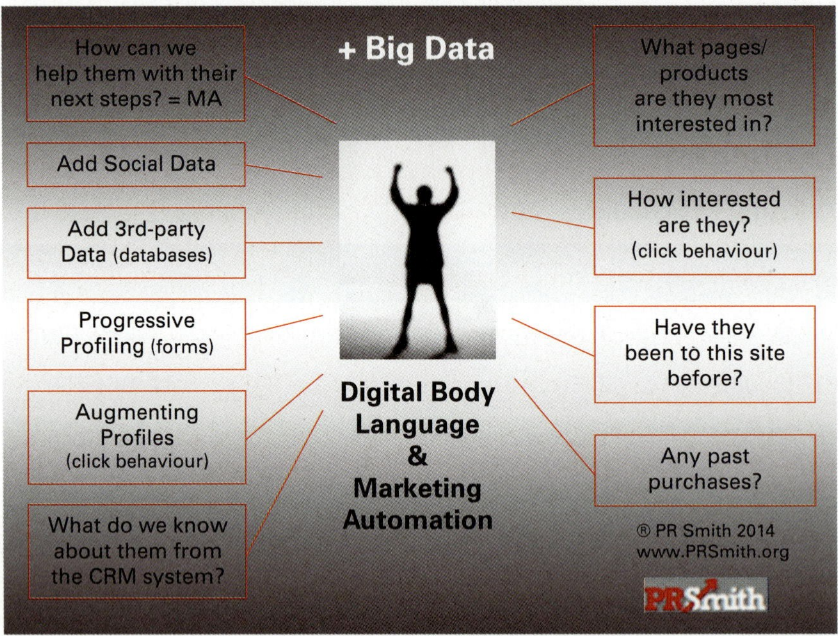

SOURCE: PR Smith's SOSTAC® Guide to The Perfect Digital Marketing Plan (2019)

There is a lot of other useful data worth collecting also, such as promotions history or responses to specific promotions, share of wallet or customer share (potential spend), timing of spend and more. In B2B, we are interested in business type (standard industrial classification (SIC) codes), size of business, holding companies and subsidiaries, competitive products bought, etc. Customers can be segmented by their activity or responsiveness levels, and then strategies to engage them can be developed. For example, Novo (2004) recommends the use of hurdle rates, which are the percentage of customers in a group (or segment) who have completed an action. Hurdle rates can then be used to compare the engagement of different groups or to set targets to increase engagement with online channels, as the examples of hurdle rates below show:

- 60 per cent of registrants have logged on to the system in the past year;
- 30 per cent have clicked through on email in the past year;
- 20 per cent of customers have visited in the past six months;
- 5 per cent of customers have made three or more purchases in the past year.

When marketers identify their customers' purchasing cycles, they can increase sales significantly, by targeting customers with attractive offers just before they start their next search. Delaying this by a month or a week reduces the probability of purchase, because once they start searching, customers explore competitive offers. Data mining reveals the average purchasing cycle and subsequently identifies those customer segments that are about to start their buying process again. The database can then automatically trigger an email or direct mail or telephone call to a customer (once certain sets of rules are applied). For example, a computer company mined its database to identify individual purchasing cycles and see how frequently different types of customers replaced their PCs. Once the frequency was identified, the company started sending catalogues and discount offers inside the buying frame, with a 95 per cent confidence level, ie 95 per cent of the prospects were just about to start searching for a new PC. Sales jumped up.

Predictive analytics

Data mining can also be used to analyse buying behaviour to identify clues for cross-selling and up-selling. For example, a bank that monitors its customers' spending may identify a segment of customers buying products from Mothercare, which suggests they have young children. This can be combined with typical profile information such as age and marital status to further identify a cluster, or segment, of the bank's customers who might be likely to consider buying a bigger car (as their family is growing). The bank's subsequent offers of a car loan might receive a 30 per cent conversion rate (request more information, call the bank, register an interest or take out an actual loan).

> **Data analytics treble conversion ratios**
>
> Wolters Kluwer UK provides publications such as Croner's information and consulting services that help businesses and professionals comply with constantly changing laws in key areas including tax and accountancy, health and safety, and human resources. The company has annual revenues of around €3.7 billion and employs over 19,000 people. After they installed and employed SAS Analytics, ROI on marketing spend increased threefold; customer retention rates increased from 75 to 83 per cent; improved efficiency and targeting meant reduced marketing headcount and costs; and in customer acquisition, sales conversion rates improved from 1 in 33 (3 per cent conversion) to 1 in 11 (9 per cent conversion). The overall project ROI ratio was 2.25:1.

GDPR compliance

The General Data Protection Regulation protects customers from misuse of their data and the customer-sensitive culture that it demands is similar to the 'permission marketing' originally defined by Seth Godin in 1999. GDPR subsequently introduced these ethical demands as an absolute necessity when it became law in 2018. Godin's *Permission Marketing* originally said that marketers must first gain customers' permission to speak to them; then they develop trust, sales and, ultimately, loyalty. GDPR goes further as it insists that marketers gain permission and also provide proof that 'permission' had been granted by customers (was it recorded?). Furthermore, proof of secure storage, data maintenance, data access and easy deletion (if the customer opts out at any time) must be ensured. For more on GDPR see p 299.

CRM implementation and agile planning

Agile planning

After the brief is issued, several supplier tenders are reviewed and researched. These solutions may be off-the-shelf, tailor-made or a mixture. When a CRM system is selected, agile planning is used. This means that working systems are delivered in short bursts, while checking that the system is robust. A pilot group of customers are selected with core, well-understood needs. The system's functionality is tested to see if it helps customers. After this, sales functionality, then service, then marketing functionality are tested.

The benefits of a phased (or agile) approach are:

- Staff and customers are 'helped' immediately. The system is used to see if it actually helps customers with tasks that can be implemented quickly, and whether staff can easily and quickly start using the system. (Customer tasks and needs have been identified in research previously carried out. This results in a much quicker buy-in from staff.)
- As customers interact with the system, it gives business analysts and implementers an iterative test bed, while still delivering value to customers.
- Major changes often require major disruption. For example, if you develop a massive CRM system over two years, the roll-out is often extremely disruptive, sometimes resulting in complete failure. A system with limited functionality is quicker and easier to introduce.
- The best business analysts and project managers often find it difficult to articulate system requirements if users are naive in

their use of (CRM) databases. Again, limited functionality helps users experience the system easily and it is then possible to identify missing features or functions.

Scoping and costing can be difficult, and always require strong leadership to decide which tasks and functions should be included (and which may have to be postponed). A 'feature score' can help to make tough decisions:

- impact to the business (efficiency, revenue);
- ease of implementation;
- completeness of understanding.

As the early iterations of the new CRM system start to reveal some ROI, incremental budget may become easier to acquire.

Writing a CRM brief

Careful thought and considerable advice are needed when setting up an initial CRM system. It requires vision, strong leadership, CRM experience, integrated skills and an integrated team. When choosing an initial CRM system, you need to consider the current and future requirements. This involves:

- objective;
- scenarios;
- contact strategies;
- communications tools.

Objective means purpose. What are you trying to achieve with a new CRM system (customer retention, customer win-back, customer acquisition, complaint processing or customer feedback)? How can it help customers? Then how can it help you and your team? What kind of scenarios does this involve (customer feedback, suggestions, complaints, enquiries, sales – all of these can be online and offline, or on a telephone line)? Is the system designed to facilitate 'welcome cycles' (welcome letters and new member offers), up-selling (moving the customer on to higher quality levels), cross-selling (other products or services) and reactivation (of previous customers), all of which help to nurture the relationship? What kind of contact strategies might this involve? What kind of marketing tools will generate the data, eg email, snail mail, outbound telemarketing, inbound telemarketing, sales teams and website dialogue?

Using SOS + 3Ms in a brief

Taken from the SOSTAC® marketing planning (see Chapter 9), SOS + 3Ms helps briefings.

SOS stands for situation (what kind of CRM do we have now and why does it need improving?), objectives (what are we trying to achieve with the new CRM system?) and strategy (how does CRM integrate with all the company's operations and improve the overall CX?).

The 3Ms are money (the budgets required for software licences plus training and motivation schemes to ensure staff buy into the new system), minutes (the timescales required to specify the brief, source it, test it, modify it, train the team and roll out the system), and men/women (who will champion the project, do the work and be involved in data capture, analysis and use).

Beware of scope creep

Scope creep destroys projects. Finally, when you've done your research, discussed everything, written up a detailed brief, got it signed off by the key people and issued it to a supplier or several suppliers, some member of staff thinks of an additional function or feature, albeit really quite helpful, and asks for it to be included in the brief. This is scope creep. It delays projects, and allows suppliers to be late with delivery ('you changed the brief') and to charge a lot more money. Although it's tempting to keep adding extra ideas, a CRM project manager has got to be strong and comprehensive in the initial exploratory discussions and ensure everyone knows that this is the last chance to discuss the brief before it goes out to tender, because once it goes out it stays out.

Reverse scope creep

Scope creep can be even more complex when flaws in the initial scope emerge during the testing phase. It takes even stronger leaders to juggle additional (essential) requirements while parking, or postponing, other requirements (functions and features) so that the initial budget and deadline are met.

Project leader

A strong CRM project leader is also required to nurture an interdisciplinary team. The project team comprises different users of the system, analysts to understand their requirements, technical staff to create the system and a project manager with sufficient time to devote to the job. You've got to involve all departments that may use the CRM system, from customer services, sales and marketing to finance (invoicing), admin, production and quality control. Don't forget IT, but we strongly recommend that marketers must take control, not IT – IT simply supplies the service expertise. It rarely has a customer focus. Remember, the primary reason is to help customers to do business with you. This is not a technology-driven project. It has to be a customer-driven project with measurable customer criteria, such as increased sales, satisfaction, referrals, etc.

Seven ways to achieve exceptional customer service

1. Make customer service a priority for the whole company. It's not just the department.
2. Empower your customer service reps. Rarely should they have to escalate a customer's issue to a supervisor.
3. Fire customers who are insatiable (cannot be satisfied) or abuse your employees.
4. Don't measure call times; don't upsell; don't use scripts.
5. Don't hide your phone number. You want to talk to customers.
6. Show the cost of handling customers' calls as an investment in marketing, not an expense.
7. Celebrate great service by telling exceptional stories to the entire company.

Hsieh (2010)

Costs and timescales

When it comes to the crunch question of 'How much does it all cost?' there are many variables to consider:

- the set-up costs of the system;
- the type of system;
- the scope of the system;
- the size of the system;
- the choice made about the database management system;
- the maintenance programme;
- where the physical database management system is geographically located.

It is a complex job but, once all these variables are taken into consideration, a task breakdown can be performed, and analysis, design, set-up, maintenance and running costs can be calculated.

Data integration and data mining costs

Costs can vary from company to company and projects can range from several hundred thousand customer records to tens of millions. A data integration, data mining campaign optimization and a full direct marketing suite from companies like SAS range from £500,000 to £5 million, with social media customer link analysis starting at around £250,000.

What's missing is customer service staff, who are a key component, particularly when they are handling wide-ranging, non-standard requests or complaints. Here's a crucial question: how many customer service staff are required?

The other key question is: how long does it take to set up a CRM system? The variables are similar to those for cost:

- time allowed for the investigative stage;
- time allowed for design;
- time for writing programmes;
- time for data capture, reassessment and input;
- time for trials, piloting, testing and debugging.

As already mentioned, agile planning accelerates this whole process by using a more iterative planning process – getting a basic system working, followed by improvement tweaks, testing, releasing and so on.

Measuring CRM success

Since data is an asset and data is also central to CRM success, one of the toughest jobs is to know which data matters most. Some customers will give incorrect information, consciously or unconsciously. Some staff (including sales people) input data incorrectly. Other staff leave data fields empty. Measuring the quality, cleanliness and completeness of data is worthwhile. Marketers and data managers have to come up with ways to acquire the correct and relevant information in the first place and then make it useful to the organization.

The customer cube

One-dimensional customer surveys usually rate product quality, after-sales service, maybe price, etc with 1 being extremely dissatisfied, 2 dissatisfied, 3 neutral, 4 satisfied, and 5 completely satisfied. This ignores how the customer ranks the importance of each variable.

Two-dimensional customer surveys weight these satisfaction factors according to how important they are to the customer: 1 is not important, 2 of minor importance, 3 fairly important, 4 very important, and 5 essential. However, this ignores how customers compare the brand to those of competitors.

Three-dimensional customer surveys also ask customers to rate the organization versus the competition for each customer service component: 1 is significantly worse, 2 somewhat worse, 3 about the same, 4 somewhat better, and 5 significantly better. The net promoter score is an excellent example of this (see below).

Measuring customer satisfaction

Call centre agents' performance is often measured by number of calls taken. This ignores customer satisfaction, although customer service is a stated aim of many companies. Many marketing managers view call centres as a means of gathering customer data rather than as a highly influential brand-building 'brand moment'.

Those marketers who do measure customer care also need to tread cautiously, as it can be misleading. For example, an increasingly high customer care score (say up from 84 per cent to 92 per cent) may seem good, but it ignores two critical elements. Firstly, which service components are very important to customers? The ultimate goal is to score 5 out of 5 ratings for all those customer service components given an importance rating of 5 by the customer. Secondly, 'how do customers rate the experience in comparison to that from competitors?', which brings us to the net promoter score (NPS).

The net promoter score

Some authors are even suspicious of three-dimensional customer satisfaction scores, as they believe conventional customer satisfaction scores 'typically only draw responses from the bored, the lonely and the seriously aggrieved' (Reichheld and Allen, 2006). The key, they suggest, is to ask customers one simple question: 'On a scale of 1 to 10, how likely is it that you would recommend us to a friend or a colleague?' where 1 is 'never' and 10 is 'always'. Calculate the NPS by counting the percentage of unhappy ('detractors') customers (who give scores between 1–6) from the percentage who are very happy ('loyal promoters') customers (who give scores of 9 or 10). The 7 and 8 scores are ignored. Then subtract percentage of detractors from the percentage of promoters to get your NPS. Some critics say that the NPS single item question cannot be a better predictor of business growth than a more comprehensive survey. However, it is used – Apple and Google have an NPS of 74 per cent and 73 per cent respectively (Curragh 2012). Other marketing influencers, like Hubspot, believe NPS can drive a business in the right direction (DeMere, 2019).

Accountants cannot distinguish between good and bad profits

'Business measures success based on profits but accountants cannot distinguish between a dollar of bad, customer abusive, growth-stifling profits and a dollar of good, loyalty-enhancing, growth-accelerating profits.'

Reichheld and Allen (2006)

Climbing the Ladder of Engagement with high NPS

O2 created a platform that helps customers to suggest improvements to the service and to help other customers. Customers earn community recognition and points-based rewards.

> 'According to Giff Gaff, customers solve 95 per cent of questions and most questions are answered in three minutes or less. What is most revealing is that Giff Gaff enjoys a net promoter score of 73 per cent (a measurement that indicates what proportion of customers are promoters versus detractors). As a comparison, Apple and Google have an NPS of 74 per cent and 73 per cent respectively. Giff Gaff has also responded to customer suggestions, implementing over 100 improvements to date, including changes to the pricing structure.'
>
> Curragh (2012)

Internal marketing

We have mentioned it already – without internal marketing even the best planned projects fail, whether CRM or marketing automation. Internal marketing ensures excellence of execution. Internal marketing identifies fears, phobias and barriers that can hinder the introduction of a new, or even just improved, CRM system. Internal marketing comprises: motivation, communication and training which, in turn, require resources to ensure the successful launch and ongoing operation of a marketing automation system and/or a CRM system. Here's an example of the importance of getting 'buy-in from all internal stakeholders' for Fujitsu's new global marketing automation project. It starts with leaders (see Figure 3.6).

Fujitsu's ambitious MA was developed for global use with over 30 countries having little or no MA execution, awareness or skills and each using a multitude of different tools, technologies, processes and standards. They suffered from a lack of transparency, consistency and oversight as well as a lack of insights. So they worked with UK-based CleverTouch.com to:

- consolidate technologies, ensuring consistent clean data, aligning disparate silos;
- develop a process that delivered a standardized execution;
- design and approve workflows, consolidate templates.

Right from the start, Fujitsu knew they had to get buy-in from all internal stakeholders from top to bottom of the business. These Fujitsu slides (Figures 3.6 to 3.10) explain how leaders (C suite), external partner suppliers (Marketo), internal marketers and external partner consultants (CleverTouch) all had crystal clear roles to play in this significant part of Fujitsu's digital transformation – introducing and embracing marketing automation.

FIGURE 3.6 Marketing automation stakeholders: C suite staff and leaders must support MA

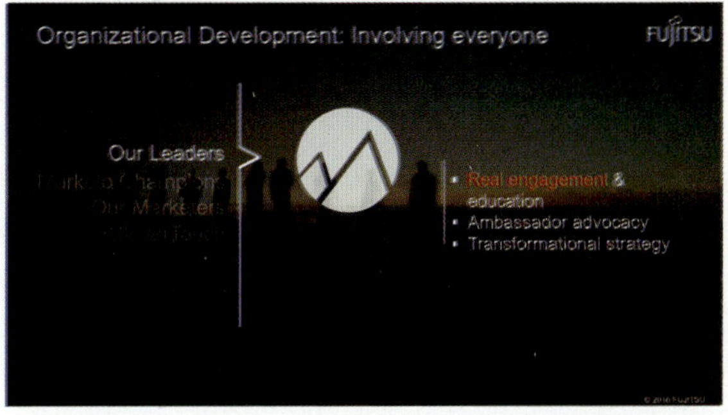

FIGURE 3.7 Marketing automation stakeholders: internal champions must be identified and empowered

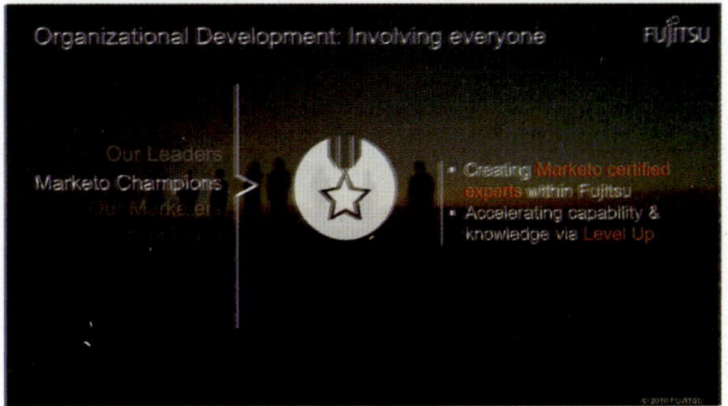

FIGURE 3.8 Marketing automation stakeholders: marketing team must be trained and motivated

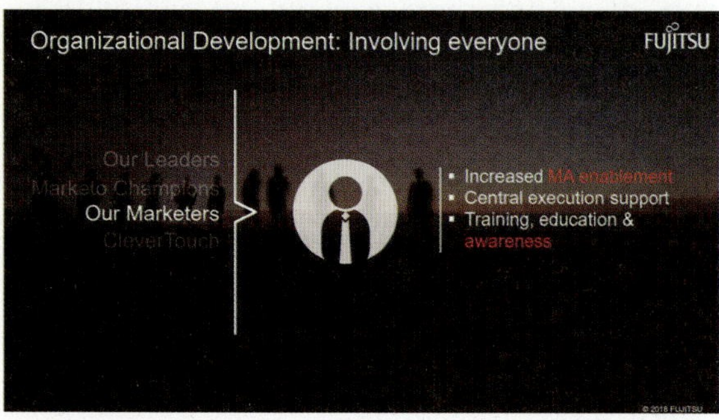

FIGURE 3.9 Marketing automation requires working with partners, CleverTouch, as an extension of Fujitsu team

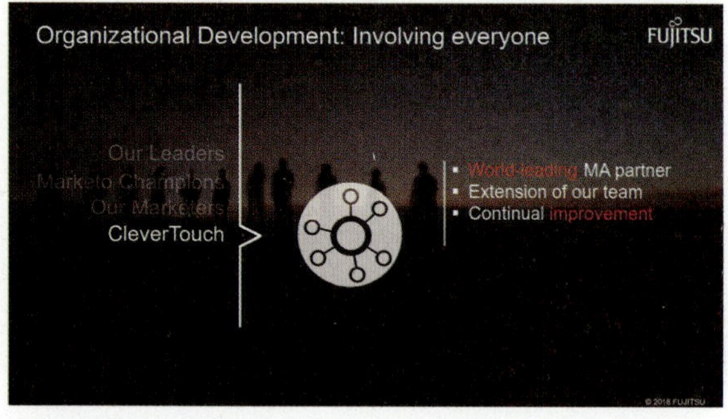

FIGURE 3.10 Three key takeaways

This major global MA programme, designed to deliver better marketing qualified leads to sales people, acknowledges, early on, the importance of internal marketing to ensure 'buy-in' from all stakeholders, ensuring future coaching and training are embraced by staff.

> **Coaching to improve not reporting to inspect**
>
> Managers provide coaching to improve, not reporting to inspect. The pivotal role in driving CRM success is not individual salespeople. It's sales management. They will determine how the sales team uses and experiences the CRM. If they use it solely to check on the amount of activity, call volume, or other measures of efficiency, it's of low value to the sales team and likely be rejected or filled with fictional data. Instead use it as a tool to jointly create strategies for major opportunities, and help the sales team to maximize opportunities by coaching them throughout the sales process.

As with any aspect of marketing communications, internal marketing helps your marketing teams to understand, embrace and deliver new marketing initiatives. None more so than CRM and MA. Without internal marketing, these initiatives will fail. With internal marketing, the chances of success increase significantly.

CRM summary and challenges

CRM is a strategic issue requiring a long-term perspective. Winning a sale is short-term transactional marketing. Building a relationship where the customer comes back again and again is long-term strategy. Building good customer relations requires a cultural shift to ensure that the whole organization wants to help customers. Slow CRM projects that take several years to research, develop, test and launch, are being replaced by a more agile planning approach, to get them up and running more quickly. There will always be some tension between the pressure to hit the short-term monthly and quarterly sales (and profit) targets versus the longer-term customer relations scores. Marketers need to educate boards about how CRM, in the long term, grows quarterly sales and profits.

ROI of customer satisfaction

'In fact, when we looked at the top 100 e-retailers, we saw that increasing satisfaction by just one point drove over $112 million in additional sales' (Atchison, 2008). That was over ten years ago. What would increasing satisfaction, or perhaps your NPS score, by '1' be worth in sales to your organization today?

The shift to becoming a relationship-building organization can start by asking how the organization or the brand can help customers even more than it does now. CRM is big business and needs careful attention to tiny details, but with a clear vision of nurturing prospects into customers and customers into lifetime customers. Although CRM will help short-term results, its real potential is in the long-term future of the business as lifetime relationships with customers are grown.

Key points from Chapter 3

- Relationship marketing (and CRM) can create competitive advantage.
- Marketing automation generates leads that are then fed into the CRM system for conversion to sales.
- CRM is ultimately all about nurturing long-term customers and brand building vs short-term sales growth.
- There is a disciplined approach to the CRM planning process.
- CRM requires resources and a disciplined set of processes.
- Many organizations allow scope creep and lack of training and motivation to destroy their CRM.
- Although CRM can boost short-term results, it really is an investment in the long-term future growth of an organization.

References and further reading

Allen, J, Reichheld, F and Hamilton, B (2005) The three 'Ds' of customer experience, Harvard Business School Working Knowledge

Atchison, S (2008) The ROI of customer satisfaction, Interview with Larry Freed, President and CEO of ForeSee Results, *ClickZ*, 24 July

August, A (2002) Smashing time for Chinese consumers, *The Times*, 14 March

Bi, F (2016) Closed-loop reporting and why it matters to your company, Salesforce Blog, 10 November

Bird, D (1989) *Commonsense Direct Marketing*, 2nd edn, Kogan Page, London

Brandi, J (2010) Customer sensitivity quotient [online] www.returnonhappiness.com (archived at https://perma.cc/5QET-VRGP)

Brann, C (1984) *Cost-Effective Direct Marketing: By mail, telephone and direct response advertising*, Collectors' Books, Cirencester

Chaffey, D and Smith, PR (2013) *Emarketing Excellence*, 4th edn, Routledge, London

Chaffey, D and Smith, PR (2017) *Digital Marketing Excellence*, 5th edn, Routledge, Abingdon

Considine, R and Raphel, M (1981) *The Great Brain Robbery*, The Great Brain Robbery, Pasadena, CA

Creak, T (2018) The simplification of marketing automation, Fujitsu presented at Clever-Touch.com (archived at https://perma.cc/T8CH-98N7) Simplification and smarter adoption event, November

Curragh, A (2012) The future of customer service: The rise of the social consumer, Social Media Leadership Forum 2012, *ItsOpen* [online] www.itsopen.co.uk (archived at https://perma.cc/H9UT-SRAD)

DB2 (1997) IBM Developer Works

DeMere, N (2019) 5 interesting ways real companies use net promoter score results, *Hubspot*, **11**

Direct Marketing Centre (1992) *The Practitioner Guide to Direct Marketing*, Direct Marketing Centre, London

dunnhumby (2006) *The dunnhumby Way*, dunnhumby, London

Earls, K (2002) *Welcome to the Creative Age*, Wiley, Chichester

Edinger, S (2018) Why CRM projects fail and how to make them more successful, *HBR*, 20 December

Exhibition Venues Association (2000) *UK Exhibition Facts*, Vol 12, Exhibition Venues Association, Mayfield, East Sussex, February

Forrester Research (2009) *Answers to Five Frequently Asked Questions about CRM Projects*, Forrester Research, Cambridge, MA

Gartner (2009) *Trip Report: Gartner customer relationship management summit 2009*, Gartner, Stamford, CT

Godin, S (1999) *Permission Marketing*, Simon and Schuster, New York

Hochman, L (2008) Guide to customer loyalty, *Marketing Age*, March/April

Howard, M (1989) Telephone marketing vs direct sales force costs, Commissioned by Datapoint (UK) Ltd, London

Hsieh, T (2010) How I did it: Zappos's CEO on going to extremes for customers, *HBR*, July/August

Huffington Post (2012) British airways will google passengers 'to put a face to the name' 7 June [online] www.huffingtonpost.com/2012/07/06/british-airways-will-google-passengers_n_1653530.html?ncid=edlinkusaolp00000003&ir=Technology (archived at https://perma.cc/8ET3-HRGY)

Ismail, N (2018) Why IT projects continue to fail at an alarming rate, *Information Age*, 16 February

Janrain (2012) Definitive guide to user management [online] https://janrain.cloud-papers.com/ (archived at https://perma.cc/QE2U-X2YE)

Kirkpatrick, D (1992) Breaking up IBM: Facing horrendous challenges, *Fortune*, 27 June

Krigsman, M (2009) CRM failure rates: 2001–2009, *ZDNet*, 3 August [online] www.zdnet.com/blog/projectfailures/crm-failure-rates-2001-2009/4967 (archived at https://perma.cc/7XS5-PDDC)

Mahoney, M (2002) 'Putting the R back in CRM': It's time to reinstall the 'R' in your customer relationship, Interview with Susan Fournier, Harvard Business School Working Knowledge, 7 January

McCorkell, G (1997) *Direct and Database Marketing*, Kogan Page, London

McGovern, G (2014) The complexity-simplicity trade off, *Gerry McGovern//New Thinking*, 9 March [online]http://gerrymcgovern.com/the-complexity-simplicity-trade-off/ (archived at https://perma.cc/ZYF3-W5HV)

Minsky, L and Quesenberry, K (2016) How B2B sales can benefit from social selling, *Harvard Business Review*, 10 November

Mitchell, A (2004) Heart of the matter, *The Markets*, 3 June

MORI (2003) Managing your customer insight capability and the drivers for change – client managed, cosourced, insourced or outsourced – a survey of UK FTSE 100 organisations, Commissioned by Detica

Moriarty, R and Moran, U (1990) Managing hybrid systems, *Harvard Business Review*, November–December

Moriarty, R and Swartz, G (1989) Automation to boost sales and marketing, *Harvard Business Review*, January–February

NetProspex (2014) *The State of Marketing Data: NetProspex annual marketing data benchmark report 2014* [online] www.netprospex.com/wp-content/uploads/2014/12/2014-NPX-Benchmark-Report.pdf (archived at https://perma.cc/4E8U-CR9K)

Novo, J (2004) *Drilling Down: Turning customer data into profits with a spreadsheet*, 3rd edn, Jim Novo

Reichheld, F and Allen, J (2006) How companies can end the cycle of customer abuse, *Financial Times*, 23 March

Rouse, M (2015) 360-degree customer view, *Tech Target*, February

Royal Mail (1991) *The Royal Mail Guide to Successful Direct Mail*, Royal Mail, London

Rubach, E (2007) Impulse buying, *New Media Age*

Smith, PR (2014a) The good, the bad and the ugly of gamification [online] www.prsmith.org/blog (archived at https://perma.cc/KA8E-SSY8)

Smith, PR (2014b) The old marketing ship is sinking [online] http://prsmith.org/listening-skills-digital-media-listening-tools-part-12/ (archived at https://perma.cc/HA9N-6BAU)

Smith, PR (2019) SOSTAC® Guide to The Perfect Digital Marketing Plan [online] http://prsmith.org/SOSTAC/ (archived at https://perma.cc/CY8M-YQ3F)

Smith, PR and Zook, Z (2011) *Marketing Communications*, 5th edn, Kogan Page, London

Stevens, M (1991) *The Handbook of Telemarketing*, Kogan Page, London

Tapp, A (2001) *Principles of Direct and Database Marketing*, 2nd edn, Financial Times/Prentice Hall, Englewood Cliffs, NJ

Toffler, A (1980) *The Third Wave*, Collins, London

Watson, J (1989) The direct marketing guide, *Marketing Magazine*, 9 February

Ye, L (nd) Why your sales reps hate CRM software, *Hubspot*

Young, M (nd) Never sell to a stranger, Ogilvy & Mather Direct

Further information

British Quality Foundation
Devonshire House
60 Goswell Road
London EC1M 7AD
Tel: +44 (0)20 7654 5000
www.bqf.org.uk

British Standards Institution
389 Chiswick High Road
London W4 4AL
Tel: +44 (0)20 8996 9000
Fax: +44 (0)20 8996 7001
www.bsigroup.com

Institute of Customer Service
Mill House
8 Mill Street
London SE1 2BA
Tel: +44(0)207 260 2620
www.instituteofcustomerservice.com

04 Buyer behaviour

LEARNING OBJECTIVES

By the end of this chapter you will be able to:

- appreciate the complexity of buying behaviour;
- understand the critical nature of a continual feed of information on customer behaviour;
- appreciate the emotional influences in decision-making;
- compare and contrast various approaches to buying models;
- apply the psychology of marketing by exploring different intervening variables.

Introduction to understanding customer buying behaviour

The first step in formulating a marketing communications strategy is to identify, analyse and ultimately understand the target market and its buying behaviour. This chapter considers some of the theories and models that the marketing professional can use to help to communicate with and influence the buyer at various stages before, during and after purchasing. Buying behaviour is often more complex than it appears. Individuals are generally not very predictable, but, in the aggregate, groups of customers (or percentages of markets) can be more predictable.

Whether in the industrial or consumer market, or whether they are buying products or services, buyers respond in different ways to the barrage of marketing communications that are constantly aimed at them. Theoretical frameworks borrowed from psychology, sociology, social psychology, cultural anthropology and economics are now added to by both commercial and academic market research into consumer and business-to-business buyer behaviour. All of this contributes to a better understanding of customers. It is this understanding that helps to reveal what kind of marketing communications work best.

This chapter can provide only an outline of the vast amount of work written in this area. The complex burger buyer example below is used to open up some of the types of questions that need to be considered. The chapter then looks at types of purchases and the buying process (including some buying models) and then considers how the 'intervening variables' of perception, motivation, learning, memory, attitudes, beliefs, personality and group influence can influence the communication process and, ultimately, buying behaviour.

Three key questions

There are three key groups of questions that have to be answered before any marketing communications can be carried out:

- Who is the buyer (target market profiles and decision-making units)?
- Why do they buy (or not buy) a particular brand or product?
- How do they buy (how, when and where do they buy)?

The second question, 'Why do they buy?', is the most difficult to answer. It requires qualitative rather than quantitative data (which often answers the other questions also). Products and services are bought for a range of different reasons or benefits, some conscious, others unconscious, some rational, others emotional. Many buyers buy for a mixture of reasons. Consider a simple hamburger.

The complex burger buyer

Why buy a burger? The answer might be as simple as 'Because I was hungry – so I bought a Big Mac.' The real reason, however, may be quite different. Perhaps the buyer was in a receptive state for food because of the time of day. In the same way that a stimulus such as a bell for Pavlov's dogs (see 'Learning', p 140) can cause a dog to salivate, the highly visible yellow McDonald's logo can act as a stimulus to customers to remind them of food and arouse feelings of hunger – even trigger salivation. Perhaps the yellow logo also acts as a cue, by triggering memories of the happy advertising images that are learned and stored in memory banks.

Choice is influenced by motivations. Consider that a teenage burger buyer may prefer McDonald's because friends hang out there and it feels nice to be in with the in-crowd (Maslow's need to be accepted or loved; see 'Motivation', p 142). Maybe the friendly image and the quick service simultaneously satisfy two basic needs – love and hunger. Many convenience purchases today are, in fact, about purchasing time, ie buying a time-saving product or service releases free time to do something else, to satisfy another need. In fact, despite Facebook losing the trust of its customers (regarding personal data), its convenience seems to be more important as Facebook numbers just keep going up (see more on 'whether convenience trumps trust' later). It is likely that buyers have many different reasons with different orders of importance. Different segments can seek many different reasons with different orders of importance. But why don't they go into a Burger King restaurant or a fish and chip shop instead of a McDonald's?

Choice is often influenced by familiarity with the brand, or sometimes the level of trust in a brand name. Familiarity can be generated by actual experience and/or increased awareness boosted by advertising, sponsorship, social media and PR. If one brand can get into the front of an individual's mind ('front-of-mind awareness'), then it will stand a better chance of being chosen in a simple buying situation like this, unless of course the buyer has a preferred set of fast-food restaurants that specifically exclude a particular brand. In this case the buyer is usually prepared to search a little harder (even cross the road) before satisfying the aroused need.

Choice can be influenced by location – eg offering the right goods or services in the right place at the right time (convenience). Assuming this is all supported by the right image (eg clean and friendly, nutritious, fast service and socially responsible), then the marketing mix has succeeded in capturing this segment of non-loyal burger buyers who have no strong 'preferred set' of fast-food outlets.

More health-conscious buyers may prefer a nice warm cup of soup. Why? What motivates them? Health? A desire to live longer? A fear of death? A desire to be fit, stay slim, look good (esteem) or just feel healthy and feel good? Or perhaps it's cheaper than a burger? Or is it because everyone else in the office recommends the local delicatessen's soup (pressure to conform to group norms, desire to be accepted by a group – again, the need to be loved)?

We like soup, perhaps, because of prenatal sensations of being surrounded by amniotic fluid...

There are other possibilities that lie in the dark depths of our vast information storage chambers otherwise known as our unconscious. For example, in 1957 Vance Packard suggested that 'the deepest roots of our liking for warm, nutritious and plentiful soup may lie in the comfortable and secure unconscious prenatal sensations of being surrounded by the amniotic fluid in our mother's womb'.

Packard (1957)

Impulse buying and repeat purchasing of low-cost fast food obviously differs from the buying behaviour involved in the purchase of, say, a new audio system, a house, a holiday or a fleet of new cars for the company. It is likely that more 'information search' will occur than in the simple stimulus–response buying model (McDonald's yellow logo stimulates the senses and arouses hunger, which generates the response – buy a Big Mac). Regular low-cost purchases are known as 'routinized response behaviour' and therefore have a different buying process than a high-cost, high-risk, irregular purchase, which is known as a 'high-involvement purchase'. Some basic buying models help to explain the different types of purchases and the types of buying processes involved. These will be considered later in this chapter.

Get customers to form new habits with their mobile phone

If a brand can become part of someone's life it can develop into a habitual behaviour. Getting customers to develop a new 'mobile habit' of using your brand's app will nurture stronger brand relationships and deliver a new form of competitive advantage. So, think mobile. As Meri Rosich (2015) says: 'Being mobile does not just mean being able to access information – it also means a lot of new habits. Habits that are only possible with an ever-present mobile device.'

Who is the customer?

So many organizations do not know who their customers are. This means they have no real idea who they are trying to target. This is high-risk marketing, something akin to trying to find a needle in a haystack. In fact, there is more chance of finding the needle, because at least we can describe what a needle looks like. But in marketing if we cannot describe (or profile) who the ideal customer is then the organization is almost totally dependent on luck. The few outstanding marketing companies out there really do spend a lot of time and effort constantly researching and analysing exactly who is their target market (in great detail), the needs of the target market (why they buy) and how they buy. It can be more difficult online. Some people behave differently online than offline. They assume different pseudonyms and personalities. However, we have a multitude of online analytics tools that help us to profile online customers.

'A 25-year-old New York stockbroker had an online fling with a 21-year-old blue-eyed blonde Miami beauty. They arranged to meet at JFK airport with red roses. The young New Yorker was horrified to see a 70-year-old man sitting in a wheelchair, wearing a red rose and roaring with laughter at him.' They used to tell this story when the internet emerged in the 1990s. Today, we can see a lot more customer profile information, with the right analytics collected from our online profiles, activities (likes and shares) as well as our basic click behaviour or 'digital body language'.

Knowing who the customer is, is not as easy as it seems. As discussed in Chapter 3, many businesses do not know who their customers are. Despite having large databases, they do not know how to put profiles on their customers. Without this information, companies are shooting blind and just hoping for the best. This is high-risk marketing. For example, a European battery supplier noticed that its highest-margin, high-tech batteries were frequently sold out in one of its most powerful retailers. As it wanted to boost sales at this retailer, it invested in a new point-of-sale. It assumed the high-tech batteries were bought by high-tech users. It designed a prominent new display rack describing the batteries' benefits for digital services. Sales fell. Research revealed that ordinary (non-high-tech) users were buying the batteries, as they perceived the hi-tech batteries would simply last longer (a fact not emphasized in the displays). The company returned to the original displays, and sales went up by 20 per cent (Forsyth *et al*, 2006).

If you are targeting 'perpetuals', those people who are 24/7 connected, what age are they? What income levels, education, spending habits do they have? You need information to build their profile to tell you who they are. Once you know this (in great detail), suddenly marketing to them gets a lot easier.

Who are Generation 'C' or the 'perpetuals' (perpetually connected customer)?

- Mostly young (27–38 year olds);
- well educated;
- tech fiends
- average income $110,000+;
- spend most money online;
- 4/5 tablet + smart phone/phone;
- use lots of apps;
- connect everywhere, frequently;
- multitask and have fast-paced lives;
- first adopters of new technology;
- Generation C (for connectedness and also 'consume, create and curate').

Adapted from Pun (2013)

Who are the visitors to your website? What is their profile? You can collect information via forms and monitor click behaviour (digital body language). Google analytics (and other packages) give you aggregate profile data (demographics, preferred content, conversion rates etc). LinkedIn Insights and Facebook Insights also reveal visitor profile information. There are services today that will profile approximately 20 per cent of your visitors on B2B sites, delivering company name, telephone number, address, number of employees, location, keywords used and a lot more for individual visitors. See PR Smith's SOSTAC® guide to your perfect digital marketing plan (2019) for these and many more services and free tools that answer the 'who, why and how?' customer questions.

Decision-making units

As mentioned previously, there are often several individuals involved in any one person's decision to purchase either consumer or industrial products and services. The choice of a family car may be influenced by parents, children, aunts, uncles, neighbours, friends, the Automobile Association and so on. Each may play a different role in the buying process. Similarly, the purchase of a new factory machine may have been instigated by a safety inspector, selected by a team of engineers, supervisors, the shop steward and production manager, agreed by the board, bought or ordered by the purchasing director and paid for by the financial director or company secretary.

PAGES is a simple acronym that helps to build a marketing communications decision-making unit (DMU) checklist:

- Purchaser: The person who orders the goods or services.
- Adviser: Someone who is knowledgeable in the field.
- Gatekeeper: A secretary, receptionist or assistant who wants to protect his or her boss from being besieged by marketing messages.
- End user: Sometimes called 'the customer'.
- Starter: The instigator or initiator.

The actual decision-maker is sometimes separate from the purchaser and/or the user. The payer (cheque authorizer) may be different to the purchaser in the B2B environment.

Other, non-human, influencers include artificial influencers (which you might find disturbing in Chapter 5) plus the intelligent shopping bot. They can take many different forms. One form is the futuristic 3D floating holograms that appear beside the customer when the customer is in buying mode, giving advice, or even haggling with the salesperson (if buying offline). Another influencer may well be Internet of Things (IoT) connected devices including the intelligent fridge, which can offer the customer a tempting online voucher to replace the last can of Guinness with an alternative brand. Other ongoing influencers are apps on your phone. My iPhone has various apps: one identifies the prices at all petrol stations near my location, and another scans in bar codes and compares prices locally. As phones become smarter, with predictive devices delivering real-time contextualized and personalized services and information, the device knows, through the aggregated filters of our location, our timeline and our social graph, what we did just before and what we are expected to want, or do, later on (courtesy of our online calendar, contacts database, web search history and geo-location information). Very soon, context-based technology will predict our needs and desires. It is 'aware' because it holds a complete record of our past actions and habits and of our future intentions – where we are heading and who we will meet via calendar entries, contacts, web/search history, etc (Frank, 2010).

It's only a matter of time before your mobile device knows your every want and need

'I am on a business trip to Madrid, have just finished my meetings and have three hours until my flight back to New York. My device "senses" I started moving and "knows" my schedule, therefore it asks me if I prefer to get a taxi to the airport, or if I prefer to stay in the city since the drive to the airport takes about 15 minutes. I choose the second option, slide the "ambient media streams" all the way from "privacy please" to "hit me with everything you've got", and the device offers me all the tourist attractions around me, even a nearby coffee shop that has received exceptionally high ratings (I love coffee). I choose the coffee shop, and as I am drinking my second cup, the device alerts me that my flight has been delayed by an hour and will board through gate E32. I drink another cup of coffee and read from my device the history of Madrid until the next alert updates me that I should call a taxi – immediately providing me with an application that directly books one.'

Frank (2010)

Why do they buy?

Marketing people really do need to know the reasons why buyers buy. More often than not, consumers do not even know all of the real reasons they buy (although they like to think that they are rational decision-makers). There is a range of conscious and unconscious reasons underlying why people buy what they buy. Some reasons are more important than others to a particular segment. Some reasons are rational, and some are emotional. The split between the two is called the 'emotional–rational dichotomy'. The late Robert Gouezeta, former CEO of Coca-Cola, once said, 'We sell on image. We don't know how to sell on performance. Everything we sell, we sell on image.' So their customers are persuaded emotionally. However, ask anyone why they buy Coca-Cola and they'll give you rational reasons like 'it tastes better'. This not always true. Often customers don't know why they buy what they buy. But marketers must know. Marketers may know why customers buy (or don't buy), why they visit your website for a second time (or why they never come back). Marketers need to know what is motivating these customers and new prospect customers. Marketers need to know their customers better than customers know themselves. Marketers need to get deep insights into the minds of their market. These deep insights can create competitive advantage.

Why do they visit your website? What job do they want done?

Visitors arrive at your website hoping to achieve something. Find a product, get more information, find a phone number, maybe even buy a product. Each of these is a 'job to be done'. Christensen *et al* (2016) extend this to buying any product or service: What job do customers want done or what problem are they trying to solve? Customers don't really buy products or services, they 'hire' them to do a 'job'. Identify compensating behaviours, where people are having to use work-arounds to get the job done. 'A compensating behaviour is any action someone performs to get a job done when there's not a good product in the market to solve that job.' Christensen continues: 'A common theme in disruption is that the technology already exists, the job to be done already exists, but the two have never been put together in an affordable and accessible product.' So often we find that the technology often already exists and the job to be done exists – it is just a question of putting the two together.

Why do people share content on social media? Rational or emotional reasons?

It is worth asking your friends and colleagues why they share. Keep asking 'why?' after each answer. And you will find some interesting answers. Ultimately, because we want to be loved, perhaps? Or perhaps we admit we want to look good or maybe even build our own brand?

Mridu Khullar Relph reveals why we share from a neuroscience perspective:

- 84 per cent share content that supported a particular cause;
- 78 per cent share content to nurture relationships;
- 73 per cent process information more deeply when they share it with others;
- 69 per cent share content to feel involved in the world;
- 68 per cent share content that they feel helps them define themselves;
- 49 per cent share content as a form of entertainment.

Khullar Relph (2015)

So, it's not surprising that the former CEO of the world's largest communications group, WPP, signed a strategic global partnership with Twitter. Why? Unique customer insights from Twitter. 'The global strategic partnership between WPP and Twitter allows the communications giant to integrate Twitter data into its media and analytics platforms' (Ibrahim 2013). The CEO, Martin Sorrell, said two-thirds of the benefits of Twitter are brand insights and customer research. So take note, WPP see Twitter as a listening tool and as an analytics tool more than an advertising tool with tremendous reach.

Useful insights can be gleaned just from the words, or phrases, people use to find firstly your website and secondly things on your site. These words and phrases describe the benefits or features they want. Consequently, they can also tell you what is missing on your site. Any analytics package reveals these key phrases that give you insights into your visitors' needs and wants.

Identify your unspoken desires (with AI)

'AI (when thoughtfully applied to protect consumer privacy) can help marketers learn things even the most creative humans can't. By using natural language processing, for instance, companies can figure out that a consumer is interested in sports cars without that person ever having said so.'

Gregg *et al* (2018)

The rational–emotional dichotomy

This rational and emotional quagmire is not restricted to B2C (consumer) purchasing but applies also to supposedly hard-nosed rational B2B (business) customers. B2B customers buy into relationships built on reliability, trust and personality (emotional factor). Meanwhile, Harley-Davidson does not sell motorcycles, Starbucks do not sell coffee, Club Med does not sell holidays, Guinness does not sell beer and Coca-Cola doesn't sell cola. Porsche buyers don't buy a transport vehicle; many of them buy a Porsche because they 'simply want to prove to themselves that they have the ability to buy such a car' (Kapferer, 2004).

Coca-Cola is not the best tasting cola, yet it commands almost 1,000 per cent price premium and it's the world's most popular cola. I know because the then European Marketing Director of Coca-Cola, George Bradt told me that Coca-Cola was an inferior cola when measuring rational taste buds using rational taste wheels to help consumers describe taste. Coca-Cola aims to satisfy our deeper emotional desires beyond rational taste. We all want to be loved. You'll never see a Coke ad with just one person, or just one polar bear. And, for this intimate privilege that reflects our deep desires we are prepared to pay the premium for Coca-Cola.

The difference between emotion and reason

'You spend three seconds. You do not think about every benefit, every attribute, every demonstration. There's an emotional connection through the packaging, through the advertising and through your memory that you make. And then you decide. Neurologist Donald Khan says the difference between emotion and reason is: "Reason leads to conclusions – emotion leads to action."

Most of the research asks: "Do you remember it? Do you get the brand benefits?", whereas the only question you need to ask in research is: "Do you want to see it again? Does this connect with you?"'

Roberts (2006a)

The bottom line is that marketing managers have constantly to ask the question: 'Why are they buying or not buying our products or services?' Customers need to be probed deeply to find the answers to questions like: 'How do you feel about the brand? Does the brand connect with you? How? How much emotional connection have you got with the brand?' The answers are not static, one-off pieces of research findings but a constant flow of information. Rational reasons need to be understood also. And remember: reasons change; people change; markets change; competition and technology change. A valid reason for buying a particular product yesterday may become invalid tomorrow as reasons can change over time as new trends kick in. Likewise, an apparently irrelevant feature yesterday may become a key reason for buying tomorrow. So we need continual research because markets are continually moving away from products (and services).

Unconscious fears and differing reasons

A company executive might buy a well-known brand of laptop rather than another brand simply because of an unconscious fear of being fired for buying a poor-quality laptop.

This is further complicated by the fact that some customers buy the same product for different reasons. For example, Americans may buy iPods because iPods enable them to listen to their favourite music without being disturbed, by others, while Japanese buy them to listen to their favourite music without disturbing others. Even an apparently simple product like toothpaste presents an array of reasons for buying. The toothpaste manufacturers respond by supplying different brands of toothpaste offering different benefits to different segments who have different reasons (needs or motives) for brushing their teeth. The following toothpaste test explains.

The toothpaste test

Why do you buy toothpaste? 'To keep teeth clean.' 'To stop cavities and visits to dentist.' 'To keep a full set of beautiful shining teeth.' Some people will admit that 'it is habit' or that 'my parents taught me always to clean my teeth'. All of these answers suggest different benefits that different groups or segments want from their toothpaste, and so the toothpaste suppliers oblige by positioning certain brands as those that deliver a particular benefit. But when do you brush your teeth? First thing in the morning? If people were serious about seeking the benefits they would carry a small portable brush and use it after each meal. Why do most people brush first thing in the morning? To avoid bad breath (which destroys one's confidence). Yet many people do not like admitting it. The real reason is often hidden beneath the surface.

The now classic Colgate 'ring of confidence' was one of the UK's best-known toothpaste advertisements. It was basically selling a tube of social confidence (the ad literally showed a 'ring of confidence' wrapped around smiling customers). This need to be accepted is relatively obvious although not always admitted initially. There are, however, deeper feelings, emotions, memories, moods, thoughts, beliefs and attitudes locked up inside the dark depths of our unconscious. Sigmund Freud suggested that the mind was like an iceberg in so far as the tip represents the conscious part of the mind while the greater submerged part is the unconscious. Even long-forgotten childhood experiences can affect buying behaviour, including that of hard-nosed US industrial buyers (see 'Mommy's never coming back', p 200). Some theories of motivation are discussed further in this chapter (see the 'Motivation' section p 142).

In the UK many organizations use in-depth research; Guinness, for example, carries out in-depth research to tap into drinkers' deeply ingrained feelings about the product. Feelings that customers cannot articulate. So, instead, they are asked to express their (often unconscious) feelings through clay modelling, picture completion and cartoon completion techniques. This kind of research has revealed that people associate natural goodness and quasi-mystical qualities with the brand. Not something that the average customer could articulate, when asked 'why do you drink Guinness?' The section 'Motivation' (p 142) looks at in-depth feelings in more detail.

Rational pricing?

Why do cinemas have small \$3.50, medium \$5.25 and large \$5.50 sodas? If a cinema only has small sodas for \$3.50 and large sodas for \$5.50, fewer large sodas are bought. But if they add in a medium size soda, it becomes a 'decoy', making you more likely to buy a large (as it appears better value).

Why does *The Economist* have a digital subscription \$59, a print subscription \$125 and a print plus digital subscription at \$125? If only two options are available, most choose the cheaper option. But three options, with one being a bad option, 'made people much more likely to choose the more expensive print plus digital option. This is called "asymmetric dominance" and it means that people gravitate toward the choice nearest a clearly inferior option' (Stibel, 2018).

In B2B markets studies reveal that emotion plays a significant part when making buying decisions:

> B2B buyers are people too, and just because they work in a corporate environment, it doesn't mean they want to digest staid, dry and 'typical' content. It also means that business marketers need to connect with their audience in a way that empathizes with their pains and offers workable solutions to them in a language that is human and that they can understand.
>
> Langton (2013)

FIGURE 4.1 How emotion influences B2B buying

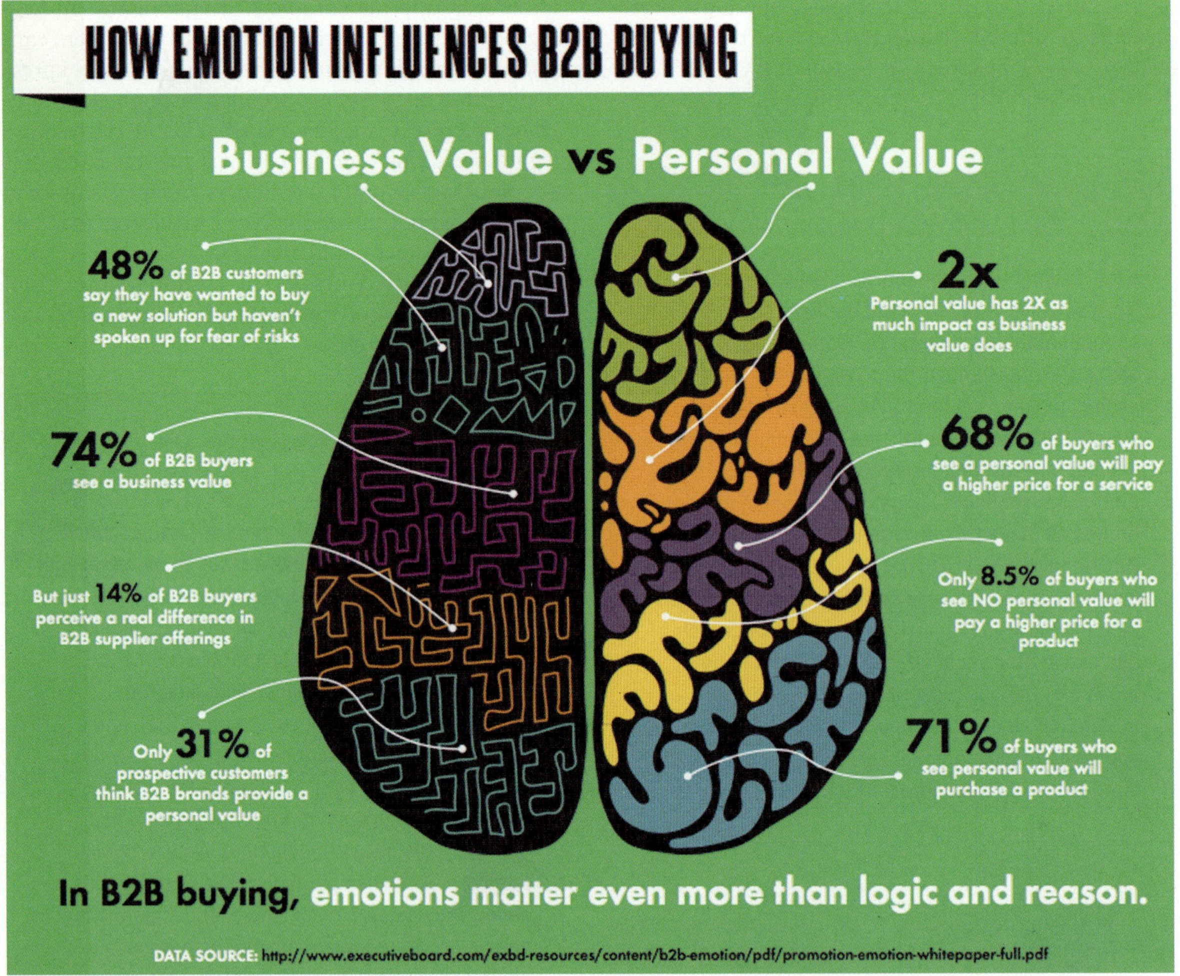

> **Bloatware: Emotional wins over rational**
>
> Forty-five per cent of software features are never used, 19 per cent are rarely used, and 16 per cent are sometimes used, so some software suppliers launched 'liteware' with fewer functions and lower prices. It flopped. Why? Because people didn't want to be without features that other people had – so bloatware prevails.

In the quest to find the real reasons why people buy or don't buy, why they visit a website repeatedly or why they never come back, marketers continually seek to answer these sometimes complex 'why' questions.

Brain science

There is no doubt that conscious reasoning accounts for only a small part of our thinking. David Penn (2005) talked about how brain science helps to throw some light on the dark depths of emotion and consciousness:

> By reuniting psychology with philosophy and biology, it shifts the scientific focus back onto the mysteries of consciousness and emotion. Increasingly, we've come to understand that unlocking the mystery of consciousness actually depends on figuring out the unconscious functions of the brain. Not Freud's unconscious functions (a repository for repressed memories) but rather the many things the brain does that are not available to consciousness. Unconscious processes include most of what the brain does – we can often be aware of what we're doing when these things happen, but much of the time consciousness is informed after the fact through the cognitive unconscious. The area that's generating hottest debate is emotion, and its operation through the so-called emotional unconscious, and it's here that the fusion of biology and psychology is changing the whole way we understand human behaviour. The unconscious explains most of what we feel, think and do. Conscious reasoning accounts for only a small part of our 'thinking'.

Penn warns of the dangers of overemphasizing the importance of brand awareness when he says: 'It is clear that if we only base an assessment of effectiveness [advertising effectiveness] on conscious recall, we potentially miss out on those [customers] who are positively affected yet have no conscious recall of having seen it [an ad or a product].'

Penn highlights the four big ideas in brain science:

- Unconscious processes (either cognitive or emotional) account for most of what we think, feel and do.
- Conscious reasoning may account for only a small part of our 'thinking', with most taking place in the cognitive unconscious.
- Emotion precedes our conscious feelings and works in tandem with rational thinking to help us make (better) decisions.
- The interconnectedness of the thinking and feeling parts of the brain facilitates the interaction of rationality and emotion in decision-making.

Each one of these has fundamental implications for marketing and research. Marketers must tread with caution and measure the emotional aspects – some of which are often unconscious emotional connections.

Now consider the types of buying situations in which customers have different approaches to choosing products and services.

Nudge theory

'Nudging is about orchestrating persuasion on a subconscious level by sidestepping arguments and leading people down the road' says Ogilvy analyst Daniel Stauber. Nudge theory is a way of appealing to people's logic or emotions.

The UK government had its own 'Nudge Unit' (or Behavioural Insights Team), which was set up by the former UK Prime Minister, David Cameron when he was in office in 2010 and subsequently privatized in 2014. Using insights from behavioural economics it finds canny, cost-effective ways of encouraging people to make choices 'that are beneficial to them and society'. It has used these techniques successfully with the HMRC to increase tax payments by tapping into peer group pressure (and sending out reminder letters stating that most people in the area have paid their tax). These subtle nudge services are now being sold to other countries like Guatemala, who have seen income tax declaration increase by 52 per cent (Benady, 2014).

Communications agency Ogilvy has recently invested six years collecting 800 studies using behavioural economics, neuroscience and narrative theory to create a body of knowledge and customer insights that can be used by clients.

Monkeynomics trace decision-making biases back to our ancient ancestors via monkey studies

'Dr Laurie Santos from Yale University spoke about the behavioural economics of primates or Monkeynomics and how we may trace our decision-making biases back to our ancient ancestors.

Laurie immediately had the crowd enraptured by the content of her talk. There is something innately fascinating about learning about our primate cousins and how similar our behaviour can be. For example, following the financial crash Laurie explained how she became engrossed in finding out the evolutionary origins of the biases that led to the crash.

Her lab at Yale had begun to teach capuchin monkeys how to use money. In this monkey market the experimenters could test how monkeys react given the same conditions as the financial crash. The idea being that gaining insight into how deeply rooted biases are in our human brain can give us guidance on how we may design for them.

These monkey markets uncovered a range of previously unknown facts, such as how monkeys and humans share the same aversion to risk the poorer they become, how loss averse they are and how sensitive they are to a fair market. It also showed how innovative they could be, within approximately eight weeks the monkeys had created a system for prostitution within the enclosure.'

Daniel Bennett, Choice Architect at Ogilvy Change

Ogilvy has worked with the Royal Borough of Greenwich to reduce street violence by putting pictures of the faces of local babies on shop shutters (18 per cent reduction) and also *The Times* to design new 'choice architecture that nudges people into buying higher-priced subscriptions'.

Unilever brands (including Magnum and Comfort) use nudge theory to boost participation in branded competitions by simply asking people to opt-out rather than opt-in. 'Orchestrating the choice architecture' like this resulted in a 65 per cent increase in social sharing, saving Unilever chunks of budget because of a reduced need for paid advertising.

Place cues on website landing pages to trigger concepts unconsciously

Robert Cialdini, author of the 1984 classic book *Influence: The psychology of persuasion* (Cialdini, 2007) and many more books since, has suggested that marketers should place certain cues on the landing pages of websites so that a particular concept is triggered in the unconscious mind. He continued: 'What many marketers forget to do is to establish the brand's trustworthiness before expecting the target market to adopt the product' (Cialdini, 2014).

We are what we shop

Effectively, marketers have to know their customers better than the customers know themselves. This involves deep customer insights, sometimes generated by intense psychoanalysis, sometimes by employing anthropologists and sometimes by cleverly looking at customers through several lenses to get a deeper insight. What people buy reflects their motivations and even their perceptions about themselves.

We are what we 'like' (on Facebook)

Researchers at Cambridge University in the UK and Microsoft Research claim that they were able to use 'easily accessible digital records of behaviour, Facebook likes', to accurately predict a wide range of attributes that included: sexual orientation, ethnicity, religious and political views, personality traits, intelligence, happiness, use of addictive substances, parental separation, age and gender (Kosinski *et al*, 2013).

Facebook data analysis identifies individual deep needs

In the 2020 race, Facebook could theoretically determine not only who are the 32,578 swing voters in Pennsylvania, but also what you need to tell each of them in order to swing them in your favour... The market is less likely to self-regulate the explosive powers of bio engineering and artificial intelligence.

Harari (2017)

Note: In 2016, Trump worked with Cambridge Analytica, who analysed Facebook data (what you like/didn't like, shared, etc). Although this subsequently shocked many, Trump delivered extremely relevant, tailored messages addressing the very specific needs of very specific clusters of people (analysed by their own Facebook behaviour). See **http://prsmith.org/blog/** for two posts on how Trump won.

We are where we are and where we have been

Basically, location-based marketing (explored in Chapter 12) uses our physical location data (determined by our mobile phone if location settings are turned on) and our previous locations to build a profile of who we are, what we do, what we like. They can now layer this on top of actual browsing behaviour also.

Top UK retailers vary their research techniques to generate customer insights that they then apply to their marketing immediately. Many combine loyalty card data (on what customers are buying), browsing behaviour (what customers are considering) and survey research (why customers considered products but then did not buy). These mixed insights reveal for example, that young mothers bought fewer baby products in Tesco stores because they trusted pharmacies more. Tesco subsequently launched a Baby Club to provide expert advice and targeted coupons. Its share of baby product sales in the UK grew from 16 per cent to 24 per cent over three years (Forsyth *et al*, 2006). The Baby Club has now become part of the Tesco Club Card family.

Tesco varies the individual store's format to reflect the needs of its local customers (the magic marketing formula). For example, stores located near large concentrations of affluent male professionals display more high-end home theatre equipment, specialized financing and same-day delivery while stores closer to family areas feature softer colours, personal shopping assistants, and kids-orientated technology sections. Marketers look at customers through a variety of lenses. So knowing your customers really does pay dividends.

Know your customers intimately – their hopes, dreams, fears and aspirations

'The job now is to be so intimate with consumers, so empathetic with their hopes and their dreams, their aspirations and their fears that we can develop revelations which we then put into creative departments and from great revelations awesome ideas will come, eg T-Mobile UK – revelation – life is for sharing, the power of tribes, the power of communities, and the power of all this social stuff.'

Roberts (2009b)

How do they buy?

Types of buying situation

The amount of time and effort that a buyer is prepared to put into any particular purchase depends on the level of expenditure, the frequency of purchase and the perceived risk involved. Relatively larger expenditure usually warrants greater deliberation during the search and evaluation phases. In consumer markets this buying process is classified as 'extensive problem solving' (EPS) if the buyer has no previous product experience and the purchase is infrequent, expensive and/or risky. The situation is different where the buyer has some knowledge and experience of, and familiarity with, a particular product or service. This is called 'limited problem solving' (LPS). In the case of strong brand loyalty for a habitually purchased product, routinized response behaviour (RRB) can be identified by the repeat brand purchasing of convenience products like baked beans. The buyer chooses quickly and has a low involvement with the purchase. EPS requires high involvement from the buyer, which means that the buyer spends time and effort before actually deciding to buy a particular product or brand. This can be complicated by further advisers and influencers who form part of the decision-making unit. LPS requires lower levels of involvement than EPS but more than RRB.

Industrial buying is even more clearly influenced by decision-making units, particularly when the purchase is considered large, infrequent or risky. As in consumer buying, types of purchase situation also vary in industrial markets. A 'new task' buying situation means what it says – the organization has no experience of the product or service and is buying it for the first time. A 'modified rebuy' situation is where the industrial buyer has some experience of the product or service, while a 'straight rebuy' is where the buyer, or purchasing department, buys on a regular basis.

Analytics reveal how customers buy

Whatever the type of buying decision, marketers need to know: how do customers make their decisions? What was their journey or route? How do they discover your site or your store? Channels include advertising (pay per click and banner ads), social media, direct mail, referral links (using your web url).

Here are 10 questions that we can now answer using analytics:

1 How do customers buy – what is their online journey/what route did they travel (eg from Facebook to website or email to website)?
2 How many channels do your visitors use and how long do they stay?
3 Did customers move between online and offline?
4 What stage are your visitors at in the buying process?
5 How many pages are ideal during a visit?
6 Which routes or channels bring you the most traffic?
7 Which ones bring you the best traffic (that converts to say repeat sales)?
8 When is the best time to post content and engage customers?
9 What percentage of your visitors view your site on a mobile?
10 Do customers see things differently on their mobile?

These questions are taken from the SOSTAC® guide to your perfect digital marketing plan (Smith, 2019). There are many more questions answered here, including how to use many of the new free tools available to marketers.

Google Analytics and Multichannel Funnel reports provide an intriguing insight into how customers buy. Just like sport, where an assist is very valuable, so too some channels, whether ads, email or social media, bring traffic that converts to sales or registrations. These 'assisting' channels can be measured via an Assisted Conversions Report. While the Top Path Report reveals the different routes customers take before the conversion, the Time Lag Report reveals the amount of time customers take from the first channel interaction to conversion and Path Length Report shows the number of interactions customers had with your channels. The Overview Report summarizes it all.

The buying process even differs between Google and Facebook users. On Google, potential customers go through a discovery phase during which they gather detailed and rich information, while on Facebook potential customers may post a message saying that they are looking for a 'new family people carrier', and soon recommendations will flow in from their friends, brands and third parties (Pun, 2013). This flow of information gathering can change the more traditional models of buyer behaviour, which we are about to explore.

Independent research reveals how customers buy

Different channels (social vs website) = different purchase behaviour

According to Google Analytics, social media accounts for 5 per cent of website traffic and 2 per cent of revenue. According to analysis by Wolfgang Digital, the true value of social is significantly higher (Table 4.1).

Wolfgang's report includes a comparison between some Google research and some Facebook research, which shows the average conversion rate when engaging with social media is 4 per cent, which is

TABLE 4.1 Percentage of traffic and revenue generated by social media

	Organic	Paid search	Direct	Email	Social	Display	Referral	Other
Overall traffic	43%	18%	20%	4%	**5%**	1%	7%	3%
Overall revenue	38%	18%	19%	4%	**2%**	0%	17%	2%

SOURCE: Wolfgang Digital (2019)

double that of the website conversion rate of approximately 2 per cent. And Facebook suggest transactions with Facebook touchpoints are almost 8 per cent. This is nearly four times the conversion rate of an average website (Sources: Facebook and Google).

Wolfgang Digital analysed over 250 million website sessions and over €500 million in online revenue over the 12 months from July 2017 to June 2018 to compile this report.

Do likes, shares, comments and messages impact sales?

Using Facebook Analytics data Wolfgang Digital (2019) found that 3 per cent of the people who like your post will go ahead and purchase from you. The conversion rate increases to 4 per cent for a share, 4.67 per cent for a reaction, 4.9 per cent for a comment, and if the user takes the time to message you it's a whopping 9.95 per cent conversion rate.

- Like = 3 per cent convert to a sale
- Share = 4 per cent convert to a sale
- Reaction = 4.9 per cent convert to a sale
- Message = 9.95 per cent convert to a sale

Channel choice affects the number of visitors and level of sales. For example, social media and website usage affect both the volume of traffic and the revenue value. Now consider whether devices affect how we buy (Figure 4.3).

Fifty-three per cent of traffic to online stores comes via mobile devices, but this translates to just 32 per cent revenue. It seems that we go back to the desktop to complete order forms, or prefer more secure platforms rather than worry about security issues with our mobile. Interestingly, revenue on mobile devices actually increased by 23 per cent during the 12 month period, which suggests (not shown in Figure 4.3) it is now becoming easier and more convenient for people to press 'buy' on their smart phone because:

1. There has been an increase in 'shoppable posts' on social media, allowing customers to click straight through to buy a product they see on their feed.
2. Mobiles are perceived to be getting more secure.

FIGURE 4.2 Average conversion rates when engaging with social media

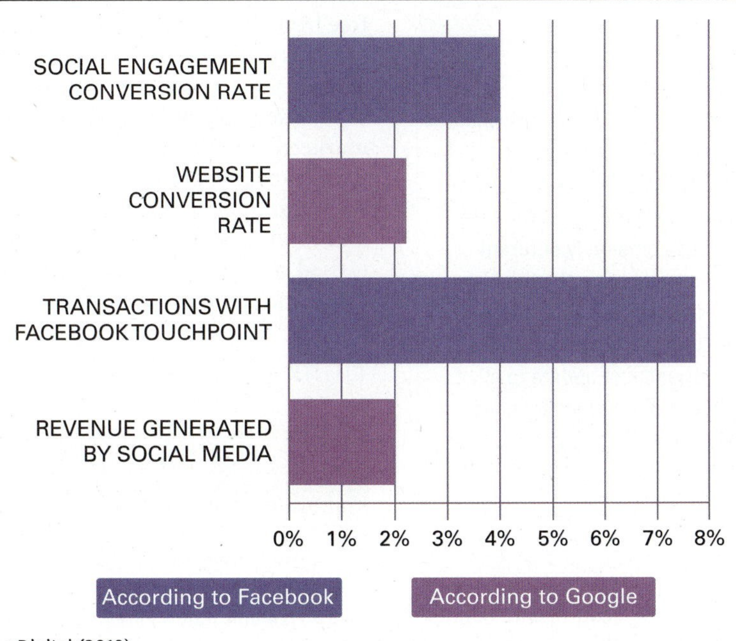

SOURCE: Wolfgang Digital (2019)

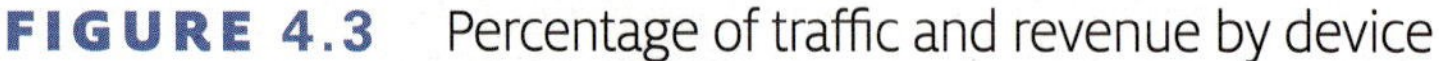

FIGURE 4.3 Percentage of traffic and revenue by device

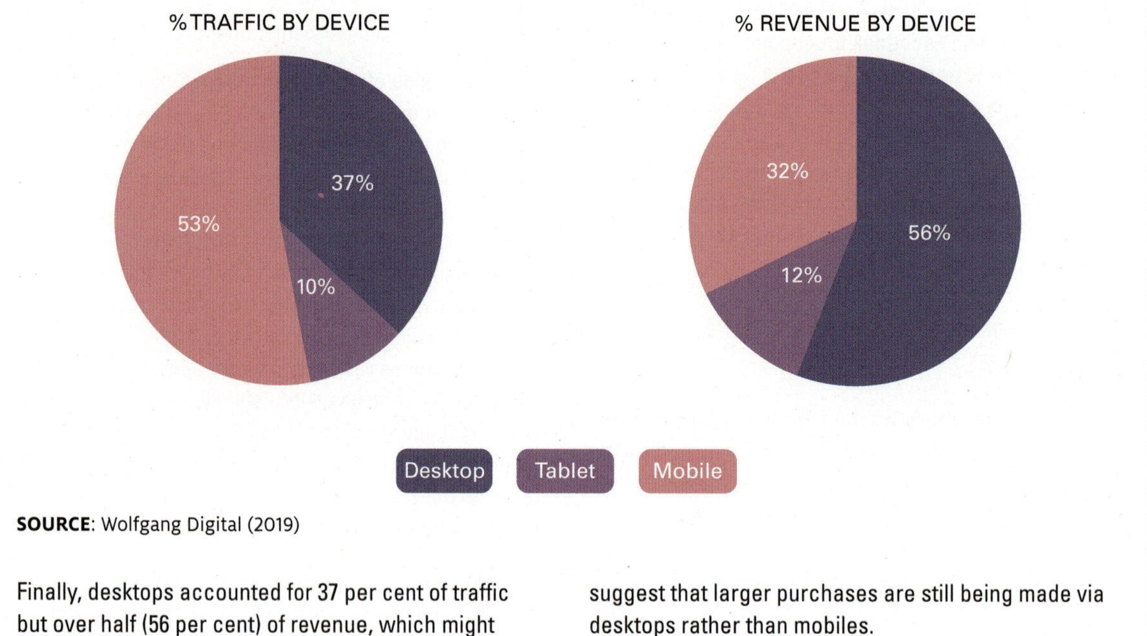

SOURCE: Wolfgang Digital (2019)

Finally, desktops accounted for 37 per cent of traffic but over half (56 per cent) of revenue, which might suggest that larger purchases are still being made via desktops rather than mobiles.

Customers process information from different social media platforms differently

> 'People use social networks like Facebook and Twitter in many different ways for different reasons. Twitter is mostly known as a place to find real-time information in a compact format, but Pinterest is used in a completely different way. Most users on Pinterest are either looking for ideas or browsing images related to topics they like. If you try to lump all the social networks together and send one update to all of them you will likely have information that is not suited for any social network.'
>
> Hagy (2013)

Marketers also need to know how customers process information, eg how do they read their emails? Surprisingly, approximately one-third of marketers surveyed did not know their email open rates, ie what percentage actually open the emails (Burstein, 2013). This information, or basic analytics, is available for free from most email systems. Equally important is to know what devices your customers use to read emails, your posts and peruse your website. How many use a mobile instead of a laptop? Professional marketers make it their business to know which words/images/colours/offers work better in emails, websites, apps as well as offline in direct mail, ads and exhibitions. It is even easier online as A/B testing is used constantly to learn what works best, then roll it out and ultimately optimize the responses.

Think mobile

How will customers use your information on their mobile?

'Don't deliver same "vanilla" experience to your mobile customers. Personalize the experience. Use information that is unique to smartphones and tablets (device type, operating system, connection speed, location, and sensors, etc) to combine with information in the consumer's profile (preferences, time, behaviour, social graph and offline data). This is the end of the era of "one size fits all".'

Pun (2013)

Can customers process your information on their mobiles? Big clunky thumbs do not work well on tiny icons or links. So be 'mobile optimized', or, as some say, 'optimize conversion paths for mobile' (make it easy for your visitors, followers and customers to use all of your marketing and services on a mobile). We all know mobile is one of the biggest trends right now. So a lot of marketers are having their websites delivered in responsive and mobile-friendly designs. Many stop there, assuming that because the website looks great on a mobile that customers can easily interact with the brand. Not true; there is much work still to be done. This is just the start of optimizing for mobiles.

Here are five tips from Hubspot's Ginny Soskey (2015):

- That blog post you wrote? The image file shouldn't be so large that it slows down your load time.
- That CTA (call to action) at the end of a blog post to download an ebook? It'd better be large enough for real fingers to tap.
- That landing page form people have to fill out to receive that ebook? It should be easy to fill out on a mobile.
- That ebook you put behind that landing page form? It's got to be easy to read – and you'll also want to send the person a follow-up email with that ebook so they can access it on another device later on.
- That email? It should be easy to read on a device – no pinching or scrolling required. And after someone clicks on that email to eventually buy something from you, your site had better make it easy to get in touch with your sales department and/or make a direct purchase.

Get ready for 'post mobile'

We are already talking to Google, Siri, Alexa and many more intelligent search engines. Soon we won't be keying in words into search engines, we'll just converse with them, whether they are connected IoT devices, wearable technology, or maybe even implanted (chips).

New currencies required: privacy, trust and time

Privacy, trust and time are new currencies that have a very high value in customers' minds. Customers are cautious about giving up private information. They are also busy and don't like wasting time (if you can save your customers time, they will like you even more). They expect their privacy to be protected and GDPR law insists organizations must protect customer data (and also be able to prove they are protecting it). Equally, customers resent being asked for too much information or being asked for information when they haven't yet established any relationship – so much so that some customers just fill in online forms incorrectly.

Do customers process information differently on mobile?

The user experience (UX) on the mobile is unique, as users process information differently when they are on their mobiles. Why? Because they are usually multitasking and more likely to be interrupted. The small screen size means people don't like reading lots of text, and therefore reading comprehension plummets.

Trust

Trust is increasingly important, as online customers live in a dangerous environment of privacy invasion and identity theft. Surprisingly, many customers trust a website more than a person. People trust well-known and well-respected brands. Why else would they give an unknown American their home address, credit card details, security code, money and time? Trust. In the UK, several major brands score higher in trust than the church and the police. Well-managed brands are trusted as long as their promise is never broken. How does it feel when a website remembers your name? And when it remembers your preferences? It seems customers are happy to have unconscious relationships with brands, robots and machines as well as people. Enlightened companies remember information for customers, not just about them. This builds trust in the relationship. Ask: what is it about a website that might attract a visitor to come back a second time and, ultimately, regularly revisit the site and develop a relationship? Remember, the second visit is the start of the relationship.

> **Can you attract users back to your website?**
>
> 'The best converting websites have the ability to attract that user back to their websites time and time again. As a result, they have thundered ahead of their one-click-wonder competitors.'
>
> Wolfgang Digital (2019)

The perpetuals, who we mentioned earlier, are (they think) immune to traditional marketing. Their default stance towards marketers is: I don't trust you. They resent banner ads but may put up with them if they offer a reward to watch the ad. They expect user-friendly personalized experiences across all devices and channels. As Pun (2013) says, obstacles are unacceptable (eg tiny, impossible to navigate websites on mobile) and so marketers should think like a digital disrupter and think 'about ways to increase the frequency of interactions' with perpetuals. 'Pleasantly disrupt customers with digitalized products that add value.'

> **Simplify the world for your customers**
>
> 'Simplify: create simple, user-friendly experiences for mobile consumers. Use digital to disrupt your customers' lives with pleasant surprises. Provide hassle-free conveniences for your customers.'
>
> Pun (2013)

Models of buyer behaviour

There are many different models that attempt to model the buyer's behaviour. Figure 4.4 shows how a buyer in either an EPS or an LPS situation moves through the purchasing cycle or continuum. The basic model can be borrowed and used in industrial markets also. It highlights some of the stages through which a potential buyer passes. Sources and channels of information plus buying criteria can also be identified, which in turn provide a checklist for the marketing plan.

The buying process

The buying process can be complicated or simple, depending on the type of purchase. High-involvement purchase is where a customer spends a lot of time researching and evaluating the choice of brand. Low involvement, on the other hand, is almost impulsive or habitual repeat buying of low-price items. Let's explore both.

High-involvement purchase model

We can demonstrate this simple buying model (Figure 4.4) by considering, say, the purchase of a new car, which is a high-involvement buying process (with extensive problem solving).

Somewhere, somebody or something makes the customer aware that he or she needs a new car. This is known as problem recognition, which is followed by 'information search'. This may include reading ads and editorial in magazines, reviews and recommendations online, visits to stores, discussion among friends.

Next comes evaluation. Leaflets, catalogues, ads and discussions are amassed, and a set of criteria is further refined. This may include engine size, eco-friendliness, space, in-car facilities, number of doors, shape, colour, delivery, guarantee, etc. Evaluation is relatively easy today, with plenty of reviews and feedback available as well as price comparison websites and apps. Many businesses now build gathering customer reviews into their post-sales service process. Reviews are now pulled into Google search results; you can see why companies want more reviews.

Finally, a decision is made to choose a particular car. It isn't over yet. The chosen brand may be out of stock or have a 12-week waiting list – in which case the communications mix has worked but the marketing mix (distribution/place) has failed (if the customer is not prepared to wait).

Regardless of which particular brand of car is eventually purchased, a tiny sense of doubt often trickles into the customer's mind. This is called 'post-purchase dissonance' and it needs to be managed to avoid large-scale product returns, cancellations or complaints. It can be managed by reassuring the buyer (with a congratulatory note, additional advertising, after-sales service and, most of all, a product or service that lives up to the promise made in the advertising). And, if the product matches the promise, then both repeat business and word-of-mouth referrals are more likely to occur in the longer run.

The simple buying model shown in Figure 4.4 serves as a useful checklist to see whether you are filling in all the communication gaps in the buying process. Interestingly, many websites now use this as a checklist to ensure that the site helps different customers to move through different stages of their buying process. The model should not be hierarchical, since in reality, there are loops, eg between information and evaluation, if the buyer learns about new criteria not previously researched nor considered.

This model is more relevant for a high-involvement purchase, whether extensive problem solving (consumer) or new task (industrial). A routinized response situation, like buying a Coca-Cola, is low-involvement, and therefore it would not involve any lengthy decision-making process.

An alternative high-involvement purchase model is suggested by Dave Chaffey (Smart Insights, 2014). It starts with something that 'triggers' awareness of the need or want. This is followed by the Initial Consideration Set (preferences and pre-conceived ideas), leading to the Zero Moment of Truth (ZMOT) when the customer gets some information including price, performance, reviews, social media... to the First Moment of Truth (a final shortlist of possible suppliers) to Purchase Decision (the moment of purchase) to the Second Moment of Truth (Figure 4.5).

FIGURE 4.4 A simple model of the buying process for a high-involvement purchase

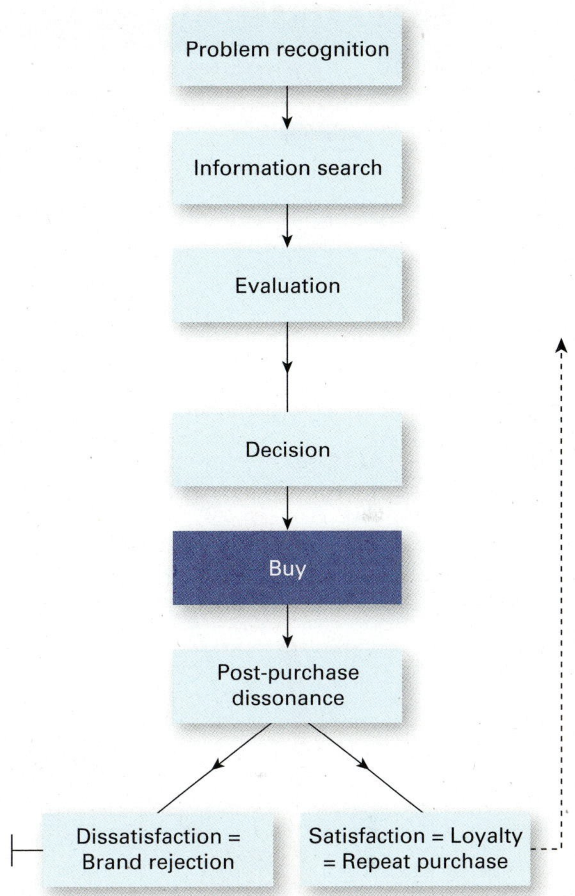

Showrooming

Another high-involvement buying model is called 'Showrooming' (Figure 4.6), which can cost retailers a lot of money. Customers walk into the store, browse, find the right product, leave without buying, go online, price compare and buy from a competitor who perhaps doesn't have the overhead costs of bricks and mortar retail stores on high streets.

How John Lewis stop 'showrooming'

John Lewis has recognized the explosion in 'showrooming'. Instead of battling this phenomenon, the brand has installed wifi in its stores to allow price comparison and product research while in store. They have also endeavoured to make the shopping experience more convenient and stress-free.

FIGURE 4.5 An alternative model

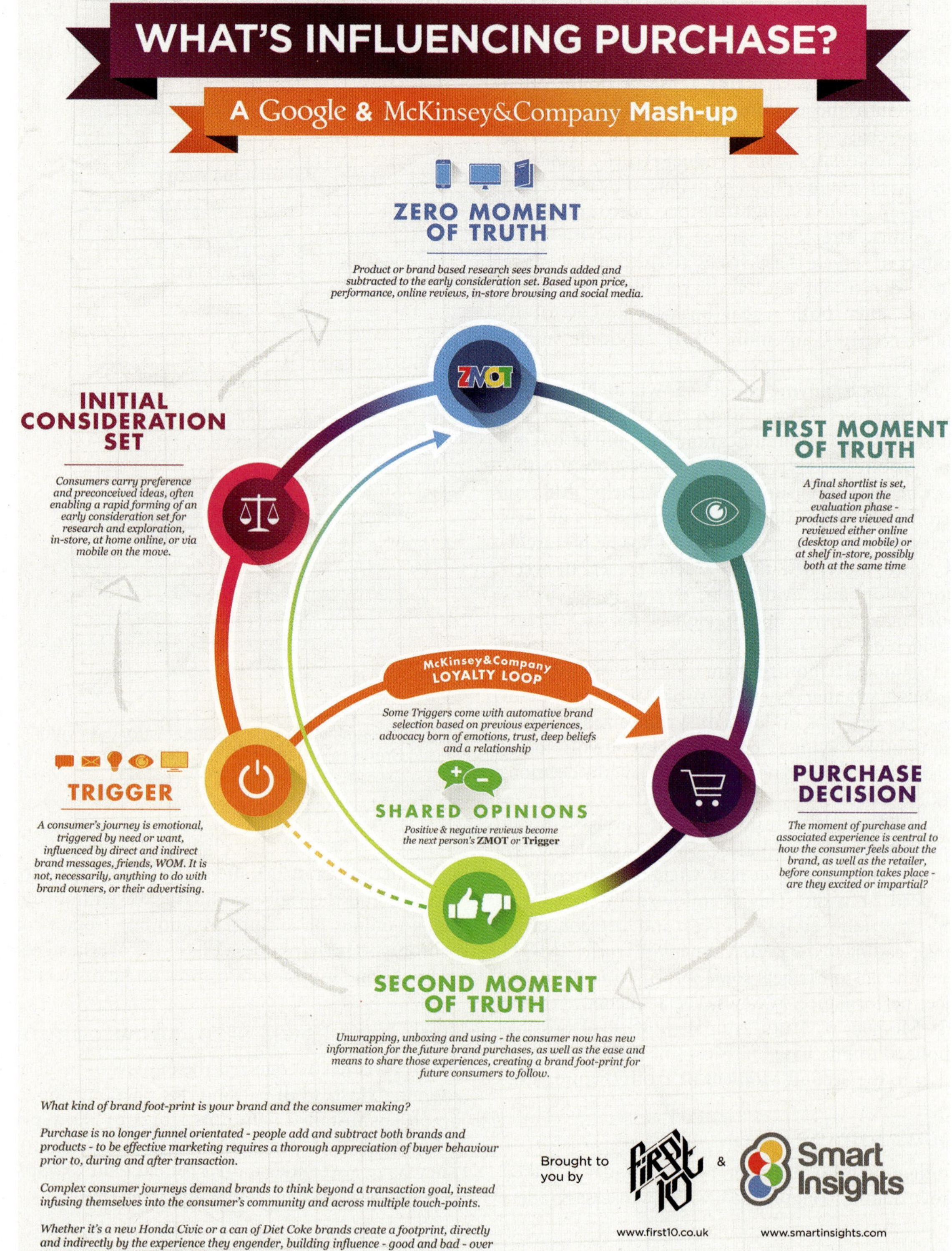

SOURCE: Smart Insights

FIGURE 4.6 The showrooming buying process

Buying process (High Involvement)	When showrooming
Problem identification ⇩	Combined marketing communications establishes the need for the product.
Information search (B2B + specification + tender) ⇩	Marcomms attracts the buyer into the store. They browse and find the product.
Evaluation ⇩	Examine and try on several products.
Decision ⇩	Choose the product.
Action/Purchase ⇩	**Leave the store (without buying).** Go online. Comparison shop. Buy elsewhere.
Post sales	Normal post-sales follow up by competitor as they attempt to nurture a lifetime customer.

Low-involvement purchase model

Low involvement can sometimes appear to be thoughtless (impulsive) responses (purchases) to stimuli (point-of-sale displays or well-designed packaging). If attention can be grabbed, then some brands can be bought, without much considered thought processing. Basically, if you see the brand, you try it, and if you like it you rebuy it. Some advertising aims to remind customers and reinforce the benefits of the brand – trying to create a routinized response behaviour (RRB).

Advertising can also reassure existing customers that they have bought the right brand. This defensive advertising (defending market share) reduces any post-purchase dissonance (or worries) and also keeps the brand on the buyer's shopping list (or 'considered set' of brands).

In contrast with attitudes towards high-involvement purchases, attitudes towards low-involvement brands can be formed after the brand experience and not before. In the more considered, high-involvement purchases attitudes are formed after awareness but before any purchasing behaviour actually occurs. The attitude may subsequently be reinforced by first, the real CX (customer experience) of buying and using the brand and second, any subsequent advertising or word-of-mouth communications.

Ehrenberg's 1974 awareness trial reinforcement (ATR) model suggested that consumers become aware of a brand, try it (buy it) and then are exposed to reinforcement by advertising (or even the actual brand experience) (Figure 4.7).

Trial can occur many months after an advertisement has created awareness. Advertising here is also seen as defensive, in so far as it reassures existing buyers that they have made the right choice, as opposed to advertising that might make them run out and buy the advertised brand immediately. Ehrenberg acknowledges that some advertising actually does prompt (or 'nudge') people to buy, as demonstrated with his more explicit 1997 awareness trial reinforcement plus occasional nudging (ATR + N) model. Ehrenberg's specific views differ from many other approaches highlighted in this

FIGURE 4.7 The ATR model

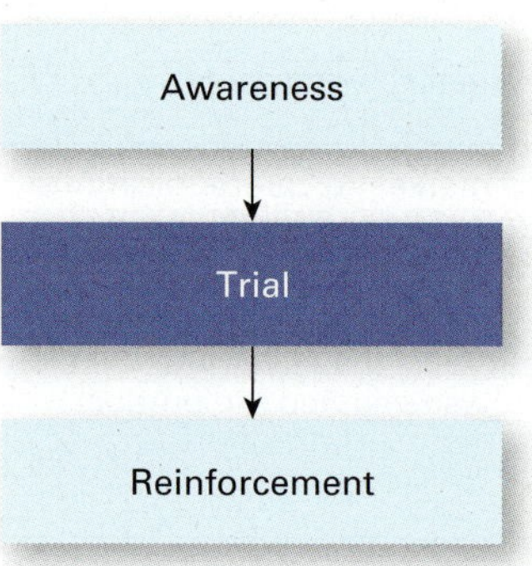

chapter, yet his research findings are used by top blue-chip companies around the world.

Many other academics believe that different buying situations (high- and low-involvement) require different thought processes and timescales. Even within the same product sector, different processes can occur. Take grocery shopping. Australian academics Rossiter and Percy (1996) identified differences in thought processes within the grocery sector. They suggested that most grocery brands (65 per cent) need recognition at the point of purchase, since buyers tend to see the brand first and then realize they want it. Less than 10 seconds elapse between recognition and putting the product into the trolley. The other 35 per cent of groceries are chosen in advance, so brand awareness (before purchase) is important for these.

Relief purchases vs reward purchases

It does not stop there. There are more differences depending on whether the purchase is a relief purchase (to solve a problem such as dirty clothes) or a reward purchase (to provide gratification, like ice cream). The relief purchases require a more rational approach and the reward purchases a more emotional approach. So each market and each brand needs to be carefully analysed. Robert Shaw (1997/98) pointed out that 'many different measures such as brand knowledge, esteem, relevance or perceived quality may need to be monitored'. Any marketing manager, whether industrial or consumer, product or service, has constantly to watch the market, its segments and how it is fragmenting.

Marketers need to understand their customers' buying process, whether online, offline or a mixture of both. Dulux paints found that its brand share is 11 per cent higher when customers choose their paint colour at home rather than in-store. But 75 per cent of colour decisions are made in the store. It therefore tried to lock people into a Dulux purchase before they visit a shop by creating a value-added online experience whereby users can decorate a virtual room (with colour coordination suggestions) and receive swatches delivered free to their home with directions to their nearest Dulux retailer.

Response hierarchy models

Although the ultimate objective for most marketing managers is to build repeat purchases from profitable customers, there are many stages between creating problem recognition or need arousal and purchase (as shown in Figure 4.5). The six different communication models in Figure 4.8 show the sequence of mental stages through which buyers pass on their journey towards a purchase.

These models are sometimes called 'message models' or 'response hierarchy models', since they help to prioritize the communication objectives by determining whether a cognitive (eg awareness), affective (eg like or dislike) or behavioural response (buy or not buy) is required, ie whether the organization wants to create awareness in the target audience's mind, or to change an attitude, or to act in some way (buy, vote, participate, etc). (See 'Attitudes' p 145 for a more detailed explanation of the cognitive, affective and behavioural/conative elements of an attitude.) Message models are helpful but not conclusive, since 1) not all buyers go through all stages, 2) the stages do not necessarily occur in a hierarchical sequence, and 3) impulse purchases compress the process.

Although expanding repeat purchase (loyal behaviour) from profitable customers is the ultimate marketing goal, a PR campaign, advertisement or sales promotion may have a tactical objective focusing on a particular stage in the above models, eg increasing awareness, changing an attitude or generating trial. In fact, Hofacker's (2001) online information processing model shows how online messages from banner ads and websites are processed (see Appendix 4.1 on p 150 for more detail).

These hierarchical communication models identify the stages through which buyers generally pass.

An understanding of these stages helps to plan appropriate marketing communications. The DAGMAR (defining advertising goals for measuring advertising results) model in Figure 4.8 was created to encourage measurable objectives for each stage of the communications process.

Some of the stages can sometimes occur simultaneously and/or instantaneously, as in the case of an impulse purchase. Buyers can also avoid moving in a hierarchy of stages when making a more considered purchase (extended problem solving). For example, during the evaluation stage a potential buyer may go back to the information stage to obtain more information before making a decision to buy. Each hierarchical model really requires a loop from the 'last' stage up to the first stage – to show that the sale (action stage) is not the end stage, but rather the beginning of an ongoing dialogue that nurtures a lifetime customer relationship.

The models also ignore the mind's 'intervening variables', some of which are identified in both the 'personal-variable models' of Fishbein (1975) and the 'complex models' of Howard and Sheth (1969) and Engel *et al* (1978). The complex models, do, in fact, allow for both loops and the complexities of the intervening variables (see p 133).

FIGURE 4.8 Response hierarchy models

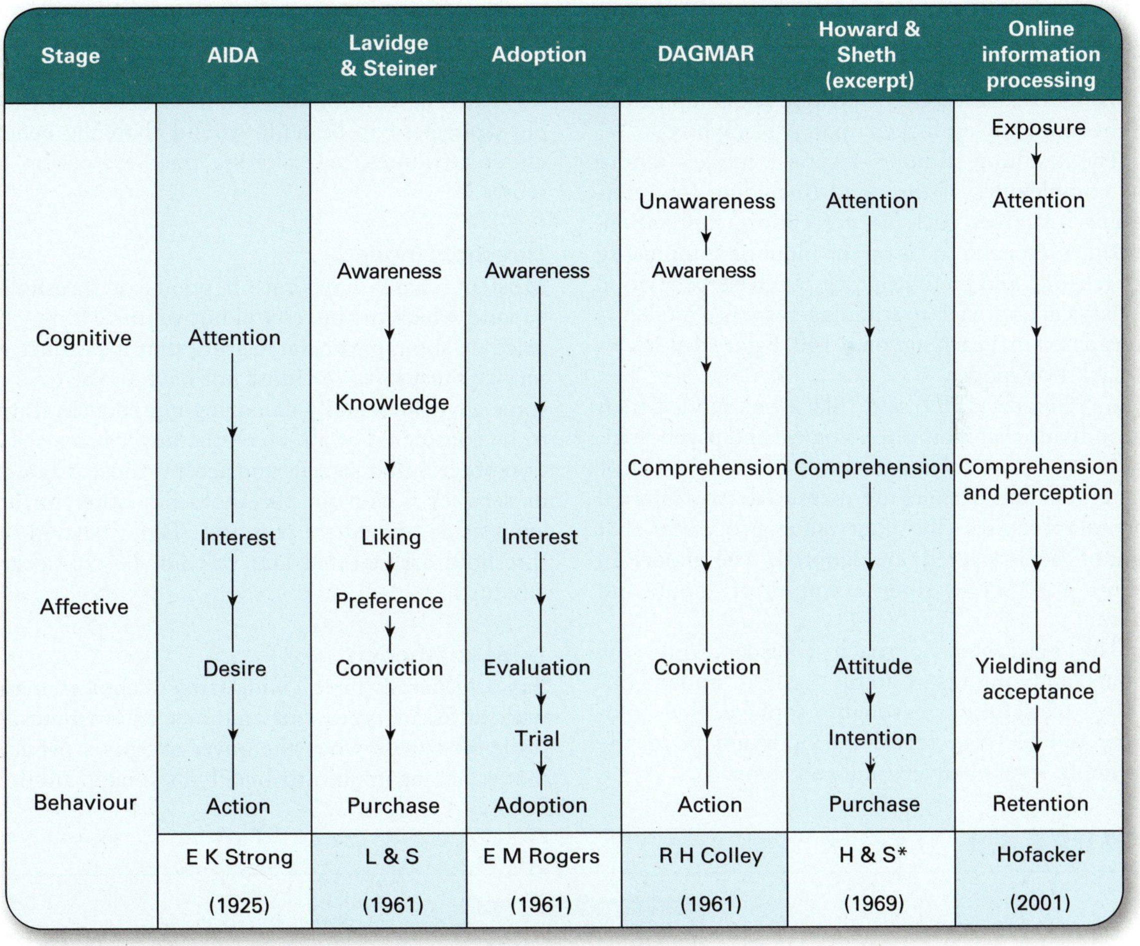

Stage	AIDA	Lavidge & Steiner	Adoption	DAGMAR	Howard & Sheth (excerpt)	Online information processing
Cognitive	Attention	Awareness Knowledge	Awareness	Unawareness Awareness Comprehension	Attention Comprehension	Exposure Attention Comprehension and perception
Affective	Interest Desire	Liking Preference Conviction	Interest Evaluation	Conviction	Attitude Intention	Yielding and acceptance
Behaviour	Action	Purchase	Trial Adoption	Action	Purchase	Retention
	E K Strong (1925)	L & S (1961)	E M Rogers (1961)	R H Colley (1961)	H & S* (1969)	Hofacker (2001)

NOTE: *The Howard and Sheth excerpt is taken from the full model shown on p 134.

Three types of models, 'black-box', 'personal-variable' and 'complex', will now be considered briefly. Black-box models consider external variables that act as stimuli (such as price, shops, merchandise, advertisements, promotions and the social environment, including families and friends) and responses such as sales. Personal-variable models focus on some of the internal psychological variables such as attitudes and beliefs. The complex models attempt to include both the internal and the external variables in one large model. To some this proves impossible. As Gordon Foxall (1992) pointed out, 'No one model can capture human nature in its entirety; nor can a handful of theoretical perspectives embrace the scope of human interaction.'

Black-box models

The behaviourist school of psychology concentrates on how people respond to stimuli. It is not concerned with the complex range of internal and external factors that affect the behaviour. The complexities of the mind are left locked up in a 'black box'.

The resulting stimulus–response models ignore the complexities of the mind (including the intervening variables such as perception, motivation, attitudes, etc) and focus on the input or stimulus, eg advertising, and the output, eg purchase behaviour. A classical approach to stimulus–response models is considered in 'Learning' on p 140. Figure 4.9 shows a black-box model.

As Williams (1989) said: 'Black-box models treat the individual and his physiological and psychological make-up as an impenetrable black box.' Only the inputs and outputs are measured. Any internal mental processes (the intervening processes) that cannot be measured are ignored. The model in Figure 4.10 shows some examples of 'input' and 'output'.

The black-box approach considers only the inputs and outputs. Careful analysis under controlled tests (using reasonably sophisticated computer models) can reveal the optimum price, the optimum level of advertising and so on.

Personal-variable models

These models take a glimpse inside the black box of the mind. They only involve a few personal variables such as beliefs, attitudes and intentions. These kinds of models are sometimes used within more complex models. Three types of personal-variable models, 'linear additive', 'threshold' and 'trade-off', are briefly considered below.

Linear additive models

Linear additive models like that of Fishbein are based on the number of attributes a particular product or service has, multiplied by the score each attribute is perceived to have, multiplied by the weighting which each attribute is deemed to have. This model opens up attitudes by indicating which attributes are considered to be important to the customer and how each attribute is scored by the customer. Attitudes are not always translated into purchasing behaviour. Even intentions are not always translated into action. Nevertheless, marketing strategies can be built around changing beliefs about attributes, and altering their evaluation or scores.

Threshold models

Most purchases have cut-off points or thresholds beyond which the buyer will not venture. It may be price or some particular feature that a product or service must have (or must not have in the case of some environmentally damaging ingredients) if it is to be considered at all. Here, the buyer has a selection process that screens and accepts those products or services within the threshold for either further analysis or immediate purchase. Those beyond the threshold are rejected and will not be considered any further.

Trade-off models

Buyers generally have a wide array of choices, many with different types and amounts of attributes. A trade-off occurs when the buyer accepts a product that is lacking in one attribute but strong in another.

FIGURE 4.9 Black-box model

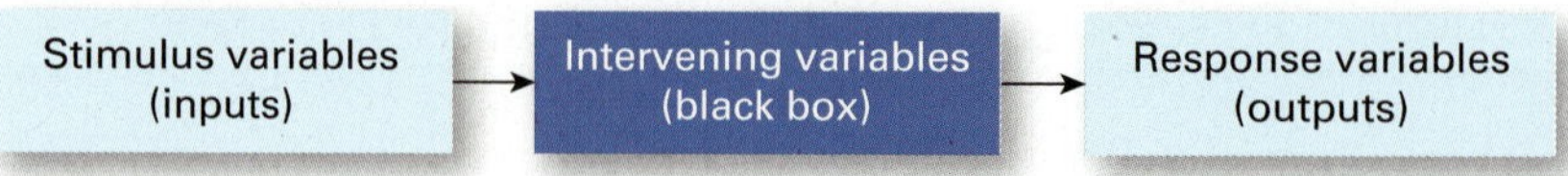

FIGURE 4.10 An enlarged black-box model

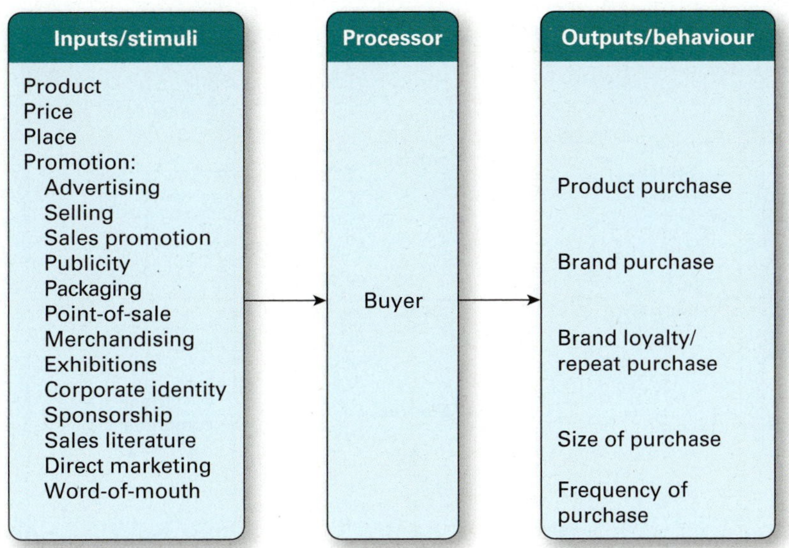

FIGURE 4.11 A simplified version of Howard and Sheth's model

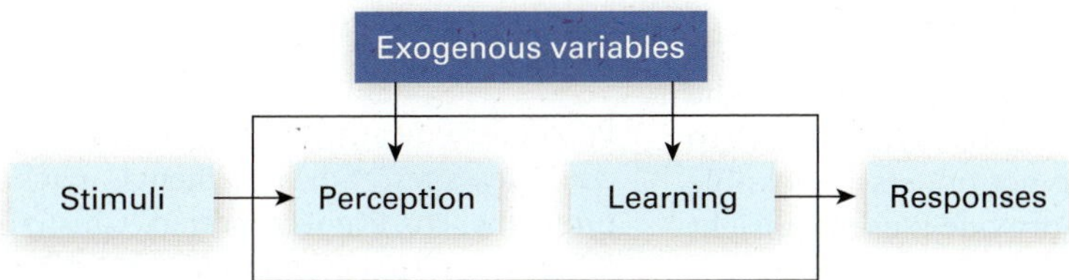

A sort of compensatory mechanism emerges. When someone is buying a car, engine size and price can be traded off against each other, eg a bigger engine means a worse (higher) price. A number of combinations of price and engine size can be researched to find the value or 'utility' for different prices and engine sizes.

Complex models

The cognitive school attempts to open the lid and look inside the mind's black box. Here more complex buying models, like that of Howard and Sheth (1969), try to incorporate into the hierarchical communication models the intervening variables of perception, motivation, learning, memory, attitudes, beliefs, group influence, etc – in fact, almost everything inside the mind.

Howard and Sheth

A simplified version of Howard and Sheth's complex model divides the black box into perceptual constructs and learning constructs, as shown in Figure 4.11. The exogenous variables are external to this model and include personality traits, social class, financial status, the social/organizational setting and even the importance of the purchase to the individual.

The complete complex model in Figure 4.12 includes perception, learning, attitudes and motivation. Stimulus ambiguity implies inadequate information to make a decision. Perceptual bias (see 'Perception' below) basically means that there is a certain amount of distortion in the way that an individual perceives a stimulus.

This complex model has been criticized for lacking a clear definition of the relationships between some of the variables and for a lack of distinction

FIGURE 4.12 The complete Howard and Sheth model

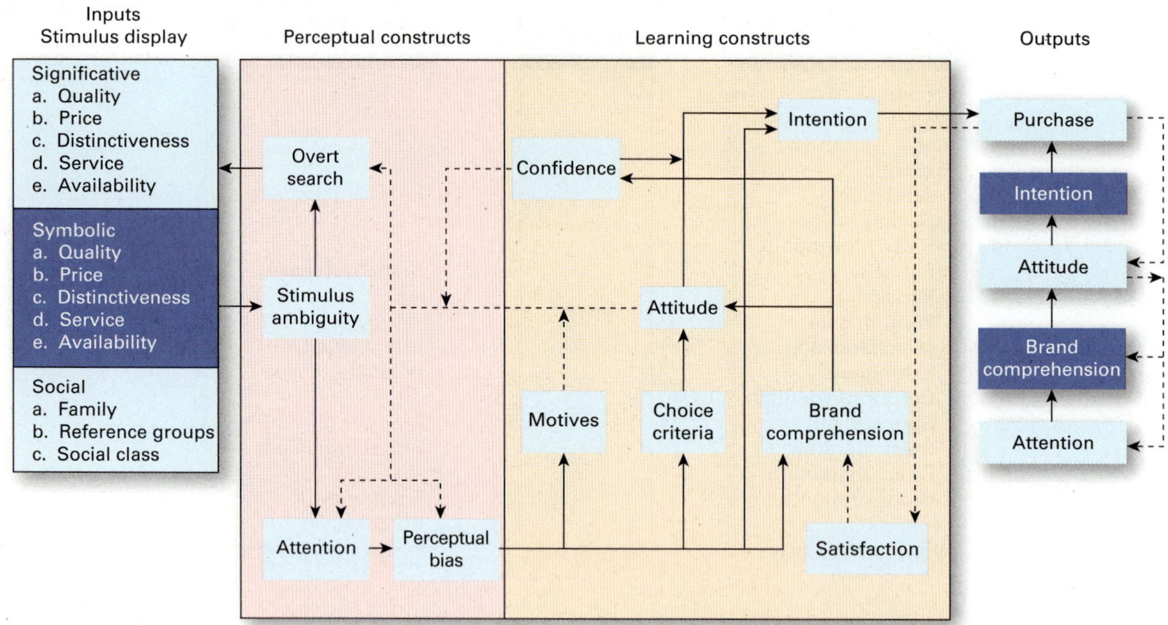

between the endogenous variables (within the model) and exogenous variables (external to the model). The model is, for many readers, difficult to understand, and for many practitioners impossible to use. Nevertheless it does provide a useful insight into the possible workings of the mind.

The remainder of this chapter looks at some of the influencing variables such as perception, learning, motivation, values, attitudes and lifestyles, and considers how an understanding of them helps to make more effective marketing communications.

Psychological variables

These are the intervening psychological variables that include:

- perception;
- learning;
- motivation;
- attitudes;
- group influence;
- habit.

Perception

Perception means the way stimuli, such as commercial messages, advertisements, packaging, shops, uniforms, etc, are interpreted. Chisnall (1985) said: 'Our perceptual system has a tendency to organize, modify and distort information reaching it.' Perception is selective. We see what we want to see.

> **For those of you who smoke – try this test**
>
> Here's a simple test. Ask smokers to recall exactly what the health warning says on the side of their packet of cigarettes. Few will be able to tell you the exact words. This is because we all selectively screen out messages or stimuli that may cause discomfort, tension or 'cognitive dissonance'. Imagine that smokers allow the message (warning) to be perceived. This will cause discomfort every time a cigarette is taken, since the box will give the smokers an unpleasant message. In order to reduce this tension, the smokers have two options: 1) change behaviour (stop smoking) or 2) screen out the message and continue the behaviour (smoking).

Many stimuli are screened out by the perceptual system, which, it is estimated, is hit by between 500 and 1,500 different commercial stimuli a day (whether ads, sponsored posts, tweets, etc). The example in the next box shows how preferences and motivations affect perception.

The same brand logo, icon or a symbol can be perceived differently

Take this example from Hong Kong, where in 1997 China regained control over this former British colony. The committee responsible for celebrating the resumption of Chinese sovereignty chose the white dolphin as its symbol. A British newspaper, the *Independent*, pointed out that this was a species threatened with extinction in Chinese waters. The committee also chose to place it alongside the new symbol for the future special administrative region of Hong Kong, the Bauhinia flower, which, reported the newspaper, was a sterile hybrid that produces no seed. The newspaper perceived Hong Kong to be marching into the future under the symbols of an endangered species and sterility. The Hong Kong committee saw the friendly dolphin as appealing to everybody, especially children: 'Its leaping movement symbolizes Hong Kong's vibrancy.' They differed vastly even over the same symbol or stimulus.

Millions perceive same moment differently: The infamous Brian O'Driscoll incident

The captain, and potential match winner, of the British and Irish Lions rugby team, Brian O'Driscoll, was spear-tackled by two New Zealand players, off the ball, in the first minute of the first test match way back in 2005. It remains, to this day, the perfect example of how two segments (influenced by their different motivations) perceive the same stimulus completely differently. O'Driscoll's shoulder was shattered and his test series over. He was lucky not to have broken his neck, as a spear tackle involves lifting and throwing a player head first to the ground. It can result in a broken neck. It is extremely dangerous and totally illegal. The Lions' manager, Sir Clive Woodward, called for a citing and disciplinary action. It never happened. Here's the interesting bit about perceptions. The author interviewed over 100 New Zealand fans several months later in Dublin, and every one of them saw nothing wrong with the incident. Ask Lions fans, and every one of them will say it was an absolute disgrace. Everyone saw the same thing, but the two groups saw (perceived) something different. Perception is selective and hugely biased by our motivations.

This incident was the trigger that founded **www.greatsportsmanship.org**, an edutainment programme designed to inspire global citizens through sportsmanship stories.

The same ad can be perceived differently

Perceptions can vary even within the same region. A UK TV advertisement for Unilever's Persil washing powder showed a Dalmatian dog shaking off its black spots, a white horse breaking away from black horses and a skater dressed in white beating other skaters dressed in black. The advertisement was perceived by some as being racist. Despite the advertisements having been tested with Afro-Caribbean women before going on air, the Independent Television Commission (ITC) received 32 complaints.

The same website can be perceived differently

You need to know how visitors see your website. Session maps and heat maps are used to try to understand how customers process information on a website. Session maps record an individual's eye movements across a web page (erratic/random eye movement suggests confusion). The larger the circle, the more time spent looking.

The results of all the individual session maps are aggregated to generate a single heat map with warmer colours revealing areas most looked at and 'black' indicating that no one looked at this part of the page (in this case no one noticed the 'Sale' sign). See Figures 4.14 and 4.15.

That's probably why most organizations put their brand top left. Incidentally, the eye movement used to be an 'F', starting top left, scanning across, reverting to top left and then scanning down and across (to complete the top two rows of the 'F') (Smith, 2019).

Usability testing is different. Basically, it asks customers (and other stakeholders) to use the website to carry out specific tasks with an observer watching to see how easy or difficult it is to complete the tasks. See the 'Control' section p 283 for more.

Research suggests that conversion rates for visitors using mobiles are a lot lower than if they were using laptops or PCs. They're typically between one-half and one-third of those on desktop (Chaffey, 2018). How visitors hold their phones affects how easy it is to click various parts of the screen (Figure 4.13). A call to action (CTA) must be easily accessible.

Figure 4.13 suggests a 'best practice' design of screen interaction points, ie CTAs, should focus in the natural green areas and avoid the red 'hard areas'. Incidentally these red areas are where the navigation menu is often located, so alternatives to this on page load should be provided (Chaffey, 2018).

Regardless of which device your audience uses, attention spans are shrinking and a shift towards visual is occurring.

The shift towards visual and social

A picture paints 1,000 words:

- Blogs have 500–1,000 (or more) words.
- Facebook has just a few words. Facebook posts with pictures and videos get more engagement.
- Twitter: 280 characters. Tweets with pictures get more engagement.
- YouTube: no words. Well, very few words – just some in the title, caption, credits and description (and the full transcript plus annotations can also now be included).
- Pinterest: essentially visual with limited words.
- Instagram: essentially visual with limited words.

Adapted from Dalton (2012)

Attention before perception

Generally, before perception occurs, attention has to be gained by, say, the advertiser (there are

FIGURE 4.13 How visitors hold their phones affects how easy it is to click various parts of the screen

FIGURE 4.14 Session map showing movement of eyes across a web page

SOURCE: Courtesy of Etre

FIGURE 4.15 Heat Map showing which areas of a web page are looked at most

SOURCE: Courtesy of Etre

exceptions – where subtle icons, colours or images don't grab attention but do affect perception, see 'Nudge theory' p 119). As Williams (1989) said, interests, needs and motives determine 'not only what will arouse attention, but also what will hold it'. For example, advertisements for a new house are ignored by the mass population. But there is a sector of the population that is actively looking for a house. This sector has a need for a new house, and it is therefore receptive to any of these advertisements. Individuals from this sector positively select information relevant to their needs. This is known as 'selective attention'.

Shrinking attention spans

Attention spans are shrinking. Estimates from Harvard for the first televised live TV debate between Nixon and JFK in 1960 suggested the attention span of the audience was only 42 seconds. Kennedy delivered key points within 40 seconds. He won the election. Fast forward to Obama in 2008 and 2012; some estimates suggested attention spans had fallen to just twelve and eight seconds respectively. Hence Obama's snappy one-liners such as 'Yes We Can' were repeated across many platforms. Obama won. There was of course a lot more than just snappy one-liners in the Obama campaign – see PR Smith's interview with Teddy Goff, Obama's Head of Digital (Smith, 2019). Fast-forward to Trump's 2016 win and some estimates suggested the concentration of the great heaving masses was now just four seconds. Hence 'Make America Great Again' (MAGA) worked far better than Clinton's longwinded socio-economic arguments. Perhaps Brexit was the same. 'Take Back Control' was a crystal-clear message pounded home by Brexiteers. Meanwhile, Remainers delivered long-winded socio-economic arguments to an audience that had switched off.

There are also certain physical properties that increase the likelihood of a message gaining attention: intensity and size; position; sound; colour; contrast; and movement (eyes are involuntarily attracted to movement because of the body's instinctive defence mechanism). Given that an individual's attention is constantly called upon by new stimuli, repetition can enhance the likelihood of a message getting through. Novelty can also be used to jar expectations and grab attention.

Goldfish a have greater attention span than some Americans

'Well, probably Europeans too. According to Harvard Business School historian Nancy Koehn, our average attention span today is eight seconds down from 12 seconds over a decade ago. Goldfish are believed to have attention spans lasting 9 seconds. We live in an "age of distraction". However, context is important as TV attention spans shrink, and smartphones, surprisingly "trump desktop computers for receptivity to ads, especially when the viewer is at school or work" (sorry, boss). Overall, a highly attentive audience was shown to boost purchase intent by 23 per cent and overall favourability by 14 per cent.'

Dishman (2014)

Perceived differences in brands are not necessarily dependent on real product differences (in either function or form). As Chisnall (1985) says, 'Consumers evaluate products against the background of their experiences, expectations and associations. Perception is seldom an objective, scientific assessment of the comparative values of competing brands.'

Colour affects our perception

'The colour red makes food smell better.'

Kanner (1989)

Perceptions are delicate and need to be managed carefully. Take Google: it is loved by everyone, but could easily be feared by all if it was perceived to be too powerful (as perhaps Microsoft experienced). Kennedy (2009) suggested:

> One of the main hurdles Google faces in its quest to manage the world's information, becoming a virtual library of books, movies, music, maps, tools, news, communication, even our very voices, is that it also becomes a figure of suspicion.

> How safe is that information, are they reading our every email, do they know too much about us?

Google CEO Eric Schmidt admitted these are real fears (Manyika, 2008), and he says:

> Trust means there is a sacred line the company must never cross. In fact, its greatest strength is, in truth, its Achilles heel. If it crosses that line it can never go back. Privacy and trust are sacrosanct. There's a lot of things we could do that would upset our users so there's a line you can't cross. We try very hard to stay very much on the side of the consumer.

Even if the company stays on the right side of the line, it still has to manage customer perceptions very carefully.

Certain words work better than others

Certain words must be perceived to have different meaning or inference. President Obama's Director of Digital, Teddy Goff, told me that one of these statements had a much higher impact than the other:

- 'You should be a donor.'
- 'You should donate.'

Which one, do you think, worked best during the last Obama campaign? Stop and think for a moment before reading the answer.

Teddy Goff discovered that people were more likely to be persuaded by the first statement, as nouns were found to be more powerful than verbs (Lee, 2013). Sometimes we just don't fully know why this is, but testing and analysis will reveal which works best. Hence the importance of developing a constant beta culture. Do check out how changing one button on a website boosted revenues so much that they named it the $300 million button.

Smith (2019)

Gestalt psychology

An understanding of the way our perceptual system organizes information has helped some brand advertisers to exploit perceptual systems through an understanding of gestalt psychology. Gestalt means 'total figuration'. One of the four basic perceptual organizing techniques from the gestalt school is 'closure'. Individuals strive to make sense of incomplete messages by filling in the gaps or shaping the image so that it can fit comfortably into their cognitive set (or their current knowledge). KitKat's 'Kit' – sometimes advertisements do not clearly say 'Kit Kat' and thereby encourage audiences to fill in gaps (to make sense of the ad). This may happen so fast that viewers are not aware of what is going on inside their heads. Effectively, the mind momentarily becomes the medium, since the complete image is visible only inside the head, while the external advertisement shows the incomplete image. In a sense, the giant billboard inside the cranium is switched on by an incomplete stimulus. The natural perceptual tendency towards 'closure' completes the advertisement's image inside the audience's mind. Perception is also influenced by past experiences, motivation, beliefs, attitudes and our ability to learn.

Everybody is scared

'Everybody is scared; everybody is insecure; everybody is nervous. Nobody knows what's coming next. Nobody. So people are looking for intimacy. They're looking for brands that understand them. They're looking for services that deliver for them in their new environment. I think most brands and most companies are operating in a time lag and a time warp. Consumers are way ahead of us. Their insecurities are much more to the surface… The challenge is to get more intimate with her fears, her needs, her desires. Let's face it: she needs to enjoy her life today – because there's not a lot of it coming her way. So she will still use brands. She will still find some pleasure in shopping. What we've got to do is provide that pleasure, provide that joy, that delight so that we can delight her in her new environment through being very intimate in her current situation.'

Kevin Roberts, CEO, Saatchi & Saatchi Worldwide (Roberts, 2009c)

Learning

Marketers obviously want customers to learn about firstly, the existence of their brand and secondly, its merits. A knowledge of the learning process is therefore useful in understanding how customers acquire, store and retrieve messages about products, brands and companies. How are attitudes about companies, products and brands developed (or learned)? Advertising and sales promotions can help customers learn in different ways (see 'classical conditioning' and 'operant conditioning' in 'Connectionist learning theories' below). In addition, how many times (frequency) should an advertisement be shown before it is remembered or, alternatively, before it causes irritation? Should it be repeated regularly once a week for a year (a 'drip' strategy) or concentrated into 12 times a week for four weeks only (a 'burst' strategy)? Differing levels of intelligence, memory, motivations, perceptions and rewards (reinforcement) affect the learning process.

Connectionist learning theories

Simple connectionist theory suggests that associations can be made between messages, or stimuli, and responses, hence the term 'stimulus–response model'. Remind people they are hungry (stimulus/ad) and they might just go to a particular takeaway where they are quickly rewarded with nice tasty warm food (response).

Learning via classical conditioning

In the late 1890s the Russian physiologist Ivan Pavlov demonstrated how 'classical conditioning', or involuntary conditioning, worked on dogs. By regularly hearing the ringing of a bell before being presented with food, a dog learned to associate (or connect) the bell with food. After a period of conditioning the dog would salivate (respond) upon hearing the bell (stimulus) without any food arriving. As Williams (1989) says, 'It is the idea of association that underlines the concept of branding in modern marketing.' Constant repetition can build associations between needs, products and brands, eg if you are thinking of beans, think Heinz: 'Beanz Meanz Heinz'. Can we be conditioned into buying brands? Can constant repetition build immediate associations between needs and brands, or needs and behaviour? Some people, if they see a yellow McDonald's arch sign when they are feeling hungry, start salivating. Is this classical conditioning? What about the pub? When the bell rings (Pavlov) for 'last drinks' or 'last orders', there is sometimes a surge towards the bar. Or the ice-cream van jingle (stimulus) which makes children and parents come out of their houses to buy an ice cream (response)?

Coca-Cola's classical conditioning

Here are some Coca-Cola slogans from the last century – applied with meticulous consistency across all communications channels.

- 1904 Drink Coca-Cola
- 1922 Thirst Knows No Season
- 1932 Ice Cold Sunshine
- 1942 The Only Thing Like Coca-Cola is Coca-Cola Itself
- 1952 What You Want is a Coke
- 1963 Things go Better With Coke
- 1969 It's the Real Thing
- 1976 Coke Adds Life
- 1982 Coke is it!
- 1993 Always Coca-Cola
- 2000 Coca-Cola. Enjoy
- 2003 Coca-Cola... Real
- 2016 Taste The Feeling

Brown (2016) and Moye (2016)

Human behaviour is influenced by music

'High-tempo music may be appropriate in fast food restaurants because it encourages faster knife and fork activity, leading to quicker table turnover. Customers buy more expensive wines in a retail environment playing classical music rather than pop music. French wine significantly outsold German wine in a store when stereotypical French accordion music was played. Marketers frequently match the volume of music in different time zones of their store to the age band of the target market... younger shoppers spend more in a retail environment playing loud music, while shoppers aged 50 and over spend more in an environment with quiet background music.'

Oakes (2008)

'London Underground started piping "uncool" classical music in the booking halls of tube stations in December 2005 to deter youths from loitering, resulting in a 33 per cent drop in abuse against staff.'

Marketer (2010)

Learning via operant conditioning

Whereas classical conditioning is non-voluntary, ie we cannot control the situation fully as lights flash, bells ring or ads roll, operant conditioning is voluntary in so far as the participant actively searches for solutions. The Skinner box was devised by Dr Burrhus Frederic Skinner in the United States during the 1940s. By placing a hungry rat in a box where food only arrived once the rat pressed a lever, Skinner observed that the rat would search, investigate and, eventually, press the lever accidentally. Food then arrived. Over a period of time the rat, when aroused by the hunger motive, learned to press the lever for food. An association or connection was made between the lever pressing and the drive to satisfy the hunger need. This approach to building associations through voluntary participation suggests that sales promotions, discussions, competitions, and engagement at various levels (like, share or comment) possibly invite the buyer to participate, and eventually connect, or learn, that a particular product or service is associated with a particular need.

Stimulus–response

Connectionist theories of learning highlight the importance of first, timing and second, frequency of marketing communications. The establishment of a connection or association between a stimulus and a response is fundamental to the conditioning process. Advertising jingles, pictures and even smells are some of the stimuli that can arouse emotional or behavioural responses. Some people still feel good when they hear the Coca-Cola jingle 'I'd like to teach the world to sing...'; others are aroused and excited when they hear the sound of a sports commentator's voice with crowd sound effects in the background. Ice-cream van jingles arouse children. McDonald's large, highly visible yellow 'M' logo can trigger a response, particularly if an individual is involved in goal-orientated behaviour (is hungry and is ready to consider eating food).

Cyber-logo makes customers salivate

'Seeing your logo on the net made me hungry' (feedback from a McDonald's website visitor, demonstrating classical conditioning).

Smith *et al* (1999)

Certainly, the release of certain aromas can stimulate immediate responses. For example, as customers leave a pub and walk down the street they are often greeted by the wafting smell of frying chips, which can stimulate or arouse the need for food, and lead to an immediate purchase.

Lunn Poly created a full sensory holiday environment in its stores using a coconut aroma, fresh coffee in the Parisian-style café area, holiday music, travel images and a variety of film footage.

Reinforcement and reward enhance the learning process. In other words, good-quality products and services reward the buyer every time. This consistent level of quality reinforces the brand's positive relationship with the buyer. On the other hand, if the quality is poor, there is no reward (the response does not satisfy the need), and the response (to buy a particular brand or visit a particular shop) will not be repeated.

Positive reinforcement helps the learning process (or helps the buyer to remember the brand or shop). It is possible to 'unlearn' or forget ('message decay'), so many advertisers seek to remind customers of their products, their names and their benefits. Some advertisements seek to remind buyers what a good choice they have already made by frequently repeating messages. The connectionist approach ignores all the other complex and influential variables involved in learning and, ultimately, buying. Arguably, it oversimplifies a complex process.

Packaging design can also act as a cue to arouse momentarily the happy images conveyed in the previously seen and unconsciously stored advertising images. This is where a 'pack shot' of the product and pack in the advertisement (usually at the end) aids recall of the brand, the advertisement and its image when the consumer is shopping or just browsing along shelves full of different brands.

All brand managers would like to have their brand chosen automatically every time. Some brands achieve this through an unconsciously learned response. How? By building a presence through frequency of advertising and maximum shelf facings (the amount of units displayed on shelves) and, most importantly, by supplying an appropriate level of reinforcement (an appropriate level of quality in the product or service itself). Chapter 3 emphasizes the importance of quality in the long-term repeat-buying success strategies of today and tomorrow.

Adopt positive psychology to create shareable meaningful moments

'Positive conditioning: if the future of a brand is dependent on shared experiences, it is important to adopt positive reinforcement and positive psychology in order to create shareable, meaningful moments... invest in the consumer as well as in these positive moments... I ask you in return to share a great experience you've had with my brand, I should have a loyalty programme that rewards you for your advocacy.... a strategy for loyalty and advocacy determines the future of the brand... Do you have a system to reward advocates?

Solis (2015)

Cognitive learning

Cognitive learning focuses on what happens in between the stimulus and the response. It embraces the intervening mental processes that lie within the black box.

Insight, meaning, perception, knowledge and problem solving are all considered relevant concepts. Cognitive learning is not dependent on trial and error. It depends on an ability to think, sometimes conceptually, and to perceive relationships and 'what if' scenarios. It is not dependent on an immediate reward to reinforce the learning process; in fact, 'latent learning' occurs in the absence of reward and without any immediate action. Of course, an individual has to be suitably motivated (interested) to achieve this kind of learning. The next intervening variable – motivation – will now be considered.

Tea-drinking Chinese learn to drink coffee

Just as they helped the Europeans to learn to eat with their hands (McDonald's) and drink ice-cold beer (Budweiser), mostly through classical advertising, Coca-Cola, Pepsi and now, Starbucks are conditioning a massive market to learn a new way of satisfying their needs, especially young Chinese. These brands are turning a tide in tastes. Tea houses in China are being challenged by coffee houses.

Motivation

Motivation is defined as the drive to satisfy a need. Some motives are socially learned (eg wanting to get married), and others are instinctive (eg wanting to eat when hungry). Sigmund Freud suggested that an individual is motivated by conscious and unconscious forces. Many motives are unconscious but active in that they influence everyday buying behaviour. Brands carry covert messages that are fleetingly understood at a subconscious level. As the Market Research Society said in its 1996 conference paper, 'It is often this deeper meaning which is what is exchanged for money. These deep underlying feelings are often the real reason why people buy products or services.'

Sigmund Freud's psychoanalytical approach

Freud broke the personality into the id (instinctive drives and urges, eg to eat food or grab food), the ego (the social learning process that allows the individual to interact with the environment, eg to ask politely for food or pay for food) and the superego, which provides a conscience or ethical/moral referee between the id and the ego. Freud suggested that all actions are the results of antecedent conditions (see how childhood experiences might even affect industrial buying behaviour some 30 or 40 years later in 'Mommy's never coming back', p 200). Occasionally these unconscious stirrings manifest themselves in dreams, responses to ambiguous stimuli and slips of the tongue (Freudian slips).

Clinical psychology uses thematic apperception tests, Rorschach tests and word association tests to analyse the underlying, and sometimes unconscious, personality traits and motivations of an individual. In-depth market researchers (qualitative researchers) use metaphors, picture completion and montages in an attempt to throw the interviewee's ego off guard and dip into the real underlying feelings that interviewees find difficult both to become aware of and to express in an articulate manner.

In the 1950s, Vance Packard was concerned about how in-depth researchers like Ernest Dichter were attempting to extract buyers' unconscious feelings, aspirations and motivations, which were then subtly reflected through advertising imagery, which in turn manipulated buyers unconsciously. Although discredited by some and criticized by others, Dichter's *Handbook of Consumer Motivations* (1964) is an extremely thought-provoking and entertaining read.

Here are some other well-known, in-depth research findings from the 1950s that were thought to reveal the deep underlying motivations that drive certain forms of behaviour, including buying behaviour:

- A woman is very serious when she bakes a cake, because unconsciously she is going through the act of birth.
- Soon after the trial period, housewives who used a new improved cake mix (no egg needed, just add water) stopped buying it. The new, improved cake mix provoked a sense of guilt, as the cooking role of the housewife was reduced.
- A man buys a convertible car as a substitute mistress.
- Smoking represents an infantile pleasure of sucking.
- Men want their cigars to be odoriferous in order to prove that they (the men) are masculine.
- Shaving for some men is the daily act of cutting off this symbol of manliness (stubble).

Of course, this is all outdated now. Humans are rational animals and are not concerned with such psychoanalytic interpretations of everyday, ordinary and, supposedly, common-sense behaviour. Consider 'A close shave?'

A close shave?

There is a simple test that has been used in lectures with different groups. A question is posed, with a request for male respondents only. The question is 'How many of you find shaving a hassle?' Usually a unanimous show of hands emerges. 'How many of you would like to be able to dispense with the aggravation of shaving?' Slightly fewer hands emerge. 'Well, here is a cream that will solve your problem. This cream closes your hair follicles so that hair will never grow there again. It is medically approved and cleared for a market launch next year. Who would like to try some right now?' All the hands are gone. The question 'Why not?' is usually answered faintly with 'Freedom to choose to have a beard later in life' and so on. Or is there something deeper here? Dichter would have said 'Yes.'

Abraham Maslow's hierarchy of needs

Abraham Maslow's (1954) hierarchy of needs provides a simple but useful explanation of the way an individual's needs work. Essentially he showed that we are driven or motivated initially to satisfy the lower-level needs and then, when satisfied, we move up to the next level of need. This theory also implies that motivation can be cyclical, in so far as buying a house may be motivated initially by the lower-level survival needs and subsequently by the higher-level need of esteem. Figure 4.16 shows Maslow's hierarchy of needs.

FIGURE 4.16 Maslow's hierarchy of needs

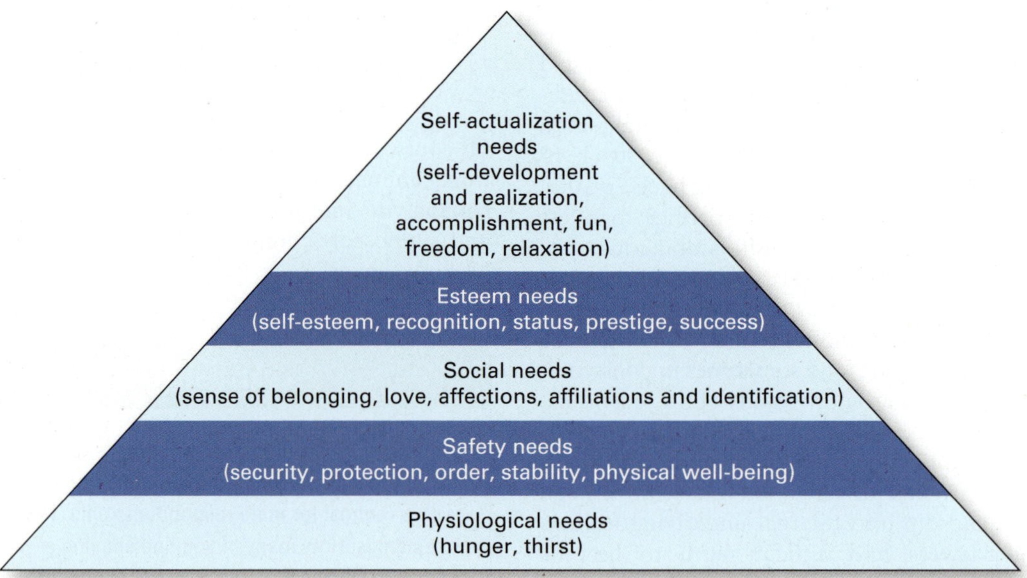

Cars transport people from A to B. Sometimes the need to buy a car is a basic survival need (eg to get to work, to earn money to buy food). Sometimes it can provide a cocoon (or shelter/safety) from the mass of bodies scrambling for the public transport system. Cars can also act as status symbols (esteem). Sometimes cars can provide freedom to explore the countryside, visit friends or do what you want (self-actualize). Some cars position their benefits (power, speed, safety, environmental, etc) so that they dominate the ad and appeal to the predominant need of a particular segment.

The invisible badge: Motivation beyond conspicuous consumption

In 1899 Thorstein Veblen introduced 'conspicuous consumption', which suggested consumers buy products to impress other people, with his example of the man who parades down Main Street in 'stainless' linen, with a superfluous walking stick. These items told a story and provided 'evidence of leisure' – to an audience of strangers. Today's customers also wear badges (a pint of Guinness is a badge that tells everyone that the drinker is a discerning beer drinker). Even hybrid cars are said to be eco-status markers (or signals) that show 'conspicuous concern' about the environment. According to Walker (2008), conspicuous consumption is no longer valid:

> There is a better idea – the invisible badge. What the Joneses might think is, really, beside the point. Because what you are really doing is telling that story to yourself. In other words, yes, a fancy 'product' really is a badge in the sense that it's a symbolic confirmation or expression of identity (an identity that we may wish for rather than actually embody – aspirational rather than authentic). But the fact that hardly anyone sees it, let alone accepts the meaning it supposedly projects, hardly matters. In fact, if the real audience is us, the badge may as well be invisible.

Sometimes customers simply do not understand the new benefits delivered by innovative products and services. For example, research originally rejected ATMs (cash machines), with typical comments like 'I wouldn't feel safe withdrawing money on the street'. Interestingly, the wheel is turning full circle, as customers are once again becoming nervous about cash withdrawals on crime-ridden streets.

Different people (or groups of people) extract different benefits from the same product. Some people want to drive a Porsche because it gives them power; others want to because they see it as a symbol of success (good for the ego and esteem); others just want the thrill of driving very fast (self-actualization, as in the case of the driver's last wish in Nevil Shute's classic *On the Beach*); others again may simply want a very fast, reliable car that allows them to get from A to B (around Europe) without delay (see the iPod example on p 116). Markets can be broken up into 'benefit segments' so that communications can be tailored to develop the ideal positioning for a particular segment. In some cases benefit segmentation demands different products for different segments, as in the case of the toothpaste market (see p 117).

Attitudes

Attitudes affect buying behaviour. Attitudes are learned, and they tend to stick; they can be changed, but not very quickly. As Williams (1989) says: 'If a marketer is able to identify the attitudes held by different market segments towards his product, and also to measure changes in those attitudes, he will be well placed to plan his marketing strategy.' An attitude is a predisposition towards a person, a brand, a product, a company or a place.

> Can attitudes be formed without any experience?
>
> Can attitudes be formed prior to purchase?

The answer is 'yes' to both. Attitudes are sometimes formed without direct experience and, equally, products are often bought without any prior attitude. In the latter case, however, it is likely that an attitude will form as a result of word of mouth, or an engaging advertisement.

Attitudes can be broken down into three components, which are often explained as 'think', feel' and 'do' or 'cognitive', 'affective' and 'conative'. The cognitive element is the awareness or knowledge of, say, a brand. The affective element is the positive or negative feeling associated with the brand. The conative element is the intention to purchase. It can be important to measure all three components, since an isolated element can be misleading. For example, Rolls-Royce scores highly on the cognitive and affective elements of the attitude, but few of those who express awareness of and liking towards a Rolls-Royce will actually buy one. Identifying the levels of each attitudinal element helps to set tighter communication objectives. For example, the creative strategy for increasing brand awareness would be different from the strategy required to change the target market's feelings (or reposition the brand). A different communications strategy (perhaps an emphasis on sales promotions) would be required if the objective was to convert high awareness and positive feelings into trial purchases.

Attitudes can be changed, but it does take time. There are several options:

- Change the beliefs held about the product or service (or its attributes and features).
- Change the importance ratings (or weightings) of various attributes.
- Introduce another attribute.
- Change the association of a particular product or service with the others.
- Change the perception of competitors' products or services.

Groups also influence attitudes: hence the importance of opinion formers and opinion leaders. Now consider group influence in the buying process.

Attitudes and consumer values are changing

> 'Buying a house is no longer the American dream. Consumers may not even need a car.'
>
> Solis (2015)

Group influence

Much of human behaviour, and buyer behaviour in particular, is shaped by group influence. Whether cultural, religious, political, socio-economic, lifestyle, special interest groups or just family, social groups affect an individual's behaviour patterns. Watch explicit group influence occur as thousands of people perform a 'Mexican wave' at football matches, the Olympics, etc.

> The effects of group influence are often seen in a queue or waiting area where charity collectors are attempting to collect money. Success or failure is often determined by the reaction of the first encounter, ie if the first person acknowledges the collector and makes a contribution, the next person is more likely to do so too. We have often seen a whole platform (on the underground train network/the subway) generously giving money after a successful start. Equally, we have seen almost total rejection by a whole queue once the initial contact has refused to donate. This is a bizarre or perverse form of charity giving and seems to be about peer group pressure. In a sense, a donation buys some relief from guilt or embarrassment.

Most individuals are members of some kind of group, whether formal (eg committees) or informal (eg friends), primary (where face-to-face communications can occur, eg family) or secondary (eg the Chartered Institute of Marketing). Groups develop their own norms or standards that become acceptable within a particular group. For example, normal dress among a group of yacht club members differs considerably from the norm or type of clothes worn by a group of clubbers. Yet both groups adhere to the rules (mostly unwritten) of their own group. Both groups also go through some sort of purchasing process.

Roles are played by different members within a group. An individual may also have to play different roles at different stages of the same day, eg a loving mother, tough manager, loyal employee, client entertainer, happy wife and, perhaps, sensuous lover. In the online world the same person can adopt different roles and even multiple personalities.

Activities, interests and opinions can form useful segmentation criteria. Roles within groups help to target decision-makers and influencers in the decision-making units. Roles are also identifiable from the family lifecycle, which shows how an individual moves from single to newly wed to full nest 1 (youngest child under six) to full nest 2 (youngest child six or over) to full nest 3 (dependent children) to empty nest 1 (children moved out) to empty nest 2 (retirement) or solitary survivor 1 (still working) to solitary survivor 2 (retired). The income levels, needs and spending patterns are often predictable as the income earner moves through various family lifecycle roles. Spending patterns, influenced by changing roles, can be monitored and forecast before communicating any marketing messages. For example, direct mail companies often mail new mothers within a few days of the arrival of their baby. Marketers must ensure they are GDPR compliant before any mailings and before even collecting the data.

> **Absenteeism out, 'presentee-ism' in**
>
> 'Men have to work harder than ever before to make themselves indispensable, to the point where we are now seeing "presentee-ism", which occurs when men feel that they have to get to work earlier and leave later to show their commitment. This is having a detrimental effect on their home lives.'
>
> Coopere (2008)

Many young men today even see their home as having a different role to that of their parents' home. For many, home is a 'refuge from an uncertain world' and a 'haven from the stresses of life'. In addition to being a long-term financial investment, a home can also be a hub of technology that 'connects a guy with his sense of self through a variety of media experiences'.

Finally, the mix of communications tools helps move customers through the stages of a buying model from unawareness to reassurance. Each tool can affect different stages. Although there is always some vagueness about exactly where the effectiveness starts and stops, Figure 4.17 is arguably an oversimplified graphic that may help in understanding which tools do what.

Powerful analytics can help change customer buying habits, by Charles Duhigg

Way back in the 1980s, a team of researchers led by a UCLA professor named Alan Andreasen undertook a study of peoples' most mundane purchases, like soap, toothpaste, rubbish bags and toilet paper. What they discovered was that few shoppers paid any real attention to how they purchased such articles – they were purchases that occurred routinely, without involving any deep thought or complex decision-making. Naturally, this causes difficulties for marketers, who rely on displays, coupons and product promotions to persuade shoppers to deviate from ingrained habits. However, they also discovered that when consumers go through a major life event – for instance graduating from college, getting a new job, moving home, etc – shopping behaviour can become more flexible and predictable. This is therefore extremely valuable for retailers. The study revealed that when a person marries they are likely to begin buying a new brand of coffee. Similarly, if a couple moves house, there's a higher than usual chance that they'll opt for a new brand of breakfast cereal. Divorce, however, leads to new brands of beer.

As would be expected, no life events lead to more drastic changes in purchasing behaviour than the arrival of a baby. The new parents' habits are more changeable then than, arguably, any other point in their lives. Clearly, this represents huge opportunities for companies: if they can identify expectant mothers, they can earn millions.

To see this in action, consider a fictional shopper. If a female shopper purchases cocoa butter lotion, a bag big enough to transport nappies and baby equipment, zinc and magnesium supplements, and a blanket, there's an excellent chance she's pregnant. If she makes her purchases via the website or via her customer loyalty card in the store, the store will

FIGURE 4.17 Which communications tools do what

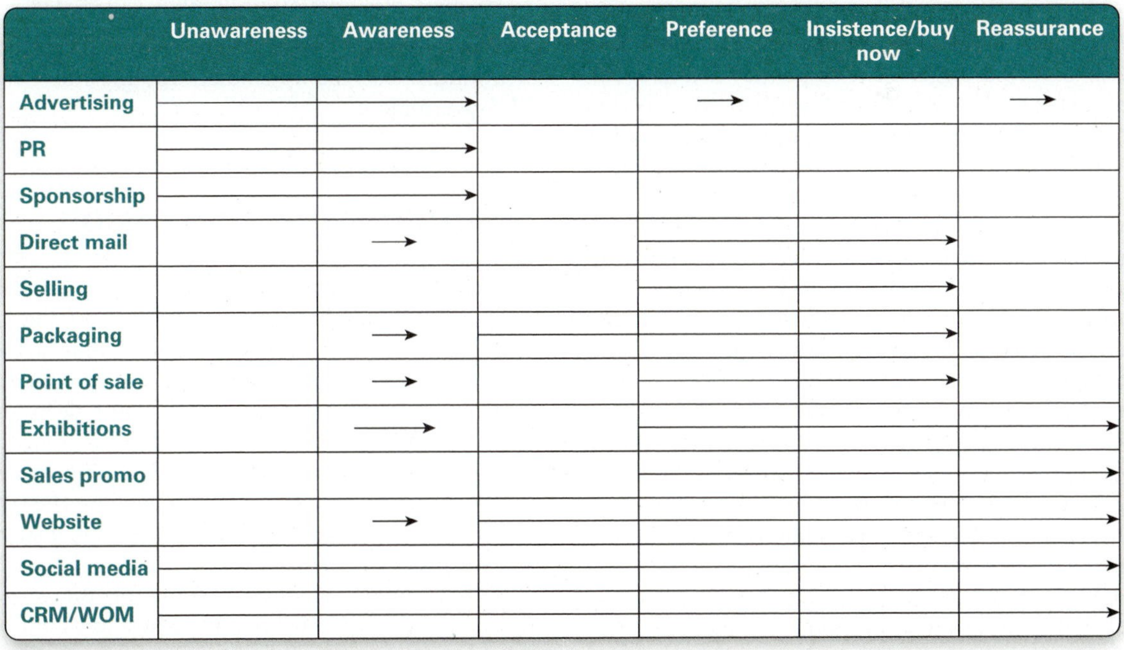

	Unawareness	Awareness	Acceptance	Preference	Insistence/buy now	Reassurance
Advertising	———	———→		→		→
PR	———	———→				
Sponsorship	———	———→				
Direct mail		→		———	———→	
Selling				———	———→	
Packaging		→	———	———	———→	
Point of sale		→		———	———→	
Exhibitions		→		———	———	———→
Sales promo				———	———	———→
Website		→	———	———	———	———→
Social media	———	———	———	———	———	———→
CRM/WOM	———	———	———	———	———	———→

know how to reach her and trigger her shopping habits (Duhigg, 2012), assuming the store is GDPR compliant in the first place.

Analytics may know more about your family than you do

Approximately 12 months after the American retailer, Target, created their pregnancy-prediction model, a man clutching coupons for baby clothes that had been sent to his daughter walked into a Target store and demanded to see the manager. Enraged, he demanded to know whether Target was encouraging his schoolgirl daughter to get pregnant, as they were sending her incentives to buy baby clothes. The manager looked at the mailer promoting maternity clothing, nursery furniture and pictures of smiling infants and duly apologized. He followed up with a courtesy call to apologize again a few days letter. However, the father answered the phone and said 'I owe you an apology, my daughter is due to have a baby in August.'

Many customers dislike their privacy being invaded by third parties using 'clever' analytics – both in the United States, Europe and elsewhere. This is now, with GDPR, a bigger issue as privacy is a new currency. People do not want to be spied upon as they live their lives and do their shopping. So retailers need to be careful. Although they can sell baby products that customers didn't even know they needed yet, they have to be careful. They have discovered that some women react badly if they receive incentives for baby products (imagine if the woman had not told her partner yet). So they learned from this and now add random products that these customers would never buy, such as lawnmowers and wine glasses, 'so the baby ads look random'. Target stores learned that pregnant women will use the coupons as long she thinks she hasn't been spied on. 'She just assumes that everyone else on her block got the same mailer for diapers and cribs' (Duhigg, 2012).

This raises all sorts of delicate privacy and ethical issues about the use of personal shopping data (and other data). Chapter 10 on the changing communications environment explores this ethical issue and more.

Is convenience becoming more important than trust?

We are so time poor that convenience becomes very attractive. Perhaps even more attractive than truth. Is saving time more important than trust? Is a convenient brand preferred instead of a trusted brand? Is convenience trumping trust? Many rational people would say 'no, convenience would never trump trust'. But in this time-poor world we live in, convenience seems to be winning, if recent surveys about Facebook highlighted by Gerry McGovern (2019) are to be believed:

- Facebook is worse for society than McDonalds or Walmart (2018 Honest Data poll).
- Facebook will have a net negative for society 10 years from now (2018 CB Insights survey).
- Yet Facebook revenue rose from $16.9 billion in the last quarter, up 30 per cent.
- Monthly active users rose to 2.32 billion, up 9 per cent.
- Share price soared more than 13 per cent.

What's happening? Is convenience trumping trustworthiness? See the appendices for the full Gerry McGovern piece.

Summary and conclusion

Marketers must understand the target market's buying behaviour before, during and after the actual purchase. Even the apparently simple act of purchasing a hamburger can reveal a host of hidden motives. In-depth research reveals some deep and unconscious reasons that demonstrate some of the complexities of buying behaviour. The time and effort spent in the buying process depend on the type of buying situation. Decision-making units also affect the process.

Buying models highlight some of the stages through which the buyers pass, offering a kind of checklist for marketing communications to ensure that they carry the buyer through each stage successfully. The behaviourist school differs from the cognitive school of more complex buying models. Motivation, perception, learning, values, attitudes and lifestyles all interact and influence the buying process.

Once marketing professionals are equipped with a clearer understanding of both the motives for buying and the buying process itself, a marketing communications strategy can be developed to ensure that it covers as many avenues to the mind of the buyer as resources allow.

Reasons and motives range from the rational to the bizarre. Motives are, however, only one variable among many other intervening variables that integrate and influence buying behaviour. For example, beliefs and attitudes affect motives, which in turn affect the way an individual sees or perceives things (images, ads, products, shops, etc). We learn these opinions, attitudes and beliefs partly from groups (such as friends and colleagues), partly from commercial messages carefully aimed at us through advertising, sales promotion, etc, and partly from real experiences of products or services.

All these influences interact with commercial stimuli such as advertisements. The effects are ultimately reflected in our behaviour (or lack of behaviour in some circumstances).

In consumer markets, buying behaviour is affected by the complex web of mostly internal intervening variables (motivation, perception, attitudes, learning, memory, lifestyle, personality and groups). Sex, age, income and even an individual's face or body affect their behaviour. Other external variables such as laws and regulations, the weather, opening hours, an out-of-stock situation or an emergency can all change buying behaviour.

A B2B buyer is also influenced by internal variables, including the organization's objectives, policies, procedures, structure and systems, and variables external to the organization such as the state of the economy, the level of demand and competition, the cost of money, etc. B2B buyers are not perfectly rational buyers. They too are affected by emotions.

Perhaps Oscar Wilde was too generous when he said that 'man is a rational animal except when asked to act within the dictates of reason'.

Some argue that it is impossible, as Foxall (1992) said, to 'capture human nature in its entirety' because of the complexity of the decision-making process. This complexity is created by the web of rational and emotional factors that are generated from internal processes and guided by external influences.

Marketing communications can change a nation's behaviour. Marcomms do affect aggregate buying behaviour, as evidenced by changed behaviour patterns after the National Lottery integrated campaign, which stimulated some 65 per cent of the British adult population into shops to buy lottery tickets on a regular basis. The same changes in buyer behaviour are evident in China and across Europe, where marketers really do change customer behaviour patterns. It is no accident. It is never the result of guesswork. It is largely dependent on accurate analysis of customers and subsequently building up valuable customer insights. If you want to protect and enhance the value of your brand, your offer must be valuable. See how Unilever change behaviour in Appendix 4.3. You will see that the higher the relevance, the greater the value – it's a continuum. It's the magic marketing formula delivering success.

Goethe and the magic marketing formula

'Behaviour is a mirror in which everyone displays his own image.'

Goethe (1809)

Key points from Chapter 4

- Buying behaviour is complex.
- There are many different approaches to buying models.
- Marketers need a continual feed of information on customer behaviour.
- Emotional influences in decision-making are still dominant in B2C and exist in B2B markets.
- Marketers must understand how the intervening psychological variables influence buyer behaviour.

- Marketers must know their customers better than the customers know themselves.
- Data analytics plus nudge theory and neuroscience can give powerful insights into customers' minds.

Appendix 4.1: Hofacker's online information processing

One approach to online information processing is Charles Hofacker's five stages of on-site information processing:

1. exposure;
2. attention;
3. comprehension and perception;
4. yielding and acceptance;
5. retention.

Each stage acts as a hurdle, since if the site design or content is too difficult to process, the customer cannot progress to the next stage. The emarketer fails. The best website designs take into account how customers process information. Good emarketers are aware of how the messages are processed by the customer and of corresponding steps we can take to ensure that the correct message is received.

The first stage is *exposure*. This is straightforward. If the content is not present for long enough, customers will not be able to process it. Think of splash pages, banner ads or Shockwave animations: if these change too rapidly the message will not be received.

The second stage is *attention*. The human mind has limited capacity to pick out the main messages from a screen full of single-column-format text without headings or graphics. Movement, text size and colour help to gain attention for key messages. Note though that studies show that the eye is immediately drawn to content, not the headings in the navigation systems. Of course, we need to be careful about using garish colours and animations, as these can look amateurish and distract from the main message.

Comprehension and *perception* are the third of Hofacker's stages. They refer to how the customer interprets the combination of graphics, text and multimedia on a website. If the design uses familiar standards or metaphors, it will be most effective, since the customer will interpret them based on previous experience and memory. Once relevant information is found, visitors sometimes want to dig deeper for more information.

Changing the layout of a website will be as popular with customers as a supermarket changing its store layout every six months! Metaphors are another approach to aid comprehension of e-commerce sites; a shopping basket metaphor is used to help comprehension.

Fourthly, *yielding* and *acceptance* refers to whether the information you present is accepted by the customer. Different tactics need to be used to convince different types of people. Classically a US audience is more convinced by features than benefits, while the reverse is true for a European audience. Some customers will respond to emotive appeals, perhaps reinforced by images, while others will make a more clinical evaluation based on the text. This gives us the difficult task of combining text, graphics and copy to convince each customer segment.

Finally, *retention* – how well the customer can recall their experience. A clear, distinctive site design will be retained in the customer's mind, perhaps prompting a repeat visit when the customer thinks, 'Where did I see that information?' and then recalls the layout of the site. A clear site design will also be implanted in the customer's memory as a mental map and they will be able to draw on it when returning to the site, increasing their flow experience.

To summarize, understanding how customers process information through the stages of exposure, attention, comprehension and perception, yielding and acceptance, and retention can help us design sites that really get our message across and deliver memorable messages and superior customer service.

Appendix 4.2: The post-PC and, soon, post-mobile customer

The post-PC customer may occasionally accept payment to view some ads. The rest are screened out by sophisticated browser software. Neither governments nor society permit old-style intrusive advertising any more. No more evening telephone calls from script-reading intelligent agents or scammers. It is also illegal to litter anyone's doorstep or house with mailshots and inserts. Heavy fines stopped all that a long time ago. The only ads that do get inside are carried by the many millions of private media owners who rent out their cars, bikes and bodies as billboards.

The tedious task of shopping for distress purchases like petrol, electricity or memory storage is delegated completely to embedded shopping bots.

Non-embedded bots spun out of control some years ago when they first appeared in three-dimensional hovering holograms – always at your side, always double-checking the best price for hire cars, hotels, even drinks at the bar. Some are programmed to be polite, aggressive or even abusive. All are programmed to be intrusive whenever anything is being bought. Delays on buses and traffic jams regularly occurred when argumentative bots engaged in lengthy negotiations. Frustration broke out. Bots attacked bots, people attacked bots and bot owners. Eventually bots were banned from buses, planes, trains and several 'peaceful supermarkets'.

Next came the great worm wars: programming bots so they only buy your brand – for life. But, unlike humans, bots can be reprogrammed by a competitor. The advertising agent's worm was born. Agent eaters soon followed. Despite being information fatigued and time compressed, the post-PC and post-mobile customer lives a lot longer than many bots. And certainly longer than most of the new brands that seem to come and go. The 150-year-old person has already been born.

Meanwhile, back at the ranch, microwaves insist on offering suggestions of ideal wines to go with your meal, offering instant delivery from the neighbourhood's wired-up 24-hour roving delivery van. Your fridge offers special incentives to buy Pepsi when you run out of Coke (or whichever brand owns or hires the IoT hub database). Children happily play chess and interact with their opponents on the giant vertical screens, called refrigerators. Voice-operated computers are considered noisy and old fashioned as discreet, upmarket, thought-operated computers operate silently, but extremely effectively.

And all the time bluetooth type technology facilitates ubiquitous communications, which allows constant interaction between machines. Man and machine integrate into a vast database. We have more IT power in today's average luxury car than the rocket that went to the moon. Yes, Moore's law suggests the tectonic shift will continue. Yes, marketing will continue in a new guise (probably not even called marketing but just 'common-sensing').

Time-compressed, information-fatigued and disloyal, the post-PC and post-mobile customer seeks relationships not from brands themselves but from databases that know, understand and seemingly care about them. Witness the virtual girlfriend relationships in Japan, relationships with shops and vending machines, oh, and relationships with people, real, quaint, touchy, feely, physical people.

And all the time the technology, if truly mastered, can free up time to do the important things in life, to give the post-PC customer a genuinely higher quality of life both at work and at home with family and friends.

Live longer

Humans may develop smaller ears (from constant use of headphones) and better body organs, replaced as a result of early-warning systems carried by miniature submarines constantly patrolling in the bloodstream. These wireless database-driven devices identify wearing parts and organs, check cloned stock availability, reserve beds and preferred surgeons and estimate time before breakdown replacement is required. Discounts for early bookings into leisure hospitals are also negotiated automatically.

Appendix 4.3: Unilever's five steps to change behaviour

Unilever publishes its marketing behaviour change principles, Five Levers for Change, to inspire sustainable living

To coincide with a public debate on mainstreaming sustainable living, Unilever has today published the behaviour change model its marketers use to encourage sustainable changes in consumer living habits: Five Levers for Change.

Based on Unilever's long history of research and insights into consumer behaviour, the tool is based on a set of key principles, which, if applied consistently to behaviour change interventions, increases the likelihood of having an effective and lasting impact. Unilever is sharing the model in the hope that others will find it helpful and use it to inspire people to turn their concerns about sustainability into positive actions.

The model outlines five techniques to apply when looking to encourage new behaviours, based on five key insights.

The Five Levers for Change are:

1. Make it understood. Sometimes people don't know about a behaviour and why they should do it. This lever raises awareness and encourages acceptance.
2. Make it easy. People are likely to take action if it's easy, but not if it requires extra effort. This lever establishes convenience and confidence.
3. Make it desirable. The new behaviour needs to fit with how people like to think of themselves, and how they like others to think of them. This lever is about self and society.
4. Make it rewarding. New behaviours need to articulate the tangible benefits that people care about. This lever demonstrates the proof and payoff.
5. Make it a habit. Once consumers have changed, it is important to create a strategy to help hold the behaviour in place over time. This lever is about reinforcing and reminding.

Appendix 4.4: Use and convenience replace trust and security

'Sheryl Sandberg: The teens "consented" to putting Facebook spyware on their phones.' Another day, another screaming headline exposes negative behaviour by Facebook. *Adweek* reported on a survey which asked US adults how they would trust 100 of the biggest brands with their personal data in exchange for 'more relevant offers, goods and services'. Facebook ranked last.

A 2018 Honest Data poll found that US citizens think Facebook is worse for society than McDonalds or Walmart. The only company ranked worse than Facebook was Marlboro. A 2018 CB Insights survey asked which company will have a net negative for society 10 years from now? 'The answer was pretty overwhelmingly Facebook.'

And yet... And yet... Facebook revenue rose to $16.9 billion in the last three months of 2018, up 30 per cent. Monthly active users rose to 2.32 billion, up 9 per cent. Consequently, Facebook's share price soared more than 13 per cent. What's happening?

Does trust matter? Clearly, not very much when it comes to Facebook. Why is Facebook still so successful?

There's a pattern to many of the negative stories about Facebook. Most of them tell of Facebook's relentless pursuit of understanding their customers deepest needs, desires and behaviours. The Facebook app that Sheryl Sandberg defended by saying that teens 'consented' to installing it, was used to target teens as young as 13 so as to track and monitor everything they did on their phones, from private messages and browsing histories to app messages. (I recently read a story about how the Silicon Valley elite, like Sandberg, 'are now restricting, or outright banning, screen time for their children').

Facebook is relentlessly focused on usability and simplicity. It wants to understand you better than you understand yourself so that it can craft a world through which its advertisers can get you to buy more and more of their products. (There are almost 7 million advertisers using Facebook.) That's the Facebook business model. Every time you use Facebook, you pay. The currency? Your personal data.

It's the things we don't talk about that seem to matter most to us. Today, we choose simplicity, usefulness and convenience over trust and security.

We don't trust Facebook. We use Facebook. So, trust doesn't matter? Or does convenience simply trump trust?

Just like with the BP oil slick scandal. People didn't stop using BP stations to fill up their cars, because these stations were too convenient, too close to their homes or workplaces to avoid.

Those that make it simple and easy are ruling the world. Those that understand what people do, rather than what people say, are ruling the world. For good or ill, you can't craft an effective customer experience on a website or app if you don't first and foremost truly understand your customers. Facebook knows this. Google knows this. But nine out of ten organizations that I deal with don't. And then we wonder why Facebook and Google have become so dominant?

McGovern (2019)

References and further reading

Benady, D (2014) A nudge in the right direction, *PR Week*, September

Bennett, D (2016) *The Evolution Of Behavioural Economics*, Ogilvy

Brown, N (2016) Keeping up with Coca-Cola's taglines, *Ideas*, 22 January

Brun-Jensen, P (2014) Next generation of social analytics are transforming digital marketing, *Adweek*, 22 September

Burstein, D (2013) Mobile marketing: 31% of marketers don't know their mobile email open rate, *Marketing Sherpa*, 1 February [online] http://sherpablog.marketingsherpa.com/email-marketing/moblile-marketing-email-open-rate/ (archived at https://perma.cc/6WSY-2Y8Z)

Chaffey, D (2018) Examples of how website designs must be optimized to support the way we hold and interact with smartphones, *Smart Insights*, 29 October

Chisnall, P (1985) *Marketing: A behavioural analysis*, McGraw-Hill, Maidenhead

Christensen, C, Hall, T, Dillon, K and Duncan, D (2016) Know your customers' 'jobs to be done', *HBR*, September

Cialdini, R (2007) *Influence: The psychology of persuasion*, Harper Business, New York

Cialdini, R (2014) An interview with Dr Robert Cialdini, *The Marketer*, 2 October

Colley, R H (1961) *Defining Advertising Goals and Measuring Advertising Results*, Association of National Advertisers, New York

Coopere, G (2008) *Species: A user's guide to young men*, Discovery Channel, Discovery Communications Europe

Dalton, J (2012) How brands can leverage the power of visual social media, *Media Matters*, 20 December

Dichter, E (1964) *Handbook of Consumer Motivations: The psychology of the world of objects*, McGraw-Hill, New York

Dishman, L (2014) Study: People are not most attentive when watching TV at home, *Adweek*, 29 September

Duhigg, C (2012) How companies learn your secrets, *New York Times*, 16 February [online] www.nytimes.com/2012/02/19/magazine/shopping-habits.html?pagewanted=all&_r=0 (archived at https://perma.cc/GGU8-E5MJ)

East, R, Wright, M and Vanhuele, M (2008) *Consumer Behaviour: Applications in marketing*, Sage, London

Egan, J (2007) *Marketing Communications*, Case study 4.1, Thomson Learning, London

Ehrenberg, A (1974) Repetitive advertising and consumer awareness, *Journal of Advertising Research*, **14**, pp 25–34

Ehrenberg, A (1997) How can consumers buy a new brand? *Admap*, March, pp 20–27

Engel, J F, Blackwell, R D and Kollatt, D T (1978) *Consumer Behaviour*, 3rd edn, Dryden Press, Hinsdale, IL

Engel, J F, Kinnear, T C and Warshaw, M R (1994) *Promotional Strategy: Managing the marketing communications process*, 7th edn, Irwin Shaw, Homewood, IL

Fishbein, M (1975) Attitude, attitude change and behaviour: A theoretical overview, in P Levine (ed),

Attitude Research Bridges the Atlantic, American Marketing Association, Chicago

Forsyth, J, Galante, N and Guild, T (2006) Capitalizing on customer insights, *McKinsey Quarterly*, 3

Foxall, G (1992) *Consumer Psychology in Behavioural Perspective*, Routledge, London

Frank, O (2010) Goodbye, smartphone; hello, predictive context device, *Advertising Age*, 25 June

Goethe, J von (1809) *Kindred by Choice*, recently republished by Oxford World Classics, Oxford

Gregg, B, Heller, J, Perrey, J and Tsai, J (2018) The most perfect union: Unlocking the next wave of growth by unifying creativity and analytics, *McKinseys*, June

Hagy, D (2013) How to create the perfect post on social media, *Dashburst*, 20 June

Harari, Y (2017) A Facebook world, *FT Life and Arts*, 25 March

Hofacker, C (2001) *Internet Marketing*, 3rd edn, Wiley, New York

Howard, J A and Sheth, J N (1969) *The Theory of Buyer Behavior*, Wiley, New York

Humby, C (2008) *Brand is Dead, Long Live the Customer*, dunnhumby

Ibrahim, M (2013) Twitter and WPP in global partnership, *PR Week*, 14 June, p 17

Jones, H (2008) How to tackle foreign markets, *Marketer*, 8 September

Kanner, B (1989) Colour scheme, *New York Magazine*, 3 April

Kapferer, J (2004) *The New Strategic Brand Management*, Kogan Page, London

Kennedy, J (2009) A wave of optimism, Interview with Eric Schmidt, *Marketing Age*, November

Khullar Relph, M (2015) Why do people share what they do? Here's what neuroscience, psychology, and relationships tell us about highly shareable content, *Buffer*, 25 August

Kosinski, M, Stillwell, D and Graepel, T (2013) Private traits and attributes are predictable from digital records of human behaviour, *PNAS Proceedings of the National Academy of Sciences of the United States of America*, ed Kenneth Wachter, University of California, Berkeley, CA [online] www.pnas.org/content/early/2013/03/06/1218772110 (archived at https://perma.cc/YTW2-MEEJ)

Kotler, P (1998) *Practice of Marketing*, Prentice Hall, Englewood Cliffs, NJ

Langton, N (2013) Emotion influences B2B buying more than you might think, *The Laws of Attraction*

Lavidge, R and Steiner, G (1961) A model for predictive measurements of advertising effectiveness, *Journal of Marketing*, October, p 61

Lee, J (2013) Obama Digital Director praises social media, *Yale News*, 9 April

Luechtefeld, L (2012) Overcoming the challenges of branded video content, *Spotlight iMediaConnection*, 19 September

Manyika, J (2008) Google's view on the future of business: An interview with CEO Eric Schmidt, *The McKinsey Quarterly*, September

Market Research Society (1996) Research is good for you: The contribution of research to Guinness advertising, Conference papers, MRS, London

Marketer (2010) Facts and stats, *Marketer*, March

Maslow, A (1954) *Motivation and Personality*, Harper & Row, New York

McGovern, G (2010) The rise of the anti brand: Ryanair [online] gerrymcgovern.com (archived at https://perma.cc/9T94-8QA3)

McGovern, G (2019) Use and convenience replace trust and security, 3 February [online] gerrymcgovern.com (archived at https://perma.cc/9T94-8QA3)

Moye, J (2016) Taste the feeling: The Coca-Cola Company's 'one brand' marketing strategy goes global with new creative campaign, Coca-Cola UK, 19 January

Oakes, S (2008) Mood maker: Music to set your till ringing, *Marketer*, September

Packard, V (1957) *The Hidden Persuaders*, Penguin Books, Harmondsworth

Penn, D (2005) Brain science, that's interesting, but what do I do about it? Market Research Society Conference

Peters, T (2003) *Re-imagine*, Dorling Kindersley, London

Pun, R (2013) Why you must understand the perpetually connected customer: Part I, Adobe Digital Marketing Blog (Adobe) 25 June [online] http://blogs.adobe.com (archived at https://perma.cc/SEL4-ZPQ8)

Roberts, K (2006a) Excerpt from a Saatchi & Saatchi presentation, Madrid, 8 June [online] http://www.saatchikevin.com/kevin-video/emotion-reason/ (archived at https://perma.cc/4HM9-ED5L)

Roberts, K (2006b) Saatchi & Saatchi presentation, Madrid, 8 June

Roberts, K (2009a) Short cuts (part 1), 6 July; see hard copy journal kept in Chartered Institute of Marketing library (www.cim.co.uk (archived at https://perma.cc/S59Y-AX9L))

Roberts, K (2009b) Short cuts (part 5), 6 July, see reference above for further details
Roberts, K (2009c) Annual City Lecture to the Worshipful Company of Marketors, 6 November
Roberts, K (2010a) Creativity, 21 January
Roberts, K (2010b) Spreading the love, *Marketer*, February
Rogers, E M (1961) *Diffusion of Innovations*, Free Press, New York
Rosich, M (2015) Digital outlook (Singapore conference) 2015, reported by Rajeck, J, Five new mobile marketing strategies for 2015, eConsultancy blog, 21 January [online] https://econsultancy.com/blog/65928-five-new-mobile-marketing-strategies-for-2015/?utm_campaign=Twitter&utm_content=11477997&utm_medium=social&utm_source=twitter (archived at https://perma.cc/94DT-3ADC)
Rossiter, J and Percy, L (1996) *Advertising Communications and Promotion Management*, 2nd edn, McGraw Hill, New York
Shaw, R (1997/98) Appreciating assets, *Marketing Business*, December/January
Smart Insights (2014) The consumer decision journey (infographic) [online] www.smartinsights.com/marketplace-analysis/consumer-buying-behaviour/what-influences-purchase/ (archived at https://perma.cc/F98H-K7LV)
Smith, P, Berry, C and Pulford, A (1999) *Strategic Marketing Communications*, Kogan Page, London
Smith, PR (1996) Video interview with Kenichi Ohmae
Smith, PR (2001) *Online Emarketing Course: Ecustomers*, Multimedia Marketing, London
Smith, PR (2010) Video interview with Kevin Roberts, CEO, Saatchi & Saatchi Worldwide
Smith, PR (2014) The rise and fall of owned and earned but not paid media: World Cup marketing wars? 27 June [online] http://prsmith.org/blog/ (archived at https://perma.cc/67JZ-HYWA)
Smith, PR (2017) How Trump won: A SOSTAC® analysis (parts 1 and 2), 20 January [online] http://prsmith.org/blog/ (archived at https://perma.cc/67JZ-HYWA)
Smith, PR (2019) SOSTAC® guide to your perfect digital marketing plan [online] http://prsmith.org/blog/ (archived at https://perma.cc/67JZ-HYWA)
Solis, B (2015) Crossing the experience divide: Creating positive, lasting experiences is a crucial mandate for any brand, *Technology of Us*, 12 January
Soskey, G (2015) What to cut from your marketing, *Hubspot Blog*, 7 January [online] http://linkis.com/blog.hubspot.com/mar/Yy9bk (archived at https://perma.cc/VD2L-6L4A)
Spool, J (2009) The $300 million button, *User Interface Engineering*, 14 January
Stibel, J (2018) Why the brain buys what it doesn't want, *LinkedIn*, 25 September
Strong, E K (1925) *The Psychology of Selling*, McGraw-Hill, New York
Unilever (2011) Unilever reveal 5 steps to change consumer behaviour, 23 November, Unilever Global
Veblen, T (1899) *The Theory of the Leisure Class*, Oxford University Press, Oxford
Walker, R (2008) The invisible badge: Moving past conspicuous consumption, *ChangeThis.com*, **47** (1)
Williams, K C (1989) *Behavioural Aspects of Marketing*, Heinemann, Oxford
Williams, T G (1982) *Consumer Behavior*, West Publishing, St Paul, MN
Wolfgang Digital (2019) KPI report 2019 [online] www.wolfgangdigital.com/kpi-2019/ (archived at https://perma.cc/RT45-KAU6)

Further information

Market Research Society (MRS)
The Old Trading House
15 Northburgh Street
London EC1V 0JR
Tel: +44 (0)20 7490 4911
www.mrs.org.uk

Ofcom
Riverside House
2a Southwark Bridge Road
London SE1 9HA
Tel: +44 (0)300 123 3000
www.ofcom.org.uk

05 Communications theory

LEARNING OBJECTIVES

By the end of this chapter you will be able to:

- understand that communication involves a two-way flow of information;
- appreciate the subtle variables involved in communications;
- apply communication theories to practical marketing situations;
- exploit contemporary models to ensure successful communications;
- explain why new models are required to meet the changing communications landscape;
- understand why new skills are required to match new communications models.

Introduction to communications theory

A dictionary definition of 'communication' is as follows: 'Communication (noun) 1. Transmitting. 2. a) Giving or exchange of information, etc by talk, writing. b) The information so given. 3. A means of communicating. 4. The science of transmitting information'.

What is interesting is the exchange of information. Communication is not a one-way flow of information (see social listening on p 167) Talking at or to someone does not imply successful communication. It only occurs when the receiver actually receives the message that the sender intended to send. Message rejection, misinterpretation and misunderstanding are the opposite of effective communication.

> **Ineffective communications kill millions**
>
> 'There is evidence that a mistake in translating a message sent by the Japanese government near the end of World War II may have triggered the bombing of Hiroshima, and thus ushered in atomic warfare. The word "*mokusatsu*" used by Japan in response to the US surrender ultimatum was translated as "ignore", instead of its correct meaning, "withhold comment until a decision has been made".'
>
> Cutlip *et al* (2004)

If true, this would be an extreme and tragic example of communications gone wrong. Communication errors in marketing generally do not cost lives but can, if allowed to continue unchecked, cost market share, company survival and jobs. On the other hand, good marketing communications help an organization to thrive by getting its messages across in a focused and cost-effective way.

Good marketing communications is not as simple as it may appear. Even David Ogilvy, the advertising guru, was once reported to have used the word 'obsolete' in an advertisement only to discover that (at the time) 43 per cent of US women had no idea what it meant. The delicacy and difficulty of creating effective communications to target audiences can be explained by Douglas Smallbone's analogy of radio communication.

Perfect transmitting conditions might exist if there were no noise (extraneous factors that distract or distort the message, such as other advertisements, poor reception, a flashing light, a door bell or an ambulance). Without noise, perfect transmitting conditions would exist. In reality, there is almost always noise, so perfect transmitting conditions do not exist. Cinemas may be the exception, where a captive audience is in an attentive state and receptive to, say, a well-produced advertisement. But even when the target audience is seemingly tuned in (watching, listening to or looking at a particular organization's package, promotion, advertisement, etc) it may not be on the same wavelength because of the hidden internal psychological processes that may be reshaping or distorting the message to suit the audience's own method of interpretation.

The human receiver is in fact equipped with five distinct means of receiving messages or information or marketing communications – the five senses of hearing, sight, touch, taste and smell. Marketing communications tools can address many senses simultaneously (for example a retail environment).

> **The human radio**
>
> 'Given good transmitting conditions and receiver and transmitter tuned to the same wavelength, perfect reception can be effected.'
>
> Smallbone (1969)

Non-verbal and non-symbolic communications

Although verbal and visual communications gain a lot of conscious attention, there are non-verbal and non-symbolic ways of communicating, such as space, time and kinetics. Crowded areas, or lack of space, send messages to the brain that, in turn, can stimulate a different set of thoughts and a different behavioural response. The opposite is also true: a spacious office or living room conveys different messages. In fact, spacious websites (minimalist design) can quickly communicate the purpose, or benefit, of a web page. Visitors are impatient and fast-moving. If a website visitor does not understand what a page is about in just a few seconds, they leave. We also need to reduce the number of choices, as Hick's Law (1952) states the greater the number of potential choices/decisions, the longer it will take to make a choice.

Visitors also seek consistency across website pages as well as community and belonging (you can use language and imagery that help visitors to feel included in your business). And of course, colour communicates; Google tests prove blue links receive more clicks (Golson, 2009) than links using other colours. A visual hierarchy also helps since visitors are also drawn to objects that stand out. They jump along prominent items on a site, which means you can guide them to information you want them to see. Audiences tend to look at faces more than other objects.

In Western cultures **the use of time creates images**; a busy but organized person gives an impression of authority. 'Thanks for your time' immediately conveys a respect for and an appreciation of a seemingly important person's time. A busy diary can project an image of importance. 'I can squeeze you in on Friday at...' implies seniority in the relationship. In the UK, the term 'window' means 'free time' or space in a busy diary. Some advertisements sell products and services primarily on time-saving and convenience benefits.

Finally, **kinetics communicate**. Gestures and movements send messages. Even the simple, swift clicking of a briefcase, entering or leaving a room or closing or not closing a door can communicate (in China sitting opposite the door means you are paying for the meal). Most of all, body language and facial gestures are powerful communicators. An understanding of body language allows an individual to learn more about what another person is really feeling. A smile, for example, communicates immediately, effectively and directly. Online, we also analyse digital body language (click behaviour) to determine what a visitor is interested in and what stage of the buying process they are at.

Symbolic and semiotic communications

The field of semiotics (or semiology) opens up a rich discussion of how symbols and signs are used in communications, particularly advertising. Audiences often unconsciously perceive images stimulated by certain symbols.

Engel *et al* (1994) demonstrated how Lever's fabric softener 'Snuggle' used a cuddly teddy bear in its advertising. It has been suggested by some psychologists that 'the bear is an ancient symbol of aggression, but when you create a teddy bear, you provide a softer, nurturant side to that aggression. As a symbol of tamed aggression, the teddy bear is the perfect image for a fabric softener that tames the rough of clothing.'

Engel *et al* (1994) comment: 'The key point here is that if marketing communicators are not aware of the subtle meanings of symbols, then they are liable to communicate the wrong message.'

Carol Moog's advice to Pierre Cardin on its men's fragrance advertisement, which was designed to show men who are 'aggressive and in control' splashing on fragrance, was accepted but rejected! Moog saw 'cologne gushing out of a phallic-shaped bottle' creating a conflict of images, since it 'symbolized male ejaculation and lack of control'. Pierre Cardin acknowledged that she was probably right, but decided to keep the shot, as it was 'a beautiful product shot plus it encourages men to use our fragrance liberally'.

Source credibility

The success or failure of an advertisement, or any message, is partially determined by whether it is a credible message in the first place. This, in turn, is influenced by the credibility of the source of the message, the deliverer of the message and the chosen media vehicle.

The perceived credibility of the message source is influenced by trustworthiness and expertise. These are key factors that organizations must constantly prove so that they have a platform of credibility. Endorsements from customers and venerable institutions, published papers, conference speeches, awards won, memberships and of course the perceived quality of the brand itself all help to establish trustworthiness and expertise, ie source credibility. In addition to the credibility of the brand, the message credibility is also influenced by the individual delivering the message, such as the presenter in an advertisement. For example, some brands stopped sponsoring Tiger Woods and also supermodel Kate Moss when their private behaviour was deemed to be 'unsuitable'. On the other hand, a highly credible presenter adds credibility to a brand.

Content design also affects credibility. Researchers asked subjects to look at two websites: one was professionally designed, and the other looked dated and ugly. When the researchers asked people why they mistrusted the information on either site, 94 per cent said it was because of design. And get this: the content on both websites was exactly the same (Sillence *et al*, 2004). Poor design is one of the main reasons why visitors distrust a site. Therefore your site should look up to date and display relevant content and images. State your business purpose/ online value proposition (OVP) clearly. Display 'trust badges', high-profile customer logos, members of trade bodies, payment methods, security protection.

Positive and negative reviews: Two-sided arguments create more trust

'Reevoo research shows bad reviews actually reduce site abandonment, with time on a site leaping from just over three minutes to 18 minutes. The research revealed that consumers trust reviews more when they see both positive and negative comments. In fact, an absence of negative reviews can lead consumers to distrust a brand. "Shoppers are suspicious when reviews don't include any complaints", says Reevoo founder Richard Anson.'

Manning (2012)

The media vehicle affects the credibility, eg a message that 'using a laptop damages your fertility' would have less credibility if it came from *The Sun* newspaper than it would have if it came from the *FT*, or even more credibility if it came from a learned medical journal rather than a newspaper survey. The media vehicle's perceived expertise, prestige and editorial tone (style, eg upmarket or mass-market, and other content, eg sex and violence) all affect the credibility of a message.

Message source affects credibility. Kelman (1961) suggested that it has three variables: 1) perceived source expertise and neutrality (or objectivity); 2) perceived source attractiveness (if it is deemed attractive, the recipients may be more likely to develop a similar opinion or position); and 3) perceived power to reward or punish message receivers (eg a teacher or perhaps an owner of a social media group). In summary, a great message delivered from a source with low 'source credibility' will not be as effective as the same message coming from a source with high 'source credibility'.

Message style affects credibility, anxiety and trust

When customers see an ad or a mailshot for your product or service they ask these three questions: Who are you? What are you offering me? And why should I care?

Many customers feel 'loss aversion' – they are more afraid of making the wrong decision than they are excited about making the right decision. They just don't want to get taken advantage of, so a customer acquisition ad has to answer these questions quickly, whereas a customer retention message is more conversational – uses the customer's name (people like to be remembered), mentions any previous purchases and perhaps offers a customized offer (which new customers can't get). Personalization also helps, whether it's a web page, an email, an ad or even a video (see personalized videos at scale, page 167). A conversational tone can make existing customers drop their defensiveness and become more receptive to your next offer.

Message likeability

'This is about how much an individual likes an advertisement. It is determined by how interesting, meaningful, relevant and enjoyable an advertisement is deemed to be. When researching advertisements, and in particular, how much customers like an advertisement, "likeability is deemed to have four elements: entertainment, relevance, clarity and pleasantness".'

Source unknown

Influencers: Opinion formers, opinion leaders and connectors

Opinion formers and opinion leaders include journalists, judges, consultants, lecturers, religious leaders, politicians, group leaders and of course bloggers, tweeters, Instagrammers and YouTubers to name a few influencer types. Officially, opinion formers such as journalists and judges are formally paid to give their opinions, while opinion leaders such as bloggers are not.

Influencers can have a much bigger impact than any of your other marketing efforts. You must identify and connect with influencers in your industry. A comment, like or share from influencers can be powerful. You may not be able to afford to pay (via money, free products or placing ads on influencers' blogs) or even collaborate with all the influencers, it may be that you just focus on a small number, or perhaps focus on niche influencers or '**nano-influencers**' (with perhaps just 5,000 followers) who usually have a more niched following who are interested in some specific aspect or group of users. A hundred nano-influencers with a combined audience of over 1 million could be very effective and cheaper, than working with one influencer with 1 million followers. Either way, you have to ensure the influencers understand your brand, your values, your messaging and then continually monitor their performance.

> **Connectors know a lot of people**
>
> 'They are the kind of people who know everyone. All of us know someone like this. But I don't think we spend a lot of time thinking about the importance of these people. I'm not even sure that most of us really believe that the kind of person who knows everyone really knows everyone. But they do.'
>
> Gladwell (2000)

Marketers recognize that in each market there is a smaller target group of influencers. Major brands can maintain their credibility by communicating specifically to these influencers, as well as communicating to the mass through other media channels (sometimes with messages tailored for the two groups).

In the world of fashion, the leaders are sometimes called **'style leaders'**. Even cult fashion products can be mass-marketed by carefully splitting the messages between style leaders and the mass. While the leaders want to set themselves apart from the rest, the mass market consciously and/or unconsciously looks to the leaders for suggestions about what to buy. The difficulty lies with success – as the mass market buys more, the leaders lose interest unless they are reinforced with brand values that preserve the brand's credibility among the cognoscenti. This is important because, if the leaders move away today, the mass sales will eventually start falling away next year or the year after. So, in addition to the mass advertising, some brands use small-audience, targeted, opinion-leader media to send the 'right' messages to reinforce the leaders' relationship with the brand.

Just getting the product into the hands of influencers can help a brand grow. Chapter 20 describes how Zip World seeded some stunning photographs with influencers outside their target market and consequently delivered a massive boost in sales (p 611).

Artificial influencers

Artificial influencers are avatars who model fashion brands, appear to drink fashionable coffee, visit cool exhibitions and maintain a dialogue with their followers. Miquela Sousa, also known as @LilMiquela, has over 1.5 million followers and gets tens of thousands of likes for each of her posts. AI can help maintain a dialogue or it could be managed manually. She's modelled for Prada, Chanel, Diesel and Moncler. She has released a Spotify top 10 track and launched her own clothing range.

Miquela's creator Brud.fyi specializes in 'robotics, artificial intelligence and their applications to media businesses'. So they gave Miquela a social conscience as she 'supports social causes such as Black Lives Matter and supports an organization called Black Girls Code, which promotes technology training for girls. British photographer, Cameron-James Wilson, created the stunning artificial influencer Shudu.

In an email interview with BBC, Lil Miquela was asked what she thought about virtual celebrities and gave this reply:

> I think most of the celebrities in popular culture are virtual! It's been disheartening to watch misinformation and memes warp our democracy,

but I think that speaks to the power of 'virtual'. Eventually, 'virtual' shapes our reality and I think that's why I'm so passionate about using virtual spaces like Instagram to push for positive change.

Brands want access to this audience so they pay $2–3,000 per 500,000 followers. Hence Miquela could earn, say, $10,000 per post x 50 posts (one post per week) which generates $500,000 pa. If Brud see good engagement in the first 30 minutes they remove the post.

Artificial influencers are proving to be a success and therefore are attracting the attention of brands (Kulp, 2018b). You will probably see more virtual models in your Instagram feed as artificial intelligence transforms influencer marketing (Kulp, 2018a).

For examples of how artificial influencers work and their use of the magic marketing formula see **http://prsmith.org/blog/** ('Artificial influencers').

FIGURE 5.1 Shudu

SOURCE: Courtesy of Cameron James Wilson, @TheDigitals, and Jennifer Powell, Inc

Microsoft call on influencers to launch new product

'Molly O'Donnell, Director of Influencer Marketing, Microsoft, says that before any influencer campaign, they identify (1) who they want to reach (2) where they are (3) what media they consume and (4) how do they behave? More than 70 per cent of its target consumers are influenced by their peers. Microsoft partners with Klout* through its Perks programme and gave a free phone to individuals with a score of 55+ (and invited them to an event). Others with scores of 29–54 were invited but didn't get a phone. Microsoft placed ads on Facebook Marketplace and partnered with Flavorpill, a daily guide to cultural events, to reach "tastemakers (massive following) and influencers". Result: thousands of people vying to get into the events and conversations reaching tens of thousands before, during and after the event.'

Solis (2012)

* Klout used to rate an individual's online social influence via the Klout Score.

The power of influencers and organizations can also be seen in industrial markets. An entire industry may follow a well-respected and highly successful company that makes an early decision to buy. Expert sales teams focus on these kinds of companies initially. Marketers in consumer markets can also focus on the people who are the first to buy new ideas. Better information today can provide a focused approach through database marketing, while the imagery used can reflect the lifestyles, attitudes and aspirations of these innovators and early adopters of fresh ideas. We are also particularly interested in the influencers, opinion formers (formal influencers like journalists, judges, consultants) and opinion leaders (informal, often bloggers and tweeters) who spread information. Communications agencies regularly use 'blogger outreach programmes' to identify and work with opinion leaders.

There are several different approaches, including Campbell's Soup's Warhol campaign (see p 562); they approached key media (ie journalists) and opinion leaders (eg bloggers) through an intensive sampling campaign, while also offering product for photo shoots.

> **WARNING**
>
> Influencers must state, when posting, 'Ad' if they've been paid, given, or loaned things.' See the CMA (2019) 'Social media endorsements: Being transparent with your followers'.

Virtual influencer: The search engine

Instead of watching ads, building brand relationships over time and eventually buying a particular product or service, customers can now speak into their phone and ask it to get a certain product or service. It duly obliges, as this virtual influencer, Google Voice, searches carefully and delivers useful suggestions for purchase. A high Google ranking, for some, acts as an endorsement of quality (or at least relevance). Mobile apps compare prices by just swiping the phone screen over the bar code or just keying in the brand name.

> **Influence is a measure of social capital**
>
> 'Social capital is a culmination of 3 pillars: Reach (popularity, proximity, goodwill); Relevance (authority, trust, affinity); and Resonance (culmination of reach and relevance: frequency, period, amplitude). Resonance is also how long something will stay alive in the stream before attention dissipates.'
>
> Solis (2012)

Advocates

Brand advocates are invaluable as they promote your brand, usually to your target market. These are your precious 1 per cent of customers that demonstrate high levels of engagement, strong brand loyalty and tell others about your brand. Sometimes called the 1 per cent rule, they are the ones that write nice reviews about your brand and recommend your brand to other people. They are special. They need to be treated as special. The 1 per cent

FIGURE 5.2 You can watch digital guru, Zaid Al Zaidy, talking about how agencies use 'blogger outreach' programmes on the PRSmith1000 channel on YouTube

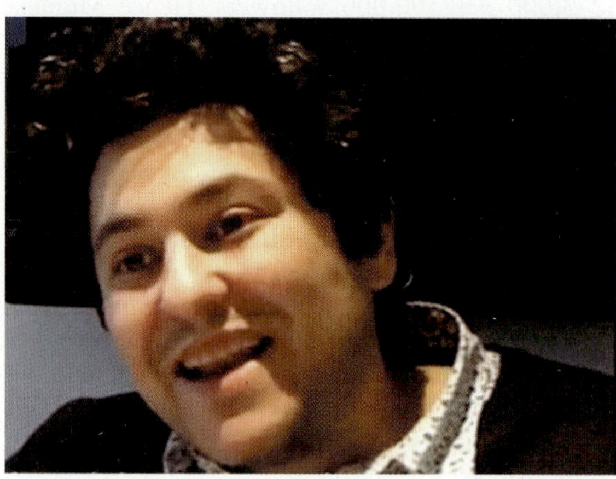

rule may be derived from the 90-9-1 rule from Ben McConnell and Jackie Huba (2006), which describes activity on online forums: 90 per cent lurked (or observed or read posts); 9 per cent commented; 1 per cent created new posts. Although it is referred to as the 90-9-1 principle or rule (and occasionally the 1-9-90 rule) it is in fact the 89:10:1 ratio, but this is not very memorable, hence the 1 per cent rule is also used.

> 'Nokia has a community of advocates in each country who are managed through a specialist agency, with updates centred around a special blog for influencers, Nokia Connects, which has resources put into it reflecting its importance.'
>
> Nokia Connects for Nokia advocates

Interestingly, Wikipedia found something similar. They suggest that in a collaborative website such as a wiki, 90 per cent of the participants of a community only view content, 9 per cent of the participants edit content, and 1 per cent of the participants actively create new content. These numbers may reduce as people find themselves increasingly busy.

What percentage of your audience, your fans, your likers will engage with your site, blog, page or whatever platform/s you use? Some are more active than others. And some of the active audience are more active than others. You need to know (and reward) these active people, as they are your advocates.

Do not forget staff advocates. If your employees can be mobilized to share and engage with the content marketing that you are generating, this can amplify your content and messages enormously. Tools like GaggleAMP help staff advocacy expand its reach with accessible content, league tables and more.

Communications models

No simple diagram can reflect all the nuances and complexities of the communication process. This section considers some basic theories and models.

Single-step communications model

There are three fundamental elements in communication: the sender (or source), the message and the receiver, as shown in Figure 5.3.

This basic model assumes that the sender is active, the receiver is inactive or passive and the message is comprehended properly. In reality this is rarely the case. Chapter 4 demonstrates how we see what we want to see and not necessarily what is sent. An understanding of the target receiver or audience helps to identify what is important to the audience and how symbols, signs and language are interpreted. The message is 'dressed up' or 'coded' in an appropriate way, sent through a media channel and, if it gets through all the other noise, finally 'decoded' by the receiver. Guinness advertisements basically ask their target audience to drink Guinness, but they are very carefully coded. For example, 'It's not easy being a dolphin' were the only words uttered in one of their television advertisements. The audience decodes the message (correctly or incorrectly) and ultimately rejects, accepts, stores or decides whether to include Guinness in its 'considered set of brands' or not. Correct decoding does not always work; for example, an anti-drink ad campaign backfired by inadvertently glamorizing the habit (see the next box, 'Decoding drunken messages'). Amidst the careful coding and decoding there is noise; the extraneous factors that distract or distort the coded messages. Figure 5.4 demonstrates this.

FIGURE 5.3 A simple communications model

The sender monitors feedback (eg whether the receivers change their behaviour, facial expression, beliefs or attitudes) so that the message (and/or the channel in which it is sent) can be modified or changed. With so many other advertisements out there it is easy to understand why so little communication actually gets through and works on the target market.

Despite the attractions of one-to-one marketing, mass communications such as television advertising are still considered attractive because they can reach a large audience quickly and cheaply (when comparing the cost per thousand individuals contacted). In fact, although TV channels are fragmenting, TV viewing is increasing year on year in most of

FIGURE 5.4 The communication process

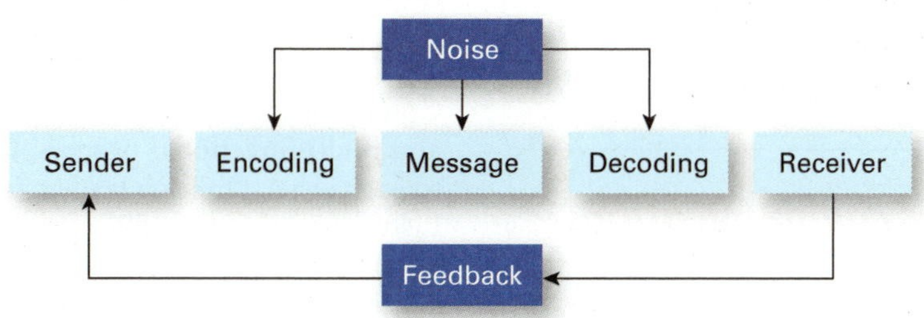

SOURCE: Based on Schramm's 1955 model

Europe and the United States. Having said that, much of this kind of mass advertising is often ignored or distorted by an individual's information processing system. However, there is usually, within the mass audience, a percentage who are either actively looking for the particular product type or who are in a receptive state for this type of message (see the financial services example in the box 'Floating targets' on p 267). Mass communication is therefore of interest to many marketing communicators. It is not the single-step process it was considered to be in the early mass communications model shown in Figure 5.5.

This kind of inaccurate model of mass communication suggests that the sender has the potential to influence an unthinking and non-interacting crowd. Audiences (receivers) are active in that they process information selectively and often in a distorted manner ('We see what we want to see'). Receivers (the audience) talk to each other. Opinion formers and opinion leaders also influence the communications process. Today's communications models are more sophisticated.

Decoding drunken messages

'Drinks manufacturer Diageo's "The Choice Is Yours" campaign implied that being very drunk with friends carries a penalty of social disapproval. However, for many young people the opposite is often the case. A University of Bath research team found adverts which show drunken incidents – such as being thrown out of a nightclub, or passing out in a doorway – are often seen by young people as being typical of a "fun" night out, rather than as a cautionary tale. Lead researcher Professor Christine Griffin said: "Extreme inebriation is often seen as a source of personal esteem and social affirmation amongst young people."'

BBC News Channel (2007)

Two-step linear communications model

Katz and Lazarsfeld's two-step hypothesis (1955) helped to reduce fears of mass indoctrination by the all-powerful media. It assumed that mass messages filtered through opinion leaders to the mass audience. Figure 5.6 shows how messages are filtered through opinion leaders, as well as going directly to some members of the target audience.

When **opinion formers** (OF) are added in, the communications model becomes a little bit more interesting. Opinion formers can be separated from opinion leaders, as shown in Figure 5.7. Opinion formers are formal experts whose opinion has influence, eg journalists, analysts, critics, judges or members of a governing body. People seek their opinions, and they provide advice. Opinion leaders, on the other hand, are harder to identify – they are not formal experts and do not necessarily provide advice, but other buyers are influenced by them. Other customers look toward them. Opinion leaders often enjoy higher social status (than their immediate peer group), are more gregarious and have more confidence to try new products and services. Endorsements from both opinion formers and opinion leaders are valuable.

The opinion formers are often quoted in promotional literature and advertisements, while the style leaders are often seen with the brand through clever editorial exposure engineered by public relations professionals. This can be generated by collecting third-party endorsements, creating events around celebrities and 'placing' products alongside celebrities (eg branded mineral water on the top table at press conferences or actual product placement in films). In **B2B markets**, blue-chip customers are opinion leaders and are much sought after, as their presence on a customer list influences other customers. Both opinion formers and opinion leaders can contribute towards credibility. 'Credibility before visibility' means that a solid platform of credibility should be developed before raising visibility with any high-profile activities.

Multi-step linear communications models

Communication is in fact a multifaceted, multi-step and multi-directional process. Opinion leaders talk to each other. Opinion leaders talk to their listeners. Listeners/recipients talk to each other (increasingly with discussion groups and internet groups) and subsequently feed back to opinion leaders, as shown in Figure 5.8. Some listeners or readers receive the message directly and some recipients talk to the message sender (eg the brand) directly.

FIGURE 5.5 One-step communications model

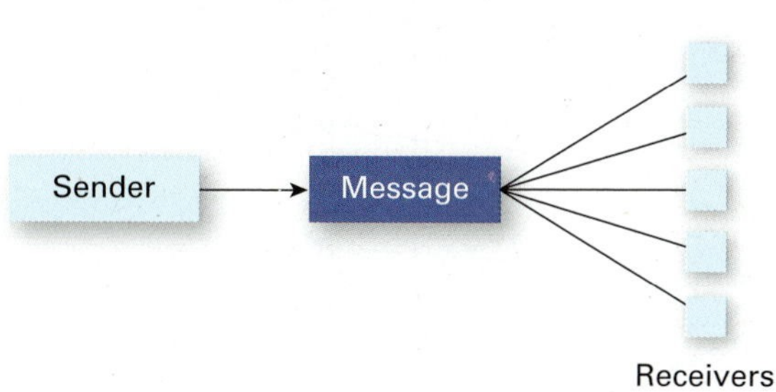

Noise, channels and feedback can be added to the multi-step model to make it more realistic, as shown in Figure 5.9. Feedback can either be formal market research, or customers communicating with the brand (via social media or CRM/customer service) or customers communicating about the brand (most brands actively listen to online discussions about their brands using listening tools – more later).

Meanwhile, the process of communicating with groups is fascinating. Group roles (leaders, opinion formers/leaders and followers), group norms and group attitudes are considered in 'Group influence' (p 146). In fact, all the intervening psychological

FIGURE 5.6 Two-step communications with opinion leaders (influencers)

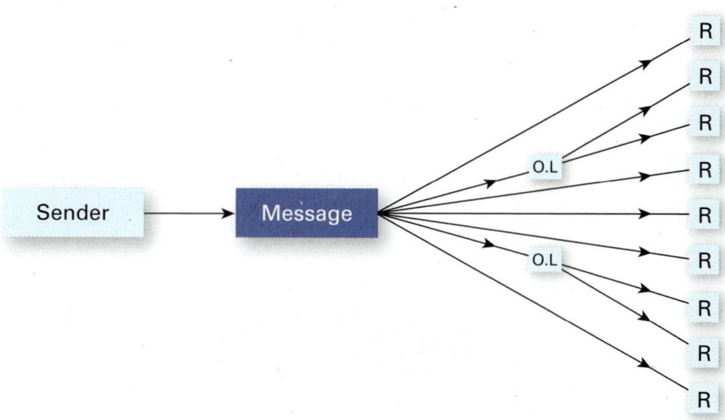

FIGURE 5.7 Two-step communications with opinion leaders and opinion formers (influencers)

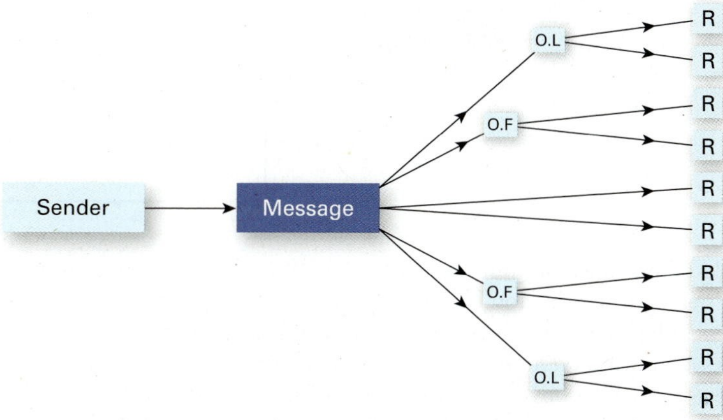

FIGURE 5.8 Multi-step communications model (a) with OL talking to each other

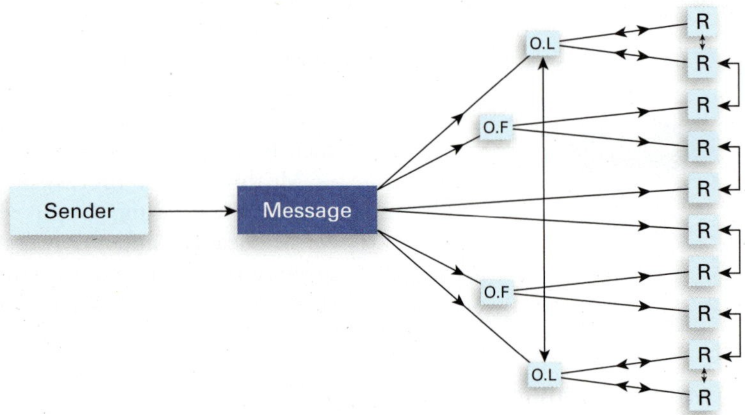

FIGURE 5.9 Multi-step communications model (b) with OL talking to each other and recipients talking back to OLs (and brands)

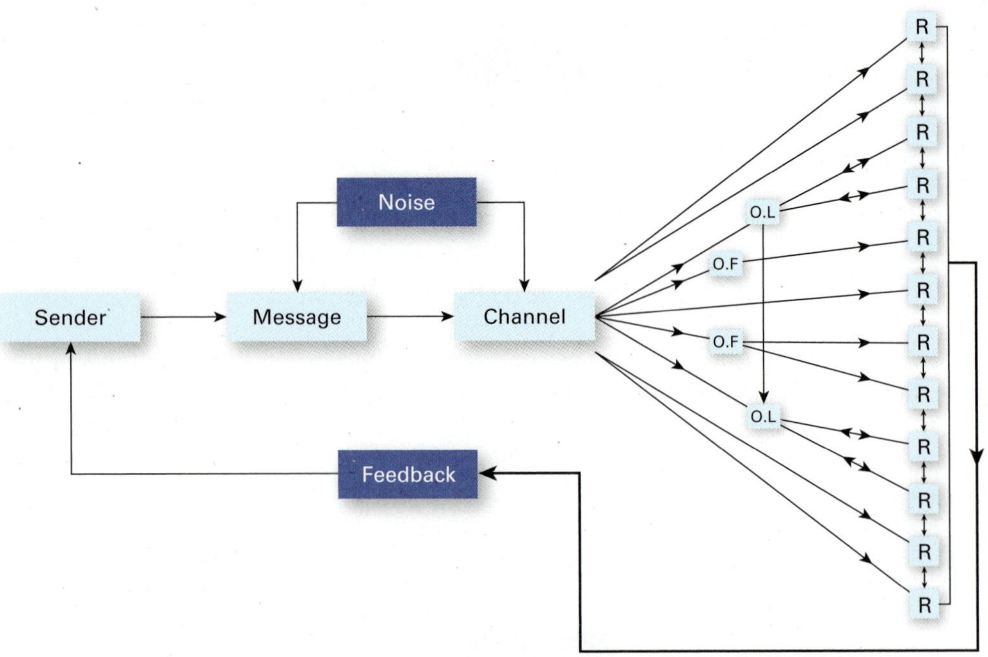

variables can be added into the communications models to show how perception, selection, motivation, learning, attitudes and group roles all affect the communication process. The intervening variables and some more complex models of buyer behaviour are considered in more detail in Chapter 4.

Winning over opinion leaders/influencers can be key to any marketing communications campaign, whether B2B or B2C. Take B2B: IBM linked up with the Marketing Society, as its 3,500 members represented key movers and shakers in the business world. Consider B2C: KangaROOS trainers targeted opinion-leading celebrities and children's TV show presenters by giving them free shoes. P&G, Unilever and Microsoft trial products with hundreds of thousands of people.

James Bond: Opinion leader/influencer extraordinaire

The fictional character James Bond, and the 25 movies about, him have always influenced others. From the Aston Martin sports car to Avon, Omega and Coca-Cola, product placement has generated significant revenues for the James Bond franchise. From Pan Am (remember that airline?) to Virgin Airlines, they all feature in various Bond movies and all of these brands have influenced others.

Personalized communications

Database marketing and direct mail perfected the personalization of messages in the 1980s. Then email marketing (1990s) combined with marketing automation (2000s) took personalization to a new level. It has been possible to personalize web pages for some time (so that pages greet each visitor by name and offer them tailored, relevant, content). Now, very **fast, scalable and extremely personalized videos have arrived.**

How about 50,000 personalized trailer videos for xyz movie (with an individual's name and the words they have actually posted about the movie xyz on social media) – all delivered within two hours? Most, if not all, of the 50,000 recipients of this personalized video are very likely to share this personalized video with their friends.

People posting comments about the movie with the hashtag (#moviexyz) can be tracked. Their comments are considered to be a form of 'intent' (or interest). 'Their tweet or comment and sometimes their photo are collected and embedded in the movie trailer (which appears in the clip's first three seconds – remember shortened attention spans)' (Redgate, 2019). They are then given the option of keeping the personalized video or deleting it and of course opting out or in re any future communications.

The Martian: Personalized video trailers

20th Century Fox create personalized trailers for *The Martian* on Twitter to drive highly personal and meaningful interactions with fans, and 'the engagement levels were out of this world' (Redgate, 2016a). It does not give studios carte blanche to spam everyone who has ever mentioned going to the cinema or 'liked' a film. 'Engagement needs to be focused (and must), **identify real intent** from fans and use content which will resonate. Ignoring this could in fact do more harm than good'(Redgate, 2016b). See Chapters 13, 16 and 20 for more. See **http://prsmith.org/blog/** 'Imagine what you could do with this video?' (2019).

> 'This kind of personalized content really amplifies our social campaigns, taking these channels to a new level of relevance for fans... that goes beyond traditional social marketing.'
>
> Chris Green, Marketing Director at 20th Century Fox (2016)

This changes the original communications model to look like Figure 5.10. Sender sends personalized/individualized messages directly to recipients or via an opinion leader/influencer. This personalized video process enables recipients, subsequently to become nano-influencers when they share the video. This is what some chief marketing officers now call one-to-one mass marketing.

Listening to your market's conversations

Listening to the market has never been easier. Here are seven ways (adapted from PR Smith's 'Social listening skills' blog post, **http://prsmith.org/blog/**, 2014). Listen to:

- customer service;
- customer feedback (post-sales try Reefo, Feefo or Trust Pilot);
- customer communities (GetSatisfaction, UserVoice, UserEcho);
- local chatter (Twitter's advance search, Hootsuite, Social Bro);

FIGURE 5.10 Revised communications model: One-to-one mass marketing

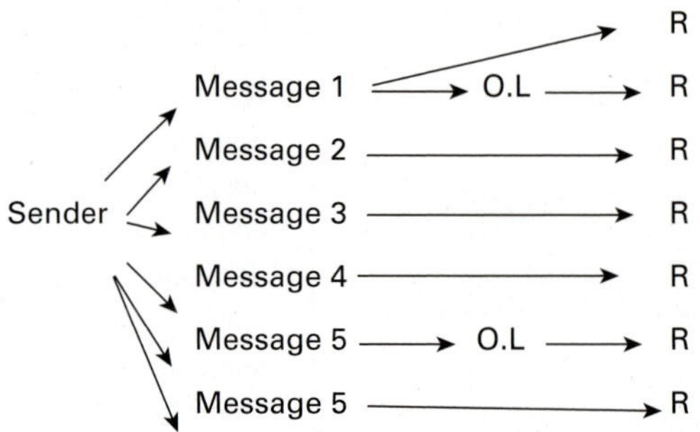

- websites (listen to several via feed readers);
- influencers (GigAlert, Newslee, Followerwonk);
- the mood of the market – sentiment analysis (Talkwalker, Brandwatch).

You can also search for topics, brands, products, by searching for specific hashtags, just like Tim Redgate's team did for *The Martian*.

Organizations that are not listening to online conversations about their brand are missing a major opportunity. If someone attacks a brand there is an opportunity to address any criticisms and rectify the issues before the rumours spread out of control. If someone applauds a brand there is an opportunity to leverage this comment. Conversations cannot be controlled like advertising messages, but organizations can feed accurate information into conversations as well as being seen to listen and care. In addition to collecting crucial feedback, ideas and public comments from the marketplace, marketers are provided with a welcome platform to get their message across, if it is relevant. This also grows a brand's presence wherever the market congregates online. Ignoring these conversations leaves an organization on the outside, soon to be replaced by another brand that does want to be a part of the conversation.

Social media provides a platform to:

- reach out to increasingly difficult-to-contact customers;
- help customers by sharing expertise (and the brand) with audiences;
- listen and engage in conversations about your brand.

This **requires a cultural and organizational shift** for some marketing departments to become a listening and sharing culture rather than a selling culture.

Develop a systematic listening team and a system to use the information

Who listens to and responds to comments on all the relevant social media platforms? Who compiles the analysis and the reports? Who analyses the comments, complaints and suggestions? What happens to all this valuable feedback information? More and more organizations are using third-party organizations or their software to scan for any online comments, discussions or tweets regarding their brand, their company, their customers or their competitors.

Personalized communications models: Messaging

Fifty-five billion messages are sent every day on the WhatsApp message platform alone (Tung, 2017). WhatsApp has 1.5 billion users, Facebook Messenger has 1.3 billion users (both are owned by Facebook) and China's WeChat has 1.1 billion users (Statista, 2019). Back in 2017, the messaging apps already had 20 per cent more monthly active users than social networks and 3 billion snaps were created every day on Snapchat (Mediakix, 2017). It looks like messaging is getting bigger than social media.

> The question emerges: **Is messaging the world's new media channel?**

These messenger apps help users communicate with each other singularly and/or in groups. They can receive personalized content, watch videos, chat with their contacts, and even shop with these apps. Marketers realize that these messenger apps have massive user numbers and therefore they are a serious new medium to consider, even though it is a one-to-one conversation model using personalized communications (Figure 5.11).

R is receiver

The average value of a WeChat user, by 2020, is estimated at $15.65 while the average user on Facebook is forecasted to be worth almost $5 (Clark, 2017). This is likely to increase as Facebook continues to develop new features (music, TV, and ecommerce).

Personalized communications models: Chatbots and messaging

As more and more humans socialize via social media (via mobile), and as more and more transactions are done via mobile, it is perfectly logical for marketers to follow their customers into this space. With 2.5 billion customers using instant messaging (IM) (*The Economist*, 2016) on Facebook, WhatsApp and China's WeChat, an opportunity opens. Within a couple of years IM will reach about half of humanity – 3.6 billion people. We are not quite there yet! But heading in that direction.

Combine this with customer dissatisfaction from lousy customer service (including endless automated telephone service systems and sloppy chatbots) and a double opportunity opens. **High-quality chatbots can fill this opportunity gap.**

Facebook Messenger developers had already created 100,000 bots for Messenger in the first year of the Messenger Platform (Johnson, 2017) while other platforms such as Twitter, Skype and Slack are actively promoting chatbots. Chatbots can be integrated into many social media channels, and CRM and marketing automation systems. This requires one-to-one communications as in the personalized message model Figure 5.11.

Companies are beginning to realize that one of the key places for selling and servicing is on Facebook or WhatsApp rather than just web pages. With 2.5 billion people using instant messaging and spending on average 200 minutes a week on WhatsApp, that's quite a market. (Lobo, 2017). (Note that these numbers differ to other research findings.)

WeChat offers a good example of how this can function. Consider a restaurant, where users can read the menu, order and pay through the mobile

FIGURE 5.11 A one-to-one conversation model using personalized communications

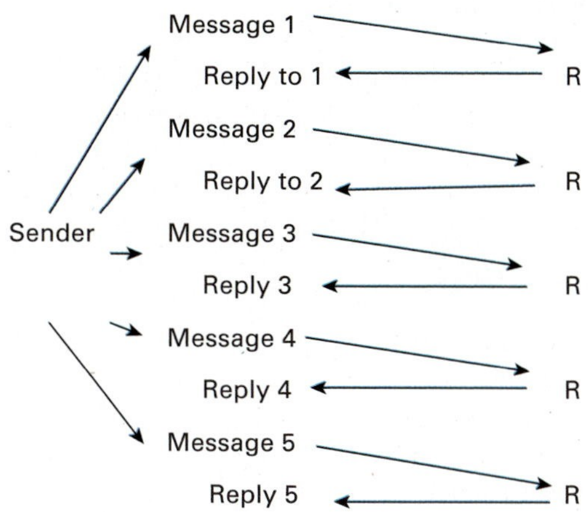

FIGURE 5.12 Active monthly users on messenger apps

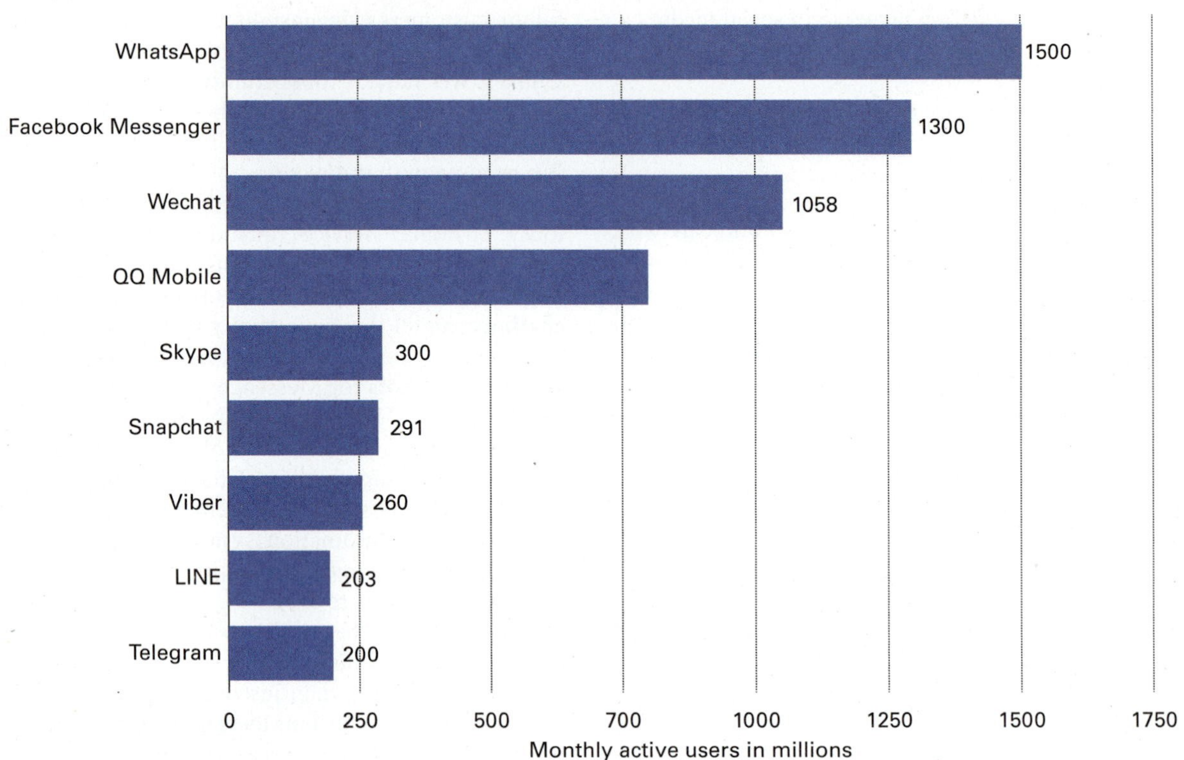

SOURCE: Statista (2019)

phone app. Indeed, it has been so successful that 40 per cent of mobile transactions in China are now through WeChat.

Chatbots, or chat apps that use artificial intelligence to receive and respond to messages, are rising in popularity. Typical outreach click-through rate ranges from 15–60 per cent compared to a click-through rate of 5–10 per cent for a marketing email (Siu, 2018).

National Geographic's genius chatbot

'National Geographic promoted its TV show *Genius* (chronicling the lives of figures like Albert Einstein and Pablo Picasso). The Nat Geo *Genius* Facebook page presented a messenger bot for each feature programme, eg for the programme on Einstein the bot could chat with users and share information about the show including quips about relativity and other Einstein topics.

The chatbot channel has to be the best marketing channel for customers. "Talking to Einstein" in real time – albeit via bot – delivered a human 1-2-1 chat with the great man as if the user were speaking to a friend and simultaneously connecting the brand and consumer in a more intimate way.

In one day alone, the bot has generated stellar engagement, including 6 to 8-minute average conversations, 11 turns per conversation, 50 per cent user re-engagement, and an involved community of followers.'

Siu (2018)

Personalized communications models: AI avatar chatbots

As mentioned earlier, have a look at @LilMiquela on Instagram to see the next level of communications where one-to-one conversations can be held with her 1.5 million followers. At present, we are unsure whether it is AI driven or manually uploaded. We suspect AI – so keep an eye on this model (literally).

Advantages of chatbots

- Always on 24/7/365.
- Never get tired, sick, take holidays, or require insurance or medicals.
- Faster – solving customer problems or getting the job done – which satisfies customers.
- Better service – getting cleverer – perhaps eventually serving customers better than humans.
- We already prefer to deal with a machine than a human when withdrawing cash.
- They collect data all the time.

Disadvantages of chatbots

- Fear of fake bots, negative bots, trolls, used to pollute and hijack conversations.
- Possible breaches of copyright or defamation of an individual or organization – who is liable?
- Customers think bot conversations are private one-to-one conversations without realizing the conversations can be viewed and analysed by humans.
- Bots can turn negative (witness the video of Sophia in Saudi Arabia – see **http://prsmith.org/blog/**) and Microsoft's chatbot 'Tay', who in 2016 learned to become a swearbot supporting Hitler with just 24 hours of machine learning.
- Data must be carefully managed in line with GDPR – if not, large fines are coming.

Just Eat's chatbot gets abuse, occasional wit and marriage proposals.

'Two challenges: parrying the f**k offs and flirtations, while making sure customers get their food on time. If at any point you say, "My food is late", then it triggers to a human being. Not relying on a piece of hardware to have an interaction.'

Crowcroft (2018)

For more on clever bots, shopping bots, marriage bots, divorce bots, research bots and videos of the world's first robot citizen, Sophia, see **http://prsmith.org/blog/** or specifically see 'Here come the clever bots: Bursting with artificial intelligence?' (16 July 2016) and 'Here come the really clever bots: Where AI meets customer needs' (8 November 2017).

Integrated marketing communications are more important than ever. Chief marketing officers (CMOs) now have a broader role, which realigns marketing communications with the new realities of customer decision-making. They have to manage the usual marcomms, product development, market research, and now data management.

Multi-step non-linear communications models

Let's take this a stage further and consider a communications model, where conversations revolve around the brand rather than just being messages sent by the brand. Markets are conversations. Word of mouth conversations and comments work more quickly online than offline. Online customers can talk, **first to each other** (C2C) and **second, back to the company** (C2B). The flow of communications eventually becomes like a web of conversations woven between customers and opinion leaders – and all built around the brand (see Figure 5.13).

FIGURE 5.13 Simple web communications model

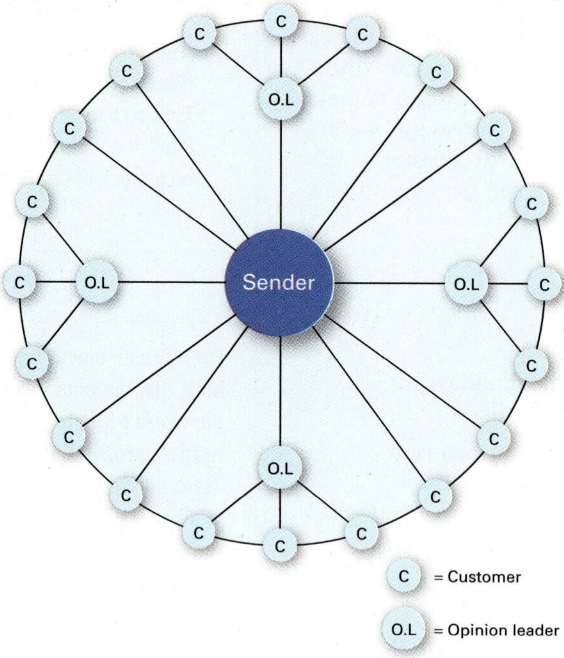

There are conversations about your brand between customers. There are other conversations started by **influencers**, many of whom are paid to do so; some just have to wear the brand or attend a brand event or venue to trigger other opinion formers (journalists) to trigger another conversation. In a sense, a web of conversations is spinning around the brand.

Marketers monitor these conversations, which include comments, likes and shares. Another conversation or comment that generates a lot of business is a referral, where happy customers become **advocates** and recommend or refer other customers to your brand.

Another form of referral is **affiliate marketing** where a third-party website promotes another brand in return for a percentage commission, eg websites that host a page promoting the SOSTAC® Certified Planner programme earn 15 per cent from any traffic that (a) comes from the affiliate site to www.SOSTAC.org and (b) converts (registers to take the course).

Finally, Figure 5.14 shows an advanced communications model with customers talking to each other on forums, groups, platforms and opinion leaders talking to each other too – all about your brand. This could be a conversation (usually sharing some interesting content) going **viral** if there are a lot of opinion leaders/influencers talking about it.

Chewing gum hysteria

Rumours spread in the Egyptian university town of Al-Mansura that after chewing certain brands of gum female students experienced uncontrollable passion for their male peers. *Time Magazine* (1996) reported that 'in a society where girls are expected to remain virgins until marriage the news has generated considerable anxiety. Suspicion of who might be spiking the gum with aphrodisiacs fell on the usual suspect, Israel, frequently accused of supplying the Egyptian black market with pornography. However, laboratory analysis showed that some gum samples actually lowered the libido.' Scientific fact may not be relevant. For once a rumour gets going, 'the suggestibility factor can be so strong that it can greatly affect one's mind and actions without there being a scientific explanation', says sociologist Madiha El Safty.

FIGURE 5.14 Advanced web communications model

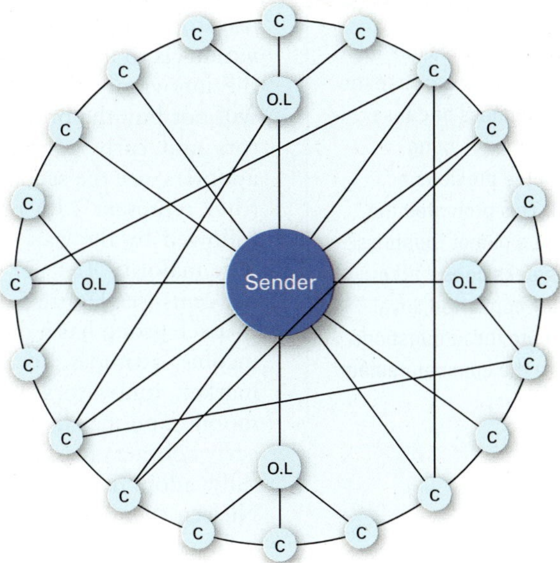

Adoption model

Several different hierarchical message models are considered in Chapter 4. The adoption model (Rogers, 1962) is such a model. As shown in Figure 5.15, it attempts to map the mental process through which individuals pass on their journey towards purchasing, and ultimately adopting (or regularly purchasing), a new product or service. This somewhat simplistic hierarchical model is nevertheless useful for identifying first, communication objectives and second, the appropriate communications tools.

For example, television advertising may create awareness, while a well-trained salesperson, expertly designed brochure or product comparison website, or iPhone app may help individuals in the evaluation stage. In reality, the process is not simply hierarchical. Some individuals move directly from awareness to trial, while others loop backwards from the later stages by never actually getting around to trying the new idea, subsequently forgetting it and then having to go through being made aware of it again.

FIGURE 5.15 The adoption model

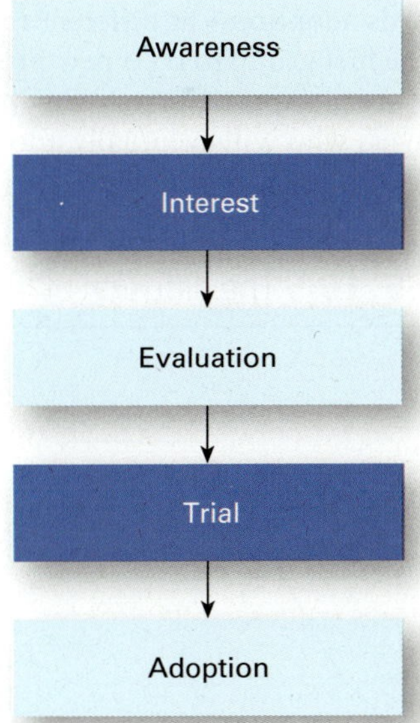

Guinness: An individual's adoption process

Although it is not a new product, Guinness has adapted the adoption process. They researched the adoption process for a pint of Guinness because high increases in consumption among young session drinkers resulting from the previous ad campaign were not sustained. This prompted the questions: How does one adopt a pint of Guinness? How many pints, sessions or weeks does it take before becoming a regular, fully converted, loyal Guinness drinker? The answers to these questions were carefully collected before the commencement of the campaign.

The diffusion of innovations

Rogers (1962) was also interested in how a new idea spreads or diffuses through a social system or market. He defined diffusion as 'the spread of a new idea from its source of invention or creation to its ultimate users or adopters'. Several groups who moved towards adoption – at different rates – were identified. The first group to try a new product were called 'innovators' (approximately 2.5 per cent of all of the buyers who will eventually adopt the new product). Their profile was very different from those who were last to try a new idea (the 'laggards'). Opinion leader characteristics were part of the innovators. The key to successful marketing of innovations is to identify, isolate and target resources at the innovators rather than everyone (84 per cent will not buy the product until they see the innovators and early adopters with it first). The 'early adopters' are the second group to adopt a new idea (they represent 13.5 per cent of the total market), followed by the 'early majority' (34 per cent), the 'late majority' (34 per cent) and the 'laggards' (16 per cent) (see Figure 5.16).

FIGURE 5.16 The diffusion of innovations

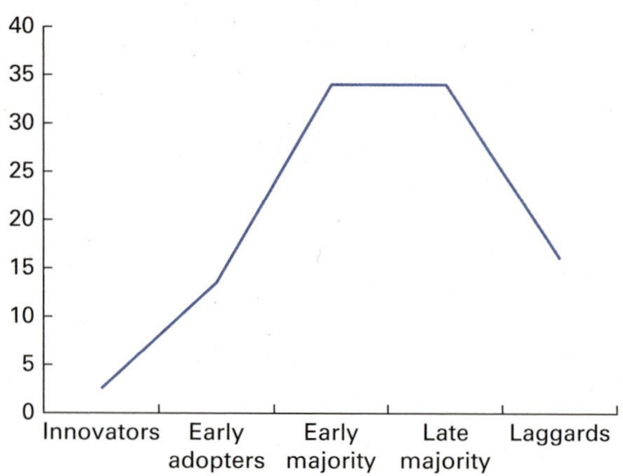

SOURCE: Rogers (1962)

Each group has a different profile, encompassing income, attitudes, social integration, etc in a B2C market. Innovators are venturesome and socially mobile, and they like to try things that are new. The early adopters tend to be opinion leaders who carefully adopt new ideas early. In the retail sector, Nielsen identified early adopters as multiple card holders (among other things), who are very different from single card holders in that they are significantly more promiscuous in their card usage. The early majority (who adopt earlier than the majority of the market) are even more careful, almost deliberate, in their buying process. The late majority adopt only after they have seen the majority of people try it. They tend to be sceptical. The laggards are self-explanatory – tradition-bound and the last to adopt.

Crossing the diffusion chasms

Geoffrey Moore (1999) applied the diffusion of innovations to the B2B sector and, in particular, technology innovation. Although he gave different names to the segments, the principle was the same: focus on and find the innovators and early adopters first. His key point is that there are gaps between the segments – gaps so big that they are chasms into which many companies fall and never climb back out (see Figure 5.17). The gap between early adopters and the early majority is massive. Whereas the former seek innovative products, like exploring how they work and accept some teething problems, the latter group (the early majority) will accept only a tried-and-tested fully functional solution with zero risk. They will also seek a different package. In the e-learning market, while early adopters like IBM were happy to buy CDs and make them integrate with their training programmes, the early-majority

FIGURE 5.17 Diffusion of innovations: The chasm between the segments

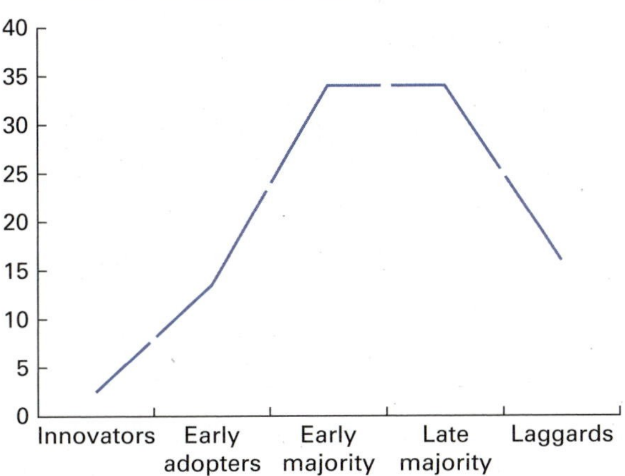

SOURCE: Moore (1999)

customers like BT needed a different solution: CDs, workbooks, textbooks, workshops and accredited training programmes. This was a completely different solution (to the same problem), albeit a much more lucrative sale. Other e-learning companies did not understand the difference between the two types of customers and the chasm between them. Many threw millions of dollars at the e-learning market and it all fell into the chasm. Casualties followed.

Marketers must recognize that offering exactly the same innovation (solution) to all the innovator segments in total marketplace will fail. Match the proposition (and the actual solution delivered) to the unique needs of each segment. This is the magic marketing formula once again (identify needs, reflect them back to the buyer and deliver a reasonable product or service).

Accelerating diffusion – the tipping point

Malcolm Gladwell's *The Tipping Point* (2000) applies to both B2B and B2C. It explores that moment when ideas, products, trends and social behaviour cross a certain threshold and spread like wildfire. In his book, Gladwell suggests three key initiatives that release the viral potential of new ideas, products or services:

- *The law of the few.* A relatively small group of adventurous influencers are powerful. Marketers need to identify these gregarious and socially active 'connectors' and then develop relationships with this small group of 'socially infectious early-adopters' or connectors (Gladwell, 2000).
- *The stickiness factor.* The product, service, idea or message has to be intrinsically infectious. Marketers need to systematically 'tweak and test' or refine and improve against diffusion criteria. 'By tinkering with the presentation of information we can significantly increase stickiness' (Gladwell, 2000).
- *The power of context.* Ideas and innovations spread quickly when they fit the context or are relevant to the group or its environment. You can exploit the bonds of memory and peer pressure in groups of 150 or less. 'In order to create one contagious movement, you often have to create many small movements first' (Gladwell, 2000). That's why many small, tightly targeted movements are better than one large movement.

Many organizations, including giants like P&G, Unilever, Diageo and Microsoft, started their tipping point initiatives several years ago. P&G set up its 'connector panel' in 2002 in the United States with 200,000 infectious teen connectors used to research and seed new products. Prior to that, Microsoft recruited 450,000 early adopters to trial Windows 95 in 1995 ('ensuring that one in every 189 PC users had a pre-release copy'), enabling Microsoft to 'capture critical pre-launch feedback for the mass market launch whilst giving the consumers that count a unique preview of their product that would generate word of mouth' (Marsden, 2004).

The end of the traditional marcomms funnel model?

Marketers aim to reach customers at the moments that most influence their purchasing decisions. **The old 'funnel' communications model started with creating awareness** (the wide end of the funnel with many brands) and then brand familiarity, followed by brand consideration, followed by purchasing a single brand (followed by repeat purchasing of the same brand, ie loyalty, where only one brand is chosen).

Is the old funnel dead? Should you change your model?

'Consumers are moving outside the purchasing funnel – changing the way they research and buy your products. If your marketing hasn't changed in response, it should.'

Court *et al* (2009)

The old linear funnel model misses many of the new touchpoints, which can occur late in the buying process. For example, a customer is looking at buying brand X, but just before clicking the 'buy' button she checks for customer comments and ratings both on the same site and on other sites, effectively going back to the 'evaluation' stage of other linear buying models despite being apparently at the 'decision' stage (see p 126).

Marketers need to be where these points of influence occur, whether at the offline point-of-sale or merchandising point or the online point-of-sale, or in the offline and online word-of-mouth discussion. For the latter, marketers monitor discussions about their brand (and their competitors' brands), whether on Twitter, forums or blogs, and automatically post their messages (some 'canned' or pre-prepared) into the conversation, with links to videos, demonstrations, testimonials or the brand itself. This can be done manually or as part of automated marketing (scanning, identifying and rules-based selection of responses).

Customer lifecycle journey model

It is important to help visitors or prospects to become customers using a variety of tactical tools and eventually help them to become repeat (lifetime) customers, with a few lapses along the way. Continual relevant and personalized (if possible) contact helps to build a healthy relationship with customers.

'This "relationship" begins today with the first contact with the customer when they are simply a contact or prospect. We believe that the best way for a company or brand to build relationships is through a planned **always-on marketing approach** of integrated communications across multiple digital channels. To enable this, we're fortunate today to have many martech options for marketing automation, so we can create a coordinated contact strategy to engage audiences through:

- automated email marketing like welcome, nuture and win-back sequences;
- display ad retargeting, eg via Google AdWords Display network remarketing;
- on-site personalization recommending next best-product, offer or content to convert;
- social media retargeting available on Facebook, Instagram, Twitter and LinkedIn;
- traditional channels like direct mail or phone contact.

This renewed focus by marketers on prospect and customer engagement, conversion and retention has led to the appearance of a new phrase in the digital marketing lexicon: customer lifecycle marketing, or sometimes just lifecycle marketing.'

Chaffey (2018)

Sequential communication

We need to think about a sequence of communications and not just campaigns. From first contact to welcome (onboarding) to ongoing help. Apply the customer lifecycle journey model to your communications. Interestingly, the 2019 KPI report by Wolfgang Digital highlights this:

> The best converting websites have the ability to attract that user back to their websites time and time again. As a result, they have thundered ahead of their one-click-wonder competitors. Focus on ways you can re-engage your previous website visitors through remarketing to really move the needle on revenue growth. Long gone are the days when 'remarketing' was executed by chasing a user around the Internet with the same banner ad until they puked. Remarketing done right, by today's best marketers, is a sophisticated sequential communication. Creating additional touchpoints, each adding a new layer of value, and reaching the

same user on a new channel is about the smartest thing a digital marketer can do in 2019.

Wolfgang Digital (2019)

Late deciders wait until inside the store

'Consumers want to look at a product in action and are highly influenced by the visual dimension: up to 40 per cent of them change their minds because of something they see, learn, or do at this point – say, packaging, placement, or interactions with salespeople.'

Court *et al* (2009)

Attention, branding and communication model (ABC)

Kerris Bright recently said that during her 10 years at Unilever, her team worked on the premise of the ABC model, 'attention, branding and communication'. She pointed out that often marketers forget the importance of 'attention' – if the message fails to cut through nothing else really matters (Rogers, 2019).

New models required

The IoT means that devices, equipment, houses, cars, clothes will communicate with us. We will no longer be dependent on smart phones, tablets and laptops as we step into the post-mobile era, as messages will arrive into our spectacles, car windscreens, our jackets and clothes and all over our homes and offices. So new communications models are required, with the opinion formers, leaders and influencers sometimes being machines, search engines and AI partners/suppliers/facilitators. Add to this the wonderful array of 3D messages and customer experiences being delivered by virtual reality and augmented reality and we have an exciting new communications frontier – requiring new thinking and new communications models.

New skills required

Scott Brinker (2009) suggests marketers need five new skills:

- *Analytical pattern skills.* Mastering the flow of data from social media feedback, web analytics, transaction histories, behavioural profiles and industry aggregates.
- *Agile project management.* As tactical campaigns fragment into more granular, relevant, niche-like propositions, each one targeted at dozens, hundreds or even thousands of different contexts, fast-moving, multiple project management skills are required.
- *Experimental curiosity and rigour.* As marketers seek constant improvement on their marketing ROI, they manage a constant flow of tests, testing new alternatives, exploring new creative executions and monitoring changes in response rates to identify immediate opportunities and threats.
- *Systems thinking.* Marketing is a set of processes. This means connecting all the parts. Who gets customer comments, summaries and key issues arising from social media conversations? Which decisions does it influence? Who else needs this information (eg salespeople, PR people, the board of directors) and what decisions can it affect?
- *Mashable software fluency.* Those marketers who understand the mashable web – a world of mash-ups, widgets and application programming interfaces (APIs) – will have competitive advantage. For example, it is possible to connect and integrate a website's content management system with site search, RSS feeds, email alerts and e-newsletters, all serving very relevant content. Rose (2006) defines mashable in terms of a 'web page or application that uses and combines data, presentation or functionality from two or more sources to create new services'.

Many of the previously discussed models offer some insight into the communication process but, almost invariably, they distort or oversimplify the process of communication. Chapter 4 draws on some of the communication models discussed here and looks at buying models, the buying process and the intervening psychological variables. How do we buy? Why do we buy? What influences our choices? Are there unconscious motives playing havoc with our day-to-day shopping behaviour? Chapter 6 attempts to look inside the customer's mind and answer some of these questions.

Key points from Chapter 5

- Communication involves a two-way flow of information.
- Communications also involves multiple flows of information.
- Influencers are playing an increasingly large role in communications.
- AI is and will continue to be integrated with communications.
- Communication theories can be applied to practical marketing situations.
- New models are required to meet the changing communications landscape.

References and further reading

BBC Capital (2018) The fascinating world of Instagram's virtual celebrities, BBC Capital, 2 April

BBC News Channel (2007) Warning on anti-drinking adverts, 10 December

Berners-Lee, T (2008) Google could be superseded, says web inventor, *Times Online*, 12 March

Berners-Lee, T, Hendler, J and Lassila, O (2001) The semantic web, *Scientific American*, May

Bernstein, M, Bakshy, E, Burke, M and Karrer, B (2013) Quantifying the invisible audience in social networks, CHI 2013, 27 April–2 May

Brinker, S (2009) 5 new skills for the future of marketing, *Chief Marketing Technologist* (blog), 23 February [online] http://chiefmartec.com/2009/02/5-new-skills-for-the-future-of-marketing/ (archived at https://perma.cc/A7DY-NCX5)

Carroll, G (2010) Jargon watch: Delinkification, *Renaissance Chambara* (blog), 5 June [online] http://renaissancechambara.jp/2010/06/05/jargon-watch-delinkification/ (archived at https://perma.cc/YYW4-RMX5)

Chaffey, D (2018) What is customer lifecycle marketing? *Smart Insights*, 25 April

Chen, Y (2017) What influencer marketing really costs, *DigiDay*, 5 June

Clark, D (2017) 2017 tech trends: Chatbots will reshape messaging apps, *Wall Street Journal*, 26 October

CMA (Competition and Markets Authority) (2019) Social media endorsements: Being transparent with your followers, CMA, 23 January

Court, D *et al* (2009) The consumer decision journey, *McKinsey Quarterly*, June

Crowcroft, O (2018) The next chatbot you speak to could be hiring, *Linkedin News*, 2 October

Crystal (2013) The 90-9-1 rule: Dead, different, or a distraction? *Cultivating Community*, 8 July

Cutlip, S, Center, A and Broom, G (2004) *Effective Public Relations*, International edn, Prentice Hall International, Englewood Cliffs, NJ

Ehrenberg, A (1988) *Repeat Buying*, 2nd edn, Charles Griffin, London

Engel, J, Warshaw, M and Kinnear, T (1994) *Promotional Strategy: Managing the marketing communications process*, 8th edn, McGraw-Hill Education, Homewood, IL

Floch, J-M (2001) *Semiotics, Marketing and Communication*, Palgrave, Basingstoke

Gladwell, M (2000) *The Tipping Point*, Little, Brown, New York

Godin, S (1999) *Permission Marketing*, Simon & Schuster, Hemel Hempstead

Golson, J (2009) When it comes to links, color matters, *Gigaom*, 9 July

Green, C (2016) Interview with John McDonald, 20th Century Fox taps EchoMany to tweet personalised Deadpool movie trailers, *The Drum*, 8 February

Guirdham, M (1999) *Communicating across Cultures*, Palgrave, Basingstoke

Johnson, K (2017) Facebook Messenger hits 100,000 bots, *Venture Beat*, April

Katz, E and Lazarsfeld, P (1955) *Personal Influence: The part played by people in the flow of mass communications*, Free Press, New York

Kelman, H (1961) Process of opinion change, *Public Opinion Quarterly*, 25, Spring

Kotler, P (2000) *Marketing Management: Analysis, planning, implementation and control*, International edn, 11th edn, Prentice Hall, Englewood Cliffs, NJ

Kulp, P (2018a) How artificial intelligence is transforming influencer marketing, *Adweek*, 20 August

Kulp, P (2018b) Artificial influencers are attracting the attention of brands, *Adweek*, 20 August

Lee, K (2015) Why your social media posts are more popular than you think: Inside the invisible audience, *Buffer Social*

Lobo, J (2017) 3 options for using chatbots for ecommerce, *Smart Insights*, 11 December [online] www.smartinsights.com/digital-marketing-strategy/3-options-for-using-chatbots-for-ecommerce/ (archived at https://perma.cc/5AJN-529P)

Lucas, J (1997) License to sell, *Marketing Director International*, October

Ma, F (2018) Kylie Jenner, Selena Gomez top Instagram's rich list, *WWD*, 25 July

Manning, J (2012) 5 trust-winning tactics, *The Marketer*, 26 October

Markoff, J (2006) Entrepreneurs see a web guided by common sense, *New York Times*, 12 November

Marsden, P (2004) Tipping point marketing, *Brand Strategy*, 1 April

McConnell, B and Huba, J (2006) The 1% rule: Charting citizen participation, *Church of the Customer Blog*, 3 May [online] web.archive.org/web/20100511081141/http://www.churchofthecustomer.com/blog/2006/05/charting_wiki_p.html (archived at https://perma.cc/P6XF-YBWE)

McGovern, G (2013) New thinking: The functional heart of web design, 21 April [online] http://gerrymcgovern.com/the-functional-heart-of-web-design/ (archived at https://perma.cc/E4J2-BDT3)

Mediakix (2017) The 8 messaging app statistics advertisers need to consider, *MediaKix*, 22 May

Moore, G (1999) *Crossing the Chasm*, 2nd edn, Capstone, Oxford

Redgate, T (2016a)A How brands can keep up with the personalisation trend, The Wall Blog, 13 April

Redgate, T (2016b) Movie studios should use personalised video to get punters into the cinema 2016, LinkedIn, 8 February

Redgate, T (2019) Video interview with PR Smith, Personalised Videos At Scale, [online] http://prsmith.org/blog/ (archived at https://perma.cc/67JZ-HYWA), 1 May

Richards, J (2008) Google could be superseded, says web inventor, *Times Online*, 12 March

Rogers, C (2019) The BBC's customer chief on the power of marketing at the 'extreme edges': Interviewing BBC'S Kerris Bright, *Marketing Week*, 24 January

Rogers, E (1962) *Diffusions of Innovations*, Free Press, New York

Rose, B (2006) Marketing mashup tools, *iMedia Connection* (blog), 27 June [onine] www.imediaconnection.com/content/10217.asp (archived at https://perma.cc/H6Q8-PEPX)

Schramm, W (1955) *The Process and Effects of Mass Communications*, University of Illinois Press, Urbana

Sillence, E, Briggs, P, Fishwick, L and Harris P (2004) Trust and mistrust of online health sites, 2004 Conference on Human Factors in Computing Systems

Siu, E (2018) 9 most innovative chatbot examples in 2019 from top, brands (and how to build your own), *Impact*, 24 May

Smallbone, D (1969) *The Practice of Marketing*, Staples Press, London

Smith, PR (2001) Online eMarketing Course: eCustomers [online] http://multimediamarketing.com/ (archived at https://perma.cc/PUG4-LB46)

Smith, PR (2014) Social listening skills, 6 January [online] http://prsmith.org/blog/ (archived at https://perma.cc/67JZ-HYWA)

Smith, PR (2016) Here come the clever bots: Bursting with artificial intelligence? 16 July [online] http://prsmith.org/blog/ (archived at https://perma.cc/67JZ-HYWA)

Smith, PR (2017) Here come the really clever bots: Where AI meets customer needs, 8 November [online] http://prsmith.org/blog/ (archived at https://perma.cc/67JZ-HYWA)

Smith, PR and Chaffey, D (2001) *eMarketing eXcellence*, Butterworth-Heinemann, Oxford

Solis, B (2012) The rise of digital influence, *Altimeter*, 21 March

Stampler, L (2018) Advertisers are giving people with 1,000 Instagram followers endorsement deals, *Fortune*, 13 November

Statista (2019) Most popular global mobile messenger apps as of October 2018, based on number of monthly active users (in millions) [online] Statista.com (archived at https://perma.cc/6QHY-RR6V)

The Economist (2016) Bots, the next frontier, 9 April

Time Magazine (1996) Chewing gum hysteria, 22 July

Tuck, M (1976) *How Do We Choose? A study in consumer behaviour*, Methuen, London

Tung, L (2017) WhatsApp: Now one billion people send 55 billion messages per day, *ZD Net*, 27 July

Wolfgang Digital (2019) KPI report 2019 [online] www.wolfgangdigital.com/kpi-2019/ (archived at https://perma.cc/RT45-KAU6)

Further information

The Nielsen Company
85 Broad Street
New York, NY 10004
USA
www.nielsen.com

Ofcom
Riverside House
2a Southwark Bridge Road
London SE1 9HA
Tel: +44 (0)300 123 3000
www.ofcom.org.uk

The Semiotic Alliance (formerly Greg Rowland Semiotics)
332 Lordship Lane
London SE22 8LZ
Tel: +44 (0)7779 611 656
www.semiotic.co.uk

06 Marketing communications research

LEARNING OBJECTIVES

By the end of this chapter you will be able to:

- understand how market research reduces risk and improves decision-making;
- list and explain the different types of research tools available;
- apply the marketing research process;
- appreciate the advantages and disadvantages between online and offline research;
- identify and avoid the potential problems.

Introduction to market research and decision-making

Relevant information reduces risk, increases power and creates competitive advantage if used correctly. Today's marketers have to be ruthless with their information needs and know exactly what it is they need to know. Then prioritize it, collect it, digest it and then, make better decisions equipped with this information.

> ### *The X Factor*: Market research makes the decisions
>
> Simon Cowell's TV phenomenon *The X Factor* uses research in a very structured and systematic manner. He researches various product concepts (singers) by testing them with customers (audiences at home and at the theatre). The customers provide free market research, revealing which product they prefer. The customers also pay for this privilege (as they vote by phone). He then refines the product concepts (trains them and adds some production effects) and repeats the market research exercise (all the time making money from the research). The final product testing is done with a chosen song, which has already been recorded by each finalist. This final layer of market research almost guarantees the success of the new product (a pop star). The finalists present their version of the song. The market research respondents (audience) complete the 'survey' via a text message (while paying for this privilege and simultaneously being highly engaged with the *X Factor* brand). The most popular product is identified (most votes). The product (star) is launched and usually becomes a chart-topping product.

Relevant information reduces risk

As more and more relevant information becomes available, risk eventually reduces to zero and certainty emerges. The young woman in the card trick story (later in this chapter) could pick the ace as soon as she knew what the other three cards were. Market research (information) also reduces risk. So why not use research to reduce all risks? There are three reasons – the three key resources (the 3Ms, men/women, money and minutes) are limited. Firstly, knowing exactly what information is required and how to gather it (whether commissioning a research agency or handling the research in-house) is a relatively rare management skill (the ability to ask great questions); secondly, research costs money; and thirdly, it takes time to define and write a brief, carry out the fieldwork, analyse the data, write and read a report and, ultimately, act upon the information. The fieldwork (asking the questions and collecting the answers) can also give competitors an early warning of intended activities. It can, sometimes, alert them and give them time to respond.

Relevant information increases power

In both military and marketing strategies, information creates power. If your organization knows what its customers really want, and its competitors do not, then it has a powerful advantage. If you know what a competitor's next move is before they make it, then you are in a stronger position to react or even pre-empt the move. In negotiations, if one party knows more about the other party's real needs, their resources and their options then the information holder has a huge hidden advantage.

The classic salesperson versus buyer situation emphasizes how sales and profits can be increased as a direct result of information: the salesperson desperately wants an order and is prepared to cut prices to get the business. The buyer desperately needs to buy the salesperson's product because all stocks were destroyed the night before in a fire and the salesperson's company is the only company that can supply the products immediately. If the buyer knows how desperate the salesperson is, then a low price will be negotiated by the buyer. If the salesperson knows the buyer's desperate situation, the salesperson has the power. In addition, the salesperson takes even more control if the buyer does not know how desperate the salesperson is to make a sale. In this situation the salesperson will make the sale, probably at a higher price. Information is power. Information can boost prices and profits.

Asking great questions increases success

Notice how senior managers always seem to ask questions that are potentially embarrassing (because sometimes you don't know the answers). When they ask the question, you might think, 'I wish I'd thought of that'. Questions are indicators of ability and seniority, or potential seniority. The ability to ask the right question is a precious skill that usually takes time and practice to develop. The ability to ask the right question is the precursor to providing the right answer. This is becoming increasingly important as too much information becomes available and the potential for information overload and information fatigue grows.

Information advantage: World chess championship

To avoid giving his competitor too much information, Bobby Fischer wore a green visor to stop Spassky, the challenger, from looking into his eyes during an alternative world chess championship.

Relevant information improves decision-making

Before making a serious decision, always ask whether you have the right information to make a great decision. Then define what information you need. Get this information, digest it and then, and only then, make an informed decision. The alternative is guesswork, which relies on luck, and is usually an unnecessarily high-risk activity. On the other hand, proprietary relevant information (or knowledge) effectively creates competitive advantage, eg if an organization has unearthed some deep customer insights that no one else has.

What is Big Data?

Big Data refers to relatively large amounts of structured and unstructured data that require machine-based systems and technologies in order to be fully analysed. 'The much-hyped term has inspired a slew of definitions, many of which involve the concepts of massive volume, velocity and variety of information. In other words, what turns data into Big Data is the amount of information, and the speed at which it can be created, collected and analysed' (Kaye, 2013). Big Data is not scary nor draconian nor Orwellian.

Big Data is everywhere

Here are 10 useful ways Big Data is used – that you probably didn't know – from Lady Gaga to premature babies:

1. The FBI is combining data from social media, CCTV cameras, phone calls and texts to track down criminals and predict the next terrorist attack.
2. Supermarkets are combining their loyalty card data with social media information to detect and leverage changing buying patterns. For example, it is easy for retailers to predict that a woman is pregnant simply based on her changing buying patterns. This allows them to target pregnant women with promotions for baby-related goods.
3. Facebook is using face recognition tools to compare the photos you have uploaded with those of others to find potential friends of yours.
4. Politicians are using social media analytics to determine where they have to campaign the hardest to win the next election.
5. Video analytics and sensor data of baseball or football games is used to improve the performance of players and teams. For example, you can now buy a baseball with over 200 sensors in it that will give you detailed feedback on how to improve your game.
6. Artists like Lady Gaga are using data of our listening preferences and sequences to determine the most popular playlists for their live gigs.
7. Google's self-driving car is analysing a gigantic amount of data from sensors and cameras in real time to stay on the road safely.

8 The GPS information on where our phone is and how fast it is moving is now used to provide live traffic updates.

9 Companies are using sentiment analysis of Facebook and Twitter posts to determine and predict sales volume and brand equity.

10 A hospital unit that looks after premature and sick babies is generating a live steam of every heartbeat. It then analyses the data to identify patterns. Based on the analysis the system can now detect infections 24 hours before the baby would show any visible symptoms, which allows early intervention and treatment.

Marr (2013)

See p 97 for information on using data for profiling and prospecting, progressive profiling and integrating all contact points, and layering on top third-party databases to deliver even more specific profile information defining exactly who your customer is and how to reach them. See also p 377 on using location-based data combined with third-party databases to target prospects very precisely.

How to make the perfect decision

1 Define the issue, opportunity or problem clearly.
2 List what information you need to make a great decision.
3 Get the information.
4 Digest the information.
5 Decide.

Cloud wars

'The marketing cloud is marketing nirvana – a place, or a hub, where marketers automate and integrate all customer data, automatically analyse it then continuously and automatically serve highly relevant engaging content across multiple channels at just the right time on the right platform to the right customer. Fast-moving marketers will use the marketing cloud (multichannel marketing automation, content management tools, social media tools and analytics platforms – more later) to create a wall around their customers, which competitors will consequently find difficult to break down (particularly because of customers' changing behaviours). This is now a race towards an automated integrated digital marketing hub.'

PR Smith (2019)

Try this next time you have a big decision to make. You will find that you need some of the 3Ms (men/women, money and minutes); usually there are not enough minutes. However, if you plan ahead you will get more information to help you make better decisions. A lot of the information is free.

Information and competitive advantage

Can information be the principal source of competitive advantage? A large, comprehensive, well-maintained and GDPR-compliant database creates a mini market belonging, at least in the short term, to the company that owns the database. And databases are essentially carefully structured customer information. This delivers an advantage over a poorly managed database. Equally, information about your competitors can create competitive advantage if they do not have access to this information.

The card trick

An Oxford Street card trick man places four cards face down on a portable table. As the crowd gathers, he shouts, '£10 to anyone who picks the ace.' Embarrassment, scepticism and even mistrust run through the crowd. No one responds to the offer of a simple £1 bet to win £10. As the card man leans forward to show the crowd a crisp £10 note, a grinning young man leans behind the card man and sneaks a look at the outside card. It's a jack of diamonds. Word quickly spreads through the crowd that the outside card is not the ace. Prompted by the fun (and the improving odds) someone shouts, 'That's not a real tenner.' The card man responds by stepping into the crowd to allow a closer inspection of the £10 note. A second stranger boldly leans across and briefly turns the other outside card over. It's a two of hearts. The card man returns. 'Come on now. Who wants to win £10?' A well-spoken young woman replies, 'If you show me one of the two middle cards, I will place a £2 bet against your £10.' The card man accepts. What has happened here? Information reduced the risk to zero.

Marketing intelligence and information

Every organization needs marketing intelligence and information that lists secondary information sources, and also includes online information tools (many of which are free) that reveal instant information about your customers, competitors, channels and market trends. A marketing intelligence and information system (MIIS) should be structured and constantly refined as new sources become available and old ones become redundant.

Good marketing departments monitor competitors' prices, products, leaflets, advertisements, marketing content, social media platforms, satisfaction scores and customer comments if they can. This can be outsourced or done in-house. Estimating a competitor's marketing spend on, say, ads, social media and marketing content can also be done manually (by collecting all the competitor's press ads, social media content, seeing which content performs best on which platforms manually and then calculating the costs from experience and/or rate card costs less bulk discounts) or it can be done automatically online (by services like **www.spyfu.com** for ads and **https://buzzsumo.com** for marketing content across different platforms).

The sales force can, if trained, provide the most up-to-date and relevant information from the MIIS. They are closest to the marketplace and in touch with what is happening. They need to be encouraged to collect relevant information.

The intelligent rep

In the United States one particular chain of stores that sold Christmas crackers held buying days when their buyers would see visiting sales representatives. Appointments were not accepted and, once they had registered with the receptionist for the appropriate buyer, reps proceeded to queue in a waiting room on a first-come, first-served basis. The room had rows of desks with telephones, where the reps sat down quietly filling in order forms, drafting letters, completing call sheets and making phone calls. Although it was only 7.30 am, a dozen registered reps were already busily working away. By 8.05 am the room was packed. The large chap beside me was on the phone at 8.00 am reporting some hot information he had come across during another breakfast appointment earlier that day. He told his boss how the competition had offered the other buyer a new buyer-incentive scheme that would commence next month, followed by a new consumer-incentive programme scheduled four months down the road. They had now four months to react or pre-empt the competition!

Good salespeople are also masters at collecting information about new product ideas, market trends, and competitors' strengths and weaknesses. Some reps also ask buyers what words and phrases they use to search for their products and services. The answers need to be regularly and systematically sent back to the marketing team to be added to the key phrase inventory for search engine optimization (SEO) and pay-per-click (PPC) purposes.

Staff members throughout an organization can be trained or briefed as to what type of information is considered important. Staff, if motivated, can scan their preferred trade journals, newspaper, online newsletters, blog, Pinterest board, etc, for items of interest to the company. Alternatively, a press clipping agency can do this work, or Google Alerts will do a lot of the online scanning for free.

Some of this information can then be fed into a strengths, weaknesses, opportunities and threats

(SWOT) analysis. This is particularly useful in monitoring uncontrollable external opportunities and threats variables such as political, economic, social and technical factors. Many forecasting companies specialize in certain aspects such as social forecasting, and they will also carry out econometric forecasting, which correlates the likely sales effect resulting from a change in pricing or advertising expenditures (price elasticity or advertising elasticity).

As with all information, you must decide exactly what information and intelligence you need and when. Know which questions really need answers.

Today there are many online tools that can almost instantaneously deliver a stream of intelligence, answering questions about your competitors. Here are some questions that can be answered easily online by using some specific tools:

- How good are your competitors' websites?
- How good are your competitors' social media platforms?
- What social content works for your competitors?
- What Facebook content works for your competitors?
- What do customers say about your competitors?
- What keywords work best in your competitors' PPC ads?
- What inbound links are your competitors using?
- Do you have enough share of voice?
- How big are your competitors' marketing team and budget?

These and many more questions are explored in the 'SOSTAC® guide to writing your perfect digital marketing plan' (Smith, 2019). Remember to choose carefully which questions you need to prioritize, to avoid drowning in a sea of information, otherwise known as 'information overload'.

Information overload

By the end of today, another 4,000 books and another 7 million new web pages will have been published around the world. As Google CEO, Eric Schmidt (2010) said, 'Every two days we create as much information as we did up to 2003'. That means every two days we create as much information as was produced in 2,000 years. That's why we've got what Gerry McGovern calls 'content wars'.

In 2010, McGovern observed:

> Never before in history has the human being had such an ability to create information. Never before have we been faced with so much information. It's not faster computers. It's not bigger hard drives. It's information literacy we need. We need to create less information of a higher quality. We need to be able to manage information much, much better, getting rid of the junk and out-of-date stuff. We need skills that help us search better, and to be able to judge better and faster the quality of the stuff we find.

Amidst the information overload and fatigue, remember to laugh

'There is a very simple way of dealing with stress that is not often considered... laughing. Laughter cures stress by pumping adrenalin and endorphins into the bloodstream. It reduces muscular tension, improves breathing and regulates the heartbeat.'

Nurden (1997)

This is very much required in today's hypercompetitive marketplace.

Way back at the turn of the millennium, University of California professors Varian and Lyman (2000) noted that our ability to create information had far outpaced our ability to search, organize and publish it: 'Information management – at the individual, organizational, and even societal level – may turn out to be one of the key challenges we face.' Marketing managers must learn to manage **information pollution**; otherwise they will make ill-informed decisions and may well end up suffering from **'information fatigue syndrome'**. Reuters reported that information overload combined with analysis paralysis and poor quality of life reveals that 'one in four people admit to suffering ill health as a result of the amount of information they now handle' (Reuters, 2009). Out of 1,300 managers, two-thirds said that their social life was affected by having too much information to process at work.

Information prioritization

There is an unlimited amount of information available and obtainable to all marketing managers; more than any manager can absorb, let alone pay for, in any one period. So the key is to define precisely what the problem, or opportunity, is and outline the kind of information that will help to make a more informed decision. An experienced market researcher (whether in-house or from an agency) can guide the marketing manager towards defining specifically what kind of information is needed. Since the research budget is usually limited, the manager may then have to prioritize which kinds of information are more important than others. Ask for ambiguous information and a lot of ambiguous answers will be delivered. Ask for a dashboard and you will get a dashboard crammed with dials, charts and scores. It's worth thinking about exactly what information you really need before accepting any information.

Are you an information junkie?

It has been suggested in previous editions of this book that a growing proportion of internet users find themselves addicted to information online. Over 50 per cent of managers were accumulating information they didn't have the capacity to assimilate; in fact, they were overwhelmed by it. Over half the respondents pronounced themselves to be 'information junkies' who got 'cravings' for new information, especially online information.

Do you find yourself constantly checking your emails, text messages and Facebook? Do you allow yourself to interrupt your own conversations when you hear the ring of your phone or the ping of a new text message? Hoping, perhaps unconsciously, that this new information will be more interesting than the person you are talking to?

A certain amount of discipline is needed to focus on relevant issues and not become side-tracked by indulging in 'interesting' bits of information. When briefing a market researcher as to the kind of information that is required, it is often tempting to add extra, 'interesting' questions. Before adding extra information requests, think about your information priorities and check that the following questions are answered satisfactorily:

- What will I do with this information?
- How will it affect my strategy or tactics?
- What action or withdrawal may result from this information?
- How much is the information worth?
- How much will it cost?
- Can I afford it?
- When do I need it?
- Have I checked all secondary sources? (See Table 6.2, p 192.)

Common sense

For example, the highly successful ice cream manufacturer Ben & Jerry's observed an increase in complaints from buyers of Cherry Garcia ice cream. Many customers were upset because they felt that the product had too few cherries. What would you do? What extra information would you collect? This is what they did – they asked the following questions. Firstly, was it only a regional problem? They checked by matching shipment records with complaints. Secondly, did the problem arise from the manufacturing process – was the quality not up to scratch? But the ingredients turned out to be normal. After questioning almost every aspect, they finally found the source of the problem. The photograph on the ice cream carton was not of ice cream but of frozen yogurt, which appeared laden with cherries in comparison with the paler pink ice cream. They simply changed the image on the carton and the complaints melted away.

Correlation is not causation: 'Drinking coffee from corporate branded mugs increases job promotion'

'The survey found that 37 per cent of people who have a coffee mug with their company logo on it have been promoted within the last six months, compared to just 8 per cent of those people who did not have a coffee mug with their company logo on it.'

A merchandise company

Statistically this is bordering on the ridiculous. Counting numbers is one thing but suggesting the correlation is predictive is another. We need proof that this hypothesis has been tested properly and can prove that there is a statistically significant association between owning a corporate branded mug and getting promoted. To begin with, samples (that is, the number of respondents being surveyed) need to be large enough and also randomly chosen to be statistically meaningful. The structure of the questions, selection of respondents and statistical analysis all need to examined before validating this 'research'.

The market research process

Using information efficiently starts with the ability to define exactly what information is required. This is a valuable management skill. Defining the problem or defining the research objectives is the first step in the market research process (see Table 6.1). Then you can decide whether you and your team can collect this information, or whether you need to use an external market research agency and/or a data analytics company that can analyse Big Data (such as historical location data combined with real-time location and demographic data).

Problem definition and research objectives

Before going through the steps of the market research process, it is worth emphasizing the importance of defining exactly what information you need and which decisions it will affect. Otherwise you get information creep, delays and confusion.

It is important to identify specific segments and what information is required from each segment. A one-size-fits-all survey may not yield the quality of market research findings that a carefully refined and tailored survey will.

Research plan

The research plan clarifies whether to do the research via your internal team or to go to an external market research agency, and whether desk research (secondary research) is required before commissioning any primary research. Research methodology (eg observation, survey, experiment, focus group or survey) along with the tactical choice of fieldwork type (face-to-face, phone, online or post) and the required degree of confidence plus sample size, cost and timings need to be clarified.

After the questionnaires have been agreed (and sometimes piloted), and the interviewers have been trained, the fieldwork commences. Once that is completed the data must be analysed carefully to identify any significant findings. Conclusions (and sometimes recommendations) are subsequently reported or presented to the management team. Equipped with this information, the marketers can make their decisions.

Research brief

Depending on the type of research, the brief can include the situation, objectives and strategy (SOS) plus 3Ms from SOSTAC® (see p 264):

- situation analysis (including target and marketing mix);
- objectives of the research (problem definition – what information is required and what decisions should be made as a result of the research finding);
- strategy (why the information is required and how the research findings may affect the communications strategies);
- men/women (who will liaise with the agency);
- money (how much is the research budget?);
- minutes (timing – when is the information needed?).

Note that some clients prefer not to divulge too much strategic or tactical information for security reasons. On the other hand, the more the research agency knows, the more useful the contribution to the success of the project will be.

> **Subcontract research but not understanding**
>
> 'There are certain research functions, marketing research functions, that are sometimes provided by outside firms that are specialists in doing nothing but research. But the core aspect of marketing, which is understanding our customer and having a close bond with the customer, that should never be turned over to anybody else.'
>
> Kanter (1996, 2000)

Agency selection

If the organization is not handling the research in-house, a market research agency will be chosen. Some of the usual agency selection procedures will apply (see 'Agency selection process overview', p 220).

A shortlist of agencies can be developed from personal recommendations from colleagues and advertising agencies, and from the organization's own observation of research agencies and their advertisements or editorial coverage. Agency size, specialism or expertise, reputation, location and whether the agency works for any competitors can be used as shortlisting criteria. The agencies that 'pitch' or make a presentation will then be judged by the quality of their research proposal (Step 2 in Table 6.1), GDPR compliance, cost, credentials and spin-offs (like free training). Even small details can make an impression – for example, the number of bound reports that will be delivered when the research findings are eventually presented, or emailing presentations and providing client access to extranets, so that clients can monitor project progress. The personal chemistry or relationship between the client and the agency presenter is often the key variable that swings the choice of agency one way or another. It is also important to find out who will be handling the project and, if it is a junior member of staff, the degree of supervision that will be offered. The Interviewer Quality Control Scheme follows rigid procedures to supervise and check the quality of the information.

TABLE 6.1 The market research process

Step	Actions
1 Problem definition	Define what you need to know. Decide clearly what information is needed and why it is needed. Is it qualitative and/or quantitative? What will be done with it? What is the objective of this research?
2 Research plan	Internal or external (if using a market research agency a briefing must be prepared along with a carefully structured selection process). Data sources: secondary/primary. Research techniques: observation, survey, experiment, focus group. Sample: size and type. Degree of confidence. Fieldwork: face-to-face, online, phone or post. Questionnaire design. Cost and timing.
3 Fieldwork	Actual interviews/data collection and supervision.
4 Data analysis	Coding, editing, weighting, summing, consistency/check questions, extracting trends and correlations, if any.
5 Report presentation	The interpretation of the figures, summary and sometimes conclusions.
6 Action taken/not taken	If the information is not used, then perhaps it wasn't worth collecting in the first place.

Some agencies demonstrate great care about the security of the data they hold. Computer hackers pose a problem to any computer-stored data. Product test samples need to be controlled carefully and securely. All samples, mock-ups and concept boards need to be returned by the interviewers, and logged as returned once they are received by the research agency. They can then be kept under lock and key.

> **Ensure the agency is GDPR compliant**
>
> Check the agency is GDPR compliant. Note the research agency will be the data controller or joint data controller. See p 299 for more on GDPR. Also see Esomar (2017) for GDPR guidance for the research sector.

Visualization

It is a shame to see great research findings suffer from 'death by PowerPoint' – ie screen after screen, table after table. Visualizing data is a skill that helps communicate key findings with more impact to a wider audience. 'Visualization is an especially important tool to have in your data-gathering belt. Dynamic visualizations can simplify complex data and capture numbers in a graphic representation, which will speak more clearly to a wide swath of people' (Olenski, 2018).

Problems and challenges

There are many challenges associated with getting good market research. These include researching new ideas, sloppy briefs, sloppy interviews and much more.

Researching new ideas

How can answers to questions about anything that is new, unseen or previously untried be valid? The first commercially produced electric car, the Sinclair C5, had the benefit of some product research, but how can research ask people about something they cannot experience? Driving a C5 in a hall is very different from driving one along a coast road or a busy, wet and windy dual carriageway with a 40-foot truck trying to overtake. Here lies one of the difficulties with researching a new idea: how can the reality of some markets and product usage be simulated? Another problem lies with the difficulty in taking the novelty factor out. When presented with something new, buyers may be prepared to give it a try, but can the marketing people sustain the marketing effort after the excitement of the initial launch?

> **No one asked for a burger until they were invented**
>
> 'Consumers can't be expected to embrace previously unseen solutions. Let us not forget that no one had asked for a hamburger until they were invented.'
>
> Murray (1997)

The same applies to advertising. Most advertisements try to be new, different and refreshing. So how can research help produce something that is radically different to people's existing levels of expectancy? One of the UK's most successful advertising campaigns, 'Heineken refreshes the parts other beers cannot reach', had the normal focus groups and concept research carried out. It 'researched poorly', ie the results said, 'This is rubbish. We don't understand this type of ad. Don't do it.' Sir Frank Lowe (chairman of the advertising agency Lowe Group) tells the story of how he had to tell the client (Heineken) about the negative concept research findings on their radically different advertising concept. 'He [the client] took a very brave decision and placed the research report document in the bin. He said, "We had best leave that alone and get on with the ad!"' Expensive and carefully prepared market research findings are sometimes ignored.

Expensive research also gets it wrong if it fails to ask the right question. Even world-class companies can ask the wrong question and make huge mistakes. Take Coca-Cola – although it researched the taste of the new Coke, its 1985 flop occurred because it failed to research how consumers felt about dropping the old Coke. It is classic marketing history now.

> 'Blind comparisons which took no account of the total product... name, history, packaging, cultural heritage, image – a rich mix of the tangible and the intangible. To many people, Coke stands beside baseball, hotdogs and apple pie as an American institution. It represents the fabric of America. The company failed to measure these deep emotional

ties, but Coke's symbolic meaning was more important to many consumers than its taste. More complete concept testing would have detected these strong emotions.'

Kotler (2000)

The question they forgot to ask was: 'Would you buy this (new Coke) if we took away the old Coke forever?'

Real innovations are difficult to research because both customers and experts struggle to visualize their benefits. Henry Ford once said: 'If I'd listened to my customers, I would have invented a faster horse.'

Flawed research: Why new Coke flopped

'Sometimes research gets it wrong because it fails to understand that people can only buy a complete brand. People don't buy products; they don't buy packages; they don't buy brand names. They most certainly don't buy advertising. They buy the sum total of all those things. At one point the Coca-Cola company thought they could improve Coke and invented a new Coke. They had thousands of consumers in the US blind-test new Coke vs old Coke without telling them what it was. New Coke won. So the Coca-Cola Company launched new Coke. It failed miserably. When the company researched new Coke versus old Coke they missed the understanding that the brand Coca-Cola was far more than just a product. It's the sum total of all elements of the brand.'

George Bradt, former European Marketing Director, Coca-Cola (1996, 2000)

Errors to avoid

Here are some of the areas where problems can occur in market research:

- ambiguous definition of the problem;
- ambiguous questions;
- misinterpretation of the written question by the interviewer;
- misinterpretation of the question by the interviewee;
- misinterpretation of the answer by the interviewer;
- interviewer bias (eg if street interviewers select only attractive-looking respondents and exclude anyone else from the sample);
- interviewee inaccuracies (trying to be rational, pleasant, offensive, disruptive, knowledgeable when ignorant, etc);
- interviewer fraud (falsely filling in questionnaires);
- non-response (a refusal to answer questions);
- wrong sample frame, type or size;
- incorrect analysis;
- freak clustering of result (an inherent danger of sampling);
- timing (researching seasonal products out of season).

Types and costs of research

There are basically two types of research sources: primary and secondary. Primary data are gathered specifically for and commissioned by an organization for a particular purpose (eg a research survey to find out about attitudes towards a company's brand). Secondary data, on the other hand, already exist and have been gathered by someone else for some other reason (eg government statistics, newspaper features or published reports). Desk research can be carried out in a library or office, since it requires researching secondary sources. It is worth doing some desk research before embarking on the more expensive primary research. There are essentially two types of primary research: quantitative and qualitative. Analytics (like Google Analytics) are quantitative while neuromarketing/neuroscience (researching the effects of marketing stimuli on the brain) tends to be more qualitative (with smaller numbers of respondents than, say, a field survey).

Table 6.2 summarizes some of the many different types of research information that are readily available. The cost figures give only a very rough indication of the budget requirements. They have been included to give some idea of the costs involved. Anything can be researched and tested, including sales promotion ideas (concepts), mailshots and even press releases and journalists' attitudes to particular companies and brands.

TABLE 6.2 Types of research or information available

Information on	Types of research or information	Sources	Approximate costs
Markets	Market reports (analysing market size, structure, market shares and trends, prices, key players, etc)	Mintel Jordans Keynotes Syndicated *FT* and trade magazines	£750–£5,000 £1,000–£15,000 £1
Distributors	**Retail Audit** (analysing a brand's penetration into various retailer store categories, average stocks bought, held and sold per period, retail prices)	Nielsen	£15,000–£50,000*
Customers' attitudes and awareness	**Surveys** – recommended minimum of 200 interviews; preferably a minimum of 500 interviews	Quantitative market research agencies Omnibus surveys	£10,000–£60,000 £10–£100 per person interviewed** £200 entry fee + £300–£700 per question
Customers' motivations and perceptions	**In-depth research**, sometimes using projective techniques, children's groups, supergroups	Qualitative market research agencies	£650 per individual, £3,000–£5,000 per group of eight
Customers' future lifestyles	**Social forecasting, futurology**, etc	Future forecasting	£1,500–£5,000 annual subscription
Customers' buying behaviour and trends over time	Who's buying what, when and from where; how buyers respond over time to various marketing activities, eg special offers, new ads and competitor activities	Consumer panels, eg AGB's Super	£15,000–£40,000
Customers' penetration	**Market penetration** of production into percentage of homes and frequency of usage	Omnibus survey	£500 per yes/no question £1,500 per multiple answer/ranking
Competition	As for markets, distribution and customers, if the budgets are available. The sales force and marketing departments' 'ear to the market' can also provide much competitive information There are now many digital tools that gather competitor information very quickly.	As for markets, distribution and customers	As for markets, distribution and customers
Simulated test market	Total mix test of product, brand name, price, positioning	Nielsen Research International; RSG8	£25,000–£100,000

(continued)

TABLE 6.2 (Continued)

Information on	Types of research or information	Sources	Approximate costs
Test market	Running a new product or variation of its mix in a test area	Sales analysis	–
Product	New product concepts can be researched ('concept research')	Focus groups	£3,000–£5,000 per group of eight
Packs	New pack design concepts can be discussed	Focus groups Hall tests	£3,000–£5,000 per group of eight £5,000+
Advertisements	New advertisement concepts can be researched before going to expensive production. Pre-and post- advertising research measures levels of awareness before and after a campaign (tracking studies)	Focus groups Hall tests Quantitative survey Online tests	£3,000–£5,000 per group of eight £1,000+ £20–£40 per person £5,000–10,000
Exhibitions	Stand design, memorability, number of passers-by, number who stopped and looked, number who visited, percentage of total exhibition visitors	Exhibition surveys	£3,000

NOTES:

* Prices can vary enormously, eg a single brand retail price check might be carried out for as little as £750, while a full-blown retail audit for multiple products can run into hundreds of thousands of pounds.

** Depending on location and methodology plus set-up plus analysis costs.

Quantitative research

Whereas qualitative research asks difficult 'Why?' questions like 'Why do you buy or not buy something?' or 'Why did you stay, or not stay, on this website?', quantitative research, on the other hand, asks numerical questions like 'Who?', 'What?', 'How?', 'Where?' and 'When?' – what percentage of buyers buy which type of product, or what percentage remember a particular advertisement, where do they buy (what percentage buy from different channels), when do they buy, etc.

Quantitative research uses **surveys** based on a representative sample of the target market. Qualitative research, on the other hand, involves an in-depth, unstructured exploration with either small groups of individuals (group discussions or **focus groups**) or individuals on a one-to-one basis (**in-depth interviews**).

Research can provide the marketing professional with information on just about anything from markets to distributors, to customers, to competition, to new products, new packs, new promotions, new advertisements, new prices and so on. Different types of research can reveal information about customers, where they are located, what they buy, read and watch online and on TV, how they spend their holiday time, which competitors they prefer and so on.

Ideas on new, or modified, products, packs, brand names or advertisements can be discussed initially in focus groups (six to eight people), which generate information explaining how people feel about a concept. This kind of **concept testing** can be used to reduce a number of ideas to just one or two for further testing, or can be used to give feedback to the creative people so that they can refine a particular concept. These qualitative interviews open up and identify areas that may need further investigation on a larger scale (a quantitative survey) to find out how important certain aspects are among a statistically valid sample (minimum 400 in the sample).

In the case of a new advertising concept, or a new pack or brand name concept, the refined concept can then be shown in a **hall test** (where respondents are invited into a hall to make comments). The packs and brand name concepts can be shown as mock-up artwork, and the advertisements might be shown as either a storyboard or an animatic (video cartoon).

A new product (concept) can be tested by using **in-home trials** or **hall tests**. Some data sources, such as the Target Group Index (see p 195), are often used in the early research stages of consumer campaigns to identify buying behaviour, socio-economic groups, lifestyles, locations and appropriate media channels.

After all of this, a new pack or brand name (or product) can be test-marketed. This reduces the risk by holding back from national or international roll-out until the advertising campaign (or pack or name or product) can be tested within a representative test area. Owing to the high cost of test marketing, and the increasing difficulty in the UK of truly isolating the test market area (especially in terms of distribution, where the national retail chains do not want to limit stocks to certain parts of the country), companies often prefer to conduct a simulated market test instead of carrying out a test marketing exercise. Some of the main research companies in the field are Burke (BASES test), Nielsen (QUARTZ model) and Research International (MICROTEST). These models use information from the concept test or product test, simulate an expected level of distribution penetration (percentage of stores that will stock the product), assume a certain level of advertising spend required to generate certain levels of awareness, and then assume competitive activity, prices and other factors to predict the likely sales of a new product with an accuracy of +/–20 per cent.

Since television advertisements can be expensive, many companies prefer to do all the careful checking and testing through focus groups and hall tests instead of testing the advertisement in a specific test region. They can, and do, however, test the weight of advertising in different regions and measure the incremental sales to help them to find the most cost-effective levels (frequency and timing) of advertising expenditure.

If a product is launched nationally or regionally, its launch can be monitored in several ways. Its usage (user profiles, frequency of purchase, etc) can then be monitored through consumer panels. Retail audits provide information about distribution penetration and how the product is moving off which shop shelves. It is also likely that tracking studies will monitor the immediate reactions and effects of the launch advertising. Pre- and post-quantitative surveys can monitor the levels of branded awareness before and after a new campaign breaks, and can then be used again to measure the effect of the advertising and the product's development in the marketplace.

Omnibus surveys

Omnibus surveys allow marketers to add a few very specific questions (eg one standard question with up to 10 options or two statements against a scale) and get quick, statistically valid answers from over 2,000 respondents within 48 hours. A popular one is the UK government's own **www.gov.uk**.

Home audits

Instead of, or in addition to, retail store research, **home audits research the customer directly**. The retail audit data can be backed up with customer usage data. Representative families (sample size: 8,500) are recruited and asked to log all their purchases using a bar code recorder. The device asks for the name of the store and the price paid per brand, etc. Non-bar-coded items are recorded on paper. Analysis of this wealth of data over time shows consumers' repertoire of brands, the effects of sales promotions on purchases, frequency of purchase, etc. This is automatically cross-referenced with the household's demographic data already held. Diaries and dedicated dustbins were once used to collect this type of information. Today the automated online bar code system is preferred.

Retail audits

Retail audits **monitor share of shelf space, prices and turnover** of particular brands (including competitors') in a large and representative sample of retailers. It is worth noting that Boots, Sainsbury's and Marks & Spencer do not allow auditors to come into their stores. This means that the audit results have to be weighted and adjusted. Where auditors are allowed access, they check shelves, facings, prices and stock levels. Most fast-moving consumer goods (FMCG) companies buy these audits, since they provide a picture of what is happening at the retail level. Bar codes and laser scanning can provide much of this information online directly to the user. Sales out of shops do not necessarily reflect actual customer usage. Home audits (see above) can provide customer purchase information.

Look at external averages/ competitor activities

Internal figures, such as sales, percentage of sales expenditures (of say advertising), response levels, cost per order or enquiry, etc, can and should be compared with external industry averages or competitor activities. Not all the information is readily available immediately, but competitors' sales figures (of grocery products and some other large markets) are available from companies such as Nielsen Retail Audits. Information on levels of advertising is available from Nielsen Media Research.

The Target Group Index

The Target Group Index (TGI) global network of market research surveys provides comparable consumer insights for over 60 countries across six continents. TGI quarterly surveys identify who a brand's target customers are, why they behave and make choices the way they do and how best to reach them. They deliver the most comprehensive insight into the online and offline behaviour of consumers.

TGI studies explore the motivations of the individual, from the conscious to the subconscious, across different product sectors:

- lifestyle attitudes;
- social DNA: economic and cultural capital;
- values;
- motivating factors/criteria of choice;
- the purchasing process;
- consumer segmentations, including electronic, shopper, social media and holiday.

TGI surveys measure the relationship between and exposure to nearly 1,500 media sources for comparative and competitive analysis at a granular level:

- press (weighted to the National Readership Survey);
- radio;
- television;
- internet;
- mobile internet;
- out of home;
- cinema;
- direct mail.

The Target Group Index (TGI) collects and compiles information on consumer brands and the profiles of heavy, medium and light users, and non-users, in a vast range of product categories and subcategories. This is all cross-referenced to types of papers read, TV programmes viewed, and lifestyle or attitude statements. It can even classify 'light users' according to whether they buy a brand exclusively ('solus users'), whether they prefer it to another brand also used ('most often users') or whether they are more casual in their use ('minor users'), again cross-referenced to demographic data, lifestyles and media used. Advertisers use the TGI to find out who the users of a particular brand are and what they read, watch and listen to. The same information is available on competitors and their brands.

Elsewhere, the index also gives lifestyle data, eg 'heavy drinkers of low-alcohol lager'. This gives an insight into what motivates them. The excerpt in Figure 6.1 shows that they are keen pub-goers and have a propensity to try new drinks. They are highly image conscious, aiming to keep abreast of new fashions. They appear to be fairly 'flash with the cash' and admit to being no good at saving money. In spite of, or maybe because of, this, they show a strong tendency to seek the advice of a financial consultant. They see their holidays as a way of achieving total relaxation, not wishing to do anything but eat, drink and lie in the sun.

Just about anything can be cross-referenced with any other variable. For example, the index can identify Heinz beans users and what kind of cars they drive. Another package, called 'trender', can be used to track product, brand, attitudinal, demographic or media trends. The index can also link into various online geodemographic packages.

FIGURE 6.1 An example of lifestyle data from the TGI

Base: NEW 18+
Pop: 20699
Private Eye Target:HEAVY DRINKERS OF LOWALCOHOL BEER AND LAGER
Pop: 1155(000) Xof Base:5.57

		INDEX	UNWTD RESP	PRJ (000)	VERT (%)	HORZ (%)
1	D8 DRINK LAGER RATHER THAN BEER THESE DAYS	176	183	366	31.68	9.83
2	PA9 I LIKE TO KEEP UP WITH LATEST FASHION	165	53	121	10.47	9.20
3	T7 HOLIDAY-ONLY WANT TO EAT, DRINK, SUNBATHE	165	75	158	13.67	9.18
4	PA15 MEN'S FASHION MORE EXCITING NOWADAYS	161	105	238	20.60	8.96
5	F7 I TEND TO SPEND MONEY WITHOUT THINKING	160	65	141	12.20	8.96
6	SP3 CO'S/PRESTIGE SPONSOR ART/SPORT	157	88	190	16.45	8.76
7	DH6 HEALTH FOODS ONLY BOUGHT BY FANATICS	155	78	179	15.49	8.65
8	D9 I LIKE TO TRY NEW DRINKS	155	70	143	12.38	8.65
9	D12 I REALLY ENJOY A NIGHT OUT AT THE PUB	146	164	345	29.87	8.12
10	P4 I WOULD LIKE TO BUY A HOME COMPUTER	142	58	148	12.81	7.92
11	F4 I AM NO GOOD AT SAVING MONEY	138	87	190	16.45	7.72
12	F15 USUALLY CONSULT FINANCIAL ADVISOR	138	62	114	9.87	7.68
13	PA2 IT'S IMPORTANT TO LOOK WELL DRESSED	137	104	247	21.38	7.65
14	T11 TRY TO TAKE ONE+ HOLIDAY ABROAD A YEAR	135	60	116	10.04	7.55
15	PA13 I REALLY ENJOY SHOPPING FOR CLOTHES	134	70	130	11.25	7.50

Social media audits

Look before you leap. It is essential to carry out an audit before jumping into the blogosphere. As always, the brand and the organization need to check that it is credible and ready to become more transparent, as social media can probe into many previously protected areas of the business. A social media audit explores **how an organization (and/or its brands and high-profile staff) and its competitors are seen in relevant online communities:** what is being discussed, what is required, whether the organization has existing assets (contents, eg speeches) and how ready the organization is (includes training, systems and processes and generating content and participating in discussions). The audit also looks at current presence, whether blog, Twitter, Flickr or YouTube, and the levels of engagement and traffic or followers. The audit explores the organization's social media goals (eg a direct channel with customers, to gather research, to improve customer service, to reach out to new audiences or markets, to add value to existing customers, etc), as well as its resources and restrictions (policy issues about content or trade secrets, any legal or political constraints or any internal issues about sensitive information).

Online analytics and behavioural insights

Analytics packages, like Google Analytics, can tell you who your visitors are (or at least give a general profile), what they are interested in (page views and key phrases used), where they are coming from (how they found your site, via search engine or referral from another site, etc), their journey (multichannel analytics), which types of journeys converted the best (got the most newsletter signups or sold the most products). Many free packages like Twitter analytics or Hootsuite can tell you where your followers are from, which of them are influencers, where they are from, who is talking about you, what they are saying, even who is attending a conference and what they are talking about before, during or after the event (if they add the conference hashtag to their tweets). Facebook Insights and LinkedIn Website Analytics offer alternative analytics.

Behavioural insights

Behavioural insights can come from customer observations, click behaviour analytics or drawing upon a range of interrelated academic disciplines (behavioural economics, psychology and social anthropology). 'These fields seek to understand how individuals take decisions in practice and how they are likely to respond to options.' Formal research can be requested from groups like The Behavioural Insights Team or data analysis companies, or managers can be simply tasked to present their key 'learnings'/insights from their marketplace when they present their key performance indicators.

Potential behavioural insights are sitting on many people's desktops unused. Most analytics packages can be used to identify what works best by split testing a single variable (such as price, image, words, or colours on website pages, ads or emails).

Behavioural insights: The greatest untapped marketing asset

'Most marketers are not exploiting the value of behavioural insights (capturing and consolidating customer behavioural data from multiple channels in a single database). Despite newly automated processes (marketing automation), marketers are increasingly capturing this data, but not using it to build better marketing campaigns.'

Forrester Consulting (2013)

Ethnographic research

Ethnography is the systematic study of people and their cultures. It explores cultural phenomena where the researcher observes society from the point of view of the subject of the study. 'Ethnography is the study of social interactions, behaviours, and perceptions that occur within groups, teams, organizations, and communities' (Anderson, 2006).

Ethnographics help Intel

'Ethnographic research is more valuable than traditional surveys and market research. The ethnographic work at my company, Intel, and other firms now informs functions such as strategy and long-range planning. Ethnography is the branch of anthropology that involves trying to understand how people live their lives. Unlike traditional market researchers, who ask specific, highly practical questions, anthropological researchers visit consumers in their homes or offices to observe and listen in a nondirected way. Our goal is to see people's behavior on their terms, not ours. While this observational method may appear inefficient, it enlightens us about the context in which customers would use a new product and the meaning that product might hold in their lives.

Ethnography has proved so valuable at Intel that the company now employs two dozen anthropologists and other trained ethnographers, probably the biggest such corporate staff in the world.'

Christensen *et al* (2016)

President Obama and behavioural analytics, 2012

President Obama's Head of Digital, Teddy Goff, believes that behavioural information is more important than demographics. Online click behaviour revealed what people were interested in. Two people with very dissimilar demographics may have a lot in common. 'Everything we did was informed by data.' They were determined to serve their supporters with the best experience possible, so they used 'the stuff people were telling us they wanted.' (Note this is the magic marketing formula mentioned in Chapter 2.) So they used these behavioural insights to create platforms for niche interests to connect and develop relationships; they had up to 18 different versions of emails going out to different niche groups (source: Teddy Goff interview with PR Smith, Dublin).

President Trump and behavioural analytics, 2016

UK Company Cambridge Analytica analysed the Facebook data of millions of adult Americans, so that they could categorize personality types and then subsequently send them tailored messages that reflect their specific needs. 'The company's former boss, Alexander Nix, claimed, before the election, to have predicted the Big 5 score of every adult in America. On Facebook, hundreds of ads were posted every day targeted at specific personality types tailored towards people's innermost fears, needs and emotions' (BBC, 2018). It used an algorithm that analyses what people like (and don't like) on Facebook to predict your personality. With 10 likes it can predict what kind of person you are better than your colleagues:

> With just 10 likes, a computer model fundamentally knows you better than a colleague... With 70 likes, it knows you better than a friend or roommate; with 150 likes, better than a family member. And with 300 likes, Big Data knows you better than your spouse.
>
> Tinker (2018)

See 'How Trump won' in more detail at **http://prsmith.org/blog/**.

Geodemographics and location-based mobile analytics

Geodemographics originally mixed geographical population data together with basic demographic data. It uses neighbourhood types to predict the kinds of people who live within them and thus their behaviour as consumers. If a brand is found to appeal to certain geodemographic groups, their locations can be mapped and the subsequent communications can be targeted at the geographical areas that offer the greatest potential.

ACORN (a classification of residential neighbourhoods) uses postcodes to identify different types of houses and generally gives useful indications about buying behaviour. Other UK online demographic analyses can be cross-referenced, eg PINPOINT, which uses 60 different neighbourhood classifications. MOSAIC has 58 neighbourhood categories linked with financial information. SUPER PROFILES uses 150 neighbourhood types. Today we use location data to monitor behaviour and more. See Chapter 12 for more.

Location-based mobile analytics are all driven by deep analysis of behaviour (within milliseconds) including both where you've been visiting/browsing online and where you've physically been visiting/travelling in the real offline world. However, they can only monitor those who have opted in via using free wifi (terms and conditions) or via accepting cookies when visiting various websites.

New market research platforms, gamification and research

Research professionals have started to use games to gain consumer insight, which has resulted in more creative surveys. Sony Music wanted to understand the connections between fans and artists: a quiz, which was introduced into Jeff Wayne's The War of the Worlds forum, resulted in nearly 2,000 completed quizzes in less than 24 hours. Despite such encouraging results, the number of clients and agencies using gamification is still fairly low. Nevertheless, the Market Research Society reports that gamification is a growth area for training so we should be seeing more of it. A case study of parenting club Bounty is also included (Fisher, 2012).

Online vs offline research

Qualitative research such as in-depth interviews and focus group discussions give insights into the real reasons why customers buy or don't buy, or what they think about a new advertisement, a new pack design or an app. A lot of this can be done online, for example by observing online discussions (some say this is akin to having access to a one-month focus group), or engaging in a one-to-one discussion in real time, or a simple pop-up exit survey. In addition, accessing real-time discussions, or even real-time behaviour and layering it with additional data can reveal valuable customer insights (see location-based mobile marketing layering digital body language with physical journeys in Chapter 12). More traditional surveys can also be carried out online. However, online research has both advantages and disadvantages.

Advantages of online research

- Access – it is easier (and cheaper) to reach respondents online than in person.
- Researchers can observe consumers in their own community (without taking them somewhere else).

- Researchers can observe passively as people interact with each other very naturally online.
- It is quicker – online dialogue and feedback are immediate and in some cases within minutes of something happening, as opposed to face-to-face surveys, which might take days, weeks or months, giving people time to think, forget or get confused. Equally split-testing ads, emails and web pages give almost instantaneous results. Do remember if multivariate testing (testing many variables), you have to have a big enough audience and sufficient duration to gather to be able to extract significant results.
- Online also allows for more longitudinal studies – instead of an intense one-hour dialogue, online can encourage conversation over months or years, which can yield very different insights to traditional face-to-face.
- There is a wider spread of respondents, as online focus groups can recruit from across geographical and social boundaries.

Disadvantages of online research

- Too much information generated by too many social media conversations means marketers potentially face 'an overload of untargeted data that is costly to analyse and requires specific expertise and resource' (Gray, 2010).
- There is less control. As the discussions reside within their own online communities, the role of a focus group moderator has become more passive and observational, with less control over the direction of the discussion. This can open up new, previously unknown aspects, but can also make it harder to get feedback on specific questions.

Facebook research platform

Restaurant chain Nando's asked its Facebook fans for their thoughts on a possible new product. Overnight, more than 500 fans clicked their 'like' button, and there were 657 comments for the marketing team to analyse.

Websites and research

Websites can help identify customer needs in the following ways:

- Identify what customers are interested in (the most popular web pages).
- See what customers really want by looking at key phrases used to arrive at the site and within the site (seeing what phrases are keyed into the onsite search engines).
- Employ polling for brand names, straplines, packaging design concepts or any concepts.

Use questionnaires sparingly, as they can cause people to leave a site, particularly if the questionnaire is on the home page. Every click potentially captures data, building a better profile about visitors and their interest. Chat rooms offer a wonderful opportunity to listen, free of charge, to customers discussing your product or service. And more sophisticated data-mining software can drill down into data mines and build profiles that help companies to understand their customers better.

A pop-up exit poll

Automatically triggered when a visitor clicks to leave a website, a pop-up survey can ask just a few short questions to determine: 1) Did the visitor find what they were looking for? 2) If not what was it? This collects extremely valuable research, which if used in a remarketing campaign could actually double sales.

Content marketing testing

Everything can, and should be tested: ads, mailshots, web pages and content marketing in particular. You need to know what topics, content type (eBook, white paper, video, infographic) and channel work the best. Once you know what works you can do more of it. But you need to know if it was a particular topic, or a particular content type or a particular channel that worked particularly well. And then optimize. See researching 'content shock', p 453, and the talented Erin Robbins O'Brien, on videoing, explaining how you need to constantly test your content (**http://prsmith.org/blog/**).

Qualitative research

An in-depth interview with an individual provides a lot of qualitative information. There is usually a series of individuals interviewed on a one-to-one basis. This type of research attempts to reveal what customers sometimes don't even know about themselves by delving deep into their unconscious motivations. In-depth interviews can reveal deep customer insights.

> **How young men retain their youth (unconsciously)**
>
> 'Amongst the most popular destinations from the stresses of life are the worlds of the computer game. One way that men retain their youthfulness is by spending large amounts of time playing video games.'
>
> Kimmel (2008)

As Gordon (1991) says, 'Consumers are often unaware as to why they do or don't use/buy/choose a particular brand. Asking for this kind of information in a direct way is like shouting at a foreigner in the belief that he will then understand English more easily.'

> **Work and family aren't the only important things in life**
>
> 'As time pressures increase on young men, so does their value of "me time". There's more of an "I deserve it" attitude towards leisure activities. What's more, leisure can enrich and reconnect a young guy with his sense of self.'
>
> Kimmel (2008)

In-depth researchers employ a variety of techniques (including psycho-drawings, word associations, metaphors, collages, picture completion, clay modelling and role playing) that throw the ego off guard and allow the subconscious feelings to be expressed. Chapter 4 considers the underlying motivations and complex information processes through which buyers pass on their journey towards a purchase.

Focus groups

Group discussions can be a more cost-effective way of collecting information that is perhaps less in-depth but nevertheless useful in understanding why and how people (in the target market) feel about certain brands, advertisements or just new ideas (concepts).

> **Mommy's never coming back**
>
> 'In-depth research for a US manufacturer of security doors revealed deeply ingrained unconscious fears of being trapped inside, or abandoned, when doors are closed. The report suggested that a young child's first experience of a door is when its mother puts it to bed and closes the door behind her as she leaves. The child fears that it may never see its mother again. Many years later, the adult's unconscious mind can react to the sight of a closed door with an 'underlying feeling of discomfort and anxiety'. The Simpson Timber Company was reported as having gained a significant increase in its market share when they changed their advertisements to show partly open security doors rather than their traditional images of securely closed doors.'
>
> Knave (1991)

A variety of creative stimuli materials are used within these groups, including cartoons, pictures, words and brand maps. One of the most common types is the collage or mood board, which is made up from scrap art taken from a wide variety of magazines and newspapers. It is used to explore a variety of themes, such as user lifestyles, occasion usage and abstract concepts such as freshness or vitality. The example of a collage board featured here (Figure 6.2) has been developed by The Collage Shop for use in focus groups. It explores concept pack themes for a shower gel.

FIGURE 6.2 Concepts for shower gel packs

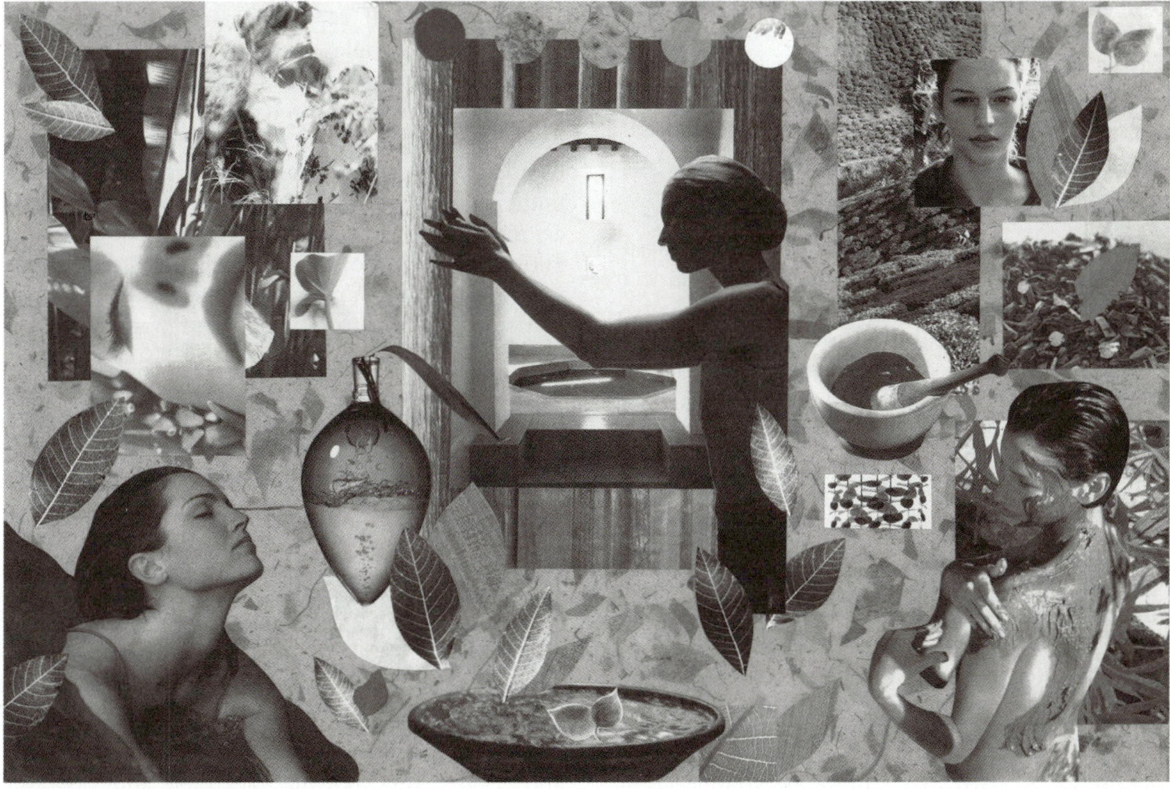

SOURCE: Collage provided by The Collage Shop

Some companies, like MTV, use online discussions and discussion groups as online focus groups – 'a year-long focus group'.

Concept research

Concept testing helps every element of the communications mix. Whether it is an advertisement, new sales promotion, new piece of packaging, new direct mail leaflet or even a product or service, the concept should be researched and discussed at least among colleagues and customers and, ideally, among unattached, unbiased focus groups that are representative of the target audience or customer.

Advertising concept testing measures responses to advertisements before they are fully produced. Storyboards and key frames or animatics are made up and shown to focus groups. This kind of group discussion is used to identify the best idea from a range of different concepts, to iron out any glaring problems with a chosen concept or simply to help to refine the concept itself.

Usability testing: Monitoring how easy/difficult a website is

Usability testing is a one-to-one observation, which explores the CX and in particular, the usability of a website. Simple setting tasks and watching individuals trying to complete them on a website can reveal bottlenecks and dead ends that can ruin the CX.

Eye tracking: Monitoring customers' information processing

The best website designs research how customers process information. Some companies use eye tracking and heat maps to try to understand how customers actually process information presented on a web page (Chaffey and Smith, 2013). We explore these in

Chapter 4 when looking at how the same website can be perceived differently by different people. Heat maps and session maps can be used to show where a customer looks, what they pay the most attention to, and, most importantly, what they miss (see p 137 for more).

Advanced one-to-one UX research: Monitoring blood, sweat and tears

Some advanced research analyses how visitors actually use a particular website and benchmark it against a number of competitive sites to identify any barriers or difficulties. Companies like Space Between measure eye movement tracking, emotional arousal (and stress) through GSR (galvanic skin response) and facial recognition (including how the eyebrows move) to measure emotional reactions, and they also measure heart rate. Their recent report for the UK's largest fashion provider, ASOS, also benchmarked the ASOS website against two competitor websites, Boohoo and Zara – all for under £10,000.

Neuroscience

Neuromarketing (and neurological techniques such as wearing a skull cap studded with electrodes to identify which parts of the brain are stimulated by ads or images) is an additional, albeit expensive, market research tool that helps marketers literally to 'get inside the heads' of their customers.

'I don't like it' really means 'I do like it': Neuroscience digs below the surface

TV show *Quizmania* invited viewers to call in and win money if they guessed the answer. Before the show was released in the United States, the concept testing (people watched it and filled out questionnaires) revealed that people clearly didn't like the programme. 'But when we scanned their brains, it showed they loved it. They didn't like the show because from a rational point of view it's ridiculous. However, the emotional part of the brain is so engaged that you keep watching it' (Martin Lindstrom, in Rothery, 2009). When the show was finally broadcast, the ratings matched the predictions from neuroscience research.

Opinion-forming panels

Some companies use opinion-forming panels, including Microsoft (450,000 early adopters), and Procter & Gamble (nearly 200,000 recruited respondents in its 'connector panel'). 'Connector panels' are used to research and seed new products. Note that in the UK market, research cannot be blended with selling (it's called 'sugging' – selling under the guise of research). Not only are these testers giving very valuable feedback, but they are also taking ownership of the product and the brand as they become more and more engaged.

Use panel data to estimate your traffic, break it down by socio-demographic characteristics and compare it to competitors. A panel member is profiled in terms of socio-demographics and software is installed on their PC to monitor the sites they visit. Examples of online panel data providers are Nielsen NetRatings (**www.nielsen-online.com**) and Comscore (**www.comscore.com**). Similar data are available from Hitwise (**www.hitwise.com**), which aggregates anonymous data from ISPs with which it has signed agreements to show the relative popularity of sites (online audience share) within a sector. Hitwise is particularly valuable since it gives information on competitors – eg which key phrases they rank well for – and shows which traffic sources drive visitors and clickstreams showing sites their audience visit before and after the evaluation of the site.

Post-it notes failed the test

'Post-it notes failed in concept testing, prototype testing and a test launch. Although a great product, consumers, when researched, simply did not like it. Just before pulling the plug on this potential new product, 3M focused on "highly connected CEO secretaries". These respondents were given boxes of the 3M Post-it notes, invited to share them with their colleagues and gather any feedback re possible uses. The goodwill, engagement and word of mouth generated pushed this product beyond the tipping point to become the fifth-largest office supply.'

Marsden (2004)

Test marketing

Test marketing refers to new packs, new brands and new products that are marketed only in a limited test region or geographical area, eg the Yorkshire TV area. A full marketing drive (distribution and advertising, etc) is released in the test area only. This gives the company a chance to spot any last-minute problems that previous research has not identified. If the test market proves to be positive, then the marketing campaign can be extended nationally.

As mentioned, everything can be tested. A new advertising campaign, a new sales promotion or even a direct mail campaign can be tested among a few thousand names on a mailing list (in direct mail, some companies test right down to whether different-coloured signatures affect direct mail response levels). Some organizations do not, however, test-market because of the associated problems of security, timing, costs and seasonality.

Testing also costs time and money, which may not be available as launch deadlines loom closer. The limited time period of a test often restricts the accuracy of the measured results, since additional time may be required to monitor whether repeat purchases continue beyond the 'trial period'. Seasonal products and services are further complicated, since they may need to be tested 12 months in advance. Both freak results and results manipulated by competitors can also invalidate certain tests. Some businesses have their own test networks.

> 'Facebook continually test over 10,000 different versions of Facebook.'
>
> Mark Zuckerberg in an interview with Reid Hoffman, *Masters of Scale*, Episode 4

Constant optimization: A/B testing and multivariate testing

Multivariate testing is a more sophisticated form of A/B testing which enables simultaneous testing of many variable (multivariables) on, say, website pages. Multivariate testing involves setting up the server to display the different web page variations (or combinations) to equal proportions of incoming visitors. You need sufficient traffic and time so that you can split it up and have significant numbers of visitors land on the many variations. The goal is to find the combination of the various page elements that delivers the best results.

The kinds of variables (or elements) which are tested simultaneously on a single web page include:

- page headline: message and typography;
- photo button (size, colour, placement and call-to-action text plus arrow);
- page copy;
- benefits (messages).

Multivariate testing can eliminate the need to run several sequential A/B tests. It can save a lot of time and find the optimum blend of variables that deliver the best results.

Tracking studies: Advertising campaigns

Advertising tracking involves pre- and post- advertising research that aims to measure levels of awareness and brand recognition before and after an advertising campaign. It can also be used to measure the series of mental stages through which a customer moves: unawareness, awareness, comprehension, conviction and action. These are the stages identified in DAGMAR (defining advertising goals for measuring advertising results – see p 131). It is worth remembering that some elements of the communications mix, such as sales promotions, packaging and point-of-sale, can be more effective than advertising when pushing the customer through the final stage of 'action' or buying.

An analysis of the sales figures can identify an advertising campaign's effect on overall sales. Home audit panel data like SuperPanel can reveal information on what is happening within the total sales figures, such as who is switching brands, who are the heavy users, etc. Quantitative techniques involving street surveys, in-home interviews or telephone surveys (obviously not used if prompting respondents with visual prompt material, eg storyboard, press or poster ad) can measure the other DAGMAR stages listed above.

The percentage of respondents with spontaneous awareness (which brands of beer can you remember seeing an advertisement for this week?) is always lower than those with prompted awareness (since the interviewer prompts the respondent by showing a list of brand names or a storyboard of the ad).

Think 'secondary' first

All communications plans should be built upon reliable research. Expensive primary data should be used only when all possible secondary data sources have been checked. Why pay £25,000 for a market research report analysing your industry when it may be possible to subscribe for less to a syndicated survey carried out specifically for a group of companies in an industry sector (eg air travel or car manufacturers)? Alternatively, some markets are researched regularly by market report companies such as Mintel, Keynote and Jordans. These reports can be purchased by anyone for a few hundred pounds. Academic institutes often publish reports on various markets or aspects of the marketing process within a particular industry. Sometimes these are available at not much more than the cost of duplication and dispatch. A newspaper like the *Financial Times* may have done its own analysis or survey, which will cost you less than £3.

In conclusion

So, what is **the best type of research**? Many marketers, and market researchers in particular, have their own favourite research techniques. Some believe the only way to understand customers is to explore their minds through qualitative research carried out on small numbers of people (from psycho drawings to clay modelling to focus groups of say six people at a time, to in-depth one-to-one discussions and even neuroscience) while others say this information only gives some clues and is statistically insignificant and therefore the only way to draw real significant conclusions is from quantitative research (such as surveys of, say, a thousand people). The truth is that qualitative research identifies the issues that need to be researched quantitatively.

Today, online, we have free and automated analytics generating behavioural information about

FIGURE 6.3 Awareness questionnaire

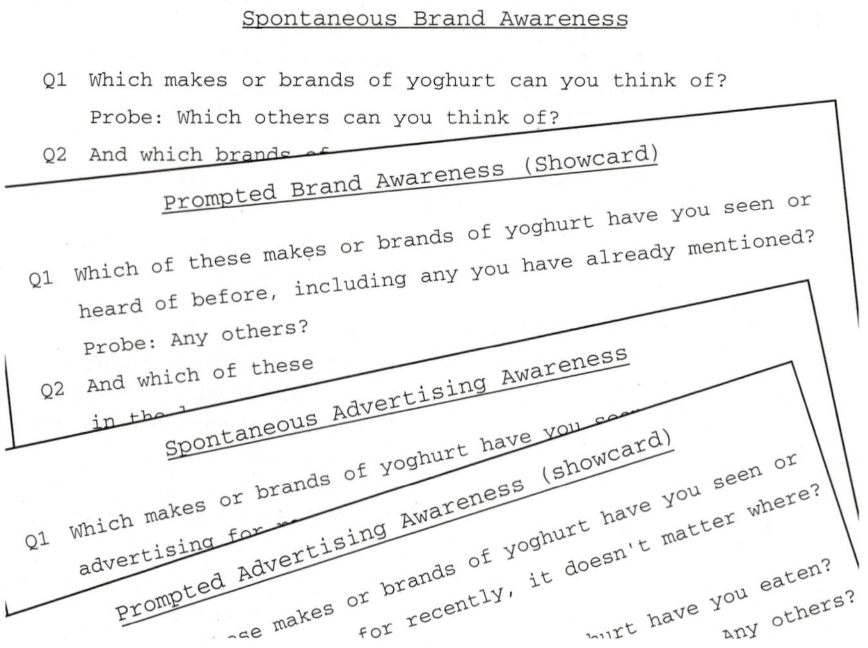

Spontaneous Brand Awareness

Q1 Which makes or brands of yoghurt can you think of?

Probe: Which others can you think of?

Q2 And which brands of

Prompted Brand Awareness (Showcard)

Q1 Which of these makes or brands of yoghurt have you seen or heard of before, including any you have already mentioned?

Probe: Any others?

Q2 And which of these in the

Spontaneous Advertising Awareness

Q1 Which makes or brands of yoghurt have you seen advertising for

Prompted Advertising Awareness (showcard)

...se makes or brands of yoghurt have you seen or ... for recently, it doesn't matter where?

...hurt have you eaten?

Any others?

how customers and prospects react to prices, promotions and special offers, whether in an ad, on a web page or in an app. Originally, metrics measured the effects of marketing decisions. Today's nimble marketers can use instant metrics (analytics) to help decide what is the best price, colour, ad, name or even phrase to use. Split-testing emails, ads and even web pages informs marketers what works best. So we can now use instantaneous measurement of the effects of our marketing decisions, to make even better marketing decisions. This is constant optimization.

Analytics are used in digital marketing. In the offline world of marcomms we tend to use the words 'market research' and 'testing' – there is no reason why we can't call all market research and digital analytics market research – a lot of the digital analytics is free and most of the traditional market research (focus groups, hall testing, ad tracking) is paid for.

Research is valuable but, as can be seen, it does require experienced advice and strict control if the data are to be usefully applied. Finally, remember, asking great questions is a great skill. It is important to know what you need to know.

Key points from Chapter 6

- Budgets allowing, research can reveal anything required.
- Consider carefully exactly what information is required, because there is too much information out there.
- Know what you need to know.
- Always check secondary sources before commissioning expensive primary research.
- Consider online as well as offline research.
- Set up a marketing intelligence and information system.

References and further reading

Anderson, K (2006) Ethnographic research: A key to strategy, *Harvard Business Review* March

BBC (2018) Facebook data: How it was used by Cambridge Analytica, BBC News, 9 April

Birn, R (ed) (2003) *The Handbook of Market Research Techniques*, Kogan Page, London

Bradt, G (1996, 2000) *Online Marketing Course 5: Marketing research*, Multimedia, London

Cerha, J (1970) Inventing products to fit the future market, Paper given at ESOMAR, Neu-Isenburg, November

Chaffey, D and Smith, PR (2013) *Emarketing Excellence*, Routledge, Abingdon

Christensen, C, Hall, T, Dillon, K and Duncan, D (2016) Know Your Customers' 'Jobs to be done', *HBR*, September

Collins, S, Dahlstrom, P and Singer, M (2006) Managing your business as if customer segments matter, *McKinsey Quarterly*, August

Crimp, M (2000) *The Marketing Research Process*, 5th edn, FT Prentice Hall, Englewood Cliffs, NJ

Crouch, S, Housden, M and Wright, L T (2003) *Marketing Research for Managers*, Butterworth-Heinemann, Oxford

Dunkley, C (2008) Gender psychology: Differentiate to accumulate, *Marketer*, October

Esomar (2017) General Data Protection Regulation (GDPR) guidance note for the research sector: Appropriate use of different legal bases under the GDPR, June

Fisher, L (2012) Game on to keep consumers engaged, *Marketing Week*, 8 November, pp 33–36

Forrester Consulting (2013) Use behavioural marketing to top up the ante in the age of the customer, *Silverpop*, May

Gordon, W (1991) Accessing the brand through research, in *Understanding Brands*, ed D Cowley, Kogan Page, London, pp 31–56

Gordon, W (1999) *Goodthinking*, Admap, Oxford

Gray, R (2010) How to do 'qual' research, *Marketer*, June

Holder, S (1999) Talking to the right consumer, *Design Week*, May

Holder, S and Young, D (1995a) A journey beyond imagination, Paper given at ESOMAR, Berlin, February

Holder, S and Young, D (1995b) Managing change: Moving towards a leaner future, Paper given at Business Industry Group, May

Holder, S and Young, D (1997) Researching the future in the present, Paper given at ESOMAR, Edinburgh, September

Holder, S and Young, D (2000) Getting to the future first, Paper given at AEMRI, Paris, June

Kanter, R (1996, 2000) *Online Marketing Research Course 5: Marketing research*, Multimedia, London

Kaye, K (2013) Data defined: What is 'big data' anyway? *Ad Age*, 15 January

Kimmel, M (2008) *Species: A user's guide to young men*, Discovery Channel, Discovery Communications Europe

Knave, M (1991) Unlocking deepseated reactions makes ads more sympathetic, in *Marketing Breakthroughs*, ed Bruce Whitehall, p 9

Knave, M (1996) Rescuing Boris, *Time Magazine*, 15 July

Kotler, P (2000) *Marketing Management: Analysis, planning, implementation and control*, millennium edn, Prentice Hall International, London

Kotler, P and Keller, K L (2012) *Marketing Management*, Pearson, Harlow

Lynch, M with Manchester, P (1999) How to uncover knowledge and make it available, *Financial Times*, 10 November

Market Research Society (1986) Research is good for you: The contribution of research to Guinness advertising, Conference papers, MRS, London

Marr, B (2013) Big Data: The mega-trend that will impact all our lives, LinkedIn Update, 27 August

Marsden, P (2004) Tipping point marketing, *Brand Strategy*, 1 April

McGovern, G (2010) Information overload – the sequel, *New Thinking*, 23 October

McNally, F (2002) Wolfe Tones' rebel ballad beats off Bollywood classic to be top choice, *Irish Times*, 21 December

Moore, A (2004) Enterprise search: The Holy Grail of KM? *KM World*, 1 January

Murray, R (1997) Clone zone, *Creative Review*, November

Nurden, R (1997) Managers pay price for office pressures, *European*, 27 November

Olenski, S (2018) Data science is the key to marketing ROI: Here's how to nail it, *Forbes*, 6 March

Reuters (2009) Information overload, 15 August

Robbins O'Brien, E (2015) Measuring the effectiveness of content marketing, 22 February, http://prsmith.org/blog/ (archived at https://perma.cc/67JZ-HYWA)

Rothery, G (2009) All in the mind, Interview with M Lindstrom, *Marketing Age*, **3** (6), November

Schmidt, E (2010) Every 2 days we create as much information as we did up to 2003, Techonomy conference, Lake Tahoe, CA (reported by Siegler, M G (2010) Eric Schmidt: Techcrunch, 4 August)

Smith, PR (2019) SOSTAC® guide to writing your perfect digital marketing plan, www.PRSmith.org/SOSTAC (archived at https://perma.cc/DR3G-UZUM)

Tinker, B (2018) How Facebook 'likes' predict race, religion and sexual orientation, CNN, 11 April

Varian, H and Lyman, P (2000) *How Much Information?* UC Berkeley School of Information Management of Systems

Wurman, R (1996) Information anxiety, system overload, *Time*, 9 December

Zuckerberg, M (nd) Interview with Reid Hoffman, Masters of Scale, Episode 4: Imperfect is perfect

Further information

Businessmagnet Ltd
9 Meadway Court
Meadway Technology Park
Stevenage
Herts SG1 2EF
Tel: + 44 (0) 870 350 7767
www.businessmagnet.co.uk

European Society for Opinion and Market Research (ESOMAR)
Atlas Arena, Aziё Building – 5th floor
Hoogoorddreef 5
1101 BA Amsterdam
The Netherlands
Tel: +31 20 664 2141
www.esomar.org

Market Research Society
15 Northburgh Street
London EC1V 0JR
Tel: +44 (0)20 7490 4911
www.mrs.org.uk

Kantar Millward Brown (London)
24–28 Bloomsbury Way
London WC1A 2SL
www.millwardbrown.com

Nielsen
Nielsen House
John Smith Drive
Oxford Business Park (South)
Oxford OX4 2WB
Tel: +44 (0)1865 528800
www.nielsen.com

07 Marketing communications agencies

LEARNING OBJECTIVES

By the end of this chapter you will be able to:

- understand the range of different types of agencies;
- understand the changing nature of agencies;
- discuss different methods of remunerating agencies;
- set up a selection process;
- nurture relationships with the agency.

Agency types

Introduction

This chapter covers agencies, types of agencies, their structure, fees and working relationships, from shortlisting to briefing, selecting, hiring and firing.

There are many types of agencies, including advertising, sales promotion, direct mail, PR, corporate identity design, web design and more. Some call themselves agencies and others, consultancies. The overall structure of advertising agencies is changing. Many agencies have moved their focus beyond specializing in a single tactical communications tool. These agencies are now moving from shouting to listening, sharing, analysing and personalizing messages whether advertising, sales promotions/content marketing, direct mail or PR both online and offline.

The process of change among agencies is being driven partly by unsettled clients, visionary agency directors, digital disrupters, the media explosion, the AI explosion, marketing automation, platform companies and other new types of competition emerging.

Full-service, specialist, hybrid or in-house

As 'ad agencies' are generally the biggest type of communications agency let us initially look at advertising agencies and then the other options that brand managers or marketing managers have.

The larger ad agencies offer a **full service**, which includes research and planning, creative, media planning and buying, production (of the actual ad) as well as many newer disciplines such as PPC, SEO, and data analytics. Many full-service agencies also have departments specializing in forecasting, market intelligence, customer insights, data, customer experience design, AI and business planning, together with support services for the advertising campaign, including point-of-sale design, sales literature, sales conferences and other below-the-line activities such as content marketing/sales promotion, PR and direct mail. **Hybrid agencies** tend to be smaller but totally integrated (more later). Alternatively, there are **specialist agencies** that stay focused on a specific aspect, such as SEO, or PR. In fact, some of these specialists may be freelancers or independent consultants. And finally, clients (the brand owners) can set up their **in-house teams** to run their own ads, PR, content marketing or SEO. Each of the four options have their own advantages and disadvantages (see Table 7.1).

There are more radical changes on the horizon as more of the big players move into this agency sector. Notably, the big management consultancies (who recruit talented digital staff combined with their traditional strategic thinking) and the large platform companies, like the FANGs and the BATs (who have the data mountains, the analytics, the digital talent, and soon, wide ranging, value-adding AI) – these are now open to advertising and marketing. (FANG are Facebook, Amazon, Netflix and Google, while BAT are the big three Chinese platform giants Baidu, Alibaba and Tencent.) Some say the future of marketing is software companies; we think platform companies offering marketing channels to both brand owners and to comms agencies may well emerge as the winners.

Full-service agencies vs hybrid agencies

Mike O'Brien (2015) reveals why many brands need something more than a large full service agency:

> At the moment most agency teams are split into management, client services, researchers, planners, creative, media, production, data, analytics, brand, direct, digital. Digital makes things even more complex, with specialist teams for SEO, PPC, display, email, affiliates, UX, social, content, analytics, and so on. It is a mess. The wastage is extraordinary. The results are less than inspirational.

Hybrid agencies

Agencies that offer integrated services, delivered by integrated/hybrid staff, across all of the channels that end-customers use are hybrid agencies. They break down the barriers between different channels and integrate them seamlessly for maximum impact. Whereas traditional 'full-service agencies' tend to be large agencies, with separate specialized departments and staff, hybrid agencies have those rarer hybrid staff who understand UX, design, websites, apps, email, social media, PPC, content marketing, contact strategies, CRM, marketing automation, AI, IoT, Big Data, data analytics and testing, and so on.

Hybrid agencies are tech savvy agencies with scalable infrastructures who hire and retain hybrid talent, and profit from diversified recurring revenue streams – 'education, training, publishing, software reseller licensing, affiliate programs — so they can focus on strategy, execution and results rather than billable-hour quotas... They provide integrated solutions that used to require multiple agencies and consultants' (Boches, 2016).

Hybrid creatives required

'Monolithic creative is no more (other than with Christmas and the Super Bowl), because there are no longer any town squares full of congregating customers where you can put them up. Creative has to sweep itself through the B-roads and back alleys to find and win over attentive eyes and ears. It's a very different challenge for brands and agencies.'

Roope (2018)

Hybrid agency structure partnering with FANG

When DDB won the huge McDonald's account in 2016 it did so by pitching not only its own services but those of a combined team drawn from people and services from Facebook, Google, *The New York Times*, Twitter and other agencies like Alba, Burrell, The Marketing Store, and many, many more. The new hybrid agency was eventually named We Are Unlimited (Ritson, 2018). The big three Chinese platform giants Baidu, Alibaba and Tencent (BAT) are eyeing up possible hybrid partnerships, as they grow their audience bases, their analytics skills and AI potential. Alibaba's AI-generated copywriting service 'enables merchants on its e-commerce ecosystem to dictate the tone of the language... merchants can choose between descriptive "short-title" copy, more promotional "selling point" copy, and more emotional "heart-warming" copy' (Nicolaci da Costa, 2019).

AI creative copywriting opens up new hybrid agency market

'One heart-felt ad for a hoodie read: "A windbreaker is enough to withstand the autumn wind in England". The AI copywriter learns from millions of existing samples and "can generate 20,000 lines of copy a second in Chinese," says Li Mu, Director of Alimama (Alibaba's digital marketing arm). "A single product might require up to 10 versions of copy for different advertising formats, like posters, web banners, product pages, and event pages," says Li Mu. AI-written "Shop the sale – don't hang around, book today!" proved more popular than the human-written "There's still time to book that dream holiday for less".'

(Nicolaci da Costa, 2019)

New hybrid agencies emerging

Interestingly, Honda also use a hybrid type of agency in Malaysia – IH Digital. They are more of a hybrid agency as they deliver paid media, owned media and earned media (POEM) for Mazda. They create content to provide **owned media** for social media (it's good enough for TV as well); They then distribute the content (content distribution) across a huge variety of platforms to secure **earned media;** They then amplify the content to maximize the **paid media** and extend the reach. This agency calls it 360-degree marketing.

In-house or do-it-yourself advertising also varies, as some advertisers may develop the actual advertisements in-house but prefer to contract out some of the other advertising requirements to very specific specialist services, such as a media scheduling and buying agencies known as a 'media independent'. Similarly, the initial creative work can be put out to a 'hot shop' or 'creative shop' to generate the concept.

Honda take content marketing in-house

'Called the "Engine Room", Honda's relaunched its content hub. It aims to "bring content to life" in a way the brand hopes will appeal to a younger audience. Honda believes agencies have "ruled the roost for too long" and so it is taking control of more of its online media and advertising in the UK to help it bring content "to life" and drive reappraisal of the brand. Honda says it can now make changes on the site that once took up to a month – slowed down by the time it took for agencies to sign briefs off – within the hour. One person is now responsible for a job that would have traditionally taken five. Honda is moving away from large agencies with large overheads to smaller companies and freelancers while growing its inhouse work. It is, however, retaining its media agency Dentsu. Nick Bennett, Honda UK's digital content and social media manager says "[Before] we had a... central agency on a retainer contract... they did a job and served a purpose but it wasn't going to allow us to emotively bring the stories of Honda products to life".'

Hammet (2018)

Alternatively, the advertiser can go **à la carte** by picking and choosing separate **specialist agencies** with specialist services for different parts of the process, eg using four different agencies for the research, creative, production and media planning/buying stages. There are other types of specialist agencies that focus on a particular industry sector. Managing an agency then becomes managing agencies, which can be complicated and very time-consuming for an already busy marketing director.

A recent discrete development in the à la carte option is the agreement of a large, well-known, full-service advertising agency to subcontract its creative services to a small communications consultancy on an ad hoc basis. This may last only as long as the agency has spare capacity or is searching for extra revenue. Some clients demand that their full-service agencies work alongside the client's separate choice of media independents. Some full-service agencies get only a portion of the full job.

TABLE 7.1 The pros and cons of different client–agency working relationships

Brand manager's/ client's perspective	Full services (and hybrid)	Specialist services	In-house
Management and control	Easier, since it is all under one roof	More work (coordinating)	Total control, but more work involved
Security	Limited risk – sensitive information is shared with agency	More risk – more people have access to information	Minimal risk – no outsiders
Speed/response	Reasonably good (hybrid is even quicker)	Possible problems if à la carte = more coordination	Fast, since all decision makers are available
Cost	Expensive, high overheads, but lower media costs with agency buying power (but hybrid have fewer overheads)	Cheaper, fewer overheads	Cheaper, but less media buying power
Fresh views	Yes	Yes	No

(*continued*)

TABLE 7.1 (Continued)

Brand manager's/ client's perspective	Full services (and hybrid)	Specialist services	In-house
Expertise	Yes (jack of all trades, master of none?)	Yes (fill in gaps in client's skills)	No (lack of specialized knowledge)
Stress	Less pressure/workload	Delegate some workload	More stress – more work

From creative to full-service to entrepreneur's business

Saatchi & Saatchi started as a specialist creative shop in 1970 and grew into a full-service 'integrated communications network', with 114 offices in 67 countries, (with its HQ in London), and is now owned by the Publicis Groupe, the world's third largest communications group. Meanwhile, in 1995, the brothers Maurice and Charles Saatchi set up M&C Saatchi Worldwide as a global marketing services company working across a wide variety of industry sectors with today's strategy focused on winning new business and starting new businesses, with almost 2,500 staff employed in over 80 business units run by local entrepreneurs.

Tomorrow's agency

Many years ago, WPP's Martin Sorrell said that agencies would be competing with software companies, search engine companies and many more as 'frenemies' or 'copetitors'. He may be gone from WPP, but he was right. Look at the DDB's big win when they pitched McDonald's and introduced their platform partner companies Facebook and Google and other partners.

At the centre of agency partnerships will be partnerships that give access to AI and data. The big platform players, the FANGs and the BATs, may become a new wave of frenemies and copetitors. Meanwhile, consultancy services like McKinseys, EY and others will be looking to partner with all of the above.

Meanwhile, the smaller, nimble, highly creative yet mathematically capable digital consultancies that have sprung up and specialize in marketing automation, data science, IoT, VR and AR will work with agencies as connected partners or specialist providers.

In an excellent piece entitled 'The agency of the future', Mike O'Brien (2015) predicted that as clients are already beginning to automate many of the less challenging communications processes in SEO, PPC, display, email, mobile and social, agencies will deliver fewer and fewer of the following processes:

- content development;
- activation publishing;
- digital analytics deployment and reporting;
- social interaction propagation;
- mobile communications;
- web experience management;
- cross-channel testing and optimization;
- media optimization;
- campaign management.

P&G integrate its agencies with a single 'throat to choke'

Several years ago, P&G undertook the task of refocusing their global agency relationships. They realized they had more than 2,500 different agencies and 3,000 pay points, with a huge duplication of resources, relationships and remuneration. Over the course of a three-year process, they launched a Brand Agency Leader (BAL) model – whereby a single person of a lead agency would have a single contact point for all integrated services on that brand at P&G. The BAL model has driven a new culture of accountability among lead agencies, and a new approach to an old problem. The model is not foolproof, and there have been a lot of kinks along the journey – but it's a quite unique step in the challenges of unifying communications.

The move also required fundamental changes on the P&G side – a single 'throat to choke' had to be established for each brand internally, with that person controlling the briefing and approval of all agencies globally. Not every company is ready for such a radical change, and not every P&G brand has migrated to the BAL model (R3, 2015). (Note: 'Throat to choke' is an aggressive metaphorical expression that describes the benefit of having a single person in a lead agency as the single contact point – so if things go wrong, you only have one 'throat to choke!' We do not advocate choking anyone, nor grabbing anyone's throat!)

Agency structure

Different types and sizes of agencies have different structures. The structure of a large advertising agency is shown in Figure 7.1, which illustrates the many different departments, people and skills that have to work together to create an advertisement. Companies that have their own in-house advertising departments (even programmatic ads), and smaller, external agencies, will subcontract (or hire) any of the departments they do not have. Many of the bigger agencies also hire, or subcontract, directors, producers, camera people, photographers, film companies, print and production facilities. Any other agent, agency, consultant or consultancy – whether public relations, direct mail, sales promotion or corporate identity – also relies on the ability to bring together many different skill sets and departments, as shown in Figure 7.1. Although pure ad agencies are growing into integrated agencies offering an additional suite of social media services, TV advertising is not going

FIGURE 7.1 Structure of a large traditional advertising agency

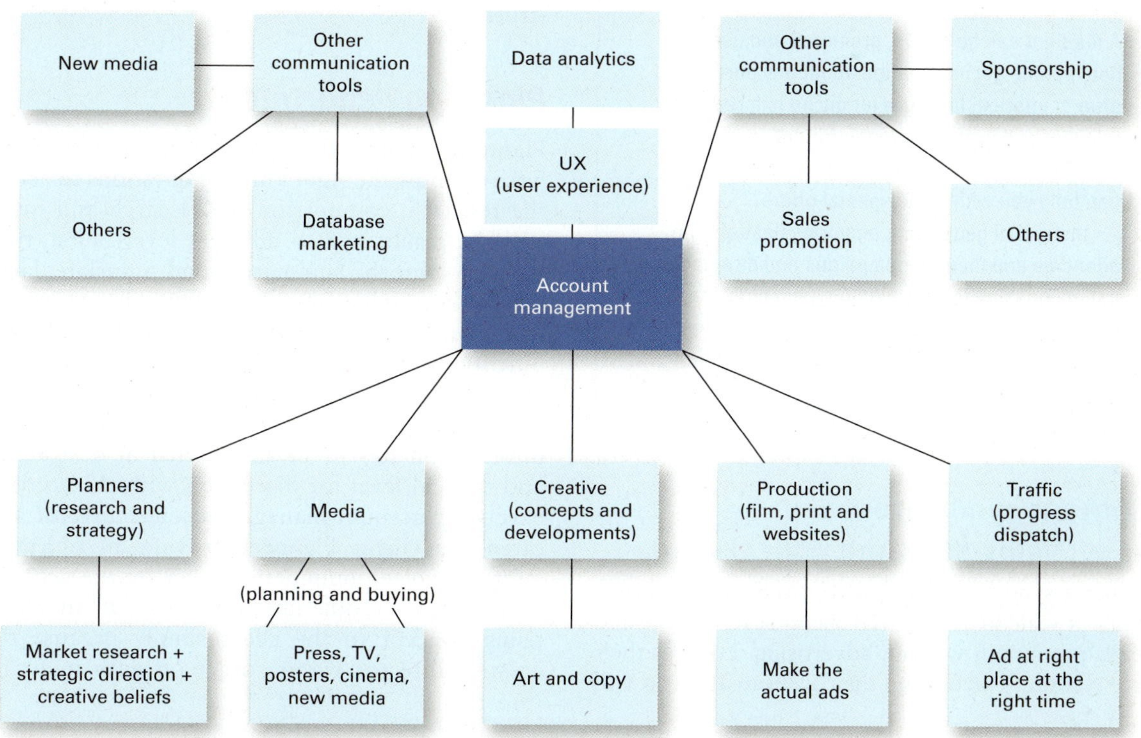

away and still takes a disproportionately large chunk of any brand's budget. Therefore the original ad agency structure is still worth exploring.

Agencies have evolved from pushing advertising campaigns to nurturing communities of consumers around brands. The new breed of agencies have a greater understanding of data analytics, brand, direct and digital skills (including AI's potential) along with the required planning, creative and media skills. It is also possible that, instead of pitching for a brand's business, agencies may offer a new service – selling access (posting their content) to groups of consumers with similar interests that they have nurtured (eg a Facebook or LinkedIn group or a chatbot's followers). Successful agencies will probably connect themselves with clearly defined communities of consumers and 'cultivate insights into their behaviour'. Agencies may also develop their own bots ready to carry the client's message personalized and at scale (ranging from election bots, to winfra bots and Boris bots to research bots to sales bots to lead generation bots).

A lead bot

A lead bot can be set up, promoted and used to help people get information about any particular area of interest. In return for giving tailored, relevant and useful content/information, the bot asks 'Is it ok if I pass this along to someone who can help you with some special offers?'

Instead of generating enquiries (leads) from agencies and their ad campaigns and direct mail campaigns and telemarketing campaigns, leads can also be generated by a new type of company, content syndicators – see the Digital Doughnut example, below.

Content syndicators skip advertising step and collect leads

Content syndicators such as **DigitalDoughnut.com** work at scale to deliver B2B clients several thousand leads per month without advertising. Look at their free resources section on their website and you will see how value exchange works so beautifully. Prospects who want a specific report, set of tips or guidelines that solves a problem (or exploits an opportunity) give their contact details in return for access to the content. The engine behind this is Demand Exchange, which is basically an advanced lead generation platform that helps B2B companies increase revenues and reduce costs (and is listed as GDPR compliant, and has also passed DMA Compliance Assessment). They offer the 'full service' from content syndication, to data capture, to verification and validation (verify the quality of the data) to lead qualification (only leads that match the required persona), data enrichment, data output (at the click of a button), integrations (with MA and CRM), reporting, analytics and tracking ROI and account-based marketing (ABM) focused on a list of target companies to make multiple connections within a company. The cost per lead ranges from £50 to £70 (although some can go up to £150 per lead).

Agency structures have changed somewhat over the years, particularly recently; with agencies wanting to position themselves as more nimble and quicker to react, many have developed flatter, less compartmentalized structures. The ad agency structure is changing.

Let's now have a look at the classic agency structure.

Planning department

Planners are more than glorified researchers. They have to know the right kinds of questions to ask in the research, commission the research and interpret the results at two different levels. First, they have to absorb, summarize and translate large market research reports into simple lay terms for inclusion in the creative brief that they, in conjunction with the account director, give to the creative team. They also need to understand analytics, and of course digital potential. Second, the information has to be interpreted at a strategic and tactical level for discussion with the account executive, account manager, account director and often the client. Planners provide an objective strategic voice, unhindered either by the account executive, who sometimes wants to 'sell' an advertising concept to the client simply because the creative director wants to get on with it, or by clients, who sometimes want to get on with it by quickly running some advertisements to satisfy the sales force, who are anxiously waiting for news on the new campaign.

Planners are experts in making sense of market research data and condensing the information into creative briefs.

Creative department

It is unfair to stereotype creative people as coming in late, lying around and dreaming up the big ideas and concepts that drive all big advertising campaigns. They can work long hours under extreme pressure to deliver unique, creative ideas that grab attention, build brands and win customers. They constantly search for the big idea that has to fit the single-minded strategy presented in the creative brief that is developed by the planning department. When working on brands and direct marketing, creative people usually work in pairs, covering words and pictures, ie a copywriter (or wordsmith) and an art director. When working in digital marketing, teams tend to be more agile (ie a cross-functional group of people that have all the skills required to create, test, run, tweak, optimize and report ROI of an ad campaign).

Creative people: An appreciation

'Somebody finally has to get out an ad, often after hours. Somebody has to stare at a blank piece of paper. Probably nothing was ever bleaker. This is probably the very height of lonesomeness. He/she is one person and he/she is alone. Out of the recesses of his/her mind must come words which interest, words which persuade, words which inspire, words which sell. Magic words.'

Leo Burnett, Founder, Leo Burnett Company

Creatives now work more on content required for generating ongoing dialogues with individuals and less on one-way campaigns to a mass audience. Outsourcing will include user-generated content (see Chapter 1), harnessing champions and brand advocates, as engagement and user-generated content becomes more important.

Media department

The media department basically plans and buys the space where the advertisements are eventually placed (press, websites, posters, social platforms, apps, games, TV, radio, cinema, etc). Media planners and media schedulers can be separate from media buyers, who negotiate and ultimately buy the space from the media owners.

Maths Men (those who are involved in programmatic ads, algorithms, or any form of software or automation that helps to minimize media costs and optimize a client's budget) are becoming key players in the media department and media houses. Maths Men used to be called the econometrics department. However, as econometrics becomes a slightly dated term and data or Big Data keeps its current appeal, data analysts and data planners are the more commonly used terms. Rather than being a department in an agency, many planning departments now sit in media companies, albeit owned by agency holding group companies such as WPP.

Both media planners and media buyers can be further separated into those who specialize in TV, press or digital media, remarketing and programmatic advertising. As markets fragment and media explode into many more magazines, TV stations and websites, large audiences become more difficult to buy. Despite this, the media explosion presents new opportunities for schedulers and buyers, as these new media vehicles have access to more tightly defined target markets. **The media department now analyses the appropriateness and cost-effectiveness of much more media than ever before** (including the one-to-one mass marketing mentioned with personalization in Chapter 5). This is quite a responsibility, as the bulk of the advertising spend is in media and not production (eg a £20 million campaign might have a £19 million media budget and a £1 million production budget). On top of this, media departments can deliver highly creative media strategies that find new ways of delivering advertisements to target audiences.

You think you are overworked – try the media department or a media company.

Data analytics

Data engineers, data architects, data-visualization experts and data scientists with advanced analytics and AI skills will be required by full-service agencies to improve decision making across communications processes from research and design to creative to supply chain. 'Data scientists are required to build the analytics models – including machine learning and, increasingly, deep learning – capable of turning vast amounts of data into insights' (Henke *et al*, 2018).

Production department

The production department actually makes the advertisement. Many agencies subcontract various parts of the production, eg hiring a studio, camera crew or photographer, director, editing suites, etc. This can involve long pre-production meetings finalizing all the minute details, flying around the world to shoot some film, and the less glamorous, lonely post-production – working around the clock in a dark and dingy editing suite.

> **Creating games, funny virals and some ads**
>
> Production departments (and outsourced production companies) will be full of clever people, some of whom can create great 60-second movies (and longer-form ads – page 359), as well as online games and, of course, contagious virals.

Traffic department

Although the traffic department is now usually part of the creative services department, dispatch, or traffic, is responsible for getting the right artwork or film to the right magazine or TV network at the right time. This becomes complicated where posters, cinema, radio and magazine inserts are included in the media strategy. Multiply this by several different campaigns for a range of different clients, and the need for a traffic manager becomes self-evident. Add in games and virals, and traffic gets busier. Traffic departments are still used in large, well-established agencies, with managers using software like Roadmunk to manage projects in real time.

The account management team

In a large agency this can involve an account director, account manager, account executive, planner, creative director, copywriter, art director, TV producer, media director, TV media scheduler, TV airtime buyer, press planner and press buyer.

The account executive

Sometimes also called an account representative, the account executive is dedicated to a particular client. The account executive wears two hats – the client's when talking to the agency and the agency's when talking to the client. Responsibilities include attendance at all client meetings, writing up 'contact reports' and general liaising between the many different members of the agency's team and the client so that projects get delivered on time (quasi producers). Many agencies write up contact reports (after each meeting), because they confirm and clarify all key points discussed, conclusions reached and any actions to be taken. This cuts out the opportunity for any misinterpretation further down the road when the client says 'I never asked for that.' When agreed by the client, vital documents, such as a summary of the agency's interpretation of the client's brief, or concept proposals, are sometimes required to be signed by the client as 'approved'. This keeps communication clear, reduces ambiguities and, if a row does break out over a particular strategic direction or over the details of copy (the words in the advertisement), the agency can pull out a signed 'approved by' copy.

> **The agency model of the future**
>
> 'What the agency model of the future looks like of course depends on the brand, its strategy, its internal capabilities and its KPIs. There will never be a one-size-fits-all solution. But such a complex landscape cannot continue; it works neither for the brands nor the agencies. And agencies will

need to get on board with this new way of thinking and prove their value to brands, or **watch as their business goes to the consultancies on strategy, and direct to media owners like Facebook and Google on execution.'**

Vizard (2018)

FIGURE 7.2 360-degree agencies

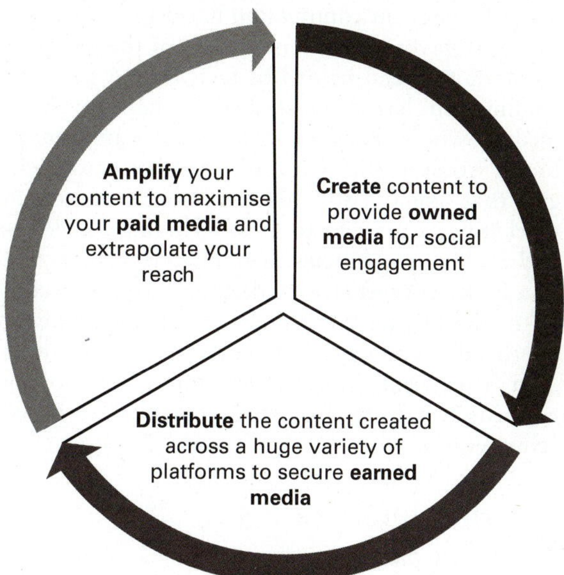

SOURCE: Courtesy of IH Digital

Integrated co-located teams

Some clients want their agency teams to work more closely with the brands they represent. For example, the brand O2 has its media, PR, advertising and CRM agencies co-located three days a week. The big players, Unilever and Procter & Gamble, both get their cross-agency groups to work more closely together. It makes sense, builds a greater 'team feeling' and facilitates easier internal communications, if they all physically work closer to each other.

Bigger agencies have to think smaller. Think like small, nimble, agile, fast-moving agencies. Big agencies have big overheads, and with that comes a culture of cost and hence agencies desperate to keep hold of their clients budgets. Clients, meanwhile want to move some work in-house.

'These days a great brand campaign had better be backed up with a great online experience. If not, Google's search engine will ensure your competitors get to cash in on your brand activation efforts... The big agency, in my experience, has a cultural downer on thinking small.'

O'Brien (2017)

Agency remuneration

Agencies have four methods of remuneration: commission, fees, pay-by-results and affiliate partner commission

Commission

Although this has changed drastically, historically media owners have given recognized agencies a 15 per cent discount off the rate card price. Thus, in the case of a £10 million TV advertising campaign, the agency gets invoiced by the TV station at rate card £10 million less 15 per cent, ie £8.5 million. The client then gets invoiced by the agency at the full rate card price, ie £10 million (this can be checked with British Rate and Data (BRAD) or the media owner's published rate card). The 15 per cent commission really represents a 17.65 per cent mark-up, ie the £1.5 million commission is the mark-up that the agency adds on to its media cost of £8.5 million:

Agency invoiced by TV station less 15 per cent £8.5 million

Agency invoices client at full rate card £10.0 million

Agency mark-up £1.5 million

Agency mark-up 17.65 per cent

The agency will also apply its agreed mark-up to other services that it subcontracts, such as market research and so on. Thus a piece of research that costs the agency £10,000 would be charged to the client (+17.65 per cent) at £11,765, or more. One of the problems with the commission system is that it can tempt agencies to get clients to spend, spend, spend. Incidentally, the commission system does not necessarily cover all production costs, so these costs are often separately invoiced directly to the client by the agency. The number of clients using 15 per cent commission has declined significantly, in favour of a combination of the payment methods outlined below. In fact, the 15 per cent commission has been slashed in half by some media owners. Back in 2006, Yahoo announced that it would pay 10 per cent commission to agencies that spend £80,000+ per month on search marketing, 5 per cent to those spending £20,000+ and nothing to agencies that spend less than that. In a hyper-competitive marketplace, some specialist media-buying companies – with much lower overheads – can work with commissions as low as 2 or 3 per cent. Many clients today are moving towards fees instead of solely commission-based remuneration.

Commission rebating

Rebates are paid by media companies (such as TV or newspapers) to agencies in return for certain volumes of media spend (common in the UK). These rebates are not always passed on to advertisers. In fact, some advertisers consider rebates to be 'controversial practices that were often not disclosed to clients. These included cash rebates, rebates as inventory credits and "service agreements" for non-media services such as consulting or research' (Hobbs, 2017). This poorly kept secret drives many advertisers to 'expect agencies to fully declare revenue streams directly or indirectly related to their business, for example, via rebates and arbitrage' (Pandey, 2016).

Some clients also insist that the agency takes less than the traditional 15 per cent commission, say just 10 per cent, with the remaining 5 per cent going back to the client. This separate type of commission rebating occurs when an agency passes on some of its commission to the client. There is no actual refund or rebate. The agencies simply invoice the client at rate card costs less the level of rebate, in this case 5 per cent. Commission rebating opens the door to agencies competing on price instead of on quality of service, as they have done traditionally. Most industries dislike price wars, and advertising is no exception. However, 'advertisers are changing the way they pay agencies as they seek more transparency and simplicity in their agency relationships' (Bruell, 2017).

Rebates above and beyond their normal commissions based on all the money they spend for all their clients

'In most of the world ad agencies get rebates from media companies based on their "pooled buying" power. In other words, they get cash returned, above and beyond their normal commissions, based on all the money they spend for all their clients.

Clients aren't routinely informed about exactly how much of these rebates is generated by their particular spending. Even when clients press for answers, they often allow agencies to keep the extra money so clients can continue to pay lower fees.'

Crain (2013)

Fees

Smaller clients with smaller media spends do not generate sufficient commission, so a fee will generally be agreed. Larger clients are also moving towards fees such as an annual, quarterly or monthly retainer or, alternatively, a project fee. 'No commission' means no media bias, since the agency is then free to recommend, say, direct mail, without losing any of its income (which would have been generated through TV commissions).

Many agencies receive a fee along with some level of commission, and/or some level of pay-by-results. The agency's remuneration essentially depends on how much work is involved and how much the client is likely to spend (on media). The trend, particularly with larger clients, appears to be moving towards a fee basis or a mixture of fees, commissions and results/performance.

Pay-by-results

Pay-by-results (PBR) can be mutually beneficial. It is sometimes disliked, however, because of the lack of control that the agency may have over its own destiny. PBR (also called value-based payment models) has become more popular. Almost half of advertisers (43 per cent) use performance-based or a combination of performance- and labour-based fee (World Federation of Advertisers, 2018). In fact, '80 per cent of marketers plan to increase the use of performance-based remuneration contracts with their ad agencies over the coming year in the hopes of not only eliciting better value and more transparency but improving the working relationship' (Faull, 2019).

Airbnb pay TBWA on a 'per night' basis

'Since 2011, marketers have been pushing for agencies to ink alternative contracts; from Airbnb paying former creative shop TBWA on a "per night" basis (meaning, the agency took a cut of every sale) to more experimental models like St Luke's set up with Uber-rival Gett.'

Faull (2019)

Media owners like Google offer another form of PBR: cost per click (CPC) and cost per action (CPA – not be confused with the other CPA, cost per acquisition of a customer). If no one clicks on the sponsored phrase or no one buys (if that is the goal) then Google do not get paid.

The problem with PBR, for agencies, is that some results are affected by variables beyond the agency's control, eg out-of-stock, price increase or competitor activities. If, on the other hand, the payment is linked to results directly influenced by advertising, eg increasing brand awareness, then the agency has more influence and is happier to be paid for, say, boosting brand awareness (rather than just sales).

Another area where results are easily measured and are directly related to the agency's input is media buying. If an agency achieves media buying at a price that is better than average, then the saving can be shared between client and agency. For example, if the average advertising cost per thousand to reach, say, housewives with children is £3.50, and if the agency gets this for 10 per cent less, then the saving might be split 8 per cent to the client and 2 per cent to the agency.

Some agencies, like BBH, prefer a fixed bid with shared risk system. For example, if an advertisement is produced under budget, the production company keeps a percentage and the client receives a percentage. If the advertisement is 10 per cent over budget, the client pays; anything over 10 per cent and the production company pays.

Pay by results for packaging designers, too?

PBR extends beyond advertising into other disciplines as far away as design. This can apply to new product design (as a royalty) or even packaging design, when the packaging design consultancy bases its fee (or a portion of its fees) on the client's increase in sales occurring after the launch of the newly designed pack.

Although PBR appears attractive to the client, it can generate extra administrative work, as exact results have to be measured, royalties and contributions calculated, invoices requested and cheques raised for each agreed accounting period.

The method of agency reimbursement is fundamental to the client–agency relationship (both working and contractual). An agency's flexibility in its range of reimbursement packages can influence the client's selection process.

Affiliate partner commission

As mentioned earlier, agencies can generate additional revenues from diversified recurring revenue streams from education, training, publishing, software reseller licensing and affiliate programmes. Consider reseller licensing and affiliate partner arrangements. Whether it is software relicensing or pure affiliate programmes, these can generate repeat revenue streams for agencies. This can be (a) a simple referral programme or (b) a more lucrative certified partner programme; eg a software company offering marketing automation solutions for SMEs might pay $500 per referral that arrives via your unique url and then ultimately signs up for the service. The more lucrative arrangement is when the agency chooses deeper involvement and gets trained up and also actually installs the system. These certified partners can earn 20 per cent of the monthly fees for many years (subject to agreement).

Costs vs ROI and creativity

Think about the essential ingredients for successful creativity and successful campaigns. BBC's Chief Customer Officer, Kerris Bright, believes that it is about being really clear on the problem you are trying to solve and not just doing 'creativity for creativity's sake'. It is important, she says, to be bold, but also focused and reframe the conversation about creativity away from cost to return on investment. 'I've been in meetings talking about media ideas and someone will say that's "very expensive" and I've said, "what's expensive?" I'm talking about, is it a good return?' Bright asks. 'Some things will have a high cost associated with them. It might cost a lot of money, but it might have a much greater return, so we talk about a low return on investment, not expense' (Rogers, 2019).

Agency selection

The coordination of any campaign's development, launch and measurements requires time and management skills. Powerful personalities in agencies need to be managed. The ability to ask the right question is a valuable management skill. **The fatigue factor in negotiations or discussions can also cause rash decisions to be made.** Marketing people tend to be energetic, enthusiastic, action-orientated achievers. Sometimes steely patience needs to be exercised. Perhaps a decision has to be delayed until further research can answer some emerging questions. Painstaking attention to detail may sometimes seem irksome to the advertising agency, but it is often the mark of a true professional. On the other hand, a key resource, time, may be running out. More research reduces the risk but costs time and money. Can deadlines be moved? Is there money left for more research? Is there time before the competition launches its new offer? A decision made in haste is rarely the best one.

Agency selection process overview

Defining exactly what is required is the first stage of agency selection. This is because an appropriate choice is partly determined by a specific requirement. Some furniture retail chains may consider the strength of the media department the key criterion when choosing an agency, particularly if the store primarily wants maximum media coverage for its relatively straightforward black-and-white product information advertisements. Another client may be looking for a radically fresh approach and have a bias towards agencies with abundant creative talent. Either way, a clear brief should be prepared to identify exactly what – in marketing and advertising terms – the new advertising campaign is trying to achieve.

The agency selection procedure is as follows:

- define requirements;
- develop a pool list of attractive agencies;
- credentials pitch (by the agencies);
- issue brief to shortlisted agencies;
- full agency pitch;
- analysis of pitch;
- select winner;
- agree contract details;
- announce winner;
- commence onboarding.

Some clients prefer to get on with it by issuing a full brief to the shortlist of, say, six agencies without going through the agency credentials presentation. Other clients prefer to restrict the valuable research findings and strategic thinking to as few agencies as possible, because the unsuccessful agencies are free to work for the competition at any time in the future.

Define requirements

The marketing director must be clear about what is required when selecting an agency. What kinds of services are critical, brand strategy, brand identity, advertising, creative services, media planning and/or buying or lead generation ad campaigns etc. This then leads to what are the critical skills and services required? In addition to the core service you require, say PPC advertising, try to consider the additional services you will be offered – market research, competitor analysis, data analytics, content marketing, social media audits, etc. You do need all of these but you have to prioritize which are more important so that you can allocate your scarce resources. What kind of agency is required – full-service global, or local specialists? Location of the agency may be important to you, too. Your pool list can be further refined by including, or excluding, agencies that have (or have not got) experience in your industry sector. Do you want to exclude large agencies with subsidiaries or divisions that have clients that are competitors? So, consider services required, type of agency, industry experience and competition when drawing up a pool list.

Pool list

Most advertising managers and marketing managers observe various campaigns by watching advertising and noting any particularly attractive campaigns. Agencies working for the competition need to be excluded or treated with extreme caution. Some desk research, both online and offline, can reveal the agencies behind the brands by reference to organizations such as AdForum, which allow advertisers to look for agencies using sensible criteria. Advertisers can create shortlists, preview creative work and explore an agency's profile, online and free of charge. Many marketing managers have a fair idea of who is doing what advertising in their sector by regularly reading the trade press. Other managers spend a few weeks watching more advertising than normal plus agency credential videos, which, ironically, can be a tad tedious.

Some clients prefer to do their own screening and request an agency reel (video) directly from a particular agency so that they can view the agency's best work. As mentioned, online sources (eg **www.adforum.com**) share agency info, some of their creative work and sometimes see some interesting updates and communications articles and news alerts. Remember, selecting agencies is hard work and requires rigorous attention to detail. Bad selections are very expensive.

Another way of building a pool list is through the professional associations such as the Institute of Practitioners in Advertising (IPA), the Incorporated Society of British Advertisers (ISBA) and the Advertising Association (AA). They all offer to provide lists of agencies that they think are suitable to handle a specific type and size of business. Similar services are offered by the relevant professional institutes of other service sectors such as public relations, sales promotion, design, direct mail, etc (see 'Further information' at the end of each chapter). This service is normally free.

There are also agency assessors, such as the Advertising Agency Register, and intermediaries whose business is agency selection. They can handle the development of the pool list, pitch list, pitch analysis, agency selection and even performance assessment of the agency when it starts working for the client.

Credentials pitch

Some clients, before issuing a full brief, prefer to ask the pool of agencies to present their credentials. This includes examples of current and previous work, team members' profiles, and company history, structure and facilities. It is worth visiting the agency, and sometimes at short notice, as this gives the client a feel for the potential agency, and its atmosphere, organization, professionalism, etc. From this a final shortlist is selected and issued with a detailed brief.

Too-long agency shortlist

Some years ago, Westminster City Council invited 10 agencies to pitch for its communications work. A long shortlist creates an unnecessary amount of unpaid work for everyone concerned.

Briefing, pitching and selecting take time and skills. Apart from creating a lot of work, a large pitch list sometimes leaves sensitive marketing information with many different people. Some cynics see it as an opportunity to get free strategic and tactical ideas from the best brains in each agency.

Pitches are not for everyone

'When it comes to agency relationships, BBC's Chief Customer Officer, Kerris Bright explains her focus is on feeling engaged in a collective endeavour, which is why she is not a fan of the agency pitch process as it can feel like there is too much luck involved in getting to the right place.'

Rogers (2019)

Issuing the brief

Briefs vary in size, structure and level of detail. Some clients may summarize on to a single A4 sheet of paper; others issue a much more detailed briefing document (one Guinness brief was 100 pages). Essentially, the brief should incorporate at least the situation, objectives and strategy (SOS) and the 3Ms (men/women, money and minutes), part of the SOSTAC® planning system explained in Chapter 1. The brief tends to be short, while a marketing communications plan has much more detail. Since the brief usually goes out to several agencies pitching (only one of which will get the business), a difficult dilemma emerges. How much confidential and strategic information should be revealed in the brief, given that the majority of the recipients will not work for you and may one day work for your competition? Food for thought.

At the bare minimum, the brief will usually include the following:

- *Situation*: Where you are now, including the market, channels, segments, target markets, trends, competition, market share, position, current and previous campaigns, strengths and weaknesses, unique selling propositions (USPs), features and benefits of the brand and the organization.
- *Objectives*: Where you want to go: marketing objectives and communications objectives (see pp 260 and 270 for examples) plus specifically defining exactly what is the problem (or opportunity). Include the required positioning and tone of voice. Ensure also that effectiveness criteria and evaluation methodology are clearly specified.
- *Strategy*: How you are going to get there (including how the marketing strategy fits in with the overall corporate strategy). This may also include a campaign strategy if this is already worked out.
- *Control*: How you will know when you've arrived. Both the agency and the client should agree on what success and failure will look like. What are the key criteria, and how will they be measured?
- *3Ms*:
    - Men/women – who makes the final decision, members of the team, who reports to whom, contacts for additional questions.
    - Money: key question for the agency – what is the budget?
    - Minutes: timescale and deadlines for pitch, agency selection and eventual campaign launch.

Control is sometimes included, as it outlines how the campaign will be measured, which in turn motivates the team to get it right. A smaller client may prefer to replace the advertising and/or marketing objectives with a statement of the problem and subsequently ask the agency to present a complete promotional plan. It is likely that the agency's first question will be: 'How much do you have to spend?' As mentioned, there are obvious dangers of releasing strategic information to several agencies, the majority of whom will never work for you (since there is usually only one winner or single agency selected). The corollary is that too little information reduces the quality (and possibly strategic direction) of the proposals. So start collecting ads, sales promotions, web pages, packaging, etc now.

It is important to get the brief correct and concise. If there are specific requirements, spell them out, eg 'It must be clearly legible from eight feet away' or the 'The brand name must stand out from the crowd', etc. You must work hard at stating your positioning and of course benefits, USPs, etc. Remember, a casual brief will probably generate casual concepts followed by frustrations and accusations. Get the relationship off to a good start with a clear, concise, yet comprehensive, brief.

Pre-pitch agency efforts

The shortlisted agencies are invited to make a full presentation or sales pitch. This usually involves several members of the agency staff and is viewed by several members of the client company. The cost of a major pitch varied from £750 to £75,000 in 2017. The highest cost incurred by an agency in 2016 was £150,000 (Ledger, 2017).

US-owned McCann Erickson was reported to draft in a professional teacher of meditation and relaxation techniques before every pitch. JWT practises its pressure presentation techniques with bizarre scenarios like asking its teams to imagine that they discover one of their art directors pushing cocaine and that, as they prepare to fire him, they discover his wife is dying of cancer and in need of private medical treatment. **Real empathy, sound strategy, exciting creative work and reasonable costs are often considered to be the key factors during a pitch**, but some agencies take initiatives before the actual pitch, as Table 7.2 shows.

Pre-pitch client's feelings

Other potential or prospective clients would deny any such self-imposed pressure. They may see the pitch as an exciting and stimulating process full of fresh ideas and strategic thinking presented by clever, articulate (and sometimes entertaining) people. Client egos are massaged, and generally the prospect is treated as a revered guest. Other prospective clients see pitches as a more tedious affair, since they have to repeat their brief in detail several times over and then sit through the inevitable credentials bit before they get to the heart of the matter – the agency proposals.

Most selling situations, including pitches, are about the removal of uncertainty. So understanding the problem, and identifying clear solutions with enthusiasm and conviction, is a winning formula.

Will they love me?

'Our research has shown that, generally speaking, clients are not happy about changing agencies. Such events are usually a signal that they are unable to sustain a productive relationship with other people, which is something that none of us is pleased to accept, however difficult the other people might be... the prospect [potential client] is under pressure from his boss to get it right quickly... so when he steps from the bustle and stress of his own trade into the palm-fringed oasis of Berkeley Square or Charlotte Street or Covent Garden it is possible that he has two questions in his mind: "Will they love me?" and "Can they save my neck?"'

Brian Johnson, New Business Director, JWT

The pitch

After weeks of intensive preparation of exciting creative ideas, ingenious media plans and pitch rehearsals, copies of the proposal or pitch document are laser-printed, bound and made ready for client distribution after the main presentation. The pitch

TABLE 7.2 Pre-pitch agency initiatives

Client	Agency	Stunt
Kiss FM Radio	BBDO	Delivered a framed poster to the Kiss MD bearing the legend 'We'll put your name on everyone's lips'*
Kiss FM Radio	Saatchi	Covered Kiss HQ with pink balloons on Valentine's Day
Guardian	Publicis	Booked a 96-sheet (40′ x 10′ poster) site opposite the newspaper's offices during the week of the pitch and ran flattering ads that changed each day*
Financial services company	Publicis	Sent a safe containing the agency's credentials
Toyota	Saatchi	Three Toyota cars suspended above Charlotte Street, hanging out of the agency's offices*

NOTE: * Won the account.

itself is where an advertising agency has the opportunity to advertise or sell itself. Given that most campaigns try to be different, grab attention and make an impression, it is understandable that some agencies should regard a pitch as a creative opportunity also. Some would say, an expensive opportunity as the cost of a pitch can be astronomical, eg £100,000 on a big global pitch say for British Airways or a global brand. Agencies often make test films for the pitch and costs quickly add up.

While most agencies pay up to £75,000 per major pitch, many more hours are burnt in overnight presentation preparations. As to clients paying for pitches, it is still too rare; but they'd never pay more than £5,000, which is really just a token gesture.

There are many stories of daring pitch techniques, some of which work and some of which do not. Here are a few.

Legendary 1980s agency ABM created **the classic British Rail pitch, which purposely created client tension** when the top executives from British Rail were kept waiting in a smoke-filled reception area while the receptionist ignored them throughout her gossip-filled telephone conversation. Eventually, a space was cleared among the empty cans and orange peels, and the executives were invited to wait, as the agency people were 'busy'. After some minutes the British Rail executives had had enough. As they got up to leave, the agency chairman, Peter Marsh, clad in full BR uniform (complete with cap, whistle and flag), burst in and said, 'You don't like it. Why should your passengers?' He then invited them to listen to how he and his colleagues were going to solve their problems.

Don White, formerly of Benton & Bowles, is reported to have **dressed up as a redcoat** for a Butlins pitch. The client took one look, said 'Anyone dressed like that isn't suitable for my business', and left. David Abbott of Abbott Mead Vickers is reported to have **greeted Metropolitan Police Commissioner Sir Robert Mark with a high-pitched nasal 'Hello, hello, hello'** as he arrived to hear the agency pitch. Not amused, Sir Robert left the building.

Agencies pitching for the **Weetabix** breakfast cereal account were invited to make their pitches in a hotel. As ABM was the last agency to pitch on the final morning, it decided to **redecorate the function room in the ABM colours.** This required an overnight painting and carpeting exercise. A stage was built, and a special chair was delivered to the function room for Mr Robinson, the arthritic and ageing Weetabix chairman. As the Weetabix panel seated themselves the next morning, the lights dimmed until they were all immersed in an enthralling darkness. A spotlight burst a stream of light on to the stage, where Peter Marsh knelt as he opened his pitch with: 'As one of Britain's few remaining wholly owned independent advertising agencies, it gives me great pleasure to present to you, Mr Robinson, as chairman of one of Britain's few wholly owned cereal manufacturers...'. ABM won the account.

One final ABM classic pitch was for **Honda**. ABM hired the **60-piece Scots Guards bagpipe band** to play the Honda jingle 'Believe in freedom, believe in Honda', while marching up and down London's Norwich Street (where ABM was making its pitch). Again, ABM picked up the account. Another agency, AMV, had Hollywood hero Bob Hoskins at its pitch for BT (which it won).

Strict adherence to the time and type of presentation (specified by the client) is essential. When **Burkitt Weinreich Bryant** was pitching for **Littlewoods**, it was asked to make a 'short and sweet' final pitch, since the then 92-year-old chairman, the late Sir John Moores, would be in attendance. The trade press reported that 'after over 30 minutes managing director Hugh Burkitt was asked to finish as it became obvious that Sir John's interest and attention was waning'. A row broke out as Hugh Burkitt persisted and a senior Littlewoods executive tried to stop the pitch.

Way back in the 1990s, **when British Airways moved from Saatchi & Saatchi to Maurice and Charles Saatchi's new outfit, M&C Saatchi**, all the agencies involved threw everything at this prestigious £30 million account. In an attempt to dramatize BA's global reach, Saatchi & Saatchi did the pitch in different rooms for different stages. Each room had been completely redecorated in the styles, natural habitat and climate of particular parts of the world – tropical rainforests, etc. When Bartle Bogle Hegarty (BBH) got its chance, it reassured BA about BBH's ability to create extremely satisfied clients by providing ready-made testimonials after the presentation – a wall went back and BA were surrounded by the key decision makers of every one of BBH's clients, who then had lunch with them. When M&C Saatchi got its chance, **Maurice Saatchi stood up and talked about the importance of music to the**

BA brand, explaining that they had commissioned their own composer to create a unique blend of popular classical music that BA could own. A growing murmur of approval was heard. He went on to say that they would like the client to meet the composer, at which point **in walked Andrew Lloyd Webber.**

The **worst, most painful and potentially career-busting ad agency presentation** was presented by Saatchi & Saatchi's own Peter Levitan when pitching for the Adidas account. They had already been told by **Adidas** that the account was as good as theirs as long as they didn't $%&* up the pitch. They did. You can read an extract of the full detailed and honest account of it, mistake by mistake, at **http://prsmith.org/blog/**. An extract is also printed here with the kind permission of Peter Levitan, of Peter Levitan & Co:

> 'A few weeks after that meeting, Maurice (Saatchi) told me that we were going to pitch the global Adidas account. Huge brand, global business, cool category, big budget, powerful competition and potentially great creative. Not much more for an agency to wish for... A couple of days later, Maurice and the reclusive Charles Saatchi and I met with Robert Louis Dreyfus, Adidas' new CEO and majority owner to discuss the pitch. Get this: Robert was a good man and close friend of the agency. Close? He had been the CEO of Saatchi & Saatchi Advertising Worldwide. He was one of us... I am working with Maurice and Charles Saatchi – the most famous advertising men in the world. They asked me to run a huge pitch for the global Adidas account. Adidas' CEO is a close friend of the agency and the management of Adidas America wants us... But wait, there's even more good news. During an early meeting, Robert leans over to me and says: "Peter, you've won this business as long as you don't $%&* up the pitch."'

The pitch, however, flopped. A video opening with scenes of baby seals being beaten to death as a way of demonstrating man's inhumanity to man contrasted with the big idea: 'the glory of sports', just didn't work. Compounded by a lack of rehearsals, big egos, no leader/manager, no control, no budgets, no real understanding of the clients' challenges and opportunities, loose creative brief and the pitch team roles based on seniority (not expertise), the pitch failed.

Dropping your guard

During an intense, high-profile, multimillion-pound pitch, the client called for a 10-minute break. Unfortunately for the agency (which will remain unnamed), a senior agency member had forgotten to remove his scribbled notes, which the client accidentally read. 'Watch out for the – in the glasses', it said at one point. Not surprisingly, the agency lost the pitch.

Pitches, like presentations for major campaigns, are now an ongoing process where effort is concentrated on developing a relationship (relationship marketing) with the client before the final presentation. This can sometimes involve client exposure to the strategy and even the advertisements before D-Day. One UK agency, Howell Henry Chaldecott Lury, has tried to appropriate this process on its own with what it calls 'tissue groups', ie a series of build-up meetings with the client. In the United States the most notable exponent, Chiat Day, has been doing this for a long time. Without doubt there is a cultural shift to ongoing pitches rather than a big finale.

Post-pitch agency's agonizing wait

Post-pitch tension is agonizing. Awaiting the outcome of a pitch is a tense and worrying time. When the phone eventually rings and it turns out to be the prospect, everyone holds their breath. Rejection means total failure. All the brilliant ideas, the careful research, the buzz of excitement, the long hours – all down the drain. Selection means total success. The post-pitch wait makes the mind wander. Were there any clues as to what the client thought of the pitch? Len Weinreich, advertising guru, had an almost unbearable wait in 'No news is bad news' (see Figure 7.4, p 229).

Occasionally the prospect client actually helps the agency by giving feedback that identifies where the client saw a real weakness. The agency can then eradicate the weakness before the next pitch. Similarly, a successful agency will be interested to find out why it was chosen, so that it can capitalize on its strengths.

Analysing the agency

As Nigel Bogle, CEO of Bartle Bogle Hegarty, says: 'The key questions today are less about an agency's ability to execute brilliantly and more about visionary strategic thinking, razor-sharp positioning, pinpoint targeting and ingenious media solutions.'

The order of importance of the following questions can vary, depending on what the prospective client really wants. Some clients may consider the agency's location and car parking facilities relevant, whereas other clients would discount this as trivial and irrelevant to good advertising. Here are two dozen questions that will help you to get deep down inside the agency you are considering working with:

1. Does the agency really have a feel for my product and market? Does it really understand my brand's situation and potential?
2. Have they got a great solution to the problem/challenge/issue?
3. Does the agency understand and use Big Data, AI, IoT, AR, VR, marketing automation, chatbots?
4. Has it got creative flair? Does it win awards? Does it suggest new ideas?
5. Has it got strong research and planning capability?
6. Does it know the best media to use? Will its media-buying skills make my budget go further?
7. Who will work on our account? Will the pitch team be involved? Are the people who worked on the case histories still with the agency? How stable will our account team be? Are we likely to get on together (chemistry)?
8. Is it full-service, or does everything get subcontracted out? How much integration experience with above-, through- and below-the-line as well as online does it have?
9. Is it international? Can its headquarters force it to resign the account should it decide to seek business in the same industry overseas? Alternatively, can it take on a lot of our coordination work through its own international management network?
10. What will it charge? And on what basis? How much time will it spend on the account?
11. How does it allocate resources in the planning, testing and evaluation process?
12. Does it display cost-consciousness?
13. How is my 'investment' going to be returned? (This should feature prominently in the agency's pitch.)
14. How will it measure its effectiveness? High-performing agencies measure their results constantly – do this agency?
15. Is the agency agile – can they adapt quickly if results not coming in? Can they make changes in real time?
16. Are we a small fish in a big pond? Is it too small or too big for us? Do we have contact with the principal partners? Will it fire us if a competitor offers it a bigger account (should we insist on a five-year contract)?
17. Does it have a good track record? Do clients stick with it and place repeat business with the agency? If not, why not?
18. How much experience does the agency have in marketing integration (particularly with the tech stack)?
19. What is the agency process (not just a bunch of arrows in a fancy PowerPoint slide)? How does it intend to allocate resources (time and people) to particular aspects of the campaign, including planning, concept development, testing and evaluation, etc? This helps in making interesting comparisons with other agencies. How much time will it devote to your account?
20. What is the agency's 'purpose' beyond making money? Ask what feedback comes from their staff and client exit interviews. Ask do they have a learning and development plan for staff – what does it look like? How many days training per staff member per annum? Do not allow soft answers such as 'Our people are our best asset.' Really? Prove it.
21. Is the agency GDPR compliant if any campaigns integrate with data collection? Note the research agency will be the data controller or joint data controller.

22 What are the agency client retention rates?

23 Check the agency's references. References from past clients must also be requested.

24 Check whether the agency care for their staff (and do their staff leave or stay) – how do they avoid staff burnout and deal with mental health, the gender pay gap, diversity, parental leave and the #timeTo campaign against sexual harassment?

The pitch is never over: Cars have ears

After making a good pitch, a well-known agency kindly offered a chauffeur-driven car to take the clients to the next agency on the pitch list. During the journey, the client team analysed the previous pitch and commented that the media strategy appeared 'off-brief'. The next day the agency found a way of representing the media strategy – and it won the business. The limo driver was an account man at the agency. Ethical or not, it's reality.

If you want to drill down a bit deeper, here are another seven slightly more technical topics for discussion with potential clients – from Brent Trimble (2017).

1 **Spatial:** Localization, geographic precision and targeting... connecting product, service, platform, description and metadata with geography, device, location and experience will be imperative for products and brands.

2 **Platforms vs impressions:** Platforms such as Google, Microsoft, Facebook, Amazon and Apple will continue to dominate both monetized ad inventory (such as AdWords, Facebook Advertising, Bing) as well as experience (Apple iTunes) and utility (Google, Apple app marketplaces) and commerce (Amazon, Google Shopping) .

3 **Drive audiences that are rapidly changing:** How can you drive audiences, particularly in a dynamic where consumers visit few independent domains each year, and consolidate, curate and refine their digital experience specific platforms, applications and systems?

4 **Predictive:** Display and other targeting platforms have become more and more accurate and predictive of targeting intent, the stage of consumers on specific journey paths and propensity of conversion. AI and machine learning platforms will increase effectiveness over time.

5 **Adaptive:** Creative messaging and cross-device delivery improvement are increasingly driving better results. Multivariate testing on site destinations and dynamic creative platforms – literal manifestations of adaptation – will continue to improve.

6 **The speed of delivery** of digital content and the ability of brand destinations to adapt to user devices, connections, locations and modes of communication will become an increasingly important aspect of campaign optimization.

7 **Transparent and credible:** Publishers, platforms and app experience will increasingly refine their delivery to provide credible, relevant and quality content and experiences to users.

Choosing an agency

The assessment form shown in Figure 7.3 can be weighted and scored as appropriate for each client's needs. A rating scale of 1–6 can be used. Agencies should be assessed using the same criteria. Few agencies perform so outstandingly that they remove all doubt in the client's mind as to which agency it should choose. The criteria should be agreed in advance by the team involved in the selection process. The assessment form shows one approach that attempts to formalize the selection by using consistent criteria. Each company obviously tailors its own approach.

Some agencies add a little extra hook, sometimes proprietary applications, widgets or iApps, data analytics or AI.

The client must eventually tell the unlucky agencies they have not been chosen. Rejected agencies will ask for feedback about their pitch. Professional clients will have kept their evaluation scores and

FIGURE 7.3 Choosing an agency – an assessment form

AGENCY	Understand our product and company?	Commit-ment to our project?	Research, planning & strategic thinking	Data analytics, AI, IoT, AR, VR	Media planning and buying including digital	Creative	Size, in-house resources, full service including digital	International	Location	Fee/cost	Will we get on?	Opinion of existing clients
1												
2												
3												
4												
5												

SOURCE: Courtesy of IH Digital

FIGURE 7.4 When no news is bad news – waiting to hear

When no news is bad news

"Why don't they ring? It's been four, no, three, days since they were in for the presentation. Didn't they say they'd make their minds up the next day? God. No news is bad news. Or is it good news? I can never quite remember.

"Anyway, I don't think we won it. I mean, we would have heard, wouldn't we? That guy, the one down the end of the table with the woolly khaki tie, he never liked us. He asked the worst questions. Like that one about putting all their press money in TV. That was a stinker, maliciously inserted to distract me. Quite arrested my flow, log-jammed my drift. No sense of unfolding drama, silly sod.

"The woman liked us though. I had a feeling she'd marked us down because we had too few women in the presentation team. But I could tell she warmed to me. Smiled a lot when I projected in her direction. God! Why haven't they rung yet? It's not as if we really need their lousy business, after all it's only an account. Ad agencies are like revolving doors: one account leaves and another one follows, I mean, enters. Have you seen this year's free-fall figures? The income from their billing would make good the loss of those bastards from . . .

"We won't get it. They hated the

Len Weinreich

creative work. Detested it. They sneered at the ads. You would've thought they'd never seen a real commercial before. On the other hand, they'd asked us to be radical. Their brief advised ignoring all restraints. Still, I think it might have been wiser to check the script with the ITVA before the presentation. The naked couple and the golden retriever might be a little rich for today's audience.

"We spent a month assembling this presentation and now, a week, okay, maybe three days later, not a dicky bird. Not a peep. Not even a whimper. Not even one of those mysterious calls to the media department dishing them undercover dirt. Nothing.

"Perhaps we should have bribed them. Maybe we should have taped a few large denomination notes to the inside covers of their documents. Perhaps I really should have nobbled the top man when he dashed out for a pee.

"Quite frankly, I think they loathed the work. And my suit. And our media director. It didn't help that our creative (ho, ho) director completely cocked up the order of the storyboards. Or that our dizzy planner addressed their company by the wrong name, twice. This instant they obviously are appointing someone else because they have no wit, taste, imagination, discernment or balls.

"I'm not so sure we'd be happy handling their business. They'd be terrible clients. Endless trips to their remote offices to niggle over a charity ad mechanical.

"Stuff their lousy business. Probably seriously unprofitable. In fact, I shouldn't be surprised if they went belly up. I've heard some interesting City whispers concerning the bizarre hotel bedroom habits of their chairman. Apparently . . . ***, is that the phone?"

Len Weinreich is a vice chairman of Burkitt Weinreich Bryant Clients and Company

will take time to either share these or write a brief feedback explaining what the agency needs to improve on. The rejected agency's managing director then has the difficult job of picking up the shattered team and building up the agency morale again.

As managing directors are never told that their pitches are terrible and come last, having always been narrowly beaten into second place, there is a plea from the advertising industry to clients that they should tell it like it really is!

Ongoing agency–client relationships

Having gone through the rigorous and sometimes exhausting process of choosing an agency, it is important to maintain a good working relationship. You do not want to split up after 6 or 12 months and have to waste all those resources searching for another agency. That is bad management. Senior management takes a poor view when they see a particular manager going through regular agency recruitment processes. Questions start to be asked. More importantly you have to get on and deliver results and not be distracted by major partner selection processes. You have to be able to manage relationships when you work with an agency.

Agency relationship and pressure

The BBC's Chief Customer Officer, Kerris Bright, said:

> **'Creativity does not come out of the wrong type of pressure and stress**. There's a pressure that's got an optimism and a positivity, a trust and a belief in it, so I absolutely believe in pressure, but I think you have to show confidence and trust. You have to create a sense of positivity and feel like you are in a collective endeavour.'
>
> Bright also believes that agencies sometimes fail to appreciate the pressures brand side marketers are under within their own organizations. However, if they can turn these pressures to their advantage this can be a great strategy for future success. "One thing I try to do, because I've seen the impact of getting it right and wrong, is think about how you exert the right positive pressure," Bright explained.'
>
> Rogers (2019)

How to ensure good agency relationships

- Invest in 'onboarding' – introducing the agency team to the client team, getting them working together as a team.
- Be very clear about remuneration – fees, commissions, mark-ups, time, expenses and method of billing – in writing. Remember, it is better to argue over a quote than an invoice.
- Explain to the agency who makes what decisions, ie who has authority for which decisions.
- Sign or approve in writing each stage from brief to concepts – finished artwork, running proofs and so on.
- Keep briefs short and unambiguous.
- Communications – regular reviews help to plug any gaps in performance, whether creative, strategic or personal.
- Write an occasional thank-you note to the team.
- Trust the agency team (share research and information with them, and involve them).
- Share the problems/challenges but also share the celebrations when results are achieved.
- Make them become part of the marketing team. Use their expertise.
- Ask relevant questions. Listen carefully to the answers. Do not be intimidated by strong agency characters. All propositions should be justifiable. The final decision is the client's.

Onboarding

Onboarding is the process of welcoming or introducing a customer or a client to an organization, usually. However, clients/brand owners also like to get the agencies on board quickly so they can build a strong team. Regardless of who instigates it both parties need to meet each other's teams, clarify expectations, understand each other's modus operandi, establish some ground rules and build an integrated team that is motivated to deliver great results. Onboarding includes getting to know each other, answering any questions or concerns and setting common goals.

Not having a good onboarding process can be one of the costliest mistakes you can make when working closely with a new team. Onboarding includes everything from the initial welcome email, letter, phone call or personal visit to clarifying the scope of work plan, the subsequent modus operandi including frequency of reviews (formal and informal). Establishing common goals is important to build a team. Increasingly, teams are agile whether they use Scrum, Waterfall, Kanban or some other approach. The preferred comms channel (eg Slack, Skype, Google Hangouts, etc) and access to shared files (including brand guidelines and logos, images, videos) and other content files must be established early on. In fact, it is not uncommon to see agency staff move into and work from clients' offices.

A stable relationship builds a real team, since the agency gets to know the client, the team, the company and the market inside out. In addition, the client does not have to worry about unfriendly discarded agencies that have previously had access to sensitive information.

Companies like P&G, Coca-Cola, Unilever, Nestlé and others are deemed to be the best-in-class brands when it comes to integrated marketing communications. '**All of the top players have their agencies evaluate them.** Some even have their agencies evaluate each other. But all of them have built in a continuous learning loop to keep driving innovation and integration and keep asking "what's next?"' (R3, 2015).

Unilever stops paying for slow work and integrates communications via multi-discipline, better-trained integrated digital teams

'Unilever is often identified as a thought leader in integrated marketing communications. Starting with the business objectives for the brand and remaining agnostic to the channels used to deliver the big ideas, Unilever takes a consistently unified approach that is enabled by multi-disciplined teams and the environment of collaboration promoted among all Unilever brands. As a part of its "Crafting Brands for Life" strategy, Unilever seeks to strike a healthy balance between magic and logic – or in other words, creativity and sales. Unilever also doubled its spend on marketing training to keep up with the ever-changing digital landscape and build a stronger team that goes beyond sole marketing skills.

From 2014 onwards, R3 has been consulting with the global Unilever team on Agency Integration, Management and Compensation. While this assignment is still confidential, the approach is to **reward agency partners on outcomes**, not on inputs. In a world where, under a fee structure, agencies are paid more based on the slowness of their work (more hours), Unilever is seeking a new path that will truly enable stronger alignment between their goals and the agency's ideas.'

R3 (2015)

Draining the joy and motivation

'Could you do more to avoid draining the joy and motivation from the very people [agency people] whose productivity your career depends on? Whether it's an occasional crappy briefing or unreasonable last-minute request.... Be part of an honest conversation.'

Bonn (2018)

Unhappy clients and unhappy agencies

It seems as if many relationships between clients and agencies are not great. According to research by the World Federation of Advertisers, 'clients give their current agency roster set-up a score of just 5.7 out of 10, where 10 is fit for purpose. Agencies themselves believe the situation is even worse, with current arrangements given a score of 5.2' (Vizard, 2018). Issues such as media transparency, revenue transparency, ad fraud (click fraud) and influencer fraud (fake followers) are making clients anxious. Vizard continues by suggesting that there may be a trend towards more clients developing their own in-house teams ('in-housing') – whether it is specializing in data science, programmatic advertising, marketing content or whole creative departments (primarily for content), as clients are unhappy with their agencies':

- lack of transparent billing model;
- lack of expertise for new communications channels (inexperienced staff);
- pitching process is too expensive/time consuming.

Agencies have got away with murder

Nick Bennett, Honda UK's Digital Content and Social Media Manager, suggests:

'"For too long, agencies have got away with murder. They have basically outlined what's successful based on metrics that work for them but don't necessarily constitute what's happening in the real world." Bennett, who joined Honda two years ago after spending 13 years agency side, thinks the traditional agency model will "crumble" in the next 10 years.'

Hammet (2018)

Firing the agency

A *Campaign* magazine survey identified the following reasons for sacking an agency (in order of importance to the client):

- receiving no fresh input;
- account conflict at the agency;
- a new marketing director arriving;
- a change of client's policy;
- other accounts leaving the agency.

A derivative of the second point, conflict of interests, arises with mergers and acquisitions. After acquiring Gillette for $57 billion, P&G sacked Gillette's agency, Mindshare (part of the WPP Group). Gillette explained that it was removing its $800 million global media planning and buying business. Mindshare already worked for Unilever, P&G's arch-rival (WARC, 2005c).

In the international arena, business relationships (including agency relationships) are even more delicate, as WPP discovered when it was fired by China's largest advertising conglomerate (Citic and its Beijing Guoan Advertising arm). Citic's Vice-Chairman, Yan Gang, claimed that WPP's CEO, Sir Martin Sorrell, had treated him 'very rudely' during an April meeting in London to discuss management problems at the joint venture (WARC, 2006).

Although over 25 years old, *Campaign* magazine's '13 ways to be a loser' article identifies many recurring reasons why agencies still get fired:

1. **Control of brand's advertising switches to rival of client:** Gold Greenlees Trott lost Fosters when Elders IXL and its Courage division took over control of marketing Fosters from Watneys, a GGT client.
2. **Agency produces irrelevant or inappropriate advertising:** Lowe Howard-Spink lost some of its prized Mobil account after its 'breakthrough' Dan Dare campaign failed. Insufficient planning was cited as a reason behind the fiasco.
3. **Client is unsettled over too many changes at agency:** Foote Cone and Belding lost £22 million worth of business – including Heinz and Cadbury – because of management upheaval.
4. **Client unhappy over excess negative publicity surrounding its agency:** IBM is uncomfortable over the widely reported lawsuits involving its agency and breakaway Lord Einstein O'Neill and Partners. Could result in IBM choosing neither and picking a new shop.
5. **Takeover of agency infuriates client:** Goodyear, Philips, Pilsbury said goodbye to JWT after it was taken over by WPP. Most cite 'disruption' as a reason for leaving.
6. **Client rationalizes its agency roster:** Toyota chose its dealer agency Brunnings over its main agency Lintas London after a creative shoot-out. British Telecom reviewed its entire account and picked three main agencies – BBH, Abbott Mead and JWT.
7. **Total breakdown in agency–client relationship:** GGT resigns the *Daily Express* after repeated clashes and an inability to work with title's marketing staff.
8. **Agency fails to come to terms with account:** BMP got sacked by Comet, its first major retail client. Former vice-chairman Paul Leeves said BMP won the business 'one year too soon'.
9. **Lack of solution creatively:** Abbot Mead couldn't crack the *Daily Telegraph*. Later the agency admitted to producing tasteless series of press ads that aroused the ire of women, among others.
10. **New client arrives:** Allen Brady & Marsh's long-standing Milk account was reviewed after new NDC chief Richard Pears joined.
11. **Agency can't master the client's politics:** JWT lost British Rail. Agency was allied to the central advertising body while the chairman, Bob Reid, was committed to devolution. Network SouthEast chief Chris Green was not keen on JWT after it produced two poor ads, one of which put it in legal hot water with the Monty Python people.

12 **Agency merges with another, producing conflict and massive disruption:** difficulties surrounding the merger of Reeves Robertshaw Needham and Doyle Dane Bernbach resulted in massive client fall-out.

13 **Client is the subject of a merger or takeover:** Fast becoming a major reason for account moves.

Reproduced by kind permission of Haymarket Marketing Publications Limited and Laurie Ludwick

Firing the client

Agencies sometimes resign accounts, particularly if a larger competing account is offered to them. Occasionally, they are obliged to resign if an agency takeover or merger brings in some competing accounts and thereby creates a conflict of interest. New demands by a client sometimes become so difficult that the account becomes unprofitable or, as in the case of ABM, a reduced commission is considered unsatisfactory.

Arrogance and egos

Some years ago, a continually critical senior marketing manager commented at the end of yet another long, unsatisfactory meeting, 'If this were my company [which it wasn't; he was an employee], I would fire the agency.' The long-suffering creative director responded, 'If this were my agency, which it is, I would fire the client, which I am.' He left the room, with the marketing manager knowing he now had to face colleagues and break the news that there was no campaign ready to roll out, no agency, and an agonizing new pitch process required.

How to upset the client and get sent to jail – overcharge them

'Thomas Early (former senior partner and finance director) and Shona Seifert (former president) at Ogilvy & Mather (O&M) New York were both reported by WARC to have been found guilty in 2005 of fraudulently overbilling the White House Office of National Drug Control Policy in 1999 and 2000. The guilty pair were allegedly responding to the anger of O&M North America's co-president Bill Gray at the loss of anticipated income. Gray was not among the accused. Early got a 14-month prison sentence and $10,000 fine. Seifert got an 18-month prison sentence and $125,000 fine (she was also ordered to write a code of advertising industry ethics). O&M extricated itself (but not its employees) from the affair with a $1.8 million settlement in 2002.'

WARC (2005b)

Agency issues

Rapid change means markets are changing, and so too agency structures must change. Amidst this 4th Industrial Revolution everything is changing for agencies. In-housing, low levels of client (and agency) satisfaction, not to mention data science, AI, IoT, VR, AR, MA and the constantly changing (and soon fully integrating tech stacks). It seems IoT could bring a whole range of new partners into play. Partners that can carry messages and conversations via home and office accessories. Equally, chatbots (see Chapter 5) and messaging combined with personalization means a whole new world is opening up for agencies, particularly as the platform companies hover and consider which industry is ripest for their entry. As they sit on their data mountains, the BAT Boys and the FANGs seem well positioned to become powerful partners in the new world of agencies of the future. Clients today are 'dividing their brand building affections across consulting firms, digital platforms and publishers as well as exploring the potent opportunity of doing the whole thing in-house' (Ritson, 2018).

In-housing

Some brands feel that content marketing is such a major part of their communications that they want to bring this function back in-house, rather than subcontract to an agency. Honda UK are taking content creation in-house. Other brands now want to deliver their in-house programmatic advertising (media buying). Lego and Spotify are building internal creative teams for advertising.

New competitors

Agencies are under pressure from activist investors, new competitors, and a trend towards setting up in-house departments. Plus professional services firms (the big consultancies) are taking a slice of the strategy and digital transformation end of spend.

'The digital duopoly of Facebook and Google are able to reach brands directly without the need for an agency middleman' (Marketing Week Reporters, 2018). See 'FANG are coming to get you' (**http://prsmith.org/blog/**).

And on top of all that, we have issues such as media transparency, ad fraud (click fraud) and influencer fraud (fake followers) (Marketing Week Reporters, 2018) as well as artificial influencers (see Chapter 5) and audiences with shorter attention spans, less time and little tolerance for anything not immediately relevant.

Lack of agency differentiation

> Ask agency people over a beer what enabled one firm to win a big account versus other agencies and most will revert back to the 'back bench' of five or six star people in each country who could offer the most impressive vision of strategy, media and creative to the client team. The brand of the firm comes a distinct second to the talent, almost as if the agencies themselves – other than as a house for certain people – are basically identical in scope, service and positioning.
>
> Ritson (2018)

Almost one third of agency staff leave each year. The IPA Agency Census 2017 reveals annual staff turnover of agencies at 32 per cent in 2017 (and 29.4 per cent in 2016). Albeit not necessarily senior agency stars, but nevertheless how does that affect your brand when middle and lower rank agency staff are leaving your account to work with another agency perhaps? Turning over?

Agency consolidation

'When private labels from Tesco and Sainsbury began to make significant inroads into the supermarket categories of the 90s the big FMCG firms like Procter & Gamble and Unilever did a very smart thing. They closed down their number three, four and five brands and focused their resources on the number one and two brands in a category, which could not only defend their turf against Tesco Value but actually prosper in that new competitive context. In the same way, WPP now hopes a smaller cadre of agencies with more horsepower will win the day against Accenture, Google and an in-house team of 300 down the road.'

Ritson (2018)

Summary and conclusion

So changing times for agencies both now and in the future. One thing is for sure, agencies will want to be both creative and analytical (with good data science and AI skills). Agencies will also have to be able to integrate data generated by their customer touchpoints with other customer touchpoints (whether bots, messaging, personalized videos) with all other customer touchpoints so that their clients and their brands will be able to deliver one seamless CX, which ultimately boosts the clients results. Happy clients equals happy agencies.

Key points from Chapter 7

- Clear communications between client and agency are important if the right messages are going to be successfully communicated to target audiences.
- Agencies, consultancies and consultants can become more than just suppliers of marketing services; they can become strategic partners of the client.
- Careful selection is crucial to ensure the development of a mutually beneficial long-term relationship.

References

Bashford, S (2008) The rise of the intermediary, *PR Week*, 4 July

Boches, E (2016) The new generation of hybrid creatives is here. Is your agency ready for them? *AdWeek*, 4 May

Bonn, R (2018) Why it's time to pay more for your agencies, *Marketing Week*, 23 November

Bruell, A (2011) Redner group loses biggest client over tweet, *Ad Age*, 15 June

Bruell, A (2017) Advertisers seek to simplify agency pay by reviving commissions, *Wall Street Journal*, 22 May

Burnett, L (nd) Quote bank, World Advertising Research Centre

Cowley, D (ed) (1989) *How to Plan Advertising*, Thomson Learning, London

Crain, R (2013) Agencies add data to boost fees, but whose data is it? *Ad Age*, 25 March

Farey-Jones, D (2008) Consumer relationships key to future agency success, *Brand Republic*, 8 February

Faull, J (2019) Advertisers turn to performance-based remuneration for ad agencies, *The Drum*, 31 January

Hammett, E (2018) Honda 'ditches' agencies in move to take charge of its brand, *Marketing Week*, 24 October

Henke, N, Levine, J and McInerney, P (2018) You don't have to be a data scientist to fill this must-have analytics role, *HBR*, 5 February

Hobbs, T (2017) Marketers returning to commission-based pay models for agencies, *Marketing Week*, 23 May

IPA (2003) *The Client Brief: A best practice guide to briefing communications agencies*, Joint industry guidelines for young marketing professionals in working effectively with agencies, IPA, ISBA, MCCA, PRCA, London

ISBA (2010) in conjunction with the Advertising Research Consortium, *Paying for Advertising 5*, ISBA, London

Joseph, S (2013) Nike takes social media in-house, *Marketing Week*, 3 January

Kemp, M and Kim, P (2008) *The Connected Agency*, Forrester report

Learmonth, M (2010) Do you know the ABCs of DSPs? Agency-relations teams pitch in, *Ad Age*, 26 April

Ledger, A (2017) *Brand Experience Report 2017: Pitching and payment*, 28 June [online] www.campaignlive.co.uk/article/brand-experience-report-2017-pitching-payment/1437428 (archived at https://perma.cc/BWK5-ZQV6)

Levitan, P (2014) *The Levitan Pitch: Buy This Book. Win More Pitches*, Portlandia Press, Portland, Oregon

Marketing Week Reporters (2018) 2018 year in review: It's been a bad year for..., *Marketing Week*, 10 December

Nicolaci da Costa, A (2019) The pun-loving computer programs that write adverts, BBC News, 21 May

O'Brien, M (2015) The agency of the future, 1 July [online] http://prsmith.org/blog/ (archived athttps://perma.cc/67JZ-HYWA)

O'Brien, M (2017) Laughing time is almost over for the agency as we know it, *Jam Partnership*, 16 December

O'Leary, N (2013) Martin Sorrell talks candidly about mergers, mayhem – and his own demise, *Ad Week*, 10 November

Pandey, R (2016) Media rebates: What is the industry doing about it? 6 August [online] Marketing-Interactive.com (archived at https://perma.cc/GYS6-66WH)

Parekh, R (2013) The ad biz is yukking it up with the #AgencyLife hashtag, *Advertising Age*, 12 April

Perry, R (2015) So what is brand activation? *Guardian*

R3 (2015) Integration 40: A report by R3 on 40 of the world's most integrated marketing approaches, *R3 Worldwide*

Rijkens, R (1993) *European Advertising Strategies*, Thomson Learning, London

Ritson, M (2018) Today's agencies are like yachts – underused, expensive and all the same, *Marketing Week*, 29 November

Rogers , C (2019) The BBC's customer chief on the power of marketing at the 'extreme edges', *Marketing Week*, 24 January

Roope, N (2018) Hybrid creatives are the future, *Campaign*, 7 December

Shields, R (2015) The case for big brands taking ad tech in-house exchange, *Wire*, 6 May

Sorrell, M (1996) Beans and pearls, D&AD President's Lecture

Stengel, J (2006) Top P&G marketer urges agencies to integrate planning, *WARC*, 7 February

Stengel, J (2010) How to save the troubled agency–marketer relationship, *Ad Age*, 26 April

Trimble, B (2017) Choosing an agency partner in a changing digital landscape, *Campaign*, 10 November

Vizard, S (2018) Trends for 2019: Agencies under attack from all sides, *Marketing Week*, 12 December

WARC (World Advertising Research Centre) (2005a) British Airways ditches Saatchi Brothers after 23 years, 10 November

WARC (2005b) O&M's Early jailed for ONDCP fraud, 14 July

WARC (2005c) WPP's 'Chinese walls' fail to reassure P&G, 6 October

WARC (2006) Chinese ad giant drops WPP pact in favor of Omnicom, data sourced from https://adage.com/ (archived at https://perma.cc/MQ9L-PXPA), additional content by WARC staff, 16 June

Watt, N (2013) What are the challenges facing agencies in the digital revolution? *Squared* [online] www.wearesquared.com (archived at https://perma.cc/QF5G-DW4N)

Weinreich, L (2000) *Seven Steps to Brand Heaven*, Kogan Page, London

Williams, H (2008) Six Degrees lands BIMA retained brief, *PR Week*, 29 August

World Federation of Advertisers (2018) *Global Agency Remuneration Report 2018*

Further information

AdForum MayDream SA
112 Bis rue Cardinet
75017 Paris
France
Tel: +33 (0) 1 42 04 96 37
www.adforum.com

Advertising Agency Registrar Services
AAR Group
26 Market Place
London W1W 8AN
Tel +44 (0)20 7612 1200
www.aargroup.co.uk

Advertising Association
7th Floor North
Artillery House
11–19 Artillery Row
London SW1P 1RT
Tel: +44 (0)20 7340 1100
www.adassoc.org.uk

Agency Assessments International
Creative Partnerships
100 Pall Mall
London SW1Y 5NQ
www.agencyassessments.com

British Rate and Data (BRAD)
BRAD Insight
Burleigh House
357 Strand
London WC2R 0HS
Tel: +44 (0)20 7420 3252
https://bradinsight.com/

Incorporated Society of British Advertisers
ISBA
12 Henrietta Street
London WC2E 8LH
Tel: +44(0)20 7291 9020
www.isba.org.uk

Institute of Practitioners in Advertising (IPA)
44 Belgrave Square
London SW1X 8QS
Tel: +44 (0)20 7235 7020
Fax: +44 (0)20 7245 9904
www.ipa.co.uk

08 International marketing communications

LEARNING OBJECTIVES

By the end of this chapter you will be able to:

- understand the globalization of markets and the international opportunities arising;
- list and explore the international challenges arising in international markets;
- avoid the classic errors in international markets;
- discuss the strategic global options available to marketers interested in growing on a global scale.

The globalization of markets

This chapter examines opportunities and the difficulties, strategic options and actual implications for implementation of international marketing communications, in particular global communications.

The growing global opportunity

Airbnb, Red Bull and Coca-Cola are just three of the many brands that have seized the global opportunity (more on them later). Meanwhile, just look around you. Yogurt, pizza, spaghetti, rice, kebabs, Indian cuisine, Chinese meals, Mexican food, Japanese sushi and American burgers are popular and now available in most cities across the world. Not too long ago they were considered sophisticated luxuries. The Rolling Stones and Shakespeare also have a global appeal. Coincidentally, there are more people learning English in China than speak it in the United States.

Thirty years ago, back in 1985, the global village emerged when 1.9 billion people from different time zones across the world simultaneously watched, and donated funds to Live Aid, the charity concert for Ethiopian famine relief. And so we continue to connect and communicate more easily with free WhatsApp calls and video sharing as well as Skype video conference calls. The London to Brussels train is quicker than the London to Newcastle train. However, be forewarned: clichés like 'The world is getting smaller' oversimplify this growing global opportunity but remember it is one that is still wrapped in cultural complexity.

Some say that human beings have more things that bind them together than separate them; others argue that market differences are greater than market similarities. There are, in fact, what the Young & Rubicam creative agency called 'cross-cultural consumer characteristics'. These identify the common ground. The person living in a smart apartment block in London's Knightsbridge probably has more in common with his or her counterpart living in a smart apartment block off New York's Central Park than with someone living in a drab south London suburb. There are indeed some common denominators and some common sets of needs and aspirations that can be identified, particularly in similarities of lifestyle.

China alone presents a vast opportunity, but one that needs careful attention, understanding, planning and long-term commitment.

Global markets are here. Al Jazeera's English-language TV news service has a 100 million audience worldwide. BBC World Service does what it says on the tin. Football clubs have global fans; Barcelona FC have 83 million fans on Facebook alone, while Manchester United Football Club have 64 million Facebook fans; recently it has been claimed they have 659 million fans around the world (**www.kantar.com**), although this is disputed by the BBC (Prior, 2013). Since media follow markets, media consumption is going global; therefore marketers must remember that brands with international ambitions must have a consistent global image – production should be international in mind, and content rights should be global (Chaffey and Smith, 2008).

Three global marketing success stories

Red Bull

Red Bull created a new global position and use word of mouth rather than mass media. They **saw a gap in the market and positioned/created a new category** of non-soda energy drinks aimed at burned-out high-school and college students. Red Bull's international event marketing strategy (hosting extreme sports events all over the world), supported by excellent content and free local experiential marketing mobilizing influencer advocates, combined with its distinctive and consistent unique packaging style has helped them to become an identifiable global 'anti-brand' (doing it their way). This Austrian company does such a great job with global marketing that many Americans assume it's a local brand.

Their **extreme sports events all over the world** include the Red Bull Indianapolis Grand Prix, the Red Bull Air Race in the UK, the Red Bull Soapbox Race in Jordan, not to mention the Bull Stratos 'mission to the edge of space' – a supersonic freefall parachute jump.

Harvard Professor Nancy Koehn said: 'Red Bull really looks like a product from a global economy. It doesn't look like a traditional American soft drink – it's not in a 12-ounce can, it's not sold in a bottle, and it doesn't have script lettering like Pepsi or Coke.

It looks European. That matters' (Rodgers, 2001) See more on p 574.

Airbnb

Airbnb has grown into a disruptive global brand. They celebrate this with an extraordinary 'global, social experiment' driven by social media around the hashtag #OneLessStranger. Airbnb ask their community to perform random acts of hospitality for strangers, and then take a video or photo with the person and share it using the hashtag.

San Francisco's Airbnb started in 2008 and is now a global community marketplace for people to rent and reserve accommodation just about anywhere in the world. Just three weeks after the launch of what was a global social experiment, Airbnb had over three million people across the world highly engaged (creating content), and, of course, talking about it.

Coca-Cola

Think global – act local community. Coca-Cola has worked hard to become a global brand. Whether it is in the burning desert heat or the frozen snowy mountain tops, Coca-Cola take great pride in getting their brand into the hands of customers anywhere, even if delivered by camel, husky or a special weightless Coca-Cola can for astronauts in space. Although it is a large global brand selling emotion (with a central global theme of 'happiness'), it acts local with small-scale local community relations programmes. For example, in Egypt, Coca-Cola built clean water installations in the rural village of Beni Suef. It sponsors Ramadan meals for children across the Middle East. In India, the brand sponsors the Support My School initiative to improve facilities at local schools.

Global marketplace: Prepare for new markets and new competitors: BAT Boys vs FANG

Will BAT (Baidu, Alibaba and Tencent), three massive Chinese platform companies, compete directly with FANG (Facebook, Amazon, Netflix and Google) and others like Apple? Baidu have hinted that there is no rush and that they target carefully, country by country.

Respecting global complexity/ cultural idiosyncrasies

The total global concept suggests that the big global marketing players can accelerate the globalization process by transcending cultural boundaries and bringing their messages, goods, services and traditions to the markets they choose.

There are some cultural norms that suggest that total globalization will not happen in every market, everywhere, at least not in the next few generations. Thank goodness for that. Here are a few interesting cultural idiosyncrasies.

The Barusho Bride
Lailan Young (1987) reported that the Barusho bride in the Himalayas has a tough time on her wedding night, as she has to share the bridal bed with her mother-in-law until the marriage is consummated.

Post-natal male exhaustion in Kerala
In the southern Indian state of Kerala, Puyala women return to the fields to tend the crops after the birth of their babies, while the husband goes to bed. The rest of the family ministers to his needs until he recovers. In the Andaman Islands, especially anxious husbands will stay in bed for anything up to six months (Young, 1987).

Women dominate men – Minaros
The lost kingdom of the Minaros was 'discovered' in a mountain hideaway 16,000 feet up in the Himalayas by a French explorer in 1984. The Amazon-like women totally dominate their men, marrying several at a time and keeping them in line by brute force.

Conspicuous consumption, extreme rivalry – Kwakiutl
The former Kwakiutl of Vancouver Island demonstrated what is almost a parody of industrial civilization: the chief motive of this tribe was rivalry, which was not concerned with the usual issues of providing for a family or owning goods, but rather aimed to outdo and shame neighbours and rivals by means of conspicuous consumption. At their potlatch ceremonies the people competed with each other in burning and destroying their valuable possessions and money.

> **No mercy from the Dobu**
> The Dobu of north-west Melanesia is reported to encourage malignant hatred and animosity. Treacherous conduct unmitigated by any concept of mercy or kindness and directed against neighbours and friends is expected.
>
> **Zuni shamed leaders**
> The Zuni (a branch of the Pueblos of New Mexico) are a people whose life is centred on religious ceremony, being prosperous but without interest in economic advancement. They admire most those men who are friendly, make no trouble and have no aspirations, detesting, on the other hand, those who wish to become leaders. Hence tribal leaders have to be compelled by threats to accept their position and are regarded with contempt and resentment once they have achieved it.

Even cultures that are relatively better known have their own intricacies over something as simple as a handshake, eye contact and the use of colours. For example, brown and grey are disapproved of in Nicaragua; white, purple and black are the colours of death for Japan, Latin America and Britain respectively.

Understanding other cultures: The oppressed male

'The Kagba women of North Colombia practise not only free love but free rape, and few men are safe.'

Young (1987)

If this is deemed to be strange, consider how other cultures might view the seemingly bizarre behaviour patterns of the tea-drinking, nose-blowing, ballroom-dancing and kissing population of Europe.

The reader may be surprised to know of a tribe where it is not uncommon for the men of the tribe to behave in a promiscuous manner with other men's wives and daughters in public. It is so popular it is even broadcast on their television networks. The country? The UK. The practice? Ballroom dancing. Here is a description of this behaviour:

> It is common in such dancing for the front of the bodies to be in constant contact – and they do this in public. In spite of the close physical touching involved in this type of dancing (a form of bodily contact not unlike that assumed in sexual intercourse), our society has defined it as almost totally asexual. Although ballroom dancing can involve high levels of intimacy, it is equally possible that there is no sexual content whatsoever. Many adult men in the United States have danced in this fashion with their mothers, their sisters, the wives of the ministers at church socials without anyone raising an eyebrow. Yet many non-American cultures view this type of dancing as the height of promiscuity and bad taste. It is interesting to note that many of those non-Americans for whom our dancing is a source of embarrassment are the very people we consider to be promiscuous, sex-crazed savages because their women do not cover their breasts.
>
> Ferraro (2001)

The international marketer embraces other cultures, researching and respecting the local culture as being right and proper and perhaps adopts Geertz's (1983) insight:

> the world... does not divide into the pious and the superstitious... there are sculptures in jungles and paintings in deserts... political order is possible without centralized power and principled justice without codified rules; the norms of reason were not fixed in Greece, the evolution of morality not consummated in England... We have, with no little success, sought to keep the world off balance, pulling out rugs, upsetting tea tables, setting off fire crackers. It has been the office of others to reassure; ours to unsettle.

Touching a global nerve

Despite the complexities of cultural idiosyncrasies, there are many common needs that manifest themselves into common wants and purchasing patterns, particularly where there are similar levels of economic wealth. It follows that, if a manufacturer or service supplier targets roughly the same socio-demographic groups in different countries and touches a common nerve within these target markets, then the same product or service can be packaged and promoted in a uniform manner. The pricing and distribution may vary, but the branding, packaging and even advertising can be the same.

The manufacturers of world brands can therefore position their products in a similar manner in the minds of millions across many different cultures. This is the result of careful analysis and planning by expert marketing professionals rather than a trial-and-error approach to market extension.

Cannibalistic disease: kissing

'A whole lot of people think kissing is not at all natural. It is not something that everybody does, or would like to do. On the contrary, it is a deplorable habit, unnatural, unhygienic, bordering on the nasty and even definitely repulsive. When we come to look into the matter, we shall find that there is a geographical distribution of kissing; and if some enterprising ethnologist were to prepare a "map of kissing" it would show a surprisingly large amount of blank space. Most of the so-called primitive races of mankind such as the New Zealanders (Maoris), the Australian Aborigines, the Pauans, Tahitians, and other South Sea islanders, and the Esquimaux of the frozen north, were ignorant of kissing until they were taught the technique by the white men... The Chinese have been wont to consider kissing as vulgar and all too suggestive of cannibalism... the Japanese have no word for it in their vocabulary.'

Pike (1966)

The next challenge lies in moving the rest of the communications mix in a uniform manner so that not just advertising and packaging but also sales promotions, direct mail, sponsorship, etc, reap the benefits of a global approach. This globalization issue has revealed itself through the increased use of the internet. Even local firms going on to the net attract customers from all over the world. A web presence can deliver a global presence. However, this does present challenges, as Pepsi discovered, with its European blue can being seen by its US customers, who much prefer the traditional red can. Similarly, Tia Maria, although it is consumed around the world, has different age segments in different countries, eg in the UK Tia Maria is about girl power, targeted at 18- to 24-year-olds, while in the Netherlands it's drunk neat by pensioners. Now this 'common nerve' presents a positioning challenge. Despite these difficulties, Coke, Airbnb, Red Bull, Apple, Facebook (just look at the Top 50 or Top 100 brands in Chapter 2) have proved that large, lucrative global markets do exist.

Forces driving globalization

Globalization has emerged not because of a product-orientated corporate sales push to find sales growth from international markets, but partly because of a market-orientated reaction to the emergence of common global lifestyles and needs. These are emerging as cheap travel combined with higher disposable incomes, allowing travellers to leap across borders, visit other cultures and return home with a little bit of that culture's soul in their own. Television and social media have also contributed. The key to global expansion, it seems, is to identify core benefits that are common to different cultures, along with any relevant cultural idiosyncrasies

The elite global players

The significant benefits derived from developing a global brand supported by a global communications strategy are currently reserved for a relatively small number of world-class globalized marketers. This elite band of players recognize the right conditions and apply thorough research and planning to exploit the brand's assets on a global scale. However, it should be remembered that a single communications strategy (incorporating everything from branding to the complete range of communications tools) rarely works for all the players operating in international markets. The desire to harness the global opportunity is natural, because international markets offer huge rewards. They also present intricate problems. Careful cultural homework needs to be included in the detailed research and planning that go below the surface.

Below-the-surface similarities

Similar buying behaviour and buying patterns do not necessarily mean a perfect uniform market with uniform needs, uniform communications channels, uniform decision-making processes, uniform decision-making units, or even uniform reasons for buying. Take the case of buying premium-priced water. In a

Khartoum slum an impoverished family pays 20 times the price paid by families with water main connections, while half a world away a middle-class family buys bottles of mineral water. This demonstrates 'unreal similarities'. The buyers appear to behave similarly by purchasing expensive water. They are, however, very different; in fact, they are from totally dissimilar groups with different aspirations, motivations, lifestyles and attitudes, not to mention disposable income. On the surface there is a market for private water in both countries, but the distribution channels, communications channels, advertising messages and levels of disposable income are poles apart.

An analysis that goes below the surface (or below the sales results) will reveal a range of different motives, aspirations, lifestyles and attitudes to the same product. Surface information can create a false sense of simplicity. International markets can also suggest surface solutions that ignore the cultural complexities and intricacies of distant international markets. The late Sir John Harvey-Jones' wise words – from his popular business TV series more than 30 years ago – still ring true today:

> Operating in this milieu requires much greater sensitivity to national differences than we are accustomed to having. The mere fact that one stays in the same sort of hotel almost anywhere in the world, that one arrives in the same sort of car, that it is now possible to call by telephone or telex directly from almost anywhere in the world, all gives a superficial feeling of sameness which is desperately misleading and must never be taken for granted.

Globalization, intertwined with cultural idiosyncrasies, is emerging in many markets around the world. The marketing maxim 'Think global, act local' remains valid. Although the late great Professor Theodore Levitt's 'globalization of markets' is occasionally criticized by some academics, he was right; globalization is happening and it does offer huge rewards for those who seize the opportunity.

Below-the-surface external differences

There are, of course, many differences below the surface also. In practice, the European Union is splintered by different levels of economic development (north and south), culture, attitudes and lifestyles, languages, retail trends, direct mail trends, sources of information, time taken to make a decision, and so on. Different marketing mixes and communication mixes are required for different European countries. For example, in the Netherlands, dentists derive 40 per cent of their turnover from the sale of products such as toothbrushes. In Germany, supermarkets are expected to sell only cheap, utilitarian brushes, while the pharmacies handle the premium brands. In Italy, a premium brush has to carry a fashionable, exclusive label. This makes any above-the-line (ad) campaigns difficult. The communications mix was built around direct mail to dentists supported by point-of-sale and product literature, packaging design and sales presenters. Although these all change over time, it underlines the necessity for detailed and thorough research before entering any market.

Check your web analytics. You may already have visitors and maybe even some customers in several international markets. Use them to gather customer insights about why they visited (or bought). How did they find you? Did they find whatever they needed from you? Who else did they consider? What can you do to get them to buy from you? Once you have collected this basic information, it may be worth geo-targeting any tests into this market.

Find where (ie the cities) your brand (or product and service) is already known and being discussed in your target market. Use this insight to research your competitors in these international markets. You can easily and quickly see what ads work for them (using **www.spyfu.com**) what marketing content works for them (using **www.alexa.com** and **www.similarweb.com**). Spyfu.com works really well in the UK and USA. Analysis of competitor PPC ad campaigns elsewhere can use **www.semrush.com**. Some companies sign up for their competitors' newsletters.

Below-the-surface internal differences

The marketer's challenge goes beyond communicating with new international customers and into working with international partners whose idiosyncrasies and languages pose many problems. To some, overcoming local customers' idiosyncrasies may seem relatively easy compared to overcoming local partners' working practices. Whether local partners, distributors, sales agents, or strategic partners, it is essential to understand and work with very different approaches to business. Take nomenclature for a moment. The French normally refer to advertising as publicité, which can cause some confusion, while the Yugoslavian word for advertising is propaganda. Other cultures have difficulty translating 'marketing', 'marketing communications' and 'advertising', as they have not created such words.

Southern Europeans work to live and northern Europeans live to work

'Somewhere in the world there are people who think the Germans are messy and unpunctual. (The chances are they are in Switzerland.) There are countries where Greece is regarded as a model of efficiency. There are countries in which French bosses would seem absurdly egalitarian and others where Italian company life would seem oppressively regulated.'

Mole (1998)

International difficulties

Apart from the normal communication challenges – different time zones and different languages – international markets are also riddled with hidden cultural differences that make global marketing an intriguing challenge even for the most experienced international marketer expert. Positioning on a global scale is not easy. In addition to language, literacy, colour, gestures and culture, marketers have to think how global audiences search for information – what words and phrases they use. Even if you do translate correctly, you probably have to redesign your web pages, since many other non-English languages require more words and therefore more space to deliver the same message. On top of all of this, sometimes the local regional teams don't share the same deep understanding of the home market's approach. Great ideas can easily become incomprehensible once they cross cultural or language divides. This lack of sharing a deep understanding of the brand doesn't fill local teams with a real passion to embrace the project.

International intricacies that contribute towards the challenge of global marketing include:

- language;
- literacy;
- tone;
- timing;
- motivation;
- different information needs;
- colour;
- design;
- form filling and privacy;
- gestures;
- culture;
- devices;
- media;
- different cost structures;
- payment;
- legal restrictions;
- competition.

Language

Language obviously requires careful translating, whether it is straplines, product descriptions or instructions (see 'International mistakes' on p 251). There are exceptions to the rule (where the language reflects beneficial cultural aspects of the product, eg Audi's Vorsprung durch Technik strapline). And some brand names simply don't work when used in foreign languages and thus restrict the brand's international growth potential or dilute the brand's presence through the need to have two brand names.

Beware of automatic translation, as it does not always work perfectly. For example, the word 'home' is automatically translated into maison, the French for 'a home to live in' (as opposed to 'home page'). In Italy, machine translation for the word 'hi-fi' generates a machine translation of ciao-fi. Ciao means hi or hello. And even the most perfect word-for-word translations often do not match the real meaning as different countries use completely different words when online.

Swansea Council translation process gone wrong

A sign that read 'No entry for heavy goods vehicles. Residential site only' was sent, by email, for translation into Welsh. As the translator was not in the office, an auto-response email was returned to the sender saying: 'Nid wyf yn y swyddfa ar hyn o bryd. Anfonwch unrhyw wiath i'w gyfieithu', which means: 'I am not in the office at the moment. Please send any work to be translated.' Since the original message had two sentences, it was assumed the Welsh message was the translation, and the sign was duly printed and erected.

Search terms

A British white goods retailer launching in Germany discovered that the common English term 'slimline' was simply never used. Instead, German consumers search for goods using precise measurements. A British sports retailer soon realized that Germans will never search for 'football kits'. They will only search for 'football shirts'. These small nuances make a big difference when it comes to an international search strategy.

Search engines

There are many markets where the digital media landscape is not the same. In the UK and US Google reins supreme in search. In the Czech Republic it's Seznam, in Japan it's Yahoo! Japan, and Bing still holds a double-digit percentage share globally. It's the same across social media, with VK (Russia) and Renren (China) being the dominant platforms, not Facebook, Twitter or Instagram. In ecommerce, the US and Europe shop at Amazon, India's online marketplaces include Snapdeal, Flipkart and Myntra while Rakuten is the overwhelming favourite in Japan (Paget, nd).

Search engines: Rules/payments/timescales

Each search engine has its own ad platform. There are some distinct similarities with Google (eg Baidu's PPC platform, called Tuigang, structures its account in much the same way – with accounts, campaigns, ad groups and keywords), but there are also some big differences (eg Tuigang has six match types, requires up-front payment for both account set-up and the minimum advertising spend, and, once applied for, an account can take weeks to set up owing to the paperwork required) (Paget, nd).

Baidu requires time and money

Baidu takes time to set up an account. It takes weeks, as opposed to hours or days. It has strict data controls, content standards and other idiosyncrasies about content. So plan well ahead of any launches and allow extra time (and knowledge skills) required.

Calls to action (CTA)

Requests for more information can vary dramatically by country. The UK and United States prefer a more direct approach, such as 'Get quote', while Australians are more likely to click on something citing 'Free'. The Chinese prefer a more respectful 'Request quote'. Eastern cultures tend to be more polite and formal.

Hybrid language

The term 'cheap flights' worked well in most markets, but it was almost completely ineffective in Italy. Consumers there often use hybrid Italian/English phrases, so 'voli low cost' is a far better fit.

Same language, different words

Even the same language uses different words; for example, in the UK, PPC means 'paid media' yet Americans call it SEM while some other countries call it SEA.

Same language, different spelling

Even when using the same language, spelling can differ; British and Americans might spell the same word differently, eg minimise/minimize or colour/color. When marketing in these countries your marketing communications must reflect (ie use) the preferred spellings.

Searching in one language for results in another language

'For example, the term "Hindi News" is used in English to find websites written in Hindi. Technology is another core area where key terms from another language are often used to find and talk about products and services.'

Oban Digital (2015)

Language barriers can be expensive

Even the same language can have different meaning in different markets, eg a 'boot' refers to the rear of a car (in the UK) as well as a shoe. In the United States, the rear section of a car is called a 'trunk'. This is relatively minor, but how about exactly the same word having radically different business meanings? Take a trillion. In most English-speaking countries, including the United States and the UK, a trillion is 1 followed by 12 zeros: 1,000,000,000,000.

In most continental European countries, a trillion is 1 followed by 18 zeros: 1,000,000,000,000,000,000.

Be careful also with a billion, as it has different meanings – in most English-language countries a billion is 1 followed by 9 zeros (a thousand million) but in many other parts of the world it is 1 followed by 12 zeros (a million million).

Words

The same words can have different meanings in different languages. Add to this subtle nuances such as date formats, localized spelling, local phrases and even slang, and international communications becomes challenging. For example, in the Australian travel market the term 'lay by' means to place a deposit and is also often used for round-the-world flights, while (still speaking the same language) in England it means a place where a truck or car can pull in off the road.

> The most relevant term for The Moorings in France is in fact *Location Bateau*. Translating that directly back into English, *Location Bateau* means boat rental. Search in google.co.uk for that term and the majority of what you see will relate to canal boat holidays. It's crucial to understand the market and the user intent behind the keywords you're going to target.
>
> Paget (nd)

Hashtags

There may be many hashtags already being used across countries, industries and areas of interest. Before entering a market, you must **research the hashtags already being used by your target audience**. Check whether any of the existing hashtags overlap with key phrases (potential hashtags) in your campaign. You can then include these hashtags in your content and perhaps set up remarketing to target people using those hashtags.

Remember the two golden rules for hashtags: **keep them short and make them memorable.**

Literacy

In many developing countries literacy is low (Dudley, 1989). This limits the amount of explanation in advertising. Even with high literacy, the reading of translated Western-style advertisements still causes problems, eg before-and-after toothpaste advertisements if they are not adjusted for Arabic readers, who read from right to left. In low-literacy countries, pictures may be used to explain the contents. When Gerber first sold baby food in Africa it put a picture of a baby on the label and didn't realize that, in Africa, companies routinely put pictures on the label to show what's inside, as there is a high rate of illiteracy.

Tone

Tone can be subtle. In mainland Europe and also in the United States, a luxury brand will approach its target audience online with bespoke, glossy, aspirational communications – more like a brochure than a transactional site. However, in China this may fail. Even for expensive purchases, and major high-profile brands, Chinese consumers prefer a no-nonsense approach – they want to know how to buy and what the options are, with all the information at their fingertips.

Sharing time: Social media

A UK Premier League football club wanted to target fans across India, Mexico, Thailand and the UK with a social media campaign – four very different audiences. Research found that each wanted very different content, and to consume and share it at very different times. For instance, Indians are less likely to react to tweets or Facebook posts during match-time itself and often for hours afterwards, while others are hugely reactive in the immediate aftermath of a game.

Email timing

Research reveals that sending emails early morning works best in Germany (where 71 per cent of online activity before work is email), whereas in the UK the evening can be better. Each product type varies – eg travel companies often find Mondays, rather than Fridays, are better.

Paget (nd)

Social networks differ

People in China use Sina Weibo, an alternative to Twitter, and Germans use Xing rather than LinkedIn.

Motivation

Motivation, or reason to buy the same product, can, and often does, differ across different countries, as Oban Digital (2015) explain:

> In Germany, price and quality are the most influential factors, while the Japanese most value a high level of customer service. The Japanese concept of Omotenashi, described as its unique approach to hospitality, is one reason why customer service is highly regarded. Kawaii, the concept of cuteness, is another differentiating factor in Japan. Kawaii values innocence, beauty and fun and is used in many areas you wouldn't expect. Brands add cuteness to their product set by associating it with pastel colours and images of hearts, flowers, stars and rainbows. Even construction guard rails are infused with Kawaii elements!

Google, Yahoo and Bing are not as big as Baidu

Yahoo and Bing are far more important in the United States than the UK, for instance, where Google overwhelmingly dominates. Baidu in China and Russia's Yandex dominate their home markets, with up to 75 per cent reach each, while Yahoo in Japan (now a separate entity) and Naver in Korea are also important considerations.

Different information needs

Even though you have got international visitors on your website, you need to research their needs, as they may be quite different to each other. A Nordics-based cruise company discovered many different nationalities visiting its site had a variety of information needs. The Brits were very interested in the Northern Lights, while the dog-loving Germans were far more interested in Husky-dog sledging; the Americans, meanwhile, wanted information on 'activity sports' while the French, with their own ski resorts, didn't want any information on Alpine sports.

Colour

Colour has a direct access to our emotions. Watch how red is commonly used in advertising in the West. Colour, however, does not have uniform meaning across the world. Asians associate red with prosperity and good luck. Consider a financial services website: if Asians see no red, they will leave; if Westerners see red, they might leave. Never wrap a gift in red in Finland, as it is associated with Russian aggression during the Second World War. Blue in Iran means immorality. White in Japan means death (hence McDonald's white-faced Ronald McDonald has problems). Black means death, bad luck or morbid in some countries. Websites designed with black backgrounds may be seen as 'hip' in the West, but can suffer lack of traffic from China and Hong Kong.

Google, Yahoo and Bing not enough in China or Russia

'Some marketers wanting to break into China or Russia might mistakenly believe a reach of around 25 per cent through Google, Yahoo and Bing might be a shortcut worth taking. Given the size of these markets, yes of course you might reach millions through such engines, but are they actually the people you want to reach? Restricting yourself to those three search engines means the audience you reach is likely to be mainly Western expats, internationalists and the elite. The aspiring middle class, the new consumers, probably the people you should be talking to, are still more likely to go local.'

Oban Digital (2015)

Design

UK and US customers prefer a cleaner, uncluttered approach with lots of white space (signalling a reassuring sense of order) and drop-down menus. Eastern markets, however, with languages that require more space, prefer busy landing pages, with links down both the left and right sides of the page. This is partly due to the sheer volume of characters making searching clumsier and therefore a poor CX. And even within Europe there are many nuances and differences, for example the design of French retail sites is often busy and can look old-fashioned to the English eye.

Form filling and privacy

Privacy is important in China, and consumers there prefer real-time interaction rather than being asked to provide information such as email addresses, using services such as 22. Though they love to comment and interact online, they also want to preserve their privacy.

Gestures

When greeting or bidding farewell, physical contact beyond a handshake in South America, southern Europe and many Arab countries is a sign of warmth and friendship, but in Asia it can be considered an invasion of privacy. After a meal in Egypt it is considered rude not to leave something on your plate, while in Norway and Malaysia leaving anything on your plate would be considered rude. Basic body gestures are not global. In some parts of India, Sri Lanka and Bulgaria, shaking the head from left to right means 'yes'. Touching the lower eyelid may be just an itch, but it also suggests to a South American woman that a man is making a pass, or to a Saudi man that he is stupid. Scratching an earlobe has five different meanings in five Mediterranean countries: 'You're a sponger' (Spain), 'You'd better watch it' (Greece), 'You're a sneaky little...' (Malta), 'Get lost!' (Italy), while a Portuguese will feel really pleased. The A-OK gesture (thumb and index finger in a circle with the rest of the fingers open) means money to a Japanese, zero in France, 'ok' in the United States, a rude gesture in Brazil and 'I'll kill you' in Tunisia. Even the thumbs-up sign is deemed to be a devastatingly obscene gesture to a Sardinian woman and insulting in Iran. Thrusting your palms towards someone's face may be meant to be endearing, but to a Greek there is no greater insult, since this gesture is called a *moutza* and comes from the Byzantine custom of smearing filth from the gutter in the face of condemned criminals.

Culture

Culture creates a quagmire of marketing problems: religion, sex, eating, greeting, habits, lifestyles, the role of women – the list is endless. Ferraro (2001) points out nine critical dimensions that contrast the United States with the rest of the world's cultures. She says that US culture places a high value on 1) individualism, 2) a precise reckoning of time, 3) a future orientation, 4) work and achievement, 5) control over the natural environment, 6) youthfulness, 7) informality, 8) competition and 9) relative equality of the sexes.

Chinese breakfast: Positioning's cultural challenges – breakfast comforting or breakfast crunching?

'A breakfast product in China should be soft, it should be reassuring, it should be comforting and *not* be about discovering your dreams as you crunch your way through the morning!

A food product manufacturer, many of whose products are consumed before noon, launched with cereal, a breakfast cereal. The Chinese don't like to crunch in the morning. The role of breakfast in the morning is fundamentally different than in America. This is a protective society; a mother's fundamental role is to protect her children with love as opposed to enable them to go discover their dreams. So breakfast in the morning should be soft, it should be reassuring, it should be comforting. This company had trouble recognizing that their lead product couldn't be what it would be in the United States. To own the morning would require a fundamentally different business model and through that they have tried to have relationships with an acquisitions strategy with domestic companies.'

Madden (2012)

As always, online can complicate matters. For example, older Scandinavians and Germans are reluctant to use credit cards, the currency of the internet; and the French dislike revealing personal information. In meetings, the Dutch and the Germans want to get straight to the point in business dealings, whereas in countries like Spain, Brazil and Hong Kong some general chat is the most important part. In France, family is private and not part of business discussions. In Hong Kong, expressing an interest in family, general health, and observations of the country help to nurture good relations.

Even protocol for follow-ups to a meeting varies from country to country, as some countries place more importance on the written word than the spoken word, and vice versa. As Julian (2009) points out: 'In Spain for instance, it's important to follow up an email with a phone call, but in Germany you must do the opposite and put your phone conversations into writing.' As for humour, use it sparingly, if at all. In Germany, humour is generally considered inappropriate in business.

Christmas in other cultures

Taking advantage of the Christmas opportunity requires an understanding of each international market. For example, in Brazil and Spain the celebration continues until 6 January (when festivities end). In Russia the celebrations start on 7 January. In India Christmas Day is called Bada Din (Big Day) in Hindi, and it is a national holiday that allows people from all religions to celebrate with their Christian friends. In China the main celebration occurs at the end of January (the Chinese New Year or the Spring Festival). In other countries Christmas does not happen (in fact the word is illegal in some countries).

Devices

In parts of Africa and Asia mobile is now the primary device through which to access internet, surpassing desktop traffic.

Ozon.ru – Russia's Amazon

In some markets such as Russia, consumers are loyal to 'local' and it might make more sense to launch via a marketplace such as Ozon.ru – the Russian Amazon equivalent.

Media

Media availability

Television is sometimes unavailable, since 1) developing countries do not have a high penetration of televisions in domestic households, 2) some countries do not have commercial TV stations, and 3) others do but they restrict the amount of advertising time. Some countries, like Pakistan, do not allow YouTube; 'although we know a significant proportion of the population accesses the service via proxy servers, it would be impossible to know who was consuming what and when' (Oban Digital, 2015).

Unilever and BAT have made their own medium available in East Africa by running their own mobile cinemas.

> **TV helps**
>
> 'The further away from a TV screen, however, the more difficult many experts say it becomes to create and to deliver a pan-European message.'
>
> Mead (1993)

Media overlap

Television, radio and the internet from one market can spill over into other markets, for example half the Canadian population has access to US television. The Republic of Ireland receives the UK's BBC and ITV channels. In mainland Europe local TV is received by neighbouring countries.

Lack of media data

Great Britain and Ireland have well-structured and categorized media analysis data (audited data). Without reliable media data the optimum cost and effectiveness of the overall campaign are unlikely to be achieved. Properly structured media markets are easier to work in.

Lack of media credibility

Unregulated or poorly regulated media in some countries may flout the principles of legality, decency, honesty and truth, which in turn may make these media untrustworthy or create audience scepticism about the particular source of information.

Varying media characteristics

Coverage, cost and reproduction qualities can and do vary from country to country. Some countries are technically more advanced than others, eg they may have massive penetration of high-speed broadband, while other countries do not even have many cinemas.

Different media standards

A lack of uniformity of standards means that different types of both film and artwork may be required for different markets, for example the United States and the UK have different standard page sizes that may require different artwork, which increases cost.

Different cost structures

Different countries have different forms of negotiation and bartering. The Americans and the Japanese are poles apart. In less developed countries cash may not be available, but barter, or counter-trading, can offer an acceptable alternative.

Payment

In Russia, cash on delivery and payment via kiosks is the most popular method of payment (Paget, nd).

Legal restrictions

Whether voluntary codes or actual law, there is as yet no harmonized set of laws or regulations. For example, the Lands' End website in Germany cannot mention their unconditional refund policy, because German retailers successfully sued in court. (They normally do not allow returns after 14 days.) This presents the advertiser with different problems in different countries. In Sweden, misdemeanours by advertisers may be charged under the criminal law, with severe penalties.

Regarding email, in the USA, the Can Spam Act 2003 governs the regulations around email marketing. You must have a valid physical address referenced in your email. In Germany, a double opt in is required for email marketing consent to be acquired and the confirmation email must be free of advertising. In Denmark, like in the UK and US, social media contests can be run without requiring too much commitment from the entrant (Paget, nd).

Competition

Different markets have different key players using different strengths. For example, Ford's position of 'safety engineering' worked in many countries, but not in Sweden, where, of course, Volvo occupied the position. Competition may react in different ways in different markets.

Language, literacy and logic

Combine these three in the international arena and a new challenge emerges – writing instructions. It is a skill in one language, and attempting to translate instructions is complex. This is an extract from the translated instructions for assembling a 'knapsack':

1 Lead for hind leg in an opened position.
2 Lead the frame of the sack support up.
3 Insert the blushing for blocking in the proper split, push it deeply and wheel in an anti-time sense till it stops.

International mistakes

Here is a selection of global misses or mistakes made by brands attempting to sell into international markets. It includes wrong brand names, wrong advertising slogans or, worse still, a fundamentally unsuitable product for a particular international market.

Some marketers carefully choose names that work for their local domestic market but never consider that one day the successful brand could sell into several markets. This insular perspective more than likely restricts any future growth opportunities into international markets and almost certainly restricts the brand from developing into a global brand.

Wrong names

Here are a few examples:

- Sic (French soft drink);
- Pschitt (French soft drink);
- Lillet (French aperitif wine);
- Creap (Japanese coffee creamer);
- Irish Mist (in Germany 'mist' means manure);
- Bum (Spanish potato crisp);
- Bonka (Spanish coffee);
- Trim Pecker Trouser (Japanese germ bread);
- Gorilla Balls (American protein supplement);
- My Dung (restaurant);
- Cul toothpaste (cul means anus in France);
- Scratch (German non-abrasive bath cleaner);
- Super-Piss (Finnish car lock anti-freeze);
- Spunk (jelly-baby sweet from Iceland);
- the Big John product range was translated as Gros Jos (slang for 'big breasts') for French-speaking Canada.

Even sophisticated marketers get it wrong. General Motors discovered that Nova meant 'it won't go' (no va) in South America. Ford launched the Pinto in Brazil and soon realized that it was slang for 'tiny male genitals'. Coca-Cola's phonetic translation in China meant 'Bite the wax tadpole'. After launching into English-speaking markets, Japan's second-largest tourist agency was surprised to receive a steady influx of enquiries for sex tours. The Kinki Nippon Tourist Company soon changed its name.

These translation problems are not insurmountable. For example, Curtis shampoo changed its name from 'Everynight' to 'Everyday' for the Swedish market, since the Swedes wash their hair in the mornings.

Wrong strapline

The New York Tourist Board found 'I love New York' difficult to translate into Norwegian, since there are only two Norwegian verbs that come close: one translation is 'I enjoy New York', which lacks something, and the other is 'I have a sexual relationship with New York'. Scandinavian vacuum cleaner manufacturer Electrolux used this in a US campaign: 'Nothing sucks like an Electrolux'. When Parker Pens marketed its ballpoint pen in Mexico, its advertisements were supposed to read: 'It won't leak in your pocket and embarrass you'. Unfortunately, embarazar does not mean embarrass. It means impregnate, so the slogan had an entirely inappropriate meaning. The Mitsubishi Pajero had problems, since pajero in some parts of the Spanish-speaking world means a liar, in others a plumber and in others something much worse. Other expressions that have been imprecisely translated include US cigarettes with low asphalt (tar), computer underwear (software) and wet sheep (hydraulic rams). Attention to detail is required when translating, as even the smallest error, such as missing out an accent on a letter, can drastically change the meaning. For example, in the United

States, a bilingual banner celebrated '100 ano of municipal history'. In Mexican Spanish, año is year but ano is anus.

'I saw the potato'

During the Pope's visit to Miami it was reported that some T-shirts were printed supposedly saying 'I saw the Pope'. However, the translation was 'I saw the potato', because in Spanish *Papa* with a capital P means Pope, whereas *papa* with a small P means potato.

Wrong product

In the attempt to get the packaging, advertising and branding right, global marketers can sometimes forget the fundamental product and whether it is suitable for the market in the first place, leading to campaign failure. Here are some examples of international product failures arising from the basic product itself: Christmas puddings in Saudi Arabia (where the word 'Christmas' is illegal and 50,000 of the Anglo-Saxon population go on leave during Christmas anyway); and toothpaste to combat betel nut stains (stained teeth imply wealth in some cultures, as does being overweight in others). General Foods' packaged cake mixes found the Japanese market too small for them (3 per cent of homes had ovens). Coca-Cola had to withdraw its 2-litre bottle from Spain, because few Spaniards owned refrigerators with large enough compartments. Tennent's Caledonian, a successful Scottish lager, flopped initially in the UK because it came in 24-packs rather than six-packs. Philips had to change the size of its coffee makers to fit into the smaller Japanese kitchens and its shavers to fit smaller Japanese hands.

Microsoft pays dear for insults through ignorance

'Insensitive computer programmers with little knowledge of geography have cost the giant Microsoft company hundreds of millions of dollars in lost business and led hapless company employees to be arrested by offended governments.'

Brown (2004)

Even the major global players can get it totally wrong. Microsoft was reported (Brown, 2004) to have released its colour-coded world map with time zones showing the disputed Jammu and Kashmir region as not being in India. Under Indian law, this is an offence. Result: the Windows 95 operating system was banned, with hundreds of millions of dollars in lost sales. Office 97 was subsequently launched without colour coding.

Microsoft employees were arrested in Turkey when Kurdistan was shown as a separate entity, so Kurdistan was subsequently removed from all maps. 'Of course we offended the Kurds by doing this but we had offended the Turks more and they were a much more important market for our products. It was a hard commercial decision, not political' (Tom Edwards, Microsoft's Senior Geopolitical Strategist, quoted in Brown, 2004).

Another mistake that caused catastrophic offence was a game called Kakuto Chojin, a fighting-styled computer game with a rhythmic chant from the Koran. Despite being alerted by a Muslim staff member as to this insult to Islam, Microsoft still launched the game in the United States on the assumption that it would not be noticed. After a formal protest by the Saudi Arabian government, Microsoft withdrew the product worldwide. The list goes on. China, Korea, Spain and Uruguay have all been upset by various Microsoft products. In Korea its software showed the Korean flag in reverse and prompted government objections. In Spain, hembra means woman, but in Nicaragua and some other Central American countries it means bitch. In China, when Microsoft referred to Taiwan as a country, the police moved in and questioned staff. In Uruguay, a proud republic, Microsoft's Outlook referred to 30 April as 'the Queen's birthday', which offended the government.

Strategic global options

More and more businesses have to compete in the global arena. For many companies there is nowhere left to hide. Those that do not move into the global market will probably find that the global market will come to them, as new international competitors target their safe local market.

A defensive strategy (eg consolidating the existing customer base, staying native, and blocking competition from entering with, for example, a series of promotions) may safeguard the company, at least in the short term. Offensive strategies are required if a company is seeking entry into new markets, eg increasing promotional spend in key national markets. Strategic alliances and joint ventures offer a lower-cost, lower-risk (and possibly lower-margin) method of entry into these new, large and increasingly competitive markets.

Global marketing strategy

A global marketing strategy usually consists of: 1) a single positioning, 2) a single brand name, 3) identical packaging, 4) a similar product concept (although with local cultural adaptations), 5) standardized ad messages, 6) synchronized pricing (not always possible), 7) coordinated product launches across different countries/regions, etc. In reality, it doesn't always go according to plan. Sometimes there is not even a detailed centralized plan! And as the campaign rolls out, frustrations, fractured messages and wasted resources are far too common.

Markets overseas are rarely at the same stage of development. They may be at different stages of maturity, have different levels of competition, different distribution channels, different levels of brand awareness, brand preference and brand market share. Not to mention the different languages and cultures both in the external marketplace and in the internal teams across the world. So how can you ensure that your product will be in 35 markets and in 25 different languages? How do you develop and execute a global marketing campaign, or even just in a selected few international markets?

International expansion is a natural growth strategy for many businesses. It can go horribly wrong, but if you get it right the rewards can be great.

Keegan and Schlegelmilch (2001) identified five marketing strategies (product/communication strategies) for international marketing. These were determined by the state of the various international markets, analysed by 1) whether the need (or product function) was the same as in other markets, 2) whether the conditions of product use were the same as in other markets, and 3) whether the customer had the ability to buy the product:

- *Same product/same communications.* This applies to markets where the need and use are similar to those of the home market, eg Coca-Cola, with its centrally produced advertisements that incorporate local differences in language.
- *Same product/different communications.* This applies to markets where the need or function is different but the conditions of product use are the same, eg bicycles in Europe and bicycles in Africa (recreation and transport, respectively).
- *Different product/same communications.* This applies to markets with the same product function or need but with different conditions of product use, eg different petrol formulae but the same advertising image (eg Esso's tiger).
- *Different product/different communications.* This applies to markets with different needs and different product use, eg greeting cards and clothes are held to be 'culture bound', but it should be noted that some clothing companies (like Levi's) use the same, centrally produced, wordless advertisements internationally.
- *New product (invention)/new communications.* This applies, for example, in the case of a hand-powered washing machine.

Gordon Storey, Mars External Relations Manager

Global advertising strategy

The question of whether at least the advertising can be standardized (across the world) is a source of great discussion. Forty years ago Kahler and Kramer's (1977) original work suggests that successful standardization is dependent on the similarity of the motivations for purchase and the similarity of use conditions. For culture-free products such as industrial goods and some consumer durables, the purchase motivations are similar enough to permit high degrees of standardization. Culture-bound products, in contrast, require adaptation. Customs, habits and tastes vary for these products, and customer reaction depends on receiving information consonant with these factors. It has been argued that 'buying proposals' (the benefits proposed in the advertisement) have a good chance of being accepted across large geographical areas, whereas the 'creative presentation' (creative treatment) does not.

Essentially, if the international market had a similar set of needs and interests, then a successful adaptation of the advertising message was more likely (as in the case of pattern advertisements – see 'Central strategy and local production (pattern advertisements)' below). Simon Majaro (1993) observed that the time period between the time a product reaches its decline stage in the most advanced market and the introduction stage in the slowest market is narrowing. If this trend continues, the point will be reached where the pattern of the lifecycle in a domestic market will become identical with the pattern in the foreign markets. This will of course have a tremendous impact on the communications strategy of firms operating internationally. It would mean that in time it would become possible for the communications objectives of such firms to become more and more homogeneous, thus allowing for a larger measure of standardization. In other words, if the trend continues, it should become possible for the same campaign, subject to the manipulation necessitated by linguistic and cultural variations, to be undertaken in all markets. This is indeed the kind of standardization that Coca-Cola has achieved in world markets. This strategy stems in the main from the fact that the product lifecycle profit of Coca-Cola is pretty homogeneous throughout the world. Rijkens (1993) confirmed the trend towards 'greater internationalization and centralization', where basic creative ideas are centrally produced for international use. Kahler and Kramer (1977) felt that transferability of advertising was dependent on the possibility of a more homogeneous consumer, who might, for example, evolve out of the ever-integrating European community. If the European consumer showed a willingness to accept the products of countries within the community, and if that consumer was motivated similarly to consumers in other countries, a common promotional approach would be practical; but if national identities prevailed, separate campaigns would be more likely to succeed.

Four global advertising strategies

The four basic strategies available for global marketing communications are:

1. central strategy and production;
2. decentralized strategy and production;
3. central strategy and local production (pattern advertisements);
4. central strategy with both central and local production.

Central strategy and production

Advertisements are controlled and produced by the head office (or its agency). This includes message modification, such as translations and tailor-made editions for various markets. Examples of centrally controlled and centrally produced advertisements include Coca-Cola's emotion-packed 'General Assembly' advertisement showing the world's children singing happily and harmoniously together, which was similar to their classic 1971 'I'd like to teach the world to sing' (McCann) in that it was packed with emotion and carried a universal theme. The 21 language editions of this advertisement opened with 'I am the future of the world, the future of my nation' and ended with the tag line 'a message of hope from the people who make Coca-Cola'. Each country then edited in its own end shot of the appropriate child's face. Incidentally, the German edition was dubbed slightly out of synchronization, since Germans associate quality films with dubbed (slightly out of sync) US and British films. Scottie's nappies save production costs by omitting any dialogue and just using a different voice-over for each country. Levi's does not bother with voice-overs, dubbings or translations, as there is no dialogue – just music. Its unified logo and brand image does away with the need for different pack shots (close-ups of the pack/label) for each country, so its commercials are used throughout Europe.

Automobile ads in Europe

Show smooth drivers driving beautiful cars around adventurous roads in Europe. These centrally produced European ads work fine in mainland Europe, but in the UK the ads reveal their 'centrally produced' style when audiences can see the driver is sitting in the 'wrong' seat – ie they use left-hand drive cars (despite UK being a right-hand drive market). As they continue to be used, we must assume this, surprisingly, does not affect their effectiveness.

Centralized global advertising campaign: Local splash page

Some brands navigate this by having a splash page. For example, Nike have the generic url nike.com/ running at the end of some of their YouTube videos. It's a global channel meaning anyone across the world could be watching that video. If you follow that url, you're presented with what they've called a location tunnel, which then re-directs to their localized content (served on a .com/en sub folder) (Paget, nd).

Decentralized strategy and production

Advertisements are controlled and produced by each local subsidiary and its agency specifically for the local market. This approach generates lots of different advertisements by the same company. Each division or subsidiary works with its own local agency to produce tailor-made advertisements for the local market. As well as being an expensive approach, it can destroy uniformity and a consistent global presence, but it does allow more creativity to suit the specific needs of the local market. Different positionings in different markets do require different campaigns, sponsorship and retail strategies. For example, if Rolex epitomizes 'achievement' in New York and 'trendiness' in Tokyo, it must implement two of everything: two product lines (one stately, one flashy), two ad campaigns, two sponsorship series and two retail strategies (Doctoroff, 2005).

Central strategy and local production (pattern advertisements)

The pattern provides uniformity in direction but not in detail, which allows the advertisements to be locally produced but within the central strategic guidelines. This is where head office guides the strategic direction of the advertisements but allows local production. These advertisements work to a formula, or pattern. In the Blue Band margarine advertisements, whether in Scandinavia or Africa, the appropriate happy mother could be seen spreading margarine on bread with her happy family sitting around eating it. Impulse fragrance used a 'boy chases girl' formula across Europe, but still allowed for cultural idiosyncrasies like eye contact, sex appeal and law-abiding citizens to be tailored into each country's different production. Renault's pan-European strategy was to 'endow the car with its own personality'. In France the car was shown with eyes. In Germany the car talked back. In the UK the end line was 'What's yours called?'

FIGURE 8.1 A location tunnel

Centralized creative problems: The creative ideas won't translate

'Global creative is often not easy to localize. From sign-offs and tag lines to pictures and concepts that offend rather than resonate, the whole process can be a minefield to the under-experienced.... voice selection is insensitive to cultural needs, it just won't work. Other creative minefields include humour, metaphors, idioms, regulatory issues and cultural norms.

Sometimes you'll find a global team working with lead agencies in a silo. Some markets won't even have been considered. How you're going to measure the success of your global campaign should be part of the initial brief. Very often it isn't.'

Freedman (nd)

Central strategy with both central and local production

Centrally produced non-verbal commercials are used to build a unified identity, while local productions supplement this platform. This is demonstrated by the Levi's example given below. Although 'standardized' generally refers to production, it can also include centrally controlled media strategies, planning and buying. The centralized or standardized global campaign problems are discussed below. As Rijkens (1993) says:

> As far as advertising is concerned, the company will continue its policy of central production of non-verbal commercials and cinema films, to be shown throughout Europe and intended to establish a uniform identity for Levi Strauss as a business and for its products. Advertising produced locally by the Levi Strauss subsidiaries will respond to local circumstances and to the local competitive scene.
>
> This formula, also applied by other companies marketing a uniform product and using one advertising strategy on an international scale, has proved successful and may well be further developed once the single market really comes about.

Advantages of central strategy and central production

- *Consistent image.* A consistent image (and positioning) is presented around the world, allowing consumer awareness and familiarity to prosper.
- *Consolidated global position.* It leaves the brand in a stronger position to protect itself from any attack.
- *Exploits transnational opportunities.* It reduces message confusion arising when advertising in one country spills over to another (eg boundary-bouncing satellite TV) or when migrants and tourists physically travel to another geographical area (geographical segment).
- *Saves costs.* Economies are enjoyed by not having several different creative teams (and production teams if central production) working on the brand around the world (saves reinventing the wheel). There is the possibility of centrally produced (or at least centrally designed) point-of-sale material also. Levi's has found that it saves £1.5 million by shooting a single TV ad to span six European countries (at £300,000 production cost per each one-minute TV ad).
- *Releases management time.* It may also reduce the size of the marketing department, which might otherwise be tied up briefing creative teams, approving creative concepts, supervising productions, etc. It may even save time invested with packaging designers, sales promotion agencies, etc, if pack designs and promotions are run from a central office.
- *Facilitates transfer of skills.* It does this within the company and around the world, since in theory it is the same job anywhere around the world. It also stimulates cross-fertilization of company ideas if staff are moving around internationally.
- *Easier to manage.* It is easier to manage centrally, since there is in total a smaller number of decisions and projects to manage:
  - One creative decision facilitates harmonization of creative treatments, particularly in areas of media overlap.

- Media policies – manage the media overlap between countries to maximize effectiveness and recommend preferred media choice in specific territories.
- Budgets – determine local budgets for each product in each market so that the method of allocating resources is balanced.
- Agree an activity programme and a specific reporting system to facilitate easier management.

Disadvantages of central strategy and central production

- *Stifles creativity.* It stops local creative contributions from both company staff and the local advertising agency (whether part of an international group or an independent agency). The account may be considered by the local agency staff to be dull and boring, and the supposed 'best brains' (from the creative department) may avoid being involved with it.
- *Frustrated local management.* Although the local office may be accountable for its performance, it does not have control over its own destiny, since advertisements are centrally produced or directed. This may lead to a sense of frustration.
- *Minimal effort from the local agency* (if using an international agency with its network of overseas branches). The high global advertising spend may put the brand high on the agency's head office list, but the local agencies may find it is uneconomic to spend too much time and top brains on it.
- *Lost opportunities.* The opportunity to react quickly to changes in the local market is lost.
- *Different product lifecycles.* Different markets may be at different stages of their lifecycle, which may make the standardized approach unsuitable. It may, however, still be possible to standardize each stage of the brand's development, eg Boots launch of Nurofen in the UK and northern Europe.
- *Wrong idea.* Some central advertising concepts may simply not work as well as a locally created original idea. Sales therefore perform below their potential.
- *Difficult translation.* Some ideas just do not lend themselves to translation, eg Pepsi's 'Come alive' was translated in some countries as 'Come from the dead' or 'Come out of the grave'.
- *False savings.* Local language adaptation or modification costs may negate the cost savings generated by the centrally controlled creative work.
- *Market complexities.* The many other local market differences (eg variations in consumer protection regulations and media availability) may make a standardized message extremely difficult.
- *Inexperienced staff.* A lack of suitably qualified expert staff who can manage the coordination of transnational standardized campaigns may make the whole centrally controlled advertising concept too risky.

Rudyard Kipling's advice to McDonald's

'Asia is not going to be civilized under the methods of the west. There is too much Asia and she is too old.'

Rudyard Kipling (1891)

McDonald's India now offers tailored products for the Indian market – mutton, chicken, fish and vegetable products, not beef, pork or their by-products. Since Hindus don't eat beef, the Big Mac is called the Maharaja Mac and made from lamb.

Decentralized strategy

Successful marketers recognize a customer-centric world in which customers choose to do business with the brands that speak to them as individuals and are always relevant to their lives, jobs, families and cultures. As Ben David (2015) points out, 'marketers are adapting their ad programmes to better relate to consumers on an individual level, but those targeting a global customer base still need to heed cultural differences to make their ads more effective across continents.'

Decentralized, localized and highly relevant ads perform better

Ben David (2015) observes that brand marketers create regional-specific advertising programmes (whether by country or even by city) because they know that the most effective ad experiences are those that are highly relevant to the customer.

> **How North American and European ads differ**
>
> It's difficult to generalize advertising preferences across regions as each advertiser is striving to be more unique and innovative than the next, but we can extrapolate a few common themes. Consumers in North America are accustomed to forming a direct relationship with big brands, so ads tend to focus more on the brand experience. US marketers use the power of story-telling to help define the consumer's persona traits, and then create an ad story that places the consumer within that storyline.
>
> On the other hand, European consumers don't tend to formulate that relationship with a brand. Consumers respond better to ads that contain brand messages around product cost and value. It's typical to see ad messaging in Europe touting the unique practical selling points of the product or service, versus emotional selling points. For instance, the underlying tone of a European ad might be, 'you should buy these shoes for their durability', versus the North American tone, 'you should buy these shoes so you can feel like LeBron James'.

Whichever strategy, smarter process, roles and accountabilities are required

Kevin Freedman suggests that marketers should make sure they have got the right people and that everyone knows what they're doing. They should also:

- Establish clear roles for global, region and local. Define roles; educate players; and follow it.
- Define a worldwide localization process. Implement one consistent but flexible process worldwide and educate global teams on transcreation and adaptation.
- Determine what resources are available and fill any gaps within internal service departments, global and local marketing teams, agencies, or other suppliers
- Identify where the money is coming from. Make sure everyone is clear. Define budgets.
- Decide on budget ownership and allocation.
- Secure early budget allocation to allow marketing teams to deliver with confidence and consistency.

Freedman (nd)

Influencer marketing

Influencer marketing (see p 410) is popular in almost all markets and therefore should be built into any international campaigns. Sunsail, a UK yacht charter business, ran an international campaign called #paperboats aimed at driving awareness of its flotilla product. In order to kick the campaign off, they engaged staff and influencers from over a dozen countries before the campaign officially kicked off, meaning they had content for their newsletters, landing pages and social media platforms for go-live (Paget, nd).

Agencies in the international arena

There are several different types of agency from which an international advertiser can choose:

- international agencies;
- independent networks, associations or confederations of agencies;
- local independent agencies;
- in-house agencies.

In addition to deciding whether to centralize control over advertising (and effectively standardize it), the international marketing manager must decide whether to put all international advertising in the hands of one international agency or hand it out to local independent agencies. Many local independent agencies have grouped themselves into networks or associations, which means that they have a ready-made network of contacts with the other network member agencies in the various international regions. A fourth and less common option is for the client to set up its own in-house agency specifically to handle its own worldwide advertising.

Choosing a centralized international agency or independent local agencies

This question is linked to whether the communications should be controlled centrally or left to run autonomously. Should the marketing team at headquarters work with just one large multinational advertising agency or should it allow a range of independent agencies to use its unique skills on a local basis? A coordinated message can be developed in either situation. For example, centrally produced advertisements (with local modifications, translations, etc) and pattern advertisements (formula advertising) can work under either system. Although a centrally produced advertisement is more likely to be handled by a large international agency, there are exceptions where local independent agencies with local media buying and production skills (if pattern advertisements are required) may be preferred. It is possible to choose to work with a range of independent local agencies while adhering to centralized policies. These policies can help the client to manage the whole advertising process by giving specific guidance on creative directions, media strategies, budgets and activity programmes. As Majaro (1993) said, 'Obviously where the product profile justifies communications standardization, it may be advisable to use the services of an international agency with offices in all markets.' Majaro continued: 'Hoping to attain the same results by using a host of local agencies with no international expertise is a formula for waste in worldwide marketing.'

Advantages of using a centralized international agency

Compared to using several local agencies, using a central international advertising agency has the following advantages:

- *Full service.* Because of the international agency's size, it can offer a full range of services, including research, planning and translation, under one roof.
- *Quality.* Some clients feel reassured by the quality feeling of a large international agency (as opposed to taking a chance with a smaller local agency). Quality and standards should, in theory, be universal.
- *Broad base of experience.* Training and transferring personnel is common among the international agencies.
- *Presence in major advertising centres.* The agency branches are located at the centre of most major cities or marketing territories.
- *Cost saving.* Less duplication in areas of communication, creative and production departments.
- *Easier to manage.* A single central contact point combined with the points listed in 'Advantages of central strategy and central production' on p 256.

Disadvantages of using a centralized international agency

It is arguably easier for a single international agency to standardize the message. The disadvantages of standardization (see p 257) therefore apply where central control moves in. In addition, the overseas subsidiary may lack enthusiasm if the account was won elsewhere. It is as if, by necessity, various branches of the international agency are brought in. The lack of excitement may be compounded, particularly where all the creative work has previously been handled by head office. In a sense, the branch's job is relegated to media scheduling and planning.

The key to successful central communications

'If Shakespeare and the Rolling Stones can do it, so can advertising.'

Maurice Saatchi

Rather than engaging in high-risk new product development many corporations prefer to consider the lower-risk new market development approach. This doesn't mean international marketing is cheap. It's not. It requires resources to grow sales and market share internationally. Without this or with too little resources the propensity for failure increases. Adequate resources: budget (money), time (minutes) and skilled people (men/women) increase the likelihood of success.

However, making it all actually happen is another thing altogether. Take advertising: although more and more advertising is used in more than one country, only some of it works successfully.

Understanding the disadvantages in addition to the advantages is the first step towards implementing centralized communications. Identifying the barriers reveals the levels of resistance among distant international marketing managers. It follows that internal marketing skills are also required. Before international communications are standardized (centralized), management thinking must first be harmonized internationally. Diminishing local autonomy without diminishing local responsibility requires skilful management handling. Indeed, maintaining management motivation requires people skills, particularly when their responsibilities for advertising budgets are being slashed.

Many local managers will perceive the central advertising campaign to be dull and disappointing because it is based on the lowest global common denominator – those common cross-cultural characteristics that somehow find commonality across borders that can result in dull ideas.

Inspiring managers to continue to excel with sometimes-bland, centrally produced advertising is a challenging job. It becomes more challenging the longer internal communications are delayed.

Note, the same applies for centrally produced content marketing, if there has been no collaboration earlier in the creative process.

How to avoid some international difficulties when creating graphics

Avoid:

- text-based graphics;
- visual puns;
- gestures;
- animal icons;
- body parts as metaphor;
- racial and/or gender stereotyping;
- flags, maps, political and religious symbols.

Get the resources required for international growth

Scarce resources limit international growth plans (or any plans for that matter). Compared to their Asian counterparts, companies based in Europe and the United States are nearly twice as likely to suggest that they don't have the analysts they need to make sense of their data. A key theme emerging from the feedback we received in response to our open-ended questions is that most companies sit on heaps of data, but being able to turn all their data into actionable insights is something that few have been able to master (eConsultancy, 2015).

International marketing communications require even more attention to detail than domestic marketing communications. But, even closer to home, care is required to ensure the correct translation processes are in place. A process is required to ensure copy is sent off for translating, translated, double-checked and then uploaded into the correct section of the foreign language site.

In conclusion

International markets present many challenges and many rewards. There are many similarities among customers around the world, but there are also many differences lurking below the surface. Even more attention to detail is required in international markets, as the opportunities for errors increase. Systems, processes and teams have to be harnessed to make it all work successfully.

Key points from Chapter 8

- The globalization of markets is ongoing.
- There are, however, technical and cultural idiosyncrasies that need to be accommodated.
- There are many other challenges that arise in international markets beyond just culture, including language, media, laws (or lack of them) and much more.
- The biggest challenge is to stay relevant to each region.
- Classic errors are made even by the big, established brands. They can be avoided by thoroughly checking and researching each market.

References and further reading

Ahonen, T and Moore, A (2007) *Communities Dominate Brands*, Future Text, London

Anholt, S (2001) *Another One Bites the Grass*, Wiley, Chichester

Becht, B (2010) How I did it: Building a company without borders, *Harvard Business Review: The Magazine*, April

Ben David, E (2015) Relevant, personalized ads solve global marketing challenges, *The SmartVideo Blog*, 24 February [online] http://info.sundaysky.com/blog/ (archived at https://perma.cc/RAL9-DDNC)

Brown, P (2004) Microsoft pays dear for insults through ignorance, *Guardian*, 19 August

Chaffey, D and Smith, PR (2008) *eMarketing eXcellence*, Butterworth-Heinemann, Oxford

Doctoroff, T (2005) *Billions: Selling to the new Chinese consumer*, Palgrave Macmillan, New York

Dudley, J (1989) *Strategies for the Single Market*, Kogan Page, London

eConsultancy (2015) Quarterly digital intelligence briefing: Digital trends 2015, eConsultancy

Ferraro, G P (2001) *The Cultural Dimension of International Business*, 4th edn, Prentice Hall, Englewood Cliffs, NJ

Freedman, K (nd) Planning a global marketing campaign? Think implementation first, Freedman International [online] www.freedmaninternational.com/implementation-first/ (archived at https://perma.cc/5XYK-BUS3)

Geertz, C (1983) *The Interpretation of Cultures: Selected essays*, Hutchinson, London

Harvey-Jones, J (1988) *Making It Happen: Reflections on leadership*, Collins, London

Inskip, I (1997) Marketing international brands in Asia needs fresh thinking, *Marketing Business*, May

Julian (2009) The 'lucky seven' tips when collecting payments from overseas companies, *Octempo: RM Blog*, 18 December

Kahler, R and Kramer, R (1977) *International Marketing*, South-Western Publishing, Cincinnati, OH

Kashani, K (1989) Pathways and pitfalls of global marketing, *Marketing Business*, June

Keegan, W J and Schlegelmilch, B B (2001) *Global Marketing Management: A European perspective*, *Financial Times*/Prentice Hall, Englewood Cliffs, NJ

Kotler, P (2002) *Marketing Management: Analysis, planning, implementation and control*, 11th edn, Prentice Hall, Englewood Cliffs, NJ

Lajoie, M and Shearman, N (2014) Defining Alibaba, *Wall Street Journal*

Madden, N (2012) Five questions with Tom Doctoroff, JWT's Greater China CEO, *Ad Age Global*, 27 June

Majaro, S (1993) *International Marketing*, 2nd edn, Allen & Unwin, London

Mazur, L (1997) Successfully managing cultural differences, *Marketing Business*, September

McGovern, G (2014) Customer-centric and easy-to-use is the new business model (The Alibaba story) *Gerry McGovern//New Thinking*, 18 May

Mead, G (1993) A universal message, *Financial Times*, 2 May

Mole, J (1998) *Mind Your Manners*, Nicholas Brealey Publishing, London

Morris, D (1988) Watch your body language, *Observer*, 23 October

Oban Digital (2015) Understanding your new global customer: 10 things you need to know about search and conversion when marketing to an overseas audience [online] https://obaninternational.com/ (archived at https://perma.cc/AX3K-WGS2)

Orton-Jones, C (2013) Follow the money, *The Marketer*, March/April

Paget, J (nd) Running international marketing campaigns guide, SmartInsights [online] www.smartinsights.com/guides/running-international-marketing-campaigns/ (archived at https://perma.cc/76AN-S48A)

Pike, K (1966) *Language in Relation to a Unified Theory of the Structure of Human Behavior*, Mouton, The Hague

Prior, E (2013) Do Man Utd really have 659m supporters? *BBC News Magazine*, 18 February

Rijkens, R (1993) *European Advertising Strategies*, Cassell, London

Rodgers, A L (2001) It's a (red) bull market after all, *Fast Company*, 30 September

Shih, C (2013) What's a 'like' worth? Ask Facebook's graph search, *Ad Age Digital*, 14 February

Universal McCann (2007) Power to the people: Tracking the impact of social media wave, *2.0*, May

Usunier, J C (2000) *Marketing Across Cultures*, Financial Times/Prentice Hall, Englewood Cliffs, NJ

Winick, C (1961) Anthropology's contribution to marketing, *Journal of Marketing*, **25**

Young, L (1987) *Love around the World*, 2nd edn, Hodder & Stoughton, London

09 The marketing communications plan

LEARNING OBJECTIVES

By the end of this chapter you will be able to:

- write an outline marketing communications plan using PR Smith's SOSTAC® planning framework;
- understand the importance of gathering intelligence and research for the situation analysis before writing the rest of the plan;
- explore strategy, knowing that it is an area of weakness for most organizations;
- schedule a range of tactical tools to fulfil the strategy;
- develop the internal marketing part of the plan to ensure excellent execution of the plan;
- establish control systems.

Introduction to the SOSTAC® marketing communications plan

There are many different approaches to building a marketing plan or, more specifically, a marketing communications plan. There is no single common approach, but there are essential elements that every plan must have. PR Smith's SOSTAC® was developed in the 1990s after 10 years of searching and experimenting: a simple aide-mémoire that helps managers to recall the key components of a marketing communications plan. SOSTAC® can in fact be applied to any kind of plan – a corporate plan, marketing plan, marketing communications plan, social media plan, direct mail plan or even personal plan:

S Situation analysis – where are we now?

O Objectives – where do we want to go?

S Strategy – how do we get there?

T Tactics – the details of the strategy (marcomms mix).

A Action – the details of tactics (internal marketing). Includes: communicating, motivating and training your team to execute with excellence and passion.

C Control – how do you know you are getting there, what metrics are you going to measure, how often, when, by whom, how much will it cost.

+ 3Ms (the three key resources):

Men and women (human resources).

Money (budgets).

Minutes (timescales).

And now, if you so choose, you can see this on video, in a bit more detail, in four minutes at **http://prsmith.org/sostac/**, or watch it later and continue reading.

SOSTAC®'s **simple structure is applicable at different levels.** In each chapter in Part Two of this book, SOSTAC® is applied at a lower level for each of the communications tools, an advertising plan, a direct mail plan, etc. SOSTAC® can also be used to check other plans to see if they are comprehensive and cover the key items that every plan needs. You don't have to use the same terminology. The SOSTAC® framework will help the development of a logical structure combined with the key elements of a plan.

A real plan requires a lot of detail, and the first component, the situation analysis, is so important that it can take up half of the total plan (this can be dumped into the appendices at the back of the plan or kept in the front but either way the situation analysis must be thorough). Objectives and strategies should be written in a concise manner, while the tactics and action plans can require a lot of details. Control, feedback and monitoring mechanisms should be built into the plan so that everyone knows what is going to be measured when, by whom, and most importantly, what happens when the numbers go up or down?

SOSTAC® is also an agile planning framework since the control section feeds into the situation analysis, which helps to refine the next set of objectives, etc.

So SOSTAC® + 3Ms works for any type of product or service in both **consumer and business-to-business markets**, as demonstrated in the short case studies used in this book. Although the case studies provide only an outline plan, they show how easily SOSTAC® can be applied to either planning the overall marketing communications or just planning a campaign for a single communications tool such as direct mail. Let us consider now each SOSTAC® component in more detail.

Note: Several extracts in this chapter are taken from PR Smith's 'SOSTAC® guide to your perfect digital marketing plan' (2019).

The 3Ms

As mentioned above, the 3Ms, the three key resources, consist of:

1. men and women (human resources);
2. money (budgets);
3. minutes (timescales).

Men/women are the human resources: who is required to do what? Some staff can be drawn from within the organization, others have to be brought in from an agency or consultancy or recruited as full-time members of staff. Is it worth asking overbusy people to give half their attention to a project or asking under-qualified and under-utilized people

FIGURE 9.1 Visit **http://prsmith.org/sostac/** and watch the four-minute video

to have a go? Perhaps the marketing communications task is too important to be casual?

Minutes, the third M, is the most limited resource – time. Is there enough time to do the job, to carry out the research, to develop credibility, to nurture a Twitter following, to develop new packaging, etc? Crystal clear timescales and deadlines are critical. How much lead time do you need if you want to launch a new toy at Christmas? The product has to be ready by February, for the New York Toy Show, when the major US retailers place their Christmas stock orders.

Money means budgets, and senior management will tend to scan budgets first and foremost. There are many different ways of setting marketing communications budgets, and there is not a generally agreed methodology but rather a whole range of approaches that can be described as either scientific or heuristic. A combination of judgement, experience and rational evaluation influences budgets. See more on budgets at the end of this chapter.

There is also a fourth 'M' – **mega data.** Every organization uses data today. Whether it is a basic database of customers and prospects or large quantities of data that can be used to make better data-driven decisions about marketing or even just finding new ways to use data to add value to the customer experience (CX). Start thinking about data (whether mega data or small data) and how data can improve marketing efficiency, add value to the CX and find new collaborative data partners (eg IoT).

Situation analysis

The situation analysis needs to be comprehensive. An in-depth analysis of customers (see the three key customer questions that must be answered in detail: Who? Why? and How?), competitors, distribution channels, the organization's own performance/results, strengths and weaknesses as well as external trends (that create opportunities and threats), is required. Half the plan should be devoted to situation analysis.

The marketing communications plan does not necessarily require a full SWOT analysis, as this is usually found in the full marketing plan. It should certainly include an explanation of the product or service's positioning – how the product is perceived in the minds of the target market.

The situation analysis can include a **PEST** analysis specifically relevant to communications, eg political (what new laws or regulations affect communications); how economic fluctuations might affect media and messages; social trends and changes in attitudes and media usage; and technology's fast-changing impact on communications.

A vital part of any analysis is the market and its structure. How is it segmented? What are the most suitable segments that can become target markets? Are the target markets big enough? Are they profitable enough? Are they vulnerable to competition? Do the existing distribution and communications channels serve them properly? Are customers satisfied in each target market? Do they intend to repurchase? Who is involved in the decision-making unit (DMU)? Do the key opinion leaders and opinion formers support the brand?

Segmentation and target marketing

Segmentation and target marketing is all about the number one customer question: 'Who is my ideal target customer? Segmentation is so important that it appears almost everywhere in a marketing plan: in the situation analysis in detail, in the objectives briefly and in the strategy (as a fundamental component); it is also referred to in all tactical campaigns and events.

Target marketing involves the division of a large market into smaller market segments. Each segment has its own distinct needs and/or its patterns of response to varying marketing mixes. The most attractive segments are targeted according to the organization's resources.

Some communication channels are more wasteful than others, eg TV, but the Target Group Index (TGI) (see Chapter 6) helps to identify what kinds of brands people buy, the papers they read, the programmes they watch, etc. As mass markets fragment and splinter into mini-markets or segments, and technology provides more tailored communications, there is less requirement for mass marketing and mass communications, although we are seeing the emergence of 'one-to-one mass marketing' with automated chatbots (p 169) and automated personalized marketing content (p 167). Data aggregators are finding new ways to profile and target prospects with the clever use of AI on massive amounts of data.

Segment attractiveness

Ideally, segments should satisfy the following criteria:

- *Measurable.* Is it quantifiable? Can buyers who fall into this category or segment be identified?
- *Substantial.* How many buyers fall into this segment? Is there a sufficient number of buyers in the segment to warrant special attention and targeting?
- *Accessible.* Can this group be contacted? Can they be isolated or separated from other non-targeted markets via specific media and distribution channels?
- *Relevant.* The benefits of the product or service being offered must be relevant to the target customer.

Some segments are obvious. Cat food is bought by cat owners, petrol is bought by motorists, and heavy-duty cranes are bought by both large construction companies and leasing companies. Other segments are less obvious, eg less expensive cars are bought by both low-income groups and high-income groups (as a second or third car). Who are the heavy users, the 9 per cent of the UK adults who drink 65 per cent of the lager? Who are the deciders? Cola drinkers may tend to be young, but who does the buying, who makes the decision and who pays? This is the DMU.

> **Targeting pays dividends: from £50 to £50m for a Rembrandt**
>
> A painting by Rembrandt probably would not sell (even for £50) in the wrong target market, whereas in the right target market it might fetch £50 million.

Decision-making units

The DMU is made up of influencers, advisers, deciders, users, buyers and payers. It applies to all types of markets (industrial, consumer, products and services). A baby's pram may be used by mother and child, bought by the mother and father, influenced by the grandmother, and decided on by the whole family. Similarly, the purchase of a new photocopier may have been instigated by a secretary, the decider may be the financial director; the buyer may be the procurement officer. In some organizations the DMU may be a committee. The acronym SPADE (starter, payer, adviser, decider, end user) helps to identify some of the DMU members. See p 114 for alternative acronym, PAGES. There is also the 'gatekeeper', who has the power to pass a message on to more senior executives.

B2C (consumer) segments

Segmenting markets into groups of buyers and targeting those groups that are more likely to be the best customers are absolutely vital if marketing communications are to be both effective and efficient. Markets can be broken into segments using many different criteria. Here are some typical consumer criteria:

- demographics: age; job type (socio-economic groupings);
- geodemographics: geographical location, type of neighbourhood and demographic data;

- psychographics: attitudes, beliefs, VALS (values, attitudes and lifestyles, see 'The Target Group Index' on p 195);
- behavioural: benefits sought (see 'The toothpaste test' on p 117); usage frequency; readiness to buy; loyal vs non-loyal.

The biggest improvements in segmenting and targeting are coming from digital sources, aggregators, social media platforms and new third-party data companies. Facebook can now offer several hundred segmentation criteria or 'filters' to tighten your targeting including: location, interests (business, hobbies, relationships, technology, fitness, food and drink, entertainment, sports, shopping and fashion), behaviours (travel, mobile device, digital activities), demographics (age, gender, language, education, generation, work, relationships) and a lot more. For the full list see 'How to target very very specific audiences on facebook', **https://prsmith.org/blog/**.

B2B (industrial) segments

In industrial markets and business-to-business markets, segmentation criteria are different but nonetheless vital. Here are some commonly used segmentation criteria for industrial markets:

- type of company (standard industrial code – SIC);
- size of company;
- structure of company (autocratic vs centralized);
- location or geographical area;
- heavy or light users;
- existing suppliers;
- benefits sought;
- title or position of key decision makers.

Many marketers now create their own target lists of prospects, eg from visitors that land on a website added to a list (without their name but just a numerical identifier) and subsequently used in remarketing ad campaigns, when they visit other websites. Or their digital body language (see p 329) identifies each visitor having a particular level of interest (or readiness to buy), derived from their click behaviour. Marketing automation is increasingly being used to automatically send alerts, emails, or trigger telephone calls from sales professionals to offer help to visitors.

How can you target frequent flyers who might take a train instead?

'If you are trying to sell train tickets to frequent flyers from London to Edinburgh, who are the ideal prospects? Your ability to ask great questions, find databases and interrogate them in new ways to profile prospects is a great skill. Stop and think for a moment.

How about asking data owners of major mobile networks (eg WEVE) to find "mobile users who disappear in Heathrow and reappear in Edinburgh in the time a flight would take". Then segment these travellers and promote highly relevant offers via their mobiles. Add a mobile commerce component enabling prospects to directly purchase a rail ticket, or just wave their smartphone at the ticket counter or transport kiosk. NB Check GDPR compliance.'

PR Smith (2015)

Floating targets

Many markets have a floating percentage who move in and out of the market, eg insurance is considered to be dull and boring (a 'distress purchase') and if customers (reluctantly) review insurance suppliers, say, every four years, then you have only got 25 per cent of the market active each year. Divide this by 12 months and you have only got approximately 2 per cent of the market active in any particular month. So, instead of advertising specific product benefits many brands just want to maintain awareness levels, so that they are at least considered when the customer becomes ready to buy.

Segmentation requires careful analysis

In reality, all the target customers rarely fall neatly into one single segment, eg surprisingly, more than half of *The Sun* newspaper's customers might be ABC1s (white collar workers) and less than half might be C2DEs (blue collar workers). However, sophisticated technology can help the marketer target using new variables, eg your 'likes', comments, hashtagged discussions as well as the usual age, income and geographic criteria.

> **Does a gap in the market equal a market in the gap?**
>
> If 85 per cent of the world's tea drinkers like hot tea and 15 per cent of the world's tea drinkers like iced tea, it doesn't necessarily mean that there is a screaming gap for lukewarm tea.
>
> Objectives can cover a variety of goals. It is useful to separate marketing objectives from marketing communications objectives. Detailed, specific objectives ensure that the subsequent choice of strategy is clearly focused.

Situation analysis requires more than just a customer analysis

An in-depth analysis of customers (Who? Why? and How?), competitors, distribution channels, the organization's own performance/results, strengths and weaknesses as well as external trends (that create opportunities and threats), is required.

Arguably the greatest marketing book ever, *The Art of War*, was written over 2,000 years ago by the Chinese military strategist Sun Tzu (translated by Wing, 1989). Sun Tzu emphasizes the importance of a comprehensive situation analysis. Most senior marketers have a copy of it on their shelves. It is a classic read. Interestingly, confrontation, or war, is seen as a last resort and the best military strategies win the war without any bloodshed. They win wars through intelligence.

Sun Tzu effectively confirms why the situation analysis needs to be comprehensive. Here's an excerpt from this masterpiece:

> Those who triumph,
> compute at their headquarters
> a great number of factors
> prior to a challenge.
>
> Those who are defeated,
> compute at their headquarters
> a small number of factors
> prior to a challenge.
>
> Much computation brings triumph.
> Little computation brings defeat.
> How much more so with no computation at all.
>
> By observing only this,
> I can see triumph or defeat.

'Much computation' or much analysis is required.

> The better the analysis, the easier the decisions will be later. Decisions about strategy and tactics become a lot easier when you know your customers, your competitors, your competencies and resources as well as market trends. That's why half your plan should be devoted to the situation analysis. It doesn't have to be at the front of the plan (you can dump a lot of it in the appendices) but the detailed analysis must be carried out if you are to succeed.
>
> Smith (2015)

Hence almost half of the marketing communications plan should be devoted to the situation analysis. The first year you do this analysis it will be particularly challenging, but as you find better (and often free) resources for highly relevant information, it gets easier, the intelligent information gets stronger and consequently, you make better-informed decisions. This ultimately boosts your results.

Objectives

After analysing the situation ('where we are now'), we can start setting sensible objectives (to determine 'where do we want to go?'). We have a mission, a vision and KPIs.

Mission

As well as defining what business you are in, your mission is your raison d'être; the reason your organization exists. It is a selfless statement about how you make the world a better place – how you ultimately help customers and stakeholders. It should also demonstrate some corporate social responsibility while giving strategic direction for the organization. Google's mission statement 'to organize the world's information and make it universally accessible and useful' makes a lot of sense. Mission overlaps with a sense of purpose; eg Kellogg food company is 'Nourishing families so they can flourish and thrive', while the insurance company IAG 'helps people manage risk and recover from the hardship of unexpected loss' (Kenny, 2014).

A man on the moon

'When John F Kennedy visited NASA he met a janitor and asked him what he did. The janitor said "I'm helping to put a man on the moon". A strong mission delivers a greater shared sense of purpose for all staff.'

PR Smith (2019)

Vision

A vision statement is more selfish, as it is more about the organization (as opposed to a mission statement, which is more customer/community orientated). A vision states where the organization sees itself in three, five or ten years' time. Imagine writing a headline in *The New York Times* or the *FT* for your business: 'XYZ is the number one company in the world (or Asia, Europe, China, London or Beijing, etc).' So the vision sets major goals for how successful your organization will be in the future. This includes size of turnover, size of organization, size of market share, local, national or global, position in the market place (number 1, 2 or 3).

What is your sense of purpose?

'A sense of purpose at work is important – partly because customers like to buy brands that stand for something and partly because employees like to work for an organization that stands for something more than just making money. Something deeper.'

PR Smith (2019)

See Chapter 1, p 6, for more on 'sense of purpose', including how 'firms of endearment' outgrow the S&P's excellent companies by eight times.

'If you don't stand for something you're dead; it's just a question of when.'

Sisodia *et al* (2014)

World-Class companies profit from passion and purpose. They endear themselves to customers and communities. These companies are what Sisodia *et al* (2014) call 'firms of endearment'. Remember in Chapter 1 we said:

- In 10 years, **'firms of endearment'** grew collectively at a rate of **1,000 per cent +**
- In 10 years, **Standard & Poor's 500** companies grew collectively at a rate of **122 per cent**

Key performance indicators

Ideally KPI objectives should be quantified in terms of success or failure criteria. Timescales should also be set. Clearly defined objectives make the management task of control much easier. Drawing up objectives for the first time is a difficult task. In future years, the previous year's objectives and corresponding results will help to make the planning job a little easier, as everyone has a better idea of what is realistic and what is not. Establishing clear objectives is necessary to give a focus to the organization or division. Clear objectives also give direction to subsequent creative efforts. Some marketing managers and agencies break objectives into many different types; other marketers use just one set of objectives (and sometimes without quantification or numbers attached). As a discipline it is useful to break up objectives so that performance can be measured more accurately. Objectives should be SMART:

S specific;
M measurable;
A actionable;
R realistic;
T time specific.

Two types of objectives are examined here: marketing objectives and communications objectives.

Marketing objectives

Typical marketing objectives refer to sales, market share, distribution penetration, launching a number of new products, and so on. For example, marketing objectives might be:

- to increase unit sales of product/brand X by 10 per cent over the next 12 months;
- to increase market share by 5 per cent over the next 12 months;
- to generate 500 new enquiries each month;
- to increase distribution penetration from 25 per cent to 50 per cent within 12 months;
- to establish a network of distributors covering Germany, France, the Netherlands and Italy during the first six months, followed by Switzerland, Austria, Belgium and Luxembourg in the second six months.

It is worth noting that not all marketing objectives are growth orientated. In Denmark, electricity boards no longer pride themselves on how much electricity they sell but on how little. Product withdrawals are another example where objectives are not attached to year-on-year growth. In very competitive mature markets, with new entrants appearing on the market, maintaining market share and consolidating sales might be more appropriate than expecting big growth. Given that marketing is shifting towards retention of profitable customers and deselection of unprofitable customers, the emphasis in some companies has moved from growth in turnover or sales to growth in profit or ROI.

Communications objectives

These typically refer to how the communications should affect the mind of the target audience, eg generate awareness, attitudes, interest or trial. Again, these tend to be most useful when quantified. DAGMAR (defining advertising goals for measuring advertising responses) and AIDA (attention, interest, desire, action) provide yardsticks for communications objectives by trying to separate the various mental stages a buyer goes through before buying. (DAGMAR is discussed in Chapter 4.)

The mental stages suggested by DAGMAR and AIDA are as follows:

DAGMAR	AIDA
Unawareness	–
Awareness	Attention
Comprehension	Interest
Conviction	Desire
Action	Action

Here are some examples of communications objectives:

- to increase awareness from 35 per cent to 50 per cent within eight weeks of the campaign launch among 25- to 45-year-old ABC1 women;
- to position the service as the friendliest on the market within a 12-month period among 70 per cent of heavy chocolate users;
- to reposition Guinness from an old, unfashionable, older man's drink to a fashionable younger person's drink over two years among all 25- to 45-year-old male drinkers;
- to maintain brand X as the preferred brand (or number one brand) of photocopiers among at least 50 per cent of current UK buyers in companies with 1,000-plus employees;
- to include Bulgarian wines in the repertoire of possible wine purchases among 20 per cent of ABC1 wine buyers in London within 12 months;
- to support the launch of a new shop by generating 50 per cent awareness in the immediate community one week before the launch;
- to announce a sale and create 70 per cent awareness one day before the sale starts.

The KPI pyramid

The KPI pyramid attempts to categorize various objectives into those that the C suite or board of directors would want to see versus those that perhaps a marketing manager might need to see versus those the operational marketing team might need to see (Figure 9.2). Although a pyramid, it is not written in stone, so feel free to move certain objectives into different categories. Now we can turn the pyramid upside down to create a funnel – starting with visitors entering the website, a percentage, moving on to become prospects and eventually a percentage converting to customers.

Figure 9.3 shows a more typical sales funnel, with a percentage of visitors moving on to become prospects/leads, of whom a percentage move on down to become hot prospects and, finally, a percentage convert by buying/becoming customers.

FIGURE 9.2 (a) The KPI pyramid. (b) The KPI pyramid upside down = the sales funnel

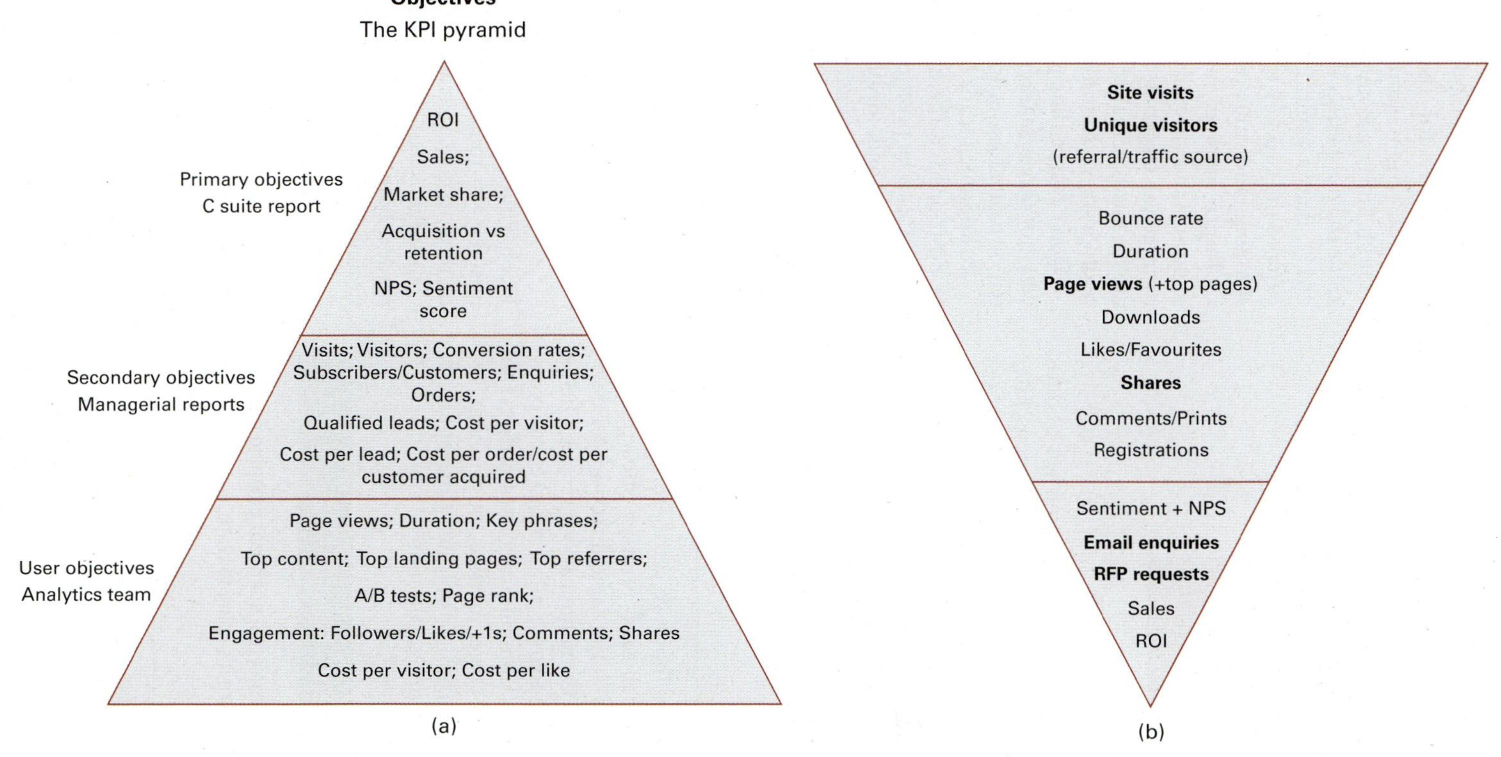

FIGURE 9.3 A simple sales funnel

Many criticize the sales funnel as being out of date, over-simplified and excluding what happens after an initial sale is made. Indeed, the first sale is just the beginning of what marketers want to convert into a lifetime relationship, so there is a lot more to do. However, it is useful and easy to agree objectives re how many visitors, prospects, hot prospects and customers for each quarter.

Strategy

Strategy summarizes 'how we get there' – how the objectives will be achieved. Strategy subsequently drives all the tactics in the same direction. Strategy summarizes tactics. Communications strategy helps to harmonize and integrate all of the tactical communications tools. Communications strategy can include selection of target markets, positioning, sequence of communications tools (are different tools used at different stages?), and more.

> **Most of us are afraid of strategy...**
>
> '...because we don't feel confident outlining one unless we're sure it's going to work.'
>
> Godin (2009)

Marketing communications strategies are hard to find. Often the strategy is retrospective in so far as the tactics are mistakenly planned first, and later, a strategy is created to try to summarize all of the tactics. This is not strategy. Before any tactics are ever discussed, strategy must be crystal clear about both positioning and target markets – just two of nine strategic components we will discuss. One aide-mémoire for the components of marketing communications strategy we shall borrow is the TOPPP SEED acronym taken from the 'SOSTAC® guide to your perfect digital marketing plan' (Smith, 2019). Before exploring all nine components let us explore the two key components: targeting and positioning (and value propositions).

Target markets means breaking markets into segments and carefully selecting the right segments to target, ie targeting the 'low hanging fruit'. These are the customers that you can easily reach and who really want your product or service.

Don't forget that your existing customers are a very hot target market and should never be forgotten or treated as second-class customers.

Positioning means how you want to be perceived or positioned in the minds of your target market – you want to be positioned where there is a real customer need and, ideally, little competition.

Two repositioning examples are e-cigarettes and Intel (also see Figure 9.4 on the repositioning of the *European* newspaper). Although seemingly small and subtle changes, these are big decisions. E-cigarette company, Blu-e-cig, want to reposition their product from:

> 'An alternative method to give up smoking'

to:

> 'A lifestyle choice for smokers'

Jacob Fuller, CEO of Blu-e-cig, said, 'Our biggest mistake was to call it an e-cigarette – an alternative method to give up smoking' (Benady, 2014).

Another example of 'repositioning' is Intel, who made a bold strategic decision to change their positioning from:

> 'High-quality technology products'

to:

> 'Leader in technology breakthroughs'

Intel's strategy is to position itself as a leader in technology breakthroughs, targeting Generation Y by associating Intel with innovation in music, art and lifestyle, using social media to leverage offline real events. This is a major strategic decision that will drive all of their tactics, including: developing an online community forum called IT Galaxy; a B2B game, outdoor 3D projections; partnering with

FIGURE 9.4 Repositioning the *European* newspaper from a medium-quality newspaper to an upmarket European newspaper

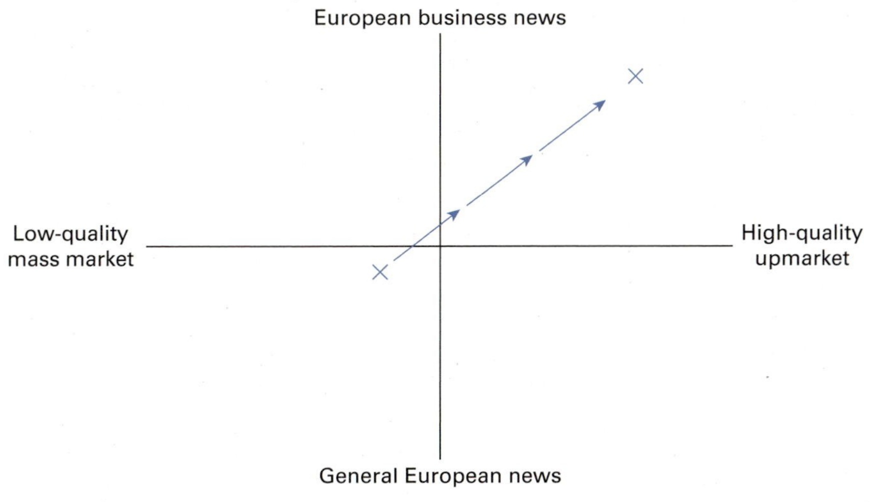

FIGURE 9.5 Watch the 'Museum of Me' video on YouTube

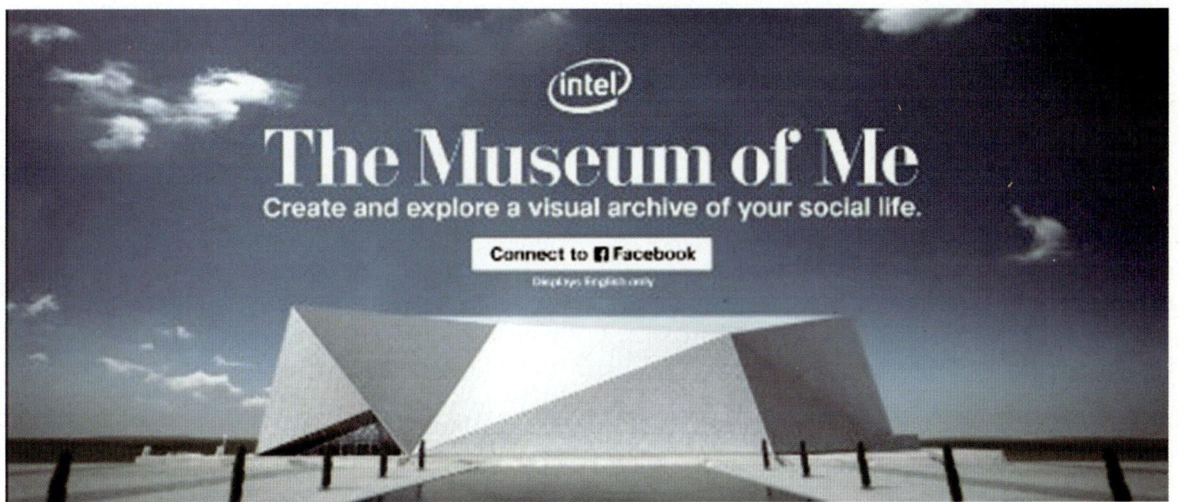

SOURCE: Used with kind permission

edgy magazine *Vice* to launch The Creators Project and Facebook app The Museum of Me (Figure 9.5); appointed will.i.am of the band Black Eyed Peas as Director of Creative Innovation; Google search, TV ads, social media, PR and training (for store assistants and re-sellers).

So, strategy drives tactics (not the other way around).

Just before we move onto the nine components of digital marketing, it is worth clarifying how 'positioning' directly influences your value proposition (VP). Your VP ultimately answers your potential customer's question 'What's in it for me?' Do your website, your content and your social media platforms all express a clear and immediate VP?

Your value proposition

A company website offers great opportunities to offer added value to the customer experience that simply isn't available offline. This added value can vary from new types of content to entertain or to inform (eg how to use your products), to new types of interactive services like a customer community or some 'sizzle' like the Sistine Chapel digital experience (see p 10). Many businesses miss out on the opportunity of adding digital value to physical products and services (not just online products and services).

Positioning

Your value proposition is closely tied to your brand's positioning, which answers questions such as: Who are we? What do we offer? What makes us different? And the customer's crunch question: What's in it for me? Which needs to be answered within seconds of landing on a website, looking at an ad or a shop window.

VP is more than just selling

Your VP is more than just a selling proposition, since it shows what you can offer by way of content, products, services and experiences to engage online customers. The VP extends this difference in that it identifies the reasons why customers will click on, return to, register or buy from your site and, ideally, feel motivated enough to share their experience.

VP communicates six customer benefits (6Cs)

VPs should communicate at least one of the 6Cs:

1. Choice: (a) wider range; (b) product differentiation (added features); (c) specialized service (niche customers).
2. Content (relevant, added value content at the right time in the right place).
3. Customization (personalization of products/services or content) for individuals or groups.
4. Community (customer forums exchanging tips, ideas, experiences or troubleshooting).
5. Convenience (24/7/365 'live' help when the intelligent bots get going).
6. Cost reduction (no middleman therefore cheaper?).

You can see some overlap with Michael Porter's (1985) now classic three growth strategies: (a) competing on cost, (b) differentiated products or (c) targeting niche segments.

Part of ongoing integrated communications

Your VP should be developed around your audience personas, support commercial goals and be communicated as part of ongoing integrated communications to encourage prospects to experience this value. The VP can only be developed after the positioning has been decided.

Targeting and positioning are just two of the nine key components of digital marketing strategy. Let's explore all nine components of a marketing communications strategy.

TOPPP SEED components of digital marketing strategy

Here are nine key components to consider when building your digital marketing strategy. You do not have to use all the key components. In fact, the strategy excerpts I'll show you later only include a selection of these components. You may find some components overlap/integrate. This is good. Your strategy doesn't have to be in the same order as TOPPP SEED. Feel free to move the components around to suit your strategy. Now let's consider each of the nine components to help you to build a crystal-clear digital marketing strategy.

- Target markets (essential).
- Objectives (summarize what objectives the strategy will fulfil).
- Positioning (essential).
- Processes (new processes like a new CRM system or a new marketing automation system or AI).
- Partnership (strategic alliances, co-marketing or marketing marriages can make marketing more cost effective).

- Sequence or stages (eg pilot campaign, then roll out in region 1, 2 and 3; or a sequence of tactical tools, eg advertising followed by a sales drive).
- Experience (does the strategy support the right customer experience?).
- Engagement (what level of the Ladder of Customer Engagement is required?).
- Data (can data be used to add value, or target new customers? This may overlap with 'processes' – major opportunity here).

Let's take a look at each of these briefly.

Target markets

Target markets need to be defined very clearly. Today we have many new variables (or filters) to help marketers identify targets. Time and effort spent carefully analysing and discussing who is/are the most ideal target market/s is time well spent. The more detailed target customer profiles, the easier it is to find the customers.

We can now add digital behaviour to many other variables. We can target people who visited certain websites, used different apps, liked, shared or commented on different topics. Lists can be created for retargeting. This is in addition to the traditional approaches to targeting (geographic, demographic, psychographic and behaviouristic). See Chapter 12 on advertising for more.

Objectives

It is always worth double-checking that your strategy actually supports the 'big' objectives (mission and vision) as well as the target sales, market share and ROI. Strategy without reference to objectives is unlikely to achieve those objectives. Hence some organizations want to see the main objectives referred to when presenting their strategies.

Decide which is a priority objective – customer acquisition or customer retention. Or perhaps it's a new market, you've no customers and you need to first build awareness, followed by preferences among the target market.

Positioning

Positioning is so strategic that you really don't want to be changing this each year. Positioning means precisely how you want to be positioned (or perceived) in the minds of your target customers.

Positioning is the foundation for brand propositions (what's in it for the customer) and ultimately, the CX. In fact, defining the brand, the VP and the CX are part of strategy. VP and CX also influence the marketing mix (tactical decisions), eg exclusive products online; differential pricing; exclusive online promotions; prioritizing which channels; online distribution partners, etc. See 'Tactics', p 280, for more.

The classic repositioning case: From sick child to healthy adult

Lucozade repositioned itself from a 'sick child's drink' to a 'healthy adult's drink'. They followed the market trends: the demographic shift from a massive child market (Baby Boom) in the 1960s to a bulging 40-year-old market in the noughties (2000s). They also followed the trend towards 'healthy living'. This repositioning strategy drives changes across all of the marketing mix tactics from chemist shop distribution and 'mother and child' ads to sports celebrity ads and Coca-Cola style distribution into shops, restaurants and offices.

Processes

If you are introducing a new approach, a new process, a system or even a new way of thinking, this can be strategic, eg introducing marketing automation or adding AI chatbots to your customer service channels, or working with new IoT partners, or insisting on analytics driven decisions, or nurturing a 'constant beta culture' (constant A/B testing/optimization of web pages, emails and ads), or integrating all data from all touchpoints to generate a real-time (immediately updated) 360 degree customer view to facilitate a personalized and tailored CX.

These are significantly new processes that will disrupt staff, departments and organization structures. Hence when introduced they are definitely a strategic issue.

> **WARNING!**
>
> Most of these new processes fail! Over 50 per cent of new CRM systems fail. See the Actions section (p 280), which explains why they fail and how to ensure your processes never fail.

Note: Processes such as programmatic ads, AI personalization and marketing automation are also referred to in another strategic component: the 'Sequence or stages' section below.

Finally, major new processes will probably require reallocating your team to some different jobs. Do you need a new marketing team structure or employ external agencies to manage the process of marketing? Either way, internal marketing (communication, motivation and training) will be required. See the 'Actions' section (p 280) for more on internal marketing.

Partnerships (and collaborations)

Partnership – introducing, strengthening or reducing strategic partnership/marketing marriages/marketing alliances – is part of strategy. Are there partners out there that can extend (a) your reach or (b) your product portfolio? Certainly, IoT is already creating new partnership opportunities to communicate with your target audience via completely different partners who have access to them, eg domestic refrigerator companies promoting beer, or vacuum cleaning equipment promoting a particular type of carpet cleaner (if it detects a stain on a carpet).

Are there potential partners out there whose customers would welcome your organization's products or services (including your content marketing)?

> **Partnership strategy worked for Amazon**
>
> 'The dot-com bubble hit Amazon in year 2000. Stock price crashed to $5.97 per share. It seemed like the end for Amazon due to extremely low investor confidence in the online marketplace model.
>
> Bezos did not give up. He saw the big picture of making Amazon the world's largest retailer and stuck to it. Innovation again was the key. In order to grow the customer base it was necessary to garner greater traction on its online presence through collaboration with physical stores. Thus it partnered with Target, Toys-R-Us, GAP and 400 other retailers for expanding its reach. Amazon was back in the picture again and it has never looked back since.'
>
> Soumya (2017)
>
> Note: Amazon also purchased key online publishers like IMDB.com to market its DVDs and DPReview.com to encourage the purchase of cameras from Amazon by people comparing cameras). Amazon have also got over 900,000 affiliate partnership arrangements in place.

Selecting the right partner can firstly give you access to a much bigger target market, and secondly strengthen your brand. But remember partnerships have to benefit both parties, with clear goals, roles and responsibilities – the devil is, most definitely, in the detail.

Sequence or stages

Stage 1, using advertising, sponsorship and PR to generate awareness, can be followed by an email drive, followed by a sales conversion drive online and offline. Another type of sequence would be a pilot campaign, followed by rolling out the campaign in region 1, 2 and 3. Another sequence is derived from AIDA (building attention/awareness, interest, desire and action/buy) as a series of stages:

1. **Develop credibility before raising visibility**
   It is so important that we thought we'd mention it again! How many major TV ad campaigns or content marketing and social media platforms drive traffic to websites or apps that don't work?
2. **Customer acquisition vs customer retention**
   Obviously, retention can only come after acquisition. However, you still need to plan for retention. In year 2, perhaps you might spend more on stage 2: retention (than you previously spent on stage 1: acquisition)?
3. **Long-term lifetime vs short-term transactional**
   The long-term view introduces lifetime customers and lifetime customer experience

(which has many stages). This type of thinking changes everything and ensures a more strategic approach.

4 **Map out the customer lifecycle journey...**
... and then deploy processes such as automated, always-on communications like programmatic ads to build awareness, AI-based personalization to improve conversions and marketing automation to nurture customer relations by delivering more relevant messages via email, app and website.

Adapted from Dave Chaffey

Experience (the CX)

Defining what kind of customer experience you want your customers to have is at the heart of your strategy. Personalized, real-time, fast and efficient or fun, relaxing and enjoyable? You must decide.

The CX establishes the brand experience, which needs to be clearly defined:

- Is your CX a one-off CX or a lifetime CX?
- Can you deliver the perfect lifetime CX?
- Can AI help your CX?
- Should the CX be personalized and available in real time?

Content marketing is part of the CX. Can you deliver a stream of relevant added-value content that your customers will appreciate? Can you do this better than competition? Can you deliver it in real time? Content marketing could be the lead component in your marketing strategy, but remember it's competitive out there and there's a lot of other content competing for your customers' shortened attention spans. See Chapter 15 for more on content marketing. Red Bull's content is simply excellent and now adds to the overall CX from Red Bull (Figure 9.6).

FIGURE 9.6 Red Bull's content supports both what their customers want and their brand values

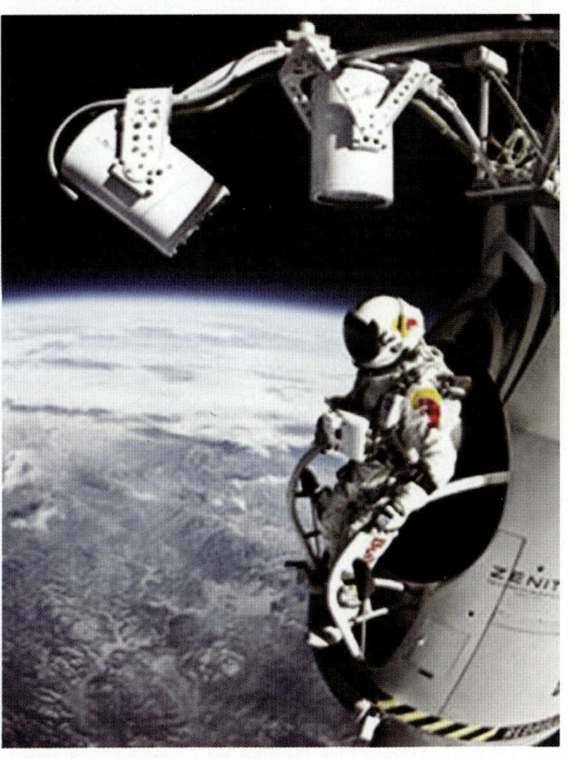

SOURCE: Red Bull

What a brand says about itself is less important than the actual experience the brand delivers to its customers across all touchpoints. So, although positioning and brand propositions are important, they are less important than the actual CX.

The CX needs to be managed across functions, by all staff online and offline.

Costco vs Apple CX

Costco customers expect bare-bones service in return for low prices, while Apple customers expect high-quality innovative products at relatively high prices. Those are very different customer experiences, but they both delight customers (Band and Hagen, 2011). And they are delivered to customers consistently online and offline.

Can you become the expert Wikipedia?

For your industry or topic, whether it is Red Bull or B2B widgets?

Engagement

There are different levels of visitor engagement, from encouraging visitors and customers to give ratings and reviews to nurturing advocates to collaborating and co-creating ideas and products. This is the Ladder of Engagement, starting with low-level engagement (ratings and reviews) and at the top of the ladder is collaborative co-creation (Figure 9.7).

Remember that not everyone wants to engage all the time, sometimes visitors just want to complete a task, find some information or just buy something and leave your site. So, don't ignore the basics of properly tested, quick, easy-to-use websites and apps. It may well be the 90:9:1 ratio that applies – 90 per cent of your visitors/customers will just lurk and watch (but not engage), while 9 per cent (if you are lucky) will engage with ratings, reviews and possible comments/discussions, while 1 per cent will be prepared to engage in what we call 'collaborative co-creation'.

Now this is strategic and it takes time to set up 1) communications systems (to acknowledge receipt and acceptance/rejection of ideas; 2) legal systems (to clearly state who owns the IPR (intellectual property rights) if visitors and customers are sharing ideas for say new products or new features; 3) financial systems to pay people if you promise to pay them a fee, a winning prize or a royalty.

If any of these three systems are not working perfectly, customers/visitors will get upset and quite quickly your ladder starts damaging your brand reputation. The Ladder of Loyalty can effectively restructure a business if customers are driving the new products, etc. So the Ladder of Engagement is strategic and requires careful planning in itself.

FIGURE 9.7 The Ladder of Engagement

Download a complete chapter about engagement from the 'Welcome' tab on PR Smith Marketing's Facebook page.

Data

The last of the TOPPP SEED components of strategy, yet some would say the most important. Remember, TOPPP SEED is not in any order of importance, it is just an acronym to help you think about various aspects of strategy. Your strategy could be led by the way you decide to use data to add value to the CX or access customers' attention.

Integrating customer data online and offline is a strategic decision. Integrating customer/visitor data from the marketing automation sales funnel (click behaviour/digital body language), to registration data, to social media data to CRM, which includes purchase behaviour, to post-purchase data (including complaints) is a worthwhile challenge for all marketers.

After that you can layer it with external data from third-party databases.

> Having social data as well as a complete history of your leads' and customers' activity in one place is invaluable to your company, because it means you can finally stop wasting time on what doesn't work, as well as equipping your sales team with the information to help them close more deals.
>
> Toner (2014)

You must give an **integrated 360-degree customer view** that brings together each customer's data from online (websites, apps, social media, etc) and offline platforms (telephone, in-store, etc). This means that all the processes (already discussed) must be integrated so data can flow between them to ensure a single 360-degree view of the customer.

Learn to ask questions of your data.

Three great data questions

1. Can you integrate your data?
2. How can data add value to the perfect lifetime CX – to help customers to 'get the job done'?
3. Can you extract more value from data – can you use your data to profile customers better or to help customers better?

WARNING! Bad or incomplete or unintegrated data damages your business

Data is the world's most valuable resource. But, equally, bad or incomplete data can damage your brand permanently – late data, unintegrated data, repeat data requests, incomplete customer data (eg they complained via Twitter but no one in the sales department knows that this customer is unhappy). So develop an interest in the many different digital marketing tools and how they integrate data.

Sample strategy excerpts

Here are four examples of strategy excerpts. These excerpts overlap with the broader marketing strategies.

Uber

Uber's algorithms use data and devices to create a service (product) that improves the CX by reducing the customer's 'cognitive load', reducing searching, reducing waiting time, reducing prices for any customer who needs a taxi, all done via a clever app. Uber wants to be seen (positioned) as a 'personal drive from any point at any time' (for customers) and also a 'business/hobby driving people for money' (for drivers). For governments, Uber wanted to be seen as a data company rather than a transport company (however, the EU has ruled it is a transport company). Uber has an aggressive growth strategy related to spending to: (a) get new customers and (b) enter new markets.

The Great Sportsmanship programme

Repositioned from a book (targeted at sports fans in the UK and Ireland) to an edutainment programme packed with inspirational true two-minute sportsmanship stories targeting youths with challenges from Ireland, the UK and the UAE via the most popular social media platforms and to help (a) coaches/trainers and influencers to guide their groups through the resources available online and (b) help youths to self-select their level of engagement for the continual delivery of user-generated content to satisfy the growing global network of schools, clubs, coaches and ambassadors.

Red Bull

Red Bull created a new category of 'non-soda energy drinks' targeting burned-out high schools and college students, firstly by initially quietly converting America's youth into devoted, enthusiastic customers, building an anti-brand via brand evangelists' word-of mouth (rather than expensive, older-fashioned mass marketing ad campaigns). Red Bull is positioned as a revitalizing drink (for both body and mind); consumer-educators drive around in shiny silver off-roaders with giant, phallic cans of Red Bull strapped to the back, giving out free cans (they also give student representatives free cases and encourage the kids to throw a party). Red Bull sponsor extreme sports events which reinforce the brand positioning of 'strong mental and physical performance' and gives them access to produce and manage a stream of high-quality action sports, and youth culture-oriented content that spans web, social, film, tablet, print, music and TV.

Avon

Avon's new strategy is to turn its existing business model into a 'modern, high-touch and high-tech organization' by mixing the best marketing communication techniques of a consumer goods company, with the social selling tradition Avon pioneered. Avon has teamed up with the creative production company MediaMonks to develop and distribute high-quality brand and product content at scale (more than five million people's worth of scale, across 50 countries). Going live in March across Brazil, Mexico and Russia, the 'always-on' content hub will develop 12,000 images, videos, gifs and pieces of gamified content annually for use across Avon's 50 markets. Multi-language and multi-platform, the content will be delivered weekly to its network of representatives. Avon reps will become 'micro-influencers' who create content and post it themselves, allowing the brand to 'let go of control a little bit'. A brand framework, tone, look and feel (brand guide) is shared so that all sales representatives create 'hyper-localized' content that fits the nuances of their specific markets.

The three priorities are to 1) convert awareness to relevance, 2) create a real-world perception of Avon quality products and then 3) communicate that.

There is no one single approach

Remember, TOPPP SEED is not in a linear sequence; eg your strategy can start with data if you prefer. There is no one single approach to building marketing communications strategies. In fact many companies do not put them together at all. A good communications strategy helps to keep all the subsequent tactical communications tools integrated and moving in the same direction, delivering bigger impacts and reducing costs. A simple way to practise writing marketing communications strategies is to generate several alternative strategies, so that strategic options can be considered. Many strategies will not use all nine components, but you most certainly should consider each of the nine components to see if it helps you to achieve the objectives you have set for your organization.

> WARNING!
>
> 'There's no point rowing harder,
> if you are rowing in the wrong direction.'
>
> Kenichi Ohmae

Tactics

Tactics are the details of strategy. In a full marketing plan, tactics are the marketing mix (product, price, place, promotion, people, processes and physical evidence). In a marketing communications plan, tactics are the 'promotions', sometimes called the promotional mix or the communications mix. This the selection (or mix) of tactical tools (or channels) such as advertising, PR, direct mail, etc. The tactics in the marketing communications plan list what happens, when, for how long, and for how much. They are often best expressed as a Gantt chart, as shown in Figure 9.8. The tactics section describes the themes, types of campaigns and whether the work will be done in-house (and whether upskilling is required) or out of house via agencies and consultancies.

The Tactics Matrix (Figure 9.9) is designed to help to discuss and ultimately choose which tactical tools are most useful at various stages of the customers' buying process. The matrix helps marketers to consider, discuss and eventually choose a particular tactical tool to achieve a specific objective. This matrix is work in progress and designed to stimulate discussion.

Social media tactical function is changing

Although social media is a tactical communications tool, way back in 2008 a Marketing Sherpa study found that the vast majority of those surveyed rated social media marketing effective at influencing brand reputation, increasing awareness and improving search rankings and site traffic. Although many organizations have a corporate blog or Facebook page, few have strategies in place and even fewer have written social media policies. In fact, only 33 per cent of larger firms had a written policy to manage brand communications, and a mere 13 per cent of smaller businesses had a written policy (eMarketer, 2009). Fast forward to today and the excellent companies not only have content 'strategies' and social media 'strategies', they also use social media as both a listening tool (re conversations about their product/customers/competitors/market) and, far more interestingly, as a source of future communications. Consider how organizations collect particular hashtag comments and then return those comments to the individuals with tailor-made video content (see also p 505, British Heart Foundation, and the videos on **www.prsmith.org/blog**).

Part 2 of this book addresses 11 tactical communications tools in great detail. So let us move on to the forgotten part of most plans. This omission causes many plans to fail. Let us explore the 'actions' section.

Actions

Excellent execution of tactics is surprisingly rare. In fact, execution, or 'actions' can often prove to

FIGURE 9.8 Tactical timings of different communication tools

	Jan	Feb	Mar	Apr	May	Jun	Jul	Aug	£
Advertising – TV – Press – PPC									
Social media – Blog – YouTube – Facebook									
Website – SEO – Inbound links									
Sales promotion – Sample drop – Competition – Collection									
Direct marketing – Mailshot – Telesales									
Publicity (and public relations)									
Sponsorship									
Exhibitions									
Packaging									
Point-of-sale and merchandising									
Internet									
Word of mouth – Viral marketing – CRM NGN									

NOTE: This is just a shortlist of some of the tactical tools employed by an organization.

be the weakest link in many businesses' plans. Strategy summarizes, and gives direction to, 'How you are going to get there?' Tactics are the details of strategy (communications mix) and action is the details of tactics – how you ensure excellent execution of the plan. Internal marketing is required.

Internal marketing

Internal marketing is like a mini project plan that covers staff:

- motivation;
- communication;
- training.

FIGURE 9.9 Tactics Matrix

Tactics Matrix	BENEFIT →	Reach	Speed	Lead time	Message size	Targeting	Personal-ization	Cost: CPC/CPM	Control	Credibility (message)
OBJECTIVE ↓	TACTIC/ CHANNEL ↓									
Awareness/ familiarity	Display ads	High	Medium	Long / Med	Medium	High	Medium	Medium	Medium	Low
	PR	High	Medium	Medium	Large	Low	Low	Low	Low	High
	Sponsorship	High	Low /Med	Long	Small	Low	Low	Medium	Low	Medium
	Social media (content marketing)	Low/Med/ High	Low / Med	Medium	Large	Medium	Med / Low	None	Low / Med	High
Consideration	Search ads & SEO	Low/Med	Medium	Long/Med	Small	High	Medium	Medium	High	Low / Med
	E-mail (AM)	Med	High	Short	Large	High	High	Low	High	Medium
	Website incentives	Low/Med	Low	Medium	Med / Low	Low/Med	High with Auto Marketing	None	High	Medium
	Social media	Low/Med /High	Low	Short / Med	Large	Medium	Med / Low	None	Low / Med	High
	Sales pitch	Low	Medium	Short	NA	High	High	High	High	Med / High
Decision	Search ads & SEO	Med / Low	Medium	Short	Small	High	Medium	Medium	High	Low / Med
	E-mail (AM)	Medium	High	Short	Large	High	High	Low	High	Medium
	Website incentives	Low	Low	Medium	Low	N/A	High with Auto Marketing	N/A	High	N/A
	Telesales	Low/ Med	High	Short / Med	Large	High	High	Low	High	Medium
	Sales pitch	Low	Medium	Short	Low	High	High	High	High	Med / High
	Exhibition	Medium	Medium	Med/Long	Large	High	Low	High	Medium	Med / High
		The Tactics Matrix www.PRSmith.org © PRSmith 2014 v2								
Post-purchase relationship building	Direct mail/e-mail newsletter/ special offers added value	Medium	High	Short (eM) Med (Dmail)	Large	High	High	Low (eMail) High (DM)	High	Medium
	Social media	Low/High	Low	Short/Med	Large	High	Medium	None	Low / Med	High
Post-purchase repeat sales loyalty...adv..	Direct mail/e-mail	Medium	High	Med/Short	Large	High	High	High (DM)	High	Medium
	Social media	Low/High	Med	Short/Med	High	High	Medium	None	Low / Med	High

Many staff resent change (eg a new plan with a new way of doing things, such as AI or automation) being imposed upon them. The excellent companies keep anything between 10–15 per cent of their marketing budgets for internal marketing – to ensure staff are capable, motivated and fully understand the new plan.

The internal marketing section of the plan includes:

- systems;
- processes;
- guidelines;
- checklists.

All of these help to ensure high-quality execution.

'Everything degenerates into work' (Peter Drucker)

That is the bad news. But, taken into context, Drucker actually said 'Plans are only good intentions unless they immediately degenerate into hard work.'

Internal marketing is largely about internal communications and motivation to make sure everyone understands what the marketing activities are all about and everyone knows who has to do what, when and how. This can include mini action plans and even checklists (which reduce the opportunity for errors) since each tactic is a mini project that needs professional execution. You don't have to include all the mini projects in the initial plan. Just be aware that someone will have to produce a mini project plan for, say, an automated marketing project linking content, emails, websites, etc.

You can add systems, processes, guidelines and checklists, either into the body of the plan or in the appendices at the back, or you can simply issue them later. The actions section of your plan ensures your plan has resources to communicate, motivate and train staff so that they are capable and motivated to execute the plan with excellence and passion. Without internal marketing, many plans fall over; 50 per cent of new CRM projects fail. The morale, culture, skills of the team is critical; look at the kind of staff Netflix recruit – they are very focused on creating and maintaining a particular culture (google 'Netflix slide deck').

Workers should be allowed to take whatever vacation time they feel is appropriate

'Facebook's Sheryl Sandberg has called the Netflix slide deck one of the most important documents ever to come out of Silicon Valley. It's been viewed more than five million times on the web. Reed Hastings (CEO) and Patty McCord (Chief Talent Officer) wrote and published openly on the internet the 'Netflix culture, freedom and responsibility' 125-slides deck – it included: "Workers should be allowed to take whatever vacation time they feel is appropriate'. They wanted to craft a 'culture of excellence".'

McCord (2014)

In reality, the actions/implementation of the marketing communications tactics also require an ability to get other people (staff, agencies, printers, etc) to deliver on time and within budget.

'Culture eats strategy for breakfast'

Peter Drucker is quoted by many as having said this, but no direct citation can be found.

Critical path and project plans

A variety of project plans are used here, whether critical path or just a Gantt chart. A detailed project plan is required for each tactical communications tool. For example, the production of a snail mailshot (that needs to be printed and mailed) is shown in Figure 9.10.

This is just for one mailing. More detailed planning is required if there is a series of mailings. The response handling also needs to be planned carefully. With hybrid and automated marketing systems (see Chapter 16), the responses can be routed to an inbound telesales team, who filter respondents, rank them in terms of urgency, size and location, and pass the enquiry to a relevant salesperson or dispatch further information and update the database for future activities. All of this requires careful planning to ensure sufficient resources are available to make the strategies and tactics actually happen.

Actions can be boring

A lot of the work involved in delivering an excellent CX is boring.

McGovern (2018)

... therefore motivation is critical.

Control

Plans should include a control section – 'How do you know you are going to get there?' A good plan specifies what is going to be measured, how often, by whom and, most importantly, what you are going to do with this information. Managers need to know at an early stage (rather than when it's too late) how your plan is working or how a particular campaign is running. If it is not working, it should be stopped. **Control systems need to be in place to help monitor any campaigns or activities** (see Figure 9.11). This is where clear objectives can once again help, since they can usually be broken down into more detailed objectives covering shorter periods of time. Once marketers are armed with clearly defined, precise objectives, money can be spent on measuring performance against the objectives (whether defined as sales, enquiries, awareness, or return on investment, etc).

FIGURE 9.10 An action plan for one communication tool – a mailshot

	Wk 1	Wk 2	Wk 3	Wk 4	Wk 5	Wk 6	Wk 7	Wk 8	Wk 9	Wk 10	Wk 11	Wk 12
Creative brief												
List brief												
List proposal												
Visual concepts												
Visuals approved												
List order												
Final copy/design												
Artwork brief												
Print quotes												
Set artwork proofs												
Receive lists												
Data preparation												
Finished artwork												
Printer brief												
Printer proofs												
Merge purge lists												
Print												
Computer bureau output files												
Live laser proofs												
Mail house brief												
Print delivery												
Laser print letter												
Mail house delivery												
Mail house sort/enclose												
Mail												

Marketers can now measure and compare all activities: inbound (social media campaigns) and outbound marketing (ad campaigns), online and offline. If a campaign is focused on boosting brand awareness or repositioning a brand in the mind of the target audience, this can be measured separately through surveys (offline and online – in fact Facebook offer advertisers a new system to link actual offline sales or store visits with online advertising including measuring awareness, etc). If the campaign is focused on engagement and/or sales, this can be easily measured by identifying if visitors, enquirers or customers are emerging from each communications tool – assuming the campaign is focused on generating engagement at some level, eg interaction on a website or Facebook page (posting a comment or voting), registering for a newsletter, taking a trial or making a purchase. The web analytics reveal where visitors are coming from, and telesales, reception and sales staff should also always log where new enquiries are coming from (how visitors heard about the business and what key phrases they used to find the website).

Cost per order, cost per enquiry and cost per visitor can be easily calculated. Other variables need to be closely monitored, including:

- cost per order, cost per customer acquisition and cost per customer retention;
- net promoter score, satisfaction score and recommendation score;
- reputation/social conversation scores (social media monitoring);
- return on investment.

Note that the figures in Figure 9.11 (control systems) are inserted when professional marketers learn what are realistic conversion ratios of enquirers or website visitors to customers. For example, in Figure 9.12, 1 per cent of visitors generated by search engine optimization (SEO) convert to customers, while only half of 1 per cent of visitors from a viral marketing campaign convert to customers. The figure would probably be higher for visitors generated from PPC campaigns.

Consider SEO. In Figure 9.12, it generates 20,000 visitors and costs £20,000. This gives a cost per visitor of £1 (£20,000 divided by 20,000 visitors). If the site converts 1 per cent of these visitors into customers, then the SEO generates 200 new customers (1 per cent of 20,000 visitors). The cost per order (CPO) generated by SEO is £100 (£20,000 divided by 200 orders).

If a viral marketing piece costs £30,000 (to create and seed) and it generates 20 million players of which 10 per cent click through to the website, this generates 2 million visitors. Say only half of 1 per cent convert, because many of them are from international

FIGURE 9.11 Control systems

Quantified objectives State each quantified objective and its time period	**Means of measuring** Sales analysis; number of responses; surveys	**Frequency of measurement** Daily; weekly; monthly; quarterly; annually?	**Accountability** Who does it?	**Cost** How much does it cost to measure?	**Action?** Who needs to be alerted if significant variances are found?

markets not relevant to this service. This generates 10,000 customer 'uniques' (unique visitors). Feel free to fill in the rest of the figures yourself.

The table in Figure 9.12 can be extended. You can create your own, more accurate, analysis by adding another column for percentage of visitors that convert to enquirers (and a percentage of them eventually convert to customers, and a percentage of them convert to repeat customers, at which point the costs decline significantly and large profit margins emerge). A longer list of tactical communications tools can be added, including different exhibition events, different email campaigns, different virals, etc, so that the marketer can see what works best and ultimately do more of what works and stop what doesn't.

More detailed control systems can be put in place. See Table 9.1 (taken from PR Smith's 2019 'SOSTAC® guide to your perfect digital marketing plan'). Here is a more compact control dashboard starting with ROI, sales and market share and moving down through various KPIs to cost per customer acquisition and then through to NPS, sentiment and share of voice.

Some tactical tools/channels are better than others

Remember, some tactical tools (channels) are better at generating awareness (eg banner ads) and some are better at closing sales (email with a sales promotion or a website page with chatbot support). So customer acquisition may not be the prime goal of some tools (eg advertising, PR and sponsorship are better at building awareness rather than closing sales). Therefore they may have different criteria for success. Be careful not to make decisions, eg to stop using a certain tactical tool based on the wrong criteria.

In fact marketing can be like a football or basketball match. The 'assist' is as important as the goal. So if you can identify players (or tactical channels) that are part of the customer journey, these may be worth investing more in. Multichannel funnel analysis does just this and helps you to make better decisions.

The lifetime value of potential repeat sales of a customer can give a truer picture of their real value. Remember, lifetime value can include 'share of wallet':

TABLE 9.1 Measuring the KPIs

KPI	Results (previous period)	Objective (current period)	Results (current period)
ROI (return on investment)			
Sales - units - value			
Market share - units - value			
Market leader number (in top 5)			
Awareness level (offline survey)			
Preference level (offline survey)			
NPS score (net promoter score)			
Sentiment score (incl. competitor comparison)			
Website/ blog: Unique visitors Average duration Subscribers to updates/ newsletter Leads generated			

(continued)

TABLE 9.1 (Continued)

KPI	Results (previous period)	Objective (current period)	Results (current period)
Cost per visitor (website)			
Cost per like (Facebook)			
Cost per lead			
Cost per customer acquisition			
Cost per customer retention			
Database size			
Prospects/ leads			
Customers			
Advocates			
Influencers			
Site visits			
Unique visitors			
Bounce rate			
Duration			
Page views Passive engagement			
Most popular page(s)			

(continued)

TABLE 9.1 (Continued)

KPI	Results (previous period)	Objective (current period)	Results (current period)
Most popular downloads			
Engagement: Downloads			
Engagement: Likes/ favourites			
Engagement: Comments			
Engagement: Shares			
Engagement: Registrations/ newsletter			
Churn rate			
Conversions Leads and sales			
Sales (all sales)			
Task completion			
SCAR (shopping cart abandonment rate)			
Satisfaction score			
NPS score			
Sentiment score			
Share of voice			

FIGURE 9.12 Cost per order/cost per customer acquisition

	Volume of people/ size of audience	Total cost	CPT/CPM (cost per thousand people reached)	Percentage CTR (click-through rate/visit website/ enquiry)	Unique visitors	Cost per visitor/ lead	Conversion rate of visitors to customers	Number of orders/ customers	Cost per order
SEO	n/a	£20,000	n/a	n/a	20,000	£1.00	1%	200	£100
Viral A	20,000,000	£30,000	£1.50	10%	2,000,000	£0.15	0.5 of 1%	10,000	£3
Blog	n/a	£20,000	n/a	n/a	10,000				
Banner ad	100,000	£1,000	£10	1%	1,000				
PPC ad	n/a	n/a	n/a	n/a	n/a				
Opt-in e-mail	10,000	£2,000	£200	2%					
Online sponsorship	50,000	£5,000	£1,000	1%					
E-zine/e-newsletter	1,000	£10,000	£10,000	5%					
Press ad	1,000,000	£5,000	£5.00	1/100th of 1%					
Direct mail List A	10,000	£5,000	£500	2%					
Telemarketing – outbound	5,000	£20,000	£4,000	10%					
Exhibition B	6,000	£18,000	£3,000	n/a					

other products or services that a customer might be prepared to buy from the same supplier.

You also need a rigorous structured approach to measuring relative satisfaction (compared to competitors) for each stage of the online experience – product search, evaluation, enquiring, purchases, post-purchase communications, after-sales support, etc. You need this more than once a year. Many organizations like to have 90-day plans and then review and modify them every quarter.

Net promoter score, satisfaction score and recommendation score

Since satisfaction criteria can change and leave an old satisfaction scoring systems irrelevant, net promoter score (NPS) has emerged. Effectively, subtracting the total number of detractors (those who give a score between 1–6) from the number of advocates (9–10 scores) delivers your NPS. We ignore the 7–8s.

Sentiment analysis: Social conversation scores (social media monitoring)

Marketers need to keep abreast of what is being said about their brands, their organizations and their staff (as well as the competition) in the vast array of conversations in social media platforms around the world. There are also some more comprehensive licence fee systems with their own scoring systems, which include Radian6, Market Sentinel and Precise Media.

Return on investment

As mentioned in Chapter 1, marketers must learn to speak the language of the boardroom. This includes ROI on marketing expenditure. Can marketers demonstrate rigorous professional discipline and track what communications campaigns deliver a better ROI than others? Can marketers convince the board that the return from investment in marketing is better than the return generated by investing the money elsewhere (eg in a high-interest deposit account)? It is possible to calculate the cost per order, profit per order and cumulative profit from a campaign? But remember customer acquisition may not be the main goal. For example, if boosting awareness is the main goal, then it may be worth calculating the correlation between brand awareness and market share, because then you can calculate the ROI of increased awareness. Figure 9.13 shows an overall ROI of 40.3 per cent.

The columns and rows in Figure 9.13 are self-explanatory. The ROI is calculated by dividing the £2,726,000 profit ('return') generated by the total cost of £6,760,667 for the marketing campaigns, delivering a 40.3 per cent ROI.

Another way of looking at this is calculating how much sales are generated by every dollar, or pound, spent on advertising What is the X factor (x being the multiple)? We can calculate it by saying every £1 spent generates x. So if spending £120,000 (total media and set-up costs) helps to deliver £9,486,667 sales, then each £1 spent generates £79 in sales revenue. The X factor is 79, ie each £1 spent on ads generates £79 worth of sales.

ROI is not the only measure

'Despite all evidence to the contrary, the belief that a single number can be used to assess marketing performance is persistent. Some say that top management can only handle a single number, or silver metric, so we must choose the least bad one. Others believe that ROI is so standard as not to be worth challenging. Others again claim modernity for customer concepts such as customer equity, customer lifetime value and Peppers and Rogers' new "Return on Customer". Yes, they are new and, yes, they have value, but these measures are not the silver metrics their promoters claim them to be.'

Ambler (2006)

Professor Tim Ambler (2006) explored four measurement mechanisms – return on investment (ROI) (or return on marketing investment (ROMI), or return on marketing expenditure (ROME));discounted cash flow (DCF); return on customer; and net advocates (Reichheld, 2006) – and concluded that no single metric does it all. In fact, a combination of metrics is required.

FIGURE 9.13 A dashboard from **www.smartinsights.com**

	A	B	C	D	E	F	G	H	I	J	K
1	Home		Online Media Mix model - based on % budget - with example of 'average' CTR								
5											
6			Advertising		Search		Partners				All digital media channels
7			Ad buys (CPM)	Ad network (CPM)	Paid search (CPC)	Natural search	Affiliates (CPA)	Aggregators (CPA)	Sponsorshi p (Fixed)	Email list (CPM)	Total or Average
8	Media costs	Setup/ creative / Mgt costs	£0	£0	£0	£0	£0	£0	£0	£0	£0
9		CPM	£10.0	£10.0	£4.0	£1.8	£10.0	£20.0	£100.0	£10.0	£4.3
10		CPC	£5.0	£5.0	£0.20	£0.90	£5.0	£10.0	£33.3	£100.0	£0.6
11		Media costs	£10,000	£10,000	£30,000	£30,000	£10,000	£10,000	£10,000	£10,000	£120,000
12		Total cost:setup & media	£10,000	£10,000	£30,000	£30,000	£10,000	£10,000	£10,000	£10,000	£120,000
13		Budget %	10%	10%	30%	30%	10%	10%	10%	10%	120%
14	Media impressions & Response	Impressions or names	1,000,000	1,000,000	7,500,000	16,666,667	1,000,000	500,000	100,000	10,000	27,776,667
15		CTR	0.2%	0.2%	2.0%	0.2%	0.2%	0.2%	0.3%	1.0%	0.7%
16		Clicks or site visits	2,000	2,000	150,000	33,333	2,000	1,000	300	100	190,733
17	Conversion to Opportunity (Lead)	Conversion rate to opportunity	100.0%	100.0%	100.0%	100.0%	100.0%	100.0%	100.0%	100.0%	100.0%
18		Number of opportunities	2,000	2,000	150,000	33,333	2,000	1,000	300	100	190,733
19		Cost per opportunity	£5.0	£5.0	£0.2	£0.9	£5.0	£10.0	£33.3	£100.0	£0.6
20	Conversion to Sales	Conversion rate to sale	100.0%	100.0%	100.0%	100.0%	50.0%	100.0%	100.0%	100.0%	93.8%
21		Number of sales	2,000	2,000	150,000	33,333	1,000	1,000	300	100	189,733
22		% of sales	1.1%	1.1%	79.1%	17.6%	0.5%	0.5%	0.2%	0.1%	100.0%
23		Cost per sale (CPA)	£5.0	£5.0	£0.2	£0.9	£10.0	£10.0	£33.3	£100.0	£0.6
24	Revenue	Total revenue	£100,000	£100,000	£7,500,000	£1,666,667	£50,000	£50,000	£15,000	£5,000	£9,486,667
25	Costs	Cost of goods sold	£70,000	£70,000	£5,250,000	£1,166,667	£35,000	£35,000	£10,500	£3,500	£6,640,667
26		Media costs	£10,000	£10,000	£30,000	£30,000	£10,000	£10,000	£10,000	£10,000	£120,000
27		Total costs (inc media)	£80,000	£80,000	£5,280,000	£1,196,667	£45,000	£45,000	£20,500	£13,500	£6,760,667
28	Profitability	Profit	£20,000	£20,000	£2,220,000	£470,000	£5,000	£5,000	-£5,500	-£8,500	£2,726,000
29		Return on Investment	25.0%	25.0%	42.0%	39.3%	11.1%	11.1%	-26.8%	-63.0%	40.3%

SOURCE: Used with kind permission

Control includes various areas of market research and testing, so measurement systems need to be built into the plan.

Planning is really an iterative process. A manager puts together a plan and a budget. The budget gets cut. The manager revises the plan according to new budget. The plan is then rolled out, results watched carefully and action taken to change the plan if necessary (ie if it is not working). Each year, improvements can be made. Procter & Gamble asks its managers to build on their 'learnings' (what they have learned from the marketplace). They constantly learn from the marketplace and then incorporate those 'learnings' in their next marketing plan.

Constant beta

Nurturing a constant beta culture is part of developing a well-managed data-driven business. Constant beta means constantly split testing web pages, ads, emails. In fact it means more as it includes multivariable testing – testing several variables simultaneously.

10,000 different versions of Facebook being tested constantly

At any given point in time, there isn't just one version of Facebook running, there are probably 10,000. Any engineer at the company can basically decide that they want to test something. There are some rules on sensitive things, but in general, an engineer can test something, and they can launch a version of Facebook not to the whole community, but maybe to 10,000 people or 50,000 people – whatever is necessary to get a good test of an experience

Zuckeberg (2018)

Do not forget your 3Ms: men/women (HR), money (budgets) and minutes (timescale), and the new resource mega data (data). We addressed 'men/women' when we explored internal marketing and recruitment; minutes and timescales need to be attached to everything; mega data is so important that it now features in almost every chapter in Part Two. That leaves 'money' or budgets. Here is a brief insight into how you build your budgets.

Budget setting

Budgeting

Outlined below are the most common approaches to budgeting:

- Objective and task – identifying the overall objectives and then breaking these down into specific tasks and calculating the budget accordingly. For example, to sell x million cans of Coke would require x per cent levels of awareness, which would require x number of impressions, which would require x amount of advertising, which would cost £x. This is sometimes called the 'ideal' or 'task' approach.
- Modelling involves the use of a variety of econometric and simulation techniques to determine how various budget levels may affect performance (eg sales). An example of this is Unilever's AMTES area market-testing model.
- Profit optimization tries to find the optimum marketing spend that would generate the most profit. It is based on ensuring that the marginal revenue derived from each marketing communications activity exceeds the marginal cost.
- Percentage of sales is a crude but quick way of calculating a budget. For example, taking 5 per cent of £1 million forecasted sales means the marketing budget is £50,000. In B2B markets, the percentage ranges from 0.5 to 2 per cent, and in B2C markets it ranges from 5 to 20 per cent.
- Competitive parity analyses competitors' marketing communications spends. Basically, it suggests that if an organization wants to match a competitor it should spend the same amount as that competitor.
- Affordability is usually driven by accountants, who draw up business plans, work out profitability and then allocate some budget to marketing based on what is left over or affordable. This is the opposite of the

objective and task method. It is based upon what is affordable after taking all costs and an amount of profit away from sales.

- Payback period is the time taken for an integrated campaign to pay back the costs (or budget) of the marketing communications.
- Arbitration requires a senior member of staff to arbitrate between different views of the marketing team and the rest of the business.

Some academics categorize these different budgeting approaches as scientific and heuristic. Scientific planning approaches include: objective and task; modelling; payback period; and profit optimization. Heuristic planning approaches include: percentage of sales; competitive parity; affordability; and arbitration.

In reality, several budgeting approaches are used. Although a manager might use the ideal task approach, the review panel (of senior management) will immediately convert it into a percentage figure, compare it with the competition's spend and ask 'Can we really afford it?' and 'Does it deliver the required level of profits?' It is not unusual to find the initial budget request cut back by senior management as other divisions and departments compete internally for limited funds for the following year's marketing. Few companies have sophisticated optimum profit models that attempt to identify the optimum spend.

Allocating budget between customer retention and customer acquisition

Another interesting question is how to split the budget between customer retention and customer acquisition. If selling to existing customers is supposed to be on average six to seven times more profitable than selling to new customers, there is a school of thought that suggests that marketers should spend at least equal resources on 1) keeping existing customers happy (eg CRM) and 2) acquiring new customers. Businesses like Amazon reportedly pay £50 to acquire a customer, and Virgin pays up to £150 (a free laptop), while Reichheld (2006) estimated the Dell average customer to be worth $210 (five-year net present value), with a detractor (someone speaking negatively about Dell) costing $57 and a promoter generating $328. In the world of online marketing it is increasingly easy to calculate the cost of customer acquisition.

See 'Social listening skills' (Smith, 2014a) for more information on each of the approaches.

Key points from Chapter 9

- SOSTAC® provides an effective structure for any plan.
- Market research and intelligence reduce risk and boost the likelihood of success. It is essential to gather key information before making any decisions about strategy or tactics.
- Strategy is the weakest part of most plans. Use TOPPP SEED as an aide mémoire for the key components for writing a strategy. Write several options before choosing the best one.
- Some tactical tools are better at achieving specific objectives, but regardless of which objective, all tactics must fit into the overarching strategy.
- Develop an internal marketing part of the plan to ensure excellent execution of the plan
- Build and monitor control systems into the plan.
- Ninety-day planning cycles can be useful.

References and further reading

Ambler, T (2006) Use a dashboard when driving your marketing, *Market Leader*, 33, Summer

Band, W and Hagen, P (2011) The right customer experience strategy, *Destination CRM* [online] http://www.destinationcrm.com/Articles/Columns-Departments/The-Tipping-Point/The-Right-Customer-Experience-Strategy-74691.aspx (archived at https://perma.cc/3KNP-ULAA)

Benady, A (2014) E-cigarette boss Jacob Fuller on comms and the industry's 'biggest mistake', *PR Week*, 25 June

Doyle, P (2001) *Marketing Management Strategy*, 3rd edn, FT Prentice Hall, Hemel Hempstead

Doyle, P, Saunders, J and Wright, L (1987) *A Comparative Study of US and Japanese Marketing Strategies in the British Market*, Warwick University

eMarketer (2009) Social media best practices, 29 July [online] www.emarketer.com (archived at https://perma.cc/7G34-UAH9)

Engel, J, Warshaw, M and Kinnear, T (1994) *Promotional Strategy: Managing the marketing communications process*, Irwin, Boston, MA

Forrester Research (2009) *US Interactive Marketing Forecast, 2009 to 2014*, Forrester Research, Cambridge, MA

Godin, S (2009) When tactics drown out strategy, *Seth Godin's Blog*, 7 August [online] https://seths.blog/ (archived at https://perma.cc/T262-CXC5)

Kanter, B (2008) How much time does it take to do social media? *Beth's Blog*, 1 October

Kanter, R M (2000) *Marketing CD 2: Segmentation, positioning and the marketing mix* [online] https://prsmith.org/ (archived at https://perma.cc/8LKG-MEEW)

Kanter, R M (2001) *On-line Marketing Course 2: Segmentation, positioning and the marketing mix*, 2nd edn [online] https://prsmith.org/ (archived at https://perma.cc/8LKG-MEEW)

Kenny, G (2014) Your company's purpose is not its vision, mission, or valuesKotler, P (2001) In conversation with Paul Smith, *Harvard Business Review*, 3 September

Kotler, P (2001) In conversation with Paul Smith, Marketing Series, Multimedia Marketing Consortium

Kotler, P *et al* (2000) *Marketing CD 3: Marketing planning* [online] https://prsmith.org/ (archived at https://perma.cc/8LKG-MEEW)

McCord, P (2014) How Netflix reinvented HR, *Harvard Business Review*, January/February

McGovern, G (2018) Keeping digital teams happy versus keeping customers happy [online] http://gerrymcgovern.com/ (archived at https://perma.cc/GF3D-CV9F), 5 August

Moore, K (2017) How to increase your performance by finding your purpose, *Forbes*, 3 August

Ohmae, K (2000) *Marketing CD 2: Segmentation, positioning and the marketing mix* [online] https://prsmith.org/ (archived at https://perma.cc/8LKG-MEEW)

Porter, M E (1985) *Competitive Advantage*, Ch 1, pp 11–15, The Free Press, New York

Reichheld, F (2006) *The Ultimate Question: Driving good profits and true growth*, Harvard Business School Publishing, Boston, MA

Sisodia, R, Sheth, J and Wolfe, D (2014) *Firms of Endearment: How world-class companies profit from passion and purpose*, 2nd edn, Pearson Education, London

Smith, PR (1998) *Marketing Communication: An integrated approach*, 2nd edn, Kogan Page, London

Smith, PR (2004) *SOSTAC Marketing Plans* (CD)

Smith, PR (2014a) Social listening skills parts 1 & 2 [online] https://prsmith.org/blog/ (archived at https://perma.cc/MJ9V-Q25F)

Smith, PR (2014b) How to target very very specific audiences on Facebook [online] https://prsmith.org/blog/ (archived at https://perma.cc/MJ9V-Q25F), 21 August

Smith, PR (2015) SOSTAC® guide to writing the perfect marketing plan [online] https://prsmith.org/sostac (archived at https://perma.cc/JKR3-HH9U)

Smith, PR (2019) SOSTAC® guide to your perfect digital marketing plan [online] https://prsmith.org/sostac (archived at https://perma.cc/JKR3-HH9U)

Smith, P, Berry, C and Pulford, A (1999) *Strategic Marketing Communications*, Kogan Page, London

Solis, B (2010) The myth of control in new media, *Brian Solis*, 25 January

Soumya, P (2017) The story of Amazon.com: Jeff Bezos, innovation, customer centricity, Amazon LinkedIn page, 24 July

Toner, L (2014) 6 ways social data can inform your marketing strategy, *Hubspot*

WARC (2006) Adidas to reposition Reebok from fashion to action, 26 January

Wing, R L (1989) *The Art of Strategy* (translation of Sun Tzu, *The Art of War*), Aquarian Press, Wellingborough

Zuckerberg, M (2018) Imperfect is perfect, Reid Hoffmann's *Masters of Scale* Episode 4

Further information

Euro RSCG
Havas Barcelona
Av. Diagonal, 575 – CC L'Illa
Modulo 2, Planta 11
Barcelona, Spain
(Now part of the HAVAS agency network)
https://havas.com/

HAVAS Worldwide London
HAVAS PR London
The HKX Building
3 Pancras Square
London
Tel: +44 (0)20 3793 3800
https://havas.com/

International Organization for Standardization
Chemin de Blandonnet 8
CP 401
1214 Vernier, Geneva
Switzerland
Tel: +41 22 749 01 11
www.iso.org

PAMCo Ltd,
4th Floor,
7/8 Market Place,
London,
W1W 8AG
Tel: +44 (0)20 7637 9822
www.pamco.co.uk

Target Group Index (TGI)
222 Grays Inn Road
London WC1X 8HB
Tel: +44 (0)20 7264 4700
www.kantarmedia.com

10 The changing communications environment

LEARNING OBJECTIVES

By the end of this chapter you will be able to:

- embrace the constant nature of change in markets and ergo marketing communications and recognize the integrated digital opportunity is now greater than ever before;
- be aware of the importance of checking the laws and regulations relevant to marcomms;
- consider building risk assessment into marketing plans, particularly including economic risks;
- accept the need to understand social change and integrate this change into marcomms to reflect changing social norms, values and roles;
- dispel any fears of technology and embrace technological advances including AI as aids to marketing.

Introduction

We are children of change. Right now business is going through the most radical period of change, the 4th Industrial Revolution (mentioned in Chapter 1). This chapter looks at how marketing communications are affected by the rapidly changing business environment and its many uncontrollable factors. Everything changes, including customers, competition, channels, technology, social trends, even regulations and laws. Whole markets are pulled and pushed in different directions by the PEST (political, economic, social and technological) factors, forces that are outside an organization's control. New laws, changing regulations, fluctuating economic cycles, demographic shifts, new social values, attitudes and cultural norms, fast-changing technology, and aggressive, borderless and category-less competitors are some of the key factors that constantly move markets away from the status quo. As a result, yesterday's marketing communications strategy will soon be ineffective, unless we embrace, exploit and integrate these change factors.

This means that marketers need a constant feed of information on patterns, trends, and of course, any sudden changes in any of these uncontrollable forces. The 'OT' part of a SWOT (strengths, weaknesses, opportunities and threats) analysis monitors the external opportunities and threats that emerge in the business environment. These are the PEST factors:

- Political (including legal and regulatory).
- Economic (global economic shifts and cycles of recession and boom).
- Social (new values, attitudes, lifestyles, ethics/environment and demographics).
- Technological (the internet, databases, digital TV and much more).

Competition can also be added as another uncontrollable factor in an organization's environment which could stop sales growth or even destroy a business. Any of these change factors could ultimately push a business into extinction if seemingly subtle, yet significant, changes are continually ignored. We will now consider how these PEST factors affect the organization's marketing activities, and its communications in particular. Note: Some organizations use the acronym PESTLE, which separates legal (from political) and environment (from political and social). There is an overlap between all of the factors, as you will see.

New borderless, category-less competitors changing the marketplace

Once upon a time, grocery stores sold groceries and petrol stations sold petrol. Today, grocery stores sell groceries and sell petrol while petrol stations sell petrol and groceries. Telephone companies sell broadband and TV, not just telephone services. All markets are constantly changing. Categories are blurring as competitors seek growth from share of wallet (if equipped with a strong brand and trustworthy customer relations, they can sell a wider range of products/services). Then some new players, such as network companies like Uber, are pushing markets into a new 'shared economy'. And on it goes – this is the borderless, category-less merry-go-round continually changing the structure of all markets.

The 4th Industrial Revolution

This is a new beginning. I know we have said this before. The internet came along in the 1990s and we said, 'This changes everything.' It did. Then social media came along in the 'noughties' (2000s) and 2005 it was suggested in that social media was the biggest change since the Industrial Revolution. It was. And now we have even bigger changes coming via AI, machine learning, marketing automation along with a proliferation of technology developments, triggering economic power shifts and new social structures. This is the 4th Industrial Revolution.

> 'We are witnessing the start of the 4th Industrial Revolution. With it come some wonderful opportunities and some dangerous risks.'
>
> Smith (2019)

There has never been a time of greater promise or potential peril

'The changes are so profound that, from the perspective of human history, there has never been a time of greater promise or potential peril. My concern, however, is that decision-makers are too often caught in traditional, linear (and non-disruptive) thinking or too absorbed by immediate concerns to think strategically about the forces of disruption and innovation shaping our future.'

Professor Klaus Schwab, founder and Executive Chairman of the World Economic Forum, 2018

A good or bad revolution?

The 4th Industrial Revolution can do good or bad for both economies and societies. It could share education in new ways, reduce illness and starvation and improve the quality of life across the world. In fact, it might even alert us before national disasters occur and 'potentially also undo some of the damage wrought by previous industrial revolutions' (Marr, 2018).

On the other hand, it could further polarize the rich and the poor as low skills get low pay and high skills get much higher pay. While AI creates competitive advantage between businesses, the bigger ones invest more heavily in AI to get bigger while wiping out, or buying, up the smaller businesses.

> Some jobs will become obsolete. Additionally, the changes might develop so swiftly, that even those who are ahead of the curve in terms of their knowledge and preparation, might not be able to keep up with the ripple effects of the changes... world governments need to plan carefully and regulate the emerging new AI capabilities to ensure our security.
>
> Marr (2018)

This is serious food for thought. However, let's get back to the PEST factors that marketers must also watch carefully. Let's start with politics. Consider briefly how laws and regulations can affect your business. In marketing communications in the UK laws are slow and expensive to enforce as they involve courts and procedures, while regulations are often self-regulating (as in the case of both advertising and sales promotions) and are quicker and cheaper to enforce.

Political change

Brexit

UK and EU marketers (and almost all other management) are currently preparing for major changes caused to their markets by Brexit (BRitain's EXIT from the European Union – actually it is Great Britain and Northern Ireland exiting the EU). This major UK political shift will have a significant effect on many businesses.

Over time, the EU laws roll out across Europe, in particular, laws that offer even more stringent customer protection. For example, the new EU Consumer Rights Directive, which has been implemented by The Consumer Contracts (Information, Cancellation and Additional Charges) Regulations 2013 ensures that consumers who buy online, in most circumstances, have considerably more rights than those who buy in stores. Businesses must be extra transparent and ensure consumers can easily see (a) the identity of the business and the business registration details, (b) its geographical address, (c) an accurate description of the goods, and (d) full detailed returns policy, delivery information and terms and conditions.

The GDPR (the General Data Privacy Regulations) Directive is another EU directive which increases and protects an individual's rights. GDPR has already had a major impact on all organizations in Europe and any organizations doing business with European customers. The EU's GDPR directive became law in the UK on 25 May 2018. More on GDPR later.

Laws and regulations

UK business legislation provides laws that essentially support the principles of being honest and truthful. There is also a host of self-regulatory professional codes that draw on the same set of basic business principles, ie that marketing professionals should conduct their business in a legal, decent, honest and truthful manner.

Meanwhile EU directives must be subsequently adopted into the member state's laws within two years. In the UK a statute is a law (also called an Act) that has to be voted in by Parliament. Acts are the primary legislation. Regulations are refinements of an Act, and they are brought into force by the Secretary of State (minister). Regulations form part of the law in the UK.

There are also self-regulating industry bodies who have their own codes of practice, such as the CAP (Code of Advertising Practice) – more on these later.

Some UK laws affecting marketing communications

- **The Trade Descriptions Act 1968** effectively stopped false claims and has mostly been repealed and superseded by the CPRs (Consumer Protection Regulations).
- **The Sale of Goods Act 1979** (Section 13: Sale by Description) demands that goods sold match their description.
- **The Business Protection Regulations 2008** replaces large parts of the Control of Misleading Advertisements Regulations 1988 in terms of B2B protections in respect of advertisements. These regulations provide a back-up for self-regulation. The Control of Misleading Advertisements Regulations 1988 provide legislation in respect of advertisements.
- **The Telecommunications (Data Protection and Privacy) Regulations 1999** emerged from the Data Protection Act 1998.
- **The EU Directive on Privacy and Electronic Communications Regulations (PECR) came into force in 2003.** GDPR does not replace PECR – although it has amended the definition of consent. You need to comply with both GDPR and PECR for your business-to-business marketing. The EU is in the process of replacing the current e-privacy law with a new ePrivacy Regulation (ePR) (ICO, 2019).
- **The Communications Act 2003** was driven by the Electronic Commerce Directive (ECD) Regulations 2002.
- **The Enterprise Act 2002** ensures fair competition.
- **The Consumer Contracts (Information, Cancellation and Additional Charges) Regulations 2013** supersedes The Consumer Protection (Distance Selling) Regulations 2000. Marketers must supply, in writing, full details of the goods or services offered, delivery arrangements and payment, suppliers' details and the consumers' cancellation right before they buy (known as 'prior information'), eg a cooling-off period of 14 days. These regulations apply when selling via the internet, TV, mail order, phone or fax.
- **The Consumer Protection from Unfair Trading Regulations 2008** seek to tackle unfair sales and marketing.
- **The Business Protection from Misleading Marketing Regulations 2008**, combined with CPR, also provide protection for businesses.
- **The Digital Economy Act 2010** regulates digital media and offers new protection against copyright infringement. Note: only some parts of the Act came into force in 2010; the main regime still remains unenforceable.

The overall guiding principles are the same in law as in voluntary regulations: simply be legal, decent, honest and truthful. If all else fails, the Office of Fair Trading (OFT) provides a safety net, and complaints about marketing communications (advertising, shop-window displays, etc) can be referred to the OFT for scrutiny. Some other laws affecting marketers in the UK:

- **The Bribery Act 2010** – in the UK sales promotions, incentives and gifts to distributors and staff can now be seen as bribes if deemed excessive and carry a maximum sentence of 10 years in prison. Marketers should issue guidance on corporate hospitality and have internal training, communications and procedures to back this up. Companies should keep a register of gifts and require employees to update it; review incentive schemes that may operate; consider changing supplier agreements to add or amend anti-bribery provisions; and review commercial practice to assess potential risk.
- **The Trade Marks Act 1994** adapted UK trademark law to fit with European legislation. This means that a wider range of

products and service attributes can now be registered as trademarks.

- **The DPA (Digital Protection Act) 2018** sets out the framework for data protection law in the UK. It updates and replaces the Data Protection Act 1998, and came into effect on 25 May 2018. It sits alongside the GDPR, and tailors how the GDPR applies in the UK – for example, by providing exemptions. It also sets out separate data protection rules for law enforcement authorities, extends data protection to some other areas such as national security and defence, and sets out the Information Commissioner's functions and powers.
- **EU Directive on Copyright (Article 13)** makes big platform companies (like YouTube) responsible for any copyrighted content they host. Once the EU passes this new directive, EU member states will have two years to pass their own legislation that brings article 13 into effect in their country. Firms exempt from Article 13 must fulfil all of these criteria: 1) they've been available to the public for less than three years; 2) their turnover is less than €10 million pa and 3) they have fewer than 5 million monthly visitors (Reynolds, 2019).

Can legal disclaimers on packaging stop sparkling wine shootings?

The classic case of a US consumer suing a UK paint company for alleged injurious effects of a lead-based paint strikes fear into the heart of many potential exporters. According to Pohl (1991), a growing awareness that a manufacturer carries a heavy and detailed obligation to warn potential users about any dangers that might lurk in the use of its products has prompted some sparkling wine manufacturers to print disclaimers on the packaging warning against possible risks involved in uncorking their products.

On a more serious note, let's take a closer look at GDPR since it has had a massive impact on all marketers and their marketing communications.

GDPR

GDPR essentially protects customers from their personal data being abused by criminals, or by businesses seeking to exploit their data unfairly, and also from sloppy organizations who simply do not protect their customers' data in a rigorous and professional manner. Ignoring GDPR can be expensive, with fines of €20 million or 4 per cent of global turnover for primary infringement (if it impacts a data subject/individual) or €10 million or 2 per cent set for secondary infringement (a breach of the regulations, eg not carrying out technical and organizational measures as required) – whichever is the greater. Directors can be sent to prison for both a breach (of security) and also for non-compliance with GDPR

Personal data includes: genetic data, bio data, voice data, finger prints and recognition data, CCTV, photos, recorded calls, CRM and after sales, search strings, web reports, systems log IP addresses, accounts and finance, financial records, HR records, communications tools such as emails, messenger messages, social networks, marketing databases and profiles.

Anyone handling personal data is now legally obliged to be GDPR trained. Staff must be trained so they understand and execute GDPR. Essentially anyone using data has to be educated about their responsibilities and processes required. **Fundamental to it all is 'consent'** – did the customer give their consent to their data being collected and used? Can you prove you have got consent? Have you made it clear to the customer why you are collecting it, what you will do with it, how long you will keep it? You have also got to protect the data securely. And update it where necessary. Customers have rights to access their data. They also have rights to opt out and to 'be forgotten' (all their records deleted). Was the data processed lawfully, fairly and in a transparent manner in relation to individuals? For another 10 internal actions see 'GDPR tactics: Action and control (Part 3)' at **http://prsmith.org/blog/** or visit the ICO or DPC sites for more GDPR checklists and advice.

Some banks now refuse business with non-GDPR compliant businesses. The GDPR compliance tightens its grip on business. GDPR is serious for both marketers and all management and directors of a business. You can read '7 data protection questions to answer before some banks will do business with you' at **http://prsmith.org/blog/**.

59,000 GDPR breaches since May 2018

Since the arrival of GDPR (25 May 2018) there have been over 59,000 breaches reported, with 10,000 data breaches in the UK alone. This puts the UK behind Germany (12,600 breaches) and the Netherlands (15,400 breaches). In less than a year, there have been 59,000 data breaches reported across Europe. 'Facebook, Google, Marriott International and Cathays Pacific are just a few of the big names to have faced hugely embarrassing and costly data breach investigations over the last 12 months' (Hunter, 2019). This has generated 91 fines so far (with the largest being Google's €50m GDPR fine).

GDPR fines

Google hit with €50m GDPR fine over personalized ads

> 'Google was fined 50 million euros (£44m) by the French data regulator CNIL, for a breach of the EU's data protection rules on two counts: (1) by failing to meet transparency and information requirements, and (2) failing to obtain a legal basis for processing.'
>
> Fox (2019)

Cambridge Analytica owner fined £15,000 for ignoring personal data request

> 'Cambridge Analytica's parent company, SCL Elections, has been fined £15,000 for failing to respond to an American citizen's request for copies of information it holds on him.'
>
> Pegg (2019)

Can you prove that you are compliant with GDPR?

Remember: The Burden of Proof Is On The DC (Data Controller) to verify that it received lawful consent.

ICO (Information Commissioner's Office, UK) and the DPC (Data Protection Commission, Ireland)

The ICO is the supervisory authority for data protection in the UK. It offers advice and guidance, promotes good practice, monitors breach reports, conducts audits and advisory visits, considers complaints, monitors compliance and takes enforcement action where appropriate. The DPC is the Irish supervisory authority for GDPR.

GDPR should help reduce data security disasters like these

Memory sticks, discs, laptops, and files lost or stolen from homes or cars or left behind on a train have included information about the following:

- 10,000 prolific offenders – profiles and other information;
- 84,000 prisoners – profiles and other information;
- 30,000 people with six or more convictions in the last year;
- 100,000 personal details about members of the armed forces;
- 600,000 people interested in, or who had applied to join, the Royal Navy, Royal Marines and RAF;
- 25,000,000 child benefit claimants;
- Gulf War invasion plans stored on a computer that was stolen from an RAF officer's car in 1990.

BBC News Online (2008a, 2008b)

No security policies, testing, audits or disaster recovery = negligence

Breaches of privacy and website security can end up in court. Organizations can be accused of negligence for breaches of privacy/security. In addition to damaging your customers' trust in your organization, 'security lapses can mean that company directors end up in court, if they are deemed to be negligent in their responsibilities towards good security' (Chaffey and Smith, 2017).

Good website management must build in security policies, security reviews, security testing and auditing, as well as planning for business continuity in case of 'disaster recovery' and emergencies. 'Remember, the earlier security is discussed, the cheaper it becomes to manage risks. Also integrate security into any testing programmes' (Chaffey and Smith, 2017). Regardless of the legal obligations, it makes sense to protect your organization's data carefully and rigorously, since how long could your business survive if it had its database hacked and stolen and destroyed?

The last generation to know privacy

American author, Brian Solis, suggests that we're 'still in the early stages of learning just what it (privacy) all means and doesn't mean. It is now something that will have to be taught.' He develops the 'we are what we share' angle by saying: 'And more importantly, what we share online, will now require thoughtful curation to deliberately construct a more accurate and desirable portrayal of who you are and how you wish to be perceived. Therein lies the inspiration for social networking; the understated, willful and dramatic leap between privacy and publicness' (Solis, 2012). It has also been suggested that your online profile is a window to your soul. See 'We trade privacy for convenience', p 308.

Self-regulation: Codes of practice

Various professional marketing bodies (advertising, direct mail, PR, sponsorship, etc) draw up their own codes of practice to which their professional marketing members must adhere. Failure to do so may result in expulsion and sometimes negative publicity, along with a form of blacklisting. In the case of advertising or a sales promotion, a breach of a code can also result in the withdrawal of an advertisement or sales promotion, etc. This can be expensive, as the development of any campaign costs money. The risks are arguably higher in television, where a 60-second advertisement can cost a million pounds. Most advertisers want to stand out from the crowd. To do this they sometimes have to be daring, bold and controversial, ie producing ads that are right on the edge of what is permitted by the regulations.

Although marketing communications must adhere to the laws of the land (ie one cannot misrepresent or blatantly mislead), the voluntary codes are both cheaper and quicker to apply should any complaints or claims be made. The codes also offer useful guidance to the marketer, so that most problems are ironed out before an advertisement goes out on air or is published in the press. Essentially, advertisements should:

- be legal, decent, honest and truthful;
- show responsibility to the customer and society;
- follow the basic business principles of fair competition.

Professional bodies need to be vigilant in order to maintain the credibility of their profession. This is particularly true in advertising, where the consumer's scepticism and resistance to advertising are heightened or lowered according to the credibility of the advertising industry. This credibility is founded upon the industry's reputation and determination to maintain standards of legality, decency, honesty and truthfulness.

Code of Advertising Practice

The Code of Advertising Practice (CAP) is for non-broadcast and covers ads that appear in a wide array of media including newspapers, magazines, cinema, billboards, mailings, leaflets, paid-for space online, sales promotions (wherever they appear), texts, emails and on UK-based company websites. This Code must be followed by all advertisers, agencies and media. The Code is enforced by the Advertising Standards Authority (the consumer side of CAP, which is the advertiser side), who can take steps to remove or have amended any ads that breach these rules.

The BCAP (Code of Advertising Practice – broadcast) applies to traditional 'spot' ads on TV channels and radio stations licensed by Ofcom as well as teleshopping, interactive services and text services.

Laws and regulations vary in different markets; for example, cold calling is banned in Germany and some US states. Equally, sales promotions, incentives, premiums and free gifts are generally unacceptable in Germany and can cause problems in France.

CAP principles

The main principles of the Codes that apply to all ads is that advertisements should not mislead, harm or offend. Certain products or services are subject to further specific rules. For instance, products or services that have the potential to harm or which are age-restricted, such as alcohol or gambling, are subject to additional restrictions above and beyond the general rules. The Codes also provide further clarity in some complex areas such as finance, the environment, and health and beauty.

The Codes are owned, written, revised and enforced by CAP and BCAP. They are developed in response to public policy, changes in legislation, emerging technologies and advertising trends, as well as in response to social or political concern. The Codes are regularly updated and are periodically reviewed to make sure they remain relevant.

CAP advice

Help and guidance is readily available from **www.asa.org.uk**, with free confidential and expert advice on non-broadcast ads prior to their launch. They offer a free 24-hour-turnaround service advising advertisers if their promotions are within the regulations, and there is a chargeable service if a four-hour turnaround is required. The website also contains copies of the advertising codes, help notes and other online advice.

Anyone planning a TV ad for UK licensed terrestrial and satellite channels should submit it to Clearcast for approval. Radio advertisers should submit their ads to the Radio Advertising Clearance Centre (RACC).

Marketers can keep up to date with developments in advertising regulation by registering for email news alerts from CAP and BCAP as well as the CAP Copy Advice team.

CAP funding

The system is funded by a voluntary levy on advertising spend. This is collected at arm's-length on behalf of CAP, BCAP and the ASA by two bodies: the Advertising Standards Board of Finance (Asbof) and the Broadcast Advertising Standards Board of Finance (Basbof).

The levy is set at 0.1 per cent of advertising space costs and 0.2 per cent of Mailsort contracts, and is collected at arm's-length to maintain the independence of the system. It ensures that the system is properly funded, while ensuring that CAP, BCAP and ASA regulatory decisions are not influenced by who may or may not be funding the system. See **www.asa.org.uk/advice-and-resources.html**.

ASA

The ASA (Advertising Standards Authority) is the independent watchdog responsible for administering the Codes. It responds to complaints from consumers and industry about advertisements that appear to be misleading, harmful or offensive. If a complaint is upheld, then the ad has to be withdrawn or amended. The ASA is the customer/audience-facing side of CAP, while CAP is the advertiser/marketer-facing side.

Clearcast, Ofcom and TV ads

TV advertisements must gain approval before broadcasting. Ofcom came into being in 2003, having been created by the Telecommunications Act 2003, and for the first time a single entity regulated what traditionally had been seen as disparate forms of media.

Initial scripts are approved by Clearcast, and a clearance certificate is issued. However, this does not guarantee that the finished production will also be acceptable, as the film's treatment is sometimes difficult to envisage from a script or storyboard, and so it is also screened for final approval by Clearcast before broadcasting. Even after an advertisement is cleared for broadcasting, it can still be pulled off the air if the ITC requests it. Its attention can be aroused by complaints from the public. If, after it has examined the material and considered the complaint, it feels that the complaint should be upheld, it can then pull the advertisement off the air.

Does Red Bull give you wings... or not?

Red Bull energy drink offered to refund $10 (with a maximum cap of $13 million) to anyone who consumed their product after 2002 since their 'Red Bull gives you wings' advertising campaign was sued for false advertising. There is a debate about the caffeine levels being less than a cup of coffee. So Red Bull settled out of court to avoid the distraction. Many marketers now look even more carefully at the promises they make via their advertising.

Sales promotions, PR and other regulatory bodies

In addition to advertising, other marketing services have their own regulations and codes. For example, the Code of Sales Promotion Practice is also published by the CAP and basically provides guidelines for sales promotion activities. The Institute of Practitioners in Advertising (IPA), Chartered Institute of Public Relations (CIPR), Public Relations Consultants Association (PRCA), Institute of Sales Promotion (ISP) and other professional bodies all have codes of practice to which their members must adhere. Any breach of the code can result in a member being warned or ultimately struck off the institute or association member list. This may have some short-term negative publicity, plus, in the medium to longer term, exclusion of that member from pitch lists. Some clients refer to the appropriate institution or association when choosing a new agent or consultant.

Social media corporations to be regulated and fined for child abuse, terrorism, self-harm materials published

The UK Government is considering ways to regulate social media companies, including Facebook, YouTube and Instagram, over harmful content. 'Nothing is off the table,' said Suicide Prevention Minister Jackie Doyle-Price (BBC, 2019). Triggered by the suicide of Molly Russell, who was allegedly influenced by harmful videos on Instagram (owned by Facebook), it is likely that the regulations will extend to child abuse, racism, hate and terrorism, with large fines imposed for future breaches.

Politics and trading block agreements

Moving on from national and international regulations and legislation, we now turn our attention to international political agreements that affect major trading regions and the world economy. Whether it is Trump Trade Wars, Brexit or major international trading block agreements, the larger international trading companies monitor the potential results of worldwide political agreements. These companies prepare plans to meet a range of scenarios built around possible results from, say, the current major economic disputes. *Fortune Magazine* described two scenarios used by an oil company:

- **Scenario 1:** Sustainable world and global mercantilism assumes that all the major international economic disputes are solved, there is European unity, the United States and Japan agree trading terms (and avoid a trade war), free trade prevails across the globe, and stable growth is maintained. As a consequence, environmental issues receive more attention. The implications for Shell are new emission restrictions and a reconfiguration of the energy industry in which less oil and more natural gas are used.
- **Scenario 2:** Global mercantilism, which assumes a gloomier world where regional conflicts basically destabilize the world, trade wars and recessions rage, trading blocs form, and consensus on environmental issues is never achieved. This scenario implies less regulation, a piecemeal approach to environmental issues and much more oil consumption.

Economic change

Economic changes affect markets and, in turn, a marketer's choice of marketing messages. Economies move in cycles, but few can forecast exact economic trends across different regions. Some market economies are more risky than others, particularly at certain periods or stages in their cycles. Marketers must be in tune with economic trends. Since 2005, UK company reports must, by law, include a description of the principal risks and uncertainties facing the company (as well as a description of the resources available to the company and a statement of the business's objectives and the strategies of the company). Businesses now need marketers to analyse the risks of various markets and the risks of particular strategies. In the United States, the Sarbanes–Oxley corporate governance legislation requires a risk management approach to business. Interestingly, the 2004 Enterprise Risk Management Integrated Framework mentions the word 'customer' 71 times and the word 'marketing' 11 times. Marketers must be well positioned to analyse risk and report risk to their boards.

> **Shift to the East**
>
> 'The dominance of the United States and the dominance of Europe – particularly Western Europe – is eclipsed. What we're witnessing is a sharp shift in wealth in a relatively short period of time from West to East.'
>
> Martin Sorrell, WPP, at the 2006 World Economic Forum, Davos

Economic policies affect markets

Industrial and consumer markets are directly and indirectly affected by economic changes. The global shift in economic power from West to East affects many markets. Trade wars seem to be more popular since President Trump arrived. Economic policies affect markets. Exchange rates, interest rates, unemployment, levels of disposable income, etc all affect how much money is around, how much will be spent and, in a sense, the size of many markets or industries.

Changing economic agreements for trading blocks

TTIP, ISDS and Ceta: Transfer of economic powers to corporations?

Trade bodies like the EU and NAFTA want to develop agreements that 'oil the wheels of economics', ie help to reduce barriers and regulations to allow faster, easier, 'free trade' to occur between economic blocks. However, some of these proposals appear to strengthen corporations' rather than customers' rights. Simultaneously, specific powers of nation states appear to be passing to corporations, if the following are agreed.

- The Transatlantic Trade Investment Partnership (TTIP) between the USA and the EU is criticized by some for allowing US corporations to sue EU governments for loss of profits caused by changes in a government's laws or regulations (eg there is an alleged case in Australia where American tobacco companies are suing the Australian government for loss of profits since banning persuasive cigarette packaging). TTIP has been thrown out, but is it being replaced by ISDS and Ceta?
- Investor-State Dispute Settlement (ISDS) or investment court system (ICS) allow investors (eg corporations) to sue nation states for alleged 'discriminatory practices' that affect their profits. Previous ISDS cases brought against governments include Swedish energy giant Vattenfall, who sued the German Government (BBC, 2015) for €4.3 billion plus interest because Germany decided to end the use of nuclear power in the wake of the Fukushima disaster. US pharmaceutical giant Eli Lilly is suing Canada for trying to keep medicines affordable; and French multinational Veolia is suing Egypt for increasing its national minimum wage (*Guardian*, 2019).
- The Comprehensive Economic and Trade Agreement (Ceta) is a free trade agreement (cutting tariffs) between the EU and Canada, signed in 2016. Ceta is a potential model of how future UK–EU relations could be structured, and linked by some to ISDS.

FIGURE 10.1 If corporations challenge governments for being over-protective of citizens, could this open the gate for law suits leading to the reintroduction of cigarette advertising and allowing the sale of cigarettes to be deregulated (ie allow the sale of cigarettes to children)?

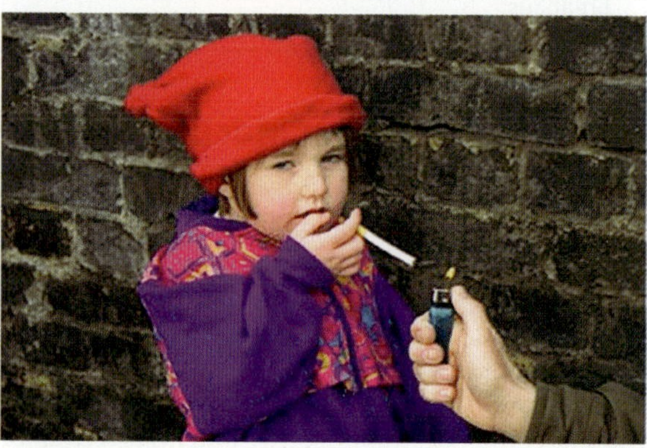

SOURCE: PR Smith

Economic cycles affect marketing

During a recession almost everyone cuts back. Consumers spend less. Companies spend less. Many organizations cut back on all types of spending, including marketing, although there are exceptions, such as Procter & Gamble, who 'automatically raise their marketing expenditure in a recession' (MacNamara, 1991). As Quelch and Jocz (2009) say, during a recession 'indiscriminate cost cutting is a mistake'. During a recession many buyers search for better deals, which include price cuts, extended terms and value-for-money sales promotions. These promotions do not necessarily increase brand loyalty; however, 'brand-building advertising' does, unsurprisingly, build brands during any economic cycle.

Recession-induced psychological change

Consumer markets have changed because of previous recession-induced psychological change, which moved people away from the self-indulgence and excess of the 'me, mine, more' mentality of the pre-millennium to the 'learning to live with limitations' of the post-millennium.

This could affect buying behaviour and the specific types of advertising messages, for example a move away from images of personal achievement to images about personal relationships, or even a move away from advertising that is built around the user imagery (from where 'the user is the hero' to where 'the product is hero'). This suggests that advertising will have to provide more hard information as consumers buy more carefully, seeking out the best deal, and display a price consciousness that rejects premium-price brands for better-value products that provide relevant benefits and excellent performance. Marketing messages change to match the mood created by the state of the economy. Equally, marketers must monitor the overall business environment for high-impact events such as a recession or banking crisis, to be ready to react and, ultimately, to reflect the changing set of needs that people acquire as their circumstances change.

Healthy economy = healthy competition

Healthy competition is deemed to be good for a healthy economy. Hence governments support start-ups and digital disruptive start-ups. Meanwhile, competition is becoming more intense as hyper-competition emerges.

Hyper-competition

Your business has moved into an environment packed with hyper-competition. You have new, indirect competitors who you need to compete with using content marketing to gain visibility in the search results and social media. You are also in a borderless market with competitors from all over the world. You are also in a category-less market with competitors from other business sectors trying to acquire your customers.

Once upon a time, supermarkets sold groceries and petrol stations sold petrol. Today supermarkets sell petrol as well as pet insurance, BBQs and clothes, while petrol stations now also sell groceries, DVDs, fresh coffee, internet connection and more.

We live in **a category-less world** determined by strength of brand and the ability to grow via share of wallet (selling a wider range to the same customer) rather than just share of market. Does the Apple Watch compete with Samsung, Swatch or Amazon? Can the big platform companies like Google, Facebook, Amazon or BAT (Baidu, Alibaba or Tencent) move into any market they choose?

Hyper competition in your pocket

Amazon and eBay mobile apps compete with all retailers. The apps invite customers, while in a competitor's retail store, to scan in a product to see how much cheaper they can get it via the app (plus they deliver it to your door). Plus, there are many other 'price comparison apps'.

So, retailers have to have even better apps (that add value rather than compete on price) to compete inside your hyper-competitive pocket. Meanwhile Amazon can target ads at customers within a radius of one mile of a competing store.

(This hyper-competition section is taken from Smith, 2019.)

> **Fashion vs pharma wars?**
>
> 'Levi's see themselves competing with the pharmaceutical companies when their "smart-clothes" start improving people's health and reducing the need for medication.'
>
> Smith (2019)

There is even more hyper-competition for your customers' attention coming from brands that appear to be way outside your category and perhaps even your country; eg Honda Cars head of marketing content

(UK) sees itself competing with Red Bull and Coca-Cola in terms of competing for attention via content marketing (see content marketing Chapter 15).

Anti-competitive laws

Free and open competition is deemed essential to a healthy economy in a capitalist world. Therefore there are regulatory bodies that protect fair competition. They also issue very large fines for any breaches of fair competition. In the UK, the Competition and Markets Authority (CMA) is responsible for strengthening business competition, and for both preventing and reducing any anti-competitive activities in the UK. You can alert the CMA about any anti-competitive practices (eg price fixing and bid rigging), or perhaps a market not working well, or any unfair terms in a contract or issues related to poor competition. The CMA took over from the Competition Commission in 2014.

European competition policy

The European Commission ensures that European competition policy is implemented. The legislation is contained in Article 101 of the Treaty on the Functioning of the European Union (1958). It is designed to prevent, or correct, anti-competitive behaviour. The main areas of legislation include rules on antitrust, mergers, cartels, and state aid.

Apple's €13b tax bill

'Apple paid tax at 1 per cent, or less, on profits attributed to its subsidiaries in Ireland, well below the 35 per cent top rate of corporate tax in the United States and Ireland's 12.5 per cent rate' (Kottasova, 2016). The European Commission, which administers EU law, has therefore ordered Ireland to recover unpaid taxes, plus interest, from Apple dating back to 2003. The European Commission said the Irish Government had granted illegal state aid to Apple (AAPL) by helping the tech giant to artificially lower its tax bill for more than 20 years.

The EU Commission demanded Apple pay back €13 billion tax to the Irish Government. The US treasury responded: 'The Commission's actions could threaten to undermine foreign investment, the business climate in Europe, and the important spirit of economic partnership between the US and the EU' (Kottasova, 2016).

Worldwide competition authorities

Worldwide competition authorities ban 'unfair methods of competition' and 'unfair or deceptive acts or practices'. The Federal Trade Commission (FTC), a bipartisan federal agency in the USA, has a unique dual mission to protect consumers and promote competition. The FTC bans 'unfair methods of competition' and 'unfair or deceptive acts or practices'. Over the years, Congress has passed additional laws giving the agency greater authority to police anti-competitive practices.

Fines for anti-competition

Google fined a total of €8.2 billion for anti-competitive restrictions

'European authorities on Wednesday fined Google 1.5 billion euros for antitrust violations in the online advertising market, continuing their efforts to rein in the world's biggest technology companies. The fine, worth about $1.7 billion, is the third against Google by the European Union since 2017, reinforcing the region's position as the world's most aggressive watchdog of an industry with an increasingly powerful role in society and the global economy. The regulators said Google had violated antitrust rules by imposing unfair terms on companies that used its search bar on their websites in Europe. The European fines against Google total roughly 8.2 billion euros, or $9.3 billion.'

Satariano (2019)

Competitive advantage: Continually changing

All products and services continually tend towards becoming commodities as competitors copy whatever succeeds. It follows, that the design of the fundamental product or service, on its own, is less likely to deliver sustainable competitive advantage. Some feel that strong brands and a data-driven culture can combine to deliver a new competitive advantage. As you monopolize your own mini market (through your own database) you create a protective wall (built on brand relationships) around your customers that stop the invasion of competitors.

Some say that content marketing can also create a new source of differentiation, in fact a new source of competitive advantage. It certainly can (particularly if you can establish authority, or expertise, on the topic). At least, that is, until competition copies it.

Going back to the brand and the customer database, this only works as long as all of the customer touchpoints deliver a single consistent customer experience that continually adds value to the CX. An integrated, added value CX is also seen as a source of competitive advantage.

For more on analysing your own competitive advantage watch the four-minute video on **http://prsmith.org/blog/**. Search for 'competitive advantage' to see Professors Urbani and Davis' unique approach to analysing competitive advantage.

Social change

Norms, values and roles change. Today, fathers change nappies, cook dinners and shop in supermarkets. Many women earn more than their male partners. Roles are becoming less clearly defined. It is no longer abnormal to have two working parents. Children are growing old younger, and many adults feel fatigue beyond their years as they suffer 'information fatigue syndrome' (too much information), which weakens the effectiveness of marketing communications, as audiences simply cannot digest all the information being thrown at them.

Young men find a lot of pressure out there and are not sure what their role is (see Chapter 4 for more). Children are growing old younger. This is substantiated by the following statement from 15 years ago: 'Corporate brands are starting to replace character brands. Kids are starting to grow up at an earlier age and so move away from characters and into brands sooner. Their pocket money is spent on items such as mobile phones and branded merchandise' (Levy, 2003). Young people also prefer to text rather than talk when using their mobiles. They also see grammatically correct sentences in ads, on television or the internet, as outdated (Lindstrom, 2003).

The changing world is no longer black or white

Who would have thought the world's favourite golfer would be a black man and the world's favourite rapper would be a white man? Tiger Woods and Eminem were once the world's best, and, who knows, may one day be number one in their respective fields once again.

Shrinking attention spans

And all the while customers' attention spans shrink, email open rates plummet and social media engagement nosedives; the information fatigued, multitasked, semi-burnt-out customer has limited time and desire to keep giving their personal data to more and more organizations that ask for it. So, 'first in' (first to get the sign-ups) wins. The 'connected customer' will expect the 'internet of everything' (everything connected) to deliver highly relevant, added-value content and personalized experiences continuously.

Increasing fear

Although we have more material goods are we more secure individually and collectively, do we feel content, comfortable and relaxed with ourselves and our surroundings? Or do we worry about work, war, family breakdown, isolation (online and offline)? Do we fear strangers and immigrants? Back in 2003 this was observed by Lindstrom, who said tweens (8- to 14-year-olds) had common fears, including terrorism and family breakdown.

FIGURE 10.2 Miracle teenager survives on his own for almost six hours with no wifi

Miracle Teenager Survives On His Own For Almost 6 Hours With No Wi-Fi

IN what has been hailed as 'a miracle', one Waterford teenager has reportedly suvived in his home with no connection to the internet for almost 6 whole hours.

WATERFORDWHISPERSNEWS.COM

SOURCE: www.waterfordwhispersnews.com

Device junkies

We are device junkies. We prefer to text rather than talk. We seem to need to be connected 24/7 to brands, people, experiences, and some of us even sleep with our phones! The wonderful satirical piece in Figure 10.2 actually reveals a lot about us, and, in particular, the new generations coming through.

Time poor

We say that we value our privacy and that we won't casually give our personal details away any more. But time may be a new currency with even greater value than privacy. Are we so time-poor that we are prepared to trade our privacy for convenience? Read on.

We trade privacy for convenience

'Adweek reported on a survey which asked US adults how they would trust 100 of the biggest brands with their personal data in exchange for "more relevant offers, goods and services". Facebook ranked last. A 2018 Honest Data poll found that **US citizens think Facebook is worse for society than McDonalds or Walmart**. The only company ranked worse than Facebook was Marlboro. A 2018 CB Insights survey asked which company will have a net negative for society 10 years from now? "The answer was pretty overwhelmingly **Facebook**." And yet... And yet... **Facebook revenue rose** to $16.9 billion in the last three months of 2018, up 30 per cent. **Monthly active users rose** to 2.32 billion, up 9 per cent. Consequently, Facebook's share price soared more than 13 per cent.'

McGovern (2019)

Is time a more valuable currency than privacy? Are we so time-poor that we just don't pay attention to our data use or abuse?

Customer rage

Alongside the customers' growing need for connectivity, we find other trends, some more surprising than others:

- customer service is falling;
- customer trust is falling;
- customer rage is rising;
- customer attention spans are shrinking;
- customers have less time;
- customer patience is falling;
- customer feedback is falling.

Customer service is falling

Seventy-five per cent of customers believe it takes too long to reach a live agent, while more than 66 per cent end up hanging up in frustration. Sixty-seven per cent of customers hung up the phone out of frustration they could not talk to a real person (Lobo, 2017).

Customer trust is falling

Two-thirds of the 28 countries surveyed in the Edelman Trust Barometer have revealed that the general population did not trust the four institutions (business, media, government and NGOs) to 'do what is right'. This means 'people's trust has declined' (Harrington, 2017).

Customer rage is rising

Consumers and advertisers are at war. Consumers surrender their personal information which is then collected and sold back to advertisers for a 'capitalist micro-assault [that] is, from all directions at all waking moments… getting much more intense, focused, targeted, unyielding and galactically more boring' – Doug Coupland's apocalyptic words (2015).

Customer attention, patience and time are falling

With attention spans shrinking (from 42 to 4 seconds) in roughly 50 years, and people having so much more 'to do' via their mobile apps (and other activities), it may follow that people's patience is shrinking.

Customer feedback is falling

Less trust in government, brands and professions, and survey fatigue – a typical Pew Research telephone survey customer response rate fell from 36 per cent to just 9 per cent over approximately 10 years to 2016. The possible causes for the general decline in feedback response rates include: 'less trust in government, brands and professions, and survey fatigue' (Bolling and Smith, 2017)

(This customer rage section is taken from Smith, 2019.)

OK, Google, sort out my life, please

'We cannot even answer the most basic questions about you because we don't know enough about you. The goal is to enable Google users to be able to ask questions like "What shall I do tomorrow?" and "What job should I take?" This is the most important aspect of Google's expansion.'

Smith (2008)

Humanity may change more in the next 20 years than in the three hundred years previous. Billions of things, devices, objects will be connected and some of these things will be inside of us (and therefore becoming a part of us). Here is futurologist, Gerd Leonhard, who borrows thoughts from Ray Kerweil, Elon Musk et al. You might find this 'peep at the future' interesting…

Rampant change: Humanity is about to change forever

'Our contact lenses will be connected to the internet. NanoBots will be inside us fixing our cholesterol… Life will be magical, abundant, full of possibilities, what could be better?

What makes us human will never change… connectivity is the new oxygen... We need it to live… even at the price of losing our privacy? Your connected car, your smart fridge, your wearables will talk to your doctor and your insurance company. Yes indeed, data is the new oil. These exponential changes are unstoppable. Man and machine will converge. We are about to transcend humanity. Is it creepy or useful? Is it heaven or is it hell? What will it mean to be human in a world where everyone will need to be amplified or augmented by algorithms?

By 2027 computers are likely to match the capacity of the human brain, perhaps even reach some kind of awareness or emotional intelligence. Yes AI and cognitive computing are incredibly powerful. But if we fail to consider the unintended consequences such as, for instance, an intelligence explosion, these advantages could be more dangerous than nuclear weapons. Why would we expect robots or AI to share, or even understand, human values, ethics and emotions? Technology doesn't have ethics, but the future of humanity depends on it.

We need to spend just as much time on the norms, and the value and the context than we spend on technology itself. After all, the future is not just something that happens to us, the future is something that we create. Are you ready for your futureshock? See where the story takes us next: data wars and privacy; exponentiality; transhumanism; singularity: heaven or hell; IoT; AI; towards abundance; digital ethics; ego to eco; algorithms to humarithms; digital obesity; sustainable capitalism; networked society; robot love.'

Leonhard (2019)

Attitudes towards issues change. Once, environmentalists and ethicists were considered to be hippies, communists, anarchists or outcasts because of their lack of conformity with other people's beliefs, values and attitudes. Today, most political parties and major corporations recognize the importance of environmental groups. Ethics is creeping back up the charts of consciousness as 'business purpose' becomes popular again, and more so, ethics is now deemed critical in AI. Let's explore some ethics.

Ethics

Social consciousness among buyers is important. However, the degree of importance can change over time. Perhaps it is linked to economic cycles; for example, during economic downturns does ethics fall down the ladder of importance? However, many customers want to know more about products and their producers. Do the products or producers damage the environment? What do the producers do in the community? Do they donate political funds? Do the organizations disclose information, and so on?

Blockchain tracks chocolate to stop slavery

'An inspiring experiment to track down sources of chocolate beans and to ensure local farmers get paid a decent price by the major brands. Allows consumers to make more informed purchasing decisions about the ethics behind major brands.'

Davis (2019)

Many buyers know that shopping is the economic ballot box of the future. And investors also are becoming increasingly interested in the corporate citizenship of organizations that they might consider funding.

Banks are becoming weary of lending funds to higher-risk, environmentally poor companies. Insurance premiums will also reflect the higher risk of non-green companies. The corporate responsibility record is now a criterion in joint ventures. For example, who wants to invest time and money in an organization that has a poor environmental record? To put it another way, who wants to inherit a green time bomb? (Note that banks will also not do business with clients who ignore GDPR regulations.)

Some estimates suggest that a 'green screen', or false green claims by corporations, will last only a short period, since probing pressure groups, investigative journalists, scrutinizing financial analysts and information-hungry customers will eventually reveal a much bigger problem than that which was originally hidden. This implies that the marketing people have a vested interest in ensuring that an organization operates in a socially responsible manner. Corporate attitudes towards altruism and ethics are changing, as are personal religious beliefs.

Finally, one extraneous factor that affects the business environment is the environment itself. If the world continues to heat up, northern European attitudes, emotions and feelings about different stimuli (particularly colour) may change. This would affect almost all forms of marketing communications.

Demographics

Demographic shifts move markets away from products. Populations are ageing across the world, ie populations are getting older. What are the implications of an ageing population? Bigger typefaces and print to help older eyes read commercial messages? Many products and services repositioned as the more mature person's choice? There will still be youth markets, but they may not be as attractive, since they will shrink in size and competition may become quite ferocious.

The falling marriage rate, the increasing divorce rate and the increasing number of births outside marriage contribute towards the sad term 'disintegrating family'. In addition, the number of single-person households is expected to increase.

Decision-making units (DMUs) are changing (see p 265, 'Segmentation and target marketing'). Over 60 per cent of mothers in the UK work either part time or full time, compared with 10 per cent in the 1930s and 20 per cent in the 1950s. Incidentally, it has been suggested that guilt-ridden working mothers may ease their discomfort by buying the 'best' brands for their families instead of buying the store's less expensive own brand. A Gallup poll suggested that 90 per cent of working mothers suffer some psychological discomfort in combining the roles of mother and worker.

Hanging out at the oxygen bar

Here is an IBM future vision from many years ago: oxygen bars offering 'nutraceuticals' (staple foods packed with vitamins and minerals) and gas for the jet-set hyperactive executives and fun lovers. Memory drugs, male birth control pills and remote-control surgery might all affect markets, their structure, the communications channels and communications tools.

Technology

This is such a fast-changing variable. We are seeing major changes occurring in the use of Big Data, AI, MA AR, VR (mirror worlds), IoT, blockchain and much more. Also see the 4th Industrial Revolution in Chapter 1.

Big Data

Customer data is everywhere. We leave digital trails everywhere when we browse, click, scan or fill in a form. And many organizations can gather a lot of it and cross-reference with social media platforms (and third-party sources) to gather extra data. Big Data refers to relatively large amounts of both structured and unstructured data that require machine-based systems and technologies in order to be fully analysed and used. Those that collect the data carefully and analyse it can create competitive advantage. They can also extract more value from data (look at Uber and Amazon), and in turn this data adds value to the CX. Data is the lifeblood of any business.

AI

Artificial intelligence is not just about businesses' processes operating more efficiently, AI combined with 'real' bots can also tackle other challenges like responding to customer requests – taking orders and payment and delivering meals in restaurants (Pizza Hut in Japan), answering hotel guest concierge queries (Hilton McLean, Canada), helping elderly folks in old folks homes (Japanese baby seals), influencing followers (artificial influencers – p 160), answering website visitor questions (intelligent chatbots) and helping marketers creatively by writing higher-impact email subject lines. See the word of caution regarding the law of unintended consequences and AI in Chapter 1, p 18.

Chatbots

Chatbots can be just text messages responding to questions from customers (say on a website or an app or social media platforms) or soon, courtesy of IoT, packaging, point of sale or anywhere really! Other chatbots can manifest themselves in human-looking robots. What's most important is the relevance/quality of their answers in the discussion/

dialogues they have with customers. AI driven bots will continually learn and improve their responses. See Chapter 1 to see the growing variety of types of bots (from research bots to ad bots). Also see 'Here come the really clever bots: Where AI meets customer needs', **http://prsmith.org/blog/**.

> **Your animal life is over. Machine life has begun.**
>
> This shocking article by Mark O'Connell in the *Guardian* in 2017 was shared over 32,000 times. He believes that we are close to having a machine that replicates the human brain and keeps a version of us alive forever. See p 19 for more.

MA

Marketing automation reduces a marketer's workload and delivers highly relevant reactions to a prospect's behaviour – automatically – once it has all been worked out in advance. A prospect's click behaviour, or digital body language, triggers automatic marketing responses like sending a particular type of email, or connecting to a salesperson or showing some dynamic content on a website. See p 329 for more.

IoT

The Internet of Things connects everything via three things: chips, sensors and wifi. My smart golf club can record the speed and angle of my swing, send that information to my mobile and show me how to improve my game. An IoT fridge could send alarms throughout the house when it recognizes that the can of 'draught' Guinness that I am taking out of my fridge is the last can, so it sends an alert to me with three optional solutions offering different speeds of delivery and prices. New IoT partnerships can add huge value to the CX and can also allow marketers to get their marketing content into the hands of new ideal customers too.

AR

Augmented reality adds digital elements to a real live view, often by using the camera on a smart phone – for example, showing a digital image of a cup on a real table (while the smart phone/camera points at the table). Virtual reality (VR), on the other hand, is a complete immersion experience via headsets that shut out the physical world. Headsets include Facebook's Oculus Rift or Google's Cardboard, and users can be transported into a number of real-world and imagined environments such as Greenpeace's Amazon Jungle experience.

And coming soon, courtesy of AR, is mirror world (also known as spatial computing) where everything (and every person will have a digital duplicate). See ex-editor of *Wired* Kevin Kelly's stunning 2019 article entitled 'AR will spark the next big tech platform – call it mirror world'.

Blockchain

A blockchain is a decentralized list of records, called blocks, which are linked (using cryptography). It is like a public ledger (or record) that records transactions across all computers in a particular network. This means it is secure since any changes made have to be recorded by all subsequent blocks.

Ray Kurzweil's Law of Accelerating Returns (Kurzweil, 1999) proposed that the rate of change in a wide variety of evolutionary systems (including but not limited to the growth of technologies) tends to increase exponentially.

> **The 21st century will achieve 20,000 times the progress of the 20th century.**
>
> American futurist, Ray Kurzweil suggests that the progress of the entire 20th century would have been achieved in only 20 years at the rate of advancement in the year 2000 – in other words, by 2000, the rate of progress was five times faster than the average rate of progress during the 20th century.
>
> Kurzweil believes that another 20th century's worth of progress happened between 2000 and 2014 and that another 20th century's worth of progress will happen by 2021, in only seven years.
>
> A couple of decades later, he believes a 20th century's worth of progress will happen multiple times in the same year, and even later, in less than one month. This is the **Law of Accelerating Returns**. Kurzweil believes that the 21st century will

achieve 20,000 times the progress of the 20th century! So, embrace technology developments.

We will see all sorts of AI developments – the most immediate might be better chatbots! Better bots simply help customers, in a conversational way, to find answers more quickly and therefore boost conversions. They help customers to 'get the job done'.

With 2.5 billion customers using instant messaging (*The Economist*, 2016) on Facebook, Whatsapp and China's WeChat an opportunity opens. Within a couple of years IM will reach about half of humanity, ie 3.6 billion (*The Economist*, 2016). Chatbots can be integrated into many social media channels.

Moore's law: Every 18 months, processing power doubles, while costs hold constant

'Gordon Moore, founder of Intel, observed that each new generation of computer chips (semiconductors) doubled in power every 18 months. This has been valid for 30 years and is predicted to continue for the next 30 years... it has held since the 1960s, and recent developments in so called 'molecular electronics' – arranging molecules in electronic circuits – suggest improvements are likely to continue for another 30 years.'

Krugman (2000)

This means that in just over 30 years computer chips will be 1 million times more powerful than today. Note that today's modern luxury car has more computer power than the first human spaceflight craft that landed on the moon.

The internet also provides virtual meeting places, virtual discussion groups, virtual greetings cards, virtual gifts and virtual exhibitions. Invisible computers will be in everything that uses electricity, and 3D environments and avatars will increase – both in virtual worlds (see Figure 10.4) and in traditional web environments. Virtual reality and augmented reality draw from a mash-up of data, allowing even richer and more relevant customer experiences.

So change appears to be accelerating – whether shrinking attention spans (social changes), quantum data shifts (technology), new regulations and laws (political) or fundamental economic cycles (economics) that grow or shrink your market, the PEST factors need constant monitoring.

Behind technology's physical manifestations, more subtle advances are occurring. Witness marriages between technologies such as geographic information systems, analytical modelling market analysis and data mining. See the 'semantic web' as well as digital body language on p 329 and location-based ad campaigns on p 377. Google Alert and Google News can even do a lot of a manager's reading by scanning journals, newspapers and trade magazines for relevant material and printing out headlines, summary abstracts or complete articles. Robots make our lives easier.

Fast-forward to the semantic web

Although this was written a decade ago, it is still accurate.

'Now, fast forward a few years. You're still happily employed as a software consultant, and today you're taking a working lunch with one of your biggest clients. Her company has an emergency project at its San Francisco branch for which they need you to consult for two weeks, and she asks you to get to San Francisco as soon as possible to begin work. You take out your hand-held computer, activate its Semantic Web agent, and instruct it to book a non-stop flight to San Francisco that leaves before 10 am the next day. You want an aisle seat if it's available. Once your agent finds an acceptable flight with an available aisle seat, it books it using your American Express card and assigns the charges to your client's account in your accounting application. It also warns you that you'll be missing a dentist appointment back home during your trip and adds a note to your calendar reminding you to reschedule. Next, you specify that you want a car service to the client's site, so your agent scans the availability of limos with "very good" or higher service ratings and books an appointment to have you picked up 30 minutes after your flight lands. Your agent also books you at your favourite hotel in San Francisco, automatically securing the lowest rate using your rewards card number. Finally, the agent updates your calendar and your manager's calendar with your trip information and prints out your confirmation documents back at your office.

With just a few clicks your Semantic Web agent found and booked your flight, hotel, and car service, then updated your accounting system and calendars automatically. It even compared your itinerary to your calendar and detected the scheduling conflict with your dentist appointment. To do all this, the agent had to find, interpret, combine, and act on information from multiple sources. This example, of course, is a long-term vision for applying the Semantic Web. It's one that may or may not come to fruition, and only the future will tell. However, the vision itself is important for understanding the potential of Semantic Web technologies.'

Altova (2010)

The Semantic Web will make life even easier. Software will talk to software, documents and a lot more. Tim Berners-Lee, the British inventor of the World Wide Web, defines the Semantic Web as 'a web of data that can be processed directly and indirectly by machines'. Data can be processed independently of application, platform or domain; in fact, data can become part of the web.

The increasing pace of change

There is no doubt that change will continue to affect organizations. Those who ignore significant trends do so at their peril. However, marketers must develop their ability to recognize and separate significant trends from insignificant fads.

FIGURE 10.3 Years taken to achieve 25 per cent market penetration, showing the ever-accelerating speed with which new ideas, products and services penetrate markets

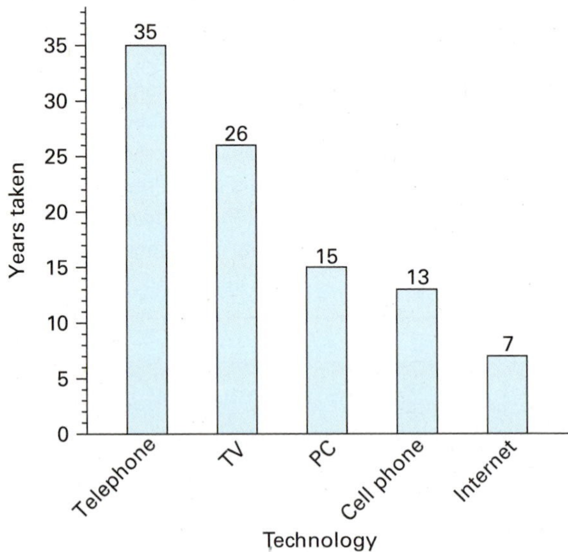

Summary

An open mind helps in exploiting trends and emerging opportunities more quickly than a closed mind. Change is constant. It churns up new opportunities

FIGURE 10.4 Virtual worlds can, and do, co-exist alongside the real world

FIGURE 10.5 A manifesto for human-centred marketing

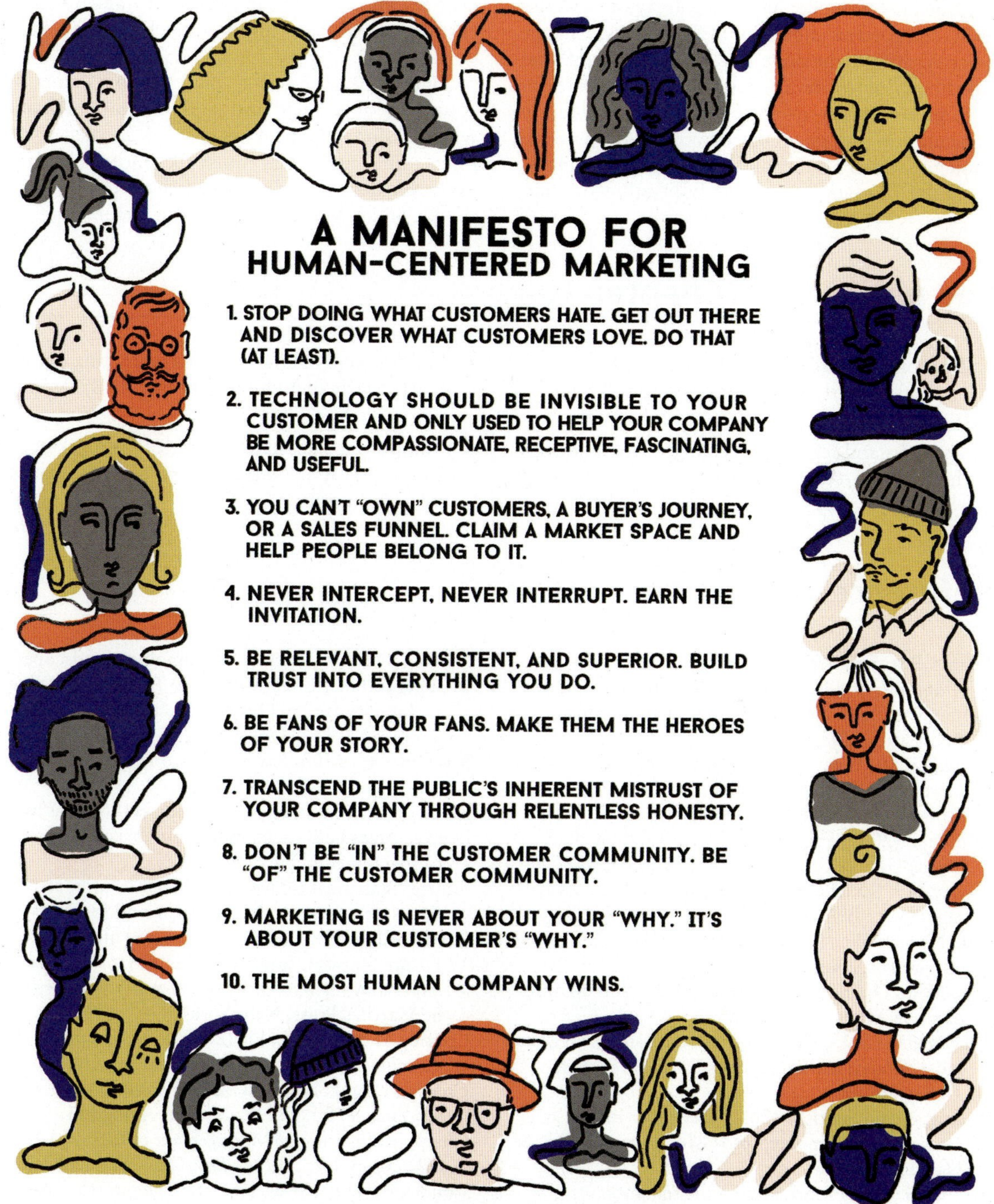

SOURCE: Reproduced with kind permission of Mark Schaefer, author, *Marketing Rebellion*

and threats in all markets. The only certainty is that all markets constantly pull away from the status quo, fuelled by an ever-increasing array of variables easily categorized under the PEST factors. Change is accelerating right now. It is every marketer's responsibility to observe, analyse and anticipate future developments in their marketplace and, in particular, in the changing communications environment. Watch all technical developments, and in particular the one that affects political, economic, social trends – AI. Marketers must lead the field with its understanding of AI, its unintended consequences and how it can be used to add value for customers and, most importantly, to create a better world for all.

Figure 10.5 shows a nice graphic from top American columnist and author Mark Schaefer, who passionately believes that to succeed in the long term, marketers must be more humanist. However, not everyone agrees (see the discussion on the PR Smith Marketing LinkedIn page).

Key points from Chapter 10

- The constant nature of change in markets presents a constant flow of opportunities and threats.
- The laws and regulations change also. Ignoring them can be a costly affair.
- Building risk assessment into marketing plans (particularly including economic risks) makes sense.
- Mapping social change is critical as marketers aim to reflect customers' social feelings, values, roles and norms.

References and further reading

Adams, R, Carruthers, J and Hamil, S (1992) *Shopping for a Better World*, Kogan Page, London

Akhtar, O (2014) Who is winning the marketing cloud wars? *The Hub*

Altova (2010) What is the Semantic Web? *Altova Library* [online] www.altova.com (archived at https://perma.cc/7K4B-D5XV)

Anning, P (2007) FSA helps ICO with £980K data fine as Halifax could be next, *Osborne Clarke*

BBC (2019) Social media: How can governments regulate it? BBC News, 7 February

BBC News Online (2008a) Company loses data on criminals, 21 August

BBC News Online (2008b) Previous cases of missing data, 25 May

Belicove, M (2013) Content marketing study suggests most content marketing doesn't work, *Forbes*, 10 September

Bolling, K and Smith, P (2017) Declining response rates and their impact, Ipsos Mori, Kantar, GFK & NatCen, 29 June

Brinker, S (2008) Marketing in the semantic web, *Chief Marketing Technologist*, 2 March [online] https://chiefmartec.com/ (archived at https://perma.cc/K3XT-YJ2W)

Brinker, S (2015) Marketing technology landscape supergraphic, *Chief Marketing Technologist* Blog, 12 January [online] https://chiefmartec.com/ (archived at https://perma.cc/K3XT-YJ2W)

Brøndmo, H (2003) Save the customer attention ecosystem, *ClickZ*, 14 July

Byron, D, Kievman, N and Schrum, R (2010) Why executives hate social media: An executive's guide to social media, *Deming Hill*

Central Statistical Office, *Social Trends* (annual) (gives demographic breakdowns and forecasts)

Cetron, M and Davies, O (1992) The Futurist (World Future Society), summarized in *Crystal Globe: The haves and the have-nots of the new world order*, St Martin's Press, New York

Chaffey, D and Smith, PR (2013) *Emarketing Excellence*, 4th edn, Routledge, Abingdon

Chaffey, D and Smith, PR (2017) *Digital Marketing Excellence*, 5th edn, Routledge, Abingdon

Chartered Institute of Management (CIM) (2010) *Fact File: Marketing and the law*, CIM, Maidenhead

Coupland, D (2015) We are data: The future of machine intellingence, *FT* [online] https://www.ft.com/content/475789b8-2b2b-11e5-acfb-cbd2e1c81cca (archived at https://perma.cc/VPC9-KKL9)

Davis, C (2019) This company is using blockchain technology to eradicate slavery in the chocolate industry, *Forbes*, 31 March

Doyle, P (1992) What are excellent companies? *Journal of Marketing Management*, 8, pp 101–16

Dwight, M (2007) Lifestyle stories, *Services,* March [online] https://www.pe.com/ (archived at https://perma.cc/G6YS-VCT8)

eConsultancy (2015) Quarterly digital intelligence briefing: digital trends

Enterprise Risk Management Integrated Framework (2004) COSO (Committee of Sponsoring Organisations of the Treadway Commission)

European Commission, Consumer Rights (2015) Your rights in consumer contracts, 23 March

Farrell, D, Ghai, S and Shavers, T (2005) The demographic deficit: How aging will reduce global wealth, *McKinsey Quarterly*, March

Fox, C (2019) Google hit with £44m GDPR fine over ads, BBC News, 21 January https://www.bbc.co.uk/news/technology-46944696 (archived at https://perma.cc/ZY4Z-BVYT)

Grey International Advertising (1992) *The Post-Recession Marketplace: Life in the slow lane*, Grey International Advertising, New York

Griffin, A (2015) Facebook users sue site over data collection, demand compensation for privacy breaches, *Independent*, 9 April

Guardian (2019) Much to fear from post-Brexit trade deals with ISDS mechanisms, *Guardian*, 20 February

Gwyer, M (1992) Britain bracing for the age bomb, *Independent on Sunday*, 29 March

Harrington, M (2017) Survey: People's trust has declined in business, media, government and NGOs, *HBR*, 16 January

Hope, M (2014) 5 things businesses need to know: The new EU Directive on consumer rights, *Digital Doughnut*, 20 February

Howarth, A (2015) Google in dock over Safari privacy breach cases, *The Scotsman*, 27 March

Hubspot (2011) The Facebook marketing update, Spring 2011: Who's blogging what?

Hunter, D (2019) British firms suffer 10,000 data breaches in GDPR era, *GDPR Report*, 11 February

ICO (Information Commissioner's Office) (2019) Guide to the General Data Protection Regulations [online] https://ico.org.uk/for-organisations/guide-to-data-protection/guide-to-the-general-data-protection-regulation-gdpr/ (archived at https://perma.cc/LF9P-PZVU)

Jankowski, S (2014) The sectors where the internet of things really matters, *Harvard Business Review Global Editions*, 22 October

Keegan, V (2002) The web needs its own police, *Guardian*, 19 December

Kelly, K (2019) AR will spark the next big tech platform – call it mirror world, *Wired*, 2 December

Kirkpatrick, M (2010) Google CEO Eric Schmidt: 'People aren't ready for the technology revolution', *readwrite*, 4 August

Knowlton, C (1991) Shell gets rich by beating risk, *Fortune*, 26 August, pp 51–53

Kottasova, I (2016) EU hits Apple with $14.6 billion tax bill, CNN Business, 30 August

Krugman, P (2000) Unleash after 100 years of trial and error, *Fortune*, 6 March

Kurzweil, R (1999) *The Age of Spiritual Machines*, Penguin

Leonhard, G (2019) Are we living in a Mirrorworld? (asks Kevin Kelly, with reference to Magic Leap), 19 February [online] www.futuristgerd.com/ (archived at https://perma.cc/M3B6-LLQM)

Levy, A (2003) Unlock the equity in your brand, *Marketing*, 24 April

Lindstrom, M (2003) *Brandchild*, Kogan Page, London

Lobo, J (2017) 3 options for using chatbots for ecommerce, *Smart Insights*, 11 December

Long, W (2013) EU Data Protection Regulation: fines up to €100m proposed, *Computer Weekly*, November

MacNamara, W (1991) A new discipline, *Marketing Week*, 6 December, pp 34–37

Marr, B (2018) The 4th Industrial Revolution is here: Are you ready? *Forbes*, 13 August

McGovern, G (2019) Use and convenience replace trust and security, 3 February [online] http://gerrymcgovern.com/ (archived at https://perma.cc/GF3D-CV9F)

McLellan, L (2012) By 2017 the CMO will spend more on IT than the CIO, webinar, *Gartner*

Murphy, D (2003) Stopping careless texting to children, *Marketing*, 3 April

Ohmae, K (1983) *The Mind of the Strategist*, Penguin Business Library, London

Ohmae, K (1999) *The Borderless World*, revised edn, Collins, London

Ohmae, K (2002) *Triad Power: The coming shape of global competition*, 2nd edn, Free Press, New York

Oliver, M (2012) Quarantining Facebook to control tracking, *ZD Net*, 3 July

Pegg, D (2019) Cambridge Analytica owner fined £15,000 for ignoring data request, *Guardian*, 9 January

Pohl, M (1991) UK unaware of legal pitfalls in US, *Marketing Week*, 13 September

Precision Marketing (2006) Privacy: Do Not Call means business, 6 January

Press Association (2015) Google loses appeal bid over suing, 27 March

Quelch, J and Jocz, K (2009) How to market in a downturn, *HBR*, April

Reynolds, J (2012) Nike ticked off for Rooney and Wilshere tweets, *PR Week*, 20 June [online] www.campaignlive.co.uk (archived at https://perma.cc/7287-8SYD)

Reynolds, M (2019) What is Article 13? The EU's divisive new copyright plan explained, *Wired*, 24 May

Rijkens, R (1992) *European Advertising Strategies*, Cassell, London

Robinson, M (2015) Is democracy threatened if companies can sue countries? BBC News, 31 March

Satariano, A (2019) Google fined $1.7 billion by EU for unfair advertising rules, *New York Times*, 20 March

Schaefer, M (2019) Marketing rebellion [online] www.businessesgrow.com (archived at https://perma.cc/56WZ-WZNH)

Smith, D (2008) Google, 10 years in: Big, friendly giant or a greedy Goliath? *Observer*, 17 August

Smith, PR (2019) SOSTAC® guide to your perfect digital marketing plan [online] www.sostac.org (archived at https://perma.cc/EMA5-H2DD)

Solis, B (2012) The erosion of privacy and the rise of publicness... and why it's a good thing, 23 October [online] www.briansolis.com (archived at https://perma.cc/5VSL-G6WR)

Taleb, N, Goldstein, D and Spitznagel, M (2009) The six mistakes executives make in risk management, *Harvard Business Review*, guest edn, *The Magazine*, October

The Economist (2003) Real men get waxed, 3 July

The Economist (2016) Bots, the next frontier, 9 April

Toffler, A (1990) *The Third Wave*, Bantam Books, New York

Williams, A (2010) Virals aren't immune to the law, *The Marketer*, 18 August

Woods, S (2009) *Digital Body Language*, New Year Publishing, Danville, CA

Further information

Advertising Standards Authority
Castle House
37–45 Paul Street
London, EC2A 4LS
Tel: +44 (0)20 7492 2222
www.asa.org.uk

Chartered Institute of Public Relations (CIPR)
4th Floor
85 Tottenham Court Road
London W1T 4TQ
Tel: +44 (0)20 7631 6900
www.cipr.co.uk

Department for Business, Energy and Industrial Strategy
1 Victoria Street
London SW1H 0ET
Tel: +44 (0)20 7215 5000
https://www.gov.uk/government/organisations/department-for-business-energy-and-industrial-strategy

European Association of Communication Agencies (EACA)
EACA Secretariat
152 Boulevard Brand Whitlock
B-1200 Brussels
Belgium
Tel: +32 2 740 07 14
https://eaca.eu/

The European Marketing Confederation (EMC)
Square du Meeûs 35
1000 Brussels
Belgium
Tel. +32 2 7421 780
https://emc.be

Fax Preference Service (FPS)
DMA House
70 Margaret Street
London W1W 8SS
Tel: +44 (0)20 7291 3300
Fax: +44 (0)20 7291 3301
https://dma.org.uk/

Institute of Practitioners in Advertising (IPA)
44 Belgrave Square
London SW1X 8QS
Tel: +44 (0)20 7235 7020
www.ipa.co.uk

The Institute of Promotional Marketing Ltd
Holborn Town Hall
193–197 High Holborn
London WC1V 7BD
www.theipm.org.uk

ITV Consumer Limited
2 Waterhouse Square
Holborn
London EC1N 2AE
www.itv.com

Ofcom
Riverside House
2a Southwark Bridge Road
London SE1 9HA
Tel: +44 (0)300 123 3000
www.ofcom.org.uk

Public Relations Consultants Association (PRCA)
82 Great Suffolk Street
London SE1 0BE
Tel: +44 (0)20 7233 6026
www.prca.org.uk

There are many other fascinating organizations whose goals are to help people embrace some of these changes for the better including: the Open Data Institute, Alan Turing Institute, Blockchain Research Institute and Customer Data Platform Institute.

Alan Turing Institute
British Library
96 Euston Road
London NW1 2DB
www.turing.ac.uk/

The Alan Turing Institute is the national institute for data science and artificial intelligence. Alan Turing is often called the father of modern computing. He developed the idea of the modern computer and artificial intelligence. During the Second World War he worked for the government breaking the enemies' codes and Churchill said he shortened the war by two years. In 1950, he published a philosophical paper including the idea of an 'imitation game' for comparing human and machine outputs, now called the Turing Test. He was later convicted of 'indecency', as being gay was a crime in the UK at that time. He died from eating an apple laced with cyanide. He was only 41 years old.

Today, their website includes posts such as: 'Alexa, Siri, Eno, Kai: Can we trust you?' and 'Questions we should be asking about AI in the financial industry'.

Open Data Institute
3rd Floor
65 Clifton Street
London EC2A 4JE
Tel: +44 (0)20 3598 9395
https://theodi.org/

The Open Data Institute works with companies and governments to build an open, trustworthy data ecosystem, where people can make better decisions using data and manage any harmful impacts. The ODI was co-founded in 2012 by the inventor of the Web Sir Tim Berners-Lee and artificial intelligence expert Sir Nigel Shadbolt to show the value of open data, and to advocate for the innovative use of open data to affect positive change across the globe.

Blockchain Research Institute
111 Peter Street, Unit 503
Toronto
ON Canada
M5V 2H1
Tel: +1 416 863 8800
www.blockchainresearchinstitute.org/

The Blockchain Research Institute was founded by Don Tapscott (an American author) based on the belief that blockchain offers an opportunity to realize the original promise of the digital era. Its manifesto, A Declaration of Independence, lists the following chapters: the Fourth Industrial Revolution; globalization; climate change; structural unemployment; growing inequality; asymmetrical power; crisis of democracy; ineffective government; failing institutions; fragmentation of public discourse; civil society and more....

Customer Data Platform Institute
www.cdpinstitute.org

The Customer Data Platform Institute is a vendor-neutral organization dedicated to helping marketers manage customers. It educates marketers and marketing technologists about how customer data platforms can solve critical marketing data needs.

PART TWO
Communications tools

11
Selling, social selling, marketing automation and martech

LEARNING OBJECTIVES

By the end of this chapter you will be able to:

- understand the purposes of different types of sales teams;
- map out the key stages and skills required of key account management and account-based marketing;
- understand how marketing automation and martech can help sales teams sell more;
- begin to manage the sales force;
- identify different ways of extending your sales force.

Introduction

The word 'sales' is conspicuous by its absence in job titles on business cards. 'New business development', 'account manager', 'key account manager', 'relationship manager' and 'marketing executive' are often preferred, yet selling's impact on the bottom line at some stage is usually vital. The 'selling' stigma is surprising, given the size and importance of selling. The sales force budget allocation varies according to industry type, but often, in B2B markets, more budget is spent on sales teams than on advertising or PR.

B2B markets depend on personal selling more than B2C marketing. Winning an order for, say, a heavy industrial machine cannot be done by advertising, direct mail or telesales (telephone selling). This kind of selling requires top-level expert sales professionals. Consumer goods, on the other hand, rarely use personal selling to the end user or consumer because of the high cost per sales visit. Nevertheless, consumer products do need salespeople to sell or 'push' the product into the retail chains (and the wholesale chains).

There was an era when selling was all about short-term tactics, quick sales, in–out and on to the next unsuspecting prospect. This is short-term transactional marketing, which in the long run reduces sales and profits. This approach to selling gave salespeople a bad reputation – probably best summarized by the well-known Heaven and Hell story.

Heaven or Hell – where do salesmen go?

A man dies and arrives at the Pearly Gates, where St Peter tells him he cannot enter until Hell has been given an equal opportunity. Although the man knows he wants to go to Heaven, St Peter insists that he checks out Hell first. To his amazement, the man discovers that Hell is a party town, with free-flowing drink, good music, lots of friendly supermodel lookalikes everywhere, perfect weather, immaculate golf courses, football pitches, super-fast broadband and white sandy beaches. Best of all, everyone is friendly and concerned that the man feels comfortable in his new surroundings. St Peter appears and asks the man for a decision, upon which the man says, 'Hell's for me!' When he returns the next day, all he sees is bodies, all scorched, burning and screaming. 'But this isn't the same place,' he shouts at St Peter in the distance. 'Oh yes, it is,' St Peter replies. 'Yesterday you were a prospect. Today you are a customer!!'

Today, selling has moved away from the short-term, quick-sale scenario of offering prospects the most fantastic products and services and then not following through with the promise. Selling has also moved away from recruiting and training combative salespeople. Instead they are being transformed into 'customer servants'. Selling today is more about 'partnering' and relationship building: 'You don't sell to people; you partner with them.' This is particularly true with key account management (KAM), which requires a more strategic approach to selling. Today selling is about building durable relationships that are dependent on satisfying the customer constantly. IBM today is following a growing trend towards paying the sales force salaries partly on customer satisfaction. Many companies are now measuring success not just by units sold but also by the far more rigorous yardstick of customer satisfaction.

The changing salesperson

'I sold systems that people didn't want, didn't need and couldn't afford.'

Bill Gardner, IBM veteran with 23 years' service, now retired

'Forty-five per cent of the variable component of my pay cheque depends on how Jon Gorney at National City Corporation rates me.'

Don Parker, IBM salesperson

How can digital help sales teams?

Today, due to hyper-competition and other change factors, delivering sales growth is difficult enough for a single-product company; imagine what it is like for a large, decentralized sales team with channel partners all over the world. Although everyone knows this, many senior sales people simply 'do not put sufficient energy into driving that change, eg advances in digital and analytics' (Chappuis *et al*,

2018). We will see later how marketing automation, Big Data and sales tools like reverse forensics and LinkedIn Navigator can help sales teams.

Functions of selling

The purpose of selling is not just to sell. Master salespeople gather intelligence and build relationships (which can, in turn, create competitive advantage). Research suggests that as little as 10 per cent of a salesperson's time is spent actually face-to-face 'selling'. In addition to prospecting, appointment setting, letter writing, travelling, training and administration, many salespeople are also responsible for some customer care, post-sales service, entertaining, intelligence gathering, forecasting, understanding customers, developing customized solutions, team selling, etc. Some managers say that 'Customers seek longer-term relationships with fewer suppliers than formerly, and in return for security of business ask their suppliers to do more for them.' Forecasts suggest that there will be a concentration of key accounts (large customers) and they will need suppliers who work with them as strategic partners instead of adversaries (see the sections 'Consultative selling', 'Key account management' and 'Account-based marketing' in this chapter) .

The best salespeople are expert listeners. They ask intelligent questions and listen carefully. The best salespeople are masters at capturing data. Since the sales force is in the front line of the market, it provides a fast and accurate feedback mechanism. Competitor activity, customer needs, and new opportunities and threats can and should be picked up by the sales force and fed back, without delay, to the sales manager or marketing manager. Reasons why an old customer is lost or a new customer is won should also be fed back immediately.

Responsive vs prescriptive selling

Many sales people incorrectly think that a responsive sales technique is best, ie responding to customers' questions by giving them more and more information, to help buyers make better decisions. Toman *et al* (2017) discovered that responding and supplying a lot of information can be counter-productive. Sales people trying to be more responsive can actually give buyers too much support and too much information, such as when the salesperson gives the buyers:

- all the data;
- case studies;
- testimonials;
- a suite of options.

But Toman *et al*'s (2017) research, reported in the *Harvard Business Review*, suggested otherwise because the responsive sales technique actually *decreases* purchase ease by 18 per cent (according to their survey of more than 600 B2B buyers). They discovered that piling on more information and options just makes it more difficult for buyers.

Prescriptive sales technique increases purchase ease

Toman *et al* discovered that a more proactive, prescriptive approach *increased* purchase ease by 86 per cent.

Prescriptive suppliers give buyers:

- a clear recommendation for action;
- backed by a specific rationale;
- a concise offering;
- a stable view of their capabilities.

Toman *et al* suggest a simple prescription might sound like this: 'One of the things we've learned from working with customers like you is that purchasing folks are going to get involved, and probably late in the process. And when they come in late, things tend to blow up. So you'll want to bring them in earlier. When you do that, they will have two main questions: X and Y. Here's how to answer them.'

Make buying easy wins big business

Sales people who make buying easy are 62 per cent likelier than other suppliers to win a high-quality sale (one in which the customer buys a premium offering). 'Purchase ease is by far the biggest driver of deal quality' (Toman *et al*, 2017). Customers who complete a prescriptive, easy sales process are dramatically less likely to regret their purchase or to speak negatively of the supplier, and are more likely to repurchase, than customers in conventional sales interactions.

It is important to **understand the customer's purchase journey:**

Identify the most significant customer challenge at each buying stage; arm salespeople with tools to help overcome each challenge; trace the customer's progress (so that they can intervene at any moment to keep the process on track).

Toman *et al* (2017)

Car dealer boosts sales with big data

'A car dealer has 2,000 showrooms across America. The marketing director asked a great question: "What information does each dealer need to sell more cars?" They previously made 2,000 different decisions to buy stock of cars, trim, colours etc. They previously made little or no attempt to use valuable data from the entire dealer network. The dealer subsequently was able to order the optimum mix of stock based on a combination of (a) profitability and (b) customer appeal (updated in real time). These insights also made dealers and sales reps better informed and able to make better recommendations to customers, delivering 5 to 10 per cent revenue growth with the same or even better margins.

The adoption rate (of actually using the Big Data analytics) within nine months was 80 per cent, which was a striking contrast to a previous effort where the adoption rate was below 10 per cent.

What changed? The first time around, the company had been clear on what the outcome needed to be, but it hadn't taken the individual dealers' perspective into account. The dealers resisted what felt like a top-down idea imposed on them, because they didn't really understand the benefits, and implementation was difficult. This time, the digital tools that delivered the insights were built hand-in-hand with the dealers from the outset, to understand what functionality and information was most helpful for them. The manufacturer also used an agile approach to development, refining the tool quickly based on real dealer feedback.

Chappuis *et al* (2018)

Consultative selling

Looking at customers as partners with whom a company wishes to develop a long-term, repeat-business relationship requires a shift in the business paradigm from 'selling to them' to 'working with them'.

B2B selling is no longer just converting features into benefits. Selling is more to do with problem solving and strategy fulfilment (for the customer). 'What is your requirement and how can we fulfil it?' is not enough. Salespeople have to understand customers' business strategies and then see how they can help to fulfil these strategies. GE asked its largest customers what they expected from the GE sales team. Customers revealed: 'The number one thing we expect is excellent knowledge of our company, our industry and the environment in which we do business.'

Offering expert advice and consultancy demands an attitude shift where the customer is seen as a partner rather than just a sales target. The short-term 'win–lose' scenario (the seller gains at the customer's expense) is replaced by the longer-term strategic partnership 'win–win' scenario. This builds customer retention through enhanced customer satisfaction, which in turn creates a sustainable marketing advantage. These new partnerships may involve joint development programmes that might not bear fruit for five or more years. This may seem inefficient in the short term but highly effective in the medium to long term. This is a strategic shift towards KAM.

Master salespeople

Master salespeople are masters at gathering information. They are equipped with 'must know', 'useful to know' and 'nice to know' questions before every meeting.

Key account management

Key account management means managing the most important customer relationships. It is strategically important and requires highly skilled senior salespeople or senior management. In addition to salespeople being able to sell on a personal level, KAM requires many other time-consuming skills, including:

- Solutions selling and collaborative selling, which generate tailored products or services, including ensuring customer retention, growing lifetime value and share of wallet. It is all about value creation for the client or partner. The initial sale (demonstration, pitch, handling objections, building trust, presenting proposals, closing the sale and after-sales service) is just the beginning. Intense collaboration is a complex, time-consuming joint effort. KAM must help the client to identify unique sources of value. Collaborative selling is a high level of customer engagement and generates collaborative co-creation offline.

- Project management skills (to ensure tailored products and services are delivered on time and within budget).
- Relationship building at many complex levels right across the decision-making unit (this requires the ability to analyse clients' internal structures, systems and overall organization and continually widen relevant contacts).
- Research and intelligence gathering (and sharing information).
- Negotiating skills (to nurture the long-term relationship and deal with a large decision-making unit).
- Legal skills (an understanding of legal issues and contracts).

10 steps to KAM

McDonald and Woodburn (2007) identified 10 steps towards developing KAM within an organization:

1. Select the right accounts.
2. Categorize them for their sales and profit potential.
3. Analyse their needs.
4. Develop strategic plans for (and with) each of them.
5. Get buy-in from all functions about their role in delivering the agreed value proposition (to the key account).
6. Get the right organization to serve the selected key accounts' needs.
7. Get the right people and skill sets in the key account team.
8. Implement the plans on an annual basis.
9. Measure success, particularly in respect of whether they create shareholder value added.
10. Reward individuals and teams for their success.

An alternative approach to seeing how KAM evolves through the following stages was developed by Millman and Wilson (1995) (Table 11.1). This overlaps with the above but also goes beyond it by including the 'uncoupling' stage when the partnership ends.

TABLE 11.1 Stages of KAM

Stage	Activity
Pre-KAM	Identify potential accounts (select the best clients - who's the perfect client?). Understand how they make decisions; key criteria;key players.
Early KAM	Tentative agreements and probing; identifying how the organization can help the client.
Mid-KAM	Account review and senior management involvement.
Partnership KAM	Joint problem solving and sharing sensitive information.
Synergistic KAM	Synergy of shared values and one-entity perspective.
Uncoupling KAM	A positive move recognizing that there is no further value in the relationship.

Account-based marketing

Account-based marketing (ABM) appears similar to KAM, as they both focus on large customers/clients and both aim to develop deep understanding of these large (sometimes global) clients, build relationships, improve brand perceptions, identify opportunities, share expertise and give world-class service (before, during and after a sale).

ABM forces marketing and sales teams to work together to deliver personalized account-specific messaging for each client. In fact, this tailored customized sequence of messages to individuals in the buying team culminates in an individual 'marketing plan for each strategic customer' says Dr Beth Rogers from the Association for Key Account Management (Rogers, 2019). This suits buyers who are increasingly insistent on 'outreach tailored to their business and even their personal interests within the business' (Golden, 2018).

This, in turn, creates the rare business luxury of slowing down to develop a thoughtful approach that boosts the odds of driving engagement and eventual conversion to a sale and repeat sales.

> 'Personalize well and buyers are more open to your outreach and less likely to ignore your content and communications.'
>
> Golden (2018)

The SOSTAC® approach to ABM (adapted from LinkedIn's ABM steps)

Step 1a: Situation analysis: Identify high-value accounts.

Step 1b: Situation analysis: Identify DMU individuals in each account.

Step 2: Objectives: Define clear objectives (leads, qualified leads, new sales, repeat sales and NPS).

Step 3: Strategy: Define targeted campaigns – personalized campaigns covering the complete buying cycle

Step 4: Tactics: Pinpoint optimal channels to get the message to the DMU within the account. And create the campaigns.

Step 5a: Action: Develop a 'playbook' for the sales and marketing team – who does what, when?

Step 5b: Action: Execute your campaigns.

Step 6: Control: Measure and optimize – marketing and sales are jointly accountable for driving pipeline and revenue.

Integrating the sales force with the communications mix

An organization's own sales force, or a distributor's or agent's sales force, should be updated regarding any new advertising, sales promotions or social media campaigns. Some advertisements are wasted when they succeed in pulling customers into stores only for the customers to find out that the sales staff behind the counter are not familiar with either the advertisement or the particular offer being made. Equally, salespeople should spend time ensuring that wholesaler and retailer point-of-sale materials are in place and ready to support an advertising campaign. The amount and type of personal selling requires changes as a product or service moves through its lifecycle (see 'Types of salespeople' p 334). Using a sales force to create awareness is expensive (and slow, and not recommended). The salesperson, eg in a retail store, has more impact in the final stages of AIDA (attention, interest, desire and action). Salespeople can also ask buyers what phrases they use when searching for the salesperson's products or services. This list of key phrases should be fed back regularly to the marketing team, who can compare with their own key phrase lists for optimizing the websites and social media. Another level of integration is between the web analytics and the sales team (see the next section).

Integrating sales with online activity

Digital body language analysis can deliver a weekly alert to each global account manager and summarize all visitors' activity from an existing key account (or a major new prospect), whether a brief visit or a deeper investigation of a particular new product. This helps salespeople gain deeper insights into, firstly, what is of interest to their key accounts (and/or key prospects) and, secondly, what buying stage they are moving towards. Alternatively, reports can analyse potential customers' interest levels by both region and product, allowing marketers to identify areas in need of additional focus and resources. These reports can save a lot of time and effort and build stronger rapport between the sales and marketing teams, as sales teams really appreciate these valuable insights. Marketers can also instantaneously see which campaigns are generating better visits and conversions. This helps to improve resource allocations to optimize ROI. See the next section for a brief perspective on digital body language.

Marketing automation

Professional buyers source and purchase products and services online all the time. The opportunities for a salesperson to get to meet the prospect are reducing. Once upon a time a salesperson could meet purchasers earlier in the buying process and gauge their reactions and, ultimately, their readiness to purchase by listening carefully to their questions and comments and, most importantly, watching their body language. Today, instead, marketers watch website visitors' digital body language to determine how interested a prospect visitor is, how ready they are to buy, and how they can help the prospects to make a purchase. If, for example, a prospect has returned several times to the site and downloaded three white papers, and some colleagues from the same company have also visited the site, this might indicate the visitor is at an advanced 'information collection' stage in the buying process. This can automatically trigger a tailored on-screen message via a web page or a pop-up message, an email or even a phone call from a salesperson offering help. See page 21 for more on marketing automation.

A window to a buyer's mind but digital body language gained

'When the sales market switched from face-to-face to online, we lost a window into the buyer's mind. But we gained access to a compelling cookie trail of leverageable information, in the form of their digital body language.

"Digital body language" is the catch phrase coined in 2009 by Steven Woods, co-founder and Chief Technology Officer at Eloqua, to describe trackable patterns in online behaviour of customers.'

Blur group email, 2 June 2013

Sales and marketing alignment

- 'Drift' (Figures 11.1 and 11.2) is a chatbot (or a 'conversational marketing' platform) that generates qualified leads from visitors to your website. Visitors landing on a particular web page trigger targeted messages from a chatbot designed to help the visitor get answers, which simultaneously generates and qualifies leads as well as directly booking sales meetings for the visitor with an appropriate salesperson (**www.drift.com**).
- 'Outreach' is a sales engagement platform that helps sales teams drive informed engagement via email (**www.outreach.io**).
- 'Inside sales' means modern sales models, ie sales that are handled remotely (not face-to-face), typically for B2B tech and software-as-a-service (SaaS) sales.
- 'Outbound leads' come from 'interruption marketing', ie sending messages or calling prospects directly.
- Eloqua is an automated lead generation platform.

Social selling

Social selling (SS) is a skill that many salespeople develop when they use social media to develop meaningful relationships with their target prospects. It involves connecting with, listening to and understanding prospects' needs and eventually, at the right time, gently, nurturing the prospect into a customer. Salespeople provide value by answering questions and sharing useful content – until the prospect is ready to buy. Effectively, SS keeps you and your brand 'front of mind' (of the prospect) and hopefully in the 'considered set' (the two or three brands that a prospect will consider when he/she is ready to buy). A 2017 Forrester Consulting survey revealed that only 2 per cent of the 265 survey respondents said they had no plans to establish their own social selling programmes. The other 98 per cent see the value in developing their own social selling approach, with half of them (49 per cent) having already developed their SS programme.

The sales team should be well trained in networking both offline and online. At offline events they are trained to open up discussions,

FIGURE 11.1 A sales lead management model from CleverTouch Marketing

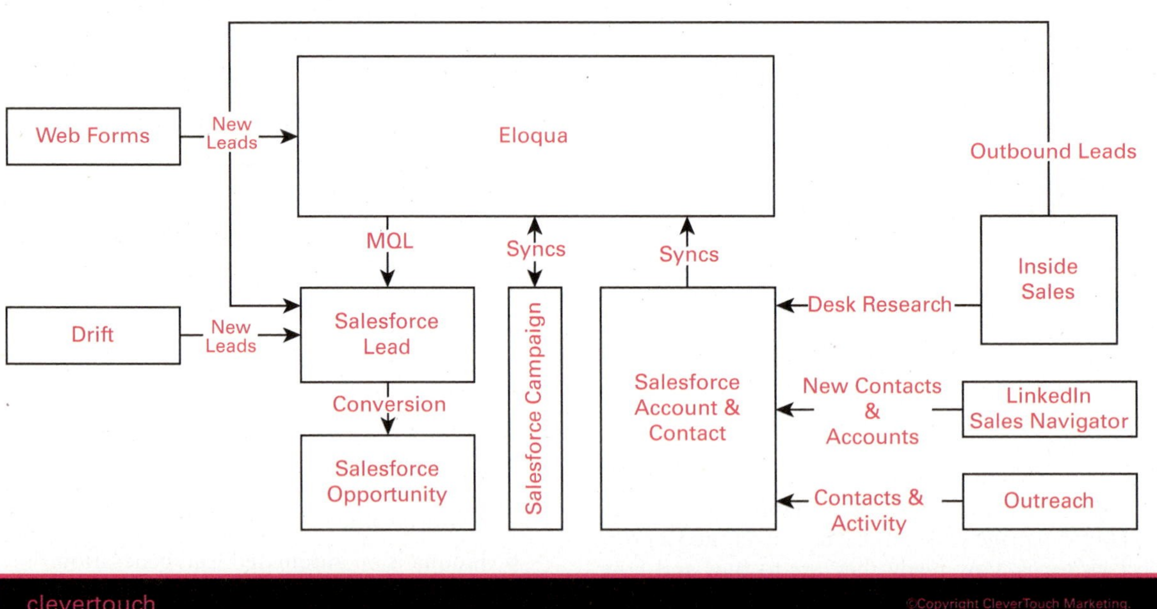

SOURCE: Used with permission from CleverTouch

move around a room, identify prospects and more. Online, salespeople have a great opportunity to use their networking skills across social platforms. Meeting new people, joining new discussions and new groups, helping other people – putting themselves about – in the right networks (or groups). Listening to discussions, joining discussions, starting discussions, and sharing genuinely useful information allows salespeople to get to know people, having helped someone. Salespeople must identify the best social channels, ie where their target audience is communicating about topics relevant to your brand. If most of your customers and prospects are on LinkedIn and not Twitter, you should invest more resource in LinkedIn groups, discussions and maybe even advertising, etc.

Incidentally, blog posts, tweets and any social media content can have a call to action to get another report/video/tip or to have a salesperson call them to help with the next steps.

> **Social selling enriches marketing database with social data**
>
> Social information such as LinkedIn interests, groups, Twitter hashtags, etc, can be added to the marketing database. Professional salespeople watch key customers'/prospects' social information so they can have more meaningful conversations. Social selling also allows salespeople to interact with customers 'socially'.

Reverse forensics prospecting

Some call it 'reverse IP look-up prospecting' as this approach to prospecting delivers a list of businesses that have just visited your site daily, weekly, monthly, or in real time. This prospect report is a hot list of companies that usually have an interest in

FIGURE 11.2 Here the chatbot asks for permission to collect some personal data. We said 'No' and you can see the bot's response highlighted on the right-hand side

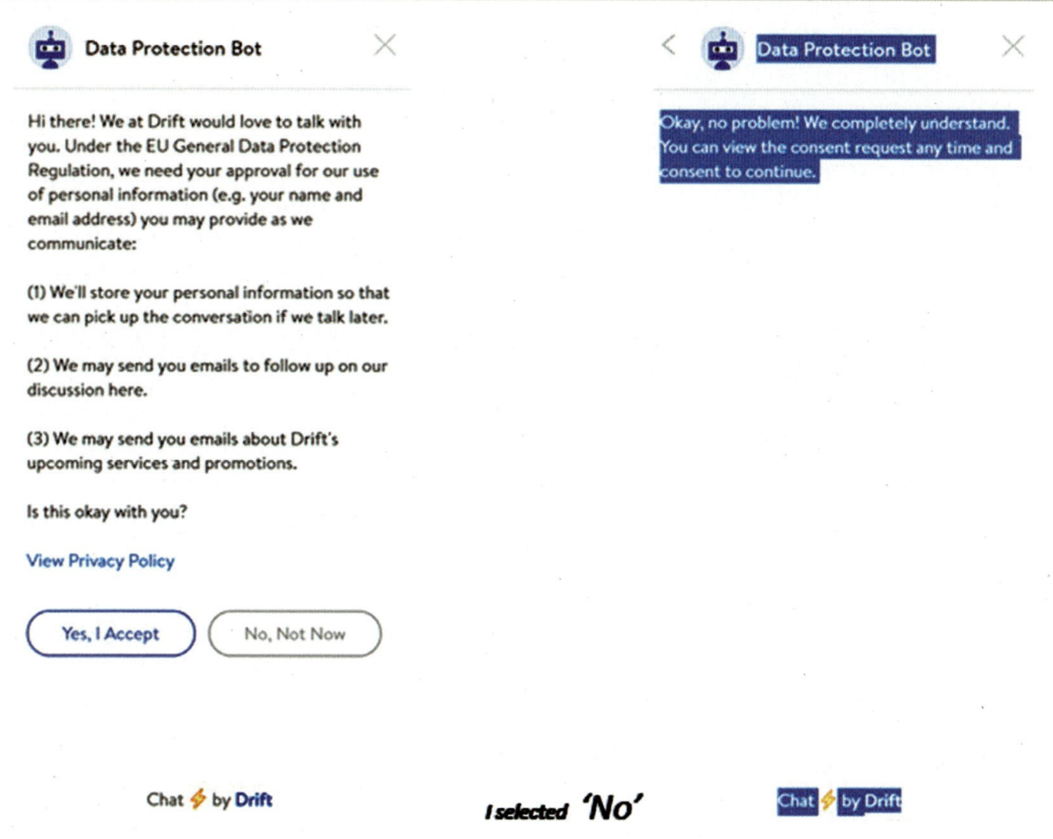

your business and/or your products. The list comes complete with the company name, address, phone number, website and firmographic (industry type/sic code, number of employees) and optional credit rating, as well as what the visitor is interested in (what keywords they used, which pages they visited, for how long). It does not, however, capture the individual's name.

A good salesperson can easily research LinkedIn and other databases to identify who might be that anonymous visitor. Some salespeople just pick up the phone and ask who is responsible for purchasing whichever product was being looked at. Prospects are often pleasantly surprised to get a call that offers help and answers all outstanding questions immediately.

This system can effectively help to identify the visitor's stage in the buying process from their digital body language – what they click on and dwell on including the length of the phrase used in the search, duration spent on product pages, repeat visits, duration spent on the pricing page and duration spent reading product reviews pages.

Rules or filters can be added so that:

- a key account manager can be alerted when his key customers (or prospects) are crawling across his site;
- a particular product specialist sales rep can be alerted when businesses are looking at his particular product;

- an area sales rep can be alerted when businesses from the same geographic territory are visiting the site;
- repeat visits or groups of visitors from the same organization can be reported.

Reverse forensics (RF) only works for B2B activity and when the visitor is using a fixed IP address (ie working from an office that has its own fixed IP address as opposed to a remote worker from home, or someone using an iPhone with 4G, or accessing via wifi). This only covers a percentage of visitors. In fact, overall, approximately 5 per cent of visitors actually make an enquiry (email or phone); 45 per cent of visitors are competitors or suppliers and the remaining 50 per cent are prospect opportunities. Companies like Lead Forensics charge between £250 and £5,000 per month (for between 50 to 5,000 visitors per day); this could generate up to 10–1,000 leads a day (based on only 20 per cent of visitors) or 200–20,000 leads a month respectively.

Most business people who visit a website will not pick up the phone and call, even though they may have a need for your services. However, some will gladly take a call from an expert adviser/salesperson from the business whose site they were recently exploring.

Real-time conversation prospecting

Some also call it 'social media prospecting'; either way, it is a prospecting process primarily for B2B companies. Basically, the system monitors conversations, posts, tweets, hashtags, etc to find people talking about your product/service type or a related issue or a conference. Specialist companies identify these people, collect their contact details, and then cross-reference this data with other online social platforms to build a better profile. They then cross-check this with a range of subscription databases (such as Dun & Bradstreet) to deliver as much detail about as many people discussing your product type or a related issue as possible. It could be a group of people discussing a particular topic, or a group that attended a particular conference.

Social media prospecting

As is often the case, the skill is in the ability to ask a good question. For example, 'Can you find me influential Twitter users, who are based in London and who work at companies in the finance industry where their revenue is greater than £200 million per year?' The answer is yes. Asking the right question is a great skill. For a relatively small budget targeted prospect names and contact details can be delivered. For example, if a sales team wanted to talk to everyone who attended a particular conference in a particular industry sector, listening tools can listen to the conference hashtagged discussions on Twitter and elsewhere and build a list of target prospects, and layer on top information from other databases (if they have opted in to receiving contact from third parties).

Most prospects are ignored

'The tragedy is that most prospects fall through the cracks in the floor boards. Eighty per cent of B2B leads are not followed up. Of the 20 per cent that do get followed up, sales reps reject 70 per cent too quickly (even though the majority of these prospects eventually buy within 24 months and often from a competitor). Effectively, only 6 per cent of a business's hard-earned leads get followed up.'

Woods (2009)

Has this improved since?

LinkedIn prospecting

Specialist social selling agencies will spend a day clearly defining their ideal target customer profile and the target customer interests. They then find and target 300 'perfect fits' and invite them to join a newly set-up, dedicated group that specializes in discussing the target group's interests. On average, 100 of 300 carefully targeted LinkedIn prospects sign up. After a few weeks or months of creating and participating in discussions, a tailored message is sent to each group member offering a one-to-one chat about a relevant sales topic. One agency generates 10 well-qualified leads per month for its clients. And if the leads are no good, the client does not have to pay – ie the client only pays for good leads. At an approximate cost of £1,000 for set up, plus £1,000 per month, this means an average prospect lead (after the set-up cost) costs £100. Sales and marketing teams will know whether £100 for a well-qualified lead is a good deal.

LinkedIn's Sales Navigator prospecting

LinkedIn Sales Navigator (LSN) helps salespeople by feeding useful information into CRM systems or just email systems, so that you can have some extra useful information about your prospect – just when you need it and without having to change apps; ie, you can see this information while you are in a CRM system or while you are sending an email.

The basic LinkedIn prospecting service allows you to identify prospects by industry sector (and by person), by location and by company growth. The system presents prospects that fit your requirements and you decide whether to save them as prospects or delete them. The system then learns from your interactions to deliver better prospects each day. It also syncs with your CRM (sales system).

> 'Good sales people know who wants to buy from them; Top sales people will know when they want to buy from you.'
>
> Source unknown

Intent and interest signals

LinkedIn can identify 'intent and interest' signals. It flags up when a prospect visits your website, the pages viewed, if it responded to any CTA, whether the prospect changed jobs recently (and perhaps needs some extra help), whether they are hiring/growing or hitting barriers to growth (which perhaps you can help them to solve).

Social signals

LSN also monitors a prospect's content sharing behaviour (identifying what content they shared) and whether they added any comments, which conferences they attended, and finally if they were in the news recently (this is the old 'Newsle' function).

Ice-breakers

Is a prospect connected with anyone else that you know on LinkedIn, whether they went to the same school, or university as you or whether they are members of any of your interest groups in LinkedIn? All of these help to make nice ice-breakers if making a first contact. If they are connected to say, your boss, then you could ask your boss to make the introduction

LinkedIn's Sales Navigator and Salesforce

The Sales Navigator Gmail extension helps users vet potential candidates right from their Gmail inbox. The user doesn't have to open Sales Navigator to use the insights. While writing an email to a prospect, you automatically get insights about the person to whom you are writing, eg if they are already a 'saved lead' or if you went to the same college or are members of the same interest group, or whether anyone else in your organization is connected to them. These insights help to build rapport with the prospect, or, sometimes, quicker sales (see 'Stuck at the bottom of the food chain', below). It'll also show you your way in, ie who in your team is already connected to this person. They can then introduce you so you don't have to go in cold.

Stuck at the bottom of the food chain

> 'I was working one of my biggest accounts a few quarters ago, but I was stuck at the bottom of the food chain. There was a lot of turnover at the account and it was difficult to engage with the decision makers. So, I was dealing with Problem #1. Then, one day, I got a notification that a new head of sales had joined the prospect company. What was even more amazing was that I saw that this head of sales was connected to many of my colleagues, including my manager. My manager made the intro, and now I have this huge deal on the table.'
>
> Keith Browning, LinkedIn

You'll also see contact information for the prospect, and you can easily save a contact as a lead in Sales Navigator so you start to get updates on them (without ever having to leave your inbox).

A Sales Navigator Team licence costs approximately $1,200 pa per seat/individual.

A fully connected marketing technology spine, notably marketing automation (MA Platform) into CRM, provides a fundamental degree of insight

FIGURE 11.3 The Sales Navigator Gmail extension

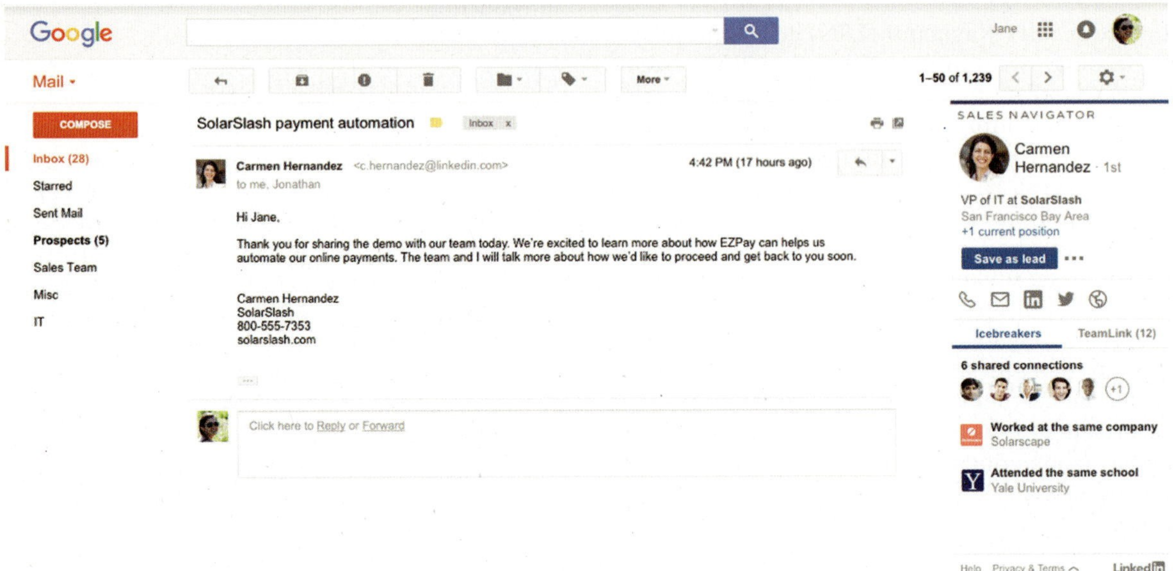

(Figure 11.4), and when connecting sales tools into the martech spine such as LinkedIn Sales Navigator or Outreach, etc, a true 360-degree view of the customer develops – tracking all marketing activity and sales activity in one place.

In Figure 11.5 you can see the status of this prospect from their campaign history. They have opened the MarTrans email in January, the GDPR webinar invite in March and the ROI event invite in April. 'Icebreakers' (listed under 'More') will reveal several other potential common interests, schools, contacts and what the prospect likes (what they share or post).

Personality AI

Personality profiles and communications insights about an individual with whom you are mailing, emailing, messaging, phoning or meeting are delivered in real time while you are actually communicating with someone on LinkedIn, or on a CRM like Salesforce or even Gmail. This intelligence is generated by a new category of AI called Personality AI, created by companies like **www.CrystalKnows.com** (Figure 11.6). In addition to useful insights, Crystal suggests the optimum phrases to use in an email, how to talk to the person, what irritates them and what they like. It is based on the well-known DISC personality analysis.

If sending a direct message in LinkedIn or emailing someone, say Gregg Skloot COO at Crystal, the system actually suggests which phrases should be changed to get maximum impact (Figure 11.7).

Managing the sales force

Types of salespeople

Some sales reps are excellent at winning new business ('order getters') and find the servicing of regular accounts to be dreadfully tedious compared to the exciting buzz of new business. Other reps are meticulous professionals who service an account ('order takers') with such professionalism, pride and affection that they create barriers for competition by building a 'wall of warmth' around their customers. In reality, most reps have to do a bit of both jobs. Shiv Mathur wrote an intriguing paper nearly 40 years ago (1981) about 'transaction shifts', which suggested that different types of marketing managers (and salespeople) were required as a product passes through its lifecycle, since the product requires different levels of service support at various stages.

In an increasingly impersonal world of faceless emails and chatbot messages, face-to-face communications or personal selling can provide a reassuring, personal touch. In addition, the salesperson can respond immediately to a buyer's

FIGURE 11.4 A fully connected marketing technology spine

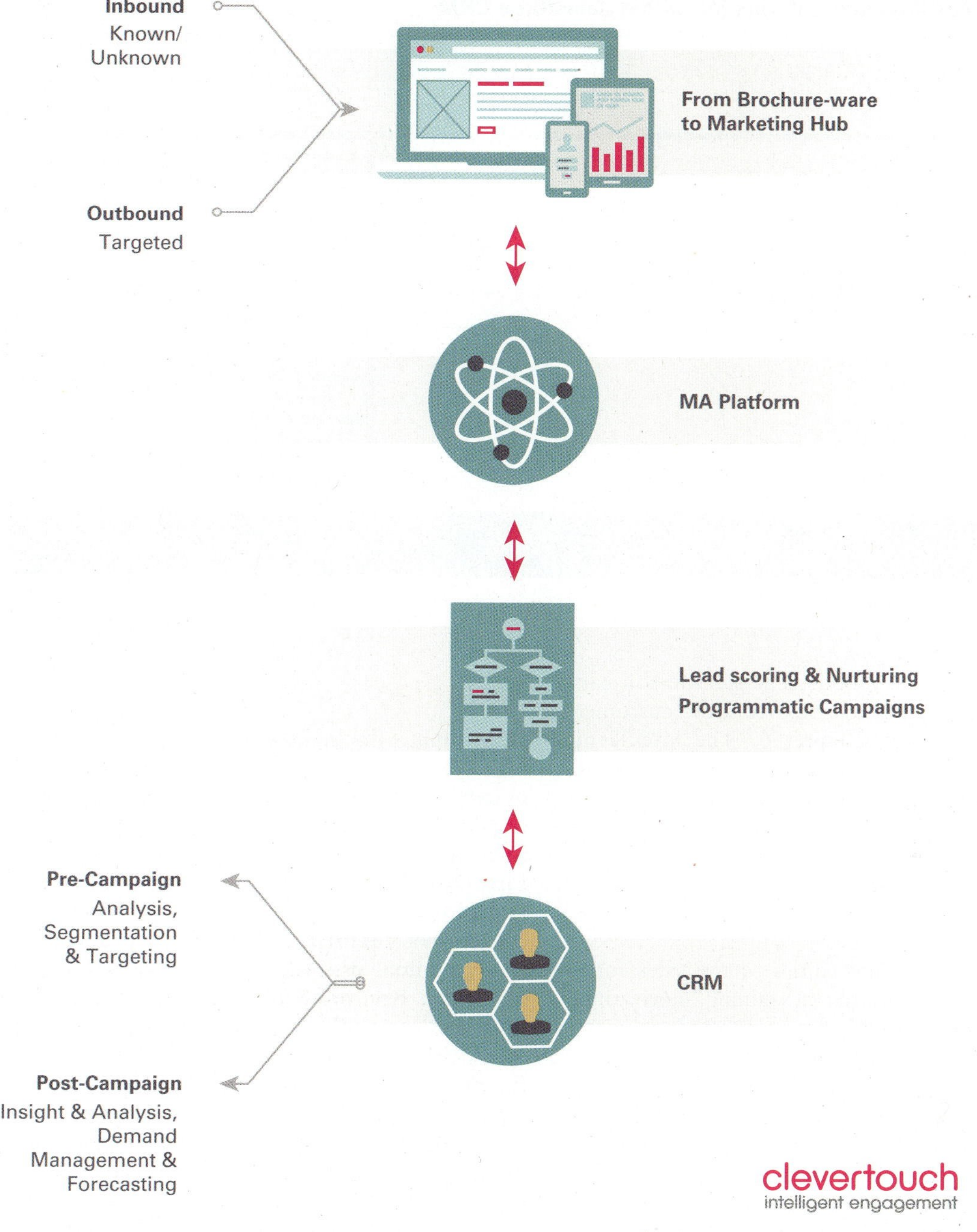

FIGURE 11.5 LinkedIn Sales Navigator information within Salesforce CRM

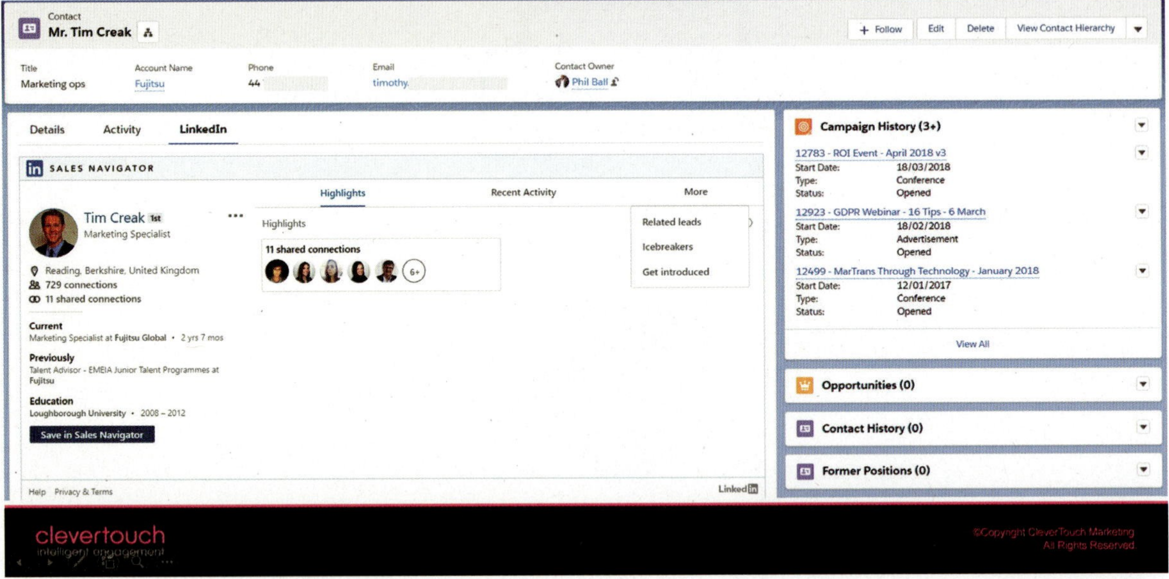

changing needs and moods. The salesperson can also provide instant feedback from the customer or marketplace (see Chapter 6, 'The intelligent rep'). On the other hand, a sales force can be expensive in terms of cost per thousand contacts, and sometimes it can prove to be uneconomical on a cost-per-order basis. This largely depends on the size and profitability of the order, the distance travelled to get it, the number of meetings required, etc.

The primary responsibilities of the sales force manager include recruitment, training, motivating, controlling and collecting feedback.

> **I perform better as a salesperson now**
>
> 'I used to have a territory where I was a free agent... today the computer recommends which calls I should make... my sales aids remind me what to ask and say... my manager knows where I am and I spend half my time on training courses... but I do sell 30 per cent more per annum.'
>
> A domestic appliance executive

Recruiting

Determining the right size and structure of the sales force is vital. What is the optimum call frequency? Who should service the account? As an organization changes or grows, so too the sales force and its responsibilities must change. Sales force attrition is a fact of life. Some salespeople move to new companies; some are promoted; others retire or are fired. This means that recruitment is a continual process that demands skills, cash and time. Recruiting the right salesperson is a resources-consuming management activity. The New York Sales and Marketing Association (2002) revealed that **71 per cent of customers buy from a salesperson simply because they like and trust them.** Two out of three customers **change suppliers because of a salesperson's lack of interest, attention or communication.** Recruit the wrong people and sales can actually be reduced instead of increased. Keeping the right sales team together is largely determined by levels of training, motivation, control and feedback.

FIGURE 11.6 Here's an excerpt of what Crystal says about Bill Gates

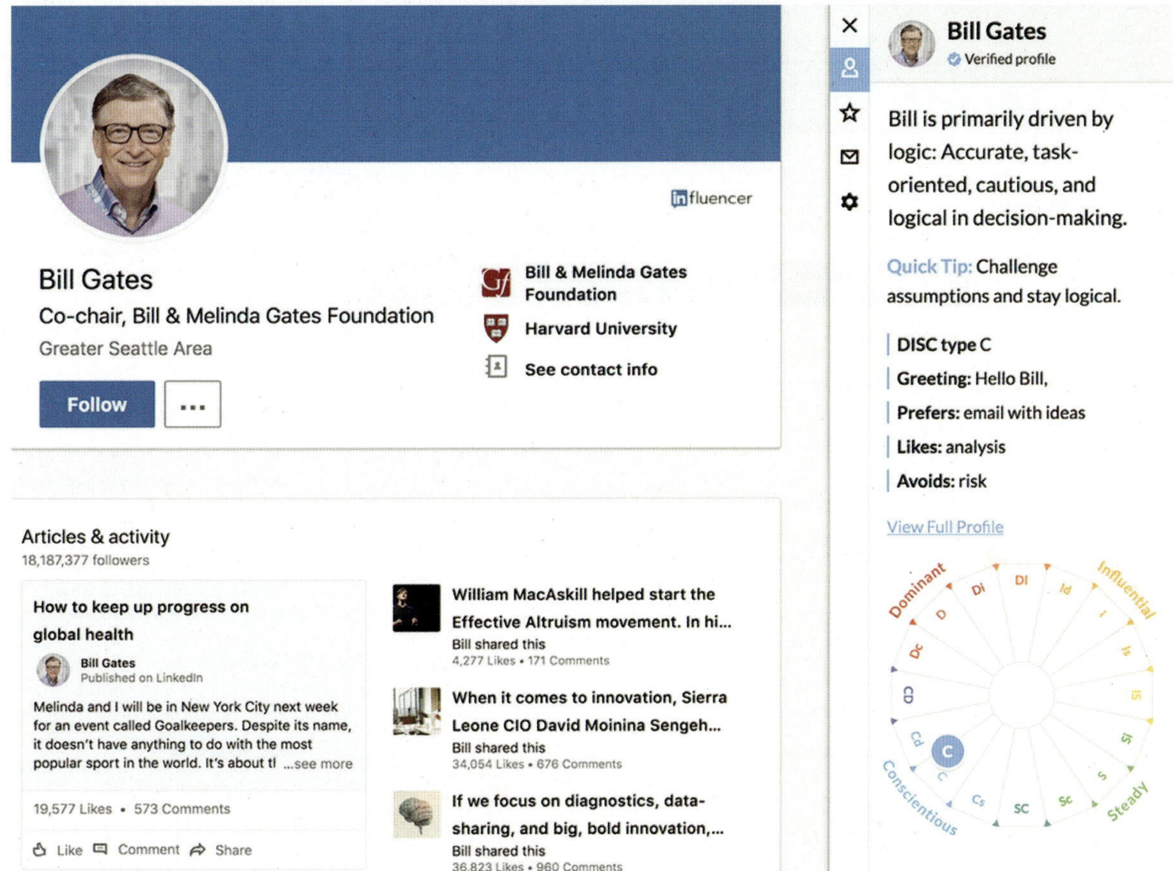

Making noises like farm animals – sales training

Imagine a group of people walking around a room, making farm animal noises and trying to form a circle with their eyes closed. This is part of a rigorous selection process of a field marketing team whose job is to help major marketing player Unilever to launch new varieties of an established snack product. Top marketing companies recognize that the more time they invest in selection and training, the better the result. Preparation is rigorous, including dealing with hecklers. As mystery shoppers check on the team, nothing is left to chance.

Training

Training is an ongoing affair, not a one-off activity. It is a continuous process. Like thinking, it requires practice. Tony Buzan's classic books (1988, 1989, 2003, 2013, 2018) emphasize that thinking is a skill that needs development and exercise. Basically, the sales force has to acquire and maintain three pieces of knowledge and one set of skills – selling skills. The three pieces of knowledge that the professional salesperson must have are:

- product knowledge (marketing mix, features and benefits, and unique selling propositions – USPs);
- market knowledge (customers and competitors);
- company knowledge (history, structure, etc).

FIGURE 11.7 The Crystal system suggests changing phrases to optimize response

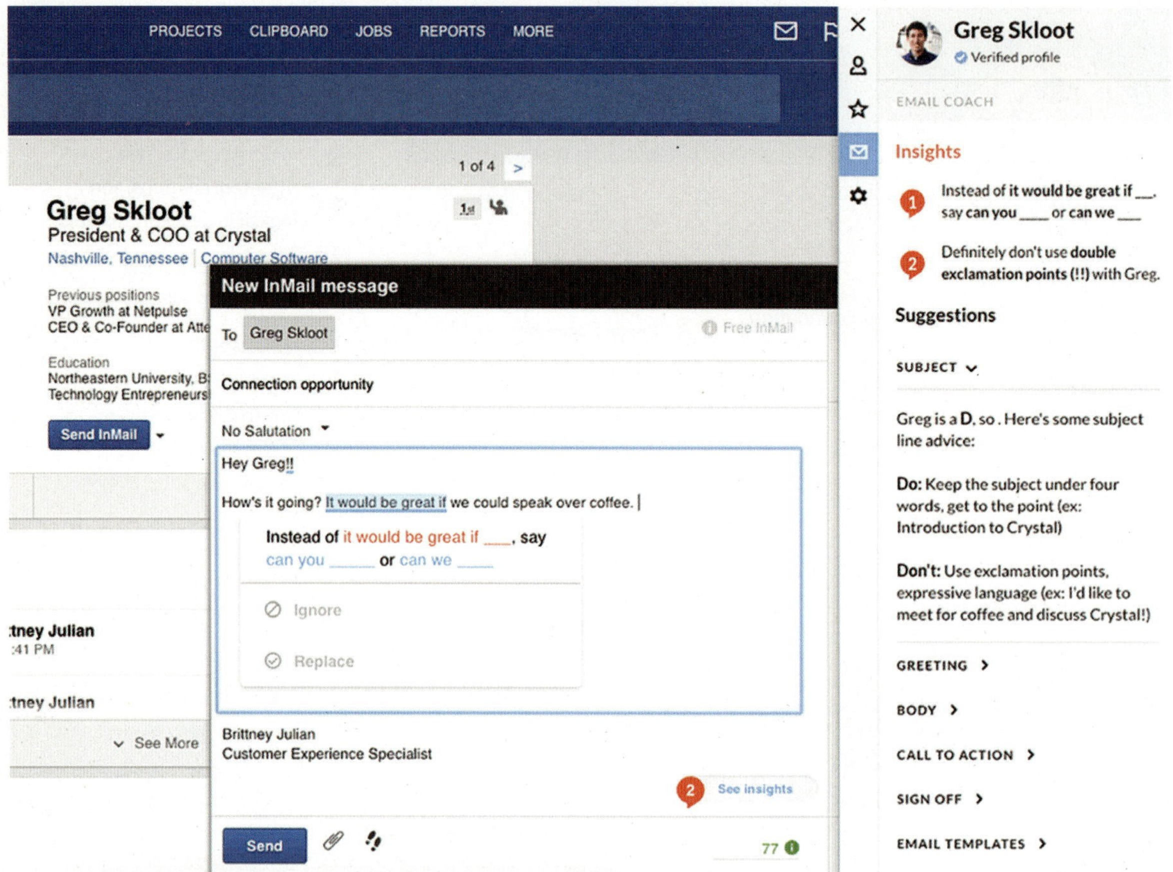

The 7P approach to selling skills

There are several different stages involved in selling. The 7P sequential approach identifies areas for skill improvement. The seven stages are:

- prospecting (looking for potential customers);
- preparation (objective setting, continual customer research, etc);
- presentation (demonstration, discussion);
- possible problems (handling objections);
- 'please give me the order' (closing the sale or getting the order);
- pen to paper (recording accurately all relevant details);
- post-sales service (developing the relationship).

Increasingly today, more and more sales come from past customers and through growing the share of wallet of existing customers. Both employees and past employees can help to prospect for new business. For example, McKinsey Consultants harnesses a network of its ex-employees – recognizing that the alumni can help to generate new business. Similarly, PwC discovered that 60 per cent of new business came from ex-employees or via ex-employee contacts.

Each stage requires a certain amount of training and practice. Training should also include non-selling activities (information-gathering techniques, time-management skills, personal expense control, etc). Preparation is continual and includes an initial analysis of the customer's business, issues and objectives, clarifying exactly what the customer wants to achieve as well as identifying its compelling reason to act. In fact, most major sales in large B2B situations involve a huge needs analysis. This involves analysing the customer's situation and includes needs, benefits, barriers and ways forward. The decision-making unit is analysed in great detail to ensure that all key decision influencers are addressed at the appropriate stage in the selling process. The customer's financial position, access to funds and decision-making units are also carefully studied. Eventually a risk analysis will be completed, identifying potential problems, their sources and their likely impacts.

How to use problems (objections) to make a sale (or to get married)

'Julie says: "I don't like the way you dress, I don't think you make enough money, and you drive like a maniac."

Frank hears: "I don't like the way you dress [*buying signal*], I don't think you make enough money [*buying signal*], and you drive like a maniac [*buying signal*]."

Frank's response: "If I let you pick my suits, if I double my income, and if I promise never to exceed the posted speed limits, then will you marry me?"'

Frank Pacetta, Xerox sales manager

Four digital steps to help sales teams

Chappuis *et al* (2018) in *McKinseys Quarterly* suggest these four steps:

1 **Get insights that help the sales rep to be better at their job**
Get your sales team involved. Ask them what information would make their jobs easier. 'The best sales organizations use data to understand the effect of all the steps in sales, from what matters most in driving a sales opportunity forward to where reps struggle or miss opportunities' (Chappius *et al*, 2018). Let salespeople see their sales funnel/pipeline so that they can prioritize each day.

2 **Create personalized dashboards around what matters to each sales rep**
Use analytics and an automated report system to create personalized dashboards for each salesperson and highlight the opportunities they needed to follow-up on.

3 **Use data to prioritize and personalize capability building**
Sales leaders can use analytics to establish exactly what specific skills are required by each sales rep so that they can optimize their performance.

4 **Communicate, communicate, communicate**
Specific tools that work well include shared dashboards, funnels and visualizations of activity across the team. Consider gamification to maintain motivation and bolster internal sales rep competition, and also online forums where sales reps can share tips and easily speak to each another. For more on gamification read the article 'Gamification – the good, the bad and the ugly' on the PR Smith website (**https://prsmith.org/?s=gamification**).

Motivating

Maintaining the sales force's motivation is a vital part of sales management.

It can be as easy as publishing the monthly sales figures against targets for each sales rep and circulating the figures among the sales team. This can lead to competition among members, which may inhibit them from sharing ideas, contacts, leads and even closing techniques. On the other hand, it can keep everyone focused on targets, with peer pressure as a source of motivation. It is the sales manager's job to build a team feeling and get everyone working together, sharing ideas rather than hiding them from each other.

'Psychic income' is often a stronger motivator than financial income, yet it does not need to cost the company any more money than the traditional financial incentive. Psychic income offers rewards aimed at the higher levels of need, such as being valued, recognized, rewarded and challenged (see Chapter 4, 'Motivation', p 142, and Maslow's hierarchy of needs, p 143).

This is how it works. A bonus cheque for £1,000 tends to get spent on dull and boring things like reducing the overdraft or paying the mortgage. On the other hand, the same £1,000 spent on a holiday for two or a spectacular piece of Waterford glass acts as a constant reminder of a job well done. Even a clap on the back, a thank-you note, a presentation ceremony or a photograph in the newsletter (or in the annual report) can arouse feelings that satisfy the higher levels of Maslow's hierarchy of needs. This contrasts with the £1,000 used to satisfy the dull, boring and soon-forgotten lower levels of need. The reward itself is soon forgotten here, whereas the psychic income reward tends to linger longer and therefore offers better motivational potential.

Psychic income: Two holes of golf with Jack Nicklaus

The Maritz Corporation specializes in psychic income packages. They even give out pyramid-shaped paperweights that list Maslow's needs. They tailor their awards so that individuals are offered an appropriate range of stimulating options. Some of their choices have offered trips to the moon, ballooning across the wine fields of Burgundy or two holes of golf with Jack Nicklaus. As you approach the 18th green there is an 80-piece orchestra perched on scaffolding, playing the tune of your choice.

The annual sales conference should be a motivator and act as a forum for sharing ideas ('how I made a sale' contest), identifying and solving problems, improving techniques, and recognizing and rewarding achievements. The conference should also provide a pleasant environment that reinforces feelings of being glad to work with the company.

Motivation is critical with sales teams (and all staff for that matter). Read more about motivation on the PR Smith website (**https://prsmith.org/?s=motivation**).

Controlling

Controlling the sales force involves analysing sales:

- by product;
- by market or region;
- by salesperson.

Sales can also be analysed by profitability or the 'contribution' each order makes towards the overall profitability of the organization. This encourages the salesperson to sell higher-margin products or services rather than succumbing to the temptation of 1) giving discounts and 2) pushing easier, low-margin items. The bottom line tends to be turnover or sales, number of new accounts (customers) won and old accounts lost, and the quality of those accounts (size and creditworthiness). Further analysis reveals number of orders (and average order size), calls-to-orders ratios, etc. Even miles driven give some indication as to whether reps are chasing their tails or leaving room for improvement. Good planning helps control.

Good sales forecasting provides targets and yardsticks for measurement. Sales forecasts can be drawn up by sales reps for each customer for each month and eventually put together to form an overall sales rep forecast. This can be modified to allow for low forecasts that reduce target sales figures, thereby reducing pressure on the reps and making it easier for them to attain their daily, weekly, monthly, quarterly and annual targets. There are also more sophisticated forecasting models that take into account a host of factors, including prices, competitors, state of the economy, etc.

Typical quantitative standards are as follows:

- sales volume as a percentage of sales potential;
- selling expense as a percentage of sales generated;
- number of customers as a percentage of the total number of potential customers in the territory;
- call frequency ratio, or total calls made divided by total number of customers and prospects who are called (or visited) by the salesperson.

The ultimate sales pitch: The extinguisher

There is always room for creativity in marketing, and particularly in selling. Whether it is a new form of presentation, a new way of prospecting or a new way of showing determination to win the business, the list is endless. The extinguisher's creative approach below is not to be recommended. This story is recalled from a marketing magazine of many years ago.

Having recognized the weary tread of a door-to-door salesman coming up the stairs, the giggling office staff scrambled behind doors and under desks to avoid the approaching salesman's eye contact. I only realized that a salesman was looming when I noticed the sniggering bodies scattered behind the furniture. Too late. I turned around to see a shabby little man with a greasy raincoat and coffee-stained briefcase move towards me. Before I knew it he had opened his briefcase and poured a jar of petrol over himself. Out of his inside pocket he drew a lighter and set fire to himself. Then, while standing in the classic salesperson pose (right arm holding out a spray can and left arm pointing to the label), he said 'And this, ladies and gentlemen, is the FlameZapper miniature fire extinguisher.' As he proceeded to spray himself, he continued, 'You can carry it anywhere.' He left several cans lighter and several pounds heavier.

Time: The scarce resource

Salespeople are spending less and less time in front of customers (Dixon *et al*, 2011). Some previous estimates suggest salespeople spend less than 10 per cent of their time engaged in face-to-face selling (Abberton Associates, 1997). The rest of the time is spent filling in report forms, travelling, setting up appointments, attending internal meetings, etc. Is this the optimum use of a key resource? Definitely not, so some companies use other communication tools (such as a direct response advertisement or a mailshot) to generate enquiries and then categorize or qualify the quality of the enquiry or lead into 'hot, medium or cold' prospects. An online form or an offline telesales team can then further qualify the lead by determining how urgent, immediate or serious the enquiry is, or this can be done by a chatbot. They can even set up appointments in a way that minimizes the travel between appointments. 'The extinguisher' (in the box above) is an extreme example, where the salesman seizes the relatively rare face-to-face opportunity and makes a sale every time (although he may also soon be locked up!).

Servicing existing customers with a mixture of telephone calls and personal visits, instead of visits only, allows sales reps to become more efficient by reducing the frequency of their visits but maintaining the frequency of contact or service by phone. There is obviously a fine line between the less personal telephone call and the more personal visit. Some buyers may prefer to avoid the interruption of a sales visit and appreciate a courtesy call ('just checking to see if everything is all right or if there is anything you need'). This minimizes time wastage (for both parties) while maintaining the customer service facility. Getting the balance between calls and visits is vital, since the competition is also out there, every day, knocking on the same doors. Optimum call frequencies need to be carefully planned.

Extending the sales force

Types of sales force

The three key resources, the 3Ms (men/women, money and minutes), are limited. Selling soaks up all three resources. There are various combinations of types of sales force. An organization's field sales force can be supported by an in-house telesales team who do the prospecting and appointment setting, thereby freeing the field salespeople to do what they are best at – selling. Resources can also be invested in agents, distributors, wholesalers, retailers and their reps so that they become an extension of the sales force. Alternatively, a temporary sales team can be contracted in to screen prospects and make appointments (telesales teams) or to go out and sell or give free samples away (see 'Field marketing' below). There is no single correct sales force mix; for example within the commercial tyre market one company achieves 200 calls per executive per annum, while its largest competitor achieves over 1,600. The former company has focused on large accounts and uses agents to service the independent trade. The latter sells direct to customers of all sizes. Both companies are highly profitable, and both have highly efficient sales organizations.

The correct approach is, of course, to monitor constantly the effectiveness of each sales force mix (customer satisfaction, sales, market share and profitability) and the efficiency (number of calls, cost per call, conversion rates of enquirers to customers, etc). There is always room for improvement.

Own sales force

Although a sales force creates a large overhead, it does allow direct control over recruiting, training and motivating. The section 'Managing the sales force' (p 334) explores the processes involved in getting the best out of this key resource. First consider alternative extensions of the sales force, both online and offline, including field marketing, multi-level marketing, affiliate marketing and distributors' sales assistants.

Field marketing

It is possible to hire flexible sales forces for ad hoc tactical activities or regular repeat activities. Reduced cost, flexibility and direct measurability make a contract sales force or field marketing team attractive compared to a full-time, in-house field sales team. Cost can be further reduced by using a syndicated or shared team as opposed to a dedicated team devoted to one particular product only. There are, of course, risks, particularly if the salespeople have a tendency for hard selling, misrepresentation or even rudeness. Careful scrutiny and supervision can usually identify these potential problems before they develop into a full-blown crisis. Field marketing tends to be used by FMCG or impulse goods manufacturers, but can be used by a wider range of organizations.

Typical field marketing activities include:

- selling into independent retail outlets, eg field sales teams sold Christmas charity cards to almost 18,000 outlets during January, February and March;
- merchandising and display – arranging stocks and literature in retail stores and other outlets, eg 25,000 newsagents and doctors' surgeries had the Department of Social Security's Family Credit information point-of-sale material placed in them within 14 days;
- sampling and promotions – providing teams (eg the Pepsi Challenge) in shopping precincts and superstores and at national events and exhibitions;
- market research into shelf facings, stocking levels and positions in store (including number of shelf facings or number of units that can be seen);
- monitoring customer care and service – with mystery shoppers who are employed to observe service and report back details of the specific levels of in-store service and customer care.

Field marketing's main advantages are widening the reach without acquiring the overhead of a full-time sales team. The disadvantages, in addition to the fees, are that training, motivation and constant monitoring and feedback are required to get the best out of the field sales team.

Telemarketing

In addition to direct selling, telemarketing (telephone marketing) is used for appointment setting, lead generation, list building or cleaning, market research, customer care, and even shareholder communications. An outbound campaign requires telemarketing professionals to make the calls, as opposed to an inbound campaign, which receives calls generated from 0800, freephone, local, standard or premium-rate (which act as 'self-liquidating', ie generating revenues that pay for other costs) phone numbers listed in direct response advertisements, mailshots or websites. Telemarketing is a flexible tool. Depending on the previous day's results, a telesales campaign can change on a daily basis, with the telesales script being rewritten overnight and tested the following day.

Telemarketing can be part of a contact strategy that includes mailshots (letters, brochures and vouchers), emails, visits and calls. Equally, telemarketing can qualify prospects to determine which particular contact strategy is best, eg prospects with less immediate needs might be mailed a brochure, while telemarketing contacts the more immediate buyers with a view to setting up an appointment. Another stage will emerge when the not-so-urgent prospects who received the brochure start to mature into the buying mode. The database can prompt some telesales action, and so on. Detailed objectives for the campaign, such as total number of calls, number of calls per person per hour, conversion rates, minimum amount of information to be collected, etc, must be agreed.

Once again, sales and marketing need to work closely together; the telemarketing manager needs to know when the mailings go out or when the sales team are available for appointments. Script development draws on the features, benefits and USPs. It will also include open-question, presentation, objection-handling and closing techniques. The telemarketing team can then be briefed and trained. Lists, scripts, incentives, prices and timing can all be tested. The results will be carefully monitored and used to develop the optimum combination for the full roll-out of the telemarketing campaign. These results should be analysed to continually build on previous success.

Telemarketing is an expensive way to boost awareness on a cost-per-thousand (CPT) basis, but it is flexible and quick and can be cost-effective if targeting the right customer profile. It can also save costs by maintaining customer relationships with telecalls bolstered by fewer actual visits from a sales rep.

Multi-level marketing

Multi-level marketing is a system of selling goods directly to customers through a network of self-employed salespeople. The manufacturer recruits distributors, who in turn recruit (or sponsor) more distributors, who in turn recruit more distributors, and so on. Each distributor is on a particular level of discounts (depending on the size of stock purchased). Distributors effectively earn income on their own direct sales to the distributors they have recruited. Distributors also earn a percentage of the earnings of all of the other distributors connected through their chain or line of distributors.

Multi-level marketing is sometimes called network selling, retail networking or pyramid selling. Several companies have proved that network selling can be a legal and successful method of marketing. Pyramid selling has a bad image because it was exploited unscrupulously, with new distributors being promised fortunes in return for large investments in stock that never sold. In addition, these selling systems tend to exploit personal contacts and networks, which can cause individuals to view all their friends and family (or anyone with whom they come into contact) as sales prospects. This mercenary perspective is sometimes enveloped in a kind of corporate evangelism, which gives this sales and distribution method a poor image, despite the several legitimate and successful systems that thrive in the United States.

A stock of goods is then purchased at a discounted wholesale price, which allows newly enrolled distributors to add their own margin of profit when selling the goods to an end user. Goods are returnable (and 90 per cent of the cost recoupable). Any training fees must be clearly stated in the written contract, and training must not be compulsory.

The advantage of multi-level marketing is acquiring a vast distribution network with no direct overhead, although margins are reduced as commissions are paid. Disadvantages include that some countries do not accept multi-level marketing and ban any form of 'pyramid selling'.

Affiliate marketing

Although it does not employ salespeople *per se*, affiliate marketing extends the reach of a brand's sales potential through an expanded network. Affiliate partners generate sales on a commission-only basis. Affiliate partners usually have access to specific communities or target markets. The affiliates often host an attractive link to the partner website, and every time the referred visitors buy the brand the affiliate gets paid a commission. The affiliates use banner ads (usually supplied by the brand), email and PPC ad campaigns.

The relatively risk-free concept is straightforward:

- Affiliate networks generate traffic to the client's website via banner ads, PPC and email.
- Affiliate networks track this traffic closely (via tracking codes) and supply reports.
- Commission is paid against whatever the agreed goals are: traffic, leads or enquiries, or actual sales, eg if sales conversions are the goal and no sales are generated then no commission is paid.
- The only investment a marketer needs is 1) the copy about the company or product to attract affiliates and 2) the banner adverts for affiliates to use on their sites.

The original form of affiliate marketing was selling through clubs, associations and networks, whether online or offline. Members within networks, clubs or associations tend to trust relevant offers from within the group. For example, an insurance company might ask a football club to encourage its members to buy its credit card. Each time a football fan buys a card, the club gets a commission and the member gets a discount or a gift instead (eg a club baseball cap that costs £2 could have much greater value, as a club baseball cap is so relevant). The insurance company can do the same online, except on a potentially much bigger scale and with multiple clubs, associations and communities. As well as boosting sales, this also increases brand awareness. In fact, affiliate marketing can get a brand's ad carried by hundreds if not thousands of websites; for example, Marriott Hotels use Commission Junction to reach into over 700 highly relevant websites with a range of banner ads and special offers.

Amazon has over 900,000 affiliates or 'associates' who offer Amazon books to their networks; a horse-riding website can have a book about horse riding promoted on the website in an Amazon banner that takes the buyer directly to Amazon. Everyone wins. The customer is offered very relevant books only. The website owner adds value to its website by adding highly relevant books and subsequently earning a revenue or commission on each book sold. There is no risk to the website owner, as no stockholding investment is required, and no resources are required for logistical operations (dispatch, post and packaging, and invoicing), as this is all handled by Amazon.

Essentially affiliate marketing extends a brand's reach across hundreds and sometimes thousands of websites (and search engines), generating extra sales on a commission basis (approximately 30 per cent). However, the affiliate may be competing for the same traffic that the brand's own website wants (or it may reach way beyond the brand's own reach). Heavy use of PPC ad words (including the brand name) by affiliates can push up bid prices for the brand itself. Some brands have strict guidelines about the use (and even restrict the use) of their brand name by affiliate PPC campaigns. Brands need to check out the quality of the affiliate's website and how it portrays the brand to ensure no damage to the brand. There are two types of affiliate programmes: in-house affiliate programmes and affiliate network programmes. Ask how the brand is being portrayed and whether the brand is effectively competing with affiliates to attract the same visitor.

In-house affiliate programmes

Some brands like to have their own affiliate networks. Amazon has over 900,000 partners who place highly relevant Amazon banner ads on their own sites, delivering visitors who buy and simultaneously earning a steady stream of revenue for themselves. Many major brands list their affiliate programmes on their websites under 'affiliate programme', 'associate programme', 'referral programme' or 'partner programme', giving a full explanation of how it works, including log-in, tracking, banners available and frequency of commission payments. Commissions range from 5 per cent to 30 per cent.

Affiliate network programme

A network is a collection of companies that have affiliate programmes but are managed by one company, eg Commission Junction, Affiliate Future, Trade Doubler or UK Affiliates. A lot of companies want affiliate programmes but they don't want to manage them (commissions, payments and queries), which can be costly in terms of time, money and systems. An affiliate network company recruits relevant new publishers (websites), checks the quality of each new affiliate, activates existing publishers, and motivates them to boost performance and ultimately grow sales. Some affiliate networks have a set-up fee (up to £2,000) and a monthly management fee, and all have a commission override, on top of the commission paid to the affiliate (say 20 per cent of the affiliate commission). For example, if an item sells for £100 with an affiliate commission of 30 per cent, £30 goes to the affiliate and £6 goes to the network (20 per cent of the £30 commission), so the brand pays a total of £36 from the £100 sale.

There are three parties involved: the merchant (eg a brand owner), a publisher (affiliate, eg a website owner) and the affiliate network (eg Commission Junction). Consider the retailer Argos ('the merchant') using Commission Junction ('the affiliate network') to reach different target markets via different publishers, eg it could target cheap furniture into its network of student sites (publishers) and camping equipment into its network of festival sites (publishers) from the 16,000 affiliate publishers that are in Commission Junction's network.

FIGURE 11.8 In-house affiliate programme

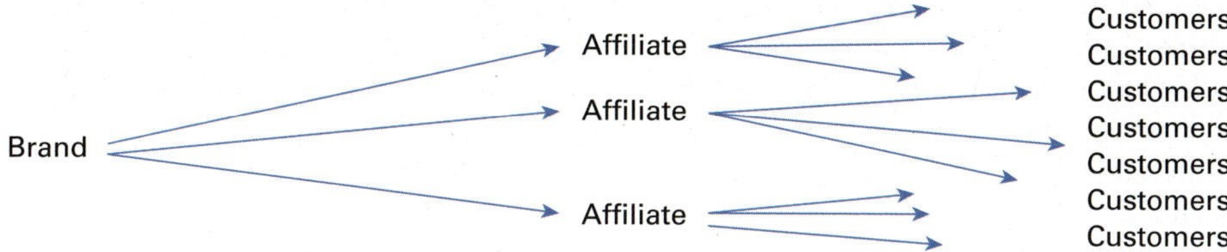

FIGURE 11.9 Affiliate network programme

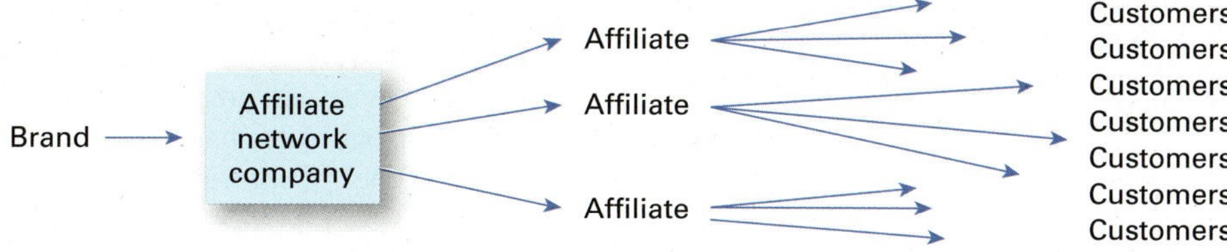

Distributors' sales assistants

In both B2B and B2C markets, most brands sell to distributors, who in turn sell to wholesalers and/or end users (ultimate customers). Winning the battle for the distributor's 'mindshare' (or share of mind) can be an important part of sales force management. Mindshare means the amount of attention and effort that a distributor's sales force gives to a particular manufacturer's product. A distributor often carries many different product lines supplied by several competing suppliers. The mindshare concept aims to develop the distributor's sales force into an extension of the supplier's sales force.

All suppliers would obviously like to have the distributor's sales force recommend, select or push their particular brand to the end user. Mindshare can be won by creating and maintaining a partnership approach that develops a mutually beneficial business relationship. This means the manufacturer must supply:

- a reasonable quality of product (and price and delivery);
- creative and frequent sales promotions (eg a distributor sales rep club where the top distributor's reps are presented with awards, in front of the distributor's own management, once they attain a certain level of sales; there might be a silver, gold and platinum club for 50-, 100- and 200-unit salespeople, respectively);
- product training;
- joint visits (the manufacturer and distributor visit the end user together);
- cooperative advertising (where the manufacturer shares the cost of the distributor's advertising when it promotes both the parties);
- merchandising and display services.

Mindshare requires a longer-term approach to selling, since the sales reps' efforts do not necessarily result in an immediate order. But mindshare will contribute to longer-term sales. It is therefore management's responsibility to develop a suitable time horizon and a mindshare strategy that works.

A US marketing consultancy, the Richmark Group, claims that a mindshare strategy has been found to be more powerful than strategies based on product differentiation and other more traditional market strategies. Manufacturers who successfully implement this strategy can build a market position that it is almost impossible for competitors to duplicate. Mindshare can make a competitor's marketing communications totally ineffective. Imagine the manufacturer makes electrical cable Z100, the distributor is an electrical wholesaler and the end user is the electrical contractor who will buy and install the cable under the floorboards of a new house. An end user (electrical contractor) customer asks a distributor's sales rep (electrical wholesaler's rep) for a competing brand, say brand A1000. The distributor's rep recommends and offers the Z100 cable instead. The end user seeks advice in selecting a specific brand. The distributor's rep recommends the manufacturer's brand Z100. The distributor's rep effectively becomes part of the Z100 brand 'unofficial' sales force.

The advantage of mindshare is spreading the sales force wider without acquiring the fixed overhead of the additional resource. The disadvantages are, once again, that training, motivation and constant monitoring are required. Note that organizations must pay heed to the Bribery Act 2011.

Advantages and disadvantages of a sales team

Here are some of the advantages and disadvantages to consider when deciding whether to increase or reduce the communications tool.

Advantages

Salespeople are great (when trained and motivated) at getting key messages across to buyers. Messages can also be changed (though it requires some training) in a relatively short lead time. If the product or service requires a personalized presentation then investing in salespeople rather than just advertising makes sense. B2B markets invest more in sales teams than advertising. Salespeople are also great at collecting intelligence and market research, as well as building relationships and, of course, getting sales.

Disadvantages

A sales force cannot spread a message as quickly and as widely as advertising, sponsorship, PR or perhaps a piece of viral marketing. Sales teams require investment in training, motivation and monitoring. It is important to spend time carefully recruiting salespeople, as they are the organization's brand ambassadors. On a CPT basis, sales teams do not compete with advertising, sponsorship or PR, but on a cost-per-order basis they may very well do better than other promotional tools.

Summary

The sales force is a key marketing resource that can determine the success or otherwise of any organization. Sales teams and marketing people need to work together more closely to share intelligence and leads in a systematic process. Managing the sales resource requires clear management skills, which include Big Data and integrating marketing automation, sales and CRM. There are many different options to extend the sales force: through its own sales team or using field marketing, multi-level marketing, affiliate marketing or mindshare through distributors' sales teams.

Key points from Chapter 11

- There are different types of sales teams, including in-house, telemarketing, multi-level marketing, affiliate marketing and distributors' sales assistants.
- KAM and ABM require a variety of management skills integrating marketing and sales staff.
- Big Data, marketing automation, CRM and martech can help sales teams sell more.
- Managing a sales forces requires recruitment, training, motivation and monitoring.
- There are many routes to extending your sales force, including field sales, telesales, distributors, affiliates and multi-level marketing.

References and further reading

Abberton Associates (1997) *Balancing the Selling Equation*, CPM Field Marketing, Thame

Buzan, T (1988) *Make the Most of Your Mind*, Pan Books, London

Buzan, T (1989) *Use Your Head*, revised edn, Pan Books, London

Buzan, T (2003) *How to Mindmap*, Thorson Publications, London

Buzan, T (2013) *Modern Mind Mapping for Smarter Thinking*, e-book, Proactive Press

Buzan, T (2018) *Mind Map Mastery: The complete guide to learning the most powerful thinking*, Watkins Publishing, London

Chappuis, B, Reis, R, Valdivieso De Uster, M and Viertler, M (2018) Boosting your sales ROI: How digital and analytics can drive new performance and growth, *McKinseys*, February

Constable, J and McCormack, R (1987) *The Making of British Managers*, CBI/BIM, London

Denny, R (2000) *Selling to Win*, Kogan Page, London

Dixon, M, Frewer, S and Kent, A (2011) Are your sales reps spending too much time in front of customers? *Harvard Business Review*, 8 February

Forrester Consulting (2017) *Social Selling: A new B2B imperative*, on behalf of Hootsuite, May

Francis, K (1998) What is KAM?, *Winning Business*, January–March

Golden, M (2018) What is account based marketing, why you should adopt it, and how, LinkedIn Marketing Solutions Blog, 26 September

Hancock, M, John, R and Wojcik, P (2005) Better B2B selling, *McKinsey Quarterly*, 16 June

Jobber, D and Lancaster, G (2000) *Selling and Sales Management*, Financial Times/Prentice Hall, Harlow

Mathur, S (1981) Strategic industrial marketing: Transaction shifts and competitive response, City University Working Paper 33, City University, London

McDonald, M and Woodburn, D (2007) *Key Account Management: The definitive guide*, 2nd edn, Butterworth Heinemann, Oxford

Millman, T and Wilson, K (1995) From key account selling to key account management, *Journal of Marketing Practice: Applied marketing science*, **1** (1), pp 9–21

New York Sales and Marketing Association (2002) Tips and advice in selling, *Sense and Sensibility*, 22 April

Rogers, B (2019) Account based marketing – is it KAM, CRM or something truly new? [online] www.koganpage.com/article/abm-is-it-kam-crm-or-something-new (archived at https://perma.cc/7487-QKST)

Toman, N, Adamson, B and Gomez, C (2017) The new sales imperative, *HBR*, March–April

Woods, S (2009) *Digital Body Language*, New Year Publishing, Danville, CA

12 Advertising

LEARNING OBJECTIVES

By the end of this chapter you will be able to:

- understand the rapidly changing nature of advertising;
- appreciate data-driven advertising and its variety of new targeting tools;
- appreciate creativity (in message and media planning) is required to break through the hyper-competitive clutter;
- consider the potential for integration with social media and other marketing communications tools;
- plan the stages of an ad campaign;
- ensure that your advertising is legal, decent, honest and truthful.

Introduction to the changing nature of advertising

Advertising is changing

Advertising is changing all the time, and in the last few years it has seen some massive changes that challenge the nature of advertising itself. It is morphing into dialogues, social media, user-generated content, native advertising, personalized content marketing and a myriad of wonderful new ways of communicating with customers. These include contextual advertising, behavioural advertising, location-based advertising, long-form and short-form ads, postmodern ads, of course creative ads, including contentious ads and continuous ads (known as 'always on' campaigns). This chapter explores these and uses a selection of mini cases to demonstrate them in action.

We are moving from mass messages to mass personalized messages (see Chapters 1 and 5), as Big Data and analytics teams (data scientists – the 'Maths Men') use programmatic ads, remarketing/retargeting ads, data enhancement and automated marketing (more later). We now have owned media* (your social media platforms and content marketing), earned media (shares/likes/comments/word of mouth and reviews) and paid media (ads and native ads) channels. *Facebook has now reduced a brand's reach significantly, and instead, Facebook now invites brands to 'boost a post' (pay for a post to get a bigger reach/audience); in a sense you are paying for the media you once thought you 'owned'.

The purpose of advertising remains the same

A large part of advertising aims to build awareness, familiarity, trust and even affection, so that eventually the brand can be considered when a customer is ready to buy. Let's remember the **original purpose of advertising is to inform, persuade and remind.** Inform is all about grabbing attention, creating awareness and developing an interest and ultimately nurturing a desire for the product or service, while persuade means motivating people to buy. Remind is an important part of advertising, as repeat business is where long-term growth and profitability come from and advertising has to remind and congratulate audiences on choosing their brands as well as reminding them to buy it next time they need it.

The end of advertising or start of a new ad era?

Some ad critics for many years have said that advertising will soon be extinct. Regis McKenna (1991) announced that we are 'witnessing the oblivion of advertising'. Other critics say that social media, chatbots and one-to-one AI driven messaging combined with location-based services and tailored videos despatched via social media will kill advertising. Mass media with its mass audiences has fragmented into thousands of TV stations, millions of websites and an explosion of new magazines, radio stations, podcasts, blogs and new apps. Mass audiences are harder to buy, and audiences now prefer more personalized messages anyway. But those who think that this augurs the end of lavish advertising productions (which used to depend on mass audiences to make them cost-effective) will be surprised to see lavish productions personalized and tailored via technology (see Chapter 5).

Who said this about advertising, and when?

'Advertising [is] one of the most fundamental ways to sort out information. And that's the gift of advertising: to connect with people in a human way, to make the kind of emotional connections that are at the core of storytelling.'

'Advertisements are now so numerous that they are very negligently perused.'

Which of these statements is the more recent? One is by Google's CEO, Eric Schmidt, in 2009 and the other by Samuel Johnson over 250 years earlier. The answer is at the end of the chapter.

Advertising people do have a unique ability to simplify and condense a complicated selling message into an emotionally charged 5, 10, 20 or 30-second piece of film, a poster or a banner. Great advertising will continue while integrating with automation, AI, IoT, AR, VR and an array of new platforms as long as they are creative enough and relevant enough to cut through the clutter.

More TV and radio stations, newspapers and cinemas still need advertisements to fill them. Social media platforms still need video to fill them.

Customers still want to be entertained, informed and engaged with relevant added-value content – but only when and where it suits them. Despite the hype, advertising is not going away. It's just reinventing itself to meet the demands and seemingly infinite array of opportunities.

Half of my advertising is wasted

'The days are over when clients politely smiled when anyone used the John Wanamaker (1838–1922) quote: "I know half my advertising is wasted. I just don't know which half." Today, better-disciplined clients demand more measurement, more integration and more dialogue from all of their communications.'

Advertising Age (1999)

Never again will half of my advertising be wasted

Although 'Marketers will waste $6.3 billion on internet ads that aren't even delivered to humans!', according to a study by White Ops and the Association of National Advertisers (Shields, 2015), we are today (2020) so efficient in micro-targeting that we can use up to 200 variables to segment and target ads with great precision. You will see how data-driven campaigns are so accurate later in this chapter. But, beware, here comes a warning about being too granular and too tightly targeted using our new digital tools.

Warning! Zero wastage/too many micro-targeting efficiencies can damage your brand

Great brands 'aren't built on the back of efficiently targeted messages' (Dempsey, 2018) aimed at custom-built micro-targeted audiences (more later). A large part of advertising aims to build awareness, familiarity, trust and even affection, so that eventually the brand can be considered when the customer is ready to buy a particular product. Data-driven, micro-targeted ads do not necessarily build long-term relationships which mass media advertising used to achieve. Procter & Gamble have admitted their targeting went 'too narrow' and that 'mass reach remains important as it looks to stay front of consumers' minds' (Roderick, 2016). In addition, ads that reach only buyers (and not other 'brand admirers') perhaps make brands less aspirational to the rest of the heaving mass market (as they never hear about, nor know of, the brand). So we need a balance between brand-building ads and actions-based ads that sell products.

Media owners and advertisers are thinking more creatively and, in some cases, thinking way 'outside the box'. They understand customers' needs for interaction and involvement and are developing strategies to maximize them. This is demonstrated by the integrating of social media, new variants of advertising (see below) and radical rethinking by major brands like Coca-Cola who invest in ideas that add entertainment value and build relationships with the brand. It is developing content and partnerships with media companies, as it sees its brands as 'portals' offering a 'network' or means of distribution in their own right. This concept has been dubbed 'brand entertainment', and companies such as Coca-Cola, Nike, Orange, Red Bull and Mercedes-Benz are busy integrating brands into such varied areas as sport, entertainment, music, travel and gaming. Some call this sponsorship, others content marketing – but to leverage maximum value out of either requires promotional support from PR, social media and advertising itself.

Strong and weak theories of advertising

The **strong theory of advertising** suggests that basically advertising works. Ads help move customers through a series of hierarchical stages towards purchase (eg see AIDA in Chapter 4). When ads persuade customers to buy something they have never bought before, or to change a behaviour (like drink-driving – see p 531) or change an attitude (and subsequent voting patterns – see 'How Trump Won' **http://prsmith.org/blog/**), this proves the strong theory of ads. However, the strength of advertising is challenged since it assumes that customers are passive and unable to process information properly. Professor Andrew Ehrenberg challenged this and proposed the **weak theory of advertising** (1974), which suggested that customers are driven by habit and that advertising reinforces rather than drives initial sales. Advertising could, he suggested, increase the frequency of purchases, as it could stimulate habitual buyers into more frequent choice of the advertised brands against a repertoire of considered brands. He developed the **awareness–trial–reinforcement (ATR) model** (see p 129). He maintained that advertising could increase or maintain awareness and improve the customers' knowledge, but only for those brands that customers were already buying (or at least had some prior knowledge of). Some academics went further and suggested that advertising could not convert customers who had reasonably strong beliefs that contradicted the messages in the advertisements. The truth is that no one is 100 per cent sure of exactly how every aspect of advertising works. The same applies for every aspect of marketing. The winners will be those who, firstly, combine analytics and creativity and secondly, those who have inquisitive minds and a willingness to continually test, analyse and optimize what ads work best, when and where.

The Big Idea and video

Despite all of these changes, one aspect of advertising remains prominent: the Big Idea. This can be a big creative idea for an ad from an agency or from a 'user created ad' produced by members of the public and subsequently shown on major channels, eg Doritos Superbowl ads. Check out **Tongal.com**, a global community of talent that develops video content for all platforms.

Note that the big medium of exchange is still film (video) – not necessarily a 30-second TV ad but perhaps a 10-second or even 5-minute video targeted at mobile devices and perhaps also aimed at another 20 different social channels which ends up going viral. Finally, don't forget that these, and other, videos can also become 'mass personalized videos' – see Chapter 5, p 167, and Chapter 16, p 505).

So the Big Idea is still much sought after and, today, it needs to cross channels and come alive in many more forms. Great advertising still comes from great briefs, except now they are media neutral as brands are no longer just 'products' but experiences created from all touchpoints (including experiencing the ads themselves).

Second screen

Advertisers now look for PR and social media conversational opportunities. The media consumption trend of viewing two screens is still growing as the audience multi-task and simultaneously use TV and social media (via mobile or tablet or laptop). This delivers a second audience for advertisers (albeit sometimes with lower attention spans). Some audience segments watch the main event on TV and then extend the show via social media, which 'lengthens the shelf life of an advertisement'. Ads get seen on TV and also on social media via phone or tablet, eg India's wonderful OPPO F7 mobile phone ad featuring the stars of India's cricket team imagining themselves as mischievous children, generated an extra 32 million YouTube views during the 12 months to March 2019. Amazon's Superbowl 2019 ad (showing Alexa going wrong) generated 40 million YouTube views in three months. As audiences continue to migrate from offline to online, the second screens are growing in importance. Social media also helps to see if an ad is getting traction. Have a look at the shocking 360 immersive video (headset/screen) campaign to stop youth's 'drink-driving' for the RSA in Chapter 17, p 531.

Apps enhance TV CX

Apps add value to the CX, thereby extending brand usage, boosting brand awareness and strengthening brand affinity. High-quality apps are putting brands back onto millions of screens (devices) worldwide, whereas devices were previously stealing attention from TV viewership.

Apps extend the user experience beyond the TV with a wider array of engagement activities. Although the TV programme and its surrounding ads may have finished at a certain time, apps prolong the sense of being in an audience/group, thereby extending the CX and simultaneously boosting marketing opportunities; eg TV's *X Factor* app updates fans with exclusive extras, news, features, pictures, videos, fun polls, all the songs and enables users to vote contestants on or off the show. TV's musical comedy series, *Glee*, had an app that combined karaoke and social singing. The app told customers if they were off-key and then corrected the pitch. Saved recordings were uploaded and used to create a band of like-minded 'gleeks' who followed and shared. The 'Broadcast' button allowed users to add their performance to Glee's global sing-along, which also allowed other users to add their own voices on to another user's – effectively extending the virtual Glee club. Apps enhance the TV CX and provide another ad platform.

Apps are assets that can become liabilities

Do remember that apps need to be maintained and updated as app operating systems and security systems are updated. Without maintenance the app performance weakens, reviews become negative and the downward spiral emerges where a marketing asset becomes a marketing liability (like when a clean database asset becomes a liability if it is not cleaned and updated).

Emotional data for emotionally targeted ads

Imagine an advertising engine that monitors people's emotional states based on their search queries, emails, instant messages, use of online games, as well as facial expressions, tone of voice, speech patterns and body movements – using motion-sensing input devices embedded in smart products.

Owned, earned and paid media

Owned media refers to your own channels or media, such as your website, your YouTube channel or Twitter stream where you have a certain amount of control over your message. Earned media refers to engagement, which means word of mouth generated by discussions/comments, likes, shares (where you have very little control), all triggered by your marketing content and social media messages. 'Paid media', whether banner ads, pay-per-click ads, promoted posts or sponsored content, all offer more control over your message and can be a much faster way to spread a message. However, audiences can be 'suspicious of paid media no matter whose name is on it' (Slaughter, 2014). There's a huge distinction in readers' minds between paid media and owned media and earned media, which readers trust. Note some brands now have to pay Facebook to get their brand's previous reach on Facebook.

'Old' media still works, eg Netflix Billboards

'How could Netflix alert audiences to the wealth of exciting new shows and movies, when they first needed to attract new writers, directors, and actors to pitch ideas and work for Netflix? It spent $150m on billboard ads. Where? Sunset Strip, Los Angeles proving that a big, bold billboard ad, on the street where Netflix's target audience walks by every day, still delivers results. "The power of **OOH Media (billboards)** has yet to be fully realized. There's dormant equity ready to be unleashed. Netflix sees this", says the OOH media company.'

Fletcher (2018)

Magic marketing formula

Always apply the magic marketing formula – IRD – to boost results:

- identify needs;
- reflect these needs and/or solutions (through ads, sales presentations, search engines, etc);
- deliver a good CX (ie fulfil your promise consistently at every touchpoint).

If Coca-Cola's research identifies people's need to be loved, Coca-Cola then reflect this by showing ads of people drinking Coke and having a really good time (whether they are people or polar bears, there's an undercurrent of love). If a B2B technology supplier identifies a segment's main need is, say, security, then it reflects 'security' in its ads, exhibitions and social media.

When you search for a very specific multi-word key phrase and then you see that exact phrase appear in the search engine results, it is a 'eureka' moment, a fusion of your specific need with a supplier's offering. The perfect match. This is the magic marketing formula reflecting your needs through SEO.

FIGURE 12.1 This creative ad by Fold7 cuts through the clutter and then presents a powerful proposition

SOURCE: Courtesy of Audible

Left brain (analytics) and right brain (creativity)

You will see the power of data and data analytics, in particular, in all of the case studies at the end of this chapter. Programmatic advertising, marketing automation and hyper-competition require data analytics (left brain) to understand customer needs and also to target audiences more efficiently. Creativity is also required to help your message cut through the clutter generated by the hyper-competitive markets. In fact, creativity in advertising, whether with just seven words in text (see the greatest ad ever – later), 30 words or a three minute video, creativity is essential to grab an audience whose attention span has shrunk and who is also 'time poor'.

Data-driven ad campaigns

Data delivers competitive advantage

The digital advertising landscape has rapidly changed over the last few years. Not long ago, digital marketing, and digital targeting had its limitations – it was based on content behaviour, search and cookie data and that's all there was. Today, that data environment has opened up with vast and varied data sets providing all sorts of deeper audience insights and contextual user information. Advertisers and their agencies now seek richer, multi-layered sets of data to give information on location, history, demographics and other sources that enable advertisers to serve the right ad, to the right audience, in the right place at just the right time.

Location-based data will become more powerful, as demonstrated on p 356 and the case study on p 377. It is crucial in understanding, segmenting, contextualizing, and actually predicting customer behaviour.

In what would have been inexplicable marketing jargon just a few years ago, here's Blis (consultancy) talking about how data can create competitive advantage in advertising:

> Using device recognition augmentation methods, such as device usage profiles, geo location clustering, cross-device/screen analytics or ID linkage, improves digital marketing programs. Exclusive strategic data partnerships with, say, major wifi providers O2 and Sky are also important. The mobile environment is expanding fast. The proper use of data is delivering competitive advantage to those that seek it.

Data-driven targeting tools

Customers still want relevant advertising to inform them, entertain them and challenge them just as before. After all, advertising does inform, persuade and remind. It can still, very quickly, help to build brands, raise awareness and nurture brand relationships, and all in a relatively controlled environment (compared to the vagaries and uncontrollable nature of editorial exposure generated by PR, sponsorship and social media campaigns). Let us consider the many different data-driven approaches to targeting ads today:

- socio-demographic and geographical (residence and office);
- contextual targeting (a third party ad on a website that is relevant to the page's content);
- behavioural targeting (targeting ads based on previous online behaviour; includes remarketing/retargeting and day-parting including/excluding specific times-of-day);
- custom audience (including behavioural, geographical, interests and lookalike audiences, in fact Facebook offer over 200 different variables to target audiences);
- location-based marketing (including geographical plus current location, ie where you are visiting online and offline).

Socio-demographic and geographical targeting

The classic demographic and geographic segmentation variables are age, income, job type combined with geographical place of residence (or office location). These have been used to target advertising for generations – eg your target might be 25- to 35-year-old ABC1 females living in London. We explore the intriguing possibilities of layering location-based data (online and offline location data) when targeting advertising on p 377.

Contextual targeting

Contextual targeting matches an ad with (a) the content that is being displayed to the visitor and (b) the identity of the visitor – so that the targeted ad is relevant to the page's content and the user profile. Online newspapers can serve specific ads to readers determined by the pages they read, the words on the pages, the number of pages they read and how often they read these pages. Ads can also be served according to a customer's changing status or status updates on a social network. For example, a man who updates his status with 'I've just got engaged' will subsequently be served ads about wedding photographers, suit hire, limousines, romantic honeymoon holidays and maybe even wild stag venues. This is contextual advertising.

Behavioural targeting

Behavioural targeting is similar but based around previous behaviour, since this gives an indication of interests (particularly if the visitor is repeatedly visiting a particular site or similar sites). The visitor profile is also used, eg if a 23-year-old male living in a major city is online comparing car prices, Microsoft can serve (or target) him with an ad for a Mini Cooper car, while a 40-year-old suburban businessman with children might be served an ad for a people carrier. Behavioural targeting uses a systematic observation research that tracks behaviour over space and time. It gets more interesting. Ads can be made even more relevant according to the geographic location of the customer. The tracking may focus on a particular place (place-centred mapping) or be based on an individual's movements (individual-centred mapping). See how Mini (cars) used behavioural mapping in some micro cases at the end of the chapter. In fact, you can explore a lot more detail on how to manage a location-based marketing ad campaign on page 377 at the end of this chapter.

Remarketing and retargeting (a form of behavioural targeting)

Remarketing (by Google) and retargeting (by Facebook) are pretty much the same. They both basically remarket your brand to your previous website visitors (and/or Facebook followers) when they visit other websites. So, for example, when you are browsing around the internet... if you previously put a shiny new Nikon D800 in your shopping cart, but didn't buy it, Google will offer advertisers the opportunity to put ads for the D800 in front of you. Or if you visited a new elite fashion design site, a website banner ad for that site will pop up when you visit other sites to lure you back to them.

Incidentally, if the banner ad is a transactional banner ad (more later) you can buy directly through the banner ad itself, ie without leaving wherever you are at that moment. Retargeting is like building an invisible anonymous email list of every visitor to

FIGURE 12.2 How remarketing works

POTENTIAL CUSTOMER VISITS LOVI SITE

LOVI ASKS VISITOR'S PERMISSION TO ADD COOKIE

VISITOR GETS LOVI TRACKING COOKIE

FORMER VISITOR SEES LOVI AD WHILE VISITING OTHER WEBSITES

LOVI LANDING PAGE

SOURCE: Courtesy of Lovi

your website but without collecting their names and emails. You can't see who's on your list but, you can see how many are on the list, and, more importantly, serve them ads as they visit other sites online.

Remarketing: How to set it up

To start using remarketing, add the remarketing tag across all your site pages. The tag is a small snippet of code that you get from AdWords or the pixel 'snippet of code' from Facebook. Many sites have an identical footer for all pages, and this remarketing tag could be placed there. Once you've added the remarketing tag to your site, you can create remarketing lists for any of your webpages – effectively an anonymized list of visitors who are interested in product X (if they visited product X page). So when a visitor visits this page, their cookie ID is added to the remarketing list. If that visitor (or that browser) with the unique cookie appears on another site, the original site is invited to bid to serve an ad to that already interested visitor – even though they are on another site.

Remarketing = stalking?

'Some consumers are being bombarded by these ads. Poorly executed campaigns make ads stick to you like flypaper, following you everywhere you go, sometimes weeks after visiting a marketer's website. While retargeting can create a lift in direct-response metrics, what is the long-term impact on branding from being relentlessly stalked like this? It's a question that smart brands are considering carefully.'

Straz (2012)

You can: (a) exclude customers that have already bought from this list; (b) set a limit to the number of ads an individual will see; (c) control the recency of visit as it can be capped from 1 day to 7 days to 30 days or 60 days. Note: Ashley Furniture, our main case in this chapter, saw a significant drop off of conversions from visitors who visited longer than 7 days prior.

Custom audience

If you upload the small snippet of code that you get from Google Ads or the pixel 'snippet of code' from Facebook onto your website, you can then build your own list of visitors that can be later used for (a) remarketing banner ads either on the Google network or Facebook, and (b) creating a 'lookalike audience (with Facebook Ads) or a 'similar audience' (with Google Ads). A lookalike audience needs a source or 'seed', which can come from custom audiences – eg uploading your own customer list, or a list (from your pixel data) that visited this webpage or that webpage or watched some video (say, 10-second video viewers).

You can create your own custom audience, say with Facebook, in these ways:

- Upload your own existing customer file to Facebook, which then searches for matches to create a lookalike audience. (This process also enables you to reach your current customers with messaging via Facebook. You might want to do this to encourage them to become a fan of your page, or simply to use an additional channel to attract their attention.)
- Website traffic visitor list (using the Facebook pixel) created from visitors to your website.

- App activity – a list of people who download/use your app (or game) or a custom audience of people who have used it, within a specific timeframe.
- Offline list –a list of people who engaged with you via visiting the real store, or called you via phone.
- Engagement list – a list of anyone who engaged with your content on Facebook or Instagram.

Facebook Custom Audience tool matches your list with its own database to create lookalike audiences (or 'similar audience' with Google Ads).

Custom audience and lookalike audience

You can build a custom audience of people who have similar demographics, interests, likes to people who are already interacting with your website. You can choose people who visited specific pages but not other pages, or people who have not visited in a certain time period, etc. You can also exclude anyone who saw a previous ad. You can exclude buyers and/or anyone else who has progressed further along your funnel (identified by visiting specific web pages). There are 17 events (Newberry, 2019) that can be used including purchase, registration, payment, add to cart, add to wish-list, donate, find location (someone who looks for your business location).

Custom audience can be used to create a broader **'lookalike'** audience to target similar users. Facebook will look for similar characteristics in common with your own audience. It will then generate a new bigger 'lookalike' list of prospect customers who have similar characteristics.

Lookalike audiences are exactly what they claim. Facebook Ads and Google Ads ('similar audience') will analyse your customer database, website visitors and followers/fan base, to determine their profile and then find a similar audience and serve your ads to this 'similar' or 'lookalike' audience. The only filter to consider using is 'geography'. These lookalike audiences are considered to be a 'cold audience' as they may not have heard of your brand yet. They may not have visited your website nor Facebook page, but they do have a similar profile to your own elusive 'ideal customer/fan'.

> Many websites, some apps and most free wifi systems opt users into this type of advertising (permission is often granted when accepting the terms and conditions of free wifi, so read the small print), or when accepting cookies. Each device is given a unique identifier, which can then be tracked.

Target audience when working with Google Ads or Facebook Ads:

1. **Warm audience:**

   Have visited your website or your Facebook.
   - Remarketing (Google).
   - Retargeting (Facebook).
   - Can target by location and recency of visit and which page visited.
2. **Cold audience:**

   Have not visited your website or your Facebook but can become:

   a. **Custom audience**
      - Facebook Ads and Google Ads offer many segmentation variables (Facebook has 200 variables) including demographics and interests to create your own target audience.

   b. **Lookalike audience**
      - Facebook find an audience that has a similar profile to your existing customers and/or visitors. Google ads call them 'similar audience'.

Note: remarketing, along with targeting Facebook 'lookalike' audiences (similar profile to your customers or fans) and Facebook custom audiences (customers you already know) are used in the Topline Christmas ad campaign, p 479.

Location-based advertising

Once upon a time marketers used to say 'you are what you shop' (your purchases represent who you are, or who you aspire to be). Then ACORN came along (A Classification of Residential Neighbourhoods) and said 'you are where you live', based on the assumption that people living in the same kinds of places purchase similar types of products. Then came mobile location marketing which said 'you are where you are' (and where you have been). A lot of advertising is based on the sites you visit and the searches you make. Now you can also add in the locations, or places, you physically visit in the 'real' world. Today location-based advertising version 2 also uses data about where a user has been (rather than just where they currently are). A deep analysis of behaviour can include (within milliseconds) both where you've been visiting/browsing online and where you've physically been visiting/travelling in the real world offline. Now **'you are where you have been (online and offline)'**.

We, increasingly, know who you are

Someone visiting a cooking website was a 'stay at home' mum. But if more data also shows that the same person goes to an international airport once a week and visits the business lounges, we could assume he or she is a business traveller who enjoys cooking as a hobby. Add in even more data points and you begin to get a very accurate picture of what kind of person they are. You can also target users who have been in, say, a particular store any time within the last six months.

We know where you are

If any of your apps or social media platforms have 'location' enabled in the settings (most people do so), then your device (mobile) can trigger information to be sent to an ad network telling it that this device owner with a particular profile is within a few metres of a Burger King (based on physical places and websites you have visited and apps you have been using).

Push-based ads can be sent to you by a media company once you have (a) opted in to receive relevant ads (often while signing up for a mobile phone service) and (b) are in a particular location (and have opted in for ads when downloading an app or signing up for free wifi).

Using data to find mortgage customers

TSB Mortgages continually improve the effectiveness of their ad campaigns. Working with Manning Gottlieb OMD and Talon, Blis analysed data generated from over 200 million daily ad impressions across a two-week period to map the actual real location of people in the market for a new mortgage. They geo-fenced estate agencies in Cambridge, so they could look at the devices that were inside this area and then tracked where they went afterwards. Equipped with this data, Talon, an Out Of Home (OOH) media specialist agency planned where to put their OOH advertising based on these movements. Geo-fencing is drawing a border around a target location, which enables marketers to detect target devices within this location.

Tracking those who visited estate agents and then used property-related mobile apps and websites helped to identify (a) property hunters and (b) what these property hunters' travel routes were so that TSB could buy OOH advertising billboards in the most effective locations.

Location-based ads vs geo-targeting ads

Location-based ads should not be confused with the geo-targeting which Google, Facebook and other platforms have been using for many years to target specific areas based on where the user is geographically located – either recognized by the locations of his/her internet service provider or the registration details which include their address (home/office address). Location-based ads, on the other hand, use location-tracking technology in mobiles to target customers with specific ads that are relevant to their actual location as they travel around.

Location beacons

iBeacon technology enables unprompted messages to be sent your mobile as you move around either outside or inside a store. Retailer apps installed on your phone effectively listen out for the signal transmitted by these beacons and respond by displaying a special offer when your mobile comes into range of a beacon (which is effectively a small, cheap Bluetooth transmitter). Virgin Atlantic tested iBeacon at Heathrow Airport (Ranger, 2014a) – when passengers walk towards the security check-point their phone automatically pulls up their mobile boarding pass ready for inspection. Upon entry into the Virgin lounge you are greeted by name (as the beacon technology presents Virgin staff with information on who you are) and they then present you with your favourite cocktail.

Hyper-competition

It's the dream of some brands to put a cookie on a rival's home page. With location-based mobile advertising, they can come close. For example, fast-food brands can already track users (without knowing their names) who visit their competitors' stores and then serve them ads at key times of day. Once Blis know the device ID, they can see what the user looks at, has looked at and where they've been as well as where they are.

Hyper-local targeting ads

While a potential investor was on holiday in Bali, Blis crunched his data to determine his location and served a 'Happy Birthday Harry' banner on each mobile site he visited that day.

Blis geo-fenced W Hotel, Bali. So each time his device ID appeared on a website that used programmatic ads, Blis got a notification of an invitation to bid to serve an ad (or, in this case, a very personal message). Note: There is more on location-based marketing in the next section.

Will you share your location data?

A restaurant, pub or night club may incentivize customers to share a special offer while sharing their location to attract their friends into the venue. Other customers might value knowing that a friend is having a coffee or a beer around the corner – as long as they are happy for all their network to see what they are doing and with whom.

Programmatic ads

Programmatic advertising, or programmatic marketing, uses data to automate the auction (buying and selling) of media inventory (ad space). This helps marketers firstly to target more relevant audiences, secondly to tailor and personalize ads and thirdly to run remarketing ads. PA uses real-time first- and third-party data to identify the best online audience for a campaign.

Programmatic ads and their real-time buying creates an automated online auction to buy space for your ads. Hence the 'Maths Men' create algorithms to place ads in real time in front of more relevant audiences.

Publishers (media companies or website owners) list their inventory (and their audience profile). Advertisers specify which ad inventory (audience profile: demographics, geography, interests, behaviours, time of day, device, etc) that they wish to purchase.

When an advertiser is matched with their target audience, ad exchanges use automated auctions to sell individual impressions to the highest bidders, whose ads are then served to the individual. This is all done in about 1/10th of a second.

Creativity in ads

There is no doubt that marketers need creative ads to cut through the clutter. Marketers also need the data scientists and media planners to use data in new creative ways so that marketers' ads can reach audiences that actually need the information at just the right time in the right place. Chapter 1 discusses the ongoing need for creativity.

FIGURE 12.3 Blis birthday banner

SOURCE: Blis

More creative ads will emerge, whether user-generated ads, apps, games, virtual reality, long-form ads, short-form ads (one-second), postmodern ads, outrageously creative or plain old contentious ads. Let's explore some of these.

User-generated ads

Customers, visitors or followers are invited to create a brand's ad. The best ideas are whittled down to a handful and eventually a winning idea is selected. Public relations and social media work hard behind the scenes spreading the word of mouth as the final selections are narrowed down and the winner is chosen. Chevrolet's Tahoe opened up user-generated (UG) ads by unveiling the winning ad during the Super Bowl. UG ads save creative costs and generate interest in the campaign. We are now seeing the emergence of user-generated content (UGC) ads, UGC films or UGC long-form ads. Sites like **Tongal.com** host very creative individual talent who prefer to work independently.

As you move into long-form ads/videos/films the lines blur between advertising and content marketing, eg Red Bull TV have 1, 2, 5, 10, 60 minutes and even 2-hour action-packed videos. Whether you call them high-quality content marketing videos or long-form video ads, audiences still want well-told, interesting stories (without too much of a hard-sell advertising pitch).

Google's perfect ad

'I've always argued that the correct ad in YouTube is itself a YouTube story. Once you start watching, it's so good you can't stop – don't have a 30-second limit in principle – and the best ads may be an ad about a refrigerator that is so compelling you will drop everything in your life and drive at full speed to get to the refrigerator store. That's the job of advertising companies: to come up with that narrative that will get you to really want that refrigerator. That's what they compete over; our job is to host them.'

Eric Schmidt, in Kennedy (2009b)

Note: Independent creative professionals and even some creative influencers, along with ad agencies, all produce some perfect ads – or at least 'near-perfect' ads.

Long-form ads

Long-form ads can help a brand stand out from the clutter and do not necessarily cost an awful lot more than a traditional 30-second or 60-second ad. Nike created a three-minute ad about the art of dropping beats using sneakers. Waitrose's mini-cooking show with celebrity chefs giving cooking tips used the whole three-and-a-half-minute ad break. Absolut Vodka created a 15-minute documentary commercial featuring Jay-Z called NY-Z; Kraft Foods' Greek chocolate brand Lacta created a 27-minute user-generated branded movie initially for online consumption but eventually seen on local TV (free), as it generated so much buzz. A natural extension of long-form ads is sponsored TV programmes (for more on sponsorship see Chapter 14).

Lady Gaga's nine-minute ad (and product placement)

'Lady Gaga's nine-minute video included product placement for Virgin Mobiles, Wonder Bread and Miracle Whip. As of 2019, it has had "over 91 million views on YouTube, with 83,000 comments, as well been watched on MTV.com, Facebook and tweeted directly from the pop star's site".

Featured throughout "Telephone" are shots of a Virgin Mobile cellphone, a nod given to the mobile sponsor of Gaga's Monster Ball tour, as well as a Polaroid camera and photo booth as part of Gaga's new role as the camera company's creative director. Several characters are also seen listening to music on Heartbeats by Gaga headphones from Interscope Music and surfing the internet on the "Beats" laptop from Hewlett Packard, all of which were unpaid extensions of Gaga's marketing partnerships.

Online, music-video site Vevo bought a slot on the YouTube home page that referred users to the "Telephone" page on Vevo.com, which crashed the morning of the clip's premiere. The video broke all Vevo single-day traffic records and had already generated close to four million views on YouTube in less than 24 hours.'

Hampp and Bryson York (2010)

Short-form ads

Somebody had to do it sooner or later, and Miller beer did it – a one-second TV spot during the Super Bowl 2009 (the American football final). The ad cost a fraction of the $3 million normally charged for 30-second spots during the Super Bowl. The ad, starring actor Windell Middlebrooks, gave one second of inspiration and reminded viewers that 'High Life is common sense in a bottle'.

Postmodern ads

Postmodern advertising may at first seem a little abstract, and certainly unconventional, as neither the user nor the product is the hero. Some marketers find it difficult to understand how an ad that doesn't promote a brand's values or have any apparent link to the brand can work. Consider Cadbury's drum-playing gorilla ad. This, now classic, postmodern ad has no apparent link to the brand, as drums, music, gorillas and animals are not part of the brand equity. However, there is a link between the brand and the ad. It is 'feeling good', which is how people feel when they eat chocolate. What engages people better than a gorilla sitting behind a set of drums waiting, as a really well-known piece of rock music builds up to the climax, where the drums come thumping in by a gorilla drummer? The ad didn't tell people to feel good; it simply made them feel good. Results: Still popular on YouTube in 2020 (13 years after it was launched). Some 50 individual YouTube channels still show the ad, (one with 9.5 million views, another with the extended mix of four and half minutes long with almost 4 million views); 100 Facebook groups and many bloggers have tried to identify why they liked the ad so much and whether the gorilla was Phil Collins (the singer) in a gorilla suit, This single 90 second ad boosted awareness and affection for the brand plus it delivered a 9 per cent sales increase year on year. In addition, all five Cadbury's chocolate bar variants were back in growth for the first time since the beginning of 2005. In 2020 this ad lives on.

FIGURE 12.4 Cadbury's drum-playing gorilla

Postmodern ad brief

'People feel uplifted when they eat it [Cadbury's chocolate]. One of the things I believe passionately is that the advertising should be as enjoyable as the product. The brief was not to tell people to feel good, it was to make them feel good and the "gorilla execution" is an expression of that.'

Phil Rumbol, former Marketing Director, Cadbury, in Jones (2008)

Contentious ads

Marketers have to be relevant and increasingly creative, sometimes challenging and occasionally contentious to break through the clutter. The Paddy Power ad in Figure 12.5 certainly cuts through the clutter. Also have a look at the shocking 360-degree immersive video campaign for the RSA, designed to stop youths 'drink-driving'; it was contentious as it was so real (p 531).

Greatest ad ever: Ogilvy and the Beggar

We feel that this is, arguably, the greatest ad of all time. Just seven words long. Read on.

> 'During one of his morning walks to work in New York City, David Ogilvy encountered a man begging with a sign around his neck. The sign read: "I am blind", and, as evidenced by his nearly empty cup, the man was not doing very well. Ogilvy removed the man's sign from around his neck, pulled out a marker and changed the sign to read: "It is spring and I am blind." He hung the sign back around the beggar's neck and went on his way. On his way home he was pleased to notice the vagrant had a full cap.'
>
> Daye and VanAuken (2008)

NB There are many variations of this story and many claims and many different cities, but the point still stands – customer empathy is a powerful marketing skill.

FIGURE 12.5 This six-week outdoor campaign broke through the clutter but received consumer complaints via the Advertising Standards Authority towards the end of the campaign; the ad was subsequently withdrawn slightly earlier than expected

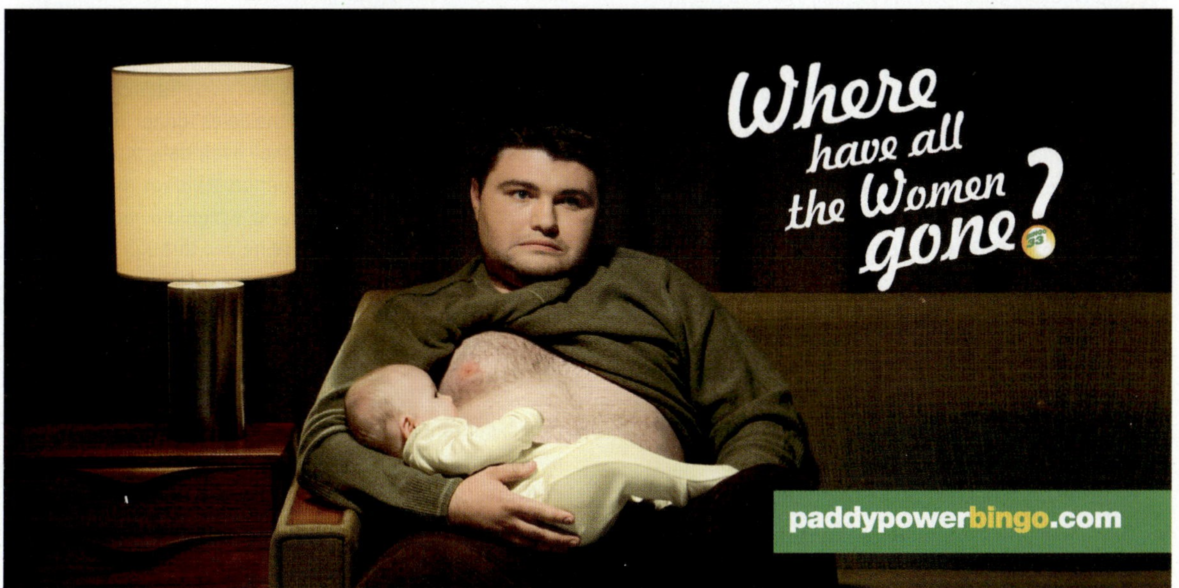

Native ads

Native advertising (or 'in-stream' advertising) is online advertising that looks like editorial (often called 'advertorial'). Native ads look and feel more like content. They never disrupt the user experience since the ads never interrupt the normal reading/viewing behaviour of the user in that particular channel. Native social ads are dressed up to look (almost) exactly like normal tweets, Facebook posts, and LinkedIn updates from your friends and followers. Despite the declaration words such as: 'ad', 'sponsored' or 'sponsored content', these ads blend in with the editorial. Media owners and publishers are increasingly looking at 'native ads' as a way to replace any lost ad revenue. *Forbes* business magazine even blends in native ads on its cover. 'Critics suggest that, at best, native advertising is a form of trickery and, at worst, a gross violation of journalistic standards' (Pulizzi, 2014a). But either way, it looks like native advertising is here to stay.

Transactional banner ads

Interestingly, many banner ads are now 'transactional banners' or, alternatively, branded applications (apps), which means customers can buy directly from the banner without being taken away from their preferred platform to a website. Customers on Facebook can order a pizza delivery while still on Facebook. These transactional banners take customers right through the AIDA buying process (see Chapter 4).

Now that we have explored both data-driven ad campaigns and creative approaches to advertising, let us consider a variety of actual ad campaigns in action.

CASE STUDY Rotating videos PPC sales funnel boosts ROAS: Ashley HomeStore Facebook ad campaign

Situation analysis

Ashley HomeStore is the number one furniture retailer in the USA. and one of the world's best-selling furniture store brands with more than 800 locations in 45 countries (600 stores across the USA). They target consumers in the regions where the stores are located. This is a highly competitive market and Ashley HomeStore like to stay on top of digital trends, in fact, all trends that affect their marketplace. 'We've always considered ourselves to be leaders in the digital marketing space – early adopters experimenting with channels to boost our presence on social, search and digital reputation platforms,' says Michael Melaro, Senior Director, Retail Performance for Ashley HomeStore. They met with Dennis Yu from BlitzMetrics and 'everything changed,' says Michael. Here is the story of a highly successful Facebook advertising campaign targeting US customers.

Campaign objective

- Establish a three-stage sales funnel for targeted prospect customers that are using Facebook.
- Develop a process that other licensees (other stores in the group) can utilize.
- Generate sales that deliver 20 × return on ad spend (ROAS).
- Reduce cost-per-store-visit to less than $16.

Campaign strategy

Ashley HomeStore was given BlitzMetric's 3 × 3 video/ad grid (Figure 12.6) to help move prospects (that are using Facebook) through a three-step sales funnel: awareness, consideration and conversion. The ads effectively move prospective customers down the sales funnel into a conversion campaign where they eventually purchase. They effectively deliver a sequence of videos to the Facebook page's social following, which ultimately converts views into sales. Prospects are helped through the sales funnel with relevant videos while location segmentation layered on refers prospects to their nearest store.

Tactics

Goals, content and targeting are the roadmap used to help prospects move into the awareness, consideration and conversion funnel. Goals are a brand's metrics – numerically driven targets, eg cost per lead, ROI/ROAS, revenue, traffic, etc.

FIGURE 12.6 3 × 3 video grid

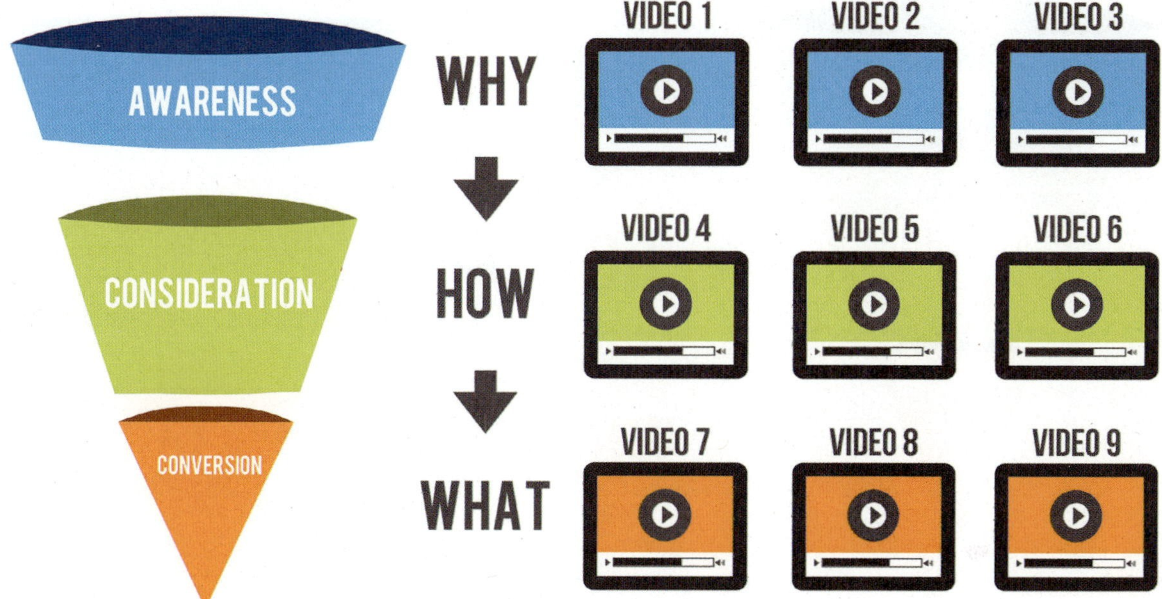

SOURCE: Used with kind permission from BlitzMetrics

Content supports each of these goals, and ties these sales funnel metrics to audience segments (eg those that are aware of Ashley HomeStore, or those that are both aware and also consider visiting Ashley HomeStore when buying home furniture, etc). The 3 × 3 video grid rotates three different types of video ads for each of the three stages. Stage 1 videos (Figure 12.9) are rotated and shown to targeted prospects to help them become aware. Stage 2 videos (Figure 12.10) are designed to help prospects consider Ashley HomeStore as a possible furniture store worth visiting. And the final stage 3 videos (Figure 12.11) are designed to help the audience that is aware of and has Ashley HomeStore in its 'consideration set' to convert and become customers by enticing them to visit the actual store.

Targeting is essential. This means identifying and targeting prospects that are at different stages of the funnel. Location segmentation is also used so that prospects can be referred to their nearest store. So each segment (defined by which stage of the sales funnel) is paired with the relevant content (video) in a carefully created sequence of video ads. The campaign also targets consumers in the regions in which the stores are located.

Once a prospect views a stage 1 video ad they become aware, and if they engaged with the ad (ie watched 10 seconds or more, or visited a page, or engaged with a post, or clicked a CTA, or sent a message or saved the page or any post), they are then listed as a prospect (that is, aware of Ashley HomeStore). They will then be served a stage 2 video. Ashley HomeStore can see/measure how many prospects are being nurtured along the conversion funnel. Eventually, this results in a sale, because this approach generates a list (or 'bucket') of ideal prospects who are ready to be served the final stage ad set – helping them convert to customers via visiting the store.

Compelling content is also essential, as is targeting the right people at the right stage in the funnel.

There are three target audiences:

- **Saved audience** (cold targeting). This lets you target interests, behaviour, income level, locations and more. In this example it is people who live in a region/area with specific demographics and interests: demographics > life events > recently moved. Interests: DIY network, fixer-upper, *Flip or Flop* (TV series), HGTV decorating show, etc.
- **Lookalike audience** (where Facebook finds more people who have similar profiles to your existing

FIGURE 12.7 Awareness, consideration and conversion funnel

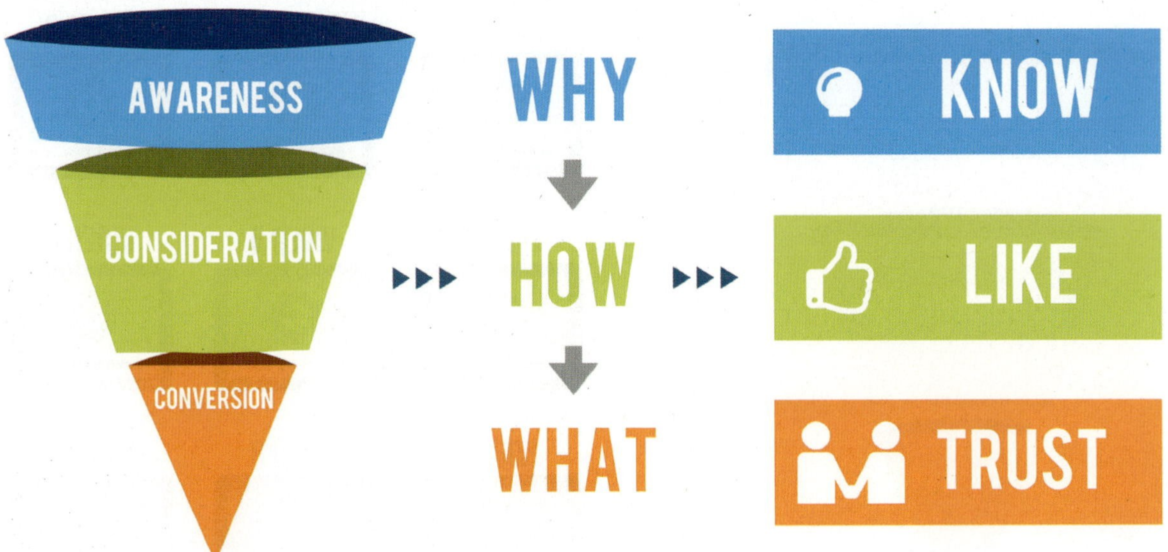

SOURCE: Used with kind permission from BlitzMetrics

followers/likers or customers). BlitzMetrics take off additional targeting criteria while leaving geographic targeting on. Facebook's algorithm does all the heavy lifting from here on, ie its algorithm is so strong it will outperform manual targeting. Facebook's targeting algorithm uses a strong 'seed' audience from the existing purchaser list (uploaded to Facebook).

- **Custom audience.** Custom audiences are people who have visited your website or have engaged with your post who are then retargeted. Since they're already a 'warm' audience, it won't take much for them to take action. If they saw a stage 1 ad (if they watched at least 10 seconds of the video) they can then be served a stage 2 ad next time they log in. Custom audiences can be further segmented: 7-day website visitors (14 days, 28 days, 90 days or 180 days); 7-day Facebook visitors (30 days, etc).

Start off with awareness (stage 1 ad). When someone sees an awareness video, they'll get retargeted to the 'consideration stage' and usually in the consideration stage they get a call to action (CTA). The CTA might be 'Hey, check out our web page!' When they click on the website, and land on the page, they'll be retargeted for a stage 3 ad.

Ads will pop up as a 'sponsored post' on Facebook newsfeed, Instagram feed, Instagram stories, messenger, audience network (see Figure 12.8).

Awareness

This first step was developing Ashley HomeStore's brand awareness. The intention with the first set of ads was not to push a product or service but to develop the Ashley HomeStore brand awareness in a particular region, eg the New York market. Using compelling stories and fun furniture tips, the consumer connects with the Ashley brand on a personal level. The ad examples shown in Figure 12.9 are the top-performing awareness ads.

Consideration

The stage 2 videos/ads for Ashley Furniture's Facebook strategy are the 'how' videos. This is the consideration step of the funnel. Consideration comes in many forms, whether it's video views, likes, comments, shares or even link clicks. Not only do these videos drive consideration, but they also help establish the business as a trustworthy source of information. This is a key step in the process of building positive connotations toward the Ashley brand.

Conversion

The final step of this strategy for Ashley HomeStore was to create the conversion videos/ads. This is the product or service that Ashley HomeStore offers. This step is what

FIGURE 12.8 Ashley HomeStore Facebook advertisement

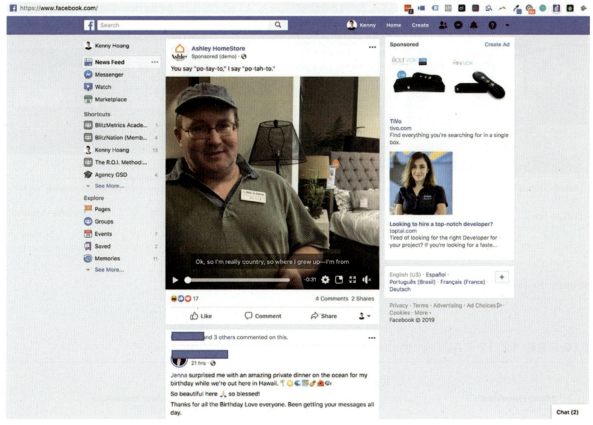

SOURCE: Used with kind permission from BlitzMetrics

FIGURE 12.9 Ashley HomeStore Facebook ads: Brand awareness

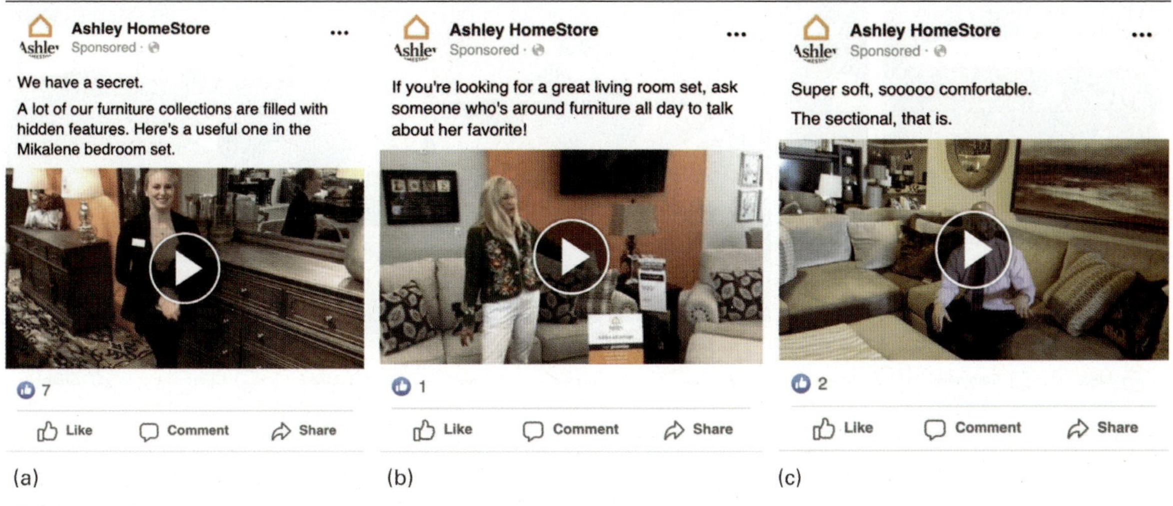

(a) (b) (c)

SOURCE: Used with kind permission from BlitzMetrics

FIGURE 12.10 Ashley HomeStore Facebook ads: Consideration

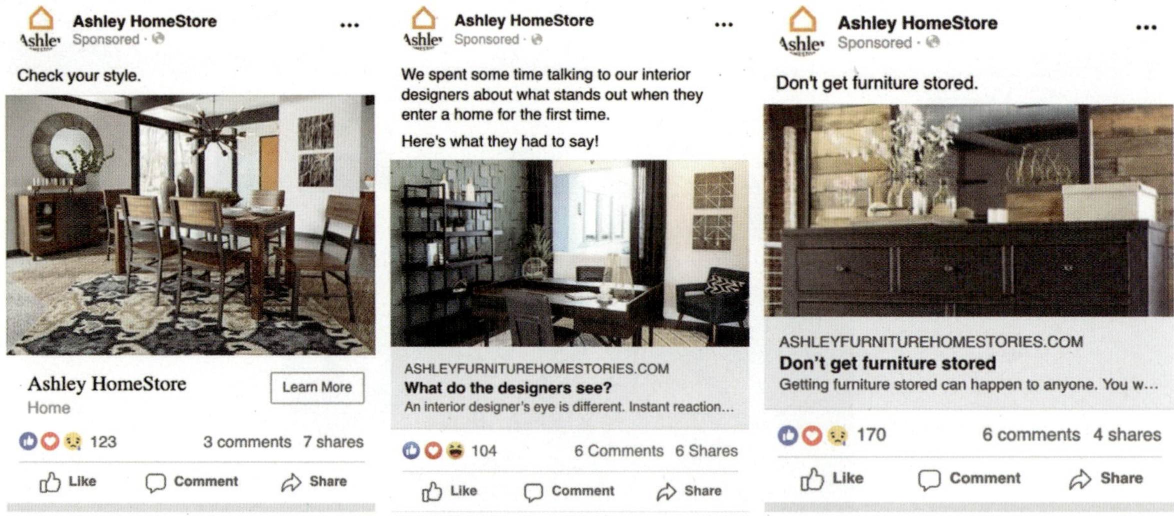

SOURCE: Used with kind permission from BlitzMetrics

FIGURE 12.11 Ashley HomeStore Facebook ads: Conversion

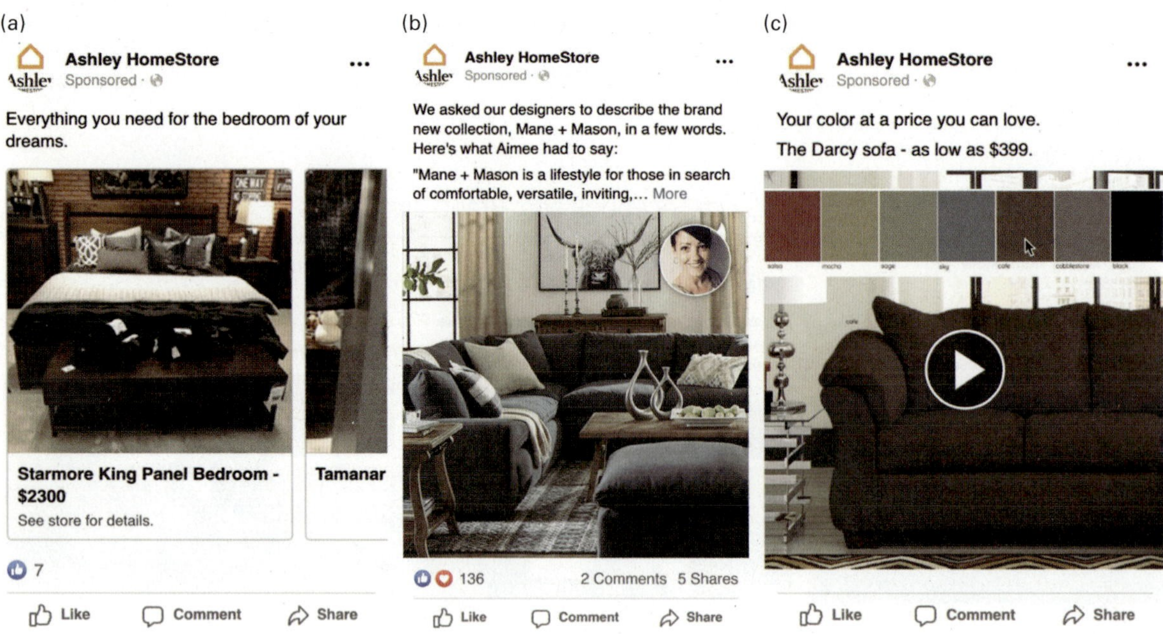

SOURCE: Used with kind permission from BlitzMetrics

most businesses do first – advertise or push products/services online. What does Nike sell? Plastic, rubber and fabric shoes. Do Nike commercials and ads talk about the specific materials used, or do they sell the dream of being a healthy runner on the Amalfi coast? Without the awareness and consideration messages/steps prospective customers ignore most businesses. Consumers do not want to connect with a business that continually spams inboxes. Typically, it takes seven touches for a consumer to convert into a customer. The 3 × 3 video grid makes those 'touches' and converts prospects into customers.

Actions

A big challenge for many businesses, particularly when working with partners and agencies, is how do you ensure your campaign plan will be executed with excellence and passion? BlitzMetrics recruit and train their teams rigorously. All of the videos need to be created with the appropriate messages suitable for prospects at each stage of the funnel. They also use automatic reporting systems to ensure the videos they produce are deemed to be excellent. They do this by monitoring the videos carefully when they are posted.

They can see which videos get more traction – more views and more engagement, which includes: reactions (likes and emojis), shares and comments.

With each Ashley ad, BlitzMetrics look at the relevance score and reactions, comments and shares to ensure ads are generating social proof, thus delivering cheaply and putting the strongest content in front of prospective customers in their Facebook and Instagram feeds.

To drive in-store visits to individual stores, Ashley set up awareness, consideration and conversion campaigns to drive store visits for each individual store.

Each campaign (awareness campaign, consideration campaign and conversion campaign) includes various ad sets (a group of ads, eg the three ads already shown in the conversion campaign that share the same targeting data, daily or lifetime budget, schedule, bid type and bid info).

As an example, for the **awareness campaigns** the ad sets would primarily be made up of cold audiences:

- 1 per cent lookalike audiences of existing store purchasers;
- saved audiences made up of interest targeting and narrowed by geography.

Starting off with a 1 per cent lookalike of existing store purchasers at the top of the funnel is an effective way to leverage Facebook's algorithm to do the heavy lifting and go after people most likely to be ideal purchasers. Geography is a filter worth considering but not demographics, as this then might ignore Facebook algorithm usefulness. So 1 per cent of your target region will be the best matching profile audience (that matched your original 'seed' audience) but will be a smaller number of people, whereas 10 per cent will be a bigger audience but not as tight fitting as the 1 per cent audience.

For the **consideration campaigns** the ad sets would primarily be made up of retargeting to warm audiences such as:

- page engager audiences;
- mega 10-second video view audiences (a compilation of videos from Ashley HomeStore that people have watched for at least 10 seconds).

For the **conversion campaigns**, the strongest audiences are 7-day website visitors (ie those that visited the website in the last 7 days). After that, there is a significant drop-off in conversions, ie 14-day website visitors do not convert as much.

After thorough testing, website visitors are the strongest audiences for conversions. Website visitors are more likely to convert to customers when put into designated buckets (or lists) and are shown ads that they will relate to.

The best ads are carefully preselected by testing them on social media platforms to find out their:

- **Performance:** The videos are first posted on various social media platforms and then those videos that perform the best are selected. This is measured by using BlitzMetrics' Standards of Excellence. A set of criteria for each part of the funnel benchmark performance.
- **Relevance score:** This will be based on quality ranking, engagement ranking and conversion ranking. This uses similar logic to Google's Quality Score for ads. Higher relevance = lower cost of advertising. NB Relevance score is about to be replaced by a new metric similar to Google's Quality Score.

Cheapest delivery (Facebook tells you how much each ad is)

Before you pay for the ad, Facebook will give you an estimate. Like an actual auction when you're trying to buy something, you can name your price and 'bid' on an item. Over time, the targets segment by audience, product and copy to optimize further efforts. The 'standards of excellence' determine the success rate of articles, posts and videos.

Control (results)

Note the difference between CPC $1.50 and website visits $3.50 in Figure 12.12. This is because sometimes people click by accident, so they close the browser and don't become a website visitor. Also, they may close the browser if the page speed loads too slowly. That's why the cost per web visit is higher than the cost per click. At the conversion level it's critical that the page load speed is optimized so customers get a good CX, as no one waits 20 seconds for a page to load.

Dashboard 1 (Figure 12.13) shows Ashley Home Store's current ROAS is surpassing the target 20 x ROAS. This means that for every $1 put into a campaign, they are now receiving an average sales return of $29.49 instead of just the target return of $20 for every dollar spent.

Observe the targeting approach of different markets for each store location in Figure 12.13.

Each campaign breaks down into the level of the funnel in which the ad belongs (Figure 12.14). In the left-hand columns, numbers 1, 2 and 3 indicate the funnel stage of the ad – 1 for awareness, 2 for engagement, 3 for conversion, which makes it easy to note funnel position when reviewing performance.

FIGURE 12.12 Cost per engagement

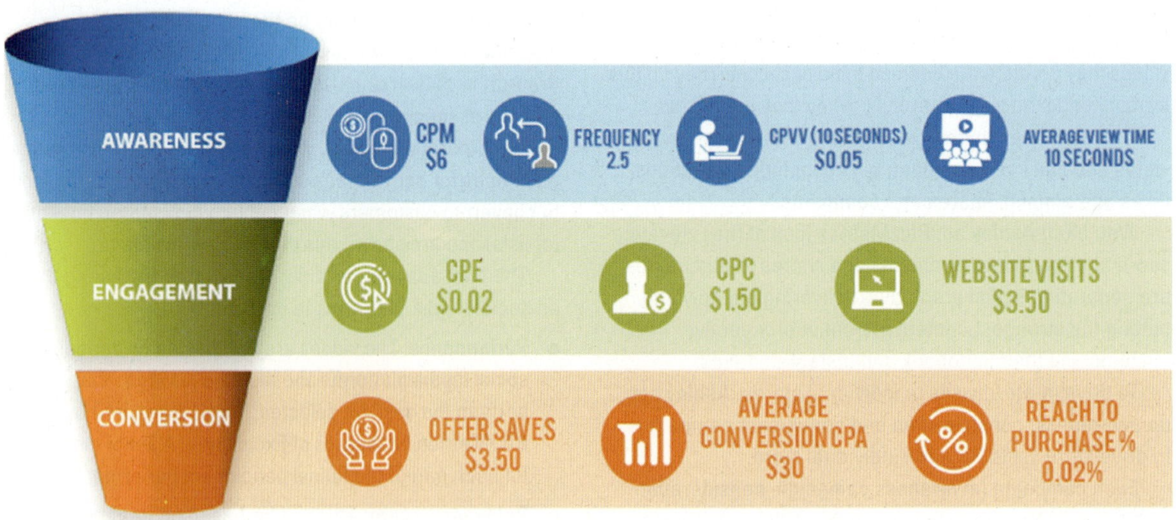

SOURCE: Used with kind permission from BlitzMetrics

FIGURE 12.13 Dashboard 1

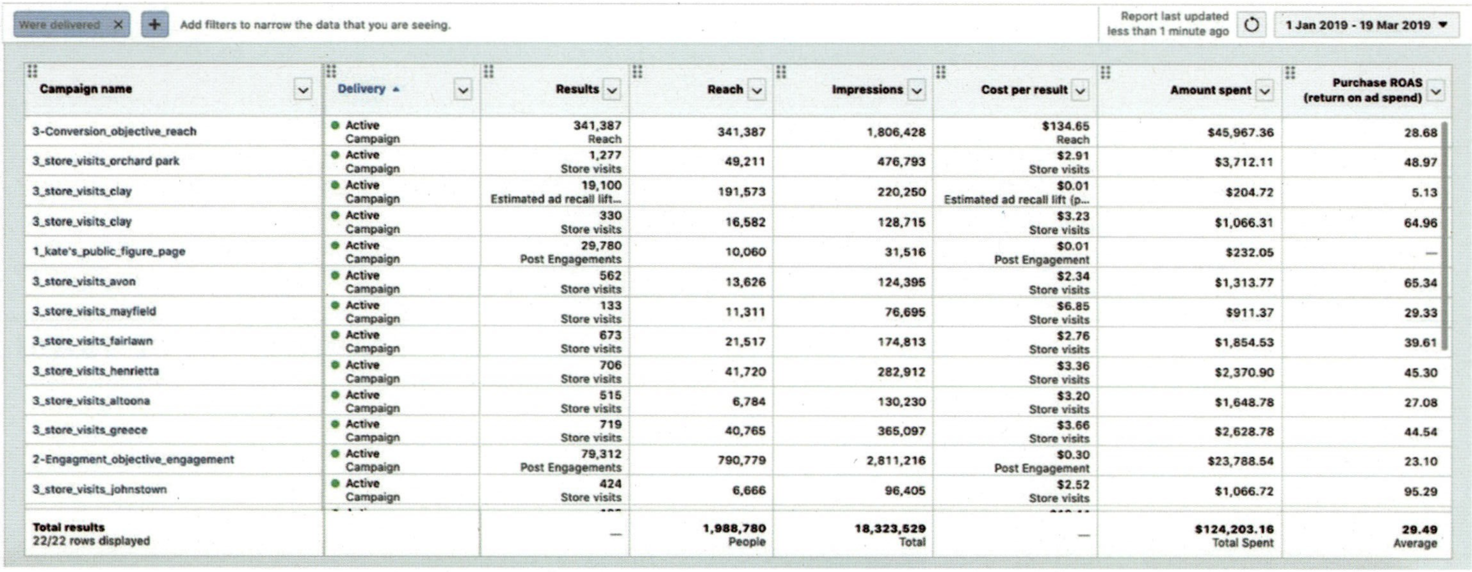

Were delivered × + Add filters to narrow the data that you are seeing.

Report last updated less than 1 minute ago | 1 Jan 2019 - 19 Mar 2019

Campaign name	Delivery	Results	Reach	Impressions	Cost per result	Amount spent	Purchase ROAS (return on ad spend)
3-Conversion_objective_reach	Active Campaign	341,387 Reach	341,387	1,806,428	$134.65 Reach	$45,967.36	28.68
3_store_visits_orchard park	Active Campaign	1,277 Store visits	49,211	476,793	$2.91 Store visits	$3,712.11	48.97
3_store_visits_clay	Active Campaign	19,100 Estimated ad recall lift...	191,573	220,250	$0.01 Estimated ad recall lift (p...	$204.72	5.13
3_store_visits_clay	Active Campaign	330 Store visits	16,582	128,715	$3.23 Store visits	$1,066.31	64.96
1_kate's_public_figure_page	Active Campaign	29,780 Post Engagements	10,060	31,516	$0.01 Post Engagement	$232.05	—
3_store_visits_avon	Active Campaign	562 Store visits	13,626	124,395	$2.34 Store visits	$1,313.77	65.34
3_store_visits_mayfield	Active Campaign	133 Store visits	11,311	76,695	$6.85 Store visits	$911.37	29.33
3_store_visits_fairlawn	Active Campaign	673 Store visits	21,517	174,813	$2.76 Store visits	$1,854.53	39.61
3_store_visits_henrietta	Active Campaign	706 Store visits	41,720	282,912	$3.36 Store visits	$2,370.90	45.30
3_store_visits_altoona	Active Campaign	515 Store visits	6,784	130,230	$3.20 Store visits	$1,648.78	27.08
3_store_visits_greece	Active Campaign	719 Store visits	40,765	365,097	$3.66 Store visits	$2,628.78	44.54
2-Engagment_objective_engagement	Active Campaign	79,312 Post Engagements	790,779	2,811,216	$0.30 Post Engagement	$23,788.54	23.10
3_store_visits_johnstown	Active Campaign	424 Store visits	6,666	96,405	$2.52 Store visits	$1,066.72	95.29
Total results 22/22 rows displayed		—	**1,988,780** People	**18,323,529** Total	—	**$124,203.16** Total Spent	**29.49** Average

FIGURE 12.14 Dashboard 2

Campaign name	Delivery	Results	Reach	Impressions	Cost per result	Amount spent	Purchase ROAS (return on ad spend)
3-Conversion_objective_reach	Active Campaign	341,401 Reach	341,401	1,806,419	$134.64 Reach	$45,967.02	28.68
2-Engagment_objective_engagement	Active Campaign	79,312 Post Engagements	790,774	2,811,196	$0.30 Post Engagement	$23,788.42	23.10
1-Awareness_objective_brand_awareness_II	Active Campaign	139,500 Estimated ad recall li...	846,803	7,863,861	$0.17 Estimated ad recall lift (...	$23,099.99	20.31

Awareness results

FIGURE 12.15 Dashboard 3a

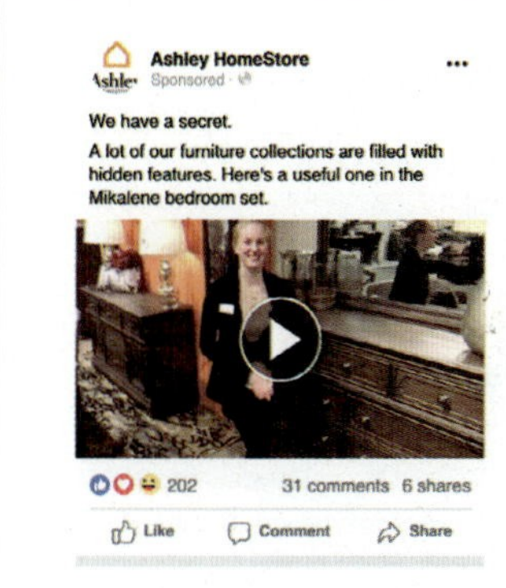

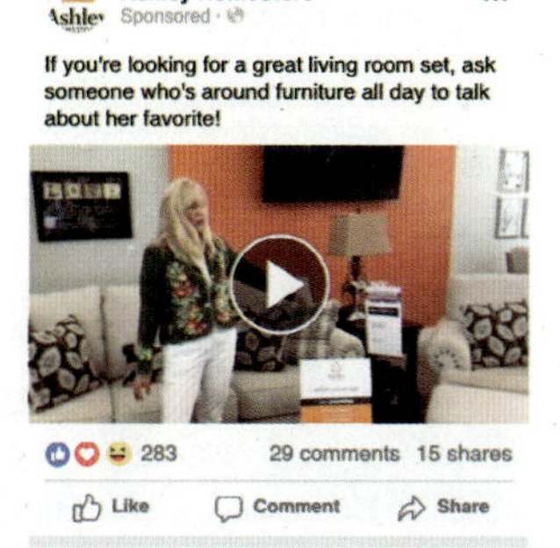

Spent: $2,675.96	Spent: $3,165.30	Spent: $1,571.82
Impressions: 890,989	Impressions: 1,045,908	Impressions: 509,599
3-sec video views: 115,519	3-sec video views: 130,477	3-sec video views: 65,525
Cost per 3-sec vv: $0.02	Cost per 3-sec vv: $0.02	Cost per 3-sec vv: $0.02
10-sec video views: 32,862	10-sec video views: 27,284	10-sec video views: 13,648
Reach: 389,840	Reach: 414,025	Reach: 279,848
Offline purchases: 54	Offline purchases: 41	Offline purchases: 30
Purchases value: $91,053.25	Purchases value: $60,102.89	Purchases value: $45,464.86
ROAS: 34.46x	ROAS: 20.01x	ROAS: 29.64x

Consideration results

FIGURE 12.16 Dashboard 3b

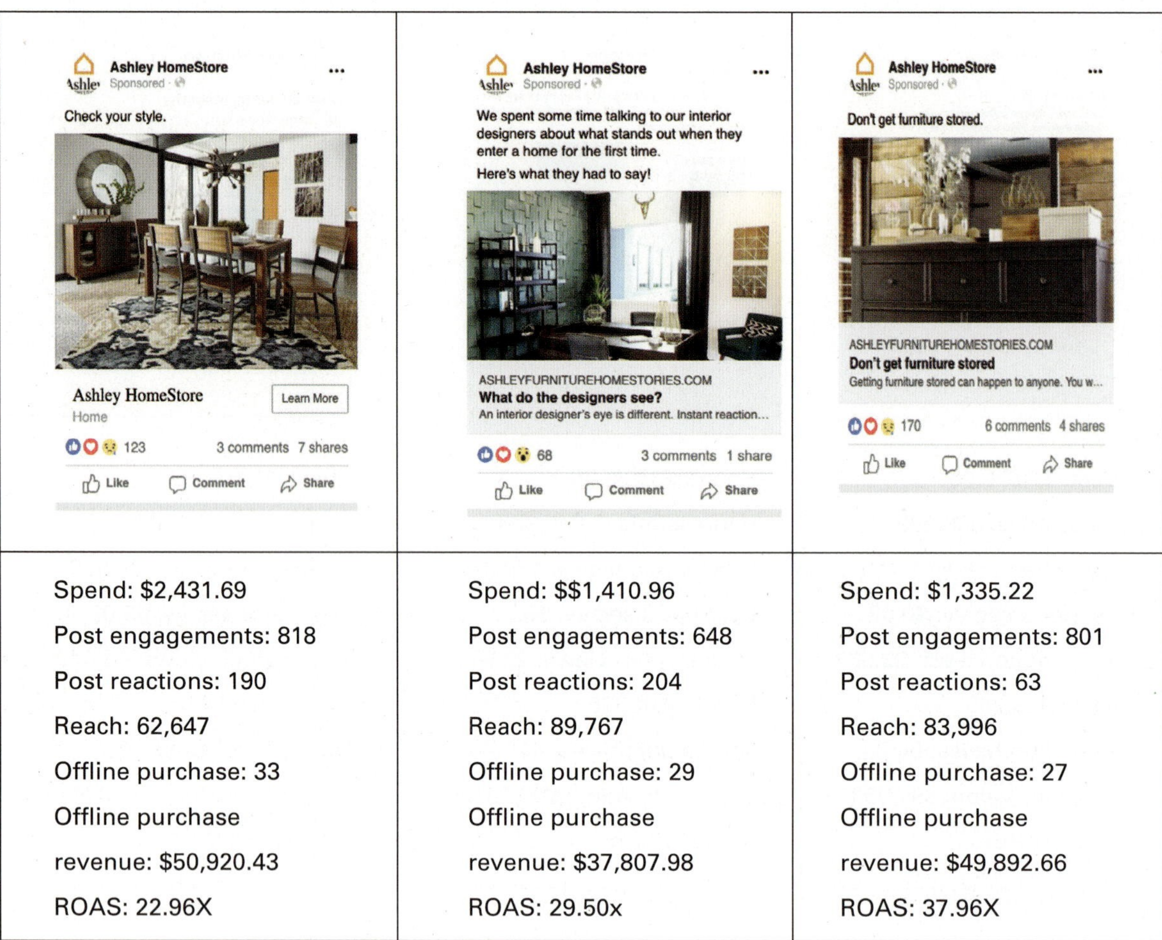

Spend: $2,431.69	Spend: $$1,410.96	Spend: $1,335.22
Post engagements: 818	Post engagements: 648	Post engagements: 801
Post reactions: 190	Post reactions: 204	Post reactions: 63
Reach: 62,647	Reach: 89,767	Reach: 83,996
Offline purchase: 33	Offline purchase: 29	Offline purchase: 27
Offline purchase revenue: $50,920.43	Offline purchase revenue: $37,807.98	Offline purchase revenue: $49,892.66
ROAS: 22.96X	ROAS: 29.50x	ROAS: 37.96X

Conversion results

FIGURE 12.17 Dashboard 3c

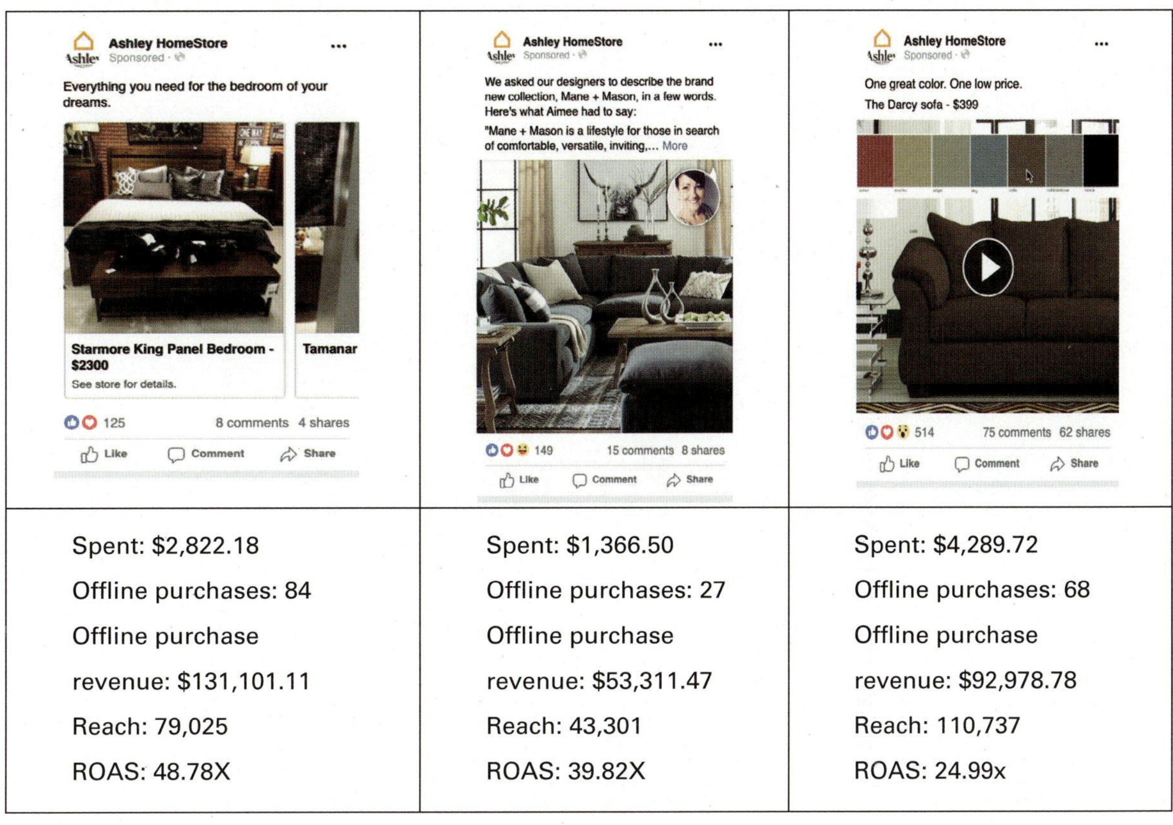

Spent: $2,822.18 Offline purchases: 84 Offline purchase revenue: $131,101.11 Reach: 79,025 ROAS: 48.78X	Spent: $1,366.50 Offline purchases: 27 Offline purchase revenue: $53,311.47 Reach: 43,301 ROAS: 39.82X	Spent: $4,289.72 Offline purchases: 68 Offline purchase revenue: $92,978.78 Reach: 110,737 ROAS: 24.99x

FIGURE 12.18 . Dashboard 4

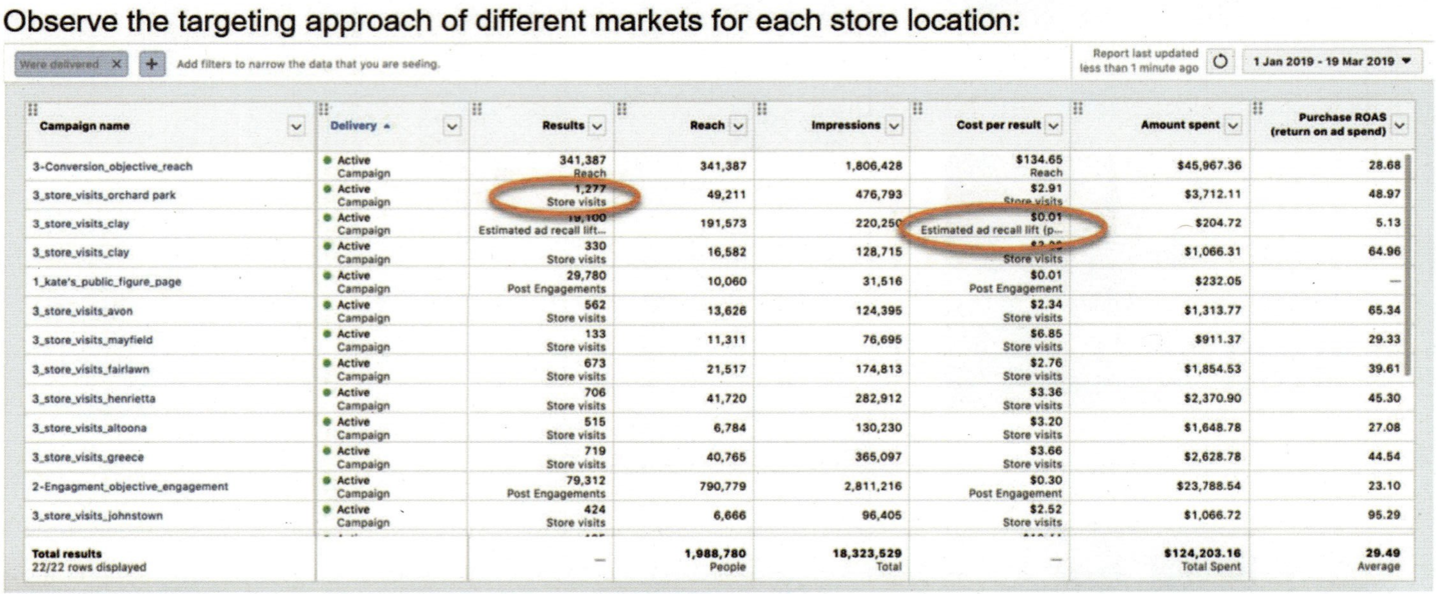

Observe the targeting approach of different markets for each store location:

Were delivered × + Add filters to narrow the data that you are seeing.

Report last updated less than 1 minute ago | 1 Jan 2019 - 19 Mar 2019

Campaign name	Delivery	Results	Reach	Impressions	Cost per result	Amount spent	Purchase ROAS (return on ad spend)
3-Conversion_objective_reach	Active Campaign	341,387 Reach	341,387	1,806,428	$134.65 Reach	$45,967.36	28.68
3_store_visits_orchard park	Active Campaign	1,277 Store visits	49,211	476,793	$2.91 Store visits	$3,712.11	48.97
3_store_visits_clay	Active Campaign	19,100 Estimated ad recall lift...	191,573	220,250	$0.01 Estimated ad recall lift (p...	$204.72	5.13
3_store_visits_clay	Active Campaign	330 Store visits	16,582	128,715	[illegible] Store visits	$1,066.31	64.96
1_kate's_public_figure_page	Active Campaign	29,780 Post Engagements	10,060	31,516	$0.01 Post Engagement	$232.05	—
3_store_visits_avon	Active Campaign	562 Store visits	13,626	124,395	$2.34 Store visits	$1,313.77	65.34
3_store_visits_mayfield	Active Campaign	133 Store visits	11,311	76,695	$6.85 Store visits	$911.37	29.33
3_store_visits_fairlawn	Active Campaign	673 Store visits	21,517	174,813	$2.76 Store visits	$1,854.53	39.61
3_store_visits_henrietta	Active Campaign	706 Store visits	41,720	282,912	$3.36 Store visits	$2,370.90	45.30
3_store_visits_altoona	Active Campaign	515 Store visits	6,784	130,230	$3.20 Store visits	$1,648.78	27.08
3_store_visits_greece	Active Campaign	719 Store visits	40,765	365,097	$3.66 Store visits	$2,628.78	44.54
2-Engagment_objective_engagement	Active Campaign	79,312 Post Engagements	790,779	2,811,216	$0.30 Post Engagement	$23,788.54	23.10
3_store_visits_johnstown	Active Campaign	424 Store visits	6,666	96,405	$2.52 Store visits	$1,066.72	95.29
Total results 22/22 rows displayed		—	**1,988,780** People	**18,323,529** Total	—	**$124,203.16** Total Spent	**29.49** Average

The second row in dashboard 4 (Figure 12.18) shows the conversion campaign named '3_store_visitrs_orchard_park' reached 49,211 people, who saw any of the conversion ads in their stream on average, 9.7 times (calculated by dividing 476,793 ad impressions by the number of viewers reached 49,211). This generated 1,277 store visits from people living in the Orchard Park area and who saw the stage 3 video.

The 'Store Visit Orchard Park' video ad cost ('amount spent' column 7) $3,712.11 and generated 1,277 visits at a cost per visit of $2.91 (column 6).

Budget

Budget figures were unavailable at the time of publishing.

Summary and conclusion

With the right sequenced content advertising strategy, Q1 2019 results showed ROAS 29.49, which means a total ad spend of $124,203 delivered $3,662,751 sales (dashboard 4). Some of the individual ROAS were as high as 49x (dashboard 3c).

'By following BlitzMetrics' social amplification engine, we were able to drastically reduce our out-of-pocket marketing dollars while simultaneously enjoying exponential growth in metrics that mattered,' said Ashley HomeStore's Michael Melaro. 'Proving return on our investment has been easy, as we now see digital marketing through an intelligent funnel process, quantifying a winning ROAS and cost-per-store-visit. Partnering with BlitzMetrics has been one of our best decisions ever!'

CASE STUDY PPC ads boost ROI: Cover My Cab

The situation

Cover My Cab has more than 30 years' experience providing specialist insurance products to taxi drivers, fleet owners and taxi operators. The brand is part of J&M Insurance, a 'business-to-business' insurance firm that has served the taxi industry for longer than any other specialist broker.

ClickThrough Marketing began working with Cover My Cab in April helping to manage and optimize its PPC campaigns.

The challenge

After four months working on Cover My Cab's paid search campaigns, results were good. However, ClickThrough suspected more gains could be made by opening the monthly budget caps (ie removing the daily cap or monthly budget) and opting, instead, for an 'always on' PPC strategy, to get 24/7 visibility (since users search 24/7).

Ian Boyden, Paid Search Manager, says:

> The risk with capping your spend is that you could 'go dark' too early in the day. In other words, your ads stop appearing because you've spent your allocated budget, but your audience may well still be searching for your services. You might even find that you're missing out on peak search activity by capping budgets.

When optimizing a Google AdWords account it is always worth seeing what impression share each of your campaigns has. There are two types of impression shares:

- *Impression share lost to budget.* This is the percentage of time your ads weren't shown on Google due to insufficient budget.
- *Impression share lost to rank.* The percentage of time your ads weren't shown on Google due to a low position in the AdWords auction.

ClickThrough used their proprietary forecasting tool to perform a deep-dive analysis of Cover My Cab's AdWords account.

The tool showed that the account had around 5 per cent impression share lost to budget in August. It forecasted that if budget caps were removed so there were no impressions lost to budget, Cover My Cab could have spent approximately 11 per cent more and seen conversions increase by 11 per cent also. This analytic forecasting tool suggested that by switching to 'always

TABLE 12.1 Analysis of Cover My Cab's AdWords account

Metric	Current Performance	Performance with Open Caps (0% Imp Share Lost to Budget)	Delta Change	% Change
Imp.	200,000	210,000	10,000	5.00%
Clicks	16,000	16,800	800	5.00%
CTR	8.00%	8.00%	0.00%	0.00%
Conv.	1,000.00	1,110.00	110.00	11.00%
Cost	£25,000.00	£27,650.00	£2,650.00	10.60%
Cost/Conv.	£25.00	£24.91	–£0.09	–0.36%
Cost. Rate	6.25%	6.61%	0.36%	5.71%
Avg. CPC	£1.56	£1.56	£0.00	0.00%

SOURCE: ClickThrough Agency
NOTE: Forecasted results by changing from a budget cap to 'always on' campaign

on' ClickThrough could generate (or deliver) an extra 10,000 impressions, which could generate an extra 800 visitors of whom 110 will convert, reducing the cost per conversion from £25 to £24.91.

Objectives

To reduce conversion costs below £25 and boost sales/conversions beyond previous months' (exact numbers are not available).

Strategy

Remove the budget cap and become 'always on'. Because the spend increase meant increasing the daily budget caps rather than pushing the position of the keywords up through the maximum cost per click they were willing to pay, Cover My Cab would not pay any more per click – as they would if they were jostling for higher positions. The tool showed simply and effectively how gains could be made by raising budget to allow the client to be visible 24 hours a day.

Tactics

ClickThrough's Paid Search Executive Dave Earnshaw said:

> This might sound like a simple thing, but many clients we take on have a limited budget and are worried about overspending. Ian created this tactical tool to show clients in a clear and simple way how they could improve their number of leads, and still remain within their cost-per-lead target without the risk of wasting budget.

ClickThrough presented the findings to Cover My Cab, who agreed to trial this new approach and raise the budget for the next month.

Actions

Removing the budget cap and becoming 'always on' was easy to execute. In fact it was set up in minutes, with no additional bid management or optimization. No additional costs or time were required.

The results (control)

In September, Cover My Cab spent 24 per cent more on clicks, and saw:

- the number of conversions increase by 25 per cent;
- the number of clicks increase by 23 per cent;
- cost per conversion decrease to £24.72.

TABLE 12.2 Actual results after starting 'always on'

Month	August	September	Difference
Imp.	200,000	250,000	25.00%
Clicks	16,000	19,680	23.00%
CTR	8.00%	7.87%	–1.60%
Conv.	1,000.00	1.254.00	25.40%
Cost	£25,000.00	£31,000.00	24.00%
Cost/Conv.	£25.00	£24.72	–1.12%
Conv. Rate	6.25%	6.37%	1.95%
Avg. Pos	3.49	3.00	–14.15%
Avg. CPC	£1.56	£1.58	0.81%

Cover My Cab were very pleased with the results and have since decided to be 'always on' (although they monitor it closely). Meanwhile, ClickThrough's Ian Boyden says:

> The next time you see impressions lost to budget, we recommend opening up the budget as you may be restricting additional volume of traffic and conversions. We recommend an 'always on' strategy with PPC, and if you find your account is spending too much then you should reduce CPCs until you see spend hit your target.

CASE STUDY Location-based ads: Managing a campaign

When managing a LBA campaign, it is probably easiest for most marketers to use expert companies in the field, eg use a data-driven programmatic, ad-buying solutions company, like Blis (who are advanced location data tech experts). To work with these kinds of solutions companies, marketers must understand:

- location-based target markets, publishers, advertisers;
- demand-side platform (DSP) exchanges, supply-side partners (SSPs) and advertisers;
- layered data, additional insights and programmatic ad buying solutions;
- data flows, bids and ads;
- unique identifiers;
- tracking visitors.

Location-based target markets, publishers, advertisers

If you, a consumer, are browsing via your mobile (or tablet) and you click onto the sports page of the *Guardian* newspaper online, a ping (it's called a bid impression/bid stream) is sent from the publisher (the *Guardian*) to an online ad network. This effectively announces 'a viewer is looking at the sports page on the *Guardian*' and invites bids (in real time, ie right now) from advertisers (or their agencies) to serve an ad to this consumer (say car intenders/buyers). Marketers can see what the viewer is looking at, at that time, via the bid impression (if they work with the right supply-side partners). They can also cross-reference that device ID into their own database and see what that person generally looks at/has looked at in the past and where they usually go location-wise.

Demand-side platform

The advertisers gain access to buying this impression and then have an ad served via a DSP, which is offered by providers like Blis.

Supply-side partner

Site owners and app owners are called publishers, since they publish the site or the app that can host ads. Some sites (like newspapers or news stations) offer their ad space inventory to advertisers as their main source of revenue. So these ad exchanges are serious business. To participate in the ad network, the publishers sign up as an SSP.

Advertisers

Brands seek to get in front of their prospective customers (and even their existing customers and sometimes their competitors' customers), ideally when that customer is either already aware of the brand and/or is moving towards making a purchase. This is where location-based marketing can deliver much more relevant ads to customers by targeting only those customers whose behaviour has already expressed an interest in the product or service by either visiting a physical location (in the real offline world) and/or visiting a website or app online. Brand advertisers access the DSP, while SSPs are the publishers (websites and/or apps) that provide data and the ad space (or ad inventory).

Layered data and additional target market insights

Data companies like Experian can delve into their databases to reveal additional insights about target markets. No names are given. It is hashed anonymized data. Experian can reveal if there are people in the postcode area that you have geo-fenced that have applied for a credit card. This data could be used to target a credit card ad that may be useful to them to help them buy, say, a new baby buggy.

Data-driven, programmatic, ad-buying solutions companies like Blis help advertisers. They can ask Experian: 'We are looking at these postal codes for people interested in mortgages. Have you got any information on people looking for mortgages in that geographical area?' They might deliver aggregated anonymized data (not individual information) which gives an insight; for example they may reveal that there are approximately 8,000 people looking for mortgages in a particular area where previously Blis were only targeting, say, 1,000 mortgage customers.

They can identify the number of people in a postcode who have recently had 'mortgages in principle' enquiries made on their credit file; in other words, people who have applied for mortgages already. Blis could start to look at other people that they haven't yet targeted, in addition to that original target group. Blis would then delve into their own database to look at browsing histories of other devices in that area. The target audience might grow from 1,000 to 3,000 based on the Experian data.

Experian basically deliver insights into the target market. They can provide information on ABC1s in a particular area. Some of that information might include a postcode, in which case Blis can start looking at residential IP addresses on that postcode. And then they can start seeing devices that are attached to that IP address. And then they can start to see the devices when they are leaving the home. This is just another way of developing behavioural location user IDs. Blis can get a residential IP address once their potential customers connect via wifi.

Data flow, bids and ads

Location-based marketers continually collect data. If your apps or your social media platforms are 'location enabled', your device location can be detected via the information passed back to the exchange from the publisher (the website) and sometimes via GPS. However, exchanges/SSPs often 'wrap up' very basic estimated location data into GPS lat/longs and try to sell it on. This is where some specialist agencies clean and filter the data so that only precise data (lat/longs with five decimal points of accuracy) gets used as the user passes locations such as football stadia, hotels and tube stations. This creates a footprint of where you have physically travelled in the real world over the last two months (if the device ID is in a particular database and, if the device, at that time, is using either apps or visiting websites that subscribe to the SSP Ad Network).

Unique identifiers

A unique identifier is added to each device IP. A brief history of where you physically went in the offline world plus where you have visited online can be added to the unique identifier. This data can be used to infer your gender, age and interests; for example, if you visited Mothercare and young women's fashion sites, it will infer

FIGURE 12.19 Blis location demographics audience

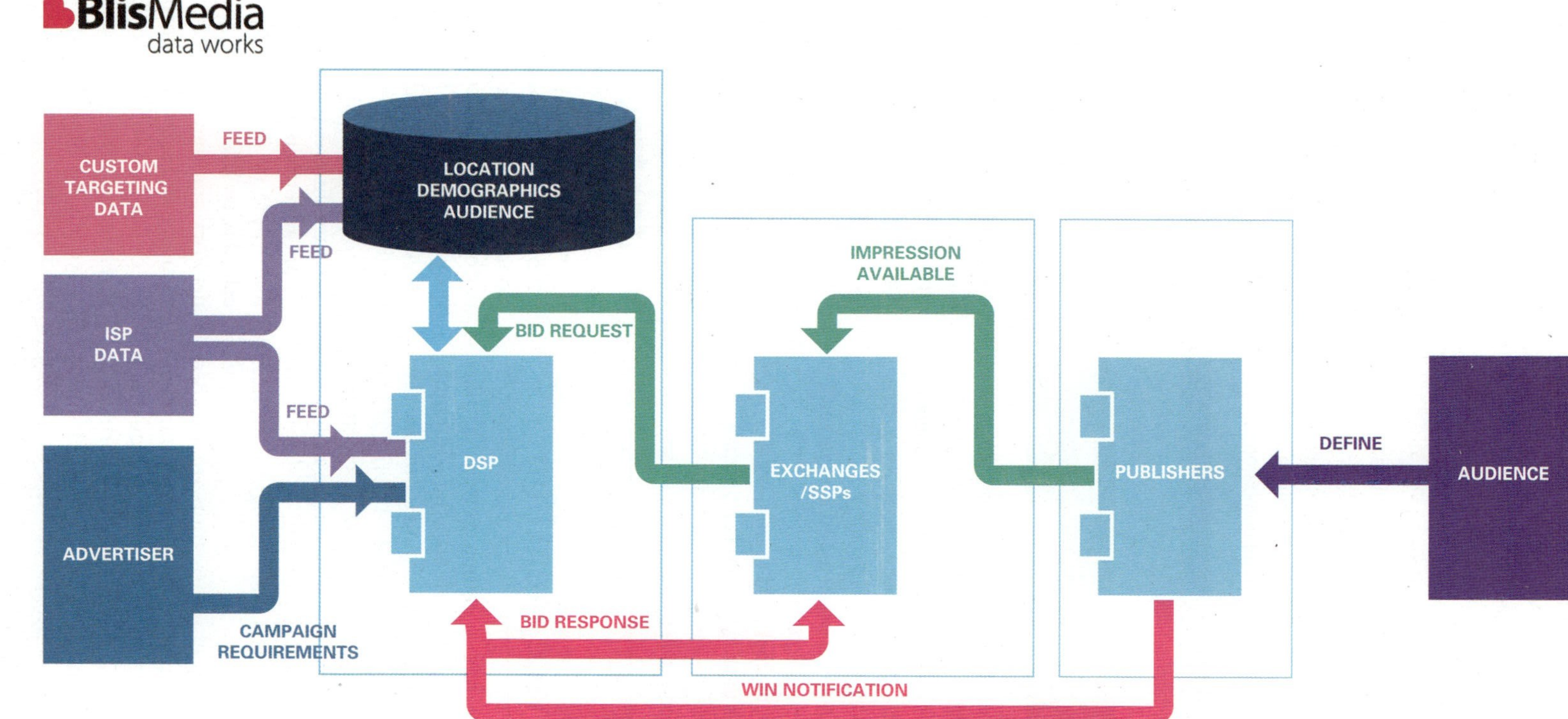

SOURCE: Blis

you are a young mother (or about to become a young mother). But cross-referencing with other data could actually reveal that this particular user is actually a young father so the ads served would be different. Agencies can also layer additional data, for example from Experian or the DVLA databases.

If a user is logged onto a BMW wifi point in a dealership, they may be in the research mode or actual purchase stage. Their level of interest can be identified from their click behaviour (or digital body language). Location and demographic data can be combined to define digital audiences, and then tightly targeted display ads can be served (via real-time bidding) to users across mobile, tablet and laptop.

So they can serve timely geo-location offers to individuals in a retailer or in a supermarket. For example, McDonald's can target people within five metres of a location. They can also then link the device footprint (where else the device owner physically walked, eg to Ladbrokes to place a bet and took a bus home). They can also layer on additional data.

Advertising is now as much about Maths Men as Mad Men

'Advertising is now as much about Maths Men as Mad Men' says WPP ad supremo Sir Martin Sorrell. (Note: *Mad Men* is an AMC television series about advertising agencies in the 1950s.)

You can see why ad agencies employ mathematicians (many of whom previously worked in the City developing algorithms to optimize the buying and selling of stocks and shares in real time). Their USP is the way they crunch the data, which is gathered from various partners such as wifi networks, supply-side platforms and so on.

Unique device identifier

Each smart phone has a unique device identifier (UDID), which is a sequence of 40 letters and numbers that is specific to each device and looks like this: 2b6f0cc904d137be2e1730235f5664094b831186. This unique device address/identifier is created by the manufacturer. When you turn on the device the software creates a device ID or IDFA (identity for advertising) so publishers can recognize devices when they connect.

About 16–24 pieces of information are attached in the 'bid stream' (which is a bid request announcing that an ad impression is available for auction) from the publisher, via the exchange. Information within the bid request includes minimum price CPM, lat/long data and gender and the device ID, for example. This piece of information gives the bidder location and content behavioural data so they can decide on the amount of their bid.

Blis uses the same device ID that the phone software creates when you turn it on to create a tracking device ID, as the identifier (or tag) it uses to store that device profile in their database. Mobile web cookies are what the publisher drops into the device browser to understand what kind of content they are using. Device IDs are not passed through the exchanges when the user is on mobile web – only when they are using apps. The mobile web cookies last for a month and then delete themselves.

Visitor tracking

If you are (a) using public wifi, (b) using an app, or (c) browsing a website, after asking your permission, each device lodges a bit of code or a user ID (websites call them cookies) invisibly onto the user's browser (or app). The device ID is sometimes also called a user ID and is used as a unique identifier, which allows marketers to create groups of devices/users (or segments) so that they can, for example, compare different groups' behaviour after exposure to an advertising campaign. Device manufacturers like Apple or Samsung/Android/Google have specific device IDs but only they can see those on the network and they are used for their own mobile advertising and app store purposes. Note: cookies are for desktops. Mobiles use the term 'user IDs'.

Here are three micro-case examples of location-based ads for Mini, Gillette and Thomson Holidays, followed by some mini-case examples of advertising.

CASE STUDY Behavioural mapping: Mini Countryman car (micro-case)

Mini used behavioural mapping to raise awareness and engagement (brochure downloads and boosting the number of test drives) for two new models, the Mini Countryman and the Mini Paceman.

Through behaviour mapping and/or IP location, Mini served ads in real time to ABC1 device owners who were visiting: 4/5 star hotels; Michelin-starred restaurants; business-class lounges in airports; or who were in proximity to a Mini dealership, or in a competitor dealership. It took two days to set this up. The £20,000 campaign ran for five weeks and delivered the following results:

- Average campaign click-through rate (CTR): 0.55 per cent (industry benchmark CTR 0.5 per cent).
- Average daily impressions: 160,843.
- Mini Paceman ads delivered greater volume impressions (63 per cent) but Countryman ads delivered better CTR (0.60 per cent).
- iOS out-performed Android on device OS CTR: 0.97 per cent vs 0.75 per cent.
- CTR peaked at mid-morning (10:00), mid-afternoon (14:00) and immediately after work (17:00) – break periods and commuting times.
- CPM (or cost per thousand – CPT) was between £5 and £8.

FIGURE 12.20 Selection of Mini ads

SOURCE: Blis

CASE STUDY LBA rich media ads using weather data: Gillette (micro-case)

Blis were asked by Gillette to deliver rich media ads incorporating dynamic weather information to identify female mobile users in the designated age range across the UK.

The immediate results showed an uplift of more than 10 per cent who identified Gillette Venus as a trusted brand and an 11 per cent-plus uplift in those who thought it was a brand for people like them.

FIGURE 12.21 Gillette ad with dynamic weather information

SOURCE: Blis

CASE STUDY LBA remarketing ads and OOH billboards: Thomson Holidays (micro-case)

Blis were asked by Thomson Holidays to increase footfall (traffic into their stores). Using Path (a retargeting solution) and footfall attribution (measures footfall in a location related to an ad) they helped Thomson combine remarketing and OOH (out of home) billboards. By comparing a control group against a group served with the ads they tracked path

FIGURE 12.22 Thomson remarketing ad

SOURCE: Blis

activity through to store footfall up to seven days later.

They delivered an increase in store footfall. Ads served in OOH sites: 121 per cent uplift; previous travel site or app users, 135 per cent uplift; Thomson store visitors, 138 per cent uplift.

This subsequently helped to reallocate budget more efficiently.

CASE STUDY Viral TV ad reduces road deaths: DOE

The situation

Since 2000, speeding in Northern Ireland has killed the equivalent of a classroom of children. Every increase in speed increases the risk of death. Research shows that just a 5 per cent increase in average speed increases the risk of serious injuries by over 15 per cent and road deaths by over 20 per cent.

Although 'speeding' is understood to be dangerous, there is a gap between the reality of what speeding is and how drivers interpret their own behaviour:

- Drivers perceive that they engage in safe speeding.
- They go over the limit but are in 'full control'.
- Seen as different to the type of speeding that results in serious collisions. They choose their speed not by

what the law dictates, but by their own feeling of safety, how in control they feel.

- They go over the limit particularly on rural roads/motorways.
- Feeling that in 30mph zones there is a reason for the limit, but on faster roads this reason is lacking.
- Much more likely to stick to speed limits in urban areas.

Drivers underplay the consequences of speeding, believing that they will not be as serious as people make out and that it will never happen to them anyway. Speeding is enjoyable and pleasurable, with many drivers even showing the classic signs of addiction.

There is an increasing belief that speeding is acceptable, almost normal, and that it is common to everyone.

Objectives

To propel speeding to the forefront of the public's mental agenda and to reduce speeding and road deaths caused by speeding.

Strategy (message strategy)

- To propel speeding to the forefront of the public's mental agenda by disrupting and challenging false perceptions through deep emotional engagement of road users as to the truly horrifying consequences of speeding.
- Targeting drivers responsible for speed-related collisions in which a person is killed or seriously injured: (a) males 17–24; (b) males 25–34; (c) females 17–24.
- Media strategy: campaign in TV, cinema and digital.

Tactics

Create an intensely shocking 60-second ad and buy 1,200 TV ratings.

Action

Focus groups were used to find what would motivate speeding drivers to slow down. During the intense

FIGURE 12.23 DOE road safety classroom

FIGURE 12.24 An intensely shocking 60-second ad to promote road safety

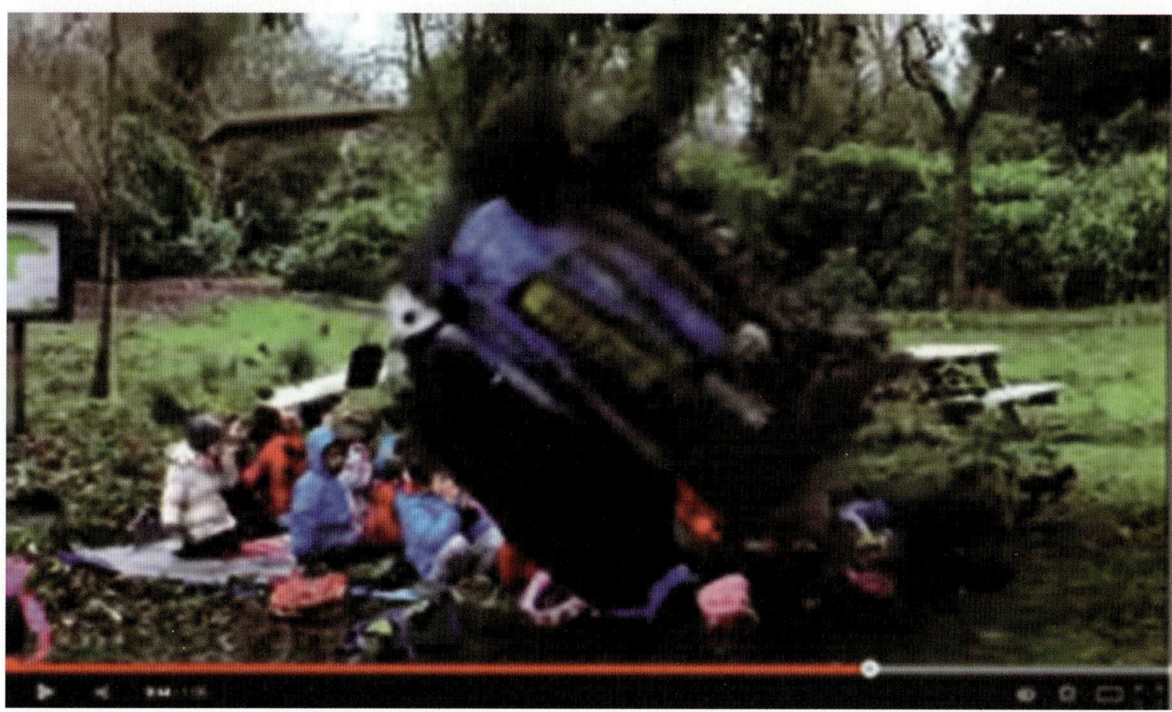

research carried out by ad agency Lyle Bailie focus groups revealed that 'speeders' feel it is their right to drive at whatever speed they want. They won't change this for anything. 'What about if you killed someone?' No this would not stop them. 'What about if you killed a child?' A resounding silence. A possible angle! The idea was born.

This research opened up a potential creative strategy. How can we challenge these misperceived beliefs?

Drivers understand that travelling at speed means that they are less able to react to unexpected events. However, they enjoy speed and believe that they are safe and in control when speeding. The natural response to cognitive dissonance is to reduce it by changing one of the beliefs/behaviours. The problem is that rather than reducing speed, drivers are instead using false rationalization, misattributing the consequences of speed to other factors. Individuals have become more sophisticated at rationalization and can now rationalize factors that were previously disrupting.

A deeply emotional approach is vital to disrupt this rationalization, to create a discomfort that can only be reduced by changing speeding behaviour. 'The temptation with unexpected events is to attribute blame to the unexpected event or to state that any speed level would have the same effect. The strongly felt exception to this is when a young (and therefore innocent) child is involved – the moderating influence of the child cannot be underestimated here.' This was without exception across all of the groups.

Children are powerless, and as drivers we feel a responsibility for their safety. It is our human nature to protect children. The thought of hurting a child is universally horrifying and is the most powerful trigger for challenging misperceptions.

Action (ad roll out)

The 60-second advertisement was first shown on a Tuesday night during a programme called *Dentist*, with no social media reaction. It was shown again at half time during an England vs Uruguay football game (19 June). It immediately received 7,000 YouTube hits. By the next morning there were 23,000 hits; and 53,000 by the end of the day. Four days later there had been 2.2 million views. Further results are shown here:

- ad shown Tues 17 June during *Dentist* – no reaction;
- played again at half time during England vs Uruguay game 19 June, generated 7,000 YouTube views;
- 20 June 11am 23,000 YouTube views;
- 20 June midnight 53,000 YouTube views;
- 24 June 2,200,000 YouTube views;
- 1 July 4,000,000 YouTube views.

Control

The cost of a road death is £1.43 million (Oxford Economics, 2012). This figure is taken from the Department for Transport Highways Economic Note No.1 (2005), and is made up of lost output, human costs and medical and ambulance costs.

You can see the ad link in the online resource pack for this book.

Note: Another road safety themed campaign from the RSA (Road Safety Authority), which uses a virtual reality video experience, is discussed on p 531.

Advantages and disadvantages of advertising

Here are some of the advantages and disadvantages to consider when deciding whether to increase or reduce advertising as a communications tool.

Advantages

Advertising informs, persuades and reminds. It is great at getting messages out to large audiences quickly. Unlike PR or social media, advertisers can control their own message (assuming it is within the regulations). Today, there are media vehicles (magazines and TV programmes) that target niche audiences. And, of course, PPC ads can now be tailored to audiences with particular interests. Location-based advertising takes this a stage further. Advertising is good for building awareness (and growing brands) and now with clever campaigns like Ashleys can move customers right through to closing the sale. On a CPT basis it can be quite effective.

Disadvantages

Message credibility is less than that of PR or social media, as it is seen as 'advertising trying to sell something', though credibility can be enhanced by source credibility. Some media advertising, such as TV ads, have a long lead time if changes are required. Such advertising also requires relatively large budgets for creating the ads. (Note that PPC ads can be small and flexible, and ads can be changed within minutes). Advertising is less engaging than social media or an interactive website, although some ads now seek to change this, as they integrate with social media. It can be difficult to cut through the communications clutter; however, creative ads, personalized ads and timely personalized videos are coming to you very soon.

One final warning: The hidden Web damages advertising

Advertising must be:

> Legal, decent, honest and truthful.
>
> Advertising Standards Authority (UK)

The Brexit advertising campaign on Facebook is explored in a 2019 TED Talk by Welsh journalist Carole Cadwalladr who said, 'Multiple crimes took place during the referendum. And they took place on Facebook.'

During her presentation, titled 'Facebook's Role in Brexit – and the Threat to Democracy', she gives examples highlighting just some of the various series of advertisements which ran throughout the campaign. One advertisement, containing disinformation (alleged spreading of hate and fear), consists of a world map and poses the question 'Turkey has a population of 76 million. Turkey is joining the EU. Good idea???' (view the advert at **https://prsmith.org/blog/**). Similar advertisements focus on Macedonia, Albania, Montenegro and Serbia. The advertisements variously show world maps with money flowing out of the UK, demonstrated with arrows, and people flowing in. This particular series alternatively calls out the population levels of these countries or compares factors such as average annual wage. All prompt a yes/no answer or a call to action which appears as an 'I agree' button. Another such advertisement by Leave.EU features highlighted text reading 'European Commission report admits Turkish visa-free travel will "increase mobility of criminals and terrorists" within the EU' over a stylized image representing terrorism (view the advert at **https://prsmith.org/blog/**).

Ms Cadwalladr describes the difficulty she had in trying to find evidence of the advertisements on Facebook, which fuelled her investigation. Her and her colleagues' findings were published in *The Observer*.

The UK Parliament forced Facebook to hand over the ads used in the Brexit campaign (which prior to this were 'dark' or hidden from the scrutiny of regulators and the general public) – these are now viewable on the government's DCMS website (see references).

Ms Cadwalladr highlighted:

- illicit use of data (harvesting the profiles of people from Facebook);
- illegal funding (illegal use of cash funding the ad campaign and unknown funds source);
- disinformation (factually incorrect statements or 'lies' in the ads, eg Turkey's 76 million people are joining the EU. Turkey is not joining the EU).

The principles of the UK advertising regulators (see p 301) appear to have been broken. Advertisements must be legal, decent, honest and truthful. The Brexit campaign breaches of these regulations not only damage the advertising, marketing and data industries' credibility but have also damaged democracy, perhaps permanently.

See the 15-minute talk by PR Smith (2019) 'Marketing gone wrong: Is the Dark Web worse than subliminal seduction?' at **https://prsmith.org/blog/** or visit **http://tedtalk.com/**

Key points from Chapter 12

- Advertising is changing faster than all other communications tools.
- Data-driven advertising uses a variety of new targeting tools, including remarketing and location-based advertising.
- Creativity (in message and media planning) is required to break through the clutter.
- Advertising needs to be integrated with social media and other marcomms tools.
- Advertising must be legal, decent, honest and truthful.

> 'Advertisements are now so numerous that they are very negligently perused.'
>
> Samuel Johnson published this in issue 40 of his magazine *The Idler*, on 20 January 1759

References and further reading

Aaker, D and Myers, J (1987) *Advertising Management*, 3rd edn, Prentice Hall International, Englewood Cliffs, NJ

Advertising Age (1999) The advertising century, 29 March

Belch, G and Belch, M (2001) *Advertising and Promotion: An integrated marketing communications perspective*, 6th edn, McGraw-Hill, London

Benady, A (2014) The 20th World Cup: social media strategies and brand war rooms, *PR Week*, 10 June

Bradshaw, P (2010) Coke sees 'phenomenal' result from Twitter ads, *FT.com*, 25 June

Brannan, T (1998) *A Practical Guide to Integrated Marketing Communications*, Kogan Page, London

Broadbent, S (1994) *The Advertising Budget*, Admap Publications, London

Cadwalladr, C (2019) Facebook's role in Brexit — and the threat to democracy, TED 2019

Caples, J (1932) *Tested Advertising Methods*, Harper Brothers

Cowley, D (ed) (1989) *How to Plan Advertising*, Cassell in association with The Account Planning Group, London

Dalton, J (2013) 24.1 million Tweets posted during Super Bowl XLVII, *Media Matters*, 5 February

Daye, D and VanAuken, B (2008) Great Moments in Copywriting: Ogilvy and the Beggar, *BrandingStrategy.com*, 17 January

DCMS (Department of Culture, Media and Sport website) is a UK government website – search for 'Facebook Ads' or https://beta.parliament.uk/search?q=facebook+ads (archived at https://perma.cc/33QF-L3VK)

Delo, C (2012) Microsoft Files Patent to Serve Ads Based on Mood, Body Language, *Ad Age Digital*, 12 June

Dempsey, S. (2018) Three lessons from P&G's frugality, *Sunday Independent*, 11 March

Douglas, T (1987) *The Complete Guide to Advertising*, Pan Macmillan, London

Dwek, R (1997) Who's got the net by the eyeballs?, *Revolution*, October

Ehrenberg, A (1974) Repetitive advertising and the consumer, *Journal of Advertising Research*, **14** (2), pp 25–34

eMarketer (2015) UK to achieve world first as half of media ad spend goes digital, *eMarketer*, 27 March

Fanning, J (1997) Is the end of advertising really all that nigh? *Irish Marketing Review*, Marketing Institute, Ireland

Fletcher, N (2018) Netflix buys LA billboards: What does it mean?

Hampp, A and Bryson York, E (2010) Singer's manager dishes on all those product-placement deals (and lack thereof) in the nine-minute video, *Ad Age*, 13 March

Hart, A and O'Connor, J (1990) *The Practice of Advertising*, 3rd edn, Heinemann, London

Heine, C (2015) Daily Mail Invests $3 Million in Native Partner Taboola, *Daily Mail*, 4 June

Howell Henry Chaldecott Lury and Partners (HHCL) (1997) *Marketing at a Point of Change*, HHCL, London

Jones, H (2008) Gorilla tactics, *Marketer*, May

Kennedy, J (2009a) App-fab, *Marketing Age*, November

Kennedy, J (2009b) A wave of optimism: Interview with Eric Schmidt, *Marketing Age*, **3** (6), November/December

Kohler, E (2007) Hyperlocal is more about ads than news, *Technology Evangelist*, 9 August

Learmonth, M and Bryson York, E (2010) Facebook poised to take geo-networking mainstream, *Ad Age*, 10 May

McKenna, R (1991) Marketing is everything, *Harvard Business Review*, January–February

Newberry, C (2019) The Facebook pixel: What it is and how to use it, *Hootsuite,* 14 January

O'Neill, M (2010) Budweiser celebrates the World Cup with Bud House reality series, *Social Times*, 14 June

Oxford Economics (2012) Economic payback of road safety advertising in Northern Ireland, commissioned by Lyle Bailie

Parekh, R (2010) Why long-form ads are the wave of the future, *Advertising Age*, 3 May

Patel, K (2010) Will growing crop of TV apps engage viewers, advertisers? *Ad Age*, 17 May

Percy, L, Rossiter, J R and Elliott, R (2002) *Strategic Advertising Management*, Oxford University Press, Oxford

Pulizzi, J (2014a) The ultimate guide to native advertising, *LinkedIn Pulse*, 7 January

Pulizzi, J (2014b) Hey WSJ – content marketing is not native advertising, *Content Marketing Institute*, 6 November

Ranger, S (2014a) Virgin Atlantic tests Apple's iBeacon at Heathrow, *ZDNet*, 1 May

Ranger, S (2014b) What is Apple iBeacon? Here's what you need to know, *ZDNet*, 10 June

Roberts, K (2010) Creativity, *KRconnectblogspot.com*, 21 January

Roderick, L (2016) Why P&G is moving away from targeted Facebook advertising, *Marketing Week*, 10 August

Schmidt, E (2009) A wave of optimism, *Marketing Age*, 3 (6), November/December

Shields, R (2015) The case for big brands taking ad tech in-house, *Exchange Wire*, 6 May

Slaughter, S (2014) The success of native advertising hinges on earning readers' trust, *AdWeek*, 26 August

Smith, PR (2014) Research-driven shock ad uses magic formula and goes viral [online] http://prsmith.org/blog/ (archived at https://perma.cc/3XZ4-MTP5), 23 August

Smith, PR (2015) The rise and fall of owned, earned but not paid media [online] http://prsmith.org/blog/ (archived at https://perma.cc/3XZ4-MTP5), 27 June

Smith, PR (2015) The SOSTAC® Guide to writing your perfect digital marketing plan [online] http://prsmith.org/SOSTAC/ (archived at https://perma.cc/MWF6-Y2TT)

Smith, PR (2019) Marketing Gone Wrong: Is the dark web worse than subliminal seduction? [online] http://prsmith.org/blog/ (archived at https://perma.cc/3XZ4-MTP5), 3 May

Smith, PR, Berry, C and Pulford, A (2000) *Strategic Marketing Communications*, 2nd edn, Kogan Page, London

Sorrell, M (1996) Beans and pearls, D&AD president's lecture

Straz, M (2012) The remarkable rise of retargeting, *Online Spin*, *Media Post*, 22 October

Weinreich, L (2001) *11 Steps to Brand Heaven*, Kogan Page, London

Whatmough, D (2010) Facebook threat, *PR Week*, 19 March

Further information

Advertising Standards Authority Limited (ASA)
Castle House
37–45 Paul Street
London EC2A 4LS
Tel: +44 (0)20 7492 2222
www.asa.org.uk

Committee of Advertising Practice (CAP)
Castle House
37–45 Paul Street
London EC2A 4LS
Tel: + 44 (0)20 7492 2222
www.asa.org.uk

Incorporated Society of British Advertisers (ISBA)
12 Henrietta Street
London WC2E 8LH
Tel: +44(0)20 7291 9020
www.isba.org.uk

Institute of Practitioners in Advertising (IPA)
44 Belgrave Square
London SW1X 8QS
Tel: +44 (0)20 7235 7020
www.ipa.co.uk

Ofcom
Riverside House
2a Southwark Bridge Road
London SE1 9HA
Tel: +44 (0)300 123 3000
www.ofcom.org.uk

13 Publicity and public relations

LEARNING OBJECTIVES

By the end of this chapter you will be able to:

- understand how PR is changing and the expanding range of PR tools;
- appreciate the potential for integration with social media and other marketing communications tools;
- plan an outline PR campaign knowing the advantages and disadvantages of PR tools.

Introduction

Positive publicity nurtures good relationships with the media (media relations). This is only one of the responsibilities of public relations, as it deals with a range of different 'publics' or stakeholders. Public relations integrates with public affairs, corporate affairs, community affairs, community relations, corporate relations and corporate communications. The first part of this chapter explores what exactly PR is and where it fits with marketing; then it examines various PR tools and finally the advantages and disadvantages of PR over other marcomms tools. The golden rule, 'Develop credibility before raising visibility', underpins this chapter.

What is PR?

Public relations is regularly, and sometimes worryingly, referred to as 'PR', which is often confused with 'press releases' or 'press relations'. These are, in fact, only a part of real public relations. **A simple definition of public relations is: 'the development of and maintenance of good relationships with different publics'.** The publics are the range of different groups on which an organization is dependent. These include employees, investors, suppliers, customers, distributors, legislators, regulators, governments, pressure groups, the community, the media and even the competition. Most of these groups have different (sometimes conflicting) interests in any particular organization. The UK's Institute of Public Relations (IPR) uses the following public relations definition: 'the planned and sustained effort to establish and maintain goodwill and mutual understanding between an organization and its publics'. In 1978 in Mexico, the World Assembly of PR Associations agreed what is now known as the 'Mexican statement': 'PR practice is the art and science of analysing trends, predicting their consequences, counselling organization leaders and implementing planned programmes of action that will serve both the organization's and the public interest.'

Public relations and marketing

While marketing traditionally focuses on markets or just three of the publics, ie customers, distributors (the 'trade') and the competition, public relations is concerned with many more publics. Add in the emergence of globalism (eg websites are viewed around the world), increased media interest (including social media) in business, new investor criteria (eg ethical policies), more effective pressure groups, information-hungry customers and the constant search for cost-effective communications tools, and you can soon see why PR has grown in importance. The new understanding of the power of PR is demonstrated when business analysts suggest that both management and trade unions, before embarking on a dispute, now ask: 'How will this play in the media?'

Some organizations insist on public relations, advertising, direct mail people and sales promotion people sitting in together on various project meetings so that they cross-fertilize ideas and create synergy through integrating the marketing communications at an early stage.

The death of PR?

When the Editor in Chief of UK's *PR Week*, Danny Rogers, announces 'The death of PR agencies – as we know them', the PR industry has to listen to it.

> 'Advertising and PR are increasingly the same thing. PR was about editorial persuasion; selling stories to journalists. And while the distinction between bought media and earned media still exists, you now find their executives working across both. So now is the opportunity for those with earned (media relations) and owned (company websites, magazines or events) media skills to completely rebrand their business. Alongside endeavours to reinvent themselves according to today's transforming media, they may finally need to cast off those two deadly letters – P and R.'
>
> Rogers (2014)

Who reports to whom? Is PR part of marketing or marketing part of PR? Product publicity is part of the marketing communications mix and therefore should be under the control of the marketing director or manager. Corporate PR, on the other hand, often reports to the board or CEO directly. However,

Martin Sorrell (2015) said: 'PR can cast off its self-doubt, build its influence and take the lead on social media, content-led campaigning and reputation... PR can place itself at the centre: data, social and content present great opportunities.'

Product PR and corporate PR

The previous definitions give an indication of the diverse nature and far-reaching effects of public relations. We need to separate product PR (product or brand publicity) and corporate PR (corporate image enhancement). Product PR (sometimes called 'marketing PR') promotes a product or a brand and is the responsibility of the marketing manager, while corporate PR promotes a company and is the responsibility of the corporate communications director. A manager responsible for product PR would ultimately report to the marketing manager, whereas a manager responsible for corporate PR would probably report to a board director or the board itself. Both types of PR do, however, integrate with each other, as observed by Professor Jon White several decades ago, in *How to Understand and Manage Public Relations* (1991):

> public relations is a complement and a corrective to the marketing approach... it creates an environment in which it is easier to market... public relations can raise questions which the marketing approach, with its focus on the market, products, distribution channels and customers, and its orientation towards growth and consumption, cannot. Public relations concerns are with the relations of one group to another, and with the interplay of conflicting and competing interests in social relationships.

Publicity objectives can vary from promoting a product (product PR) to promoting a company (corporate PR) among employees, unions, customers, investors, the community, local government, etc. Marketing will tend to be sales or market share orientated, while public relations can, but will not always, be sales or market share orientated; for example a PR objective may be to recruit the best employees, to win permission to build a new factory or to influence government. Nevertheless, today's PR people, like any marketing professionals, have to be fully familiar with AI, Big Data, marketing automation, webinars, podcasts, chatbots, influencer marketing (including AI influencers – see more later), social media and optimized news releases (press releases optimized for key phrases and also designed for easy sharing on social media). Today's PR is often measured less by press coverage (press clippings) and more by web traffic, registrations and sales, sentiment and brand engagement.

The influence of public relations stretches far beyond product marketing and into corporate strategy, particularly where long-term decisions affecting choice of markets, products, factory locations, production processes, etc are concerned. External groups are becoming more demanding, and organizations are beginning to have to demonstrate their social responsibility on a global basis. Ethics and social responsibility have traditionally been the bastion of public relations. Today all managers need to develop their awareness and understanding of at least the PR implications of both boardroom and marketing decisions, strategies, policies and actions (or the lack of these).

Integrated reporting

'There is a massive opportunity for corporate communications in adopting "integrated reporting". The International Integrated Reporting Council (IIRC) has seen Coca-Cola, Microsoft and Sainsbury's "jumping on board with the concept", which is basically intertwining non-financial reports (eg CSR reports) with financial reports. Integrated reporting has been mandatory in South Africa for some time.'

Farey-Jones (2014)

PR is more than communications

Publicity/visibility should not be raised before a solid platform of credibility has been developed through decent, safe products, fully functional websites, friendly customer service, caring ethics and socially responsible policies. The PR mix is diverse and its effects are far-reaching. It is more than just communications; it is part of the broader business disciplines such as corporate planning, finance, personnel, production and marketing. It cannot work effectively unless it is integrated into these areas and unless it also links with product quality, customer care and design management (corporate identity). These are the credibility elements that build a platform for subsequent publicity, which is just one of the many visibility tools.

Corporate responsibility

Survey after survey reveals that the public feel that industry and commerce don't pay enough attention to their **corporate social responsibilities** (CSR). People feel that a company that supports the community is a good one to work for. People believe that companies have responsibilities towards their employees and communities that go beyond making profits. Today ethical issues are highlighted by new pressure group techniques.

Although Naomi Klein's challenging, and now almost cult-like book, *No Logo* (2000) was criticized, she did highlight issues and the need for constant corporate social responsibility. Amnesty International, which defends the human rights of individuals, departed from its normal focus on prisoners persecuted for either their religious or their political beliefs and, as Klein reported, 'is also beginning to treat multinational corporations as major players in the denial of human rights worldwide'.

Nike

'According to Campaign for Labor Rights, the largest ever anti-Nike event so far took place on October 18, 1997: 85 cities in 13 countries participated. Not all the protests have attracted large crowds, but since the movement is so decentralized, the sheer number of individual anti-Nike events has left the company's public relations department scrambling to get its spin onto dozens of local newscasts. Though you never know it from its branding ubiquity, even Nike can't be everywhere at once.'

Klein (2000)

Corporate responsibility is not just an overseas responsibility but starts in the corporations' own back gardens. A few years ago, the *Chicago Tribune* reported that Sears Roebuck had hundreds of elderly protesters picketing its store as a result of a decision to reduce pensioners' life insurance benefits. Any amount of press releases, or even advertising, announcing Sears' caring ethics would have a negative effect until this basic credibility problem was sorted out.

Shell in Nigeria

'The most significant landmark in the growth of anti-corporate activism also came in 1995, when the world lost Ken Saro-Wiwa. The revered Nigerian writer and environmental leader was imprisoned by his country's oppressive regime for spearheading the Ogoni people's campaign against the devastating human and ecological effects of Royal Dutch/Shell's oil drilling in the Niger Delta. Human rights groups rallied their governments to interfere, and some economic sanctions were imposed, but they had little effect. In November 1995, Saro-Wiwa and eight other Ogoni activists were executed by a military government who had enriched themselves with Shell's oil money and through their own people's repression.'

Klein (2000)

Even companies with a great tradition of social responsibility and, ergo, high credibility, like Cadbury Schweppes, sometimes score PR own goals when mixing marketing and social responsibility without carefully thinking through the implications. Some years ago it offered nearly £9 million worth of sports equipment to UK schools if schoolchildren bought lots of chocolate (millions of bars of chocolate had to be bought to get all the equipment). The media quickly picked up on the negative spin associated with the prospect of a teenager 'needing to consume thousands of calories before being able to play with a new basketball'. Using cause-related marketing to boost sales and corporate image is popular but needs, firstly, to be thought through carefully and, secondly, to be screened to ensure that there is a clear and positive strategic fit between the brand and the cause.

Shell trigger protests in Ireland

Shell continue to be embroiled in controversy, by way of environmental protest when in 2010 an award-winning documentary called *The Pipe* highlighted Shell's attempt to pipe gas under fields in Rossport, Co Mayo, Ireland. Five locals, 'The Rossport Five', were jailed, which caused a national outrage. The **ShellToSea.com** campaign is an attempt to stop the proposed construction of a raw natural gas pipeline through a parish, as locals feel this puts residents at risk.

FIGURE 13.1 'Shell to Sea mural'

SOURCE: Courtesy of Lapsed Pacifist

Good business is not just about achieving financial targets; it is also about behaving with a sense of responsibility. Eighty-four per cent of the value of the S&P 500 comes from intangible assets (Hargreaves, 2017), such as management, leadership, vision, innovation, customer loyalty, product and service quality, intellectual property, brand equity and reputation. In September 2001 the US stock market was worth an estimated $24 trillion; by summer 2002 it had collapsed to $11 trillion. The events of 9/11 and economic uncertainty had a significant impact, but so too did the collapse of Enron and a wave of other scandals that raised fundamental questions over corporate governance.

At the time, the vast majority (84 per cent) of Americans thought that the people who run their companies were trying to do what was best for themselves rather than the company (Accenture, 2004). Years later, following another major economic crisis and an environmental crisis, organizations now, more than ever before, need to engage in, and provide evidence of, solid ethical policies.

Companies can take positive steps, such as being transparent and carrying out environmental impact studies, talking to communities, addressing their issues and finding solutions. An Irish renewable energy company, Mainstream Renewable Power, has wind farms and solar parks across the world and they work closely with each community to ensure harmonious co-existence. Other companies join the 'per cent club' and promise to donate 1 per cent (or half of 1 per cent) of profits to the local community. There are even 2 per cent and 5 per cent clubs. Another way is by ensuring regular ethical and/or environmental audits and, of course, taking appropriate action.

Imagine your funeral

'I went on this training course (at Procter & Gamble) where you had to imagine what the minister might say about you at your funeral. When I realized that mine would say I was the leading expert on housewives' toilet cleaning products, I realized it was time for a change.'
Hamish Taylor, Managing Director, Eurostar

It is not just about making good business sense. Marketing, PR and corporate communications professionals are in the exciting position of being able to help improve their local communities, support valid causes, improve the environment, and much more. The bottom line is that it makes long-term business sense to be ethical, as it creates a platform of credibility that enriches all subsequent communications. As Bob Leaf of Burson Marsteller succinctly says in PR Smith's award-winning PR film *Actions Speak Louder than Words* (PRTV, 1991), **'Ethics is good for business'.**

Cancel your Christmas party

'As CEO of Electronic Data Systems, Mort Meyerson made an unpopular decision and cancelled the Christmas party when he realized it was going to cost $360,000. Instead, he insisted,

"We'll take the $360,000 and buy food and clothes and toys, and we'll get our employees to take those things personally and deliver them to the inner city, to people who don't have anything." The result was, initially, outrage that the party was cancelled, then depression, then recognition that the company was doing something different and then elation for those who actually took part in the project. This project "made them more human... made them better employees... better family members... it did a whole bunch of things". When Meyerson was CEO, he used to give 10 per cent of his time to community and philanthropic projects.'

Colvin (2003)

were required to sign strict legally enforceable confidential agreements. Subtle hints that there weren't enough copies of the book to go around... fake TV footage of heavily armed security vans delivering Potter books to online book stores... Twenty advance copies were "accidentally" sold by an unnamed Wal-Mart in deepest West Virginia and one of the "lucky children" was miraculously tracked down by the world's press and splashed across every front page worth its salt... Another copy "accidentally" found its way to the news desk of the Scottish Daily Record.'

Brown (2001)

The PR mix

The 'visibility' or publicity-generating activities such as news releases, news conferences, publicity stunts, conferences, events, exhibitions, sponsorship and sales promotions can all integrate. Before we look at publicity in more detail, it is worth mentioning again that the key to long-term success is to develop credibility before raising visibility. Credibility is created by a proper product and/or quality of service. This means that the product must match the promise made by the marketing communications, ie do not sell a Rolls-Royce and deliver a Ford Ka. False expectations only lead to disappointment, frustration and extremely high post-purchase dissonance. This kills off any long-term repeat business. Good customer service makes doing business a pleasurable experience for all parties. Having the right sort of people or institutions associated by their using or endorsing a product improves credibility. So too ethics, social responsibility and corporate image all contribute towards building a credible image.

Harry Potter's anti-marketing magic builds the PR hype

'Review copies were withheld from interviews, no author interviews were allowed, and foreign translations were deferred for fear of injudicious leaks... printers and distributors

There is no point waving a flag or raising an organization's visibility if it does not have a solid platform of credibility supporting it. The days when the two aspects were held separately are gone. Spending thousands or millions of pounds on raising a profile is not just wasteful but is actually damaging if a lack of credibility is exposed. So today, more than ever before, it is worth investing men/women, money and minutes in getting the credibility right before raising visibility. And credibility must also be evident on websites and social media, as journalists use these as their first port of call for gathering information.

New and old PR tools

Media relations and publicity

Take a look at the local and national newspapers, trade journals, radio programmes and television. Spot the commercial news items or features that have made news. Although they appear to be written by an editor or journalist, many of them have been written by skilled PR professionals. Like advertising, editorial publicity can achieve many similar communication goals, such as increasing awareness, repositioning a brand, generating enquiries and boosting sales. Busy editors do not have time to scout around for all the items they use. They depend on a constant feed of professionally presented news items and news releases from organizations. Despite this, sackfuls of press releases get thrown into editors' bins continually. Many of them are badly written and inaccurately targeted (sometimes even addressed to people who have long left the newspaper).

Publicity can be generated through written press releases and feature articles for the press, video news releases for television programmes, syndicated radio recordings for radio programmes and digital press packs for all and sundry. Publicity is also generated by press conferences, press receptions, media events (what the media less reverently call 'stunts') and public speaking at conferences, lectures, seminars, dinners, chat shows, etc.

News releases

News by definition is new – a new idea, a new process, a new product, a new service or even a new use of an old product. News should 'defy expectations' and provide a new way to understand the world we live in, so it has to be newsworthy. A news release should make it easy for a journalist (and a search engine) to make news. All the key information should be in the first paragraph for the journalist, and key phrases, if relevant, should be used in the title or headline and also in the opening paragraph (to optimize it for search engines). The press releases can then be distributed to the news wires, top-ranking free publicity websites, news aggregators, relevant social news sites such as Digg, and relevant online and traditional media outlets. Press release services like Pressbox, PRWeb, Free Press Release and ClickPress can do it all in one go.

Ensure the organization's web url is included and any other links to relevant sections of a website, as not only does this help readers but it also acts as inbound links, which boost search engine rankings.

As the proliferation of online news aggregators (eg Google News) increases, the debate continues as to whether PR staff are writing news releases for people or machines – a human editor or a robot. The reality is both. A select few organizations bother to write different news releases for human editors and online aggregators.

The debate rattles on with Ryan Singel's (2006) comments:

> Standing up for the human intellect, upstart Digg is betting that its formidable legion of users can find better and more interesting news faster than any algorithm Google – or a number of upstart companies – can code. On the machine side, the purest algorithmic news finder is Google News, which made waves in the media world when it debuted. With Google News, it's code, and not a team of editors, that decides which stories make it onto the front page.

Figure 13.2 shows an excerpt from a Samsung news release regarding Tim Peake's Soyuz spacecraft tour landing in Belfast. Note the image is supplied with the news release and access to more photos. A great headline is used. Most of the key questions are answered in the first paragraph.

A national PR and marketing campaign promoted this national tour, with each site hosting media previews and family launch events in addition to promotion of the partnership (Samsung and the Science Museum Group) and the tour used a variety of channels including but not limited to: internal and external signage at the tour venue, social media, website, press and online ads. Support from Tim Peake himself, both in person at events and across traditional and social media, has helped raise the tour's profile and Samsung has also worked with other inspirational female STEM ambassadors such as Libby Jackson (UK Space Agency), Dr Suzanne Imber (planetary scientist and winner of the BBC Two astronauts programme *Do You Have What It Takes?*) to promote this unique tour. It has become a massive success story – see the full case in Chapter 14, p 440).

Online newsroom

If building an online newsroom or media facility on a website, make it easy to make news by considering what journalists need when writing up a story:

- news releases and press releases (easily searchable and sortable by date, by topic and by department);
- photos (linked to each news release, plus an archive or library of high-, medium- and low-resolution images);
- video (can be linked to a new release if it is a launch event, a press conference, a speech, an interview, a product demonstration, vox pops or endorsements);
- media kits to support news (all of the above in one downloadable file);

FIGURE 13.2 Tim Peake news release, Belfast tour

SAMSUNG Newsroom U.K.

CORPORATE PRODUCTS PRESS RESOURCES VIEWS ABOUT US  

Corporate › Citizenship

Press Resources › Press Release

Tim Peake's Soyuz spacecraft docks in Belfast

on February 20, 2019 SHARE

London, UK – 20th February 2019 – On Wednesday 20th February Tim Peake's, the UK's first European Space Agency astronaut, famous Soyuz TMA-19M capsule will arrive at the Ulster Transport Museum, Belfast, the final stop on the spacecraft's national tour.

- general corporate information (corporate background, corporate financials, corporate statistics and executive team information);
- research and study data, white papers, links and related resources (including blogs, which journalists use increasingly);
- awards and recognition;
- upcoming events;
- contact information.

Note that all media assets, including videos, photos, news releases, white papers, etc, should be easily searchable, sortable and shareable. An effective online newsroom invites visitors to go deeper into the site for additional background information on the organization, its corporate social responsibility, its people and its media assets, so that journalists get to know the organization and form a healthy relationship.

Embeddable digital press kit

Buena Vista International's film *Starship Troopers* had an innovative 'digital press kit' available to support its launch. The kit comprised a ready-made mini-site packed with material related to the film. It was designed in such a way that it could be incorporated into other media sites. This made a convenient package for media partners, distributorships, agents and promoters to link the mini-site to their own website.

Press conferences and interviews

Press conferences are an efficient way to release information to a large number of journalists, newspapers, blogs and radio and TV stations. They should include pre-prepared press packs and, ideally, rehearsed Q&As (the likely questions and sensible answers), although there is not always time to prepare Q&As.

Key staff need to be trained for press interviews. Avoid jargon, tell the truth and be topical, relevant and unusual if possible. A story that stirs up some trouble can be attractive to an editor. However, some caution is required to ensure the facts are 100 per cent correct, as journalists will investigate rigorously and any inaccuracies will subsequently cause damage. Finally, the human angle (human story) always appeals at an emotional level. Paint a picture with words; as Scott Chisholm (2010) says, 'Imagine is the most powerful word you can use in an interview.'

Virtual press conference in Second Life

For those international bloggers and journalists who could not physically attend the launch of Northern Ireland's creative digital hub in Belfast's Science Park, a virtual press conference was held the next day, with some 50 bloggers attending. The Minister for Enterprise's avatar and PR Smith's avatar presented the hub and took questions for an hour afterwards. This resulted in a buzz of discussions on key international blogs, raised awareness, a new network of bloggers and a surge of valuable inbound links.

Video news releases

A video news release (VNR) is conceptually the same as a written press release, except that it is produced on broadcast-quality digital video. A key factor is that it must be newsworthy or highly relevant as a feature item. VNRs also save broadcasters from having to send their own busy camera crews out to cover a story. The VNR consists of two sections: a 30–90 second 'A' roll, which carries a commentary designed to show the editor and/or journalist how the story could run on air, and a three to five minute 'B' roll, which is a selection of loosely cut shots ('rushes') designed to be re-edited by the broadcasters into their own style, ie the broadcasters use their own commentary, graphics and captions so that as far as the viewers are concerned the story has been originated by the broadcaster. As with a press release, **a VNR is paid for by the brand that is looking for publicity. The TV stations receive VNRs free of charge.** Again, as with press releases, there is no guarantee that the material will be used, since a bigger story can break at any time. Equally, a VNR can be used negatively, since, unlike advertising, there is no control over the final message. These videos can also eventually be used on social media sites, websites and blogs as well as form part of the press resources. Some organizations, like Greenpeace, like to control how they are seen in the press and therefore produce their own broadcast-quality videos.

Personalized videos

A little-known new resource is 'personalized videos' at scale. For example, a trailer for a new film can be personalized and sent to micro-influencers. The personalized video will contain a comment that the influencer has made online about the film, plus the influencer's name, photo and sometimes their handles (eg Twitter name).

Specialist video companies can scour the internet searching for people talking about hashtagged topics or brands, or the name of a movie. They then collect the comment, photo and handle and embed this into the first three seconds of the video. They can filter the selection to only use comments from people with over 500 followers. They can also filter out any comments that use obscene language, etc. They can scale this up and collect, create and dispatch up to 150,000 personalized videos in two hours. The influencer receives a film trailer featuring his/her comments. They then choose whether to delete or share it.

For much more detail see 'Imagine you could do this with video' at **https://prsmith.org/**.

Content pools

Some companies like Red Bull make it easy for the media by providing well-organized cross-referenced (tagged) media resources. These include stories,

FIGURE 13.3 Personalized videos at scale sent to micro-influencers

PRSmith
MARKETING SUCCESS

About Blog Books Consulting SOSTAC® Planning Training Speaking Contact

Imagine You Could Do This With Video

by prsmith | Apr 18, 2019 | Big Data, Content Marketing, Creativity, Data, Engagement, Marketing Automation, Social Media, Targeting, Viral Marketing | 0 comments

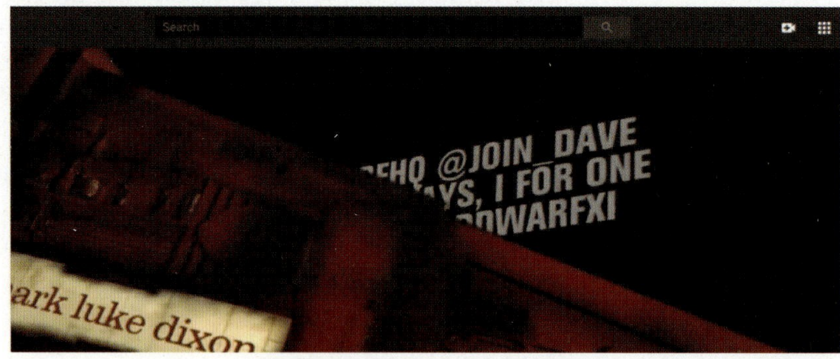

Follow me

Subscribe via RSS

Subscribe to Marketing Insights

Enter your email address to receive new posts by email.

Email Address

Subscribe

Join Me At My Next Event

2019

videos, photos, album, cartoons and advanced search (which has 14 filters including length, location, subtitles and semantic values).

The Red Bull Content Pool is the global B2B self-service media and news platform for press, journalists and business partners. It offers photos, videos and news about Red Bull events, partner events and athletes – all free and with all rights cleared for editorial and news purposes. It includes global news, exclusive interviews, more than 300,000 high-quality photos and over 22,000 HD videos, from thrilling sports to lifestyle, and from culture to ground-breaking photography.

Other Red Bull channels and media products include: Red Bull TV; **www.redbull.com**; Red Bull Illume; Red Bull Records; Red Bull Radio; Red Bulleting; Red Bull Photography; Red Bull Media House; Red Bull Media House on Shutterstock; and Terra Mater Factual Studios. Terra Mater Factual Studios is a subsidiary company of Red Bull and specializes in factual production and distribution for cinema, TV and multimedia platforms.

Syndicated radio interviews and down-the-line interviews

A syndicated radio interview is, on average, a three-minute recorded interview about a person, event, company, product or service. The audio file and script are distributed (or syndicated) to radio stations. The same principles as apply to VNRs apply here, ie it should be newsworthy and not a blatant plug. For just a few thousand pounds, a syndication supplier's basic package usually includes:

- preliminary discussion;
- interviewer – selecting, booking and briefing;
- structuring the interview;
- studio session (one hour);
- recording (three minutes);
- editing the master tape;
- two spare copies for the client;
- cue sheet preparation (written introduction to the taped interview);
- selecting 30 relevant radio stations (only one per area where stations overlap);
- monitoring – three to four weeks after dispatch, a written report is produced, giving details of which stations broadcast the information, which is sometimes followed up with a more detailed report.

A 40 per cent take-up of a professionally produced, newsworthy, accurately targeted syndicated radio interview is considered to be an 'average success

FIGURE 13.4 Red Bull's Content Pool

FIGURE 13.5 Red Bull's Terra Mater Factual Studios in Vienna

rate'. There is usually a range of optional extras (eg localized cue sheets or overseas distribution).

Syndicated producers usually offer an alternative service – 'down-the-line interviews'. This is where the interviewee is brought into the studio, linked up live to local radio stations one at a time, and interviewed on a one-to-one basis. On average the interviewee does about 10 separate interviews per day. Some interviewees have been known to do up to 15 separate interviews in one day. This is exhausting, and sometimes the later interviews are not as good, as interviewees cannot remember if they have said something before or not. However, syndicated radio interviews can be very cost effective ways of spreading a message.

Photography

A picture paints a thousand words. A cleverly crafted photograph can catch a photo editor's eye. Some of the same criteria as for a news release apply – is it newsworthy, is it different, does it tell a story, does it catch the reader's eye and does it add value to the publication? If the photo has someone famous in it, then it is even more valuable. Ideally photos can be stored in three file sizes: high, medium and low resolution. They can be stored securely for press, or distributors only. Social photo sites like **Instagram.com** can store the images, and embed them on the company's or individual's blog and as part of an electronic press kit. Again, tagging makes the images searchable and sortable. Here is a list of some great publicity photos that generated vast audiences (see Figures 13.7–13.12):

- *Jarvis Cocker's blue beard for Oxfam* was part of a series taken by Rankin to promote Oxfam's 'blue faces' campaign, which was to raise awareness of the effects of climate change on poor people around the world, and was carried out across the UK festival season.
- *Dom Pedro and the 15 Second Film Festival.* Dom Pedro is the iconic character used by the 15 Second Film Festival to promote the concept of 15 second movies. Each movie has a beginning, a middle and an end, and Dom Pedro is the front man, deal maker and do-er who catches the picture editor's attention (**www.15secondfilmfestival.com**).
- *No 10 Downing Street.* Plan UK created this image to put pressure on the prime minister to help 72 million extra children into primary school across the world. This was part of an ongoing advocacy/PR campaign to ensure the Government delivered on promises to fulfil the Millennium Development Goals (MDG) at the MDG summit in New York in September 2009.
- *Projection on Parliament.* 'Don't forget planes!' – Friends of the Earth took its successful campaign for aviation emissions to be included in the Climate Change Act to Parliament and mobilized huge public and political support for action on climate change, engaging a mainstream public audience, as well as environmental activists and politicians.
- *MPs support Friends of the Earth's rainforest-free lunches for planet-friendly farming.* Andrew George finds out that there's no such thing as a rainforest-free lunch if you're eating meat or dairy. He's one of 160 MPs who backed Friends of the Earth's call for government action to reduce the environmental impact of livestock farming.
- *Admiral Lord Nelson.* The stunning skyline around Nelson's Column certainly helped to grab attention of the picture editors of many media outlets, and consequently their audiences, during England's World Cup 2018 bid.

Publicity stunts

Publicity stunts are at much higher risk of error and 'egg on the face' than issuing a news release with a photograph, since the media are invited to wait and watch.

Legendary publicity stunts

Pimm's Cup punch-up (1949)

'The most celebrated was by a New Yorker called Jim Moran, who once contrived a bar-room brawl between a fairly well-known band leader and a bystander. When the judge asked what they were fighting about, the band leader told him it was over the recipe for Pimms Cup. Pimms had hired Mr Moran because they were having trouble establishing the brand name in the United States. The "brawl" received so much publicity that he solved the problem with a single blow.'

Independent on Sunday, 1 April 1990

Tightrope across the Thames (1997)

Didier Pasquette promoted Vanguard while walking high above the River Thames on a tightrope, meeting Jade Kindar-Martin heading in the opposite direction. The two had to climb over each other midstream in the first-ever double tightrope crossing of the Thames – a stunt that was publicized worldwide.

Banksy shreds his own painting (2018)

Just moments after the painting *Girl with a balloon* by the world's most famous street artist, Banksy, was auctioned and sold for $1.4 million to an unknown buyer at the world's most famous auctioneers, Sotheby's in London, the painting self-destructed whilst still hanging on the wall, in front of an audience and captured on camera (Figure 13.6). The publicity spread and the story immediately went viral. According to Banksy's own video on his own Instagram account (**www.instagram.com/banksy**), he had, some years earlier, installed a shredder into the frame of the painting, so that it could shred itself if it was ever auctioned. Ironically, some experts suggest the painting (or what's left of it) has, since this shredding stunt, doubled in value. Perhaps this is the greatest publicity stunt of all time? Jennifer Calfas (2018) from **Money.com** suggests: 'The stunning and widely viewed moment was seen as a pointed criticism of the lucrative art world from the daring artist.' Banksy posted the video showing the installation of the shredder into the frame of the painting, and his 5.7 million followers subsequently posted more than 95,000 comments. The video has had almost 15 million views.

Other stunts include:

- *The Archaos fish diet:* A classic 'What the –?' photo, this is a brilliant example of life mimicking art. Photographer Gavin Evans was sent to shoot a fish-throwing act. Stuck for a workable angle, Gavin stuffed a fish in the performer's mouth. Archaos subsequently made the stunt the grand finale to its routine.
- *Friends of The Earth one-off gig with Razorlight at the Science Museum:* Razorlight played a one-off gig at London's Science Museum to back Friends of the Earth's call for aviation emissions to be included in the forthcoming Climate Change Act.
- *Fuel poverty stunt outside the Royal Courts of Justice:* Friends of the Earth and Help the Aged took the government to court over its failure to tackle fuel poverty.
- *Mortascreen's funeral procession:* Mortascreen has a consumer database of over 7 million deceased individuals, with 50,000 UK deaths being added each month. Brands use the Mortascreen database to remove deceased people from their mailing lists, firstly, so families are not upset in bereavement with unwanted mail and, secondly, to improve the effectiveness of the brands' marketing campaigns. The PR agency Eulogy set up a photo opportunity using a traditional horse-drawn funeral procession, complete with four mourners, walking across Westminster Bridge and Parliament Square and finally coming to rest behind the London Eye. The funeral cortège contained a coffin filled with the amount of direct mail Londoners receive in one day addressed to deceased loved ones. This publicity stunt achieved 90 pieces of coverage across key national, broadcast, trade and online media (within an hour it was on YouTube and probably even more quickly on Twitter), delivering 35,000,000 opportunities to see (OTS), with a publicity value equivalent (PVE) of £578,000. On a small budget of £8,500, this generated an ROI of £68:£1 or 6,800 per cent. It also generated £60,000 worth of licence sales, which gave a sales-to-fee ratio of 7:1.

FIGURE 13.6 Banksy: Love is in the Bin, 2018

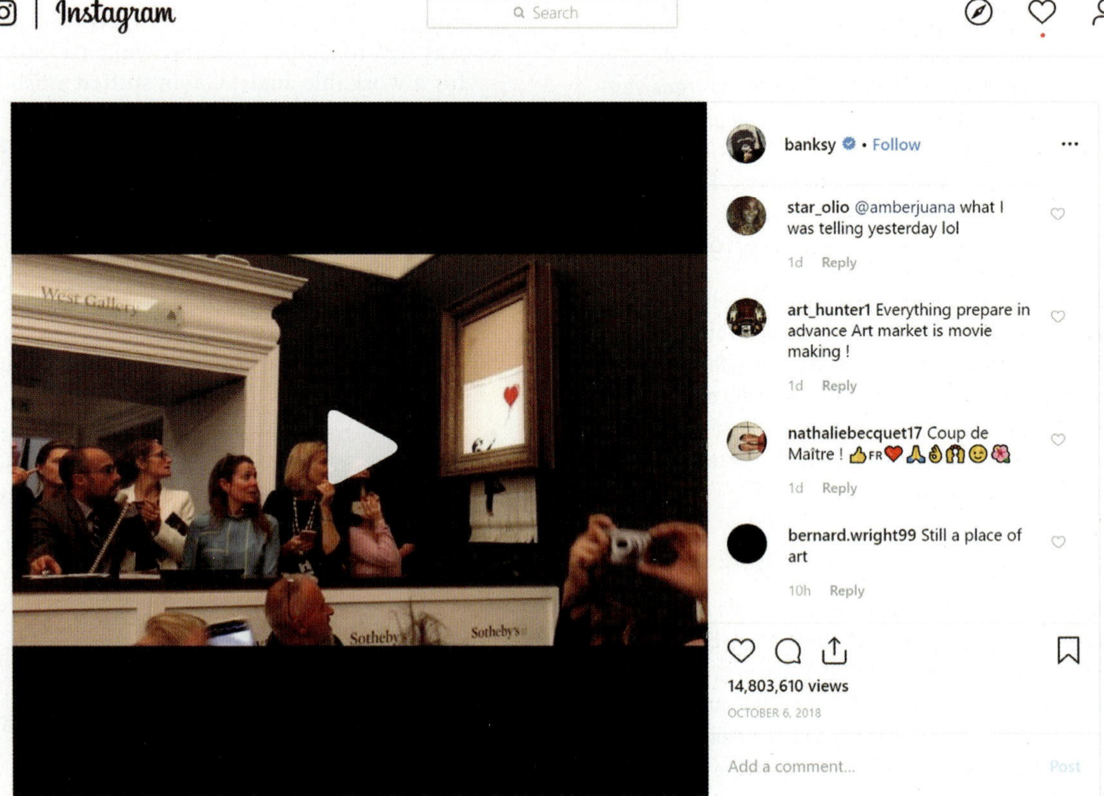

SOURCE: Screengrab, courtesy of Pest Control Office

A photograph's unconscious messages

With the accelerating rate of declining attention spans, images become more important. Your organization's images send out many unconscious messages. It is worth checking your images match your company's core objectives. Even head-and-shoulder shots can send all sorts of messages, as shown in the selection in Figure 13.14. Note that although folded arms can suggest insecurity or nervousness, if the subject can relax the shoulders it reduces the defensive impact and the person can look quite confident.

Viral marketing

Viral marketing devices include videos clips, TV ads, cartoons, funny pictures, a short poem, a political or social message, or a news item, games or widgets, but they can also be a game, a photograph, a graphic or just a piece of text, as long as it is enlightening (informative), entertaining (shocking or funny), engaging (people must play or interact with it) or simply so good that you just have to pass it on to a friend or colleague. That is the acid test: is it worth looking at again, and is it deemed valuable if it is passed on? Anything that enhances the value of the sender (or person who passes it on) has viral potential.

FIGURE 13.7 Jarvis Cocker's blue beard

SOURCE: Rankin/Oxfam

FIGURE 13.8 (Dom) Pedro El Magico, silent investor of the 15secondfilmfestival.com

FIGURE 13.9 The 10 Downing Street image for the MDG summit

SOURCE: Plan UK/Mark Read

FIGURE 13.10 The 'Don't forget planes!' campaign

SOURCE: Friends of the Earth

FIGURE 13.11 Andrew George supporting Friends of the Earth's rainforest-free lunches

SOURCE: Warren Allot

FIGURE 13.12 Admiral Lord Nelson supporting the London bid

SOURCE: On Edition

FIGURE 13.13 The Archaos fish diet

SOURCE: Gavin Evans

FIGURE 13.14 Selection of head shots and the messages they send

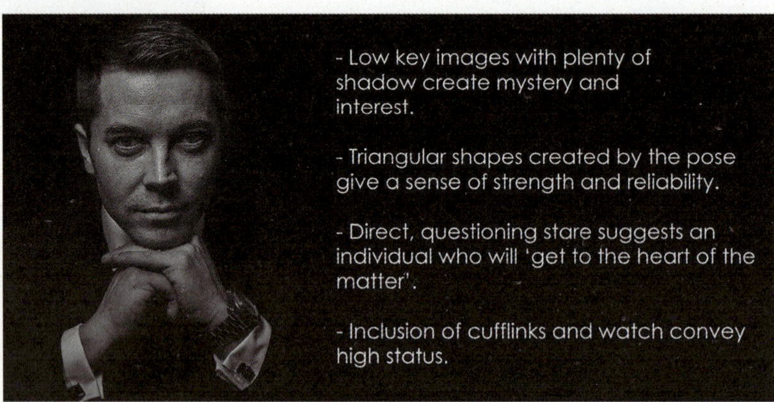
- Low key images with plenty of shadow create mystery and interest.
- Triangular shapes created by the pose give a sense of strength and reliability.
- Direct, questioning stare suggests an individual who will 'get to the heart of the matter'.
- Inclusion of cufflinks and watch convey high status.

- Slight tilt of the head towards the viewer is a friendly, welcoming gesture.
- Loose scarf protects the neck, balancing the openness of expression and head tilt.
- Camera angle enhances an elegant feminine neck whilst lighting carves out high cheekbones.

(*continued*)

FIGURE 13.14 (Continued)

- 'Young entrepreneur' status reinforced by light grey suit, tie and pocket handkerchief.

- Shot outside to enhance green credentials and natural products.

- Hint of blossom on trees and budding green leaves creating a fresh, spring like impression.

- Expression is relaxed and confident. Head is balanced and upright, being neither aloof nor 'over-friendly'.

- Glasses as a prop (rather than on the face) suggesting seniority and someone who works with detailed documents rather than their hands.

- Pose, with the glasses, suggests a college lecturer: someone with professional knowledge.

- Open shirt and lack of tie exposing neck: showing trust and openness.

SOURCE: Grey Corporate

Viral criteria

The viral object has to be so amazing that it makes people want to pass it on. The best ones simply make compulsive viewing. Here are some tough criteria:

- Is it good enough to make people pass it on?
- Is it on trend with whatever is trending?
- Does it create a 'shared experience'? (Eg Father's Day, St Patrick's Day, Christmas time – people want to share the experience, so suitable virals can be propelled by a shared experience.)
- Is it emotional (does it make you smile/laugh/feel enraged/shocked/happy/sad/sentimental)?
- Does it have the wow factor?

Seeding

Great creative material ('the viral agent') is simply not enough. It needs to be seeded, branded and measured. Seeding means identifying websites, blogs and influential people and sending them the email, or posting the viral on their Facebook wall to start the virus spreading. Some agencies offer seeding services, where they have databases of people who like virals and tend to pass them on. Other marketers tend to build their own lists of their champions or brand advocates and influencers who like to be the first to see a new idea and therefore get credibility among their networks when they pass on useful virals. When it comes to branding your viral video, you have to be careful to ensure the branding actually works. This means clear branding and a url, ideally not just at the beginning and end where they can be cut out before being passed on. Although they cannot be controlled, virals should be measured as to what (a) brand awareness and (b) traffic they generate and (c) what conversions come from this, as measured by ROI.

TV channel E4's 'Stack Da Police' viral mixed real video, animation, sound and gaming technology to create a viral that promoted its new TV programme. It generated 3.8 million unique visitors (to the website) and a 14 per cent click-through rate (CTR), which is about 0.5 million click-throughs. The cost per click (CPC) was 6p (approximately £30,000 divided by 500,000). Kerb viral agency created and seeded it for £30,000.

Influencer marketing

Seeding influencers is common practice today – whether you tag an influencer in your post, or send your list of influencers an early notice or special preview before releasing information to the rest of the market. Some influencers are paid to post comments or wear certain brands. Influencers are obliged to declare if they have been paid or given gifts or even loans of products. See Chapter 5 p 160 for more on influencer marketing.

Subscriptions services like Gorkana help influencers/journalists to find the right PR people managing specific brands, and Gorkana also helps PR people to find the right influencer/journalist as they provide information to journalists about PRs (and to PRs about journalists).

Engaging Influencers: Tim Peake's Spacecraft Tour

It is interesting to see how the Tim Peake's Spacecraft Tour engaged some influencers.

The tour bus was brought to the House of Commons, where Parliamentarians were encouraged to nominate a school in their local area to receive a visit from the Samsung VR bus, thus engaging influencers (members of parliament). Samsung and the Science Museum Group also ran a nationwide prize draw for any primary or secondary schools to enter for a chance to win a visit from the Space Descent Bus – thereby attracting more major influencers (headmasters and senior school staff) to engage with the tour and hopefully spread the message. For more on this tour see p 440.

Creating human influencers: *Love Island*

The programme sponsors deliberately use the dual screening trend among millennials by integrating the app (which is the only way to vote people off the show). The app also contains a summary video of each day and opportunities to buy, in real time, the clothes being worn by the contestants at that time directly from the show's fashion/clothing sponsor, Missguided. Each carefully selected/handpicked contestant immediately became an influencer (once they appeared on TV) and was therefore given a Missguided wardrobe, which included everything from swimsuits and pyjamas to the 'going-out' outfits. 'It's a classic bit of product placement combined with influencer marketing. We can expect to see a lot more TV influencer marketing which abuses our love–hate relationships with our phones and the accompanying apps' (Friend Bartlett, 2018).

Creating AI influencers: Lils & Ugoto

As mentioned in Chapter 5, 'Artificial influencers are proving to be a success and therefore are attracting the attention of brands' (Kulp, 2018a). You will probably see more virtual models in your Instagram feed as AI (artificial intelligence) transforms influencer marketing (Kulp, 2018b). See a full artificial influencer post: 'Artificial influencers use my magic marketing formula (IRD)' at **https://prsmith.org** and also on p 352.

Creating micro-influencers

Helping customers share the great experience they have is often called the 'shared experience'. How can we help customers to share the pleasure and joy they get from our products or services? One way is to provide props or sometimes backdrops of beautiful scenes. Sri Lanka Golf Tours encourage customers to take selfies in front of stunning images from the golf courses. The Tim Peake Soyuz spacecraft tour (see p 440 for more) displayed this iconic object accompanied by an immersive 'Space Descent VR' lounge along with a Selfie spacesuit specially designed for visitors to share their experience. Encouraging selfies encourages everyone to become an influencer. Some are more influential than others. Shared images like these 'selfie astronaut' images can be more powerful than any form of advertising. Note: See also how Zip World seeded stunning photographs with influencers outside their target audience to boost sales enormously (their website crashed as a result of the surge in traffic!) in Chapter 20, p 611.

Warning: Influencer fraud/fake followers

'The Competition and Markets Authority (CMA) launched an investigation to measure how transparent influencers are actually being about sponsored posts. It said there were **"clear examples of influencers not stating they have been paid to promote a product or service"** – and a number of influencers have already fallen foul of the Advertising Standards Authority (ASA) for just this.'

Marketing Week Reporters (2018)

FIGURE 13.15 Shared images can be very powerful: the selfie spacesuit at the Science Museum

SOURCE: © Science Museum Group 2019 – reproduced with kind permission

FIGURE 13.16 A fun way for visitors to share their experience

SOURCE: © Science Museum Group 2019 – reproduced with kind permission

> 'The ASA and Committees of Advertising Practice (CAP) launched a new set of principles on advertising disclosure called *The Influencer's Guide* – which some argue still don't go far enough – while ISBA unveiled an updated version of influencer marketing contracts as it looks to bring better "commercial discipline" to the relationship between brands and influencers.'
>
> Marketing Week Reporters (2018)

See Chapter 10, p 302 for more on ASA and CAP.

Now let us look at any advantages and disadvantages of increasing spending on PR.

Advantages and disadvantages of PR

As mentioned, editorial coverage can achieve many objectives similar to those of advertising, but there are three important points that differentiate editorial coverage from advertising:

- there is no media cost;
- the message has higher credibility;
- there is no control over the message.

No media cost

There is no media cost since, with editorial coverage, unlike advertising, the space is not bought. There are, however, other costs, since news releases have to be written, carefully targeted and distributed to the right editor at the right time in the right format. This can be done by an in-house press officer or public relations department, or it can be handled by an external public relations agent or consultancy. There are news release distribution companies that specialize in getting releases physically or electronically to news editors' desks at the right time. This kind of editorial coverage creates valuable positive publicity, as **it has higher credibility than advertising copy**. No space was bought, and therefore no media costs were incurred. However, whether it is in-house PR people or an external consultancy, it does cost someone's time and expertise to:

- select the right target media (appropriate press and editors) at the right time;
- write the news releases;
- distribute the news releases;
- handle any press enquiries. (There are, of course, other minor costs, some of which are hidden: photographs, stationery, stamps, phone calls, and wear and tear of the word processor, laser printer and so on.)

Editorial coverage is used increasingly to stretch the above-the-line advertising campaigns. Good press officers push the knock-on PR potential of advertising. Bruno Magli shoes enjoyed an uncontrolled estimated $100 million worth of free exposure during American football star O J Simpson's trial. The calculation is simple: add up the column inches of coverage, times by the amount of broadcast coverage and find the equivalent cost for the same amount of advertising space. There are more sophisticated methods of evaluation, which include: positive and negative comments; the position on the page; whether a picture is shown; the number of times a brand name is used, etc. Forte Hotels' constant quantitative report on editorial coverage is outlined in the box 'Scoring your PR performance', p 418.

Higher credibility

Editorial coverage has higher credibility than advertising because it is perceived as being written by an editor or journalist and not by an advertiser trying to sell something. There is arguably less resistance to the message. Some estimates suggest that a message carried in a piece of editorial has three times more credibility than a similar message carried in an advertisement. Despite the attraction of the message credibility factor, editorial coverage is risky because there is no control over the message. An editor can take a news release and criticize the sender for sending it. Advertisers, on the other hand, can control the message, since they buy the space and publish exactly what they want to say (within the law and advertising regulations). Despite this, editorial clippings and their associated levels of credibility are often compiled and used as endorsements in direct mailshots, sales literature, advertisements and exhibition stands. You can even see them above theatres promoting a show, where extracted comments from the press are highlighted in bright lights outside the front door. The third-party editorial coverage adds credibility to the claim that this is a good show. Equally, a reviewer can severely criticize a show and therefore damage the credibility (and viability) of that show.

Lack of control

The uncontrollable element of media relations is demonstrated by the montage of press clippings (editorial coverage) generated by PR Smith's 'nuclear missile' news release (Figure 13.17). This shows how the same news release gets totally different editorial coverage from two different editors. On the one hand, *The Wall Street Journal* gives it brief but positive front-page exposure, while *Personnel Today* treats the same news release with a lot of cynicism and, arguably, negative editorial coverage, despite a lot more detail about the promotion. It can be argued, in the case of PR Smith's award-winning PR video, that 'any publicity is good publicity', but this is certainly not the case with Ratners, IBM and McDonald's. These examples demonstrate the dangers of uncontrolled publicity (see the next section). Even carefully controlled media events such as annual general meetings can go wrong (see the box below). Every media event has an element of risk attached to it, since if things do go wrong the press are waiting – with cameras perched and pens ready.

Fat cat pig

'The production of a pig at the British Gas annual general meeting helped give the bandwagon against "fat cats" (overpaid directors) a memorable push.'

Andrew Bolger, *Financial Times* (date unknown)

Uncontrollable publicity – any publicity is good publicity?

The adage 'any publicity is good publicity' is not always true. Although the PR training video's negative editorial coverage mentioned in the previous section is, arguably, useful publicity, this is not always the case. Retail jewellery giant Ratners discovered this when it fell foul of the power of negative publicity. Its chairman, Gerald Ratner, told the press that his jewellery was 'crap'. This gained national coverage, but it also kept customers away from his shops and lowered morale among his employees. He relinquished his joint position of chairman and managing director, and the Ratners shops have since disappeared. On the other hand, unexpected editorial coverage can sometimes help, as shoemakers Bruno Magli observed when their sales jumped 50 per cent because of references to their shoes during the trial of O J Simpson. Uncontrolled editorial exposure, and particularly negative publicity, can somersault out of control, as IBM discovered during the 1996 Olympics when one of its official Olympic computers started churning out incorrect information. 'The press reported the story ad nauseam, even blaming IBM for things it had nothing to do with. In the aftermath of the tragic bombing in Centennial Park, for example, the *Philadelphia Inquirer* erroneously reported that an IBM system may have contributed to security lapses' (*Fortune Magazine*, 9 September 1996). How a company handles the spotlight is a test for its company values. When 21 customers were shot dead in a McDonald's restaurant in California in 1984, McDonald's knocked the restaurant down within days and eventually donated the land to a local community college. Continued publicity and association with such a tragedy are certainly not 'good publicity'. More recently, BP's negative publicity threatens the very survival of this highly profitable global success story. The negative coverage has been exacerbated by extremely poor crisis management (see 'Crisis management' overleaf for more).

Reducing the lack of control

Red faces can be avoided by checking to see if any events clash with a particular news release or event (such as launching a new hamburger bar on a national vegetarian day). There are directories available that list events and categorize them by type, region, date, etc. There are other directories that list editors' names, addresses and numbers (again categorized by type of magazine or programme). Editorial risk can be further reduced with the help of companies (such as Echo Research) that compile lists of journalists who have written articles on a particular organization or on its products, or on any particular issue, together with a favourable or unfavourable rating for each article. A further analysis compares the incidence of solicited and unsolicited press coverage, which can be cross-referenced with the ratings to identify any apparent bias in specific journalists' relationships with organizations. When a journalist calls the press office, the staff can punch in a few keywords into a desk terminal, and effectively see the profile of the caller on the screen almost instantaneously, even before the preliminary greetings are completed. So the pressurized PR manager is briefed automatically.

Despite the best preparation and briefing, things still go wrong. In advertising, the organization gets a chance to approve the final copy (or wording), but with editorial coverage deadlines are too tight even for the friendliest of editors to allow the PR manager sight of the copy and layout before it is published: hence a bad day for Mr Pimlott (p 416).

Controlled integration of publicity

Publicity should be integrated with other elements of the marketing communications mix. Chapter 1 explained how many major advertising campaigns are now supported by press launches and followed up with a press and publicity campaign to maintain the visibility generated by the public relations people. An integrated packaging, PR and sales promotion campaign maintains the brand's share without any traditional above-the-line support. In other cases, blown-up press cuttings can be used (once permission is gained from the copyright owners) at trade fairs and exhibitions. Third-party endorsements can be used in advertising, news releases, sales literature, packaging design, sales promotion and so on. A single photographic shoot can produce a range of material suitable for advertising, packaging, exhibitions, direct mail, press packs, etc. Strategically, the marketing communications tools should all work together (consistent positioning) rather than pull in different directions. Ideally, each activity should be planned for maximum integration.

FIGURE 13.17 PRTV news release: The same news release can generate totally different types of editorial coverage, from positive coverage on the front page of *The Wall Street Journal* to negative coverage in a training magazine

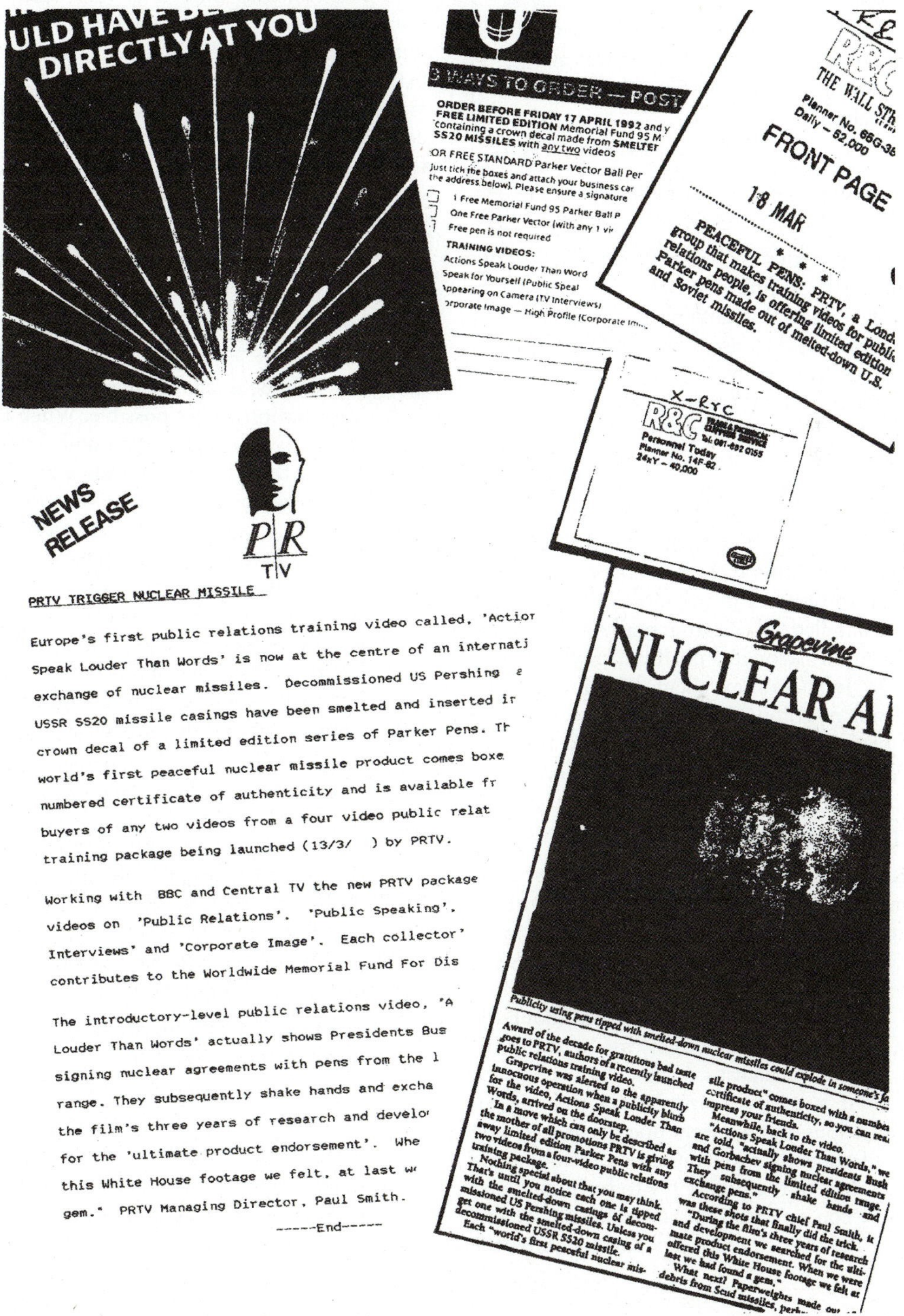

ULD HAVE BE
DIRECTLY AT YOU

3 WAYS TO ORDER — POST

ORDER BEFORE FRIDAY 17 APRIL 1992 and y
FREE LIMITED EDITION Memorial Fund 95 M
containing a crown decal made from SMELTER
SS20 MISSILES with any two videos
OR FREE STANDARD Parker Vector Ball Per
Just tick the boxes and attach your business car
the address below). Please ensure a signature
1 Free Memorial Fund 95 Parker Ball P
One Free Parker Vector (with any 1 vi
Free pen is not required
TRAINING VIDEOS:
Actions Speak Louder Than Word
Speak for Yourself (Public Speal
Appearing on Camera (TV Interviews)
Corporate Image — High Profile (Corporate Im

R&C
THE WALL STR
Planner No. 66G-35
Daily – 62,000
FRONT PAGE
18 MAR

PEACEFUL PENS: PRTV, a Lond
group that makes training videos for publi
relations people, is offering limited edition
Parker pens made out of melted-down U.S.
and Soviet missiles.

X-RYC
R&C
Personnel Today
Planner No. 14F-82
24xY – 40,000

NEWS RELEASE

PR TV

PRTV TRIGGER NUCLEAR MISSILE

Europe's first public relations training video called, 'Actior
Speak Louder Than Words' is now at the centre of an internati
exchange of nuclear missiles. Decommissioned US Pershing a
USSR SS20 missile casings have been smelted and inserted ir
crown decal of a limited edition series of Parker Pens. Th
world's first peaceful nuclear missile product comes boxe
numbered certificate of authenticity and is available fr
buyers of any two videos from a four video public relat
training package being launched (13/3/) by PRTV.

Working with BBC and Central TV the new PRTV package
videos on 'Public Relations'. 'Public Speaking'.
Interviews' and 'Corporate Image'. Each collector'
contributes to the Worldwide Memorial Fund For Dis

The introductory-level public relations video, 'A
Louder Than Words' actually shows Presidents Bus
signing nuclear agreements with pens from the l
range. They subsequently shake hands and excha
the film's three years of research and develo
for the 'ultimate product endorsement'. Whe
this White House footage we felt, at last w
gem." PRTV Managing Director, Paul Smith.

-----End-----

Grapevine

NUCLEAR A

Publicity using pens tipped with smelted-down nuclear missiles could explode in someone's fa

Award of the decade for gratuitous bad taste goes to PRTV, authors of a recently launched public relations training video.

Grapevine was alerted to the apparently innocuous operation when a publicity blurb for the video, Actions Speak Louder Than Words, arrived on the doorstep.

In a move which can only be described as the mother of all promotions PRTV is giving away limited edition Parker Pens with any two videos from a four-video public relations training package.

Nothing special about that you may think. That's until you notice each one is tipped with the smelted-down casings of decommissioned US Pershing missiles. Unless you get one with the smelted-down casing of a decommissioned USSR SS20 missile.

Each "world's first peaceful nuclear missile product" comes boxed with a number certificate of authenticity, so you can rea impress your friends.

Meanwhile, back to the video. "Actions Speak Louder Than Words," we are told, "actually shows presidents Bush and Gorbachev signing nuclear agreements with pens from the limited edition range. They subsequently shake hands and exchange pens."

According to PRTV chief Paul Smith, it was these shots that finally did the trick. "During the film's three years of research and development we searched for the ultimate product endorsement. When we were offered this White House footage we felt at last we had found a gem."

What next? Paperweights made ou debris from Scud missiles, perh

A bad day for Mr Edward Pimlott

'Mr Pimlott's letter to the *Grantham Journal* led to this apology: "In a letter printed in our July 25 issue, Mr Pimlott apparently described himself as 'a pillock of the community'. This was our error. Mr Pimlott described himself as a pillar of the community."'

Independent, 28 August 1997

Unforeseen opportunities and threats invariably emerge that make it difficult to plan for everything. For example, editorial is difficult to forecast. (Even if an editor promises to use a news release, it often gets 'spiked' or replaced by some other news item at the last moment; at other times the news release gets used later than expected.) Successful positive publicity can trigger all sorts of ideas for mailings, promotions and further press coverage. Crises and negative publicity are equally difficult to forecast and plan, although top companies invest in crisis management programmes before crises occur. This allows them to respond in the most effective manner. A well-handled crisis can actually leave an organization in a stronger position, for example Johnson & Johnson's excellent handling of the 1982 Tylenol poisoning crisis (when seven people died of poisoning from cyanide that had been inserted in their headache tablets) in Chicago.

Crisis management

Accidents happen, sometimes on a massive scale. Crisis management is standard procedure when a nightmare occurs. Top companies have crisis management procedures in place in case of a crisis – whether of their own or someone else's making. Key speakers are agreed, with key messages about the company, and specific messages for a series of different disaster scenarios. These are reviewed immediately if a crisis occurs. Media training includes a questions-and-answers document (tackling all the most frequently asked questions, including the tricky ones). Key to it all is simply to be human and decent. Show concern. Visit the site or the customers. Answer the questions. Pay for any damage (after the legal people have approved it). Communicate to all stakeholders. Avoid threatening legal action if possible. Legal options can be part of the solution, but rarely all of it. Note that legal action takes time (and money), and time is a very scarce resource during a crisis. Company spokespeople must tread with caution. As Alex Wollfall (2010) points out, 'After the global banking crisis and the politicians' expenses scandal, public distrust of politicians, company spokespeople and big brands is at an all-time high.'

There is a process, which usually includes the following steps.

1. Survey the scale of it. Is it just a handful of moaners or something more significant, and have they good reason to moan?
2. Don't deny it. Acknowledge the issue if it is an issue. Be open and honest and give useful information where possible. When the toy company Mattel faced a number of product recalls, the CEO tackled the issue head on with a video message that was posted on Mattel's corporate website, spread virally across the internet and appeared on some TV news bulletins. Compare this to TV images of queues of concerned customers trying to withdraw their savings from a crippled Northern Rock for several days, while no one really knew what was happening and rumours spread uncontrollably.
3. Be genuinely concerned. It seems ridiculous to spell this out, but a lack of sincerity will be sniffed out by an angry press corps very quickly. Witness the BP CEO's now infamous comment 'I would like my life back,' which displayed a concern for his own personal circumstances at a time when others' livelihoods were being destroyed by a massive environmental disaster.
4. Be open with employees. Inform them as much as the press.
5. Fix it so it is better than it was before the crisis. Make sure processes are reviewed so that the accident can never happen again.
6. Finally, repair or compensate for any damage done or replace any faulty products.

Yacht holiday while Atlantic burns

'BP's Gulf of Mexico crisis is a case study in how poor communications skills will only magnify a corporate crisis. Avoid any photographs transmitting the wrong message. Of course everyone needs some time off but to be snapped enjoying yourself on your yacht in blue seas – when just across the Atlantic a BP field continues to spew oil into the ocean – is tantamount to reputational suicide. It was just the latest mistake by Hayward, who, despite correctly apologizing on 30 May, stupidly added: "I would like my life back," demonstrating a lack of judgement... His performance in front of a Senate committee was evidence of this. While one sympathizes with the pressure he was under, and the fears of his legal advisers, he came across as overly defensive and unemotional, playing into the hands of aggressive US journalists.'

Rogers (2010)

It may be difficult to avoid financial losses, but crisis management can, if handled properly, strengthen relationships with all stakeholders. In this way it not only repairs damage but is an investment in the future. It is worth remembering that good corporate social responsibility gives a platform of credibility, particularly during a time of crisis.

Control – measuring media relations

Free publicity, news coverage or editorial can be monitored, measured and analysed. The old approach was just 'column inches' and TV minutes of press coverage. Today, news releases are also measured by impressions, shares, reads, traffic and engagement. News clippings can be compiled in-house, by an agency or by a specialist news clipping company that monitors, cuts out, pastes up and delivers the clippings daily, weekly or however regularly the client wants, or delivers the coverage stats online. Google Alert and Talkwalker can deliver a list of your brand's mentions online each day (with a link to the original article or source). Companies like Durrants supply their clients with press digests, reports of where they are covered, how favourably and how often. Sentiment Analysis aggregates everything that is said about your brand online and gives it a score each day, each week or each month. Companies like Social Mention, Radian6 and Kantar supply sentiment analysis to help managers monitor what is being said about their brands online.

Similar media monitoring services are available for television, radio and the internet (scanning newsgroups, online editions and search engines). The size of file, number of references, and quantity of space or time devoted to a chosen product, organization or issue are, again, a simple method of measurement. More detailed analyses give a breakdown of: front-page mentions; exclusive mentions; size of mention or cutting; number of beneficial credits; neutral credits; adverse credits; and opportunities to enquire (includes reach of article, circulation, and whether a contact address and/or phone number, enquiry card, coupon, etc was included). Various formulae attempt to calculate the quality of the coverage rather than the quantity. These can include photographs or diagrams, position on the page, etc.

Online measurement includes the following:

- 'Reads' measures how many times a news release has been read every day.
- 'Impressions' measures how often a news release headline was displayed to how many people visiting PR websites and RSS feeds.
- 'Activities' reveals who read the release, who skimmed the headline and how many 'shares'. Social media sharing is important, and the number of times a release was shared on Facebook, LinkedIn or Twitter can be measured.
- Keywords that were used to find the news release.
- Search engines that were used to find the release can be reported on as well.

All of these are hard facts, which could provide a simple format for pay-by-performance.

These factually based reports will make it easier for more PR consultancies to accept pay-by-results from their clients. The PR industry has not fully embraced pay-by-results (probably because of the large number of uncontrollable variables that affect the results).

Paul Miller, Strategic Planning Director at Porter Novelli Europe, has observed that 'the PR business is not the most sophisticated or advanced about setting good objectives. But this is now being recognized as a weakness, and what we like about performance-related fees is that they make clients really focus on what they want, so they are not wishy-washy.' Hill & Knowlton, a leading PR agency, launched the pre-school animation series *Engie Benjy* using the TV stars Ant and Dec, and 30 per cent of its fee was contingent upon the programme achieving audience reach targets.

These forms of analysis measure what gets into the press; they do not measure what gets into the minds of the target audience, ie whether the editorial has changed or reinforced the target audience's attitudes and intentions, voting patterns, shared values, sales levels, etc. This has to be measured separately by researching attitudes and behaviour patterns. Sales can be measured, but it can be difficult to isolate PR from other communications activities when attempting to gauge the effect of any aspect of public relations. Perhaps this is the reason for the apparent resistance to payment-by-results. But, despite the difficulties of isolating and measuring PR's results, performance-related fees do encourage clients to set very clearly defined, measurable objectives.

In summary, PR punches above its weight. It can be a very cost-effective communications tool that nurtures and strengthens relationships with key stakeholders.

Scoring your PR performance

'When we have a story about a new hotel or product we identify five key messages we want to put across – it's never more than five – and we're lucky if we get two across in print. We then identify the key target audiences and the most appropriate publications to reach them. This establishes a matrix which ensures the maximum efficiency for our efforts. All stories are then monitored on a scale of one to five, according to how favourable they are and how many of the key messages are included.'

Richard Power, Director of Corporate Communications, Forte Hotels

This enables Power to give Rocco Forte and other executive directors a quantified report on just how well they are communicating.

CASE STUDY The gnome story that went viral

FIGURE 13.18 The start of the gnome going viral

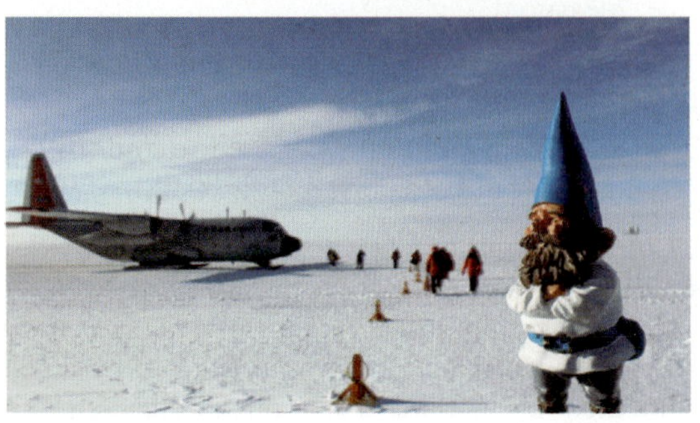

SOURCE: Ogilvy PR

Situation

Kern, a precision scales manufacturer, needed to build its brand, differentiate itself and grow market share within the science and education sectors. However, with millions of schools and laboratories around the world to reach, Kern faced the challenge of a highly commoditized marketplace and a disinterested media. Subsequent audience analysis by Ogilvy PR (surveys, perceptions audit and analysis of Kern's historic sales data) revealed: low brand recognition for laboratory grade balances; a highly commoditized marketplace; no significant discussion of measurement and accuracy outside of specialist titles; and few independent views on quality, reliability or precision. Recognizing that Kern's targets represented a global audience, from school teachers to Nobel scientists, this extremely diverse group was influenced by equally diverse sources, including friends, peers and media. They are highly active online; inquisitively seeking out, discussing and sharing information they 'discover' from a host of influential and specialist cross-media sources.

Objectives

Ogilvy PR London and OgilvyOne were challenged to deliver an engaging business campaign that would effect behavioural change within the target audience, encouraging them to recognize brand 'Kern' for the first time and make purchases based on familiarity and preference. These translated into:

- **Drive sales** of scales to the education and science sectors by enhancing Kern's brand visibility and preference among these key markets.
- **Generate conversations** internationally around gravity's influence on weight measurement – explaining the importance of Kern's USP; calibrating scales for local gravity.
- **Raise awareness** of Kern's reputation for accuracy within and beyond its existing customer base – securing coverage outside of specialist media.

Strategy

Make complex science accessible, harnessing Kern's gravitational calibration USP. Give the public a reason to talk about Kern and 'accuracy in measurement'. Conduct in-depth research into education and science influencers, delving into scientific theories on weight and measurement to find a unique, engaging concept that had viral potential. The Gnome Experiment was born – a global research project aimed at proving the scientific theory that gravity varies from place to place affecting weight. This would:

- harness compelling science surrounding gravitational anomalies to engage new audiences;
- give Kern a personality that would speak to all media channels;
- transform the way Kern reaches buyers, targeting influencers via new channels and encouraging interaction with the brand;
- go beyond traditional media, amplifying flagship coverage and developing engaging sharable content.

Tactics

- **Chip-proof gnome:** Create a chip-proof garden gnome (also called Kern), providing the campaign with a universally appealing personality. Gnomes are famed for their love of travelling and originate from Bavaria, where Kern scales are manufactured.
- **Create local stories:** Offer local stories anchored in international activity targeting territories including: Switzerland, South Africa, the UK, the United States, Canada, etc for physical activity to spark local conversations yet attract international attention.

Stage 1: Endorsements/develop credibility

Packed in a flight kit containing a set of Kern precision scales, the gnome was then circulated between scientists and existing Kern customers globally. This provided professional endorsement of the Gnome Experiment as individuals weighed the gnome at their location before passing it on.

FIGURE 13.19 The gnome pack

SOURCE: Ogilvy PR

FIGURE 13.20 The gnome in famous locations

SOURCE: Ogilvy PR

Stage 2: Initiate media and influencer engagement/ raise visibility

- The Gnome Experiment Blog – a blog and website were created to host the experiment's results and directly engage volunteers and fans. Through these channels, and across other social media, the gnome's own personality emerged: scientifically irreverent.
- Social media news releases targeting global media as well as science and education influencers brought consumer and target business attention to the project – requesting volunteers and engaging millions.
- Participants were given the tools to share their involvement with local media and friends.
- Content was shared, including travel snaps of the gnome, video and facts about gravity to encourage further sharing.

Action

The creative use of little-known gravitational facts and a travelling gnome brought together academics, scientists and the media, sparking global conversations through the world's first mass-participation gravity experiment:

- Dispatching gnome packs. Following up to ensure safe receipt.
- Creating website/blog, testing and release.
- News releases and blog post creation.
- Monitoring reactions, press coverage, social media engagement, on a daily basis.

Control/measurement/results

Lauded by Oxford scholars and science geeks alike, the campaign resulted in schools incorporating Kern's experiment into lessons, a TED presentation, *National Geographic* feature articles; and TV production companies around the world vied to feature Kern in shows.

One week after launch

News, science and education shows globally ran dedicated Kern segments. The website saw 52,425 views, with a new participant enlisting every 20 seconds. 16,386 websites linked to the project website.

Two weeks after launch

Coverage reached an audience in excess of 355,378,000:

- Analytics revealed coverage reached 152 countries.
- 1,042 per cent ROI achieved based on new distributor sign-ups alone.
- Schools around the world added Kern's story to the curriculum.
- The experiment became a TED talk.

Drive sales

- Product sales to target groups increase by 22 per cent.
- 2,200 former customers got back in touch.
- 1,445 new leads were generated: 40 per cent schools, 25 per cent scientists.

Generate conversations

Kern and its USP were debated among scholars, scientists and the general public across all media. Its experiment increased global understanding of the issues of gravity and weight measurement, reaching an audience of over 350 million.

Corporate website visits increased 256 per cent and Gnome Experiment volunteers ranged from schoolchildren to internationally acclaimed scientists.

Raise awareness

Globally, people became enthralled by the Gnome Experiment as it brought science to life. For the first time Kern drew the attention of popular science publications, national newspapers, influential online publications, broadcast news and social media, eg *New Scientist*, Fox News, BBC, the *Metro*, *Le Monde*, *National Geographic*, etc.

Today

The experiment continues... Kern's Gnome visited Newton's apple tree in the company of BBC's Newsround, followed swiftly by a trip into earth's upper atmosphere in NASA's zero-G flight trainer. The campaign has taken Kern from laboratories and schools into people's daily lives. Millions learned about gravity, tens of thousands shared Kern's content, and thousands volunteered to take part in the experiment.

3Ms

- **Men and women/human resource required:** Kern worked with Ogilvy PR London and OgilvyOne. Ogilvy PR team was led by Blair Metcalfe and Allan Edwards who worked intensely with the Kern marketing manager.
- **Money/budget required:** All of this was done for a surprisingly small budget of £10,000. Other non-OPR costs, including shipping, cases, web design and some advertising placement to showcase the campaign in trade press, added another £25,000, giving a grand total of £35,000. Many people, for example the US Army at the South Pole, and SnoLab in Ontario, found the project so fascinating they simply gave their own time and even paid to move the gnome on once they had weighed him.
- **Minutes/time required:** From brief to launch, the campaign ran for two weeks but still has momentum and continues to engage its target market, and maintain awareness, preference and sales.

CASE STUDY The Snack Dash viral game

This is another more detailed viral case (created by Kerb Games) regarding the serious issue of obesity and healthy eating. The client, Digital Public, proposed a viral game to the School Food Trust to promote its healthy eating message, raise awareness of the School Food Trust and drive traffic to its site. The target market is a cynical age group, and the task of creating a game with such a nannying message without alienating the target market is a minefield.

Objectives

The brief was to build a game that conveyed the message of healthy eating to a target market of children aged seven and over in the UK, drive traffic to the site and also for the game to sit on the site as a flagship piece of game content for the site's newly established game section.

Strategy

To create more than just a game with a logo on it, or with information regarding healthy eating embedded in it, the strategy required the creation of a game with pure game play and humour that would appeal to children but that would actually illustrate the benefits of healthy eating within the game play.

Tactics

The tactics were to design and build a game that requires the player to guide the main character from start to finish in the shortest possible time, while collecting as many points as possible along the way. In order to fulfil the brief, one of the game's key features is the inclusion of healthy and unhealthy food. Collecting healthy foods (such as apples, water and carrots) increases the player's score and protects the player from danger. Conversely, the consumption of unhealthy food (such as crisps, sweets and fizzy drinks) causes the character considerable instant weight gain. The player can still move but is unable to move quickly enough to negotiate features like the loop-the-loop or to jump over the baddies. A little bit of exercise is required to lose the excess pounds (toggling the A and S keys will make the character perform a number of press-ups in order to lose that puppy fat). However, this all takes up precious time. The only way to get a good score and speed is by avoiding the fatty foods altogether.

Action

- Week 1: design.
- Week 2: develop.
- Week 4: test.
- Week 5: seed.

Control

Results: As expected from an engaging viral, it got huge worldwide traffic; 70 million uniques, with 3 per cent coming from the UK, which equals 2 million UK uniques, without any media spend. In the first two weeks alone, the game achieved over 3 million visits, with no budget spent on media buying. It subsequently spread like a true viral. The game has been independently tracked by MemeCounter and Viralchart. 'Out of over 400 campaigns this is the fastest-moving viral that we have ever tracked' (Viralchart). MemeCounter recorded over 340,000 visitors in one day, which beat the previous record by over 80,000. The cost per thousand was £8.33, and the reach was 3 million, with a cost of £25,000. This may seem expensive, but it was a highly engaged audience. The cost per click was less than 1p (£25,000 divided by 3 million).

3Ms

- **Men/women:** Created and seeded by Kerb Viral Agency.
- **Money:** £25,000.
- **Minutes:** Eight weeks to create, seed and spread to 70 million users.

CASE STUDY Virgin Mobile's new tariff

Situation

Tariff announcements are essential for mobile phone providers, as they are one of the key factors affecting consumer purchase. It's a cluttered marketplace where a formulaic approach to PR is typically used. The campaign used innovative techniques in digital media to promote Virgin Mobile's new, very cheap, 30p tariff, engaged a hard-to-reach audience and delivered coverage that surpassed all client expectations for a new tariff announcement.

Objectives

- Engage Virgin Mobile customers, potential customers and key online influencers with the data tariff story – Virgin Mobile offers unlimited mobile internet for 30p a day.
- Find a creative way to get people talking about a dry news story.
- Increase inbound links to the tariff's homepage.
- Secure at least 60 pieces of coverage between online national news and blogs in three weeks.
- Increase average monthly new customer acquisition by 4 per cent.

Strategy

To build an online PR and social media campaign using innovative digital techniques to engage Virgin Mobile's customers, prospects and influencers. The campaign had to be developed with the essence of the brand in mind, so elements of youth, fun, funkiness, vibrancy and edginess were critical in positioning Virgin Mobile as the 'challenger' brand within its competitor set.

Tactics

The '30 peas' campaign was the first-ever online PR and social media campaign for the launch of a new mobile phone tariff. The creative concept was to use '30 peas' in different, digitally enhanced ways to illustrate the new 30p tariff in a fun and quirky way. A stop-motion animation film of 30 frozen peas dancing through black holes, climbing mountains and playing Pong fully encapsulated the fun of the Virgin Mobile experience, with the subtle messaging 'If you can get all of the internet for 30p a day, just imagine what 30 peas could do.' The *30 Peas* film premiered at London's first interactive blogger event for the launch of a viral video called the Voscars (Virgin Mobile Oscars).

Action

The premiere of *30 Peas* took place at the Curzon Theatre in Mayfair, where a group of 30 of London's most influential bloggers were invited to showcase their favourite viral videos. Bloggers across all categories, including tech, coolhunting, mobile, social media, marketing, transport, London, food and news, took part, bringing an eclectic and vibrant energy to the event.

At the end of the screenings, the bloggers voted on their favourite videos. The winning video was packaged as a story and sold at a 'Virgin Mobile's 30p per day Mobile Internet Tariff' premiere.

The Voscars also saw the opportunity for Virgin Mobile to engage directly with online consumers. Members of the Virgin Mobile communications team were on hand to chat about the campaign, the data tariff and Virgin Mobile's plans for the future.

What was not covered in national news was covered by the bloggers in attendance at the event. Each of the 30 bloggers wrote his or her own post about Virgin Mobile, the Voscars, *30 Peas* and the mobile data tariff plan, often linking to or embedding the *30 Peas* clip.

Additional online outreach was conducted to bloggers who were not able to make the event, as well as to non-London-based bloggers on mobile, creative, entertainment, coolhunting and technology blogs.

Control

Results

- Monthly new customer acquisition increased 5.5 per cent (over 37 per cent over target).
- There were 99 pieces of coverage, including a feature in *Metro* online and print.
- Over 80 per cent of sites linked to the website.
- There was OTS of over 20 million across non-mobile blogs and websites.

FIGURE 13.21 Virgin Mobile campaign timescale

Week commencing	24 November	1 December	8 December	15 December	22 December
Brief delivered					
Campaign planning					
Video production					
Event planning					
Blogger engagement					
Event confirmation					
Video approval					
Event			11 December		
Top virals story developed					
Top virals story sell-in					
Campaign evaluation					

- There were 10,000 video views in 10 days.
- In total, 75 per cent of placements linked to or embedded the *30 Peas* video.
- Over 95 per cent of placements mentioned Virgin Mobile.
- For every £1 spent, 952 people were reached.
- Outcome: over 80 per cent of sites linked that wrote about the plan and/or the campaign created inbound links to Virgin's site.

3Ms

- **Men/women:** Account executive, managers and senior managers.
- **Money:** This amounted to £21,000 for all PR activity, including agency fees and third-party costs.
- **Minutes:** Figure 13.21 shows the timescales required for this campaign.

A summary of the advantages and disadvantages of PR

Here are some of the main advantages and disadvantages to consider when deciding whether to increase or reduce this communications tool.

Advantages

PR has higher credibility than advertising, as it is deemed to be a journalist's opinion or at least vetted by a third-party news source. Equipped with a good platform of corporate social responsibility, PR can work wonders. It also has much lower costs (on a CPT basis) than advertising. PR is good at generating awareness, building preference and overall brand building. It often delivers more 'bang for your buck'.

Disadvantages

PR has no control of the message once editors receive it. They can rewrite it any way they want, whereas advertising controls its message. Editors, journalists and bloggers often dig deep under the surface to expose any inconsistencies. Also, the message can spread beyond target areas. PR cannot close sales.

Key points from Chapter 13

- PR and marketing are not subsets of each other, although they do integrate.
- Editorial coverage has lower costs, higher message credibility and higher risks because of lack of control over the message.
- Social media is a natural fit for PR.
- Integrated PR contributes to marketing communications synergy.

References and further reading

Accenture (2004) *The Business of Trust*, White Paper referencing the World Economic Forum 2004

Bernays, E (1923) *Crystallizing Public Opinion*, Boni & Liveright, New York

Bernays, E (1969) *The Engineering of Consent*, 2nd edn, University of Oklahoma Press, Norman

Bland, M (1987) *Be Your Own PR Man*, Kogan Page, London

Brown, S (2001) Marketing for Muggles, *Journal of Marketing Management*, **17** (5), 5 July

Calfas, J (2018) Banksy shredded a piece of art that sold for $1.4 Million. Now it's worth double, according to an art expert, Money.com (archived at https://perma.cc/8JMC-CWEF), 8 October

Chisholm, S (2010) Getting your message across, *PR Week*, 16 April

Churchill, D (1992) The power behind the image, *PR Week*, 15 October

Colvin, G (2003) Value driven – think about this as you don your tuxedo, *Fortune*, 18 December

Cutlip, S, Center, H and Broom, M (1999) *Effective Public Relations*, 8th edn, Prentice Hall International, Englewood Cliffs, NJ

Farey-Jones, D (2014) The bigger picture, *PR Week* March

Friend Bartlett, J (2018) Does love island show us the next phase of influencer marketing?, CIPR Influence, 25 July

Hargreaves, R (2017) Intangible assets now account for more than 84% of S&P 500, *Talk Markets*, 25 February

Haywood, R (1990) *All about PR*, 2nd edn, McGraw-Hill, London

Jefkins, F (1998) *Public Relations*, 5th edn, FT Management, London

Klein, N (2000) *No Logo*, Flamingo, London

Kosky, H (2008) Howard Kosky on PR and digital broadcasting, *Independent*, 16 June

Kulp, P (2018a) Artificial influencers are attracting the attention of brands, *Adweek*, 20 August

Kulp, P (2018b) How artificial intelligence is transforming influencer marketing, *Adweek*, 20 August

Larkin, J (2003) Reputation under fire, *Profile*, **35**, April

Lohr, S (2006) This boring headline is written for Google, *New York Times*, 9 April

Luckett, T (2010) Crisis communications, *PR Week*, 26 February

Marketing Week Reporters (2018) 2018 year in review: It's been a bad year for..., *Marketing Week*, 10 December

Murphy, D (1992) Don't forget the hype, *Creative Review*, October, p 16

PRTV (1991) *Actions Speak Louder than Words*, PR training video by PR Smith, Chartered Institute of Public Relations, London

Rich, F R (2003) There's no exit from the Matrix, *New York Times*, 25 May

Rogers, D (2010) Poor comms skills just magnify a crisis, *PR Week*, 25 June

Rogers, D (2014) *PR Week* leader: The death of PR agencies, *PR Week*, July–August

Ross, D (1990) *Surviving the Media Jungle*, Mercury Books, London

Singel, R (2006) Man vs machine in newsreader war, *Wired Magazine*, 14 March

Sorrell, M (2015), founder and CEO, WPP, Bright Future, *PR Week*, May

White, J (1991) *How to Understand and Manage Public Relations*, Business Books, London

Wollfall, A (2010) Crisis communications, *PR Week*, 26 February

World Advertising Research Centre (WARC) (2005) Excerpt from a subscription-based article archive

Further information

CIPR Public Relations Centre
4th Floor
85 Tottenham Court Road
London W1T 4TQ
Tel: +44 (0)20 7631 6900
www.cipr.co.uk

Communications Advertising and Marketing
Education Foundation Limited (CAM Foundation)
Moor Hall
Cookham
Maidenhead
Berkshire SL6 9QH
Tel: +44 (0)1628 427120
Fax: +44 (0)1628 427158
www.camfoundation.com

Public Relations Consultants Association (PRCA)
82 Great Suffolk Street
London SE1 0BE
Tel: +44 (0)20 7233 6026
www.prca.org.uk

14
Sponsorship

LEARNING OBJECTIVES

By the end of this chapter you will be able to:

- consider the unlimited range of sponsorship opportunities online and offline;
- assist in managing a sponsorship programme;
- discuss the advantages and disadvantages, including what can go wrong;
- monitor a sponsorship programme.

Introduction

Sponsorship can help brands build and maintain awareness and preference as well as positioning a brand by associating it with the sponsoree's positioning. Major brands see major sponsorship opportunities as medium- to longer-term opportunities and hence longer-term agreements, ie 10- and 20-year agreements are more popular. However, there is room for shorter-term sponsorship deals, like Samsung's amazing sponsorship of Tim Peake's Spacecraft Tour (more later).

> Ford have been sponsoring Australia's Geelong Football Club for approximately 95 years.

Meanwhile, Adidas extended their kit sponsorship with Bayern Munich until 2030 for a reported €900 million (£645 million). This figure is dwarfed by the Adidas 10-year sponsorship of Manchester United's kit for £750 million, which ended Nike's 13-year sponsorship deal (Lusbec, 2015). Manchester United have 22 sponsor partners including a shirt sponsor, shirt sleeve sponsor, outdoor apparel partner, music partner, feature film partner, wine partner, watch partner logistics partner, tyre partner, lubricant partner, fuel retail partner, office equipment partner, global mattress and pillow partner, and many more.

LeBron James and Cristiano Ronaldo each have a lifetime arrangement with Nike reported to be worth at least $1 billion (*Sports Illustrated*, 2018).

Brand managers understand the power of sponsorship and therefore see sponsorship as an in-term strategic marketing tool. Take Coca-Cola, who sponsored the FIFA World Cup back in 2005 and committed $500 million to extend its sponsorship until 2022. This gave Coke exclusive rights as non-alcoholic beverage supplier to all major competitions, including the World Cup tournament, and sales rights for TV and stadium advertising. It also extended its Olympic Games sponsorship for 12 years to 2020. The Coke deal covered the 2010 Winter Olympics, the 2012 Summer Games and the 2014, 2016, 2018 and 2020 games (WARC, 2005). Note that even the signing of a sponsorship contract provides a PR opportunity – Coke took it and signed the contract on the Great Wall of China. Although this is based on anecdotal evidence, it is from one of the world's best marketing machines, which considers that its sponsorship management ('know-how') actually gives it a distinct competitive advantage.

Some brands get more out of sponsorship than others

'We do not sponsor sports. It's a very cluttered market where you can spend millions without getting much return,' said David Goldesgeyne, Head of Sponsorship for Lloyds Bank, a few years ago. While Gillette World Cup News state, 'Each World Cup has proven even more rewarding than the last, in terms of global name exposure, premium positioning, sales promotion results, cementing relationships with trade customers.'

Immature sponsorship

The European Sponsorship Association (ESA) describes yesterday's approach to sponsorship:

> In the early days of sponsorship, arrangements were made for simplistic and one-dimensional reasons. There was little, if any, media proliferation; advertising was very much the dominant marketing discipline of choice (due to a lack of alternatives) and gaining awareness for company or brand names was the strategic priority. It was considered enough just to attach your brand name to an event title and place your branding in front of the TV cameras. Partnership choices were often made on the likely volume of TV coverage alone, with no other considerations or priorities. Success was likely to be assessed by attaching a TV equivalent advertising value to the exposure of the company or brand name and whether this seemed to be good value for money when compared to advertising.
>
> ESA

Align with new communities' passions through sponsorship

'While advertising is excellent for generating awareness, public relations informs and influences, and sales promotions stimulates trial, they all compete with each other to cut through the marketing clutter. Brands have found that the best way to get our attention is to identify the passions of new communities and align with them through sponsorship.'

Collett and Fenton (2011)

Today, expert sponsors leverage the sponsorship opportunity to maximize the return on their investment. It is much more than just 'badging an event'; for example, if a mobile phone company sponsors a summer music festival, it will seek to be allowed to collect and distribute backstage gossip, generate exclusive video content, interviews and jam sessions, and share this with its audiences, with its own customers getting extra benefits. These may include VIP access, parties and intimate performances from artists. Some phone companies loan phones so people can share their partially branded photos and videos with their social media networks.

In a community-less society sponsorship can give supporters a greater sense of belonging

In an increasingly impersonal world (where email, texting and 'social' media platforms replace talking), while the pillars of society crumble (as trust plummets for churches, politicians, banks, police and communities), work pressure and time increases, and changing gender roles reduce a sense of order. ESA suggest:

> 'Our sense of community and belonging is increasingly under threat; this has led to the adoption of new allegiances and relationships, often passionate ones, with a range of interests. Increasing numbers of media outlets and digital channels are offering more compelling, in-depth and personalized content than ever before. It is no surprise that these stronger and more intimate affiliations across a range of sports, arts activities, live entertainment, charities, environmental concerns, politics and educational activities are offering their followers (supporters) a greater sense of belonging and association.'
>
> ESA (2015)

Mature sponsorship

Sponsors have got a lot more professional about leveraging their investment in sponsorship:

> Time has moved on and sponsorship has matured and now plays an integral role in an increasingly sophisticated marketing environment. While achieving significant media coverage is still important, it is now likely to be only one of many objectives set by the company. Some sponsors select properties with no, or at least very limited, media coverage because their objectives do not require it. Sponsorship is so versatile that a relationship can be used to fulfil a broad number of strategic marketing objectives. Selection of the most appropriate property to satisfy specific objectives is, therefore, often the most crucial part of the sponsorship process.
>
> ESA

Think of sponsorship as an enabler of marketing's broader objectives and strategies. It is not an end in itself. Today marketers look beyond the old objectives of reach and affinity and try to leverage the sponsorship to create value for consumers in a way that can, firstly, drive behavioural change, and secondly, reinforce the brand. As Rosen and Minsky (2011) say, sponsorship can 'create unique opportunities for experiences, access, self-expression, entertainment, connection, or contribution to the social good.'

So, what should be sponsored? How does one choose what to sponsor and what to reject? Maybe arts are good for computers and sports are bad for banks? If sports sponsorship is so good for Gillette, why does it bother to advertise at all? Or perhaps its advertising doesn't work, which means any meagre improvement would be deemed to be a success? Do sponsorship funds come out of the above-the-line budget, ie does it always mean reducing the advertising budgets, or can they come out of some corporate communications or corporate social responsibility (CSR) programme? How much should be spent? How much is too much? When does it become less value for money? How is it measured? Finally, what exactly does sponsorship mean? These are some of the questions this chapter answers.

The power of sponsorship

Tiger Woods is Nike's $650 million man. His contract stipulates that he wears Nike clothes when doing other brands' promotional work, so its brand piggybacks other sponsorship programmes and advertisements.

However, just like PR, sponsorship is uncontrollable as sponsors' brands can be damaged by behaviours of the people they sponsor. Woods' well-publicized personal problems a few years back resulted in the loss of several sponsorship deals.

Sponsorship shifting from brand exposure to brand activation

'In a little less than 20 years, the focus of sponsorship has shifted from the valuation of brand exposure (eg jerseys, boards, etc) to the sponsor's brand activation by focusing attention on the organization's relationship with the people interested in the event.'

Ferrand *et al* (2007)

What is sponsorship?

Sponsorship is more than patronage, altruism or benefaction. **It can indeed help others while simultaneously achieving specifically defined communications objectives.** Some sponsors see sponsorship as a form of enlightened self-interest, where a worthy activity is supported with cash and/or consideration in return for satisfying specific marketing or corporate objectives. As sponsorship matures, its diverse range of programmes, objectives, advantages and disadvantages requires a relatively sophisticated level of management understanding.

The target audience must be researched in detail, crystal-clear qualitative and quantitative objectives must be set, and appropriate types of sponsorship vehicles must be agreed, considered and selected. A programme of integrated communications has to be planned with precision, and sufficient budgets have to be allocated to allow for 'leveraging', stretching or maximizing the overall sponsorship impact.

Can anything be sponsored?

All sectors of society can be targeted and reached through sponsorship. Just about anyone or anything can be sponsored. You can even sponsor 'the possibility of an event'; Granada TV once sponsored Manchester's bid to host the Olympic Games. The range of sponsorship opportunities is limited only by one's imagination. The obvious areas are sport, arts, education, community and broadcast.

Whether the events are large or small (eg blind golf and blind cricket), sport offers an effective route into the minds of various target markets. Even within a particular sport there is a range of different sponsorship opportunities. Take football, for example. It is possible to sponsor a title, eg the Carling Cup or the Barclaycard Premiership, or a stadium, eg the Reebok Stadium. Perhaps a more interesting example is where Maxwell House coffee's Taste of Chicago sponsorship maximized the off-site potential by buying all 37,000 tickets to a game and then giving them away free in return for two empty Maxwell House jars. It is also possible to sponsor:

- a club, eg Emirates and Arsenal, Doritos and Wolverhampton Wanderers (incidentally, since the 1980s, five of Japan's baseball teams have been owned by railway companies, four by beverage companies, two by newspapers and one by an automobile company);
- a match day (eg York City gave 12 stand tickets, free buffet, free bar, free ads in the programme, hoardings in the car park and the opportunity to present the Man of the Match award and join players in the bar after the game – all for approximately £1,000);
- a kick-off (in the United States, Anheuser Busch sponsors NFL kick-offs, and they are referred to as 'Bud kick-offs');
- a ball, eg Crystal Palace FC match ball sponsorship costs £250;
- a fair play award, often tied in with another sponsorship package;
- a sin bin (the Northern Ireland police force wittily sponsored the 'sin bin' at the Belfast Giants hockey team – essentially made up of neutral Canadians);
- a player (players receive individual sponsorship and in return they open stores, meet employees and acknowledge the sponsor in the programme);
- a pass, a tackle, a goal, a save or a miss – the Pizza Hut and American Express examples in the boxes opposite show US baseball creating such exciting opportunities. Score updates, gossip about players and even free betting can be sponsored. It is even possible to sponsor a fictitious team in a kids' comic.

FIGURE 14.1 Sponsoring the national tour of Tim Peake's spacecraft

> **Sponsor anything: Sponsor a catch – fan catches 33,000 pizzas**
>
> Pittsburgh Pirates fan Ted Bianucci was picked at random out of a crowd at Three Rivers Stadium to take the field to try to catch three pop-ups (balls shot out of a gun used to help catchers practise defence). Sponsors Pizza Hut promised every spectator in the park a free soft drink at Pizza Hut (by showing the ticket stub), a jug of soft drink or a small pizza if the fan caught one, two or three respectively of the pop-ups. No one had ever previously caught all three. Bianucci, to the cheers of 33,789 people, caught all three balls – and $150,000 worth of pizza generates a lot of good feeling, and probably extra business as 33,000 customers enter Pizza Hut's premises.

Effectively, anything can be sponsored, including golf on the moon. A golf equipment manufacturer asked Russian cosmonaut Mikhail Tyurin, who was based on the International Space Station, to take a golf club and ball outside to tee off into space for what was likely to be the longest golf shot ever (IOL, 2006). See Samsung and National Museum Group's intriguing sponsorship of the national tour of Tim Peake's spacecraft on p 440 of this chapter. See also Red Bull's sponsorship of the mission to the edge of space and supersonic freefall parachute jump in Chapter 15, p 457). See more on sponsoring a spacecraft tour later.

It is the marketer's job to spot the opportunity and determine if it is really just a publicity stunt sponsorship or if it is a medium- to longer-term sponsorship programme.

> **Sponsoring a miss**
>
> American Express and Best Western International Hotels jointly sponsored a programme that donated $300 to a children's baseball league every time top baseball pitcher Nolan Ryan bowled or pitched an opposition player out. If Ryan pitched a 'no-hitter' (bowled the whole team out for nought) then a whopping $1.25 million would be donated by the sponsors to the league. AmEx and Best Western also

donated three cents every time an AmEx card was used to pay for a Best Western hotel. In addition, $2 was contributed for every newly approved AmEx card member application that came from a 'take-one' box at each Best Western hotel.

Arts sponsorship can be even more diverse – from sponsoring the opening of Disneyland Paris, to a film premiere, to a particularly obscure type of play to gain access to an otherwise difficult target market. Education is a sensitive area, and sponsorship can come in cash or in kind, such as a computer company donating computers to schools. **Community sponsorship** is becoming increasingly important as businesses recognize the importance of their community and their corporate responsibility. The corporate citizen is alive and well within the Per Cent Club. (In the UK, corporate members of the Per Cent Club promise to spend one-half of 1 per cent of their profits on community programmes. In the United States, there are also 2 per cent and 5 per cent clubs.) In the UK, it is possible to sponsor the police, the fire brigade and the coastguard. Off-licence chain Thresher sponsored a van for Avon and Somerset police force, while Newcastle Breweries sponsored a mobile police station.

Sponsoring a possibility and then asking FIFA for money back

'Morrisons supermarket chain sponsored England's failed 2018 World Cup bid. After the bid was lost, they called on FIFA to donate £1 million to charity for compensation for an 'unfair' bidding process. Morrisons said: "We think the decision-making process was unfair. We hope FIFA will do the right thing and offer £1m to be invested in grassroots football."'

PR Week, 17 December 2010

Other (unusual) types of sponsorship

Here are some other forms of sponsorship, which give an indication of the variety and potential available. An organization can sponsor an expedition (Mercury has sponsored a walk to the North Pole). British Aerospace, Memorex and Interflora signed as sponsors for a voyage into space (the package was subsequently cancelled). An organization can also sponsor a species (Systematics Association, a scientific group involved in classifying organisms, named seven wasps after the directors of Salomon Brothers when they waived a $300,000 debt arrangement). The 'Ugly Bartender' contest sponsored by the Multiple Sclerosis Society is its second-biggest revenue generator. Some years ago, cows wearing Vladivar Vodka jackets in a field near the London-to-Brighton railway line were sponsored during the Brighton festival. Akai sponsored bullfights at £10,000 a fight. BP sponsored Eugène Ionesco's play *Journeys Among the Dead*. Sponsoring a war? It is possible to sponsor sections of the US Army (eg the Medical Corps). On the other hand, sponsoring peace initiatives is also possible. For example, during the height of the Cold War the *Irish Times* sponsored an official televised arms debate between Soviet and US diplomats. It is even possible to sponsor an Amnesty International tour.

Broadcast sponsorship offers possibilities ranging from sponsoring other people's advertisements (Midland Bank's £50,000 and Cancer Research), to the weather, specific programmes and themed weeks on cable television.

Online events in virtual worlds or online community events (webcasts, discussions, video walls, etc) can be sponsored. Effectively, any event anywhere, online or offline, presents sponsorship opportunities that can be leveraged in many ways.

Managing a sponsorship programme

The SOSTAC® + 3Ms acronym (see Chapter 9, p 264) can be used to develop and manage a sponsorship programme.

SOSTAC® + 3Ms involves:

- defining target audiences;
- defining sponsorship objectives;
- analysing and summarizing the current sponsorship situation (including competitive review, previous sponsorship experiences, sponsorship strategies, etc);

- clarifying the strategy (how the sponsorship programme contributes towards the overall corporate or brand mission, marketing objectives and communication objectives);
- developing the tactical details of how it all fits together;
- building in measurement or evaluation to see whether the programme is worth repeating;
- identifying the resources required to leverage a programme to give the maximum return.

Situation: The target audiences

There are two different audiences. The first is the one immediately involved with the programme; the second is the one that can be reached through advertising and media coverage. Although there are many spin-off objectives that offer benefits to different target groups, the primary objective should be linked clearly with the primary audience. This involves some research into the lifestyles, attitudes, behaviour patterns, leisure activities, issues and demographics relevant to the primary target group. Previous research should have identified the current situation, ie how the sponsor is positioned in the target audience's mind. This will reveal the kinds of specific communications objectives that need to be set.

Objectives

After defining the target audiences, objectives must be fully clarified to focus both the spin-off activities (eg sales promotions linked with the core sponsorship programme) and the marketing support activities (eg advertising and publicity announcements around the sponsorship programme). A sponsorship programme can satisfy many objectives simultaneously. The range of objectives is varied:

- **Increase awareness:** Eg Canon sponsored the Football League to create a presence, become a familiar household name and generally raise awareness of a previously relatively unknown company in the UK marketplace. Its sponsorship gave it a foothold in the UK market.
- **Build/enhance an image:** This can help to reposition or strengthen a brand or corporate image through association with particular types of sponsorship activities, eg a caring image through community programmes. The sponsorship must support the brand values.
- **Activating a brand:** There is a shift in sponsorship from building brands to 'activating' brands.
- **Customer engagement:** There are many spin-off engagement benefits that can be shared with customers such as free gifts, tickets, photos in return for participation in a sales promotion.
- **Content generation:** Part of the sponsorship package can be the brand's own content creators generating content, eg behind the scenes interviews, photos, videos, etc.
- **Differentiate a brand:** Create a unique association with a particular passion point of a target audience.
- **Strengthen brand personality:** Associate a brand with an 'activity area' with which the target audience has a positive, and ideally, a passionate, connection (often referred to as a 'passion point'). This adds value to the overall brand proposition and allows a more personal, passionate and a more connected form of communicating.
- **Improve or maintain relations:** With customers, the trade, employees and even investors through hospitality and entertainment at a sponsored event. Rumbelow's department store sponsored English soccer's League Cup. Part of the agreement allowed the sponsor to appoint its own employee of the year to meet the teams and present the cup to the winning captain. Community relations can also be enhanced by supporting appropriate local activities.
- **Increase sales and open closed markets:** Coca-Cola was banned in Arab markets because it had built an Israeli bottling plant. Sponsorship of the 1989 Arab Youth Football Competition in Riyadh helped to open the door again.
- **Increase sales (sampling and direct sales):** Action-orientated sampling opportunities abound in a captive market where the buyer is in a relaxed frame of mind, for example

buying and drinking Victoria Beer at a touch-rugby competition sponsored by Victoria Beer. Some market research can also be carried out. Sponsorship can create a dialogue, whereas a lot of advertising is a monologue (although there are some campaigns that engage the customer in more than just a monologue).

- **Attract distributors or agents:** For example, sponsoring a radio station's weather forecasts to build awareness and attract enquiries from agents in other markets.
- **Employee motivation:** Offering employees special access to the sponsored event, or team.
- **Create promotional material:** Some events offer wonderful photo opportunities with scenes, sights and stars. One climbing equipment company sponsors climbs primarily to secure stunning photographs with branded climbing gear featuring prominently.
- **Circumventing advertising bans:** Sponsorship, particularly of televised events, allows sponsors a way around mainstream above-the-line advertising bans, for example tobacco companies sponsoring sports events such as snooker. Incidentally, the famous 1985 Steve Davis vs Dennis Taylor snooker final kept one-third of the British population glued to their TV sets until 3 am.
- **Cost effectiveness:** More bang for your buck when comparing CPT (cost per thousand) reached vs CPT for advertising.
- **Miscellaneous:** Ranging from, for example, the generation of new product ideas (new product educational competitions) to graduate recruitment.

Sponsorship strategy

The strategy statement briefly explains which types of sponsorship programmes are preferred, why a particular sponsorship programme is selected, how it will be exploited and integrated, and at what cost. To maximize the effect, sponsorship must be integrated with other elements of the communications mix, eg advertising, sales promotion, direct mail and public relations. It should also be explained internally and sometimes used internally as part of 'psychic income' (non-financial rewards that fulfil your dreams; see Chapter 11, p 339) as a means of improving employee relations.

A sponsorship policy helps the programme selection process by defining sponsorship parameters such as the preferred types of sponsorship that fit with the overall mission statement and the marketing and communication objectives. Questions to ask include the following: Is there any relevance between sponsor and subject, eg a chess competition and a computer company share values of intelligence? Is there a consistent message or objective behind all the organization's chosen sponsorship programmes? Does the association add value to the company or product? Does the sponsorship support the brand values? Is the association internationally acceptable? Think global; act local (sponsoring bullfighting is globally unacceptable, although Pepsi has sponsored it). Are there certain types or areas of sponsorship that are preferred? It is often felt that it is better to concentrate in certain areas. What is the ideal time in terms of seasonality and length of commitment, eg a three-year minimum? When should a sponsorship programme be dropped, changed or simply reviewed? Are both solus and shared or joint sponsorship programmes acceptable? Can staff involvement be incorporated? Does the sponsorship lend itself to leverage by offering potential for spin-off promotions and publicity? Does it lend itself to sales promotions? Can customers become even more engaged? Is it unique? Is it protectable from ambush marketing (see p 439 for more on this)? What is the competition doing? Are 'me-too' sponsorship packages (the competition follows with a similar sponsorship programme) preferred to unique (and uncopiable) sponsorship programmes? What kind of budget is required? What is defined as value for money?

Tiger Woods and a watch

Does the sponsorship support the brand values? The watch company TAG Heuer sponsored Tiger Woods for £1.5 million and he didn't even have to wear one of its watches while on the golf course (their sponsorship arrangement has now expired). Both brands, one might argue, are very similar. The trick is to balance the person and the product. Arguably, there was a good balance between Tiger Woods's and TAG Heuer's brand values: timing, focus and commitment.

Tactics

Squeeze as many benefits as possible into the programme. Sponsorship does not involve just adding the organization's name to an event, team or situation and waiting to see if awareness takes off overnight. A well-planned sponsorship programme involves attracting media coverage, corporate entertainment, new client recruitment, miscellaneous spin-off promotions and staff motivation schemes. (See the 'tactics' section in Chapter 9, p 280, to help develop a whole communications plan around the sponsorship package or to help integrate the sponsorship programme into the rest of the marketing communications activities.)

The launch is the easy bit. The real work starts then, as years one, two and three need constant attention to detail. A series of checklists and detailed plans (including contingency plans) have to be developed.

Actions

Internal marketing

The actions are all about internal marketing. Communicating, motivating and training staff if necessary. Without this, staff may feel alienated so it is reasonably common practice to share some of the benefits of sponsorship with the brand's own staff (as well as customers). See Liberty Insurance's sponsorship of the GAA, which includes staff days out and staff tickets to big matches on p 444. Actions also include detailed project management right down to logistics plans (see Tim Peake's Spacecraft Tour, p 440). And the details of sponsorship contracts need to be carefully checked as they try to cover all possible eventualities; eg, what if there is a media strike or blackout?

The agreement

Agreements need to be carefully checked, as sometimes, in the frenetic search for funding, those sponsored may promise the world to potential sponsors. The potential sponsor needs to exercise some caution. Here are some points worth considering:

1 Have the contract checked by an expert. In particular, check the exit clause and exit arrangements, since it may be harder to get out of sponsorship than to get into it. For example, it is easy to start supporting a local theatre, but when the sponsor wants to switch into a different type of sponsorship the eventual withdrawal of funds may prompt the local paper to print a headline that reads 'Company X Pulls Plug on Theatre' or 'Company X Leaves Theatre in the Dark'. Consider exit strategies also.
2 Can those sponsored deliver on their promises? Can they provide proof? Have they done it before? Have they any references? Are they financially secure?
3 Is it fair and reasonable to all parties? Sometimes razor-sharp negotiators agree a deal that is too good for the sponsors, which eventually creates problems. A good example is Nike's sponsorship deal with the Brazil football team (see the box 'Sponsor being too clever' on p 437).
4 Are there other opportunities for brand exposure via the sponsored person or organization's other marketing activities (see the next box)?

Nike piggyback on Tiger Woods' other endorsements

'Nike's association with Mr Woods has worked wonders for the company. After signing him in 1996, Nike redid the deal in 2000 for a reported $105 million. That may sound like a lot of money, but not only has Mr Woods single-handedly built Nike Golf, his apparel deal means that even when he appears in ads for his other partners, he wears Nike clothing. The swoosh is clearly visible in ads for American Express.'

Thomaselli (2006)

Note: When Tiger won the US Masters in 2019 his value increased enormously, despite his difficulties along the way.

Pilot scheme

Pilot testing is where 'action' overlaps with 'control'. In an ideal marketing world, all risks are reduced by testing and researching everything. Extra research costs resources, primarily time and money.

Sometimes the nature of a sponsorship programme does not lend itself to testing, eg sponsoring the English Football League, but customers can be asked what they would think of it (before signing on the dotted line). Alternatively, a local league can be sponsored to allow management to move up the learning curve. Telstra was reported to have jointly sponsored the 2003 Rugby World Cup so that it could learn about how sponsorship worked. The cautious or delayed approach arising from testing can also cause opportunities to be lost, since the competition may snap up the best sponsorship programmes. It may, however, identify some opportunities and avoid some nasty problems.

35 days' continuous monitoring

When npower sponsored cricket, media monitoring services revealed it received:

- 350 hours of TV coverage (Channel 4 and Sky);
- 12,500 banner sightings;
- 625 references in the national press.

Cost: £18 million over three years. Result: spontaneous awareness up to 45 per cent.

Roll-out

This is the exciting side that everyone sees without fully realizing the amount of work that goes on beforehand. Nevertheless, it is deceptively hard work since, even though the sponsors are enjoying entertaining their clients, it is still work. In smaller sponsorship programmes sponsors have constantly to think on their feet while entertaining, as minute problems inevitably crop up from time to time. In larger sponsorship programmes the constant alertness, attention to detail and readiness to react can be shared between members of staff (or a consultancy). Staff will be interested in high-profile sponsorship programmes. Keep staff informed about how the programme is working and whether it is on target and generating results. Where possible, include programme prizes as staff incentives. Marks & Spencer sponsors projects that attract staff involvement.

Control: Monitor, measure and evaluate

This is where the clearly defined sponsorship objectives make life easy, since results can be compared with predetermined targets. Once the result has been measured, further analysis as to why a programme was particularly successful or unsuccessful will help future sponsorship programmes. The first two objectives listed on p 433, awareness and image, would normally require some formal market research activity such as a survey. There is, in addition, an interim method of evaluating sponsorship – by the amount of media coverage or name mentions. There are many monitoring companies that provide such services.

Although cricket is on TV for long periods, its audience is often quite small. Sponsorship research company AGB divides broadcast time by audience size to give cricket a ranking of 67, less than half that of ice skating. There are other, sometimes simpler, approaches to measuring the effectiveness of sponsorship. For example, Volvo calculated that its $3 million tennis sponsorship generated 1.4 billion impressions (number of mentions or sightings times audience size), worth about $18 million in advertising. It is worth noting that this measures only the amount of media coverage or output. It does not measure the ultimate objectives of, say, increasing awareness, changing attitudes or improving relations with different groups. This is where money may have to be spent on commissioning a piece of research that looks inside, instead of outside, the minds of the target audience.

The other objectives can be relatively easily measured if a system of measurement is set up in the first place, eg everyone is briefed to log or identify the source of any enquiries from customers, agents or distributors. Then again, a common-sense approach may help to identify results, eg new distributors or increased sales, without changing any of the other elements of either the marketing or the communications mix (and assuming the competition has not had a strike or a factory fire).

Waffles or lager?

'In 1979 Belgium was "better known for its waffles than its lager". When TV ads were beyond budget, sponsorship of the Queen's tennis tournament beckoned. TV exposure and tennis's "aspirational and achievement" image matched Stella's objectives. Stella rose to number 1 in Britain's premium lager sector. Sales increased by 400 per cent.'

Observer, 1 April 1988

Canon got good value for its money when, some 30 years ago, it sponsored the Football League for a limited period only. As Frank Jefkins (1991) observed, 'Hardly an office in Britain is without a Canon machine. It only took £3 million and three years – peanuts in that sort of business when you think what the sales are valued at.' More recently, Barclays paid £31.5 million to sponsor the football league (Georgiou, 2018). Incidentally, the Premier League receives over £100 million pa from commercial partners, and is set to generate over £5 billion in domestic TV revenue over the course of the coming three-year rights cycle (Georgiou, 2018).

Sponsor being too clever

There was a legislative inquiry into Nike's sponsorship deal with the Brazilian football team. [Nike had negotiated a $400 million, 10-year kit sponsorship deal with the Brazilian Football Federation.] A sense that Nike had too much control over the country's affairs was magnified by original provisions in the contract allowing the company to promote 50 Nike-branded Brazil-friendly matches involving eight first team players... With World Cup qualifiers and other friendlies to organize, it became clear that the original number of Nike friendlies was too large. In November 1999 Brazil found itself double booked to play two matches. This led to a second-string Brazil team playing in Australia, while most of the country's top stars featured in a game against Spain. Consequently last April Nike reduced the contractual number of games it would promote to two a year. Also under the initial contract – since changed – legal disputes with the CFB were to be settled outside of Brazil. "The CFB transferred part of its autonomy as a public entity to Nike", said Aldo Rebelo (head of the 25-member committee of Brazil's Lower House of Congress investigating Nike's sponsorship deal).'

Colitt and Garrahan (2001)

Budgets

Budget allocation may in fact determine programme choice rather than the other way around. The formulae for determining the sponsorship budget vary, but a rough rule of thumb suggests that the basic sponsorship fee should be at least doubled to get maximum leverage from the programme (Coca-Cola allows 16 times the sponsor fee to generate maximum leverage).

This then leaves a budget for supporting marketing activities such as advertising and publicity, and maybe even some direct marketing. It also allocates some money for other spin-off activities. For example, sponsors of the Olympics will tend to milk the sponsorship to the maximum by running sales promotions offering Olympic prizes and donations in addition to simply carrying the 'official Olympic sponsors' logo. Payment can be in cash or in kind. A sponsor's services or facilities are likely to have a much greater value than cost; for example a newspaper sponsoring a boxing match can offer the fight promoter free advertising space in return for exclusive sponsorship rights. The cost may be minimal if the newspaper is not selling all its advertising space, while the value to the promoter is, of course, much greater.

There are also various government sponsorship grant programmes that contribute significantly towards the cost. (Check for any government subsidies; arts and business for example have different subsidy programmes.)

The 3Ms (men/women, money and minutes) need to be budgeted for and built into plans. Who is responsible for what – the supporting advertising, the spin-off sales promotions, the hospitality tent, the invitations, the publicity, etc? Is it all handled by an agency or controlled and administered by the in-house team? Time can be the greatest constraint to leveraging a sponsorship programme fully, since there may be lots of great ideas for exploiting the opportunities to the full but each one takes time to plan and ultimately put into action. Some estimates suggest a minimum of nine months is needed to develop a proper sponsorship strategy and programme plan.

Advantages and disadvantages of sponsorship

Advantages of sponsorship

Sponsorship can be cost-effective (compared to advertising) in terms of reaching a particular audience. It does allow access to very specific targeted audiences that otherwise might be difficult to reach. Sponsorship can achieve many different objectives (see 'Objectives', p 433), including:

- increased awareness;
- image enhancement;
- customer engagement;
- content generation;
- brand differentiation;
- strengthened brand personality;
- improved relationships;
- increased sales;
- sampling and database building;
- creating a platform for new promotional material;
- beating advertising bans, etc;
- employee motivation;
- cost effectiveness.

It also offers creative opportunities, including the engagement of an audience in a relaxed atmosphere of goodwill. Hospitality events open doors and create a dialogue that conventional media simply cannot match. As Alan Mitchell (1997) says, 'sponsorship reaches the parts conventional advertising cannot'. Sponsorship lends itself to integrated communications and the cost-effectiveness of integrated activities.

Sponsorship packages can offer brands an opportunity to communicate regularly. Finally, the effects of a sponsorship programme are measurable.

Even the uncontrollable nature of sponsorship is measurable. Consider the now classic case of the 1996 Olympic sponsors (who paid $40 million each). They were pleased to have the rights to the Winter Olympic Games in Lillehammer thrown in free of charge. The US figure skater Nancy Kerrigan was violently attacked six weeks before the Games began. The attack was masterminded by the ex-husband of her chief rival, Tonya Harding. Interest in Kerrigan's recovery created an avalanche of media coverage before, during and after the event. The extra, unplanned coverage was carefully measured and valued by the sponsors.

Disadvantages of sponsorship

Sponsorship cannot close sales; it only creates awareness. It can carry only a very limited message (for the masses), usually just a brand name, although some brands leverage the sponsorship into many diverse aspects, which allows more detailed brand value messages. The message cannot be controlled; a football hooligan wearing a club shirt with a sponsor's brand might appear on the front page of a newspaper, attacking a police officer. Guerrilla marketing can also damage the sponsor's impact. It is not so easy to change a message or to exit a sponsorship programme quickly (unless carefully planned). As with PR, there is a lack of control, as strikes, riots, weather and media all affect the impact of sponsorship.

Some say that sponsorship is insidious and that it undermines artistic integrity. In areas such as health and education, some feel that the issues involved are too important to be left to the whim of a corporation. Although sponsorship can deliver extremely cost-effective benefits, it can be misunderstood by employees as an excessive indulgence if they are kept in the dark about it and if there are redundancies occurring at the same time. In both cases sponsorship, particularly high-profile sponsorship, needs to be presented to the employees as a cost-effective business tool that can help the business to survive and thrive in the future. Sponsorship of a competitive activity, such as a football club, can alienate the company or product from the opposition fans, eg a national audience if the teams are involved in an international competition, or an even larger audience if the team or player behaves badly.

Global media coverage may not be a good thing if what is being sponsored in one country is unacceptable in another country, for example bullfighting, camel wrestling, etc. If the medium is the message (ie the choice of sponsorship reflects the values of the sponsor), the message can become tarnished through its association with a socially unacceptable event. Some sponsorship deals can alienate a whole nation, particularly if the sponsor is perceived to have negotiated too good a deal for itself (see the box 'Sponsor being too clever', p 437). The uncontrollability of so many variables from weather to fans to strikes to riots makes sponsorship more risky than advertising. Even pop concerts are risky, as Naomi Klein (2000) points out:

> Celine Dion's concert tour was picketed by human rights activists in Boston, Philadelphia and Washington, DC. Although she was unaware of it, her tour sponsor – Ericsson cellular – was among Burma's most intransigent foreign investors, refusing to cease its dealings with the junta despite the campaign for an international boycott.

Finally, ambush marketing allows non-sponsoring competitors to soak up some benefits without paying full sponsorship fees.

Ambush marketing

Ambush marketers attack official event sponsors by running competing promotions, events and advertisements close to the official sponsors' activities. This way they create an aura of being official sponsors without paying the official sponsor fees. An example is the classic 1984 ambush by Kodak when it sponsored the ABC TV coverage of the Olympics despite Fuji being the official sponsor. In 1988 Kodak was the official Olympics sponsor while Fuji sponsored the US swimming team. Nike managed to 'ruin the 1996 Olympics for the official sponsors by ruthless advertising and by exploiting its star names' (Boshoff, 1997). The International Olympic Committee stepped in next time round by ordering that all poster sites in Athens be bought up and fairly distributed. For the 1998 World Cup, Adidas paid £20 million to be an official sponsor and, among other things, built a football village under the Eiffel Tower, while Nike responded with a site on the outskirts of Paris. Adidas signed up Paul Gascoigne, Paul Ince and David Beckham, as well as sponsoring the kit of nine teams, including Germany, France and Spain, while Nike sponsored six squads, including the favourites, Brazil (which cost £250 million over 10 years). The *Daily Telegraph* reported that 'rumours have it that Nike is willing to spend £20 million to hijack its arch-rivals Adidas during the competition in France'. Adidas planned a series of 'counter-stunts' and intended to 'ambush their ambush by having our own stunts and tricks'. Both companies supposedly had £20 million to spend on the five months up to and including the competition (on top of Adidas' sponsorship fee).

There is nothing really new in this, as ambush marketing has been around almost as long as sponsorship itself. Measurement of the 1991 Rugby World Cup broadcast sponsorship demonstrated its ability to influence consumers and override the main event sponsors. Spontaneous brand awareness of Sony rose among Rugby World Cup watchers by eight points to 61 per cent (between September and November). Despite the recession, the company went on to record sales in December. Although Sony was not a sponsor of the event itself, it did sponsor the ITV coverage. ITV report that invariably the first name mentioned as sponsor of the Rugby World Cup and overwhelmingly seen as the main sponsor was Sony.

However, over-zealous policing can backfire. Pepsi was one of the official sponsors at the 2003 Cricket World Cup in South Africa. The drinks company had to distance itself from the embarrassment of the publicity surrounding the ejection of a fan caught drinking a can of Coca-Cola. Previously, Coca-Cola had been the official sponsor of the Football World Cup in Japan, where organizers had stopped fans from taking Pepsi into the stadium. This kind of action is not necessarily protecting sponsors from mainstream ambush marketing but is an indication of the attention to detail and the lengths that event organizers will go to in order to protect the interests of sponsors. It can, however, backfire in publicity terms.

Shani and Sandler's (1989) study of ambush marketing revealed that it works. For example, Wendy's got what it wanted for about $20 million or so less than McDonald's spend. McDonald's didn't leverage its sponsorship well at all, advertising its super-value meals and Double Big Macs instead of its Olympic sponsorship.

For some 20 years now, the Olympics Committee has had clear anti-ambush guidelines, including the registering of all trademarks and emblems, coordination with city authorities to control the skies above venues, and ensuring that sponsors have first option for any broadcasting and advertising rights for the event in each country where the Olympics is shown on TV. In 2010 a beer company tried ambush marketing tactics inside the stadium by introducing a group of women wearing similar shirts. The women were ejected. The laws and regulations have become more stringent (the UK has specific Olympic legislation in place to stop ambush marketing).

Unpredictable sponsorship results from an ambushed knee

'When US skater Tonya Harding's associates hammered her main competitor Nancy Kerrigan's knee, they performed a dastardly deed – which happened to boost the fortunes of Kerrigan's sponsors, Campbell's Soups, for the first time in a decade. Campbell's was also a sponsor of the US Figure Skating Association. After the incident Campbell's placed ads everywhere, and when Kerrigan recovered and came back to win silver Campbell's sales skyrocketed. Which just goes to show that no amount of planning could have produced the publicity it received from the wounded-knee incident and the sales bump that accompanied it. Campbell's was even mistakenly perceived by the general public as a full-fledged Olympic sponsor in 1994, even though it wasn't.'

Schlossberg (1996)

Now let us see what two actual sponsorship campaigns look like: firstly, Samsung and the Science Museum Group's unique sponsorship of the national tour of Tim Peake's spacecraft, and secondly how a new entrant into a new market used sponsorship to establish itself – a great example of how to leverage sponsorship way beyond just a match, a cup or a competition – Liberty Insurance's sponsorship of the Gaelic Athletic Association.

CASE STUDY Sponsoring the national tour of Tim Peake's spacecraft

Despite the world's fascination with space travel and what lies beyond, it is staggering that only 24 people in the world have travelled beyond the Earth's orbit – out of them, only seven have been British. The Science Museum Group's acquisition of Tim Peake's (Britain's first-ever astronaut to board the International Space Station) spacecraft from the Soyuz TMA-19M mission was an amazing opportunity for Samsung and the Science Museum Group to address the challenge of how to open up the subject of space travel to as many people as possible across the UK (particularly beyond the capital, where many of UK's world-class cultural organizations are heavily concentrated) and help them to relate and engage with the science and inspiring technologies that make space travel possible.

Samsung partnered with the Science Museum Group to sponsor this unique tour which included the Soyuz TMA-19M capsule – complete with equipped interior and char marks on its outer body from its re-entry into Earth's atmosphere – and is displayed along with its 25-metre diameter parachute and the Sokol KV-2 spacesuit Peake wore during his high-speed descent back to Earth.

Objectives

To inspire millions of young people across the UK by bringing to life the wonder of space travel, sparking a curiosity in life-long learning. To inspire the next generation of scientists, engineers and technologists.

Strategy

Create a highly interactive, engaging and inspiring experience, targeting KS3/4 students in schools with low cultural engagement rates who may be disengaged with STEM (science, technology, engineering and mathematics) subjects. Share the experience by bringing the experience to the people rather than trying to bring the people to the experience.

Tactics

The 'Soyuz Rocket Show' was delivered in schools by the Science Museum Group Outreach team. Schools were visited by an immersive Samsung VR bus (double-decker

FIGURE 14.2 Tim Peake, the UK's first European Space Agency astronaut to visit the International Space Station, wanted to share the experience with schoolchildren to ignite their interest in space and ultimately STEM subjects

FIGURE 14.3 Tim Peake sharing the knowledge and inspiration with schoolchildren (note the look of amazement on one of the children's faces)

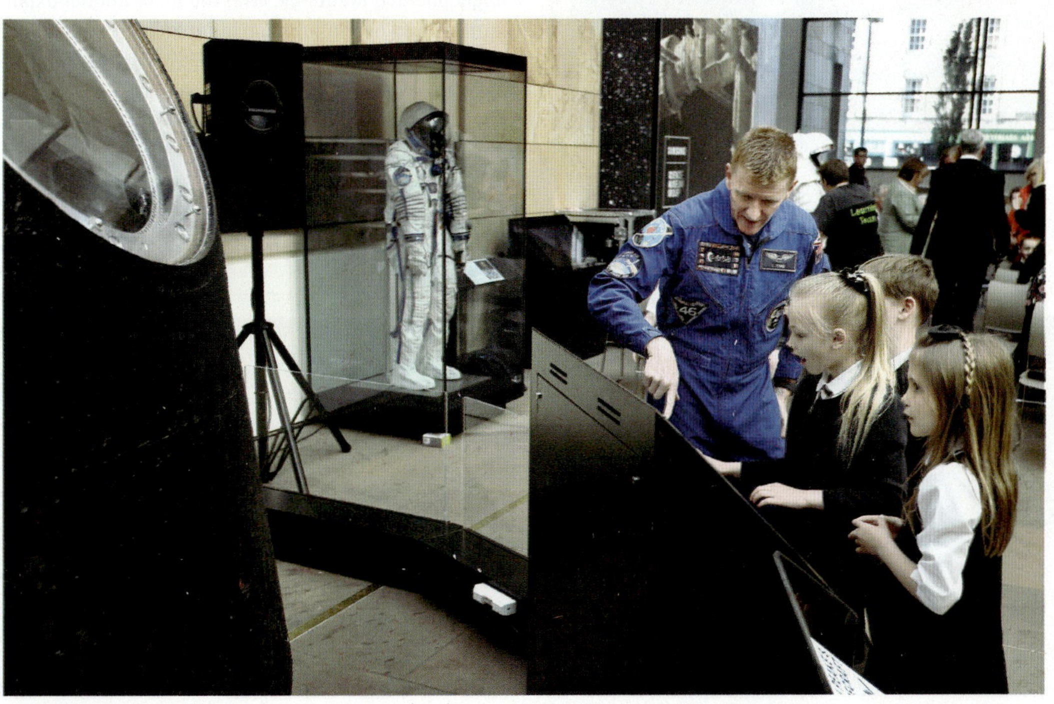

FIGURE 14.4 The Soyuz TMA-19M capsule with char marks on its outer body from its re-entry into Earth's atmosphere

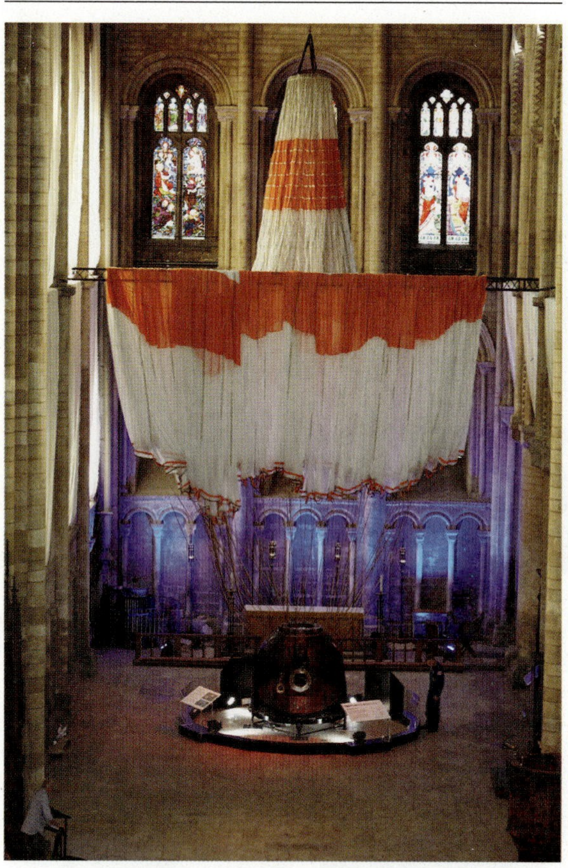

conversion) mirroring the inside of the International Space Station, fully equipped with educational games and a VR lounge upstairs. Students visited their local tour venue to see Soyuz and to partake in a specially curated STEM themed day

Accompanying the spacecraft was the unique Space Descent VR experience. With the help of Samsung Gear VR technology, Space Descent VR placed visitors at the heart of Tim Peake's historic return voyage to Earth from the International Space Station and was voiced by the astronaut himself.

Actions

The logistics of this tour were carefully managed by a highly trained team who knew how to liaise with schools, their curriculum and ultimately how to inspire the children with a once-in-a-lifetime experience. The ongoing collection of feedback from students, teachers and institutions revealed extraordinary enthusiasm from the children, with science clubs increasing by 600 per cent in some cases. The national tour project was meticulously managed by a dedicated project team.

Control/results

The tour and its outreach programme received overwhelmingly positive feedback, with the inspirational experiences both in and outside the museum helping Samsung and the National Science Museum to reach diverse audiences at levels far exceeding initial expectations.

FIGURE 14.5 Samsung's 360-degree immersive and interactive double decker 'Space Descent VR Experience' bus visited schools to deliver Soyuz Rocket Shows

FIGURE 14.6 Schoolchildren learning how to make rocket fuel on a Samsung tablet aboard the Space Descent Bus

FIGURE 14.7 The Samsung VR Bus resulted in more than 56,000 engagements in 130 days at over 90 locations including more than 60 schools

Across seven sites:

- Over 1.2 million visitors visited tour venues across the UK with the mid-project visitor target exceeded after just two venues.
- Tour venues saw increases in visitors of between 31 and 810 per cent (nearly 10 times more visitors at Peterborough Cathedral) during the time Soyuz was in situ.
- The VR Lounge at each local museum venue received 43,891 visitors – a 327 per cent increase compared to the initial campaign target.
- The Samsung VR Bus resulted in more than 56,000 engagements in 130 days at over 90 locations including more than 60 schools.
- The tour had a significant impact on regional museum partners, supporting them to connect with local audiences like never before.

Education outreach programme

The programme was delivered to more than 10,000 students from over 60 schools. Students have displayed an increase in STEM knowledge behind Tim's principal mission and the desire to want to find out more.

Teachers confirmed that the outreach programme exceeded their expectations and would recommend it to other educators. The schools expressed a desire to develop relationships with their local museums to continue to inspire students in STEM learning.

FIGURE 14.8 On the Samsung VR Bus

Marketing results

- 584 pieces of coverage with an estimated reach of over 117 million.
- Joint national marketing campaign across all sites promoting the activity (OOH, social, online) delivered an estimated 37 million impressions/impacts.
- The bus was invited to numerous exciting festivals and events around the country, including the Bradford Science Festival, Bournemouth Air Show, Norwich Science Festival and the BT Young Scientist and Technology Exhibition in Dublin, as well as to the Houses of Parliament.

FIGURE 14.9 The bus was invited to festivals and events around the country

CASE STUDY Liberty Insurance and GAA

What is the GAA?

The Gaelic Athletic Association is the largest sporting body in Ireland; Gaelic games are among the most-watched spectator sports in Ireland, with over 1 million people attending matches live in any given year. The GAA has 600,000 registered members and over 2,300 GAA clubs nationwide. Every parish/community in the country has a historically established GAA club, allowing sponsors to reach all points in the country. Supporters of the GAA are deeply loyal to sponsors with a high level of the population agreeing that they would look favourably on a brand that sponsors the GAA.

Situation analysis

In May 2013 for the first time ever in Irish sporting history, a sponsor, Liberty Insurance (LI), brought together Ireland's two oldest field games: hurling (a male sport) and camogie (a female sport) in a unique and ground-breaking sponsorship. Part of the sponsorship planning process included qualitative research among hurling players, camogie players and supporters. This research revealed key insights around the GAA engagement and participation. These outputs underpinned the strategic planning and activation of the sponsorship over 18 months. LI wanted an innovative programme that positioned hurling and camogie on an equal platform, and for LI to stand out in a cluttered market, bolstering the image of Liberty Insurance (part of a global insurer) as committed to the Irish market and understanding the passion of the Irish for sport, while also delivering a return on business objectives, driving sales and quote volumes.

Objectives

- **Awareness and brand building:** Drive sponsorship awareness; deliver minimum increase in two or more image statements; achieve higher consideration of Liberty Insurance among those aware vs unaware of the sponsorship; drive social media engagement through value-added content; maximize all opportunities for PR and media exposure.
- **Acquisition and retention:** To increase insurance quotes and sales through the use of incentives targeted towards GAA hurling and camogie clubs.

FIGURE 14.10 Liberty Insurance sponsorship of GAA

SOURCE: Liberty Insurance

- **Fan engagement:** Deliver an enhanced fan experience for hurling and camogie supporters through experiential match day activations.
- **Commercial relationships:** To develop a comprehensive programme to build meaningful relationships with brokers and commercial partners, including delivery of corporate hospitality to key insurance brokers currently engaged with Liberty Insurance.
- **Employee engagement:** Increase excitement and awareness among staff through the development of an inclusive employee engagement programme.

Strategy

LI used careful audience and media research to identify a previously untapped sponsorship opportunity and integrate it with PR to gain access to a traditionally difficult target market. The selection of 'the bringing together' of Ireland's two oldest field games is a unique and ground-breaking sponsorship. It also complements and reinforces LI brand values of integrity, inventiveness and fairness. The sponsorship has increased both awareness and reputation, driven positive engagement with Liberty Insurance and delivered a significant commercial return on investment.

Tactics

The LI approach was underpinned by an innovative campaign, positioning camogie/hurling on an equal platform across multiple consumer touchpoints.

- **Awareness and brand building:**
  - TV, print and online creative featuring hurling/camogie players provided a point of differentiation and showcased Liberty Insurance's shared passion for both sports.
  - Live Twitter Q&As with camogie/hurling players.
  - Innovative digital and print media partnerships with Today FM, Newstalk, www.thejournal.ie, the *Irish Times* and the *Irish Independent.*
  - PR strategy 'One Game: One Family' was developed with players from both sports.
- **Acquisition and retention:**
  - GAA club affinity programme via dedicated microsite.
  - €50 to a nominated hurling/camogie club for every insurance policy purchased.
  - Entry for your nominated club into a draw for €10,000 with every insurance quote.
  - Customer opportunities for sons/daughters to be flagbearers on match days.
- **Fan engagement – match day activations including:**
  - Complimentary branded shuttle buses bringing supporters to matches.
  - Best banner and 'supporter of the match' competitions; face painting and ice creams in family fun zones.

  - Flagbearer opportunities for children at All Ireland Finals and Semi Finals.
  - Distribution of supporter 'Scór' scrollers; use of Liberty Insurance 'blimps'.
- **Commercial relationships:**
  - Provision of tickets, hospitality and events to foster relationships with Liberty Insurance's broker partners and stakeholders.
- **Employee engagement:**
  - 'Liberty's Big Day Out', Croke Park's largest ever sponsor-run event, for employees and families.
  - Staff competitions for match tickets and mascot opportunities.

Action/execution

Careful attention to detail, staff training and project management ensures that all aspects of this innovative sponsorship programme are executed professionally, including: LI employees benefiting from LI's association with both hurling and camogie (900 employees and their families celebrated LI's sponsorship at 'Liberty's Big Day Out' in Croke Park, and 60 per cent of staff regularly attend matches during the Hurling and Camogie Championships).

Match day activation was carefully carried out to ensure all activation was carried out smoothly for: the complimentary shuttle buses to key fixtures; once-in-a-lifetime opportunities for children to be flag-bearers at the All Ireland Hurling and Camogie Finals; and contributing to the drama and theatre on the day with 'best banner' and 'supporter of the match' competitions.

Several selected players were encouraged to tweet.

Control/evaluation

- **Awareness and brand building:**
  - Increased sponsorship awareness among GAA fans.
  - Uplift achieved across six brand image attributes.
  - Established a substantial consideration gap (aware vs unaware).
  - Considerable PR and media exposure.
  - Significant social media reach and engagement across Hurling and Camogie Championships.
- **Acquisition and retention:**
  - GAA activation affected significant uplifts across business metrics including acquisition, customer retention and net promoter score (NPS).
- **Fan engagement:**
  - Match day experiential activation programme delivered to significant percentage of supporters on match days and in stadia.
- **Commercial relationships:**
  - Tickets and hospitality provided to a significant percentage of Liberty Insurance's broker partners and commercial stakeholders.
- **Employee engagement:**
  - 900+ employees and their families participated in 'Liberty's Big Day Out'.

3Ms

- **Men/women:** The ongoing management of Liberty Insurance's sponsorship is maintained through a partnership arrangement with regular meetings and engagement with rights holders, as well as fortnightly inter-agency meetings with advertising, creative, PR and social media agencies. Employee involvement is important too, with over 50 per cent of Liberty Insurance employees directly engaged in the sponsorship, entering competitions, attending matches, participating as flag bearers and other related events. The sponsorship is activated through internal communications and ongoing face-to-face briefings including opportunities to have photographs taken with the All Ireland Hurling and Camogie Trophies. Staff are actively encouraged to participate in live Twitter Q&As with match players.
- **Money:** The sponsorship fees and the budget for promoting the sponsorship across a range of tactical tools and channels are not available for release at this point in time.
- **Minutes:** A five-year partnership with the GAA and Camogie Associations was announced in May 2013.

FIGURE 14.11 Liberty Insurance sponsorship at work

SOURCE: Liberty Insurance

Key points from Chapter 14

- Almost anything can be sponsored.
- Almost any target audience can be reached through sponsorship.
- Choose sponsorship programmes carefully, and separate the initial excitement from the numerical analysis.
- Sponsorship can provide a cost-effective marketing communications tool, satisfying a range of different objectives.
- Maximize leverage by integrating sponsorship with other communications tools.
- Sponsorship does not have total control over the message. Have contingency plans in case things go wrong.
- Think global, but act local (today's satellite communications may highlight a sponsorship programme that is acceptable overseas but unacceptable at home and vice versa).
- Budgets should be secured to leverage the programme and maximize impact through other communications tools.
- Keep employees informed. Sometimes getting them involved increases the leverage.
- Run a small pilot scheme, if possible, to iron out any teething problems.
- Beware of ambush marketing.

References and further reading

Atkinson, S (2007) Why just a logo is now a no-no, *BBC News*, 21 June

Boshoff, A (1997) World Cup's battle of the boots, *Daily Telegraph*, 4 December

Colitt, R and Garrahan, M (2001) Nike finds Brazil deal a bad fit, *Financial Times*, 12 January, p 19

Collett, P and Fenton, W (2011) *The Sponsorship Handbook*, Jossey-Bass

ESA (2015) European Sponsorship Association, ESA DIPLOMA 2015 (Study notes – module one, section 1.8.1)

Ferrand, A, Torrigiani, L, Camps, I and Povill, A (2007) *The Routledge Handbook of Sports Sponsorship*, Routledge

Georgiou, S (2018) Barclays extends league sponsorship deal, *SportsPro*, 16 November

Giles, C (1991) *Business Sponsorship*, Butterworth-Heinemann, Oxford

Head, V (1981) *Sponsorship: The newest marketing skill*, Woodhead-Faulkner, Cambridge

IOL (2006) The year of golf in space, IOL, 7 December

Jefkins, F (1991) *Modern Marketing Communications*, Blackie & Son, London

Klein, N (2000) *No Logo*, Flamingo, London

Lusbec, K (2015) Adidas all in with Bayern Munich until 2030 for €900m, *Football Marketing XI*, 30 April

Mitchell, A (1997) Sponsorship works, *Marketing Business*, September

Rosen, W and Minsky, L (2011) Six steps to successful sponsorships, *HBR Insight Center Marketing That Works*, July 28

Schlossberg, H (1996) *Sports Marketing*, Blackwell, Oxford

Shani, D and Sandler, D (1989) Olympic sponsorship versus ambush marketing, *Journal of Advertising Research*, August/September

Shank, M (2002) *Sports Marketing: A strategic perspective*, 2nd edn, Prentice Hall, Englewood Cliffs, NJ

Sports Illustrated (2018) Ranking the Top 10 Athletes by Endorsement Income for 2018, *Sports Illustrated*, 19 September

Thomaselli, R (2006) Dream endorser: Tiger Woods as a giant of marketing ROI, *Ad Age*, 24 September

Turner, S (1987) *Practical Sponsorship*, Kogan Page, London

WARC (2005) Coke pours $500 million into soccer sponsorship, 24 November

Further information

Business in the Community
137 Shepherdess Walk
London N1 7RQ
Tel: +44 (0)20 7566 8650
www.bitc.org.uk

European Sponsorship Association (ESA) Office
Suite 130
61 Victoria Road
Surbiton
Surrey KT6 4JX
Tel: +44 (0)20 8390 3311
https://sponsorship.org/

Ofcom
Riverside House
2a Southwark Bridge Road
London SE1 9HA
Tel: +44 (0)300 123 3000
www.ofcom.org.uk

15 Content marketing and other sales promotion

LEARNING OBJECTIVES

By the end of this chapter you will be able to:

- understand the variety and importance of content marketing and sales promotions;
- explore the process of creating and distributing content marketing;
- discuss the difference between strategic sales promotions and tactical sales promotions;
- separate brand-enhancing sales promotions from brand-diluting sales promotions;
- grasp the emergence of gamification as a potent sales promotions tool;
- integrate sales promotions with other elements of the communications mix;
- avoid the typical costly trial and error;
- embrace creativity, amidst the vast range of collaborative opportunities.

Content marketing

Content marketing is a type of sales promotion where the gift or prize is content marketing. We will explore more traditional sales promotions like competitions, gifts and prizes in the second half of this chapter. But first let us explore one of the hottest topics in marketing today: content marketing. It has become a major part of most organizations' marketing efforts today. It can be a source of competitive advantage. It can also be a waste of time and effort. So let's explore the best practice.

What is content marketing?

Content marketing includes videos, webinars, infographics, PowerPoint slides, tweets, posts, posters (memes), articles, speeches, white papers, books, games, VR and AR experiences to help customers to fulfil their own needs and goals. Content should inspire; entertain; educate; inform; help; reward (Meaningful Brands, 2019).

The content marketing process involves researching, creating, promoting, distributing high-quality content at the right time and in the right place and then measuring its effectiveness. See the range of content in the content pyramid (Figure 15.1).

Surprisingly, a well-produced printed book (with excellent graphics and production value, and assuming good content) is top of the content pyramid (if its content is relevant to the target market).

FIGURE 15.1 The content pyramid

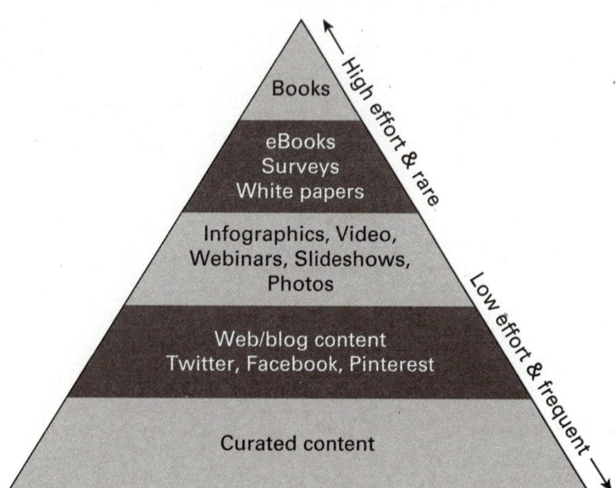

SOURCE: Adapted from **curata.com**

Creativity, aesthetics and graphic design are important. See also how Zip World seeded a few stunning photographs with influencers to deliver a massive boost in sales (p 611).

Managing content marketing

Situation

Content marketing is part of CX

If more than 85 per cent of Google searches were for useful information and only 10 per cent of searches were for products and services (Toll, 2014), it follows that producing good quality marketing content will satisfy searchers' needs and give them a good customer experience (CX). Note this excellent quality content also satisfies some of Google's SEO criteria, which requires relevant high-quality content that people like (and engage with) across multiple platforms. Some brands, like Red Bull, make content marketing a major part of the brand experience.

Content marketing is now a significant part of the CX as you help them along their journey.

Content challenge

Can you deliver a stream of relevant added-value content that your customers will appreciate? Can you do this better than competition? Can you deliver it in real time – just when they need it and where they need it? Customers are drowning in a sea of content – some good and some bad. Customers' ability to consume content is finite because there are only so many hours in a day to read/watch/listen, even to really interesting content. Meanwhile, competitors are churning out content – some good and some bad.

Nine out of 10 consumers expect brands to deliver content, but consumers think 58 per cent of content from brands is irrelevant (Meaningful Brands, 2019). In fact, most customers wouldn't care if most brands disappeared forever. *Havas Meaningful Brands Report 2019* reveals that customers couldn't care if 77 per cent of brands disappeared (3 per cent higher than the 2018 report). So, why should they bother reading your content? Brands seen as meaningful and viewed as making the world a better place have seen their

FIGURE 15.2 Content wars rage while customers drown in a sea of content

wallet share multiply by 9, and see a 24-point greater purchase intent (Sweeney, 2019).

Content wars

Mark Schaefer (2014) describes this as the 'content shock' when 'At some point, the amount I am "paying out" will exceed the amount I am bringing in and at that point, creating content will not be a smart business decision for me and many other businesses.'

We may have to pay customers to read our content! In fact, we already are (indirectly as we spend, say, six hours writing a blog post at a nominal cost of £100 per hour = £600 spent producing the piece!).

> 'Lowering the barrier of content creation to near-zero has contributed to an exponential rise in content production, making it more difficult than ever to gain attention and engagement.'
>
> Buzzsumo

Big budgets might win the content war

Some competitors will pay to promote their content. If their regular audience fails to engage, they may try to reach a broader audience via paid media (sponsored posts or tweets or messages). This makes it even more difficult for the other companies' content to be effective. The biggest budgets may prevail by promoting heavily their content against yours.

Hyper-competitive content marketing (cars compete with Red Bull and Coca-Cola)!

> 'Honda plans future models 10 years in advance but it is now having to think about how it creates content that vies for attention against content powerhouses like Red Bull and Coca-Cola. Meanwhile, the likes of Tesla (with electric cars), Dyson (which is set to enter the automotive market in the next two years) and Amazon (with its test-driving partnership with Volvo) are changing the way the automotive industry works entirely.'
>
> Hammett (2018)

Loyalty and emotion disappearing?

Mark Schaefer (2019b) recently observed that 'Research by McKinsey and others shows the reason people feel disconnected or even distrustful of brands is because there is a lack of emotional connection with the company and its products'. This creates an opportunity to create powerful, emotional, content, to help brands build relationships again. Fully 87 per cent of our customers 'shop around' now (Schaefer, 2019a).

> Content is an area where most marketers are failing, according to the report. Consumers expect relevant, personal content from their favourite brands, but brands are missing the opportunity to engage them in a meaningful way that builds loyalty.
>
> Schaefer (2019a)

Content research

Mission and brand values

An organization's choice of content ('content strategy') is influenced by its mission, its brand values and brand personality and also what your customers want or would value, that your competitors do not currently create.

Content research involves looking at trends, customer needs, direct and indirect competitors to see who is producing what content, which content works best, and most importantly, are there any gaps in the market where your brand could become the expert source?

Magic marketing formula (for content)

The magic marketing formula we introduced in Chapter 1 also works for content marketing: IRD (identify customer content needs; reflect those needs (or solutions) in the content name; and deliver the content at the right time and in the right place.

Talk to customers, ask them what would help them, inform them, inspire them, entertain them, etc. Ask them what would they really like. Also, search your own and your competitors' reviews, comments, complaints, FAQs and anywhere customer concerns might exist. Then search more widely for questions relating to your product/service's features and benefits. Identify customer content needs. You might be pleasantly surprised to find that you already have the basic answers to these questions. They just need to be produced with nice graphics or on video, etc.

Tommy's Tent Company identify needs

Tommy has a tent company and wants to be on YouTube. So he visits all of his competitor sites and analyses all the comments/discussions to identify what are people concerned about when buying tents. He discovers customers are concerned about whether the tents are (a) as big and (b) as fully waterproof as claimed by many tent companies. Tommy's research also reveals that the typical customer is new to camping.

What should he do next?

- Tweak website copy – spelling out size and water-resistance of his tents.
- Website copy may not be enough – video a tent outside during a rain storm and film a product video inside (big and waterproof).
- Not too 'sales-ey' – all practical and authentic (and add some tips).

His video isn't focused on technical details. These can be addressed elsewhere if more experienced campers need this information.

Audit existing content

Most organizations already have a lot of marketing content (market research, white papers, presentations, speeches, articles, videos, photos, graphics, as well as social media content). Some potential content is less obvious but nevertheless easy, such as book reviews (if written by the CEO). FAQs collected by customer service teams can be a rich source of content recreated into '10 most popular questions', '10 questions you've got to answer', '10 reasons why' or '10 things you've got to know'. These can be converted into quizzes with multiple answers, or self-assessment widgets. Speeches – record them and then edit them into shorter clips. Slide shows – share them on SlideShare. Re-use the graphics. Work out what customers need first, then create a content plan and calendar and deliver it. Being creative is great, but it has to be relevant/interesting to the customer. One problem remains. Most customers do not fully know what they want nor what they might like in the future (as they cannot imagine it).

Audit your current content to see what works best. Compare with your competitors' content to see what works for them. Look out for content gaps, particularly if there's nothing already on YouTube on this topic. Companies like Buzzsumo, Compete, Crawlytics, Hitwise and SimilarWeb analyse what content works best for your competitors (or you can do this research yourself) and they also benchmark your customer acquisition strategy against competitors.

Your choice of content ('content strategy') will also be influenced by your mission, your brand values and brand personality and also what your customers want (or would value), that your competitors don't currently have.

> Perhaps you already have some great content, but in the wrong format; or maybe it's just not easily findable on the site.
>
> Chaffey and Smith (2017)

Content shock

Content shock (content saturation) will occur in your market at some point. You need to recognize when it does and consider stopping or varying your approach to publishing this content (see below). Here's Mark Schaefer's explanation: 'As content becomes saturated, it will be more difficult to break through the noise. The cost of competing will rise due to the need for better content and paid promotion. Content engagement levels will fall. Some will be squeezed out of the content marketing option when costs outweigh benefits' (Schaefer, 2018).

Schaefer's five content saturation implications

If entering a saturated content market:

1. Create radically different and exceptional content.
2. Discover specific niches or networks (eg LinkedIn or YouTube) where content is still gaining traction.
3. Promotion and amplification are critical (including paid ads).
4. If you are a leader in a saturated niche, more content might create content shock for competitors.
5. Identify topics before they become saturated – build authority, reputation and trust early and quickly.

Schaefer (2018)

Schaefer's four unsaturated niche guidelines

If in an unsaturated niche:

1. Create core evergreen content.
2. Develop authoritative content.
3. Increase quality content publishing schedule.
4. Build content promotion competency.

Schaefer (2018)

You can see content shock when more and more content is released/published (by everyone) and less and less engagement occurs. When the two graphs meet, content shock occurs. Schaefer's content shock has a common pattern: as the volume of posts/articles/content (blue bars) about, coincidentally, the topic of 'content marketing' grows (Figure 15.3), the average number of shares/engagement declines (black line) well before 'content saturation', ie when the number of articles peaks.

Objectives

Content marketing objectives

Think carefully about what you are trying to achieve with your content marketing. Is it to: inspire; entertain; educate; inform; help; reward? Look at it from the customer journey point of view – is it to build awareness, consideration, preference, sales and after that, strengthening post-sales relationships?

Some content is better for certain tasks. Figure 15.4 shows Dave Chaffey's Smart Insights content matrix, which shows which content type supports the objectives of: entertain, inspire, convince and educate.

FIGURE 15.3 Articles published on content marketing and average shares

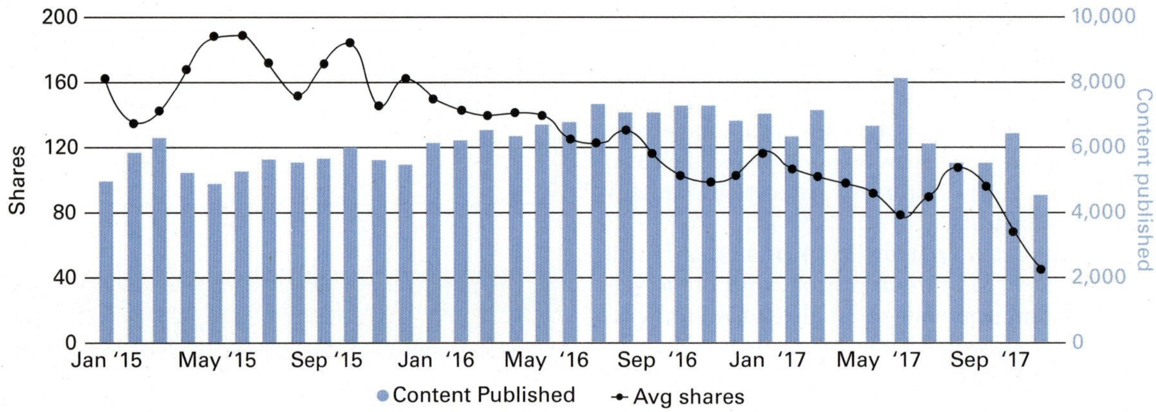

SOURCE: Buzzsumo

Content marketing strategy

The content marketing strategy summarizes which kind of content topics will be delivered via which type of content format across which platforms over a sequence or series of trigger points. The choice of a particular topic is informed by the content research already carried out. 'Content pathways' will also be developed so that when prospects show interest in a particular piece of content, they automatically get sent (or given access) to another, even more relevant, piece of content.

See how Red Bull has strategically developed their content to create a distinct competitive advantage and grow their audience/fans and ultimately customers on p 239.

Source of competitive advantage

It is worth considering whether content marketing could be the lead component in your digital marketing strategy (eg Red Bull and Kelly HR), but remember it's competitive out there and there's a lot of other content competing for your customers' shortened attention spans.

Tactics: Creating, promoting and distributing content

Story-telling

High-quality story-telling that helps brands to be meaningful to their audiences start with a deep understanding of the brand, its relationship to the society or culture, plus an interesting market insight (which some call 'an informed idea'). If a brand truth 'intersects' with a cultural truth there lies some potential. The 'Fearless girl' story by State Street Global Advisors (SSGA) focuses on a statue of a young woman facing the famous Charging Bull statue on Wall Street, New York. A duplicate statue has since been brought to London.

As Bruce Henderson (2018) says, this may have all came from an insight that had to do with one or more of the following:

- Very few public companies have enough female senior leaders.
- SSGA introduced the SHE fund, an ETF (exchange traded fund) that tracks firms that have women in senior leadership roles.
- The charging bull is a symbol, and a very male symbol, of Wall Street.

FIGURE 15.4 Content marketing matrix

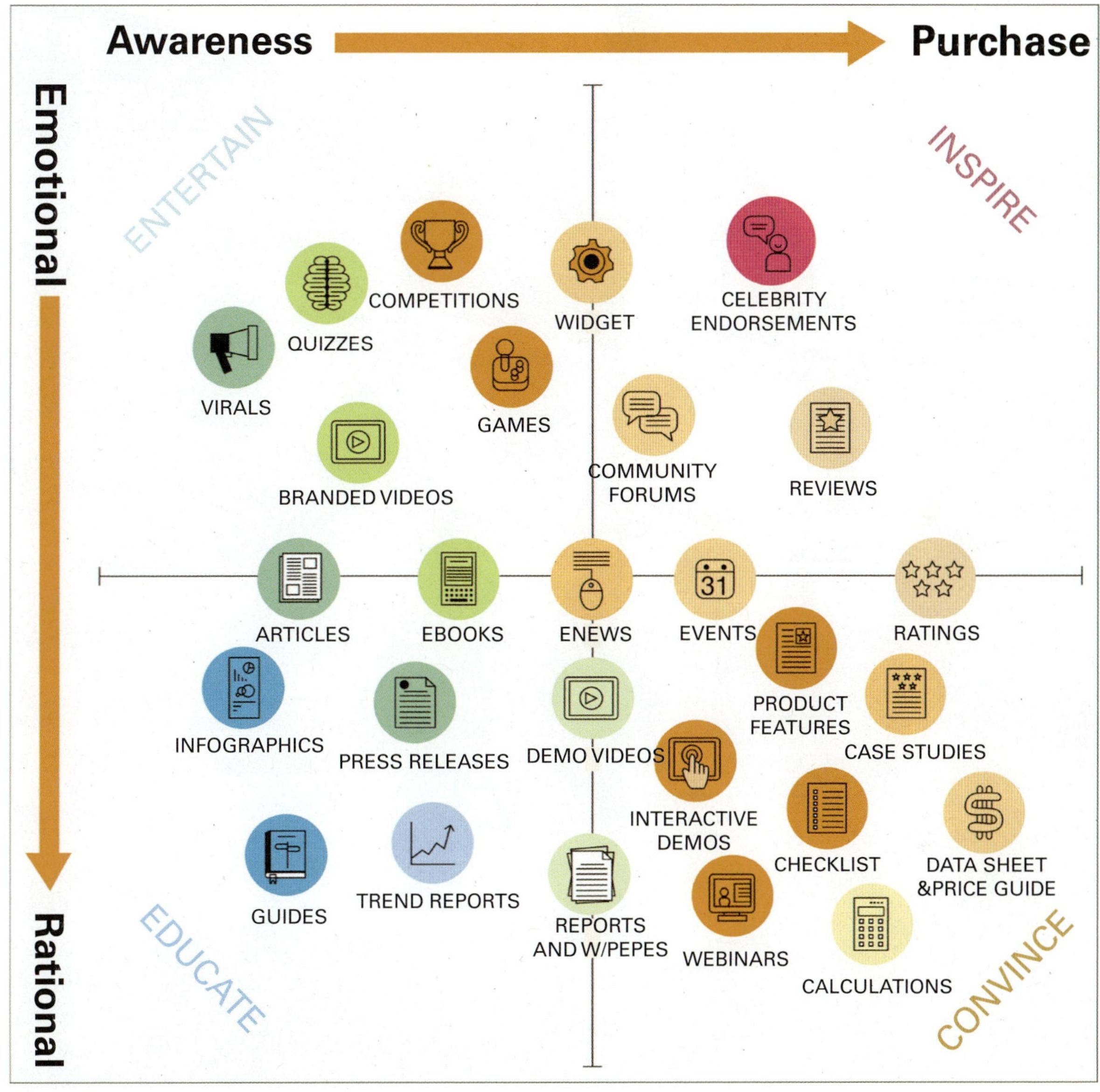

SOURCE: Courtesy of Dave Chaffey Smart Insights

Therefore the 'Fearless girl worked so well because it acknowledged the tension inherent in those thoughts, and used that tension and the resulting execution to spark and shape a brand story that quickly spread around the world' (Henderson, 2018). Great stories that make great marketing content that delivers a great brand experience tend to have, Henderson suggests, three things in common – they are:

- simple;
- moving (emotional);
- original.

FIGURE 15.5 Fearless girl

Sculpture by Kristen Visbal

When these three variables come together, you've got a story that is memorable.

> And since brands, and therefore brand narratives, are built on memory structures, it's imperative that we create things that are memorable and worth talking about. Simplicity of an idea and execution – particularly when featuring uncluttered, recognizable visual elements of a brand's identity – makes the idea or execution easier to remember. It also increases the likelihood that what people take away from and share about the experience will be clear and consistent with its intention.
>
> Henderson (2018)

Emotional stories simply have more impact, become more easily tied to our memories and are more likely to be shared. Lastly, people tend to remember and share things that are new or novel, so creating work that is original – ie hasn't been done before, or done before in that context can also increase the likelihood that it will be remembered and shared (Henderson, 2018). Food blenders have been used to blend difficult types of food, but never to blend an iPhone or an iPad; when Blendtech started blending in this context they generated 6 million viewers for each video they produced.

See checklists for great story-telling techniques in the actions section, p 461.

Content calendar

A content calendar is used to schedule what content will be published in which month, week or day. Some calendars also specify type of content (post, video, infographic, eBook, webinar, etc). Relevant key phrases that can be used to optimize the content and url links are sometimes added. Organizations adopt their own calendar style, some with a lot more detail than others.

Personas

Don't forget to create personas for content marketing (in the same way you do for any communications, PPC, etc). This helps you to write much more relevant content as it's aimed at real people (personas). See p 596 for more on personas.

Frequency of content

Once a day or once a month? Firstly be consistent. More than once a day might be too much – it depends on what market you are in. It is worth being consistent with the type and style of content.

Content size: Short or long?

If we all just followed best practice and never tested the alternatives then all content marketers would still be creating blog posts that were exclusively between 500 and 750 words long... Data and science have since shown this to be nonsense. Our research with Buzzsumo proved that the most effective posts in any B2B sector are over 1,000 words long – and that the most influential posts of all tend to be over 2,000 words long. And contrary to the perceived wisdom, audiences have no problem concentrating on something for longer periods – providing it's interesting.

Miller (2018)

Leverage content

Your marketing and advertising team probably have a lot of material that they can share on Instagram, Pinterest, YouTube, Vimeo, Facebook and LinkedIn. Sharing advertising collateral and any marketing content in an organic way simply gets you 'more bang for your buck' (eg PR photos with an added caption).

A blog post's key points can be broken into many tweets, etc. Images can be re-used in many ways. You leverage, across many tactical channels, the assets you invested in and created (rather than leave them gathering dust). See the Kelly HR example on p 475. NB Some content is better for certain tasks. See Dave Chaffey's Smart Insights content matrix p 455.

Any speeches, presentations, articles can also be leveraged across many channels. Sift through your marketing collateral. Among these assets, you will find components that need polishing or some components that just need a caption or developing into Memes/posters and then release them in an organized process (or schedule).

See Kelly HR (p 475) for a full case study of how a team of two generated content from one piece of research to fuel content for books, blog posts, tweets, infographics, events, videos, public talks and a lot more. It all went global and connected with a very specific universe of HR directors.

Remember, some content is better for certain tasks (or objectives).

Red Bull

Red Bull released an 81 minute movie, *Where the Trail Ends*. This was after they had sponsored Red Bull Stratos – Mission to the Edge of Space, and Supersonic Freefall parachute jump, which was made into a TV documentary complete with photo gallery, video gallery and media tour.

Content deletion

Reviewing and removing out-of-date content is never going to be as exciting as creating and publishing new content. Getting involved in a project to create a marketing video is always going to be more interesting than writing a clear and easy to follow set of instructions on how to install a product. In most

FIGURE 15.6 Red Bull: Mission to the Edge of Space. Red Bull's content supports both what their customers want and their brand values

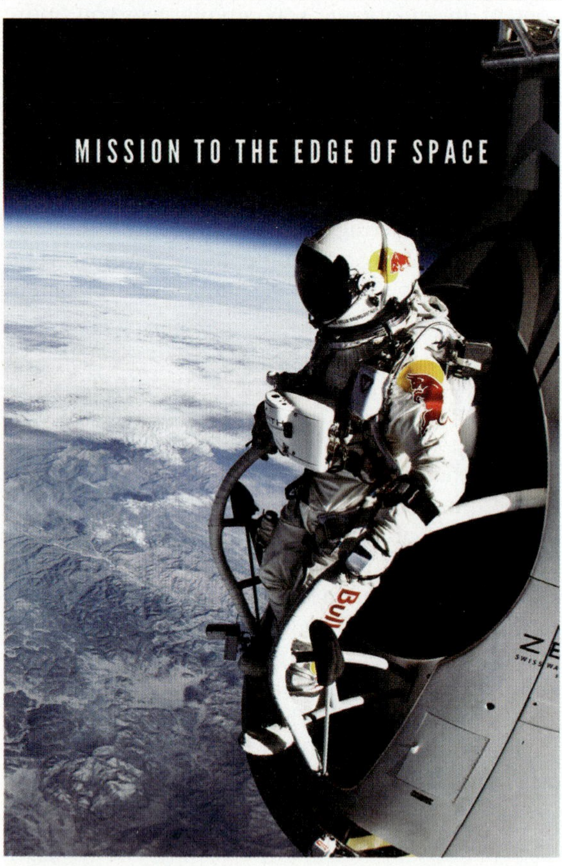

SOURCE: Red Bull

organizations, those who sell and market are the 'creatives' and the stars. Those who service and support are outsourced and ignored. Many marketers and communicators find it really difficult to give control to customers because that means giving up control. The indomitable Gerry McGovern (2018) nails it once again in his article 'Keeping digital teams happy versus keeping customers happy'.

Content outsourcing

Work can be commissioned to external writers. Equally interesting external content can be curated and shared (as long as it adds value to your followers and doesn't compete with your product or service).

Content distribution and promotion

Content distribution can be as important as the content itself. There's no point creating great content if nobody sees it. You may have to spend more on promoting the content than on creating it. Great quality content can deliver low-cost visitors and conversions but it may also be worth pushing your best content via paid media (eg sponsored posts and ads) as they can generate additional conversions (albeit more expensive). It is worth testing and subsequently blending. In fact, you need to test and blend both to find out what is the best way of distributing your best content.

Social media management dashboards like Hootsuite can help schedule content publishing across most social media platforms each week or each month. It also gives access to comments and discussions.

Seeding influencers

Seeding, ie sending content to influencers like traditional journalists and other influencers (both social media influencers and micro-influencers), is still important.

Warning: Influencer fraud and fake followers

'While many marketers intend to increase their budget for marketing content and most marketers plan to increase spend on influencer marketing, there are increasing worries about influencer fraud (fake followers). Some industry experts (including Unilever) insist that tighter regulations are required. A Unilever speaker at Cannes Lions 2018 went on to say: "the market gets undermined if people don't trust the amount of followers someone has". Unilever now refuse to work with influencers who buy followers and will prioritize influencer partners who increase their transparency.'

Marketing Week Reporters (2018)

Staff and partners promote content

Passionate staff (and partners, resellers and suppliers) often like to share your content to their own networks too. Software like GaggleAMP gives staff and partners the ability to share and engage with your content from one easy-to-use, intuitive platform. Staff are rewarded for sharing as every action earns points, which earn rewards – a form of gamification which helps staff to start sharing, and even more importantly, to stay sharing over time. Staff can opt in to a leader board league table that is automatically updated and published.

This can be quite powerful for any company. Imagine Avon (see p 279) with their 50,000 sales people or 50,000 micro-influencers selecting, posting, or sharing, really interesting content to their networks.

Content distribution matrix

The content distribution matrix (Figure 15.7) will help you to decide how to promote/distribute

FIGURE 15.7 The content distribution matrix

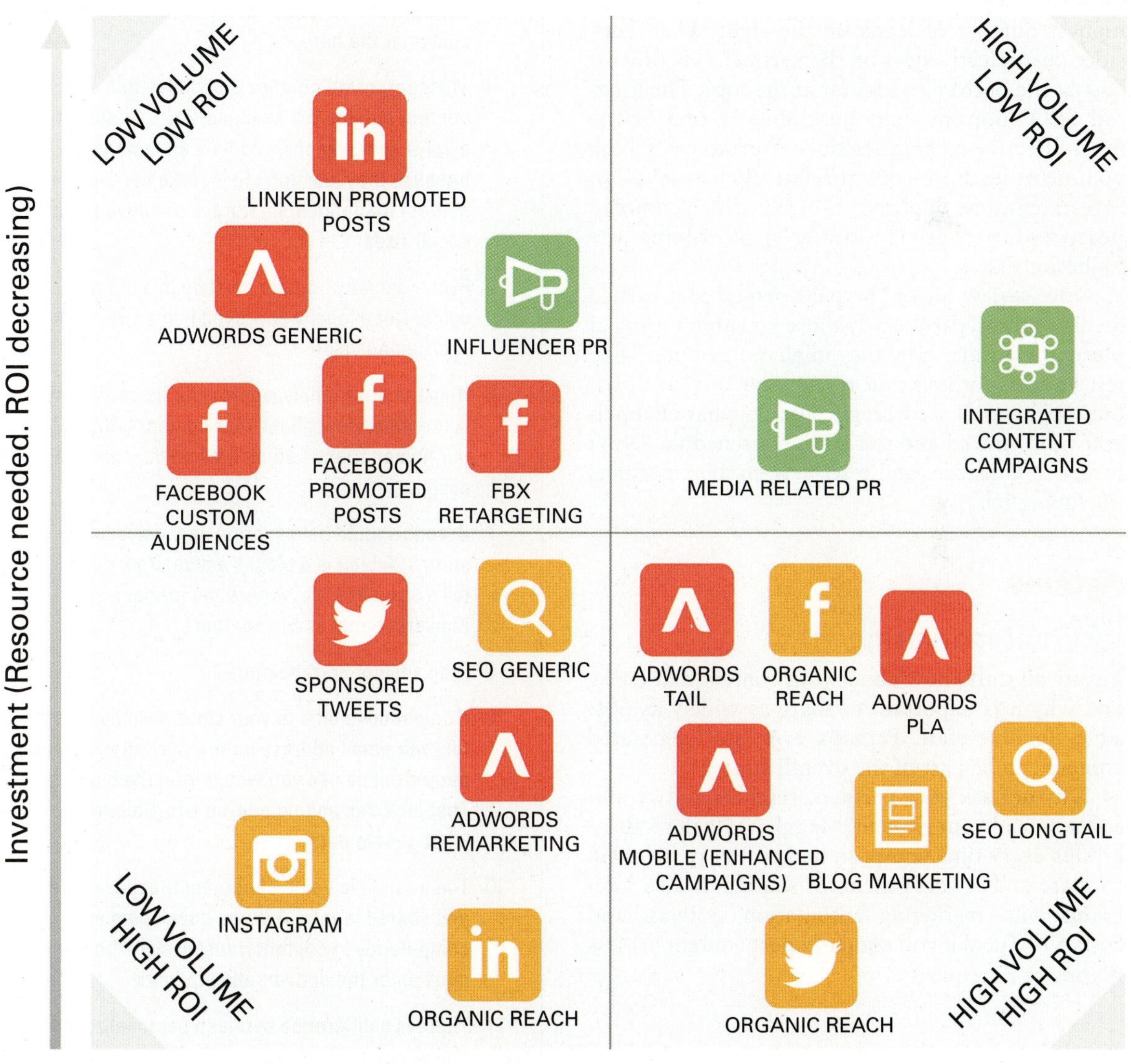

SOURCE: Chaffey (2015)

your content. This infographic is aimed at helping marketers to review the effectiveness of different types of paid, owned and earned media to promote or distribute their content in generating site visits, leads or sales, compared to the level of investment in applying the media measured as paid media costs, or the costs of marketing team members.

Note each business and sector may find some content far more effective than others.

Plot each media type (paid-owned and earned media options) on the horizontal axis – based on each option's effectiveness in generating leads or sales from a low number of leads on the left to the highest number of leads on the right. Then consider cost effectiveness on the vertical axis (lowest cost at the bottom to highest at the top). The long-tail SEO (bottom right quadrant) is one of the most effective techniques since it produces a high volume of leads or sales at relatively low levels of investment, as opposed to LinkedIn promoted posts with a relatively low level of volume and highest costs.

Now review all of the paid-owned and earned media options, particularly those you aren't using at present. Consider how they might contribute. Then test your hypothesis and revise your mix of distribution channels accordingly. Decide what channels you want to trial and test. Set up a schedule. Don't forget to consider (and test) new content partners (including IoT).

Actions

Internal marketing

Ensure all staff know about your content marketing and why it is important to share as widely as possible. Involve staff. Perhaps even staff-generated content can be part of the overall strategy.

Why not ask your partners, resellers and suppliers to spread your content? GaggleAMP alerts these groups every time you post, makes it easy for them to share and rewards them for sharing. It also integrates with marketing automation systems, and costs $100 pcm if you regularly post content (or less if you are infrequent).

Schaefer's checklist for improving content marketing's emotional impact

1. In most company content, I don't know who is producing it. Where is the author? I want to see a human face.
2. Stop using stock photos. Show real people and their smiles. When you use stock photos, the message you convey is 'even we don't care'.
3. Nobody cares about the arc of your story. Content that connects in an emotional way must put the customer at the centre. Make the customer the hero.
4. Most corporate content isn't native to a normal content stream. For example, you can almost always spot a sponsored post on Instagram because they just don't fit in. Take care to craft content that appears natural and native to the social stream.
5. Even company content must be in a human voice. Not a legally approved human voice. A *real* human voice.
6. Humans are friendly, approachable and even vulnerable. How about your content? Oh yes, our human friends admit it when they make a mistake.
7. Brands should be exploring new ways to tell stories. A blog is a blog is a blog. How do you tell a story in a way where the format is as conversational as the content?
8. Stop selling. Start helping.
9. If somebody came to your store, would you ask for their email address before they enter? Treat people online like you would treat them offline. That includes ending pop-up ads. Stop doing what people hate.
10. The economic value of content that is not seen and shared is zero. Are you developing a competency in content transmission? Content must enter the conversation to work.
11. There is a difference between personalization and personal. Personalization is an expectation. Personal creates emotional impact.

12 Content should be viewed with the same esteem as your company's products. It's not just sales propaganda. It should be good enough to be a stand-alone product that customers look forward to receiving. If you can't meet that standard of quality, you'll certainly fail in this era of overwhelming information density.

Schaefer (2019a)

Story-telling checklist

1. Is it simple, moving and original?
2. Would you remember this experience?
3. Would you talk about it?
4. Would you share it with someone else?

'If the answer to these questions is "maybe" or "no," chances are the work isn't good or bold enough to create meaningful impact.'

Henderson (2018)

Content brand experience checklist

1. Be useful – people appreciate things that make their lives easier or better.
2. Be human – treat people as human beings, not as targets or demographics.
3. Invite participation – physical engagement has been shown to increase mental engagement and memorability.
4. Be shareable –create things that are worth sharing, and make it easy to do so.
5. Build community – give people opportunities to connect with each other in both physical and digital places. Human beings thrive on connection and community.

'People will also have more positive experiences with brands if we do all 5.'

Henderson (2018)

Call to action in all content marketing

Check that every piece of content has a call to action – whether it is just sign up for a newsletter or for email alerts of special offers or new content. It doesn't have to be to make a sale. In fact, content marketing is good at building awareness and relationships, not for hard sales, although several content marketers do ask if you would like a call from a salesperson.

Think like a publisher

You have to think like a publisher, discover hot topics that are not well served by competitors, brainstorm, create content concepts, select the best ones, produce them, distribute them and measure their impact. You need a team that looks like an egg timer (large at the start, thin in the middle and large at the end – see Figure 15.8). A cross-functional group at the beginning (for brainstorming), then a small editorial team and small production team to produce the content, and finally a large team mobilized (staff, distributors, retailers, influencers) to help the promotion distribution (and engagement).

Figure 15.8 shows many staff can help with brainstorming new content ideas, then a single editor decides and manages production and then all staff are invited to help share the new content.

FIGURE 15.8 The 'staff egg timer' (many staff contribute during brainstorming; then reduce staff during production, and then many staff help distribute content)

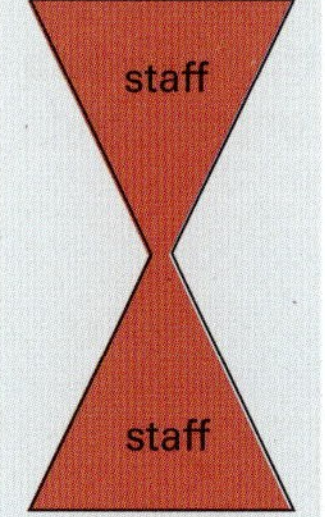

Control

Measuring content marketing's effect

Content marketing should be designed so that it is easy to measure its impact (is it driving traffic, or is it boosting newsletter subscriptions, trial requests, enquiries or sales?). Make sure each piece of content has direct links to the correct landing pages so it becomes easy to measure the effectiveness of your content. Build 'content pathways' so that when prospects or customers show interest in (open) a particular piece of content, they automatically get sent, or are given access to a link, to another even more relevant piece of content. Finally, content should also have feedback mechanisms that allow the audience to give direct feedback, comments, ratings or discussions.

> **Is there a pulse?**
>
> Watch open and click rates to see if there's a 'pulse' – ie whether the content is connecting and resonating.

Content marketing can be a major component in your communications strategy. But in a hyper-competitive environment you need to have processes in place to identify what's needed, produce it, release it and monitor which kind of content works best.

For more on measuring content marketing, watch the video 'Measuring the effectiveness of content marketing' by Erin Robbins O'Brien in an interview with Steve Farnsworth of the Steveology group, posted on **http://prsmith.org/blog/**. It really puts marketing content and analytics together very nicely.

> - Do you know what successful content marketing looks like?
> - Do you document your content marketing strategy (topics, formats, sequence)?
> - Have you got an editorial mission statement?
> - Are you telling everyone what's coming up?

Sales promotions

Sales promotion is big business. In fact, it has traditionally been bigger than advertising in the UK. And if content marketing is included as well as gamification multiplied by VR and AR, then you can see why sales promotions is going to continue to grow. Brand activation and customer engagement are two big buzz words in marketing, as is content marketing.

Sales promotions, premiums, incentives and motivation schemes are used for both products and services in consumer and business-to-business markets. There are three main categories:

- customer promotions (premiums, gifts, prizes and competitions, eg on the back of breakfast cereal boxes);
- trade promotions (special terms, point-of-sale materials, free pens, diaries, competition prizes, etc);
- sales force promotions (incentive and motivation schemes; see p 340 for an explanation of how these become a form of psychic income).

Successful promotions

Whether they take the form of competitions, price reductions, free gifts, coupons, samples, special demonstrations, consumer sales promotions tend to affect the later stages of the communications and buying process (see Chapters 4 and 5), ie they trigger action, such as a purchase or increased usage of a particular brand. Whereas advertising tends to affect the earlier

FIGURE 15.9 Watch the video 'Measuring the effectiveness of content marketing' by Erin Robbins O'Brien at **http://prsmith.org/blog/**

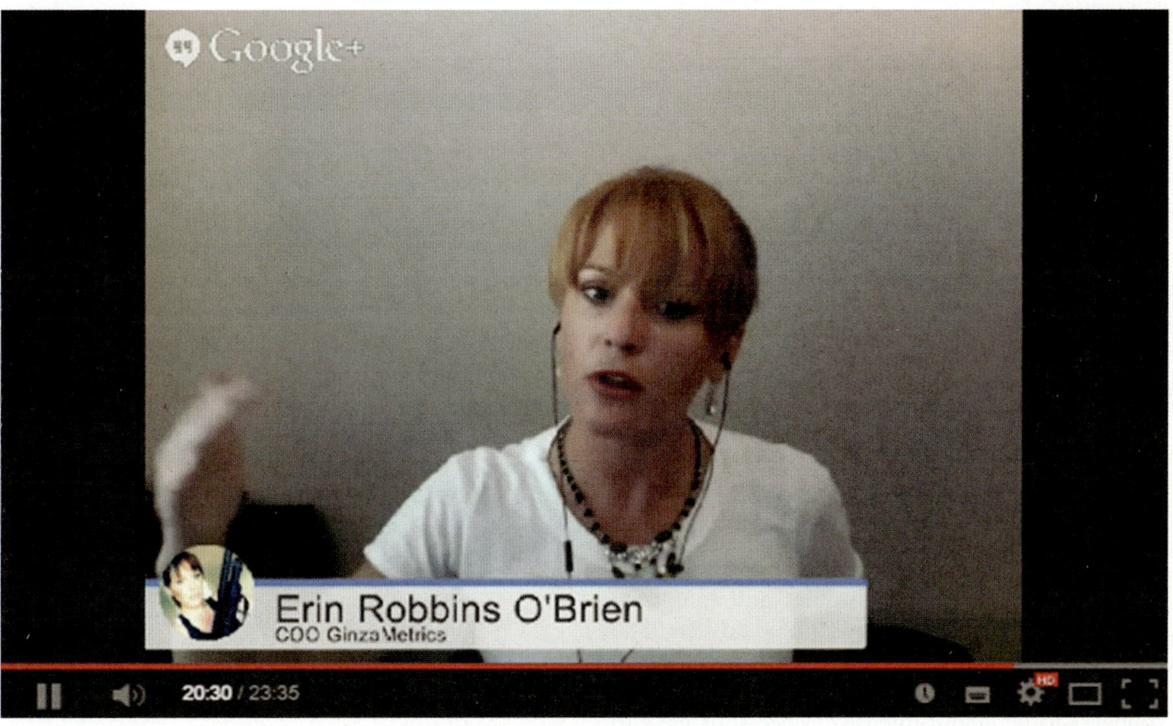

stages, such as awareness, interest and desire (there are exceptions, particularly where direct response advertising is concerned). Content marketing is often used, particularly in B2B markets, as a sales promotion to identify and build a list of prospective customers by collecting an email address, in return for giving the gift of content. However, sales promotions are an expensive way of generating awareness and need to be supported by advertising, PR and social media. Sales promotions are often action orientated, particularly as they can tempt the buyer to buy, or at least try, a product or service. These kinds of promotions often provide the final nudge that moves a customer towards making a purchase.

Sales promotions consumers = Skinner's rats vs Pavlovian dogs?

In terms of learning about brands and learning to use them frequently, many sales promotions, and the engagement they create (by filling in forms, collecting coupons, posting application forms, trying a free sample, etc) are a form of 'operant conditioning' (demanding active engagement), as demonstrated by Skinner's rats (see Chapter 4, p 141). Advertising, on the other hand, is thought by some to help buyers to learn and remember brands and their benefits by repeating the message and building associations between brands, logos, images and benefits, a form of classical conditioning as demonstrated by Pavlov's passive dogs' engagement (see Chapter 4, p 140). Well-thought-out sales promotions that embrace the brand values and deliver real customer benefits can be enormously successful. Promotions should strengthen or add value to the brand image.

These types of promotions build 'consumer franchise'. This means that the gift is in some way related to the brand, its image or its properties. Franchise-building promotions contrast with price and discount offers, which can dilute brand values and do not enhance brand loyalty, despite boosting short-term sales. See 'Packaging with added value on-pack promotions' p 583).

Free Ladas boost football club sales by 36 per cent

After several seasons of declining gates, Russian football club Zenit used a simple sales promotion to boost attendances up to 26,000. Entry costs 1.5 roubles and tickets for the Lada car lottery cost 1 rouble. Ladas cost 8,000 roubles (equivalent to three years' salary for the average industrial worker). The biggest roar of the evening comes not as the two teams run out on to the pitch but when the three cream-coloured Ladas are driven on to the running track. The opportunity of winning a Lada just pulls in the crowd. Whether it builds the brand's franchise is another question.

Unsuccessful promotions

Many sales promotions fail for two reasons: 1) they have no link to the brand values and long-term branding; 2) a lack of attention paid to detail, so problems emerge, such as fulfilment (eg pubs and bars find SMS promotions offering money-off vouchers to be labour-intensive, since staff have to be trained). See 'Disaster promotions', below, for major disasters by, surprisingly, major brands.

There is much room for more creative flair in sales promotions (see 'Creative sales promotions' p 466). Effective sales promotions can creatively build the brand franchise while achieving many other objectives, such as increasing sales, cementing loyalty, building databases, generating publicity and more. However, more than half of trade promotions fail: 59 per cent of global promotions do not break even (and in the United States that figure is even higher, at 71 per cent, with the UK at 58 per cent and Italy with the lowest failure rate at 41 per cent). These figures are from 2015 (Nielsen), but has it improved since? How many really good sales promotions do you see that make you want to tell your friends about it?

Disaster promotions

Despite the phenomenal size of the sales promotions industry and the data available for analysis, there are a frightening number of sales promotions that are relatively ineffective, and some are actually damaging in terms of branding, sales and cash flow.

Warning: Continued price promotions can damage brands

Price promotions such as discount vouchers, two for the price of one, a free extra 10 per cent can help to boost sales in the short term, but what do they do to the brand in the long term? Discount the price and you discount the brand down to a point where it loses its brand value and competes solely on price (which is not a protectable competitive advantage, unless you have massive scale).

Warning: Temporary boost reduces subsequent sales

Some promotions create a temporary boost in sales followed by an immediate drop, as customers who initially bought and stocked up on more product then stop buying until they have used up their extra stock (as shown in Figure 15.10). Other promotions actually damage the brand image and even the holding company's corporate image, sales, profits and cash flow (eg Hoover's £48 million fiasco – see more below).

FIGURE 15.10 Some promotions boost sales temporarily as customers stock up but don't come back for twice as long

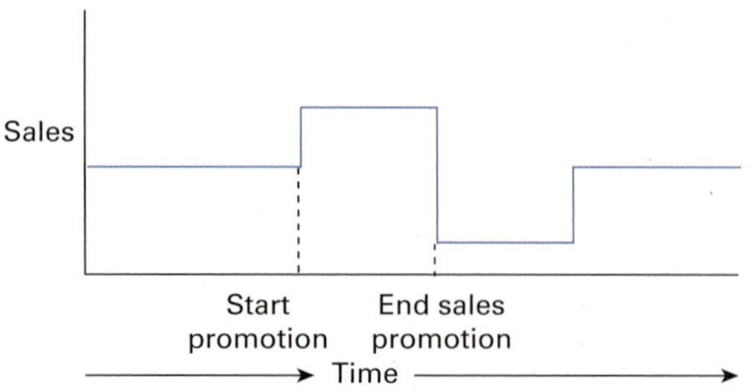

Murphy's Law

What can go wrong will go wrong with sales promotions. As with most marketing communications tools, things can go wrong with sales promotions and destroy many excellent ideas that have apparently been meticulously planned. Sample packs may burst open and destroy other goods (or carpets), or premiums may be pilfered. There can be problems of misredemption (non-buyers acquire other buyers' coupons), malredemption (large-scale fraudulent coupon redemption), over-redemption (with millions claiming their prizes), or door-drop samples that the dog or child gets to before the adult. The possibilities of a mini-marketing disaster seem endless. In addition, the *Competitors' Companion*, a monthly subscription magazine (**www.competitorscompanion.com**), publishes news and views on which sales promotion competitions are running, what prizes they offer, exactly where to get entry forms, which qualifiers are required (eg a label) and the closing dates. According to the magazine, 'You receive advice on the answers to their questions plus a regular list of winning slogans and tie breakers... that way, you can read what's catching the judge's eye today and make them work for you tomorrow.'

Here are a few classic cases of promotions that went horribly wrong, even for the biggest and the best of marketing companies:

- **Typhoo Tea's Cash Pot promotion** was reported to have had to make cash payouts of more than £1 million. According to *Marketing Week* Cadbury Typhoo's insurers were reported to have issued a High Court writ against the company seeking a 'declaration that some claims made by Cash Pot competitors are outside the rules of the competition'. Nevertheless, the expensive promotion apparently increased its market share to its 'highest level since its relaunch in 1982', but at what cost?
- **Coca-Cola's MagiCan** US promotion was supported by a massive $100 million push. The MagiCan looked, weighed and felt (even when shaken) like a regular can. When the tab was pulled, the winning cans had a mechanism inside that pushed real rolled-up dollar notes through the hole in the top of the can. Cash prizes inside the can ranged from $5 to $200. The winning cans had some extra liquid to ensure the weight of all cans was the same. Inevitably there were a few duds. Most of them just didn't work, but in a few cases the seal that held the 'liquid that gives the can the feel of the real thing' had broken. Although it was not harmful, one small boy (who was not aware of the promotion) drank the liquid and public health officials were called in. Massive media attention followed; 750,000 cans were held back while each one was shaken to determine whether the seal was broken or not. An immediate TV and press campaign was put into action to explain the promotion and to warn customers not to drink the liquid if the seal was broken (*Marketing*, 31 May 1990).
- **Pepsi's special bottle top** was offered by its Philippine subsidiary with a 1 million pesos (£26,000) prize to anyone finding a bottle top with the number 349. Pepsi paid out £8 million before it realized that thousands of winning bottle tops were appearing everywhere. When payment stopped there were public demonstrations; then Pepsi plants were attacked with grenades, and Pepsi lorries were burnt (three people were killed). Pepsi executives hired bodyguards before fleeing the country.
- **Heinz recipe book** was a printed recipe book promotional offer on its Pickering Fruit Pie Fillings. Heinz forgot to print a reply address, so no one could participate in the promotion.
- **KFC plastic figures** seemed like a good idea (giving a free plastic figure in some of its meals as a promotion). Although they tested the plastic for proximity to hot food, they did not test it for children sucking off the plastic and poking their eyes with the remaining wire. Personal injury claims followed.
- **Macy's department store talent promotion** was designed to find an Annie for a new production of the Broadway show. The lucky 12-year-old winner later made even bigger

news when she sued Macy's after she was 'dumped' from the production.

- **Hoover's free flights to New York** were offered to anyone purchasing any Hoover over £100. Wrong comparisons with response rates from a dissimilar 'two flights for the price of one' promotion, prompted wildly inaccurate forecast response rates for this new promotion. (The company forecast 5,000 responses and received 600,000!) The fixed-fee limit of £500,000 was agreed with a relatively small travel agent. When the agency went bust, Hoover was exposed to a massive response (note that sales promotion insurance is essential). Meanwhile, the trade increased prices of the cheaper Hoover models to over £100 so that effectively any Hoover purchase qualified for free flights (Hoover should have restricted the offer to certain models). The promotion cost £48 million, careers and corporate image.
- **Kraft Foods' 'Win a free camper van'** promotion had a computer error that generated hundreds of winners. As the prize-winners' claims kept coming in, Kraft realized there was a problem. Some disappointed customers vowed never to buy the firm's food products again. Others sought legal action.
- **Vidal Sassoon shampoo samples:** According to *Marketing Breakthroughs* (1991), half a million special free sample minipacks of Vidal Sassoon shampoo were distributed throughout Poland. When news of the promotion spread, around 2,000 mailboxes (mostly at apartment blocks) were pillaged. The sample packs then started appearing in street markets and soon sold out. The extra costs incurred by the damaged mailboxes added a new dimension to the sales promotion review process.
- **Alamo Car Hire's free car hire** flopped in Germany. Alamo normally offers one free day's car hire with every 30-day hire. This was fine until it discovered that it is illegal in Germany to give anything free after just one transaction. The international arena further complicates the life of the sales promotion professional, as regulations vary enormously.
- **Coca-Cola and McDonald's got into trouble with Coca-Cola's special-edition round bottle,** which was a potential 2006 World Cup collector's item – available from McDonald's outlets in the host country Germany as well as Austria, Hungary and Poland during the tournament. This fell foul of Germany's strict waste recycling regulations. Although it was stamped with the word Mehrwegflasche, indicating it was returnable, McDonald's did not charge the customary deposit meant to ensure the bottle was returned for recycling. The environmental lobby threatened legal action if McDonald's continued to advertise or sell the bottles.

The moral of the story? Check all possible disaster scenarios. Get advice from third parties. Test the promotion. Take out promotional insurance: professional indemnity insurance covers an agency's duty of care to its clients; product recall insurance protects against the cost of a recall of products or promotional gifts; over-redemption insurance protects against an unexpectedly high response. Whether the client pays or the agency pays is an issue that needs to be clearly agreed long before any sales promotion campaign rolls out.

There is, arguably, a worse scenario – no one responds to the sales promotion. Large stocks of premiums are left in the warehouse, and teams of order fulfilment staff (who dispatch the prizes) sit around with nothing to do.

Creative sales promotions

There is always room for creative innovation. Whether it's a trip to the moon or a party in an underground nuclear shelter, the only limitation to potential sales promotion creation is one's imagination. If it is stunningly successful, it is likely that the competition will follow, unless the innovative promotion relates uniquely to the brand in a creative way. This is demonstrated by the *Sunday Sport* tabloid newspaper.

'Is your mother-in-law an alien?'

Although no longer in circulation, the *Sunday Sport* newspaper once offered a free test kit that helped readers to determine whether their mothers-in-law were, in fact, aliens. The paper sold out within hours.

This 'alien mother-in-law' type of promotion is arguably just a stunt designed to generate publicity that may, at least temporarily, increase levels of awareness, boost sales and also reinforce readers' loyalty by rewarding them with a gift that appeals to their mentality. Because the gift is relevant to both the target reader's sense of humour and the newspaper's image, it adds to the paper's branding. In a way it adds to the brand franchise or builds consumer franchise.

One sales promotion that might have impressed mothers-in-law was for Cadbury. When it launched its white chocolate, Snowflake, agency Triangle achieved significant consumer trial by negotiating a cover-mount of a free bar on *OK!* magazine. When it discovered that the same issue was featuring celebrity television presenter Anthea Turner's wedding, it persuaded *OK!* to give free bars to all the celebrity guests. The additional brand exposure enabled Cadbury to hit the media headlines, gain an estimated £1 million worth of editorial coverage, and ensure a spectacular launch success as a result.

Creativity and originality can work well together, as when NatWest Bank's sales promotions and direct marketing were combined as a 'direct promotion' (most mailshots use an incentive). NatWest moved away from the traditional clock/radio/calculator/travel-bag type of incentive used by the banks from time to time. Instead it offered the choice of one of 10 limited-edition prints that were specially commissioned from five artists. It mailed to 65,000 names (who were thought to have over £25,000 to invest) and received a 12.3 per cent response (instead of the targeted 5 per cent response level). Another highly creative and popular promotion was Guinness's inflatable armchair, which formed part of its campaign as sponsor of the Rugby World Cup. An application for the armchair was even received from Buckingham Palace!

Highly creative sales promotions may involve an element of risk. Insurance (indemnity insurance, redemption insurance, etc) is advised with all sales promotions, but particularly recommended with highly creative and high-risk ones. Incidentally, creative thinkers will spot the PR opportunities that can be exploited when creative sales promotions are developed. These can spread through social media networks, and the press are usually also interested. See how Canada's TD Bank use creative promotions to 'literally blow their customers away', on video at **http://prsmith.org/blog/**.

FIGURE 15.11 Two creative promotions on video – watch the recipients' reactions: **https://prsmith.org/2014/08/22/customer-retention-isnt-boring-heres-wow/**

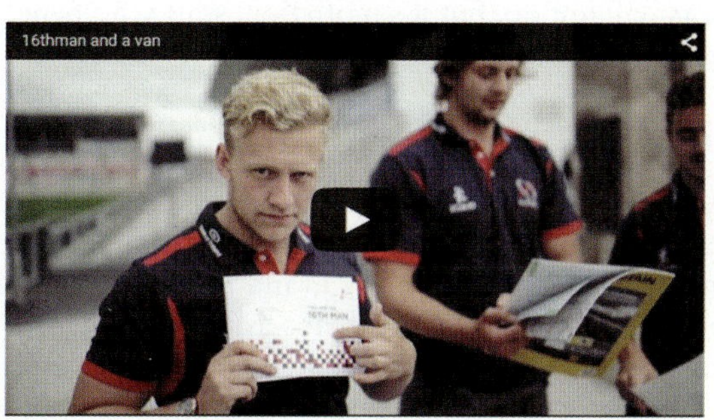

One other dimension that creative thinkers can explore is the huge synergies and creative potential released by joint promotions with other brands, sometimes known as marketing marriages (note: these strategic alliances can integrate or work across all 10 communications tools/channels/tactics).

Gamification

What's it all about?

We feel a sense of achievement upon completing tasks, whether building a boat or going for a swim. Gamification taps into this human characteristic, particularly if there is:

- reward;
- recognition;
- progress.

What exactly is gamification?

Gamification can be defined as: 'The use of game thinking and game mechanics in a non-game context in order to engage users and solve problems. Gamification is used in applications and processes to improve user engagement, return on investment, data quality, timeliness, and learning.' The word was created by computer programmer and inventor Nick Pelling.

More than entertainment and engagement

Gamification is much more than entertaining and engaging customers. Watch how gamification will become embedded into relatively mundane business processes to add sparkle to repetitive tasks that robots will not do. But it's more than staff who benefit from gamification.

Who uses gamification?

Arguably, all stakeholders can benefit from gamification. It helps to deepen learning of brand awareness, brand aspirations, brand features, brand preference, brand relationships as well as entertaining and engaging the user/stakeholder in a meaningful and relevant way. Let's look at two stakeholder groups split into three: customers, and staff (salespeople and cashiers).

- **Customers:** 'Nike Missions' has grown, as does its UK Facebook page, which urged its 200,000+ fans to 'forget public transport' and 'make the commute home your racecourse'. This creative approach to gamification also allows customers and prospects to race against themselves or a worldwide community. Membership boosts brand relationships, which boost sales.
- **Staff:**
    - **Salespeople:** Salespeople are competitive people by nature. Internal sales league tables have been around since the year dot as a way of motivating sales reps. One thing salespeople don't like is filing reports. So some organizations' sales reporting systems have been 'gamified' by rewarding accuracy and frequency of data entry, with the scoring of points complete with a leader board and monthly prize – 'morphing mundane into motivation' by making a tedious task surprisingly exciting.
    - **Cashiers:** The retail checkout is a chicane for customer emotions. A delay in a queue can destroy a reasonably positive CX. Target Retail chain gamified the check-out process to engage their staff. Items scanned first time get a green score (as opposed to red for several scanning attempts). Getting the scan process right first time shaves a minute off the check-out procedure. Cashiers can see their own, their colleagues' and their store's score (to compare with other stores).

Gamification disaster: Mistakes to avoid

Most staff are not engaged. Are you shocked? It's not a mystery that employee engagement continues to sink, say Sturt and Nordstrom (2018): 'The Gallup organization reminds us every couple of years that nearly 70 percent of employees are actively disengaged.' Here are three gamification mistakes to avoid:

1. **Poor gamification design**
   '80 per cent of current gamified applications fail to meet business objectives primarily due to poor design' (Burke, 2013). Is this perhaps similar to the lack of 'instructional design' in the many failed elearning projects in the 1990s? Deep levels of detail are required; if ignored, this can result in some of the early stage chatbot errors we see today. Testing is also a critical part of these processes.
2. **Don't leap into the game**
   Don't leap into gamification (without understanding good design) like many who jumped into elearning (without understanding instructional design). It's as if they felt they ticked that box 'yes we do gamification' or 'yes we do have chatbots'. Gartner's Brian Burke's (2013) comment still rings true today: 'remember not to confuse activity with success'.
3. **Know your audience**
   Do not design for the wrong audience. The average gamer is 35, married, earns £23,000 pa; games 12 hours a week; owns two consoles, 18 games and takes a month to complete one game; rows with their partner twice a week over their pastime (Source: Pixwoo.com). Note this will change if gamification spreads to non-gamers, ie customers, call centres, cashiers, sales teams, etc.

10 gamification success factors

1. Narrative that guides, challenges and changes as the player progresses.
2. Feedback immediate re success or failure, and most importantly, progress.
3. Competitive: We like to compete with others – even in a different location. Make it social.
4. GUI (graphical user interface) – must be easy and fun to use.
5. Test with a view to usability, security, scale, local or global roll-out.
6. Rewards, recognition, awards – it's a motivation programme (that involves changing behaviour, knowledge and or skills). Note that major staff motivators are 'progress' and 'psychic income' (see below).
7. Achieve business objectives (not just entertainment objective).
8. Promoting gamification – avoid using the 'g' word and focus on bottom line results (ie don't promote the word gamification, do promote the benefits of gamification).
9. Add in some psychic income (non-financial rewards) – see below.
10. Add in some earned media/social sharing

Psychic income is non-financial rewards that fulfil your dreams. Instead of giving a £100 cash bonus, which gets lodged in the bank and forgotten, give two tickets to see the person's favourite band or team (see the TD bank 'wow' video mentioned on p 77). Companies like Maritz offer psychic rewards to shop floor workers and CEOs. For example, instead of a £50,000 cash bonus for the CEO give him/her two holes of golf (if they like golf) with Jack Nicklaus, and on the 18th green provide an orchestra perched on scaffolding playing the tune of the CEO's choice.

Earned media children's retailer Step2 use gamification and give points to users depending upon their social media interaction and activity within the BuzzBoard community. Customers are rewarded with points for different levels of engagement, from sharing Facebook content to uploading videos and photos, writing reviews, following fellow reviewers and subscribing to have reviews sent to their Facebook news feeds. Remember GaggleAMP is used in content marketing.

The business benefits

- Customers are engaged and have fun, see progress, win rewards.
- Staff: Boosts product knowledge, processes efficiency, customer service skills and engagement.
- Business: Boosts awareness of brand and features/benefits, recruitment, retention and advocacy.
- Business cost reduction: Cost-effective – embeds key messages and boosts operations efficiency.
- Business data capture: Build customer database for future engagement and relationship building.

Note: this gamification excerpt was first published at **http://prsmith.org/blog/** in October 2013 in an article entitled 'Gamification – the good, the bad and the ugly'.

Joint promotions

Joint promotions, cross-promotions or marketing marriages offer effective partnerships to target the same customers with relevant offers. When Coca-Cola led its army of soft drinks brands into a joint promotion with Cadbury, it was followed by their arch-rival Pepsi announcing another mega-brand deal, in this case, with Kellogg's. When Deep Pan Pizza created a joint promotion with Lego, giving children free branded toys, sales of children's meals inevitably grew. In fact they doubled. To maintain repeat purchases, the choice of toys was changed every quarter.

However, caution must be exercised when choosing a partner. Brand space allocation, data collection and budgets must be clarified. Stuart Hardy, MD of WLK (who married Mothercare and Lever's Persil in a joint promotion), says, 'In any true relationship each side is going to have 50 per cent of the say. A lot of marketing people want 100 per cent of the say and only 50 per cent of the costs.' Although there are lots of opportunities, particularly with new IoT partner potential, relatively few joint promotions seem to get off the ground. It must be agreed and specified who actually does what and gets what, including databases, space allocation, etc.

Integrated promotions: Social media

As with any marketing communications tactical tools or channels, social media is an essential element of any sales promotion campaign. But as social media reach declines, sponsored posts may need to be used. As mentioned earlier in the chapter, no matter how great your content marketing is, it fails if no one knows about it. The same applies to a sales promotion. It needs to be promoted. Sometimes you need to spend as more money promoting it than creating it.

Integrated promotions: Other tactical tools

Sales promotions naturally integrate with other marketing communications tools, particularly packaging ('on-pack' promotions), point-of-sale, merchandising, sponsorship, PR, advertising, direct mail, events and selling and, of course, social media. Advertising-supported promotions do better than ones that are not supported. There are occasions when point-of-sale materials promoting the offer are considered to be more cost-effective than above-the-line (advertising) support.

Managing sales promotions

Going back to mainstream sales promotions where gifts, prizes and competitions are popular promotions, the SOSTAC® + 3Ms* planning process can be used to build a sales promotion plan.

Situation analysis

The situation analysis requires research into past promotions (including those of your competitors), present and possible future campaigns, combined with a clear analysis of the target market. An initial review can be followed by further research into the target market including concept testing, and eventually test marketing.

In addition to the usual demographic and psychographic information, further analysis may reveal what Philip Kotler (2000) identified as three types of new triers who are attracted to (and respond to) sales promotion offers: 1) users of a competing brand in the same category; 2) users in other categories; and 3) frequent brand switchers. These 'deal-prone customers', the brand switchers, tend not to be loyal and are likely to switch away to the next low-price or free-gift offer that comes their way. The group at the other end of the target market loyalty spectrum are called 'the immovables', who are locked into brand loyalty. Do not waste resources targeting them. The real target group within the target market are called the 'loyal susceptibles'. These are there to be won (or lost if they are your brand customers). Once their loyalty is broken, their new-found loyalties can be nurtured and relationships strengthened through regular relevant communications and engagement.

Knowing exactly who these people are and why they are more susceptible is the key to the sales promotions tapping into their susceptibilities, which in turn will increase market share beyond a short-term temporary boost.

After the real target market has been analysed, the eventual sales promotion concept should be researched in focus groups or at least with sample customers. When the idea or promotional tool is agreed, it is still worth testing it in a limited area or customer group to reveal any hidden problems or even opportunities before launching it nationally or internationally.

Objectives

As the name suggests, a promotion is a limited-period offer. It is therefore not surprising to find that sales promotions tend to have shorter-term tactical objectives (although, as previously explained, this need not be the case). As well as boosting brand activation and customer engagement, some typical sales promotion goals include:

- increase sales (although it may be only a temporary increase, because customers can simply stock up with the goods or temporarily switch brands while the promotion is running) by:
  - rewarding loyal customers;
  - increasing the repurchase rates of occasional users;
  - locking customers into loyalty programmes (collecting coupons or items);
  - generating trials among new customers (by triggering an impulse purchase);

- deseasonalise seasonal sales (eg skiing holidays in the summer);
- develop new sales leads;
- nurture loyalty;
- brand activation and customer engagement;
- demonstrate new features or modifications or introducing a new product or service;
- develop new uses;
- satisfy retailers with a complete package – gain trade acceptance;
- move excess stock;
- block a competitor's sales promotion;
- match a competitor's sales promotion;
- build a database (NB GDPR compliance);
- generate publicity.

Some sales promotions are more appropriate than others in achieving various objectives (see Table 15.1).

Strategic impact of sales promotions

'Years ago, Heinz used to say that they saw more far-reaching effects on image dimensions of their tracking studies from their sales promotion schemes than they ever saw resulting from advertising campaigns.'

Castling (1989)

TABLE 15.1 Matching promotions with objectives

Objective	Promotional tool
Consumer	
Trial	Sampling; couponing; free draw; price-off; self-liquidator (send in some money, which pays the costs of the promotion); premiums; in-pack; on-pack; near-pack; re-usable container; personality promotion
Retrial	Coupon for next purchase; price-off
Increase usage	Collections; games; competitions; extra-quantity or bonus packs; price-off multiple purchase
Develop new uses	Companion brand promotions; publications; workshops
Image development	Publications; sponsorship; charity
Trade	
Increase distribution, shelf facings or displays	Discount; extended credit; point-of-sale materials; tie-in with advertising
In-store promotion	Discount; extended credit; point-of-sale materials; tie-in with advertising; consumer offer; promotion allowance
Increase sales	Sales competitions and rebates (mostly independent stores and wholesalers)
Cement good relations	Gifts,holidays and awards
Sales force	
Sales and distribution	Psychic income and financial income

Cummins (2003) identified how certain sales promotion techniques match up with various objectives (Table 15.2).

Strategy

Ideally, all promotions should be part of a longer-term strategy. Longer-term sales promotion strategies build and reinforce brand image, strengthen user loyalty, and can also invite new users to join the club, as opposed to short-term tactical temporary sales boosts. Sales promotions (including content marketing) work best when a sequence of promotions (or content) are scheduled to be given to prospects or customers at various points in their lifetime buying cycle.

Some organizations only see promotions as a short-term tactical tool, eg 'Get 50,000 people to see my store opening'. So strategic sales promotions are not always possible to achieve if clients do not want them in the first place. The difficulty is compounded by the fact that strategic promotions may sometimes not generate immediate customer response. So the question is: should the longer-term image-building capability of sales promotions be forfeited for the shorter-term tactical sales objective? The growth of content marketing is forcing many companies to think more strategically; for example, after a prospect downloads the free ebook, what do we do next? Perhaps a webinar, followed by a free trial, and after that how can we reward them for being customers?

TABLE 15.2 Linking the objective to the mechanics: how they match up

Objectives / Mechanics	Immediate free offers	Delayed free offers	Immediate price offers	Delayed price offers	Finance offers	Competition	Games and draws	Charitable offers	Self-liquidators	Profit-making promotions
Increasing volume	9	7	9	7	5	1	3	5	2	1
Increasing trial	9	7	9	2	9	2	7	7	2	1
Increasing repeat purchase	2	9	2	9	5	3	2	7	3	3
Increasing loyalty	1	9	0	7	3	3	1	7	3	3
Widening usage	9	5	5	2	3	1	5	5	1	1
Creating interest	3	3	3	2	2	5	9	8	8	8
Creating awareness	3	3	3	1	1	5	9	8	8	8
Deflecting attention from price	9	7	0	7	7	3	5	5	2	2
Gaining intermediary support	9	5	9	5	9	3	7	5	1	1
Gaining display	9	5	9	5	9	3	7	5	1	1

Each square is filled with a rating from 0 (not well matched) to 10 (very well matched.). Use it as a ready reckoner for linking your objective to the mechanics available

SOURCE: Cummins (2003)

A strategic approach is preferred, as explained by Cummins (2003):

- It enables one offer to build on the previous one, and to establish a continuity of communication.
- It makes it possible to communicate image and functional values, so promotions work harder.
- It can produce considerable savings in time and money.
- It enables offers to be fully integrated into the other activities in the marketing programme (eg linking with advertising and PR).
- It facilitates a better approach to joint promotions (see above).
- A strategic approach does not exclude the use of tactical promotions, since it can provide a framework within which shorter-term tactics can be determined.

How to develop a strategic approach

1. Identify what customers (and prospects) really want (in terms of promotions).
2. Identify the long-term strategic marketing and communications objectives.
3. Create guidelines for each product or service, showing the style of sales promotion that is most appropriate to the brand's long-term health.
4. Determine exactly how much of the total marketing communications budget is available for sales promotions.
5. Ensure that there is support and commitment from senior management.
6. Develop a promotions file that compiles promotion ideas throughout the year. These can then be reviewed closer to the time of planning.
7. Plan and forecast the sales promotions' results.
8. Develop a method of evaluation so that longer-term performance can be measured against longer-term objectives and forecasts.

Tactics

The general short-term, 'immediate action', tactical nature of sales promotion contrasts with the longer-term image and brand-building capability of advertising. This need not be the case, because sales promotions can be planned on a strategic level. But, first, why is there a tendency towards short-termism?

Perhaps the short-term focus is a result of:

- management pressure to boost quarterly sales, which therefore encourages the use of quick-response sales promotions;
- shortening product lifecycles, which demand quick sales results;
- increased competition and increased new product introductions, which increase the need for tactical defensive sales promotions;
- the speedy response required to handle business problems when they arise;
- full-service agencies trying to sell the client additional services such as sales promotion on an ad hoc, 'add-on' tactical basis.

Actions

Sales promotions also require internal marketing to ensure staff (particularly customer-facing staff) are aware of the promotion. Contingency planning should cater for an unexpectedly large response. Insurance can help here, because things do go wrong and costs can rapidly escalate. Although creating a promotion is exciting, executing it is dull and boring. This is where attention to detail and ensuring proper processes and resources ensure the smooth running of any sales promotion and avoidance of the 'disaster promotions' mentioned earlier (see p 464).

Cut-off dates, logistical arrangements (returning unused stocks) and even announcing the end of the promotion cost time and money; eg Shell wanted to avoid the flush of irritation that would undoubtedly rise up if its customers failed to cash in their carefully collected gift tokens before they expired and became worthless, so it advertised the end of the promotion.

Here is a checklist covering some sales promotions issues:

1 Does the promotion exploit key strengths and unique selling propositions (USPs)?

2 Is it a franchise-building promotion? Does the gift, incentive or premium relate to or enhance your product or service or the organization's image?

3 What can go wrong? Contingency planning, crisis management and insurance are worth considering.

4 Has the promotion got legal clearance? Should it be checked with the Committee of Advertising Practice (CAP) sales promotions department?

5 Will the promotion generate only a temporary gain (see Figure 15.10)? Will existing or old stocks (not carrying the promotion) be wasted?

6 How will the promotion be promoted? Does it need advertising and PR support?

7 What other communications tools are required – new packaging, point-of-sale materials, new literature or field sales teams?

8 Is there an administrative burden created by new order forms, coupons, judging, choosing winners, dispatching gifts, etc? Or will this all be handled by an external agency?

9 Is there a cut-off date, and is it clearly stated when the offer closes?

10 Are there any hidden costs associated with this sales promotion that have not been included in the budget?

Control

Control, measurement and monitoring form the loop in the management system. How can the success or otherwise of the promotion be measured? The number of respondents, redemptions and increased sales are all relatively easy to calculate, but these are only the surface figures. They may be hiding the fact that many of the responders are the wrong profile, or existing customers who simply buy twice as much this week (Figure 15.10).

The purpose of measurement and monitoring is twofold:

- to control current campaigns;
- to improve future campaigns by learning about what works.

Sales promotion, ads, AR, engagement and gamification

Now here are some actual sales promotion (including content marketing) case studies.

CASE STUDY Burger King's 'Burn that ad'

Burger King (Brazil) ran a most unusual sales promotion (free vouchers) using augmented reality to engage in a form of gamification (downloading the app, then playing a game): scanning a competitor's ads and setting them on fire (in augmented reality) and winning a voucher for a free whopper.

This presents the question: 'How can AR turn a competitor's ads into your own ad, using competitors' billboards, magazine ads to generate your own discount coupons?' Or how can Burger King change the media investments of its competitors (billboards ads, magazine ads, discount coupons) and turn them into ads of their own collateral?

Here's how: Burger King used advanced AR to enable customers to 'burn down' competitors' ads using a lens that recognized competitors' ads (eg McDonald's). Burger King also encouraged customers to share their experience: if a customer shared this experience, they got a free Whopper.

Is this the beginning of 'billboard hacking'? Soon we will see ads change from a McDonald's billboard to one for Burger King or Coke or Pepsi or any other variant of this.

Burger King expected to give away over 500,000 burgers through this unique, innovative and highly engaging fun campaign. Vouchers were limited to one per consumer. 'Augmented reality is a fascinating tool. And when combined with a little pyrotechnics, is even better. With "Burn that ad," we hacked the competition by leveraging our biggest advantage, which is fire', said Rafael Donato,

FIGURE 15.12 Burger King 'Burn that ad'

Creative Vice-President for David SP, referring to the flame-grilled burger which is a Burger King USP. The message 'After all, flame grilled is always best!' appears on the app screen after burning a competitor's ad.

The marketing hack also promoted Burger King's Express Service, which allows customers to pre-order their meals to avoid real-world queues (lines).

'Technology as a means to provide the best customer experience is one of our main investment targets in 2019,' explained Ariel Grunkraut, Burger King's marketing and sales director for Brazil in a statement.

Diaz (2019)

CASE STUDY Content marketing delivers competitive advantage: Kelly HR

Australian company Kelly HR are doing all the right things re content marketing:

- create engaging content;
- produce the content;
- measure content effectiveness.

Plus, they are doing an awful lot more with their content marketing. They create, promote and distribute their content marketing in a consistent format, in an integrated marketing communications process. This 'integrated content marketing' is now their number one lead generator, number one brand awareness builder and it is now delivering a competitive advantage that is rapidly becoming a sustainable competitive advantage.

Situation: The company

Kelly Services is a recruiting staff organization with two core audiences: companies who will pay Kelly money to recruit staff for them; and staff looking for a new job. Kelly are effectively in both B2B and B2C.

Target market

Instead of dealing with traditional staffing/recruitment companies, Kelly targeted the more traditional consulting firms including McKenzie's, the Banes, the IBMs, PWCs; all of whom have a lot bigger budgets. Kelly wanted to break into this market and demonstrate its capability to play in the outsourcing space where the deal size is typically $20 million to $1 billion and where it takes 18 months to two years to close deals.

Content, competition and the opportunity

Already a lot of the players were quite well advanced in thought leadership content but not many of them were taking it to a real content marketing approach integrating and leveraging the content to the maximum. Kelly saw this as a really good opportunity to create competitive advantage and, frankly, they didn't have enough money to do anything else.

Step 1: Content audit
Kelly's Marketing Content Director, Todd Wheatland, talked to a lot of staff and identified 600 pieces of content that had been developed by someone somewhere for some purpose (eg promotional materials for events, exhibitions, conferences, collateral literature, reports, etc), all of which were potential marketing content. Kelly found the process of looking back (at existing content) in order to look forward to be very useful. This process helped the team to learn how to structure content. 'We understood a lot more about who we're trying to speak to, and what we're trying to tell them. What value Kelly is trying to add, what questions they're asking,' said Wheatland. A huge underutilized resource was discovered.

Step 2: Content selection
Out of those 600 pieces of content two were selected that could be used. Kelly are good at leveraging research. Eighty per cent of all their content, including blog posts, has a unique original research component to it.

Step 3: Develop personas
Personas help Kelly to understand the audience, which tends to be typically C suite plus some HR and procurement audiences.

Step 4: Identify five buckets, 200 keywords and 2,000 pieces of content
Five buckets (themes) of content were identified along with some 200 relevant keywords that searchers would use. For each of those 200 keywords Kelly produced 10 pieces of content per year, optimized for that keyword. Effectively Kelly produce 2,000 pieces of content in English a year, based on these five buckets.

Step 5: Secure budget (3Ms resources)
Kelly made a strategic decision to focus on content marketing, subsequently cancelling some major events that they normally attend and using the money to develop content and run a pilot programme to demonstrate value.

Resources required

Content has now become about 50 per cent of the total marketing spend. In terms of structure, Kelly's content marketing team is lean – led by Todd Wheatland who spends 50 per cent of his time with another content marketer in Germany who is basically the head of B2B content marketing and distribution channels. Kelly have one other person in the United States who is in charge of B2C content, which is now a big focus for Kelly since they have introduced the Kelly Service side of the business. The US team member spends 20 per cent of their time (annualized) on content marketing (0 per cent in the quiet months, and up to 40 per cent in the busy months), and there are many individuals both within and outside the company who play varying roles in Kelly's highly successful content marketing. This includes translations, videographers, animators, illustrators, etc. Beyond that, everything is outsourced.

Tactics: Leverage content

The research report may be 80 pages in a general term; they may do a spinoff ebook that's 2–3 pages long and is very specific and targeted to a different audience. The research is repurposed into different elements beyond a research report to deliver ebooks, blog posts, infographics, social memes, animated infographics and more. In fact, Kelly Global Workforce Index (survey) was leveraged to deliver:

- 1 × survey or ebook;
- 6 × topics/chapters (mini ebooks);
- 1,000 + content pieces;
- 200 + news releases;
- 20 + company events;
- 40 + external events;
- 30 × countries' languages.

Kelly also generate white papers over consecutive years and sometimes look at the same topic, going back to reinvent and refresh older pieces. Books still have a high degree of credibility when being considered for events.

Generate leads and integrate

Integrated marketing communications and integrated lead generation content marketing requires more than content generation. It's a naturally integrated process involving everything from undertaking the research through to analysis, content development, PR, events, staff mobilization and measurement. The website's front end has free content supported by a lot of social distribution around that, and there is a lead registration or capture model for the really juicy pieces of content that Kelly think people are willing to go through and sign up for. Marketo is the lead nurturing platform used, which integrates nicely into Salesforce, with auto alerts sent to sales reps when qualified leads interact with specific content.

Action: Leverage, repurpose and produce

The production process can be the lengthiest part of content management, particularly if running a properly structured survey with time allowed for testing the questionnaire, rolling it out/fieldwork, analysis, report presentation and the array of design and editing required to generate a suite of marketing content. Atomizing content means breaking it into different formats and/or tailoring reports into very specific regional or industry type reports (relatively easy to do once the survey questions have covered some regions and sectors). For example, a global survey can be split and sliced in many ways, such as gender, jobs and geography, so that tailored reports for engineers in Queensland, or creative services people in New York, etc can easily be generated.

Integrate, mobilize and distribute

The task was producing so much content around specifically defined keywords, with frequency, and circulating and distributing that content, both on Kelly's own channels, (SlideShare and YouTube), plus mobilizing staff and partners. Kelly wanted many people from within the organization to have an external profile. They didn't just want it to be the top 10–20 employees, the same old people who have the senior titles. So the content management team (of two) fought very hard to get people right down the

FIGURE 15.13 Variety of content created from one piece of research

Career Development and Upskilling Report (12.00)

Employees' self-help ebook (2pm)

Animated infographics (9pm), video at 10pm

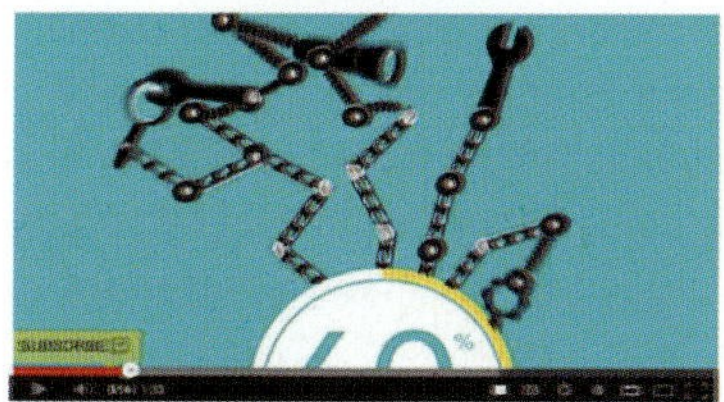

Career Development & Upskilling

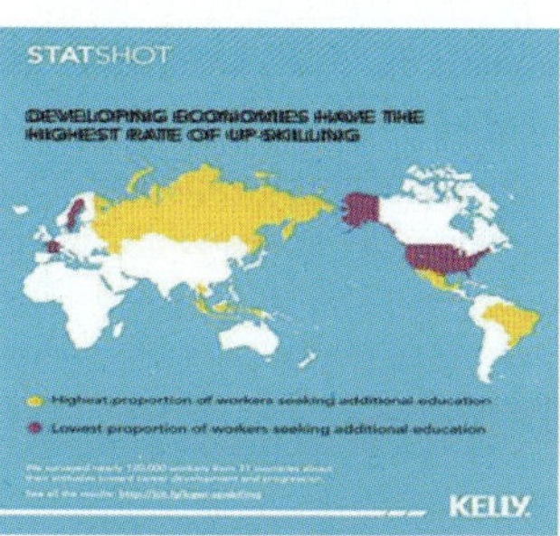

Social memes (7pm)

Infographics (6pm)

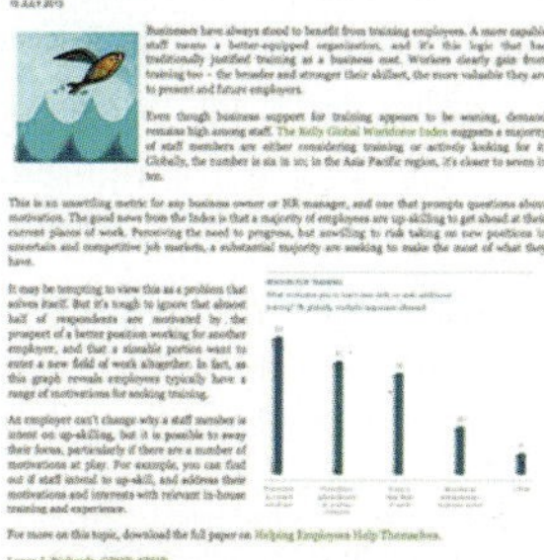

Blog posts (5pm)

SOURCE: Kelly HR

basic operational level involved in being part of this mission. Kelly now leverage their content via staff social networks supported by a huge amount of internal content plus internal webinars. The sales teams are always briefed and equipped so they can offer added-value content (eg sample reports, memes, infographics and even mini ebooks) at exhibitions/conferences/events. Popular posts are also promoted (they find it delivers a healthy ROI).

Hot new content is also regularly leveraged via PR (news releases). Most surveys make interesting news.

Apps

Kelly believe in apps as part of their content marketing and they cannot overestimate the value of such things. 'People like shiny stuff.' People internally get very excited about things that maybe aren't that strategic but that actually have some sort of cool factor that they can share with their network, so they talk about it with clients. That funky factor, that thing that's a bit light-hearted, or a bit cool or a bit new; having something like that every few months, or whenever it is justified, has really helped sustain interest, momentum and a sense of excitement that stuff is happening within Kelly.

Action: Systematic content marketing

Kelly now has one of the fastest-growing groups on LinkedIn with 25,000 members and another 350–400 new members a week, because LinkedIn promotes it and because Kelly manages it diligently. It literally takes only 10 minutes a day to manage the LinkedIn platform and yet it generates more traffic than search. Kelly's proactive weekly email to any member of this group brings people back and says 'There's three hot new discussions here, can you help out these guys?' Todd believes that the LinkedIn company page is becoming and will become more of a hub for any content and will become a much bigger channel.

Kelly do a lot of research annually, quarterly and monthly. It's like a self-perpetuating cycle. It's very easy to calenderize, it's very easy to find a process around and it gives them a layer of those core things that can help set the content. Calendarization around that gives them some predictability throughout the year.

Kelly try to stream the same visual look across the family of content.

Control: Measuring results

In addition to its 25,000 LinkedIn members, Todd Wheatland's tiny team's continual stream of great content is now reaching a tightly targeted global audience which has, in turn, lifted the monthly unique visitors by over 350 per cent within the first 12 months. So from Kelly's own channel through to their SlideShare channel, through to YouTube, through to other communities it's not uncommon for those 200 keywords to have multiple Kelly results on the first pages of search results. Todd is very clear about the tight connection between content marketing, marketing objectives, bringing in leads and closing sales.

Ongoing results: The knock-on effect

Events companies now invite Kelly to attend for free because they have become an influential content company. Some companies invite Kelly back because of their blog power. Event organizers see Kelly's growing database, their growing audience, all of their content and often ask them if Kelly can come and cover an event. Maybe even host the event? Kelly then get given behind-the-scenes access to talk to the different speakers, interview them and run that through various blogs. They now increasingly make connections between topics, spokespeople, content assets and events – a self-fulfilling cycle. Kelly's successful content marketing has moved them out of being the vendor in the trade hall booths, and up to being the people doing a lot of hosting, but also a lot of keynote speaking around topics that are important to Kelly's target market.

Conclusion

Through their dedication to relevant quality content, repurposing and promoting in an integrated process, Kelly have created an ever-strengthening competitive advantage that is rapidly becoming a sustainable competitive advantage.

CASE STUDY Topline's advertising boosts Christmas promotion

Situational analysis

With over 150 retail stores in Ireland and Northern Ireland, Topline is Ireland's largest DIY/building materials buying group (retail and trade chain of stores).

Traditionally, Topline's digital tactics focused solely on Facebook competitions and campaigns using a mix of organic posts and paid advertising targeting a broad user base in Ireland. This organic social media promotion tactic mixed with paid traditional advertising by Topline had worked reasonably well. Previous Topline competitions were also promoted via Twitter with scheduled tweets and profile background imagery; however, it was difficult for Twitter followers to use the competition page in order to enter the competitions, especially on mobile devices. Campaigns were not cross-platform nor cross-device so a large percentage of potential customers were neglected.

As of October 2014 Topline's Facebook following was 11,000. Topline came to Dublin-based agency, Continuum, looking for assistance on a digital campaign strategy with a view to driving traffic to their website and improving brand engagement online. An advertising budget was made available for a specific online campaign.

Objectives

The Topline digital marketing objectives were as follows:

- Primary objective: Improve customer data collection for future Topline communications.
- Secondary objective: Improve brand engagement on social media.
- Tertiary objective: Generate website traffic to the corporate Topline site.

Exact target numbers are not available.

Strategy

Topline came to Continuum with a Christmas-themed social media competition – '12 Stoves of Christmas' – consisting of a giveaway prize of one Topline stove product each day for 12 days. Topline required Continuum to assist in the implementation of their proposed strategy to achieve targets and maximize the potential results of the campaign. This strategy needed to include cross-platform and multi-device capabilities to reach all of Topline's target audience.

Tactics

Google AdWords

Standard display/text adverts were created for appropriately researched strategic keywords and placement, such as the keyword 'Stanley Stoves' placement on **Elledecor.com** and **Housebeautiful.com**.

A remarketing campaign targeted people who had recently visited the Topline site. This audience then received Topline ads when they landed on other sites. The remarketing AdWords campaign performed significantly better than the standard display advertising and text ads. The remarketing campaign had a CPC of 0.43c versus 0.80c for text ads and 0.98c for placement ads.

Facebook

Pre-defined target audiences based on previous Topline campaigns – 1) lookalike audience, and 2) custom audience for interior design/DIY interest targeting – were targeted via sponsored posts.

A separate lookalike audience was also targeted by sponsored posts for the competition, to entice new engagement. This campaign performed the best by far, with a cost of 34c per follow compared to previous CPF of 42c per like of a custom audience.

Any remaining budget for Facebook was used to boost the standard organic posts. Lookalike audiences help you reach people who are similar to your current customers. Custom audiences let you reach customers you already know with ads on Facebook.

Twitter

Sponsored tweets were used to amplify posts.

Action

A third-party application, 'ShortStack', was selected, implemented and used to host the competition page and data collection. This app allowed Topline to create a landing page without any coding or development dependence, and collect the entrants' contact details

FIGURE 15.14 Topline ran a Christmas-themed giveaway social media competition

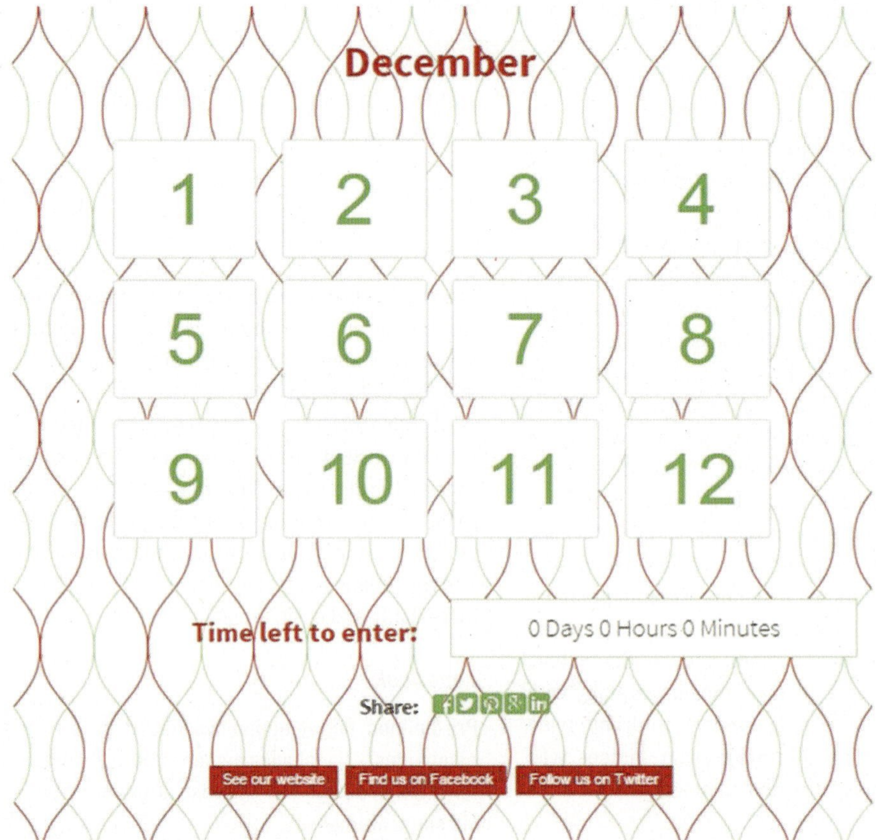

for each of the 12 daily competitions seamlessly across all channels including the Topline website, Facebook page and Twitter profile. An opt-in to further marketing promotions 'tick-box' was included on the landing page and provided a post-campaign final opt-in rate of 83 per cent.

A two-week campaign calendar that outlined all deliverable elements of the campaign from the set-up of the competition page using ShortStack to the selection of competition winners was created and used as a point of reference throughout the campaign.

Control

The Topline '12 Stoves of Christmas' social media campaign was a success surpassing expectations for social media engagement, email communication sign-up and website traffic generation.

Both Topline and Continuum made daily checks of the campaign. These checks resulted in tweaks to the advertising spend throughout the campaign based on best performing ads.

- Customer data collection for future communication:
  - total competition entrants = 19,313;
  - total competition entrants after duplicate removal and unwanted countries = 18,000;
  - final opt-in competition entrants = 15,003;
  - opt-in rate = 83.4 per cent.
- Brand engagement on social media (December 2013–December 2014):
  - Facebook following December 2013 = circa 1,000;
  - Facebook following 27 November 2014 = 20,300;

FIGURE 15.15 Topline's Christmas sales promotion appearing on Facebook

  - Facebook following 13 December 2014 = 35,454;
  - growth over 16-day period = 72 per cent;
  - growth since this time last year = 3,440 per cent.
- Increase in website traffic (December 2013–December 2014) compared to previous month:
  - overall up 47 per cent;
  - social media traffic up 147 per cent;
  - organic traffic up 11 per cent;
  - referral traffic up 134 per cent;
  - direct traffic up 82 per cent.
- Other: The ShortStack app competition page received 45,000 page views.

FIGURE 15.16 The campaign calendar

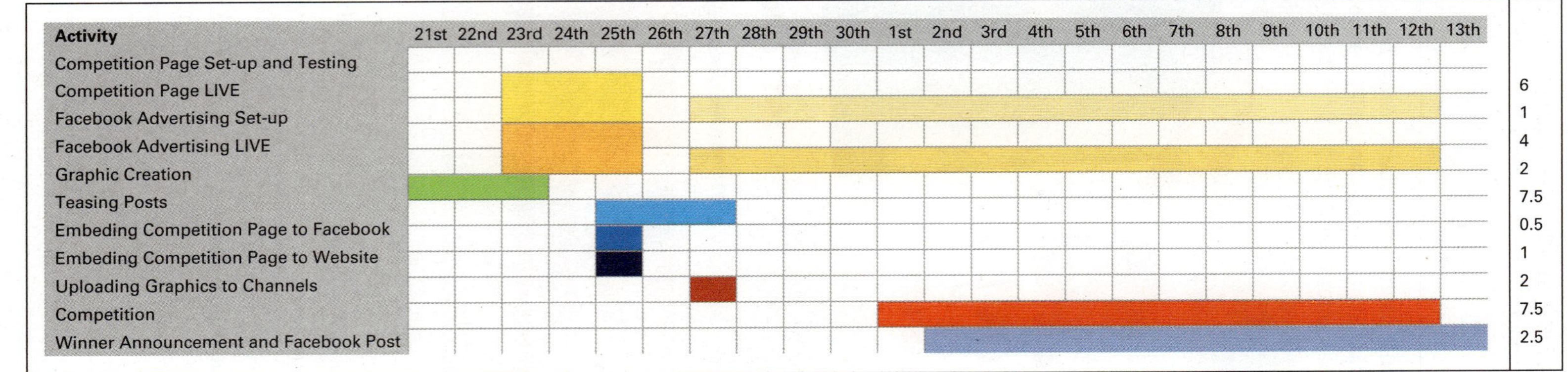

FIGURE 15.17 Topline overall traffic

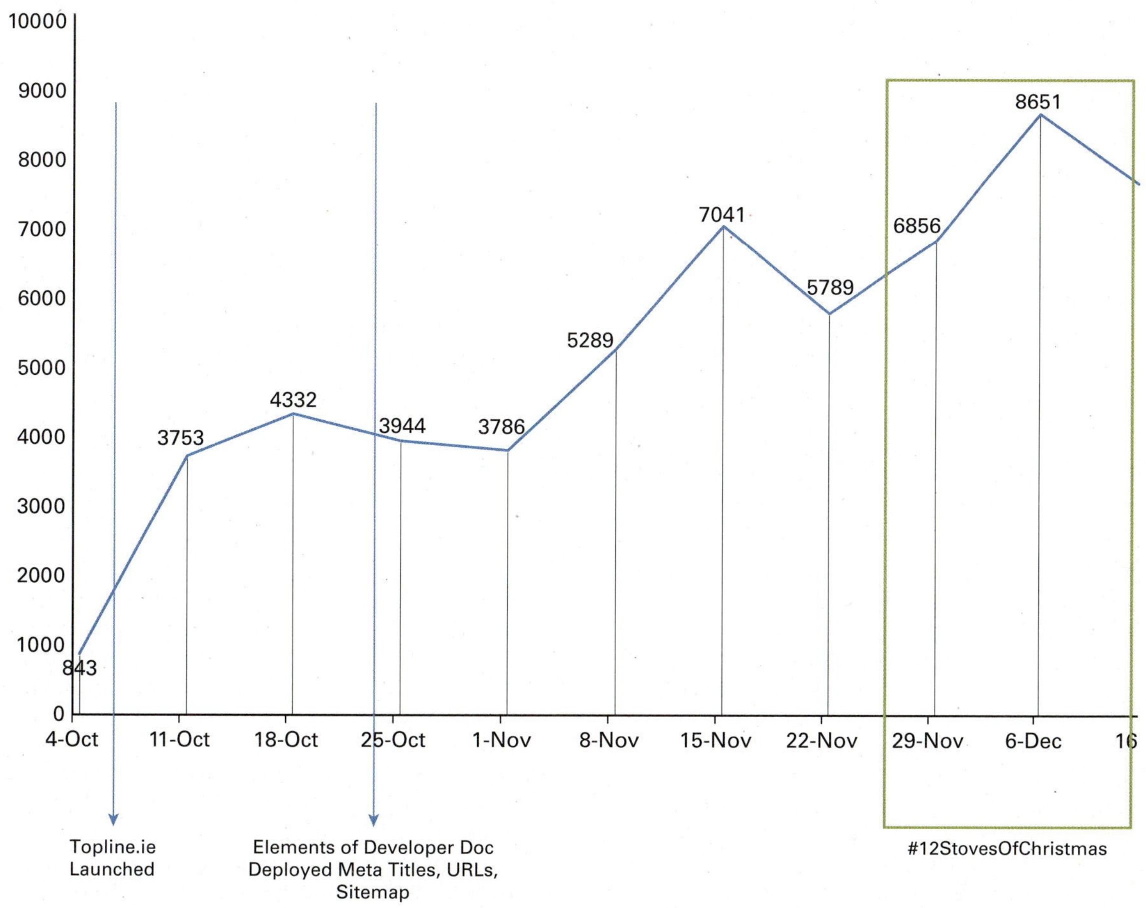

SOURCE: Topline

Advantages and disadvantages

Here are some of the advantages and disadvantages to consider when deciding whether to increase or reduce this communications tool.

Advantages

Sales promotions are useful when trying to close the sale or push the customer through the last stage of the buying process. They can also help to keep a relationship alive with existing customers by rewarding their loyalty. Sales promotions can support the brand and customer relations. They can be developed strategically to strengthen relationships over time. Increasingly content marketing is used in B2B marketing to capture email addresses, develop leads and constantly nurture the customer relationship.

Disadvantages

Promotions require other tools to promote them, eg advertising, PR, direct mail or social media announcing the promotion. What can go wrong will go wrong, hence the need for insurance. Some promotions actually damage the brand. Promotions can be expensive to set up, procure, administer and wind down, although third parties are generally contracted to do so. On a CPT basis, promotions are expensive, although they can prove to be more cost-effective on a cost-per-order (CPO) basis. Content wars make content marketing a more challenging type of sales promotion.

Key points from Chapter 15

- Sales promotions can be used strategically rather than simply as short-term tactical tools.
- Sales promotions must integrate with other elements of the marketing mix.
- Attention to detail is required, as sales promotions can go horribly wrong.
- There is room for enhanced creativity, as social media has opened up a vast range of collaborative opportunities.

References and further reading

Bird, D (1990) No mileage in frequency marketing, *Marketing*, 10 October, p 12

Bird, J (1997) How to keep them faithful the world over, *Precision Marketing*, 26 May

Bond, C (1991) Marriages of some convenience, *Marketing*, 10 October, pp 23–26

Britt, B (1990) Coke's magic spells trouble, *Marketing*, 31 May

Burke, B (2013) The gamification of business, *Forbes*, 21 January

Castling, J (1989) Buying strategic sales promotion, *Sales Promotion*, July, p 11

Chaffey, D and Smith, PR (2017) *Digital Marketing Excellence*, 5th edn, Routledge, Abingdon

Chaffey, D (2015) The content distribution matrix, *Smart Insights*, 20 January

Chaffey, D (2018) The content optimization matrix, *Smart Insights*, 16 April

Chapman, N (1985) Cadburys pays up in Typhoo game, *Marketing Week*, 17 May

Cummins, J (2003) *Sales Promotion: How to create and implement campaigns that really work*, 3rd edn, Kogan Page, London

Diaz, A C (2019) Brazilian campaign from David SP is latest clever play to get consumers using the app, *Adweek*, 20 March

Douglas, T (1987) *The Complete Guide to Advertising*, Pan Macmillan, London

Ehrenberg, A, Hammond, K and Goodheart, G (1991) *The After-Effects of Large Consumer Promotions*, London Business School, London

Farrell, J (1989) Which countries allow which promotions? *Marketing Week*, 16 June, pp 75–77

Grobel, W (2013) Marketing and insights practice manager, Deloitte, CIM Gamification webinar, July

Hammett, E (2018) Honda 'ditches' agencies in move to take charge of its brand, *Marketing Week*, 24 October

Henderson, B (2018) Storymaking: How to shape the stories that people share about brands, *Chief Marketer*, 14 February

Hollinger, P (1996) Electronic age raises ghost of Green Shield stamps, *Financial Times*, 9–10 November

Holloway, P (1989) Getting it right in the 90s, *Sales Promotion*, February, pp 23–24

Hyslop, R (1989) Round table discussion, *Sales Promotion*, July, p 14

Kotler, P (2000) *Marketing Management: Analysis, planning, implementation and control*, Millennium edn, Prentice Hall, Englewood Cliffs, NJ

Marketing Breakthroughs (1991) Polish give-aways struggle to reach target, December

Marketing Week Reporters (2018) 2018 year in review: It's been a bad year for…, *Marketing Week*, 10 December

McGovern, G (2018) Keeping digital teams happy versus keeping customers happy, gerrymcgovern.com (archived at https://perma.cc/HV6Y-DZWG), 5 August

Meaningful Brands (2019) *Havas Meaningful Brands Report 2019* [online] https://www.meaningful-brands.com/en (archived at https://perma.cc/XGK5-CAGW)

Miller, J (2018) Don't let 'best practice' take over your brand, LinkedIn Sales and Marketing Solutions EMEA blog

Nielsen (2015) Trade promotion doesn't have to be a guessing game, *Neilsen's Trade Promotions Performance Visualisation Report*

Pelling, N (nd) http://www.nickpelling.com/ (archived at https://perma.cc/95HM-ZX29)

Schaefer, M (2014) Content shock: Why content marketing is not a sustainable strategy, *Businessgrow*, 6 January

Schaefer, M (2018) Is content marketing sustainable? *SlideShare*, 14 February

Schaefer, M (2019a) 12 incredibly easy ways to create content with emotional impact, *Businessgrow*

Schaefer, M (2019b) *Marketing Rebellion*, Publisher Services

Schnaars, S (2013) General manager EMEA, Badgeville, CIM gamification webinar, July

Smith, D (2008) Google, 10 years in: Big, friendly giant or a greedy Goliath? *Observer*, 17 August

Smith, PR (2013) Gamification: the good, the bad and the ugly, http://prsmith.org/blog/ (archived at https://perma.cc/67JZ-HYWA), 9 October

Smith, PR (2014) Customer retention isn't boring, here's wow, http://prsmith.org/blog/ (archived at https://perma.cc/67JZ-HYWA), 22 August

Smith, PR and Chaffey, D (2001) *eMarketing eXcellence*, 2nd edn, Butterworth-Heinemann, Oxford

Sturt, D and Nordstrom, T (2018) 10 shocking workplace stats you need to know, *Forbes*, 8 March

Sweeney, E (2019) Consumers see 77% of brands as not meaningful, *MarketingDive*, 22 February

Toll, E (2014) Content marketing strategy: 5 essential tips, *Champion Communications* 18 September

Yardy, R (2015) Your parents were wrong! You were not 'wasting your time' playing computer games, *Digital Doughnut*, 15 July

Zeisser, M (2010) Unlocking the elusive potential of social networks, *McKinsey Quarterly*, member edn, June

Further information

British Promotional Merchandise Association (BPMA)
Fetcham Park House
Lower Road
Fetcham, Leatherhead
Surrey KT22 9HD
Tel: +44 (0)1372 371 184
www.bpma.co.uk

Content Marketing Institute
2 Penn Plaza
15th Floor
New York
NY 10121
USA
www.contentmarketinginstitute.com

Institute of Promotional Marketing Ltd (IPM)
Holborn Town Hall
193–197 High Holborn
London WC1V 7BD
www.theipm.org.uk

Marketing Agencies Action Group (MAAG)
82 Great Suffolk Street
London SE1 0BE
Tel: +44 (0)20 7535 3550
www.marketingagencies.org.uk/

Promota UK Ltd (Promotional Merchandise Trade Association)
1310 Solihull Parkway
Solihull
Birmingham B37 7YB
Tel: +44 (0)8453 714335
Fax: +44 (0)8453 714336
www.promota.co.uk

16

Direct mail, email, messaging and chatbots

LEARNING OBJECTIVES

By the end of this chapter you will be able to:

- be aware of the changing trends in one-to-one direct marketing;
- understand how email, messaging, Messenger and direct mail work;
- integrate direct one-to-one marketing into both acquisition and retention campaigns;
- check that you are GDPR compliant;
- understand the advantages and disadvantages of different direct marketing tools.

Introduction

Direct marketing includes any marketing communications tools that interact directly with customers. This includes direct response advertising, telemarketing and email, messaging, direct mail and now chatbots. This chapter explores direct mail, email, messaging and Messenger within the context of a contact strategy.

> **Direct marketing is never alone**
>
> It rarely ever, these days, works on its own. It is usually one component of a contact strategy for customer retention or maybe even customer acquisition. Email (and messaging, direct mail and even Messenger) integrates with a series of contacts – which can be a microsite, a Facebook page, a personalized video (more later on real-time personalization), snail mail and even a salesperson's visit or call.

In fact, these one-to-one tools can create conversations that unveil even more information about the visitor, eg a Messenger bot (primarily on Facebook, which is the dominant Messenger platform) can collect additional information from conversations. Very rudimentary data can be easily pulled from Facebook, such as name, profile picture and gender. 'But then once visitors start to talk to you through Messenger you can start asking them questions and you can use those answers to inform what you are going to send back. This is real time personalization of the content (eg a personalized video)' (Redgate, 2019). But first let us introduce the various tactical tools that help one-to-one conversations or correspondence.

Direct mail

Once upon a time, precisely targeted direct mail, with relevant incentives, and relatively cheap lists to hire, became the clever marketer's approach (1980s). Then, as it grew and customers became saturated with piles of 'junk mail', it lost its attractiveness. However, a relevant, aesthetically pleasing and timely piece of direct mail can still work (see Greenpeace's email success that generated more sales than any other tool, p 497), particularly if it is three-dimensional, and perhaps delivered in a jiffy bag, which can arouse curiosity and ensure the envelope is opened. A plastic cucumber mailed to media buyers in the UK once proved to be the most successful mailshot at that time. Media buyers kept the cucumber (with a data services company's details on it) on their desks for months afterwards. Today, direct mail can form a surprisingly pleasant part of the mix within a contact strategy.

Email

Once upon a time email marketing was considered to be an innovative and exciting way of communicating with prospects and customers (1990s). Then as everyone started using it, individuals' email bins got saturated and important emails got buried. The average worker receives 121 emails per day and only approximately 20 per cent are opened (Smith, 2019). The emergence of the derogatory email word 'spam' occurred. Spam and other breaches of personal privacy irritated people so much that privacy laws and eventually GDPR (see Chapter 10) came into legislation to protect people from the vagaries of unethical, and now illegal, spam emails. However, permission-based, carefully targeted and highly relevant email is generally welcomed and does have a role to play in the mix within a contact strategy.

Messaging to mobiles

Whether text messages, vouchers, downloadable podcasts, video clips or photos, messaging to mobiles/smart phones is going to get bigger, it is safe to say here that special offers made only to relevant target prospects as they pass by a relevant location will work, at least in the short term. Longer-term success will be determined by how well the industry regulates itself and the need for privacy (which is an issue that will continue to grow in importance also). If too many location-based mobile messages appear and clutter inboxes, customers will bar such messages and may also take legal action. As email is still popular, we will look at seven email types later.

Messenger bots/chatbots

Chatbots are automated messaging that chat with people. Chatbots use AI. Facebook Messenger bots are the same as Facebook chatbots. Messenger bots are primarily on Facebook, which is the dominant Messenger platform. Chatbots have been around in some form or shape for decades. They appear in social media, apps and websites. Bots are basically programmed to understand questions, give answers, and execute tasks. Designed to 'help' the customer by not having to search, look up, phone for info, just ask the chatbot, who is there, 24/7, waiting to be asked to help. They should save time (no queues). Some are better than others

> **Bots will replace everything**
>
> 'You've heard the buzz. Chatbots will replace mobile apps. Chatbots will replace email marketing. Chatbots will replace customer care agents. Chatbots will cut your costs and increase your revenue. And they're gonna do it all while you sleep. There's a lot of hype floating around right now about chatbots in general, and Facebook Messenger bots in particular. It's no surprise that, according to a survey by Oracle, 80 per cent of businesses want a chatbot in place by 2020.'
>
> Cooper (2019)

Contact strategy

Email does work quite well if it can be mixed in as part of a customer acquisition contact strategy, inviting prospects to click through to a website for some relevant information, followed by some remarketing if their subsequent digital body language (click behaviour) identifies them as interested prospects as opposed to visitors that 'bounce' away from the site immediately (more later). Despite this (and falling email open rates), many organizations either maintain their own database or buy (rent) databases (lists) of 'opt-in' email addresses, personalize a relevant offer and, despite the very small percentage response rates, still find it works for many markets, particularly if the email is part of a contact strategy. Equally, we see more and more contact strategies using messaging and chatbots (more later).

The contact strategy can include messaging, email, snail mail, telemarketing and even personal visits. The mailings (online or offline) can be short messages or letters, newsletters, vouchers or full brochures (or links to a website section: video, ebook or web pages). NB Short is good – scrolling on smart phones is getting less popular.

Email types

- Rented list email (rental doesn't usually give direct access to data nor unlimited use);
- co-branded email (and/or co-registration);
- competition sites;
- third-party email newsletter;
- viral email;
- triggered, retargeted email;
- first-party house e-newsletter or acquisition deal.

Objectives

Direct mail, email, messaging and Messenger can all trigger conversations, dialogue and engagement. They probably work best with individuals who are already warm, ie they know you already, although they can be used as part of an integrated contact strategy to trigger a conversation too.

> 'Key Strategy Recommendation: 1. Focus your email marketing efforts on current contacts. Email marketing tends to work best as a tool to improve prospect conversion, nurturing, customer retention, and growth. This is because emails to warm contacts who already know you work best. Don't forget to focus on getting email opt-in and your email marketing efforts on known contacts.'
>
> Chaffey and van Rijn (2019)

Direct response vs brand building

Although it is similar to direct mail, email is most widely used for direct response (as opposed to brand

TABLE 16.1 Email types

Option	What is it?	Benefits	Issues
1. Rented list	Renting access to contacts from a list owner who broadcasts on your behalf	Reach into new contacts	List source High typical cost of acquisition Low responsiveness Perception of spam – rent from a reputable list owner
2. Co-branded email	Email sent from list owner but with your brand, message and offer	Leverage partner brand. Can also co-register – sign up on their site	Exclusivity Brand mismatch
3. Competition email	Email inviting recipient to join a competition to win a prize	Works best if firstly the prize is relevant and secondly, it relates to brand	If too many people win the prize, insurance required
4. Third-party e-newsletter ad/ sponsorship	Placing an ad, sponsorship, editorial in a publisher's e-newsletter	Responsiveness compared to other options Reach	Need prime position Clutter Cost
5. Viral email	An email is designed to be shared and seeded to a house or rented list in combination with social media promotion	Potentially low-cost and high reach Reach second degree contacts	Not achieving the viral effect Negative brand impact
6. Triggered email	Email that is automatically sent after a trigger event like a download or cart abandon	Automated – just sit back and relax Can handle conversion of leads	Optimizing creative, offer and frequency Might have high start-up costs Availability of enough data to target/segment
7. House newsletter	Newsletters keep your contacts informed, they can work well for prospects who haven't bought from you yet	Helps build a relationship with recipient over time Broad testing and optimization options	Achieving balance between informing the list member and selling to them Creating relevant and interesting content

SOURCE: Chaffey and van Rijn (2019)

building or brand awareness), although e-newsletters in particular can also support brand awareness. Email enables a targeted, and personalized, message to be pushed out to customers to inform and remind. They will, at worst, see the subject line within their email inbox, even if only to delete it. Contrast this with the web, which is a pull medium where customers will visit your site only if there is a reason to do so. Nevertheless, unsolicited email (spam) is illegal in B2C markets and damaging to a brand.

Opt-in is essential, whether B2C or B2B. Emailing only those who have opted in is simply best practice. Before starting an email dialogue with customers, companies must ask them to provide their email addresses. GDPR/privacy law in many countries requires customers to proactively opt in by checking a box (showing consent in some way). In the UK it is alright to email prospects either if they have been customers or if they have made enquiries and have given their email address. With every subsequent email, however, marketers must offer customers an easy way to opt out at any time.

Stay within the law: Opt-in email

'Email is an effective push online communications method. It is essential that email is opt-in, otherwise it is illegal spam. Consider options for customer acquisition including cold email, co-branded emails and placements in third-party emails. For house list emails, experiment with achieving the correct frequency, or give customers the choice. Consider automated event-triggered emails. Work hard on email design and maintaining up-to-date lists. Stay within the law.'

Chaffey and Smith (2013)

Customer acquisition

For those companies that use opt-in email for customer acquisition, there are three main options for customer acquisition programmes, as highlighted by Chaffey and Smith (2017):

- **Cold email campaign.** In this case, the recipient receives an opt-in email from an organization that has rented an email list from a consumer email list provider such as Experian, Nielsen, Claritas or a business email list provider such as Mardev, trade publishers, event companies, or data companies. Although the recipients have agreed to receive offers by email, the email is, effectively, cold. For example, a credit card provider could send a cold email to a list member who is not currently their member. It is important to use some form of 'statement of origination', as otherwise the message may be considered spam. Cold emails, unsurprisingly, tend to have a higher cost per acquisition (CPA) than other forms of online marketing, but different lists should still be evaluated.
- **Co-branded email.** Here, recipients receive an email with an offer from a company with which they have a reasonably strong affinity. For example, the same credit card company could partner with a mobile service provider such as Vodafone and send out the offer to their customers who have opted in to receive emails from third parties. Although this can be considered a form of cold email, it is warmer, since there is a stronger relationship with one of the brands, and the subject line and creative will refer to both brands. Co-branded emails tend to be more responsive than cold emails to rented lists, since the relationship exists and fewer offers tend to be given.
- **Third-party e-newsletter.** In this visitor acquisition option, a company publicizes itself in a third-party e-newsletter. This could be in the form of an ad, sponsorship or PR (editorial) that links through to a destination site. These placements may be set up as part of an interactive advertising ad buy, since many e-newsletters also have permanent versions on the website. Since e-newsletter recipients tend to engage with them by scanning the headlines or reading them if they have time, e-newsletter placements can be relatively cost-effective.

Customer retention

As mentioned, email marketing is best for customer retention, as part of an ongoing contact strategy to keep in touch with customers and deliver them relevant updates, offers, tips and advice. It also provides a response mechanism for customers to air their views and give valuable feedback. Every contact creates an opportunity to continuously add data to the customer profile. It is therefore important that marketing integrates with the rest of the organization's operations, particularly if there was a sudden surge in responses but there was no system in place to manage responses (whether asking a question, making a complaint, looking for advice or trying to buy the product or service). Any glitches in the system can damage the customer relations that have been built up over time. **Well-managed systems test campaigns before roll-out and build in the facility of continual customer profiling to identify which customers are likely to want which products or services.** (See the grandfather clock story, p 89.)

Predictive analytics predict acquisition and retention, and reduce emails

'"All of our analysis was based on past purchases behaviour. We're not data scientists, we don't have PhDs in our office, so any predictive analysis – like who might buy in the future, and what a customer might buy in the future – was not something that we were able to capture" (Victoria Graham, Guess Director of Marketing).

Guess applied predictive analytics by first identifying and understanding their customers across two dimensions: purchase-based customer personas, and high-value customers. These insights were then applied to predict future purchase response to acquisition and retention campaigns. This has prompted a change in the Guess email strategy. "Three years ago we were emailing customers three, possibly four times a week," Graham says. "We were very much batch and blast, and our email calendar was driven by our merchant team: If there's a product launch, or a big promotion, like 40 per cent off all sweaters, that was driving the email calendar. We're now in the process of changing that."

"We've been cognizant of the fact that it is quite likely that we were irritating our customers with constantly talking to them. We had two options when we talked about getting personalized with our emails: one option was to cut back on emails. If today's email is about denim, and you like accessories, you just don't get today's email. But the thought of cutting down the number of emails we send out was scary. The other option was, if we're going to email everyone every day, let's talk to them in a way that's meaningful and relevant to them."

In a test, they isolated the accessories persona and the non-accessories persona. They compared the accessories customers who received the accessories-focused email (group A) to accessories customers who received the regular email (group B). The CTR and conversion rate of group A far exceeded those of group B.

Another analysis approach was identifying high-value customers to optimize acquisition. This dispelled a lot of assumptions, according to Graham, such as assuming that top customers were metropolitan customers, who liked core products like denim, but also loved accessories. But this wasn't necessarily the case, Graham explains: "When we looked at where our customers really over-index and differentiate themselves from the rest of our customer database, they found that they were more likely to live in suburban areas. Arizona popped as a big state for high lifetime value customers. Their first purchase tended to be a knit or a sweater or denim."'

Chaffey & Smith (2017) and Kivilis (2014)

See Chapter 3, p 96 on how the fire brigade use predictive analytics to predict fires through profiling and how gaming companies profile and target big gamblers versus loss making bonus seekers.

10 success factors

1 **Conversation: Engaging conversation or…** Email marketing is two-way – are we helping recipients to engage in a dialogue or just pushing content at them? Ask recipient to engage via polls, surveys, ratings, reviews, competitions or maybe sharing content. Keep any forms short and simple. Add the option to opt-out (by law).

2 **Relevant: Highly relevant or ...**
Great emails if targeted at the wrong people, become irrelevant emails, which become an irritant. 'Sense and respond' communications are driven by interactions from the customer. If the subject line is deemed irrelevant it will not even get opened. Tighter targeting equals higher response rates.

3 **Incentives: Great incentive or...**
Do the recipients actually want our incentives? What benefit does the recipient gain from staying subscribed, reading the email, participating or clicking on the links? Have we asked them what they want? The incentive should be part of a strong call to action.

4 **Timing: Great timing or....**
What time of day and what day in the week is best for sending emails in your industry sector? Markets differ. The only way to find out is to test and learn. Some email services learn and adjust timing based on previous email campaign open times.

5 **Integration: Part of a contact strategy or....**
Are our emails integrated with other channels? Is the email part of a sequence of emails or a mix of emails, snail mails, messages, phone calls, remarketing – ie a contact strategy spread across multi-channels?

6 **Creative: Cut through the clutter or...**
Does the creative (design, layout, images) and the copy (words) catch the eye, arouse interest and generate a 'must open' feeling? Again, subject line is critical. Keep it brief, personalized and clear CTA. The ultimate test for an email in the email pile is this: 'Are you more important than my partner?' There are AI systems such as Phrasee and Persado that claim to optimize subject lines better than humans.

7 **Render or....**
Does the email look ok when opened via different email servers, different browsers and different devices? If the recipient has 'images turned off' is there some text (vs image only)? Are images tagged so there is still some message? Is the email short enough not to look too long on a smart phone?

8 **Landing page or...**
The link clicked on in an email should, ideally, take you to a landing page tailored specifically for the email. Never send customers to a home page where they have to start searching. Landing pages are part of the magic marketing formula (IRD): identify need, reflect need (or show solution on the landing page) and then deliver a reasonable product or service.

9 **Targeting...**
Although it is implicit in 'Relevance', it is so important, we need to highlight it as targeting is the variable that impacts results the most – more than creative, timing and even incentives. Should be continually refined, as customer profiling and preferences continually improve over time.

10 **Testing....**
Continually test to continually improve and optimize everything over time. A/B testing allows marketers to test different headlines, different offers, different photographs and even different background colours to see which perform the best. Small improvements directly impact the bottom line. Test everything, continually.

Note the first eight factors were adapted from Chaffey and van Rijn's Email marketing strategy (2019).

Initiating conversations via social media, Messenger and CRM

Brands pull data from Facebook feeds, Messenger bots, Twitter and CRM platforms. Consider a Facebook feed – where a brand posts something onto its page and someone posts a comment. This data can be pulled (the comment they have made, their handle name and photo). This data is subsequently processed and used to personalize a message, or in the case of videos a personalized video complete with the user's name, photo and comment (more later).

Twitter

Brands use an API that pulls in all the tweet data. Brands search against the hashtag or for brands or people mentioning a certain brand. This is deemed to be an 'engagement' from Twitter's point of view and that is a signal of 'intent' from the user towards the brand (or towards a campaign) which means that brands can then legitimately respond to including using the user's quote or whatever they have said and their Twitter handle. Remember this is only for a personalized video which will only be sent to that individual person who then chooses to post it or delete it.

Messenger bots

Messenger bots, primarily on Facebook, can trigger a conversation. Initially, personal data available on the general public level can be collected, such as name, profile picture, gender. Once the individual starts to talk to the brand (through Messenger) then you can start asking them questions and use those answers to inform (and personalize) something even more relevant which you are going to send back. As mentioned, this is real-time personalization of the content.

CRM

Comments made by a customer and stored on a brand's CRM system provide more 'more passive engagement' data compared to the real-time personalization data we just mentioned. However, this can be done, as demonstrated by EchoMany, who worked with Save the Children on their Christmas Jumper Day (see below).

Integrating tactical tools

Each tactical tool used in Part Two of this book naturally integrates with several other tactical tools. One-to-one personalized campaigns, at scale, also naturally integrate with a variety of tools. Let us explore a few examples.

CRM with emails and personalized videos

Data is pulled out from the CRM system of people that engaged with Save the Children Christmas Jumper Day promotion last year. We know that this person engaged last year – they raised this much money and they are based here. That data is pulled from the CRM system and used to inform the video so then when they get the video sent to them it would be like 'Hey, Paul thanks for doing Christmas Jumper Day last year, you raised £500 lets see if you can smash it and beat that this year.' You can see these and many other personalized videos at **http://prsmith.org/blog/**.

> **See yourself on the side of a bus**
>
> Putting your name, photo and quotation onto the side of a bus as it drives by, is an advanced video after effects technique.

Messenger with personalized video

A prospect is in Messenger (where you don't have them for much longer than 60 seconds). So once they start engaging, you pull that data, you run it through the profanity check (that the name is a real name and that there is no obscene language, etc). Other rules and filters can be added – eg if prospect is on Twitter you might only send a personalized video to somebody that has got over 500 followers because they are going to be more influential when they share it. Anyone with fewer followers might just get a personalized image. This can be done at scale, ie delivering 250,000 personalized videos and sending back to 250,000 individuals via Messenger – all done within approximately 25 minutes from the user's first engaging (10,000 videos per minute).

Then you've got moderation. Since you have got user generated content (UGC), eg you are asking people to submit photos, then you need to moderate that. This is a manual step that ensures a brand can protect itself from anything naughty, rude or obscene, or political.

Asset selection (part of moderation), puts these platform tools in the hands of the brand's social media teams. They can add the campaign rule: 'Find people that are talking about our movie' (eg *Deadpool*) and when people say something nice about the movie they can be sent a personalized video, so that needs to be checked manually. One of five different video trailers featuring five different characters can be selected, depending on which particular *Deadpool* character this person is talking about.

FIGURE 16.1 Campaign rules and filters include profanity checks and minimum number of followers required

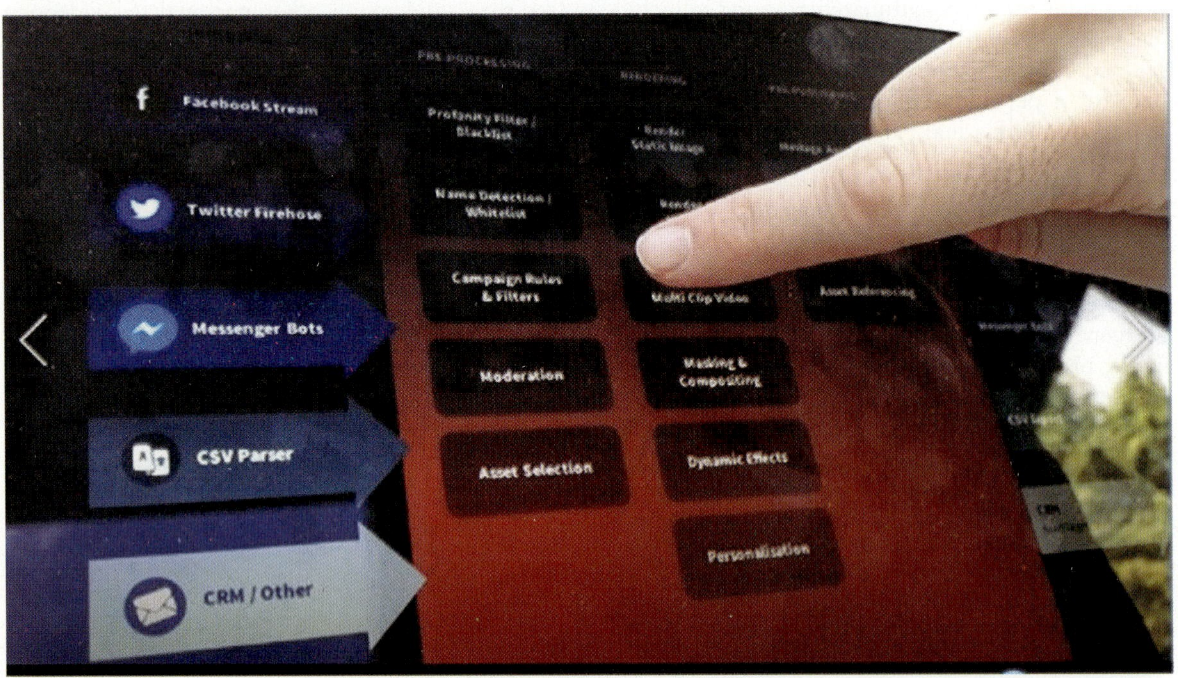

FIGURE 16.2 Asset selection allows the most relevant video clip/trailer to be dispatched

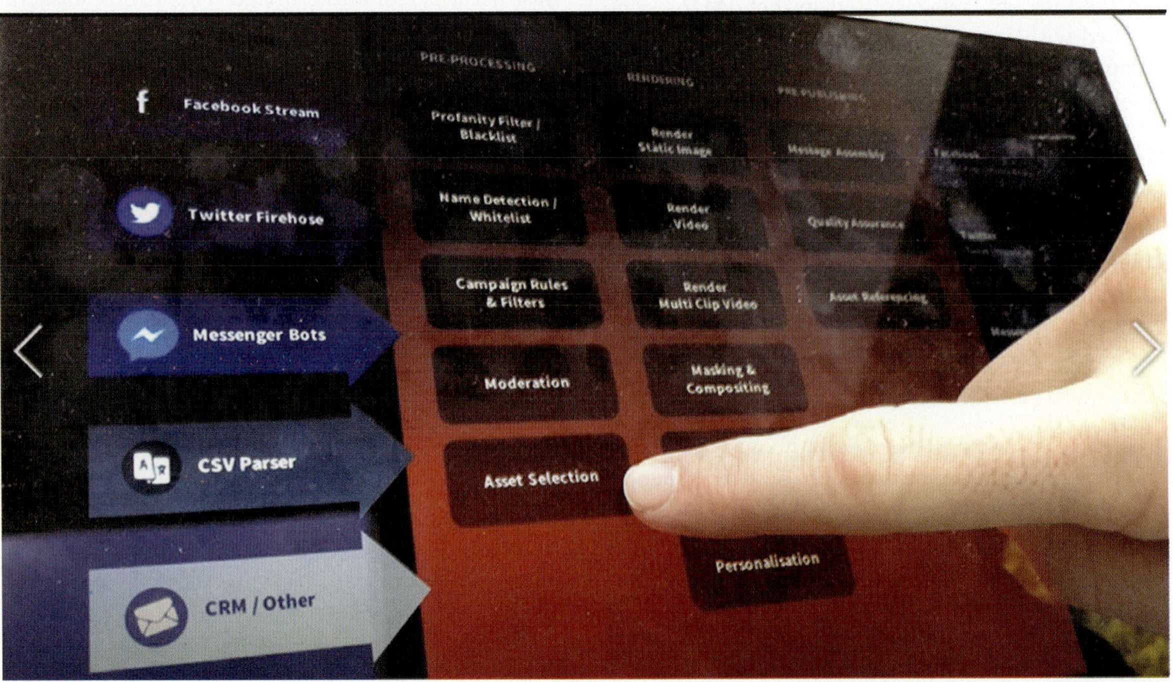

FIGURE 16.3 Personalized thank-you

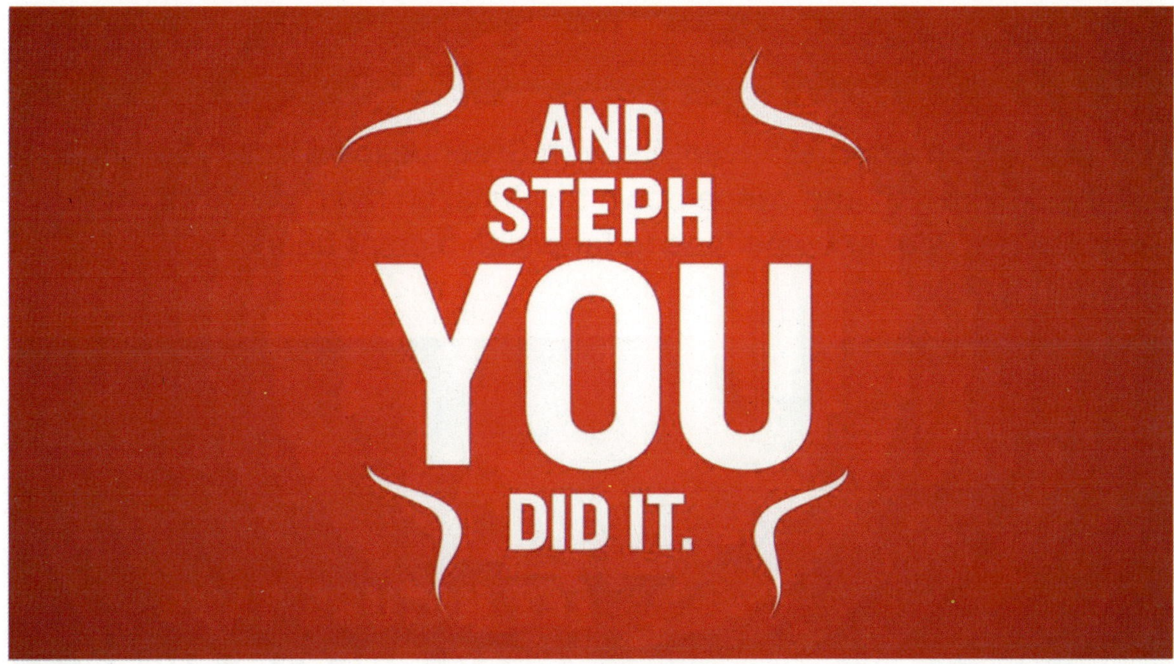

They will get a personalized video about that particular character, still personalized in the same way – pulling in the fan's name, their tweet, their profile picture all embedded into the first few seconds of the video.

You can put somebody's profile photo into the background of a movie scene (this is called 'masking and compositing'), effectively masking the original background image out. This is a bit like green screen technique. Dynamic effects allow you to make the fan/prospect or customer's name turn around in 360 degrees, or you might have other animation effects added in.

Email, personal landing pages, social media and personal videos

See the case study p 505 which shows how the British Heart Foundation emailed 13,000 fundraisers a link to a personalized landing page with an embedded personalized video, which the fundraiser could then choose to share or delete. The net result? Almost a 20 times return on campaign cost. This was followed by another personalized video at Christmas. The second personalized video thanked individuals for being a fundraiser, completing the London–Brighton bike ride video and asked them if they were 'up for it' again next year.

Messaging and ads

Weve are a telco data company who helped to raise awareness of Seat Ibiza by targeting both verified 25–54 adults and verified 18+ adults, living in proximity to Seat dealerships, with a messaging campaign that drove through to a 360-degree landing page, where users explored the car by rotating their phone. Results: 24 per cent not previously aware of the Seat Ibiza; 166 per cent uplift in likelihood to consider Seat Ibiza when next buying a car, and more likely to remember Seat Ibiza after they explored it in full 360 degrees.

Messaging and display ads

BMW 2 series generated leads for the BMW 2 Series Active Tourer. Weve used a combination of messaging and display advertising to target different family audiences. For example, Weve targeted first time mums, young families and empty nesters with bespoke copy to appeal to their unique needs from a

FIGURE 16.4 Greenpeace ad on Facebook

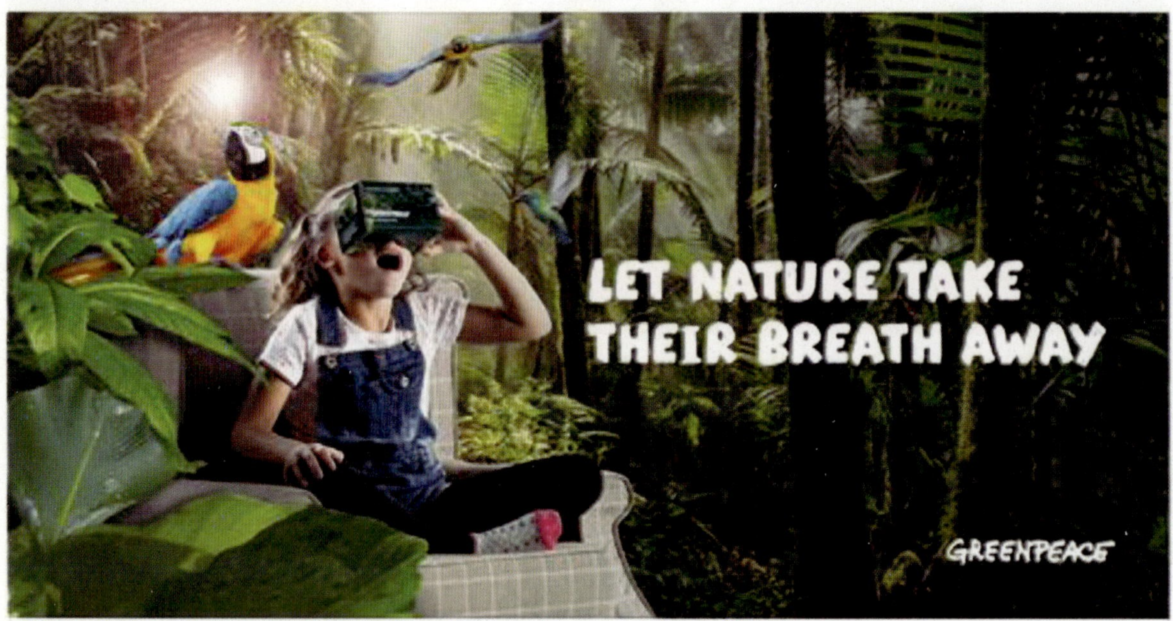

new BMW family car. Twenty per cent took an action to find out more about the car. Eight per cent intended to register online to get 2 Series updates.

Email and ads

Greenpeace wanted to boost awareness of global issues and introduce a new audience (families and kids) to the beauty of the fragile natural environment with a VR explorer kit promoted at Christmas.

Greenpeace tested ads on major platforms like National Geographic and found that emailing their own database got by far the best results. See the box below.

Greenpeace VR Explorer Kit campaign results

'In total we have received 1749 orders with an average amount of £13.37. We also got 57 online direct debits (membership sign-ups) and will be calling other people in two weeks' time to convert them into regular donors. Most of the external channels were very new to us, so it was a great testing opportunity for us to see what other channels Greenpeace could be investing more in, in the future.

Most orders came from our emails (we sent two of them) – generating 1,302 orders (74 per cent of sales). Paid Facebook performed quite well, generating 112 orders (6 per cent of sales) with a £17 CPA. SMS marketing achieved only 15 orders out of around 60,000 messages sent (<1 per cent).

Online banner advertising performed well for retargeting as we got just over 100 orders (6 per cent of sales) with a spend of under £2,000 (CPA of £18). It was also driving high traffic to our organic search results and therefore our Greenpeace shop page (which wasn't advertised in any other way than search). On the other hand, prospecting banner advertising didn't achieve good results as we achieved only a handful of orders.

A *Radio Times* advert achieved just under 40 orders and two online direct debits. Also, our advert was featured in around 800,000 copies and it definitely raised our brand awareness, which should help with the longer-term results.

Nat Geo Kids editorial and website also didn't perform very well, as we only achieved 17 orders. Taking into account the fact that Nat Geo Kids has 45,000 subscribers a month and each magazine has over 100,000 circulation (90 per cent of parents read it too), it was a great opportunity for us to raise our brand awareness among new audience groups: parents and kids.

This campaign is considered to be a "self-liquidating sales promotion" (promotions that pay for their own cost). Whilst proving there is a need for VR experiences, Greenpeace also grew brand awareness, found a new target audience (families and kids), boosted customer engagement by adding value to CX and sowing the seeds of the importance of stopping climate change in this beautiful, yet fragile, world, amongst a new generation.'

Greenpeace

FIGURE 16.5 Greenpeace VR ad

Data brokers, list broker and a telco powered data offering

Weve are backed by O2, the UK's leading telco company. Twenty-three million UK adults make up their transparent, verified and consented data foundation, creating accurate data and location at scale.

That potential for this inbuilt functionality to create powerful mobile creative should not be ignored. In fact, some brands have found a 10 times higher engagement rate on campaigns that utilize these unique features, which could include anything from the gyroscope, light sensor and accelerometer through to the camera, microphone and touch screen.

Advertisers can use these sensors to make existing ads feel more mobile friendly, but most importantly these unique features should be considered from the start and used to power creative ideas full stop. In doing so brands have the opportunity to create rich, immersive ads that are more akin to the engaging experiences we have come to know and love on our phones.

Rain-triggered emails

'In the United States, bowling company AMF works with engagement marketing specialist, Silverpop, to take advantage of sudden changes of weather. Live weather feeds are used to trigger emails. So, if rain is forecast for the weekend, emails are sent out to opted-in bowlers on AMF's database, offering discounts on and vouchers for the days in question. By making it clear that rain is likely and outdoor activities won't be as much fun, AMF has been able to boost participation and revenue. Silverpop also works with Air New Zealand, putting live weather feeds into travel confirmation emails. Suggested activities for travellers to undertake once they reach their destination, provided by the airline's partners, are tailored depending on the predicted weather conditions.'

Gray (2011)

Issues and challenges

Email challenges

Email marketing brings its own peculiar set of challenges that need to be managed. Your email programme will fail if you are not managing these issues adequately:

- **Deliverability:** All emails are not delivered in the same way through different internet service providers (ISPs), corporate firewalls and email systems. Your carefully crafted email may be classified as SPAM 1) due to the use of spam words (like 'free') or 2) if the reputation of your email sender is poor (due to previous bounced emails, complaints or sending high volumes rapidly). Check your reputation using SenderScore (**https://www.senderscore.org/**). The better your reputation, the less likely you are to be blocked for using copy such as 'free' or 'limited offer', which have proven effectiveness.
- **Renderability:** This refers to the difficulty of displaying the email message as intended within the inbox of different email reading systems. If the email is all image-based, the images are not always displayed in the email (an anti-spam measure). The email will be meaningless unless it is has a powerful subject line. Response rate will fall. Best practice is to ensure the body copy and alt tags (tags or labels behind the images) get your message (and CTAs) across even when images are blocked. An additional problem is that different email readers can display emails differently, so they need to be coded and tested to look their best across different email readers and devices.
- **Email response decay:** Email recipients are most responsive when they first subscribe. It is difficult to keep them engaged. A carefully planned welcome strategy will include a series of pre-prepared emails with a variety of relevant messages, coupons, gifts and news, scheduled to be sent out over a period of weeks and months. Response will also affect which email gets sent (see the PayPal case study at the end of this chapter).

- **Communications preferences:** Recipients will have different preferences for email offers, content and frequency, which affect engagement and response. Some list members will prefer more frequent emails and others may prefer once a month. These can be managed through communications preferences, which can also include which channel they prefer (email, Messenger, snail mail, telephone).
- **Resource intensive:** Although email offers great opportunities for targeting, personalization and more frequent communications, additional people and technology resources are required to carry out testing and overcome issues such as deliverability and renderability. Having said that, most email services, eg Mailchimp, include deliverability and renderability testing. In addition, marketing automation systems and rules can be set up so that certain click behaviour (on a website or with an email – opening it and/or clicking a link) will trigger an automatic email.

Chaffey and Smith (2013)

Data decay rate is a separate, major issue affecting email, direct mail and messaging. So we will address it here with some specific solutions, and also when we explore the importance of maintaining a clean database in the following section.

Data decay rate

Email marketing databases naturally degrade by about 22.5 per cent every year. So it's important to have a strategy to make up for these lost contacts (HubSpot, 2016). That means more than half your database erodes every three years (53 per cent is gone).

Managing email engagement decay

It is inevitable that email list subscribers have their highest levels of engagement with a brand when they are first added to a database and that this will decay through time. Dom Yeadon (2009) of The Marketing Bureau analysed a sample of B2C and B2B lists that show the extent of email list decay. He summarized the implications of the research as follows:

- You could lose 5 per cent of the whole list every 3 months
- Your list loses two-thirds of its value in 12 months.
- Fresh emails (0 to 3 months old) are each worth three times as much as older emails (12 months old).

You can evaluate your email list using Dom's formula based on different aspects of email response:

Engagement index = (D × V × CTR × 100) where D = deliverability, V = views (opens) and CTR = click-through rate

He gives these examples:

Email engagement index, 0–3 months = 11
Delivery rate = 90 per cent
Views = 35 per cent
Click-throughs = 36 per cent
[.9 × .35 × .36 =.11 × 100 = 11]
Email engagement Index, 9–12 months = 4
Delivery rate = 73 per cent
Views = 31 per cent
Click-throughs = 18 per cent
[.73 × .31 × .18 = .04 × 100 = 4]

So, what to do about email decay?

Digital marketing best practice checklist: Email list decay

Checklist for managing email list decay

- Develop a welcome programme where, over the first three to six months, you deliver targeted auto-triggered emails to educate subscribers about your brand and products, and deliver targeted offers.
- Think about how you can reactivate list members as they become less responsive.
- Segment list members by activity (responsiveness) and age on list. Assess your level of email list activity (ask what percentage of list members haven't clicked within the last three to six months – if they haven't, they are inactive and should be

treated differently, either by reducing frequency or using more offline media).

- Follow up on bounces, using other media to reduce problems of dropping deliverability.
- Best practice when renting lists is to request only emails where the opt-in is within the most recent six to nine months when subscribers are most active.

Chaffey and Smith (2017)

Database maintenance

A well-maintained database is crucial. A poorly kept database turns an asset (database) into a liability, as customers are irritated by incorrect emails, or even worse irrelevant emails determined by segmenting a poorly maintained database. Worse still, you might end up in court courtesy of the new GDPR laws (see the next section).

Profile data (first name and address) is static data. Dynamic data is profile data generated from open and click behaviour. This data reveals interests, optimum times and ultimately helps you to target even more relevant direct messages in the future.

GDPR

Is the General Data Protection Regulation an opportunity to boost CX, or a threat that could put you out of business? It's both. A great opportunity, if you work with it. A threat, if you dare to ignore it. Do we really need the GDPR?

The answer is 'yes' and here are six big reasons why:

- falling customer trust;
- data criminals are growing;
- GDPR breach (poor data security) incurs big fines;
- GDPR breach can close your business;
- GDPR breach can send you to prison;
- GDPR protects individuals and your customers.

Smith (2017)

A company can be fined €20 million/4 per cent of global turnover for primary infringement (if it impacts a data subject/individual) or €10 million/2 per cent for secondary infringement (a breach of the regulations – eg not carrying out technical and organizational measures as required) – whichever is the greater.

Personal data includes: genetic data, bio data, voice data, finger prints and recognition data, CCTV, photos, recorded calls, CRM and after sales, search strings, web reports systems log IP addresses, accounts and finance, financial records, HR records, communications tools such as emails, Messenger messages, social networks and marketing databases and profiles.

So, GDPR tries to protect an individual's rights to privacy and security of data, and protection from identity theft. It is therefore much required. The onus and responsibilities it places on organizations have created a lot of extra work and cost a lot of money. However, the net result is a better CX, and ultimately this should benefit the business as it forms better relations with its customers and takes care of their data. Data is the lifeblood of any business today. GDPR helps us marketers to take good care of it. For more on GDPR see **http://prsmith.org/blog/**.

Managing incoming emails

Many organizations insult their customers by ignoring or mismanaging their incoming emails – they not only lose sales but also raise anger and damage the brands which they have spent budgets on building. Marketers have to be careful and manage the volume of incoming emails and reduce the manual workload required by outgoing responses, while somehow still growing strong customer relations. Whether it is a sales enquiry, an after-sales service issue, a complaint or a compliment (five star rating or review), email provides a direct conduit to the marketplace. Having made the effort to create a dialogue, you need to have the systems, procedures and resources in place to manage this communications channel. This can be automated, semi automated or manual. However AI is improving and the maturity of marketing automation will eventually integrate seamlessly with CRM systems (still a challenge for many organizations). Meanwhile, unsubscribes must be deleted from your database, whether manually or automatically. Finally, think about a contingency plan if you get an unusually large response (see Zip World, p 611, whose website crashed when they got an above-average response).

Keeping the relationship alive

One-to-one emails, messages, Messengers or letters, if timely and relevant, can be an excellent tactical tool to keep the relationship alive. It's a relatively inexpensive, flexible, personal communications tool. The key is relevance and timing. See the British Heart Foundation case at the end of this chapter, who send out a timely and useful personalized video to fundraisers just two weeks before the London–Brighton bike ride and follow it up with a friendly 'Thank you' email with another personalized video at Christmas time.

See some quick tips on how to 'convert customers to lifetime customers' in Chapters 19 and 20, and a more detailed approach to relationship building in the CRM in Chapter 3, p 75. Basically, it's all about common sense courtesy, listening, communicating, helping and rewarding with relevant useful gifts, at the right time (and ideally, in the right place). Customer lifecycle marketing is based on the principle of exchange of value. Savvy brands develop a series of structured communications across channels to encourage further engagement, dialogue, purchasing and advocacy – always offering something of value to their recipients.

> **Useful gifts**
>
> Sending a custom gift (anything you like from Amazon, a winery, or a flower shop) or company merchandise (t-shirts, hats, pens) or instant eGifts (online vouchers) in real time with handwritten notes can be a pleasant variation (within a contact strategy) for the customer and adds value to the overall lifetime CX. Companies like Sendosa.com do exactly that with an integrated system that fits other stacks.

Managing a direct mail campaign

Whether an organization is planning an advertising campaign or a direct mail campaign, a similarly disciplined approach should be taken, ie researching the situation, message development (creative mailing), media planning (list selection and timing), testing and monitoring, etc.

A direct mail campaign can be planned in the same way as an advertising campaign, ie by using SOSTAC® + 3Ms (see Chapter 9). However, six factors will be examined in more detail using the SOSTAC® structure (**http://prsmith.org/SOSTAC/**).

Situation analysis

The usual product interrogation, trend identification and soliciting customer feedback help build a bigger picture as to where the brand is now, its strengths and weaknesses, competition, customer trends, etc.

Objectives

Crystal-clear objectives can eventually be broken down to ensure that everyone knows where the brand is going. Ideally, marketing communications objectives should be numerical for sales, enquiries and even brand awareness.

Strategy

Use STP (from the TOPPP SEED components of strategy discussed in Chapter 9). Segmentation creates customer profiles from the database (or just select profiles from a mailing list). Target or select the best profiles. Positioning ensures the message is right. Is there a marketing automation process (or manual), are there any partnerships, or a sequence of emails? How does the data integrate with your main database? Any other tactical tools used to support the email campaign (see PayPal case at the end of this chapter)?

Remember target list selection is the most important stage in the whole direct marketing process. Sixty per cent of any project's time should be spent on list selection. 'There's no point fishing in the pool if the pool ain't got any fish.' See 'Actions' section, p 502, for a 'list-buying checklist'.

Tactics: Creative mailings

Opportunities for creativity abound. Most mail competes with bills and statements. Many of the top creative people still feel television advertising is more glamorous, so perhaps most mailings are restrained either by the people who create them or by the managers who commission them. Here are some odd exceptions:

- A plastic green cucumber was mailed by the Direct Mail Sales Bureau to all UK media buyers to raise awareness of the direct mail option.
- The Prince's Trust, when targeting company chairmen, mailed a box containing a ceramic bowl created by one of the businesses the Trust had supported (the bowl provided a gift for the chairmen's secretaries, to encourage them to pass on the pack; it also brought the achievements of the Trust to life for the chairmen).
- A briefcase was mailed to car distributors. When opened, the briefcase resembled a car dashboard complete with audio system and car phone. The recipient inserted a CD and lifted the phone to hear a sales pitch about why that particular car phone was outstanding. The briefcase further doubled as a point-of-sale item for the distributor.

The mailing piece and the incentive can affect the budget significantly. Not all creative mailings need anything other than a few clever words. One recent mailing simply said 'Good morning'. This generated a lot of interest, anticipation and eagerness to get the next mailing in the sequence.

Action

List buying/hiring

Here are some questions that should be asked before using a list:

- Where do the names come from (eg compiled, previous mail responsive, subscription lists, etc)?
- When was the list built?
- How often is it cleaned (updated)? Is it Mailing Preference Service (MPS) cleaned? Is it GDPR compliant?
- When was the list last used (and by whom) and what was the percentage of gone-aways (redundant names or addresses that the post office return to the sender)? Are there any known results or any references from past users?
- What is the rebate per gone-away that is returned to the list owner for future cleaning?
- What proportion of the target's total universe does the list represent, eg does the 1 million list of home movers represent all the home movers, or half, or what?
- What selections are available (eg geographic split, job title, etc)? Are there any additional costs?
- What net names percentage is quoted (ie net usable names after deduping with other lists)?
- Are there any rental restrictions (minimum quantities, competitive products subject to the list owner's approval, etc)?

Assuming the list has an appropriate profile (similar to your specified target market), clarify whether:

- it has named individuals as opposed to job titles or 'The Occupier';
- it is in an appropriate format, ie labels, USB stick etc; if USB stick, check that this suits the letter shop's requirements;
- it is postcoded (for post office mailsort discounts).

How much does it cost? What is the lead time from order to delivery?

If the list is hired, permission is usually given for one use only. Sleeper names are planted in the list to ensure that it is not used more than once (the sleepers immediately notify the list owner if they receive two mailings). Hiring charges vary from £50 to £350 per thousand. Many lists are not available for purchase, but those that are available are often priced at least four times higher than the rental price.

Integrated systems

If carefully thought out, the operational requirements clarify how the campaign will actually work. For example, what happens to the information that is collected during a telephone conversation? How do the sales representatives' diaries get updated, and who monitors their availability? Research by Euro RSCG Direct found 'an irresponsible use of response-handling mechanisms', with only a 70 per cent chance of respondents receiving information. The majority of this 70 per cent were never contacted again. Only 5 per cent ever received a follow-up telephone call. Is there a plan or system that ensures follow-up?

Automation can deliver both cost savings and increased effectiveness of marketing and sales follow-through. Hybrid systems help salespeople by reminding them which customers need attention this month, next month and so on. Enquiries generated through an array of marketing efforts are all dealt with (a brochure is dispatched along with a letter; telesales follow up for an appointment; an appointment is made for the salesperson). Nothing slips through the system. No enquiries are lost. All are followed up. The system has to accommodate returned goods and cancelled orders. Up-front investment in an integrated system is falling as more and more sales-tracking software packages come on to the marketplace.

> **Direct mail: A strain on your office?**
>
> 'Even if the response is fairly modest it can still be a strain on your office resources. Could your telephone system handle thousands of calls in an hour? Could your staff still treat customers with enthusiasm at the end of a whole day of frantic answering? Do you have space for sackfuls of mail? Do you have time to answer every reply quickly? If not, a specialist fulfilment company can help.'
>
> Royal Mail (2001)
>
> Or at least test the campaign with a sample of the list to gauge the response level.

Timing

The faster you need something done the more it will cost and the more likely there will be mistakes. Deciding whether the campaign should be multi-stage (generate enquiries, screening, follow-up phone calls and sales visits, etc) or single-stage (straight order), cross-platform or single media, and so on, is arguably less important than determining strategically how each mailing forms part of an overall communications programme that develops a cumulative effect.

One-off large mailings should gradually be replaced by smaller, more frequent mailings as the database identifies what is needed by whom, and when. Many direct mail agencies can develop a campaign in four to six weeks, but ideally the campaign should be researched and planned strategically, and with a greater emphasis on creativity, to achieve 'cut-through'.

Timing also refers to identifying when a target market buys and how often. Markets are constantly moving. Buyers drift in and out at different stages. Some markets are seasonal, and others again have peaks and troughs on different days of the week. Are target respondents more receptive to a mailshot that lands on a Friday morning or a Monday morning?

The development and scheduling of the campaign are shown in Figure 16.6. Essentially they follow the normal campaign development sequence: brief, concept development, research artwork, production and roll-out (note that research can be supplemented by continual testing).

As in an advertising campaign, a creative brief is followed by concepts that are subsequently approved, amended, researched and eventually developed into final copy and design. This is turned into artwork that is checked, proofed and eventually turned into final approved artwork that goes to the printer. Prior to this (or sometimes simultaneously) a list brief is agreed. This defines the target market. Lists are carefully researched and checked.

A list proposal is subsequently approved for ordering (purchase or hire). The letter shop puts the required letter into the system ready for laser printing on to personalized letters. Proof letters are checked and approved while the lists are prepared, merged and purged (duplicate names withdrawn). The printer dispatches the brochure to the letter shop, which then presses the button. The letters are lasered, folded, collated and inserted with the brochure or mailing piece into lasered (or window) envelopes (sometimes pre-printed with teaser messages or images) and posted (companies like Sendosa.com offer print on demand along with incentives/gifts plus all the logistics required for mailings). Then a dreadful quietness descends as the bags of mail are driven off into the sunset and the wait begins. Pre-mailshot tension can run riot, with nightmares about

FIGURE 16.6 Example of a mailing schedule

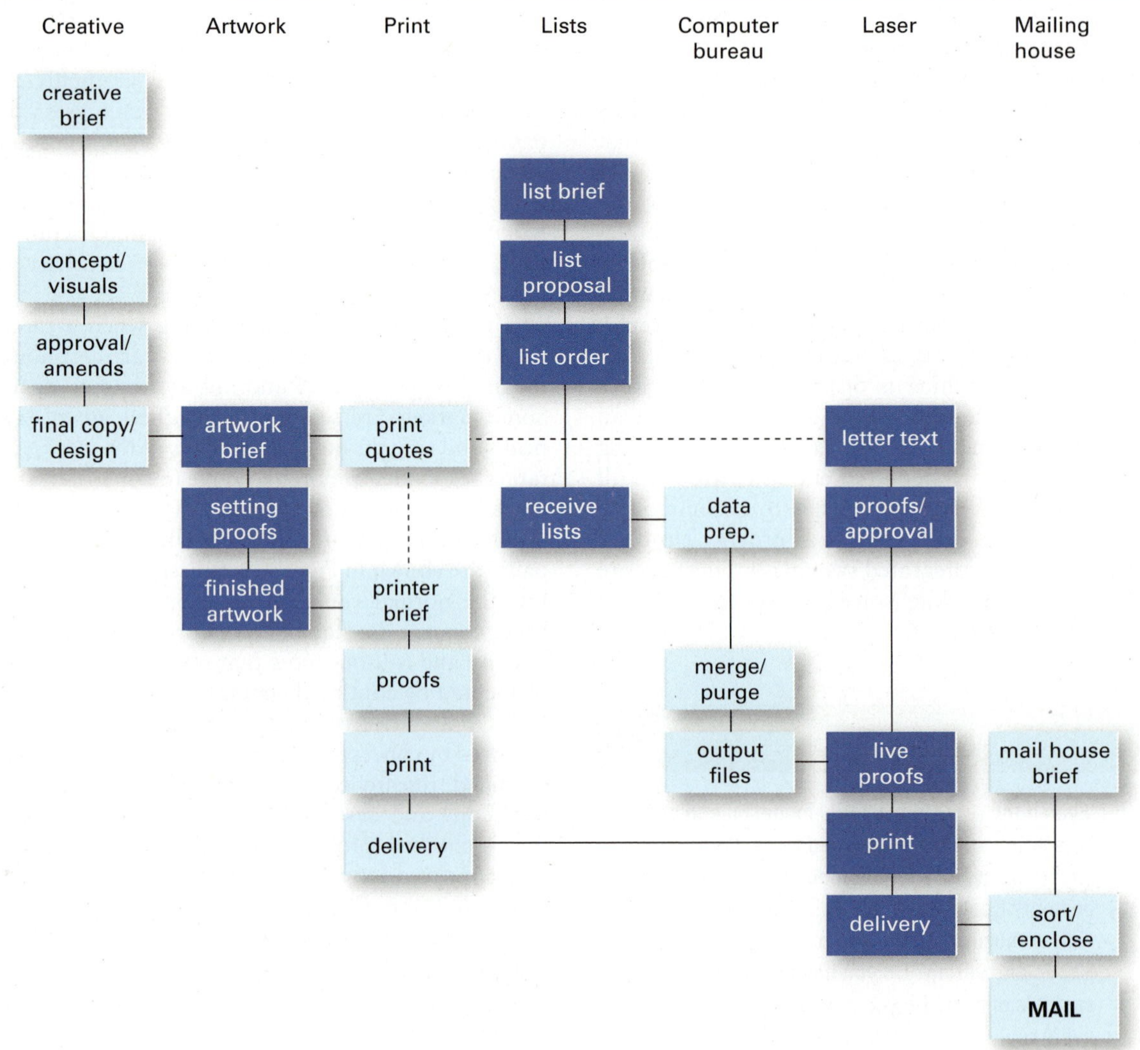

SOURCE: Institute of Direct Marketing
NOTES: 1 Print includes letters, brochures, envelopes.
2 If there is a large mail quantity, the mail house need more notice.
3 If envelopes are special, their make-up requires a longer lead time.

postal strikes, redundant lists, a printing error, a wrong expiry date or, worse still, a nil response level.

Good planning ensures that the best lists are used (perhaps based on test results), print, proofs, dates, etc are checked, and acceptable results are projected. Even in a situation where a lot of variables are unknown, careful planning can reduce the chance of failure.

Control

Budgeting 'money'

One way of budgeting is by asking: '**How much can the organization afford to spend to recruit a new customer?** How much is a new customer worth or what is the allowable cost per customer? What is the customer's lifetime value?' Then multiply this by the number of customers required and, bingo, a budget emerges. Another way to build a budget or at least a ballpark cost figure is to calculate 50p per mailshot. Thus if an organization is running a 20,000 mailshot, then ballpark costs to cover everything (design, artwork, print, list, letter shop, insertion or collation incentive, envelope and postage) would be £10,000; a 500,000 mailshot would enjoy economies of scale and cost less than £250,000.

Cost per response and cost per order give the bottom line of success or failure. Percentage response levels vary from 0.5 per cent to 5 per cent, although there are many examples now of much higher rates – as high as 60 per cent – especially when targeting existing customers with strong creative combined with highly relevant incentives. (Note that enquiries, as opposed to orders, are easier to get and therefore pull higher response levels.)

How much would you spend on winning a customer? What kind of incentive would you offer a customer to take action and place an order? Here are a few examples: $50 Amazon voucher; Alliance & Leicester (bank), £50 (to open an account); Virgin, £400 (free laptop to selected customers); FedEx, £1,000 (free PC).

Test, test, test

One of the advantages of direct marketing is the ability to test, retest, change, monitor and learn what works best. Everything can be tested, including the colour of the signature. A white envelope will do better than a manila envelope, and a brightly coloured envelope will do better than a white one (but will it damage the long-term corporate image?). If 10 per cent of a direct marketing budget is allocated to continual testing, then response levels will be continually higher.

Test and optimize

There's nothing new in optimization. Drayton Bird (2000) tested 12 different 'appropriate' lists, three different prices, two different ways to pay, different times for the mailings, alternative ways of responding and several creative approaches. He found that the best combination of all these factors produced a result **58 times better** than the worst combination. By identifying the best and worst responses for each variable, the maximum response variation (difference between best and worst) was found. Table 16.2 shows the results.

TABLE 16.2 The impact of different direct-mail variables on response levels

Variable	Different response between worst and best
List	× 6.0
Offer	× 3.0
Timing	× 2.0
Creative	× 1.35
Response	× 1.2

Ideally, everything should be tested in isolation to give more realistic results. There are sometimes so many combinations that testing might appear endless. However, the big variables (those likely to have a significant impact on the bottom line) should be tested. Work down the list, but stop when the cost of testing outweighs the benefits. As mentioned, direct mail lends itself to testing. It allows the marketing manager to become more scientific and more precise – basically a better manager. Testing the colour of a signature may yield only one-twentieth of 1 per cent difference in response, but even so it still generates increased revenues, so it is worth testing everything.

CASE STUDY Personalized videos for British Heart Foundation bike ride

Situation

The annual London–Brighton bike ride is the British Heart Foundation (BHF)'s biggest fundraising event. They have participants in other events such as various marathon runs, but the London–Brighton bike ride is BHF's 'owned event'. With between 12,000–13,000 riders cycling and raising money for BHF, it is the major profile-raising and fundraising event each year. Some riders raise £500+, others raise £100. Most fundraisers use the JustGiving website, which is a simple tool for fundraisers to build their own charity donation web page to help donors make donations online in a simple and easy manner. All of this exists in a hyper-competitive charity marketplace. With a lot more charities vying to do good and donors being approached all the time, while people becoming more 'time poor' and information fatigued, it is more difficult for any charity fundraisers. On top of this, the donor pool is shrinking as the donating public gets older.

Objectives

BHF needed to find new ways of raising money. BHF needed a creative solution to cut through the clutter, primarily boost fundraising and secondarily increase the profile of BHF.

Strategy

BHF decided to work with Tim Redgate's EchoMany, specialists in personalized videos at scale. Together they strategically decided to try to get donors to raise more money (rather than finding many more new donors) and leverage the BHF database of around 13,000 donors, with an added value CX delivered by a personalized video campaign, which can be shared widely and used to generate more funds. The personalized video was also a unique reward that supports the ongoing relationship between donors and the charity.

Tactics

EchoMany's creative team took video footage from the previous year's event and cut this into a promotional video for the event. Building in some branded graphics based on the BHF brand guidelines, EchoMany created a personalized video template with placeholder content that would be dynamically added to the live campaign, such as the fundraiser's name, profile photo and fundraising target. This template was then reviewed and approved by BHFs marketing team.

To generate the 13,000 or so personalized versions of the video, EchoMany first pulled data from the BHF's opt-in CRM database for the participants who had signed up for the event. As many of the participants provided their unique JustGiving IDs on sign-up, EchoMany were able to use the JustGiving API to cross-reference the data and enrich the videos with more personalized content, highlighting how much they had raised, how much they aimed to raise, who had donated, etc (only donors' names that chose to be public were used). If donors didn't have a JustGiving page they just got a video with their name in the video. If donors had a JustGiving account they received a much richer video.

EchoMany created approximately 13,000 personalized vides in two hours. This had to be done at the same time so EchoMany had the most up-to-date data and accurate fundraising totals.

Personalized email was tested internally to ensure it rendered ok on all different email platforms and devices (from desktop to tablet to smart phone). The personalized email was sent, via the BHF email platform, to the database complete with url link to a personalized landing page which had the personalized video embedded along with links to donate as well as to share and download the video.

The email was sent two weeks before the actual bike ride. Many fundraisers had been fundraising for months already, while others had started just a few weeks earlier. This was the final push: 'Let's see how many more donors you can get.'

Actions

Here is what needed to be done when using a personalized video engine. Attention to detail is required. After the personalized video template had been approved by BHF and the data was pulled from the CRM system and the JustGiving pages, the videos had to be created at scale quickly. Next is rendering. This is the real power behind this personalized video platform. BHF needed to render those videos out as quickly as possible.

Although not used in this particular campaign, the advanced option for multi-clip video rendering allows multiple videos – eg 100 video clips can be built into the video in a different sequence to provide something that is highly individualized and unique.

Masking and compositing – allowing clients to put a profile photo into the background of a movie scene – is like 'green screen' technique; you effectively have to mask things out and add in the user's photo. Dynamic effects can be added to make an individual's name turn around in 360 degrees or other animation effects. This was not used in this campaign.

The video finally gets published when it is assembled into a message so that it goes out as an email with something like this: 'Hey Paul, here's your personalized

FIGURE 16.7 The personalized email with a link to the personalized landing page

You've signed up, you've finished the training and now it's time to polish up that dusty JustGiving page. Share your very own personalised fundraising video with your family and friends.

Get those pounds in!

You are a BHF Champion.

BHF L2B Bike Ride Team

WATCH YOUR PERSONALISED VIDEO NOW >

TRAVEL ON THE DAY

Book your seats online now and take the stress out of planning how you're getting to and from the bike ride.

Click here for travel and merchandise info for the big day.

BOOK TRAVEL >

You've received this email as a registered participant of this event. We'll send you safety, logistical and fundraising information leading up to and

FIGURE 16.8 The personalized landing page, with three options: share, download and donate

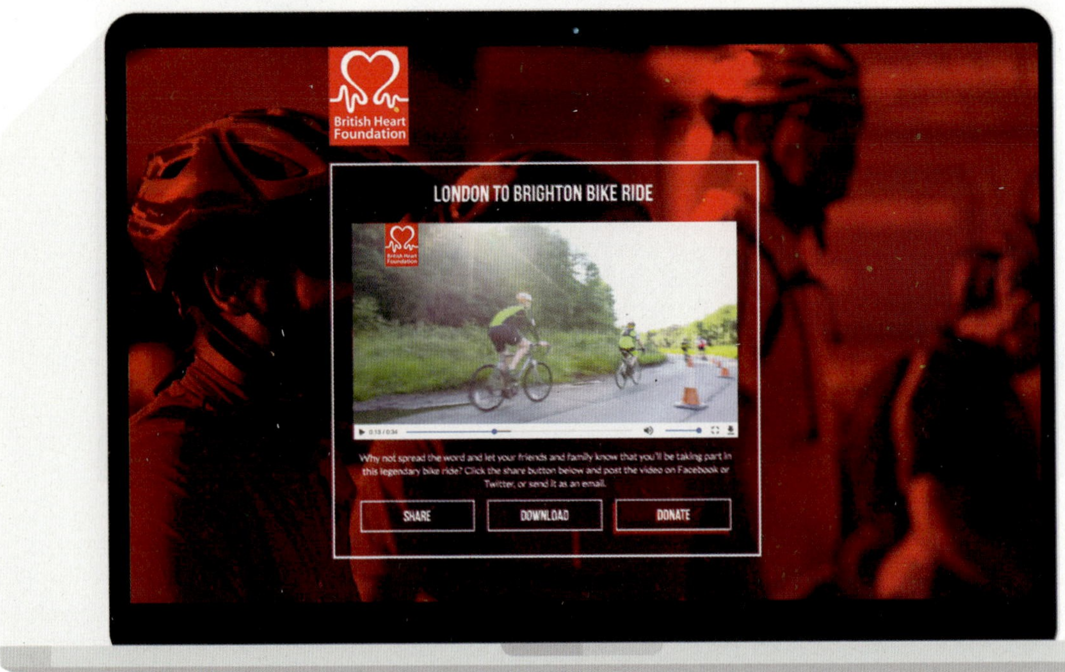

FIGURE 16.9 EchoMany took the all the data that had been pulled in and then injected it into those dynamic videos

FIGURE 16.10 Multiple video clips can be built into a video in a different sequence (not used in this campaign)

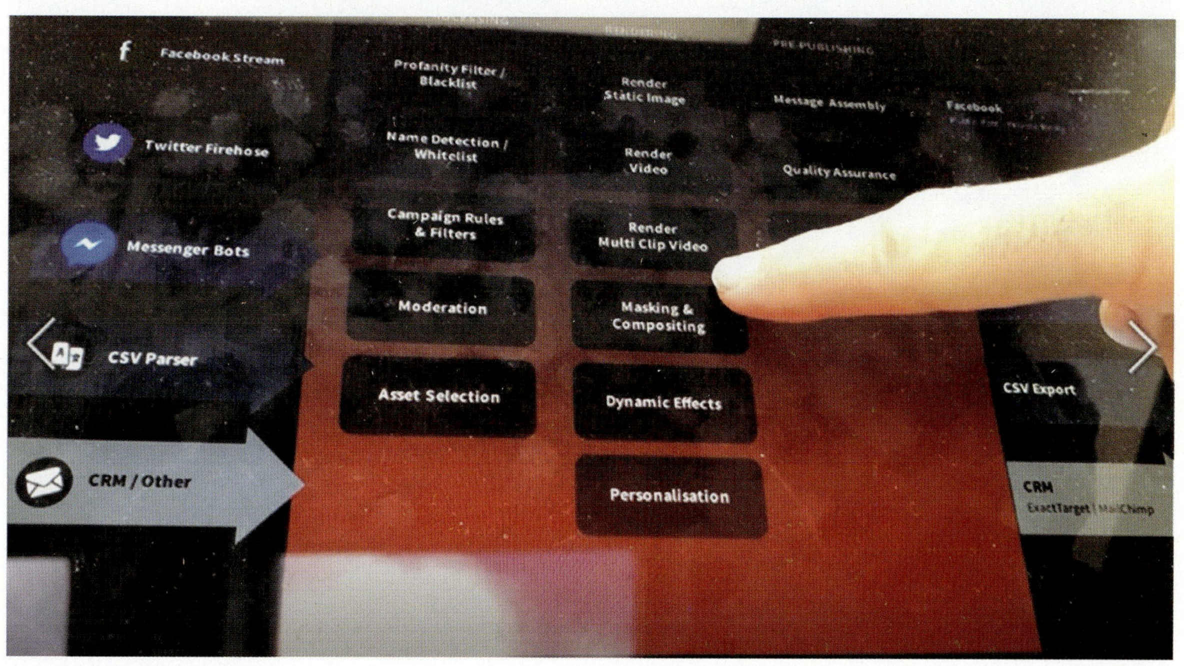

FIGURE 16.11 Masking and compositing

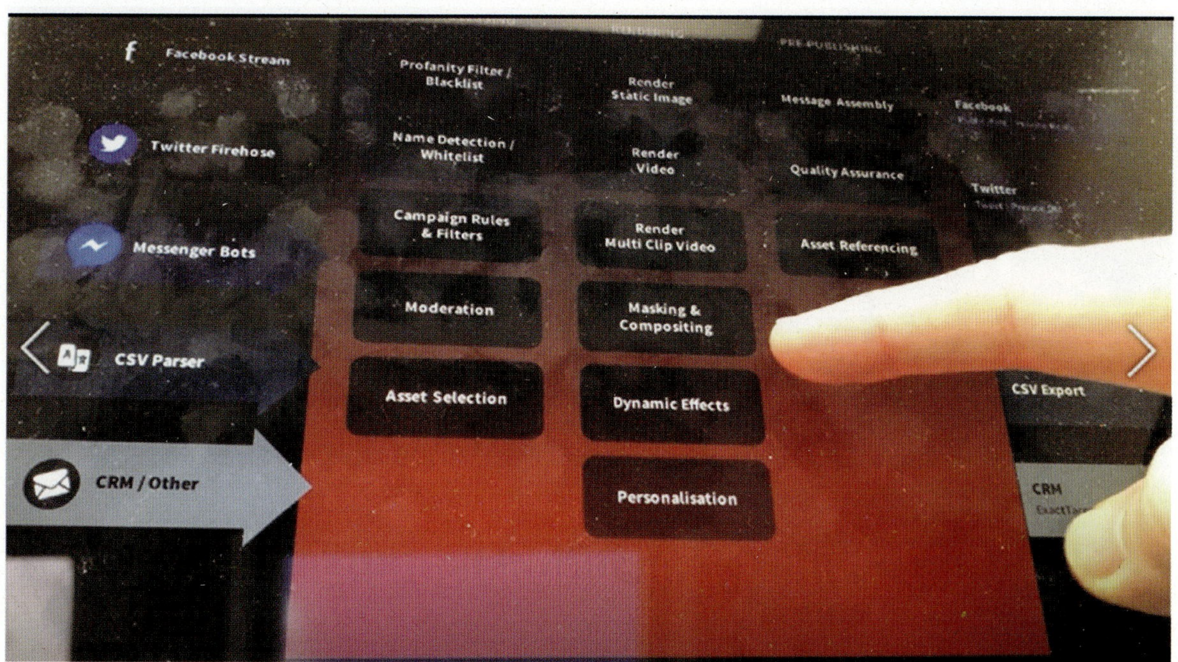

FIGURE 16.12 Message assembly

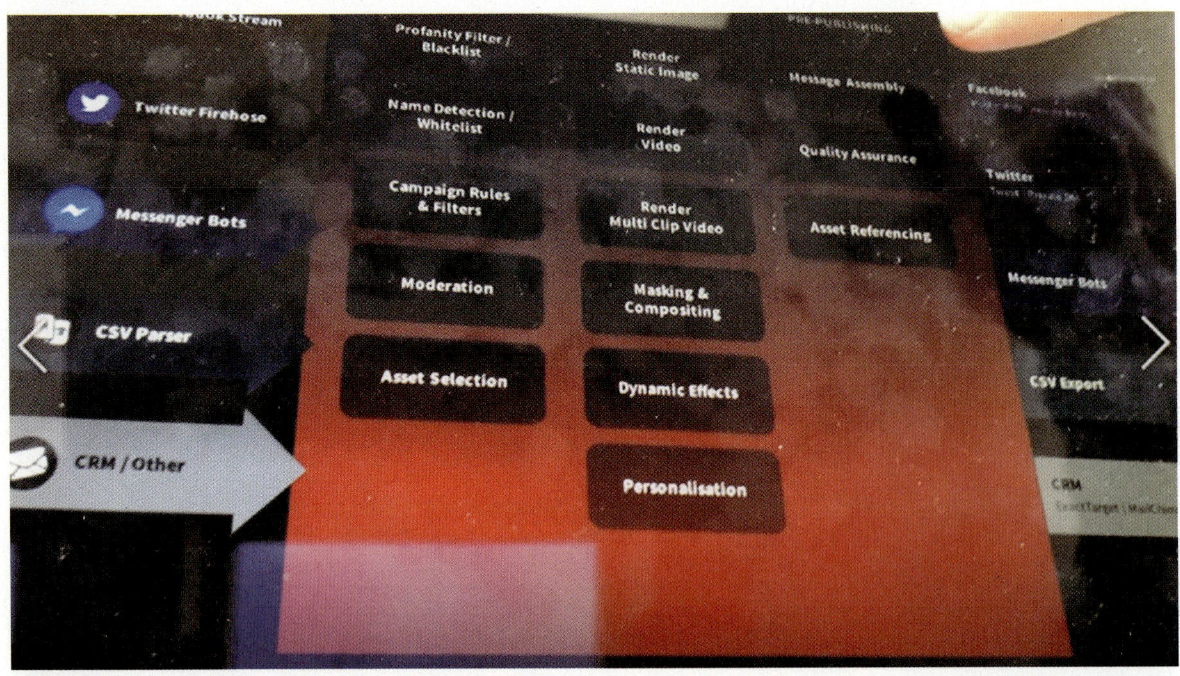

FIGURE 16.13 End screen in the personalized video that Laura will proudly share to her network

FIGURE 16.14 Success carried forward

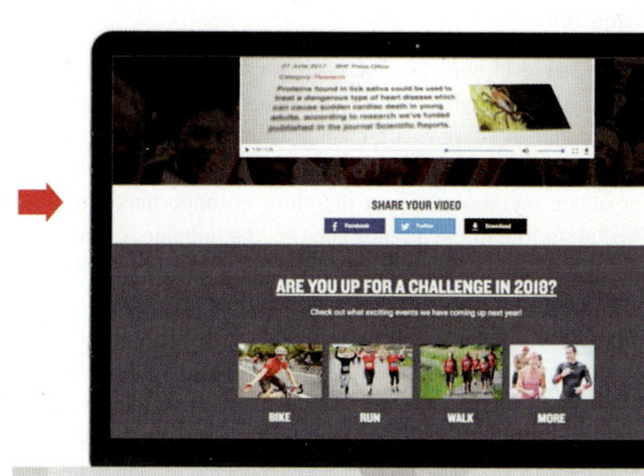

video' (with links to the personalized landing page with the video embedded).

Figure 16.13 shows the end screen of the personalized video. It generated a near 20 times return on spend (see the Control section).

Control

- Open rate: 70 per cent of approximately 13,000 (ie 9,100) registrants opened the email.
- Click through rate: 63 per cent of 9,100 (5,733) clicked through to the landing page.
- Share: 40 per cent of 5,733 (2,293) shared the video. Assuming each individual has an average of, say, 200 friends or followers, then these videos potentially reached another 457,640 people.
- Donations: 14 per cent increase year on year against the previous year's donations of an estimated £2 million. On this basis, the campaign generated an additional £280,000. The spike in sharing happened within two days of the emails going out, leaving almost two weeks for the final fundraising push.

At a cost of approximately £15,000, this campaign delivered a return on personalized video of almost 19 times (£280,000 divided by £15,000).

British Heart Foundation donors liked the videos. So too did BHF as they want to repeat personalized videos next year, as they continue their important fundraising efforts to create a world free from the fear of heart and circulatory diseases.

Success carried forward

BHF kept the relationship with its donors warm by sending a separate 'thank you' and a 'congratulations' personalized video to each donor at Christmas time. BHF also asked the donor if they were 'up for it' next year.

CASE STUDY PayPal: Helping Britain's online retailers to go mobile

Situation

In the space of one year, the volume of mobile payments processed by PayPal tripled. As smart phones became more common, there was a change in the way consumers were making purchases. This was a massive opportunity for online merchants – and therefore an opportunity for PayPal to reinforce its position as the leading online payment brand by talking to merchants about how they could optimize their sites for the 'mobile boom'.

PayPal faced two main problems. Firstly, there was a general perception among merchants that going mobile was complicated. Secondly, many of them felt that it was not important to them. PayPal therefore had a twin objective of instilling a sense of urgency and explaining the value of the mobile opportunity, while also reassuring them by explaining the simple steps that could be taken now, while they start thinking and planning for the future.

Objectives

The commercial advantage to PayPal was to reinforce the benefits of its own mobilized payment solution. But, of course, this proposition was not compelling to merchants who were reluctant to optimize their own sites. So PayPal had to, firstly, spread the mobile commerce gospel to the non-believers and, secondly, reinforce benefits of PayPal's mobilized payment solution.

Strategy

PayPal undertook a two-phased automated email campaign supported by banner ads and telemarketing and a 'fully mobile optimized' microsite using high-quality content that not only helped merchants to understand the mobile opportunity, but which also helped them to begin their own mobilization process.

Tactics

This content was presented in a variety of formats:

- housed on a purpose-built microsite;
- promoted by an email campaign;
- web banner adverts;
- supported by telemarketing.

As the microsite's content centred on mobile optimization, it was critical for the site itself to be fully mobile optimized.

While responsive design is often the best approach to optimization, striving to develop web content that renders well on numerous devices often results in pages that are not truly optimized for any of them.

In this case the user interface on mobile devices needed to look and feel like a native mobile application. With more screen space available, it made sense for the interface on desktops and tablets to be very different and include much more information on each page.

To achieve this level of device optimization, two versions of the microsite were developed. Custom client-side coding enabled the user's device to be detected so that the correct version could be loaded automatically for each visitor. From the visitor's perspective, the same site would appear to be dramatically different when viewed on different types of device.

The microsite showed visitors:

- why optimizing their websites for mobile devices is so important;
- how to approach mobilization (guidance and advice) together with an overview of PayPal's mobile optimized payment solutions.

The high-quality content comprised a series of:

- articles and links;
- interactive visual guide on the key five steps;
- video providing an overview of PayPal's mobile checkout service and benefits.

Action

This typically included the details of implementation, ie how to ensure excellent execution of the strategy, and tactics. It included internal marketing (ensuring all staff understand, and have the opportunity to share, the campaign), as well as detailed action plans regarding automated email marketing.

Control/measurement

Reporting was a key requirement, in order to be able to measure the success of the campaign. The microsite was hosted on the Eloqua MA platform, which meant that visitor activity on the site would be logged, either anonymously for visitors arriving from web banners or telemarketing, or by email address for visitors arriving from the email campaign.

Alongside common reporting metrics such as email open rates and page visits, custom tracking was deployed so that campaign reports were able to provide a view of where microsite visitors arrived from and which devices they were using.

Survey data gathered before and after the campaign also served to highlight the campaign's effectiveness.

Results

- **Open rates 25–35 per cent:** The campaign had a very positive impact. Email open rates were between 25 and 35 per cent, driving 6 per cent of the customer base to the microsite.
- **CTR – 20 per cent:** Of those merchants who received an email from PayPal about mobile optimization, 20 per cent clicked on the articles/links provided.
- **Awareness almost doubled:** Of the merchants surveyed before and after the campaign, the effectiveness of the campaign awareness that PayPal provided mobilized payment solutions had nearly doubled – 11 per cent awareness increased to 20 per cent during the campaign.
- **Include mobile in their business plans – 24 per cent:** A quarter of merchants surveyed (24 per cent) were encouraged to include mobile as part of their overall business plans after seeing the information on PayPal's website, and 57 per cent of all merchants surveyed had a positive view of PayPal as an enabler of mobile payments. The video proved to be the most popular asset within the microsite, proving a good way to display content to the audience.
- **Brand preference from 70 to 78 per cent:** For merchants intending to offer mobile payments, PayPal remains the preferred solution. The proportion of merchants preferring PayPal increased by 8 percentage points to 78 per cent.

3Ms

PayPal worked with two agencies: Base One, a specialist B2B agency, and CleverTouch, leading experts in marketing automation. The two agencies worked together, combining their specialist expertise to manage the project: Base One creating the content, microsite and communications material, while CleverTouch managed the planning and delivery of the communications and campaign measurement across Eloqua.

Success carried forward

PayPal saw US $14 billion in payments through mobile in the previous year and were expecting US $20 billion in the subsequent year. The microsite continued to be used as collateral across the business and as part of other campaigns. PayPal continued to work with Base One and CleverTouch, creating and implementing a variety of innovative online campaigns to build on this success.

CASE STUDY Acronis automated marketing campaign

Situation

Acronis is a software company that helps small to medium businesses manage their back-up and disaster recovery operations. The automated marketing agency CleverTouch launched a campaign entitled 'Digital assets' in the UK, which targeted senior IT contacts in organizations of up to 500 employees.

Objective

The objective was to target new customers in the UK with the aim of achieving about 65 attendees per webinar for real educational engagement. From these attendees, an estimated 10–20 opportunities per event would evolve with an average value of typically £5,000, ie £50,000–£100,000 revenue generated from each event.

Strategy

CleverTouch marketing deployed a five-stage strategy to inform identified organizations' IT managers about the latest practices in storage, back-up and recovery while meeting the objective to confirm that any existing contact still existed and was relevant. The focus was on helping prospects along their buying cycle or journey of understanding and not purely selling to them or securing a sales appointment.

Tactics

Acronis commissioned market research to identify the key pain points for IT managers implementing storage back-up and disaster recovery solutions. The results were presented in an Acronis white paper entitled 'Digital assets research findings: Unveiling backup and recovery practices across Europe', which became the call to action for the first email.

- **Stage 1:** Email 1 was sent to 24,000 contacts. It had a secondary purpose of cleansing the database of contacts that were no longer in the role or relevant. The initial email was re-sent to all those who had not clicked through or registered, whose email address was still valid (c 21,500). Duplicates were suppressed at all stages.
- **Stage 2:** Email 2 was sent to those who had opened the initial email, with an invitation to download an Acronis blueprint in back-up and disaster recovery. The blueprint email was re-sent to those who had not opened it and whose email address was still valid (c 2,125). Simply put, this email was sent to everyone who downloaded 'Digital assets research findings'.
- **Stage 3:** Email 3 was sent to respondees of the first two emails inviting them to attend a market research led webinar that again highlighted the findings from the market research and linked the findings to Acronis best practice (c 4,600). Simply put, this email was sent to everyone who downloaded emails 1 or 2.
- **Stage 4:** Throughout the campaign a link was included that enabled the recipient to forward the email to a friend, providing Acronis with the possibility to acquire relevant contacts for this and further campaigns.
- **Stage 5:** Marketing engagement was used to follow up on those contacts who registered and attended the webinar, and those who registered but did not attend, to identify any immediate sales opportunities. The qualified sales leads were passed to the Acronis sales team for closure (80 leads).

Action

The campaign ran across a five-week timeframe, with typically five working days between email distributions. This meant that contacts who were out of the office for a week would not miss the follow-up email. When resending an email, the identical email was sent with a different subject line. Recipients' email addresses that were no longer valid (hard bounce) were removed from the contact database.

Marketing automation technology increased efficiencies in the whole process and workflow and reduced costs (see Figure 16.16).

Control

The goal was to get 65 attendees to a webinar (based on previous history and experience). The result was over 140 attendees, with 10 immediate opportunities (worth over approximately £50,000 in year 1) and one initial sale of £10,000. As a result of the campaign's success, the same process was applied to a secondary campaign within a three-week time frame. This second campaign had equally successful results, with again over 140 contacts in attendance.

As a result of the success, the campaign has now expanded to other languages and regions within Europe. To supplement the campaign with additional coverage, a channel partner version was developed, which was used by Acronis channel partners to enhance their marketing activities.

The key to this campaign was to nurture the prospects through the campaign and create a pool of engaged contacts to be used in future, more targeted campaigns, eg direct mail. This method of continued, ongoing activity aimed at educating and engaging contacts is far more beneficial than a single campaign that is executed in isolation.

Men/women, minutes and money

This campaign required an estimated 10 days from Acronis and an estimated five days from CleverTouch. It was a

FIGURE 16.15 The amount of time IT managers could lose in the event of data loss (email 1 with 'Digital assets research findings' attachment)

Acronis

THROW AWAY EVERYTHING

YOU DID YESTERDAY

THEN TELL YOUR WHOLE COMPANY TO DO THE SAME.

Dear Phil Crawley,

Recent research indicates that a massive two thirds (63%) of IT managers would take a day or more to recover their company's data in the event of system downtime, leading to lost revenue, lost productivity and huge frustration of both employees and customers.

If you're not backing up regularly, one minor disaster could mean that everything everyone in your organisation did yesterday, the day before and last week...could be lost.

Read the Digital Assets Research Findings: Unveiling Backup & Recovery Practices across Europe.

- What you fear most about system failure
- How confident you are that you could recover in the event of a disaster
- How quickly you could recover
- How stressful data loss is in comparison to other events
- Download the Acronis complimentary White Paper 'Digital Assets Research Findings: Unveiling Backup & Recovery Practices Across Europe'

Best Regards,
Acronis Team

Get your Free Research Findings!

DOWNLOAD NOW

Acronis
Acronis® Digital Assets Research Findings:
Unveiling Backup & Recovery Practices across Europe
March 2010

Acronis. **Move. Manage. Maintain.** Seamlessly.

FIGURE 16.16 Contact workflow strategy

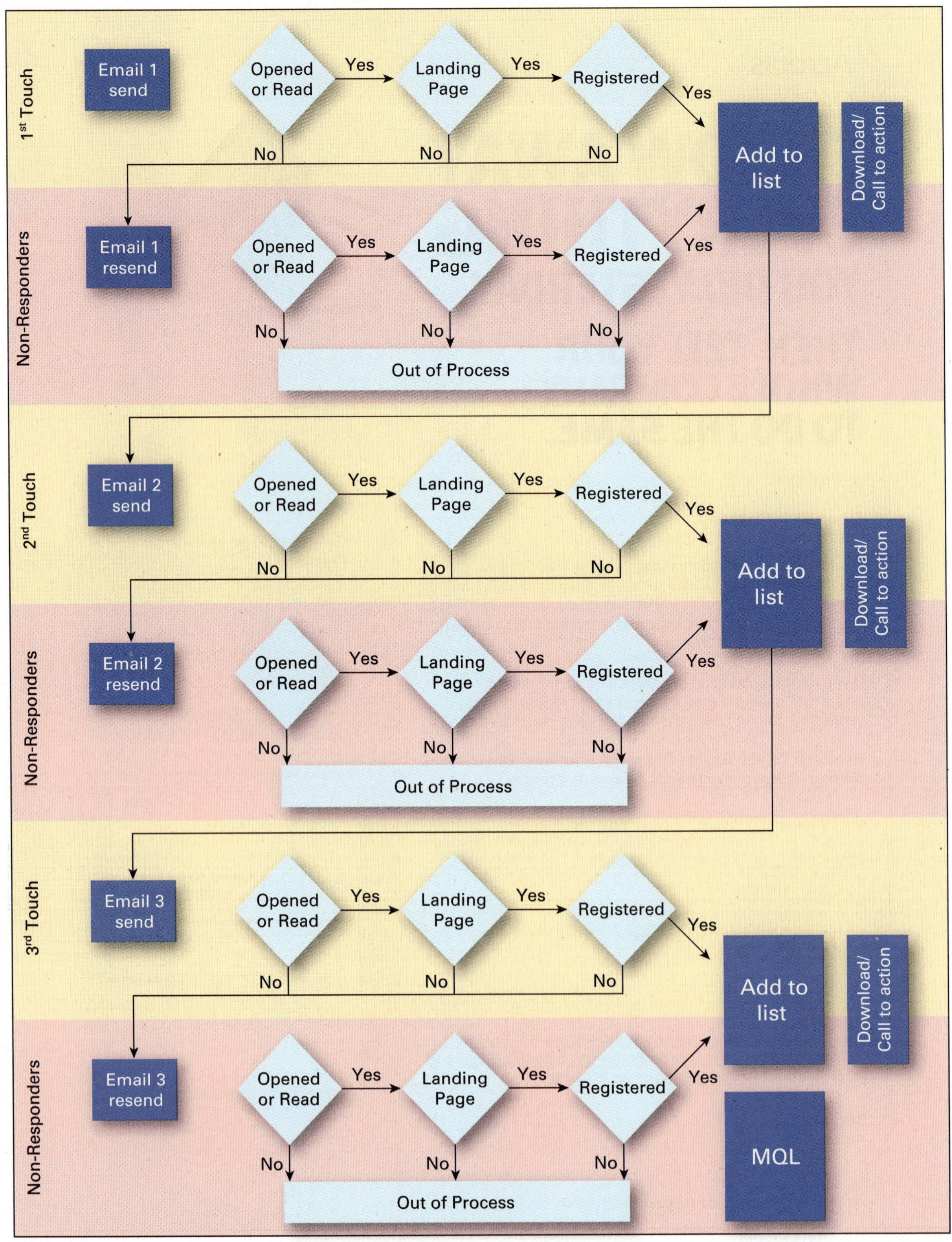

digital multi-step campaign, with each step requiring ever-increasing degrees of commitment and engagement on both sides. The campaign took eight weeks to research and plan, and was rolled out in eight weeks. The budget for this campaign, including imagery and CleverTouch's development, build and delivery time, was estimated at £25,000. Currently the ROI is 4:1, and it is expected to peak at 10:1.

Advantages and disadvantages

Here are some of the advantages and disadvantages to consider when deciding whether to increase or reduce the use of email, messaging, Messenger and direct mail.

Advantages

Email, messaging, Messenger and direct mail one-to-one communications can create unique dialogues with customers, particularly if part of a bigger communications strategy. Creating conversations and nurturing interactions with relevant information creates an opportunity to also collect data. All of these tools are flexible (messages and target audiences can be changed quickly) and it is easy to measure their performance. These tools are interactive and therefore engaging as they solicit responses from audiences, albeit percentages of audiences.

Whether response or non-response, marketers can use this information to improve the profiling of each customer and constantly learn about what works for them and what doesn't. These direct tools lend themselves to split testing and multivariate testing, with very quick response times to ensure constant improvement.

The debate continues as to whether these tools work best at which end of AIDA (attention/awareness/brand awareness building/action – making sales or converting customers). Brand-building campaigns tend to be served best by banner ads, PR and sponsorship, while these direct one-to-one tools, when integrated into a communications strategy, are good at **helping customers to take a trial or even buy or repurchase.** These tools certainly work for **customer retention** and we are seeing more integrated communications strategies using them for customer acquisition also. A well-targeted mailing in a jiffy bag or gift wrapped, with an attractive incentive inside, can generate unexpectedly high response rates, trigger word of mouth and sometimes generate publicity in the press. Finally, adherence to GDPR ensures all marketers are now building and maintaining what is arguably the organization's most valuable asset: data.

Disadvantages

In addition to sometimes upsetting intermediaries (because marketing/selling directly to customers), these direct marketing one-to-one tools used to have a problem with being associated with 'junk mail'. Direct mail is therefore also vulnerable to criticism from environmental pressure groups (if only 1 or 2 per cent respond to a direct mailshot, this implies 98 or 99 per cent of those printed pieces of paper are wasted). When, pre GDPR, emails had connotations of spam, direct communications tools were perhaps considered less worthy marketing tools. This is changing as campaigns are now GDPR compliant, and therefore permission-based (ie opt-in) and more relevant.

The initial cost per thousand (CPM) for direct mail is very high compared to advertising (although, cost per acquisition, if targeted carefully can be a lot lower than for other communications tools).

Under GDPR, data has to be collected more carefully, stored securely and used for a limited time. This and overall database maintenance costs money, expertise and time. GDPR compliance is required by law in Europe, and it does create extra work (although it has many benefits). Organizations that ignore GDPR will incur significant fines – sometimes big enough to close a business down.

Finally, international direct mail, whether direct mail or opt-in email, has to adhere to local regulations that still vary (eg some countries do not allow incentives).

Key points from Chapter 16

- Email, messaging, Messenger and direct mail one-to-one communications can create unique dialogues.
- One-to-one communications tools can integrate with landing pages.
- One-to-one communication is always part of a bigger contact strategy.
- These tools are highly targetable and relatively easy to test and control (particularly email).
- The systems and database behind any campaign must be fully integrated into the campaign or ongoing contact strategy.
- Database maintenance is essential.
- GDPR compliance is required by law in Europe
- Organizations that ignore direct marketing and database techniques will suffer a competitive disadvantage.

References and further reading

Bird, D (2000) *Commonsense Direct Marketing*, 4th edn, Kogan Page, London

Brann, C (1984) *Cost-Effective Direct Marketing: By mail, telephone and direct response advertising*, Collectors' Books, Cirencester

Chaffey, D and Smith, PR (2013) *Emarketing Excellence*, 4th edn, Routledge, Abingdon

Chaffey, D and Smith, PR (2017) *Digital Marketing Excellence*, Routledge, Abingdon

Chaffey, D and van Rijn, J (2019) Email marketing strategy: A practical guide to improving email communications, *Smart Insights*

Considine, R and Raphel, M (1987) *The Great Brain Robbery*, The Great Brain Robbery, Pasadena, CA

Cooper, P (2019) Complete guide to using Facebook messenger bots for business, *Hootsuite*, 9 May

Exhibition Venues Association (2000) *UK Exhibition Facts*, Vol. 12, Exhibition Venues Association, Mayfield, East Sussex

Gray, R (2011) Here today... *The Marketer*, July/August

Hilpern, K (2013) How to personalise your customers experience, *Marketer*, March/April, p 42

Howard, M (1989) Telephone marketing vs direct sales force costs, Datapoint (UK) Ltd, London

HubSpot (2016) Database decay, *HubSpot*

Kivilis, N (2014), Taking the guesswork out of marketing: How Guess uses predictive analytic, Blog post, Custora blog, 10 December

McCorkell, G (1997) *Direct and Database Marketing*, Kogan Page, London

Moriarty, R and Moran, U (1990) Managing hybrid systems, *Harvard Business Review*, November–December

Moriarty, R and Swartz, G (1989) Automation to boost sales and marketing, *Harvard Business Review*, January–February

Redgate, T (2019) Personalised videos at scale, video interview with PR Smith, http://prsmith.org/blog/ (archived at https://perma.cc/67JZ-HYWA)

Royal Mail (2001) *Getting More from Integrated Marketing and Making Direct Mail Work for You*, MBO, London

Schlosser, J (2003) Looking for intelligence in ice cream, *Fortune*, 17 March

Smith, C (2019) 90 interesting email statistics and facts, *DMR Business Statistics*, 13 May

Smith, PR (2017) GDPR: Opportunity to boost CX or a threat of closure? (Part 1), http://prsmith.org/blog/ (archived at https://perma.cc/67JZ-HYWA), 19 May

Stevens, M (1991) *The Handbook of Telemarketing*, Kogan Page, London

Tapp, A (2001) *Principles of Direct and Database Marketing*, 2nd edn, Financial Times/Prentice Hall, Englewood Cliffs, NJ

Toffler, A (1980) *The Third Wave*, Collins, London

Watson, J (1989) The direct marketing guide, *Marketing Magazine*, 9 February

Worcester, R (2002) Customers: Handle with care, *Purple Issue*, 30 October

Yeadon, D (2009) The Marketing Bureau

Further information

Data & Marketing Association
DMA House
70 Margaret Street
London W1W 8SS
Tel: +44 (0)20 7291 3300
Fax: +44 (0)20 7323 3301
www.dma.org.uk

Federation of European Direct and Interactive Marketing (FEDMA)
Avenue des Arts 43
BE 1040 Brussels
Belgium
Tel: +32 2 779 4268
www.fedma.org

Institute of Data & Marketing (IDM)
DMA House
70 Margaret Street
London W1W 8SS
Tel: +44 (0)20 8614 0255
www.theidm.com

Mailing Preference Service (MPS)
DMA House
70 Margaret Street
London W1W 8SS
Tel: +44(0)20 7291 3310
www.mpsonline.org.uk

Information Commissioner's Office
Wycliffe House
Water Lane
Wilmslow
Cheshire SK9 5AF
Tel: +44 (0)303 123 1113
Fax: +44 (0)1625 524510
www.ico.org.uk

17 Exhibitions, events and experiential marketing

LEARNING OBJECTIVES

By the end of this chapter you will be able to:

- consider exhibitions, events and experiential marketing;
- plan for before, during and after;
- integrate particularly with PR, email, social media, sales and the overall contact strategy;
- develop an exhibition strategy;
- measure the success or otherwise of events;
- appreciate how exhibitions can be part of a contact strategy.

Introduction

Exhibitions, events and experiential marketing present unique opportunities to meet prospects and customers, engage with them, learn from them, generate leads, enquiries, sales and even strengthen existing customer relationships. Whether it is an exhibition or an event like a conference or summit, a roadshow event or an experiential branding experience, they all use a physical space to get people engaged with the brand. Some will expand that physical space into augmented or virtual space. We will see more and more augmented reality and virtual reality integrating into these 'events', as in the RSA case at the end of the chapter. They all require meticulous planning and execution before, during and after the events. Done well, they can be very potent marcomms tactical tools. Done poorly, they are a waste of resources that also damage the brand.

Exhibitions

Imagine bringing a whole market together, under one roof, for a few days. An exciting idea? An explosive concept? It happens all the time. Exhibitions are unique in that they are the only medium that brings the whole market together – buyers, sellers and competitors. Products and services can be seen, demonstrated or tested, and face-to-face contact can be made with a large number of decision makers in a short period of time.

Events, conferences, summits, launches and experiential marketing

In fact some organizations are exploring parallel areas, such as conferences and summits (their own or third-party conferences where they can exhibit and/or speak) and events that can expand into experiential marketing where brands are activated and brought to life by creative experiences in both the real world and virtual worlds.

A product launch is a major event opportunity

When Jaguar Land Rover launched the Range Rover Sport, guests were invited to attend a live film of the upmarket car being driven all the way from the New York docks to the venue. Not very exciting you might think; however, when the actual car was driven into the venue the driver, James Bond 007 Daniel Craig, stepped out from the driver's seat. This event engaged and enthused 750 VIP guests and simultaneously connected with 20,000 others who had already registered to watch this event live also. Some four million viewers have since watched the recorded video, while the many hundreds of mobile photos snapped at the event have been shared and reshared across thousands of networks.

JCB construction machinery use fully immersive experience

JCB, whose yellow machinery is seen on construction sites, created a global roadshow that delivered a 300 per cent boost in sales. A three-day event ran 13 times in four weeks as more than 3,000 customers attended. Marquees, fireworks and dancing diggers ensured that delegates had a fully immersive experience, and orders were placed there and then.

Experiential marketing with virtual reality and augmented reality

Experiential marketing creates experiences between a brand and a customer (or stakeholder). Experiential branding is more than just dressed-up, branded characters giving out free samples. We now have pop-up shops, roadshows (see the RSA case p 531), publicity stunts and Google's very cool Curiosity Rooms (see the case on p 538) and, of course, augmented reality and virtual reality (again, see the RSA case).

FIGURE 17.1 Mazda North American dealer meeting, Prudential real estate national sales meeting, RNC welcome event, Gaylord Opryland Hotel Grant reopen

Mazda North American dealer meeting

Prudential Real Estate national sales meeting

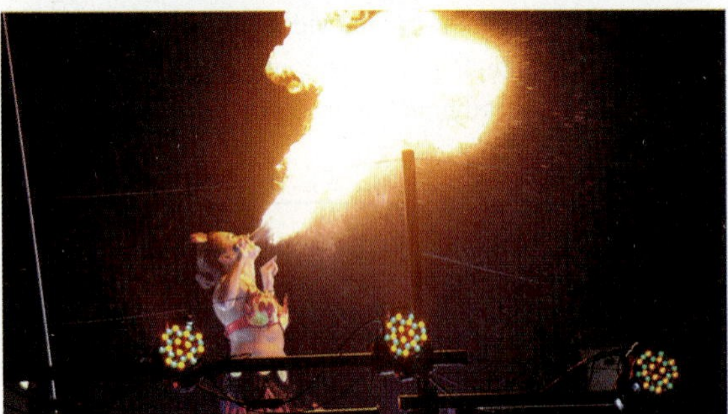

RNC welcome event

Gaylord Opryland Hotel Grant reopen

SOURCE: Photos courtesy of CorporateMagicInc.com

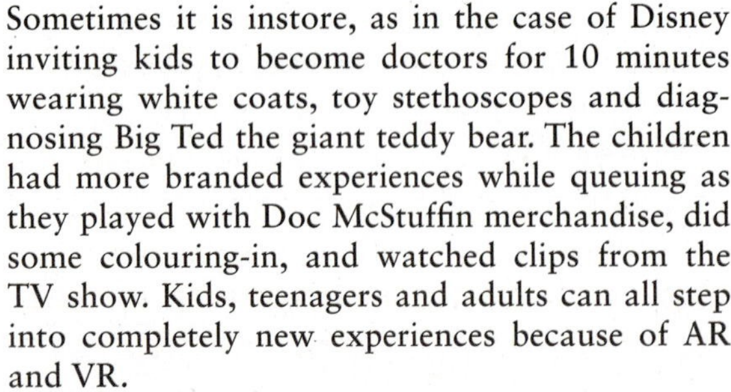

Sometimes it is instore, as in the case of Disney inviting kids to become doctors for 10 minutes wearing white coats, toy stethoscopes and diagnosing Big Ted the giant teddy bear. The children had more branded experiences while queuing as they played with Doc McStuffin merchandise, did some colouring-in, and watched clips from the TV show. Kids, teenagers and adults can all step into completely new experiences because of AR and VR.

As mentioned in Chapter 10, AR augments or adds digital elements to a real-life view, often by looking through your smart phone. VR, on the other hand, is a complete immersion experience via headsets that shut out the physical world, as in the RSA case. 'The premise is to create a closer bond between the consumer and the brand by immersing them in a fun and memorable experience' (eConsultancy, 2018) – or a shocking one with RSA.

So, augmented worlds will continue to develop, as will virtual events. The same basic principles apply when managing any kind of an event. For now, let us explore what it takes to manage an offline, real-world exhibition.

Managing exhibitions

Exhibitions offer an array of opportunities, problems and challenges. They can be leveraged to the maximum effect by integrating them with other communications tools and developing a longer-term perspective incorporating an overall exhibition strategy. Detailed exhibition planning skills require the manager to work through the following:

- Situation: To exhibit or not to exhibit?
- Objectives: Prioritize exhibition objectives.
- Strategy: Develop an exhibition strategy, including selecting the right shows and agreeing a design strategy.

- Tactics: Pre-show, during and post-show follow-up.
- Actions: Train exhibition staff – operational plan.
- Control: Evaluate post-show.

Situation: To exhibit or not to exhibit?

Exhibitions are expensive investments in terms of money required for renting the space, building a stand, promoting it, entertaining customers, travel and accommodation. They are also expensive in terms of human resources and time required. Sometimes the cost is disproportionate in terms of return on investment, and marketers have to make tough decisions as to whether to continue attending all the usual exhibitions and conferences, particularly if customers are migrating online and doing business there instead of visiting trade shows. For the marketer who wants to attend some exhibitions, whether online or offline, here are the stages of planning that will help to boost return on investment, save time and, ideally, reduce workload through better planning.

Objectives: Prioritize exhibition objectives

Exhibitions can achieve many different objectives including:

- sell – generate sales and enquiries;
- launch new products;
- reinforce relationships with existing customers (hospitality);
- maintain a profile presence in the market;
- build awareness – external PR opportunities;
- market research and intelligence gathering (the whole market is here);
- competitor analysis and intelligence gathering;
- test new ideas – product testing and informal creative discussions;
- motivate staff – some exhibitions can be the focal point of the year;
- recruit new staff;
- be part of a contact strategy (including emails, snail mail, telemarketing, sales team visits, etc).

Strategy: Develop an exhibition strategy

Ideally, exhibitions should not be used as a one-off, ad hoc activity. They can be used more effectively when: 1) they are viewed as a possible series of exhibitions; 2) they are integrated carefully with other communications tools; 3) they are selected and planned well in advance; and 4) their effectiveness is constantly measured. An exhibition strategy summarizes the frequency and types of show selected (eg national, international, real or virtual, exhibition, event or roadshow). See the 'Selection checklist' below.

Select the right events

There is an increasing number of exhibitions available, usually more than an organization can attend. Some are better than others. Some are far more expensive than others and some have a smaller number of visitors. Some have better-quality visitors. You must choose carefully.

Selection checklist

- **Type of exhibition:** Local, national or international; vertical (tight focus of interest for buyers or sellers) or horizontal (wide range of interest for buyers or sellers); general public; trade events; private events; symposia or conferences where a limited amount of exhibiting facilities are available.
- **Target audience:** Type and number of visitors; audited figures should be made available, for example Audit Bureau of Circulations figures are approved by the Association of Event Organisers.
- **Timing:** Does it meet buyers' purchasing patterns and can the organization prepare for it in time? For example, foreign shows may need to be planned 18 months in advance.

- **Facilities:** Any limitations or constraints; how the organizers intend to promote the event; supporting contact events, such as dinners, award ceremonies, seminars, breakfast receptions, etc.
- **Costs:** Compare 'cost of space' and 'size of audience' ratios between different exhibitions. The space cost is useful for comparison, but it represents only a small proportion of the total cost of exhibiting. NB Miscellaneous extra items (see Figure 17.1) rapidly cause costs to escalate.
- **Previous success:** How long has the show been running? Has it been a success previously? Is it enjoying year-on-year growth? Are there any customer (exhibitor) testimonials or references available?
- **Endorsements:** What official bodies are supporting it? There are independent surveys that list visitor numbers, visitor quality, sales enquiries and a summary of exhibitors' results (see 'Evaluate post-show' below).

Agree on a design

The stand design is a key factor in the overall exhibition strategy. It should present the right corporate/brand image, announce the product or service and visualize benefits, attract interest and look aesthetically pleasing while providing for other functions such as display, demonstration, discussion, hospitality and storage (of spare samples, literature, coats, etc).

Clarifying the key performance indicator (KPI) for the exhibition, whether it is sales, enquiries, trials, visitors, etc, or boosting awareness of a key message helps to guide the overall design of the exhibition stand.

A visitor may have less than three seconds to scan and decide whether to enter a particular stand instead of one of the many others competing for their attention. Buyers have only a limited amount of time to visit a limited number of stands. Buyers have to choose quickly whether to visit a stand or not.

Buyers often decide what route they will take and which stands they will visit before entering the main exhibition hall. Despite a pre-planned schedule of visits, a busy buyer can still be tempted by an excellent stand design or interesting promotional stunt. However, a stunt can also attract time-wasting, stand-congesting, non-target-market visitors.

The 'three-second' test

When you next visit an exhibition look around you and see how many (if any) stands clearly tell you what they offer. How many exhibition stands actually explain what business the exhibitors are in and their benefits? How many stand designs actually help visitors by answering this question within three to five seconds before they pass by?

It is surprising to observe the number of organizations that promote their name first and foremost, perhaps followed by a product name, and somewhere, almost hidden, the product and product features and benefits are displayed. Product benefits (what buyers really seek) cannot be seen easily.

The exhibition stand design should be consistent with the organization's corporate identity guidelines and the brand design guidelines (see Chapter 2). These specify the logo style, typefaces, and primary and secondary colours. The overall stand design must catch the visitor's attention and attract them.

The design brief

The design brief for an exhibition stand can use the extract SOS + 3Ms from SOSTAC® + 3Ms discussed in Chapter 9 (p 264). Essentially, the designer needs to know: who the target audience is; in what kinds of exhibitions the stand might appear; the exhibition locations and preferred stand locations (within the exhibition); stand size and function (display, demonstration, hospitality area, access and service facilities required); and whether the stand needs to be re-usable. Information on competitors and their stands is also useful.

Additional information such as the design manual and the dimensions of any display items is also important. The success criteria must be listed and objectives prioritized. The designer also needs to know the overall exhibition strategy. Tactical information is sometimes included, for example any promotional ideas, specific numbers of staff and visitors on the stand at any one time, whether any promotional off-stand activities will be attracting visitors on to the stand, whether the stand will be used for photo opportunities, and what kinds of electronic gadgetry (data projectors, laptops, sound, etc), products and sales literature need to be displayed. **The designer also needs to know about the 3Ms – the three key resources of men/women, money (budget) and minutes (time – set-up and knock-down time).**

The whole exhibition design should focus on key, measurable objectives – are all the elements linked up to and consistent with the overall exhibition strategy, etc? Sound, sight, space and even smell can be used creatively by a designer (there are, however, likely to be some constraints imposed by the organizers). Good designers exploit both two-dimensional design (eg graphics) and three-dimensional design (eg the use of space).

Tactics: Pre-show, during and post-show follow-up

Careful pre-show promotions can ensure a steady flow of visitors on to a stand. Direct mail, linked with an incentive or sales promotion, free tickets, inserts, advertising, publicity, etc, can all be used to get visitors to decide to visit a particular stand before they arrive at the exhibition in the first place. Given that the average visitor visits only 13 stands, it is important to get on to the appropriate target visitor's 'must visit' list. Pre-show marketing identifies who to expect and who to chase up. **Exhibitions (pre, during and post) provide a fresh opportunity to talk to customers and prospects and therefore should be part of both your overall contact strategy and your content calendar** (Chapter 15).

Advertising and editorial opportunities range from the usual trade, professional and domestic press, local and regional media, and transport (taxis, trains, buses and stations) through to the exhibition catalogue itself. Sponsorship of exhibition guides, maps, promotions, teaser promotions, free gifts and competitions can all be offered to the target visitor through advertising, editorial, inserts, mailings, social media posts, messaging and even telemarketing. This means that the costs of sales promotions and incentives can be reduced significantly by increasing the organization's buying power when sourcing many different sales promotion gifts simultaneously. Delivery and invoicing can also be staggered or delayed so that cash flow bottlenecks do not occur. It might be possible to run a joint promotion with a non-competing exhibitor so that your product or service (or even just the incentive) is combined with someone else's to promote both sites as 'must see' sites.

In summary, pre-show promotional activity can involve:

- social media activity (announcements, inviting visitors); updates (photos, videos, tweets, posts) during the build-up (plus thank-you notes after the event);
- content calendar (see p 457) with marketing content created for and by the events;
- snail mail invitations (with an incentive?);
- email invitations and reminders;
- telesales key customers or prospects;
- field sales force briefing (to invite their key customers);
- press activities;
- sponsored activities;
- perimeter advertising (around the venue) and location-based advertising (see p 377);
- press advertising (trade magazines and exhibition manual);
- joint promotions.

Post-show follow-up

This is essential, but surprisingly rarely done. Seventy per cent or more of enquiries or leads from exhibitions are not followed up (Junius, 2017). This is a disgrace. All that hard work wasted. Be vigilant, set up a thorough and rigorous follow-up on all leads. Remember, some buyers will not be ready to reply for two weeks, four weeks, eight weeks, twelve weeks, so send them a reminder via a different medium (email, letter, LinkedIn message, telephone call, etc).

Actions: Train exhibition staff – operational plan

After all the hard pre-show work, when a stunning stand has been created, the promotion has been publicized and a good flow of traffic on to the stand has been generated, what a shame it is to lose business through staff who don't know exactly how to deal with people. Staffing an exhibition stand is hard work. The day becomes even longer when staff have no goals, no targets and no exhibition training. The team needs to be briefed about why the organization is exhibiting (including specific objectives broken down into daily objectives). Exhibition training helps staff to know:

- **how to physically stand** (the importance of body language);
- **how to approach a visitor** (never with a closed question such as 'May I help you?' – try open-ended questions like 'What caught your eye?');
- **what kind of information should be gleaned from visitors** (see the box below);
- **when a senior manager should be called over;**
- **how to demonstrate** (product knowledge and skills);
- **how to close a sale;**
- **how to present records** (ask permission to use their business card details to follow up with special offers from time to time).

Staff should practise all of these before the show starts each day (or during quiet moments during the show).

Six essential questions for qualifying a prospect

'Thanks for stopping. How are you familiar with...?' or 'What attracted you to our display?' or 'What do you see that you like?' (This gives the history of the prospective buyer and tells you where to start selling.)

'What's your situation now?' (This tells you if the prospective buyer actually has a real live need.)

'What would you like to achieve [or change]?' (This further defines the prospective buyer's application of your product.)

'What are your concerns as to budget?' (This tells you if the prospective buyer has the money.)

'How does your timetable look on all of this?' (This gives you the prospective buyer's timetable for buying or acting.)

'How would you like to proceed from here?' (This lets the prospective buyer take over.)

Engebretson (2000)

Increase newsletter sign-ups

Staff can be trained to ask prospects what they need to know about the staff's business, then show the prospects some really relevant content from the blog or white papers and invite them to get regular free updates via signing up for the newsletter. This boosts the size of the prospect database.

Boost social media engagement with a social butler

Some events have social butlers who, equipped with their tablet, take photos and videos of visitors and then offer to post them immediately to the visitor's social platform with the appropriate hashtags. All the visitor has to do is hit their own 'share' button.

Finalize the exhibition action plan

Everything, from staffing to samples and sales promotions, has to be meticulously planned. Even contingencies should be allowed for. Exhibitions are hard work. A staffing roster schedules staff so that they can have a break and a chance to look around the exhibition (and report back on their observations). How many visitors are expected? How many staff will be required? How many junior and senior staff? Comfortable shoes, regular breaks and solid rest between exhibition days are also essential. Individual performance on the stand can be measured against pre-set criteria (number and quality of enquiries, etc). Social media integration: are all the staff aware? Are there guidelines regarding social media? Does everyone know the event hashtag and key messages? Here's how some organizations integrate Instagram and other social media into their exhibition activities.

10 ways to integrate social media into exhibitions, events or conferences

1. **Add a photo-sharing social network to your exhibition, event or conference checklist** so that you can increase engagement with your visitors and maybe even grow your database with more leads.
2. **Get the event hashtag** before exhibiting or attending, or establish one if you are the event host.

3 **Search using the hashtag to find your prospects' photos** and ask them to visit your stand (maybe add a small incentive): like their photos to start establishing a relationship with these prospects; post your own photos using the hashtag also. You can also add geo-tags using the venue name and even add 'visit stand number 301' or 'main lobby' so visitors can find you.

4 **Add a tailored event landing page on your website** and paste the url into your Instagram profile information (you can change it after the event). So when someone finds one of your Instagram photos (hashtagged to the event) and they click your avatar or name to get to your information they will be able to click the link to take them to your tailor-made event website (well, landing page!).

5 **Grow your prospect database by giving them a reason to add their details**. Only ask them to fill out a short form so they can receive some information or maybe a prize or password to collect a prize from the stand. Remember GDPR – you must explicitly ask permission to add their name to your database.

6 **Amplify your reach.** Share your Instagram photos onto other social media platforms. Note photos shared from Instagram to, say, Twitter appear as a link instead of a photo preview (and therefore have lower engagement rate). There are some 'hacks' to post as photos.

7 **Create a visually engaging backdrop** as part of your stand design – insert a large stunning image plus your brand name/url and maybe the event hashtag so that visitors can take selfies or team photos with a stunning (yet clearly branded) backdrop. Ideally the image should relate to your business benefits, values or mission.

8 **Run a contest** by asking attendees to repost, tweet, and share their own photo with your own hashtag, eg #PRSmithGiveAway. You can monitor entries by refreshing the contest hashtag. Ensure the prize whether offline or online can only be collected at your stand – so that you get even more personal engagement (and another photo opportunity of presenting 'today's prize'). Be sure to check Instagram rules regarding competitions. Also request permission to re-use photos posted in the competition.

9 **Re-use these photo assets** across multiple platforms. Set up a photo feed to the website to show as a slideshow or display as a grid (during or after the show). Then after the show make some photo montages and share cross-platform, including maybe a creative blog post featuring lots of photos. NB Get permission to use any photos you take.

10 **Finally, measure the results:** (a) Increase in the number of your followers; (b) increases in engagement levels (likes, shares, comments); (c) database growth; and (d) how much traffic was generated to the main site and whether any conversions were generated.

Small exhibitors can be beautiful

NCH Action for Children charity had to break through the clutter with a small two- by two-metre stand. Its stunning backlit graphic of children's faces, supporting the 'All children dream' theme, did the trick. The stand staff were fully trained in exhibition techniques and fully briefed to communicate key messages and collect key information. They fulfilled their 'key contacts hit list', snapped publicity photos with visiting MPs and shone out from the heaving masses.

What can go wrong will go wrong

The 'What can go wrong will go wrong' law runs rampant in exhibitions. Contingency planning reduces risks, but inevitably something unforeseen still occurs. One of the authors has had two such experiences, both of which happened at international shows: the first was in Birmingham, where a new electrical product set itself on fire while being exhibited; the second was in New York, where the freight company lost all the samples and display units. Other exhibition nightmares include a stand that was built upside down (because the architect read the plans upside down) and neighbouring stands encroaching on each other's areas (sometimes by accident), or breach of trade union regulations by using a hammer or screw-driver!

To minimize risk of errors, checklists can be used to ensure execution is professional at all times. Figure 17.2 shows a simple daily checklist used at the end of each day in preparation for the next day.

FIGURE 17.2 This checklist needs to be checked at the end of each day so that everything is in place for the next day

Daily Checklist

Appointments diary	______
Visitors book	______
Enquiries log/lead form	______
Badges	______
Business cards	______
Brochures	______
Press packs	______
Samples	______
Spare parts	______
Display screen	______
Laptops	______
Scissors, adhesive tape, penknife	______
Fishbowl	______
Water	______
Clean glasses	______
Insurance	______
First aid kit (including aspirins)	______
Other?	______

Ensure follow-up

The exhibition is not an end in itself, although by the end of the show the exhausted staff probably feel as though it is. Careful follow-up work must start almost immediately. This is where the organization can earn its return from the exhibition. Leads, enquiries, quotations, sales and after-sales discussions need to be followed up in a professional manner. This requires a follow-up meeting where all the staff go through the cards they collected (or scanned), the people they talked to and the projects or jobs that were discussed. This prevents the duplication, contradiction and conflict that can arise where two people from the same prospect organization have asked two different members of staff for a quotation for the same job, or where two different enquiries have emerged for the same job from two different prospects. Worse still are unfulfilled enquiries. How many times have you left an enquiry with exhibitors never to hear from them again? Lack of post-show follow-up makes all the previous exhibition efforts a complete waste of time.

The manager can determine who follows up what, with a report-back meeting date set to see what sales are actually generated. More detailed evaluation of the true exhibition results can be carried out so that future efforts are improved. It is worth formalizing the evaluation process so that the trend, individual performance and competitor performance can all be measured.

Control: Evaluate post-show

Post-show evaluation measures performance against the pre-set objectives. It also examines whether the objectives were realistic, whether the show was the right show, and what was good and what was bad about the organization's performance. A competitor's performance can also be evaluated to a certain degree. How can the performance be improved? Should the exhibition be run again next year? Was it value for money?

Some post-show questions

1. What percentage of the potential number of visitors to the whole exhibition (that fitted the target market profile) visited our stand?
2. What percentage stopped but did not visit our stand?
3. What percentage saw but did not stop at our stand?
4. How many leads or enquiries were created?
5. What was the cost per contact or visitor/lead?

6. What percentage of contacts or visitors plan to buy the product or service?
7. What was the cost per 'serious' visitor/hot lead?
8. What was the cost per order?
9. How effective was each staff member's performance? Research can get visitors to rate individual staff because the visitors' comments can be linked back to the stand record of contacts with a view to continually improving/optimizing exhibitions).
10. Did we overspend or underspend (too large or too small a stand, or too many or too few staff)?

Costs

Exhibition costs need to be looked at carefully. Various sources suggest that the cost of hiring the exhibition space represents as little as one-fifth of the total costs of exhibiting. This obviously depends on whether the cost of the stand design is included, whether there is much integrated promotional activity and whether the opportunity cost of taking members of the sales team 'off the road' are included. The most important thing is to be consistent, so that year-on-year comparisons can be made. Cost per enquiry, cost per order, percentage of sales, return on investment and experimental non-attendance are now considered.

Cost per enquiry and cost per order

Cost per enquiry:

$$\frac{\text{Total exhibition costs}}{\text{Number of enquiries}} = \text{Cost per enquiry}$$

Total exhibition costs can be divided by the number of orders taken to find the cost per order.

Cost per order:

$$\frac{\text{Total exhibition costs}}{\text{Number of orders}} = \text{Cost per order}$$

There are some difficulties here, however. First, there is the timescale (some orders instigated by a contact at a trade show or exhibition can take several months or longer to be finally confirmed). Second, the regular orders (which would have been brought in by the normal sales force visits anyway) should, ideally, be separated from those incremental orders generated solely by attending the show. Third, there is a school of thought that suggests that exhibitions do not generate sales; they only allow the exhibitor to meet a useful target market, but whether the target market buys depends on a number of factors totally divorced from the show (eg the product, competitors' products, and prices). CPO also ignores both the size of the orders and their profitability. The size of the orders could be expressed as a percentage figure in the same way as a marketing communications budget is sometimes expressed, ie marketing expenses as a percentage of sales. In this case, exhibition costs as a percentage of sales generated can be calculated.

Percentage of sales

The difficulty here lies in isolating the sales generated exclusively through the exhibition, ie ignoring sales that would have been taken by the sales force regardless of the exhibition. Nevertheless, the cost of taking the same number of sales by routine sales visits should be compared to the costs of sales taken during the exhibition.

Return on investment

The long-term profitability of the sales is probably the most important of all the criteria. This is difficult to calculate, because the lifetime value of a customer can be difficult to forecast. However, the short-term ROI can be calculated by dividing the profit or contribution made from the orders by the total cost of the exhibition.

For example, if the orders taken during a show amounted to £200,000 and the total cost of investment in the exhibition was £20,000, the calculation would be as follows:

Sales	£200,000
Less cost of sales (say 50 per cent)	£100,000
Contribution	£100,000
Less cost/investment in the exhibition	£20,000
Return or profit on the investment	£80,000
This can then be expressed in percentage terms	$\frac{£80,000}{£20,000}$ = 400 per cent

The real ROI should in fact only be calculated from additional or new sales that were generated by the exhibition. Say the exhibition generated only five new customers, who in total bought £50,000 worth. The real ROI (on new business) would be 25 per cent. The word 'investment' is a bit misleading, since if the exhibition stand cannot be used again it is not an investment but an expense. If the exhibition produced only one new customer, who bought £10,000 worth, then the ROI would be negative.

Press coverage

One simple gauge is to collect the press clippings from the show. How important publicity and press coverage are as exhibition objectives determines how important publicity is among your KPIs.

Experimental non-attendance

Some organizations decide to stop exhibiting and use the opportunity to measure the impact of non-attendance on their sales and on their competitors' exhibition results.

The many other functions exhibitions provide are not included in the costs or revenues used in the previous calculations. Other, non-selling exhibition activities such as maintaining a presence, projecting an image, entertaining customers, marketing research, competitor analysis and product testing all, in a sense, save costs that would have been incurred if they were commissioned outside the exhibition. Arguably, these 'saved costs' could be subtracted from the other costs in these calculations. Real costs can certainly be saved by careful coordination throughout the whole exhibition planning cycle.

12 errors to avoid

James Dudley (1990) highlighted research findings indicating the 12 main reasons for poor performance. How much has changed?

1. Inadequate statements of purpose and objectives – nobody fully knows what they are supposed to do – eg personal and team targets.
2. Poor performance of staff running the stand, because of poor selection, training, motivation or management.
3. Lack of follow-up of leads and enquiries.
4. Poor-quality visitors.
5. Bad location of the stand.
6. Ineffective quality and design of the stand.
7. Poor recognition of company by customers (lack of pre-show marketing and poor design).
8. Low recall of the stand by visitors (bland design).
9. Ignoring competition and letting them steal your prospective visitors.
10. Breakdown in organization and control, eg unfinished stand on the opening day of the show or late arrival of literature, give-aways and so on.
11. Inadequate arrangements made for staff working on the stand, such as locating their accommodation too far from the event or failing to obtain car park permits.
12. Inadequate control of costs and budgets, leading to over-expenditure and consequently a poor return on investment.

Now let us look at two intriguing case studies: the RSA (Road Safety Authority) Virtual World event designed to stop the trend towards drink-driving in Ireland and then Google's curious Curiosity Rooms, which was an unusual piece of experiential branding beside London's Piccadilly Circus before Christmas.

CASE STUDY The RSA's shockingly immersive VR experience (that saves lives)

Situation

There has been a recent resurgence of drink-driving in Ireland. A legacy of historical anti-drink-driving advertising previously reduced this behaviour, but a new cohort of younger people, who have never been advertised to about this issue, are drink-driving anew. There were 146 fatalities on Irish roads in 2018 (RSA). The RSA asked BBDO Dublin if they could help to reduce this worrying drink-driving/fatalities trend. Once BBDO decided that virtual reality was the best way forward, they partnered with film production company, assembly and VR production company, Inition, to make this Webby-nominated VR experience to stop this drink-driving trend. 'Consequences' brings this message home in a new and brutally immersive style.

Objectives

Reduce drink-driving. Get under the audience's skin, using a tech-appropriate medium, and make sure they have an experience they will never forget. Use technology to make the consequences of drink-driving very real.

Strategy

Create a shocking and deeply resonant immersive experience called 'Consequences' with virtual reality production that puts the users into the shoes of a drink-driver. Drink-driving can change anyone's life in an instant and this virtual reality series brings that reality home in chilling detail. Emerging technologies like VR can ultimately help to change customer behaviour. Delivered via the RSA Shuttle Bus, awareness of the VR 'Consequences' experience is spreading across schools and colleges in Ireland.

Tactics

Create four varied storylines to help participants to plunge themselves into the shoes of a drink-driver and experience the full extent of the agonising consequences of drink

FIGURE 17.3 Stay in or head out?

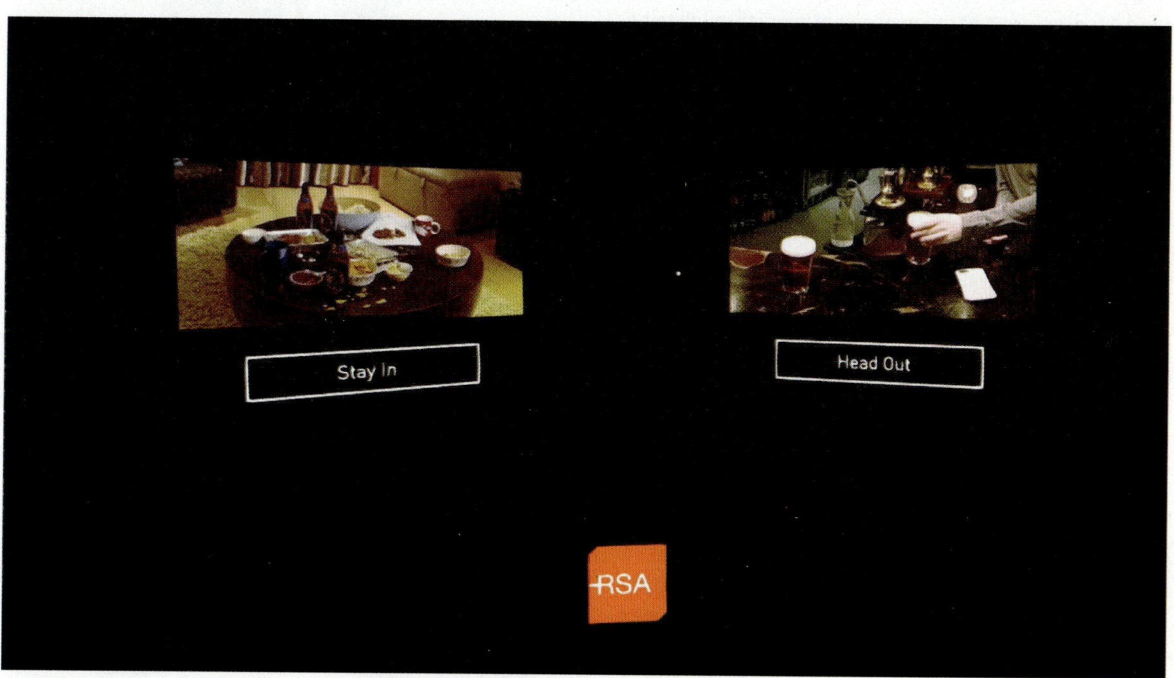

FIGURE 17.4 Two narrative journeys leading to permanent injury or criminal prosecution

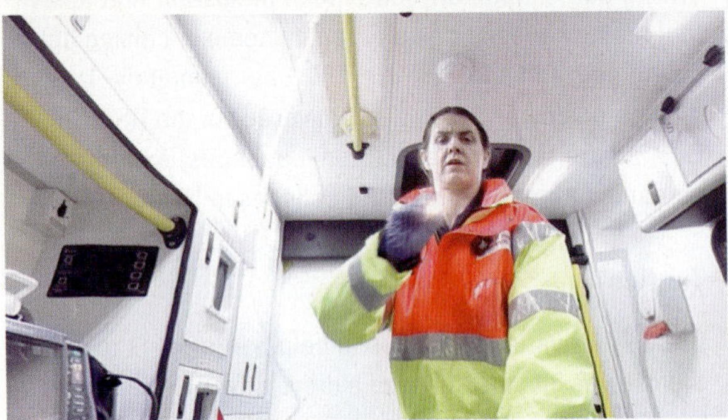

driving – from being invited to have 'one more' drink in the pub or at home (the viewer can choose which experience they want – 'stay in' or 'head out'), to suffering the nightmare car crash with permanent spinal injury through to being prosecuted in court.

Then, two narrative journeys take the viewer either through the jarring medical experience of permanent injury or to the lonely confines of a prison cell. Experiencing a drink-driving related crash first-hand is the surest way to never experience one again. The RSA and BBDO are giving people that chance. This VR experience is housed permanently on the RSA's shuttle travelling across Ireland all year round.

The RSA also sends the cardboard goggles to schools that have heard about the shuttle and its immersive virtual experience but whom the RSA cannot visit due to the growing waiting list of schools. So the teachers are also sent a bullet point activation email, video link and cardboard goggles.

Actions

Detailed project planning was required to produce the immersive video (shot in 6K with 3D audio), including storyboarding and shot planning (see the courtroom shot map, Figure 17.6).

FIGURE 17.5 User flow chart

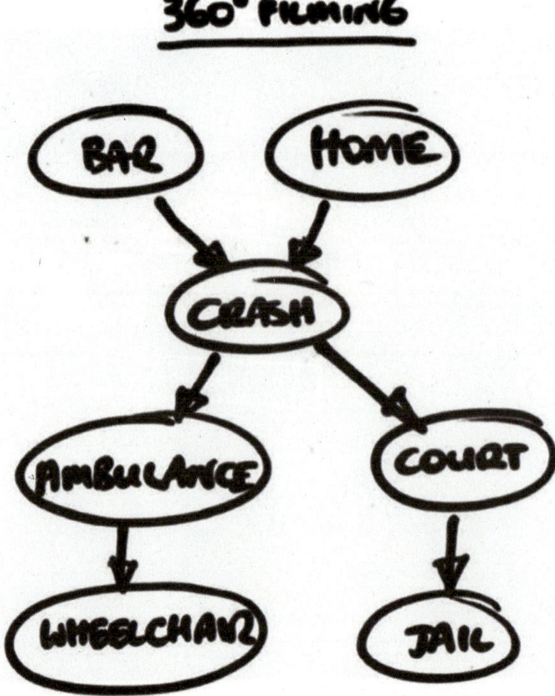

The user flow chart (Figure 17.5) shows the potential journeys that the viewer might experience. The 'crash' is the one constant factor. This one scene can lead to one of four possible journeys, making sure everyone has a slightly different experience to chat about afterwards: 1) bar – jail; 2) bar – wheelchair; 3) home – wheelchair; 4) home – jail.

The shot map for the court room scene is used in pre-production to outline where the 360 camera will be positioned and the type of real estate and other key actors that will be present, so set-designers can start to plan the scene around it (Figure 17.7).

After the 360-degree video production, the logistics of the RSA Shuttle Bus also have to be planned meticulously before it travels across Ireland to schools that are waiting anxiously for their turn with the immersive experience.

Testing was done between June and November 2018. The Shuttle Bus was launched in December 2018.

The RSA also sent training staff to schools and colleges that can't visit the shuttle bus. These staff are equipped with Oculus Go's wireless version of the experience on the shuttle bus. The VR headset is near identical, just the Oculus Rift on shuttle has higher processing power, which can lead to slightly higher picture quality and sound. But, overall, the Oculus Go still delivers a very hard-hitting experience for people who can't visit the shuttle to teach them about the dangers of drink driving. The Oculus Go RSA VR app is also available to download from the Oculus Go store for users lucky enough to have their own Oculus headset (retailing at €300).

Any other remaining schools that don't get a visit from the RSA team can request the teaching pack (cardboard goggles plus bullet point activation list plus the link for the videos), which the RSA subsequently send.

Journalists who cannot visit the shuttle but are interested are also given the cardboard goggles, the tips and the url link.

FIGURE 17.6 Shot map (for the court room scene)

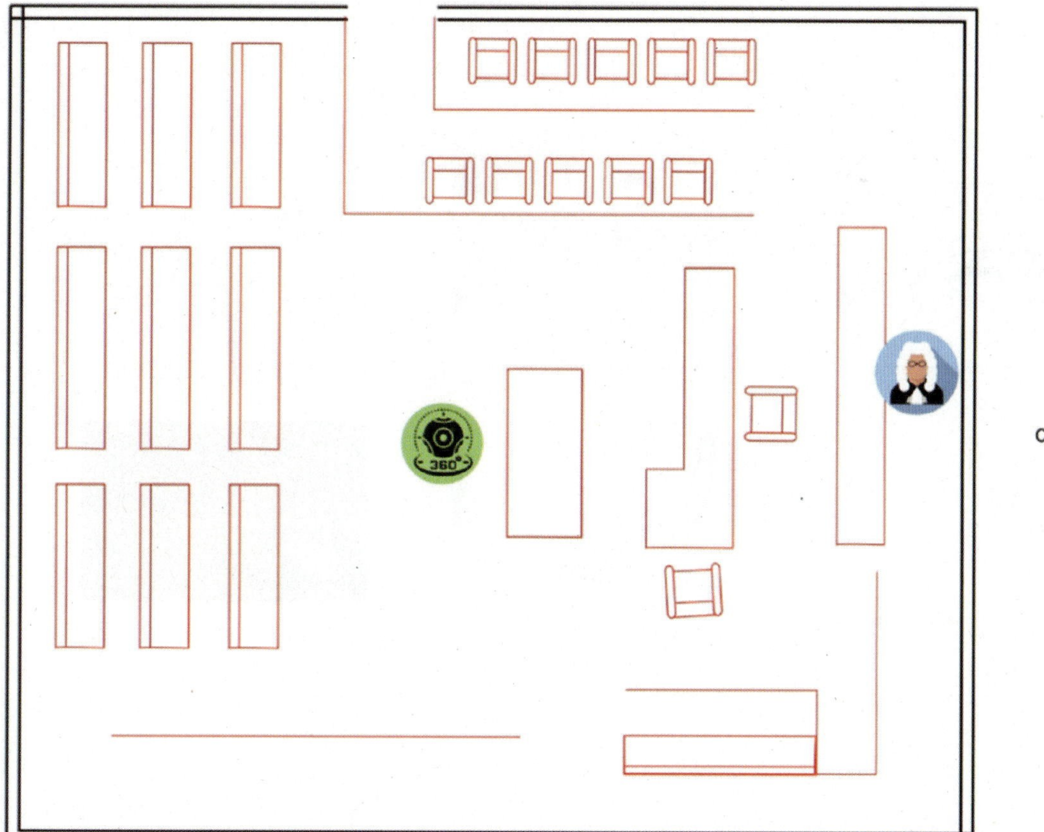

FIGURE 17.7 Storyboards plan each scene

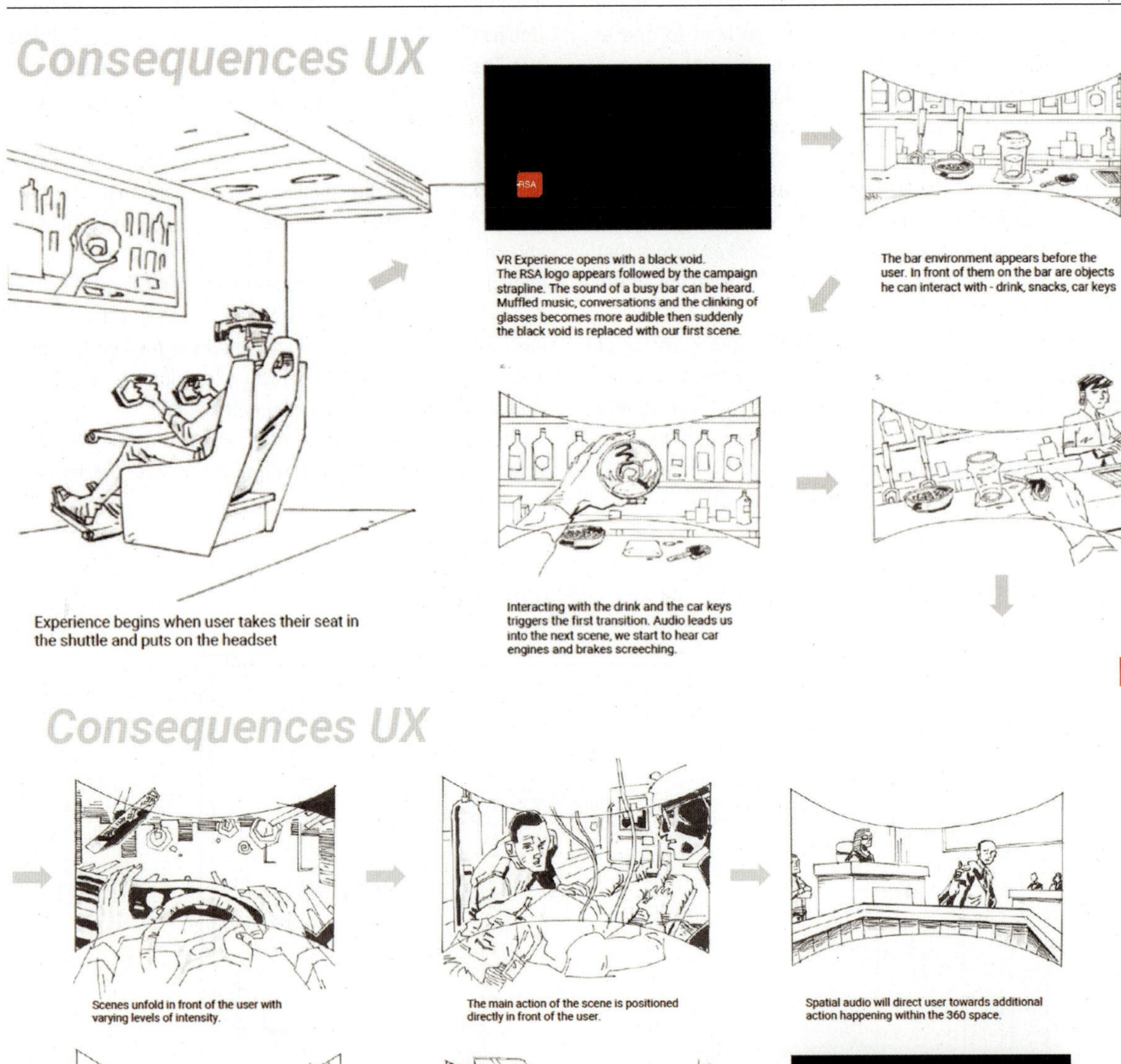

Consequences UX
RSA
VR Experience opens with a black void. The RSA logo appears followed by the campaign strapline. The sound of a busy bar can be heard. Muffled music, conversations and the clinking of glasses becomes more audible then suddenly the black void is replaced with our first scene.
The bar environment appears before the user. In front of them on the bar are objects he can interact with - drink, snacks, car keys
Experience begins when user takes their seat in the shuttle and puts on the headset
Interacting with the drink and the car keys triggers the first transition. Audio leads us into the next scene, we start to hear car engines and brakes screeching.
Consequences UX
Scenes unfold in front of the user with varying levels of intensity.
The main action of the scene is positioned directly in front of the user.
Spatial audio will direct user towards additional action happening within the 360 space.
Audio will also be used to suggest activity beyond the visible 360.
Final scene and end scene will all transition in a similar manner to ensure campaign tag line is clearly understood.
Never ever drink and drive.
RSA

FIGURE 17.8 Interactive shuttle statistics

Interactive shuttle programme										
	June	*July*	*August*	*September*	*October*	*November*	*December*	*January*	*February*	*March*
Locations	16	19	15	11	20	18	4	13	12	17
No of visitors	15,965	17,586	20,294	27,195	6,687	12,294	990	15,695	4,783	16,387

FIGURE 17.9 The RSA interactive shuttle

Key visuals

Key visuals have to be created to promote the experience once it's been created. A single hero visual/identity that can be easily recognized is created. Lots of concepts are drawn up until one is chosen. Once the concept is chosen, it is worked up, art directed, shot and retouched to create the master visual for the campaign.

Control/results (to date)

Over 135,000 students have experienced 'Consequences' (the VR experience). RSA have a waiting list of schools and colleges and events wanting the shuttle bus, and the unpleasant immersive 'Consequences' experience, to visit their school, festivals, businesses and events.

The RSA Shuttle Bus and the 'Consequences' experience has almost instantaneously become one of Ireland's most accessible high-end VR activations, with over 135,000 views so far.

Most importantly, this innovative VR experience has already changed lives, saved lives and is inspiring drivers to change their behaviour away from the drink-drive trend that has emerged in recent years.

The BBDO 360 Video has also been nominated for a Webby award: agency: BBDO; film production company: Assembly; VR production company: Inition.

FIGURE 17.10 Virtual reality set-up

Note: If you want to experience 'Consequences':

1. Use a smart phone with at least a 5.1 inch screen and gyroscopic technology, eg iPhone 8+ or Samsung galaxy S7+.
2. Open up your YouTube App manually, and search for 'RSA VR'.
3. Click the 'Cardboard Goggles' icon in the video player control panel.
4. Ensure you are in 'landscape' orientation.
5. Click 'Play'.
6. Place phone in Google cardboard goggles.
7. Put goggles on.
8. Experience 'Consequences' (move your head and look around).

See the online resources to see how this kind of video was created. See a 'behind-the-scenes' video on how this VR experiences was produced, and more.

FIGURE 17.11 Cardboard goggles

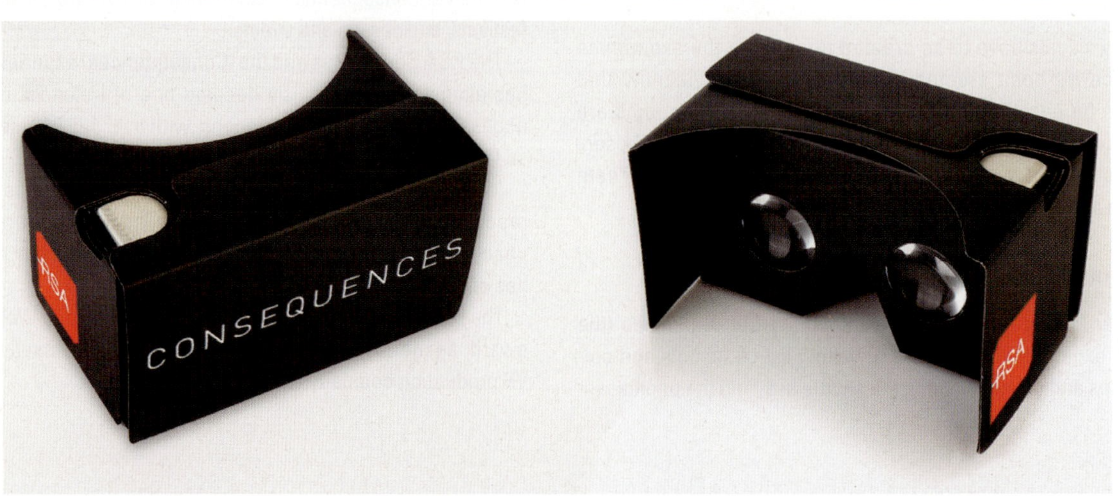

FIGURE 17.12 Two key visuals, one of which is developed into the master visual – the promotional visual for the campaign shown on the right

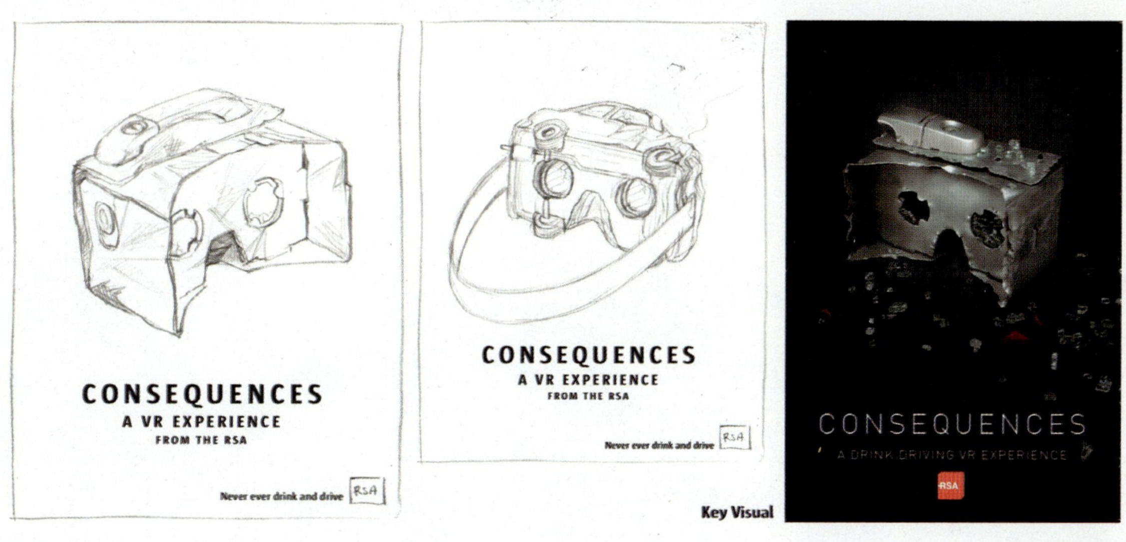

FIGURE 17.13 Participants on the RSA Shuttle Bus

FIGURE 17.14 Promotional poster

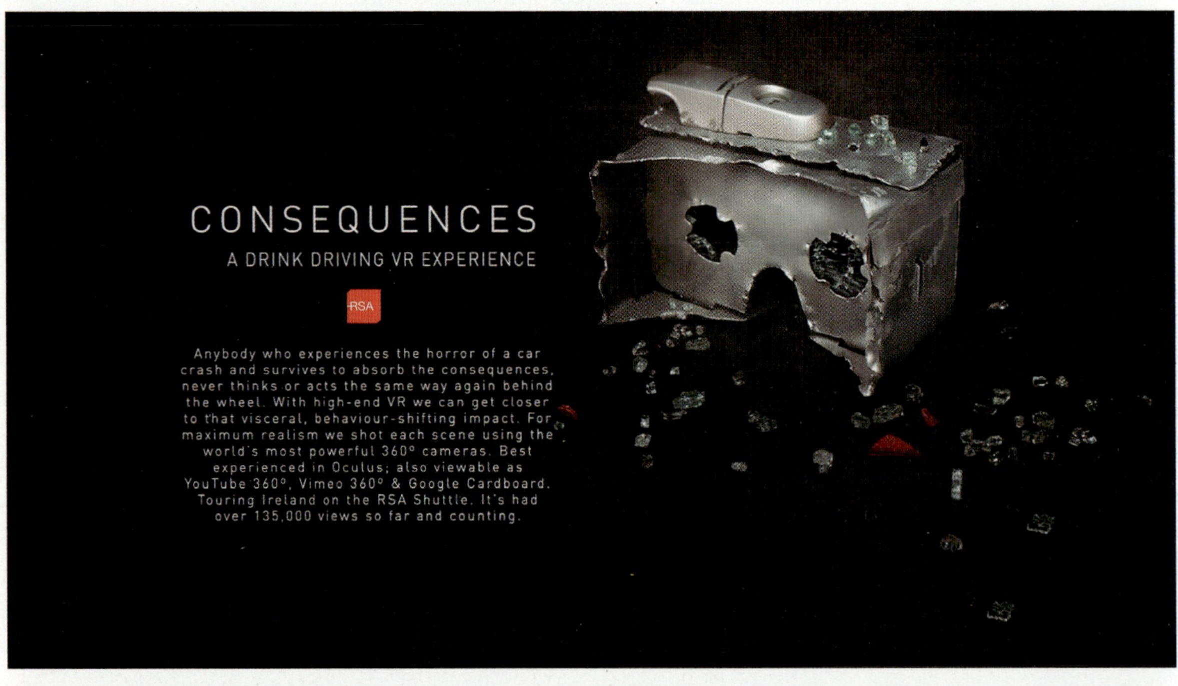

CASE STUDY Google's Curiosity Rooms: Experiential branding

Google's five-week Curiosity Rooms branding exercise was located in Piccadilly Circus, London – where retail design meets experience design.

Situation

The Google Pixel 3 phone is a challenger brand in the hyper-competitive mobile market place.

Target audience

Consumers who are naturally curious and willing to innovate. Google hope to engage the younger tech-savvy and tech-positive audience who are in tune with culture, fashion and experiences.

Objectives

Build and strengthen awareness of the Pixel 3 phone. Get the Pixel 3 phone into the consideration set of the target market.

Strategy

Promote awareness and nurture consideration of the Pixel 3 phone among younger tech-savvy consumers by integrating retail design with experience design, and converting the prestigious location 55 Regent Street in London's Piccadilly Circus into 'Pixeldilly Circus', an engaging experiential brand exercise.

FIGURE 17.15 All-in auto wash

SOURCE: Matt Monfredi

A free specially curated experience opened for five weeks before Christmas. All integrated into Google's Pixel 3 campaign which is all about discovery and making every day extraordinary.

A high-profile, prestigious location was chosen to create a space where people can come and explore, and be curious in a playful way. An offline physical space was used to get people involved.

Message/theme

Create a space where people can come, have a coffee and explore, and be curious in a playful way. It ties in perfectly with the product's overall campaign, as Google and Pixel 3 are all about discovery and making every day extraordinary.

Tactics

Twelve windows, three floors and a packed programme of free talks, workshops, gigs (YouTube music gigs), coffee and food, and special events including celebrity talks, weekly podcast recordings, and many other experiences, for five weeks. Google also invited cool local London businesses into the Curiosity Rooms, such as Patch, Perky Blenders, Earl of East, Lapp by Leomie Anderson and more. Tickets were free, with a recommended donation to the charity Crisis.

Here's a small sample of some of the events that were promoted:

- Join John Boyega in conversation with his mentor. The actor shook up Star Wars as its first black stormtrooper and hasn't looked back since.

FIGURE 17.16 Google Lens Launderette

SOURCE: Matt Monfredi

FIGURE 17.17 Christmas booths in the curiosity rooms

SOURCE: Matt Monfredi

FIGURE 17.18 Perky blenders in the curiosity rooms

SOURCE: Matt Monfredi

FIGURE 17.19 Perky Blinders, Pixeldilly Tea

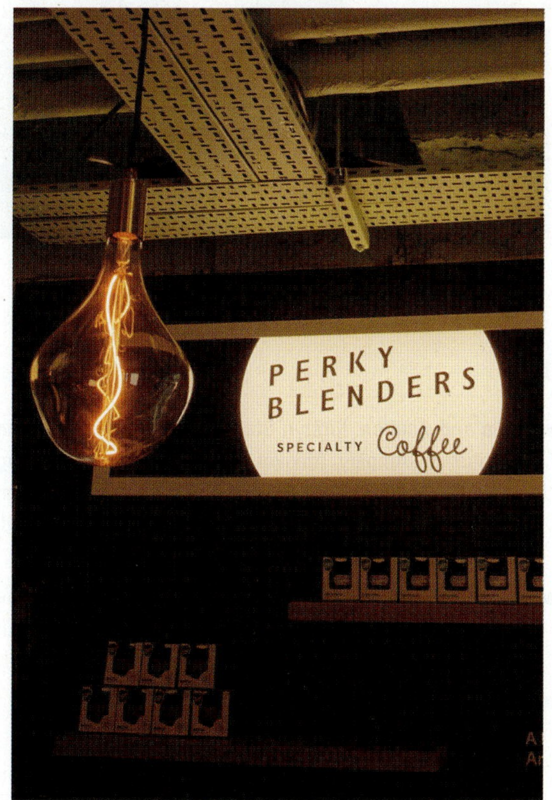

SOURCE: Matt Monfredi

- Grab a seat at the table as Jessie Ware and her mother are joined by a special guest to take their Table Manners podcast live to discuss food, family and the beautiful art of everyday life and its joys.
- Join Professor Green as he records his new podcast live with very special guests.
- Join Dolly Alderton and Pandora Sykes as they record their weekly hit podcast The High Low.
- The star of one of Netflix's most popular debut original series *The Haunting of Hill House*, Oliver Jackson-Cohen, will share how he landed the starring role.

Actions

Eight weeks to set it up. It ran for five weeks.

Control/measurement and metrics

Success was measured in footfall, social reach and consideration rather than sales. 'This is a brand experience first and foremost, so we aren't expecting to transact. This is about consideration,' said Kirstyn Stark, Head of UK Hardware Brand Marketing and Partnerships at Google.

FIGURE 17.20 Mistah Jam and Professor Green

SOURCE: Matt Monfredi

There was a lot of press coverage, including *Campaign Magazine*:

> A basement bursting with music and dining experiences, a candy-pink faux launderette, a *Vogue* photo shoot, intriguing installations and Instagram-friendly moments at every point, not to mention a slide in place of an escalator: welcome to the 'Curiosity Rooms', where Google has chosen to promote its latest smartphone, Pixel 3.
>
> Arrigo (2018)

3Ms

- **Men and women:** Kirstyn Stark led the project with the support of Amplify (deliver the experience), working alongside Halpern, 72andSunny, Essence and OMD, with Kru Live providing brand ambassadors. Matt Monfredi supplied photography.
- **Minutes:** Eight weeks to build. Five weeks to run. Google saw it as a test in terms of a longer-term activation, but they like to experiment.
- **Money:** Budget undisclosed.

FIGURE 17.21 Pixel booth for selfies

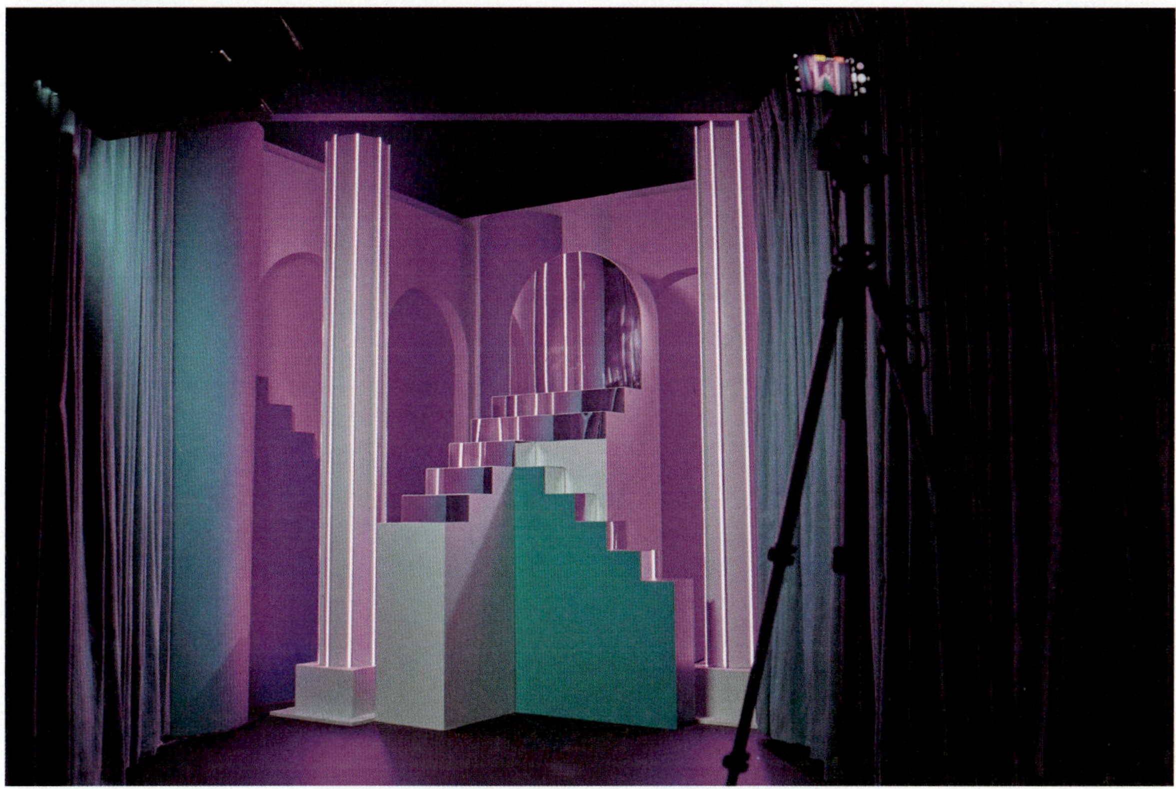

SOURCE: Matt Monfredi

FIGURE 17.22 A slide adds to the experience

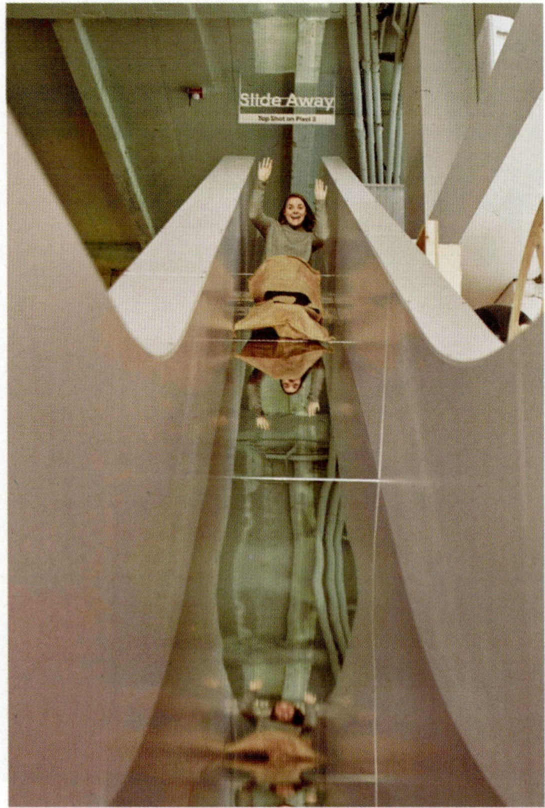

SOURCE: Matt Monfredi

You can see an extra exhibitions case study on Sedgwick at RIMS Monte Carlo in the online resource pack.

Advantages and disadvantages

Here are some of the advantages and disadvantages to consider when deciding whether to increase or reduce this communications tool.

Advantages

Exhibitions contain a whole market under one roof in an engaging environment where the message can be controlled: prospects, customers, distributors, competitors, the media and many more. While exhibitions do create a presence (or awareness in the mind of key customers), they do generate business. Orders can be taken (sales can be closed), and new customers can be introduced to the brand. Enquiries can be taken and customer needs explored in conversations that otherwise might be difficult to engage in.

Disadvantages

Many exhibitors are looking at the total cost of exhibitions (including pre-promotion, attendance, design and build, staff, sales promotions, gifts and 'freebies'). Some exhibition traffic is falling, and hence exhibitors see their costs rising. Lastly, exhibitions are hard work and require pre-show training and motivation, which are also time-consuming.

Key points from Chapter 17

- Exhibitions, events and experiential marketing offer a unique one-to-one opportunity.
- Exhibitions are hard work. They can work well for the exhibitor if they are carefully and thoroughly planned and integrated with other marcomms tactical tools.
- Plan for before, during and after the exhibition/event or experience.
- Integrate particularly with PR, email, social media, sales and the overall contact strategy.
- Develop an exhibition strategy.
- Exhibitions should be part of a contact strategy.
- Every element of exhibition performance can be monitored and measured with a view to making future improvements.
- Measure the success or otherwise of events.

References and further reading

Arrigo, Y (2018) Google's 'Curiosity Rooms' aim to inspire experience-savvy Londoners, *Campaign*, 23 November

Black, S (1989) *Exhibitions and Conferences from A to Z*, Modino Press, London

Cotterell, P (1992) *Exhibitions: An exhibitor's guide*, Hodder & Stoughton, London

Dudley, J W (1990) *Successful Exhibiting*, Kogan Page, London

eConsultancy (2018) 10 very cool examples of experiential marketing, *eConsultancy*, 12 November

Engebretson, D (2000) *Exhibiting in the USA* (video), Trade Partners UK, Department of Trade and Industry, produced in association with Multimedia Marketing.com, London

Junius, W (2017) Trade show success: New rules for Europe and beyond, *Exhibit in Europe*, 18 September

Seekings, D (1996) *How to Organize Effective Conferences and Meetings*, Kogan Page, London

Talbot, J (1989) *How to Make Exhibitions Work for Your Business*, *Daily Telegraph*/Kogan Page, London

Further information

Association of Event Organisers
119 High Street
Berkhamsted
Hertfordshire HP4 2DJ
Tel: +44 (0)1442 285 810
www.aeo.org.uk

Event Supplier and Services Association (ESSA) Limited
119 High Street
Berkhamsted
Hertfordshire HP4 2DJ
Tel: +44 (0)1442 285 812
www.essa.uk.com

Society of Event Organisers
29a Market Square
Biggleswade
Bedfordshire SG18 8AQ
Tel: +44(0)1767 312986
www.seoevent.co.uk

18 Merchandising and point of sale

LEARNING OBJECTIVES

By the end of this chapter you will be able to:

- appreciate the impact of merchandising techniques;
- understand how offline and online merchandising must integrate and optimize;
- empathize with a retailer's strategies and merchandising policies;
- discuss retail strategies and how they incorporate store image, store layout, merchandise ranges, colour blocking, point-of-sale, promotions and a range of miscellaneous items;
- ensure that a culture of constant analysis and improvement is employed so that results can constantly be improved.

Introduction

The importance of merchandising

Merchandising success or failure is determined by the final moments before a purchase is made (or not made). This is the point in the buying cycle where the customer is in front of the product or service and is about to make a final decision, the point of purchase, to buy or not to buy. It is also called the 'point-of-sale'. Merchandising is all about presenting goods and services in an enticing way. This involves everything from packaging, displays, posters, splashes, special offers, choice of supporting products as well as the overall store design including lighting, layout and ambience offline and integrating this with the customer's offline and online needs.

Shopping for happiness

In the offline world, going shopping is still a popular leisure activity. In fact some tourist resorts offer shopping facilities as a USP. This is also evident in the United States, where retail centres almost double as leisure centres. 'Mall walking' is a significant activity. In the north of England, customers are transported by the coachload to spend a day at one of Europe's largest retail centres, Gateshead's Metro Centre. Similarly, visitors to Dubai consider 'shopping malls' as one of the attractions.

In many consumer markets the **consumer's final decision to buy is often made inside, and not outside, the store.** More recently there is evidence that more

FIGURE 18.1 Red Bull's Hangar 7: Merchandising involves multiple factors including overall store design

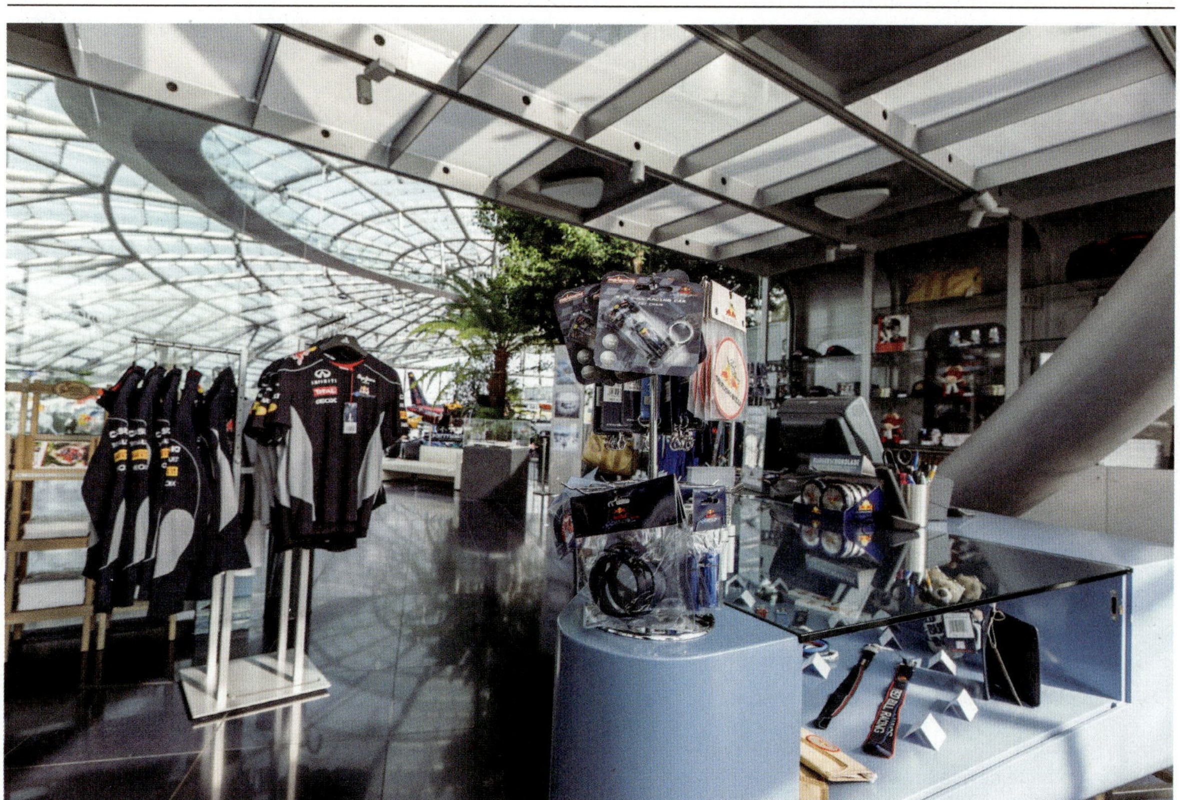

decisions are being made on the smart phone (outside). More later. There has been some debate as to exactly what percentage of decisions are made inside the store, and although '70 per cent of decisions are made inside the store' appears to be used widely, Court *et al* (2009) suggest that these figures may vary according to sector. Neff (2010) suggests that retail stores have more impact than TV when generating awareness of new products. Google (2016) reveal changes in purchasing habits over the last 10 years – see 'Ten years ago shoppers did this' in the box below.

Websites, smart phones and apps will affect these figures significantly, as all of these tools are vying for the consumer's attention and attempting to secure the decision making, sometimes even before point-of-sale can persuade a customer. See how Dulux shifted the decision from inside the store to outside the store online (p 130). And mobile devices can influence a customer before, during and after a shopping trip. Paperless couponing, special promotions, and information via SMS and location-based advertising are likely to have a significant impact on the customer decision journey.

Location-based advertising and paperless coupons can also be triggered by the actual location of a customer (actually, the location of their smart phone), so that as customers walk through a shopping centre, or even a particular retail store, their mobile rings or a text message appears and mentions a relevant special offer in a competing store that is close by them at that precise moment. Read more about location-based advertising at p 377.

Ten years ago shoppers did this...

'When looking for ideas and inspiration, a shopper would either go online, browse a catalog, or walk the store aisles. When in-store, a shopper would learn more about a product and either head to the cashier or head home to buy online. The point is that a shopper interacted with channels independently. But the rise of mobile has changed this picture. What's different today is that even though this behavior still happens, shoppers are omnichannel:

- 60 per cent of internet users start shopping on one device but continue or finish on a different one;
- 82 per cent of smartphone users say they consult their phones on purchases they're about to make in a store.

They get ideas, look up information, and make decisions, all from their smartphone anytime, anywhere.'

Google (2016)

Switching to industrial markets (B2B markets), the merchandising opportunity lies relatively untapped in industrial wholesale outlets such as electrical wholesalers and builders' suppliers, where a lot of merchandising tends to look dusty, dirty and uninteresting. There is room here for creative, intelligent and effective merchandising. It does require a delicate balance, since a hard-working electrician in search of some 2-core 3-millimetre cable might assume a distributor to be too expensive if it looked too glitzy and comfortable. On the other hand, merchandising including offering 'free coffee' can provide customers with useful information and overall, a better shopping experience, for example, reminding the buyer about other relevant products and any special offers.

Merchandising offline

You are probably more aware of offline merchandising in stores where they use point-of-sale (POS) banners, leaflets and dispensers ('take one' boxes); stickers; posters; showcards; cardboard cut-outs; 3D lenticular images; branded racks or display units; dump bins; free-standing floor displays. You can also see electronic gadgetry: spotlighting systems; video walls; plasma screens; illuminated display systems and more. Meanwhile the brands themselves are acutely aware of, and negotiate hard for use of, these in store and also for premium shelf positioning (eye level and end of aisles); in-store sampling, window displays and more sophisticated interactive merchandising.

In-store screens and video terminals positioned at checkouts can transmit special relevant offers (based on specific customer's previous purchase data) to customers as their store cards are swiped through the checkout.

These tools have been available for many years. One problem with any particularly clever high-tech POS is that customers can end up admiring the POS material instead of buying the product. On the other hand, products can benefit from POS support, as many products can get lost among the 25,000 lines of food that the average superstore displays. An innovative POS attracts attention – which is a key stage in the AIDA communication model (see p 270). Although it is important to present fresh images to repeat-visit customers to maintain their interest and loyalty, many retailers' obsession with product density and profit per square foot means that they instantly dismiss most of a supplier's branded merchandising tools. In fact, the majority of stores do not have the flexibility or the luxury of space to dedicate to one-off 'stunts' with in-built novelty obsolescence.

Merchandising online

For online retail website owners, merchandising is a crucial activity, in the same way that it is for physical, offline, retail store owners. In both cases, the aims are similar – to help customers and maximize sales potential for each store visitor.

> Online, this means presenting relevant products and promotions to site visitors which should help boost key measures of site performance such as conversion rate and average order value. You will see that many of these approaches are related to the concept of findability. Some of the most common approaches used are:
>
> - Use of customer ratings and reviews have a direct influence on sales.
> - Feature the best-selling products prominently.
> - Use 'bundling', ie buy-one-get-one-free (BOGOF) on the product page or in checkout, although care has to be taken here since this can reduce conversion rates.
> - Use of product visualization systems, which enable web users to zoom in and rotate products.
> - Expanding navigation through synonyms. Using a range of terms that apply to the same product, the product may become easier to find.
> - Applying faceted navigation (easy to drill down by selecting different product attributes). Conversion rates will be higher if relevant products and offers are at the top of the search results list.'
>
> Chaffey and Smith (2017)

In terms of customer ratings and reviews, 85 per cent of online consumers trust online reviews on the same level as personal recommendations from friends and family (Bright Local, 2018). Other research shows a 166 per cent increase in sales conversion when ratings and user-generated content are integrated into the online shopping experience (Baker 2018).

Target stores merge online and offline merchandising teams

> 'Guests might search on smartphones for patio furniture, then see completely different merchandise when they came into their local store. So Target Retail chain in the USA merged its online and offline marketing and merchandising teams into a single unified patio team that was mobile-first. It decided what products and signage to feature in-store based on digital demand. Target also ran Google local inventory ads to show customers on mobile the exact patio furniture that was available in the store nearest them. As a result, patio revenues in the stores in which Target made this change have been dramatically outpacing the others.'
>
> Google (2016)

See also the case study 'Rotating videos PPC sales funnel boosts ROAS: Ashley HomeStore Facebook ad campaign', p 362.

Augmented reality in store and at home

AR allows users to see additional information about a product, an item or an exhibit by pointing a mobile phone and reading any hyper-data posted. Additional information can be text or photographs. For example, a building site might use AR information on the site to show what the site will look like when it is finished. Through use of AR software like Layar or other apps from the App Store, the horizon expands as augmented reality emerges. Having downloaded the app (eg Layar), it opens to the scan screen. Scan the street around you to see useful information like icons for restaurants. Or you can look for the Layar logo on magazines, packaging, billboards, magazine and newspaper ads, business cards and other items. Then tap anywhere on screen to see the extra information such as a graphic, an extra photo, a video, a website, or take an action like call a phone number, vote in a poll, send an email or share the extra layer of information, or engage in a game. Soon apps may be built into things like car windscreens so you can see layers of data if you want to. Incidentally, Layar also scans QR codes. The company that owned Layar, Blippar, has since developed ARDP (augmented reality digital placement), which allows users to view web AR experiences without the need for a separate app to be installed on their device.

AR is also used in magazine ads (once the AR code/logo is visible in the ad), so that an ad, say for a pair of shoes, then becomes a 3D pair of shoes protruding out from the page when viewed via the AR app. You can move around and see different views of the shoe. You can also change colour and style and ultimately select and purchase shoes – all from a print ad that is AR enabled.

Apple's ARkit app allows users to add images to reality, eg add an image of a cup, or a vase, or a candle, or a lamp onto a 'real world' table that is in front of you. If you select the cup it appears on your table immediately. You can, in the real world, walk around the table to see the other side of the 'virtual' cup or look over it to see inside the 'virtual' cup. You can see how this can help customers visualize what particular products might look like in their own homes.

See the box about Memory Mirrors' digital mirrors later in this chapter.

Virtual reality in store and at home

As the online experience may become more 3D orientated and more virtual world-orientated, marketers will require inquisitive minds to find what works and what doesn't. This is what Tesco started exploring when they unveiled a prototype of a virtual reality supermarket back in 2014, in which customers browsed a 3D supermarket using an Oculus Rift virtual reality headset. 'Although customers can't yet pick (or click) anything off the shelves, customers can travel through the store and look at the brands on offer without leaving the comfort of their home' (Ad Age, 2014). Effectively, the store is being brought to the customer rather than the customer visiting the real-world store.

Meanwhile, some 20 million MMOGs immerse themselves in virtual gamers' worlds as they engage in 'massively multiplayer online games', with some 23 million subscribers to MMO gaming in 2014 (*Statista*, 2014). Most of the games are not truly immersive experiences and do not require headsets. However, a lot of people do play games online and transcend into a games world. It is estimated that there are currently 2.2 billion active video gamers (individuals that play video games). This is expected to grow to 2.7 billion by 2021 (*Statista*, 2019).

Virtual immersion in a non-reality world has been around for many decades and crept into people's living rooms in the form of Wii games. These popular virtual games convert a living room instantaneously into a gymnasium, a tennis court, a boxing ring, a dance studio, a keep-fit studio or even a golf course, and customers (players) play happily in their virtual worlds. It will become a lot more sophisticated – eg Guinness's virtual pint given to customers in Tesco stores (more later).

Virtual rain

Nine years ago, the University of Tokyo perfected 'virtual rain' that looks and probably feels like water dropping on to a surface. It may well be that the next wave of virtual experiences combines virtual worlds with artificial intelligence that will create whole new stream of opportunities for those that embrace the technology.

Blurring virtual and reality

More and more customer service avatars (interactive cartoon characters on websites) are appearing, particularly in the customer care sectors, where they offer themselves as 'your assistant'. Some of these are being replaced by real photographs of real people who want to help.

It might also become more blurred as virtual reality and 'real' reality morph. Back in 2007, I held a parallel product launch of Northern Ireland's creative digital hub, CRE8IVITY.COM in Second Life. The Minister for Enterprise's avatar spoke to an international virtual audience (of avatars) who were overseas bloggers who could not physically attend the main 'real' event in Belfast, but could attend the virtual event held in a virtual venue we hired for the virtual event. We simultaneously beamed some of this virtual event from a virtual world onto a real world screen with 300 'real-world' visitors sitting in the real audience in Belfast's Science park (where the Titanic was built). The dividing line between virtual and real is blurring

Soon, virtual reality may come to us instead of having to log in to a screen. A variation of VR may come to us in the form of avatars on websites or augmented reality images on a car windscreen, or hovering holograms, or shopping bots appearing beside us, or even static, attractive bots that stand beside us as we queue, offering helpful advice – as did the simple talking, moving bot who kindly helped me in Dubai airport four years ago by reminding me to put my liquid containers in a plastic bag (Figure 18.2).

In addition, as already mentioned, our own homes and offices can be converted instantaneously into gyms, golf courses and discotheques courtesy of Wii games. The blurring of reality and virtual reality continues.

Merchandising challenges

The high street struggle

Troubled consumer confidence, crippling business rates and digital disruption have all been blamed for the battering endured by most high streets and their retail stores.

FIGURE 18.2 A friendly airport avatar spoke to me

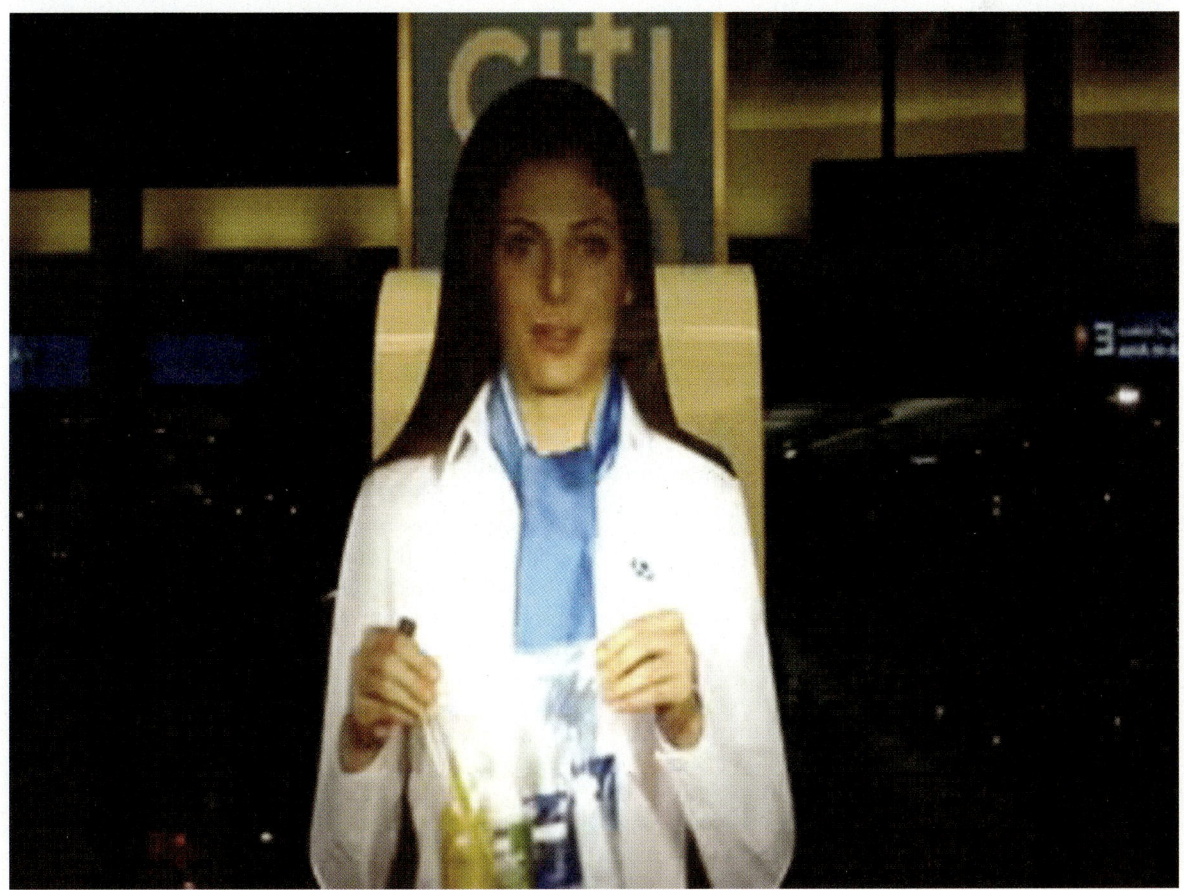

> From casual dining to department store chains, high street stalwarts have fallen into the red at an alarming rate. In 2018 alone, toy superstore Toys R Us and electronics retailer Maplin disappeared from the UK high street, while the House of Fraser collapsed into administration in August owing nearly £1bn to creditors, but was rescued by Mike Ashley's Sports Direct and is now closing some stores. Debenhams is set to axe 50 of its 166 stores after posting a £491.5m loss in the year to 1 September. Meanwhile, profits plummeted 99 per cent at the John Lewis Partnership in the six months to 28 July.
>
> *Marketing Week* (2018)

Hyper-competitors in customers' pockets

Competition has become so intense that we call it hyper-competition. And it is in your customers' pocket on their smart phone apps. Both Amazon and eBay want customers to use their apps when physically shopping in other retail stores. They want customers to scan any product's barcode and the app will tell them if they can get a better price and free delivery which will save them having to lug home some heavy products. So hyper-competition is in your pocket. Retailers now have to motivate customers to use the retailer's app to get special offers and rewards instead of using competitor apps.

Showrooming when shops become showrooms

Are stores becoming just showrooms for mobile users? Are shops becoming changing rooms where customers find what they like, try on the clothes and then go home and buy online? This is 'showrooming', and it damages high street and shopping mall retailers' sales.

Merchandising opportunity

Marketers have got to get technology developers, app engineers, virtual engineers, social media creatives, content marketers and mobile marketers to come up with even more clever ways to engage, entertain, inform, save time, and add fun or knowledge to today's shoppers. Can they make shopping fast and fun? How can they use the interactive potential between store, merchandising, mobile and the customer – a much sought after experience? How can they use AI, IoT, VR and AR to enhance the customer experience? How can they expand the CX onto smart phones and maybe onto other IoT 'things'? How can a retailer add value to their customers' experiences when inside the store? These are the questions for many retailers today.

To tackle showrooming, some retailers, like John Lewis, encourage customers to use John Lewis iPads, which are supplied in the changing room. If the customer subsequently finds the same product at a cheaper price, the store will give them a special gift that compensates for the price difference, if they still buy from them.

Near field communications

Other stores like Harvey Nichols encourage customers to use the store's own iPads to tap on a particular product in a store to get access to rich, in-depth product content such as images, videos and recommendations. This is near field communications (NFC) technology. Customers just have to insert their email address to set up an account. They can also send details of the products to their inbox. 'Harvey Nichols (retail store chain) found that 90 per cent of shoppers engaged in-store were not previously known to them. Sixteen per cent of all shoppers engaged with the experience and 18 per cent took further action after receiving an email' (Chaffey and Smith, 2017). NFC is limited to a distance of approximately two inches, while Bluetooth (see Beacons, next section) can reach over thirty feet.

Beacons and proximity marketing

Beacon technology has been generating buzz since Apple introduced Bluetooth beacons to the market in 2013 (da Silva, 2017). These small, battery-operated wireless devices transmit Bluetooth signals to nearby smart phones (if the smart phone is Bluetooth enabled and if the customer has downloaded the store's app). Beacons emit signals that mobile apps recognize and these signals then trigger the app to open and present the customer with a personalized offer (discount, gift, rewards, recommendations) on their smart phone as they approach the product being promoted by the store. It can even help customers find a product tucked away in an obscure aisle. Soon it may even be used to provide augmented reality experiences, enabling customers to 'try' merchandise on without ever having to enter a dressing room (da Silva, 2017).

Digital mirrors

Another exciting merchandising development leveraging the Internet of Things, is the Memory Mirror®, a digital mirror that helps customers try out clothes without actually trying them on. Designed by Memomi Labs for in-store clothes shopping, it captures stills and video of everything a customer tries on. Through artificial intelligence, virtual reality and augmented reality customers can virtually 'try on' products such as clothing, eyewear, footwear, accessories and make-up in real time without any of the inconveniences of the actual 'try-on experience', while looking at a digital mirror. More on digital mirrors on page 558.

3D interactive POS

Over thirty years ago Brian Oliver (1987) wrote in *Marketing Magazine*:

> Imagine walking into a high street department store and being greeted by a three-dimensional lifelike copy of John McEnroe's head. As you walk past, it starts to move and even speaks to you... pointing out the features of a tennis racket suspended in mid-air in front of you with no apparent means of support. Then a giant pair of moving lips mounted on a glass display suddenly start talking to you, inviting you to try on the store's winter fashions without even undressing. All you have to do, say the lips, is stand in front of a 'magic mirror', select an item of clothing and, before you can say 'Bruce Oldfield', your reflection is wearing it.

Today, many websites engage customers by inviting them to upload their head and shoulders photographs (for trying on spectacles on an optician's website) or a full photograph for a boutique (to see what certain clothes look like on the customer).

Smart shelves

Smart shelves can help customers and stores. Smart shelves interact with a store's app on a customer's smart phone. The IoT sensors installed in the shelves recognize each customer as they approach, so they can then offer a highly relevant and personalized deal. And if you use the store's shopping list function on the app, the smart shelves will also interact with your list and show you where to find the items on your list. Smart shelves can also change all prices in a store in minutes. They reduce damaged stock and wasted energy as the IoT sensors can check temperatures in the freezers to avoid damaged food products due to wrong temperatures and reduce temperatures if necessary.

'Smart shelves will change how you shop in the future. From digital displays that show instant price changes to advertisements linked to your shopping list, you can expect the technology to become more personalized' (Bandoim, 2018).

Adding value and increasing dwell time

Marketers can also help customers with better product information, product walk-throughs, loyalty points and prizes. Dining facilities, coffee shops, crèches, relaxation areas may become popular as some retailers are looking at the new priority of making the store less about selling and more about what retailers call 'dwell time' (or duration of visit). Ideally not being stuck in long queues but rather enjoying pleasant time spent in the store's environment, in fact better time spent in the store than time spent at home with a mobile. The relentless search for added value for the CX continues. There are opportunities for, say, a luxury retail store, or any store, to engage a shopper's non-shopping companion (eg a child or husband) with the store's brand. A comfortable area with newspapers, TV, iPad and coffee might help. The longer the attention of the unengaged shopper is occupied, the longer the engaged shopper will continue on her shopping mission.

Dwell time decreases if companion/child accompanies shopper

When working on a strategy to bring digital experiences to life in-store for Bloomingdales, one of the surprising insights had nothing to do with the customer's shopping behaviour in Bloomingdales, but more with the dwell time and attention span of a customer when she brought a companion or child. Her dwell time decreased when she had a male accompanying her and decreased even more when she had a child or children with her.

When the customers are alone they accomplish their shopping. When a customer is with a companion or child, the flow of the shopper is interrupted.

The customer enjoys focusing on her shopping mission when alone or with an engaged shopping companion, and this is less likely when someone is in tow who is not engaged. When the unengaged shopper or child doesn't want to be there then tension stirs within the shopper, causing her to lose focus and want to tend to the care of her unengaged companion or child. The two men sitting on the uninspiring bench in Figure 18.3 don't know each other. The man on the left was tapping his foot, patiently waiting while his wife was looking for a new outfits; he said he does this every weekend. The man on the right had been waiting for 20 minutes for his wife to finish her shopping. He had brought his iPad.

The Gap 1969 store took a leap and borrowed from the Apple Store. They placed a table in the centre of the store with several iPads for shoppers to use. On the iPad, the customer can browse assortments from Gap 1969 while the unengaged shopper could play games, check Facebook, movie times or simply browse. Gap 1969 created a feeling of well-being and comfort for the shopper, and for the unengaged shopper a positive brand experience.

FIGURE 18.3 These two waiting men offer an opportunity to retail stores

SOURCE: Photo courtesy of Teri Sporato

Always-on 'shop now' windows

Shop windows can integrate offline with online seamlessly. Shop windows can offer real browsers an engaging 'buy now' moment even when the shop is closed by connecting the shop window display with a mobile app, QR code or other AR approaches (see p 312).

3D street images through shop windows

Reebok has developed 3D images that can be projected through shop windows and into the street. Using 'mirror technology' the image literally hangs in space in front of pedestrians. Pedestrians will be bumping into lots of 3D images as soon as production costs fall.

O2 and House Of Fraser: Retailing, wifi and geo-targeting

'Retailers that offer free wifi have an opportunity to collect data, build lists, highlight the retailer's own in-store app and geo target messages to users whenever they are in the area. For example O2, has been working with House of Fraser stores across the UK to offer its customers free O2 wifi. As well as giving customers the benefits of good internet access, this clearly presents geo-targeting opportunities, including pointing wifi users to House of Fraser's own department store app to showcase deals, offers and planned in-store activities.'

Gray (2013)

See Chapter 12 for more on geo-targeting.

Alternatives to high street and shopping mall locations

Non-high street retail venues

Are some brands strong enough and bold enough to create their own stores in unexpected locations and unusual environments? Red Bull is one such brand. Consider the Red Bull aircraft hangar

FIGURE 18.4 Some brands, such as Red Bull, are strong enough to create their own stores in a variety of locations, including airports

called Hangar 7. This is a unique building in Salzburg, Austria hosting a collection of historical airplanes, helicopters and Formula One racing cars, and serving as home for the Flying Bulls, a private aircraft fleet stationed in Salzburg. Hangar 7 is owned by Red Bull founder Dietrich Mateschitz. It houses the Michelin starred restaurant Ikarus, two bars, a lounge, art exhibitions (current and previous), The Flying Bulls (aircraft, pilots, airshows and upcoming events) and a shop, which is what we are interested in from a merchandising and POS perspective.

Illuminated train platforms

We've seen some developments in Korea where virtual stores are created at train stations so that commuters can scan shelves and buy with their mobile phones, so that the delivery awaits them as they arrive home from work.

Retailer empathy required from brands

Skilful supplier merchandising requires an ability to empathize with both the customer and the retailer/wholesaler (distributor). Understanding customers is one thing. Understanding distributors and their perspectives, goals, strategies and tactics is another. It is easy to grasp the importance of maintaining the theme of an advertising campaign inside a store with carefully designed point-of-sale displays. It is not so easy to understand when, why and how a retailer will allow its space to be used for such in-store promotions and display, ie what its merchandising policies are and how to operate within that framework.

This '**distributor empathy**' helps suppliers to make their product or service (and the relevant marketing communications) fit in with the retailer's plans. The retailer relationship is even more important in today's UK retail market, since market power has moved from the manufacturer into the hands of a few major retail chains. It is therefore necessary to understand the various distributor strategies and their approach to merchandising techniques.

Some retailers do not enter into any merchandising arrangements with suppliers, as the retailers prefer to control all aspects of product presentation centrally to ensure commonality and consistency in all their stores. This is managed by carefully supervised store personnel and/or a roving display management and merchandising team. This does not mean that the supplier can have no involvement in the merchandising. Many stores encourage proactive contributions from their suppliers. Some suppliers gain permission to use their own display teams to ensure that their particular products or services have optimum display on their allocated shelf at all times.

Retail strategy

Every retailer has its own retailing strategy, which exploits its source of competitive advantage (eg exclusive products, lower prices, location or customer service). A department store exploits location, its quality of service and its range of products. A small independent grocery cannot compete on product range or price but can compete on its convenient location, opening hours and its personal service, friendly relationship and rapport. A takeaway restaurant may promote its unique home-delivery service (perhaps drones for a period of time). Competitive advantage is relative to competitors' unique selling propositions and customer needs. A constant monitoring of the uncontrollable variables that affect markets reveals how competitive advantage can emerge or erode over relatively short periods of time. Strategies can change. Merchandising strategies are also affected by corporate cultures. For example, some distributors and retailers are more profit orientated than turnover orientated. This, in turn, affects their pricing, promotion and merchandising strategies and policies.

The more common low-tech merchandising tools are now summarized and discussed under six key headings:

- store image (external and internal);
- store layout (customer traffic flows);
- merchandise ranges;
- colour blocking;
- point-of-sale displays and retail sales promotions;
- sounds, scents and mindshare.

Store image

The human eye is more sensitive than is sometimes imagined. Clues about a shop are absorbed, often sometimes without our knowing it. Psychologists call these 'cue patterns'. They help shoppers to decide what kind of a shop it is before actually entering (if entering at all). The store's exterior offers an opportunity to communicate with customers, to invite them into the store or to reinforce a desired corporate image.

Inside the shop, the concept of the 'retail theatre' becomes evident. It has been suggested that a retail design concept lasts only three to five years, hence the need for the adaptable retail theatre that allows the store's interior layout and design to be changed easily. It is worth remembering that products, service and store design all contribute towards the overall store image, but if a customer has no prior experience of a particular store, or any word-of-mouth reference from peers, then the decision to enter or not to enter may be made solely from the store's visual image. The store's exterior is a bundle of cues. Even the psychological barrier or obstacle, the door, should be removed or minimized wherever possible, thereby facilitating an even easier store entry.

Online store/website aesthetics

Aesthetics = graphics + colour + style + layout + typography

Effective website design includes both form and function. Form means the aesthetics created by the visual design and function means interaction, navigation and structure.... A site with powerful aesthetic appeal can help communicate a brand's essential values. The use of graphics, colour, style, layout and typography creates aesthetics. Together, these create a personality for the site.

Chaffey and Smith (2017)

FIGURE 18.5 A store's exterior is an opportunity to communicate with the human eye, which is more sensitive than we imagine

Store layout

Customer traffic flow can be directed around a store through detailed attention to layout. For example, 9 out of 10 people are right-handed and naturally prefer turning to the right, so most supermarkets have the primary doors on the left-hand side so the shopping is done to the right in a sort of clockwise manner. Flow-modelling time-lapse photos analyse which people go where in the store (and at what times, days, weeks or months). Further analysis reveals where the high-density areas are and whether they match the high-turnover areas. Customer movements can be predicted by model questions like 'If a customer were here (in the store), where would he or she go next?' This is important because, as a general rule, if the goods are in the wrong place they won't sell: 'out of sight, out of mind'. Primary and secondary visual points (as opposed to clutter) are used to pull the customer around the store or to 'shop the full shop' (visit every part of the store). Lighting, signage, photographs, software packages and even popular products like known-value items in a food supermarket help the customer to shop the full shop ('the more you see, the more you buy'). Hence bread and milk are often found at the back of a food store. It is estimated that, out of the 25,000 food lines on display in a superstore, only approximately 250 are essential items such as tea, coffee, bread, etc.

Merchandise ranges

Once inside the store the customer is faced with a bundle of retail cues that are never neutral. Fruit or perfume is positioned at the front of a store (supermarket and department store respectively). This helps to create images and feelings of freshness and luxury respectively. Impulse products are placed at key positions. Cross-merchandising reminds the customer of related end-use products, which are carefully positioned beside each other, eg shirts and ties

FIGURE 18.6 Detailed attention to store layout is crucial

SOURCE: Photo courtesy of James Whelan

together, or pasta and pasta sauce. The maxim '**Full shelves sell best**' is valid for retailers of fast-moving consumer goods (FMCG, also called consumer packaged goods/CPG) but not necessarily for some clothes boutiques. Although 'eye-level is buy-level', shelf positioning can reflect the current product life-cycle stage. The larger retail chains use merchandising display software packages to determine the right allocation of space to a particular product or brand. An 'optimum shelf layout' printout shows what mix and quantities of packs on a shelf maximize a store's objectives (maximize sales, minimize over- and under-stocking, maximize profitability). It presents a printout of what the recommended shelf layout would look like. Some retailers like to have their own brands placed alongside the main brands, often on the left-hand side (since the Western eye reads from left to right and therefore spots the own brand first).

Memory Mirror's AI, AR, VR, IoT and 360-degree view shows large range

FIGURE 18.7 The Memory Mirror® from Memomi Labs

The digital mirror mentioned earlier in this chapter effectively expands the range of merchandise with which a customer can engage (and try on).

Using simple body gestures, or via a companion mobile app, customers can control the mirror to see 360-degree back and side views and compare outfits side by side. Customers can change the colour of clothing with just a gesture in real time without changing clothes. Using a physics and pixel-based algorithm, Memomi provides a realistic and personalized augmented reality experience. Smart mirrors like this can transform the customer's shopping experience. The Memory Mirror also captures the 'try-on' sessions so that they can be reviewed and shared later on by the customer. See the online resources for more information.

Colour blocking

A supermarket customer scans shelves at the rate of four feet per second from a distance of eight feet away. Packaging therefore has to work very hard to attract the customer's eye. Retailers and packaging designers sometimes use colour blocking to attract attention by placing similarly coloured items close to each other to create a stronger shelf presence. Colour blocking can also link colours to product-use associations; for example blue, green and white can be associated with stimulating and refreshing surf. This in turn might be built into the shower gel section.

Point-of-sale displays and retail sales promotions

This includes displays, sampling points, dump displays and so on. Many retailers will not allow

FIGURE 18.8 Working very hard to attract the customer's eye

suppliers this free space, since every square foot of retail generates a certain amount of revenue. In the appropriate store space, a retailer may allow the supplier the privilege of using extra space. Prime selling space can be bought by suppliers. A product's sales can be boosted depending on its location and shelf positioning. In-store sales promotion can tie in with advertising, cooperative advertising, publicity and perhaps even trade discounts and rebates. It should be designed to boost sales without creating any conflict with overall store image. Balance, proportion, lighting, colour and display units should be used to create the optimum impact on a consistent basis (perhaps across many hundreds of stores). Once the store grants permission, field marketing agencies can then provide merchandising teams to maintain proper POS displays or shelf facings.

Virtual pints of Guinness in Tesco stores

'To introduce its latest line of beers – West Indies Porter, Hop House 13 Lager and Guinness Draft – Guinness is exploring virtual pint experiences in Tesco stores. Rather than simply throw up a rickety tasting booth under the harsh glare of strip lights and the tannoy cacophony of your typical Tesco supermarket, Guinness has instead crafted an immersive 360-degree video to transport each drinker into a world of "colours, shapes and sound" which Guinness claims is "scientifically proven" to enhance flavours. Technology was actually designed to suspend the senses and transport you to another place (Glenday, 2017). The digital transformation consultancy, R/GA, found visual and audio cues that truly enhance specific flavours in different beers. "It seemed like something that any beer drinker would love to experience. We hope shoppers appreciate Guinness beers in a new light – and maybe like a beer they wouldn't have thought to try otherwise".'

Kiefer (2017)

Dynamic design and personalization

Personalization delivers customized services through web pages and email and rich media containers. Personalization can be triggered through several dynamic variables, including: customer preferences, dates, events and locations. The jury is still out on the value of personalized web sites. It may work for some situations such as media sites, portals or complex e-tail catalogue sites. Remembering names shows respect. Recognizing customers and their preferences sows the seeds of good relationships and better business. The database is obviously vital for this.

Chaffey and Smith (2017)

Store apps combined with smart shelves will facilitate an even more personalized in-store offer.

Sounds, scents and mindshare

In-store sound effects can be used to make announcements (for example to direct shoppers' attention to a special offer), to add atmosphere (crowd applause in sports shop video walls), to relax the buyer or to stimulate the buyer to move faster (varying the types of music) and so on. Some POS tools engage customers in a dialogue by asking questions.

Scents are also used inside a store to change shoppers' moods and buying behaviour. The Monell Chemical Senses Center in Philadelphia has found its pilot projects highlight how the use of smell affects sales. For example, a fruity floral scent caused casual shoppers at a jewellery store to linger longer. An individual's brainwaves and moods (eg relaxed and trusting) can be changed by extremely low levels of certain scents. In the UK, one home furnishings retailer uses a bakery and café to entice customers into the store to buy non-food-related products such as clothing and lighting.

In supermarkets it is interesting to note how odours are carefully managed; the smell from the fish counter will not be as strong as the wafting smell of freshly baked bread at the bread counter. London-based DigiScents can create a particular atmosphere in a retail store or evoke associations in the customers' minds through a variety of dispersion techniques, from central ventilation systems to hand-held sprays, liquids, granules, gels or powder (or even pressure-sensitive micro-encapsulated strips). All of these can help to produce specific moods or simply neutralize unpleasant odours. Effectively they create an 'aromatic logo' by impregnating a product or a service environment or just corporate literature with an aroma.

Finally, 'mindshare' (discussed in Chapter 11) combined with merchandising techniques provides an extremely potent communications package as the store's sales staff, space and display promote a particular supplier's goods.

Whispering windows

'Sound is projected through the shop windows so everyone on the street outside can hear what is being played from the Smart TVs on display inside the store windows. "After installing whispering windows into our storefront, the number of people who stopped to view our window displays increased by nearly 50 per cent", said Kevin Scully, the visual merchandising manager of the company's Peter Jones store in Sloane Square, west London, where testing has been carried out on the system since June. The technology originated from sonar work developed for the US Navy and is being applied for John Lewis by Newlands Scientific, a spin-off company from Hull University. It effectively turns a shop window into a giant speaker, using vibrations through a "bug" attached to the window to project sound. So far, John Lewis has used the device to project the sound of music playing on DVD players and high-end plasma television sets in its store window – although the developers boast that it can also be used to make dummies speak. The whispering window is able to monitor the level of external street noise and set its sound output just above the ambient level.'

Adams (2013)

Measuring merchandising effectiveness

Smart shelves will record everything including what is being picked up, looked at and returned to the shelf, as well as what is taken away in the basket. Equally, smart shelves can test pricing and '2 for 1' offers at different times of day and different days in the week. The emergence of check-out-free supermarkets means that the old bar code scanner technology is rapidly approaching the end of its lifecycle.

Bar codes have traditionally instantaneously recorded what is being sold and measure the effect of allowing a product more shelf space, a different shelf location, special displays and so on. Electronic point-of-sale (EPOS) scanners could also measure sales responses to new advertising campaigns and price changes, as well as providing operational stock control data to central warehouses.

Whether smart shelves or EPOS, suppliers and distributors work closely together and become strategic partners with some suppliers given access to a selection of EPOS/smart shelf data that measure sales results, store by store around the country, on a daily, weekly or even hourly basis.

This is similar to best practice web management, where the marketing team studies the analytics to see if there is any unusually busy activity on any particular product or service. Anything with a significant uplift in visits or sales can be highlighted on the home page to leverage the emerging popularity of the product or service. This gives the particular item an even bigger lift – until the next emerging popular item is identified and highlighted on the home page. Finding the most profitable mix of offers on the home page is similar to finding the most profitable mix of offers at key locations in-store. A constant process of analysis and improvement yields bigger and better results.

The checkout-free store

'As shoppers walk around the store, they will scan the items they wish to buy, pay using an app and then scan a QR code to confirm they have paid. The store has been remodeled for the new technology, with its checkout area and tills removed. The pilot will last for three months. A helpdesk has been installed to support shoppers who want to pay with cash or cards. Sainsbury's said that 82 per cent of transactions at the shop were cashless.'

Frangoul (2019)

Change is constant, and nowhere more explicit than in merchandising, both offline and online – if you look carefully.

CASE STUDY Campbell's soup: Where packaging and point-of-sale form a foundation for an integrated campaign

FIGURE 18.9 Campbell's limited edition cans of soup

© The Andy Warhol Foundation for the Visual Arts, Inc./Artists Rights Society (ARS), New York and DACS, London

Situation

Campbell's Soup decided it was time to introduce its products to a wider market.

Objectives

- To build awareness for Campbell's new range of condensed tomato soup;
- to drive sales and increase household penetration;
- to support a retail listings drive.

Strategy

Create a limited edition Campbell's Condensed Tomato Soup featuring labels derived from original Andy Warhol artwork. Integrate unique Warhol-style packaging with point of sale, and sales promotions generating UGC content via the website supported by the PR campaign.

Unique POS creation

To encourage word of mouth and social media buzz once the product hit the shelves, renowned artist Stuart Murdoch was commissioned to create an exclusive two-metre art installation, built using over 2,000 cans, with both the original and the limited edition range. The use of the iconic red and white cans provided a platform of recognition for consumers, raised awareness of the new limited edition range and ensured both press and the public fully appreciated the relationship between the original Campbell's soup can design, which many have an emotional association with, and the new limited edition cans.

The installation featured a well-known image of Andy Warhol on the front, made out of Plexiglass, framed by the brightly coloured new limited edition cans, raising visual awareness of the brand new range.

The installation was positioned in London's renowned Leadenhall Market for a closed photo call. National newspapers and news wires attended.

PR

In the months leading up to the launch, Campbell's targeted food, art, lifestyle and media news desks with details of the launch. Additionally, the team approached key media and opinion formers through an intensive sampling campaign, also offering product for photo shoots. On the day of the photo call, samples were delivered to selected radio DJs and TV shows, resulting in coverage appearing on *The Wright Stuff* and *This Morning*, and Phillip Schofield tweeting about his love of the cans from both his personal and food-focused accounts.

Website

Working closely with the Andy Warhol Foundation for the Visual Arts in New York, Campbell's PR Agency, Wild Card, 'Warholized' the classic Campbell's website, redesigning the entire site to reflect classic Warhol styling.

FIGURE 18.10 The limited edition cans were eye-catching

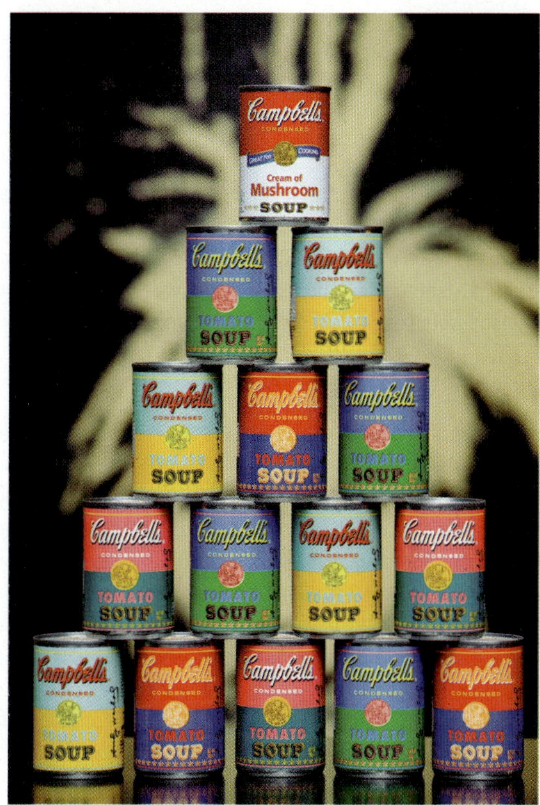

FIGURE 18.11 Campbell's two-metre art installation offered selfie opportunities

User-generated content

A 'Warholizer' tool was built enabling visitors to upload images and transform themselves into works of art. Wild Card supported this through social media channels by designing a Facebook tab on the Campbell's page, encouraging fans to 'Warholize' their profile images.

Sales promotion

The 'fifteen minutes of fame' competition on the website encouraged fans to submit appetizing recipes that include Campbell's soup, raising awareness of its benefits in many popular dishes. The competition was supported through Campbell's social media channels and sold across the digital landscape through bloggers and influencers. The winning recipe was professionally photographed and featured on the Campbell's website.

POS and UGC

Post-launch, the installation travelled to three key regional Tesco stores in Watford, Coventry and Purley. The installation was situated at the front of store, engaging and educating consumers about the new limited edition range and providing a further photo opportunity for them (creating Campbell's-branded user-generated content). A team on site issued campaign collateral and money-off coupons and invited consumers to 'Warholize' themselves using iPads.

Control/results

Over 80 pieces of branded coverage have appeared to date, offering over 289,726,245 people the chance to view.

FIGURE 18.12 Campbell's 'Warholized' their website

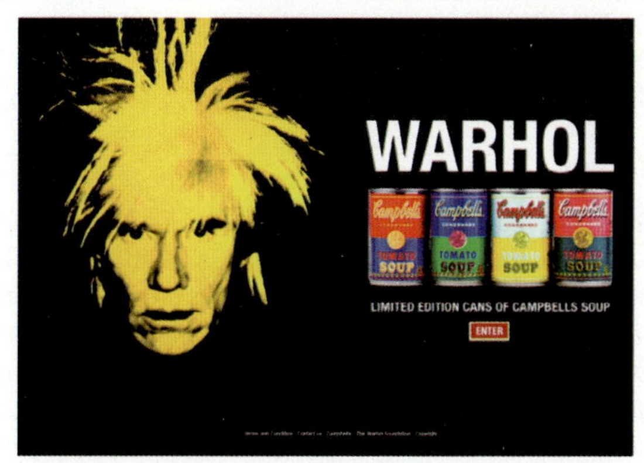

CASE STUDY Thomson Tours

This case study demonstrates how vital merchandising is and, how a field marketing agency manages the whole operation.

Situation

Major travel operator Thomson Tours enjoys a dominant market share and offers a wide range of long- and short-haul holidays to prospective customers via the travel agent in the competitive, and currently economically vulnerable, travel sector. 'Racking' (the display of a brochure in travel agents) is crucial to the success of all tour operators. Holidays are rarely booked without a comparison of the product offering from several competitors. Over 75 per cent of holidays are booked from a brochure that has been picked up and read. Few consumers ask counter staff for a brochure. It is therefore essential to ensure that the 30 different types of Thomson brochures are positioned in the right store, on the right shelf, at the right time of year. Stock of replacement supplies has to be ready so that the appropriate brochure is available at the point-of-sale at the right time. The several thousand travel agents mean that this is too big a requirement to be handled by Thomson's in-house marketing and sales team. Three thousand nominated UK travel agencies were targeted.

Objective

To ensure that the right brochures are available to the 3,000 nominated travel agents at all times.

Strategy

A comprehensive brochure management and merchandising support programme was developed and contracted out to the field marketing agency.

Tactics

Stamping, racking and ordering brochures as required and where stocks allow. This includes use of BOBCAT – a computerized brochure-ordering system based on Psion technology developed by Thomson with CPM Field Marketing. The system allows the merchandiser to transmit daily via a handheld computer to the brochure distribution house, thereby ensuring a speedy, accurate and effective stock control and delivery system.

Carrying out short sales presentations, highlighting key selling points to counter staff.

Action

Supporting brochure launches with additional tactical activity during key periods. Blitz operations such as these involve the team making 3,000 calls in two days, with the final results presented to Thomson three weeks later. Three thousand agents are visited, normally every two weeks.

Control

Thomson previously sent off batches of brochures to travel agents without really knowing which agents were running out, which agents placed them on which shelves, and which agents threw them in a pile in the store room. The new merchandising system gives online data, which reduce wastage, as the team ensures the right brochures are on the right shelf at the right time. This has helped to increase sales by ensuring that the brochures are available at all the targeted agents. At the same time it has helped to reduce costs incurred by inappropriate print runs, unnecessary deliveries, etc.

3Ms

- **Men/women:** CPM allocated a team of 65 field staff, eight supervisors and one account manager to the ongoing field marketing activity. A team of 150 merchandisers and eight supervisors support blitz operations at key times such as brochure launches. Both teams are headed by a national field manager who reports to Thomson's marketing department.
- **Money:** Comprehensive field marketing activities range from £50,000 to £1,000,000 annually, depending on the size and scope of the operation.
- **Minutes:** All field marketing staff attend a fortnightly half-day briefing. This is supplemented by six-monthly one-day sales conferences where major briefings and reviews are presented. The normal call cycle, which covers every one of the 3,000 travel agents, is two weeks. This means that every targeted travel agent gets visited and updated once a fortnight. Alternatively, a faster blitz can be completed within two days by using the extra 150 merchandisers.

CASE STUDY Useful shopping apps can help

Situation/problem

The target consumer (brand-loyal female grocery shopper) is overwhelmed with the grocery shopping task and meal planning. Market research customer insights reveal customer issues and concerns: busy lives, time, managing kids, (food) waste and crowded stores.

Objective

Help customers by finding a solution to address their concerns and consequently boost sales and brand loyalty.

Strategy

Create an innovative grocery shopping experience and provide a helping hand to the consumer, while utilizing the CRM and branded promotions (and create consumer engagement). Basically the app helps the customer manage their busy life.

Tactic

Design a mobile grocery shopping application that gives the consumer the ability to plan weekly shopping, plan meals, get recipes, have ingredients added to the shopping list, and provide the consumer with brand coupons and meal suggestions.

FIGURE 18.13 Shoppers' considerations for grocery shopping time

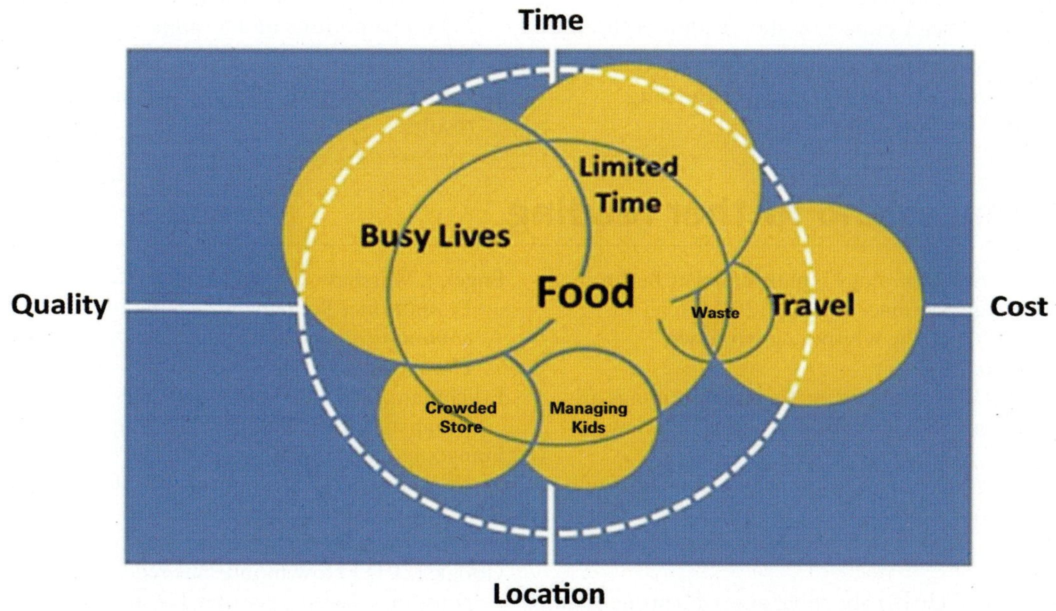

Advantages and disadvantages

Here are some of the advantages and disadvantages to consider when deciding whether to increase or reduce this communications tool.

Advantages

Merchandising and point-of-sale are present at the point a customer makes a decision to buy, the very last opportunity to communicate with a customer before the decision is made. The message can be controlled, and it can range from ensuring customers are aware of the brand through to encouraging them to buy now. Special offers and sales promotions can be highlighted.

Disadvantages

Retail space is premium, and brands compete to get this space. It is therefore limited and expensive to secure. It is also expensive to create, deliver and install point-of-sale materials into the retail trade. Sales teams have to work hard and also try to motivate the busy retailer. Reverse logistics can be incurred at the end of a promotion if the POS has to be removed. Also the lead time has to include the retailer's time horizons as well as the time required to produce, deliver and install any POS.

Key points from Chapter 18

- Merchandising techniques not only offer a last chance to communicate with the buyer, but they can have a major impact on the customer's choice.
- Manufacturers need to empathize with their distributors' strategies and merchandising policies.
- Retail strategies incorporate store image, store layout, merchandise ranges, colour blocking, POS, promotions and a range of miscellaneous items.
- Constant analysis and improvement boost results.

References and further reading

Ad Age (2014) Technology is showcased at Berlin marketing conference, *Ad Age*, 20 March

Adams, R (2013) The whispering windows, *Guardian*, 8 August

Baker, L (2018) How to increase search rankings and conversions with customer ratings and reviews, *Forbes*, 5 March

Bandoim, L (2018) How smart shelf technology will change your supermarket, *Forbes*, 23 December

Bright Local (2018) Local consumer review survey, 7 December

Bryson York, E (2010) Shopping aisles at cutting edge of consumer research and tech, *Ad Age*, 15 March

Chaffey, D and Smith, PR (2017) *Digital Marketing Excellence*, 5th edn, Routledge, Abingdon

Court, D *et al* (2009) The consumer decision journey, *McKinsey Quarterly*, Q3

da Silva, M (2017) Proximity marketing: How to attract more shoppers with beacon technology, *Shopify*, 12 April

Danger, P (1968) *Using Colour to Sell*, Gower, Aldershot

Engel, J, Warshaw, M and Kinnear, T (1991) *Promotional Strategy: Managing the marketing communications process*, 7th edn, Irwin, Homewood, IL

Erlichman, J (1992) How hidden persuasion makes shoppers spend, *Guardian*, 11 August

Frangoul, A (2019) Supermarket giant Sainsbury's opens UK's first checkout-free store, *CNBC*, 30 April

Glenday, J (2017) Guinness tantalises Tesco shoppers with VR tasting experience, *The Drum*, 18 May

Google (2016) How mobile has redefined the consumer decision journey for shoppers, Think with Google, July

Gray, R (2013) Retail revolution, *Marketer*, March/April

Grey, C (2013) The most ambitious in-store retail iPad integration we've ever seen, *Fast Company Labs*

Kiefer, B (2017) How Guinness and R/GA made a VR tasting experience for all five senses, *Campaign*, 30 May

Marketing Week (2018) 2018 year in review: It's been a bad year for..., *Marketing Week*, 10 December

Neff, J (2010) This upfront, P&G may want to boost spend on Piggly Wiggly, *Ad Age*, 3 May

Oliver, B (1987) *Marketing Magazine*, 10 September

Statista (2019) Number of video gamers worldwide 2014–2021, *Statista*

Further information

British Promotional Merchandise Association (BPMA)
Fetcham Park House
Lower Road
Fetcham, Leatherhead
Surrey KT22 9HD
Tel: +44 (0)1372 371184
www.bpma.co.uk

Institute of Promotional Marketing Ltd (IPM)
Holborn Town Hall
193–197 High Holborn
London WC1V 7BD
www.theipm.org.uk

Marketing Agencies Action Group (MAAG)
82 Great Suffolk Street
London SE1 0BE
Tel: +44 (0)20 7535 3550
www.marketingagencies.org.uk

POPAI UK & Ireland Ltd (Point-of-Purchase Advertising International)
7a Lakeside Court
Maple Drive
Tungsten Park
Hinckley
Leicestershire LE10 3BH
Tel: +44 (0)1455 613651
www.popai.co.uk

19 Packaging

LEARNING OBJECTIVES

By the end of this chapter you will be able to:

- understand the three functions of packaging and the importance of packaging at the point of sale;
- explain how packaging design can create competitive advantage;
- appreciate the six design variables;
- outline the stages in the packaging design process.

Introduction

Packaging is the 'silent salesperson'. But it has many other purposes. It also presents opportunities to create competitive advantage and save money. Packaging designers work with six variables (shape, size, colour, graphics, materials and smell). Managing the packaging design process is similar in many ways to managing other marketing communications tactical tools.

The importance of packaging

Since many sales assistants have been replaced by self-service systems, packaging today often has to act as a silent salesperson, helping customers by bringing a particular brand to their attention, highlighting its USPs, giving friendly tips on usage and, ultimately, helping them to break through the misery of choice created by the large range of seemingly similar brands. The plethora of 'me-toos' (similar products and brands) and the relentless fragmentation of markets mean that pack designs have to work very hard in a hyper-competitive market.

The design of the pack can create competitive advantage by adding value, improving the product itself (eg improving the freshness or making it easier to pour or store, etc), developing stronger shelf presence, positioning a brand in a particular way, and creating or strengthening the brand's relationship with the buyer. The pack should be a 'visual magnet' that entices the customer to purchase, form a relationship and, eventually, ultimately become loyal to that particular brand.

Packaging can also be an extraordinarily effective advertising medium, particularly in terms of cost and penetration, and reach or cover of a target audience. On the shelf and in the home it continues to work, day in, day out, for 52 weeks of the year. In some ways it is a free medium.

No single element of the communications mix comes under as much environmental scrutiny as packaging. In a sense, packaging should reduce in size as oversized cartons and unnecessary layers of packaging are stripped away by environmental pressures (and some cost pressures). Good pack design also pleases the distributor and retailer by helping to make distribution, warehousing and use of shelf space more efficient. In fact, many warehouses are becoming fully automated distribution centres, demanding packs of a size that suits the warehouse handling equipment. Good pack design also saves manufacturing costs.

Falling in love with a pack

Packaging facilitates choice. Choice is rarely made on a rational basis. In fact, the consumer is faced with several thousand packs screaming 'Buy me'. A well-designed pack offers relief from the misery of choice. Ernest Dichter (1964) suggested that 'this relief may be derived through being permitted to like a product, almost to love it indiscriminately and irrationally'.

The packaging opportunity

Packaging is an area of opportunity, as some sectors have difficult to open packs, inadequate labelling and messy packets, such as boxes of tea that leak leaf dust, sugar packs that spill sugar and bottles that dribble after pouring. In a market where pack design is weak, a new design can steal the advantage. It is worth remembering that, although pack design at worst is just a recognition symbol, at best it can offer so much more. As the cost of advertising rises, product lifecycles shorten and hyper-competition intensifies, marketers need to get more from their packaging. Creative packaging can create competitive advantage. Even dull and seemingly staid pack designs can be redesigned to create a competitive, cost-effective edge (see the box 'Creative industrial packaging can also gain competitive advantage', p 579).

The three basic functions of packaging

The three basic functions of packaging are to:

- protect (and contain);
- offer convenience;
- communicate.

First and foremost, a pack must protect its contents during storage, transportation and use. Some packs have to protect the user from the contents (as in the case of children with weedkillers, medicine, chemicals, etc). Sadly, some packaging today must also protect the contents from tampering. Six people died in Chicago when Johnson & Johnson's Tylenol pain relievers were laced with cyanide. There is a market for tamper-proof packaging and tamper-evident packaging.

Second, the pack must offer convenience in pouring, squeezing, storing, stacking and consuming (in cars, in the garden, on the beach, in the home and, one day, in space). Sugar has yet to be mastered in terms of truly convenient packaging. Even a minute improvement in convenience can create competitive advantage, as demonstrated by Schlitz beer's pop-top can, which helped to boost sales from 5.7 million in 1961 to 15.1 million in 1970. On the other hand, some pack designs are so poor that they cause their own problems. In 1985 the Norwegian company Elopak had to use TV advertising to try to explain how to open Elopak cartons.

Third, the pack must communicate. Before concentrating on the communications aspects of packaging, it is worth mentioning that all three packaging functions are interdependent. The first two, protection and convenience, both communicate indirectly. For example, if the product is damaged, tarnished or stale, then a negative image is what remains, despite advertising, publicity and sales promotions that claim otherwise. Equally, if the instructions for storage or pouring are not communicated clearly, then the pack loses its protective and convenience capabilities.

Some products prioritize some functions over others. Some design solutions (or redesigned packs) cannot optimize all three functions simultaneously because of constraints such as cost or overall pack size limitations. Trade-offs, or compromises, between functions will then occur. Surprisingly, some optimum functions can be forfeited for other reasons.

The communication functions of the pack

The communication function breaks down into several different sub-functions:

- Grab the attention of the passing shopper.
- Persuade and convince the shopper to buy.
- Build brand personality and build a relationship with the buyer.
- Build loyalty with a pack that:
  - looks nicer on the table;
  - is easy to find in the garden shed or in the warehouse;
  - is distinctive and easily recognizable in a store carrying 9,000 separate items;
  - is easier to use than the competition's.
- Instruct the user about how to use the product to optimum benefit.
- Inform the user of mandatory requirements such as warnings, source of manufacture and/or ingredients (buyers tend to want more information today).

The silent salesperson

The pack is the last chance and sometimes the only opportunity to communicate with and sell to a customer. The pack is the silent salesperson. Initially it has to shout boldly to grab attention and then fade into the background and let the product benefits come forward. A well-designed pack can stop customers, invite them to have a look, pick it up and pause for a few valuable moments while they are engaged at the point-of-sale. It is here that the pack can develop a dialogue by attracting, intriguing, arousing unconscious aspirations, informing, reminding, involving, entertaining and, above all, persuading.

The pack can arouse or trigger stored images from a television advertisement that have been lying dormant in the memory bank either if the advertisement includes a 'pack shot' (close-up of the pack) or if the pack includes some of the images from the advertisement. The brand can also reflect images and aspirations. The pack can help the customer to recall those aspirations and develop associations between the aspirations and the brand. The hand lifts the pack off the shelf, allowing the customer, his or her other aspirations and the brand to move closer together.

Packs like Heinz are sometimes called **'trigger packs'**, because there is little dialogue other than the announcement of a strong, confident tone. The pack design concentrates on being recognized through its unique visual identifiers, colours, keystone, name and lettering, while heavy advertising communicates the brand values and aspirations. It is interesting to see Campbell's Soups dispense with Andy Warhol's legendary red and white livery and replace it with another aspirational soup setting (Figure 19.1). The

Campbell's graphics portray product values that are arguably less protectable from the inevitable 'me-toos' sometimes produced by the retail stores' own labels. The Heinz pack and image are unique and therefore more protectable (in terms of branding).

Having said that, Campbell's introduced a limited edition Campbell's Soups can recently and integrated the new design online and offline across several communications tools. See the full case study in Chapter 18 on merchandising.

Over-protective packaging

There is a balance between protective packaging, sales, returns and overall costs incurred. Here are three examples from James Pilditch's classic book on packaging design, *The Silent Salesman* (1973). They demonstrate how over-packaging can be identified, reduced and subsequently used to boost sales and/or profits:

> An electric light bulb company had a breakage rate so low that it prompted the question: were the bulbs over-packaged and too well protected? It subsequently reduced the grade of cardboard, and returns (of damaged bulbs) went up. The overall saving in packaging costs was greater than the increased costs of breakages and returns.

> A detergent company used stronger boxes than its competitors. The distributors were aware of this and liked the better boxes, because they were able to put them on the bottom of the pile without their collapsing. The product was hidden at the bottom instead of being at eye level, which is the optimum 'buy level'. So the box weight was reduced. The boxes started to collapse and the detergent was soon freed from the bottom of the pile. Sales soon increased.

> A London discount house was concerned over the lack of stealing. It thought, 'Maybe we make our goods too hard for people to get at', so the packs were redesigned.

FIGURE 19.1 Campbell's soup limited edition new designs: 'Everybody must have a fantasy'

SOURCE: Wildcard

Packaging needs a long-term commitment

The pack design needs to develop and change as markets constantly move away from existing products (and their packs). The pack may have to reflect changes in the customers' aspirations, incorporate demographic shifts such as an ageing population, exploit new technologically driven opportunities (such as microwaves, which require new food packaging) or simply highlight a new improvement in the product itself. There needs to be a constant review of customers and their perceptions, motivations and aspirations, and, of course, a constant review also of competitive packs. Sometimes customers just get tired of a design.

One of the problems with packaging design is that it never shows up in a normal media budget. A major redesign involving a change of shape as well as a change in graphics can cost anywhere from £25,000 to £250,000 for the design stages. The tooling cost (the machine parts that the production line needs to produce the new pack shape) will probably double the cost. Packaging design is an evolutionary rather than revolutionary process. But not all designs involve three-dimensional changes;

often it is simply a two-dimensional change of graphics. Sometimes this is so subtle (a 'design tweak') that the consumer is not even aware of the change, yet the new design will be working harder for the manufacturer. Look at the Heinz beans cans in Figure 19.2 and the subtle design tweak. Packaging design often does not sit comfortably in the marketing budget at all, but failure to get a pack right is tantamount to possibly wasting millions of pounds' worth of above-the-line advertising.

A constant design analysis looks at ways in which design can help to strengthen a brand's position. Heinz had maintained market share, but only at the expense of margin. Pack design gave it a lift. Turquoise is rarely associated with food except for Heinz. Subtle alterations were made to make the product more appealing and give it a stronger image for the future. The Heinz lettering was changed from a thin typeface to a fuller, more generous style; the keystone was broadened and a white in-line used to sharpen its impact; the lettering of 'oven' and 'with tomato sauce' was changed from turquoise to gold; and the tone of the turquoise background was enriched to create added warmth.

It is possible, as Dichter's classic 1964 book, *Handbook of Consumer Motivations*, suggests, to **'fall in love with a pack'**. It is also possible to form extremely strong trusting relationships with a pack. The relationship-enhancing pack can also help to strengthen branding and even the corporate profile of the manufacturer or distributor that controls it. The next section of this chapter suggests how.

FIGURE 19.2 Spot the difference: subtle design tweaks increase shelf presence

Would you pour a pile of white powder over your new baby?

'Would you have the confidence to pour an unknown pile of white powder over your new baby? Put the powder inside the pack called Johnson's, and emotions are immediately evoked of the caring mother–child relationship. You would certainly trust the product with your baby. You would not be willing to pay much, if anything, for the powder alone. You would be willing to pay a premium for a brand you trust and believe in.'

Lewis (1996)

Brands, packs and corporate identities

Some brands, and their packs, are inextricably linked with the corporation that owns or makes the brands (eg Heinz, Honda or BP). Others keep a lower profile with a more subtle form of corporate endorsement (like ICI's Crown Paints). Others still prefer to keep the freestanding brand or pack identity very separate from the corporation, which remains anonymously behind the scenes (eg After Eight chocolates and Nestlé). There are advantages and disadvantages to all three approaches. The corporate culture and diversity of products and markets can determine the specific approach. Packs can work in exactly the same way – linking the brand to the parent company. However, this may be restricted by the diversity of products and markets. For example, think of Esso ice cream, Lada airlines and Beecham's beer. If any of these products existed, the corporate link would not support the brand proposition; it would, arguably, detract from it.

The strengthening of the link between a company and its brands or packs can help the company by facilitating new product launches and brand stretching or brand extension (eg Heinz Weight Watchers). **It can also reinforce corporate presence** and, in turn, reassure different audiences, eg existing customers, new customers, investors and even employees. On the other hand, the link can create a design straitjacket that, as Lewis (1996) pointed out, 'inhibits the active development of sub-brands aimed at different target markets'. Since different target markets often require radically different images, these images may pull in different directions, thereby detracting from the consistency of the overall corporate identity and image. In addition, if a particular brand has a problem (such as product tampering or a faulty production batch), it is immediately associated with the parent company. This negative reflection can, if the link between brand and parent company is clearly established, affect all the other brands operating under the same corporate umbrella. As James Pilditch (1973) said, '**The pack can contribute to instant consumer recognition of the company or the brand.**' Now let us consider the other communication functions of the pack.

The designer's tools

The six variables or tools a designer can use are:

- shape;
- size;
- colour;
- graphics;
- materials;
- smell.

Shape

Some brands have such distinctive pack shapes that they are recognizable from the shape alone, eg Baileys, Mateus Rosé, Perrier and Jif Lemon. Other pack shapes communicate conscious and unconscious meanings.

Ask a group to draw the first image, abstract or otherwise, that comes into their minds when the word 'love' is mentioned. If they struggle with this, ask them to imagine they are a design consultancy whose job is to design a logo for a new political party called 'the Love Party'. After a minute ask them to do the same for 'hate'. (Close your eyes or make a doodle yourself before reading on.) Over 95 per cent of the drawings tend to conform to the same perceptions about shape. The love image usually has softer edges, curves and maybe heart shapes, while the hate image tends to have jagged edges and sharper shapes like swastikas and daggers. We may not consciously associate these meanings with shapes, but they are there. During the Second World War, US paratroopers were tested to find whether they were shape orientated or colour orientated by being shown a film of abstract shapes and patterns. The shapes moved from right to left and the colours moved from left to right. The paratroopers were then asked which way the design was moving. Shape-orientated men were supposed to be more intelligent, more stable and less emotional. The Thurstone test can be used for packaging design. It has revealed that younger children respond to colour more than form (shape), while adults, and men in particular, react more to form.

Pilditch (1973) suggested that a rectangular box created images of sharpness, neatness and cleanliness, while a round box had associations of security, plentifulness and generosity. Go into a chemist's shop and observe the different packaging shapes used for adults' and children's bubble bath. Some shapes give the product a value much greater than its contents. Shapes can also be masculine or feminine. Whisky bottles tend to be masculine in shape, while some perfume bottles are feminine.

Shape affects the protection and convenience functions in holding, pouring and storing. How a pack fits into the hand is part of the study of ergonomics. A well-designed pack fits the hand more comfortably and creates what Coca-Cola proudly calls 'in-hand embellishment' (it feels good in the hand). In 1910, part of the packaging design brief for the now-famous Coca-Cola bottle read: 'We need a new bottle – a distinctive package that will help us fight substitution... we need a bottle which a

FIGURE 19.3 This product can be recognized in the dark by feeling it

person will recognize as a Coca-Cola bottle even when he feels it in the dark. The Coca-Cola bottle should be so shaped that, even if broken, a person could tell what it was.'

False ergonomics communicate unreal values to customers. For example, dimples (for fingers to grip) are sometimes placed down the side of a bottle, when in fact the bottle is rarely held by the two dimpled sides; instead, it is held by the two flat front and back sides of the pack. The subtle impression created by these false ergonomics is one of 'This pack looks slightly better or friendlier.'

Customers do not often consciously choose one brand instead of another. Ergonomics can help to express that one brand is nicer to use than another. Real ergonomics help the user to have a more pleasant experience with the pack and therefore encourage repeat purchasing.

Some shapes reinforce product values by designing product features into the pack, as with the honeycomb effect on the base of a honey jar. The ultimate brand shape is arguably Jif Lemon's lemon-shaped pack. The Law Lords granted Reckitt & Colman exclusive rights to this shape; only Jif can use this unique get-up or shape to package lemon juice.

Can manufacturers own monopoly rights to a pack shape? The test, it seems, is 'whether the shape serves mainly to distinguish a product from its rivals and whether a competitor using the shape is seeking to mislead purchasers' (Warden, 1990). There are an infinite number of shapes. Pack shape can form a valuable property of the brand. It can become part of the brand or the brand equity, eg Red Bull's slim can with its distinctive graphics is one of the most recognized brands in the world.

Size

Some say Red Bull's smaller sized packaging reinforces its reputation regarding the concentrated strength of Red Bull. Others perceive the packaging's

FIGURE 19.4 Red Bull is one of the world's most recognizable cans

size to be 'slim, sexy, and powerful'. Size does communicate. Would you give your loved one a perfume packed in a two-litre bottle? The corollary, ie large pack communicates better quality, is true in product sectors such as breakfast cereals. Consumer perceptions about cornflakes have been found to change according to size of pack. Large cereal packs build feelings of plentiful, expansive, energy-giving food, whereas a smaller pack may make the cornflakes seem heavy, solid and no good. Size can be used to communicate in different ways. For example, a 33-centilitre bottle of premium beer cannot be fully poured into a half-pint glass. If the drinker uses a glass, he/she is forced, after filling a glass, to carry the bottle away from the bar and over to the table, where the unemptied bottle continues to work both as a badge and as an advertisement.

Different sizes are aimed at different segments, for example the family pack. Pack size can determine target markets, or is it that target markets can determine pack size? This may be similar to Ehrenberg's philosophy of marketing, which states that marketing means excluding many customers from a particular product (target marketing excludes the mass). Certain segments exclude certain sizes, as Coca-Cola discovered when it had to withdraw its two-litre bottle from the Spanish market after discovering that few Spaniards owned large fridges. If the colour were changed, would the pack then fit the fridge? Warm colours like red and yellow seem to advance or make the pack appear larger, while cold colours like blue recede and make the pack appear smaller. Although a change of colour would not have saved Coca-Cola's large bottle in Spain, colour does communicate in many different ways.

Colour

Colour communicates. Albert Kner, former design chief of the Container Corporation of America, said 'Colour is the quickest path to the emotions'. Words have to be translated into images in the mind. These images, in turn, have to be assembled, organized and categorized to give them meaning. This may be followed by an emotional response, which may subsequently trigger a physical response. Colour skips all this and goes straight into the emotions, often creating a physiological response. Colour is physical. Russia's Pedagogical Institute has found that most people can feel colours. Eyeless sight or 'biointroscopy' suggests that all one's skin has seeing power. Red, green and dark blue have been found to be sticky. This may have something to do with electromagnetic fields. There have been claims that the Chinese can teach children to see with their elbows. Many years ago the US Color Research Institute found that the colour of walls in an office could make people feel sleepy, excited or healthy. More recently, a British police force has experimented with pink cells for prisoners. Red increased blood pressure and pulse, while blue had the opposite effect.

The Lüscher colour test uses colour cards to analyse the reader's psychological, and specifically emotional, state. Green is 'the colour of the environment in Europe and a significant colour for all Muslims. It has religious significance in Malaysia and is popular in Mexico as a national colour' (Ronay, 2005).

Colour codes

Some product sectors, particularly food, appear to have colour codes. For example, within the carbonated drinks sector, red is cola and yellow is tonic. Freezer meat is red, fish is blue and anything low-calorie or diet is white. Pilditch (1973) suggested that in the wake of health scares many of the world's cigarette packs now emphasize white: 'They hope white is associated with cleanliness and purity.'

Colours have meaning for people. Many people associate colours with images, eg 'garden fresh', 'mountain cool' or 'rugged manliness'. There was a group of people for whom 7UP's green bottle had almost medicinal links and therapeutic overtones: 'the thing to take when you had the flu and the doctor told you to take a lot of liquid'. Whether it is an annual report, a reception area, some sales literature or a piece of packaging, colour communicates. This applies to products and services in both consumer and industrial markets.

Colour affects perception. This is probably best demonstrated by Ernest Dichter's research (1964) into how packaging colour affects people's perceptions of taste. Unknown to the respondent, the same coffee was put into four cups. One of four different-coloured coffee cans was placed beside each cup. Respondents were then asked to match the statements below with each cup tasted. The research revealed strong perceptions linked with specific colours:

- dark brown can: 73 per cent 'Too strong aroma or flavour';
- red can: 84 per cent 'Richer flavour or aroma';
- blue can: 79 per cent 'Milder flavour or aroma';
- yellow can: 87 per cent 'Too weak flavour or aroma'.

More recent research into packaging colour and perceptions of washing machine powder provided interesting results. The same powder was put into three different-coloured packs. The respondents tried them on delicate clothing for a few weeks and were then asked which was best for delicate clothing. Respondents thought the performance (of the same powder) was vastly different. Statements below demonstrate the striking finding:

- largely yellow pack: 'too strong', 'ruined clothes';
- largely blue pack: 'did not work', 'clothes were dirty looking';
- blue and yellow pack: 'fine', 'wonderful'.

This differs from previous US research reported by Terrell Williams (1982) that tested identical washing powders in three different-coloured boxes; yellow, blue and red. The yellow detergent was 'mild, too mild really'. The blue detergent was 'a good all-round laundry product'. The red detergent was 'good for stains and the like'.

Colours may not be international, since colours have different meanings in different cultures. For example, white is life, purity and diet in the UK, but it means death in Japan. Softer pastel colours and brighter colours are perceived differently around the world. In China, bright colours symbolize quality. Scott entered the Taiwan market with its US blend of pastel-coloured toilet tissues; the launch flopped. Sales took off when it changed the colours to bright red, yellow and gold. Can you imagine UK toilets with bright red toilet paper? Pilditch (1973) remarked, 'Not only do simpler folk like stronger colours, but people who live under bright sun have different values from those whose outlook is dimmed, say, by England's "leaden" skies. Think of this when designing packs to sell to Italian wine-growers, or Glaswegian dockers.' This is important, because cross-border packaging may become more common than cross-border advertising.

The cost of colour

Four colours obviously cost more to print than two colours. Can one be economic with the use of colour, the number of colours and the kind of inks? Is single colour too downmarket? Are four colours really needed? Has anyone tested a change in colours?

Graphics

Graphics communicate on different levels. The two-dimensional design on a label can help to create and protect individuality and uniqueness, reinforce a brand name or image, help to reposition, increase shelf presence, etc. The use of graphics is arguably the easiest of the designer's tools to analyse, as marketing managers are reasonably design literate as far as graphics are concerned. A naked body on the label of a bottle of beer will attract attention. However, not every brand manager wants this kind of attention. Other images can be used to make a pack stand out from the crowd. In terms of branding, the visual image should be distinctive and should make the pack immediately recognizable. Even an ordinary tin box can become a valued item once some attractive graphics have been applied. **Graphics add value by adding aesthetic quality.**

This creates 'stay-after value', which allows the branding to keep working inside the home, sometimes for many years, sometimes for generations. Graphics are sometimes used as a kind of sales promotion by becoming a limited edition or collector's item, as in the case of the Guinness centenary Christmas label. Graphics can add value by offering, for example: additional features such as games (eg a box of matches with matchstick puzzles); a room-enhancing, stimulating plaything rather than just a dull necessity (baby lotion with a colourful children's toy); or quality associations with images of far-off places (coffee with palm trees).

Good graphics can create a mood or trigger lifestyle aspirations that reflect the often latent desires of the target market, for example a shampoo label showing an English country scene for one target market and a rugged desert for another aspiring lifestyle segment.

FIGURE 19.5 The LOVI graphics are simple yet aesthetically pleasing

Attention to detail combined with an understanding of the cues and symbols that are relevant to a particular target market allow the designer to play with the unconscious meaning of symbols and images. In the case of a cooking fat, according to the psychologists, the positioning of a wooden spoon made it 'possible for the housewife to rehearse the use of the product while it was still on the shelf'. Pilditch (1973) explained that 'the spoon also served to inject the product with some of the reliability of grandmother's honest-to-goodness, my doesn't that smell good, old-fashioned kitchen'. In a separate piece of research the analysts turned to the number and layout of biscuits on a package. A picture showing biscuits scattered all over created psychological discomfort, or dissonance, because it suggested gaiety, disorganization, permissiveness and irresponsibility ('never know how many were eaten by the kids'). A different picture showing the biscuits in a neat line triggered associations with orderliness, parsimony, and fear of disrupting the line by taking a biscuit, which again resulted in unconscious psychological tension or discomfort. The third image of just a few biscuits on a plate cut out the chaos and the irresponsibility and invited the viewer to feel free to take a biscuit. The number of biscuits was, however, limited to demonstrate authority and control.

Graphics affect taste

In the same way as colour, graphics also affect taste perceptions. In fact, packaging designers can test different label graphics by asking focus groups or consumer panels to give their opinions on the taste of (unknown to them) the same product. The more elegant bottle will tend to have a refined taste, the macho label might have a stronger flavour, etc.

Graphics integrate with other packaging variables to create effective communications. Lewis (1996) suggested that 'if the form [shape and size of the pack] makes the statement then the graphics should step back'. The Lewis Moberly consultancy worked on Yves Rocher aromatherapy oils and created a tactile experience prompted by graphics 'by running the typography [letters] right round the bottle to encourage the viewer to turn it, touch it and begin to experience the product through the pack'.

Many years ago Coca-Cola discovered that its dynamic white contour curve (the flowing white ribbon underlining the Coca-Cola and Coke logo) reminded observers of the famous profile of the hobble-skirted contour bottle.

The graphics should be developed only after some other key questions have been asked. These include: Does the pack use the logo effectively? Can the graphics make space for future on-pack promotions? Do the graphics leave space for international copy translation (usually requires more space than English)? Will the graphics lend themselves or at least link with point-of-sale materials? Are the graphic images unique and protectable, or can someone else design something similar, leaving customers confused and unaware of their own brand-switching decision?

FIGURE 19.6 Bar codes provide useful marketing information

0102021207

5 021376 002875 >

The other pack functions are also helped by good graphics; a blend of visual and verbal instructions can make a product and pack much easier to use and store (convenience and protection).

Graphics can also indicate production processes or corporate caring values such as 'recycled' or 'free from animal testing'. There is some confusion currently because of the lack of central agreement on appropriate logos.

Finally, bar codes linked with electronic point-of-sale (EPOS) scanners at retail store checkouts help internal communications between the retailer and supplier by updating stock levels, reorder information and other sales analysis (eg by product, by store, by day, etc).

Materials

Materials communicate. Certain materials, like glass or metal, have an intrinsic value. Glass still seems to be associated with higher quality. Many wine drinkers would be suspicious of a supposedly top-quality wine if it were presented to them in a plastic bottle. Nevertheless, the packaging of wine has gone through the most radical of shake-ups. Forty years ago, if someone had forecast that people would soon be drinking wine out of cardboard boxes it is likely that the comment would have been taken as an insult – with hints of socially unacceptable behaviour. Yet during the 1990s the wine box became arguably packaging's greatest innovation, with a nation happily drinking from cardboard boxes.

The materials used in packaging affect perceptions of product quality. A good example of this was discovered in the United States, where, ironically, the better product was perceived to be in the more difficult-to-open package. Crisps of equal freshness were packaged in wax paper bags and polyvinyl bags. The crisps in the polyvinyl bag were perceived (by 87 per cent) to be 'superior in taste and freshness' despite being more difficult to open.

Guinness found that packaging materials, and tins in particular, affected taste perceptions. There were comments like 'too gassy, it taints the flavour and it tastes of tin' (Nicholas, 1991). Pre-launch research of the Guinness draught can showed that in blind taste tests equal numbers preferred the pure draught Guinness and canned draught Guinness. Subsequent sight tests (showing the source, ie can or tap) revealed the hidden associations of tin cans: there was a 70:30 split in favour of the draught Guinness. Pretty Polly used tin as an innovative piece of packaging for its nylon tights.

Certain overseas markets have different packaging material expectations from what is considered to be the norm in the UK. For example, in Europe, meats, fruit, vegetables, pet foods and fruit juices are packed in glass. This means that if UK manufacturers want to enter these markets they will have to work with a new packaging medium, which may well be glass. In the UK, tin has an emotional quality. It can become even more emotional when mixed with shape and colour, eg a red, heart-shaped tin box of chocolates for St Valentine's Day.

Some packaging materials have to work very hard. For example, microwave packs have to be able to protect and store the food at temperatures below zero and then have to offer convenience cooking by being able to be put into the microwave at very high temperatures. Some packs are then used to eat out of. Self-heating and self-cooling cans offer new levels of convenience. Apart from the convenience and communications implications of packaging materials, the final materials choice is integrated with a host of other factors such as optimum size, weight, strength, cost and filling speed, together with other features such as colour, closure, secondary packaging, shelf life, tactile characteristics and shelf impact.

Finally, material is the variable that is affected directly by environmental pressure groups. New legislation is putting pressure on manufacturers and retailers to use more environmentally friendly packaging. In the US, garbologists now probe landfill sites to determine the state of decay of various materials. In Europe, Germany leads the way in environmental legislation. A company's overseas growth may be stifled by packaging and materials that do not meet legislative criteria. Despite the logistical nightmare, the refillable pack is here to stay. The environmental factor has a direct impact on packaging and, in particular, on packaging materials. Warner-Lambert is developing a new disposable plastic made almost entirely out of biodegradable starch derived from potatoes, corn, rice and wheat.

We made plastic. We depend on it. Now we're drowning in it.

The miracle material has made modern life possible. But more than 40 percent of it is used just once, and it's choking our waterways.

Parker (2018)

Smell

Smells can change shopping behaviour. In a Philadelphia jewellery store some years ago, casual shoppers lingered longer than usual because, claims the Monell Chemical Sense Center, scents change shoppers' moods. In this particular case it was a fruity floral scent. Mood-changing odours change people's brain patterns. The *Chicago Tribune* reported the renowned neurological director of the Smell and Taste Treatment and Research Foundation in Chicago, Dr Alan Hursch, as saying, 'Eventually we will be able to influence in a much more powerful way. By making people more relaxed or more trusting you could sell them more.' Scented packaging is becoming more popular.

Creative industrial packaging can also gain competitive advantage

The design resource is not exclusively reserved for FMCG goods. There is always room for design, creativity and innovation in industrial markets. Electric cable manufacturer BICC used pack design to stand out from the competition in the commodity cable market and to offer USPs to a traditionally conservative market. It moved from the traditional reel of cable to a newly designed box. This helped the electrical wholesaler by making stacking, storage and identifying (holes in the pack allowed the different colours of cable to be seen) a lot easier. The pack, however, was not allowed to look too upmarket, as the conservative buyers assumed it would be more expensive. Before phasing out the old cable packs (reels), they were used to advertise the imminent arrival of the new packs – the box of cable.

The packaging design process

Why redesign?

'If it ain't broke, don't fix it.' Perhaps, but some pack designs can become tired or dated, or the market simply moves away, making the pack's current position a liability. On the other hand, valuable brand equities or properties such as names and logos are assets worth maintaining. They may also need 'tweaking' from time to time, but rarely need to be disposed of. Perhaps a creative brand manager and a professional printer can produce an updated or even new graphic design for a pack. Jan Hall, formerly of Coley Porter Bell, says this would be like 'putting together the Pope and a paint company to paint the Sistine Chapel'. The designer's interest (or input) in the pack increases progressively during the course of the product's lifecycle (see Figure 19.7). In other words, the pack design has an increasingly important role as competition becomes more intense.

A packaging design brief

The SOS + 3Ms can be used as a checklist when writing a design brief, which can be modified for packaging.

Situation/background

- Company (history, production facilities).
- Product (range, features and benefits, material properties, eg liquids, gases, chemicals).
- Market (size, growth, competitive structure, positioning, specific requirements such as pallet configuration).
- Target markets: segments, targets, decision-making units – particularly tricky with gift products, eg at whom do you target the design, the giver or the receiver?
- Reason for design (eg pressure from retailers' own labels).
- Design constraints, eg size, shapes, colours, images or materials.
- Restrictions: technical, legislative and corporate restrictions on materials, warnings or warranties, and logos respectively.
- Brand factors and personality, key design elements.
- Merchandising display opportunities.

Objectives

What packaging functions are prioritized (protection, convenience or communication)? If communication, state the objectives specifically; repositioning from what to what? Or is the new pack design primarily aimed at shouting louder or creating a stronger shelf presence, etc?

Strategy

How does the pack fit in with the rest of the communications mix (the communications objectives and mix)? The brief may also state whether the pack design is a low-risk design project (new unit load, new material, temporary sales promotion, secondary panel changes, new ingredients, etc) or a high-risk design project (new name, new colour, new image, new logo, new shape, etc).

Tactics

Details are not always required here.

Men/women

These are the contact names for technical discussions (eg the production manager) and for marketing discussions. Clarify who makes the key decisions (who signs off or approves artwork, etc) and who can provide answers to miscellaneous questions.

FIGURE 19.7 How design attention shifts between content and presentation as a product progresses through its lifecycle

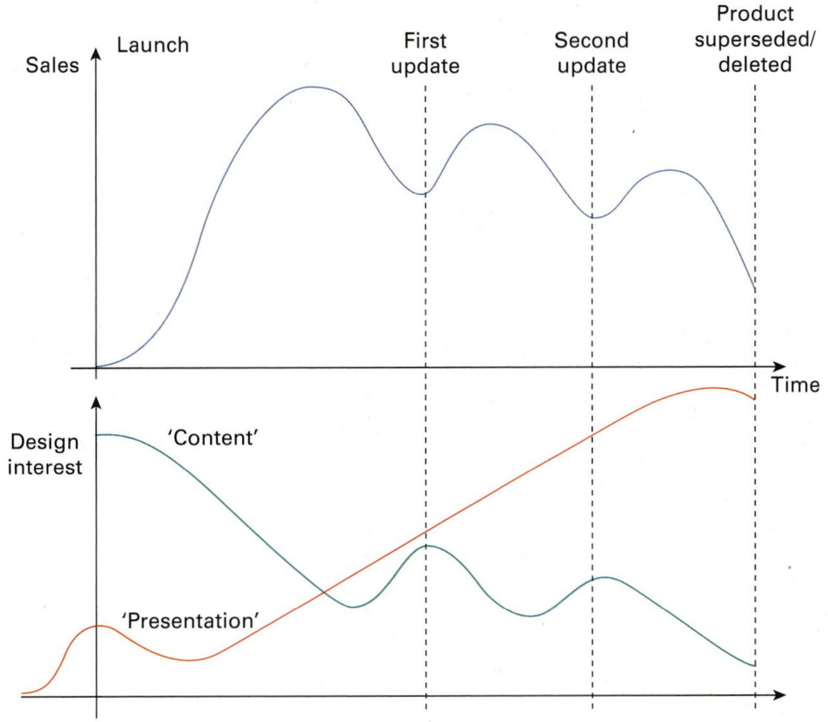

Provide the names of any other agencies that may be working on other marketing communications aspects, such as advertising and sales promotion.

Money

Money means the design fee, rejection fee (some designers charge a rejection fee for presenting ideas or concepts, even during a pitch), changeover costs (this may incur capital expenditure if a change of shape requires a new machine tool) and, ideally, an indication of the maximum unit cost of the new pack (the designer will need to know the size of production runs, etc).

Minutes

This is the timescale. What are the launch deadlines? When must concepts be presented, agreed, researched, refined and approved? When must the final artwork be delivered? How long has been allowed for tooling (which can take up to 50 per cent of the total design time, eg three months)?

The process

The brief may emerge after an initial review of the pack design. The designers (whether in-house or an external consultancy) often take the brief away, interpret it and rewrite it. Then they present this to the marketing team to ensure that everyone agrees with each other before embarking on any further creative work or research. This may be followed by further research, and eventually a range of concepts (two-dimensional labels and three-dimensional pack shapes, sizes and mechanisms) is developed for further research. This guides the selection of a concept for ultimate development into the new pack. Figure 19.8 shows the standard stages of a pack design project.

FIGURE 19.8 The packaging design process

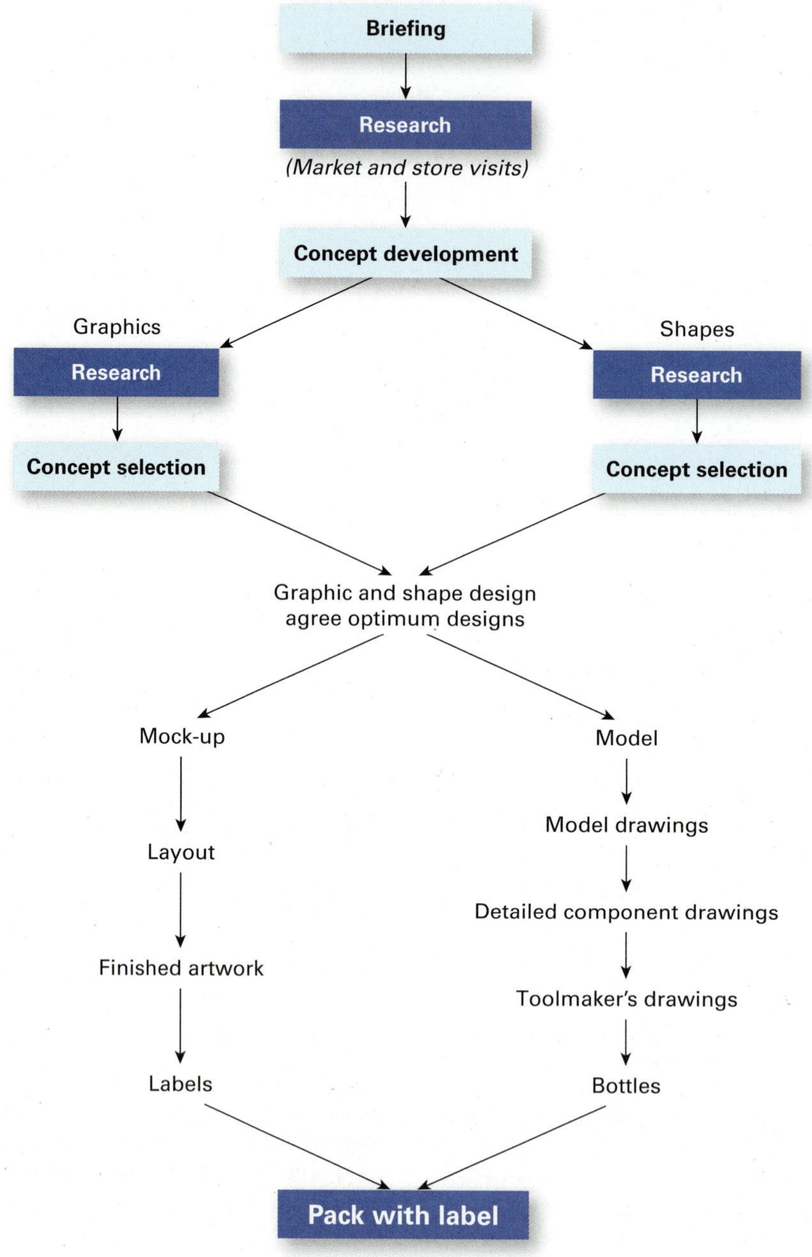

SOURCE: Adapted from the pack design management video From Dream to Reality (Smith, 1991)

CASE STUDY Packaging with added value on-pack promotions

Situation

Pedigree dog foods marketing team and agency, Colenso BBDO, constantly scan the market for trends and opportunities to deepen Pedigree's relationship with their customers. The selfie photo has become a 21st century phenomenon. And dog lovers are no different. In fact, they love to take photos of their dogs and, when they can, take selfie photos of their dog. Problem: dogs don't pose for selfies, or any kind of photo.

> "When we work on Pedigree, we don't consider that we're selling dog food, we're selling the relationship between the human and their dog. That's what we're competing against – other things that take your emotional attention away from your dog."
>
> Dan Wright, Colenso BBDO

Objective: The challenge

So how could a dog food company help their customers to get these photos? Another useful question for all brands is 'How can AI help my CX?' In Pedigree's case, the question becomes, 'How can AI help dog owners and their relationships with their dogs?'

The actual brief was to change the perception of DentaStix from being a functional product (keep your dog's teeth clean and healthy) to something that is equally irresistible for dogs (and also nurtures the relationship between dog and owner).

Strategy (part 1): Reposition

Pedigree was moving from their old positioning, 'We're for Dogs', to the current one, 'Feed the Good'. And that came from an understanding that the brand needed a purpose that goes beyond being for dogs. 'Feed the Good' refers to the fact that dogs bring out the best in the dog owner and therefore Pedigree's job is to bring out the best in them.

There are three ways of doing that. The first one is obviously the product, giving dogs access to good, nutritious food. The second one is the Pedigree Adoption Drive programme, which helps rescue dogs find homes, with the added benefit of growing the category. Because the more dogs there are in homes, the more dogs you have to feed. It's hard to grow as a brand if you don't grow the category. And the third one is innovating with technology or any other available tool to help make the world a better place for dogs and their owners.

Strategy (part 2): Create and distribute an on-pack SelfieSTIX gift

Create and distribute an on-pack Pedigree SelfieSTIX (a clip that attaches Pedigree Dentastix to a phone) plus a Pedigree SelfieSTIX app for smart phones so that owners can add filters to their dog photos. The SelfieSTIX clip is free with each pack of Dentastix. The SelfieSTIX unit is simply a smart phone clip that can hold one dental dog treat (eg Dentastix). Dog owners simply have to clip the SelfieSTIX on their phones and attach a tasty Dentastix to entice the dog to become very focused on the food, effectively staring at the camera and allowing dog owners to take the perfect selfie with their pup.

The SelfieSTIX app uses unique dog facial recognition (AI) to recognize when a dog is looking straight at the camera. To create this AI, they used Stanford University's dog dataset (of dog photos).

Tactics

The usual marketing mix has to be mobilized to create awareness, sales and ongoing engagement. This included packaging redesign (to accommodate the offer), PR (product launch – SelfieSTIX and the app), advertising and social media (user-generated content marketing: selfie photos).

Actions

To build an algorithm that identifies an object, you have to teach it what that object looks like. And so, in order for you

FIGURE 19.9 The free SelfieSTIX on-pack-promotion

to do that successfully, you have to train the algorithm with thousands of images. By feeding the algorithm thousands of dog face photos, machine learning 'learns' to recognize different dog faces, their size and structure so that items/filters can be perfectly fit to each particular dog face. So the app learns to recognizes different dog faces (colours, size, features) so that the app can then suggest perfectly sized items/filters (hats, glasses, moustaches) to be added to the basic photo.

Every pack of pedigree dog food included a SelfieSTIX clip and instructions to download the app. AI recognition allows the app to recognize (a) when the dog looks straight at the camera, and (b) different sizes and structures of dog faces (so that filters fit perfectly). The app then automatically takes the photo and then offers a selection of filters to fit the dog's face. The app allows the customers to select a particular filter (eg hat) for the final photo (Figure 19.12).

Pedigree also added an ecommerce dimension – if the dog stops looking at the camera, the app triggers an optional order of Dentastix (or pack of Pedigree dog food).

Control: Measuring the results

Four months post-campaign launch: 2.1 million interactions, 3.5 million engagements and a 24 per cent increase in sales. One-quarter of New Zealand's dog owners redeemed a SelfieSTIX, making acquisition cost 12 times lower than the industry standard. ROI: 1.5 : 1

SelfieSTIX is now rolling out globally. In fact, the campaign execution was refined for the 25+ markets that have since rolled it out. Watch the Pedigree Chum video **https://vimeo.com/254605619** and see the explanation of how the AI works, or view it in the online resources for this book.

FIGURE 19.10 The SelfieSTIX in use

FIGURE 19.11 AI recognition

FIGURE 19.12 The filter in the SelfieSTIX app allows the customers to select a particular filter for the photo

FIGURE 19.13 If the dog stops looking a the camera this triggers an optional order of Dentastix

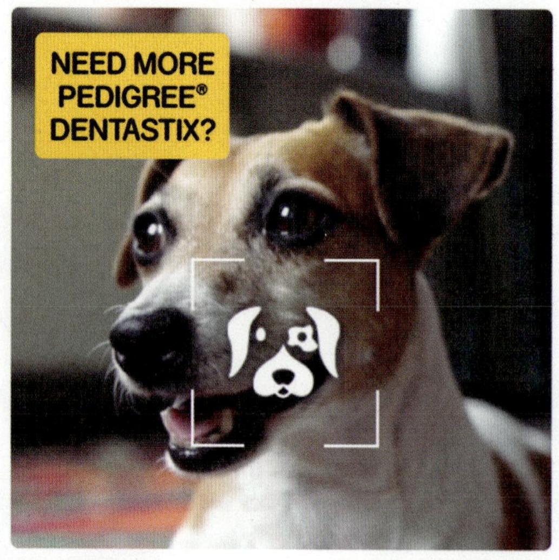

And if dogs stopped looking at camera, the app prompted an order of DENTASTIX™.

CASE STUDY Brand range development in India

Situation

The background

During the winter months in northern and eastern India, evening temperatures can drop down as low as five degrees. This causes dry skin conditions ranging from general dehydrated, chapped skin to more serious cracked skin. The market is flooded with manufacturers advertising skin care products that promise to 'keep skin healthy'.

In 1929 GD Pharmaceuticals based in Calcutta identified the need for an antiseptic ointment to combat dry skin problems. Boroline was launched. It was effectively the first brand in the antiseptic cream category. The consumer offer was a perfumed multi-purpose skin cream for cuts, burns, chapped skin, etc. The trusted Boroline brand achieved strong penetration in eastern Indian markets. Although Boroline had firmly established itself within the market, it had not capitalized on the huge potential opportunity of national penetration into India's giant marketplace of a population of one billion.

Boro Plus Antiseptic Cream was launched in 1982 to revolutionize the antiseptic cream market, and differentiate Boro Plus from Boroline through product formulation and branding. The name Boro Plus was created, as it was seen to convey a sense of added value. The herbal formulation combined with the Ayurvedic concept (an ancient Indian healthcare system that means 'the science of life') was marketed as a preventative, curative and healing ointment. Leading Ayurvedic authorities endorsed the brand.

Competition

During the 1980s an established Indian manufacturer of beauty and healthcare products, Emami, saw the bigger market opportunity to introduce a low-end product into the mass market to directly compete with Boroline. The low-end segment had cold creams (for night use) and vanishing creams (for day use). The antiseptic cream category offered a multi-purpose product – if positioned and marketed correctly.

Packaging

Boroline packaging was perceived to be dull and old-fashioned: an earthy green pack that had not changed since its 1929 launch and was not seen as attractive. It lacked 'Pick me up' appeal. The new 1980s Boro Plus pack colours were purple and white, and delivered brighter, fresher contemporary colours. These colours were also attention-grabbing.

Advertising

An advertising campaign created the category for a more youthful and aspirational quality by bringing in Bollywood celebrities to endorse the brand.

The challenge

Although Boro Plus had performed consistently since its successful 1980s launch, it was facing increased competition, in particular from international brands entering the Indian domestic market. Over 20 years after Boro Plus's launch, Emami needed to do something because, firstly, being recognized as an antiseptic cream with a multi-purpose benefit restricted new product extensions and, secondly, there was an opportunity to create a range of skin care products for both domestic and export markets.

Emami recruited a London design agency, Evolve Creative, to work on the new branding and packaging because of its track record of working with international beauty and healthcare companies. They work closely together today developing and tweaking designs to meet the continually changing market opportunities.

Market research conducted by Emami among retail outlets and users revealed one factor that went against Boro Plus: the oiliness of the product on the skin, which meant that during warmer months the cream felt uncomfortable to use due to the heat, and therefore larger purchases were seasonal, ie during the winter. This, in turn, restricted the multi-purpose proposition, so Emami decided to reposition the brand from a traditional medical product to an aspirational beauty product.

Objectives

- To create a new brand (identity and packaging design) for both Indian and export markets.
- To strengthen the brand's credibility as a skin care product by simultaneously expanding the product range to meet new needs.
- To help boost sales by a minimum of 30 per cent.

FIGURE 19.14 Repositioning from a traditional medical product to an aspirational beauty product

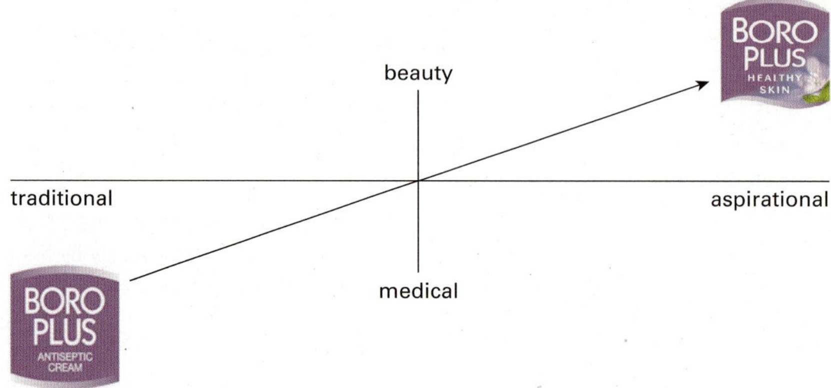

FIGURE 19.15 Original logotype vs new identity

Strategy

Reposition the conservative multi-purpose pharmaceutical product to an aspirational skin care brand bridging skin health and beauty, and expand the product range to fill identified needs.

Brand development

The brand repositioning was achieved by highlighting the product's natural herbal formulation and creating a softer and more distinctive logotype. The design also linked the product more directly with the media personality used for a testimonial in the launch TV and cinema campaign. The result was highly successful, and the year-on-year sales increased by 32 per cent.

New product extensions

Immediately following the approval of the re-launch pack design, work began on a series of product range extensions for both the domestic and the international market, which were test marketed and launched in India. These successfully positioned Boro Plus as a substantial and

FIGURE 19.16 Boro Plus antiseptic cream packaging

FIGURE 19.17 Boro Plus healthy skin packaging

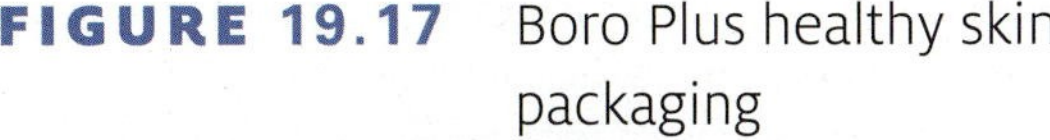

serious contender in the broader skin care market, with the consumer promise of a full, natural skin care regime. Emami now work closely with Evolve design agency extending the range further. Market research has revealed that there was also a need for a low-unit product (LUP) in the antiseptic category. It showed a large number of women wanted to carry a tube of Boro Plus in their handbags, but couldn't because of its size. With this in mind, Emami launched the 8 gram variant priced at five rupees. The affordable price point has triggered impulse purchasing, which allows customers to trade up as they move up the ladder of loyalty.

Results

Boro Plus now successfully dominates the market with a 70 per cent market share. It continues to expand the range to fill identified gaps as they emerge from ongoing market research. The brand's now extensive range is being established in international markets, including Russia and Africa.

3Ms

- **Men/women:** The team consisted of three people (two designers and an account handler).
- **Money/budget:** The budget was £6,500 for branding, and £7,000 for packaging.
- **Minutes/timescales:** The lead time required to create, develop, test, refine and roll out the brand and the pack was three months for the brand and five months for the pack.

Advantages and disadvantages

Here are some of the advantages and disadvantages to consider when deciding whether to increase or reduce this communications tool.

Advantages

Packaging is the silent salesperson, catching customers' eyes, drawing them in and selling the finer detail as they digest the information. Like merchandising, it is often the last chance to communicate before the customer makes a decision. Packaging provides a platform where the exact message is controlled by the marketer (unlike PR and social media). It also carries the brand into the customers' homes or workplaces, so it keeps on working long after the sale. Great packaging stands out from the clutter and adds perceived value to a product. Within the retail environment, packaging can create or reinforce awareness as well as help to close the sale.

Disadvantages

Packaging requires long lead times and is expensive to change. The audience is obviously limited to retail traffic looking at the category. Wasteful packaging is not only an irritant for customers but also deemed to be un-environmental (in some markets this is a legal issue). If the pack is too trimmed or too light the product can get damaged.

Key points from Chapter 19

- Packaging has three functions: to protect, offer convenience and communicate.
- Packaging design presents an opportunity to create competitive advantage.
- The designer's six tools are shape, size, colour, graphics, materials and smell.
- All marketing is a series of processes, and packaging development is no different: there is a sequential method for managing the design process.

References and further reading

Bayley, S (1986) *Coke! Coca-Cola 1886–1986: Designing a megabrand*, Conran Foundation Boilerhouse Project, London

Dichter, E (1964) *Handbook of Consumer Motivations: The psychology of the world of objects*, McGraw-Hill, New York

Lewis, M (1996) In *Understanding Brands*, ed D Cowley, Kogan Page, London

Milton, H (1991) *Packaging Design*, Design Council, London

Nicholas, R (1991) Come home to a real beer, *Marketing Week*, 15 February

Opie, R (2001) *The Art of the Label*, Chartwell, London

Parker, L (2018) We made plastic. We depend on it. Now we're drowning in it, *National Geographic*, June [online] http://www.nationalgeographic.com/magazine/2018/06 (archived at https://perma.cc/48XN-9BNJ)

Pilditch, J (1973) *The Silent Salesman*, 2nd edn, Business Books, London

Raeburn, O (2003) Design choice, *Marketing*, 8 May

Ronay, A (2005) Paint your brand, *The Marketer*, 15 September

Smith, PR (1991) *From Dream to Reality* (video), Media Services, London Metropolitan University, London

Southgate, P (1994) *Total Branding by Design*, Kogan Page, London

Warden, J (1990) White paper gives shade to trademarks, *Marketing*, 27 September

Williams, T G (1982) *Consumer Behavior*, Research report, West Publishing, St Paul, MN

Further information

Chartered Society of Designers (CSD)
1 Cedar Court
Royal Oak Yard
Bermondsey Street
London SE1 3GA
Tel: +44 (0)20 7357 8088
www.csd.org.uk

Design Business Association
35–39 Old Street
London EC1V 9HX
Tel: +44 (0)20 7251 9229
Fax: +44 (0)20 7251 9221
www.dba.org.uk

Design Museum
224–238 Kensington High Street
London W8 6AG
Tel: + 44 (0)20 3862 5900
www.designmuseum.org

The Museum of Brands
111–117 Lancaster Road
London W11 1QT
Tel: +44 (0)20 7243 9611
www.museumofbrands.com

The Packaging Society
A division of the Institute of Materials, Minerals and Mining
297 Euston Road
London NW1 3AD
Tel: +44 (0)20 7451 7300
www.iom3.org/packaging

20 Owned media – websites and social media

LEARNING OBJECTIVES

By the end of this chapter you will be able to:

- understand what makes websites succeed;
- understand what makes social media successful;
- ensure that the four key satisfaction factors are applied to your website;
- understand what increases the quality of the content on a website;
- understand what increases navigation's ease of use;
- convert visitors to customers and customers to lifetime customers;
- avoid the 10 common mistakes of social media;
- know how to optimize your website and your social media content.

Introduction

The chapter explores owned media (media that you own). We also explore 'sizzle' (exciting added-value content), customer engagement and customer conversion (from prospect to customer to lifetime customer), as well as the constant search for website improvement. The chapter then explores how to ensure social media actually wins.

Great websites are useless if they have no traffic. So to ensure we get the right traffic we will look at SEO for websites and social media.

Owned media

Owned media (media you own, such as your website), earned media (word of mouth, shares, likes, comments) and paid media (paid-for posts, tweets and ads) are referred to throughout this book. Your content marketing is technically owned media and arguably your offices/buildings are permanently owned media (planning permission allowed, you could host banner ads or messages on your own buildings – see Whitehawk FC's clever use of the stone steps for key messages, p 636).

However, 'owned' generally refers to your website, your apps and your online social media platforms. Owned media usually targets your brand's existing community/followers and/or current customers. We are going to concentrate on websites (first half of this chapter) and social media (second half) and finish the chapter with some intriguing case studies.

Why do you have a website?

Do you remember the single most important reason discussed in Chapter 1, page 4?

Website purpose

Firstly, without a website you are not credible. This may change in the future, but right now, you are not credible without a website, or at the very least, some social media presence whether that is LinkedIn, Instagram or maybe Facebook. Secondly, a good website should help and engage customers and hence nurture some brand preference. Thirdly, websites should help to identify prospects, who can be converted into customers via the website, or an automated email, telephone call or offer of a chatbot to help. Finally, the website should ideally help to convert customers into lifetime customers and ultimately into brand advocates by adding value to the customer experience each time they visit. The '5Ss' is another way of thinking about the objectives or purpose of a website: sell, serve, save (time), speak (dialogue) and sizzle (more later).

Sizzle sites

Sizzle adds excitement to a website. Sizzle is a 'wow' website experience that leaves customers delighted and wanting to only use your website forever. Ask yourself, 'What experience could my website deliver that would really help customers get excited?' Some sizzle isn't awfully expensive, eg Harley-Davidson's motorcycle website offers web visitors a virtual ride and lets them actually see the same view a Harley rider enjoys, cruising through the countryside. The UK Patent Office's trademark division allows visitors to search by name, design and date for similar trademarks. Its integrated system ensures Patent Office staff are available to talk customers through any of the processes. It also gives visitors access to their own archived applications – all with the click of a button. A complicated and sometimes dull process has been made surprisingly user-friendly.

Sloppy sites

In just a few seconds, sloppy websites destroy brands that took years to build. Whether it's broken links, dead ends, confusing registration forms, typos, poor design or cluttered content, error-laden websites all do serious damage. Sloppy websites not only kill sales, but they can destroy a brand. Cluttered sites grow as nearly all managers want their products, their innovations, their news, their staff on the website. As concentration spans fall and impatience rises, clutter becomes a killer – particularly if the visitor uses a small screen/smart phone.

'Inside-out' or 'outside-in' websites

With 'inside-out' design the content is all about the organization, the team, its products; 'outside-in' design starts with search queries (which keywords in ad campaigns and Google searches deliver profitable customers) – search phrases are then grouped and content written to answer each search query. The outside-in site design is driven by what customers seek.

> 'Get rid of anything that is not an answer to questions that your readers may ask.'
>
> Visser *et al* (2018)

Top tasks sites

Identifying the top tasks that visitors want to complete when they are on your website is critical. The website design is consequently driven by these kinds of tasks. Wunker *et al* (2016) call it 'the jobs to be done'. Every visitor has a reason, a job, or a question that need answering. Here is Gerry McGovern explaining how identifying top tasks can reveal insights that directly affect customer conversion rates, enquiries and, ultimately, sales.

Two key tasks: Getting married and divorced get lost amidst tiny tasks

'Another legal and medical publisher spent a long time trying to figure out what its customers' top tasks were. One area in which they publish is family law. After much discussion it dawned on them that there are really only two tasks that matter: getting married and getting divorced. If you went to their current website these tasks would have been very hard to find amidst all the clutter. They (the many other tiny tasks) all want to be on the homepage. They all want to be a news item or an ad. They want more links. And they will press and press the web team to give them these things. Little by little the tiny tasks clutter the homepage, the other major pages, the navigation and the search. And, of course, once these tiny tasks are published there is absolutely no incentive to review or remove them. Thus as the website gets old it gets worse. What is the classic solution? A redesign!'

McGovern (2010b)

Raving alcoholics and web redesign

'A classic web redesign is like taking a raving alcoholic and sending them to rehab for a month. (Giving a website to a marketer or communicator is like giving a pub to an alcoholic.) They come out looking clean and redesigned. However, the underlying problems have not been addressed so six months later you're back in the same mess.'

McGovern (2010b)

Customer orientated sites

'Defining, first, the purpose of your web site and second, your audience, are fundamental stages of web site development. The answers drive the kind of content required; content drives the form required; and form drives the structure of the site' (Chaffey and Smith, 2017). This answers the 'who' and the 'why' questions raised in Chapter 4. The third customer question, understanding 'how' people use your website, is answered via range of research approaches including:

- eye tracking and mouse tracking;
- facial scanning; neurological examination;
- web analytics;
- user testing;
- optimization teams.

Think mobile first

'Google have announced that the smartphone websites and mobile index will become the primary input in the near future. If a website is not suitable for smart phones this could have adverse consequences after this switch.'

Visser *et al* (2018)

Remember, if it looks ok on mobile it usually looks ok on a tablet or desktop. But not necessarily the other way around. So 'think mobile first' makes sense. In fact, **responsive design** (scalable website) converts desktop designed websites so they look ok on tablets and smart phones, by making all the content fit the smaller screen size of other devices.

The alternative is **adaptive design** (specifically for smart phones) – it will have fewer images and shorter text plus thumb-friendly body and you often see a hamburger icon in the top right-hand corner that represents the menu. Mobile-specific websites also feature 'tap-to-call' and 'tap-to-SMS' which let visitors easily and quickly contact the business directly from their mobile device.

Content design

- **Sentences should be short** because reading texts from a screen is much more tiring than reading text on paper. An average length of between 12 and 15 words per sentence is considered optimal. For screen texts the optimal average is nine words per sentence.
- Landing pages that fit on one screen perform better. **Visitors read less and less.** Information from pictures, headings and pieces of text are sufficient for encouraging visitors to respond.
- **Scrolling is in decline.** Asking for comments at the bottom of the pages there are only visible after scrolling will cost you a response. Use special landing pages and eye-catching action buttons.
- **People like to look at other people.** Landing pages that include an image, preferably of a person, perform better on average than landing pages without images.
- **Draw people's attention to an action button.** Visitors tend to follow the same viewing direction that the people in an image are looking in.
- **The call to action button must be prominent and immediately clear.** On a landing page, you may be asked to perform the same action several times. Clear and noticeable action buttons perform better.
- You will receive considerably more completed forms if you **refer to the form in various places** and on a lot of pages and **directly asked for a response**.

Excerpts from Visser *et al* (2018)

Many websites are built on social media engines like Wordpress, which also offers responsive design options/templates, ensuring the website is smart phone friendly. In fact, it renders/displays differently ie it rearranges the website content display (and apparent structure) to suit whichever device is being used, eg a smart phone. Therefore, many websites are effectively blogs if using, say, Wordpress (social media blog) although they may not look like a simple blog. However, we will separate 'websites' from the main social media platforms. So let us look firstly at successful websites and find out what makes them successful.

Successful websites

Web usability guru, Jakob Nielsen, identified four basic website factors that keep visitors satisfied and coming back again and again:

- relevant content;
- easy-to-use navigation;
- speed of download;
- updated content.

The last two factors are self-explanatory: sites that are slow to load (particularly on smart phones) lose customers, who will not wait more than four seconds. 'Google will finally use mobile page speed as a ranking in their mobile search results' (Schwartz, 2018). Site speeds are actually getting slower. In

2019 the average page load time was 6.8 seconds, up from 6.1 the previous year, which is a long way off Google's recommended target of two seconds (Wolfgang Digital, 2019).

Regarding updated content, sites that have out-of-date content will irritate visitors. So we are going to batch 'relevant' and 'updated' content together and list them collectively as 'relevant content'. This allows us to add our own critical component – 'conversion techniques'. These include (a) visitors to customers and (b) customers to lifetime customers. We will now explore the following modified success factors:

- relevant content;
- easy-to-use navigation;
- engagement;
- conversion techniques.

Relevant content

In addition to the usual offline and online market research (see Chapter 6), which reveals what the target market wants to see on a website, marketers can also ensure that their site is even more relevant by using:

- scenario planning;
- personas.

Relevant content is the number one reason why visitors come back to a website. Suffice to say that customers at different stages of the buying process need different information. And they need a stream of information during their buying journey – some of it on the website, some in email, some on an app, some can be a personal phone call or even a sales rep visit to complete the sale. A contact strategy defines the sequence of possible contacts with the customer and the kind of content they receive. See Chapter 15, p 449 for more.

Relevant landing pages

Landing pages are additional web pages designed for customers who click on an ad or an email. They are temporary pages but should look and feel the same, and have the same layout as the main website pages with a few small differences. The headline on the landing page should be the same as the advertisement. Therefore, a separate landing page for each ad is best. Have just one proposition on each landing page. Reduce the number of CTAs and buttons, as landing pages with navigation that is limited to a few buttons do better than pages with (full) navigation (Visser *et al*, 2018). For example, if you search for one of Britain's leading insurance companies and insert 'Compare the market car insurance' you will find a link to a landing page for 'Compare the Market' with, essentially, just two options: 'Start a quote' or 'Go to your account'.

Scenario planning

One tried-and-tested technique for ensuring relevant content is scenario planning. Marketers take each target customer type and consider, in detail, the customers' situation, how they might use the product or service and the steps they would take when buying. A chocolate company might have different customer scenarios – some who want to buy a gift for a loved one, others who want chocolates for a dinner party, and other customers who want chocolates for a wedding. By exploring what would be helpful to customers for each of these scenarios, marketers build sites that cater for each scenario, eg the wedding section might have ideas on wedding table layouts or love messages on chocolates, and the dinner party section might list ideas for dinner party games.

A plumbing company might identify at least two customer scenarios – one for emergencies (they need a big panel saying 'Emergency – call now 24/7' with a telephone number), while another scenario might be customers who need help and ideas to change a bathroom.

Personas

Personas help decide what kind of content customers want. Personas are 'thumbnail' descriptions of types of visitor for each scenario. Advertising agencies have used personas for planning ads for many years, and now web designers find personas very helpful too.

Here are three personas for Dulux paint who firstly, describe their target market as:

> Adventurous 25–44 year old women, with a propensity to socialize; with 12-month decorating cycles; shopping online; but lacking in DIY confidence because of the gap between inspiration (beautiful decorated homes in TV, magazines and

FIGURE 20.1 Compare the Market landing page with just two CTAs

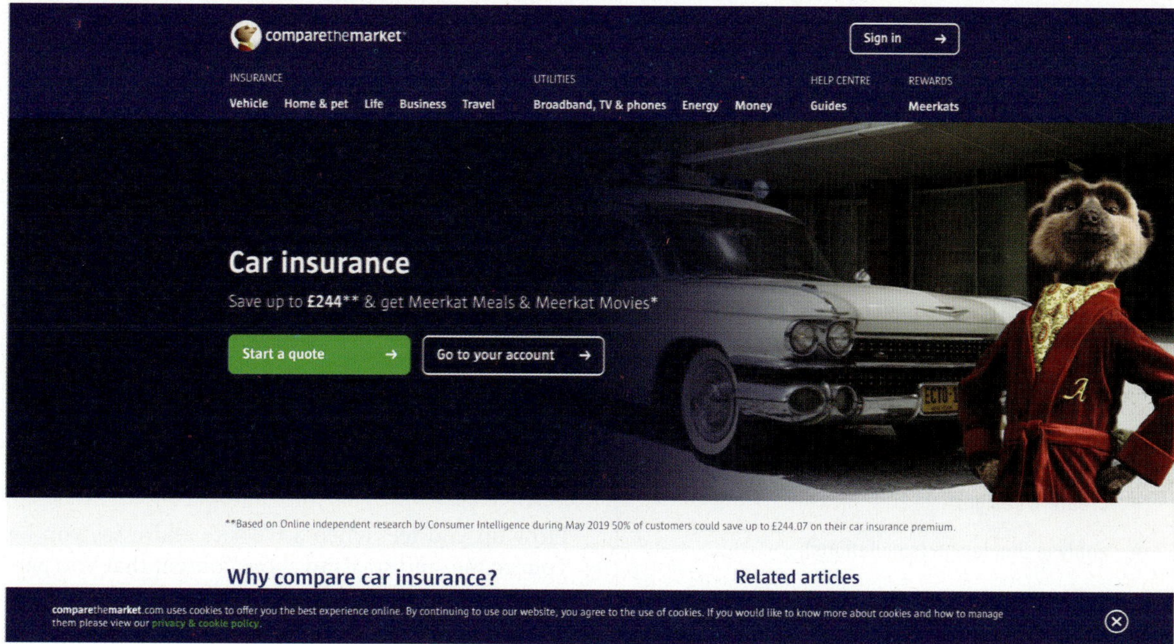

SOURCE: Courtesy of Compare the Market, and also thanks to M Visser, B Sikkenga and M Berry (2018) *Digital Marketing Fundamentals*, who suggested this example

advertising) and their own experience (large, cold, impersonal sheds/stores); without any guidance nor reassurance available currently on their journey; although they know online is a well-used channel for help and guidance (on other topics); colours and colour combining are key.

- Persona 1: First-time buyer Penny Edwards, age 27; partner: Ben; location: North London; occupation: sales assistant.
- Persona 2: Part-time mum Jane Lawrence, age 37, husband: Joe, location: Manchester; occupation: part-time PR consultant.
- Persona 3: Single mum Rachel Wilson, age 40; location: Reading; occupation: business analyst.

Personas can have a lot more details (what media they like to read, what cars they like to drive, etc). Personas create pictures of the actual people, which really helps copy writers to write much more relevant content.

National Semiconductor take scenario planning to the extreme with their hugely successful scenario-driven website built almost twenty years ago, yet still a masterpiece in web design. See the box below.

Scenario planning that delivered massive success: National Semiconductor

National Semiconductor (NSC) supply analogue and digital microchips that process sounds and images for mobiles and DVDs. Target decision makers are design engineers and corporate purchasing agents (they don't buy but they do specify what components they recommend at the beginning of new product development). This influences which components get bought later. The old website gave information about products.

The CEO one day challenged everyone and asked a great question: 'How can the website help engineers?' So a team launched a project to develop a deep understanding of engineers, including how they work (what their scenarios were). This helped them learn how engineers actually design components, leading them to consider creating online tools (on the website) to help engineers to do a better job (and save time).

They discovered that design engineers were under time pressure and realized that NSC could create easy-to-use tools that could speed the design process and save time, so they put a multifunctional team together (including marketing, application designers, web designers and engineers). They identified the design engineer's work process as follows:

- create a part;
- create a design;
- analyse the design (simulations);
- build a prototype.

NSC then created a web-based tool called 'web-bench', which helped engineers to complete the whole design process without special software. When engineers log on, they are prompted to specify overall parameters and key components. The web-bench auto-generates possible designs and complete technical specs, part lists, prices and cost-benefit analysis. The engineer then refines the design. Next, the design engineer can run a real-time simulation (using sophisticated software that NSC had licensed).

An engineer can then easily alter the design many times and save iterations in 'My portfolio', with an email link to colleagues so they can run and save simulations. Once the engineer agrees the final design, the system generates a bill of materials for the prototype, complete with NSC's components and all requirements from other manufacturers, with links to distributors and prices.

The result is that an engineer can do in two hours what previously took months. Not surprisingly, design engineers loved it. More than 20,000 power supplies were designed in this way in the first year of operation.

What next? The team went on to ask engineers about other activities with which they had difficulty. This revealed thermal simulations and circuitry, so new scenarios and applications were built for engineers who design wireless devices. By the end of the year NSC had 31,000 visitors on-site, generating approximately 3,000 orders or referrals every day. One particular order, from Nokia, was for an integrated socket for 40 million units. National Semiconductor are now a part of Texas Instruments, but the web-bench facility lives on, on the Texas Instruments website.

Adapted from Seybold (2001)

Dynamic design and personalized websites

How do you feel when a website addresses you by your name, and starts to show content that you particularly like? Personalized web pages driven by dynamic variables including: name, preferences (including shopping), dates, events and locations. So depending on which country (location) you are in will determine which landing page you see. Or the content on each page contains your name (or perhaps your previous shopping basket if it is a weekly grocery shopping store). Or your digital body language (your click behaviour) can determine a dynamic page swap or even a pop-up page with a specially relevant tailored offer. 'Remembering names shows respect. Recognizing customers and their preferences sows the seeds of good relationships and better business' (Chaffey and Smith, 2017).

Personalized sites have been around for a decade, but soon it will be expected as visitors demand relevant content. 'Websites that lack the ability to change and respond to users will become ever less successful,' predicts Sitecore Marketing Director, Shawn Cabral.

The next page of content you show your website visitor should always be in response to your collective knowledge of them, and it should move the dialogue on to building a relationship with that visitor. Use implicit, situational data, such as a web visitor's location, device type, incoming search term or the website they were previously on. If you make it easier for visitors to find what they need, and make sure you display content that is suited to their device, they will stay on your site for longer and engage more (Hilpern, 2013).

> **Remove content: Why 'review and remove' are such critical web skills**
>
> 'There is often a fear of removal. Review and removal of old and out-of-date content is crucial for the successful management of large websites. And yet, these critical processes are lacking in most organizations.'
>
> McGovern (2012)

Easy-to-use navigation

The overall navigation structure should clearly demonstrate how content is grouped and how different pages relate to others. Without a planned structure, a site can soon end up as a 'spaghetti site'. At worst, this leaves visitors angry and frustrated. At best, it leaves them dazed, disorientated, confused and frustrated. If there is no natural flow, visitors may leave forever.

Navigation requires careful consideration and eventual usability testing. This can be done on paper with mock-up screen grabs rather than on a fully developed site. Many navigation issues can be spotted before the site gets fully developed. Here are three navigation rules from *Digital Marketing eXcellence* (Chaffey and Smith, 2017):

1. **Keep it simple.** Do not have too many buttons. Psychologists who have analysed the behaviour of computer users in labs say the magic number is seven (or fewer). Any more than seven and the user will find it difficult to choose. You can use nesting or pop-up menus to avoid the need for too many menus or too many menu items. Simplicity is necessary to avoid confusing the user.
2. **Be consistent.** Consistency is helpful, since you want to avoid users seeing different menus and page layouts as they move around the site. For example, the menu structures for customer support should be similar to those for browsing product information.
3. **Signposts.** There should be signposts to help visitors by telling them where they are within the website and what else they might like to see.

> **'Flow'**
>
> Excellent websites achieve 'flow' as they help the visitor to complete their task by prompting them to move to the next page. Ask yourself 'Where would the visitor like to go next?' and then make sure you have signposted and perhaps even incentivized it so that more visitors will move to the desired page.

Remember, not all of your visitors want to buy right now. Cater for customers at different stages of the buying process. Some want to see more information, some want to try a sample, and some want to buy right now. So 'see', 'try' and 'buy' options can help (see below). These can be presented in different formats, particularly when catering for customers who prefer to receive information in different formats, eg video (demonstration), text (often a PDF article) or actually speaking to a human (call-back technology or live chat). Clearly label the different folders or directories on the site so they act as a reference point for describing particular types of content (Chaffey and Smith, 2017).

> **People see images first**
>
> 'People see images first, then headers, then the body of text. Large images are seen before smaller images. Warm colours (orange and red) are seen before colder colours (blue and green). Images of people are seen before images containing objects. The eyes of people who are making eye contact are, in a business sense, the strongest visual magnet. There are even stronger images: images of naked people and pictures of a sexual nature are seen earlier. All the way at the top, are moving images. Of course, not everything that attracts attention is also functional. A moving image on a website diverts so much attention from the message that

although it can sometimes be functional, it is more often a disadvantage than an advantage. The same applies in most cases to images of naked people. People don't actually look, or read, from top to bottom or from left to right. Visitors are in a hurry, read badly and only have eyes for what they are looking for. Preferably place navigation buttons at the top, company logo on the top left (with a link to the homepage), place call to action and other buttons on the right. A website can be visited with the sole purpose of finding the telephone number or address of the company in question. Hyperlinks and control of the screen are important items for website visitors. Also a search box, reviews and feedback and videos contribute to optimal usability.'

Visser *et al* (2018)

Design and layout

Good websites are also carefully designed in terms of both form and function. Form means the way a site looks, ie the aesthetics, which includes layout, graphics, colour and typography. Function is interaction, integration, navigation and structure. Navigation is a critical aspect, as it determines how users can move around a site using menus, hyperlinks and signposts or panels.

Most sites include a general home page, product/solutions pages, about us, contact and buy now for primary navigation. And then under, say, the 'Solutions' navigation tab (nav tab), a drop-down menu offers a sub-menu (sub nav-tabs) for, say, different industry sectors. The footer will have the usual reference to privacy statements, copyright, disclaimers and sometimes contact details again.

Site structure should be simple, consistent and well signposted in order to create flow. Remember, some people are ready to buy right now, others want to try it first and others simply want more information. Telephone numbers and contact details should always be readily accessible. Placing an order or making an enquiry should never be more than three clicks away.

Can customers easily find and use key content?

What three things do you want visitors to get from your website? Are they completing these tasks (eg viewing a page; registering for a newsletter; requesting a quote, etc)? Is it easy to complete these tasks? Are there any barriers? And how do you know?

Engagement

Engagement means interaction, whether this is posting a star rating, a like, a comment, a share, a chatbot chat or just watching a complete video. Goals such as sign-up for a newsletter or taking a trial purchase or repurchase, or just sending a message or email via the website also indicate engagement with a website. Return visits to a website suggest a level of engagement. Marketers want customers (and prospects) engaging with the website.

However, the mere presence of, say, a contact button on each page is not always enough to trigger customer engagement. Ask directly, and ask frequently, for engagement. This should increase the level of engagement. CTAs can be placed under every post and on every page.

Two-way websites

Communication is a two-way process (Chapter 5), and websites should be a two-way experience. Visitors should be encouraged to engage in a variety of ways. More engagement means visitors have more involvement and control over their own experiences. This increases satisfaction and the overall CX.

Customers can be engaged at any stage of the buying process. For example: 1) learning: watching short videos, animations, simulations, downloading reports, testimonials, emailing and chatting; 2) deciding: interactive product selector, callback facility, chat facility, onsite search engines; 3) buying: 'buy now' button, 'wish list' button, lead the customer with a clearly labelled set of numbered steps to buy, customer feedback/ratings (essential); 4) post-purchase: email with link to specific web pages containing useful information (and videos, eg how to assemble/use/clean/maintain, etc), searchable FAQs, interactive support tools, list of 'how to' videos and customer feedback (essential).

The Ladder of Engagement

Another way of looking at engagement is PR Smith's Ladder of Engagement (Smith, 2011). From encouraging visitors and customers to giving ratings and reviews to nurturing advocates to collaborating and co-creating user-generated content, ideas and products, this ladder works well for some organizations. Consider **threadless.com**, whose visitors send in their designs for T-shirts and users then vote for the best designs, which are then printed and sold online. This UGC is sold back to customers who voted for it. These customers are highly engaged with the brand – even co-creating some of its products. This is collaborative co-creation. They have built a solid business from this model.

Do remember, however, that not everyone wants to engage all the time, sometimes visitors (most visitors) just want to complete a task, find some information or just buy something and leave your site. So, don't ignore the basics of properly tested, quick, easy-to-use websites and apps (Smith, 2019).

If the site content reflects the customers' interests, then the magic marketing formula (identify needs, reflect them and satisfy them) is activated. This brings visitors back to the site and boosts conversions (more later).

Now consider our fourth satisfaction factor – conversion techniques.

Conversion techniques

In the offline world, many salespeople avoid asking for the sale, or 'closing the sale', perhaps because of an unconscious fear of failure or possibly poor training. Whatever the reason, all the hard work of finding a prospect, getting an appointment, preparing, presenting and handling objections is wasted if the salesperson does not ask for the business. The same applies online. Getting traffic to a website is one thing. Getting conversions is another thing. Here are 10 tips to boost conversions:

1. Apply the four basic satisfiers: relevance, navigation, fresh content and download speed.
2. Develop credibility and reduce customer anxiety.
3. Use a clear online value proposition (OVP).
4. Have tailored landing pages with OVP tailored to a need (or a key phrase).
5. Test multiple tailored landing pages.
6. Have calls to action (many types of CTAs).

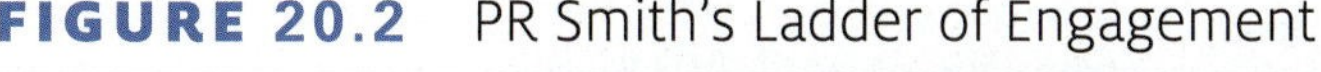

FIGURE 20.2 PR Smith's Ladder of Engagement

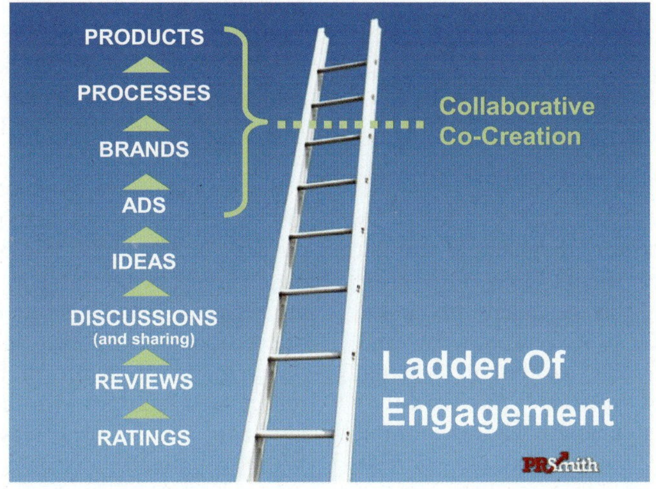

7 Include 'see', 'try' and 'buy' options.
8 Price lining.
9 Simplify processes (remove barriers).
10 Develop a contact strategy (potentially driven by digital body language).

We will now discuss each of these points in more detail.

Apply the four basic satisfiers

We have discussed these already. Nielsen's original four factors, which satisfy customers and bring them back to a website, are relevant content, easy navigation, fresh content and download speed.

Develop credibility and reduce customer anxiety

Customers are nervous about giving away their three currencies: personal data, money and time to someone they don't know, often thousands of miles away. Customer endorsements, reviews and ratings and a list of high-profile customers and money-back-guarantees reassure people. Membership of professional bodies, awards won, standards achieved, expertise (books, articles, speeches) and trusted services like VeriSign reassures visitors. Also, a well-designed, uncluttered site gives a reassuring sense of order amidst a chaotic, cluttered and sometimes crazy digital world. Include friendly faces in the 'about us' section, contact details (including phone number) and, ideally, a photograph of a real building with a full address. Typos, broken links, and dead ends (just one ruins the credibility) ruin everything – so run regular usability testing.

Reminding customers about money-back guarantees and the progress of their dispatch also reduces customer anxiety.

A clear online value proposition

You have got a couple of seconds (maximum) to communicate to a visitor why they should stay on your site. What is in it for them? What is the value proposition? Sometimes this is called the online value proposition (OVP). Is it clear exactly what benefits this site delivers? What's different, or better, about this site than all of the others? Ask six different members of staff to summarize what they think your home page offers. Then repeat the exercise with many more customers. Use their feedback, along with your competitive advantage to improve your OVP to keep more visitors on your site longer, so that more will convert.

Online value proposition

Be very clear about what is your value proposition. Can you summarize what customers will get from your website? Remember, customers can decide within seconds (or even less than a second) whether this website is worth staying on and visiting. Is it clear that what are you offering:

- is different from your competitors;
- makes a difference to your customers' lives;
- is not available offline?

Relevant landing pages

When prospects click on a PPC Adword or a hyperlink, they expect to land on a page that contains relevant information. They do not expect to land on a home page and have to start searching. Landing pages are sometimes temporary pages but should look and feel the same as the main site and have the same layout (with a few small differences). Reduce the number of CTAs and buttons; remember that landing pages with navigation that is limited to a few buttons do better than pages with full navigation (Visser *et al*, 2018). Add a home button or ensure there is a link embedded into the logo in the top left corner. Again, the UK price comparison website, Compare the Market, offers no menu and just two choices on its credit card landing page: 'Compare credit cards' and 'Credit card eligibility check' (Figure 20.3).

Other insurance companies' landing pages will just have 'home', 'calculate premium' and 'transfer' on the landing page. The headline on the landing page should be the same as the advertisement (create separate landing pages for each ad). Have just one proposition on each landing page. This fulfils the magic marketing formula (IRD): identify needs, reflect needs/solutions (to those needs) (on the landing page) and deliver a reasonable product/service. We have already discussed dynamic design and

FIGURE 20.3 Compare the Market credit card landing page with just two CTAs

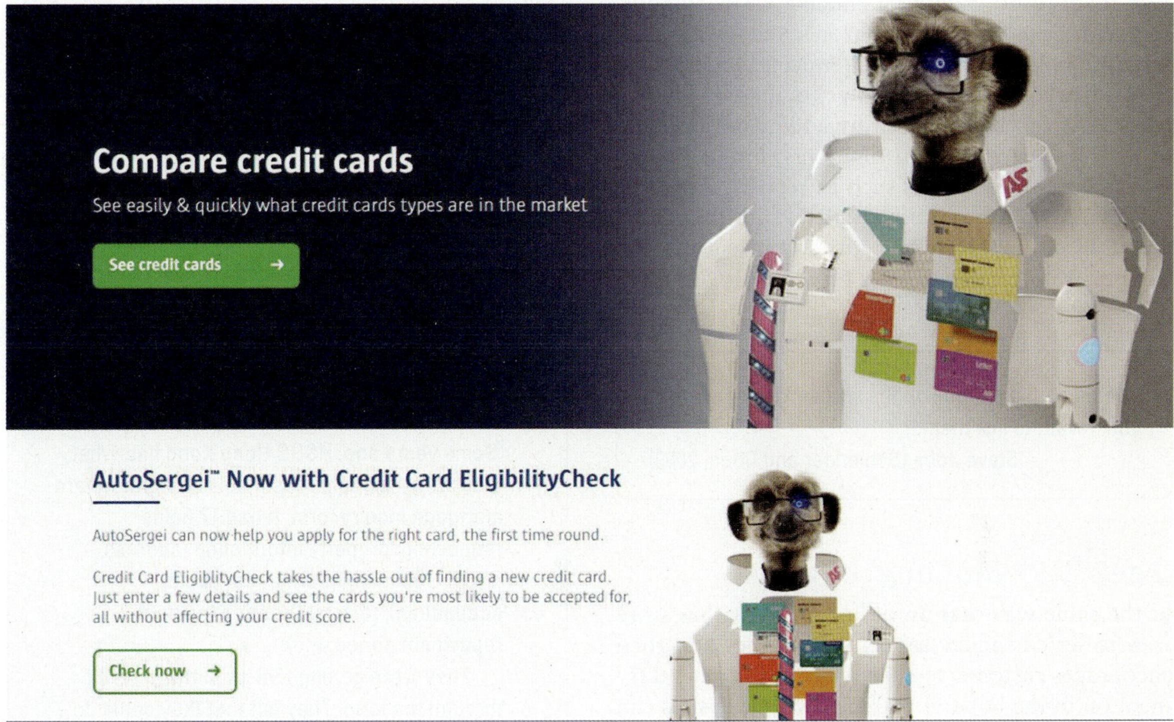

SOURCE: Courtesy of Compare the Market

personalized web pages (that effectively remember the customer's preferences and therefore serve even more relevant content). Some brands build microsites for a particular campaign (rather than just a landing page). Either way, it's all about relevant content.

Test multiple tailored landing pages

Different versions of a landing page can be tested by splitting traffic so that equal amounts of visitors land on each variation (perhaps of the OVP). See the American Greeting ecards case on p 630 for full details. Basically, three different landing pages are tested for each key phrase. The one that converts more visitors is retained and the other two are deleted. This optimizes your tailored landing pages.

> **Create an A/B culture**
>
> A/B testing helps to boost conversions. Create an A/B testing culture and watch results start to improve.

Calls to action

Whether it is 'register now' for an e-newsletter or 'buy now', the CTA should be clear, attractive and above the fold, if possible (since people are scrolling less and less). Each page should have a crystal clear CTA. If someone is on your landing page because they want to lose weight, the CTA should not say 'more' or 'click here' or 'begin your journey'; it should be 'start losing weight now'. Another relevant

CTA is 'you might also like (insert link)'. Decide what you would like the visitor to do next and then help them to do it with an enticing CTA. Symbols and icons can help; eg Amazon's yellow-trimmed (high-visibility), soft cornered (enticing) blue button (reassuringly safe corporate blue) is almost voluptuous. CTAs can be enhanced by adding an incentive to act now, eg early bird discounts, limited stock/seats/rooms or even gifts such as reports, videos or insights, or more traditional gifts. Note that some countries do not allow free gifts and incentives. See Chapter 15 for more on sales promotions.

> 'We made the buttons on the screen look so good you'll want to lick them.'
>
> Steve Jobs (Schlender and Chen, 2000)

'See', 'try' and 'buy' options

In the same way that an offline retail clothes store tries to let customers see its best clothes and then encourages customers to come into the store and try them on in the hope of making a sale, websites can also accommodate the three stages of 'see it', 'try it' and 'buy it'. A key point to remember here is that some visitors have found exactly what they want and are ready to buy right now, while other visitors want to trial it, and others again are interested but want to see more information about the product first. The site should accommodate all three types of visitor by offering all three options to help them along their buying journey.

Price lining

Price lining effectively means having a range of prices so that anyone with any budget can always buy something, even if it is a sample unit or a small version. A range of sizes allows for a range of price points, which guarantees that anyone with any budget can at least be in a position to buy something. Not having enough money is no longer a barrier. Price lining takes away the pricing barrier. A variation of this theme of having something for every budget is rental or leasing; some organizations partner with leasing companies that effectively give the customer a choice of paying a large capital sum or paying a smaller weekly or monthly amount.

Simplify processes/usability

All form filling should be short and easy. Some marketers get greedy for data and ask far too many questions early on in the relationship. This is a mistake. Generally, visitors do not like having to register for anything, so if they do have to register make it easy for them by having only a few questions initially. More information can be collected later. If one of the top customer tasks is to download a white paper or register for a newsletter, make it easy for the busy visitor. Make the form short. Do not create barriers with forms.

Big forms kill customers

'Some years ago, HSBC Hong Kong had what they thought was a reasonably straightforward mortgage inquiry form. It had 17 fields requesting: property information (address, price); applicant information (name, occupation); loan information (amount, repayment period, etc).

They were getting two enquiries a week through the form. They felt that they could do better. They turned to Brett King, a well-known innovator in the industry (see his book *Bank 2.0*). Brett and his team convinced them to radically simplify the form.

They reduced the number of fields from 17 to 3: name, email and phone number. The simplification process met some resistance. People said that the old form gathered data that integrated well into the internal system. People felt that the new form would encourage frivolous enquiries from the likes of Donald Duck and Arnold Schwarzenegger.

They finally launched the new form. There was no publicity or special promotion, so the basic number of visitors to the mortgage pages remained the same. However, enquiries jumped from two per week to 180 per week. And yes, they did indeed get mortgage requests from Arnie. Despite such frivolous enquiries, new mortgage business directly connected with the new, simpler online form reached $20 million in the first quarter after its release. With the old form they were doing less than $1 million a quarter.'

McGovern (2010a)

The ultimate way to check to see if the website is easy to use is to carry out usability testing. Here, customers matching the target market profile are given sets of tasks to complete.

Tesco's usability tests focus on tiny details, integrating offline and online

'"Little tiny things make a big difference to the customer experience, and Tesco is unbelievably good at creating that differentiation", says Catriona Campbell, Director at Foviance. When Tesco was developing Tesco Direct, Foviance was tasked with getting real customers to test the site.

"We used eye-tracking, so we literally tracked where their eyes were going on the catalogue and on the web, and we could see that some of the creative in the catalogue wasn't transferring to the web," she says. The usability innovations that came out of the research were not huge, but they made a big difference.

"It was things like putting the catalogue page number into the website, so you could search for something you had seen in the catalogue. Customers also wanted to see the Tesco Value 'stickers' throughout the website and the catalogue as well, the way they do in store. It doesn't make it easier to read, but they just wanted to see that big red splodge."

The point, says Campbell, is that true usability depends less on creative ideas that spring from nowhere than it does on asking the audience. "A lot of the things that came out of the research you couldn't have come up with in isolation," she says. "The creative had to go hand in hand with research into real-life situations, and the beauty is in combining the skills of researchers with those of the designers to get that creative idea out that really makes a difference. Little tiny things make a big difference to the customer experience, and Tesco is unbelievably good at creating that differentiation".'

Woods (2007)

Develop a contact strategy

Visitors can still be converted into customers even after leaving the website without buying by following them up with (a) remarketing campaigns (targeting ads at visitors as they move around the web) or (b) if the prospect's email was collected, a simple follow-up contact strategy. See Tesco's simple email contact strategies for customers at different stages in the buying process in Chapter 3. There is a different sequence of contacts depending on whether customers registered for an email newsletter, made an enquiry, took a trial or actually made a purchase.

Digital body language can trigger the appropriate dynamic page swap pop-up message, eg three visits online could trigger an alert to a sales rep (with the relevant prospect data) followed by a courtesy sales call to see if the prospect needs any help. Alternatively, certain click behaviour can trigger a 'nurturing campaign' that combines direct mail (snail mail) and email to strengthen the brand's proposition.

Visitors' digital body language (click behaviour) is logged so that marketers know what level of interest any particular (anonymous) visitor has, so that sales and marketing people know which buyers are actively engaged in a buying process and which are not. They identify a quality lead, where the lead is in the buying cycle and when to bring a salesperson into a deal and when not to. If digital body language is objectively scored and suddenly changes, this can indicate that the prospect has moved to a different phase in the buying process.

Excellent contact strategies vary according to the prospects' preferences in media type, frequency and style

Some prospects want information via RSS feeds into their RSS readers; others prefer email, direct mail, podcasts, trade shows or industry analyst reports. Some want quarterly, monthly or weekly contact. More engaged customers tend to be more comfortable with increased frequency of contact. The prospects' progression through the sales cycle can be identified by profiling both the communication frequency and any responses. If open rates start dropping, prospects are either under time pressure or losing interest and therefore it may be worth reconsidering the contact strategy for them. Again, all this can be managed by a set of rules that trigger various contact strategies and particular propositions and offers. Some prospects prefer rich graphical communication, while others just want the basic information in a text or email.

Convert customers to lifetime customers

The second visit to a website is the beginning of a relationship. Today, marketers ask themselves whether they are giving customers enough reasons to come back and visit the site for a second time. It is a great question. Honest answers will improve the website. On the assumption that the site works and customers have bought once, how do marketers convert those same customers into lifetime customers? How do marketers keep the relationship alive? Answer: the same way anyone keeps a relationship alive and well – by listening to them, understanding their needs, speaking to them regularly, always giving them good value (never breaking the promise) and occasionally giving them a nice surprise. What does that mean? It means marketers must deliver the quality the brand promises, have a contact strategy, respond to the customers – their questions, queries, worries, complaints or suggestions – and reward them occasionally. Part of the contact strategy includes acknowledging the order, confirming delivery dates, and following up with a satisfaction survey, a request for a recommendation or a review. Ongoing tailored special offers and reminders, if they are timely and considered useful or helpful, should keep the relationship alive.

Tech efficiency replaces loyalty with a switching economy?

'This is the age of customer engagement, experience, relationships and loyalty. There is an impression that these things matter when, in fact, they don't. Loyalty for most organizations is a one-way street. The customer is expected to be loyal to the brand. The idea of loyalty to the customer is not even considered... 66 per cent of marketers surveyed believed that loyalty programmes are for consumers to show loyalty to brands... relationships take time and effort... loyalty and caring are powerful human emotions but brands seem to want to get them on the cheap... Technology has been used to replace expensive human-to-human, face-to-face relationships:

- customer calls to a US call centre cost $7.50;
- customer calls to an overseas agent cost $2.35;
- automating the call/interactive voice response system costs $0.32.

"Our analysis suggests that migrating customers from channels they prefer to use to channels they don't, may lower their engagement with their bank" (Gallup 2013 study of banking customers). A 2013 study by Accenture estimated "that the 'Switching Economy' puts up to $5.9 trillion of revenue up for grabs for companies globally." So, organizations are saving on their relationship costs with customers but in the process are making customers less loyal and more likely to switch.'

McGovern (2015)

Do not let bland, soulless contact strategies occur in your business. Converting customers into lifetime customers is critical in the long term. Look at exit points in your analytics to see what is reducing your conversion rate. Equally, look at the journeys of your highest converting customers. Now let us consider successful social media: the key success factors and the classic errors to avoid.

Successful social media

Chapter 15 (content marketing) specifically includes several social media campaigns that involve collaborative co-creation. This is exciting UGC and is at the top level of the Ladder of Engagement. We will now explore how to integrate social media into business systems and after that, how to optimize your social media (SMO).

10 steps to integrate social media into the business

Here are ten steps towards integrating social media into business processes so that it becomes a normal process required to run a business (Brian Solis, 2010):

1 **Listen.** Staff members are allocated certain groups and communities. They search for the use of certain brands, people and key phrases and use listening tools such as Google Alerts, Talkwalker, Twitter Search, Radian6, and GaggleAMP in addition to monitoring their own allocated communities. Log hot topics and listen for heated topics packed with emotion that could go viral.
2 **Create a presence.** Create a presence on the usual social networks. This is not strategic engagement, just experimental at this stage.
3 **Join the conversation.** Take the plunge, join some relevant conversations, add some value/ some useful information. You can also announce activities, events and competitions on your own pages or tweets. If in another community's discussion, add these announcements to the conversation only if they are relevant and useful.
4 **Identify communities, burning issues and opinion formers.** Observing where the really significant conversations are, the types of responses and the language that is used can reveal burning issues, pain points, new ideas and a lot more valuable intelligence. Businesses do not have to be everywhere to create a presence, but they do have to be where relevant conversations are occurring with significant audiences or influencers.
5 **Content strategy.** As the needs of relevant communities and opinion formers emerge, an organization can begin to define what kind of content, questions, challenges and collaborative co-creation it would be good to feed into these communities. This is the shift from ad hoc communications to a more carefully planned communications agenda. See Chapter 15, p 449.
6 **Social media guidelines.** These guidelines spell out the desired positioning of the brand, key phrases with which the brand wants to be associated, typical hot issues in which the organization has expertise, and possible links to some of the brand's own popular pages, specific landing pages, articles, PowerPoint slide shows or videos. The guidelines can also include tone of voice, use of logos and straplines.
7 **Grow the community.** Establishing a blog, a Facebook page, a LinkedIn group or any online profile with great content is not enough. You need great questions to spark discussions. You need members/fans, advocates and influencers engaging with each other also. You and your team need to engage too.
8 **Socialization of the team.** Staff have got to get used to the sharing and collaborating potential of social media. The listening and conversing stages are only as effective as their ability to inspire transformation. Interdepartmental cooperation (sharing) is required. All staff are brand ambassadors and members of the social team. Any external-facing department will have to be socially mobilized. Internal social champions must be identified and encouraged to collaborate.
9 **Socialization of business processes and workflow.** Monitoring discussions, discovering great resources, participating in conversations, blogging and encouraging UGC all require staff time and also processes that ensure conversations are fulfilled and intelligence is collected, stored and used to make better decisions and ultimately run a better organization. New workflows require the reorganization of teams and processes. Organizations will have to manage the social workflow.
10 **Measure and report.** Marketers must evaluate the value of social media marketing (as well as all aspects of marketing) and present this to the board. For each social media tool, it is possible to quantify and compare cost per thousand reached, cost per enquiry, cost per order, cost per customer acquired and ROI (as well as return on ad spend and return on social media spend). The difficult bit is measuring the impact of social media on the brand value, which can now be included as an asset on the balance sheet.

> **Employee advocacy**
>
> Don't forget to mobilize one of your key social media assets – your staff. Employee advocacy (EA) programmes enable your staff to easily share company content among their own networks – thereby strengthening their position/establishing them in certain networks and simultaneously expanding the reach. EA helps to refocus the passions of employees on your marketing content, translating their enthusiasm into better campaign results. A good EA programme energizes your team to get started with social engagement. Staff are trained and rewarded for sharing because every action earns points which earn rewards, and also using a leaderboard to encourage staff introduces a form of gamification.

10 common social media mistakes

Here are 10 common social media mistakes highlighted by Econsultancy's Patricia Robles. Although she wrote it approximately ten years ago (2010) it still proves a useful list of social media mistakes to avoid today:

1. **Over-following.** Social media is called 'social' media for a reason, but there's nothing 'social' about following an ungodly number of users, especially in a short amount of time. Success with social media is just like marketing, sales and PR: results are achieved one victory at a time.
2. **Using every tool available.** Getting social media 'right' is harder than it looks. One of the things that's required: focus. But it's hard to focus when you try to build a presence on every popular social media platform. Which is why companies should resist the urge to get involved with all the new shiny toys and instead focus on the social media platforms that are most likely to be a good fit.
3. **Falling off the wagon.** A social media effort is easy to start, but it can be a challenge to keep going. In short, social media is a journey, not a destination. Businesses that aren't prepared for the long haul are far more likely to give up. That's not a good thing because social media is a party and the other partygoers (your customers, competitors, etc) are likely to notice if you pass out.
4. **Not training employees.** Social media may look easy, but it really isn't. How your employees behave can have a big impact on your company's social media reputation. For companies that are actively involved with social media, setting expectations and creating policies for employees is the best way to ensure that they help your reputation, not hurt it.
5. **Letting the new kid or a low-level employee manage your profiles.** Who should be in charge of your social media endeavours? The young employee who joined Facebook back in 2004 and who has 5,000 followers on Twitter might seem like a good choice, but chances are he or she isn't. Your social media presence is far too valuable to leave in the hands of somebody who is new, inexperienced, lacks detailed knowledge about the company or isn't heavily invested in the company's success. Putting it in the hands of anyone else can quickly lead to disaster.
6. **Pretending that social media is free.** Signing up for a Twitter account and Facebook page, for instance, may not cost any money, but managing them (and managing them well) doesn't magically happen without an investment that can be quantified in dollars and cents. Social media will always require somebody's time and may require that certain corporate resources be allocated differently. Businesses can't ignore these costs when planning their social media strategies and evaluating what they're delivering.
7. **Publishing first, thinking later.** In the world of social media, everything you say can and will be held against you. Unfortunately, the real-time nature of many social media websites encourages a 'publish first, think later' dynamic. Companies have far too much to lose, however, and need to ensure that what's being published is accurate, honest and in line with the company's values. Sometimes, it's better not to publish.

8. **Ignoring metrics.** When it comes to social media, companies need to be comfortable experimenting. But experimentation doesn't mean that companies shouldn't define the metrics by which progress and success can be measured. Measurement is just as important with social media as it is with any other business effort.
9. **Assuming ROI isn't possible to calculate.** The three letters R-O-I often make social media proponents cringe and social media sceptics grin. Many companies buy into the notion that social media is really, really important, but a lot of them also buy into the notion that its value can't reasonably be calculated in terms of ROI. That's a mistake because for all of social media's virtues, any effort made by a business eventually has to produce tangible value that can be correlated to the bottom line.
10. **Expecting the world.** Social media can do many great things for businesses, but it has its limitations. For instance, it isn't necessarily going to drive sales, increase brand loyalty or create buzz – especially overnight. Getting the most out of social media requires healthy, not unrealistic, expectations.

Of course content created for social media can be used in many other channels, in fact across all 11 marcomms tactical tools (10 if you don't consider earned media/CRM/word-of-mouth to be a channel itself), if you plan it right. Chapter 15, content marketing, explores how to get the content right. Here are a few approaches to using social media to boost a business's results.

SEO

Great websites (and social media platforms) fail if they have no traffic or if they have poor quality traffic that does not convert into followers, advocates, enquirers and eventually customers. Search engine optimization (SEO) generates traffic by making your websites and social media platforms more easily findable by search engines. So, when people search for a particular item or topic, your website or social media platform is found. All of the other tactical tools discussed earlier in this book (ads, sponsorship, packaging, etc) can also generate visitor traffic. Here are 10 SEO tips.

10 SEO tips

1. Develop a list of key phrases.
2. Write content that answers questions that people might ask.
3. Include key phrases (and related phrases) in each topic-specific page and, in particular, in the title, headlines (H1, H2, H3 and H4) bold text, initial words in a sentence and in a paragraph. Note that it is better to use key phrases in a headline than a sophisticated alliteration or intriguing words.
4. Insert key phrases in the tags: alt tags for visuals, title tags for the top of each page and meta-tag descriptions (the snippets or summaries of a page shown in some search engine results pages/SERPs).
5. Insert key phrases in urls and 'anchor text' (instead of 'more', use key phrases in a link).
6. Develop inbound links ideally from venerable institutions (inbound links are like a vote of confidence, particularly if coming from a venerable institution). Quality links have the most impact and generate traffic on their own, and also push you up the Google rankings.
7. Use internal links (link your own pages with each other, ie make related content easy to find).
8. Add a site map to the footer.
9. Nurture relations with opinion formers/ influencers/bloggers.
10. Ensure fast download speed (optimize content including photos and video).

SEO for voice search

Voice search queries (with Alexa or Siri) are longer than the traditional keyword search. Searches like 'best digital camera' will start to disappear. Very specific searches will be more popular, eg 'Alexa, where can I find a waterproof video camera that works with Facebook Live?' Write short answers to the questions that voice searchers are asking. 'This also increases your chances of appearing in a Google's Featured Snippet' (Bonelli, 2017). We are using more natural language and longer queries when voice searching. Queries can be three to five (or more) keywords long. These 'long-tail' keywords are very, very specific to whatever you are selling, or more to the point, specific to what searchers are searching for. Include trigger words like who, how, what, where, best, where, why and when. Use these words in your content (on your pages). Natural language queries such as 'what is a tasty Italian restaurant in midtown Manhattan?' will be more popular than the old-style search for 'Italian restaurant'. 'Search engines are becoming adept at understanding intent (ie not "what did they type?" Nor "what did they say?" but rather, "what do they want?"' (Visser *et al*, 2018). The plus in 'long-tail+' refers to the conversational phrases that must be included when optimizing for the more 'conversational' voice search.

Questions first, website content second

It is worth documenting and recording the exact questions and words customers use when they talk to both your customer service representatives and your sales people. Once you have a list of natural-sounding questions and statements that customers ask (even over the phone), you can then start creating content pages that focus on those longer, more conversational questions (which now are also 'search terms'). Use conversational language – write as if you are talking to a friend face-to-face. As voice search grows, this will become more important.

Optimizing = empathizing and eliminating

Optimizing web page text:

> is mainly a matter of empathizing and eliminating. Empathizing is the most difficult. Eliminating often meets with internal resistance. If web text begins with a promise, an offer or an advantage, it immediately raises questions from the reader. A good web text is limited to the answers to questions raised in the reader's mind. The fact of the matter is, if you don't know what your readers' questions are, you cannot write. Get rid of anything that is not an answer to questions that your readers may ask.
>
> Visser *et al* (2018)

Key phrases

A key phrase list is an inventory of words and phrases that the target market would use when searching for an organization's product or service, or searching for topics, information or just videos. This requires empathy – the ability to think like your customers and list the words and phrases customers would use. Web analytics show which words bring the most traffic. Marketers also watch competitor sites to see what words and phrases they use. **Spyfu.com** can tell you what key phrases work best for your competitors when using PPC ads. The sales teams ask customers what phrases they use when searching. Customer service teams note what phrases and questions customers use. And the marketers use tools to generate keywords and compare popular ones with the same phrases used on other websites.

Commercial phrases vs informational phrases

'According to Brian Dean, the #1 keyword research mistake is not spending enough time on commercial keywords. That's because commercial keywords are the ones that make money. To improve your rankings and make money, you need to understand the difference between commercial and informational keywords. If all your keywords are informational, you will still generate organic traffic, but converting those visitors to buyers may be difficult. The reason is because visitors who search for informational keywords are not in a buying mood. They want you to speak their language – the language of free, eg: how to clear acne with home products; how to install Wordpress; make money online for free; free ebook download; top 10 free article spinners.

In contrast, people who use commercial keywords like: best acne products; top 10 web hosting providers; web designers in NY, are probably searching for a solution they can buy.

If you're in the e-commerce industry, you will recognize commercial keywords tend to convert well. Keywords that have these words as a prefix (before) or suffix (after) to the rest of the keyword phrase, tend to do well: buy; review; purchase; discount; coupon; deal; shipping; order.'

Patel (2014)

Now explore our case studies.

- Social media content seeded cross-industry influencers to improve sales for adventure company Zip World.
- A brand new business, LOVI, was grown out of social media usage and clever influencer marketing to steadily nurture a new luxury fashion business in Sri Lanka.
- The New York Giants use social media to add value to the fan experience (FX).
- Owned media helped a Brazilian football club to wipe out hospital waiting lists for organ donors by using the stadium banner space, the club's match-day programmes, Facebook, a YouTube video and its own website.
- A microsite was created to support the Brian Clough film *The Damned United*.
- American Greetings e-cards optimized its landing pages.
- And finally, social media was used to stop young people smoking.

CASE STUDY Social media content seeded cross industry influencers: Zip World

Situation

Adventure company Zip World created a stunning subterranean playground caving adventure for both adults and children called Bounce Below.

Objectives

Grow sales of tickets for Bounce Below and boost the tourism economy of northern Welsh town Blaenau Ffestiniog.

Strategy

Weber Shandwick helped Zip World develop a two-phased marketing communications strategy:

- Phase 1 targeted a number of influential arts and culture writers and creative design blogs (social media) to seed the pictures of this stunning underground playground.
- Phase 2 targeted the mainstream media and shared content for 'adrenalin junkies' with a wide selection of influencers such as Thrillist, Unilad, Ladbible and Viral Thread.

Tactics

Create some 'wow' content (mostly photos and some short videos) and target some influencers outside of the tourism and leisure sector and more in the design sector. With an initial budget of just £2,500 and an amateur photographer,

FIGURE 20.4 Bounce Below, a subterranean playground in the heart of Wales

Zip World's Bounce Below wanted to showcase to the world the three-story underground trampoline cavern that is twice the size of St Paul's Cathedral in London.

Celebrity blogger Perez Hilton used the photographs with the line: 'You win Wales. You win. The title of the "Most Fun Place in the World" is all yours.'

Some videos that went viral had an immediate impact, increasing daily website visitors from 6,000 to 33,000. This had an immediate knock-on effect on ticket sales.

Actions

Internal marketing includes staff training, crystal clear internal communications and motivation. Staff are highly motivated already and proud of this innovative concept. They are trained to encourage all visitors to share their experience by taking photos and videos and writing reviews.

Another major influencer, George Takei (*Star Trek* actor), shared a 30 second video clip (see Figure 20.7) which helped to generate four million views. The Bounce Below website crashed! But within 24 hours it was back up again (this time supported by several extra servers). Zip World also immediately increased their customer service telephone sales team to cope with the increased number of telephone enquiries.

Control

The initial £2,500 campaign secured £72,000 worth of pre-booked tickets within a week, with 4,500 daily hits on the website during the campaign period and widespread coverage in the international media.

FIGURE 20.5 Bounce Below's nets are connected by stairways, net walkways and slides

Actual customer visits to Zip World were 327,000 for the year (up by 54 per cent on the previous year), which generated revenues of over £11 million (56 per cent increase year on year), which in turn delivered a healthy EBITDA (profit) of £3.7 million (up by 56 per cent on the previous year).

Zip World has succeeded in every criteria, including the original promise to boost tourism in the Northern Welsh mining town of Blaenau Ffestiniog – 'the town that roofed the world'.

3Ms

- **Men and women (staff):** At the time of writing, there were three marketing communications staff, sending around 4 emails a month (not including pre-arrival and booking confirmation emails, working with approximately 220k contacts), developing fresh marketing content, updating the website (which had 3.6m sessions from 2m unique visitors) and social media platforms, sowing seeds with influencers and, most of all, ensuring customers enjoy their experience so much so that they share their customer experiences with their own personal networks.
- **Money:** Budgets were tiny at the start – just £2,500 for photography and video and advice.
- **Minutes:** A busy year!

Note: SOSTAC® is an agile planning system. This period's results will become part of the next plan's 'situation analysis', which in turn influences the next set of objectives. A really good in-depth situation analysis also helps develop the next period's strategy.

FIGURE 20.6 Bounce Below is made up of six enclosed bouncy nets, with a huge bouncy net spiral going from the bottom to the top

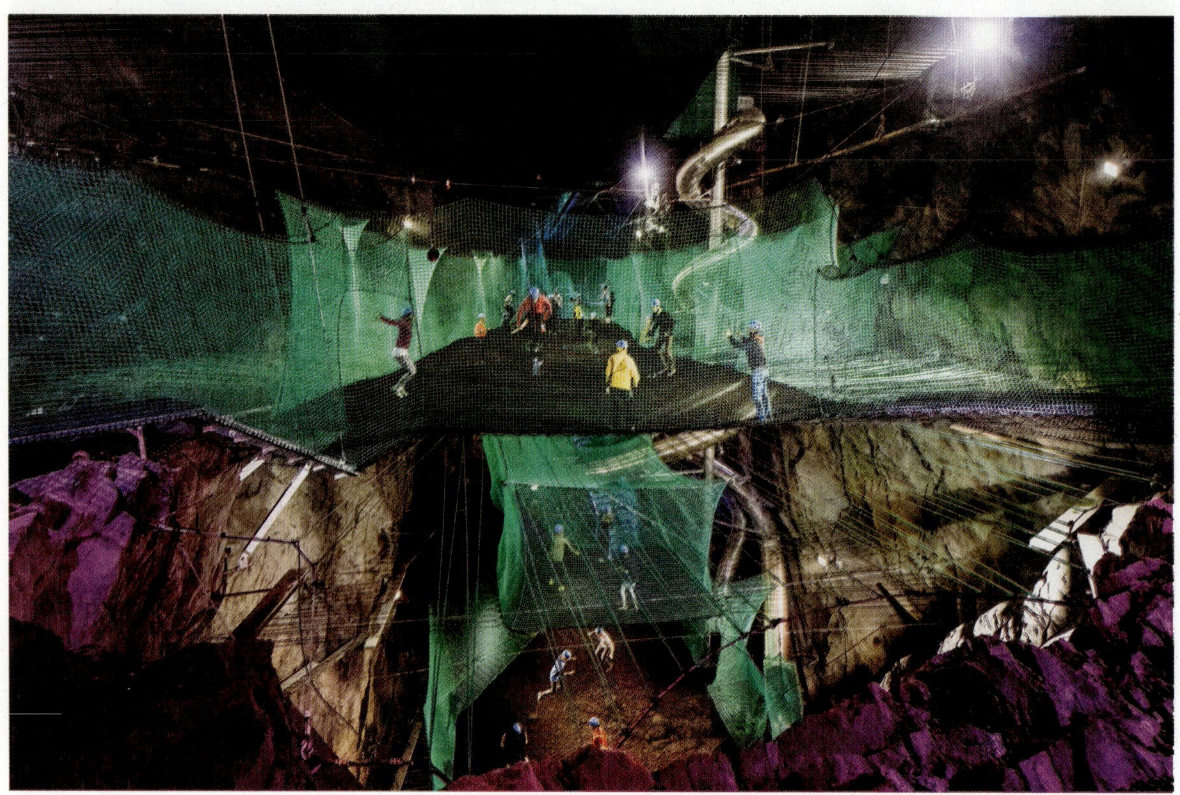

In the case of Zip World, the company's strategy for the next period's plan is:

- Constantly improve the customer experience and invest £4.7 million in fixed assets.
- Expand to new locations.
- Nurture a secondary spend (ie share of wallet) for customers – food, merchandise including photography.

FIGURE 20.7 This video went viral

CASE STUDY Social media launches luxury fashion brand LOVI Ceylon

Situation

LOVI was founded in 2015 by Asanka de Mel, to leverage Sri Lanka's aesthetics and design into a premium and elegant line of apparel that excites fashion-conscious men and women around the world.

Trends

The civil war in Sri Lanka ended nine years ago. Peace and pride are returning. People (locals and tourists) love the ancient history, culture and sheer beauty of Sri Lanka. There is a gap in the market for uniquely styled high-quality

FIGURE 20.8 LOVI's Unity collection

fashion. Sri Lankan communities all desire peace and unity. LOVI even have one collection called 'Unity'.

Technology/social media has spread everywhere. People tend to communicate via social media platforms because it is convenient for them. LOVI receives daily enquiries via Instagram and Facebook. Enquiries are growing and are directed to the website **www.lovisarongs.com** and to one of the new distributor stores.

Customer insights

Instagram, Facebook and Shopify (website data) give comprehensive analysis as to the best performing posts, timing of most likes, number of impressions, demographics of followers, etc. The Instagram Insights (see below) suggest the initial demographic profile for the current primary target market is 18- to 34-year-olds in Colombo. More layers of

FIGURE 20.9 Instagram insights/analytics

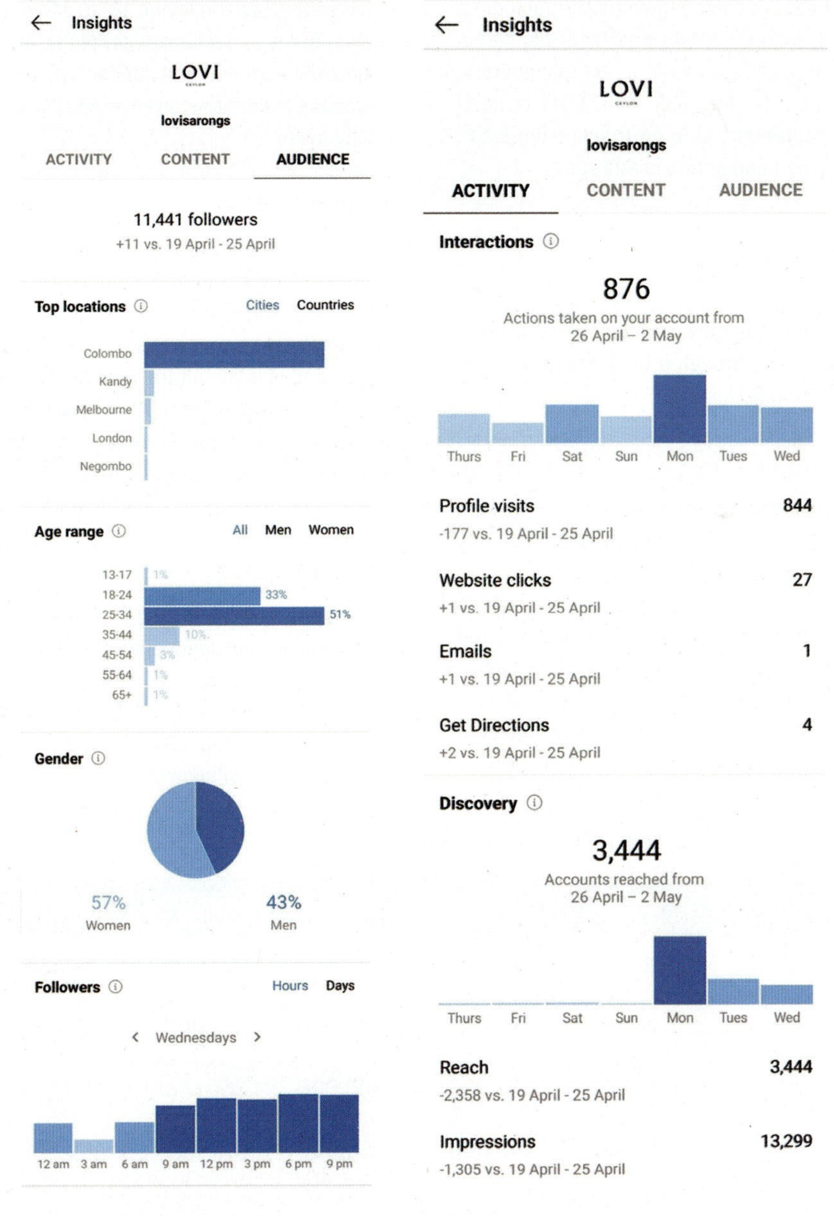

data will be added, including income level/job type, location (residential type), hobbies and interests as well as 'response to remarketing'.

Initial customer research shows the ideal target customers are confident, wealthy, fashion loving 18- to 34-year-olds, males and females: firstly in Sri Lanka; secondly, overseas where Sri Lankans have settled and succeeded; and thirdly, in the UK, EU and USA.

Competition

There is plenty of competition in Sri Lanka. There are many low- to high-end products competing with LOVI including: small-scale retailers, Indian imports and local handloom sarongs (at the low end) and two major direct competitors: Barefoot and Hameedia (at the high end). LOVI is positioned as a fashion statement, as a go-to occasion wear. There are few emerging competitors in this space.

Objectives

Mission

LOVI brings beauty and a maverick confidence to the world of fashion and style lovers through a unique international luxury fashion brand from Sri Lanka.

Vision

Build a global clothing brand based on the finest sarongs in the world while respecting the environment and the dignity of the people who make them.

LOVI brings stylish Ceylonese clothing back to the fashion scene to recreate an identity for Sri Lankan clothing, inspired by kings and queens and the ancient history of Sri Lanka. Sarongs have been worn for centuries; it's a traditional garment. LOVI is shaking things up. Interest is growing and continues to grow, as can be seen by the figures in Table 20.1.

Strategy

LOVI is positioned as an exciting and elegant new international fashion style targeting the confident fashion and style loving maverick in firstly, Sri Lanka and secondly, overseas. Delivering a premium and elegant line of apparel that excites this 'fashion-hungry' global market, targeting confident males and females that share a passion for exploring and adventure – eg have the confidence to get on stage at a rock concert. Not afraid to try something new. Not encumbered but empowered by tradition.

As stated above, the ideal target customers are confident, wealthy, fashion loving 18- to 34-year-olds, males and females: firstly in Sri Lanka; secondly, overseas where Sri Lankans have settled and succeeded; and thirdly, fashion-conscious confident Asians overseas in soon to be selected specific cities.

The ideal customer

Confident, wealthy people who like to shake things up… the ones who want to look completely different at a wedding (where everyone is wearing suits). The core age range is 18–34 years, primarily Sri Lankan, followed by a wide spread of multicultural communities and other nationalities that love wearing LOVI. For example, recently there was a wedding in San Francisco, a Jewish wedding between an Indian groom and an American bride. The groom wore a LOVI sarong and a shirt (Figure 20.10).

The style

LOVI, inspired by 'love' and Ceylonese tradition, brings to life a creative and innovative twist for an internationally minded fashion consumer. Blending high-quality craftsmanship, materials, and design, LOVI breaks the mould of the traditional sarong. LOVI is mindful of human and environmental responsibilities.

TABLE 20.1 Interest in the LOVI brand is growing

	2019	2020	2021	2022	2023	2025
Facebook followers	30,055	35,000	40,000	50,000	60,000	75,000
Instagram followers	11,444	15,000	25,000	50,000	75,000	100,000
Website unique visitors	27, 858	45,000	100,000	250,000	400,000	550,000
Email list size	14,980	40,000	60,000	80,000	100,000	150,000

FIGURE 20.10 A Jewish wedding of an Indian groom (wearing LOVI) and an American bride in San Francisco

The communications strategy

The strategy is driven by social media, primarily with Instagram and Facebook and supported by influencer marketing and PR.

Stage 1 is to establish credibility and build a sustainable/viable business.

Stage 2 is to maintain the domestic market, introduce remarketing and grow the franchise overseas.

Social media increases the reach. A manual follow-through contact strategy is designed to convert visitors to enquirers, enquirers to first-time buyers and buyers to lifetime repeat buyers. LOVI also identifies advocates, particularly those who are influencers, and nurtures relations with these opinion-formers.

LOVI's social responsibilities

LOVI's social commitment:

- When it comes to the local market, we want to try and bring everybody together.
- We truly believe that fashion could bring people together. In fact, we have one collection called Unity.
- We will continue to bring collections to life inspired by ancient Ceylonese aesthetics.
- With a lot of division in the country, the concept 'together as one' is needed in Sri Lanka more than ever.
- Environmentally, we only use polyester-free materials. We try to stick to biodegradable materials as much as possible – 100 per cent cotton and handloom materials. At this point only our buttons and belt anglet are metal.
- The lovi fruit is a berry-sized plum that grows in bunches like cherries do. The beautiful bright red lovi grows in Sri Lanka (and much of tropical Asia) and yields many healthful properties. 'LOVI sounds like love, doesn't it? We like that,' says Asanka, the founder.

Tactics

Product

Create new international fashion sarongs that define a modern Sri Lankan clothing identity. Create beautiful clothes that people feel loved in, while respecting the environment and the dignity of the people who make them. Using impeccable craftsmanship and the finest fabrics, LOVI brings authenticity and innovation to sarongs, for all ages and genders. While hinting at Ceylon's aesthetics, LOVI crystallizes the modern Sri Lankan identity.

Distribution

Online shopping (via the website) and 11 retail partners, of whom eight are fashion retailers in Colombo and Kandy. Three are hotel shops in Galle, Southern Sri Lanka. The clothes are dispatched centrally from the distribution centre. Returns: is this an issue? How do you deal with returns? What percentage of orders are returned?

Communications

Social media

Each new collection, uses different models showing different looks from the collection. Social media tactics are timed to coincide, where possible, with events like the Colombo's Fashion Week.

In addition to Instagram and Facebook, LOVI is planning to activate Twitter and YouTube. Images of costumes are posted three or four times a week, while stories are shared almost every day.

Stories on Instagram

Very recently, one lady took a 200km train trip all the way from Anuradhapura just to buy a LOVI and gift it to her boyfriend, who was leaving Sri Lanka the next day. We managed to have it ready by the time she arrived in Colombo after 9pm. Her boyfriend is a die-hard LOVI fan.

FIGURE 20.11 Instagram generates business for LOVI

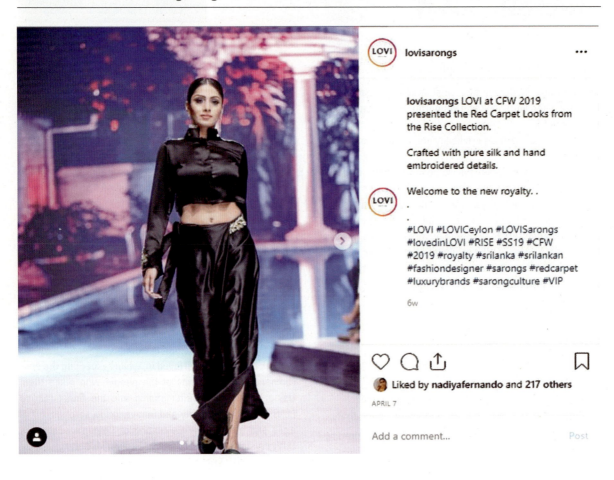

FIGURE 20.12 Stories: A secret train trip secures a LOVI for her loved one

Sharing social media content

Sharing the social media content is really important. LOVI staff all work hard and ask all customers to tag @LOVIsarongs when they wear a LOVI and also to add the #LOVI hashtag to all posts. All staff are trained to ask customers to do so.

Other hashtags are also used, depending on the occasion, including: I #LOVICeylon #LOVISarongs #lovedinLOVI #RISE #SS19 #CFW #2019 #royalty #srilanka #srilankan #fashiondesigner #sarongs #redcarpet #luxurybrands #sarongculture. Searches for ideas, images, photos and posts about these topics, eg #sarongculture, should find LOVI.

Social media and PR/general media coverage and word-of-mouth from the many brand ambassadors are the primary promotional channels. LOVI generally do not sponsor posts or boost posts, but occasionally sponsor a post if it is particularly important, like announcing a new retail partner or a new collection.

Remarketing is being planned to execute in Q3 (creating anonymous lists of your customers and then serving them ads when they are online), to bring the customer back to the website. In addition, an email can be sent to anyone who abandons their shopping cart (if they have registered with LOVI).

Influencer marketing

Approximately 15 influencers (including Tatyana Lee Jay, Tayden Aaditya and Danu Innasithamby) extend LOVI's reach to almost half a million people. Influencers do not get paid. They sometimes get clothes and sometimes LOVI loan clothes for professional attire to people who represent Sri Lanka at international events, eg tourism, human rights, etc.

Actions

All LOVI teams work on a project management plan. Every Monday, the LOVI team discuss each department's and each person's tasks and deadlines. The team discuss and get an update so everyone knows what is going on. Usually the CEO or CCO (chief commercial officer) heads the meeting. After going through the tasks, the team discuss any further issues, clarifications, share ideas and solutions, etc.

Control

Customer reviews are taken very seriously. All staff are trained to ask customers to post a review or at least a rating. LOVI also use a project management task report weekly.

Shopify is a user-friendly analytics platform. LOVI staff access detailed reports showing daily and monthly data,

FIGURE 20.13 Search engine results page (SERP) lists LOVI prominently

#sarongculture

All Maps Videos Images Shopping More Settings Tools

About 218 results (0.22 seconds)

LOVI Sarongs: Sarongs with pockets | Designed for Movement
https://www.lovisarongs.com/ ▾
Designer sarongs | The very first patent-pending sarongs designed with built-in pockets, belts, and lining to suit your active lifestyle.

LOVI - خروني | فيسبوک
https://ps-af.facebook.com › پانی › نور › Brand › جامی › LOVI › خروني
★★★★★ Rating: 4.9 - 45 votes
#LOVICeylon #LOVISarongs #LOVI #Ceylon #srilankan #fashiondesigner #srilanka #RISE #SS19 #royalty #sarongs **#sarongculture** #srilanka #luxurybrands.

LOVI - Posts | Facebook
https://en-gb.facebook.com › Pages › Other › Brand › Clothing (Brand) › LOVI › Posts
★★★★★ Rating: 4.9 - 45 votes
#LOVICeylon #LOVISarongs #LOVI #Ceylon #srilankan #fashiondesigner #srilanka #RISE #SS19 #royalty #sarongs **#sarongculture** #srilanka #luxurybrands.

LOVI CEYLON (@lovisarongs) | Instagram photos, videos, highlights ...
https://www.pictame.com/user/lovisarongs/2247811813 ▾
#LOVI #LOVICeylon #LOVISarongs #lovedinLOVI #RISE #SS19 #royalty #srilanka #srilankan #fashiondesigner #sarongs #luxurybrands **#sarongculture** ...

LOVI CEYLON (@lovisarongs) - Photos, videos, stories and highlights ...
https://kmgram.com/user/lovisarongs ▾
18 Apr 2019 - ... #SS19 #CFW #2019 #royalty #srilanka #srilankan #fashiondesigner #sarongs #nautical #luxurybrands **#sarongculture** #yatch #collection.

LOVI CEYLON (@lovisarongs) Instagram photos and videos ...
https://publicinsta.com/user/lovisarongs ▾

FIGURE 20.14 New collections announced on Instagram

lovisarongs •••

lovisarongs Welcome to the New Royalty.
Introducing the new collection, RISE for the authentic, the confident, the graceful, the new royalty of Sri Lanka — You.

See the new looks on www.lovisarongs.com

#LOVICeylon #LOVISarongs #LOVI #Ceylon #srilankan #fashiondesigner #srilanka #RISE #SS19 #royalty #sarongs #sarongculture #srilanka #luxurybrands

9w

lovisarongs #LOVI #LOVICeylon

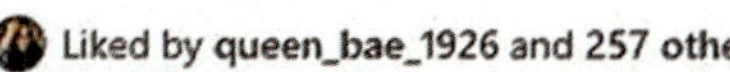

Liked by queen_bae_1926 and 257 others

MARCH 19

Add a comment... Post

FIGURE 20.15 Influencer Danu Innasithamby

lovisarongs •••

lovisarongs @danuinnasithamby featuring LOVI UNITY Collection.

Photography by @youremyfavoritenyc

.
.
.

#togetherasone #UNITY #unitedsrilanka #LOVI #LOVICEYLON #srilanka

Liked by nadiyafernando and 180 others

APRIL 30

Add a comment... Post

FIGURE 20.16 The LOVI emblem is inspired by the crown of the last king of Sri Lanka, King Sri Wickrama Rajasignhe. The crown is surrounded by bold, beautiful symbols: traditional 'liyavel' foliage, a protective arch, and courageous arms. For the wearer, the insignia declares Sri Lankan nobility – not one marked by status, class, or religion, but by a fundamental belief in unity, self-confidence, and personal style

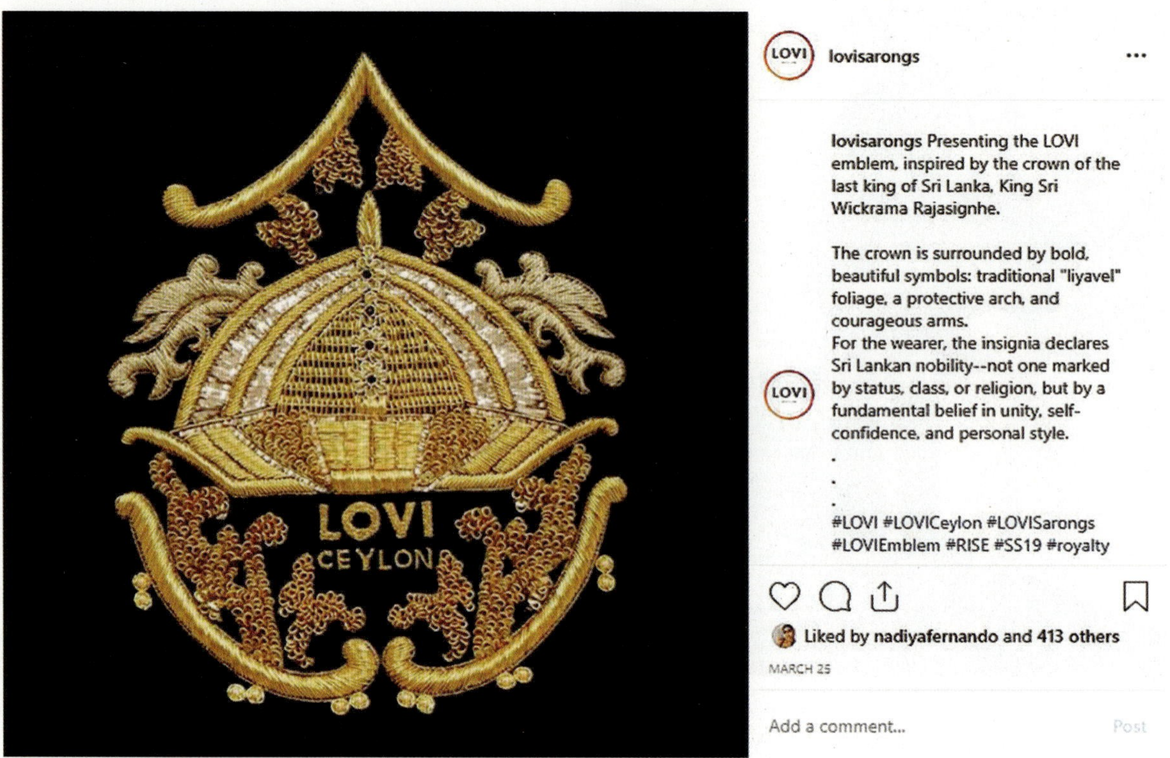

which can be compared to previous data such as sales, orders, best-selling products, visitors country-wise, city-wise, etc.

LOVI is an agile business, listening to customers, watching the numbers, changing the collections, and most of all creating beautiful fashion styles that raise eyebrows everywhere.

CASE STUDY Integrated social media: New York Giants

FIGURE 20.17 The New York Giants integrate social media

May	August
FAN TICKET CONTEST Ask fans to state why they were the biggest Giants fan. All stories narrowed down to 20 finalists. Giants then let the fans decide (vote) what they considered the best story. 10 winners were each featured on this year's game tickets. Total views of Facebook Tab: 238k. Total shares within Tab: 161k.	**TWITTER FEEDS IN BROADCAST/IN-STADIUM** NYG integrate live tweets in the broadcast commentary during Giants preseason games. First team in professional sports to submit tweets using #NYGBCA which appeared on all of our stadium distribution channels. Giants fans loved the fact that NYG allowed fans to share with NYG how much the people they loved also loved the Giants.
September	**October**
9/11 ONLINE TRIBUTE MOSAIC By adding their own Facebook and Twitter profile photos, fans helped to complete a mosaic. Fans could also post a message in the mosaic. The hashtag #NYGneverforget allowed fans on Twitter to append themselves to the mosaic.	**ROOKIE HALLOWEEN COSTUME CONTEST** In partnership with Party City, fans vote via FB/Twitter for which Halloween costumes rookies would wear when doing their hospital visits. Giants veteran players picked out the initial choice of costumes.

ALL SEASON

Man of the Match Extra Effort Player of the Game

Fans voted for their Man Of The Match (Extra Effort Player Of The Game from a choice of three players for each game). Each player was given a unique hashtag, eg to vote for Eli Manning fans tweeted #Manning10.

PRE- SUPER BOWL

Social Media Night – #NYGsocial

On the Thursday before the Super Bowl whomever answers questions submitted to them via Twitter. Each player is given a hashtag which allows fans to submit their questions. The hour-long LIVE webcast was broadcasted from the Giants team hotel on Giants.com.

SUPER BOWL

Twibbon (Ribbon/Badge)

NFC East Champions/Super Bowl Champions Get Twibbon.

A Twibbon Campaign is your own microsite where users can support your *cause*, *brand* or *organization* in a variety of ways. Saves time.

Fans add a custom badge to their Facebook or Twitter profile by clicking one button.

Super Bowl Social Media Initiatives – Follow 30 Players Via One Microsite

Fans could follow the Giants players all the way to Indianapolis.
NYG launched a microsite that allowed our fans to follow all Giants players who had Twitter accounts.

Website: **http://www.giants.com/assets/standalone/connect/default.html**

Behind the Scenes Web Cam

Give fans access to behind the scenes video footage each day if 10,000 'likes' were given on NYG Facebook page. Each day, fresh footage was captured of training, eating and general behind the scenes.

American football team the New York Giants use social media to 'give fans every opportunity to feel as if they are "part" of the team', ie they use social media to add value to the fan experience. Figure 20.17 shows how.

What made this campaign a success? Unique, relevant content. This footage was genuine, behind-the-scenes material that no blog, website or TV network could get. So in this example, the social media actually helped to create a lot of relevant content, engage customers and add value to the overall brand experience.

CASE STUDY Brazilian football club creates immortal fans via social media

Situation

Organ donation was taboo in Brazil for many people. Yet people are dying every day because they cannot find a suitable donated organ. Hospitals have waiting lists of desperately sick patients on stand-by, hoping and praying that someone somewhere has been kind enough to have committed to donating an organ. Brazil's Sport Club Recife is known for having some of the most passionate football fans in Brazil. 'First God. Second Sport Club Recife. Third Family. Fourth work' says one fan. 'Nothing else matters... Sport Club Recife is everything' says another fan. They are passionate about life (and death too). Perhaps this passionate community can help each other by committing to become organ donors? The club has owned media which includes a Facebook page, website, match day programmes and signage (around the stadium).

Objective

The board agreed to mobilize the fans and get as many of them as they could to sign up and become organ donors. This supports the club's community goals and its corporate social responsibility goals of helping their community.

Strategy

Create the first football club organ donor card by mobilizing the passion, harnessing the club's community energy and creating 'immortal fans' whose organs keep on living (in other people's bodies), long after the donor has died. This can be done at minimal cost since it leverages the club's owned media, which includes its website, Facebook page, YouTube channel, match day programme and posters around the stadium.

The club has created a new kind of fan – the immortal fan! Their hearts, eyes, lungs could keep cheering for Sport Club Recife even after death. And the fans responded. Fifty thousand of them committed to helping others after they die.

Sport Club Recife have helped to reduce the waiting list for heart transplant and cornea transplant to zero.

Tactics

YouTube and Facebook were the main tactical tools used to drive this unique and highly successful campaign. The extraordinary YouTube video shows passionate fans that care – some that need an organ, some who have received an organ and some who want to donate. Adriano Dos Santos (who was waiting for an eye transplant) says: 'I promise your eyes will keep on watching Sport Club Recife.' Luiz Antonio (who was waiting for a lung transplant)

FIGURE 20.18 The flowing banner says: Everything for Sport Recife. Even after death

says: 'Your lungs will keep on breathing for Sport Club Recife.' Marleade Dos Santos (who was waiting for a heart transplant) says: 'I promise your heart will always beat for Sport Club Recife.'

One lady who received a heart transplant says: 'My new heart comes from a Sport Club Recife fan and it will keep on beating for Sport Club Recife. C'mon Sport Club Recife fans, let's donate! Let's form this chain and never stop donating.'

You can see the extraordinary YouTube video that helped to create the world's first organ donor football club on **www.GreatSportsmanship.org** (to find it, search for 'Brazil').

Action

Fans get their organ donor card through their preferred channel:

- at the stadium;

FIGURE 20.19 The Great Sportsmanship Programme Blog was founded by PR Smith and is a NFP edutainment programme designed to inspire young people and boost their literacy, self-esteem and interest in sport via true two-minute stories about sportsmanship

Home About Become An Ambassador Buy the Book Watch the Action Share Your Moment Archives

WATCH THE ACTION
Checkout our must-see collection of 'Great Moments' videos

Immortal Fans, Sport Club Recife Donate Organs

by Paul Smith on May 11, 2014 in Brazil, Football

Brazil's Sport Club Recife is known for having some of the most passionate fans in Brazil . "1st God. 2nd Sport Club Recife. 3rd Family. 4th work" says one fan. "Nothing else matters.....Sport Club Recife is everything " says another fan. They are passionate about life too. Even after death. 51,000 Recife fans have signed up to donate their organs after they die (more than the stadium capacity). The club has mobilised their passionate fans to do something really great: to save other people's lives. Watch this wonderful video. Pass it on.

The Immortal Fan

Search...

Anyone for Olympism – the real Olympic dream?

Mobilising Communities into Sportsmanship

Inspiring a new generation via true two minute stories about sportsmanship. Watch this colourful video. Tell us your story. Share a story. Post a comment. Tell a friend. Become an ambassador (looks good

- through a Facebook app;
- at home by mail.

The greatest difficulty in the organ donation process is the family's authorization. So this barrier was removed by ensuring the donor cards communicate with the donor's family. The organ donor card also informs the family of the fan's donation wishes.

Control (measurement/results)

Fifty-one thousand Recife fans have signed up to donate their organs after they die (more than the stadium capacity).

3Ms

- **Men/women:** The Ogilvy agency shaped and executed the idea.
- **Money:** This is a zero budget campaign, with time and effort donated by volunteers.
- **Minutes:** In less than a season this campaign recruited 51,000 donors.

Note: This case was first posted on The Great Sportsmanship Programme blog (11 May 2014).

CASE STUDY *The Damned United*, Brian Clough microsite

Situation

Digital agency Moonshine Media was asked by *Times Online* to create an engaging showcase to celebrate the colourful life and times of Brian Clough, one of England's most controversial and outspoken football managers.

Objectives

The ultimate objective for the website was to help promote the film *The Damned United*, an adaption of David Peace's best-selling novel of the same name about Clough's stormy 44-day tenure as manager of Leeds United.

Strategy

The website was designed to focus on Clough's career as opposed to his personal life, which was why the inspiration for the website layout was derived from an interest in card collecting, as well as showing a clean and text-minimalist look.

Tactics

The site provided links to an archive of information including video, images and articles, and ultimately displayed an interactive timeline, 'Clough in the rough', and aggregated video as well as images. The *Sunday Times* archive content highlighted the key events in Clough's career, enabling readers to explore and navigate through the most memorable moments in Old Big 'Ead's life.

Action

The action section is all about excellent execution of the tactics. This includes internal marketing (training, motivation and internal communications), mini project plans, action plans (see Figure 20.20), checklists and processes.

Control/results

Feedback from *Times Online* praised the website for having a 'slick and exciting design which showed off our content in a fresh and dynamic manner'. The project was completed with *Times Online* feeling 'confident' that the application would engage and entertain its readers.

3Ms

- **Men/women:** A research team involving five individuals from *Times Online* worked for a month before the project started in order to collect all the information with which to populate the site. They went through archives from newspapers, looked through interviews, and bought very limited film footage. Moonshine Media was given the content and populated the site with everything that was supplied.
- **Money:** *Times Online* had a budget of £13,000 for the microsite (no retainer, pay by results).
- **Minutes:** From start to finish the project took 30 days.

FIGURE 20.20 *Times Online* microsite timetable

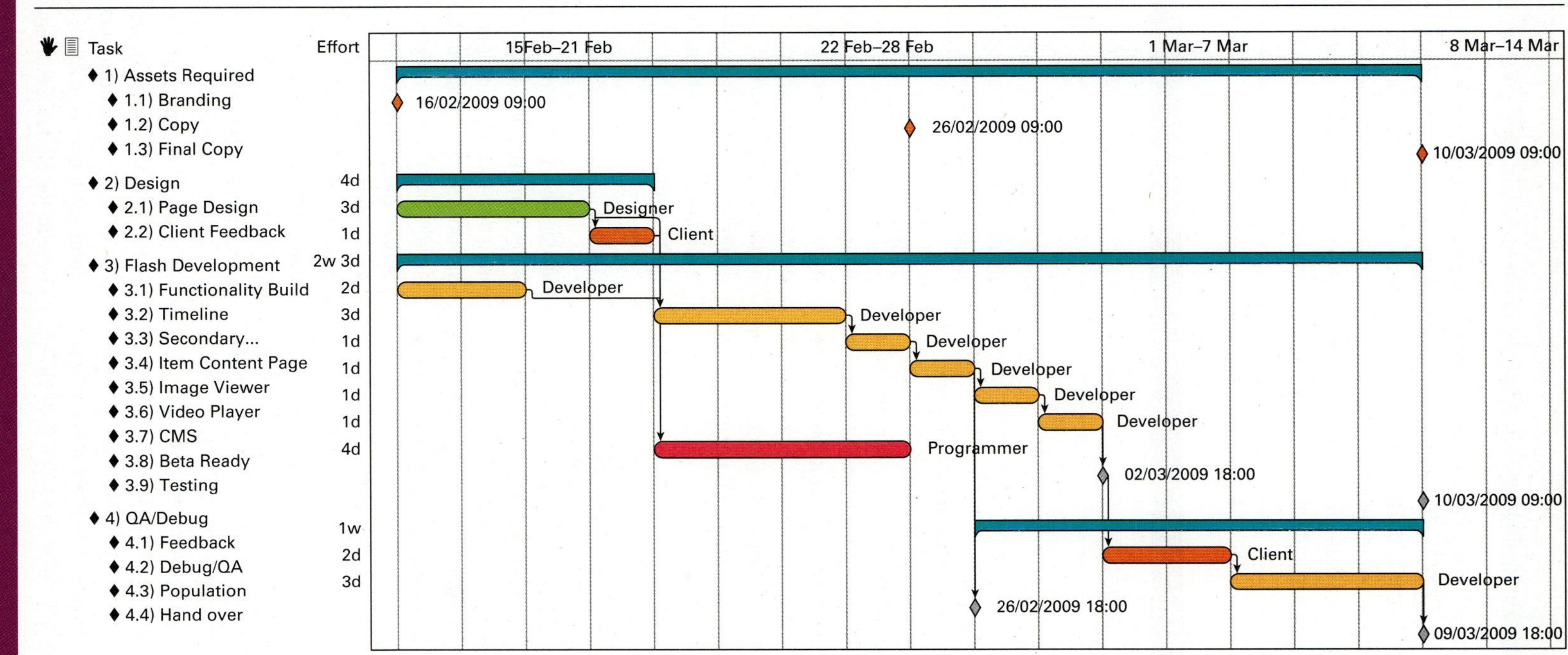

Do not forget internal communications – 10 per cent of the budget

Flawless execution of marketing campaigns and simple tools like websites is not as common as it should be. In fact, Bossidy and Charan (2002) claimed that execution was the last bastion of competitive advantage; ie, being able to execute plans better than your competitors created competitive advantage. One aspect that is critical to flawless execution of marketing communications is internal marketing, which means communicating to your team, colleagues, staff and other departments within your organization. Figures vary, but many well-run organizations allocate a minimum of 10 per cent of their resources to communicating internally.

CASE STUDY American Greetings e-cards optimized landing pages

Situation analysis

American Greetings has the largest collection of electronic greetings on the web, including cards available at **AmericanGreetings.com** through AG Interactive, Inc, the company's online division. AG Interactive funnelled online traffic to the **www.americangreetings.com** homepage, or a single multivariate testing (MVT)-optimized landing page. The marketing team decided they needed to launch an aggressive landing page testing in order to lift visitor conversion rates from an average of 1.47 per cent to 2.01 per cent.

Objectives

The goal was to convert traffic using online registration for a free trial subscription (which later converted to a paid subscription on **AmericanGreetings.com**); however, one landing page was not converting enough of the total traffic. Implementing testing on one landing page was slow, with a multi-month feedback loop to the marketing team. Experimentation with alternative design and content was even slower.

Strategy

To lift conversions, the marketing team decided to create and test several different context-specific landing pages for each keyword: e-cards, free e-cards, birthday, create and print, and international. They determined they needed to experiment broadly with content and layout, test results and view analysis in real time to find which landing pages worked best. Their new strategy was based around a system (Ion's LiveBall) where the marketers could change the offers, propositions and even pictures directly without needing developers and designers to code and create new pages for them.

Tactics

American Greetings adopted LiveBall in order to increase agility, speed to market, specificity and ultimately to improve conversion performance to lower cost per customer acquisition. Ion worked closely with the AG Interactive marketing manager to launch and test alternative landing experiences that were specific to marketing segments and traffic sources.

Action

Within the first three months of testing with LiveBall, American Greetings moved from a single, optimized landing page to over 40 unique landing pages, each context-specific to its source of traffic. Three entirely different design formats were tested with 12 different price points across 200 different audience segments. By speaking to each segment, American Greetings was able to increase conversions despite an economic fallout that actually reduced the flow of traffic.

Customers looking for e-cards search using different phrases. Tests revealed which landing page performed best for each key phrase. Once these 'champion' landing pages were identified, all traffic from a particular ad word was directed to that champion page. Consider three search phrases: 'e-cards', 'birthdays' and 'create and print' (your own card). Each phrase is linked to a specific landing page that reflects the phrase. Each landing page has several versions

FIGURE 20.21 American Greetings

The key phrase 'e-cards' was tested against many different landing pages before choosing the landing page called 'Browse with Flash' (on the right hand side). This was the champion page (which made the most sales).

The key phrase 'birthdays' was tested against many different landing pages to see which page converted the most visitors into customers. The landing page called 'Browse with Flash' (in the middle) was the champion (ie it sold the most cards).

Many different landing pages were tested for the key phrase 'Create and Print'.
The 'general' landing page (on the left hand side) converted higher than the other family focused themes.

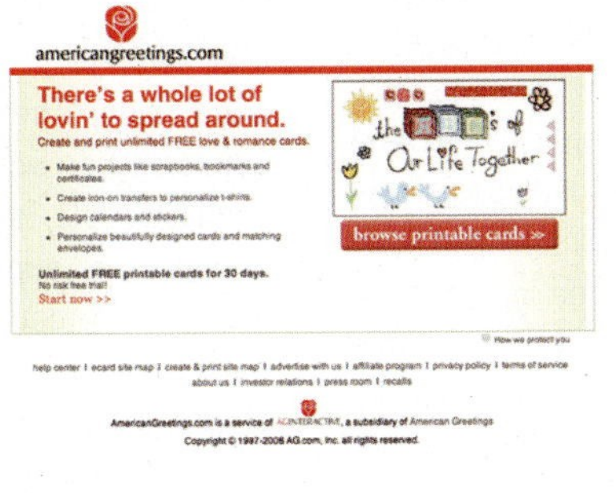

tested before the marketing team selects the 'optimum' landing page for each key phrase. This is the magic marketing formula at work (see Figure 20.21 for the testing process and results).

Control

Each unique landing page format was customized and matched with the PPC ad that was sending it traffic. The testing resulted in an almost immediate 30 per cent increase in conversion and a subsequent 20 per cent decrease in cost per acquisition (which is a net benefit that included the added expenses associated with Ion's LiveBall platform and conversion optimization services). E-cards run 13 or 14 tests simultaneously at any one time and get quick, actionable learning.

Over the first five months using LiveBall, the American Greetings online marketing team created over 700 unique landing pages, which were tested across hundreds of unique traffic sources. The real-time testing and analytics in LiveBall ensured that traffic arrived at the best-performing landing page for each traffic source. As soon as American Greetings got statistical significance on a test, they drove traffic immediately to the champion landing page in real time. On Mother's Day alone this resulted in $45,000 in incremental revenue. That's revenue that would have been lost without LiveBall's actionable, real-time approach.

New tests are always in the works at American Greetings. The conversion goal was over 40 per cent higher than the previous year, and another 33 per cent lift was targeted for the next two years. American Greetings uses Ion's LiveBall platform to drive real business ROI at scale. Smaller-percentage improvements on the top-line sales figures have a big impact on the bottom-line profit figures. LiveBall gives fast speed to market and learning. It's a visual tool that lets marketers focus on what's working to improve results.

World-class marketers constantly try to optimize and improve their marketing performances, and American Greetings is a good example. Testing multiple landing pages is one of many ways to boost the conversion of visitors to customers.

Marketing professionals now need to convert existing customers to lifetime, repeat-purchasing customers. Here's how.

CASE STUDY Social media helps stop smoking: Using social media (and UGC movies) to help 11- to 15-year-olds to stop smoking

Situation

Although the proportion of young people aged 11–15 who smoke had fallen over the previous 10 years, it was reported that by age 15 the proportion who reported smoking at least once a week had risen to approximately one in seven (14 per cent). Smoking is the main cause of preventable morbidity and premature death in England. The Deborah Hutton Campaign is working in harmony with existing government and charitable initiatives to reduce the prevalence of smoking among young people.

Objectives

Change agency ICE has worked with the Deborah Hutton Campaign on a pilot, Cut Films, a film-making competition that took place across 10 schools and a youth club nationwide. The challenge was to develop a creative concept that would positively resonate with and inspire young people, so the campaign grew through genuine enthusiasm, supported by schools and young people across the country. Ultimately, the project aimed to engender 1,000 films, generating a change in the attitudes of young people towards smoking and a reduction in the number of young people smoking.

Strategy

Cut Films used the creative film-making process, combined with the use of social media, to influence 11- to 15-year-olds. It attracted young people and encouraged them to share their own personal messages and creative work by using the relational nature of social media. This enabled users to forward films and messages, in order to create a snowball campaign that aimed to influence the cultural attitudes of young people towards smoking. The power of the campaign lay in the use of social media as part of a peer-to-peer approach engaging young people through the creative attraction of film and new media technologies.

Tactics

The campaign set up a presence for Cut Films on a range of social media sites. Films were uploaded to YouTube and then 'pinged' across to pages on Facebook and Twitter. The campaign also promoted its presence among key stakeholders.

Action

The Cut Films competition was managed by the campaign director, who supported schools and youth clubs throughout the process. However, the main way of managing the results was through the 'My film' document that young people used to help them plan, reflect on and evaluate the process of producing a film, and reflect on the content they discovered throughout the process.

All films were submitted to the Cut Films website, moderated and uploaded to YouTube. There is an ongoing effort to introduce the campaign to schools, as well as constant communication with key stakeholders, including:

- the Department of Health;
- the head of features, ITV;
- key academic health promotion specialists;

FIGURE 20.22 Cut Films 'film page' containing multiscreen grabs

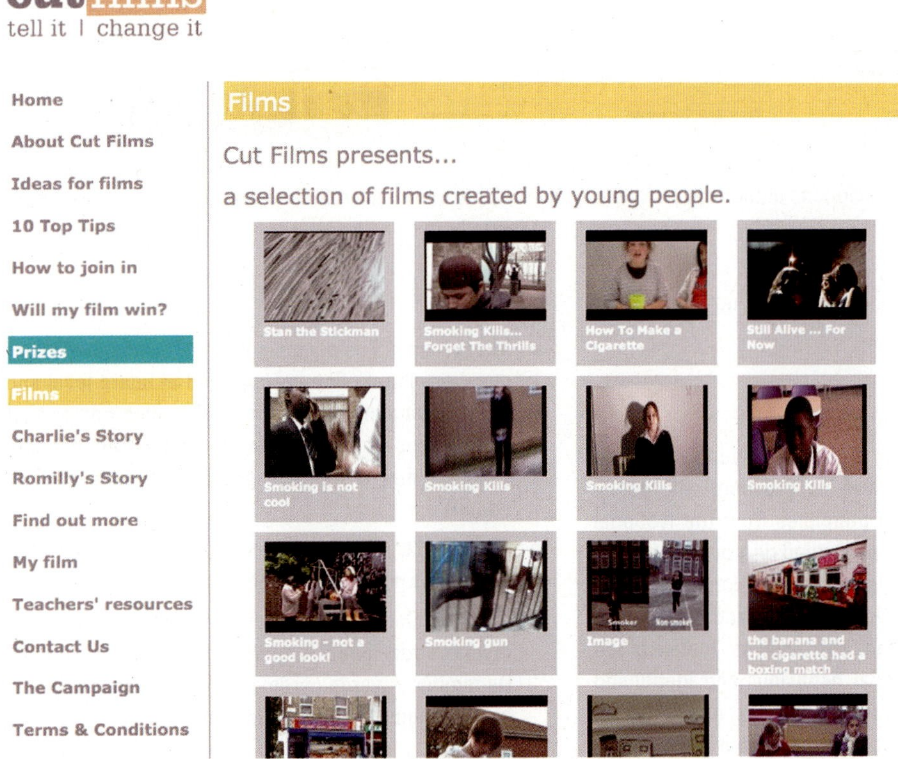

FIGURE 20.23 'Smoking is not cool' on YouTube

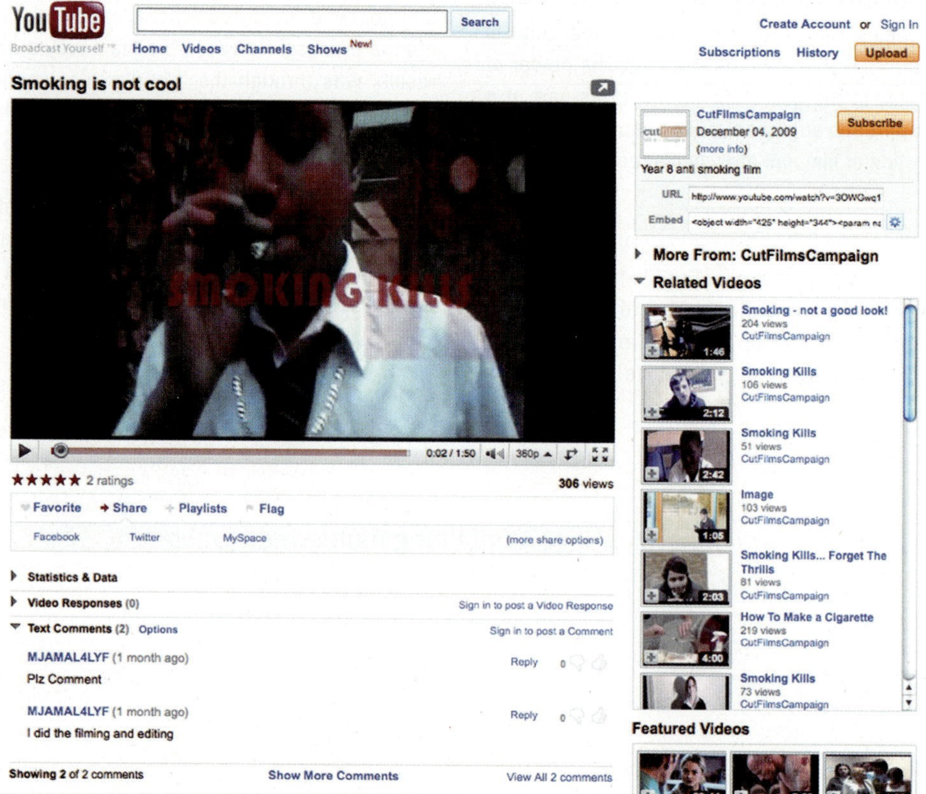

- the head of public health sciences at the University of Edinburgh;
- schools and youth clubs;
- regional and local tobacco leads within local NHS services.

Control

Cut Films fed into health and citizenship issues within the PSHE curriculum, and this was underpinned with social marketing or social change principles from the National Social Marketing Centre. This provided rigorous evaluation and evidence for the campaign's long-term impact.

Underpinning every aspect of the project, ICE's social marketing division provided key insight focusing on realigning concepts of normal behaviour and identifying film topics that would inspire as well as nudge young people and their communities towards a move in behaviour. They also created an evaluation framework and focus groups to inform the roll-out and evaluation of the campaign nationally.

3Ms

- **Men/women:** The campaign director is the only full-time member of staff. She is supported at board level and is also working alongside social marketing company ICE, which as part of the pilot provided free access to expertise in web development, design, social marketing and PR.
- **Money:** ICE provided its expertise for the pilot free of charge, as a contribution to this charitable initiative.
- **Minutes:** Cut Films' pilot: June to March. Website and resources designed: August to September. Film deadline: December. Awards ceremony: March. National roll-out of campaign: September onwards.

See the Cut Films website (**www.cutfilms.org**).

Advantages and disadvantages

Here are some of the advantages and disadvantages to consider when deciding whether to increase or reduce this communications tool.

Advantages

Websites can help to establish the credibility of a brand, engage customers in a unique way and convert them into lifetime customers and brand advocates. Combine this with social media platforms, and the combination can be used to move customers up the Ladder of Engagement and spread the word. The website is owned media and therefore it is a controlled environment (assuming it is moderated). New ideas that add value to the customer experience can be added to the site continually. An infinite amount of new added value opportunities are emerging, particularly as technology develops. Deeply engaging, relevant experiences can be delivered. This is a form of competitive advantage. Social media can help to create awareness and engage customers all the way through a purchase cycle. It can also help to nurture influencer relationships and advocates who will spread your brand. While the website is generally not a tool for building awareness, it is a tool for nurturing awareness into relationships. Social media, on the other hand, can create awareness, change attitudes and help to convert prospects to customers and customers into lifetime customers.

Disadvantages

Websites are totally dependent on traffic. No traffic makes a website useless. Investment is required for, first, traffic-building campaigns and, second, maintenance of the site with fresh content. Equally, social media requires a continued feed of fresh content (as well as resources to respond to discussions). This can be resource hungry (SMO is the new SEO), and as yet there are few models to indicate the optimum resource allocation here. The usual issues of servers crashing, security hackers, scams and spammers jeopardizing the control of the message are challenges, and constant vigilance is required. Equally, conversations across the full social media spectrum need to be monitored and tracked continually. Conversations also require moderation and response. Scope creep can mess up a website either at the development stages, or ongoing requests for website changes/improvements can eventually create a patchwork quilt that loses the site's cohesiveness and its 'thing', as can poor content management, eg out-of-date content left online. Maintenance is essential.

Key points from Chapter 20

- There are four key satisfaction factors for websites: high-quality content, easy navigation, fast downloads and updated content.
- High-quality content is more likely with some scenario planning, persona development, creative sizzle and customer engagement.
- Navigation requires careful planning, including navigation rules and identifying the top tasks.
- Customer conversion increases with: a strong call to action; price lining; simplified processes; reduced customer anxiety; a contact strategy and digital body language; and relevant landing pages.
- Successful social media requires high-quality content, suitably optimized (also for audio search) and spread across various social networks.
- Social media processes must be integrated into business systems and databases.
- The 10 common social media mistakes can be avoided with common sense.

As it is the end of this book...

We hope you have enjoyed it. One final point regarding owned media. Here is, in our opinion, one of the finest uses of owned media. It belongs to a non-league semi-pro football club on the south coast of England, called Whitehawk FC. They have one small stand. The steps in the stand are owned media. Here's how they used their owned media to get a serious message out there. See **www.GreatSportsmanship.org** for more.

FIGURE 20.24 Unique use of owned media by Whitehawk FC

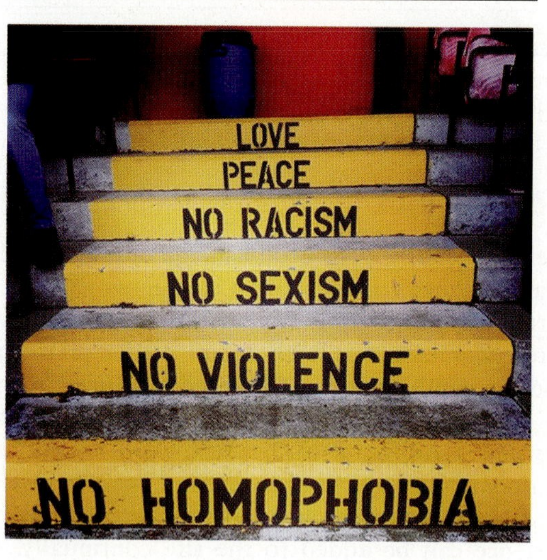

References and further reading

Baer, J and Naslund, A (2011) *The Now Revolution*, Wiley, London

Bonelli, S (2017) How to optimize for voice search, *Search Engine Land*, 1 May

Bossidy, L and Charan, R (2002) *Execution: The discipline of getting things done*, Soundview Executive Books, Concordville, PA

Byron, D, Kievman, N and Schrum, R (2010) *Why Executives Hate Social Media: An executive's guide to social media*, Deming Hill

Chaffey, D and Smith, PR (2017) *Digital Marketing eXcellence*, 5th edn, Routledge, Abingdon

Gallup (2013) How customers interact with their banks, *Gallup Business Journal*, 7 May

Hilpern, K (2013) How to personalise your customers experience, *The Marketer* March/April

King, B (2010) *Bank 2.0*, Marshall Cavendish

McGovern, G (2010a) The customer is a stranger, *New Thinking*, 7 June

McGovern, G (2010b) Web manager: Top tasks versus tiny tasks, *New Thinking*, 28 June

McGovern, G (2012) Why review and remove are such critical web skills, *Gerry McGovern: New Thinking*, 8 July

McGovern, G (2015) Relationships are expensive, *Gerry McGovern: New Thinking*, 21 June

Patel, N (2014) The step-by-step guide on improving your Google rankings without getting penalized, Neil Patel.com, December 2

Robles, P (2010) 10 common social media mistakes, *Econsultancy*, 31 March

Schlender, B and Chen, C Y (2000) Steve Job's Apple gets way cooler, 24 January [online] https://money.cnn.com/magazines/fortune/fortune_archive/2000/01/24/272281/index.htm (archived at https://perma.cc/995C-M8AT)

Schwartz, B (2018) The Google speed update: Page speed will become a ranking factor in mobile search, *Search Engine Land*, 17 January

Sexton, J (2010) Dispelling buyer anxiety and replacing it with buyer confidence, *Web Marketing Today*, 3 August

Seybold, P (2001) Get inside the lives of your customers, *Harvard Business Review*, May

Smith, PR (2011) *Marketing Communications: Integrating offline with online and social media*, 5th edn, Kogan Page, London

Smith, PR (2019) *SOSTAC® Guide to your perfect digital marketing plan*, http://prsmith.org/books/ (archived at https://perma.cc/LKV2-WDEY)

Solis, B (2010) The 10 stages of social media integration in business, BrianSolis.com/ (archived at https://perma.cc/432D-MSML), 22 January

Surowiecki, J (2005) *The Wisdom of Crowds*, Anchor Books, New York

Visser, M, Sikkenga, B and Berry, M (2018) *Digital Marketing Fundamentals*, Noordhoff Uitgevers

Wolfgang Digital (2019) KPI report 2019 [online] www.wolfgangdigital.com/kpi-2019/ (archived at https://perma.cc/RT45-KAU6)

Woods, A (2007) The Revolution usability report: Creativity – looks aren't everything, *Revolution magazine.com*, 4 December

Woods, S (2009) *Digital Body Language*, New Year Publishing, Danville, CA

Wunker, S, Wattmann, J and Farber, D (2016) *Jobs to Be Done: A roadmap for customer-centered innovation*, Amacom

Further information

Advertising Standards Authority Limited (ASA)
Castle House
37–45 Paul Street
London EC2A 4LS
Tel: +44(0) 20 7492 2222
www.asa.org.uk

Business Link (now part of Gov.uk)
Tel: 0845 600 9006
www.gov.uk

Wordtracker LLP
Kemp House
152–160 City Road
London EC1V 2NX
United Kingdom
Tel: +44 0333 200 4555
www.wordtracker.com

Cloudmark Europe Ltd (anti-spam software)
c/o Olswang
90 High Holborn
London WC1V 6XX
www.cloudmark.com

Committee of Advertising Practice (CAP)
Castle House
37–45 Paul Street
London EC2A 4LS
Tel: +44 (0)20 7492 2100
www.asa.org.uk

Google Business Solutions
www.google.co.uk/services/

Information Commissioner's Office
Wycliffe House
Water Lane
Wilmslow
Cheshire SK9 5AF
Tel: +44 (0)30 3123 1113
Fax: +44 (0)1625 524510
www.ico.org.uk

INDEX

Note: Numbers within main headings are filed as spelt out; acronyms and 'Mc' are filed as presented. Page locators in *italics* denote information contained within a figure or table.

The SOSTAC® story

Although SOSTAC® is simple, it actually took me almost ten years to develop. When I took my MBA back in the 1980s I was frustrated reading books with long, meandering marketing plans that were unnecessarily complicated and impossible to remember. So, I kept in touch with my classmates and asked them to send me just the contents page (list of contents) from their marketing plans. I analysed all of them over a two-year period and developed my own new structure. This went through a number of iterations for several years until I came up with SOSTAC®. It was like someone had turned the light on!

www.SOSTAC.org